RACIAL PROVERBS

By the same Author
THE ELEVEN RELIGIONS and their Proverbial Lore

RACIAL PROVERBS

A Selection of the World's Proverbs arranged Linguistically

By

SELWYN GURNEY CHAMPION, M.D.

WITH AUTHORITATIVE INTRODUCTIONS TO THE PROVERBS OF 27 COUNTRIES AND RACES

New York

BARNES & NOBLE, INC.

First published 1938
Second edition 1950
Reprinted 1963
Reprinted 1966

"*It may be true what some men say;*
it must be true what all men say."

PRINTED IN GREAT BRITAIN

CONTENTS

CONTENTS

PROVERB COLLECTIONS:

CONTENTS

INTRODUCTION

I AM frequently asked by people of education and culture, " What is a proverb ? " or " Did you invent these sayings yourself ? " One cannot help wondering whether the same profound ignorance does not obtain in many other Occidental countries. This ignorance of racial aphorisms is becoming more and more profound and universal, and I feel firmly convinced that the time is not far distant when the proverb, so far as the Occident is concerned, will be entirely forgotten. The reason is not far to seek. I can conceive of no greater mental punishment than to be compelled to wade through a collection of so-called proverbs which almost invariably consists of a heterogeneous conglomeration of sayings, colloquialisms, idioms, slang, bon mots, rhymes, riddles, and a mass of stupid, silly, commonplace proverbs, producing in my unfortunate translators and myself a boredom verging on tears, but fortunately, " He who catches one fishes on ! " It is hardly surprising that in my quest for choice proverbs (it is by now, I hope, understood that I prefer the wheat to the chaff) in the British Museum, London Library, etc., a paper-knife was even more essential than a pen ! " e multis paulum fructus collegi ".

I wonder what the result would have been had those three brilliant compilers, Burton Stevenson, Gurney Benham and John Bartlett included in their classical collections a mass of stupid, inane, commonplace quotations ? These books would, like so many books of proverbs, be little read, and would never have reached a second edition, instead of which they are in universal demand and on the shelves of every library.

The late celebrated scholar Woislav Petrovitch, who did an enormous amount of invaluable work for me, was of the same opinion, as the following extract from one of his letters to me shows :

> " . . . I had to wade wearily hour after hour through dozens of pages to find ONE PROVERB worth retaining. Let me take for example the Bulgarian sources which I used in translating for you : Slavikov's two volumes containing some 22,000, Cholakov's collection with some 8,000 and Altmann's selection with some 4,500. Out of these I found only 340 proverbs worth retaining. This is 1%. . . . I read Wander's collection (*Sprichwörter Lexikon*) some twenty years ago and was so enraged that had the five huge volumes been my property, I should have shoved them into the furnace and had a warm bath on them, for they contained sheer stupidities, often imbecile sayings of which cannibals would be ashamed. Yet they were dear to him, so dear, indeed, that one insipid saying (often indelicate, coarse, rude, nauseous) he would repeat hundreds of times in all the possible dialects one after another through whole pages (and those

pages in his collection are not small, two columns in each), and I who was never a great master of the German language, had often consulted dictionaries to find out the meaning of the next proverb, when lo ! I found the same insipid proverb in a dialect spoken in some God-and-devil-forsaken hole ! "

In confirmation let me quote my own experience in the translation of Karl Wander's monumental *Sprichwörter Lexikon* by Miss E. Hyla Greves and Dr. M. Armfield. Out of some quarter of a million German proverbs and some thousands from other sources, we could only find 1,100 German worth retaining. One could go on multiplying this fact *ad infinitum*, but one further example must suffice : out of Adalberg's *Księga Przysłow Polskich*, containing some 30,000 proverbs, my translator, A. Przybyszewski, could only find just under 400 worth retaining. Not only has this very loose method of compilation existed in the past, but still obtains to-day, and in our own country, evidence of which can be found in two recent publications : *The Oxford Dictionary of English Proverbs*, by Wm. Geo. Smith (Oxford, 1935), and also *English Proverbs and Proverbial Phrases*, by G. L. Apperson (London, 1929). May I quote a few examples of " English Proverbs " taken at random from these works :

Old Nick.
Wait till you're asked.
John Bull.
Hard Cheese.
Home Rule, Home Rule !
Judge's Wigs.
Merry England.
I told you so.
Silly Billy.
Simple Simon.
Can't you hit the door ?
John-a-Nods.
Mum for that.
Noah's Ark.

It must surely be obvious that these are not proverbs at all, but simply trite, commonplace remarks. There are many true and beautiful English proverbs in these volumes, but one is compelled to sift a rubbish heap to find them. Is it to be wondered at that the average reader has neither time nor inclination to do this ? How much the seeker would benefit if compilers realized the wisdom of the Hindi Proverb : " Wheat has chaff on every grain." One of these volumes contains in addition a mass of foreign proverbs : Irish, Scottish, Hebrew, Greek, Arabic, Latin, French, Chinese, Italian, etc., e.g. :

Let the buyer beware. (Latin.)
He who rides on a tiger can never dismount. (Chinese.)
If a word be worth one shekel, silence is worth two. (Hebrew.)
Truth lies at the bottom of a well. (Greek.)
There are no fans in hell. (Arabic.)

There are hundreds of these. On what conceivable assumption does the compiler justify the inclusion of foreign proverbs which he classifies as such in a work of English Proverbs ? The only reason which I can suggest is that someone once quoted them in England. But does a rabbit become a dog if it is put into a kennel ?

Perhaps the inclusion of such an amazing conglomeration of extraneous material in compilations of proverbs can be partly accounted for and excused by the fact that there is, so far as I am aware, no clear and exact definition of a proverb. A proverb in my opinion is a racial aphorism which has been, or still is, in common use, conveying advice or counsel, invariably camouflaged figuratively, disguised in metaphor or allegory. I have been to considerable pains to trace the etymology of the word " Proverb ", and I give here a list of derivations and meanings of the word in various languages and dialects.

In ARABIC, " mat͟hal " or " tamt͟hal " signifies a proverb or simile and means a resemblance, " to make like ". It is essentially a " similitude " or " parable " describing human conduct in word pictures.

The word for " proverb " in BULGARIAN and SERBO-CROATIAN is, as in Russian, " poslovitsa " ; this is derived from the Slavonic " slovo ", meaning " word ", and begins with a prefix which may be represented by the English word " by ", and may be translated literally as " by-word ".

CHINESE consists of two almost distinct languages, the literary and the colloquial. The literary term for proverb in Chinese is " yen " or " yen yü ", elegant or accomplished words. In colloquial speech, " su-hua " (common talk) or " su-yü " (common saying).

The word for proverb in CZECH (plural and singular) is " přísloví " : " při "—" by ", " slovo "—" word " = a by-word, and " pořekadlo " and " říkadlo " = a saying.

EFÏK—" ñ'-ke " = a traditional story, a fable, parable, allegory or metaphor.

In ESTONIAN, " vana-sona " means an " old word ".

In FINNISH the word " sanalasku " (proverb) means the " dropping of a word ". " Sana "—" word " and " lasku "—" drop or let fall ".

The word for proverb which has established itself in modern literature in GEORGIA or SAK 'ART 'VELO, is " andaza ". This however is a Persian word " andāz " and denotes " example ", " form ". In ancient times the Georgian word " igavi " was used for both proverb and parable —also " moko ", which also denotes " allegorical ". " Igavi " is derived from " gav ", a later popular variant of " sgav ", the modern " gav-s " (it) resembles.

The GERMAN word " Sprichwörter " = (proverb) from " Sprach " (speech) and " Wort " (a word), " Redensart " = a figure of speech.

The GREEK " paroemia "—a trite roadside or wayside saying or expression or a " by-word ".

" Karim magna " is the HAUSA word for proverb, aphorism, by-play with words, turning and twisting the meaning of a word. The Hausas say : " This is the beginning of words which are taken and jumbled up (that a man may not know their meaning), and such is called ' Habaichi '—proverb."

In HEBREW, " mashal ", the word for proverb, has the same interpretation as in Arabic, viz. " to make like ", a proverb, a simile, or resemblance.

The HUNGARIAN "koz-mondas"—"common saying"; "pelda-beszed"—"example talking"; "koz-szolas"—"common or general sentence"; "szokas-mondas"—"usual saying".

Proverb in ICELANDIC is called "Orŏ̃skviŏ̃r".

In the IRISH—"sean fhocal", literally "an old word", but "word" in the primitive sense of a "saying". Hence "sean fhocal" is an ancient saying that has come down on the lips of the people from time immemorial.

In ITALIAN, as in Latin, the word "proverbio" signifies a proverb, "detto", saying. The Tuscan rendering being "dettato", i.e. something repeatedly said, this being a frequentative verb, for one generation tells it again and again to another for perpetual remembrance.

JABO word for proverb is "da'le'kpa"; same word is used for a "parable". The literal meaning of "da' le'kpa" is derived from "da'de'kpa", which means "old matters take"; to take old matters, apparently means to take an old situation and apply it to the present.

In JAPANESE we have "koto-waza" or "words that work", signifying a proverb.

In the LATIN—(from "pro"—"publicly" and "verbum"—"a word"). "Proverbium" signifies a saying in which a figurative expression is used in place of the plain word "proverbo".

In LETTISH, "proverb" is "sakamvārds"—"vārds" means "word" and "sakam" is really short for "sakamais", which is a kind of participle of the word "sacit". "Sakamais" would correspond in English to "repeatable" or "sayable". A proverb is therefore a sayable or repeatable word.

The word for proverb in LITHUANIAN is "partarle", derived from the verb "tarti"—"to say", "to utter".

The word "proverb" is usually expressed in MALAY by the word "umpama-an" or "pĕr-umpama-an", derivatives of the word "umpama". Wilkinson, in his Malay-English Dictionary, gives the meanings of "umpama" as "likeness, similarity, resemblance; a similar case; an example or instance". He gives the meanings of "umpama-an", or "pĕr-umpama-an", as "a proverb; a parable; a metaphorical example or story to illustrate a point". Proverbs are frequently introduced in writing by the expression "sapĕrti kata arif" = as say the wise; or by one of the following words, "sapĕrti" or "laksana" or "ibarat" or "bagei", all of which have the meaning of "like as", or "as it were".

The MAORI word for a proverb is "whakatauki", apparently composed of "whaka tau", to address in a formal speech, and "ki", to speak. ("Whaka" is a causative prefix.)

The MOORISH word for proverb is "miṯāl", plural "miṯālāt", meaning "similitude", also "similar".

In PERSIAN, as in all Muslim languages, the word for proverbs is "amsāl"; this is the plural of the Arabic word "masal". The root means in the first place to resemble or to reproduce. A proverb is therefore a saying which recalls something else.

In POLISH, " przysłowie " has exactly the meaning of the Greek " paroemia ", viz. " a trite roadside or wayside saying or expression " or " a by-word ".

The RONGA word for proverb is " šiga " (cp. Zulu " is-aga ", defined by Bryant as a " current saying or proverb, which suggests a second meaning not literally that of the words ") ; this definition fits the Ronga proverbs excellently.

The RUSSIAN word for " proverb " is " poslóvitsa " and for " proverbial expression ", " pogovórka ". The first-named may be translated literally as " by-word ", while the second could be rendered as " by-talk ".

A proverb in SANSKRIT is called " su-bhāsita ", meaning " well spoken word " or " fine saying ".

SERBO-CROATIAN (*see* BULGARIAN).

Proverbs are in SIĀM ranged under the generic designation of " sup'hāsit " (" subhāsit ", from the Pāli " su-bhāsito ", which has the same meaning as in Sanskrit, viz. " well spoken word ", " fine saying ".

In SPANISH, " refran ", which is a " referendo " from its frequency of repetition. " Proverbio " in Spanish signifies an apothegm, a maxim —not a proverb.

The word proverb in SWEDISH is " ordspråk " : " ord "—" word " and " språk "—" language ".

In SWAHILI the word for proverb is " methali ", " mathali ", " methili " or " misli ", from the Arabic, and is the same in the singular and plural, meaning emblem, parable, allegory or similitude.

The TURKISH word for a proverb, " atalar sözü ", literally means " grandfather's sayings " or " ancestral sayings " or " words " or " elder's words ".

The WELSH " dihareb " or " dihaereb " (plural " diarhebion ") means " a saying "—" to affirm or assert ".

In YORUBA " owe " = proverbs. " Alo " = riddles or play-upon words.

The Swedes have a saying which seems to me to be a very true interpretation—" A proverb says what man thinks."

Some of these old folk-sayings are of immense antiquity : the sayings in the *Book of the Dead* were in general use in Egypt as far back as 3700 B.C. Ptah-hotep in his precepts over 3,000 years before the Christian era has recorded many proverbs. Aristotle, one of the first known collectors of proverbs, more than 2,000 years ago spoke of them as " fragments of an elder wisdom ". To me their most striking characteristic lies in the extraordinary number which embody warnings against consequences (evidence of this will be found by reference to the Subject-matter Index) :

" It is the melancholy face that gets stung by the bee." (Japanese.)

" One half of the troubles in this world can be traced to saying ' yes ' too quick, and ' no ' not soon enough." (American, U.S.A.)

" If you look at men's faults you will have no friends." (Tamil.)

" The error of one moment becomes the sorrow of a whole life. (Chinese.)

" The sad man rose to enjoy himself but found no room." (Egyptian and Arabic.)

" What you have put into your kettle comes afterwards into your spoon." (Turfan and Arabic.)

These old saws are a strange medley of deep, indifferent *Opportunism*—

" Dawn does not come twice to awaken a man." (Arabic.)

" Always take the fee when the tear's in the eye." (Scottish.)

" The morning hour has gold in its mouth." (German, Estonian Livonian, etc.)

" Take the ball as it bounces." (French.)

" Be jogging while your boots are green." (English.)

" Winnow while the wind blows." (Tamil, Hindi.)

Fate—

" After the game the king and the pawn go into the same bag." (Italian and English.)

" What will be, will be." (Urdu.)

" What ever way you take, there is a league of bad road." (Spanish.)

" The beginning and the end reach out their hands to each other." (Chinese and other countries.)

" One passes by the cemetery so often that in the end one falls into it." (Russian.)

" Are the lines of the hand ever rubbed out ? " (Hindi.)

and subtle *Diplomacy*—

" When a neighbour is in your fruit garden, inattention is the truest politeness." (Chinese.)

" One ' No ' averts seventy evils." (Indian.)

" If you cannot shut the door again, do not raise the latch." (Turkish.)

" The wise man sits on the hole in his carpet." (Oriental.)

" Give over while the play's good." (Scottish.)

" Pick up the hen and you can gather all her chickens." (Ashanti warrior saying—Oji.)

added to which is a remarkable combination of *Courtesy*—

" Behave to everyone as if receiving a great guest." (Confucianism.)

" If your wife is small, stoop down and whisper in her ear." (Hebrew.)

" Bowing to a dwarf will not prevent your standing up again." (Hausa.)

" If we could all be courteous for even a single day the hatreds of humanity would turn to love." (Confucianism.)

" If you bow at all, bow low." (Chinese.)

" Being polite means taking nothing amiss." (Chinese.)

Charity and Kindliness—

" Don't look at a torn dress." (Malagasy.)

" When a friend asks there is no to-morrow." (English, etc.)

" Reconcile the offended, sew up the torn." (Hindi.)

" One good word can warm three winter months." (Japanese.)

" If given with love a handful is sufficient." (Telugu.)

" A kind word is like a Spring day." (Russian.)

" Blessèd man who says and does, his feet I hold close to my heart." (Chinese.)

" A good heart always does a little extra." (Chinese.)

Philosophy—

" Sour, sweet, bitter, pungent, all must be tasted." (Chinese.)

" Gnaw the bone which is fallen to thy lot." (Hebrew.)

" The wine is drawn it must be drunk." (French.)

" Want a thing long enough and you don't." (Chinese.)

" There's crust and crumb in every loaf." (English.)

" If you tickle yourself you can laugh when you like." (Russian and other countries.)

" A butting ox is better than a lonely bed." (Punjabi.)

Parœmiographers in the past have invariably arranged their material alphabetically according to the first letter of the first word of each proverb. Others have in addition grouped the proverbs according to subject-matter, such as : friendship, love, God, enmity, etc., etc. Some have included at the end of the book an index of the chief words, but the appalling amount of time wasted in searching for a particular proverb can be imagined when one realizes that there are over four hundred entries under one heading alone, all of which may have to be waded through before one can find the proverb one wants, as in the case of the *Oxford Dictionary of English Proverbs*. G. L. Apperson in his book, *English Proverbs and Proverbial Phrases*, has adopted a method of indexing based upon an extraordinary mixture of subject-matter and so-called " first significant word, with cross-references to exceptions ". The following list has been taken at random from this book :

I know what I do when I drink.
I made of my friend my foe.
Every man wishes water to his own mill.
Desperate diseases must have desperate cures.
No knaves and fools, if there were, all the world would be alike.
The best mirror is an old friend.
Cold as charity.
He that goes to bed thirsty riseth healthy.
In a quandary.

In no single case can be found any cross-references, nor are the proverbs arranged under any obvious subject-matter heading, and they are not arranged, in my opinion, under their very definite " significant words ". Could any of the above italicized words by any stretch of imagination be called " significant " ? To quote a few examples for which I was searching : " Desperate diseases must have desperate cures " I quite expected to find under " diseases ", but there is no mention of it under either " diseases " or " cures ", and after a prolonged search it was eventually found under " desperate ". " A broken apothecary, a new doctor " does not appear under " apothecary " or " doctor ", but is indexed under the adjective " broken ". " Never sigh but send " is under " never ". " Nothing is more easily blotted out than a good turn " is under " nothing ". With regard to the latter proverb, it is curious to note that there is one other proverb indexed under " Good turns "—" Good turns, One never loseth by doing " : if one, why not both ? Similar examples could be quoted *ad nauseam*, and the most extraordinary fact which strikes one is that a mass of material is correctly indexed under definite and obvious chief or " significant words ".

Intermittently, Mr. Apperson transposes parts of the proverbs apparently to bring the " first significant word " at the beginning, e.g. " *God* or a painter, He is either a, for he makes faces," and again—" Gropes in the dark, He that, finds that he would not." This most unfortunate transposition of the words completely spoils the beauty and rendering of the proverbs and makes the reading wearisome to a degree. It is much to be deplored that in this erudite and monumental compilation such a vast amount of interesting and beautiful material should be so inaccessible to the reader.

I hope I am not cherishing a delusion in believing that this work on Racial Proverbs (which embodies the first and second series of " Wayside Sayings ") will have the desired effect of supplying a long-felt readable, referable, want. My sole aim has been to select mainly the best, most interesting, and less-known proverbs, without including the commonplace or palpable truisms. I have, however, included a few idioms solely because of their beauty, e.g. " To sleep in the inn of the stars " (i.e. out of doors) (Spanish). " To smell of the baby " (i.e. not to outgrow one's childish ignorance) (English). " To make little loaves " (i.e. to say little in an important manner, to pay court to a woman) (French). " To drive the fairy chariot on a long journey " (i.e. to die) (Chinese). A considerable number will be found in the African section because the African proverbial speech is often expressed idiomatically. In addition I have included a section under " Religions ", to which an intensely interesting Introduction by P. Macleod Yearsley will be found on page lxxxviii, and an equally interesting extract from the preface to Robert Hume's *Treasure-house of the Living Religions* precedes this section. I realize that I am laying myself open to criticism in doing this, as, strictly speaking, a large number of the sayings of these old religious teachers have never, so far as I know, previously been designated as proverbs ; but on the other hand, many of the sayings of Confucius, Lao Tzŭ (founder of Taoism), Buddha and Mohammed are undoubtedly proverbial and in common use in the East. The same applies to the majority of the sayings taken from the Old and New Testaments and Apocrypha, many of which are in common use in our own country to-day. Christ Himself said (St. John xvi.), " These things have I (Jesus) spoken unto you in proverbs, but the time cometh when I shall no more speak unto you in proverbs." In St. Mark iv. is recorded—" Without a parable spake He not to the people." In the Korân is found (*chap.* ii. *v.* 24), " Verily, Allah disdaineth not to make any mathal (proverb) whatsoever, a gnat, yea, and less than that." Those sayings which cannot be designated as true proverbs I have, as in the case of the idioms, included because of their extreme beauty.

With regard to the collection under American, U.S.A., I realize that these, in the strict sense of the word, are not true proverbs, but rather " Americanisms " or colloquialisms, but in fact they are racial sayings and in common use in America. The South American proverbs were probably originally Spanish, but are and have been long current in South America.

A collection will be found in the Asiatic section entitled " Oriental ". This is a very loose classification, the proverbs being collected from varied sources and the exact country of origin unstated—simply designated as Oriental or Eastern. The same applies to India. A separate collection will be found in this section labelled " Indian ". The majority of these proverbs cannot be placed in their respective provinces, as I found them simply designated " Indian ".

In this work of mine, in order to facilitate easy reference, the proverbs belonging to different countries, races, or tribes, have been arranged linguistically, as far as possible, according to their country of origin, and put in Continental sections, the African section being preceded by a " language-family " index. A language-family map of Africa has also been included. In the case of one or two collections some difficulty has arisen with regard to their Continental placing, e.g. Romany, spoken wherever gipsies have wandered, I have placed in the Asiatic section, their origin being Hindu. Negro presents rather greater difficulty. The bulk of these proverbs originated in America and the West Indies, so have been included for convenience in the American section and not in the African. I have placed Arabic according to its Continental origin—Asia. Yiddish, being a jargon based on middle-high German, has been included with Europe.

Each proverb is arranged alphabetically through each collection according to the chief or catchword and subsequent word or words, so that each collection is therefore a complete index in itself. (A modified form of this method was adopted by Dr. Anderson and Mr. Cundall in their *Jamaica Negro Proverbs and Sayings*, London, 1927, and this book is certainly the most readable and referable proverb work I have ever read.) Where there are two or more chief words of equal importance the first has been chosen. I have further tried to avoid the use of any qualifying word immediately preceding the chief word. The late W. S. Stallybrass of Geo. Routledge & Sons, strongly advised me to index in the foregoing way, and he was, I believe, the first to introduce this method of indexing, which he used in his books of quotations, and which he claimed was the chief cause of their great popularity. I would, however, be very glad if any reader would be kind enough to suggest any method which would be an improvement on this. In order to make this work more referable and of greater utility to parœmiographers I have included a Subject-matter Index. Not in the manner compilers usually adopt of indexing under literal headings such as animals, trees and plants, utensils (kettles, ladles, etc.), which are only intended to be metaphorical or figurative and are not subject-matter at all. To illustrate this point let me quote a few examples taken from a delightful collection just published, Dr. Henry H. Hart's *700 Chinese Proverbs* (Stanford University Press, California, and London, 1937).

1. "The great tree attracts the wind." (Is under the heading Trees and Plants.)
2. "Don't loose the falcon until you see the hare." (Animal Kingdom.) (Advice to take ready money.)
3. "When eating bamboo sprouts, remember the man who planted them." (Food and Drink.)
4. "The crow does not roost with the Phœnix." (Animal Kingdom.)
5. "Crows are black the whole world over." (Animal Kingdom.)

The obvious subject-matter headings to the above are:

1. Vulnerability of position in life.
2. Materialism or Diplomacy.
3. Gratitude.
4. Inequality.
5. Instinct or heredity.

To take only one of these examples (No. 3), who would ever think of looking for a proverb of gratitude under "Bamboo sprouts" or "Food and drink"? By far the majority of compilations of proverbs are indexed in this extraordinary way. The method which I have adopted has been by no means easy, as in many cases not only is the metaphorical application obscure, but exactly the same proverb often occurs in different languages with a totally opposite or different application. One great difficulty which I have encountered (often insurmountable) is to interpret certain proverbs (and/or the application of such), the meaning of which is doubtful, but I have found in so many cases that compilers differ in their interpretations of the same proverb, and very often no explanation or application is given, as will be seen in the three examples given below:

(1) "The bullock does not get tired of his horns" [i.e. she is welcome back to his house]. (If a married man complain of his wife to her father and say that he is going to divorce her, this is the father's reply.) (Moorish.)

"Bull horn never too heavy for him head" [i.e. it is a bad sheep that is too lazy to carry its own fleece]. (Creole.)

"The elephant is not weighed down by his tusks" [i.e. the rich do not feel their wealth as a burden]. (Giryama and Ndau.)

"No elephant is overburdened by his own trunk" [i.e. a man won't admit a failure of his own idea]. (Zulu.)

"No elephant is overburdened by his own trunk" [i.e. a man is capable of bearing his own troubles]. (Xhosa.)

"An elephant is not borne down by its own tusks (or belly)" [i.e. a man is not borne down by his own responsibilities—family, money or troubles]. (Thonga.)

The same proverb occurs in Hindi, Swahili, Pedi, Haytian, Mauritius and other countries, with uncertain applications.

(2) " Under the lamp it is dark " [i.e. a good man has some blemish]. (Marathi.)

" There is darkness under the candle " [i.e. a good king, but bad ministers ; a good master but bad servants]. (Kashmiri.)

This proverb also occurs in Kumauni and Garhwali, Japanese, Chinese, Persian, Pashto, Turkish and others with uncertain application.

(3) " Coal gives birth to ashes " [i.e. a clever man may beget a fool]. (Thonga.)

" Fire begets ashes " [i.e. a father's deeds are often contradicted by his son]. (Thonga.)

" The fire leaves only ashes, and the rain leaves only roses " [i.e. children will be like their parents]. (Moorish.)

" Life, like fire, begins with smoke and ends with ashes " (Fate). (Arabic.)

The same proverb also occurs in Swahili, Lango and others with uncertain application.

Obviously, owing to their antiquity, the meaning of many of these old sayings we can only conjecture, and apply them as we think the circumstances demand.

In addition to the Subject-matter Index, there will be found an Alternative Chief-word Index, as very many proverbs contain two, three, four or more equally important chief, or catchwords, e.g. the Russian proverb—" Bread and salt together but each his own tobacco," is chief-worded under Bread, and alternatively under Salt and Tobacco. My one and only concern is that these unique, little-known and appreciated, earliest recorded thoughts of mankind should not suffer the inevitable tragic penalty of neglect and disuse—the gulf of oblivion. Immense numbers of proverbs have been saved from this fate—the result of the labours of parœmiographers, but in spite of this it is utterly impossible to compute the huge number lost. Even among such primitive people as the Sechuana of Bechuanaland, proverbial speech is fast dying out. In the Preface to Mr. Solomon J. Plaatje's book of Sechuana Proverbs, published in 1916, is to be found the following statement : " It is the author's belief that had these aphorisms been collected thirty years ago, this book could have been enlarged to nearly three times its size. With the spread of European speech and thought in South Africa, these primitive saws are fast being forgotten." " Vox audita perit, littera scripta manet."

Patrick Pichi Sun in his foreword to Dr. H. H. Hart's *700 Chinese Proverbs*, published in 1937, mentions that on the authority of Scarborough there are as many proverbs current in China as in the whole of Europe—over 20,000. An amazing statement ! A reference to Stephen and Bonsor's Bibliography of proverbs would at once show how utterly wrong and misleading such a statement is. This bibliography records some, but by no means all, of the European compilations ; the number of proverbs contained in them runs into millions. The writers of the Introductory Forewords in my book give definite information regarding this point. Colonel Bäckström has made a collection of thirty thousand Swedish proverbs which he states contains nothing like all his country's proverbs. Mr. A. Guershoon states that there are more than sixty thousand recorded in the Great Russian language. Mrs. Tuomikoski tells us that the Finnish Literature Society and Dictionary Endowment have now in their possession one million, four hundred and fifty thousand Finnish proverbs. Over one hundred and ten thousand Estonian proverbs are in the possession of the Estonian Folk-Lore Archives. In 1880 Karl Wander brought out his *Sprichwörter Lexikon*, which contains some forty-five thousand German proverbs in each of its five volumes. The recorded proverbs of these five European countries alone amounts to nearly two millions.

Proverbial wisdom is exactly the same all the world over, differing only in the rendering. " Men are all made of the same paste " (Dacian). Fundamentally, psychologically, they are the same, Oriental or Occidental, pigmented or white. Love, hunger and fear are the basic factors that rule mankind, primitive or cultured ; factors uninfluenced by environment or civilization. All the civilization of the ages will not eradicate the primary instincts of mankind. A study of proverbial racial folk-lore provides overwhelming evidence of this similarity. The same proverb conveying the same piece of advice recurs again and again in the indigenous aphorisms of all tribes and races. Hundreds of examples could be quoted, but a few only will suffice now to emphasize this point :—

(1) " Health goes in puds and comes back in zolotniks " (pud = 40 Russian lbs. ; zolotnik = 1/96th of a lb.). (Russian.)

" Diseases come on couriers' horses, but go away on tired oxen." (Estonian.)

" Ill luck enters by fathoms and departs by inches." (Spanish.)

" Evil comes to us by ells and goes away by inches." (English.)

" It comes through an elephant's mouth and goes through an ant's." (Hindustani.)

Variants of this proverb occur in Russian, Sindhi, Creole, French, Serbo-Croatian, Siamese, Swedish, Chuana, Walloon, Dutch, German, English, Italian, French, Mauritius, Jamaican, Polish, Wallachian, Spanish, Marathi, Slovakian and others.

(2) " You a lady, I a lady, who is to bed the sow ? " (Galician.)

" I am an esquire, you are an esquire, who will harness the horses ? " (Turkish.)

" If I am a master and you are a master, who shall drive the asses ? " (Arabic.)

" I stout [i.e. proud] and thou stout, who shall bear the ashes out ? " (English.)

" If I am to be prince, and you are to be prince, who is to drive the donkey ? " (Egyptian.)

" If I be a queen and thou be a queen, who will bang the butter ? " (Punjabi.)

" You a lady, and I a lady, who will milk the cow ? " (Serbian.)

"I master, you master, who shall clean the boots?" (German.)
"I a gentleman, you a gentleman, who then is the carrier of the sack?" (Estonian.)

Variants of this proverb occur in Kashmiri, Kumauni and Garhwali, Danish, Telugu, Armenian, German, Finnish, Hindustani, Swedish, Slovakian, Czech and others.

(3) "One day a guest, two days a guest, the third a nuisance." (Urdu.)
"Fresh fish and new-come guests smell in three days." (English.)
"Guests and fish will get old on the third day." (Estonian.)
"After three days fish and a guest who tarries become odious." (Czech.)
"After three days, a woman, a guest and the rain become very tiresome." (Latin.)
"Guests and fish stink on the third day." (Montenegrin.)
"One day a guest, two days a guest, the third day a nuisance." (Mohammedan).

The same proverb occurs in Slovakian, Punjabi, Marathi, Montenegrin, Dutch, Danish, Basque, Portuguese, Swiss, Hindi, Hindustani, Spanish, French, Italian, Scottish and others.

Archbishop Trench in his book, *On the Lessons in Proverbs* (London, 1854), Chap. 2, talks of the versification, borrowing and mutual interchange of proverbs between nations. "A free giving and taking, in which it is often hard and oftener impossible, to say which is the lender and which the borrower. Thus the quantity of proverbs not drawn from antiquity, but common to all, or nearly all of the modern European languages is very great." He attempts to prove, *inter alia*, that an old Greek proverb is the father of proverbs in other languages when they express the same piece of counsel or advice. "There is indeed nothing in the study of proverbs, in the attribution of them to their right owners . . . which creates a greater perplexity than the circumstances of finding the same proverb in so many different quarters, current among so many different nations . . . (it is) impossible to determine to what nation it first belonged." This view is shared by many other parœmiographers, I think quite erroneously.

I firmly believe that the similarity or parallelism of racial proverbs is the main reason which has influenced parœmiographers of the past to conclude that these old folk sayings have been borrowed or transfused by one nation or tribe from another, but as Elliot-Smith said, "similar conditions lead to similar cultures"—"As the country, so the proverb." (German). "As the people, so the proverb" (Scottish). The Masai say, "The bark of one tree will not adhere to the bark of another tree" (i.e. the people of one tribe cannot assimilate the customs or proverbs of another).

It is beyond the realms of possibility that the Occident borrowed from the Orient, or vice versa, and yet these proverbial sayings are exactly the same, differing only in the figurative expression or metaphor. A certain small amount of diffusion undoubtedly has taken place where one nation or tribe conquered another or as a result of intermarriage.

If Proverbs have been borrowed, surely it must necessarily follow that Fairy-Tales have also been borrowed and that " The Story of Cinderella " has been actually borrowed by sixty-four different nations, and variants of it by three hundred and forty-five others (on the authority of Miss M. B. Cox in " Cinderella ", 1893). This would suggest that this delightful fairy-tale has been the subject of an orgy of borrowing —viz. four hundred and nine times ! There are more than four hundred variants falling into three groups. " Cinderella ", the ill-treated heroine, recognized by a shoe or a ring. " Catskin ", the heroine who flies from an unnatural father, and " Cap o' Rushes " which embodies the King Lear Judgement and connects up with " The Outcast Child " cycle of stories. These stories are, " Cindrillon " (French) ; " Rashin Coatie " (Scottish) ; " Catskin ", " Peu d'Âne " (L'ile St. Maurice and Corsica) ; " Cap o' Rushes " (Irish and English) ; " La Sendrarœula " (Palermo) ; " Loving like Salt " (Venice) ; " Turkey Girl " (Azenais) ; " Johnny of the Bark " (Spain) ; " Salt and Bread " (Sweden) ; " Value of Salt " (Italy, Rome) ; " Blear Eye " (Italy) ; " Story of the Candlestick " (Bologna) ; " Screw of Salt " (Abruzzi) ; " She Sweeps the Oven " and " Dirty Skin " (Belgium), and others from Swabia, Haute Bretange, Jersey. Cinderella also has affinities with Hestia (Roman " Vesta "), the Greek " Hearth Goddess ", daughter of Cronos and Rhea (who was the daughter of Uranus and Ge), who probably represents the earth, so that it is impossible to say how far she goes back before she becomes encrusted with later ideas. The Joseph story in the Old Testament is one of this group, and there is one in Brazil, others in Persia, India, Kashmir, Serbia, Russia, etc. Similar stories occur among the Hausas and Red Indians (the most beautiful of the Cinderella stories comes from the Mic Macs—a branch of the Algonquins). It is impossible to say which is the oldest version of Cinderella, it is such a medley of folk tale, showing such diversity. There is the outcast child part which itself is pretty old ; the " youngest best " which takes one back to the inheritance by the youngest (" Borough English "). Not only " The Story of Cinderella " but many other fairy-tales are common to many nations. They all connect up with other tales and especially with the helpful beast motif and many classical and other tales.

If one takes the Bluebeard and Forbidden Chamber cycle the similar world-wide ideas are found—and with Greek, Tuscan, Basque, Russian, Red Indian, Italian, Tyrolese, Swiss, Icelandic, Gaelic, Sicilian, Slavonic, African, Malagasian, English, Lithuanian (as " Mary's Child ") variants, some showing Christian influence.

Similarly the Separable Soul and Life-Token Tales are world-wide, as are also Rumpelstilzchen and the Swan Maidens. No doubt these tales have been handed down for ages (indeed the Separable Soul Story of " The Two Brothers " is found in the d'Orbiney papyrus of about the fourteenth century B.C.). I think it is quite permissible to suggest that the incidents they tell may have been invented separately.

A study of the religious beliefs of the world reveals the same striking similarities found in proverbs and fairy-tales. There is no saying of Christ which is not paralleled in earlier religions. The foundations of all religions are practically identical (this subject has been very ably dealt with in Macleod Yearsley's scholarly *Story of the Bible*, London, 1933). Where one gets identity of phrasing in the sacred literatures it may suggest borrowing, but it does not necessarily mean that the fundamental idea was borrowed, but merely the clothing of the idea may have been taken as more suitable, ornamental or apt. As Swift said, "They are only the same garments more or less embroidered."

My greatest difficulty in compiling this work has been translation. Not only with regard to the material, but also in discovering suitable translators, in which I have been more than fortunate, because, as the Italians say: "Translators—traitors." My translators have made it a rule to translate literally and thus maintain the original sense and beauty of the proverbs, but it must be realized that it is often absolutely impossible to render into English many primitive and Oriental proverbs without completely spoiling them.

A bibliography will be found at the beginning of this book. This is by no means representative, as there are several hundred other books which I have read and had translated, from which I obtained no material whatever. Many of these books contained only European equivalents, which I have omitted entirely, as they are not translations. Further, many hundreds of the proverbs included in this work of mine have been supplied by collectors, teachers, missionaries, doctors, clergymen, playwrights, authors, librarians, etc., from private collections which, as far as I know, have never been previously put into print, having been collected from the lips of the people. I myself have collected many in this way. In addition, a number have been given by my patients, taken from novels, books of travel, newspapers, journals, periodicals, etc. These sources could not of course be included in the bibliography. A very large number of the proverbs have never before, so far as I am aware, been translated into English nor published in this language, e.g. The late Rev. W. E. Taylor's collections of Swahili and Giryama proverbs, translated by the late Professor Alice Werner. During his lifetime, the Rev. W. E. Taylor also supplied me with a large cosmopolitan collection which was never before published. A Columbian collection was given by Dr. A. J. Restrepo. The entire Estonian collection and also most of the Livonian collection (both hitherto unpublished) were supplied by Professor Osker Loorits, Director of the Folk-Lore Archive, Eesti Rahva Museum, Tartu, Estonia. Dr. Lionel Giles sent me his own unpublished collection of over a thousand Chinese proverbs. The late W. M. Petrovitch, B.A., supplied an unpublished collection of Montenegrin which he collected from the lips of the peasants of that country, together with other Slavonic ones. Dr. A. Worsley of Birmingham, a Sudanese collection. The entire Yoruba collection was supplied by N. A. Fadipe; many of the proverbs he collected from the lips of the natives, the remainder we owe to his translations. Dr. T. Browning of Kilkee, Co. Clare, Ireland, an Irish collection. Miss

Marion S. Stevenson, a Kikuyu collection. P. Macleod Yearsley, Jersey and Guernsey collections. Miss W. Jakibickova of the Czech Legation, a Czech collection. J. Schnyder of Lucerne, Switzerland, a Swiss collection and others. Lieut.-Colonel C. Bäckstrõm, a Swedish collection. Two works on Irish proverbs—" *Seanfhocail na Muimneach* ", by An Seabhac, Dublin (Cork, 1926) and " *Sean Fhocal Uladh* " by Henry Morris (Dublin, 1907) (the former translated by the author and the latter by James Gallaher) have never before been translated nor published in the English language, so far as I am aware. The same applies to the majority of the Finnish proverbs translated by Mrs. A. Tuomikoski of Tampere, Finland ; the majority of the Russian and the whole of the Kalmyk translated by A. Guershoon, LL.B. ; the majority of the Polish proverbs translated by A. Przybyszewski ; C. A. Mackehenie, a Peruvian collection ; the entire Lettish collection translated by Miss M. Grosvald of Riga, Latvia. The same can probably be said of a large proportion of the proverbs of many other countries.

I owe a deep debt of gratitude to the foregoing collaborators, especially to the late Professor Alice Werner of the School of Oriental Studies, without whose invaluable aid in supplying material in the African section, advice as to arrangement, grouping and classification, and for years past translating and correcting translations, I do not think it would have been possible to have produced an accurate and representative African section. Since her untimely decease her sister, Miss M. H. Werner, has filled the gap and (with the collaboration of other African authorities) has completed the work which Professor Alice was unable to finish ; she has also assisted with the language map of Africa. It is difficult to find words to express my thanks for this most invaluable assistance. The Language Map of Africa is based on Cust's Map and the drawing up of it was done by Dr. A. N. Tucker of the School of Oriental Studies. He has also given very valuable assistance with the whole African section. I am most grateful for his kind services. I should also like to make special mention of equally valuable services rendered by Andrew Ivanovich Guershoon, LL.B., Medallist of St. Petersburg University, who was born in Russia and spent his youth and early life in that country. He is responsible for almost the whole of the Russian translations and Kalmyk translations, and for many years he has helped and advised me in other directions. A very interesting and informative Foreword from his pen will be found to the Russian collection on page xcv. He has my most grateful thanks.

It would not have been possible to have compiled this work without the aid of *Proverb Literature*, a bibliography of works relating to proverbs, by W. Bonser, B.A., Ph.D., and the late R. A. Stephens (London, 1928). This unique and masterful compilation of the world's proverb literature is indispensable to the parœmiographer.

A similar meed of praise must be given to S. C. Coles of Messrs. Kegan Paul, Trench, Trubner & Co. of London, who for many years has rendered the greatest service in discovering for me an enormous amount of little-known Oriental and foreign proverb literature, and who has been of invaluable assistance in supervizing the classification and arrangement of the whole work.

I wish to thank the writers of the various Introductions. These invaluable contributions have added in a very great measure to the interest of this work, and I value and appreciate immensely their kind services.

I acknowledge with grateful thanks the services of the Librarians and Secretaries of many Libraries and Societies in the British Isles, and abroad, also Consuls and Secretaries of all Consulates and Legations in London, and the following translators, collaborators and helpers :

Ali Riza Bey. School of Oriental Studies, London (Turkish translations).

Dr. T. G. R. Andringa. Amsterdam. (Information, Dutch.)

Professor Aarne Anttila. Secretary, Society of Finnish Literature, Helsinki, Finland. (Information, Finnish.)

Dr. M. M. Armfield. Bournemouth. (German and other translations.)

N. T. Balabanov. Sofia, Bulgaria. (Information and advice and material, Bulgarian.)

Professor J. Balčikonis, of University of Vytantas the Great, Lithuania. (Information and assistance, Lithuanian.)

E. A. Reynolds Ball. Supplied Italian material.

Late Sir J. Ballinger. National Library of Wales, Aberystwyth. (Supplied books and information, Welsh.)

Lieut.-Colonel C. A. Bäckstrõm. Stockholm. (Sent collection, Swedish. Wrote foreword to Swedish collection.)

Risdon Bennett, M.A. Broadstone, Dorset. (Latin translations.)

M. Beza. Roumanian Legation. (Sent own book, Roumanian.)

Professor Emilio Bodrero, Ph.D. Professor, Royal University of Padua. (Wrote introduction to Italian proverbs.)

Miss O. Bottomley. Bournemouth. (Rendered invaluable clerical assistance for past twenty years.)

Dr. T. Browning. Kilkee, Co. Clare, Ireland. (Supplied an Irish collection hitherto unpublished.)

Mrs. G. Butt (*née* Yates). (My secretary.) (Many years' all-round valuable assistance.)

T. Clifford. Bournemouth. (Dutch translations.)

Rev. Henry Coles. Hastings. (Material and translations, Gogo.)

A. R. Cook, B.A., B.Sc. (Luganda translations.)

Sir J. Howard Cook. (Material and translations, Luganda.)

Rev. W. A. Crabtree. Cambridge. (Luganda translations.)

R. D. Crail. Consul-General, Siamese Consulate, London. (Sent collection, Siamese, also information.)

Rev. F. L. Cross. Oxford. (German translations.)

Frank Cundall, O.B.E., F.S.A., F.R.Hist.S. Librarian of the Institute of Jamaica. (Wrote introduction to Negro proverbs.)

P. W. Cushion, B.A. Bournemouth. (Translations, Greek.)

Canon Godfrey Dale. (Material and translations, Swahili and Bondei.)

W. Ll. Davies, M.A. Librarian, National Library of Wales, Aberystwyth. (Assistance, Welsh.)

Professor J. H. Driberg. Cambridge. (Assistance, African.)

Miss Margaret S. Demchevsky. Sofia, Bulgaria. (Bulgarian translations.)

Rev. V. Ellenberger. Basutoland, S. Africa. (Sent book, Sechuana, also translated and supplied material, Se-Suto.)

Professor Aurelio M. Espinosa, Ph.D., Litt.D., LL.D. Professor of Romanic Languages. Stanford University, California. (Wrote introduction to Spanish proverbs.)

N. A. Fadipe. School of Oriental Studies, London. (Sent own collection, Yoruba, also translations. Assistance, West African classifications.)

Mrs. A. H. Forster. Bournemouth. (Over twenty years' valuable assistance in obtaining material.)

Professor R. Firth, M.A. School of Economics, London. (Information, advice and material, Polynesian.)

C. A. Franklin, of Messrs. George Routledge & Sons. (Interest and help during preparation of this work for publication.)

James Gallaher. Donnybrook, Dublin. (Irish translations.)

Miss D. Galtin. School of Slavonic Studies, London. (Information, Slavonic.)

Dr. Moses Gaster. (Information, Roumanian.)

Professor H. A. R. Gibb, M.A. Professor of Arabic at the University of Oxford. (Wrote introduction to Arabic proverbs.)

Lionel Giles, M.A., D.Litt. British Museum. (Wrote introduction to Chinese proverbs and contributed large private collection. Also valuable assistance and supervision.)

Miss E. Hyla Greves. Bournemouth. (Invaluable service in translation of most European languages [except Slavonic] for past twenty years.)

Dr. Otto V. Greyerz. Bern. (Swiss information.)

Miss Marguerite Grosvald. Riga. (Translations, material and information, Lettish. Wrote introduction to Lettish proverbs.)

Andrew Ivanovich Guershoon, LL.B. London. Medallist of St. Petersburg University. (Many years' invaluable assistance. Responsible for translation of practically whole Russian collection, also Kalmyk. Advised *re* Slavonic classification. Wrote foreword to Russian collection.)

A. Gugushvili. (Wrote introduction to Georgian proverbs.)

A. W. Hamilton. Chislehurst, Kent. (Assistance, Malay. Sent own book.)

K. Hanbergs. Riga. (Books and information, Lettish.)

Professor Aage Hansen, Ph.D. Charlottenbund. (Translations and information, Danish.)

Miss M. M. Hasluck. London. (Assistance, Albanian.)

A. Hegedus. London. (Hungarian translations.)

Miss S. G. A. Henriques. Gillingham, Kent. (Supplied Persian material.)

Melville J. Herskovits. Associate Professor of Anthropology, N.W. University, Evanston, Illinois, U.S.A. (Information, Negro.)

Professor Otto Höfler. Professor of History of German Literature at Kiel University, Germany. (Wrote introduction to German collection.)

E. S. Hose, C.M.G. Guildford, Surrey. (Assistance, Malay. Wrote foreword to Malay proverbs.)

Rev. J. A. Houlder. Worthing. (Information, Malagasy.)

Miss W. Jakubickova. London. (Sent own collection, Czech, also responsible for translation of most of Czech collection.)

F. Johnson. Librarian, University College Library and Folk-Lore Society Library. (Rendered valuable assistance for many years, granting me free use of both libraries.)

J. J. Jones, M.A. Deputy Keeper of the Department of Printed Books, National Library of Wales, Aberystwyth. (Wrote introduction to Welsh proverbs.)

Professor T. Gwyn Jones. Aberystwyth. (Information, Welsh.)

Professor N. B. Jopson. Professor of Comparative Philology, Cambridge University. (Information and assistance, Slavonic.)

Professor Kochi Doi. Professor of Literature Tohoku Imperial University, Japan. (Wrote introduction to Japanese proverbs.)

Professor K. Kraus. Prague. (Assistance, Czech.)

Dr. Carlos Larroude. Lisbon. (Advice and material, Portuguese.)

R. le May. London. (Information *re* Siamese and Tai.)

Professor Osker Loorits. Director, Estonian Folk-Lore Archive, Easti Rahva Museum, Tartu, Estonia. (Supplied entire Estonian collection, also most of Livonian. Wrote foreword to Estonian collection.)

C. A. Mackehenie. Peruvian Consulate, London. (Sent own collection, Peruvian, also advice.)

Rev. G. T. Manley and Mrs. C. Manley. (Sent books and material, Hindi and Hindustani.)

Robert R. Marett, D.Sc., LL.D., F.B.A., M.A. Rector of Exeter College, Oxford. (Wrote introduction to African section.)

J. Marshall. Belfast. (Collections and assistance, Irish.)

M. Martinez-Moles. Havana. (Sent own book, Cuban.)

Rev. W. R. Miller. Nigeria. (Assistance, Nigerian.)

Dr. W. A. Morison. School of Slavonic Studies. (Slavonic and Eastern European information.)

Henry Morris, M.A. Dublin. (Information and assistance, Irish. Wrote foreword to Irish collection.)

Miss O. Murray Brown. Librarian, School of Oriental Studies. (Valuable assistance for many years, granting me free use of Library.)

J. Musleg. Academia Romana, Arhiv de Folklor, Cluj. (Sent book, Roumanian.)

Late Rev. C. N. Nowers, M.A. (Translations and advice on various sections.)

A. F. McDonnell. Auckland, N.Z. (Sent book, Maori.)

Late W. M. Petrovich, M.A. (Translations and assistance, Montenegrin, Serbian, Albanian, Bulgarian, Bosnian, Herzegovinian, Croatian, Slovenian, Ukrainian, Czech.)

Sir Bernard Pares, K.B.E., M.A. School of Slavonic Studies, London. (Revised Russian translations.)

A. Przybyszewski. London. (Translations, Polish. Wrote foreword to Polish collection.)

Dr. H. N. Randle, Ph.D., M.A. India Office. (Valuable assistance, supervising and classifying Indian collection. Wrote foreword to this section.)

Dr. A. J. Restrepo. Delegate to League of Nations, Geneva. (Sent own collection, Columbian, also own book.)

Sir E. Denison Ross, C.I.E., D.Litt., Ph.D. School of Oriental Studies. (Wrote introduction to Persian proverbs.)

Darío Rubio. Mexico. (Sent own book, Mexican.)

Professor Denis Saurat, D. ès L. Professor of King's College, London. (Wrote introduction to French proverbs.)

J. Schnyder. Lucerne, Switzerland. (Supplied most of the Swiss material and translations, and wrote foreword to Swiss proverbs.)

An Seabhac. Dublin. (Translation own book, Irish.)

TOWNLEY SEARLE. London. (Sent own book, Chinese, also material.)

REV. J. SHARMAN. Tananarive. (Advice *re* Malagasy.)

BISHOP SIBREE, D.D., F.R.G.S. Madagascar. (Translated and advised *re* Malagasy and Betsimisarak.)

DR. L. SIMA. (Hungarian translations.)

Late W. S. STALLYBRASS of George Routledge & Sons, London. (Invaluable all-round assistance and interest in material, classification, indexing, etc.)

MISS MARION S. STEVENSON. (Sent own collection, Kikuyu.)

MRS. I. H. A. STURT. Librarian, Church Missionary Society Library. (Valuable assistance for many years granting me free use of the Library.)

Late REV. W. E. TAYLOR. (Sent collections of Swahili and Giryama, also Negro, Dyak and other collections and translations.)

PROFESSOR VILMOS TOLNAI. University of Pécs. (Wrote foreword to Hungarian collection and supplied Hungarian material.)

S. TOPALIAN. School of Oriental Studies, London. (Wrote introduction to Turkish collection.)

A. N. TUCKER, Ph.D. School of Oriental Studies, London. (Assistance, classification African, also assistance and supervision, African Map.)

MRS. AINO TUOMIKOSKI, M.A. Tampere, Finland. (Finnish material and translations. Wrote foreword to Finnish collection.)

COUNSELLOR TURKISH EMBASSY. London. (Supplied Turkish material, also advice.)

LIBRARIAN VAJIRAVUDH. Royal Institute of Literature, Archæology and Fine Arts, Bangkok, Siam. (Advice *re* Siamese.)

PROFESSOR J. VERCOULLIE. Ghent. (Information, Flemish and Walloon.)

A. VIDAKOVIC. Belgrade. (Selection and supervizing Serbian translations.)

IDA WARD, D.Litt. School of Oriental Studies, London. (Assistance, West African section, also language map.)

Late PROFESSOR ALICE WERNER. School of Oriental Studies, London. (Supervision, entire African section, also innumerable translations and vast amount of material supplied.)

MISS M. H. WERNER. School of Oriental Studies, London. (Supervision, African section and language map of Africa. Varied translations.)

PROFESSOR EDWARD WESTERMARCK, Ph.D., LL.D. (Wrote introduction to Moorish proverbs.)

L. C. WHARTON, M.A. Librarian, School of Slavonic Studies, London. (Information *re* Slavonic section.)

MISS AUDREY WHITE. Central Literature Committee for Moslems, Cairo. (Information *re* Arabic.)

PROFESSOR IFOR WILLIAMS. University College of North Wales, Bangor. (Supplied Welsh material and information.)

W. D. WILLIAMS. Swansea. (Welsh translations.)

REV. H. W. WOODWARD. Orange Free State. (Sent Bondei and other African proverbs.)

DR. A. WORSLEY. Birmingham. (Supplied a Sudanese collection hitherto unpublished.)

C. F. WORTERS. Croydon. (Sent various books and materials.)

DR. DUDLEY WRIGHT. Oxford. (Translations, Tamil and others.)

SIR HAGBERG WRIGHT. Librarian, London Library. (Rendered valuable assistance to myself and translators.)

P. MACLEOD YEARSLEY, F.R.C.S., F.Z.S., London. (Supplied Jersey and Guernsey material. Wrote foreword to Religions.)

I am afraid that a number of names may have been inadvertently omitted from my lists of kind helpers and collaborators, but over twenty-five years have elapsed since I first started on this big task, and I tender them my sincere apologies and would crave their indulgence for this omission.

I would be most grateful if any parœmiographers would very kindly send me any good proverbs, not included in this work, or if possible lend me any collections they may possess. It is inevitable that in a work of this size and complexity errors must occur, and I would greatly appreciate any criticism, advice or suggestions that would help to make this work more attractive and of greater utility as a book of reference, so that in the years to come parœmiographers may not find " Racial Proverbs " on the dusty shelves of libraries with its pages uncut, as was frequently the case with many works of reference which we consulted in most of the libraries !

Although these twenty-six thousand proverbs have been selected from one hundred and eighty-six languages and dialects, I would like it to be clearly understood that this work makes no claim to be a full and complete compilation of the world's best racial aphorisms. Some languages and dialects are not represented at all ; others are numerically inadequate. This is due to the dearth of written material in some cases, and the impossibility of discovering competent translators for the less-known languages and dialects.

I further realize that the value of this book would have been enhanced had the material been given in the originals as well as translations, but in many of the works consulted and in collections given only translations were supplied, and I consider that it would not have been satisfactory to have provided on the one hand originals and translations, and on the other hand translations only, so I very reluctantly decided to omit the originals.

Before the sands run out, it is my hope and ambition to compile a book of idioms as distinct from a book of proverbs. Another work which I feel ought to be undertaken is to make a comparative study of proverbs, but this, I fear, is quite beyond my limited capabilities, and is a task only for the expert.

SELWYN GURNEY CHAMPION.

FRAMFIELD,
SUSSEX.
APRIL 1938.

INTRODUCTION TO THE PROVERBS OF AFRICA

By ROBERT R. MARETT, D.Sc., LL.D., F.B.A., M.A.

WHILE I am entirely in sympathy with Dr. Gurney Champion's object in introducing to the public the proverb as a vehicle of the world's culture in its most concentrated and communicable form, I am not sure how far my own studies fall into line with his, and can but hope that the following remarks will be found to be more or less relevant.

An anthropologist is a tedious fellow who finds almost as much grist for his mill in bad proverbs as in good ones. It is not for him to extract the gold from the dross, so long as the material is authentic evidence of how a given people actually speaks, thinks and believes. Nay, what from a civilized point of view seems crude, or even downright stupid, may yet for the folk concerned be the very quintessence of their peculiar wit and wisdom.

Again, translation into a polite tongue may prove wellnigh impossible where the native idiom indulges in obscure figures, or in allusions to current custom, so that a line of text calls for a page of commentary. One is apt to forget, too, that a primitive proverb, if it be of the home-grown type, usually has a special context, divorced from which it loses half its meaning.

It may make all the difference to the sense to know who says it ; and when, where and why it is said just so. Often some pregnant byword represents the pith of a long story, as when a whole beast fable of the kind dear to the African heart, is echoed in a few words put into the mouth of the animal in question—*verbum sapientibus*, in fact.

Apart from such considerations which bear directly on interpretation as a pre-requisite of appreciation, the anthropologist has many reasons for regarding proverbs as among the most important of his data. For one thing, a key to linguistic usage is to be found in them, more especially as their crystalline quality, so to speak—the fixed and enduring shape to which folk-memory aided by folk-humour, has reduced them—causes them to be retentive of ancient forms that may be of great philological interest.

Or again, a whole cultured anthropology may be written round them in so far as they contain references to religion, magic, marriage, government, law, arts and crafts, and in short, every element that enters into the social life. Above all, they can serve as documents of a history, otherwise unrecorded.

Given a real proverb—not merely a happy phrase invented for the occasion, but a recognized adage that has become the property and pride of the collective intelligence—it is to be reckoned an integral part of the tribal life, and as such can testify to the development of that life as moulded partly by internal and partly by external forces. Thus, if it bear all the marks of an indigenous origin, it is a fair inference that it belongs to a culture well enough established to have attained to a certain individuality.

If, on the other hand, there are foreign counterparts that point to diffusion from some common centre, which may or may not be the area responsible for the version with which we are more particularly concerned, ethnic contacts have to be postulated which must involve the tracing of the movements of peoples over a wide region.

It is well known that stories, songs, riddles and so forth, are objects of spiritual barter even between artless folk for whom bilingual communications must offer considerable difficulty; and there is no reason why the wise saw should not be swapped in like manner when the representatives of alien groups foregather. Nay, to chase a proverb home might invite a world's tour; while, since time no less than space must be traversed in such a quest, one might have to seek back from the cottager to the cave man for the true authorship of some pawky sentiment on which simple minds have ever since been content to ring the changes.

As for Africa, none of the five great continents is more heterogeneous in its ethnic composition, so that its proverbial philosophy cannot be but on the face of it a cento—in other words, a patchwork of precious fragments from numberless tribal wardrobes rejoicing in as many distinct patterns and hues of raiment. As in some museum we may treat an assortment of art treasures as a general guide to the æsthetic standards of an epoch, regardless of the plurality of styles that it may comprise, so from the African collection we may gather that up and down Africa the mind of man reacts as shrewdly as elsewhere to vital situations which, for unsophisticated folk, at any rate, do not greatly differ over the surface of the globe.

Thus, whatever the diversity of human manners, morals are more uniform than one might expect, as witness these very proverbs.

Whether we put our faith in certain eternal values or not, a survey of the actual valuations of character and conduct to which mankind has been led by sheer experience of the conditions of the good life and its opposite brings out the fact that, racially, we have one and all eaten of the same tree of the knowledge of good and evil. Proverbs, indeed, are the fruit thereof, served delicately in succulent morsels.

So too, then, these African specimens, flavoured though they be by the soil in which they were grown, derive their magic power from that universal faculty of plain common sense that has kept our species not only alive but dominant down the long ages.

R. R. MARETT.

RECTOR OF EXETER COLLEGE,
OXFORD.

INTRODUCTION TO THE PROVERBS OF ARABIA

By PROFESSOR H. A. R. GIBB, M.A.

THE Arabic "mathal" is essentially a "similitude" or "parable", which describes human conduct in word-picture, usually taken from the animal world. In such terse and allusive phrases the Arabs of the desert, sharp-eyed observers of the world around them, found scope for that play of the imagination which is a natural craving amongst all races of men. The emotional appeal of the vivid and apposite simile is to be seen in all that has come down to us of their poetry, and even in the Korân, where the same device is constantly employed to drive home both arguments and precepts. "Verily Allah disdaineth not to make any 'mathal' whatsoever, a gnat, yea, and less than that" (Korân, chap. ii, v. 24).

The "mathal" as proverb and the "mathal" as simile thus shade into one another, and it is often difficult to draw the dividing-line between them. For the art of the Arab has always been his speech, and with that intense feeling for words that is his birthright, the striking simile coined for the occasion by poet or orator rapidly acquires currency as a proverb. The element of simile is present also in the large and characteristic class of Arabic proverbial phrases formed of reminiscences of historical or legendary persons and of comparisons on the model of "More open-handed than Hātim Tai." But alongside these there is a host of maxims, especially on matters of social relationships, in which the proverb, though still called "mathal", has completely emancipated itself from the simile. All these sayings show the same vigorous terseness and the same rhythmic phrasing. The proverb need not be strictly metrical, and is in fact rarely so except in poetical citations which have passed into popular use. The rhythmic effect is more often produced, as in the corresponding Hebrew "mashal", by a harmonious arrangement of syllables, or by parallelism between the halves of the phrase, which, in Arabic, is generally reinforced by internal rhymes. For example, the proverb translated below "[Choose] your neighbour before your house, and your companion before [taking] the road" is in the original: "Al-jār qabl ad-dār, war-rafīq qabl at-tarīq."

This earliest stratum of proverbial sayings, which comprises the most typically Arab proverbs, naturally reflects the social conditions of desert life, and the aloofness, pride and stoical endurance of the nomad. But it includes also a great many sayings which share the common characteristics of proverbial philosophy elsewhere, with its emphasis on self-reliance, prudence and the pagan virtues, and its sceptical attitude towards the world and the motives of one's fellow-men. It is not surprising, therefore, to find amongst them sayings which can be exactly paralleled in the proverbs of widely separated peoples, where no suspicion of borrowing can be entertained.

With the rise of Islam, however, a completely new current of ideas was injected into Arabic proverbial lore. Most of Mohammed's teaching ran directly contrary to the old maxims, and those of his sayings which passed into proverbs introduced a stratum of ethical precepts, afterwards supplemented by his followers and successors. Though there is still an Arabian flavour about some of them, such as "Bless the date-palms, for they are your aunts," the majority belong to the circle of Jewish and Christian teachings, and some are even literal translations of scriptural sayings. There is a corresponding change in the style of these proverbs ; they are in general more prosaic, less vivid in phrase, direct rather than allusive.

But this by no means completed the development of the Arabic proverb. When the Arabs occupied the homelands of the ancient Oriental civilizations, and mingled with their populations, in Egypt, Syria, Mesopotamia and Persia, it was inevitable that the proverbial lore of these regions also should be re-fashioned in their speech. Here again there were two conflicting elements : the one consisting of popular sayings handed down from time immemorial, the other of the relatively recent Christian or Zoroastrian overlay. And to these four strata there was in course of time added a fifth, made up of sayings of later origin and of fragments of verse from the post-Islamic poets, such as al-Mutanabbi (d. A.D. 955), who either coined new phrases and similes or clothed the old in new and more expressive forms.

It is not, of course, always possible to assign a given proverb to a definite group, especially as the sayings of Mohammed and his followers and the proverbs of Jewish and Christian origin share the same ethical character as against the more pagan worldly wisdom of the ancient sayings within and without Arabia. Amongst any people other than the Arabs it might have been expected that the later importations would drive out or largely supplant the earlier proverbs. This was undoubtedly the case to a certain extent, but the natural conservatism of the Arabs brought about rather a fusion of the different stocks. Another factor also operated to secure the survival of the traditional Arabian lore. At a very early period after the Islamic expansion there arose an active school of Arabic philologists, who, in their endeavour to search out and place on record all that could be gleaned of the ancient Arabian usage, naturally gave their attention to the old proverbial sayings. Out of this interest came a very extensive Arabic proverbial literature, probably running into hundreds of works, of which a considerable number are still extant. The oldest dates from about A.D. 775, and the most famous is that of al-Maidāni (d. 1124), which has been translated into Latin with an exhaustive commentary by G. W. Freytag (*Arabium Proverbia*, 3 vols., Bonn, 1838–43). The proverbs of Mohammed were collected separately, while a very few of the learned (including al-Maidāni) admitted an appendix of post-Islamic proverbs to their works. But it is only within the last century or so that European and Oriental scholars have seriously attempted to collect the proverbial sayings in the living speech of the people, from which Dr. Gurney Champion's selection has been made.

From this brief historical survey it will be seen that the store of Arabic proverbs is almost incredibly large, and composed of the most heterogeneous elements. That so many thousands of sayings should have remained in circulation down to our own times is due to the frequency with which they entered into the speech of both ignorant and learned, and to the different stocks of proverbs current in the various Arabic-speaking countries as well as, to some extent, in different social circles. Until recently they were the seasoning of all conversation and argument, " a proverb is to speech ", it was said, " what salt is to food ". But the influence of modern education has been as fatal to this practice in the East as in the West, and the younger generations are rapidly losing their fathers' memory of and taste for proverbs.

In view of their heterogeneous components, one would scarcely be justified in accepting the Arabic proverbs in the lump as an index to the mentality of the Arab peoples. Yet it is possible to single out some characteristic traits. In accordance with the popular notions of Mohammedanism current in the West, one would expect to find a fatalist outlook expressed or implied in many of these proverbs. But it is not so; the fatalist sayings are far outnumbered by those which, as in the proverbial philosophy of other peoples, lay stress on the responsibility of the individual. Proverbs drawn from the operations of husbandry are rare, except among the Syrian and Egyptian cultivators; on the other hand, those in which trading and commercial terms are figuratively applied are very prominent. Perhaps the most striking feature is the survival through so many centuries of the ancient Bedouin emphasis on the duty of hospitality, offset, it is true, by repeated warnings to the guest to speed his departure. Concision and aptitude in expression may generally be taken for granted, but wit in the narrower sense is relatively rare, and usually caustic. True humour, as we understand it, is probably to be found only in the Egyptian proverbs.

H. A. R. GIBB.

Professor of Arabic,
University of Oxford.

INTRODUCTION TO THE PROVERBS OF CHINA

By LIONEL GILES, M.A., D.Litt.

We all know what a proverb is, yet there are few things more difficult to define. The best we can do is to point to certain qualities which a proverb must possess in order to be considered good of its class. Most people will agree that the perfect proverb must be short, that it must embody a sagacious or witty reflection on some aspect of life, and that it must be expressed in such a way as to arrest the attention. Chinese proverbs vary much in their degree of excellence, but a large proportion of them may be said to fulfil all these requirements.

Human nature being much the same all the world over, it is only to be expected that similar proverbs will be found in different languages. We are accustomed to think of the Chinese as differing widely from ourselves in habits of thought, yet it is remarkable how many English proverbs have their counterpart in Chinese. It may be interesting to compare a few of these, always remembering that the great difficulty in translating proverbs is to preserve the terseness of the original. We say, " Look before you leap " ; the Chinese : " Before you hit the dog, look at its master." " Nothing venture, nothing win " may be paralleled by " If you do not scale the mountain you cannot view the plain " ; " Don't meet troubles half way " by " Wait till you come to the river before pulling off your shoes." Here the Chinese versions, though slightly longer, conjure up a more lively image. The reverse is the case in the following : " What is truly within will be manifested without " ; " If something is done for you, it must always be reckoned as good." These are obviously inferior to " What's bred in the bone will come out in the flesh " and " Don't look a gift-horse in the mouth." Honours, perhaps, are even in such proverbs as " You can't get ivory out of a dog's mouth " (" You can't make a silk purse out of a sow's ear ") ; " One hand cannot make a clap " (" It takes two to make a quarrel ") ; " Ice is not frozen three feet thick with one day's cold " (" Rome was not built in a day "). Quite a number of proverbs, English and Chinese, not only have the same root idea but are practically identical in form. The following will at once suggest their counterparts : " Luck does not repeat itself, but misfortunes never come singly " ; " Deep waters run slowly " ; " Ten birds in the tree are not worth one in the hand " ; " Partitions have cracks, and walls have ears " ; " Planning rests with man, accomplishment rests with God " ; " If there are too many cooks, the dog's flesh will never get done " ; " Once bitten by a snake, and the well-rope is a three years' terror." A striking coincidence, too, may be noted between " If one blind man leads another, they will surely fall into a ditch " and Matthew xv. 14.

Brevity is essential to a proverb ; anything superfluous must be cut away. It is noticeable that a language which is rich in particles and inflexions tends to drop these as far as possible when it begins to coin proverbs. We do not say, for example : " A thing that is easily acquired is apt to be easily lost," but " Lightly come, lightly go." Now, in Chinese there is no grammar to shed. As is well known, the language consists of monosyllabic words (each represented in writing by an indivisible character) which are entirely free from any sort of inflexion ; there are no cases or conjugations, no persons, moods or tenses. Moreover, auxiliary parts of speech are comparatively few, the meaning of a sentence being largely determined by position or the logic of the context. Consequently, Chinese composition can be reduced to a terseness which is quite unattainable in European languages, and is admirably suited for the formation of proverbs. Consider the following, for example : " Chihnan pao tê huo," " You can't wrap fire in a paper parcel " ; " Chih chih pu tai," " He who knows when to stop does not come to grief " ; " Ch'un wang ch'ih han," " When the lips are gone the teeth feel cold." The last is an historic saying often applied to the seizure of key territories on the Chinese frontier.

The ancient philosophers of China have always favoured simple, dogmatic statements rather than complex reasoning, and some of the oldest Chinese proverbs are derived from them. The teachings of Confucius and Lao Tzŭ, in particular, abound in pithy utterances, many of which have passed into proverbial use : " Rotten wood cannot be carved, mud walls cannot be plastered " ; " Virtue cannot live in solitude : neighbours are sure to grow up around it " ; " Study without thought is vain, thought without study is perilous " ; " The soft overcomes the hard, the weak overcomes the strong " ; " To see oneself is to be clear of sight " ; " By many words wit is exhausted " ; " In the track of great armies there must follow lean years " ; " The further one travels the less one may know."

There is often an element of quaint or humorous exaggeration in Chinese proverbs which enhances their charm : " He who rides on a tiger can never dismount " ; " Men love their own compositions and other men's wives " ; " A maker of images never worships the gods " ; " An honest official has no fat subordinates " ; " A dragon in shallow water becomes the butt of shrimps " ; " Nails are not made from good iron, nor soldiers from good men." This last may also serve as an example of a favourite type of proverb consisting of two clauses complementary to each other. We find the same sort of thing sometimes in English : " Two blacks do not make a white, two wrongs do not make a right." This balanced structure is highly characteristic of Chinese composition, both prose and verse. The simplest form of it occurs when two converse statements succeed each other : thus, Lao Tzŭ said : " Those who know do not speak, those who speak do not know." Other examples of parallelism will be found in such proverbs as " Our pleasures are shallow, our troubles are deep " ; " When the flight is not high the fall is not heavy"; "Fish see the bait but not the hook; men see the profit but not the peril." Here is an excellent maxim for the student: "Be not afraid of going slowly, be only afraid of standing still"; and for the business man: "If small sums do not go out, large sums will not come in."

Alliteration, which plays a conspicuous part in English proverbs (e.g. "Where there's a will there's a way"; "A miss is as good as a mile"; "One swallow doesn't make a summer"; "Practice makes perfect") does not seem to come so naturally to the Chinese, and is replaced to some extent by rhyme, for which there is almost unlimited scope in this monosyllabic language of comparatively few sounds. Thus we get "Hsien ju wei chu," a Chinese equivalent of "First come, first served"; "Chün tzŭ i yen, k'uai ma i pien," "A single word to the wise man, a single lash to the swift horse"; "Jên tê i shih fên, chung shên wu nao mên," "By controlling the anger of a minute you may avoid the remorse of a lifetime"; "Huo ts'ung k'ou ch'u, ping ts'ung k'ou ju," "Out of the mouth calamities fly, in by the mouth all sicknesses hie." This, as well as the next, is a rhyming translation by Mr. Scarborough, one of the first compilers of Chinese proverbs: "Jên wu shên ling, ts'un pu nan hsing," "Men without divine assistance cannot move an inch of distance."

In the main, as the reader may have observed, the common maxims of the Chinese are ethically sound; but on occasion they are tinged with a not unpleasing cynicism: "Money covers a multitude of sins" (lit. "a hundred uglinesses"); "If you want to enjoy peace, first square the magistrate"; "A clever man will build a city, a clever woman will lay it low"; "If you want to see black-hearted people, look among those who never miss their prayers." And of course we find the world-wide aphorism: "So long as you have wine and meat, you will have many close friends; but when you are in sore distress, do you see a single person coming to your door?" This is most familiar, perhaps, in its Latin dress: "Donec eris felix, multos numerabis amicos; Tempora si fuerint nubila, solus eris." But Colonel Joyce's lines are even more epigrammatic, and nearer to the Chinese: "Feast, and your halls are crowded; fast, and the world goes by."

The quoting and sorting of proverbs is a pastime that grows upon one, especially when there is a choice yet inexhaustible fund to draw upon, but this foretaste of what will be found in the following pages must suffice. "Until you approach a deep ravine you do not realize the thickness of the earth"; and only after dipping into Dr. Champion's monumental work will one be able to grasp and appreciate the enormous wealth of proverbial lore created by the Chinese and still in current use among them.

LIONEL GILES.

KEEPER OF ORIENTAL
PRINTED BOOKS AND MANUSCRIPTS,
BRITISH MUSEUM,
LONDON.

INTRODUCTION TO THE PROVERBS OF ESTONIA

By PROFESSOR OSKER LOORITS

THE word " proverb " in Estonian (" vana-sona ") means " an old word ".

In trying to understand the peculiarities of the meaning and wording of Estonian proverbs attention must be paid, above all, to two factors that play a decisive part in Estonian poetical thinking and its form of expression : they are parallelism of thought and alliteration. The parallelism of thought strives after the impressive elaboration in different colours and different directions of a word picture created by repeated (and frequently gradated) figures. Here only two parallel pictures are often not considered sufficient, and we get three, four, or even more :

Õige hõlma ei hakka ükski,	No one gets at the skirts of the righteous one,
vaga veri ei värise.	Pious blood does not tremble.
Naer ei riku nahka, tühi jutt ei võta tükki.	Laughter does not spoil the skin, Empty gossip does not take a piece [off you].
Puhas süda, puhas suu ja puhas käsi käivad kõigest ilmast läbi.	A clean heart, a clean mouth and a clean hand Go all through the world.
Varandus kadunud—vähe kaotatud, jõud kadunud—pal ju kaotatud, au kadunud—kõik kaotatud.	Fortune gone—little lost, Strength gone—much lost, Honour gone—all lost.
Uhke läheb hukka, kõrk läheb kõrva, käre läheb kärna, hiljuke läheb edasi.	The proud one will perish, The haughty one will go astray, The hasty one will go mangy, The wary one will go on.

Such parallelisms of thought often lose all their poetical attractiveness in translation, for their constructive basis is the untranslatable alliteration, i.e. the sameness of initial vowels and consonants. That alliteration springs from the characteristic stressing of the first syllable in Estonian, and its mesmeric influence reaches everywhere in Estonian poetical creation, up to the most recent times, guiding the development of images and the trend of thought pictures as well as influencing even the innermost meanings. Translated into any foreign tongue the sayings that have their birth in parallelism of thought and alliteration must needs often appear quite unintelligible or flatly nonsensical, while to the Estonian mind and world of thought they are all the more organic and natural, e.g.

Otsa peal on orja täid,	On the forehead are the serf's lice,
pea lael on laisa täid,	On the top of the head are the sluggard's lice,
kõrva ääres kõrgi täid.	Near the ear are the haughty one's lice.

About the strength-giving power of certain dishes the following picture has been sketched :

Kiisliga saab kindad kätte	Gruel gets the gloves on,
Kördiga köie rekke,	Broth the rope to the sled,
Pudruga poole sülla puid koju.	Porridge half a fathom of wood home.

A weather forecast after the departure of birds of passage says :

Haned lähevad—halvad ilmad,	The geese go—bad weather,
kured lähevad—kurjad ilmad	The cranes go—evil weather,
luiged lähevad—lumi maas.	The swans go—snow on the ground.

Change of weather in connection with certain saints' days of the calendar is given in a whole series of pictures :

Mihkel mõtleb,	[St.] Michael thinks,
Mart matab,	[St.] Martin buries,
Kadri katab,	[St.] Cathrin covers,
Andres arutab,	[St.] Andrew reasons,
Nigul niisutab,	[St.] Nicholas moistens,
Lutsi pühib luuaga kooku,	[St.] Luke sweeps a broom,
Peeter pistab pulga ette,	[St.] Peter sticks a plug in,
Simm teeb silla soole peale,	[St.] Simon makes a bridge across the bog.
Toomas tore mees tuiskab taga taaripuuga laiali ja sõidab üle silla.	[St.] Thomas, fine man, blizzards after with a mead-stick and drives across the bridge.

Alliteration has also coaxed forth several puns and nonsensical sayings like the following characterization of the days of the week :

Esmaspäev enesel oldi,	On Monday one used to be by one's self,
Teisipäev teole mindi,	On Tuesday one used to go to work,
Kolmapäev koera tapeti,	On Wednesday one used to kill the dog,
Neljapäev nahka nuliti,	On Thursday one used to skin him,
Reede rasva riisuti,	On Friday one used to skim the lard,
Poolpäev putru keedeti ja	On half-day [Saturday] one used to cook porridge and
Pühapäev peeti püha	On Sunday one used to have a holiday.

As to the contents of the stock of Estonian proverbs, the bulk of them are original, partly very old. Many of them are common to the

Estonians and their two most closely related peoples—the Fins and the Livs. Of course the Estonians have translated and re-created also the proverbs of alien nations, and here the two highways of culture from the East and the West are most clearly to be traced. Most of the proverbs of alien nations have reached Estonia via the Germans, and in a lesser degree via the Russians, and fewer proverbs still have been translated from Swedish and other languages. Collecting proverbs and old sayings was started by the grammarians (H. Göseken, 1660 ; A. Thor Helle, 1732 ; A. W. Hupel, 1818 a.o.m.) ; at present the Estonian Folk-lore Archives possesses over 110,000 variants. The greatest printed collection with a German translation is F. J. Wiedemann : *Aus dem inneren und äusseren Leben der Esten* (1876).

OSKER LOORITS.

DIRECTOR,
ESTONIAN FOLK-LORE ARCHIVE,
EASTI RAHVA MUSEUM,
TARTU, ESTONIA.

INTRODUCTION TO THE PROVERBS OF FINLAND

By AINO TUOMIKOSKI, M.A.

As the translator of the greater part of the Finnish proverbs included in this great collection of Dr. Champion's, I am taking this opportunity of stating some facts concerning them.

The Finnish " sanalasku " (" proverb ") can be translated—" sana " —a word, " lasku "—drop or let fall.

The Finnish nation has always had a very great confidence in the might of the word. Already its national *epos*, the " Kalevala ", contains many witnesses of the immense power of the word, whether it be expressed with the accompaniment of music or without it.

Professor Elias Lönnrot, M.D., collected the songs of the " Kalevala " and in addition published the greatest part (about 7,000) of the Finnish proverbs known in 1842.

The Finnish proverbs that are contained in this collection of Dr. Champion's are translated from a collection published in 1906 by Professor A. V. Koskimies, who based his work on the collections of Suomalaisen Kirjallisuuden Seura (The Finnish Literature Society). In the introduction of his work he writes :

> " The chief distinctive feature of a proverb is its general acceptability or the quality of revealing and reflecting the ideas and ideals, the opinions and observations, the conclusions and estimations about everything that in the circle of the visible and invisible world has become clear to the physical and mental eye of the nation."

Since the above-mentioned publications of Finnish proverbs, Suomalaisen Kirjallisuuden Seura (The Finnish Literature Society) and Sanakirjasäätiö (The Dictionary Endowment) collected Finnish proverbs on a large scale and have now in their possession proverbs and bywords and different variations of them (Suomalaisen Kirjallisuuden Seura 250,000 and Sanakirjasäätiö 1,200,000) at present unpublished.

Much of the charm of these proverbs is invariably lost in translation because the Finnish folk-lore is especially inclined to express its thoughts and feelings in an alliterative and poetical form as also in the proverbs and riddles. Yet I hope that even these specimens will give some feeble idea of the Finnish proverbs.

AINO TUOMIKOSKI.

TAMPERE, HALLITUSKATU 14,
FINLAND.

INTRODUCTION TO THE PROVERBS OF FRANCE

By PROFESSOR DENIS SAURAT, D. ÈS L.

Two things strike me about French proverbs, and indeed all proverbs, although I do not like to generalize about them. The first is that in any question in life which has to be decided there are always proverbs which can be quoted on both sides, thus making them appear contradictory. For instance, we say :

" A chaque jour suffit sa peine,"

but we also say :

" Ne jamais remettre à demain ce qu'on peut faire aujourd'hui."

We say :

" Tel père, tel fils."

But we say also :

" A père avare, fils prodigue."

This merely means that proverbs are crystallized forms of human experience, and as human experience gives no definite solution to any problem, proverbs cannot do so either. This does not for a moment imply that they are of little use in deciding life's difficulties, but rather are they of the greatest help to mankind in that they present clearly both sides of any question, thus putting the choice on man himself.

The second point which strikes me in French proverbs is that they are not particularly French. Indeed, I doubt whether any proverbs are truly national ; except for some topical references which may be imbedded in the expressions used, but the ideas are universal. Proverbs are obviously a form of literature which appeals to the widest public of all, and the widest public is only reached by getting down to the lowest and therefore the broadest possible level. This again does not mean that proverbs have no value or that French proverbs are not typical of France. But it means that they are typical of that part of the French which is similarly a part of the psychology of any other people. This must be specially true of peasant proverbs which, I suppose, are fundamentally the same, from France to China, wherever there are peasants. Perhaps in the case of French proverbs we can see merely that general tendency which is so visible in French literature to reach after universal statements, statements which can be regarded as valid for the whole world.

These personal remarks are no doubt extremely controversial, but are meant to induce the readers to study for themselves Dr. Champion's collection of French proverbs, when they will be better able to appreciate the points which I have raised.

DENIS SAURAT.

Institut Français du Royaume-uni,
London.

INTRODUCTION TO THE PROVERBS OF GEORGIA (SAK 'ART 'VELO)

By A. GUGUSHVILI

To my own great surprise, I find myself writing an Introduction to Dr. S. Gurney Champion's collection of "Racial Proverbs"—a subject which, a month or two back, was to me *terra incognita*.

Lest curious friends should question this divergence on my part, or suspect me of posing as an authority on Proverbs, I feel it my bounden duty to offer an explanation.

A telephone call started it. An inquiry by that philosopher and guide of Oriental book lovers—S. C. Coles of the Oriental Department of Kegan Paul, Trench, Trubner & Co. He wanted some information on a minor point connected with Dr. Champion's Georgian collection, and I became greatly intrigued, so intrigued, in fact, that I shortly found myself in contact with the compiler himself, who eventually not only requested my co-operation in checking over his Georgian proverbs, but also—to my infinite amazement—asked me to write an Introduction to his collection. I was flattered and agreed. But, later, a sense of guilt came over me, as it dawned upon me that I had committed myself to something for which I was ill-prepared. Who was I to write about Proverbs? What was a Proverb, anyway? Had I ever read anything about Proverbs? In fact I felt—and a Georgian proverb comes to my assistance—like our proverbial hen who scratched, and scratched, and scratched among the ashes, until she scratched up the knife which cut her own throat.

A strange notion, this, to collect proverbs from every country on God's earth! What queer hobbies people have! But it behoved me to stop casting such reflections and to get down to my task. What proverbs did I know? Surely enough, as I racked my brains, they gradually came to my mind. I examined each critically. What a golden mine of moral or practical precepts! How curt, precise and vigorous their form of expression! I was captivated. Now the mist had cleared and I saw wherein lay the fascination for Dr. Champion. I realized how convenient a channel this pointed proverbial expression was, through which to hand down to future generations "the most precious fruits of wisdom" of past ages. Proverbs are, indeed, "capsules" containing "doses" of wisdom which, thus easily absorbed, strengthen our discerning judgment in the practical concerns of Life.

But I digress. I was not asked for a treatise on proverbs, but to write a short history of Georgian proverbs, to quote the Georgian word for proverb, and to explain its origin.

Lacking the requisite knowledge, I turned for information to the library of my friend and Maecenas, W. E. D. Allen—a library containing the richest and (as far as I am aware) the largest collection of Georgian books in Great Britain. Here—in this my sanctum where I hold spiritual communion with my country's past—I searched in vain for an historical sketch on Georgian proverbs. Lists of Georgian proverbs were there in plenty—Abkhasian, Svanian, Megrelian, K'art'lo-Kakhian, Ingiloan, etc.—published in various books and periodicals on Georgian ethnography, but lists only.

Proverbs, I found, were receiving due attention in Georgia as early as the second half of the seventeenth century. Among those showing a great interest in the subject at this time, stands out the name of Sulkhan Saba Orbeliani, a Georgian famed as a writer, lexicographer, legislator and diplomat of that century, of whose book, *The Wisdom of Lies*, Z. Avalishvili writes,

> "Orbeliani appears to attach great value also to proverbs and short maxims. Sometimes these are explained; sometimes cloaked in anecdote. For instance, in No. 54: 'The Indian King and the Barber, the saying "his foot stood on the treasure" is explained as meaning "the moment was favourable for gaining his purpose." (See A. Tsagareli, *Kniga Mudrosti*, etc., St. Pb., 1879, p. 188.) Also, in No. 1, what is said about the donkey's common sense appears in connexion with a proverb. (Cf. N. Marr, *Sbornik Pritcht Vardana*, St. Pb., 1899, vol. 1, p. 536, g. 542.)'" [1]

Now, in regard to the Georgian equivalent for the word "proverb". The word which appears to have established itself firmly, at least in modern literature and among the people in Eastern Georgia, is "andaza". This, however, according to D. Tchubinov's (=Tchubinashvili's) *Georgio-Russo-French Dictionary* [2] is a Persian word, "andâz", and denotes "example, form". In Persian itself, according to a *Modern Persian Conversation-Grammar* in my possession, a proverb is "masal", derived from Arabic, "mathal". The Georgian "andaza", however, is not translated as meaning proverb in either Tchubinashvili's *Dictionary*, referred to above, or in the older *Georgian Dictionary* of Sulkhan Saba Orbeliani.[3] In the latter it is interpreted as denoting "anything formed or designed as a guide or model for making things, particularly boots, gloves", etc. The word which Tchubinashvili translates as meaning "proverb", in his *Dictionary* mentioned above, as well as in his *Russo-Georgian Dictionary*,[4] is "igavi", which also denotes a "parable". "Igavi", according to Sulkhan Saba Orbeliani's *Dictionary*,[5] is "a word

[1] See Avalishvili's Introduction to the German translation of *The Wisdom of Lies*: *Die Weisheit der Lüge*. Gesprochen von Sulchan Saba Orbeliani. Übersetzt von Dr. M. von Tseretheli (Georgische Bibliothek, herausgegeben von A. Metreweli, Berlin, 1933).

[2] Published in St. Petersburg, 1840, s.v. p. 20.

[3] Published by Professors I. Kipshidze and A. Shanidze, Tiflis, 1928, s.v. p. 13.

[4] My copy, unfortunately, has neither date nor place of publication, s.v. "poslovitsa", p. 533, and "prittcha", p. 570.

[5] s.v. p. 147.

example" ("sitqwit' magalit'i"). In Svanian (Svanet'i, a northern mountain province in West Georgia), too, both "proverb" and "parable" are rendered, according to I. I. Nizharadze's *Russo-Svanian Dictionary*,[1] by the word "igav", which is, of course, the Georgian "igavi". In Megrelian (Megrelia, a province in Western Georgia, the Lazica or Colchis of classical writers) it is rendered, according to I. Kipshidze's *Megrelo-Russian Dictionary*, by "moko", which also denotes "allegorical"; e.g. "mokot' itchiebu", he speaks allegorically.[2] In Abkhasian (Abkhasia, north-western part of Georgia) it is rendered—so the writer is informed by I. Shervashidze (= Sharashia), an Abkhasian —by "avitsw."[3] In *A History of Abkhasia*,[4] by D. Gulia, a noted Georgian historian, I find, however, "Azzhwa-p'qak'wa" as the word denoting proverb in Abkhasian.

The word "andaza", however, appears to be widely used also in Megrelia. The Georgian "igavi", which evidently, judging from the dictionaries quoted above, was used in ancient times in the sense of both "proverb" and "parable", is derived, according to N. Marr and M. Briere's *La Langue Géorgienne*,[5] from "gav", a later popular variant of "sgav", the modern "gav-s" = (it) resembles. The use of the word "igavi" in these two senses is not peculiar to Georgian alone, for I observe from Professor H. A. R. Gibb's introduction to Dr. Champion's collection of Arabic proverbs, that Arabic "mathal" also denotes both "proverb" and "parable", and so also does the Persian "masal" quoted above.

Proverbs are short sayings which reflect not only moral conceptions and rules of worldly wisdom, deduced by people from experience and observation, but also reveal traces of culture, nature and theogonic myths, and of historical events. As such, they constitute important ethnological material and command a significant historical value. Judging Dr. Champion's collection of Georgian proverbs from this point of view, compiled though it undoubtedly is with great acumen and from a good source, it nevertheless falls short of being fully representative. Therefore, I take the liberty of supplementing his Georgian collection of proverbs with a few more of decided historical value. The proverbs I give below are taken from the late Professor A. S. Khakhanov's (=Khakhanashvili's) *Sketches from the History of Georgian Literature* (in Russian).[6] I also follow his system of classification.

[1] See *Sbornik* (*Collection*) *of Materials for the Description of Places and Tribes of Caucasia* (*in Russian*), Tiflis, 1910, vol. 42, s.v. "poslovitsa", p. 325, and "prittcha", p. 350.

[2] See I. Kipshidze, *A Grammar of Megrelian* (*Iberian*) *Language*. With a Chrestomathy and a Dictionary (in Russian), St. Petersburg, 1914, s.v. p. 281. See also pp. 176–80, which contain 127 Megrelian proverbs.

[3] I am indebted for this information to my friend, Mr. D. Gatserelia of Paris.

[4] Published in Russian in Tiflis, 1925, p. 170.

[5] Published in Paris, 1931, s.v. p. 640.

[6] Vol. I (no date or place of publication), pp. 118–22.

I. Proverbs of mythological character :

" A momentary sleep overtakes even a river."

representing rivers, like living beings, as capable of giving themselves up to sleep.

" If the moon is on my side, what need have I of the stars ? "

reflecting planet-worship and indicating the pre-eminence of the Moon as a deity.

" Death said : ' Whomsoever I have killed, I lay the blame on other causes.' "

representing the personification of Death.

" From Fate one escapeth not."
" Give me Luck and throw me on the muck-heap."
" The [rolling] stone overtakes the unfortunate, even uphill."

characterize belief in the insuperable power of Fate.

" Though himself a giant, of brains he had but few."
" Large head, little brain ; small head, great brain."

reflecting a belief that there existed at one time a people of giants and a people of dwarfs. The giants lacked sufficient intelligence to feed their huge horses from mangers placed on the ground ; they had the idea that the horses could not bend their heads and therefore placed the mangers on the roofs of the houses. The dwarfs, however, excelled them in intelligence.

" There was no wine, yet the demons inflated the wine-skins."
" The man who worked for a demon was ruined by God."
" Devils take possession of an abandoned church."

represent a survival of belief in demons, i.e. traces of demonology.

" Soul knows soul."
" Keep in good health until his coming."

reflect belief in the possibility of the surviving souls returning to carry away the living relations ; the cult of the Dead.

" Even a priest may make a mistake in saying ' alilo '."

reflecting a worship of some pagan god in whose honour " alilo " was sung.

II. Under the influence of the Christian religion, proverbs gained currency which replaced belief in Fate with faith in God. Such are :

" God is bountiful ; pauper, do not despair."
" Widows and orphans, God visits thrice a day."
" Like priest, like people."

III. Historical events are reflected in the following proverbs :

" The Erzerum Tartar disputes with me the sucking-pig's head."

reflects the relations of Georgia with Turkey and the latter's persecutions of her sons.

" Came a Meskh and ousted the native [autochthon]."

reflects the abandoning by the Meskhs of their native province, in consequence of its occupation by Turkey, and moving into another province of Georgia.

" Let there be honey and a fly will come from Miletus."
" Countless, like the Milesian people [said at the sight of a diverse concourse of peoples]."

represents traces of relationship between Georgians and Greeks in far-off times.

" By asking the way, one can go as far as India."

an allusion to India.

IV. Proverbs relating to the Feudal system, or to the relations between a lord and his vassal :

" If the lord says that apples grow on oak-trees, believe."
" The anger of a lord against a serf is a sign of favour."

reflects submission to, or accordance with, the will of one's lord.

" Though neither a serf nor a serf-holder, old wine and bread lasted through the year."

reflects the consciousness of the dignity of a free man.

V. Proverbs relating to social-political life :

" God's voice—people's voice." (Cf. " vox populi ; vox Dei.")
" If the King be angry with you, go to the ' T'emi ', and if the ' T'emi ', too, is angry, ostracize yourself." (" T'emi " is a popular council, court.)

assert supremacy of the people's will.

" A man should be a saw and cut out in both directions, and not an axe to cut only in his direction."
" A man should have two names, one for that world, and one for leaving behind in this."

reflect man's duty to Society.

" Mountains and plains cannot be levelled up."

asserts the inequality of social classes.

" Bribery illumines even hell."

illustrates corrupt justice.

" Beat me a hundred times, only let me speak the truth."

reflects love of the people for truth and justice.

" He who speaks the truth must have a saddled horse " [that he may escape swiftly].

" Run after the truth and lose the world."

illustrate how unwelcome is the truth.

" He who flatters is the demon's messenger."

reveals people's hatred of flattery.

" Even a stone will remember bread and salt."
" To visit a house is your business ; to leave it is your host's."
" If the host be not gay, the guest's spirits fade."

illustrating people's appreciation of hospitality.

" A theft of a needle or of an ox is a theft nevertheless."

expresses condemnation of stealing.

" To the end of your life, do not tire of learning."

shows the respect and appreciation of the people for learning.

A great number of proverbs derive their origin from literary sources, and particularly from Shot'a Rust'aveli, a great Georgian poet of the twelfth century. We shall quote here only a few of these :

30, 4. " An evil man loves an evil word [1] more than his soul or heart."
39, 4. " The lion's whelps are equal, be they male or female."
50, 4. " What thou givest away is thine, what thou keepest is lost."
526, 4. " To do true justice makes even a dry tree green."
781, 4. " Better a glorious death than shameful life."
1232, 4. " If a crow finds a rose, it thinks itself a nightingale."

A. GUGUSHVILI.

LONDON.

[1] See *Vep'khis Tqaosani* ; the English translation : *The Man in the Panther's Skin.* A Romantic Epic by Shota Rustaveli. A close rendering from the Georgian attempted by Marjory Scott Wardrop. Published by the Royal Asiatic Society, London, 1912.

INTRODUCTION TO THE PROVERBS OF GERMANY

By PROFESSOR OTTO HÖFLER

In proverbs is to be found the philosophy of the people : the experience, handed on from old to young, of countless interlocked generations—pitiless realism and prudence drawn from life's experience, side by side with devout idealism, witty unveiling of false pretence, together with the profound wisdom of old age, that pierces through the commonplace of daily life into the dim mysteries of existence—fierce scorn bordering on cynicism and the smiling wisdom of charity.

The realm of the Proverb is rich and broad as the soul of the people—it is a treasury to which centuries have contributed—and in this treasury dwell sayings that have their source in the Bible, others coined from classical antiquity, yet others that have their home in the Germanic North distant—what is foreign has been welcomed into the community, the produce of the home soil lives unchanged throughout the centuries.

In the case of many proverbs, the very form points to ancient origin. Along with sayings characterized by the rhymed ending so prevalent since the Middle Ages (e.g. " Wer den Heller nicht ehrt, ist des Talers nicht wert "—" He that honours not the penny is not worthy of the pound "), tradition knows many in which the style and structure of old German heathen poetry still lives, the alliterative style, that is to say, the correspondence of the beginning sounds in the stressed words. This so-called alliteration exists not merely in formal combinations in popular parlance (e.g. " über Stock und Stein laufen "—" To run up hill and down dale " ; " Kind und Kegel "—" Kith and Kin " " Frank und frei " (" Point blank—in plain language "). In the proverb, too, this immemorial old Germanic form exists to this day (e.g. " Glück und Glas, wie bald bricht das "—" Luck is fickle as glass is brittle " ; " Hoffen und Harren macht manchen zum Narren "—" Hoping and waiting makes a fool of many a man " or " To hope and to tarry makes much to miscarry "). The older principal of alliteration is often joined to the later, namely, that of the rhymed ending, symbolizing the intimate union of past and present in the German Proverb.

Proverbs, like so many popular traditions, delight in emphatic form. Antithesis, the special pride of witty modern prose and polished epigrammatic poetry, is a regular popular favourite in the wise sayings of the people. We will quote only one or two out of the thousands of examples.

"Jung gewohnt, alt getan"—"Practised in youth, performed in old age"; "Wie du mir, so ich dir"—"As thou to me, so I to thee"; "Böses kommt geritten, geht aber weg mit Schritten"—"Ill is swift to come, slow to go." The parallelism of the antithetic halves of such sayings is often carried to the uttermost, as for instance in that most concise expression of the instability of all things human—four words, no more: "Heute rot—morgen tot"—"Red to-day, dead to-morrow"—"Heute" and "Morgen" are contrasted, and in the same way the word "Rot", symbolic of hale and hearty life, is contrasted and rhymed with "Tot".

The Proverb is a masterpiece of concentrated symbolism, unsurpassed by the choicest, the most refined verse epigram, and it is only in rare and fortunate moments that our so-called philosophy attains to the simple crushing force that gives immortality to many a proverb. The customs and affairs of mankind, their follies, their faults are illustrated by simple, self-evident comparisons from life in general or from everyday experience. "Der Apfel fällt nicht weit vom Stamm"—"The apple falls not far from the tree"; "Früh krümmt sich, was ein Häkchen werden will"—"Early a crook, what means to be hook"; "Kein Feuer ohne Rauch"—"No fire without smoke"; "Keine Rose ohne Dorn"—"No rose without thorn"; "Wer anderen eine Grube gräbt, fällt selbst hinein"—"He that digs a pit for others often falls himself therein"; "Zeit frisst Stahl und Eisen"—"Time devours steel and iron"; "Nach Regen kommt Sonnenschein"—"Sunshine after rain."

The concise but self-evident word-wisdom of the people has a further advantage over all abstract school-philosophy. It loves in modest simplicity to set its knowledge, its insight, its experience into the golden frame of humour. It speaks not with the cold voice of reason, but with the warmth of the full heart, which knows joy and sorrow, can smile and forgive. Mere intellectual cleverness isolates and separates—the proverb reconciles and unites; in the proverb, as nowhere else, appears the blessed gift we call gemüt (humanity). Even where it shows an unerring insight into human weakness (and for this it has a more piercing vision than all the learned psychologies) it retains after all, above and beyond the penetration of its intuition, the humanity of its understanding for the heights and depths.

If wisdom is more than cleverness and if humour belongs to wisdom, it must follow that the Proverb belongs to the class of gifts that are most beneficient to mankind, because in the investigation of the soul it does not end in sceptical nihilism. In spite of all, the Proverb sees the good in man and believes in this good.

OTTO HÖFLER.

KIEL UNIVERSITY,
GERMANY.

INTRODUCTION TO THE PROVERBS OF HUNGARY

By PROFESSOR VILMOS TOLNAI

HUNGARIANS are even nowadays considered an exotic people in Europe, though they have lived more than a thousand years on the banks of the Danube. This is easy to understand, because the Hungarian (or more correctly, Magyar, pronounced Madyar) people and language is almost absolutely isolated between foreign peoples, e.g. westwards, the South-German Austrians ; northwards, the Slovaks, Poles and other Slavonian races ; eastwards, the Roumanians, who belong to the Latin stock ; southwards, more South Slavonian tribes. The Hungarian language belongs to the Ugro-Finnish family, and came, after grave adversities, from the South-Ural, through the wide South-Russian plains to his present country. On this long journey the Hungarian was often in political, cultural and ethnographical connexion with several Turkish tribes ; one of them, the Kabarian, joined the seven Hungarian tribes when they conquered the Danubian country. This occurred at the end of the ninth century B.C., and about the year 1000 the first Hungarian king converted his people to Christianity. Since this time the frightened Hungarians became the " Shield of Christianity " against the pagans.

The fate of the Hungarians must be mentioned in order to understand the many parts of their culture and language, and in connexion with it their wayside sayings or proverbs. One can discover therein old relics of the Ugro-Finnish era. There are also to be found many indications of Turkish origin ; old Bulgarian, Pechenegues, Kasars, Comans, also the newer Osmanli-Turkish. There are also indications of the peoples in the neighbourhood—Germans and Slavs—and of Latin of the Middle Ages.

The history of Hungarian wayside sayings teaches us that the proverb is to a great extent an international wanderer which has not been restricted by the boundaries of languages, cultures, or peculiar characters of national feature ; only to a lesser extent is it the sole possession of a nation, closely bound to its life, country, special state, customs, etc. This explains why there are so many analogous, even identical proverbs in sense and form among the languages. This matter has been dealt with by Dr. Champion in his Introduction.

The most frequent denominations of the Hungarian " proverb " are : " köz-mondás "—common saying ; " példa-beszéd "—example talking ; " köz-szólás "—common or general sentence ; " szokás-mondás "—usual saying.

It must be understood that the value of the Hungarian wayside sayings is above all in their intellectual contents and sense, depicting life, while the metaphors and figurative expressions are merely ornamental disguises of speech. In addition the proverb often appears in poetical form, rhythm or rhyme, because, rendered in this way, it is more easily remembered.

The proverbs most frequently used are :

(*a*) Those dealing with the everyday things of life, e.g. " pénz beszél, kutya ugat ", i.e. " Money talks, dogs bark " ; " Rövid farsangnak hosszú a böjtje ", i.e. " Short carnival has long fasting " ; " Sok kéz hamar kész ", i.e. " Many hands make quick work."

(*b*) Those which embody a judgment with a fact, e.g. " Jobb ma egy veréb, mint holnap egy túzok ", i.e. " Better to-day a sparrow than to-morrow a buzzard " or " A bird in the hand is worth two in the bush " ; " Okos ember tovább lát az orránál ", i.e. " A wise man sees farther than his nose."

(*c*) Those which convey counsel and advice for life, e.g. " Lassan járj, tovább érsz ", i.e. " Go slowly and you can go farther " or " More haste, less speed " ; " Ahol nincs, ott ne keress ", i.e. " Where there is nothing, there is nothing to look for " ; " Akinek nem inge, ne vegye magára ", i.e. " Whose shirt it is not, may not put it on."

The proverb or wayside saying is always isolated and independent, and is never in syntactical connexion with the text, like a citation, e.g. it is an old truth—we all know that—everything proves it : " Man proposes, God disposes." This is so in all languages of the world ; while other stylistical formations are firmly bound in with the text and follow strictly the grammatical structure.

In common with all others, the Hungarian wayside sayings know not their author who quoted the first sentence which became the possession of the people, of all humanity. Formerly, proverbs were born every day, perished every day. One knows the thousand-years-old specimens and the more modern recently coined ones, but with civilization their popularity slowly decreased, like the popular song. The original old-fashioned country life has given place to the condensed life of the towns and cities, and to-day thousands of proverbs live only in old books.

There are some hundreds of collections of Hungarian proverbs (not mentioned in the largest foreign bibliographies). Here it will be enough to point out the most valuable. (1) Decsi, János (John Decsi), *Adagiorum . . . ungaricorum chiliades quinque*, Bartphæ, 1598. His model was the herculean work of Erasmus, Basileæ, 1574. He did not translate the quotations, sentences, citations of Erasmus, but substituted them mostly by original Hungarian wayside sayings. (2) Dugonics, András (Andrew Dugonics), *Magyar példabeszédek*, i.e. Hungarian example talkings or proverbs, Szeged, 1820. About 12,000 specimens in 49 material groups. (3) Erdélyi, János (John Erdélyi), *Magyar közmondások* (Hungarian Proverbs), Pest, 1851. He ranges his material according to the most significant chief- or catch-word and gives also the Latin, German, French, etc., synonyms. (4) The greatest collection is by MARGALITS, EDE (Edward Margalits), Budapest, 1896—twenty thousand specimens; the real quantity is far lower, because the author mentions every proverb under every presumable catchword, e.g. " The *higher* the *mountain*, the *deeper* the *vale*," is cited under the four italicized words. In this way every proverb is easy to find, and this is very practical, but the collection has a great fault that the origin is never recorded, and without chronological, geographical, ethnographical, etc., designation, a collection of proverbs has not its complete scientific worth.

VILMOS TOLNAI.

PÉCS UNIVERSITY,
HUNGARY.

(Theory and bibliography of the whole Hungarian literature of proverbs : TOLNAI, VILMOS, " A szólás ; szóláshasonlat, szólásmód és közmondás ", *A Magyarság Néprajza*, III, 397–433. Budapest, 1935, i.e. " Theory, Bibliography and History of the Hungarian Phrase, Metaphor, and Wayside Saying ". See : *The Ethnography of Hungarians*, III, 397–433. Budapest, 1935, and reprint.)

INTRODUCTION TO THE PROVERBS OF INDIA

By H. N. RANDLE, Ph.D., M.A.

INDIAN languages which borrow from Sanskrit denote proverbs by some such term as " lokokti ", " folk-saying ", underlining thus the popular character of these profitable sayings : as, I think, the Greeks intended to do in their designation *παροιμία*, which, despite Hesychius (*λόγος παρα τὴν ὁδὸν λεγόμενος*), may rather have connoted what a neighbourhood (*πάροιμος*) says than what is said by the way (*παρ' οἶμον*). But, as Dr. Champion insists, *vox populi* tends to teach by examples ; and it is this aspect of the proverb that is emphasized in the designations given to them by Indian languages which borrow from Persian and Arabic—" misal " or " naql " (the terms commonly used in such languages, signifying likeness or exemplar). The Malay names mentioned by Dr. Champion, which also seize upon this aspect of the proverb, appear to be loan-words from Sanskrit : " upamā " or " upamāna " meaning " similarity " or " analogy ", while " laksana " is a " characteristic " or, in Indian logic, the " middle term " which sets inference moving. That familiar device of Indian reasoning, the " laukika nyāya ", or popular ruling, is closely related to this aspect of the proverb, consisting as it does in an appeal to some popular fable or instance illustrative of a general truth. Thus an Indian who wished to inculcate the Hobbesian doctrine of the war of every man against every man in a " state of nature " would probably cite in evidence the " matsya-nyāya ", the rule of the fish—one eats the other. But a " laukika nyāya " is not a full proverb, as it stands, but only the vestige or potentiality of a proverb.

Readers who look for anything very philosophical in Indian proverbs will be disappointed. The Indian's proverbs, like the proverbs of all other folk, do not give forth directions at large. They are practical and often personal ; the common butts of their personalities being barbers, Brahmans, banais, physicians, and above all women. I suspect that, in this last matter, the professed philosopher may have had a bad influence on the village philosopher ; for if there was one thing that Indian philosophers disliked more than they disliked everything, it was Woman. It is the more gratifying, therefore, to find one wiseacre rising above the general level of his tribe in the really excellent saying that " a man thinks he knows ; but a woman knows better ". On the whole it is perhaps the practical folk who make the best proverbs, since what they say is too close to experience to stale with repetition. Thus the first proverb that many Europeans learn in India is that " the eye of the master makes the horse fat" ; and it does not lose its force. It may surprise, and possibly disappoint, some readers to find how very practical the Indian is in his proverbs. India, moreover, is a land of villages, and the wit of its folk is often bucolic wit ; which is to be judged by its own standards—since (to quote a proverb from the Kumauni and Garhwali collection) "You must look at the country of the one-eyed with one eye". Really philosophical proverbs are, I think, reasonably suspect, as being either not popular currency or other than proverbs. One Tamil adage is exactly "quem Deus vult perdere prius dementat" : and it has a strangely un-Indian sound. The Sanskrit collection necessarily includes literary commonplaces, since Sanskrit was not a speech of any folk : and the commandment in which India has tended to find the golden rule of life—"ahimsā paramō dharmah"—"the cardinal virtue is to do no harm"—is more than a "lokokti"

H. N. RANDLE.

INDIA OFFICE,
LONDON.

INTRODUCTION TO THE PROVERBS OF IRELAND

By HENRY MORRIS, M.A.

THE Irish word for a proverb is "Sean-fhocal", literally "an old word", but "word" in the primitive sense of a "saying". Hence, "Sean-fhocal" is an ancient saying that has come down on the lips of the people from time immemorial.

The Irish people had a great wealth of proverbs, which have been only partially collected. In a few areas the collection has been fairly complete; in others partially so; while in many large areas there has been no systematic collection. Thousands of proverbs have been lost owing to the decay of the Irish language, for probably not more than five per cent of them have been translated into popular English speech, and have continued in use in an English dress. From purely English sources a number of proverbs in English have come into use, but these would not represent in number a tenth of what was lost, so that an English speaker in Ireland to-day has a very small repertoire of proverbs compared to what his grandfather or great-grandfather had a hundred years ago.

Causes, however, other than the change of language have also contributed to this end. Modern life with its continuous excitement and sensations, fed by travel, the press, broadcasting, cinemas, the daily post, etc., has almost completely destroyed that repose of mind in which proverbs flourished. The man of some centuries ago had a narrow horizon. His world was a small area a few miles around his home, and his knowledge of life within that small area was far-reaching and exhaustive. He could trace the genealogy of the families in that area back for several generations, and had heard the characteristics of these families and their vicissitudes as a direct resultant of these characteristics discussed on hundreds of occasions. Thus he could hardly help being somewhat of a philosopher, and continually tracing effects to their causes. All this is now gone, even in Ireland. We have become cosmopolitan in mind and outlook, but have lost in depth what we have gained in superficies.

The Scotch proverbs are probably the nearest in character to those of Ireland, but the Irish proverbs compare unfavourably with those of Scotland in wit and humour. The Scotch proverbs are much more humorous, ours more serious. This may be due to our unfortunate modern history—seven centuries of almost continuous warfare. And again, unlike the Scotch, comparatively few of our Irish proverbs have any reference to features of modern Irish life, which would suggest that the vast bulk of them are at least several centuries old.

Another characteristic of them is that a large proportion are in metre. Just as several lines of the poetry of Pope, Tennyson and other English poets have become proverbs, so many of our Irish proverbs may have been lines of ancient poems that no longer exist. This metrical character can be observed in Irish proverbs even when they consist of only a single line each, owing to the internal rhymes in almost every line of modern Irish poetry. Let me give as an example—" Or like men in retreat from the field of disaster, who beseech the black *night* on their *flight* to fall faster." In the last line the words *night* and *flight* are internal rhymes, while " retreat " and " field " give us simple vowel rhymes in the first line.

Hundreds of Irish proverbs have these internal rhymes. Needless to say, in translation into English, all this literary artistry is lost. It suffers almost the same as a beautiful gold trinket would if melted in a crucible. The melted mass would contain all the gold, but the artistic form had vanished. Hence, no translation can do justice to Gaelic proverbs. A good deal of what Dr. Nicolson has written of Scotch Gaelic proverbs is equally true of the Irish ones :

> " Their view of human nature is keen but kindly ; critical, but not contemptuous. The number of them that can be condemned on the score of morals or bad taste is singularly small. With much natural reverence for religion, our Celts have combined a freedom of criticism on the ministers of religion. The proverbs of Italy and France specially abound in insinuations against priests and women. In both respects the Gaelic ones form a contrast to them, which testifies equally to the character of the people, their priests, and their women."

The Irish people in their proverbs, as in their ordinary speech, could curse heartily, but they were never blasphemous or profane. The common use of such terms as " damned ", " hell ", " bloody ", etc., so common in vulgar English speech, was quite unknown to the humblest and most ignorant Irish speakers, and as a consequence their proverbs are free from that kind of profanity.

Irish proverbs were not used merely to spice conversation or writing : their chief use was for the philosophy they supplied in a convenient form.

Having left more than three score years behind me, I have seen two generations pass away, and can recall numerous instances where important affairs of life were settled or determined by reference to a proverb.

" [The wisdom of] the proverb cannot be surpassed " is one of our sayings. So an apt proverb opportunely quoted silences all opposition.

The disappearance of proverbs may not be felt by the cultured and educated classes, but it will certainly be a serious loss to those who have not had time or opportunity for intellectual development. Hence, a collection of proverbs such as this volume contains is most valuable. Who knows, but there may be a reaction to the present inanity of popular life, and that people mentally sickened by it may begin to search again for the wisdom and serenity of their forefathers. Should that time come, these collections of proverbs by Dr. Champion will then be sought after for their wisdom, as the bee seeks the flowers for their honey.

HENRY MORRIS.

OFFICE OF NATIONAL EDUCATION,
DUBLIN,
IRISH FREE STATE.

INTRODUCTION TO THE PROVERBS OF ITALY

By PROFESSOR EMILIO BODRERO, Ph.D.

If proverbs really contain the wisdom of peoples, then it must be said that this wisdom is very uncertain, since from the contrast between *Dulcis in fundo* and *in cauda venenum,* and so on, one observes that there is no proverb that has not another one to contradict it. On the other hand, the variety of the vicissitudes of human nature are such that with the exception of a few fundamental principles that form the basis of life, every one of our experiences offers us contrary aspects in which the good and the evil, which may be observed or deducted in any event, are disciplined.

In this argument Italian proverbs present numberless slight differences. This could not be otherwise when one considers that they are the creation of a people who from the disembarking of Aeneas on the shores of the Tyrrhenian Sea can count thirty-two centuries of civil life and who in addition to that has seen enacted on its soil the most glorious as well as the most tragic deeds that history can relate, and who has known every form of government and experienced every joy and every misfortune.

There is no type of man or society that does not find its archetype or counterpart in Italian history, and that has left in the minds of our people the dregs of an experience which they express in their proverbs with perspicacity. Moreover, for millenniums the Italian people has been accustomed to universal grandiose ideas, as were in the past and still are in the present those two Roman ideas of Empire and Papacy, which have given this people the inclination to seek and form other universalities, as, for example, those moral and psychological which find their codification in proverbs. It must also be added that Italy is geographically in the centre of three continents. If we place before us a map of Europe and fix the one point of a compass on Rome and the other on the coasts of the Atlantic Ocean, and then describe a circle, we shall see that Rome is approximately at equal distance from the Ocean, from Asia Minor, from the Baltic and from the Sahara desert. The Mission therefore of Rome and Italy in past centuries has been to concentrate and diffuse the spirit of the most diverse civilizations, from the Germanic to the Arabian, from the Byzantine to the French, from the Barbarian to the Asiatic, from the Greek to the Etruscan, making it one with its own education of humanity which in this case is equivalent to "Romanita".

In addition to this the land of Italy is the most varied, I don't think any other territory can show a more extensive and more complete collection of samples of climate, cultivation and scenery. Italy is in part made up of a continent, peninsular and various islands, some of which are of a considerable size. In the northern part of Italy it is as cold in winter as in Northern Europe ; in Sicily it is as warm in summer as in Africa ; there are lakes and rivers, seas that wash shores of sand and rocky coast ; there are plains and hills and very high mountains ; every kind of cultivation is carried on by us as well as every industry. The trees vary from the firs of the Alps to the palms of the South, and those trees which may be called our national trees grow with a special luxuriance—these are the pine, the holmoak, the olive and the cypress. Each of our cities has its own particular character given to it by its history—thus Rome, Florence, Venice, Palermo, Naples, Milan, Turin, Genoa, Ravenna, Siena, Bari, Bologna, and many more are profoundly different the one from the other not only from the physical, material and artistic point of view but also from the psychological. In the science of proverbs Italy should therefore occupy a notable place. Our language and our popular literature are full of them, the more so since with us not only quotations from the Bible and the Gospels have become proverbs, as in all other Christian countries, but also verses from Virgil, Horace, Dante and Plutarch. With us the populations of the islands are very sententious, even Cicero noticed that the Sicilians " grandes sunt verbis et crebri sententiis ".

Amongst our proverbs there are many that are common to all parœmiographical literatures ; these are the ones relating to human nature, certain characteristics of woman, certain vices, the value of money, social differences and similar arguments, others relate to the seafaring life, the life of husbandry or handicrafts of the various populations, and these are the most characteristic. Others contain laws arrived at through millenniums of experience, and which science has attempted in vain to contradict, they are all the more right and exact the more the phenomenon with which they deal escapes from the discipline of human reason. The psychological proverbs and those relating to the professions are accompanied by the political ones, which are very numerous with us. They nearly always imply a criticism of government since Italy for many centuries was either wholly or partially subject to the foreigner, thus the government was always hated because it represented servitude, oppression and exploitation.

In all these categories animals have a notable allegorical function, not alone on account of the Æsopian and Phœdrian tradition, but from the sympathy that the Italians have always had for animals and from their powers of observation.

To a great extent our proverbs present a comic and ironic character ; they are very rarely bitter or sarcastic. One would say that from the kindliness of the climate, the beauty of the sky and of nature, the Italian people are inclined to optimism. I should say that the majority of those Italians who are fatalistically pessimists are those who came from the national zones of the slopes of the Tyrrhenian, the part most subject to earthquakes and volcanic eruptions. These populations have lived and still live bearing in their subconscious minds the terrified expectation of a terrific catastrophe. This gives them, together with the sense of the uncertainty of human life, an acute desire for joy and at the same time a mysterious melancholy. It is to this ever-present danger that are owed their songs, which are very frequently sad, and certain of their superstitions, as for example the evil eye.

It is natural that it should be so with a people who have always before their eyes great mountains like Vesuvius and Aetna, whose rumblings they hear and from which they see lava and cinders pouring out, remembering the tragic cataclysms caused by their caprices. It is natural that it should be so with a people who live on ground often shaken by slight shocks and which during prolonged periods destroyed whole cities with thousands upon thousands of victims.

But apart from these particulars, Italian proverbs are serene and often gay. They give definitions which are in themselves a training and more rarely a rule of conduct. Sometimes they are sceptical, sometimes even cynical, due to the length of our experience which has constantly reproved the futility of struggling against certain ills. Many, on the other hand, express a profound morality and an exquisite kindness which are the special virtues of our people, who possess in such a high degree the sense of citizenship.

The family, the nation, religion and property are glorified in our proverbs as a patrimony which they wish to preserve as the unassailable conquest of our civilization, and in this is the most honourable element of that spontaneous expression of the wisdom of our people.

EMILIO BODRERO

Professor, Royal University of Padua,
Italy.

INTRODUCTION TO THE PROVERBS OF JAPAN

By PROFESSOR KOCHI DOI

THE earliest traditions of Japan were handed down in the unlettered ages by the so-called " story-telling clan " ; and at some festivals these traditions were probably recited and represented in mimetic plays. As the years went on the gists of these traditions were crystallized into short sayings, which were called " koto-waza " or " words that work ". Such words were the earliest proverbs.

" Beware a returning arrow " (No. 11) seems to have been originated from the custom of shooting an enemy with the same arrow that he had first used, and in the eighth century it was a time-honoured proverb.

When Buddhism and Confucianism were introduced to Japan the essence of those doctrines was given to the illiterate as proverbs. Nos. 33, 47, 213, 231, 421 were probably Buddhistic, while Nos. 111, 116, 256, 268, 384 sound like Chinese origin. Chinese proverbs were often expressed in parallelism. One might argue that these were not purely Japanese proverbs, but they went home into the heart of the people and remained there for several centuries. We may regard them as ours.

The Japanese poems of 31 syllables, or of 17 syllables, seldom became real proverbs. An eighth-century poem :

> " What use to me silver, gold and jewels ?
> No treasure can surpass children "

is almost a proverb in cultured society, but the proverb is

> " Children are poor men's treasures " (No. 51).

A subtle verse of the seventeenth century :

> " After speaking lips are cold in the autumnal wind "

may pass as a proverb in a literary circle, but the people would have as theirs :

> " Open lips make cold teeth " (No. 378).

Even folk-songs supplied few proverbs, for they were not made in a dancing mood. I meet with only two such in the collection.

> " Drink and sing, an inch before us is black night " (No. 88).
> " Things never change since the time of gods, the flowing of water, the way of love " (No. 417).

Those which belong to the above-mentioned categories will be less than ten per cent. of the present collection. The majority seem to have been the creation of the common people, hard-living in town or in country. These people had undergone all the miseries of life, and had grown very cautious, and they were very bitter against gay and talkative women. They knew, however, all the bitters and sweets of their humble world, and were very human and shrewdly observant.

Sometimes wise sayings were used, and when these served as a caution or encouragement they naturally became proverbial, and have been handed down through the ages.

> " Seven falls—eight rises " (No. 112).
> " An insect an inch long has half an inch of soul " (No. 193).
> " There is a piece of fortune in misfortune " (No. 242).
> " A child brought up by its grandmother is three hundred farthings cheaper " (No. 46).

Such sayings bring back to my memory the hardy country people who poured these words into my childish ears. I have heard almost all of these proverbs here gathered in Dr. Champion's big work on Racial Proverbs. I was brought up in the country, but I suppose these proverbs were current in towns as well, until the recent deluge of printed matters.

I believe that in this book the racial proverbs are very well chosen, and they represent the people who were never mentioned in elegant literature, nor came in touch with the Western tourists.

In my boyhood children had playing-cards which were fifty in number. On each of them there was a proverb illustrated. Someone had to read out a proverb, and we rivalled each other to find the card which had that proverb printed. I recollect the following were on those cards :

> " Fortune will call at the smiling gate " (No. 132).
> " If in haste go round " (No. 166).
> " The heart of a child of three years remains until he is sixty " (No. 174).
> " After victory tighten your helmet cord " (No. 407).
> " Three men together are as wise as Manjusri " (No. 271).

KOCHI DOI.

PROFESSOR OF LITERATURE,
TOHOKU IMPERIAL UNIVERSITY,
JAPAN.

INTRODUCTION TO THE PROVERBS OF LATVIA

By MISS MARGUERITE GROSVALD

A Lettish proverb says, " Poor in goods, rich in joys," and anyone acquainted with the history of Latvia will agree with me that a more fitting motto could hardly be found for the collection of Lettish proverbs which are here presented to the English public for the first time. The fact that in the past the nation was " poor in goods " explains the sad note we frequently come across, while their variety and charm leave us in no doubt as to the mental faculties of those who produced them and were, owing to their folk-lore, " rich in joys ".

Latvia is a new country, but her seafaring people have inhabited the shores of the Baltic since the beginning of the Christian era. Their geographical situation early brought them into contact with other nations, and numerous finds of Arabic, Roman and Scandinavian coins speak of flourishing trade relations. Engaged in peaceful pursuit (chiefly husbandry and apiculture), they seemed destined for a peaceful life in peaceful surroundings. But another fate was in store for them. Beginning with the thirteenth century, their coveted territory was invaded by a succession of foreign armies, and their liberties were destroyed one by one until, by the eighteenth century, such liberties had ceased to exist.

The above events could not but leave a lasting mark on the folkloristic treasure of the nation, of which Latvia is justly proud. Life was too hard, perhaps, for some long *epos* to be composed ; but there was no lack of shorter tales or of folk-songs, sung to shorten the endless hours of drudgery or to test the wits of rival poets in a duel of song when friends assembled for some spinning-bee, and proverbs were coined whether the sky was serene or whether thunder-clouds threatened.

The hardships the Letts suffered served to sharpen their powers of observation and made them anxious to let others profit from their experience. If book-learning was at that time out of their reach, practical wisdom was not, and it was stored up in their proverbs.

Until the second half of the nineteenth century Latvian proverbs were learnt from memory and handed down by word of mouth. Even now only part of them has been collected. In their character, their aspirations and the lessons they teach, they may not differ from others. All proverbs tell one what to do and how to do it in a manner suitable to all times and all nations. But for all that the proverbs of Latvia have an aroma of their own. They speak of the peaceful life on a Latvian farm, of its animals, of the tricks its inhabitants play on each other, of the dense woods and undulating fields which provide one with one's daily bread, of the master's exactions, of ways and means how to weather a storm. They grow sarcastic over the fate of those who disregard good advice and, finally, they talk of Sundays, when people drive to church a long way off and enjoy their hours of leisure, since according to another Lettish proverb, "Where there's a church, there's an inn not far away."

Before I let the proverbs of my country speak for themselves, there is another point I would advance in their favour—their extreme brevity. The Lettish language, which is said to be akin to ancient Sanskrit, seems to say a great deal in a very few words. But in order to render their meaning in English, I have often been obliged to employ double the number of words used in the original. I can only hope that part of their charm at least has survived.

MARGUERITE GROSVALD.

Aspazijas Bulvari 2,
Riga,
Latvia.

INTRODUCTION TO THE PROVERBS OF MALAY

By E. S. HOSE, C.M.G.

It is fitting that in a comprehensive work of this kind a selection of Malay Proverbs should be given a place. The Malay, with his innate courtesy, not unmixed with a certain veiled sense of superiority, will always adapt himself to the manner of speech of any foreigner, and in such circumstances he will carefully refrain from the use of aphorisms or proverbial sayings that might not be understood. But in the intimacy of the family and the village, proverbs and similes are indispensable to any discussion or argument. Indeed, without a fairly extensive knowledge of proverbial expressions and their application, the stranger in a Malay household would find it quite impossible to follow the meaning of a conversation, although he might have a sufficient vocabulary to chatter fluently enough to any Malay whom he might meet.

So deeply embedded are proverbs in Malay thought and speech that it is only by a careful study of local sayings, and their judicious use in conversation, that a foreigner can hope to break down the barriers of reserve, and win the confidence and friendship of this lovable and warm-hearted people.

The selection of Malay Proverbs made by Dr. Champion for the purpose of this work is of necessity limited, but is sufficiently wide in scope to be quite characteristic. One cannot help regretting, as in all other languages, the inevitable loss in vitality and pithiness from setting the proverbs down in a bald translation, without the subtle charm and poetry of their native dress, but one realizes that conditions of space, if nothing else, are imperative, and that for purposes of comparison there is everything to be said for the use of a common language.

Perhaps a word should be said about the "pantun", or rhyming quatrain, that is so often made the means of conveying some well-known wise saying or adage. The first two lines of such quatrains are generally little more than a nonsensical jingle, the true meaning being contained in the last two lines. Often in conversation a Malay will quote the first line of a familiar "pantun", which to his *vis-à-vis* will convey a proverb appropriate to the occasion, while to the uninitiated it will have no sort of meaning. It is regrettable that examples of "pantun" could not be given in this selection of Malay proverbs, but it is essential to their proper appreciation that they should be given in their own language.

E. S. HOSE.

Manor House,
Normandy,
Guildford.

INTRODUCTION TO THE PROVERBS OF MONTENEGRO

By THE LATE WOISLAV M. PETROVITCH, M.A.

THE following views on proverbs in general, and Montenegro in particular, were extracted from the letters to me of the late Mr. W. M. Petrovitch, who did so much invaluable work for me in translating from many languages, and who was to have written a foreword to this collection and the Serbian.

" In compiling the collection of Montenegrin proverbs which I am sending to you, I consulted Vuk Karadzic's collection of Serbian Popular Proverbs (where he has designated in parenthesis those which he picked up in Montenegro and Herzegovina. Vuk Karadzic is the father of our literacy and the Dr. Johnson of the Yugoslavs, and has collected some 8,000 proverbs from the Yugoslav countries a hundred years ago ; other collections have been made since). I had at my disposal no other books of proverbs properly so called, but only general literary works of :

(1) Prince-Bishop Petar Petrović-Njegoš : *Gorski Vijenac*, etc.
(2) Stjepan Mitrov Ljubiša : *Narrations*, etc.
(3) Ljubomir P. Nenadović : *Djela*, etc.

but the majority I collected from the lips of the Montenegrin peasants during my travels through Montenegro and Herzegovina. A number of them I heard from the late King Nikola of Montenegro, Major Marko Popović, Dušan Osmokrović, The Herzegovinian, and others.

" As regards your theory that a nation creates her own proverbs, I agree. Nations do so, but when a nation conquers and subjugates another, the more civilized of the two, whether victor or vanquished, imposes its culture to the more barbarian. This is almost a constant law in history. The ancient Greeks, although conquered by Rome, not only imposed to the rough Romans their refined Hellenic culture, but even made them think in the Greek way. Examples are innumerable. When the fanatical, but not exactly civilized Turks, conquered the rather advanced Serbo-Croats-Montenegrins, not only could they not impose the Turkish language to the indigens, but, in order to live in amity with those Christians, they set down and learnt our language to an astonishing degree of perfection. What is more, most Turkish families actually forgot Turkish. However, Constantinople, alarmed at that Serbification, as it were, of its Ottomans, kept on sending hodjas, dervishes, mufties and softas to those provinces, who, while unable to make the Bosnians and Herzegovinians speak Turkish, certainly made them think in the Moslem (Mohammedan) way ; thus they transplanted the Arabic wisdom in those provinces. You will seldom find a Bosnian or Herzegovinian Christian quoting a Christian proverb; nay, if he cites anything at all, he will say an Arabic proverb, or at least a Serbian redaction of it. Therefore, it is, I am sure, most difficult to advance a candid opinion on the subject. The Bosnians and the Herzegovinians, taken on the whole, are either Serbians, Croatians or Montenegrins (the reigning dynasty of Petrović-Njegoš in Montenegro came only two hundred years ago from Herzegovina), ergo, Slavs *par excellence*; they are proud of their origin—but they still sigh for the departed Padishah's rule from Bosnia and Herzegovina. So deep was their reverence of the clean teaching of the Mohammedans—which were chiefly, as I said, Arabians! The Slavs and, indeed, all the other Christians, may live another 2,000 or 10,000 years, but they will never engender a thought worth comparing with those which the East produced. That is why Mehmed Beg Kapetanovic gave in his collection such a prominent place to the Oriental sayings amongst his Christian and Mohammedan countrymen in Bosnia and Herzegovina.

"Of course, you, as a student of folk-lore, will surely know that no definite line could be fixed to delimitate the territory within which a proverb, respectively a fairy tale, or a myth, or a legend, has been created; still less could any province legitimately claim their ownership, monopoly or exclusiveness, which proves, better than anything I know, the oneness of the Arian race. All nations—not only those belonging to the Arian race, but *ALL* nations of the human gender—think alike, have same or similar desires, aspirations, and even humour, satire, etc. If they do not all express themselves as eloquently as some naturally witty nations (such as English, Irish, Chinese, Russians and such other naturally gifted nations), that is not to be inscribed as a drawback, for they most often atone with their other qualities (such as genuineness of feelings, sincerity, bluntness, naïveté, etc.) for their lack of wittiness, sharpness, astuteness, biting sarcasm (which qualities are not quite free of sadism and sometimes utter perversity). Proverbs are the mirror of a nation's soul, and the folk-lorist's duty is not to *edit*, but *register* the national aphorism such as he hears it from the single-eyed people. The Germans, for example, say: 'Such country—such proverbs.' This is utterly absurd, for the country may be inhabited next day by another, cleverer or duller people. What they really meant is, 'Such *people*—such proverbs,' because it is the people, not the countries, who make the proverbs.

"It would be as ridiculous to claim the monopoly of some international, universal, truths as it would be if any nation claimed the story of *Cinderella* as its exclusive possession, for Mr. J. G. Frazer informed me, at the time of the first appearance of my work, *Hero Tales and Legends of the Serbians* (Harrap, London, 1914), that he had seen that story in not less than 64 languages!

"In my estimation a proverb ought not to contain only a dose of national wisdom, but also *de l'esprit*; unless a proverb is witty it runs the risk of becoming a dull, flat solecism. Such do not, of course, live to see a second edition ; *sacre il sera car personne n'y touchera !* to use Voltaire's famous saying (which he addressed to Empress Katharine II, when she bored him with her poetry, in lieu of all criticism of the verses which he returned untouched to the Imperial versifier, alluding to the Vestal maidens ! . . .)"

INTRODUCTION TO THE PROVERBS OF MOROCCO

By PROFESSOR EDWARD WESTERMARCK, Ph.D., LL.D.

The Moorish proverbs (or "mitālāt", sing. "mitāl") amounting to nearly two thousand, which I have collected from the mouths of the people and published in my book, *Wit and Wisdom in Morocco*, are to a large extent sentences conveying a statement of a more or less general character which is either literally or metaphorically applicable to individual cases, but the statement of some particular event, real or imaginary, may also be a proverb, though only on condition that it may be applied figuratively to other events reminiscent of it. Proverbs have become proverbs only by being used in definite concrete situations.

The Moorish proverbs, like proverbs generally, have a strong tendency to make use of figurative language. They abound in metaphors, which imply the application of a name or descriptive term to an object to which it is not literally applicable; and in similes, which introduce an object or scene or action with which the one in question is compared, but not identified, and is usually connected by a comparative conjunction such as "as". A trope that is particularly congenital to the nature of proverbs is the hyperbole, that is, an exaggerated statement not meant to be taken literally. It conduces to shortness, definiteness, and impressiveness; and proverbs are essentially sparing of words, categorical in their pronouncements, forcible in their expressions. They avoid modifying adverbs, like often, sometimes, mostly, scarcely; they state as a universal truth what is true on the whole or even what is true in exceptional cases; and they exaggerate not only the frequency of events but their quality and, generally, anything they are intended to express: "What the devil does in a year an old woman does in an hour"; "A hundred drunkards are better than one gambler"; "Everything is useful, except that lies and slander bring no profit." Another trope implying a statement that is not meant to be taken literally is irony. But while the hyperbole gives vigour and intensity to the expression by exaggeration, irony does so by making use of language that in its literal sense is opposite to the meaning attached to it; and while the hyperbole is serious in its purpose—though it may itself unintentionally become an object of ridicule by degenerating into rant—derision is the very essence of irony: "Dress up the little piece of wood, it will become pretty" (said of an ugly woman who wears a fine dress); "Generous, except with regard to his own field" (said when a person who has been invited to a wedding takes with him several uninvited guests); "Get what you want, may God curse your female neighbour" (said of a person who speaks badly of another who has done him a favour).

The proverbs of a people may be studied under different aspects. Their study has been the pursuit of philologists who have been mainly interested in the linguistic side of the subject; thus various eminent scholars have made use of proverbs for their study of modern Arabic dialects. Another method of studying proverbs is to examine their diffusion: peoples have at all times taken sayings from each other. The wanderings of proverbs are a fascinating study, but one beset with considerable difficulties. It must always be borne in mind that the resemblance between proverbs may have another cause than diffusion, namely, the uniformity of human nature, which makes men in similar situations think and feel alike. The real test of a common origin is therefore not the mere similarity of ideas and sentiments expressed in the proverbs, but the similarity of formal expression, with due allowance for modifications that are apt to occur when a saying is adopted from another language and transplanted into a new soil. Among the nations of Europe we find a very large number of identical, or almost identical, proverbs that obviously have a common origin; and Arabic-speaking peoples have also in common a store of sayings, partly derived from the Mohammedan traditions but largely of secular origin.

Besides those two methods of investigating proverbs there is a third, which is primarily concerned with their contents as a subject of sociological or psychological interest. It is a traditional view that the proverbs of a people are a safe guide to its character and temperament, opinions and feeling, manners and customs; Bacon said that "The genius, wit, and spirit of a nation are discovered by their proverbs." This view has of late been subjected to criticism, not altogether undeserved. It has been pointed out that a very large number of proverbs are international common property, and that most of the sayings of different nations are so similar that they must be regarded as expressions of general human nature. This is perfectly true. But besides similarities there are also differences, and even in substantially similar proverbs there may be shades of dissimilarity that correspond to national characteristics. Such characteristics may also to some extent show themselves in what the proverbs of a people speak of and what they are silent about, in the degree of popularity a certain proverb, or class of proverb, has gained among a people, and in the frequency or paucity of proverbs dealing with a particular subject. It has further been argued that the proverbs of a people have to a large extent come to it from other peoples and cannot, therefore, be indicative of its peculiarities. But it should be noticed that a foreign proverb is scarcely adopted by a people unless it is in some measure congenial to its mind and mode of life; that it is apt to be modified so as to fit in with its new surroundings; that, when sufficiently deeply rooted, it may in turn influence the native habits of thought and feeling; and that, if it does not succeed in being acclimatized in its adoptive country, it will wither and die. These facts are of great importance on account of the frequent difficulty, or impossibility, of separating indigenous proverbs from others, which have crept into the language from abroad ; and a very similar answer may be given to the objection that proverbs are not creations of a group of people but of individuals. At the same time there is a point to be remembered in this connection, which is of the utmost importance for the whole study of proverbs : in order to gain reliable information about people from its proverbs it is necessary to possess intimate knowledge of it derived from other sources, foremost of which is personal experience. I venture to think that I have acquired some qualification for such a task during the nine years I have spent in Morocco for the express purpose of studying its natives. Goethe wrote :

> " Sprichwort bezeichnet Nationen,
> Musst aber erst unter ihnen wohnen."

Proverbs are not only reflections of life, but also play an active part in it. This functional aspect should by no means be neglected by the student ; he should learn what use people make of their proverbs—when and how and why they use them.

Most Moorish proverbs are expressive of feelings or opinions, or intended to influence people's wills and actions. One of the feelings which figures very prominently in them is dissatisfaction. The world is full of evils of many kinds. The innocent is punished for the fault of the guilty : " One eats beans, and for another they swell in his stomach." A good deed is often rewarded with evil : " He who has done good will have colic in return." Good servants or workmen are dismissed to give place to bad ones : " The tables were turned upside down, and the earthenware pots sat up." What a difference between a poor man's life and a rich man's : " If a wealthy man speaks unjustly they say to him, your speech is gold ; if a poor man speaks the truth they drive him away and in addition spit on him." But while the proverbs express sadness and despair, they also give hope and consolation : " However long the night may last, there will be a morning " ; " After every affliction there is enjoyment." Everybody will get what he deserves : " An innocent person's invocation to God has no curtains " (it will be heard at once) ; on the other hand, " He who sows thorns must walk on them barefoot." A poor man who has many worries is given the comfortable advice : " Put the troubles in a net, some will fall and some will remain." It may be said that even pessimistic proverbs give some comfort in suffering by reminding the sufferer that there are others as badly situated as himself.

Dissatisfaction often leads to disapproval or reproach ; and here again a proverb is a very suitable vehicle for giving vent to one's feelings. On the one hand, it gives censure a semblance of public opinion ; on the other hand, it makes even a sarcasm less offensive by making it less personal. A person who makes a show of friendship but hides enmity in his heart is told : " Fire underneath the straw." Someone who does not do his work properly: "A work rises only in the hand of its master." A person who interferes in other people's affairs: "Enter your own market, don't enter the markets of others." But the reproof is not always equally polite. A man of low extraction who pretends to come from a good family may hear the remark: "A wick does not come from a rag." A person who quarrels with his guest: "None but a dog bites in his own house." And as proverbs are suitable means of censure they are also, for the same reasons, useful weapons of defence. When an indocile apprentice is beaten by his master, and his father complains of it, the master may say: "The thorn is not removed with cotton." If a person denies the truth of a statement made by another, he may have the reply: "The clouds are not hurt by the barking of dogs." A thief excuses himself by repeating the saying: "Lack of work is a misfortune."

Generally speaking, the Moors are a polite race. If anyone shows you a thing he has bought you should say it is good, whatever you may think of it: "If you see him riding on a bamboo-cane say to him, Good health to your horse." Indeed, this is not a matter of mere politeness: there is an idea that the spoken word brings about its own realization. And there is another superstition that has been conducive to politeness, and at the same time to the use of proverbs as polite answers, namely, the belief that a person by refusing a request exposes himself to the danger of being hurt by the other person's evil eye or his curse. Now it is obvious that a request cannot always be granted, and people often prefer running some risk to doing what they are asked to do; but they may lessen the danger by politely couching the refusal in a proverb. In a country where charity is a cardinal duty it does not sound well to say "no" to a beggar; it is much better to convey one's denial by making an excuse: "What will death take from an empty house"; or, "Our sickness is the same, and the one who cures is God." In spite of their politeness, however, the Moors are an excitable people and, when enraged, hurl at each other the most terrible curses. There are also curses among their proverbs. But, on the other hand, the use of an appropriate proverb may serve to cool the rage, stop the quarrel, and make those who were cursing each other a moment before rejoice and shake hands with each other. Once when two of my servants from Tangier quarrelled I had only to recite the proverb, "The quarrel of a native of Tangier is like fumigation with benzoin" (which only lasts for a moment)—and the angry look was changed into a friendly smile.

EDWARD WESTERMARCK.

Professor of Sociology, London University, and
Professor of Philosophy,
University of Helsingfors,
Finland.

INTRODUCTION TO THE NEGRO PROVERBS

By FRANK CUNDALL, O.B.E., F.S.A., F.R.Hist.S.

The Negro Proverbs of Jamaica, as of the rest of the West Indies, may be divided into four classes: those that have their origin in Africa, those originating in the West Indies, those adapted from European proverbs, and those that are frankly European proverbs expressed in Negro language.

Appended is a list of works giving examples of West India proverbs. The most complete collection of West India Proverbs known to the present writer, is that made by the Rev. James Speirs of Demerara, which numbers 1,069. A comparison shows that several of the proverbs most often heard in Jamaica, e.g. "Greedy choke puppy"; "Rocktone a riber bottom neber know sun hot"; "When black man tief, him tief half a bit; when bockra tief, him tief whole estate"; "Ebery John Crow tink him own picknie white", etc., are common to several of the colonies. The last-named in the French colonies is rendered in patois—"Macaque pas jamais ka die iche li laide" ("Monkey never says its young is ugly").

No collection of Negro proverbs could hope to be exhaustive. As they improvise some verses to their songs as they sing, so the negroes improvise proverbs and proverbial sayings. For this reason one meets with two or three renderings of the same saying, and very often the same idea clothed in different words. Sometimes they are in direct opposition, as "Man mus' die, but wud neber die," and "Wud mus' die, but man mus' lib." Their riddles have a family likeness to their proverbs.

In the West Indies, European proverbs are turned into meanings more readily understood by the people, e.g. "A cat may look at a king" becomes "Darg hab liberty fe watch gubnor." Similarly, "Hard words break no bones" becomes "Cuss-cuss neber bore hole a me 'kin," and "Les absents ont toujours tort" becomes "Behind darg, it is 'Darg'; before darg, it is 'Mr. Darg'"; or in the patois of the French islands, "Deier chien ce 'Chien'; douvant chien ce 'Missier Chien'." "Familiarity breeds contempt" (which the Italian expresses by "Don't play with the bear if you don't want to be bitten" becomes in Jamaica, "If you play wid puppy, puppy lick you mout"; and "Honesty among thieves" is rendered by "Darg no nyam darg".

"Ebery man know wha' him own house a leak," obviously, is a rendering of the English proverb dating from the time when negroes wore no shoes to pinch their feet. "He laughs loudest who laughs last" becomes "Fus' laugh a no de ending". "All is not gold that glitters" becomes "No ebery ting wha' got sugar a sweet," which is especially applicable in the lands of the sugar-cane.

There are but comparatively few proverbs which can be traced to their African origin.

In Demerara, though not in Jamaica, the Negroes have proverbs telling of elephants. These are obviously of African origin. In Jamaica there are no monkeys, but monkeys figure in many of their sayings; the explanation being no doubt the same. Tigers are also sometimes mentioned in their proverbs, as they are frequently in their Annancy stories.

Those proverbs that have frankly been taken from the English are of interest in showing the class of thought that appeals to the Negro mind. In the same way, some Annancy stories of European origin have an interest second only to those of undoubted African source.

Some proverbs have one or two different renderings. Some say, "Big words break nobody's skin," others say, "Big words neber break man jawbone." Many phrases, it will be noted, are more or less Biblical in character.

In so far as they touch upon morals and manners, the proverbs of a race seldom display its good points. They are practically the race's criticisms of its own salient defects. If taken seriously, therefore, the proverbs of a race are apt to give an impression of its faults rather than of its virtues. In the case of the West Indian negroes, those defects on which most stress is laid are: hasty conclusions, improvidence, insincerity, greediness, want of foresight, interference, ingratitude, insolence, vanity, and presumption.

With the spread of education, the use of proverbs has a tendency to lessen, and the Negroes display a certain amount of diffidence about using them, at all events before "bockra". If asked the meaning of a somewhat obscure one, they will not infrequently plead ignorance. "Me no know," "Dat's only a sayin'." Some of them affect surprise, or even indignation, when a proverb is quoted against them, and will say, "Hi, wha dis Bockra get all dem old-time saying?" It seems fitting, therefore, that those which can be collected should be put on permanent record.

One sometimes hears it said of some proverbial saying that it is "not a true proverb". The first definition given of "Proverb" in the New English Dictionary—"a short pithy saying in common and recognized use"—seems wide enough to include all the sayings included in a Jamaica collection. They are at all events, all sententious and quaint, and interesting as illustrative of Negro thought and character.

In the Negro pronunciation of English words, the initial "s" before a consonant is usually lost (e.g. "'tand" for stand); "h" often disappears after " t " (" t'ink " for think) ; " him " stands for he or his ; " for " (fe) often marks the infinitive mood ; " in a " takes the place of " in " ; " da " of be ; " a " of is, and so on.

FRANK CUNDALL,
O.B.E., Officier d'Academie (France), F.S.A., F.R.Hist.S., Honorary Corresponding Member of the Institut Historique et Heraldique de France, the American Antiquarian Society, the American Jewish Historical Society, the Hispanic Society of America, the Ontario Historical Society.
SECRETARY AND LIBRARIAN OF THE INSTITUTE OF JAMAICA.

INTRODUCTION TO THE PROVERBS OF PERSIA

By SIR E. DENISON ROSS, C.I.E., D.Litt., Ph.D.

The Persians are past masters in the art of conversation, and they love to introduce appropriate quotations on every possible occasion. Proverbs naturally play a very large part, but many of those current in Persia are translations from the Arabic, which is exceptionally rich in this respect, and educated Persians are fond of quoting such proverbs in the original. Consequently in order to understand Persians and to enjoy the full savour of their company the foreigner should possess more than a passing acquaintance with their classic literature and with the homely sayings which illustrate their philosophy of life. In this introduction to Dr. Champion's collection of Persian proverbs I propose to deal with (1) proverbial expressions dealing with universal truths; (2) brief aphorisms associated with anecdotes; (3) examples of the wisdom of the world set to verse by the wit of a poet—often simply platitudes in fine clothes; and (4) some Persian idioms.

Space will not permit me to enumerate more than a very few of the commonest of the many proverbial expressions in use among the Persians. Many of these have, naturally, their counterpart in other languages. Some, on the other hand, appear to be exclusively the property of Persia. It must be borne in mind that, as in the proverbs of all countries, half the point lies in the phraseology, and this, of course, is difficult to reproduce for English readers.

Let me take a few examples at random. "Beyond black there is no colour" is an original way of saying that the limit has been reached in some particular direction. An unfortunate man is described as being so unlucky that he "breaks his teeth when eating jam". Persian literature contains many examples of the truth of the saying, "A wise enemy is better than a foolish friend"; and of the advantage of doing in Rome as the Romans do: "If you do not wish to be insulted, behave like the rest of the company." To live beyond one's means is called "putting one's foot outside the coverlet"; and the following examples are also characteristic: "A thousand leagues divide Love and Patience"; "The foot of the lamp is dark"; "If Fate does not adjust itself to you, adjust yourself to Fate"; "Two dervishes can sleep on one carpet, but a whole empire cannot hold two kings"; "If you wish to make yourself dear [valuable] you must either die or go on a journey"; "Reflection before speech is better than repentance afterwards."

The Arab sage Loqman is frequently made the author of wise sayings; and the equivalent of "carrying coals to Newcastle" is in Persian "to teach wisdom to Loqman". (This idea is also expressed by the saying "to carry the leg of a locust to Solomon".) Someone once inquired of Loqman from whom he had learnt manners; he replied: "From the mannerless." A certain man, happening to meet Satan, addressed him with the pious remark, "May your end be well" ("Aqibat bikhair"). Satan replied, "Hardly" ("Mushkil"). A man, meeting the Prophet Mahomet, addressed him in the following words: "O thou best of all creatures!" The Prophet replied: "That was Abraham." The ostrich which hides its head in the sand in the hope of becoming invisible has its counterpart in the partridge which puts its head in the snow. A child who has once been burnt and ever afterwards fears fire is replaced in Persian by "A child who has been bitten by a snake fears every rope." Such are a few examples of the first two categories I mentioned.

The words of the poet Sa'di, like those of our own Shakespeare, are "full of quotations". Let me enumerate a few of these as examples of versified wisdom. They must necessarily, of course, lose in translation. "In the sea are treasures without number, but if it is safety you desire, that is on the shore"; "A lie told for a good purpose is better than a truth which brings misfortune"; "If the fireworshipper keeps the sacred fire burning even a hundred years, he will be consumed should he happen to fall into it." Somewhat related to this in sentiment is the verse of Sa'di which says, "I have taught no one the art of the bow who did not in the end make me his target." "If the builder sets the first brick awry the wall will be crooked although it reach to the Pleiades" is another good example.

I must now refer to one or two purely Persian idioms. Quite recently I noticed in a Persian newspaper an expression which seemed to translate admirably the word "snob"—namely, "Did-na-did"—literally, "He saw, he did not see." A man whose presence in a company is unwelcome is called "Sar-i-khar". "Sar-i-khar" means "head of a donkey" and signifies a scarecrow, as a donkey's skull is often set up on a stick for this purpose. On the other hand, of a person whose absence is much regretted they say, "His place is very green," referring obviously to a picnic on the grass.

Finally, let me tell two well-known and characteristic camel stories: They said to the camel, "Why is your neck crooked?" The camel replied, "What part of me is straight that you should complain of my neck?" A mule once inquired of a camel: "How comes it that you never stumble, whereas I am always knocking my hoofs against stones, and run the risk of falling with my pack?" The camel replied, "You always look on the ground and pay attention to mean things; that is why you stumble against them. Do as I do; hold your head high and look upwards, and then the mean things can do you no harm."

A selection of Persian proverbs such as this volume of Dr. Champion's contains is not only most interesting, but of great value to any student of folk-lore, and I, for one, warmly welcome the author's efforts to preserve these old folk-sayings and help, even in some small measure, to prevent their being entirely ignored in Europe.

E. DENISON ROSS.

School of Oriental Studies,
London.

INTRODUCTION TO THE PROVERBS OF POLAND

By A. PRZYBYSZEWSKI

No student of Slavonic traditions, customs, and thought will fail to give Dr. S. Gurney Champion a very warm welcome, for it is his love of proverbs, the work and passion of a lifetime, that has given us this important ethnological material, collected and edited in such a complete form, and in so carefully prepared a manner, and in so far as I may be allowed to bear testimony to the Polish section, for the first time in the English language.

The mental development of a nation is nowhere so well represented as in the popular sayings of the crowd. Naturally, the life of an essentially childlike and primitive people is more concisely expressed in proverbs than in any other way.

The full measure of the joys and sorrows of the peasant, of the achievements and misdeeds of the gentleman, of the virtues and vices of the priest—not to mention the measure of that genius of rural commerce and finance, the village Jew—is eloquently and sometimes crudely voiced in these axioms.

In a nation more fully developed and with a more sensitive literary consciousness, though not necessarily greater richness of literature, proverbs tend to be forgotten or mistrusted. But to the Pole they are what the nursery rhyme is to the child : something which contains in an easily memorizable and easily digestible form some simple moral content—which, in fact, may be quite as easily contradicted by some other proverb.

In Liddell and Scott's *Greek-English Lexicon*, I find under " *παροιμία* ", as the first English equivalent, " a by-word ", which is exactly what the Polish " przysłowie " means. A by-word ! Can it be something to have " by you ", some little talisman to help you along on the stony path of life ? Does it perhaps explain the more contented attitude towards things in general of the Slav peasant than that of the industrial worker of the Western " civilization ", although the former is actually confined to a lower standard of living ?

This much to the serious student.

To the man-in-the-street, to whom the Pole, maybe, is only known as one of the happy or unhappy members of the League of Nations, or the delighted owner of two things, equalled only by the Loch Ness Monster in publicity value, such as the Polish Corridor and the Jewish Question, I will say with Montaigne, " C'est icy un livre de bonne foy."

It is not the vacuous dictums of the professional politician ; it is not the subversive sayings of the hired traveller ; it is not the glamorous maxims of the neurotic novelist : it is the fount and true essence of Polish wisdom and tradition.

To the casual reader to whom neither science, nor politics, nor travel, nor the new morality means anything, let me recall Shakespeare's " Patch grief with proverbs." And here it should be of especial satisfaction to the Author that whereas in his professional sphere as physician it must have often been his good fortune to bring relief to the body in anguish, it is now in this work that he has accomplished, consciously or unconsciously, a much more important task, that is, to carry assistance to the soul in torment.

I commenced with a word of praise. Thus it will be in keeping if I conclude with a word of regret, or to be precise, two words of regret : one, that it has been found impracticable to print the Polish original by the side of the translation ; two, that owing to my mistaken notions of propriety a number of " choice " sayings are omitted as " untranslatable ".

A. PRZYBYSZEWSKI.

LONDON.

INTRODUCTION TO THE RELIGIONS

By P. MACLEOD YEARSLEY, F.R.C.S., F.Z.S.

Any mention of the current proverbs occurring in the teaching of the major religions of the world at once calls to mind those to be found in that of one's own country, and the fact that there is incorporated in the Christian Bible a special section which deals with them under the appropriate title of The Proverbs. A few remarks upon this particular book may, therefore, furnish both a useful introduction to the study of these sayings and of religious proverbs in particular, and also reveal certain significant facts as to their origin and distribution.

The origin of The Proverbs, which is a collection of sayings of wise men, loosely strung together to form a single book, can be traced to two distinct historical times, its oldest part belonging to the Persian Period, while its present form dates from the Greek Period. The sayings it contains are attributed to Solomon, to Agur the son of Jakeh, to King Lemuel and others. The attribution to Solomon is in all probability due to the fact that, in common with many other notable national heroes, much that is wholly mythical accumulated around him. Tradition is rife concerning him and wonderful things are told of him in the Korân, but his fame rests on no surer foundation than tradition, and the stories concerning him are those of the after-growth of legend. Certain of the *Psalms* are assigned to him, while the *Song of Songs* (a love poem of the Persian Period) was attributed to him merely because it contains his name, while the celebrated Judgement of Solomon is a widespread Eastern Legend, one version of which appears in the literature of the Jains of India and another is told of Buddha. To the Jews, Solomon was the "Great King" who united Israel and founded the Temple, and it was but natural that they should glorify his more worthy acts and keep a discreet silence as to those which were unworthy.

Apart from other considerations, the paramount interest of The Proverbs is the way in which the sayings it contains gained entry into the religion of Israel and thus became later current in Christian religious literature. In the time of the Persian kings there was settled at Elephantine, in Egypt, a colony of Jews. In that locality were discovered, in 1904, some nine or ten perfectly preserved rolls of papyrus. These important documents relate mainly to the affairs of the colony, but among them exists one which is of considerable importance to the subject which concerns us here. It is entitled "Sayings of the Wise and Skilful Scribe, Ahikar by name, which he taught to his Son". This Ahikar was prime minister of Assyria in the reign of Sennacherib, by whom he was sent to Egypt. There he distinguished himself in a trial of wits with the Pharaoh, a form of contest which was always, and still is, very popular among Eastern peoples. The manuscript found at Elephantine was probably written for the Jewish Colony there some five hundred years before the Christian Era, but the "Sayings of Ahikar" preserved therein are much older than this particular copy. They were well known and much prized by the Jews and are mentioned in the apocryphal Hebrew *Book of Tobit.* It would appear —and this is an important point—that a number of these sayings were incorporated in THE PROVERBS and, as illustrating this fact, the following examples from the latter may be given side by side with extracts from Ahikar for the sake of comparison.

Proverbs.	*Ahikar.*
Withhold not correction from the child; for if thou beat him with a rod he shall not die. Thou shalt beat him with a rod, and deliver his soul from Sheol.	If thou strike him with a rod, he does not die. But if thou leave him to his own will, he becomes a thief, and they take him to the gallows and to his death.
A stone is heavy, and the sand is weighty; but a fool's vexation is heavier than them both.	Son! I have lifted iron and I have lifted stones upon my shoulders, and it was better for me than to dwell with the ignorant and the fool.
Rejoice not when thine enemy falleth, and let not thine heart be glad when he is overthrown.	My Son! Envy not the prosperity of thine enemy, and rejoice not at his adversity.

The interest of this comparison is that it demonstrates clearly the interchange of proverbial sayings between the teachings of different peoples, and shows the universality of the proverbs which are met with everywhere. This, I think, can be amplified and corroborated by a study of the sayings, many of which are to all intents and purposes proverbial, to be found in other religions, and the following survey, made as succinct as possible, will, I hope, make this clear.

Taking first the religion of *Ancient Egypt,* the high code of ethics which the Egyptians evolved is shown by the texts in their *Book of the Dead.* The origin of this ritual is lost in antiquity, but it was believed by the Egyptians themselves to have been compiled by Thoth, and it was certainly in general use as far back as 3700 B.C. It would be superfluous to give more than a few quotations from this wonderful work, and the following excerpts are sufficient to show their high character.

> "I have not caused pain—I have not let any man hunger—*I have made no man to weep*—I have not committed murder—I have not committed fornication—I did not encroach upon the fields [of others]—I have not added to the weights of the scales—I have not taken milk from the mouths of children."

Of all these, out of many, protests to be made by the soul before the Judgment Seat of Osiris, the finest and most comprehensive is that which I have italicized. The Egyptian code of ethics contained every essential which is usually supposed to make a "good Christian"; whether it was lived up to as much by the one as by the other is not the question: the code itself was there.

Besides the *Book of the Dead* are other ethical works which contain what are practically proverbs. These are the *Instructions* of Ke'gemni (3998 B.C.) and of Ptah-Hôtep (3550 B.C.). From these the following are sayings readily comparable with those found in all religions. K'gemni has:

"If a man be lacking in good fellowship, no speech hath any influence over him."

"Beware of making strife, for one knoweth not the things which the God will do when he punisheth."

In Ptah-Hôtep occur:

"Be not proud because thou art learned, but discourse with the ignorant man as with the sage."

"If thou desire that thine actions may be good, save thyself from all malice, and beware of the quality of covetousness."

"He that obeyeth becometh one obeyed."

"Take not any word away, neither add one; set not one in the place of another."

But of all the ethical sayings of Egypt, none are more striking than those of the Reformer-King, Akhnaten (1386–58 B.C.), the founder of a theology which was the forerunner of the later monotheistic religions. Specially important as showing the composite nature of the Christian Bible is Akhnaten's "Hymn to Aten", the Sun-God, which bears a striking resemblance to *Psalm* civ., as the following three extracts will show:

Akhnaten.	*Psalm* civ.
How manifold are all thy works. Thou didst create the earth according to thy desire—men, all cattle—all that are upon the earth.	O Lord, how manifold are thy works. In wisdom hast Thou made them all. The earth is full of Thy creations.
Thou makest the seasons. Thou hast made the distant heaven in order to rise therein—dawning, shining afar off, and returning.	He appointed the moon for certain seasons, and the sun knoweth his going down.
The world is in thy hand, even as Thou hast made them. When Thou hast risen, they live; when Thou settest, they die.—By Thee man liveth.	These wait all upon Thee. When Thou givest them [food] they gather it; and when Thou openest Thy hand, they are filled with good. When Thou hidest Thy face, they are troubled. When Thou takest away their breath they die.

In *India*, Hinduism or Brahmanism is the result of the growth of centuries from the primitive religion of the Aryan invaders, mixed with Animism. It is unique among the world's great religious systems in having no personal founder nor hard-and-fast creed, and from it sprang Zoroastrianism and Buddhism. From its sacred books, the *Vedas*, I have picked out the following as furnishing striking parallels with the precepts of other religions : and precepts are so closely akin to proverbs that the dividing-line is difficult to define.

" In the beginning there arose the source of golden light."

" Purity of body comes by water, purity of mind by truthfulness. The lamp of truth is a lamp of the wise."

" Let him not do evil to others who desire not that sorrows should pursue himself." (The Golden Rule.)

" Absolve us from the sins of our fathers, and from those which we have committed with our own bodies."

The other great religion of India is *Buddhism*, which claims so many peoples in the East. From its sacred writings, the *Tripitaka*, may be culled the following flowers of precept :

" Conquer anger by mildness, evil by good, falsehood by truth."

" Be not desirous of discovering the faults of others, but zealously guard against your own."

" To the virtuous all is pure."

" To be pure, temperate, to persevere in good deeds ; these are excellences."

" The gem of the sky is the sun ; the gem of the house is the child ; in the assembly shines the brow of the wise man."

Zoroastrianism.—The teachings of Zarathustra, or Zoroaster, the reputed founder of the Parsis religion, are contained in the *Zend-Avesta*, and his cult was certainly founded before the Conquest of Bactria by the Assyrians. Its teaching rests upon the dual conception of a good and an evil principle in ceaseless conflict. The Zoroastrian ethics are essentially practical, emphasizing active charity, useful deeds, kindness to animals, courage and uprightness, in a creed which is noble and uplifting. It is an important event in the evolution of Christianity that the Jews came in contact with the teachings of Zarathustra at the period of the Exile and obtained therefrom the ideas of a future life and a personified evil principle, from the latter of which the conception of Satan evolved. It is not surprising, therefore, to find in the *Zend-Avesta* sayings which have their parallels in Christian precepts. I give three examples.

" Hear with your ears what is best, perceive with your mind what is pure, so that every man may for himself choose his tenets before the great doom. May the wise be on our side."

" Those old spirits who are twins made known what is good and what is evil in thoughts, words, and deeds. Those who are good distinguished between the two, not those who are evil-doers."

"Purity is for man, next to life the greatest good. That purity is procured by the law of Mazda to him who cleanses his own self with Good Thoughts, Words, and Deeds."

In *China*, besides Buddhism, there are two systems, Taoism and Confucianism, neither of which can be strictly called religions. Taoism, founded by Lao Tzŭ, has become a mere chaos of magic and animism and is the creed of only the uneducated. Lao Tzŭ (600–500 B.C.) was a noted sage who contemplated the futility of human life and the best way to cope with it. A didactic moralist rather than an active and practical reformer, his precepts (which form the nucleus of Taoism) contained much that was current before his time, and his teachings were passive. The following may be taken as typical specimens:

"He who is self-displaying does not shine."
"He who is self-approving is not held in esteem."
"He who is self-praising has no merit."
"He who is self-exalting does not stand high."
"When in the world beauty is recognized to be beautiful, straightway there is ugliness. When in the world goodness is recognized to be good, straightway there is evil."
"Recompense injury with virtue [kindness]."

A far different man was Kung-Foo-Tsze, the founder of Confucianism, and better known under his Latinized name of Confucius (551–487 B.C.). As he was never deified his teachings have not suffered from the corrupting influence of a priesthood. His memory is venerated as a man of great and pure mind and integrity and his precepts, which are essentially rationalistic and humanist, hold a prominent place in Chinese education and are learned by heart. In the following is the best definition of the "Golden Rule".

"Tsze-Kung asked saying, Is there one word which may serve as a rule of practice for all one's life? The Master said, Is not *reciprocity* such a word? What you do not want done to yourself, do not do to others."
"When you know a thing, to hold that you know it; and when you do not know a thing, to acknowledge that you do not know it—this is knowledge."
"To see what is right, and not to do it, is want of courage."
"The real fault is to have faults and not try to amend them."

We may pass over the sayings of the Greek philosophers, merely drawing attention to certain outstanding precepts, like that of Alcidamas: "God sent all men to be free; Nature made none a slave"; the wisdom of Socrates in "Know thyself," and his exposition of the Golden Rule in "You should be to others what you think I should be to you"; Plato's "The temperate man is the friend of God, for he is like to him," and Aristotle's "In justice are comprehended all the virtues" and "The worst man is he who works evil as regards himself and others; the best is he who works good not only for himself, but for others—truly a hard task." Callimachus, for twenty years chief librarian to the library at Alexandria, is notable for "Not to every one doth Apollo manifest himself, but only to the good."

Similarly, a passing note must be taken of the wisdom of Rome. Cicero gave the world two sayings :

> "The unruly passions of anger and desire are contrary and inimical to reason."

and approaches the "Golden Rule" in

> "Nature ordains that a man should wish the good of every man, whoever he may be, and for this reason—that he is a man."

Other interpretations of the "Golden Rule" occur in Lucretius, "Violence and wrong enclose all who commit them in their meshes, and do mostly recoil on him from whom they began"; Seneca, "You must live for another if you wish to live for yourself"; Epictetus, "What ought not to be done do not even think of doing"; Ælian, "Not only is he who does evil bad, but also he who thinks to do evil"; and Marcus Aurelius, "No mere talk of what the good man should be. Be it", and "That which is not good for the beehive cannot be good for the bee."

Finally, there is the youngest of all the Great Religions, that founded by Mohammed (A.D. 571–632), with its sacred book, the *Korân*. It is difficult to select passages for quotation from the Mohammedan scripture, but the following give some conception of its vigorous language and sound ethic.

> "Bestow on me wisdom, and join me to the just, and give me a good name among posterity."
>
> "The fate of every man have I bound about his neck."
>
> "O Believers ! avoid frequent suspicions, for some suspicions are a crime ; and pry not : neither let the one of you traduce another in his absence. Would any of you like to eat the flesh of his dead brother ? Surely you would loathe it."

The "whole duty of man" appears in the precept of Mohammed's son-in-law, Abou Bekr :

> "Be just : the unjust never prosper. Be valiant : die rather than yield. Be merciful : slay neither old men, children, nor women. Destroy neither fruit trees, grain, nor cattle. Keep your word, even to your enemies."

An admonition which seems specially to be required at this present time of political unrest.

This short summary of the teachings of the great religions and the ancient philosophers will, I hope, prove my point. The passages quoted may not all answer the reader's conception of the word "proverb", but it is undeniable that the difference between a proverb and a religious direction or admonition is sufficiently imperceptible to make it difficult at times to distinguish the one from the other. It would seem that the trend of man's thought has, from the earliest times, run on fundamentally similar lines. Speaking generally, the cultures developed by primitive man in every part of the globe show such basic similarities. If, for example, his implements, both of peace and war, be considered, they show developments on parallel lines, interpreting the experiences which, governed to a certain extent by the exigencies of geographical and climatic environment, must have moulded his mental development. In like manner, his experiences in human relationship must have led him to much the same ideas of conduct and ethic, so that his best rules of life with comparatively slight modification due to race and environment, were strikingly alike and developed in the slow course of ages, from nebulous conceptions that certain actions entailed certain results affecting his welfare, into the one great central idea of Reciprocity, that " Golden Rule " which permeates practically every proverb and every surviving creed, not to mention those that have decayed and disappeared. The pity of it is that so universal and ancient a precept as Reciprocity should not have proved sufficient guidance for humanity without spoiling its simplicity with the crude incrustations of different theologies. It has ever been—perhaps must ever be—that man has always been prone to think better than he can practice, to conceive ideals to which he cannot attain. This is nowhere better demonstrated than in his religious proverbs.

MACLEOD YEARSLEY.

GERRARDS CROSS,
BUCKS.

INTRODUCTION TO THE PROVERBS OF RUSSIA

By ANDREW IVANOVICH GUERSHOON, LL.B.

THE word " Proverb " translated into Russian is " Poslovitsa " (" By-word "), the " Proverbial Expression " is " Pogovorka " (" By-talk "). The first recorded collection of Russian proverbs dates back to the seventeenth century.

As an introduction to Dr. S. G. Champion's Selection of Great-Russian Proverbs, the following remarks may be of interest.

Every country, every district, every region in the world has its Proverbs and uses them. These sayings of the people are sometimes so old that their origins cannot be traced, while others are comparatively new and mirror the latest developments in civilization.

By studying the Proverbs of a people one studies that particular people, although it is true that the Proverbs of various nations do not present equal possibilities of acquiring knowledge of the people themselves.

Some nations seem to have lost many of their oldest Proverbs. Some are poorer than others in proverbial lore and do not give the student a full chance of getting a complete picture of their people's characteristics.

The study of Great-Russian Proverbs, as distinct from those of other nations, shows that the Russian people are marvellously portrayed in their Proverbs. Hardly anywhere else can such wealth of material and so truthful a picture of national life be found, as in Russian Proverbs. The whole of the vast country of Russia, with its millions upon millions of homogeneous people, has for centuries contributed to the treasury of national Proverbs. There are more than sixty thousand recorded in the Great-Russian language.

Almost everyone is different from the others and is purely Russian in its origin. One of the reasons for this abundance and originality is the Russian's innate love for Proverbs. Centuries of oral wisdom, practically unhampered by any precepts, examples, or book-learning, have placed the Proverb in a lofty position in the Russian mind. Proverbs, fairy-tales and songs have been the only vehicles of the Russian man and woman's creative mental power. (In so far as the people's folk-lore is concerned, and as distinct from the advance of education in the cities and towns.)

When I speak of homogeneous people I mean the Great-Russian nation, as different from other Slav entities inhabiting the extreme western and the southern parts of Russia. There are over one hundred million Great Russians living to-day. They occupy the vast plain east of the Vistula and stretch right up to the Pacific. Apart from the Ural and the ridge in Eastern Siberia, there are no mountains to separate the people ; no dialects, no peculiarities of speech to act as handicaps to the free dissemination of folk-lore. I trust that I may be forgiven for reminding the reader of the well-known, albeit wonderful fact that what is spoken in Smolensk on the Polish border is spoken in Vladivostok on the Great Ocean, many thousands of miles away. A Proverb current where the sun rises in the extremities of Asia, is found intact where the sun sets over the Western rivers, on the fringes of other European countries.

Such a possibility for the preservation and safe keeping of Proverbs over time and space has not presented itself to any other nation in the world. If other Proverbs have become obsolete, nay forgotten, or if they mirror purely local, hemmed-in interests, this is certainly not the case with those of Russia. In other countries learning, the Press, books, periodicals and the like have tended to displace Proverbs. This is not so in Russia. Even to-day the innate love of the Russians for their Proverbs remain. Only those dealing with the Tsar and partly those dealing with the Deity have lost currency. The overwhelming majority are still in common use, and will be current for centuries to come. There are one or two things to be said why the Russian man and woman are, perhaps subconsciously so, fond of their Proverbs ; why the people at large constitute themselves involuntary and unconscious keepers of Russian Proverbs for posterity. Firstly, they feel them to be their own national treasures. During the last centuries, almost anything of an authoritative nature, practically everything connected with philosophy and standard precepts regulating the problems of how to live, have been brought into Russia from abroad. The Christian religion came from Byzantium, learning from the West of Europe. The folk-lore, however, is Russian through and through. Whilst songs are usually women's expression of lore, and fairy-tales belong in the main to the children, Proverbs, and *only* Proverbs, are the whole country's unaided acquisition and possession.

I agree entirely with Dr. S. G. Champion that every nation creates its own Proverbs and that adaptions of foreign ones are really of no account, although they undoubtedly exist. It is therefore clear that the riches in Russian Proverbs, both as to number and diversity of subject-matter, are pre-eminently a Russian achievement.

There are other quite important aspects of the interesting part played by Russian Proverbs in any parœmiological collection. Unfortunately many of these aspects get lost in the process of translation. I was often sorry when submitting my translations of these old folk sayings to Dr. Champion, to note the loss of rhyme, rhythm, alliteration, dramatization, witticisms, *jeux-de-mots*, and so forth. However, these losses being unavoidable, they need not be regretted in this foreword to Dr. Champion's selection. Suffice it to say that these fanciful embellishments are ever-present in the originals, and that they have greatly helped in the preservation of the actual Proverbs to this day. When speaking of losses in the rendering of Proverbs of another nation, I ought to mention that other ornaments are fully able of being retained. I refer to allegories, metaphors, comparisons, parallelisms, contrasts, personifications, studied omissions, incongruities (apparent) exaggerations and a host of other genuine devices serving to enliven and preserve a Proverb. All these ornaments are to be found in Dr. S. G. Champion's selection. After these very general remarks a reader will readily appreciate why Dr. Champion chose to select and to give room to a great number of Russian Proverbs in his monumental work.

Undoubtedly he was prompted by the consideration that if a people's Proverbs are strong and virile, if the subject-matter is all-encompassing, if the creators, the common people of Russia, are proud and fond of them to this day, then a certain prominence should be given them.

The Russian nation's Proverbs are wholesome, devoid of morbidity and entirely free of sarcasm. They are brief, smooth and easy to understand. They undoubtedly portray the ordinary Russian man and woman's soul and outlook.

If I have succeeded in assisting Dr. Champion during the six years of our collaboration on Slavonic and, more particularly, on Russian Proverbs, even in a small measure, I shall feel very gratified. A selection of Russian Proverbs in the English language has never been published before. We must exclude two or three brief anthologies the authors of which never intended to give a representative selection. The reason why I so warmly welcome the publication of Dr. S. G. Champion's work is that owing to his labours a good selection of the Proverbs of a great nation will for the first time be presented to the English-speaking reader.

A. GUERSHOON.

LONDON.

INTRODUCTION TO THE PROVERBS OF SPAIN

By PROFESSOR AURELIO M. ESPINOSA, Ph.D., Litt.D., LL.D.

The proverbs of Spain constitute one of the most important branches of Spanish and European folk-lore. They are the philosophy of the common people, the judgments based on the experiences of the race, and expressed in brief artistic forms, both prose and verse. The people, both young and old, use them in their daily conversation, as their ancestors have used them for centuries, and consider them as traditional and authoritative opinions on most of life's problems. So many of them express such universally admitted truths, and are at the same time rendered in such beautifully artistic forms, that they have found their way into formal literature.

Spanish proverbs and proverbial expressions are, of course, in a great measure, the Spanish forms of similar materials that are common to the folk-lore of Europe, and even to universal folk-lore, but many are fundamentally and typically Spanish in origin and form, and depict very accurately some of the outstanding traits of Spanish character. Their deep philosophic and religious content and rendering, particularly those that deal with the most tragic problems of human life, such as wealth and poverty, youth and old age, love and hatred, death and the future life, is a clear indication of the Roman, Christian and Arabic heritage of the Spanish people.

The fact that we find the Spanish proverbs in such beautifully artistic forms, with varied metrical renderings as early as the fourteenth and fifteenth centuries aside from their similar prose forms, is clear proof of their antiquity. By the middle of the fifteenth century even the learned Marqués de Santillana, the aristocrat who had despised the popular ballads or romances *de que la gente baja e de servil condición se alegra*, had appreciated the Spanish proverbs to the extent of collecting and publishing what is probably the first European collection of proverbs, his universally famous *Los proverbios que dizen las viejas tras el fuego*. By the beginning of the seventeenth century, when Gonzalo de Correas published his monumental *Vocabulario de refranes y frases proverbiales*, the proverbs of Spain had already become the philosophy of the people, and they had been accepted as such even by the greatest men of letters. When the Marqués de Santillana published his Refranes they had already been utilized in literature by the novelists, such as Martínez de Toledo in his *Corvacho* or *Reprobación del amor mundano*, and after that we find them extensively cited in *La Celestina*, in the picaresque and other novels, and to some extent even in lyric poetry.

The popularity of proverbs in Spanish literature, however, found its greatest expression in the Don Quijote of the immortal Cervantes. It is generally believed that only Sancho Panza cites proverbs, but as a matter of fact Don Quijote cites them also and frequently. In his great novel Cervantes gives us abundant proof of the popularity of proverbs and ballads, both with young and old, learned and illiterate.

Generally speaking, after Cervantes, proverbs, like ballads, were not extensively used in literature, but were relegated to the common people, who have treasured them always in popular tradition, often in the same linguistic and artistic forms of the sixteenth and seventeenth centuries, or earlier, and who often altered them to add new and variant poetic forms to the traditional ones. It is not rare to find the old traditional proverbs cited side by side with their new forms, even by the same individuals. The seventeenth-century and modern *coplas populares* give expression to the older prose and poetic forms.

Because the proverbs of Spain have been the philosophy of the common people, who have treasured them always in the original and in new forms, and because they have been so extensively used in literature, reaching their greatest literary prestige in the *Don Quijote* of Cervantes, they are worthy of being studied by all students of literature, and particularly by those who study the literature and history of Spain. They are a true and direct expression of the psychology of the Spanish people.

PROFESSOR OF ROMANIC LANGUAGES,
STANFORD UNIVERSITY,
CALIFORNIA.

AURELIO M. ESPINOSA.

INTRODUCTION TO THE PROVERBS OF SWEDEN

By LIEUT.-COLONEL CARL A. BÄCKSTRÖM

PROVERBS are as old as the community, as old as the thinking human being. The collected experience of humanity lies, one may say, in proverbs.

What is a Proverb?

There are many different opinions as to that. Antiquarians do not give the same answer or the same explanations.

My belief is that you come nearest the truth if you say that a proverb is a short, pithy and visually picturesque aphorism, which lives on the people's lips and expresses an observation from the practical life, a universal experience, a rule dictated by prudence, or an upright rule of life.

One of our Swedish authors writes about the proverb, that it is a clever opinion, a lesson or phrase of knowledge expressed in few words and put into a certain euphonious style, that it may be easily learned and remembered, and which has lived and lives on the people's lips.

Proverbs speak of life's happiness and misery, sorrow and joy, riches and poverty, honour and disgrace, beauty and ugliness, power and weakness, greatness and smallness. They comfort and deplore, mock and praise, joke and speak with pathetic seriousness.

Generally the lesson which they contain is spiced with a certain quaint humour. In proverbs treasures of sound judgment are bestowed, practical wisdom, justice, sympathetic and often poetical comprehension, also witty satire. But in many you will find the contrary qualities.

Proverbs of a people constitute a source which is not insignificant for the knowledge of its national character and customs, which are faithfully reflected in them. Besides, they provide a great interest in point of language.

You will find many of the same proverbs with almost all civilized people, but in different places they generally have a national diverging wording.

The people's sense of justice is in proverbs, and there is scarcely any vice which is not scourged in them, no virtue which will not be elevated.

Our old Swedish proverbs contain a treasure of great value, not only for the antiquarian, but even for the historian of civilization, the social politician, the judge of art and the poet.

They are the first and most simple fruits of a primitive poetry, that have arisen and lived on the people's lips, the remains of ancient poetical work. They constitute an old national inheritance, which have passed from generation to generation, and deserve nevertheless to be preserved as other paternal estates, which are taken good care of and protected.

A great number of the Swedish proverbs contain direct rules of life, and that statement is easily verified, scarcely has any country from its pagan olden times more excellent gnomical poetry, philosophy of life in song and proverb, than those which belong to the Scandinavian people.

Regarding the collections of Swedish proverbs it can be said that already in the seventeenth century several collections were published, and among them *Svenska ordsedker eller ordsaghor.*

He who first collected and compared the Swedish proverbs more closely was Chr. Grubb-Mayor. His work, *Penn Proverbial* was printed the first time in 1656, and is in its way of pioneering significance.

Jesper Swedberg has in his work, *Ludus Literarius*, adopted a number of our most characteristic proverbs. He worked at the end of the seventeenth and in the beginning of the eighteenth centuries.

Johan Ihres' great work, *Glossarium Sviogothicum*, even deals with Swedish proverbs.

In 1807 Lars Rhodin published his collection of Swedish proverbs, amounting now to three thousand.

H. Renterdahl published in 1840, *Old Proverbs in Latin and Swedish*, and in 1865 the same author published *The Swedish Book of Proverbs.* During 1857–86 K. Strõmbãck compiled a Swedish-Northern dictionary of proverbs, comprising Swedish proverbs in alphabetical succession, compared with Danish, Norwegian, Icelandic, Faroese, German, English, French, Italian and Greek.

The Dictionary is in the Royal Library in Stockholm, unprinted. A textual critical edition of old Swedish proverbs was published 1889–94 by Axel Kock and K. af Petersėns under the title of *East-Northern and Latin Proverbs of the Middle Ages.*

Several unknown authors have published smaller collections during the past years.

In 1926 Fredrik Strõm published *The Swedes in their Proverbs*, including seven thousand Swedish proverbs.

The writer of this foreword presented in 1928 to the Royal Library in Stockholm, his collection of proverbs which he worked out during many years, comprising about 30,000 proverbs in Swedish, German, French and English.

The Swedish proverbs are alphabetically arranged, the others are entered in the Swedish where similarity, agreement and spiritual meaning are in accordance. A catch-word register worked out by me, helps to find a desired proverb easily.

CARL A. BÄCKSTRÕM.

STOCKHOLM.

INTRODUCTION TO THE PROVERBS OF SWITZERLAND

By J. SCHNYDER

A COLLECTION of good proverbs is a breviary of wise and understandable sayings, conveying useful views and suggesting counsel and advice; coined and expressed in an inimitable way by unknown, but surely clever and witty men, and which have therefore come into popular and universal use.

These Swiss proverbs which Dr. Champion has chosen have been selected from a private collection I began in early years and completed in the course of time from the lips of the peasantry and from different Swiss and German compilations. The essentially Swiss part of these sayings are, with many variations, at home in the alemanic dialects of our valleys and cantons, but a great number of the proverbs used in Switzerland have currency in a more or less varied form in Germany and other German-speaking countries, and vice versa. I found in the immense *Deutsches Sprichwörter-Lexikon* of C. F. Wander (five volumes, 1867–80, Leipzig, ed. Brockhaus) a multitude of sayings fundamentally common to both regions. In studying other foreign works on proverbs I had often occasion to recognize that the best Swiss and German proverbs are not known abroad, and I would be delighted if the specimens I presented to Dr. Champion might encounter some interest.

J. SCHNYDER.

KRIENS,
LUCERNE.

INTRODUCTION TO THE PROVERBS OF TURKEY

By S. TOPALIAN

SIXTY years ago Ahmet Mitat, a well-known Turkish writer, published in Constantinople a collection of Turkish proverbs, the largest of its kind, containing four thousand three hundred proverbs, arranged in alphabetical order but without any classification or comment. The book was soon out of print and forgotten, as to-day it does not appear in the list of the author's works. However, in 1897, Rev. E. J. Davies of Alexandria, realizing its value, reprinted the text in London, at the same time translating it into English, under the title of *Osmanli Proverbs and Quaint Sayings*, thus he saved the text which still remains as the main source for these proverbs, but his translation, owing to a large number of errors, is almost useless.

Dr. Gurney Champion, in preparing his present collection, has utilized modern small texts. Although his collection comprises only a fraction of the available material, it gives a fairly good idea of the nature of the Turkish proverbs. No translation, no matter how carefully done, can convey the true form and charm of the original. Brevity and rhyme play a very prominent part in the proverbs of all nations, and these often have to be sacrificed in translations.

Turkish proverbs are generally very short, this being due to the fact that the language lacks altogether the relative pronouns. With the exception of a few comparatively modern ones they are mostly very old, dating from early centuries when the Turks were leading a nomadic and agricultural life in Central Asia before their victorious march to the West in the Middle Ages. This can be proved by the figurative rendering of many proverbs which frequently refer to country life and domestic animals, especially the latter ; animals constitute the main metaphorical feature of Turkish proverbs. In this collection we find the following animals mentioned in one or more proverbs, i.e. the horse, 92, 125, 166–169, 215, 221, 270, 292 ; the lion, 156, 189, 141, 119 (with the fox) ; the dog, 73–76, 307, 309 (with the wolf) ; the sheep, 256, 257, 288 ; the bear, 13–15 ; the ass, 137, 167 ; the camel, 34, 35, 57 ; the falcon, 202, 97 (with the goose and hen) ; the crow, 50 ; the raven, 237 ; the cock and the hen, 44, 162 ; the mule, 167 ; the serpent, 253, 259 ; the fish, 110, 111 ; the bird, 131 ; etc.

Dr. Gurney Champion's work will show that the human mind reacts more or less in the same way all over the world. This is reflected in the proverbs of different peoples which vary so much in their rendering of the same idea owing largely to the influence of environment and climatic conditions. In England there is not enough sunshine, but plenty of rain, so " Make hay while the sun shines," but in Central Asia it is just the opposite, so " Fill the jars while it rains " (176), or " The water of a new jar is cold " (177) will say a Turk, where an Englishman says, " A new broom sweeps clean." In England " There is no smoke without fire ", a picture of the cold climate ; in Turkey, " No leaf moves without a wind " (183), a picture of open-air pastoral life.

In trying to understand a proverb the peculiarities of its language should be taken into consideration. This will explain many points that might appear at first obscure or grotesque. In English proverbs there is a reasonable contrast of one with two, " One bird in the hand is better than two in the bush," or, for the sake of rhyme, " One stitch in time saves nine " ; but on all similar occasions the Turkish has " a thousand ". " One accident teaches more than a thousand good counsels " (1, 32) ; " A thousand worries do not pay one single debt " (58) ; " Measure a thousand times before cutting once " (199) ; etc. A superficial explanation will attribute this to Oriental exaggeration, but the true explanation lies in the fact that the Turkish words for a thousand and one, " bin, bir ", have an alliteration and euphonic charm almost too strong to resist.

Turkish proverbs are very remarkable in expressing highly complex ideas in a simple way ; for instance, the Utopia of Communism and human equality is brushed aside simply by saying (you see) " Five fingers are not equal " (105). In Turkey no conversation takes place without one or more proverbs being mentioned, and it is amazing to see the influence that they make on an audience ; as soon as a proverb is recited all heads nod in approval and all arguments cease, a suffering or loss becomes bearable and even death loses its sting, for proverbs embody the crystal truth found by long and painful experience, and even though it may sometimes be bitter, it is in an acceptable form.

Turkish proverbs with their idyllic rendering remind one of the teachings of Christ, who took his similes from shepherds and lambs, from flowers and seeds, and this perhaps explains the reason why they are cherished so much by the Christian subjects of the former Ottoman Empire, who hold them in great respect and affection. There can be no fear of their being forgotten, for they will live as long as the Turkish nation and language live, because men and women need them in their daily life as they need their daily bread, for " He who does not heed proverbs, will not avoid mistakes " (236).

S. TOPALIAN.

School of Oriental Studies,
London.

INTRODUCTION TO THE PROVERBS OF WALES

By J. J. JONES, M.A.

The etymology of the Welsh word for proverb " dihareb " (plural, " diarhebion ") is perfectly analogous with that of proverb itself and of the corresponding terms in many other languages. That is to say, it shows that the general significance of the word is that of " a saying ". The final element of the word, " -eb ", is from a verbal root which is still used in Welsh in such forms as " ebr ", " ebe ", " eb ", all meaning " he says ". The etymologically correct form of this root is " heb ", and there are indications that " dihareb " was at one time pronounced " diarheb ". The dissyllabic prefix is intensive in force, so that to all intents and purposes we have in Welsh an exact equivalent, as far as the meaning goes of the Latin " proverbium "

A plausible attempt has been made to give another etymology of the word. This is based on the supposition that the primary form is " dihareb ", which, as it also appears in the form " dihaereb ", gave rise to the suggestion that the second syllable was from the verb " haeru ", " to assert ", the first syllable still retaining its intensive force.

But whatever be the true etymology, it is clear that the Welsh conception of what constituted a proverb is the same as that of other races. And the proverbs themselves have the general characteristics of all proverbs the world over. This is only what is to be expected, for proverbs are the expression of the wisdom of the folk, and the value of a comprehensive collection of proverbs lies in its preserving vivid examples of the native sagacity of man. Accidental circumstances of environment or history may sometimes be detected in the metaphors which the folk uses to clothe its thought, but all over the world, given the intellectual level which it is requisite for him to reach before he can create proverbs, man, faced with the occurrences and perplexities which are the universally common lot, reacts in the same way. It is this fact, and not mutual borrowing, that explains the parallels that can often be found between the proverbs of one nation and another. Actual borrowing there has been, of course, but this would seem to date chiefly from the comparatively modern age of written, and the still more modern age of printed literature.

The true nature of proverbs is well expressed in the title of one of the first books to be printed in Welsh. This is the book called *Oll Synnwyr Pen Kembero ygyd*, being a collection of proverbs made by the Welsh poet Gruffydd Hiraethog, and published some time between

1546, the date of the first Welsh book, and 1553. The translation of the title is " All the sense in a Welshman's head ".

What is peculiarly and permanently national in a collection of proverbs is the idiom of their original language. But in such a comprehensive collection as that of Dr. Champion it would be wellnigh impossible to publish each section in its respective language. To do so, it would be necessary also to provide translations, which would result in an impossibly bulky volume.

Leaving, therefore, on one side the question as to what national characteristics, if any, the selection of Welsh proverbs here published show, it will be profitable to dwell on one or two especial features of Welsh proverbs which derive from the genius of the Welsh language itself. First, there is the tendency for the proverb to be expressed in an alliterative form. Alliteration has always been one of the most characteristic of Welsh poetic devices. The fixed and complicated rules governing the repetition of consonants in the line was, and continues to be, a main part of Welsh bardic discipline. Examples of such alliterative proverbs, though not necessarily in accordance with the strict bardic rules, but sometimes consisting rather in a jingling of consonantal sounds, are " Edau rhy dyn a dorr " (" The tighter the string, the sooner it will break ") ; " Diwedd y gan yw y geiniog " (" The end of the song is money ") ; and " Arf glew yn ei galon " (" The weapon of the brave is in his heart ").

Another poetic element sometimes found in the composition of proverbs is the internal rhyming of vowels. One example is " Peswch sych diwedd pob nych " (" A dry cough ends all ills "), and another, " A ddwg wy a ddwg fwy " (" He who will steal an egg will steal more ").

A true poet can, of course, create lines which appeal to the folk as summing up some experience of its own, and many proverbs undoubtedly originated in this way, as they are sometimes seen to be created in modern times both by poets and by orators or writers of prose. But the reverse process is also possible. The wise saying of the folk may be taken up and refashioned in poetic form by the poet. Many of the lines of Edmwnd Prys (1541–1623), for example, have the ring of true folk proverbs. There is his " Llwybr pawb yw lle bo'r pant " (" Where the valley is, there is everyman's path "), which is not far removed from the Welsh proverb translated in this selection as " Every path in a gorge leads to the same place ". The sight of the tumbledown hedge, everywhere a sign of slothful husbandry, leads to much the same reflection by the poet as by the folk. The former sums up the matter by saying " Llwm yw'r yd lle mae'r adwy " (" Scarce is the corn where is the gap "). The latter says, " Better the shelter of a hedge than its place."

Again, in the " Myvyrian Archæology of Wales " there are nearly eighty of what are called " Englynion y Clywed " or " Stanzas of what is heard ". Some examples translated in the notes to her *Mabinogion* by Lady Charlotte Guest will make clear to the English reader what these were :

1. Hast thou heard what was sung by Hual,
   The son of Kaw, whose saying was just ?
   Often will a curse fall from the bosom.
2. Hast thou heard what Geraint sung
   The son of Erbin just and skilful ?
   Short lived is the hater of the saints.
3. Hast thou heard what Garselit sang
   The Irishman whom it is safe to follow ?
   Sin is bad when long pursued.

It is unnecessary to point out the proverbial character of the third line of each of these stanzas. Other stanzas contain as third lines some of the proverbs actually found in the present collection.

These stanzas are anonymous and traditional. Also traditional is the ascription of the sayings to the heroes named, warriors and bards of the sixth century A.D. For in Wales, as in other countries, proverbs are often fathered on men of legendary wisdom. Many, for example, are put down to the authorship of Catwg Ddoeth, the Welsh equivalent of Cato Dionysius, and one of the few triads given by Dr. Champion is to be found in the Welsh collection of sayings which correspond more or less to the "Districha" of Cato. The triad in question is, "Three things will drive a man from his house ; a leaking roof, a smoky chimney, and a quarrelsome wife."

No discussion of Welsh proverbs would be complete which did not contain some reference to triads. Examples of triads may be found among other nations, but nowhere do they form such a large portion of a nation's literature as they do in Wales. They are found among the oldest literature, but they were more especially developed in the sixteenth and seventeenth centuries, and deal with all sorts of topics from domestic economy to theology. Indeed, they may be taken to represent the sum total of all that was known.

Other examples of triads in the present collection are : "The three opportunities of all things—time, place and kind" ; "In three things a man may be deceived, in a man till known, in a tree till down, in the day till done" ; and, "Three pillars of judgment, bold purpose, frequent usage and frequent erring."

This is not the place to discuss the origin of the triads. Suffice it to say that there is but scanty evidence for the theory that they were of Druidic origin. There is greater probability in the theory that men were urged to this mode of expressing their thoughts by the influence of the doctrine of the Trinity. At least this influence seems to be apparent in the case of the Irish triads. Finally, there is the possibility that they are due to some mental trait which makes the folk conceive some virtue in odd numbers—the same belief which Pythagoras developed in his philosophy of numbers, making three the perfect number.

For the rest, these proverbs of Wales are marked by a high moral tone, as all true proverbs are. Based as proverbs are on the observations of experience, on the due regarding of cause and effect, the consolidated wisdom of the folk could hardly express other than what was true and good. Typically Welsh humour may be discerned here and there, sometimes cynical but always moral. There are also proverbs markedly religious in tone, and such as those which contain references to Paradise and the Mass may be supposed to date from pre-Reformation days. But on the whole, the religious proverbs are the fruit of experience, not the considered statements of dogma. They are such as could be fashioned anywhere where a simple trusting belief in God prevailed.

J. J. JONES.

Deputy Keeper of the Department
of Printed Books,
National Library of Wales,
Aberystwyth.

AUTHORITIES CONSULTED

I AM indebted to the following authorities for material found in their works :

*ABRAHAM (Capt. R. C.). *The Tiv People.* Lagos. 1933.

ADALBERG (S.). *Ksiega c Przyslów Polskich.* (*Polish Proverbs.*) Warsaw. 1889–94.

**Ādi Granth, The, or The Holy Scriptures of the Sikhs.* Translated by Dr. E. Trumpp. (W. H. Allen.) London. 1877.

AFANASIEV (A.). See SNEGIREV.

AHMAD MIDHAT. *Osmanli Proverbs . . .* with English translations by Rev. E. J. Davis. London. 1898.

AIPHT (MOSES O'R). "Proverbs of Brittany." (*Celtic Review.* Vol. 1.) Edinburgh. 1904–5.

AKIYAMA AISABURO. *Japanese Proverbs and Proverbial Phrases.* (Japan Welcome Society.) Kyoto, 1935.

*ALBERTI (LEONORA DE). *Proverbs in Portuguese and English.* (Hill.) London. 1920.

*ALLAN (Rev. C. W.) and SCARBOROUGH (Rev. W.). *A Collection of Chinese Proverbs.* Revised and enlarged by the Rev. C. W. Allan. (Presbyterian Mission Press.) Shanghai. 1926.

ALMASY (JANOS). *Hatezer Magyer Kozmondas.* (*Six thousand Hungarian Proverbs.*) Budapest. 1890.

ALTMANN (Dr. J.). "Uber die Sprichwörter der Russen." (Published in *Magazin für die Literatur des Auslandes.*) Berlin. 1854.

ALTMANN (CARL F. J). "Die Sprichwörter der Bulgaren." (Published in *Jahrbuecher fuer Slavische Litteratur.*) Bautzen Schmaler. 1853.

*ANDERSON (I.) and CUNDALL (F.). *Jamaica Negro Proverbs and Sayings.* (Institute of Jamaica.) 2nd Edition. London. 1927.

APPENDINI (F.). *Grammatica della Lingua Illirica.* 3rd Edition. Ragusa. 1838.

*APPERSON (G. L.). *English Proverbs and Proverbial Phrases.* (A Historical Dictionary.) (Dent.) London. 1929.

ARATCHY (ALEXANDER MENDIS SENANAYAKA). *A Collection of Sinhalese Proverbs, Maxims, Fables, etc.* Colombo. n.d.

ARTHABER (A.). *Dictionario Comparato di Proverbi e Modi Proverbiali.* Colombo, Milano. 1929.

ASTON (W. G.). *Japanese Proverbs.* ("Phœnix.") London. 1872.

BAERLEIN (H.). *The Shade of the Balkans.* Compiled by P. Slaveikoff and E. J. Dillon. London. 1904.

*BALABANOV (N. T.). *Narodna Mudrost.* (*Bulgarian Proverbs.*) Selska Bibliotheka. No. 5. Sofia. 1928.

BALFOUR (M. C.). *County Folk-Lore.* Vol. 4. Printed Extracts. No. 6. "Concerning Northumberland." London. 1904.

*BALL (E. A. R.). *Unknown Italy—Piedmont and the Piedmontese.* London. 1927.

BANFIELD (A. W.). *Gạ̀mặ̆gạ̀ Nyạ́ Nupe.* (*Nupe Proverbs.*) (S.P.C.K.) Shonga, Nigeria. 1916.

BANFIELD (A. W.) and McINTYRE (J. L.). *A Grammar of the Nupe Language.* (S.P.C.K.) London. 1915.

BARTEN (J.). *English and German Proverbs.* Hamburg. 1896.

BARTLETT (J.). *Familiar Quotations.* Boston. 1900.

BARTLETT (J. R.). *Dictionary of Americanisms.* (Bartlett & Welford.) Boston. 1879.

BASDEN (G. T.). *Among the Ibos of Nigeria.* (Seeley.) London. 1921.

BASHFORD (Bishop J. W.). *China, an Interpretation.* New York. 1916.

BASKERVILLE (Mrs. G.). *The King of the Snakes, and other Folk-lore Stories from Uganda.* (Sheldon Press.) London. 1922.

Basque Proverbs : Refranes y Dichos Populares. (Collected by various people.) (" Anuario de la Sociedad de Eusko-Folk-Lore." Vol. 1.) Vitoria. 1921.

BATES (W. C.). " Creole Folk-Lore from Jamaica." *Jnl. of American Folk-Lore.* Vol. 9. Boston. 1895.

*BAUER-CZARNOMSKI (F.). *Proverbs in Polish and English.* London. 1920.
Proverbs in Russian and English. (Hill.) London. 1920.

BAYAN (Rev. G.). *Armenian Proverbs.* Venice. 1889.

*BAZIN (R.). " Tuareg Proverbs." From *The Life of Charles de Foucauld.* (Burns, Oates & Washbourne.) London. 1923.

BECKWITH (M. W.). *Jamaica Proverbs.* Collected by M. W. Beckwith. (Publication No. 6 of the Folk-Lore Foundation.) New York. 1925.

BEECH (M. W. H.). *Aids to the Study of Ki-Swahili.* (Kegan Paul.) London. 1918.

BEIDERBECKE (H.). " Omiano vi Ovaherero, or, Proverbs of the Overherero." (*South African Folk-Lore Jnl.* Vols. 1, 2.) Cape Town. 1880.

*BELL (Sir C.). *The People of Tibet.* (Clarendon Press.) Oxford. 1928.

BENDER (C. J.). *Proverbs of West Africa.* Kansas. 1924.
" Die Volksdichtung der Wakweli." (*Zeits. für Eingeborenen Sprachen.* Part 4.) Berlin. 1922.

*BENHAM (Sir W. G.). *Cassell's Classified Quotations.* (Cassell.) London, New York. 1924.

BERNEKER (E.). *Zeits. des Vereins für Volkskunde.* Berlin. 1904.

BERNSTEIN (I.). *Jüdische Sprichwörter und Redensarten.* (Krauffmann.) Zweite Auflage. Warschau. 1908.

*BEVERIDGE (A. S.). *The Bābur-Nāma.* (Luzac.) London. 1922.

*BEZA (M.). *Rumanian Proverbs.* (Philpot.) London. 1921.

Bible. The Old and New Testaments and Apocrypha.

BIGELOW (J.). *The Wit and Wisdom of the Haytians.* New York. 1877.

*BIRKERTS (P.) and BIRKERTS (M.). *Latviešu Sakāmvārdi un Parunas.* (*Latvian Proverbs.*) (Valtera un Rapas, AKC., Sab Izdvums.) Riga. 1927.

*BISHOP (Mrs. J. F.). *Unbeaten Tracks in Japan.* (Murray.) London. 1900.

BISHOP (Rev. H. L.). " A Selection of Sironga Proverbs." (*South African Jnl. of Science.* Vol. 19. 1922.) London. 1922.

BLADE (J. F.). *Proverbes et Devinettes Populaires Recueillis dans l'Armagnac et l'Agenais.* (Champion.) Paris. 1879.

BLAGDEN (C. O.). See SKEAT.

Blanco y Sánchez (Rufino). *Refranero Pedagógico Hispanoamericano.* 3rd Edition. Madrid. 1920.

Bland (R.). *Proverbs taken from Adagia of Erasmus.* London. 1814.

Blooah (G. G.). See Herzog.

Boas (F.) and Simango (C. K.). "Tales and Proverbs of the Vandau of Portuguese South Africa." (*Jnl. of American Folk-Lore.* Vol. 35.) 1922.

Bohn (H. G.). *A Hand-Book of Proverbs.* (Bell.) London. 1855.

A Polyglot of Foreign Proverbs, etc. (Bell.) London. 1857.

*Bonnevie (M.). *Ord Som Lever.* (*Norwegian Proverbs.*) (Some & Co.) Oslo. 1928.

Bonser (W.) and Stephens (T. A.). *Proverb Literature, etc.* (Glaisher.) London. 1930.

Bourke (Rev. U. J.). *The College Irish Grammar.* Dublin. 1868.

Bowen (T. J.). *Grammar and Dictionary of Yoruba Language.* (Smithsonian Contributions to Knowledge. Vol. 10.) 1858.

Bownier (C.). *Étude sur les Proverbes.*

Bowring (Sir J.). *A Visit to the Philippine Islands.* London. 1859.

Boyle (Major C. A.). *Naqlūna* (*Some Pushtu Proverbs and Sayings*). Allahabad. 1926.

Bridge (J. C.). *Some Cheshire Customs, Proverbs, and Folk-Lore.* (Simpkin.) London. 1910.

Cheshire Proverbs and Other Sayings and Rhymes. (Phillipson & Golder.) Chester. 1917.

Britten (J.). Proverbs and Folk-Lore from Wm. Ellis's *Modern Husbandman.* (Folk-Lore Record. Vol. 3.) London. 1880.

*Brown (B.). *The Wisdom of the Chinese.* (McKay.) New York. 1922.

Brown (J. T.). *Among the Bantu Nomads.* (Seeley.) London. 1926.

Brunot (L.). *Proverbes et Dictons Arabes de Rabat.* (Hespéris. Tome 8.) Paris. 1928.

Büergi (E.). *Sammlung von Ewe-Sprichwörter* (Archiv für Anthropologie. N.F. Bd. 13.) Braunschweig. 1915.

Bulbena y Tusell (Antoni). *Aforismes e Proverbis Historichs e Tradicionals . . . d'en Antoni Tallander.* Barcelona. 1900.

*Bullock (C.). *The Mashona.* (Juta.) Cape Town. 1927.

Burckhardt (J. L.). *Arabian Proverbs, or The Manners and Customs of the Modern Egyptians.* (Murray.) London. 1830, 1875.

Burke (R. U.). *Sancho Panza's Proverbs.* London. 1872.

Burne (C. S.). *Shropshire Folk-Lore.* (From the Collections of Georgina F. Jackson). (Trubner.) London. 1883.

Burton (Capt. R. F.). "Proverbia Communia Syriaca." (*Jnl. Royal Asiatic Society.*) London. 1871.

Burton (Sir R. F.). *Wit and Wisdom for West Africa.* (Tinsley.) London. 1865.

Burton (Capt. R. F.). *Lake Regions of Central Africa.*

Buslaev (T. I.). See Snegirev.

Bystron (Prof. Jan St.). *Przÿstowia Polskie.* (A Treatise on Polish Proverbs.) Cracow. 1933.

Caillot (A.). *Nouveau Dictionnaire Proverbial Satirique et Burlesque.* (Dauvin.). Paris. 1826.

Canziani (E.). "Piedmontese Proverbs in Dispraise of Woman." (*Folk-Lore.* Vol. 24.) London. 1913.

Through the Apennines and the Lands of the Abruzzi. Cambridge. 1928.

CAPE (Rev. C. P.). *Benares, the Stronghold of Hinduism.* London.
CARR (Capt. M. W.). *Telugu and Sanskrit Proverbs.* (Trubner.) London. 1868.
A Selection of Telugu Proverbs. (C.K.S.) Madras. 1869.
CASALIS (Rev. E.). *The Basuto.* London. 1861.
CASSIDY (J.). "A Chapter on Indian Proverbs." (*Westminster Review.*) London. 1905.
CERULLI (E.). *The Folk-Literature of the Galla of Southern Abyssinia.* (Reprinted from *Harvard African Studies.* Vol. 3.) Naples. 1917.
CÉSARD (R. P.). "Proverbes et Contes Haya." (*Anthropos.* Bd. 24.) Sonderabdruck. 1929.
CHAMPION (S. GURNEY) and MAVROGORDATO (E.). *Wayside Sayings.* 1st and 2nd Series. (Duckworth.) London. 1922, 1924.
CHEALES (A. B.). *Proverbial Folk-Lore.* 2nd Edition. London. 1875.
CHEVIOT (A.). *Proverbs, Proverbial Expressions, and Popular Rhymes of Scotland.* (Gardner.) Paisley and London. 1896.
CHOLAKOV (VASILI). *Blgarski Naroden Sbornik.* (Bulgarian National Collection.) 1872.
CHRISTIAN (J.). *Behar Proverbs.* (Kegan Paul.) London. 1891.
*CHRISTIANSEN (R. TH.). *Gamle Visdomsord.* (*Norwegian Proverbs.*) (Steenske.) Oslo. 1928.
CHRISTY (R.). *Proverbs, Maxims, and Phrases.* 2 vols. (F. Unwin.). London. 1898.
CLARIDGE (G. C.). *Wild Bush Tribes of Tropical Africa.* (Seeley.) London. 1922.
CLEWS, afterwards PARSONS (ELSIE WORTHINGTON). "Riddles and Proverbs from the Bahama Islands." (*Jnl. American Folk-Lore.* Vol. 32.) Lancaster. 1919.
CLIFFORD (Sir HUGH). "Malay Proverbs." (*Jnl. Royal Asiatic Society,* Straits Branch. No. 24.) 1891.
COHEN (Rev. A.). *Ancient Jewish Proverbs.* (Murray.) London. 1911.
COHEN (Rev. H.). *Talmudic Sayings.* (Bloch.) Cincinnati, Chicago. 1894.
COLEMAN (A. N.). *Proverbial Wisdom.* (Eckler.) New York. 1903.
COLENSO (W.). "Contributions towards a Better Knowledge of the Maori Race." (*Trans. New Zealand Institute.* Vol. 12.) Wellington. 1880.
COLLINS (J.). *A Dictionary of Spanish Proverbs.* (Whittaker.) London. 1823.
COLLOCOTT (E. E. V.) and HAVEA (J.). *Proverbial Sayings of the Tongas.* (Bishop Museum.) Honolulu. 1922.
*COOK (Dr. A. R.) and PILKINGTON (G. L.). *Engero za Baganda.* (*Luganda Proverbs.*) (S.P.C.K.) London. 1901.
COUPLAND (W. C.). *Thoughts and Aspirations of the Ages.* London. 1895.
COWAN (F.). *A Dictionary of Proverbs and Proverbial Phrases of the English Language relating to the Sea.* (Oliver.) Greensburgh, Pennsylvania. 1894.
COWPER (F. A. G.). *Italian Folk Tales and Folk Songs.* Chicago. 1923.
COX (M. B.). *An Introduction to the Study of Folk-Lore.* London. 1897.
Cinderella. London. 1893.
CRAWFORD (D.). *Thinking Black.* London. 1912.
CRISP (W.). *The Bechuana of South Africa.* (S.P.C.K.) London. 1896.

*CUNDALL (F.). See ANDERSON.

*CUNHA (ALFREDO DA). *Ditames e Diterios, etc.* (*Portuguese Proverbs and Sayings.*) 3 vols. Lisbon. 1929, 1930, 1931.

DAL (VLADIMIR IVANOVICH). *Proverbs of the Russian Language.* 2nd Edition. St. Petersburg. 1879.

*DALE (Capt. A. M.). See SMITH, Rev. E. W.

DALMEDICO (ANGELO). *Proverbi Veneziani.* Venice. 1857.

DANIČIÉ (G. J.). *Poslovice.* (*Hungarian Proverbs.*) Zagrebu. 1871.

DATTA (RAJ. CHANDRA). *Some Chittagong Proverbs.* Compiled as an example of the dialect of the Chittagong District. Calcutta. 1897.

DAVIS (Rev. E. J.). *Osmanli Proverbs and Quaint Sayings.* London. 1897.

DAVIS (Sir J. F.). *Chinese Proverbs translated from the original.—Proverbs and Moral Maxims.* (Murray.) London. 1822.

DAWSON-GRÖNE (H.). *Ming Hsien Chi. Being a Collection of Proverbs and Maxims in the Chinese Language.* (Kelly & Walsh.) Shanghai. 1911.

DEGEORGE (J. B.). " Proverbs, Maximes et Sentences Tays." (*Anthropos.* Bd. 27.) Wien. 1927.

DEJARDIN (J.). *Dictionnaire des Spots ou Proverbes Wallons, etc.* Liége. 1863 and 1891–2.

DENNYS (E. M.). *Proverbs and Quotations from many Nations.* (Simpkin.) London. 1890.

D'ISRAELI (I.). *Curiosities of Literature.* London. 1823.

DITLEVSEN (SOREN). *Danske Ordsprog.* (*Danish Proverbs.*) Copenhagen. 1912.

DITTMER (G. W.). *Te Tohunga—The Ancient Legends and Traditions of the Maoris.* (Routledge.) London. 1907.

DOKE (C. M.). " Lamba Aphorisms." (*Bantu Studies.* Vol. 4.) Johannesburg. 1930.

DOMBAY (VON FRANZ LORENZ). *Popular-Philosophie der Araber Perser und Türken, etc.* Agram. 1795.

DOOLITTLE (Rev. J.). *Social Life of the Chinese.* (Harper.) New York. 1867.

A Vocabulary and Hand-Book of the Chinese Language. (Rozario Marcal.) New York. 1872.

*DOUGHTY (C. M.). *Travels in Arabia Deserta.* (Cape.) London. 1921.

*DOUGLAS (C. N.). *Forty Thousand Quotations.* London. 1921.

DOZON (L. A. H.). *Manuel de la Langue Chkipre ou Albanaise.* (*Albanian Proverbs.*) Paris. 1878.

*DRIBERG (J. H.). *The Lango.* (F. Unwin.) London. 1923.

DUNDAS (Hon. C.). *Kilimanjaro and its People.* (Witherby.) London. 1924.

DUPLESSIS (M. G.). *La Fleur des Proverbs Francais recueillis et annotés.* Paris. 1851.

Bibliographie Paremiologique, études bibliographiques et Litteraires. Paris. 1847.

DÜRINGSFELD (IDA VON) and REINSBERG-DÜRINGSFELD (O. F. VON). *Sprichwörter der Germanischen und Romanischen Sprachen.* Leipzig. 1872 and 1875.

EDDEN (Mrs. E.). " Chinese Chapters " from the Book of Stanley. Tientsin. 1935.

EDE (Dr. M.). *Hungarian Proverbs and Standing Phrases.* (Szerzó Sajátja.) Budapest. 1910.

EDELMAN (H.). *The Path of Good Men.* London. 1852.

EDWARDS (E. D.) [translator]. Li-Shang Yin. The Miscellanea of I-Shan. (Bulletin of School of Oriental Studies. Vol. 5.) London. 1928–30.

EHMANN (P.). *Die Sprichwörter und Bildlichen Ausdrücke der Japanischen Sprache.* Tokyo. 1927.

EISEN (Prof. M. J.). *Eesti Vanasônad.* (Eesti Kirjanduse Seltsi Kirjastus.) Tartu. 1929.

ELLIS (A. B.). *The Yoruba-Speaking People of the Slave Coast of West Africa.* London. 1894.

The Ewe-Speaking Peoples of the Slave Coast of West Africa. London. 1890.

ELLIS (G. W.). *Negro Culture in West Africa, etc.* (Neale.) New York. 1914.

ELMSLIE (W. A. L.). *Studies in Life from Jewish Proverbs.* (Clarke.) London. 1917.

EPERNII (T.) and SCALIGERI (J. J.). *Proverbiorum Arabicorum, etc.* Liedæ. 1614.

ERMAKOV (N. JA.). *Proverbs of the Russian Nation.* St. Petersburg. 1894.

ESPINOSA (A. M.). "Spanish Folk-lore in New Mexico." (*New Mexico Historical Review.* Vol. 1.) Sante Fé, N.M. 1926.

EVSTAFIEV (P. V.). *Ancient Russian Literature.* St. Petersburg. 1901.

FAÏTLOVITCH (J.). *Proverbes Abyssins, etc.* (Geuthner.) Paris. 1907.

FALLON (S. W.). *A Dictionary of Hindustani Proverbs.* London and Benares. 1886.

FARRER (J. A.). *Primitive Manners and Customs.* London. 1879.

FARROW (S. S.). *Faith, Fancies, and Fetish, or Yoruba Paganism.* London. 1926.

FAYE (C.). *Zulu References for Interpreters and Students.* (City Printing Works.) Pietermaritzburg. 1923.

FERGUSSON (D.). *Scottish Proverbs.* 1641.

*FIELD (D.). *The Religion of the Sikhs.* (Murray.) London. 1914.

FIELDING (T.). *Select Proverbs of all Nations.* London. 1824.

FINAMORE (G.). "Proverbi Abruzzesi." (*Romanische Forschungen.* Bd. 2.) Erlangen. 1901.

*FIRTH (R.). *Primitive Economics of the New Zealand Maori.* (Routledge.) London. 1929.

"Proverbs in Native Life, with special reference to those of the Maori." (*Folk-Lore.* Vol. 37.) London. 1926.

FOKKEN (VON H.). *Spruchweisheit der Masai.* Leipzig. 1914.

FOSTER (Rev. E.). (Supplemented by Rev. J. G. Pilkington.) *The Dictionary of Illustrations adapted to Christian Teaching.* London. 1881.

FRANCK (H. A.). "Jamaica Proverbs." (*Dialect Notes.* Vol. 5, Part 4.) New Haven. 1921.

FRASER (D.). *Winning a Primitive People.* (Ugoni, Senga, and Tumbuka People of Central Africa.) London. 1914.

FROELICH (R. A.). *Theoretisch-Praktische Taschen Grammatik der Illirischen Sprache.* Vienna. 1850.

FULLER (T.). *Gnomologia; Wise Sentences and Witty Sayings.* London. 1732 and 1819.

*GADEN (H.). *Proverbes et Maximes Peuls et Toucouleurs.* Paris. 1931.
GAISFORD (T.). *Paroemiographi Graeci, etc.* Oxinii. 1836.
GAJUMAL (ROCHIRAM). *A Hand-Book of Sindhi Proverbs.* Karachi. 1895.
*GALLOP (R.). *Book of the Basques.* London. 1930.
GALVIN (D. J.). "Proverbs and Sayings from North Cork." (*Gaelic Jnl.* Vol. 6.) Dublin. 1895.
GANGADATTA UPRETI. *Proverbs and Folk-Lore of Kumaun and Garhwal.* Lodiana. 1894.
GANG-AR-AMA (Rai Bahadur) *Punjabi Agricultural Proverbs and their Scientific Significance.* Lahore. 1920.
GEIL (W. E.). *The Great Wall of China.* London. 1909.
GERINI (Col. G. E.). "Siamese Proverbs and Idiomatic Expressions." (*Jnl. Siam Society.* Vol. 1.) Bangkok. 1904.
GILES (H. A.). *A History of Chinese Literature.* (Heinemann.) London. 1901.
Gems of Chinese Literature. (Kelly & Walsh.) London and Shanghai. 1884.
*GILES (LIONEL). *The Sayings of Lao Tzŭ.* (Murray.) London. 1904.
GOLDMAN (M.). *Proverbs of the Sages.* (Goldman & Steinberg.) New York. 1911.
GOMME (Sir G. L.). *The Hand-Book of Folk-Lore.* London. 1914.
GORDON (Mrs. E. A.). *Clear Round.* London. 1903.
GÖSEKEN (H.). *Manuductio ad Linguam Oesthonicam Anführung zur Ehstnischen Sprache.* (*Estonian Proverbs.*) Reval. 1660.
GRANT (C. F.). "Negro Proverbs collected in Jamaica." (*Folk-Lore.* Vol. 28.) London. 1917.
GRATET-DUPLESSIS (P. A.). *Bibliographe Paremiologique, etc.* Paris. 1847.
GRAY (J.). *Ancient Proverbs and Maxims from Burmese Sources.* London. 1886.
GREEN (L. S.). *Hawaiian Stories and Wise Sayings.* (Publication No. 3 of the Folk-Lore Foundation.) New York. 1923.
GREY (Sir GEORGE). *Ko nga whakapepeha me nga whakaahuareka a nga tipuna o aotea-roa.* (*Proverbial and Popular Sayings of the Ancestors of the New Zealand Race.*) Cape Town. 1857.
GRIFFIS (W. E.). *The Mikado's Empire.* New York. 1876.
Corea—The Hermit Nation. London. 1882.
GUITERMAN (A.). *Betel Nuts. What they say in Hindustan.* San Francisco. 1907.
GURDON (Major P. R.). *Some Assamese Proverbs.* (Assam Secretariat Printing Office.) Shillong. 1903.
GUTCH (Mrs. E.) and PEACOCK (M.). *County Folk-Lore.* Vol. 5. Printed Extract. No. 7. "Concerning Lincolnshire." London. 1908.
GUTCH (Mrs. E.). *County Folk-Lore.* Vol. 2. Printed Extracts. No. 4. "Concerning the North Riding of Yorkshire, York, and Ainsty." London. 1901.
County Folk-Lore. Vol. 6. Printed Extracts. No. 8. "Concerning the East Riding of Yorkshire." London. 1912.

HAHN (J. G. VON). *Albanesische Studien.* Part 2. Jena. 1854.
HALDAR (NEEL-RUTNA). *The Kobita-Rutnakur, or Collection of Sanskrit Proverbs in Popular Use.* Calcutta. 1872.
HALDEMAN-JULIUS (E.). *Proverbs of Arabia.* Kansas.

HALLER (Dr. J.). *Altspanische Sprichwörter und Sprichwörtliche Redensarten, etc.* Regensburg. 1883.

*HAMILTON (A. W.). *Malay Proverbs.* (Proof Copy.) (Printers, Ltd.) Singapore. 1937.

HANKI (JOSEPH). *A Collection of Modern Egyptian Proverbs.* (Al-Baian Printing Office.) Cairo. 1897.

HANUŠ (I. J.). *Bibliotheka Slovanského Přislovnictvi Svazek.* 1, *etc.* Praze. 1853.

Hao Ch'iu Chuan, or The Pleasing History. London. 1761.

HARBOTTLE (T. B.) and HUME (M.). *Dictionary of Quotations.* (*Spanish.*) New York. 1907.

HARFOUCH (M. J.). *Le Drogman Arabe, etc.* Beyrouth. 1894.

HARRIS (M. C.). "Japanese Proverbs." (*The Chrysanthemum.* Vol. 1.) Yokohama. 1881.

HARRISON (W.). *Mona Miscellany.* Douglas, I.o.M. 1873.

HART (H. H.). *700 Chinese Proverbs.* (Stanford Univ. Press.) London. 1937.

HAVEA (J.). See E. E. V. COLLOCOTT.

HAYDEN (T.). "Sean Fhocail." (*Gaelic Jnl.* Vols. 14 and 15.) Dublin. 1905–6.

HAYWARD. See PALMER.

HAZLITT (W. C.). *English Proverbs and Proverbial Phrases.* London. 1907.

HEARN (LAFCADIO). *Gombo Zhebes. Little Dictionary of Creole Proverbs.* New York. 1885.

In Ghostly Japan. London. 1899.

HECKLINGER (P.). "Duala Sprichwörter, etc." (*Zeits. für Eingeborenen Sprachen.* Bd. 11.) Berlin, Hamburg. 1921.

HEDOG-JONES (D.). *West Indian Studies.* Grenada. 1916.

HELLE (A. TH.). *Kurtzgefasste Anweisung zur Ehstnischen Sprache.* Halle. 1732.

HENDERSON (A.). *Latin Proverbs and Quotations.* London. 1869.

HERBERT (G.). *English Poems.*

Outlandish Proverbs. London. 1640.

Jacula Prudentum, or Outlandish Proverbs, Sentences, etc. London. 1651.

Including Jacula Prudentum, New impression. Longmans Green, 1911.

*HERTZOG (G.) and BLOOAH (C. G.). *Jabo Proverbs from Liberia.* (Oxford Univ. Press.) London. 1920.

HERVÉ (Abbé). See HINGAUT.

HESSER (P. J. VON). *Sprüchwörter Phrasen und Redensarten.* (Druck und Verlag der Missions Druckerei.) Tsingtau. 1909.

HILLELSON (S.). *Arabic Proverbs, Sayings, Riddles, and Popular Beliefs.* Khartoum. 1921.

HINGAUT (Abbé) and HERVÉ (Abbé). "Proverbs of Brittany." (*Celtic Review.* Vol. 1.) Edinburgh. 1904–5.

HISA (MICHITARO). "Some Japanized Chinese Proverbs." (*Jnl. American Folk-Lore.* Vol. 9.) Boston. 1896.

HISLOP (A.). *The Proverbs of Scotland.* Edinburgh. 1870.

Hitopadesa—Fables and Proverbs from the Sanskrit. [Translated by Sir C. Wilkins.] London. 1885.

HOCHSTETTER (FERDINAND VON). *Neu-Seeland, etc.* Stuttgart. 1863.

HOFFMAN (W. J.). "Folk-Lore of the Pennsylvanian Germans." (*Jnl. American Folk-Lore.* Vol. 2.) New York. 1889.

HOLLIS (Sir A. C.). "Nyika Proverbs." (*Jnl. African Society.* Vol. 16.) London. 1916–17.

HOLLIS (Sir A. C.). *The Nandi—Their Language and Folk-Lore.* Oxford. 1909.
"Taveta Sayings and Proverbs." (*Jnl. African Society.* Vol. 9.) London. 1909–10.
The Masai—Their Language and Folk-Lore. Oxford. 1905.
HOOD (E. P.). *The World of Proverb and Parable.* London. 1885.
*HOPPÉ (E.). *In Gipsy Camp and Royal Palace.* London. 1924.
*HOSE (E. S.). *Malay Proverbs.* Singapore. 1933.
HOULDER (Rev. J. A.). "Madagascar and its Proverbs." (*Antananarivo Annual.* Vol. 5.) (London Missionary Soc.) Antananarivo. 1896.
Ohabolana, or Malagasy Proverbs, etc. Antananarivo. 1915.
HOWELL (J.). *Proverbs.* London. 1659.
HOYT (J. K.) and WARD (A. L.). *New Cyclopædia of Practical Quotations.* London. 1923.
HULBERT (H. B.). "Korean Proverbs." (*Korean Repository.* Vol. 4. No. 8.) Seoul. 1897.
HULME (F. E.). *Proverb Lore.* London. 1902.
HUME (M.). See T. B. HARBOTTLE.
*HUME (R. E.). *Treasure-House of the Living Religions.* (Charles Scribner.) New York and London. 1933.
HUPEL (A. W.). *Ehstnische Sprachlehre.* Mitan. 1818.
*HUREL (R. P. E.). *La Poésie chez les Primitifs ou Contes, Fables, Recits, et Proverbes du Rwanda.* (Lac Kivu.) (Bibliothèque-Congo. Tome 9.) (Goemaere.) Bruxelles. 1922.
HUXLEY (H. M.). "Syrian Songs, Proverbs, and Stories." (*Jnl. American Oriental Society.* Vol. 23.) New Haven. 1902.

ILIĆ (LUKA). *Narodni Slavonski Običaji, etc.* (i.e. National Slavonic Customs, etc.). (Agram.) Zagreb. 1846.
INWARDS (R.). *Weather Lore, etc.* London. 1898.
ITOTIA (JUSTIN). "Kikuyu Proverbs." (*Africa.* Vol. 1.) London. 1928.
ITTMANN (J.). "Sprichwörter der Nyang." (*Zeits. für Eingeborenen Sprachen.* Bd. 22. H. 2, 3, 4.) Berlin. 1931–2.
IVENS (W. G.). *The Island Builders of the Pacific.* (Seeley.) London. 1930.
IZZET (HAMID). *Proverbes Turcs et Français.* Constantinople. 1923.

JACKSON (H. C.). "Sudan Proverbs." (*Sudan Notes and Records.* Vol. 2.) Cairo. 1919.
JACOB (Col. G. A.). *A Handful of Popular Maxims in Sanskrit Literature.* Bombay. 1907.
JACQUES (A. A.). See H. P. JUNOD.
JAMSHEDGI (NASARVANJI PITIT). *Gujarati Proverbs.* Bombay. 1903.
JANEŽIĆ (ANTON). *Cvetje Slovanskega Naroda* (i.e. *The Flowers of the Slovenian People.*) Celovac. 1852.
JENINGS (F. H.). *The Proverbial Philosophy of Confucius.* New York and London. 1895.
JENSEN (H.). *A Classified Collection of Tamil Proverbs, etc.* London. 1897.
JEWETT (J. R.). "Arabic Proverbs and Proverbial Phrases." (*Jnl. American Oriental Society.* Vol. 15.) New Haven. 1891.
JOHNSON. (H. K.). *Proverbs.* New York and London. 1885.
JOHNSON (W. F.). *Hindi Proverbs with English Translations.* Allahabad. 1898.

JOHNSON (The Ven. W. P.) (Archdeacon of Nyasaland). *Chinyanja Proverbs.* (Smith.) Cardiff. 1922.

*JONES (H. P.). *Dictionary of Foreign Phrases and Classical Quotations.* (Grant.) Edinburgh. 1923.

*JOYCE (P. W.). *English as we speak it in Ireland.* (Talbot Press.) London and Dublin. 1920.

Jüdische Sprichwörter und Redensarten, etc. Warschau. 1908.

JUDSON (A.). *The Judson Burmese-English Dictionary.* (Government Printing, Burma.) Rangoon. 1914.

*JUNOD (H. A.). *The Life of a South African Tribe.* (Macmillan.) London. 1927.

* *Quelques Proverbes Thonga.* Lausanne. 1931.

*JUNOD (H. P.) and JACQUES (A. A.). *The Wisdom of the Tonga-Shangaan People.* (Central African Press.) Pretoria. 1936.

KALLSTENIUS (G.) and RUGMAN (DOMINO JONA). " Proverbia Islandica." (*Kungel, Humanistiska, Vetenskaps-Samfundet i Uppsala-Skrifter.* Bd. 22.) Uppsala. 1922.

KAMARDAS (DEMETRIUS). *Saggio di Grammatologia comparata sulla Lingua Albanese.* 2 parts. Livorno. 1864.

KAPETANOVIĆ-LJUBUŠAK (Mehed Beg). *Narodno Blago* (i.e. *National Treasures*). Sarajevo. 1887.

KARADZIČ (VUK STEFANOVIC). *Srpske Narodno Poslovice.* (*Serbian National Proverbs.*) Belgrad. 1900.

**Kashf Al-Mahjúb, The, of al-hujwírí.* The Oldest Persian Treatise on Súfiism. [Translated by R. A. Nicholson.] (Luzac.) London. 1936.

KAZUMOVIĆ (IVAN). *Hrvatske i Srpske Narodne Poslovice Spram Grskih i Rimskih Poslovica i Krilatica.* (Jugoslovenska Akademija.) Zagreb. 1911–12.

KELLY (J.). *A Complete Collection of Scottish Proverbs.* London. 1721 and 1818.

KELLY. *Life and Adventure in the Land of Mud.* London.

KELLY (W. K.). *Proverbs of all Nations.* London. 1859.

KHAN L'EMIR KAMURAN BEDIR. See L. PAUL-MARGUEITTE.

KIDD (D.). *The Essential Kaffir.* London. 1904.

KINCAID (C. A.). *The Tale of the Tulsi Plant.* Bombay. 1908.

KING (Mrs. L.). [Rin-chen Lha-mo.] *We Tibetans.* (Seeley.) London. 1926.

KING (W. F. H.). *Classical and Foreign Quotations.* (Whitaker.) London. 1889.

KITCHING (Rev. A. L.). *On the Backwaters of the Nile.* London. 1912.

KNOWLES (Rev. J. H.). *A Dictionary of Kashmiri Proverbs and Sayings.* (Education Society Press.) Bombay. 1885.

KOELLE (Rev. S. W.). *African Native Literature.* London. 1854.

Outlines of a Grammar of the Vei Language. London. 1854.

Korân, The, or El-Korân. [Translated from the Arabic by J. M. Rodwell.] London. 1876.

KÖRBER (K.). *Vanna Rahva Moistusse Konned ja Targad Sannad.* Tartu. 1869.

*KOSKIMIES (A. V.). *Valikoima Suomalaisia Sananlaskuja.* (*A Selection of Finnish Proverbs.*) (Suomalaisen Kirjallisuuden Seura.) Helsinki. 1929.

KOTVICH (V.). *Kalmyk Riddles and Proverbs.* St. Petersburg. 1905.

*KRAUS (K.). *Czech Proverbs.* Prague. 1931.
KREBS (G.). *Militarische Sprichwörter und Redensarten, etc.* Wein. 1895.
KUHN (G.). "Sotho-Sprichwörter." (*Zeits. für Eingeborenen Sprachen.* Bd. 20.) Berlin. 1929–30.

L'AMY (J. H.). "Patois Proverbs and Ditons of Jersey." (*Jersey Folk-Lore.*) Jersey. 1927.
LAKERU (Rev. J. A.). *Awọn owẹ ile wa* (*Yoruba Proverbs.*) E.N.A. Press.) Abeokuta. 1916.
LANDBERG (C.). *Proverbes et Dictions du Peuple Arabe.* Leide. 1883.
Proverbes et Dictions de la Province de Syrie. Leide. 1883.
LANDIS (Dr. E. B.). "Some Korean Proverbs." (*Korean Repository.* Vol. 3, No. 10.) Seoul. 1896.
LANE (Lt.-Col. J. G. M.). *A Collection of Hindustani Proverbs.* Madras. 1870.
LANGDON (S.). "Babylonian Proverbs." (*American Jnl. Semitic Languages.*) Chicago. 1912.
LAVAL (RAMON A.). *Paremiologia Chilena.* 2nd Edition. Santiago. 1928.
LAZARUS (J.). *A Dictionary of Tamil Proverbs.* Madras. 1894.
LEAKE (W. M.). *Researches in Greece.* London. 1814.
LEAN (V. S.). *Lean's Collectanea.* Proverbs, Folk-Lore, Superstitions, etc. London. 1903.
LEATHER (E. M.). *The Folk-Lore of Herefordshire.* Hereford and London. 1912.
LE COQ (A. VON). "Sprichwörter und Lieder aus der Gegend von Turfan, etc." (*Baessler-Archiv.* Beiheft 1.) Leipzig and Berlin. 1911.
*LEE (C.) and MOORHEAD (J. K.). *A Dictionary of Quotations.* Vol. 2. (Dent.) London. 1928.
LEEDER (S. H.). *Modern Sons of the Pharaohs.* (Hodder & Stoughton.) London. 1918.
LEGGE (J.). *The Life and Teachings of Confucius.* (Trubner.) London. 1875.
LELAND (C. G.). *The English Gipsies and their Language.* London. 1873.
LENNEP (H. J. VAN). *Bible Customs in Bible Lands.* London. 1875.
LEONARD (Major A. G.). *The Lower Niger and its Tribes.* London. 1906.
*LETHEM (Sir G. J.). *Colloquial Arabic.* Shuwa Dialect of Bornu, Nigeria and other regions of Lake Chad. (Government of Nigeria.) London. 1920.
Lettish Proverbs. Published by the Literary Section of the Jelgava Lettish Society. Part 2. (A. Reinbergs.) Jelgava. 1893.
Lettish Proverbs. A Collection published by the Commission of Science of the Riga Lettish Society. (Sieslack.) Jelgava. 1890.
*LEVY (Rev. S.). *Treasures of the Talmud.* (Mazin.) London. 1925.
LEWIN (Dr. M.). *Aramäische Sprichwörter und Volkssprüche.* Berlin. 1895.
LEWIN (Capt. T. H.). *Hill Proverbs of the Inhabitants of the Chittagong Hill Tracts.* Calcutta. 1873.
LINDBLOM (G.). "Kamba Folk-Lore. III. Kamba Riddles, Proverbs and Songs." (*Archives d'études Orientales.* Vol. 20.) Uppsala. 1934.
LINTON (M. MCINTOSH). "Madagascar Proverbs." (*Atlantic Monthly.* Vol. 139.) Boston. 1927.
LISTER (A.). "Chinese Proverbs and their Lessons." (*China Review.* Vol. 3.) Hong Kong. 1874–5.

LLOYD (J.). "Ulster Proverbs contributed to the *Gaelic Jnl.*" (*Gaelic Jnl.* Vols. 4, 6, 7, 12.) Dublin. 1894–1902.

LONG (Rev. J.). *Eastern Proverbs and Emblems.* (Trubner.) London. 1881.

Oriental Proverbs in their Relations to Folk-Lore, History, Sociology. (Royal Asiatic Society Publication.) London. 1875.

"On Russian Proverbs, as illustrating Russian Manners and Customs." (From the *Trans. Royal Society of Literature.* Vol. 2. New Series.) London. 1875.

"Proverbs in the Zenana." (*Jnl. National Indian Association.*) London. 1880.

Popular Bengali Proverbs. Calcutta. 1868.

Bengali Proverbs. Calcutta. 1851.

"Proverbs English and Keltic, with their Eastern Relations." (*Folk-Lore Record.* Vol. 3.) London. 1880.

"Oriental Proverbs and their uses in Sociology, Ethnology, Philology and Education." (*Trans. International Congress of Orientalists.* Vol. 2.) London. 1876.

LONG (W.). "Popular Proverbs, Co. Kerry." (*Gaelic Jnl.* Vol. 5.) Dublin. 1894.

LOREY (E. DE) and SLADEN (D.). *Queer Things about Persia.* London. 1917.

LOSCOMBE (A. R.). "Jamaica Wit and Wisdom." (*Gentleman's Magazine.* Vols. 2, 5, 9.) London. 1903.

LUFTÌ MUZZAFFER. *Turk Atalar Sözü* (i.e. *Turkish Ancestors' or Grandfathers' Sayings*). (Matabaai Ebuzziya.) Constantinople. 1928.

*LYALL (L. A.). *The Sayings of Confucius.* (Longmans.) London. 1925.

LYON (J. J.). "Sean-Raidte." (*Gaelic Jnl.* Vols. 8, 9.) Dublin. 1897–8.

LYS (ODETTE ST.). *From a Vanished German Colony.* London, Dublin. 1916.

*MACADAM (J. H.). *A Collection of Proverbs of all Nations on Bread and Baking.* (MacLaren & Sons.) London. 1924.

MACCULLOCH (Sir E.). *Guernsey Folk-Lore.* London. 1903.

*MACDONALD (T. D.). *Gaelic Proverbs and Proverbial Sayings.* (Mackay.) Stirling. 1926.

MACFINLAY (CONAL). "Proverbs—Ulster." (*Gaelic Jnl.* Vol. 8.) Dublin. 1897.

MACINTOSH (Rev. W.). *Gleanings from the Talmud.* (Swan Sonnenschein.) London. 1905.

MACKIE (Rev. G. M.). *Bible Manners and Customs.* London and Edinburgh. 1908.

MACON (J. A.). *Uncle Gabe Tucker—Reflection, Song, and Sentiment in the Quarters.* Philadelphia.

MACONACHIE (R.). *Punjab Agricultural Proverbs.* Delhi. 1890.

MCCABE (DANIEL). Irish Proverbs contributed to *Gaelic Jnl.* Vols. 4, 5, 7. Dublin. 1893–7.

MCCARTHY (P.). "Proverbs—Munster." (*Gaelic Jnl.* Vols. 5, 6.) Dublin. 1895.

MCDONNELL (A. F.). *Maori Songs and Proverbs.* Auckland. 1923.

MCINTYRE (J. L.). See BANFIELD.

MAETERLINCK (L.). *Nederlandsche Spreekwoorden.* Gent. 1903.

MAIR (J. A.). *A Handbook of Proverbs, Mottoes, Quotations and Phrases.* London. 1874.

MALARET (A.). *Diccionario de Americanismos.* 2nd Edition. San Juan. Puerto Rico. 1931.

MANIOGLU (KEMAL) and SCHEURRMANN (LUDWIG). *Turk Atalar Sözü.* (Buchhandlung Erich Kalis.) Istanbul. 1936.

MANWARING (Rev. A.). *Marathi Proverbs, etc.* Oxford. 1899.

MARIETTE (A.). *French and English Idioms and Proverbs.* (Hachette.) London and Paris. 1896.

MARIN (FRANCISCO RODIGUEZ). *Refranes Castellanos.* (Revista de Archivos.) Madrid. 1926.

MARKOVITCH (O. V.). *Ukrainski Prikazki, Prisliviya i taki Inse* (*Ukrainian Proverbs, dicta, and such-like*). St. Petersburg. 1864.

MARTIN (W. G. W.). "Traces of the Elder Faiths of Ireland." (*Ulster Jnl. of Archæology.* Vols. 5, 6.). London. 1902.

*MARTINEZ-MOLES (MANUEL). *Contribución al Folklore.* Habana. 1928.

MARTIN-LEAKE (WM.). *Researches in Greece.* London. 1814.

*MARVIN (D. E.). *Curiosities in Proverbs.* (Putnam.) London and New York. 1916.

The Antiquity of Proverbs. (Putnam.) London and New York. 1922.

MAVROGORDATO (ETHEL). See S. GURNEY CHAMPION.

MAXWELL (Sir W. E.). "Malay Proverbs." (*The Jnl. Straits Branch, Royal Asiatic Society.*) Singapore. 1878–9.

MAYO (ISA F.). *Stories and Sayings of Japan and China.* (Daniel.) London.

Stories and Sayings of Southern Europe. London. 1912.

Stories and Sayings of the Continent of Africa. London.

Old Stories and Sayings from India, Ceylon, Burma, and Near East. London.

MAYR (FR.). "Zulu Proverbs." (*Anthropos.* Bd. 7.) Vienna. 1912.

MEAKIN (JAS. ED. BUDGETT). *An Introduction to the Arabic of Morocco.* London. 1891.

*MEEK (C. K.). *A Sudanese Kingdom.—An Ethnographical Study of the Jukun-Speaking Peoples of Nigeria.* (Routledge.) London. 1931.

MELLAND (F. H.). *In Witch-Bound Africa.* (Seeley.) London. 1923.

MENDIS (N.). *A Number of Singalese and European Proverbs.* Colombo. 1890.

MERRICK (Capt. G.). *Hausa Proverbs.* (Kegan Paul.) London. 1905.

MERY (M. C. DE). *Histoire Générale des Proverbes, Adages, Sentences, Apophthegmes.* Paris. 1828–9.

METELKO (FRANZ SERAPH). "Lehrgebaeude der Slowenischen Sprache." (*Koenigreiche Illytien und in den Benachbarten Provinzen.*) Leibach. 1825.

*MIGEOD (F. W. H.). *A View of Sierra Leone.* (Kegan Paul.) London. 1926.

*MILNE (Mrs. L.). *Shans at Home.* (Oxford University Press.) Oxford. 1910.

* *The Home of an Eastern Clan—A Study of the Palaungs of the Shan States.* (Oxford University Press.) Oxford. 1924.

*MOLEMA (S. M.). *The Bantu, Past and Present.* Edinburgh. 1920.

Monografia sobre los refranes, adagios y Proverbios Castellanos, etc. Madrid. 1891.

MONTET (E.). *Choix de Proverbes, Dictions, Maximes et Pensées de l'Islam.* Paris. 1933.

MOORHEAD (J. K.). See C. LEE.

MORAWSKI (J.). *Proverbes français anterierrs au XVe Siècle.* (Champion.) Paris. 1925.

MORISON (Mrs. O.). "Tsimshian Proverbs." (*Jnl. American Folk-Lore.* Vol. 2.) New York 1889.

MORRIS (H.). *Sean Fhocla Uladh* (i.e. *Proverbs of Ulster*). Dublin. 1908.
* "Farney (Co. Monaghan) Proverbs and Sayings." (*Gaelic Jnl.* Vols. 8, 12.) Dublin. 1902.
MÜGGE (M. A.). *Serbian Folk-Songs, Fairy Tales, and Proverbs.* London. 1916.

NARASIMHA (CHARLU A.). *A Collection of Telugu Idioms, Colloquial Expressions, and Proverbs.* Madras. 1882.
NEGRIS (A.). *A Dictionary of Modern Greek Proverbs, etc.* Edinburgh. 1831.
NICHOLSON (A.). *Gaelic Proverbs.* Edinburgh. 1881.
NILARATNA SARMAN (called HALDAR). *The Robita-Rutakur, or Collection of Sungskrit Proverbs, etc.* Serampore. 1830.

O'BRIEN (E.). *Glossary of the Multani Language.* (Revised by J. Wilson and Pandit Hari Kishen Kaul.) Lahore. 1903.
OBRIEN (J.). "Sean Fhocail." (*Gaelic Jnl.* Vol. 16.) Dublin. 1906.
O'DALY (J.). *The Irish Language Miscellany.* Dublin. 1876.
O'DONOGHUE (T.). "Seanfhocail na Muman." (*Gaelic Jnl.* Vol. 7.) Dublin. 1896.
"Sean-Raidte, Sean-Ranna." (*Gaelic Jnl.* Vol. 7.) Dublin. 1896.
O'LEARY (P.). "Sean-Raidte, no Sean Fhocail." (*Gaelic Jnl.* Vols. 4, 5.) Dublin. 1890–4.
*O'RAHILLY (T. F.). *A Miscellany of Irish Proverbs.* (Talbot Press.) Dublin. 1922.
OKOSHI (N.). "Japanese Proverbs." (*Trans. and Proc. Japan Society.* Vol. 2.) London. 1895.
OLD (W. G.). *The Shu King.* New York. 1904.
OLDHAM (C. E. A. W.). "The Proverbs of the People in a District (Shāhābād) of Northern India." (*Folk-Lore.* Vol. 41.) London. 1930.
OOST (LE R. P. J. VAN). *Dictions et Proverbs des Chinois, etc.* Shanghai. 1918.
OPDYKE (G. H.). *The World's Best Proverbs and Short Quotations.* Chicago. n.d.
*OSSENDOWSKI (F.). *Slaves of the Sun.* (Allen and Unwin.) London. 1928.
OTTO (Dr. A.). *Die Sprichwörter und Sprichwörtlichen Redensarten der Römer.* Leipzig. 1890.

PADDON (E. M.). "Hausa Proverbs and Hausa Character." (*Moslem World.* Vol. 5.) London. 1915.
PALMER (FRANK and CECIL) and HAYWARD. *National Proverbs—Arabia, Belgium, China, England, France, Holland, India, Ireland, Italy, Japan, Russia, Scotland, Serbia, Spain, Wales.* London. 1912–20.
PARSONS (E. C.). "Riddles and Proverbs from the Bahama Islands." *Jnl. American Folk-Lore.* Vol. 32.) 1919.
*PAUL-MARGUERITTE (L.) and KHAN L'ÉMIR KAMURAN BEDIR. *Proverbes Kurdes.* (Berger-Levrault.) Paris. 1937.
PAULINUS (A SANCTO BARTHOLOMNEO). *Centum Adagia Malabarica, etc.* Romæ. 1791.
*PAYEN-PAYNE (DE V.). *French Idioms and Proverbs.* (Oxford University Press.) Oxford. 1924.
PEACOCK (M.). See Mrs. E. GUTCH.
PERCIVAL (Rev. P.). *Tamil Proverbs.* 2nd Edition. Madras. 1874.

PERRIN (Mrs). *Tales that are Told.*
*PETRIE (W. M. F.). *Religion and Conscience in Ancient Egypt.* (Methuen.) London. 1898.
PETRINI (Prof. PODALYRE). *Choix de Proverbes et de Locutions Proverbiales.* Livorno. 1913.
*PETROVITCH (W. M.). *Montenegrin Proverbs.* (An Unpublished Collection.) "Wit and Wisdom of the South Slavs." (*Notes and Queries.* Vol. 165.) London. 1933.
PETTINEN (A.). "Sprichwörter der Aandonga." (*Zeits. für Eingeborenen Sprachen.* Bd. 17.) Berlin. 1926–7.
PEUGOT (P.). *L'Esprit Allemand, etc.* Paris. 1885.
PFOUNDES (C.). "Folk-Lore of Old Japan." (*Proc. Birmingham Philosophical Soc.* Vol. 2.) 1881.
PHILLOTT (Lt.-Col. D. C.). "Persian Saws and Proverbs." (*Memoirs of the Asiatic Society of Bengal.* Vol. 1.) Calcutta. 1906.
Philosophy. "African Proverbial Philosophy." (*Putnam's Magazine.* Vol. 4.) New York. 1854.
*PILKINGTON (G. L.). See Dr. A. R. COOK.
PILKINGTON (Rev. J. G.). See Rev. E. FOSTER.
PINKERTON (Dr.). "Russian Proverbs." (*Youth's Instructor and Guardian.* Vol. 14.) London. 1835.
*PLAATJE (S. T.). *Sechuana Proverbs.* (Routledge.) London. 1916.
PLOPPER (C. H.). *Chinese Religion seen through the Proverbs.* (China Press.) Shanghai. 1926.
POLANO (H.) [Translator]. *The Talmud. Selections from its Teachings, Commentaries, etc.* London. 1877.
POWELL (F. Y.). *The First Nine Books of the Danish History of "Saxo Grammaticus."* [Translated by Oliver Elton.] London. 1894.
PRIETZE (R.). "Bornu Sprichwörter." (*Sonderabdruck aus den Mitteilungen des Seminars für Orientalische Sprachen zu Berlin.* Berlin. 1915.
PRIMROSE (A. J.). *A Manipuri Grammar.* Shillong. 1888.
"Proverbs Ancient and Modern." (*Quarterly Review.* Vol. 125.) London. 1868.
"Proverbs English and Keltic, with their Eastern Relations." (*Folk-Lore Record.* Vol. 3.) London. 1880.
Proverbes et Devinettes Populaires, Recueillis dans l'Armagnas et l'Agenais, etc. Paris. 1879.
"Proverbs." (*Jnl.American Folk-Lore.* Vol. 32.) Lancaster and New York. 1919.
Proverbs. "Servian Proverbs." (*Fraser's Magazine.* Vol. 51.) London. 1855.
Proverbs. "Tuscan Proverbs." (*Fraser's Magazine.* Vol. 55.) London. 1857.

RADA (GIROLAMO DE). "La Bandera dell Albania" (i.e. "The Albanian Flag"). (*Fiamuri Arberit.* Anno 1. Nos. 3, 4, 6.) Carigliano calabro. 1883–7.
RAMSAY (A.). *Scottish Proverbs.* Edinburgh. 1818.
RATTRAY (Capt. R. S.). *Some Folk-Lore, Stories, and Songs in Chinyanga.* (S.P.C.K.) London. 1907.
* *Hausa Folk-Lore, Customs, and Proverbs.* (Vols. 1 and 2.) (Clarendon Press.) Oxford. 1913.

*Rattray (Capt. R. S.) *Ashanti Proverbs.* (Clarendon Press.) Oxford. 1916.

* *Ashanti.* (Clarendon Press.) Oxford. 1923.

* *Religion and Art in Ashanti.* (Clarendon Press.) Oxford. 1927.

Raverty (Major H. G.). *The Pushto Manual.* London. 1880.

Reed (Sir E. J.). *Japan: Its Traditions and Religions.* London. 1880.

" Refranes y Dichos Populaires." " Basque Proverbs." (*Annuario de la Sociedad de Eusko-Folk-Lore.*) Vitoria. 1921.

Rehatsek (E.). " Some Parallel Proverbs in English, Arabic, and Persian." (*Jnl. Bombay Branch, Royal Asiatic Society.* Vol. 14.) Bombay. 1878.

Reinsberg-Düringsfeld (O. F. von). See Düringsfeld (Ida von).

*Rhys-Davids (T. W.). *Buddhism.* London. 1925.

Rigel (Rev. J.). *A Grammar of the Tulu Language.* Mangalore. 1872.

Ris (Rev. H. N.). *Grammatical Outline and Vocabulary of the Oji Language.* Basel. 1854.

Risley (Sir H.). *The People of India.* Calcutta and London. 1908.

Roberts (T. R.). *The Proverbs of Wales.* (Jones.) Penmaenmawr. 1885.

*Rodd (F. R.). *People of the Veil.* London. 1926.

Roebuck (T.). *A Collection of Proverbs and Proverbial Phrases in the Persian and Hindustanee Languages.* Calcutta. 1824.

Rogers (Capt. T.). *Buddhaghosha's Parables.* Translated from Burmese. With an Introduction containing *Buddha's Dhammapada* or *Path of Virtue*, by F. Max Müller, M.A. London. 1870.

Rorie (D.). " Scottish Proverbs bearing on Medicine." (*Caledonian Medical Jnl.* Vol. 14.) Glasgow. 1929.

Roscoe (Rev J.). *The Baganda—Their Native Customs and Beliefs.* (Macmillan.) London. 1911.

*Rother (K.). *Die Schlesischen Sprichwörter und Redensarten.* Breslau. 1928.

Rotta (N.). *Albanische Sprüche und Redensarten.* Vienna. 1914.

Rowling (Rev. Canon F.) and Wilson (Rev. C. E.). *Bibliography of African Christian Literature.* London. 1923.

Rowling (Rev. F.). *A Guide to Luganda Prose Composition.* (S.P.C.K.) London. 1921.

*Rubio (Darío). *La Anarquia del Lenguaje en la América Española.* (2 vols.) Mexico. 1925.

Rugman (D. J.). See Kallstenius.

*Ruskin (E. A.). *Proverbs, Fables, Similes, and Sayings of the Bamongo.* Bongandanga. 1897.

* *Mongo Proverbs and Fables.* (Congo Balolo Mission Press.) Bongandanga. 1921.

Sadáshew Wishwanáth. *Select Proverbs of all Nations.* Bombay. 1858.

Sagen (E.). " A Few Norwegian Proverbs." (*Folk-Lore.* Vol. 22.) London. 1911.

Sakhokia (Th.). " Les Proverbes Georgiens." (*Revue des Traditions Populaires.* Tomes 17 and 18.) Paris. 1902–3.

*Samain (R. P. A.). " La Langue Kisonge." (*Revue Generale de la Colonie Belge.*) Brussels. 1923.

*Samenhof (L. L.). " Proverbs in Esperanto and English." From *Zamenhof's Proverbaro.* (Hill.) London. 1926.

Sánchez (R.). See Blanco y Sánchez.

Sapir (E.). " Some Gweabo Proverbs." (*Africa.* Vol. 2.) London. 1929.

SBARBI (DON JOSÉ MARÍA). *Diccionario de Refranes, Adagios, Proverbios de la Lengua Española.* 2 vols. Madrid. 1922.
Monografia Sobre los Refranes, Adagios y Proverbios, etc. (Hernando.) Madrid. 1891.
SCALIGERI (J. J.). See EPERNII.
SCARBOROUGH (W.). *A Collection of Chinese Proverbs.* Shanghai. 1875.
*SCARBOROUGH (Rev. W.). See ALLAN.
SCHEIBLER (P.). and ZEIGLER (J.). "Basa-Sprichwörter." (*Zeits. für Kolonialsprachen.* Bd. 8.) Berlin. 1917–18.
SCHEUERMANN (L.). See K. MANIOĞLU.
SCHLENKER (Rev. C. F.). *A Collection of Temme Traditions, Fables, and Proverbs.* London. 1861.
SCHOENHÄERL (J.). *Volkskundliches aus Togo, etc.* Dresden and Leipzig. 1909.
*SCOTT (G. I. W. R.). *The Foundations of Japan.* New York and London. 1922.
*"SEABHAC AN." *Seanfhocail na Muimhneach.* (Gaelic Proverbs and Folk Sayings from Munster.) Dublin, Cork. 1926.
*SEARLE, (T.) *Strange News from China.* (A First Chinese Cookery Book.) (Ouseley.) London. 1932.
SEILER (F.). "Deutsche Sprichwörter Kunde." (*Handbuch des Deutschen Unterrichts, etc.* Bd. 4. Tl. 3.) Munchen. 1922.
SEKESE (AZARIẸLE). *Mekhoa le Maele a Ba-Sotho.* (*Customs and Proverbs of the Basuto.*) Morija. 1931.
SETON (Mrs. G. T.). *Yes, Lady Sahib.* London.
SHORTLAND (E.). *Traditions and Superstitions of the New Zealanders.* London. 1856.
*SIBREE (Rev. J.). *Fifty Years in Madagascar.* ? 1923–4.
SIMANGO (C. K.). See BOAS.
SIMPSON (D. C.). "Hebrew Book of Proverbs." (*Jnl. Egyptian Archæology* Vol. 12.) London. 1926.
SINGER (Mrs. A. P.). *Arabic Proverbs.* (Diemer.) Cairo. 1913.
SIRISAKA (ANDOR). *Magyar Közmondások Könyve.* (*Hungarian Proverbs.*) Pecsett. 1891.
SKARPA (V. J.). *Hrvatske Narodne Poslovice.* (*Croatian National Proverbs.*) Sibenik. 1909.
SKEAT (W. W.) and BLAGDEN (C. O.). *Pagan Races of the Malay Peninsula.* (Macmillan.) London. 1906.
*SKRINE (C. P.). *Chinese Central Asia.* (Methuen.) London. 1926.
SLAVEIKOV (PETKO RACHEV). *Blgarski Pritchi i Poslovici.* 2 vols. Sofia. 1889 and 1897.
SMITH (A.). *Proverbs and Common Sayings from the Chinese.* (American Presbyterian Mission Press.) Shanghai. 1914.
*SMITH (Rev. E. W.) and DALE (Capt. A. M.). *The Ila-Speaking Peoples of Northern Rhodesia.* (Macmillan.) London. 1920.
*SMITH (Rev. E. W.). *A Handbook of the Ila Language.* (Macmillan.) London. 1907.
*SMITH (W. G.). *The Oxford Dictionary of English Proverbs.* (Clarendon Press.) Oxford. 1935.
SNEGIREV (I.). "Russian Proverbs." (*Archive for Historical and Legal Knowledge.* Part 2. Additions by A. Afanasiev on materials supplied by T. I. Buslaev.) St. Petersburg. 1850.

SNELLMAN (J. V.). *Kokoelma suomen kansan sananlaskuja.* (*Proverbs of the Finnish People.*) (Finnish Literature Society.) Helsinki. 1906.
SOCIN (A.). *Arabische Sprichwörter und Redensarten.* Tubingen. 1878.
*SOGA (J. H.). *The Ama-Xosa—Life and Customs.* (Lovedale Press.) South Africa and London. 1931.
SPANO (G.). *Proverbii Sardi Transportati in Lingua Italiana.* 2nd Edition. Cagliari. 1871.
SPEIRS (Rev. J.). *The Proverbs of British Guiana.* Demara. 1902.
SPENCE (J.). *Shetland Folk-Lore.* Lerwick. 1899.
SPIETH (J.). *Die Ewe-Stämme.* (Material zur Kunde des Ewe-Volkes in Deutsch-Togo.) Berlin. 1906.
STAGLIENO (DA MARCELLO). *Proverbi Genovesi.* Genova. 1869.
STANNUS (H. S.). "Yao Proverbs." (*Harvard African Studies.* Vol. 3.) 1922.
STARR (F.). "Proverbs of the Upper Congo Tribes." (*Proceedings of the Davenport Academy of Science.* Vol. 12.) Davenport. 1909.
STEENACKERS (F.) and TOKUNDSUKÉ (UÉDA). *Cent Proverbes japonais.* Paris. 1886.
STEERE (E.). *Swahili Tales.* London. 1922.
STEIN (V. J.). *Üks Kubu Vanu-Sõnu ja Vanu Kõnekombeid.* Tartu. 1875.
STEPHENS (T. A.). See BONSER.
STEVENS (Capt. J.). *Spanish and English Dictionary.* London. 1706.
STEVENS (Rev. H. J.). *Cantonese Apothegms, etc.* Canton. 1902.
*STEVENSON (B.). *Stevenson's Book of Quotations.* London. 1934.
*STEVENSON (Mrs. S.). *The Heart of Jainism.* (Oxford Univ. Press.) London. 1915.
*STEVENSON (M. S.). *Specimens of Kikuyu Proverbs.* 1926.
STIRLING (Sir W.). *Proverbial Philosophy of Scotland.* Stirling. 1855.
STIRLING (W.). Review of *Wit and Wisdom of West Africa.* Compiled by R. F. Burton. London. 1865.
STOCKINGER (Dr. J.). *Ungarische Sprichwörter in Deutscher Sprache.* Wien. 1919.
*STOETT (Dr. F. A.). *Nederlandsche Sprukwoorden, Spreekwijzen, Uitdrukingen en Gezegden.* 2 vols. (Thiem.) Zutphen. 1923–5.
STORBECK (Dr. F.). "Fulsprichwörter aus Adamaua Nord-Kamerun." (*Zeits. für Eingeborenen Sprachen.* Bd. 10.) Berlin and Hamburg. 1919–20.
STRAFFORELLO (G.). *La Sapienza del Monjo Ovvero Dizionario Universale dei Proverbi di Tutti Popoli.* 3 vols. Torino. 1883.
*STRÖM (F.). *Svenskarna i Sina Ordspråk.* (Bonnier.) Stockholm. 1926.
*STUCKI (KARL). *Schweizerdeutsche Sprichwörter.* (Rascher.) Zurich. 1918.
STUHARDT (J. GUNTHER). "A Collection of Zulu Proverbs." (*Nada.* Nos. 3, 8, 9.) Salisbury, Rhodesia. 1930–1.
SUTPHEN (M. C.). *A Collection of Latin Proverbs.* Supplementing Otto's *Sprichwörter.* Baltimore. 1902.
SWAINSON (C.). *A Hand-Book of Weather Folk-Lore, etc.* Edinburgh and London. 1873.
SWETTENHAM (Sir F. A.). *British Malaya.* London. 1907.
SYKES (E. C.). *Persia and Its People.* London. 1910.
Through Persia on a Side-Saddle. London. 1898.
*SYKES (E. C.) and SYKES (Brig.-Gen. Sir P.). *Through Deserts and Oases of Central Asia.* London. 1920.

*TALBOT (P. A.). *The Peoples of Southern Nigeria.* (Clarendon Press.) Oxford. 1926.
TALLANDER (A.). Pseud. of BULBENA Y TUSELL.
*TAYLOR (Prof. A.). *The Proverbs.* Cambridge, Mass. 1931.
TAYLOR (Rev. R.). *Te ika Maui, or New Zealand and Its Inhabitants.* London and New Zealand. 1870.
*TAYLOR (W. E.). *African Aphorisms, or Saws from Swahililand.* (Sheldon Press.) London. 1891, 1924.
TEMPLE (Capt. R. C.). "North Indian Proverbs." (*Folk-Lore.* Vol. 3.) London. 1885.
TEMPLE (Sir R. C.). "Some Punjabi and other Proverbs." (*Folk-Lore Jnl.* Vol. 1.) London. 1883.
THEAL (G. McCALL). *Kaffir Folk-Lore.* London. 1882.
*THEAL. *The Breeze in the Moonlight.* (Allen & Unwin. London. 1926.
THIESSING (J. B.). "Eine Auswahl der Gebräuchlichsten Languedocischen Sprüchwörter, Reimhaften Formeln und Redensarten." (*Archiv für Neueren Sprachen.* Bd. 43.) Braunschweig. 1868.
THISTLETON-DYER (T. F.). *Folk-Lore of Women.* London. 1905.
THOMAS (W. N.). *Anthropological Report on the Ibo-Speaking Peoples of Nigeria.* (Harrison.) London. 1913–14.
THORBURN (S. S.). *Bannu, or Our Afghan Frontier.* London. 1876.
**Times* (*The*). Persian Art No., Jan. 5, 1931. By Sir E Denison Ross.
TOKUNDSUKE (UÉDA). See STEENACKERS.
TREMEARNE (A. J. N.). *The Tailed Head-Hunters of Nigeria.* London. 1912.
Hausa Superstitions and Customs. (Bale.) London. 1913.
TRENCH (R. C.). *Lessons in Proverbs.* London. 1854.
Turkish Proverbs. Venice. 1868.
Turkish Proverbs translated into English. (Armenian Monastery of St. Lazarus.) Venice. 1844.
Turkish Proverbs. A Pocket Dictionary of the English, Armenian, and Turkish Languages. Venice. 1843.
TYLER (E. B.). *Primitive Culture.* London. 1891.

*UDAL (J. S.). *Dorset Folk-Lore.* Hertford. 1922.
URBAS (W.). *Sprichwörter des Slovenen.* (Verein für Oesterreichische Volkskunde. Jahrgang 3.) (Tempsky.) Wien, Prag. 1897.
USBORNE (C. F.). *Punjabi Lyrics and Proverbs.* Lahore. 1905.

VÁMBÉRY (H.). *Sittenbilder aus dem Morgenlande.* Berlin. 1876.
*VAN VECHTEN (C.). *The Tiger in the House.* (Heinemann.) London. 1921.
VASSALLI (M. A.). *Motti Aforismi e Proverbii Maltesi.* Malta. 1828.
VAUGHAN (H. H.). *British Reason in English Rhyme.* London. 1889.
VELIMIROVIČ (NIKOLAJ). *Serbia in Light and Darkness, etc.* London. 1916.
VIVIAN (H.). *Tunisia and the Modern Barbary Pirates.* London. 1889.

WADDELL (L. A.). *The Buddhism of Tibet, or Lamaism.* London. 1895.
Lhasa and Its Mysteries. London. 1905.
Wainamoisen Kannel. (The Harp of Wãinãmõinen.) Helsinki. 1909.
WANDER (K. F. W.). *Deutsche Sprichwörter-Lexikon.* 5 vols. Leipzig. 1880.
WARD (C.). *National Proverbs and Phrases in the Principal Languages of Europe.* London. 1892.

WAUGH (F. W.). "Canadian Folk-Lore from Ontario." (*Jnl. American Folk-Lore.* Vol. 31.) New York. 1918.

WEBSTER (N.). *International Dictionary.* London. 1907.

WEEKS (J. H.). *Among the Primitive Bakongo.* London. 1914.

WELLS (C.). *The Literature of the Turks.* London. 1891.

*WELMAN (C. W.). *A Preliminary Study of the Nzima Language.* London. 1926.

*WERNER (Prof. A.). *The Language Families of Africa.* (Kegan Paul.) London. 1925.

*WESTERMARCK (Prof. EDWARD). *Wit and Wisdom in Morocco.* London. 1930.

Ritual and Belief in Morocco. (Routledge.) London. 1926.

WIEDEMANN (F. J.). *Aus dem inneren und ausseren Leben der Ehsten.* St. Petersburg. 1876.

WILDE (Lady J. F. S.). *Ancient Cures, Charms, and Usages of Ireland.* London. 1890.

WILKINSON (R. J.). *Malay Proverbs on Malay Character.* Kuala Lampur. 1907.

WILSON (Rev. C. E.). See ROWLING.

WILSON (Rev. C. T.). *Peasant Life in the Holy Land.* London. 1906.

WILSON (J.). *Grammar and Dictionary of Western Panjabi.* Lahore. 1899.

WINSTEDT (R. O.). *Papers on Malay Subjects and Malay Literature.* Part 2. Kuala Lumpur. 1907.

WINTEMBURG (W. J.). "Folk-Lore Collected in the Counties of Oxford and Waterloo, Ontario." (*Jnl. American Folk-Lore.* Vol. 31.) New York. 1918.

"W. K." *Swahili Notes.* Part 4. Proverbs. (Universities Mission Press.) Zanzibar. 1899.

WOOD (G. W.). "On the Classification of Proverbs and Sayings of the Isle of Man." (*Folk-Lore.* Vol. 5.) London. 1894.

WOOD (Rev. J.). *Dictionary of Quotations from Ancient and Modern English and Foreign Sources.* (Warne.) London. 1909.

WOOD-MARTIN (W. G.). *Traces of the Elder Faiths of Ireland.* London. 1902.

WOODWARD (Rev. H. W.). *Stories in the Bondei Language, with some Enigmas and Proverbs.* (S.P.C.K.) London. 1894.

WORK (MONROE N.). "Geechee and other Proverbs." (*Jnl. American Folk-Lore.* Vol. 32.) 1919.

WORTABET (J.). *Wisdom of the East, Arabian Wisdom.* London. 1910.

*YEARSLEY (P. MACLEOD). *The Story of the Bible.* (Watts.) London. 1936.

* *The Folk-Lore of Fairy Tale.* (Watts.) London. 1924.

YOE (SHWAY). *The Burman, His Life and Notions.* London. 1896.

YOFFIE (LEAH RACHEL). "Yiddish Proverbs, etc." (*Jnl. American Folk-Lore.* Vol. 33.) Lancaster, Pa., and New York. 1920.

YOSHITAKE (S.). *Some Mongolian Maxims.* (Bulletin of School of Oriental Studies. Vol. 4.) London. 1926–8.

*YOUNG (Rev. T. CULLEN). *Notes on the Customs and Folk-Lore of the Tumbuka-Kamanga Peoples.* Livingstone. 1931.

ZÁTURECKÝ (A. P.). *Slovenská Přislovi Peřekadla a Úslovi.* Prague. 1896.

ZBIRNIKI (O. B. M.). *Collections of Ukrainian Proverbs.* By O. V. Markovitch and others. St. Petersburg. 1864.

ZIEGLER (J.). See SCHEIBLER.

ZIMMERMANN (Rev. J.). *A Grammatical Sketch of the Akra or Ga Language.* Stuttgart. 1858.

ZOYSA (L. DE). "Specimens of Sinhalese Proverbs." (*Jnl. Ceylon Branch, Royal Asiatic Society.*) Colombo. 1870–1.

ZULU MISSIONARY, A. *Zulu Izaga Proverbs, or Out-of-the-way Sayings of the Zulus.* Durban. 1880.

* These authors, compilers and publishers have granted me permission to use material from their works, and I wish to express my appreciation of their courtesy and kindness.

PROVERBS AND SAYINGS ABOUT PROVERBS

PROVERBS AND SAYINGS ABOUT PROVERBS

EUROPE

BASQUE

Old sayings contain no lies.

Old words are wise words.

BOSNIAN

Proverbs in conversation—torches in darkness.

BRITISH ISLES

ENGLISH

A good maxim is never out of season.

All the good sense of the world runs into proverbs.

Proverbs are the children of experience.

Proverbs are the wisdom of the streets.

Proverbs lie on the lips of fools.

It may be true what some men say;
It must be true what all men say.

Infinite riches in a little room. (*Marlowe.*)

A proverb is the half-way house to a thought. (*Geo. Meredith.*)

There is hardly a mistake which in the course of our lives we have committed, but some proverb, had we known and attended to its lesson, might have saved us from it. (*Archbishop Trench.*)

'Tis as sooth as gospel. Ay, they that set these by-words a-rolling had eyes and tongues, and tongues and eyes. Before all the world give me an old saw. (" *The Cloister and the Hearth.*" *Charles Reade.*)

With a little hoard of maxims, preaching down a daughter's heart. (" *Locksley Hall.*" *Tennyson.*)

A good saying is a good thing, and a proverb sometimes fits into a fancy better than a foot into a shoe. (*Marie Corelli.*)

A frequent review of proverbs should enter into our reading. (*Isaac D'Israeli.*)

A proverb is much matter decocted into few words. (" *Worthies of England* ", *Ch. 2.* *Thomas Fuller.*)

Centuries have not worm-eaten the solidity of this ancient furniture of the mind. (*Isaac D'Israeli.*)

For I am proverbed with a grandsire phrase. (" *Romeo and Juliet,*" *Act I.* *Shakespeare.*)

In ancient days, tradition says, when knowledge was much stinted,
When few could teach, and fewer preach, and books were not yet printed.
What wise men thought, by prudence taught, they pithily expounded,
And proverbs sage, from age to age, in every mouth abounded.
O, blessings on the men of yore whom wisdom thus augmented,
And left a store of easy lore for human use invented.

Jewels five words long, that, on the stretched forefinger of time, sparkle forever. (*Tennyson.*)

BRITISH ISLES (ENGLISH)—*contd.*

Nothing tells us more of the spirit of a people than its proverbs.

Patch grief with proverbs. ("*Much Ado about Nothing*", *Act V. Shakespeare.*)

Short sentences into which, as in rules, the ancients have compressed life. (*Johann Agricola. 1558.*)

Proverbs were anterior to books, and formed the wisdom of the vulgar, and in the earliest ages were the unwritten laws of morality. (*Isaac D'Israeli.*)

Grounding their fat faiths upon old country proverbs. ("*Wit Without Money.*" *Beaumont and Fletcher. 1639.*)

I said that I loved the wise proverb, brief, simple, and deep;
For it I'd exchange the great poem that sends us to sleep.
I'd part with the talk of a neighbour that wearies the brain,
Like the rondo that reaches the end, and beginneth again.
(*Bryan Waller Proctor.*)

The genius, wit, and spirit of a nation are discovered in its proverbs. (*Francis Bacon.*)

The people's voice the Voice of God we call; and what are proverbs but the people's voice? Coined first and current made by common choice? Then sure they must have weight and truth withal. (*Preface to* "*Collection of Proverbs.*" *Howell.*)

The proverb is something musty. ("*Hamlet*", *Act III. Shakespeare.*)

The proverbs of a nation are the great book out of which it is easy to read its character. (*Paxton Hood.*)

The wit of one man; the wisdom of many. ("*Mackintosh Memories.*" *Lord John Russell.*)

There is often more true spiritual force in a proverb than in a philosophical system. (*Thomas Carlyle.*)

"Hang 'em"!
They said they were an hungry, sighed forth proverbs;
That, hunger broke stone walls; that, dogs must eat;
That, meat was made for mouths; that, the gods sent not corn for the rich man only;—with these shreds they vented their complainings.
("*Coriolanus*", *Act I, Scene 1. Shakespeare.*)

But then their saving pennie proverbe comes. ("*Two Angry Women of Abingdon.*" *Porter, 1599.*)

The guiding oracles which man has found out for himself in that great business of ours, of learning how to be, to do, to do without, and to depart. (*Mr. Morley's* "*Definition of Proverbs*".)

It is a wise and sooth fast saw,
Half roasted never will be raw.
No dough is baked again to meal,
No crock re-shapen at the wheel;
And, having tasted stolen honey,
You can't buy innocence for money.
("*Motto*" *to* "*The Profligate*". *Sir Arthur Pinero.*)

The wise make proverbs and fools repeat them. ("*Curiosities of Literature.*" *Isaac D'Israeli.*)

A man of fashion never has recourse to proverbs and vulgar aphorisms. ("*Advice to His Son.*" *Lord Chesterfield.*)

IRISH

Nothing can beat a proverb.

Proverbs cannot be contradicted.

Though the old proverb be given up, it is none the less true.

What everyone says must be true.

The old saying cannot be excelled.

[The wisdom of] the proverb cannot be surpassed.

BRITISH ISLES—*contd.*

SCOTTISH

As the people, so the proverb.

Common proverb seldom lies.

Don't quote your proverb till you bring your ship into port. (*Gaelic.*)

The old saying, long proved true, shall never be belied. (*Gaelic.*)

Wise men make proverbs and fools repeat them.

Old saws speak truth.

It may be true what some men say; it must be true what all men say.

WELSH

Every proverb is truth; every report a lie.

Old proverbs are the children of truth

The common sayings of the multitude are too true to be laughed at.

True is every proverb; false every superstition.

What everyone says is true.

DUTCH

Proverbs are the daughters of daily experience.

ESTONIAN

A proverb has contents of gold.

A proverb does not tell a lie; an empty pipe does not burn.

Old saw—old silver.

The proverb does not lie.

Old saws—wise saws.

A proverb is the key of the thought.

A proverb makes a thief wise.

A proverb is an old word.

FRENCH

A good proverb is made to remember.

GERMAN

Proverbs are like butterflies, some are caught, others fly away.

As the country, so the morals; as the morals, so the proverbs.

A proverb deceives not; the heavens fall not.

A proverb never lies; it is only its meaning which deceives.

As the country, so the proverb.

Death and proverbs love brevity.

Proverbs are taught through experience.

Proverbs are the wisdom of the ages.

Proverbs are the wisdom of the streets.

When a poor man makes a proverb he does not break it.

There are many blunt proverbs, but they have good meanings.

In whatever language it may be written, every line, every word is welcome that bears the impress of the early days of mankind. (*Max Muller.*)

It is the manner of proverbs that we realize their meaning only when we experience it ourselves. (*Rückert.*)

GREEK

Proverbs are wayside sayings.

Remnants which, on account of their shortness and correctness, have been saved out of the wreck and ruin of ancient philosophy. (*Aristotle.*)

HUNGARIAN

Proverbs are common sayings.

ICELANDIC

All old proverbs are spread abroad.

All old sayings have something in them.

ITALIAN

Proverbs are so called because they are proved.

Proverbs bear age, and he who would do well may view himself in them as in a looking-glass.

LATIN

The voice of the people is the voice of God.

Proverbs are salt-pits from which you may extract salt and sprinkle it where you will. (*Cicero.*)

POLISH

Proverbs are not vain words.

RUSSIAN

Proverbs are butterflies; some are caught, others escape.

Proverbs are the coins of the people.

Proverbs are the people's wisdom.

Proverbs do not lie.

The proverb comes from the intellect and the intellect from the proverb. (*Slavonian.*)

There is no proverb without a grain of truth. (*Slavonian.*)

The word of the Tsar is a proverb.

There is no disputing a proverb, a fool, and the truth.

For the sake of a proverb a peasant walked to Moscow.

A good proverb does not strike one in the brow, but full in the eye.

SPANISH

A proverb is a short sentence, sententious and true, long since accepted by common consent. (*Capriano de Valera.*)

Proverbs are little gospels.

A proverb is the voice of God.

It seems to me, Sancho, that there is no proverb which is not true, for they are all opinions formed from the same experience, which is the mother of all knowledge. (*Cervantes.*)

Proverbs are short sentences drawn from long experience. ("*Don Quixote.*" *Cervantes.*)

There are no proverbial sayings which are not true. ("*Don Quixote.*" *Cervantes.*)

SWEDISH

A proverb says what man thinks.

SWISS-GERMAN

A beautiful proverb in the memory is like a golden piece in the money-chest.

A proverb characterizes nations, but must first dwell amongst them.

A proverb is shorter than a bird's beak.

A proverb places the words in one's mouth.

A saying of the people is often a salutary warning.

Great consolation may grow out of the smallest saying.

In a proverb you buy with your ears a good lesson at the cheapest price.

SWISS-GERMAN—*contd.*

In proverbs the conscience of the people sits in judgment.

Proverbs are like butterflies; some are caught and others fly away.

Proverbs are often in themselves beautiful little allegories.

Proverbs are constantly warring against each other.

Proverbs are the echoes of experience.

Proverbs are the wisdom of the alley.

We have many coarse proverbs, but their meaning is good.

ASIA

ARABIC

That a proverb is to speech what salt is to food.

Proverbs are the lamps to words.

There is something wise in every proverb.

APOCRYPHA

Despise not the discourse of the wise, but acquaint thyself with their proverbs, for of them thou shalt learn instruction, and how to serve great men with ease. (*Ecclesiasticus viii.*)

BIBLE

And he (Solomon) spake three thousand proverbs: and his songs were a thousand and five. (*1 Kings iv.*)

A word fitly spoken is like apples of gold in pictures of silver. (*Proverbs xxv.*)

To understand a proverb and its interpretation; the words of the wise, and their dark sayings. (*Proverbs i.*)

And Israel shall be a proverb and a by-word among all people. (*1 Kings ix.*)

Behold everyone that useth proverbs shall use this proverb against thee, saying, "As is the mother, so is her daughter." (*Ezekiel xvi.*)

He gave good heed, and sought out, and set in order many proverbs. (*Ecclesiastes xii.*)

And thou shalt become an astonishment, a proverb, and a by-word among all nations. (*Deuteronomy xxviii.*)

Therefore it became a proverb, is Saul also among the Prophets? (*Samuel x.*)

The legs of the lame are not equal: so is a parable in the mouth of fools. (*Proverbs of Solomon xxvi.*)

Without a parable spake He not to the people. (*St. Mark iv.*)

These things have I (Jesus) spoken unto you in proverbs, but the time cometh when I shall no more speak unto you in proverbs. (*St. John xvi.*)

CHINESE

Proverbs are "common talk" or "common sayings".

Everyone who has a proverb to contribute is worthy of attention, whether he be a mandarin or a coolie.

CHINESE—*contd.*

When one has read the book of proverbs, no effort is needed to speak well.

The truest sayings are paradoxical. (*Lao Tzŭ. The founder of Taoism.*)

HEBREW

What everyone says must be true.

A man's life is often builded on a proverb.

A proverb is the interpretation of the words of the wise.

What flowers are to gardens, spices to food, gems to a garment, and stars to heaven, such are proverbs interwoven in speech.

The wise man delights to seek out the mysterious meaning of proverbs.

INDIAN

General report is generally true. (*Hindi.*)

Time passes away, but sayings remain. (*Hindi.*)

The voice of the people is the drum of God. (*Punjabi.*)

If there is falsity in a proverb, then milk can be sour. (*Malayalam.*)

JAPANESE

Everybody's voice is God's voice.

MONGOLIAN

When one has read the book of proverbs no effort is needed to speak well.

ORIENTAL

The voice of the people is God's kettle-drum.

PERSIAN

A proverb is an ornament to language.

He is the proverb of the age.

Proverbs are the adornment of speech.

SANSKRIT

Proverbs are well-spoken words.

SIAMESE

Proverbs are well-spoken words.

TURKISH

Who does not heed proverbs will not avoid mistakes.

The fox has a hundred proverbs to tell about ninety-nine fowls.

YIDDISH

A proverb is a true word.

AFRICA

HAUSA

This is the beginning of words which are taken and jumbled up (that a man may not know their meaning), and such is called " Habaichi ", proverb.

IBO

The proverb is the leaf that they use to eat a word.

Proverb or parable is the broth of speech.

KONGO

Proverbs are the affairs of the nation.

MASAI

The bark of one tree will not adhere to another tree.

[i.e. the people of one tribe cannot assimilate the customs or proverbs of another.]

NANDI

There is no saying without a double meaning.

OJI

When a fool is told a proverb the meaning of it has to be explained to him.

When a poor man makes a proverb it does not spread abroad.

When the occasion comes the proverb comes.

RUANDA

A proverb comes not from nothing.

YORUBA

A proverb is the horse of conversation; when the conversation droops, a proverb revives it. Proverbs and conversation follow each other.

A wise man who knows proverbs reconciles difficulties.

It is he who is as familiar with proverbs as he is with the matter in hand who usually arbitrates.

AMERICA AND AUSTRALASIA

MAORI

Hold fast to the words of your ancestors.

NEGRO

Hi! Where this book get all them old-time sayings? (*West Indian.*)

EUROPE

ALBANIAN, OR CHKIPRE

1. Sharp **acids** corrode their own containers.
2. As much as you **advance,** so much will you retreat.
3. The **apple** does not fall far from the apple-tree.
4. Who finds fault with an **ass** buys it.
5. The lame **ass** feels its wounded foot.
6. Because he cannot beat the **ass,** he strikes his saddle.
   [i.e. He takes revenge of the great on the insignificant.]
7. Who has a **beard** has also a comb.
8. It is better to be **beaten** by your own man than kissed by a stranger.
9. As you **bed** yourself, so will you be covered.
10. **Blood** cannot be turned into water.
    [i.e. Blood relations are inextinguishable.]
11. A dry **bone** is never licked.
12. There is no **bravery** without a brave company.
13. With thy **brother** eat and drink, but have no business.
14. **Brotherly love** for brotherly love, but cheese for money.
15. Two **brothers** are but neighbours.
16. As you **call,** so will you be answered.
17. Human life is like a **candle.**
18. A **cat** is a lion to a mouse.
19. Who has not the **chicken** has the crow.
20. Neither have we any **chickens,** nor do we quarrel with the fox.
21. White **coins** for dark days.
22. When you have no **companion,** consult your walking-stick.
23. When you have something to do you find no **companion,** take your stick and go slowly.
24. Let your prayers for a good **crop** be short and your hoeing long!
25. If you follow a **crow** long enough you light on carrion.
26. The **devil** was not long in finding man.
27. Many wash before **dinner,** but few dine.
    [i.e. Many are called, but few are chosen.]
28. A tail-less **dog** cannot express his joy.
29. Caress the **dog** that he may soil you with his paws!
30. An old **dog** will learn nothing.
31. Eat with the **dogs,** howl with the wolves.
32. Tell the **door** so that the window may hear it.
    [i.e. Beat the saddle so that the ass may see and meditate.]
33. Wants to **drink** by two spouts.
34. Who has been almost **drowned** fears not the rain.
35. Who roasts does not **eat.**
36. Better an **egg** to-day than a hen to-morrow.
37. Happy the **endurer!**
38. The **evil-doer** shall weep.
39. **Fear** came into the world before man.
40. He has many **feathers** and little flesh.
41. When you have **figs** in your haversack everybody seeks your friendship.
42. **Fire** is a good slave, but a bad master.
43. **Fire,** water, and governments don't understand mercy.

44. **Fish** begin to stink from the head.

[i.e. All corruption comes from the upper classes.]

45. For a **flea** he burnt his blankets.

46. The **flesh** cannot be torn away from the nail.

47. If one hundred men call a sage a **fool,** he becomes one.

48. Leaf by leaf—a **forest.**

49. The **fox** will eat even marked chicken.

50. The sons eat the **fruit,** and their fathers slip on the peel.

[In the Albanian vendetta, the young men commit the murder, and the elders have to pay for it with their own blood.]

51. The first **game** belongs to children, the second to heroes.

52. Do not plant **garlic** with the great.

[i.e. Do not have dealings with powerful personages.]

53. **Glory** to your feet.

[Common form of road greeting.]

54. The **goat** eats and pays.

55. If you fear **God** you will not fear man.

56. One bunch of **grapes** sees the other, and becomes black.

57. When you shake hands with a **Greek,** count your fingers.

58. One **hand** washes the other ; both the face.

59. With what you **handle** you get soiled.

60. No matter how long a **hare's** tail grows, it will not be longer than its mother's.

61. You cannot have **harmony** without noise.

62. The **hasty** leaps over his opportunities.

63. **Hatred** is worse than murder.

64. Hard **heads** suffer much.

65. The walking **hen** comes back with full crop.

66. Even the **hen** looks towards heaven when she drinks water.

67. Don't call the **hens** if you have none.

68. Young **hens** lay eggs ; old cows give milk.

69. Who **hesitates,** regrets.

70. Mending and doing without keep the **house.**

71. If the **husband** gathers with a fan, and the woman scatters with the spoon, there will never be a heap.

72. The **idiot** has no horns [to be distinguished by].

73. What a **kid** can jump over, a goat can.

74. More **lambs** are slaughtered than sheep.

75. He wants roasted **larks** to fall from the sky on his plate.

76. One natural **law** follows another, and the wolf the sheep.

77. Who has no head has **legs.**

78. **Lend,** and lose the loan, or gain an enemy.

79. Say what you **like,** but take even what you do not like.

80. It is hard to **live,** but it is harder still to die.

81. **Losses** are for the living.

82. Eat the **lunch,** and cook for supper.

83. Who **marches** fast remains on the road.

84. To covered **milk** no flies.

85. More than a hood and a sad face is necessary to make a **monk.**

86. He dreads a **moth,** who has been stung by a wasp.

87. With your **mother,** as far as the sea ; with your husband, across the sea.

88. If you don't obey your **mother** you'll obey your stepmother.

89. **A mother-in-law** near the door is like a cloak near a hedge.

90. In the time of **need** the pig is called uncle.

91. If your **neighbour** is an early riser, you will become one.

92. The **neighbour** is nearer than the relative.

93. A faithful **neighbour** is the best guardian.

[i.e. of your property.]

94. Better a **neighbour** over the wall than a brother over the sea.
95. A small piece seems a big piece in your **neighbour's** hand.
96. Where you have given **nothing,** ask for nothing.
97. The **pear** falls under the pear-tree.
98. The **pear** has its stalk behind.
99. A **pig** won't spare even the most beautiful fruit.
100. The **ploughman's** hands are black with earth, but his loaves are white.
101. **Poverty** and wealth are twin sisters.
102. Who can **read** and write has four eyes.
103. The **rose** came out and hid the violet.
104. The **satiated** does not believe the hungry.
105. He who throws into the **sea** finds it again in salt.
106. He who **seeks,** finds everywhere.
107. God will give you plenty of **sheep,** but you must secure the fold.
108. A darned **shirt** and a stomach full of drugs can't last long.
109. When you have the plate and spoon, there is no **soup.**
110. The empty **stomach** cannot jump well; the full one not at all.
111. The **stomach** has no windows.
112. The **sun** at home warms better than the sun abroad.
113. Who does not wish to soil his hands and feet will have inactive **teeth.**
114. The **thread** is cut where it is thinnest.
115. He who is not **tipsy** on Sunday is not worth shaking hands with on Monday.
116. Who has the **tongs** does not burn his fingers.
117. If you do not keep your **tongue** at rest it is often in contact with an aching tooth.
118. The **tongue** has no bones, yet breaks its own skull.
119. The **tongue** is boneless, but breaks bones.
120. It is better that a **village** should fall than a custom.
121. The **village** that can be seen needs no sign-post.
122. Free **vinegar** tastes better than bought honey.
123. Into a big **vineyard** take a small basket.
124. All **virtues** spring from honour.
125. From the drop of **water** through the roof, and death through the door there is no escape.
126. We see the **wolf,** and yet we look for his trace.
127. The **wolf** changes his hair, but not his skin.
128. An old **wolf** is the dogs' laughing-stock.
129. The **wolf** likes the fog.
130. Nurse the **wolf's** pup to devour thy hand!
131. There was never a conflict without a **woman.**
132. The singing **woman** needs a husband.
133. **Words** are feminine, deeds are masculine; words won't make the wheels of a mill go round.
134. **Work** as a slave, and eat as a lord.

BASQUE

1. Old **bachelors** and old maids are either too good or too bad.
2. When one is **Basque** and a good Christian, when one has two mules he needs no more.
3. The **Basque** is faithful.
4. In the house of the **blacksmith** there is a stick for a spit.
5. Every man pushes the embers near to his own **bread.**
6. The judgment of **children**—what they hear at home.
7. The **devil** himself was learning the Basque language for seven years and then he only learned three words.
8. I command the **dog** and the dog commands his tail.
9. An old **dog** does not howl at the stump of a tree.
10. To be worth a hundred ducats the **donkey** must have appearances.
11. Many **donkeys** need much straw.
12. As many **doors,** as many catches.
13. One **eye** is sufficient for the merchant, but a hundred are scarcely enough for the purchaser.
14. The reward for a **favour**—a stick behind the door.
15. A house without **fire** is a body without blood.
16. Heavy is the hand of **foreigners.**
17. **A foreign land** is a land of wolves.
18. When the **fox** starts preaching look to your hens.
19. One **gift** awaits a better one.
20. To **give** to the needy is not to give but to sow.
21. The languid **goat** is always thin.
    [Said of people who don't listen to conversations and then ask what it was about.]
22. Everything comes from **God** except the fear of God.
23. **God** is a good worker, but He loves to be helped.
24. A fish and a **guest** go bad on the third day and must be thrown out.
25. The empty **house** is full of noise.
26. "**If I had**" and "If I were" go hand in hand.
27. To **know,** take, to learn, give.
28. That which one sees, one **learns.**
29. **Mountain** needs not mountain, but man needs man.
30. **A poor man** double labours.
31. Is there any **river** with clear water?
    [Any wealth honestly acquired?]
32. Old **sayings** contain no lies.
33. When the **shepherds** quarrel the cheese shows it.
34. **A tailor** is not a man, he is in fact only a tailor.
35. There is never **trust** without loss.
36. The December **wind** goes in search of old clothes.
37. Cover yourself not with the skin of a **wolf** if you would not be considered a wolf.
38. He who marries a **wolf** often looks towards the forest.
39. Satisfy a dog with a bone and a **woman** with a lie.
40. Gold, **women,** and linen should be chosen by daylight.
41. Beware of **women** with beards and men without beards.
42. **Words** and feathers are taken by the wind.
43. Old **words** are wise words.
44. The **world** for the daring and Heaven for him who wins it.

BELGIAN

WALLOON AND FLEMISH

1. The **beautiful** is less what one sees than what one dreams. (*Flemish.*)
2. In a **bet** there is a fool and a thief. (*Walloon.*)
3. He who throws away his straw throws away his **bread.** (*Walloon.*)
4. He who doesn't know how to cut **bread** doesn't know how to earn it. (*Walloon.*)
5. His **bread** is baked for his lifetime. (*Flemish.*)
6. To **build,** one must have two purses. (*Walloon.*)
7. There are more foolish **buyers** than sellers. (*Walloon.*)
8. You can go to bed with two **candles.** (*Flemish.*)
9. He is the fifth wheel to the **carriage.** (*Flemish.*)
10. **Children** have a hair of their father. (*Flemish.*)
11. Too many **children** never broke the roof of a house. (*Walloon.*)
12. Those who **counsel** do not pay. (*Flemish.*)
13. The less seen, the more **coveted.** (*Flemish.*)
14. Little **crows** have the largest beaks. (*Walloon.*)
15. God heals and the **doctor** gets the money. (*Flemish.*)
16. Where there is sunshine no **doctors** are wanted. (*Flemish.*)
17. What is said in a **drunken** state has been thought out beforehand. (*Flemish.*)
18. He who is not satisfied by **eating** will not be by licking. (*Walloon.*)
19. **Excuses** are made to be made use of. (*Walloon.*)
20. If they **fear** you in your presence, they speak ill of you in your absence. (*Walloon.*)
21. You must look through the **fingers.** (*Flemish.*)
22. What one throws on the **fire** one finds again in the cinders. (*Walloon.*)
23. Do what you will but be the **first.** (*Walloon.*)
24. It isn't in a coal-sack that one finds white **flour.** (*Walloon.*)
25. One is only betrayed by one's own **friends.** (*Flemish.*)
26. The **friends** of my friends are my friends. (*Flemish.*)
27. **Friendship** descends more than it rises. (*Walloon.*)
28. Everyone has enough to do in weeding his own **garden.** (*Flemish.*)
29. He who has never risked has never been **hanged.** (*Walloon.*)
30. What lies on my **heart** lies on my tongue. (*Flemish.*)
31. I like his **heels** better than his toes. (*Walloon.*)
    [i.e. prefer to see him go.]
32. **Honour** is better than honours. (*Flemish.*)
33. He who lives with **hope** dies with desire. (*Walloon.*)
34. The **horse** must graze where it is tethered. (*Flemish.*)
35. It is not always the **horse** that earns the oats that eats them. (*Walloon.*)
36. Where can one be better than in mother's **kitchen ?** (*Flemish.*)
37. A large **lantern** with a small light. (*Flemish.*)
38. No one is so active as a **lazy man** when he sets to work. (*Walloon.*)
39. Hidden **life**—happy life.
40. He who does not wish **little things** does not deserve big things. (*Flemish.*)

41. He who only tastes one **loaf** doesn't know what the other tastes like. (*Walloon.*)
42. "**Loss and gain**" are brother and sister. (*Walloon.*)
43. He who has once had **luck** cannot always call himself unlucky. (*Walloon.*)
44. An ounce of **luck** is better than a pound of knowledge. (*Walloon.*)
45. **Luck** is flying about; who catches it, gets it. (*Flemish.*)
46. **Love** that blushes is a flower; love that pales, a tragedy of the heart. (*Flemish.*)
47. The first **man** is a friend, the second a man, the third a master. (*Flemish.*)
48. Three are too **many** and two are too few. (*Walloon.*)
49. He who suffers **misfortune** may well look out for another. (*Flemish.*)
50. With **money** one buys cherries. (*Flemish.*)
51. It is a hard job to make old **monkeys** pull faces. (*Flemish.*)
52. One doesn't open one's **mouth** any wider to tell a lie than to tell the truth. (*Walloon.*)
53. Don't make use of another's **mouth** unless it has been lent you. (*Walloon.*)
54. Happy **nations** have no history.
55. In the end a **needle** weighs heavy.
56. Don't make yourself **one-eyed** to make another blind. (*Walloon.*)
57. One does not see **oneself** if one doesn't look at oneself. (*Walloon.*)
58. He who has been in the **oven** knows how pears are dried. (*Walloon.*)
59. No one seeks another in the **oven** unless he has been there himself. (*Flemish.*)
60. Nothing **passes** without re-passing. (*Walloon.*)
61. "**Perhaps and nearly**" are cousins germain. (*Walloon.*)
62. He who comes too late finds the **platter** turned over. (*Flemish.*)
63. A rich man's sickness and a **poor man's** pancake are smelt a long way off. (*Flemish.*)
64. Better the head of a **rat** than the tail of a lion. (*Flemish.*)
65. Where one can't **reach** one throws. (*Walloon.*)
66. No grass grows on every man's **road.** (*Flemish.*)
67. One **sees** no farther than the candle lights. (*Walloon.*)
68. **Self-interest** is the touchstone of men. (*Flemish.*)
69. Whilst the **sheep** bleats it loses its mouthful. (*Flemish.*)
70. When the **sheep** has put itself into the shepherd's hands it must let itself be shorn. (*Walloon.*)
71. The **shirt** is nearer than the skirt. (*Flemish.*)
72. With a woman's tongue and a curé's hate one makes a wonderful pair of **shoes.** (*Walloon.*)
73. Don't mock at an ill-shod person, your own **shoes** may tear. (*Walloon.*)
74. **Sickness** comes riding on horseback and goes away on foot. (*Walloon.*)
75. Who **sieves** too much, keeps the rubbish. (*Flemish.*)
76. **Small folks** gain nothing by frequenting the society of great folks. (*Walloon.*)
77. One **spot** spots the whole dress. (*Flemish.*)
78. The first **step** is the only difficult one. (*Flemish.*)
79. No **stone** ever falls alone. (*Walloon.*)
80. One never throws a **stone** into the water that doesn't return to the daylight. (*Walloon.*)
81. He who **strikes** first, strikes twice. (*Walloon.*)
82. One **sword** keeps another in the scabbard. (*Flemish.*)
83. The **table** stands near the door.
84. To hear, watch, keep silent and endure, **teaches** you everything without asking. (*Flemish.*)

85. He who **thinks** far, goes far. (*Walloon.*)
86. **Time** spoils everything that has been done, and the tongue all that is to be done. (*Flemish.*)
87. A **tree** falls the way it leans. (*Walloon.*)
88. **Truth** seldom finds a lodging. (*Flemish.*)
89. Grow **twenty years,** bloom twenty years, stand twenty years, fade twenty years. (*Flemish.*)
90. It is better to **warn** than to be warned. (*Walloon.*)
91. There is no **water** so troubled that it doesn't end by becoming clear. (*Walloon.*)
92. **Weeds** never perish. (*Flemish.*)
93. A young **wife,** new bread, and green wood, devastate a house. (*Flemish.*)
94. A **woman's hands** should never be doing nothing any more than a horse's mouth. (*Walloon.*)

BOSNIAN

(Including Herzegovinian)

1. When an **ant** gets wings it loses its head.
2. Man **approves** only those who are like him.
3. They invited an **ass** to the wedding feast and he said: "Assuredly they want some more wood and water."
4. Whose **back** is heavily loaded his steps are short.
5. **Bagdad** is far away, but the foot-rule is here.
   [Said to a boastful person.]
6. It is the empty **barrel** which resounds.
7. While in **battle** you cannot lend your sword.
8. When people praise someone, few **believe** it, but when they blame him all believe it.
9. The more a man progresses, the deeper he goes into **danger.**
10. If the **day** be short, the year is not.
11. **Day** by day passes until the last one stands behind the door. (*Herzegovinian.*)
12. Beware of him whom your heart **despises.**
13. If one **door** is closed another is opened.
14. Consider more the **end** than the beginning.
15. If the **evil** will not leave you, leave it.
16. Every deceiver's **eyes** are full of tears.
17. The first stage of **folly** is to consider oneself wise.
18. A man without a **friend** is like the right hand without the left.
19. If you suspect your **friend** you give him reason to suspect you.
20. Affluence will bring you many **friends**; adversity will drive away even those whom you inherited from your father.
21. Who fears **God** fears nobody else.
22. **Good humour** is man's wings.
23. **Haste** and rue are brother and sister.
24. The **head** is older than the book. (*Herzegovinian.*)
25. Who has a clean **heart** has also a clean tongue.
26. Mending and doing without keep the **house.** (*Herzegovinian.*)
27. The real **housewife** is at once a slave and a lady.
28. When one is **ill** one's mind is also ill.

29. Who **lies** for you will lie against you.
30. There are **lies** more credible than truth.
31. A fettered **lion** will be attacked by hares.
32. Who sees his own **mistakes** has no time to consider those of others.
33. If " **Mr. Won't** " won't, " Mr. Will " will.
34. Mix thyself with bran and thou shalt be eaten by **pigs.**
35. Do not scratch a **pimple** lest it become an abscess.
36. The great **poet** must be either gifted or exiled.
37. Why use **poison** when you can kill with honey?
38. Beware of a **poor man's** tear. (*Herzegovinian.*)
39. **Proverbs** in conversation—torches in darkness.
40. Eat and drink with your **relatives,** but do no business with them.
41. Before you go, think of your **return.**
42. Two things rule the world: **reward** and punishment.
43. The **rose** grows out of thorns; the thorns out of roses.
44. Beware of him to whom you have rendered the greatest **service.**
45. An evil **spahi** drives away one cow, a good one two.
46. **Solitude** belongs only to God.
47. In one **stable** there may be a steed and an ass.
48. A man's beauty is the sweetness of his **tongue.**
49. General **tribulation** is not hard to bear.
50. Where there is **up-hill** there is also down-hill.
51. The **victor** is always justified.
52. **Wealth** is a slave to the wise, a master to the fool.
53. After **weeping**—laughter; after laughter—weeping.
54. If you hearken to your **wife's** first word, to her second one you must listen for ever.
55. A hundredweight of **wine** mixed with one drop of impurity will become a hundredweight of impurity. (*Herzegovinian.*)
56. All **women** and cats are black in darkness.
57. A brave man's **wounds** are seldom on his back.
58. With whom **you are**—such you are.

BRITISH ISLES

ENGLISH

(Including Anglo-Saxon, Berkshire, Cambridgeshire, Cheshire, Cornish, Derbyshire, Devonshire, Dorset, Hampshire, Herefordshire, Lancashire, Lincolnshire, Monkish, Norfolk, Northumberland, Oxfordshire, Shropshire, Somerset, Suffolk, Sussex, Wiltshire, Yorkshire)

(Proverbs marked " *G. H.*" are taken from George Herbert's collection, *Outlandish Proverbs*)

1. Go **abroad** and you'll hear news of home. (*Dorset.*)
2. **Abundance** maketh poor.
3. It would take an **acre** to keep a peewit. (*Cheshire.*)
4. **Affairs,** like salt fish, ought to be a good while a-soaking.
5. No **alchemy** like saving.
6. Good **ale** is meat, drink, and cloth. (*Cornish.*)

7. He that preacheth giveth **alms.**
8. **Almsgiving** never impoverished, stealing never enriched, and prosperity never made wise.
9. Never so little **alone** as when alone.
10. If thou seest ought **amiss,** mend it in thyself.
11. Who goes **a-mothering** finds violets in the lane.

    [Violets were sent as gifts from daughters away from home to their mothers on Mothering Sunday—4th Sunday in Lent—together with a Lambert Simnel cake.]
12. The **anger** is not warrantable that has seen two suns.
13. Two things a man should never be **angry** at: what he can help and what he cannot.
14. A broken **apothecary,** a new doctor.
15. A waiting **appetite** kindles many a spite.
16. An **apple** at night puts the dentist to flight.
17. There is small choice in rotten **apples.**
18. Who sets an **apple-tree** may live to see its end; who sets a pear-tree may set it for a friend.
19. Go round the **apple-trees** till you find a crab. (*Marriage proverb. Dorset.*)
20. **April** and May the keys of the year.
21. Where **argument** fails, try abuse.
22. All the **art** lies in making the best of a bad market.
23. An **artist** lives everywhere.
24. I stout [i.e. proud] and thou stout, who shall bear the **ashes** out?
25. The highest price a man can pay for a thing is to **ask** for it.
26. An **ass** loaded with gold climbs to the top of a castle.
27. The **ass** that drinks wine carries water.
28. If all men say that thou art an **ass,** then bray.
29. An **atheist** is one point beyond the devil.
30. Kick an **attorney** downstairs and he'll stick to you for life. (*Legal proverb.*)
31. If you rock the cradle empty, then you shall have **babies** plenty. (*Sussex.*)
32. To smell of the **baby.**

    [i.e. not to outgrow one's childish ignorance.]
33. Better bend the **back** than bruise the forehead.
34. The **bait** hides the hook.
35. Be not a **baker** if your head be of butter.
36. When the **bale** [evil] is hest [highest], thenne the bote [remedy] is nest [nearest].
37. The golden **ball** never goes up but once. (*Oxfordshire.*)
38. Put not thy hand between the **bark** and the tree.

    [i.e. between husband and wife.]
39. Empty **barns** need no thatch. (*Suffolk.*)
40. Every **bean** has its black.
41. **Beauty's** only skin deep, but ugly goes to the bone.
42. A **bee** was never caught in a shower.
43. **Beech** in summer and oak in winter.

    [i.e. if a beech tree is felled about midsummer, the wood of it will last three times longer than that felled in winter.]
44. The **beggar** is never out of his way.
45. In every **beginning** think of the end.
46. Beware **beginnings.**
47. You'll **beguile** none but those that trust you.
48. They that think no ill are soonest **beguiled.**
49. Hungry **bellies** have no ears.
50. Give her **bells** and let her fly.

    [Bells taken off a worn-out hawk which is set free.]
51. In a full **belly** all the devils dance. (*Monkish.*)

52. The **belly** hath no ears.
53. The **belly** teaches all arts.
54. If it were not for the **belly** the back might wear gold.
55. A **bellyful** is one of meat, drink, or sorrow. (*Cornish.*)
56. The last **benefit** is most remembered.
57. There is no grace in a **benefit** that sticks to the fingers.
58. **Benefits** bind.
59. The **best** is behind.
60. **Bind** so as you may unbind.
61. If every **bird** take back its own feathers you'll be naked.
62. Noble **birth** is a poor dish at table.
63. Above **black** there is no colour, and above salt there is no savour.
64. **Black** will take no other hue.

    [i.e. vicious people are seldom or never reclaimed.]
65. He that **blames** would buy.
66. On the wrong side of the **blanket.**

    [Said of the birth of an illegitimate child.]
67. A common **blot** is held no stain.
68. It takes two **blows** to make a battle. (*Shropshire.*)
69. Every man gnaws on his own **bone.**
70. Gnaw the **bone** which is fallen to thy lot.
71. **Bones** bring meat to town.
72. They that are **booted** are not always ready. (*G. H.*)
73. The man in **boots** does not know the man in shoes.
74. We are **born** crying, live complaining, and die disappointed.
75. **Botch** and sit; build and flit.
76. What is **bought** is cheaper than a gift.
77. Three things are thrown away in a **bowling-green,** namely: time, money, and oaths.
78. One **boy** is a boy; two boys are half a boy; three boys are no boy at all. (*Lancashire and Yorkshire.*)
79. If the **brain** sows not corn, it plants thistles.
80. The **brains** don't lie in the beard.
81. Some have been thought **brave** because they were afraid to run away.
82. Crumb not your **bread** before you taste your porridge.
83. Much **bread** grows in a winter night.
84. Charity **bread** has hard crusts.
85. Eaten **bread** is forgotten.
86. **Bread** is the staff of life, but beer's life itself.
87. What **bread** men break is broken to them again.
88. Give **bread** to the poor, but bar the door.
89. You must go behind the door to mend old **breeches.** (*Cornish.*)
90. Let every man praise the **bridge** he goes over.
91. Better spare at **brim** than at bottom.
92. To hang out the **broom.**

    [i.e. to signify that the wife is away from home and that the goodman's friends may come freely to visit him.]
93. Sweep the house with the **broom** in May and you'll sweep the luck [or head] of the house away. (*Sussex.*)

    [In olden days a bunch of the twigs of Cytisus or broom was used by housewives for sweeping, hence the name " broom " still used for a brush.]
94. It is a good thing to eat your **brown bread** first.
95. He that hath more smocks than shirts at the **bucking** [washing] had need be a man of good forelooking.

    [i.e. more smocks than shirts means more daughters than sons.]
96. **Building** is a sweet impoverishing. (*G. H.*)
97. The spirit of **building** is come upon him.
98. He that **builds** on the people builds on the dirt.

99. He that **bulls** the cow must keep the calf. (*Legal proverb, dating from Henry IVth's time.*)
 [i.e. illegitimate child.]
100. A light **burden's** heavy if far borne.
101. The citizen is at his **business** before he rises.
102. They who have much **business** must have much pardon.
103. **Butter** is mad twice a year.
 [i.e. when very hard and when very soft.]
104. **Buy** at a fair and sell at home.
105. **Buying** and selling is but winning and losing.
106. Who always **buys** and sells feels not what he spends.
107. He that **buys** land buys many stones; he that buys flesh buys many bones; he that buys eggs buys many shells, but he that buys good ale buys nothing else.
108. He who **buys** pays.
109. Turn the **cake** in the pan.
 [i.e. attend to the whole of your business.]
110. **Cake** is dough.
111. He that will have a **cake** out of the wheat must tarry the grinding.
112. He who has carried the **calf** will be able by and by to carry the ox.
113. A **calf's head** will feast the hunter and his hounds.
114. A **candle** lights others and consumes itself.
115. A good **candle-holder** proves a good gamester.
116. Many can pack the **cards** that cannot play.
117. You may know a **carpenter** by his chips. (*A proverb of great eaters. Suffolk.*)
118. Such **carpenters,** such chips; such lettuce, such lips.
119. No **carrion** will kill a crow. (*Yorkshire.*)
120. It is time to yoke when the **cart** comes to the capples. (*Cheshire.*)
 [" Capples " is a Keltic word meaning horses.]
121. Never was **cat** or dog drowned that could but see the shore.
122. You can have no more of a **cat** than her skin.
123. A cast is not a **catch.**
124. Old **chains** gall less than new.
125. When your **character** is made you may lie a-bed. (*Dorset.*)
126. Send your **charity** abroad wrapped in blankets.
127. The third's the **charm.**
128. He that **cheateth** in small things is a fool, but in great things is a rogue.
129. **Cheese** and money should always sleep together one night. (*Cheshire.*)
 [Said of old when payment was demanded before delivery.]
130. After **cheese** comes nothing.
131. Eat not **cherries** with the great.
132. Woe to the house where there is no **chiding.**
133. Better a little **chiding** than a good deal of heartache.
134. Many kiss the **child** for the nurse's sake.
135. A **child** may have too much of his mother's blessing.
136. When you've got one [**child**] you can run, when you've got two you may go, but when you've got three you must bide where you be. (*Sussex.*)
137. With one **child** you may walk; with two you may ride; when you have three, at home you must bide. (*Cornish.*)
138. **Children** be first a yearm-ache [arm-ache] and a'terwards a heart-ache. (*Wiltshire.*)
139. A man among **children** will long be a child; a child among men will soon be a man.
140. Forced put is no **choice.** (*Dorset.*)
141. From a **choleric man** withdraw a little; from him that says nothing, for ever.
142. Let the **church** stand in the churchyard.
143. It is the men, not the houses, that make the **city.**

144. A great **city**, a great solitude.
145. Do not dwell in a **city** where a horse does not neigh nor a dog bark.
146. You cannot **climb** a ladder by pushing others down.
147. An old **cloak** makes a new jerkin.
148. Twice **clogs**, once boots. (*Lancashire.*)
149. **Cloth** must we wear, eat beef and drink beer, though the dead go to bier.
150. Ever since we wear **clothes** we know not one another.
151. When a man's **coat** is threadbare it is easy to pick a hole in it.
152. Who eats his **cock** alone must saddle his horse alone.
153. Ill fares the hapless family that shows a **cock** that's silent and a hen that crows.
154. An hour's **cold** will suck out seven years' heat.
155. The **comforter's** head never aches. (*G. H.*)
156. They that **command** the most enjoy themselves the least.
157. **Commend** or amend.
158. All **complain.**
159. **Congruity** is the mother of love.
160. No man is **content.**
161. He who wants **content** can't find an easy chair.
162. He that studies his **content** wants it. (*G. H.*)
163. Spread the table and **contention** will cease.
164. All in a **copse.** (*New Forest—Hampshire.*)
    [i.e. indistinct.]
165. Mad men and lame men **copulate** best.
166. Clover is the mother of **corn.**
    [i.e. where a full crop of clover has grown, the next crop of corn will be better for it.]
167. The more furrows, the more **corn.**
168. In good year's **corn** is hay; in ill year's straw is corn.
169. Sow early and have **corn**; sow late and have straw.
170. All **Cornish** gentlemen are cousins. (*Cornish.*)
171. That which **costeth** little is less esteemed.
172. Examine well the **counsel** that favours your desire.
173. A friend in the **court** is as good as a penny in the purse.
174. It is at **courts** as it is in ponds; some fish, some frogs.
175. Full of **courtesy**—full of craft.
176. Pluck not a **courtesy** in the bud.
177. He that asketh a **courtesy** promiseth a kindness.
178. All **covet,** all lose. (*G. H.*)
179. The **covetous** spends more than the liberal.
180. A blethering **cow** soon forgets her calf. (*Yorkshire. East Riding.*)
    [i.e. excessive grief does not last long.]
181. A blaring **cow** soon forgets her calf. (*Dorset.*)
182. Milk the **cow** that standeth still.
183. Some folks never gets the **cradle straws** off their breech. (*Yorkshire. East Riding.*)
184. First **creep,** then go.
185. He who laughs at **crooked men** should need walk very straight.
186. Every **cross** has its own writing [inscription].
187. A **crowd** is not company.
188. Cleave to the **crown** though it hang on a bush.
    [Alluding to the crown of Richard III, which was hidden by a soldier in a hawthorn bush at Bosworth, but was soon found.]
189. A **cur** will bite before he bark.
190. He that bewails himself hath the **cure** in his hands.
191. Past **cure,** past care.
192. Once a use and ever a **custom.**
193. **Custom** without reason is only an old error.
194. **Customs** must be indulged with custom or custom will weep.
195. **Danger** and delight grow on one stock.

196. Better face a **danger** once than be always in fear.

197. Without **danger** we cannot get beyond danger.

198. **Day** and night; sun and moon; air and light; everyone must have and none can buy.

199. One may see **day** at a little hole.

200. Who sees thee by **day** will not seek thee by night.

201. Two fine **days** and a thunderstorm.
[i.e. an English summer.]

202. An inch in an hour is a foot in a **day's work.**

203. Stone-**dead** hath no fellow.

204. Bread and cheese be the two targets against **death.**

205. **Death** keeps no calendar.

206. After **death** the doctor.

207. Every door may be shut but **death's** door.

208. There is never a **debt** is paid so high as that which the wet owes to the dry.

209. A poor man's **debt** makes a great noise.

210. **Deeds** are males, but words are females.

211. Launch out into the **deep,** for 'tis good fishing in deep waters.

212. A small **de-merit** extinguishes a long service.

213. First **deserve** and then desire.

214. **Desire** hath no rest.

215. He begins to die who quits his **desires.**

216. Happy is the man whose father went to the **devil.**

217. He that labours is tempted by one **devil**; he that is idle is tempted by a thousand.

218. He who hath shipped the **Devil** must make the best of him.

219. He who has the **Devil** on his neck must give him work.

220. Paint and putty make angels of **devils.** (*Painters' proverb.*)

221. A man may **die** old at thirty and young at eighty.

222. He that **dies** pays all debts.

223. A **dimple** in the chin, your living comes in; a dimple in the cheek, your living to seek.

224. No man can harm me, I have **dined** to-day.

225. That which covers thee **discovers** thee.

226. Whatsoever was the father of the **disease,** an ill diet was the mother. (*G. H.*)

227. A **disease** known is half cured.

228. The first **dish** pleaseth all. (*G. H.*)

229. Remember to **distrust.**

230. **Disuse** is sister to abuse.

231. The best way to see **divine light** is to put out your own candle.

232. **Do** as most men do and men will speak well of thee.

233. **Do** it well that thou mayest not do it twice.

234. The **doctor** dressed his wounds, but God healed him.

235. Eat leeks in March, garlic in May; all the rest of the year the **doctors** may play. (*Sussex.*)

236. If the **dog** bark, go in; if the bitch bark, go out.

237. A lean **dog** for a hard road. (*Cheshire.*)

238. Every **dog** hath his day, and a bitch two afternoons.

239. When a **dog** is drowning everyone offers him water. (*G. H.*)

240. The saddest **dog** sometimes wags its tail.

241. The **dog** that fetches will carry.
[i.e. he who gossips to you will gossip of you.]

242. Hang the **dog** that has no excuse. (*Dorset.*)

243. A man can cause his own **dog** to bite him.

244. Fiddlers, **dogs,** and flies come to feasts uncalled. (*Yorkshire.*)

245. Scornful **dogs** eat dirty puddings.

246. **Dogs** must eat.

247. In every country **dogs** bite.

248. A **dog's** nose and a maid's knee are always cold.

249. What can be **done** at any time is never done at all.
250. Don't put stones into **donkeys'** ears. (*Cheshire.*)
251. He must stoop that hath a low **door.**
252. However far a man goes he must start from his own **door.**
253. A creaking **door** hangs long on its hinges.
254. An open **door** may tempt a saint.
255. Make not the **door** wider than the house.
256. When in **doubt** do nought. (*Cheshire.*)
257. Put in with the **dough** and come out with the cakes.
258. He that's **down,** down with him. (*Sussex.*)
259. **Drought** never brought dearth to England. (*Cheshire.*)
260. If you would know the value of a **ducat,** try to borrow one.
261. The **eagle** does not catch flies.
262. You cannot fly like an **eagle** with the wings of a wren.
263. **Eagles** fly alone.
264. **Earth** must to earth.
265. **Earth** produces all things and receives all again.
266. **Earth** receives all that falls from Heaven.
267. **Earth's** the best shelter.
268. Of little meddling comes great **ease.**
269. He that is at **ease** seeks dainties. (*G. H.*)
270. Too far **east** is west.
271. The further you go **east** the more certain you are that the Wise Men never came from there. (*Cornish.*)
272. If you hate a man **eat** his bread; and if you love him do the same.
273. Either you **eat** it or it eats you. (*Norfolk.*)

    [Said of the east wind.]
274. **Eat** peas with the king and cherries with the beggar.
275. If you **eat** till you are cold you will live to be old. (*Oxfordshire.*)
276. Good **eating** deserveth good drinking.
277. He who **eats** until he is **ill** must fast until he is well.
278. The **ebb** takes back to the sea not all that the flow brings in.
279. The **ebb** will fetch off what the tide brings in.

    [i.e. the uncertain weltering world ebbs and flows like the sea.]
280. **Economy** is the easy chair of old age.
281. Won with the **egg** and lost with the shell.
282. An **egg** and to bed.
283. An **egg** of an hour's laying, bread of a day's, flesh of one year's growth, fish of ten, a woman of fifteen, and a friend of a hundred years' standing.
284. Take **eggs** for money.

    [i.e. bear insults.]
285. From th' **eggs** to th' apples.

    [Old Roman custom of commencing a feast with an egg and ending with an apple. This proverb refers to a speaker who monopolizes the conversation from soup to dessert.]
286. The safest antidote against sorrow is **employment.**
287. An **empty bag** cannot stand upright.
288. If you had no **enemies** it is a sign fortune has forgot you.
289. No worse pestilence than a familiar **enemy.**

    [i.e. a member of one's own household.]
290. Save a stranger from the sea and he'll become your **enemy.**
291. Every man will shoot the **enemy** but few will go to fetch the shaft.
292. You may find your worst **enemy** or best friend in yourself.
293. In an **enemy** spots are soon seen.
294. Never Cardinal or Legate brought good to **England.**
295. **England** is a little garden full of very sour weeds.
296. **England** is a ringing island.
297. The **English** love; the French make love.

298. First an **Englishman** and then a Whig.

299. Few are fit to be **entrusted** with themselves.

300. **Error** is always in a hurry.

301. Every age confutes old **errors** and creates new ones.

302. **Eternity** has no grey hairs.

303. There's many a thing as belongs to **everything.**

304. **Evil** comes to us by ells and goes away by inches.

305. Welcome, **evil,** if thou comest alone.

306. **Experience** is the mistress of fools.

307. What is **extraordinary,** try to look at with your own eyes.

308. Every **extremity** is a fault.

309. Please the **eye** and plague the heart.

310. You should never touch your **eye** but with your elbow.

311. The light is naught for sore **eyes.**

312. The **eyes** have one language everywhere.

313. Blue **eyes,** true eyes.

314. He who gives **fair words** feeds you with an empty spoon.

315. Pin not your **faith** on another's sleeve.

316. **Faith** sees by the ears.

317. If a man once **fall** all will tread on him.

318. Don't **fall** before you're pushed. (*Wiltshire.*)

319. He that is **fallen** cannot help him that is down.

320. **Families** go from clogs to clogs in three generations. (*Lancashire.*)

321. A **famine** in England begins at the horse-manger.

322. **Fancy** is a funny dog if you feed him well. (*Dorset.*)

323. **Far-fetched,** dearly bought. (*Cheshire.*)

324. The eyes, the ears, the tongue, the hands, the feet, all **fast** in their way.

325. Is there no mean but **fast** or feast?

326. **Fat** with the lean.

327. Where no **fault** is there needs no pardon.

328. Everyone puts his **fault** on the times.

329. **Faults** are thick where love is thin.

330. Wink at small **faults** unless you can cast the first stone.

331. The **faulty** stands on his guard.

332. **Favour** will as surely perish as life.

333. Our **fear** commonly meets us at the door by which we think to run from it.

334. Small cheer and great welcome make a great **feast.**

335. We are often shot with our own **feathers.**

336. Better **fed** than taught.

337. Where your will is ready your **feet** are light.

338. No **fence** against a flail.

339. It is no advantage for a man in a **fever** to change his bed.

340. In the house of a **fiddler** all fiddle.

341. A man that will **fight** will find a cudgel in every hedge.

342. A pruned **fig-tree** never bears.

343. Better a **finger** off than one wagging.

344. Long **fingers** count out money. (*Dorset.*)

345. The **fingers** have got pretty close to the thumb. (*Sussex.*)
[Refers to a father being able to get several of his children into the same employ.]

346. Skeer [rake out] your own **fire.** (*Cheshire.*)

347. Base terms are bellows to a slackening **fire.**

348. You must know a man seven years before you can poke his **fire.**

349. **Fire** is half bread.

350. **Fire** is love and water sorrow.

351. Make no **fire,** raise no smoke.

352. **Fire** that's closest kept burns most of all.

353. Better a little **fire** to warm 'ee than a great one to burn 'ee. (*Dorset.*)

354. There is always a **first time.**

355. A **fish** begins to stink at the head.

356. A **fish** follows the bait.

357. Dead **fish** go always with the stream.

358. **Fish** must swim thrice.
[i.e. in water, sauce, and wine.]

359. **Fish** swim best that are bred in the sea.

360. It is no use **fishing** in front of the net.

361. There is no such **flatterer** as a man's self.

362. After your **fling** watch for the sting. (*Cheshire.*)

363. A **flow** will have an ebb.

364. You must lose a **fly** to catch a trout. (*G. H.*)

365. A **fog** cannot be dispelled with a fan.

366. There's nought so queer as **folk.** (*Lancashire.*)

367. He who physics himself poisons a **fool.**

368. He who treats himself has a **fool** for a patient.

369. Enjoy your little while the **fool** is seeking for more.

370. If thou play the **fool,** stay for a fellow.

371. Better a witty **fool** than a foolish wit.

372. The **fool** wanders, the wise man travels.

373. **Fools** are weatherwise, and those that are weatherwise are seldom otherwise.

374. Learn to shave on a **fool's** head.

375. He that has no **fools,** knaves, or beggars in his family, was begot by a flash of lightning.

376. We are **fools** one to another.

377. If **fools** went not to market bad wares would not be sold.

378. Measure yourself by your own **foot.**

379. Whoso stretcheth his **foot** beyond the blanket shall stretch it in the straw.

380. Do not put out your **foot** farther than you can draw it back again.

381. The difficult thing is to get your **foot** in the stirrup.

382. Tread on the ball [of the **foot**], live to spend all. (*Dorset.*)

383. Some men go through a **forest** and see no firewood.

384. He that gets **forgets,** but he that wants thinks on.

385. We have all **forgot** more than we remember.

386. **Four things** are most to be desired: a good neighbour, a window to every man's heart, that men's tongues and hearts should go together, and an house on wheels.

387. We can have no more of the **fox** but the skin.

388. The **fox** is taken when he comes to take.

389. The brains of a **fox** will be of little service if you play with the paw of a lion.

390. When the Ethiopian is white the **French** will love the English.

391. To burn the paper he **fried** in. (*Devonshire.*)

392. There is no better looking-glass than an old **friend.**

393. Live with your **friend** as if he might become your enemy.

394. When a **friend** asks there is no to-morrow. (*G. H.*)

395. It is not lost that a **friend** gets.

396. An old **friend** is a new house.

397. He quits his place well that leaves his **friend** there.

398. Make not thy **friend** thy foe.

399. By requiting one **friend** we invite many.

400. Wheresoever you see your kindred make much of your **friends.**

401. It's good to have some **friends** both in heaven and hell.

402. We can live without our **friends** but not without our neighbours.

403. When **friends** fall out the truth doth appear.
404. God defend me from my **friends,** I'll keep myself from my enemies.
405. Falling out of **friends** is the renewal of love.
406. **Friends** may meet but mountains never greet.
407. All **friends** round the wrekin. (*Shropshire.*)
408. **Friends** tie their purse with a cobweb thread.
409. There is flattery in **friendship.**
410. Hedges between keep **friendship** green. (*Cheshire.*)
411. No **friendship** lives long that owes its rise to the pot.
412. For every fog in March ther's a **frost** in May.
413. Take away **fuel** and you take away fire [or flame].
414. A **full cup** must be carried steadily.
415. To **gain** teacheth how to spend.
416. Better play at small **game** than stand out.
417. No **gaping** against an oven.
418. None says his **garner** is full.
419. **Gay** go up, gay go down.
420. Ill-gotten **gear** wilna [will not] enrich the third heir.
421. The **generous man** pays for nothing so much as what is given him.
422. The **giant** loves the dwarf.
423. A man's **gift** makes room for him.
424. He that gives me small **gifts** would have me live.
425. To **give** a thing and take a thing is to wear the devil's gold ring.
426. The hand that **gives** gathers.
427. He that **gives** to be seen will relieve none in the dark.
428. **Giving** is fishing.
429. A broken **glass** can't be hurt.
430. The **goat** must browse where she is tied.
431. At wits' end is **God.**
432. He that after sinning mends, recommends himself to **God.**
433. He that sows trusts in **God.**
434. Soon tod [toothed], soon with **God.** (*Lancashire.*)
435. The nest of the blind bird is made by **God.**
436. Think and thank **God.**
437. **God** and enough. (*Ancient Druid maxim.*)
438. **God** gives His anger by weight, but His pity without measure.
439. They are poor whom **God** hates.
440. **God** hath often a great share in a little house.
441. **God** helps the rich man that the poor man may beg.
442. Where there is peace **God** is. (*G. H.*)
443. **God** is better pleased with adverbs than with nouns.
444. The grace of **God** is gear enough.
445. **God** is where He was.
446. **God** looks to clean hands, not to full ones.
447. **God** promises a safe landing, but not a calm passage.
448. The charitable give out at the door and **God** puts in at the window.
449. **God** send you readier meat than running hares.
450. **God** sends fortune to fools.
451. He is a **god** that helps a man.
452. There is **God** when all is done.
453. Spend and **God** will send.
454. Get thy spindle and thy distaff ready and **God** will send thee flax.
455. **God** writes straight on crooked lines.
456. **God's** a good man.
457. Out of **God's** blessing into the warm sun.

    [i.e. from austerity into luxuriousness.]
458. Many meet the **gods** but few salute them.
459. No pillow so soft as **God's** promise.

460. The **gods** sell all things at a fair price.
461. He talks **gold** but pays copper. (*Sussex.*)
462. What cannot **gold** do?
463. A man may buy **gold** too dear. (*Dorset.*)
464. When we have **gold** we are in fear; when we have none we are in danger.
465. That is **gold** which is worth gold.
466. In **Golgotha** are skulls of all sizes.
   [i.e. as there are none too old for eternity, so there are none too young for mortality.]
467. There is not the thickness of a sixpence between **good** and evil.
468. **Good** finds good.
469. Du zummat; du **good** if ye can, but du zummat. (*Somerset.*)
470. Do **good,** thou dost it for thyself. (*Cornish.*)
471. He that brings **good news** knocks hard.
472. Nothing is more easily blotted out than a **good turn.**
473. Where **good's** been found, there look again.
474. A man far from his **goods** is nigh his harm.
475. Heavy **goods** lack heavy payment. (*Devonshire.*)
476. A man has no more **goods** than he gets good by.
477. A wild **goose** never lays a tame egg.
478. A **goose-quill** is more dangerous than a lion's claw.
479. Standing **gossips** stay the longest. (*Dorset.*)
480. There is a devil in every berry of the **grape.** (*Doubtful English proverb.*)
481. **Grape** on grape, corn on corn.
   [i.e. better to drink brandy after wine; whisky or gin after beer.]
482. He that gives to a **grateful man** puts out to usury.
483. **Gratitude** is the least of virtues; ingratitude is the worst of vices.
484. All **griefs** with bread are less.
485. A fish and a **guest** after three days are poison.
486. Fresh fish and new-come **guests** smell in three days.
487. It is time to part with your **guide** when you have got your boots off.
488. **Habits** are at first cobwebs, at last cables.
489. Beware of "**had I wist**".
   [i.e. after-regrets.]
490. The **hailer** [receiver] is as bad as the stailer [thief].
491. Long **hair** and short wit.
492. The soil of **Hampshire** requires a shower every day, and on Sundays two. (*Hampshire.*)
493. One **hand** for the owner and one for yourself. (*Sailors' proverb.*)
494. Put your **hand** quickly to your hat and slowly to your purse, and you'll come to no harm.
495. Take things always by the smooth **handle.**
496. **Hanging** and wiving go by destiny.
497. All worldly **happiness** consists in opinion.
498. **Happiness** is an home-made article.
499. All **happiness** is in the mind.
500. We are never so **happy** or unfortunate as we think ourselves.
501. Good **harvests** make men prodigal; bad ones, provident.
502. When thou hast well done, hang up thy **hatchet.**
   [i.e. to cease from one's labours and rest.]
503. A **hat** is not made for one shower.
504. Pull down your **hat** on the wind side.
505. **Have** is have, however men do catch.
506. He that would **have** what he hath not should do what he doeth not. (*G. H.*)
507. Too low for a **hawk,** too high for a buzzard.

508. One **head** and a thousand anxieties.

509. Shade your **head** and go east. (*Cornish.*)

510. We are usually the best men when in the worst **health.**

511. If you can be well without **health** you may be happy without virtue.

512. **Hear** all, say now't, take all, pay now't, and if thou does ow't for now't, do it for thysen [thyself]. (*Yorkshire.*)

513. The country for a wounded **heart.**

514. Set your **heart** at rest.

515. What comes from the **heart** goes to the heart.

516. Where a man's **heart** is, there is his God.

517. A sighing **heart** never breaks. (*Dorset.*)

518. He that gives his **heart** will not deny his money.

519. Slow are the steps of those who leave their **hearts** behind.

520. The **heart's letter** is read in the eyes.

521. The way to **heaven** is by Weeping Cross.

522. The **hedge** abideth that acres divideth. (*Anglo-Saxon.*)

523. Where the **hedge** is low, there every man treads down.

524. Better keep under an old **hedge** than creep under a new furze-bush.

525. The fork is commonly the rake's **heir.**

526. **Hell** and chancery are always open.

527. They that be in **hell** think there's no better heaven.

528. Little **hemlock** is sister to the big hemlock.

529. It is a sad house when the **hen** crows louder than the cock.

530. The **hen** reveals her nest by cackling.

531. If the **hen** does not prate she will not lay.

532. A sitting **hen** gets no feathers. (*Sussex.*)

533. If you would have a **hen** lay you must bear with her cackling.

534. He that is born of a **hen** must scrape for a living.

535. The **highway** is never about.

536. To steal the **hog** and give the feet for alms.

537. A **hog** upon trust grunts till he is paid for.

538. Near **home** some people can see no good.

539. Never go **home** without stick or stone. (*Berkshire.*)

540. There is more **honesty** in a penny than in five pounds. (*Shropshire.*)

541. All the **honesty** is in the partings.

542. He that hath no **honey** in his pot, let him have it in his mouth. (*G. H.*)

543. Lick **honey** with your little finger.

544. Where there is no **honour** there is no grief.

545. **Honour's** train is no longer than his foreskirt.

546. A **hook** is well lost on a salmon.

547. He gains a good deal who loses a vain **hope.**

548. Though **hope** be a small child she can carry a great anchor.

549. **Hope** is a good breakfast but a bad supper.

550. **Hope** is as cheap as despair.

551. **Hope** is the poor man's bread.

552. Walk with **hope** or you walk backwards. (*Devonshire.*)

553. If it were not for **hope** the heart would break.

554. Wear a **horn** and blow it not.

555. Let the **horns** go with the hide.

556. A man, a **horse**, and a dog are never weary of each other's company.

557. The old **horse** must die in somebody's keeping.

558. When two ride on one **horse** one must sit behind.

559. The **horse** that draws after him his halter is not altogether escaped. (*G. H.*)

560. It is a sin against **hospitality** to open the doors and shut up the countenance.

561. The fairer the **hostess,** the fouler the reckoning.

562. The fed **hound** never hunts.

563. There is an **hour** wherein a man might be happy all his life, could he find it. (*G. H.*)

564. A **house** built by the wayside is either too high or too low.

565. The first year let your **house** to your enemy; the second to your friend; the third live in it yourself.

566. Fat **housekeeper** [or kitchen], lean executors.

567. There is but an hour a day between a good **housewife** and a bad.

568. When gnats dance in February the **husbandman** becomes a beggar.

569. Good **husbandry** is good divinity. (*Northumberland.*)

570. Trust not one night's **ice.**

571. **Ignorance** is a voluntary misfortune.

572. **Ill-doers** are ill-deemers.

573. He that hath no **ill-fortune** is troubled with good.

574. **Ill-luck** is good for something.

575. Let an **ill man** be in thy straw and he looks to be thy heir.

576. He that does you a very **ill turn** will never forgive you.

577. Great folks' **illnesses** and poor folks' bacon smell a long way off.

578. **Injuries** we write in marble, kindnesses in dust.

579. **Innocence** itself sometimes hath need of a mask.

580. The **Italians** are wise before the deed; the Germans in the deed; the French after the deed.

581. The galled **jade** will wince.

582. Be **jogging** while your boots are green.

583. For a morning rain leave not your **journey.**

584. A man knows his companion in a long **journey** or a little inn.

585. One year of **joy,** another of comfort, and all the rest of content. (*Marriage wish.*)

586. **Joy** was born a twin. (*Wiltshire.*)

587. Had **Judas** betrayed Christ in Scotland he might have repented before he could have found a tree to hang himself on.
[Refers to the tree-less condition of Scotland then.]

588. He hath good **judgment** that relieth not wholly on his own.

589. The used **key** is always bright.

590. All **keys** hang not at one man's girdle.

591. The **king** and his staff be a man and a half. (*Devonshire.*)

592. At the end of the game the **king** and the pawn go into the same bag.

593. An illiterate **king** is a crowned ass. (*Quoted by Henry I.*)

594. The **king** is the top-sawyer. (*Devonshire.*)

595. The **king's** cheese goes half-away in parings.
[The Courts of Princes are seldom free from pilferers, pickpockets, and thieves in places of trust.]

596. A **king's** face should show grace. (*A favourite proverb of King Henry VIII.*)

597. Do not make me **kiss** and you will not make me sin.

598. **Kisses** are keys.

599. A crafty **knave** needs no broker.

600. Better kiss a **knave** than be troubled with him.

601. It is better to **knit** than to blossom.

602. Where the **knot** is loose the string slippeth.

603. It is almost as necessary to **know** other men as ourselves.

604. He that **knows** thee will never buy thee.

605. **Labour** is light where love doth pay.

606. The **labour** we delight in physics pain.
607. You should lie down with the **lamb** and rise with the lark.
608. If you desire to see my light you must minister oil to my **lamp.**
609. He that buys **land** buys stones; he that buys flesh buys bones. (*Devonshire.*)
610. There is good **land** where there is a foul way. (*Northumberland.*)
611. No **land** without stones, or meat without bones.
612. A lisping **lass** is good to kiss. (*Cheshire.*)
613. **Lasses** are lads' leavings. (*Cheshire.*)
614. It's easy holding down the **latch** when nobody pulls at the string. (*Cheshire.*)
615. He that **laughs** when he is alone will make sport in company.
616. Like **lavender,** grow sweeter as you grow older. (? *Lancashire.*)
617. **Law** cannot persuade where it cannot punish.
618. He that goes to **law** holds a wolf by the ears.
619. In a thousand pounds of **law** there's not an ounce of love.
620. **Laws** catch flies but let hornets go free.
621. New **laws,** new frauds.
622. The fall of the **leaf** is a whisper to the living.
623. The three **learned professions** live by roguery on the three parts of man. The doctor mauls our bodies, the parson starves our souls, and the lawyer ensnares our minds. (*Devonshire.*)
624. Raw **leather** will stretch.
625. A broken **leg** is not healed by a silk stocking.
626. It is no good lifting your **leg** until you come to the stile.
627. Everyone stretches his **legs** according to his coverlet.
628. **Lend** not horse, nor wife, nor sword.
629. **Lend** not unto him who wears no breeches in January.
630. He that **lends,** gives.
631. In a **leopard** the spots are not observed.
632. What can't speak can't **lie.** (*Norfolk.*)
633. Tell your friend a **lie,** and if he keeps it secret, tell him the truth.
634. A **lie** has no legs, but a scandal has wings.
635. A **lie** stands upon one leg, but truth upon two.
636. **Life** and misery began together.
637. There is always **life** for the living.
638. We must not look for a golden **life** in an iron age.
639. **Life** is half spent before we know what it is.
640. **Life** lieth not in living, but in liking.
641. Look at the **light,** not at the lantern.
642. "**Likely**" lies in the mire when "unlikely" gets over.
643. **Likeness** is the mother of love.
644. A man is a **lion** in his own cause.
645. Free of her **lips**—free of her hips.
646. What costs **little** is little esteemed.
647. He that hath **little** is the less dirty. (*G. H.*)
648. From a **little** take a little; from a lot take a lot.
649. Mind what you must **live** by.
650. **Live,** horse, and thou shalt have grass! (*Lancashire.*)
651. We shall **live** till we die.
652. He that **lives** most, dies most.
653. We know not who **lives** or dies.
654. There's crust and crumb in every **loaf.**
655. Give a **loaf** and beg a shive [slice]. (*Shropshire.*)
656. A slice off a cut **loaf's** never missed. (*Lancashire.*)
657. A borrowed **loan** should come laughing home.
658. You must **look** where it is not, as well as where it is.
659. In the name of the **Lord** begins all mischief.

660. A nod from a **lord** is breakfast for a fool. (*Lancashire.*)
661. Give **losers** leave to talk. (*G. H.*)
662. He that **loseth** is a merchant as well as he that gains.
663. He that is not sensible of his **loss** has lost nothing.
664. Many things are **lost** for want of asking. (*G. H.*)
665. Cold pudding settles **love.**
666. Throw your rubbish where you throw your **love.** (*Dorset.*)
667. **Love** and hunger rule the world.
668. Whom we **love** best, to them we say least.
669. A man has choice to begin **love,** but not to end it.
670. He who has **love** in his heart has spurs in his heels.
671. **Love** is full of busy fear.
672. A penny-weight of **love** is worth a pound of law.
673. **Love** makes a good eye squint.
674. They **love** most who are least valued.
675. Next to **love,** quietness.
676. They that lie down for **love** should rise for hunger.
677. Of soup and **love,** the first is the best. (*? English.*)
678. Where there is much **love** there is much mistake.
679. As **love** thinks no evil, so envy speaks no good.
680. **Love** will creep where it may not go.
681. Men are best **loved** furthest off.
682. He **loves** not at all who knows when to make an end.
683. **Luck** is the idol of the idle.
684. **A maid** that laughs is half taken.
685. "Well, well" is a word of **malice.** (*Cheshire.*)
686. **Malice** is mindful.
687. The **man in the moon** drinks claret.
688. One **man,** no man.
689. Where there is a **man,** there do not thou shew thyself a man.
690. The grey **mare** is the better horse.

    [i.e. the wife wears the breeches.]
691. Nothing is lost in a good **market.**
692. A **marriage** between a young man and a young woman is made in heaven; a marriage between a young man and an old woman is made by the devil; a marriage between an old man and a young woman is made on earth. (*Monkish.*)
693. More belongs to **marriage** than four bare legs in a bed.
694. The **married man** must turn his staff into a stake.
695. He that **marries** a widow with three daughters marries four thieves.
696. **Marry** a down pillow and you have a feather bed.
697. Never **marry** anybody outside the sound of your parish bells. (*Dorset.*)
698. **Marry** first and love will follow.
699. Honest men **marry** soon; wise men not at all.
700. Everyone is **master** and servant.
701. Reserve the **master-blow.**
702. He that is a **master** must serve. (*G. H.*)
703. **Masters** are mostly the greatest servants in the house.
704. Don't be between two parishes at **meal times.** (*Dorset.*)
705. Never be ashamed to eat your **meat.**
706. **Meat** and mass [or matins] hinder no man's journey [or work].
707. Much **meat,** much malady.
708. **Meat** was made for mouths.
709. **Medicines** be not meat to live by.
710. Time and straw make **medlars** ripe.
711. **Mends** is worth misdeeds.
712. Every **mile** is two in winter.

713. Nothing turns sourer than **milk.** (*Lincolnshire.*)
[i.e. a mild man is most determined when provoked.]
714. The **mill** stands that wants water.
[Said of lawyers who work only for payment.]
715. An honest **miller** has a thumb of gold.
716. What is man but his **mind ?**
717. The mother of **mischief** is no bigger than a midge's wing.
718. **Misery** loves company.
719. **Misfortunes** come on wings and depart on foot.
720. **Misfortunes** tell us what fortune is.
721. If you would make an enemy, lend a man **money** and ask it of him again.
722. **Money** and bread never brought plague.
723. Ready **money** is a ready medicine.
724. **Money** is often lost for want of money.
725. **Money** talks.
726. Of **money,** wit, and virtue, believe the fourth of what you hear.
727. A **moneyless man** goes fast through the market.
728. God saves the **moon** from the wolves.
729. No **moon,** no man. (*Cornish and ? Dorset.*)
[In Cornwall when a child is born in the interval between an old moon and the first appearance of a new one, it is said that it will never live to reach the age of puberty.]
730. The **morning** for speed.
731. A misty **morning** may have a fine day.
732. When in **motion,** to push on is easy.
733. Dun as a **mouse.**
734. It is a cunning **mouse** which nesteth in the cat's ear.
735. Half the pleasure of the **mouth** is in the nose beforehand. (*Devonshire.*)
736. **Muck's** the mother of money. (*Cheshire.*)
737. The way to keep a man out of the **mud** is to black his boots.
738. He that lives with the **muses** shall die in the straw.
739. **Must** is a king's word.
740. After meat, **mustard.**
[When there is no more use for it.]
741. One shoulder of **mutton** drives another down.
[i.e. appetite comes with eating.]
742. One **nail** [fire or love] drives out another.
743. Drive the **nail** that will go.
744. He must have **nails** who scratches a bear.
745. He who lives according to **nature** will never be poor, and he who lives according to opinion will never be rich.
746. **Naught** is never in danger.
747. **Necessity** is coal-black.
748. He that is **needy** when he is married will be rich when he is buried.
749. The way is an ill **neighbour.**
750. A good **neighbour,** a good morrow.
751. You may love your **neighbour** and yet not hold his stirrup.
752. There is talk of the Turk and the Pope, but it is my next **neighbour** doeth me hurt.
753. Love your **neighbour,** yet pull not down your hedge.
754. You must ask your **neighbour** if you shall live in peace.
755. Know yourself, and your **neighbours** will not mistake you. (*Cumberland.*)
756. Better be stung by a **nettle** than prickt by a rose.
757. Every **new thing** has a silver tail. (*Cornish.*)
758. An oven and mill are nurseries of **news.**
759. **Night** brings the cows home. (*Lancashire.*)
760. **Night** is the mother of counsels.
761. The **night** is the mother of thoughts.

762. **Nits** will be lice. (*Said to be Oliver Cromwell's favourite proverb.*)

763. There be three things that never comes to **no good**: Christmas pigs, Michaelmas fowls, and parsons' daughters.

764. An inch in a man's **nose** is much.

765. He that is won with a **nut** may be lost with an apple.

766. Every **oak** has been an acorn. (*? English.*)

767. The first in the boat has the choice of **oars.**

768. They that are bound must **obey.**

769. When you have no **observers** be afraid of yourself.

770. He that can stay, **obtains.**

771. **Occasion's** head is bald behind.

772. The **offender** never pardons.

773. They that buy an **office** must sell something.

774. **Old maids** lead apes in hell.

775. An **old man's** end is to keep sheep.

776. **Old men** and travellers may lie by authority.

777. **Old** young and old long.

778. **One** is no number.

779. Some men plant an **opinion** they seem to eradicate.

780. When **Our Lady** falls in Our Lord's lap, then may England look for a mishap.

781. A little wood will heat a little **oven.**

782. He who has been in the **oven** himself knows where to find the pastry.

783. The good wife would not seek her daughter in the **oven** unless she had been there herself.

784. Old **ovens** are soon heated.

785. Whither shall the **ox** go that he shall not labour?

786. An **ox** is taken by the horns and a man by the tongue.

787. An **oyster** may be crossed in love.

788. **Pain** is forgotten where gain follows.

789. **Pains** to get, care to keep, fear to lose. (*G. H.*)

790. He who would enter **paradise** must have a good key.

791. The very best men stand in need of **pardon.**

792. It takes a shrew to sow **parsley.** (*Devonshire.*)

793. **Parsley** fried will bring a man to his saddle and a woman to her grave.

794. **Parsley** grows only in the gardens of henpecked husbands. (*Hampshire and Dorset.*)

795. Where the mistress is the master, the **parsley** grows the faster. (*Monmouthshire.*)

796. **Parsley** seed goes nine times to the devil. (*Yorkshire.*)

[i.e. it must be sown nine times, for the devil takes all but the last sowing.]

797. **Patch** side by side be neighbourly, but patch upon patch be beggarly. (*Sussex.*)

798. Every **path** hath a puddle. (*G. H.*)

799. Sweet appears sour when we **pay.**

800. What will you have? **Pay** for it and take it.

801. Fore **pay** is the worst pay. (*Dorset.*)

802. **Pay** with the same dish you borrow.

803. He that **payeth** another remembereth himself.

804. There are two bad **paymasters**: he that pays too soon, and he that does not pay at all.

805. **Pen** and ink never blush.

806. Lazy and good tempered makes a good **pensioner.** (*Naval proverb.*)

807. **Peril** and pleasure grow on the same tree.

808. Honour a **physician** before thou hast need of him.

809. Every man is a fool or **physician** to himself at least.

810. An inward sore puts out the **physician's** eye.

811. **Physicians'** faults are covered with earth, and rich men's with money.

812. Feed a **pig** and you will have a hog.

813. A **pig** in a poke.

[This proverb has probably wandered from Greece. During Moslem ascendancy in Greece, the people were not allowed to sell the pig as it was an unclean animal; hence it was offered for sale in the night season, hidden in a bag.]

814. One **pig** pays for his brother.

815. Living at the best end of the **pig-trough.** (*Cheshire.*)

816. A **pigeon-pair** is as bad as a single. (*Dorset.*)

["Pigeon-pair" is a boy and a girl.]

817. In a calm sea every man is a **pilot.**

818. He that will not stoop for a **pin** will never be worth a pound.

819. When the **pirate** prays, hide your silver.

820. **Pitch** and pay.

[i.e. trust none.]

821. He that **pities** another remembers himself.

822. **Pity** without help is like mustard without beef. (*Yorkshire. East Riding.*)

823. **Plain dealing** is dead, and died without issue.

824. Pluck not where you never **planted.**

825. **Plant** the shortest—pull the longest. (*Dorset.*)

[Refers to the day of the year to plant and gather shallots, the last day of June and December.]

826. If thy cast [hand] be bad, mend it with good **play.**

827. **Play** off your dust.

828. It signifies nothing to **play** well if you lose.

829. If you be not **pleased,** put your hand in your pocket and please yourself.

830. Fly that **pleasure** which paineth afterward.

831. **Plenty** brings pride, pride plee, plee pain, pain peace, peace plenty.

832. **Plenty** makes poor.

833. Never let the **plough** stand to catch a mouse.

834. A **ploughman** on his legs is higher than a gentleman on his knees.

835. There dies a **poet** with every man.

836. We give to the rich and take from the **poor.** (*G. H.*)

837. **Poor** and liberal, rich and covetous.

838. **Poor** and pert. (*Cheshire.*)

839. **Poor** folk fare the best.

840. Whenever a **poor man** helps another poor man, God Himself laughs.

841. The **poor man** pays for all.

842. **Poor men** seek meat for their stomachs; rich men stomachs for their meat.

843. A **post** of yew will outlast a post of iron. (*New Forest, Hampshire.*)

844. I will either make a **post** or shaft of it.

845. When the **pot** boils over it cooleth itself.

846. One **pot** sets another boiling.

847. A **pot** that belongs to many is ill stirred and worse boiled.

848. The **pot** will boil over before long. (*Lincolnshire.*)

[Said when a quarrel or scandal is anticipated.]

849. There is no virtue that **poverty** destroyeth not.

850. **Poverty** is an enemy to good manners.

851. **Poverty** is the mother of all arts and trades.

852. **Poverty** is the mother of health.

853. **Poverty** is the sixth sense.

854. Neither great **poverty** nor great wealth will hear reason.

855. **Poverty** parteth fellowship.

856. Old **praise** dies unless you feed it.

857. None ever gives the lie to him that **praiseth** him.

858. **Pray** and work.

859. **Pray** devoutly but hammer stoutly.

860. He that wishes to learn to **pray** must go to sea.

861. Once on shore we **pray** no more.

862. **Prayer** and provender never hindered work.

863. **Prayer** knocks till the door opens.

864. A short **prayer** reaches heaven.

865. A man may say even his **prayers** out of time.

866. **Prayers** should be the key of the day and the lock of the night.

867. He **preaches** well that lives well.

868. Whose **presence** does no good, their absence will do no harm.

869. He that bringeth a **present** findeth an open door.

870. **Prettiness** dies first.

871. Ask but enough and you may lower the **price** as you list.

872. **Pride** costs us more than hunger, thirst, and cold.

873. It is **pride,** not nature that craves much.

874. Young **prodigal** in a coach will be old beggar barefoot.

875. The **prodigal** robs his heir, the miser himself.

876. No one was ever ruined by taking a profit. (*Stock Exchange.*)

877. When a man repeats a **promise** again and again, he means to fail you.

878. Penny-pouched is **promise** broken.

879. **Promise** is debt.

880. The **promised land** is the land where one is not.

881. Don't throw your **property** out through the door with a spade, while your husband is bringing it in through the window with a spoon. (*Shropshire.*)

882. **Prospect** is often better than possession.

883. Adversity is easier born than **prosperity** forgot.

884. **Prosperity** gets followers, but adversity distinguishes them.

885. **Prosperity** lets go the bridle. (*G. H.*)

886. He who swells in **prosperity** will shrink in adversity.

887. **Proverbs** are the children of experience.

888. Wise men make **proverbs** but fools repeat them.

889. **Proverbs** lie on the lips of fools.

890. **Providing** is preventing. (*Shropshire.*)

891. He that puts on a **public gown** must put off a private person.

892. He that praiseth **publicly** will slander privately.

893. **Pudding** still before praise.

894. Painting the **pump** will not clean out the well.

895. Open thy **purse** and then open thy sack.

[i.e. receive thy money and then deliver thy goods.]

896. When **quality** opens the door there is poverty behind. (*Cornish.*)

897. He that can make a fire well can end a **quarrel.** (*G. H.*)

898. You can't gather **rabbit-meat** without finding nettles. (*Lincolnshire.*)

899. The **race** is got by running.

900. A wet **rag** goes safely by the fire.

901. The **raven** chides blackness.

902. **Reason** lies between the spur and the bridle.

903. **Reasons** are not like garments, the worse for the wearing.

904. No **receiver,** no thief.

905. No man's **religion** ever survives his morals.

906. **Religion** is a stalking-horse to shoot other fowls.

907. Common **report,** common liar.

908. The sting of a **reproach** is the truth of it.

909. **Reputation** is commonly measured by the acre.

910. Most men worship the **rising sun.**

911. All **rivers** do what they can for the sea.

912. **Rivers** need a spring.

913. The other side of the **road** always looks cleanest.

914. The **robin** and the wren are God Almighty's cock and hen.

915. Many speak of **Robin Hood** that never shot his bow. (*Yorkshire. North Riding.*)

[i.e. many talk of doing great things they can never accomplish.]

916. For the **rose** the thorn is often plucked.

917. **Rosemary** only flourishes where the missus is master. (*Herefordshire.*)

918. If you lie upon **roses** when young, you'll lie upon thorns when old.

919. What does not float is **rotten.**

920. He that is carried down the stream need not **row.**

921. All men **row** galley way.

[i.e. towards themselves.]

922. To **row** with the oar one has.

923. It's a poor **rule** that doesn't work both ways.

924. What boots **running** if one is on the wrong road.

925. You may know by a handful the whole **sack.**

926. An empty **sack** cannot stand upright. (*Cumberland.*)

[i.e. if you are hungry you cannot work.]

927. Many a **sack** is tied up before it be full.

928. The measure of our **sacrifice** is the measure of our love.

929. There is a time when nothing may be **said;** a time when something may; but no time when all things may. (*Monkish.*)

930. Young **saint,** old devil.

931. The **saint** who works no miracles has few pilgrims.

932. They that know one another **salute** afar off. (*G. H.*)

933. There is a **salve** for every sore.

934. Seek your **salve** where you got your sore.

935. The fragrance of **sanctity.**

936. **Saturday's moon** comes a day too soon.

[i.e. an unlucky day for a new moon.]

937. The **Scot** will not fight till he sees his own blood.

938. The **sea** refuses no river.

939. Thy **secret** is thy prisoner.

940. Do not speak of **secret** matters in a field that is full of little hills.

941. If you would know **secrets,** look for them in grief or pleasure.

942. One year's **seeding** — seven years' weeding. (*Cheshire and other counties.*)

943. Tho' **seeing** is believing, feeling has no fellow.

944. **Seldom** comes the better.

945. **Self** do—self have.

946. **Self's** always at home. (*Suffolk.*)

947. **Sell** in May and go away. (*Stock Exchange.*)

948. While the dust is on your feet, **sell** what you have bought.

949. Never sigh, but **send.**

950. Be a **serpent** save in the poison.

951. It is good to strike the **serpent's** head with your enemy's hand.

952. Men shut their doors against a **setting sun.**

953. Every time the **sheep** bleats it loses a mouthful.

954. Coupled **sheep** drown each other.

955. Old **sheep** shouldn't dress lamb fashion. (*Dorset.*)

956. The difference is wide that the **sheets** will not decide.

957. A **ship** leaks somewhere.

958. A bad **ship** never casts her anchor in port.

[Said to those who speak evil of a bad man who has had the good fortune to die in his bed and not on the gallows.]

959. Meddle with your old **shoes.**

960. He who once hits will be ever **shooting.**

961. We see not what sits on our **shoulder.**

962. He who was never **sick** dies the first fit.

963. Tell a man he is **sick** unto death and you tell him to die.

964. To put one's **sickle** into another man's corn.

965. **Sickness** cometh on horseback but goeth away on foot.

966. **Sickness** is felt, but health not at all.

967. The **sickness** of the body may prove the health of the soul.

968. Study **sickness** when you are well.

969. Little **silver**—much love.

970. **Silver** will have a silver sound.

971. **Sin** that is hidden is half forgiven.

972. He that **sings** worst, let him begin first.

973. The greater the **sinner,** the greater the saint.

974. **Sins** and debts are always more than we think them to be.

975. That man **sins** charitably who damns none but himself.

976. When all **sins** grow old, covetousness is young. (*G. H.*)

977. Poorly **sit,** richly warm. (*Gloucestershire.*)

978. Try your **skill** in gilt first, then in gold.

979. If the **sky** fall we shall have many larks.

980. Nature requireth five hours' **sleep**; custom taketh seven; idleness takes nine; and wickedness eleven. (*Shropshire.*)

981. He sups who **sleeps.**

982. A broken **sleeve** keepeth [or holdeth] the arm back.

983. A **slut** always carries her duster in her pocket. (*Dorset.*)

[Said of a person who uses a pocket handkerchief instead of a duster.]

984. Keep touch in **small things.**

985. Of all **smells,** bread; of all tastes, salt.

986. **Smoke** follows the fairest.

987. Use **soft words** and hard arguments.

988. A **solitary man** is either a brute or an angel.

989. **Something** old, something new, something borrowed, something blue. (*Marriage proverb.*)

990. A mother's **son** is not her own until he has had the small-pox.

991. If you make **songs** about yourself, you can't blame other people for singing them. (*Dorset.*)

992. Small **sores** require slender medicines.

993. You will have to sup **sorrow** by spoonfuls before you die. (*Yorkshire. North Riding.*)

[Said to a rebellious child.]

994. **Sorrow** is always dry.

995. When **sorrow** is asleep, awake it not.

996. A fat **sorrow** is easier borne than a lean one. (*Norfolk.*)

997. If thou hast a **sorrow,** tell it to thy saddle-bow, and ride thee, singing, forth.

998. It is no use laying **sorrow** to your heart when others only lay it to their heels. (*Lancashire.*)

[Said to those who grieve over the ungrateful.]

999. When **sorrows** come, they come not single spies, but in battalions.

1000. Providence always greases the sides of a fat **sow.** (*Norfolk.*)

1001. **Sow** dry and set wet. (*Northumberland.*)

1002. **Sparing** is the first gaining.

1003. Who **speaks** sows; who keeps silent reaps. (*Sussex.*)

1004. He who **speaks** well fights well.

1005. Do not all you can; **spend** not all you have; believe not all you hear; tell not all you know.

1006. That we **spent** we had; that we left we lost; that we gave we have.

1007. All the speed is in the **spurs.**

1008. To break no **squares.**

[i.e. to do no harm; to make no difference.]

1009. Small **stake** makes cold play.

1010. If you **steal** for others you will hang for yourself.

1011. The hardest **step** is over the threshold.

1012. The greatest **step** is that out of doors.

1013. Too high for the **stirrup** and not high enough for the saddle. (*Oxfordshire.*)

1014. The **stone** that lieth not in your way need not offend you.

1015. The **stone** which is fit for the wall will not be long on the road.

1016. Who remove **stones** bruise their own fingers. (*G. H.*)

1017. Boil **stones** in butter and you may sup the broth.

[i.e. good ingredients will make even impossible things savoury.]

1018. Set thy **stool** in the sun; if a knave goes an honest man may come.

1019. **Stop** a little to make an end the sooner.

1020. If **strokes** are good to give they are good to receive.

1021. **Suffer** and expect.

1022. Of **sufferance** cometh ease.

1023. That which **sufficeth** is not little.

1024. A dry **summer** never begs its bread. (*Somerset.*)

1025. A **summer's evening** is as long as a winter's day.

1026. It is day still while the **sun** shines.

1027. The **sun** shines on both sides of the hedge.

1028. Come day, go day, God send **Sunday.** (*Yorkshire. North Riding.*)

[Said by indolent workers.]

1029. He who **sups** late sups well.

[Said of one who marries late in life.]

1030. Be slow to be **sure.** (*Norfolk.*)

1031. The last taste of things gives them the name of **sweet** or sour.

1032. **Sweet-meat** must have sour sauce.

1033. **Swine,** women, and bees cannot be turned.

1034. At a round **table** there's no dispute of place.

1035. Make not thy **tail** broader than thy wings. (*Dorset.*)

1036. A **tailor** is the ninth part of a man.

[The word "tailor" is a corruption of "tellers": see under "tellers" for explanation.]

1037. As yt **is tak** [take] yt. (*Carving on the wall in the Beauchamp Tower, Tower of London.*)

1038. Everything is as it is **taken.**

1039. **Talk** much, err much.

1040. **Talking** comes by nature, silence by understanding.

1041. It takes nine **tellers** to mark a man. (*Dorset.*)

[An old Dorset custom, to strike the passing bell when a death takes place to indicate the age and sex of deceased—thrice for a girl, four times for a boy, six for a spinster, seven for a matron, eight for a bachelor, nine for a married man. (This old custom still in use in Dorset fifty years ago.)]

1042. All **temptations** are found either in hope or fear.

1043. He that is busy is **tempted** by but one devil; he that is idle by a legion.

1044. Once in **ten years** one man hath need of another.

1045. My dame fed her hens on **thanks,** but they laid no eggs.

1046. It is opportunity that makes the **thief.**

1047. The hole calls the **thief.**

1048. **Thieves** are never rogues among themselves.

1049. Old **thieves** make good gaolers.

1050. They are not all **thieves** that are barked at by dogs.

1051. The **third time** pays for all. (*Cheshire.*)

1052. A **thistle** is a fat salad for an ass's mouth.

1053. It early pricks that will be a **thorn.**

1054. Wherever a man dwells he shall be sure to have a **thorn bush** near his door.

1055. The **thorn** comes forth with the point forwards.

1056. While thy shoe is on thy foot tread upon the **thorns.**

1057. There are **three ways:** the Universities, the sea, the Court.

1058. The groundsel [**threshold**] speaks not, save what it heard of the hinges.

1059. Winter **thunder,** rich man's food and poor man's hunger.
[i.e. it is good for fruit and bad for corn.]

1060. **Tie** it well and let it go.

1061. **Time** and I against any two.

1062. **Time** is a file that wears and makes no noise.

1063. **Time** is the father of truth.

1064. The **time** that is to come is no more yours than the time that has gone by.

1065. **Tithe** and be rich.

1066. In **to-day** already walks to-morrow.

1067. **To-day** is yesterday's pupil.

1068. Now is yesterday's **to-morrow.**

1069. **To-morrow** is a new day.

1070. If you keep your **tongue** a prisoner, your body may go free.

1071. The **tongue** is the very last means a woman has of making herself understood with her husband.

1072. The **tongue** talks at the head's cost.

1073. **Touch** pot, touch penny.
[i.e. no credit given.]

1074. There is but one road out of the **Tower** and that leads to the scaffold.
[i.e. Tower of London.]

1075. He that hath a **trade** hath an estate.

1076. **A trade** is better than service.

1077. **Trade** is the mother of money.

1078. A handful of **trade** is worth a handful of gold.

1079. He who changes his **trade** makes soup in a basket.

1080. One cannot **trade** without holding a candle to the devil. (*Lancashire.*)
[i.e. tricks of trade.]

1081. To **travel** safely through the world a man must have a falcon's eye, an ass's ears, a merchant's words, a camel's back, a hog's mouth, and a hart's legs.

1082. A **travelled man** has leave to lie.

1083. If you no but say "**treacle**" she'll lick. (*Lincolnshire.*)

1084. As a **tree** falls, so must it lie.

1085. He that loves the **tree** loves the branch.

1086. He that plants **trees** loves others besides himself.

1087. It must be **true** that all men say.

1088. **Trust** is the mother of deceit.

1089. **Truth** always comes by the lame messenger.

1090. Deem the best in every doubt until the **truth** be tried out.

1091. **Truth** comes back where she has once visited.

1092. **Truth** finds foes where it makes none.

1093. **Truth** has a scratched face.

1094. He who follows **truth** too close upon the heels will, one time or other, have his brains kicked out.

1095. **Truth's** best ornament is nakedness.

1096. **Tuck** it in May, tuck it away.
[i.e. unlucky to short-coat a baby in May.]

1097. **Turkeys,** carps, hops, pickerel, and beer, came into England all in one year.
[Believed to be 1520.]

1098. Things don't **turn up,** they must be turned up.

1099. Things not **understood** are admired.

1100. Nothing is certain but the **unforeseen.**

1101. **Ungirt,** unblessed.

1102. **Unkissed,** unkind.

1103. Unknown, **unkissed.**

1104. Three **unreliable things:** a horse's health, a woman's word, and a boy's love.

1105. He lives **unsafely** that looks too near on things. (*G. H.*)

1106. It is lost that is **unsought.**

1107. **Upbraiding** turns a benefit into an injury.

1108. The **vale** best discovereth the hill.

1109. **Varnishing** hides a crack.

1110. The **vessel** that will not obey her helm will have to obey the rocks. (*Cornish.*)

1111. Every **vice** fights against nature.

1112. What maintains one **vice** would bring up two children.

1113. Great **vices** and great virtues make men famous.

1114. One may smile and smile and be a **villain.**

1115. **Virtue** now is in herbs and stones and words only. (*G. H.*)

1116. **Virtue** which parleys is near a surrender.

1117. **Virtue** would not go far if a little vanity walked not with it.

1118. He that walketh with the **virtuous** is one of them.

1119. Men's **vows** are women's traitors.

1120. He that goes and comes maketh a good **voyage.**

1121. The **vulgar** keep no account of your hits, but of your misses.

1122. **Walls** hear without warnings.

1123. There is no woe to **want.**

1124. **Want** is the whetstone of wit.

1125. All weapons of **war** cannot arm fear.

1126. Pleasing **ware** is half sold.

1127. He that is **warm** thinks all so. (*G. H.*)

1128. **Wash** your hands often, your feet seldom, and your head never.

1129. Half of the **washing** is to wipe in the water and wash in the towel. (*Dorset.*)

1130. He who has **water** and sleep has no cause to grumble. (*Sailor's proverb.*)

1131. **Water,** fire, and soldiers quickly make room.

1132. Clean **water** often comes out of a mucky spout. (*Lincolnshire.*)
[i.e. a good person may spring from a disreputable family.]

1133. There's always some **water** where the heifer drowns.

1134. Although it rain, throw not away the **watering-pot.**

1135. People with **wax heads** shouldn't walk in the sun. (*Cornish.*)

1136. **Wealth** is enemy to health.

1137. A man's **wealth** is his enemy.

1138. **Wealth** makes wit waver.

1139. Bear **wealth,** poverty will bear itself.

1140. A man of courage never wants **weapons.**

1141. Everyone is **weary:** the poor in seeking, the rich in keeping, the good in learning. (*G. H.*)

1142. No **weather** is ill if the wind be still. (*Northumberland.*)

1143. Woo in haste and **wed** at leisure.

1144. Early **wed,** early dead.

1145. Better **wed** over the mixen than over the moor. (*Cheshire.*)

1146. More **wedders** than pot-boilers. (*Yorkshire. North Riding.*)
[i.e. many marry without sufficient means.]

1147. Dance barefoot at the **wedding.**
[Said of an elder unmarried sister.]

1148. **Wedding** and ill-wintering tame both man and beast.

1149. In the **wedding cake** hope is the sweetest of the plums.

1150. Age and **wedlock** bring a man to his nightcap.

1151. He that bites on every **weed** must needs light on poison.

1152. Who hath none to still him must **weep** out his eyes. (*G. H.*)

1153. Learn **weeping** and thou shalt laugh gaining. (*G. H.*)

1154. If **well** and them cannot, then ill and them can. (*Yorkshire.*)

1155. Cast no dirt into the **well** that hath given you water.

1156. Drawn **wells** are seldom dry.

1157. I **wept** when I was born, and every day shows why.

1158. When all is **wet** to the skin, hold out yet. (*Derbyshire.*)

1159. Save something for the man that rides on the **white horse.**
[i.e. old age.]

1160. Marry a **widow** before she leaves mourning.

1161. A smoky house and a railing **wife.**

1162. He that takes not up a pin slights his **wife.**

1163. He that will thrive must ask leave of his **wife.**

1164. Three things are men most likely to be cheated in: a horse, a wig, and a **wife.**

1165. A man who tells his **wife** all is only newly married.

1166. When the husband drinks to the **wife,** all would be well; when the wife drinks to the husband, all is well.

1167. A man must not choose a **wife** in Westminster, a servant in Paul's, or a horse in Smithfield, lest he choose a queen, a knave, or a jade.

1168. He that goes a great way for a **wife** is either cheated or means to cheat.

1169. A man who keeps a **wife** is like a man who keeps a monkey; he is responsible for her mischief. (*Legal proverb.*)

1170. The **wife** is the key of the house.

1171. In a narrow house with an ugly **wife** you are secure of your possession.

1172. A **wild goose** never laid a tame egg.

1173. A **willow** will buy a horse before an oak will pay for a saddle.

1174. The **wind** hath a draw after flying straw. (*Devonshire.*)

1175. The **wind** in one's face makes one wise.

1176. A little **wind** kindles, much puts out the fire.

1177. He that will use all **winds** must shift his sail.

1178. It is a good wind that blows a man to the **wine.**

1179. He that is fit to drink **wine** must have sugar on his beard, his eyes in his pockets, and his feet in his hands.

1180. Good **wine** needs no bush.
["Bush"—a wisp of straw stuck upon the top of a country house to show that ale was sold there. If the ale was good, people went there, though there was no "bush".]
[The association of the "bush" with wine is seen in the "Bush-House". A bough was used as a "bush" as a sign for a tavern; and a bunch of ivy was the sign of a vintner's shop. "Bush" was also a term for a spray of rosemary or other herb which was laid in the bottom of a drinking-cup by publicans. A "bush" was hung out at the top of mines to show that they were at work.]

1181. **Wine** sets an edge to wit.

1182. Of **wine** the middle, of oil the top, and of honey the bottom is best.

1183. **Winter** finds out what summer lays up.

1184. **Winter** is summer's heir.

1185. **Winter** never died in a ditch.

1186. The life of man is a **winter** way.

1187. **Winter's** thunder is summer's wonder.

1188. The most manifest sign of **wisdom** is a continual cheerfulness.

1189. **Wisdom** sails with wind and tide.

1190. **Wisdom** sometimes walks in clouted shoes.

1191. The least foolish is **wise.**

1192. If the **wise** erred not it would go hard with fools.

1193. A **wise man** may live anywhere.

1194. The **wise man** must carry the fool upon his shoulders.

1195. Bout's **[without's]** bare, but it's easy. (*Cheshire.*)

1196. Bought **wit's** best.

1197. They that **wive** between sickle and scythe will never thrive. (*Suffolk.*)

1198. **Wives** are young men's mistresses and old men's nurses.

1199. **Wives** be like pilchards—when they be good they be only middlin', and when they be bad they be bad. (*Cornish.*)

1200. The dust raised by the sheep does not choke the **wolf.**

1201. He that hath a **wolf** for his mate needs a dog for his man. (*G. H.*)

1202. Man is a **wolf** to man.

1203. Who keeps company with a **wolf** will learn to howl.

1204. Pluck a hair of the same **wolf.**

1205. A whistling **woman** and a crowing hen is neither fit for God nor men. (*Northamptonshire.*)

1206. A fair **woman** and a slashed gown find always some nail in the way.

1207. **Woman** conceals only what she does not know.

1208. He that hath a **woman** has an eel by the tail.

1209. A **woman** hath none other weapon but her tongue.

1210. An ugly **woman** is a disease of the stomach; a handsome woman a disease of the head.

1211. A **woman** is an angel at ten, a saint at fifteen, a devil at forty, and a witch at fourscore.

1212. A morning sun, a wine-bred child, and a Latin-bred **woman** seldom end well. (*G. H.*)

1213. He that does not love a **woman** sucked a sow.

1214. Beware of the forepart of a **woman,** the hind part of a mule, and all sides of a priest.

1215. Trust your dog to the end; a **woman** till the first opportunity.

1216. **Woman** to man is either a god or a wolf.

1217. A **woman** will laugh in your face and cut your throat.

1218. Fools are wise men in affairs of **women.**

1219. **Women** and bridges always lack mending.

1220. **Women** and music should never be dated.

1221. **Women** are necessary evils.

1222. **Women** are saints in church, angels in the street, devils in the kitchen, and apes in bed.

1223. **Women** be forgetful, children be unkind.

1224. Weal and **women** cannot pan, but woe and women can. (*Derbyshire.*)

1225. **Women** grow on the sunny side of the wall.

1226. **Women** in mischief are wiser than men.

1227. Two **women** placed together make cold weather.

1228. **Women,** priests, and poultry have never enough.

1229. **Wooers** and widows are never poor.

1230. **Wood** half burnt is easily kindled.

1231. A **wool-seller** knows a wool-buyer.

1232. A **word** and a stone let go cannot be called back.

1233. "Take", "have", and "keep" are pleasant **words.**

1234. **Work** hard and be poor; do nothing and get more. (*Dorset.*)

1235. Quick at **work,** quick at meat.

1236. If anything stay, let **work** stay.

1237. It is working that makes the **workman.**

1238. It is the ordinary way of the **world** to keep folly at the helm and wisdom under the hatches.

1239. It is a **world** to see.

1240. The **worth** of a thing is best known by the want.
1241. A green **wound** is soon healed.
1242. A **wreck** ashore is a beacon at sea.
1243. He that is thrown would ever **wrestle.**
1244. An old **wrinkle** never wears out.
1245. **Write** with the learned, but speak with the vulgar.
1246. Obey orders and do **wrong.** (*Stock Exchange proverb.*)
1247. A snow **year,** a rich year.
1248. The **year** doth nothing else but open and shut.
1249. A daisy **year's** always a lazy year. (*Lancashire.*)
1250. **Years** know more than books.
1251. "**Yes**" **and** "**no**" are the cause of all disputes.
1252. No man can call again **yesterday.**
1253. **Yesterday** will not be called again.
1254. They who would be **young** when they are old must be old when they are young.
1255. Take heart of grace, **younger** thou shalt never be.
1256. Mind other men, but most **yourself.**
1257. What **youth** is used to, age remembers.
1258. **Youth** will be served.

IRISH

(Including Armagh, Carlow, Cavan, Clare, West Clare, West Connaught, Connemara, Cork, North Cork, West Cork, Derry, Donegal, Farney, Galway, South Galway, Kildare, Kerry, Macauber, Mayo, Meath, Monaghan, Munster, Tyrone, Ulster, Wexford)

An Introduction to this collection by Henry Morris, M.A., will be found on page lxii.

1. He **acts** well who acts quickly. (*Galway and Mayo.*)
2. One **advice** bought is worth two advices gratis.
3. Be duly **afraid** and there is no danger.
4. Young people don't know what **age** is, and old people forget what youth was.
5. The third generation is never seen in an **ale-house.**
6. The **angels** know each other. (*Kerry.*)
7. **Apples** will grow again. (*North Cork.*)
8. The thing that often occurs is never much **appreciated.** (*Armagh.*)
9. An **art** is better than a heritage.
10. Better is an **ass** that carries you than a horse that throws you.
11. **Asthmatic** people live long.
12. Aristotle could not divine what an **autumn** night would do.
13. A grassy **autumn** presages a spring of many deaths.
14. Always touch a new-born **baby,** or when it grows up it will lift its hand against you.
15. The "**bad drop**" runs in a family for seventeen generations. (*Armagh and Donegal.*)
16. Care beheads **bad luck.**
17. What is got **badly** goes badly. (*South Galway.*)
18. At the mouth of the **bag** is the economy possible.
19. It is not in the bottom of the **bag** that one may do the housekeeping but at its mouth. (*South Galway.*)

20. Keep the **bad man** on your side. (*South Galway.*)
21. He is like a **bag-pipe,** he never makes a noise till his belly's full.
22. Everyone is winding-in his own **ball.** (*West Clare.*)
23. **Bareness** is better than misfortune.
24. Go to a man who is in a difficulty and you'll get a **bargain.**
25. An empty **barn** needs no roof.
26. It is a hard-fought **battle** from which no man returns to tell the tale.
27. There has not been found, nor will there be found, a juster judge than the field of **battle.**
28. **Beauty** does not make the pot boil. (*Armagh.*)
29. One **beetle** knows another.
30. If you don't give the **beggar** anything, don't tear his bag.
31. A constant **beggar** gets a constant refusal. (*Kerry.*)
32. The **beggar** is in no danger from the robber.
33. The **beginning** of a ship is a board; of a kiln, a stone; of a king's reign, salutation; and the beginning of health is sleep.
34. The **beginning** of a ship [is] a plank; of a kiln, stones; of a prince, welcome [i.e. preparation for his coming]; of health, sleep. The end of a ship [is] drowning; of a kiln, burning; of a prince, fault-finding [after his departure]; of health, a sigh. (*Armagh.*)
35. When the **belly** is full, the bone likes to stretch.
36. A **belly** to the sun is often empty. (*West Connaught.*)
37. **Bend** with the tree that will bend with you.
38. Woe to him whose **betrayer** sits at his table.
39. Don't let anyone take the **bit** out of your mouth. (*Farney.*)
40. Cut the **binding** that is nearest to the throat.
41. You'll never get from the briar but a **blackberry.**
42. A **blanket** is the warmer from being doubled. (*Ulster.*)
    [Said when relations marry.]
43. A **blessing** does not fill the belly.
44. In the world of the **blind** the one-eyed man is king.
45. 'Tis a little drop of **blood** that's not warmer than water.
    [i.e. even a distant relationship is better than none.]
46. There's no crime in the **blow** that has not been struck.
47. There is another side on the **boat.**
48. What's in the **bone** is in the marrow.
49. He whose **boot** pinches thinks the world too narrow.
50. The man with **boots** doesn't mind where he puts his foot.
51. There is no welcome for one who **borrows.** (*West Connaught.*)
52. Every **branch** blossoms according to the root from which it sprung.
53. **Bravery** is not lasting. (*Munster.*)
54. It takes no butter off your **bread.**
    [i.e. the circumstance does not affect you.]
55. Eaten **bread** is soon forgotten. (*Ulster.*)
56. Eaten **bread** is sour.
57. It is easy to make **bread** [knead] near the meal. (*Kerry.*)
58. If you give the loan of your **breeches,** don't cut off the buttons. (*Armagh.*)
59. A new **broom** sweeps clean, but the old brush knows the corners. (*Farney.*)
60. The first drop of the **broth** is the hottest. (*West Meath.*)
61. Let **broth** boil slowly, but let porridge make a noise.
62. The shelter of the **bush** is not noticed till it is gone. (*Galway.*)
63. A house [**business**] can't be kept without talk [lit. tongue]. (*Kerry.*)

64. 'Tis he who has **butter** gets butter.

65. **Butter** is usual [or natural] on buttermilk.

[Hence fair dealing is natural for an honest man, cheating for a rogue.]

66. He who eats the **butter** takes the colour of the crock.

67. **Butter** to butter is no kitchen. (*Farney.*)

[Said of two girls kissing.]

68. I hate **buttermilk** after I have had my fill.

69. I don't cook my **cabbage** twice.

[Said when a person is asked to repeat a remark or tale.]

70. A full **cabin** is better than an empty castle.

71. He's eating the **calf** in the cow's belly.

72. The rain is best for the **calf**; the wind for the lamb; the sun for the foal. (*Farney.*)

73. Good **care** never yet destroyed anything.

74. Grass and **carelessness**. (*Farney.*)

[The peasantry say this is the best rule for rearing young cattle. They believe that too much attention does them more harm than good.]

75. Better bring a **case** before the judge's beard than to the elbow-bone.

[i.e. a fight.]

76. What should you expect from a **cat** but a kitten? (*Donegal.*)

77. What can you expect from a **cat** but her skin?

78. To please himself only the **cat** purrs.

79. What would a **cat's** son do but kill a rat?

80. The third time's a **charm.**

81. Give to the **child** and it will visit you again.

82. A woman is better of a **child** but worse of twins.

83. A **child** desires [what fills] his eye.

84. An old **child** has a long recollection. (*West Connaught.*)

85. The **child** has but as he hears. (*Munster.*)

86. Woe to the person who rears not a **child** of his own.

87. There is no anguish of soul till one has **children.** (*West Cork.*)

88. **Choose** before you speak. (*Armagh.*)

89. "Are you a **Christian**?" asked the priest of the man. "I am not," he replied; "I'm a Connachtman." (*Said only in Ulster.*)

[The traditional dislike of Ulster for Connacht is nearly two thousand years old.]

90. There's no mark of a **Christian** on him except that he walks the road without a halter.

91. He who is nearest to the **church** is the last coming in to Mass.

92. The yellow **clay** comes up.

93. The **closed hand** gets the shut fist.

94. Clean and whole make poor **clothes** shine. (*Cork.*)

95. She burnt her **coal** and did not warm herself.

[Said when a woman marries a bad husband.]

96. If you give away an old **coat,** don't cut off the buttons.

97. He is a big man, but a small **coat** fits him.

98. From the crow o' **cock** till the song o' the redbreast.

99. What keeps out the **cold** will keep out the heat.

100. A **combed head** sells the feet.

[i.e. the hair well dressed covers the defects of the feet.]

101. **Comfort** is not known if poverty does not come before it. (*West Connaught.*)

102. Fire and tow are dangerous **companions.**

103. The man beyond does not know the **condition** of the man on this side.

104. The **Connachtman** has thirteen hearts. (*Ulster.*)

105. The heaviest ear of **corn** is the one that lowliest hangs its head. (*Ulster.*)

106. Wide is the door of the **cottage.** (*Ulster.*)

107. Everyone is a **counsellor** until he begins to quarrel.

108. Two-thirds of help is to give **courage.**

109. If you go to the **court,** leave your soul at home.

110. **Covetousness** bursts the bag.

111. Don't trust the son of the **cow.**

112. Many a **cow** did not follow cow nature.

113. Everyone is affable until a **cow** goes into his garden. (*Galway.*)

114. It is from her head the **cow** is milked. (*Farney and Ulster.*)

115. Some **cow** will bear some calf some day. (*Macauber.*)

116. The **cow** which has the loudest bellowing has the slenderest tail. (*Kerry.*)

117. Better be a **coward** than a corpse.

118. A **cow dung** is wider when trodden on.

119. Easy, Oh woman of three **cows** !

120. Far-away **cows** wear long horns.

121. **Credit** till harvest, and credit for ever.

122. No one ever **cried** but for something that pinched himself. (*Connaught.*)

123. The economy of the **crow.** (*Farney.*)

[The crow in summer time spends half a day perhaps and travels over miles of country searching for a potato. On unearthing it she generally flies off with it, but, if in her flight she happens to let it drop, she flies on and the result of all her toil is lost.]

124. When the **cuckoo** comes on a leafless tree, sell your cow and buy corn. (*Farney.*)

125. Chew your **cud** where you have worked. (*South Galway.*)

[i.e. keep the advantage you have gained.]

126. Break not a **custom** and invent not a custom. (*West Cork.*)

127. Better sup with a **cutty** than wait for a spoon.

["Cutty" is a short or broken spoon.]

128. Good care takes the head off the **danger.** (*Farney—Co. Monaghan.*)

129. It is many's the big **darkness** comes and with little rain. (*Farney—Co. Monaghan.*)

130. Many a big **darkness** comes with little rain. (*Donegal.*)

131. The **day** always finds fault with the work of the night.

132. Praise the **day** at evening.

133. It is the **deaf people** that make the lies. (*West Connaught.*)

134. He has not tasted food who will not also taste **death.**

135. What is there that seems worse to a man than his **death,** and yet he does not know but it may be the height of his good luck.

136. **Death** has him under lock. (*Armagh.*)

[Said of one in a fatal illness.]

137. Sleepiness is the sign of **death** in a man, and watchfulness in a woman.

138. **Death** is the master of the world. (*Armagh.*)

139. **Death** is the poor man's best physician.

140. **Death** never comes untimely.

141. Two who never believe the report of your **death**—the person who hates you and the person who loves you. (*Farney and Armagh.*)

142. Better old **debts** than old grudges.

143. The **deed** will praise itself. (*Ulster.*)

144. Your own **deeds** will be long baptized on you. (*Cork.*)

145. If you're **depending** on one mouthful, have a hen's egg: if you're depending on one garment, have a greatcoat.

146. Never give the **Devil** good-morrow till you meet him.

147. The **Devil** never grants long leases.

148. Give a thing, take a thing is the **Devil's** gold ring. (*Ulster.*)

149. The poor man's cow and the rich man's son are the two things that will **die.**

150. A **dimple** in the chin, a devil within.

151. The man that stays long out, his **dinner** cools.

[Applied to anyone who remains too long from home.]

152. He that hath a **dinner** [to give] can have a witness.

153. A long **disease** does not always tell a lie.

[i.e. it will kill at last.]

154. At the beginning of the **disease** do not delay, as the herb that is not used in time has no virtue.

155. Every **disease** is a physician. (*Munster.*)

156. Patience is the [best] cure for old **diseases.** (*Cork.*)

157. Better have a cloak on your shoulder than have the **doctor's** horse at your door.

158. One who is cowless must be his own **dog.**

[i.e. a poor man must forage for himself.]

159. One **dog** can't fight.

160. Keep the bone and the **dog** will follow you.

161. The **dogs** follow the man who has the bone.

162. 'Tis for the sake of the company the **dogs** go to church.

163. Threatened **dogs** live long.

164. A **dog's nose,** a man's elbow, and a maid's knee are always cold. (*Ulster.*)

165. Never bolt your **door** with a boiled carrot.

166. The **doorstep** of a great house is slippery.

167. The **dowry** goes with the wind, and the ugliness stays with the wife.

168. Where there is **dowry** there is danger. (*Ulster.*)

169. As wet as **drammock.**

[Drammock is raw oatmeal and water.]

170. Cool [the beverage] before you **drink.**

171. If you don't **drink,** don't be rubbing your back to the alehouse. (*Armagh.*)

172. Take the **drink** for the thirst that is yet to come.

173. A **drink** is shorter than a story. (*Ulster and Donegal.*)

[Said to a story-teller or bearer of news before he begins his narration, a drink being then handed to him.]

174. The **drink** of the door. (*Farney.*)

[i.e. the parting drink.]

175. Thirst is the end of **drinking,** and sorrow is the end of love.

176. Alas for him who is **drowned** in the storm which soon gives place to sunshine.

177. Time enough lost the **ducks.**

178. Everybody understands his own **dumb person.**

179. No one knows which is best, **early** or late.

180. Woods have **ears** and both sides of the fences.

181. Do not put the **ease** before the hardship.

182. A man's business will give him an **education.** (*Kerry.*)

183. An **egg** is a mouthful of wine, but a mouthful of poison if spoiled.

184. Blow not on dead **embers.**

[i.e. do not attempt a hopeless task.]

185. Burning **embers** are easily kindled.

186. Beware of the horns of a bull, of the heels of a horse, of the smile of an **Englishman.**

187. About **evening** a man is known.

188. The **evening** is a good prophet.

189. **Evening** is speedier than morning.

[i.e. better do a thing in the evening than postpone it till next morning.]

190. What **everybody** says must be true. (*Ulster.*)

191. **Everybody's** body and nobody's bit.

[i.e. all things to all men.]

192. Unwillingness easily finds an **excuse.**

193. An **eye** is blind in another man's corner.

194. A hungry **eye** sees far.

195. The **eye** should be blind in the abode of another.

196. It is the master's **eye** that feeds the steed. (*Cork.*)

197. The **eye** will note what it is used to.

198. A man never **fails** among his own people.

199. Don't lift me till I **fall.**

200. **Famine** never came from drought. (*South Galway.*)

201. What goes **far** grows cold. (*Cork.*)

202. He who has water and peat on his **farm** has the world his own way.

203. A long **fast** and want of shoes make young folk sensible. (*Kerry.*)

204. The body would like well to leave **fasting** to the soul.

205. **Fate** is stronger than rearing.

206. **Fear** is worse than fighting.

207. If you go to a **feast** uninvited carry your own stool with you.

208. Three **feasts** due to everyone—the feast of baptism, of marriage, and of death.

209. Seeing's believing, but **feeling** is God's own truth. (*Ulster.*)

210. Think of the sore **feet.** (*South Galway.*)

[i.e. look before you.]

211. A combed head hides ugly **feet.**

212. When you have a desire to do anything your **feet** are light. (*Farney.*)

213. Never speak to the **feet** while the head is alive. (*Farney.*)

[i.e. you should not approach nor address a subordinate while a superior is present.]

214. Praise **field,** and do not praise young crop.

215. You can't **find** a thing except in the place it is. (*Kerry.*)

216. Putting a thing on the long **finger.**

[i.e. postponing it.]

217. If you don't want to cut your **finger** don't put it before the hook.

218. Why burn your **fingers** when you have a pair of tongs? (*Ulster.*)

219. There's no want like the want of **fire.**

220. Have your own **fire,** or trust to the sun for a warming.

221. Who steals the **fire** steals the blessing.

[Old Gaelic proverb, which has its origin in Druidical days. The "wee people" (fairies) go off with the fire if it goes out.]

222. It's the **first drop** that destroyed me; there's no harm at all in the last. (*Armagh.*)

223. The man who gets the **first share** is neither thankful [satisfied] or unthankful. (*Galway.*)

224. It is not a **fish** until it is on the bank.

225. There are white flowers on the **fisherman's** garden.

[i.e. the sea. Said when the sea is white with breakers.]

226. A closed **fist** gets a closed eye.

[i.e. if you are not generous people will pretend not to know you.]

227. A shut **fist** gets only a closed hand.

228. A **fist-full** of a man is better than a gad-full of a woman. (*Kerry.*)

["Gad"—an osier or twig used for tying bundles.]

229. **Flowing** and ebbing, it spends the day. (*Galway.*)

230. The short way to the **food,** and the road-about to the work.

231. When one is absent, his **food** is allowed to grow cold.

232. It is better to be in search of **food** than of appetite. (*North Cork.*)

233. There is no **fool** who has not his own kind of sense. (*Galway.*)

234. A thorn in mud, a hound's tooth, a **fool's** word—the three sharpest things at all. (*Ulster.*)

235. The **foot** at rest meets nothing.

236. Slow is every **foot** on an unknown path.

237. The moving **foot** will get what the idle foot will not.

238. Let every man praise the **ford** as he finds it. (*Ulster.*)

239. What occurs but once will be **forgotten** for ever. (*Cork.*)

240. **Fortune** comes in a slender stream, but misfortune in a torrent.

241. Every **fortunate** person is fair.

242. The thing that is not eaten and is not stolen will be **found.** (*Ulster.*)

243. What is not taken away will be **found.**

244. The **fox** never sent out a messenger better than himself.

245. Without store, without **friend.**

246. It's not lost what a **friend** gets.

247. Don't put your **friend** in your pocket. (*Cavan.*)

248. A **friend** is better than ale.

249. Your **friend** is in your pocket. (*Kildare.*)

250. The three best **friends** and the three worst enemies—fire, wind, and water. (*Farney.*)

251. "Gift-gaff" makes good **friendship.** (*Ulster.*)

["Gift-gaff" means give and take.]

252. Reckoning up is **friendship's** end.

253. **Frost** is the forerunner of mud. (*Cork.*)

254. When all **fruit** fails, welcome haws.

255. 'Tis the hope of satisfaction that ruins the **gambler.**

256. Guarding is [a good] part of the **game.**

257. Any fool can see the **gatehouse,** few see the house.

258. A hard **gathering,** a wide scattering. (*Armagh.*)

259. After a **gathering** comes a scattering.

260. When we're not **gathering** we're spending.

261. **Generosity** which is dilatory is worth going to meet.

262. Take **gifts** with a sigh; most men give to be paid.

263. A Sunday **girl,** or a summer calf.

[i.e. deceptive appearance.]

264. If you only have a **goat,** be in the middle of the fair with it.

265. All good has an end save the goodness of **God.**

266. **God** curses haste.

267. **God** did not tell everything to His Mother.

268. **God** does not pay debts with money.

269. The help of **God** is nearer than the door. (*Armagh, Donegal, and Farney.*)

270. **God** likes help when helping people.

271. **God** opens the mouth of the grave to take the wretched in [to rest].

272. Far-off—**God** sends.

273. It is far away what **God** sends. (*Farney—Co. Monaghan.*)

274. **God** shares the virtues about.

275. **God** never sends a mouth but He sends meat for it.

276. **God** never closed one gap that He did not open another. (*Ulster.*)

277. Make a good beginning and **God** will help you. (*Munster.*)

278. If they are **good** at all, they are good together. (*Kerry.*)

279. **Good** is never late.

280. The **good**-that-was go out; the good-that-is come in.

281. In slender currents comes **good luck,** but in rolling torrents comes misfortune.

282. Many a time a **good man** fell on a cow-dung.

283. Many a time a **good man** had only a torn breeches.

284. Bad **goods** never yet went to the market that some blind market-man did not buy.

285. A **good word** never broke a tooth.

286. A wild **goose** never laid a tame egg.

287. If you have a **goose,** you'll get a goose.
[i.e. money goes to money.]

288. Who **gossips** to you will gossip of you.

289. Don't say **grace** for your meat till you've got it.

290. A **grain** often came whole from the grinding.

291. Without taste, without **gratitude.**

292. No man ever wanders far from his **grave-sod.**

293. You are blindfolding the **graveyard** for a long time.

294. **Greatness** knows gentleness.

295. A **greyhound** finds its food in its feet.

296. **Grief** has no cure but to kill it with patience. (*Kerry.*)

297. Better a **grip** than a blow. (*Kerry.*)

298. A man of reading understands **half a word.**

299. The blow of one **hammer** is light.

300. Prosperity on your **hand,** and may God always leave the stretch in it.
[i.e. may you always have something to give.]

301. When the **hand** ceases to scatter, the mouth ceases to praise.

302. Where the **hand** goes the foot must follow.

303. The **hand** of readiness. (*Farney.*)

304. The back of my **hand** to you.
[Used by one person when reproaching another.]

305. If you stretch out with your **hand,** you will seek out with your foot.

306. **Happiness** follows simplicity.

307. God give you better meat than a running **hare.** (*Tyrone.*)

308. The **hares** sleep.

309. **Harvest** is green.
[i.e. don't praise prematurely.]

310. There never was a **harvest** without a spring to follow that would eat it.

311. The race of the hound through the bog is the **harvest night** falling. (*Farney.*)

312. When your **haste** is greatest your delay is greatest. (*South Galway.*)

313. The age of an old **hat** is in the cock of it.

314. The life of an old **hat** is to cock it. (*S.E. Counties.*)

315. One must pay **health** its tithes.

316. He does not **hear** what he does not like.

317. Live in my **heart** and pay no rent.

318. He who fills the **heart** fills the eye. (*Armagh.*)

319. A **heart** is better than jaws.

320. What is nearest to the **heart** is nearest to the mouth. (*Armagh and Farney.*)

321. A sore **heart** makes a feeling one.

322. Happy must be the **hearth** where her light will shine.

323. The three kinds of people who will quickest get to **heaven** after their death—a young child after baptism, a young priest after ordination, and the poor tiller of the soil.

324. Do not turn your back on anything but on going to **hell.** (*Cork.*)

325. No one ever went to **hell** without sixpence at the time of his death.
[A relic of pagan burial custom.]

326. The biggest **help** is help, and even the smallest help is help.

327. There is no luck in the hen-house when the **hen** crows.

328. Never sell a **hen** on a wet day.

329. The **hen** with the chicks never yet burst her craw. (*Ulster, Farney, and Armagh.*)

330. The law of **heredity** runs through the cat's eyes. (*Munster.*)

331. **Heredity** will come through the hoofs, and the greyhound will pursue the hare.

332. The people go, but the **hills** remain.

333. Don't desert the **highway** for the short cut.

334. The **hob** is a good anchor. (*Kerry.*)

335. There's a **hole** in the house. (*Meath.*)

[i.e. there's a tell-tale listening.]

336. **Holy water** is not found in the foreign churches.

[i.e. Protestant churches.]

337. When the **honey** ceases falling the flower hardens.

338. Though **honey** is sweet, do not lick it off a briar.

339. **Hope** is the physician of each misery.

340. **Hope** protects the oppressed. (*Cork.*)

341. Sell the cow, buy the sheep, but never be without the **horse.**

342. Buy at three and sell at seven and you will always have a good **horse.**

343. It is easy to comb a little **horse.** (*Ulster.*)

344. 'Tis "rest yourself" lost the **horse.**

345. A borrowed **horse** has hard hooves.

346. A white **horse** is always white. (*Farney.*)

347. An eating **horse** never founders.

348. The man who is bad for entertainment or **hospitality** is good for directing you on the road. (*Ulster.*)

349. Every **hound** is a pup until he hunts.

350. A **hound** is worth whistling for.

[i.e. one should not be afraid to ask a favour.]

351. Thank God that the right side of the **house** is out.

[Said on a very wet day.]

352. Alas for the **house** where there are no men.

353. Seldom are **hunger** and thirst together.

354. **Hunger** after grace.

355. The best **hurler** is always on the ditch [fence].

356. Keep your **hurry** in your fist.

357. Hold your **hurry** in your hand. (*Ulster.*)

358. An eye, a knee, and an elbow, the three easiest things to **hurt.**

359. A misty winter, a frosty spring, a varied summer, and a sunny harvest [an **ideal year**]. (*Farney and Ulster.*)

360. **Idleness** muses many things. (*Cork.*)

361. Long are the dregs of an **ill deed.** (*Cork.*)

362. **Influence** is better than riches.

363. The bare right is almost **injustice.**

364. **Instinct** comes through the claws. (*Farney—Co. Monaghan.*)

365. What does not **interfere** with you, don't interfere with it. (*Farney.*)

366. Every **invalid** is a physician.

367. An **Irishman** half intoxicated, an Englishman with his belly full, and a Scotsman hungry.

[i.e. their best form.]

368. A **joint pot** does not boil. (*Armagh.*)

369. Prayer and provender hinder no man's **journey.**

370. Two **journeys** to you.

[i.e. to Purgatory and Heaven.] (Roman Catholics believe that few, if any, die pure enough to enter Heaven without a cleansing term in Purgatory). (A good prayer—those condemned to Hell have only one journey.)

371. One "**Keerog**" knows another "Keerog".

["Keerog" = beetle.]

372. **Kernels** taste bitter in the evening.

373. He has a **kick** in his gallop.

[Said of a man who is crooked in his dealings.]

374. Don't **kick** till ye're spurred.

375. Everybody [is] as it is "**kind**" for him. (*Munster.*)

376. A **kind word** never broke anyone's mouth.

377. He who can follow his own will is a **king.**

378. The first year—the **kissing** year; the second year—the fisting year. (*Marriage proverb.*)

379. Out of the **kitchen** comes the tune.

[Much of the success of matrimony depends on good cooking.]

380. You tied a **knot** with your tongue that your teeth cannot loose.

[Used chiefly in reference to betrothals.]

381. A person [often] ties a **knot** with his tongue that cannot be loosed by his teeth. (*Ulster.*)

382. What you don't **know** will do you no harm. (*Ulster.*)

383. Questioning is the door of **knowledge.**

384. One must yield to one's **lameness.** (*Kerry.*)

385. Everyone is foolish until he buys **land.**

386. Everyone is a **landholder** until it comes to debts.

387. Seldom is the **last** of anything better than the first.

388. Few things more **lasting** than a human being.

389. **Laugh,** when your sting is inserted. (*Cork.*)

390. May your **laughter** be from God.

391. A good denial—the best point in **law.** (*Farney.*)

392. A sign of an old **law** is an old song.

393. Neither break a **law** nor make one.

394. **Laziness** is a load.

395. The rotten **leather** is the first that cracks [or breaks].

396. **Leave** is light.

397. The law of **lending** [is] to break the borrowed article. (*Cork.*)

398. They can **lick** thumbs to the elbow. (*Ulster.*)

[Said of persons who are "tarred with the same brush".]

399. A **lie** goes but on one leg.

400. A **lie** looks the better of having a witness. (*Ulster.*)

401. Don't give the **lie** till you are ready with the blow. (*West Connaught.*)

402. **Lies** only last for a while.

403. He who has spent a [long] **life** has many a story.

404. **Life** is a queer man.

405. **Life** is but a vapour.

406. I have but **little,** and that is wholesome for myself. (*Cork.*)

407. We **live** as long as we're let.

408. A continual **load** is better than a too heavy load.

409. No **load** to a man is his garment, nor to the steed his bridle, to the sheep its fleece, to the body its reason. (*Kerry.*)

410. Cut your own **loaf** and you'll never be hungry.

411. A long-continued **loan** usually confers ownership.

412. Better a **lock** [i.e. security] than doubt.

413. He who is bad at giving **lodgings** is good at showing the road.

414. Even contention is better than **loneliness.**

415. **Loneliness** is better than bad company.

416. The three **longest lives**—the life of a yew, the life of an eagle, the life of the Hag of Beara.

417. Your **Lord's rent** or your child's life.

418. There's no physician or physic for **love.**

419. 'Tis hard to escape the bonds of **love.**

420. **Love** all men barring an attorney.

421. A woman's first **love,** a woman's second.

422. The **love** disease and thirst know no shame, but the itch beats them hollow.

423. When the view leaves the eye, **love** leaves the heart.

424. Throw your rubbish where your **love** lies. (*Ulster.*)

425. **Love** lives a short while, but hate lives for long.

426. **Love** pursues profit.

427. There was never great **love** that was not followed by great hate.

428. Give your **love** to your wife and your secret to your mother.

429. When the hand weakens, **love** weakens. (*Cork.*)

430. A man **loves** his sweetheart the most, his wife the best, but his mother the longest.

431. Often has **luck** attended a slow traveller.

432. Good **luck** beats early rising. (*South Galway.*)

433. He who gets the little **luck** gets the big luck.

434. There is **luck** in complaining. (*Kerry.*)

435. There is **luck** in sharing a thing.

436. There's no **luck** when the stranger that comes in doesn't put a hand to the churn.

437. Late was often **lucky.**

438. It is not the one way everyone goes **mad.**

439. **Majesty** knows modesty. (*Cork.*)

440. Every **man's mind** is his kingdom. (*West Connaught.*)

441. **A man's will** is his life, if he avoids evil. (*Cork.*)

442. The **mare** that kicks is the one that squeals.

443. No feast is without a roast piece; no real torment is experienced until **marriage.** (*Kerry.*)

444. **Marriage** at the dung-heap, and sponsorship far away. (*Clare.*)

[i.e. it is best to marry a neighbour and to have one's godparents far away.]

445. **Marriage** comes unawares like a soot drop.

446. Not **married** till bedded.

447. **Marry** a glen woman and you marry the whole glen.

448. **Marry** a mountainy woman and you'll marry the whole mountain. (*Armagh.*)

449. **Marry** an island woman and you marry the whole island.

450. If you **marry** at all, marry last year.

[i.e. get it over quickly.]

451. When you **marry** a woman, don't do it with a pig's ring.

[i.e. don't be mean in your marriage arrangements.]

452. It is unlucky to **marry** for love.

453. If you wish to be reviled, **marry**; if you wish to be praised, die. (*Armagh.*)

454. The day you **marry** your wife you marry your children. (*Farney.*)

455. The **master's eye** is the best curry comb.

456. The **master's eye** puts meat on the horse's ribs.

457. The sweetest part of every **meal** is its first part.

458. 'Tis easy to knead near the **meal sack.**

459. The flavouring of all **meat** is salt.

460. Long is the **memory** of an old child.

461. Little said is easy **mended,** nothing said needs no mending.

462. The son of a widow who has cattle, the foal of an old mare at grass, and the dog of a miller who has meal, are the three **merriest creatures** living.

463. The three **merriest things** in the world—a cat's kitten, a goat's kid, and a young widow. (*Farney.*)

464. If the **messenger** be cold, the answer is cold.

465. The raven-**messenger** from the Ark. (*Kerry.*)

[Said of a slow messenger—a raven-messenger is one who never returns.]

466. You'd be a good **messenger** to send for death.

[Said to one who loiters.]

467. The slow **messenger** will be better if you go meet him. (*Kerry.*)

468. Who loves the **midden** sees no motes in it.

469. The **milk** froth is more lasting than the soup.

470. The **mill** that is always going grinds coarse and fine.

471. Smaller than a fleshworm is the mother of **mischief.** (*West Connaught.*)

472. The mother of **mischief** is no bigger than a midge's wing.

473. The **miser's wedding** — a potato and a herring. (*West Connaught.*)

474. There is nought in this world but **mist.** (*Munster.*)

475. **Money** swore an oath that nobody that did not love it should ever have it.

476. The **money-maker** is never tired.

477. An old **moon's** mist never died of thirst. (*Ulster.*)

478. Peaceful is a shut **mouth.**

479. Sweet is the silent **mouth.**

480. Melodious is the closed **mouth.**

481. A shut **mouth** catches no flies.

482. A close **mouth** is as good as a priest's blessing any day.

483. A silent **mouth** is musical.

484. A shut **mouth** makes no enemies.

485. Musical is the **mouth** that is wont to be closed. (*Cork.*)

486. Never take the full of your **mouth** out of anybody. (*Farney.*)

[i.e. never do your enemy as much harm as you might.]

487. Anything will fit a **naked man.** (*West Connaught.*)

488. **Natural** qualities live long.

489. **Nature** is stronger than rearing [training]. (*Clare.*)

490. There is no law for **necessity.** (*Armagh.*)

491. Our **neighbour's** care hangs by a hair.

492. You never had **neighbours** as good as boundary fences. (*Armagh.*)

[i.e. because they (fences) prevent so many quarrels and lawsuits.]

493. A little **nest** is warmer than a big nest.

494. " This " is better than the thing we **never had.** (*Donegal.*)

495. It is almost as good as bringing **news** not to bring bad news. (*South Galway.*)

496. The **night** and the day are as long as ever they were. (*Farney.*)

497. One's **nonsense** makes great company for one. (*South Galway.*)

498. An inch is a great deal off a **nose.** (*Ulster.*)

499. Often a person's mouth has broken his **nose.**

500. Your own **nose** will yet advise you.

[i.e. if you go wrong ways your nose will get broken.]

501. There is **no talk** about what is neither seen nor heard. (*Ulster.*)

502. Every **nursling** as it is nursed; every web as it is woven.

503. When the **nut** is ripe it must fall.

504. " **Often** " does not receive honour.

505. [He who comes] **often** is not honoured. (*South Galway.*)

506. Live, **old horse,** and you'll get grass. (*Ulster.*)

507. Buy an **old thing** and you will be without anything. (*Cork.*)

508. The three best **old things**—an old lamb, an old piglet, and old seaweed.

509. The **ordinary** are often amiable, and the beautiful unfortunate. (*Cork.*)

510. **Ourselves** for ourselves. (*Sinn Fein.*)

511. How small a thing **outlives** a man.

512. On an unknown **path** every foot is slow. (*Ulster.*)

513. **Patience** will get its relief.

514. Towards the warlike man **peace** is observed.

515. **Peace** is worth purchasing. (*Kerry.*)

516. The **peace-maker** never lost.

517. Fly pride says the **peacock.**

518. The three worst **pets**—a petted parson, a petted beggar, a petted pig.

519. All men are **physicians** after being cured.

520. What can you expect from a **pig** but a grunt? (*Ulster.*)

521. If you catch a **pig,** catch it by the leg.

522. The fat **pig** gets the most grease.

523. Smoke your **pipe** and be silent, there's only wind and smoke in the world.

524. He who has **plenty** gets more.

525. Late **ploughing** is better than no ploughing.

526. A **ploughman** is taller on his feet than a lord on his knees.

527. There is no good in putting a hand into an empty **pocket.** (*West Connaught.*)

528. Many a big defect is seen in the **poor man.** (*Ulster.*)

529. A **poor man** is fain o' little.

530. A **poor man** must chew hard morsels. (*Connemara.*)

531. **A poor man** never had children enough.

532. Never scald your lips with another man's **porridge.**

533. The end is the thickest of the **porridge.**

534. **Possession** satisfies.

535. A man of **possessions** is never tired.

536. Little **possessions,** little care.

537. What's **postponed** too long becomes cold.

538. Help is good, but not round about the **pot.**

539. You must take the little **potato** with the big potato.

540. The **potatoes** would be dug, washed, cooked and eaten by the Ulsterman while the Munsterman would be saying "potato".

[i.e. Ulster people speak fast, Munster people slowly.]

541. Between **poverty** and riches there is but one year. (*Armagh.*)

542. Don't **praise,** don't disparage yourself. (*Armagh.*)

543. **Praise** not lest you should find fault. (*West Cork.*)

544. **Prettiness** makes no pottage.

545. The **pride** of women and the pride of priests, the two things that will ruin Ireland.

546. There is pain in **prohibition.** (*Cork.*)

547. **Promise** much, and there will be many in search of you. (*West Connaught.*)

548. One puff of the wind of **prosperity** is better than if you sweated yourself off the bones all your life.

549. Nothing can beat a **proverb.**

550. [The wisdom of] the **proverb** cannot be surpassed.

551. Though the old **proverb** may be given up, it is none the less true. (*Ulster.*)

552. **Proverbs** cannot be contradicted.

553. A little often fills the **purse.**

554. A **quarrel** is like buttermilk, once it's out of the churn, the more you shake it, the more sour it grows.

555. Better be **quarrelling** than lonesome. (*Armagh.*)

556. The solution of every **question** is [to be found] in itself. (*Ulster.*)

557. **Quietness** is worth buying.

558. A **rag** upon every bush.

[Said of a young man who pays attention to more than one young lady at a time.]

559. **Rain** abates wind.

560. The comfort of a ship of the sea is the evening **rainbow.** (*Armagh.*)

561. It will not be always **raining.** (*South Galway.*)

[Refers to misfortune.]

562. Long **raining,** long fair.
563. It is no use throwing water on a drowned **rat.**
564. No cure for **regret** but to kill it with patience.
565. A half is better than a complete **refusal.**
566. 'Tis only at home you have **relations.**
567. Better a little **relationship** than much acquaintance.
568. The heart knows a **relative.** (*Farney.*)
569. Prowess at arms is better than a **reputation.**
570. A hasty **retreat** is better than a bad stand. (*Kerry.*)
    [Like James II at the Battle of the Boyne, 1690.]
571. **Reverence** ceases once blood is spilt.
572. When a thing is put anyway **right** at all, it takes a vast deal of mismanagement to make it go wrong.
573. Might overcomes **right,** and right dies in peace with poverty. (*Cork.*)
574. He that is not in the habit of **riding** forgets the spurs.
575. Be the **road** crooked or straight, the highway is the short cut. (*Ulster.*)
576. The longest **road** that brings you out is the shortest road that brings you home. (*Armagh.*)
577. A pair shortens the **road.** (*Armagh.*)
578. Every **rod** on the branch does not grow alike, and all the nuts in a cluster are not full.
579. When the **rod** grows it is not easily bent.
580. The **rod** that will hang him is growing.
581. The **rook's** portion is what she gathers.
582. He has got the two ends of the **rope** and leave to pull. (*Ulster.*)
583. The **rubbish** [or chips] are only where the tree is felled. (*Kerry.*)
584. **Rule** according to instruction. (*Cork.*)
585. **Rule** [is] according to learning.
586. Better a good **run** than a long standing.
587. 'Tis the man who **runs** that falls.
588. An empty **sack** can't stand, nor a dead cat walk.
589. A **sage** slips.
590. Help me to **salt,** help me to sorrow.
591. **Salt** is sweeter than sugar.
592. The old **saying** cannot be excelled.
593. A **scabby head** is easily bled.
594. The **sea** does not wait for a man with a cargo. (*West Clare.*)
595. The loan of the oyster-catcher to the **seagull.** The loan that was never returned.
    [The seagull was originally without web-feet, and she asked the oyster-catcher for the loan of her webs for one day, but having got them she never returned them.]
596. Don't make an enemy of your **secret.**
597. A **secret** is a weapon and a friend.
598. Don't tell your **secret** to a ditch till you have a look over the top. (*West Connaught.*)
599. Tell not your **secret** to a fence.
600. What is **seldom** is tasty.
601. A **sensitive man** is not often wealthy.
602. He is a bad **servant,** but the want of him is worse.
603. A bad **servant** to himself is often a good servant to another. (*Kerry.*)
604. A **service** not asked for, neither God nor man is thankful for.
605. The saying of a fool, a thorn in mud, and a soft woollen thread that cuts to the bone, are the three **sharpest things** in the world. (*Ulster.*)
606. A black **sheep** is first sometime. (*Munster.*)
607. Every man is a **sheriff** on his own hearth.

608. Don't be after breaking your **shin** on a stool that's not in your way. (*Ulster.*)

609. There is not much comfort in turning a dirty **shirt.** (*West Connaught.*)

610. A buckle adds much to an old **shoe.**

611. She has got the length of his **shoe.**
[i.e. knows how to manage him.]

612. He whom the **shoe** is pinching has the most right to rip it. (*Kerry.*)

613. There is no overtaking the **shot** once fired.

614. Bare is the **shoulder** that has not a brother.

615. Cold **shoulders** speckles the shins.

616. A man is **shy** in another man's corner.

617. A man's last **sickness** is attended by sleep; a woman's with the contrary.

618. Let him cool in the **skin** he heated in. (*Ulster.*)

619. Don't show your **skin** to the person who won't cover it. (*Farney.*)

620. The bottom has fallen out of the **sky.**
[i.e. great rain.]

621. One **sleeps** tranquilly on the hurt of another. (*Ulster.*)

622. A man **sleeps** very soundly on another man's wound.

623. There never was an old **slipper** but there was an old stocking to match it. (*Carlow.*)

624. A **sloe** year, a woe year. (*Wexford.*)

625. The three **small things** that are best—a small bee-hive, a small sheep, a small woman.

626. It is not usual [or natural] to have **smoke** without fire, nor fire without people. (*Ulster.*)

627. Don't be bare with the **soil** or the soil will be bare with you.

628. Good **soles,** bad uppers.

629. **Soles** make bad uppers.

630. One good pair of **soles** is better than two pairs of uppers.

631. Your **son** is your son to-day, but your daughter is your daughter for ever.

632. Take care to lay by for the **sore-foot.**
[i.e. prepare for adversity.]

633. There's no cure for **sorrow** but to put it underfoot.

634. A cure for all **sorrows** is conversation.

635. **Souls** will not enter heaven in each other's shade.

636. The face of everything to the **south.** (*Macadam, Ulster.*)
[A ploughman in Ireland uniformly turns his horses' heads to the south when yoking or unyoking them. The glass is always sent round the table from left to right, or with the course of the sun. This custom is derived from pagan times.]

637. Better to **spare** in time than out of time.

638. The more the **speed,** the less the collection. (*Cork.*)

639. Every **spider** winds his own ball of thread.

640. That's a **spoon** in another man's mouth.
[Said when someone in an office dies or resigns.]

641. It was put on the **spoon** for him. (*Ulster.*)

642. If you don't make **sport** when young, you'll not do it when old.

643. Two days in the **spring** are as good as ten days in harvest.

644. A speckle-shinned **spring** makes an envious harvest-time.

645. A black nose to every **spring** morning and a filly's tail coming behind.

646. The warm side of the **stone** always turns up on Saint Patrick's Day.
[March 17th. An omen of good weather.]

647. On **St. Patrick's Day** in the spring there is a nest in every wood, a trout in every pool, and a heifer calf in every cow-paddock in Ireland. (*Ulster.*)

648. The **stars** make no noise.

649. Mind the **step**; the bottom one's the lowest. (*Ulster.*)

650. A dropped **stitch** is soon a hole.

651. What is not **stolen** is found. (*Clare.*)

652. Boil a **stone** in butter and its juice will be drunk.

653. A **storm** does not go beyond Sunday, nor a spring-tide beyond Wednesday. (*Kerry.*)

654. An old **story** and rust on it.

655. However long you remain away from home, don't bring home a bad **story** about yourself. (*Ulster.*)

656. [Always put] the **stranger** near the danger.

657. Better knot **straws** than do nothing.

658. Better **strife** than solitude. (*Kerry.*)

659. Come a day, go a day, God send **Sunday.** (*Ulster.*)

660. It is better to be **sure** than sorry. (*Ulster.*)

661. The day you go **surety,** put your hand in your pocket.

662. It is the **sweat** of his own brow that burns or scorches everyone.

663. The three **sweetest sounds**—the sound of the quern, the lowing of the cow, the cry of a child.

664. Who brings a **tale** takes two away.

665. **Talk** brings on talk. (*South Galway.*)

666. People pay no tolls [custom] for **talking.**

667. It is the little that **tastes.**

668. After **tasting** you will want it.

669. Avoid the **tavern,** or limpets are your food. (*Kerry.*)

670. Whoever is king, **tea** is queen.

671. **Tears** bring nobody back from the grave. (*Ulster.*)

672. Never show your **teeth** unless you can bite. (*Farney and Ulster.*)

673. The first **thread** is not part of the yarn. (*West Clare.*)

674. The **three steps** of decency. (*Armagh.*)

[i.e. when seeing a friend away from your house you should accompany him at least three steps from your own door.]

675. The **three steps** of mercy. (*Armagh.*)

[i.e. everyone was expected, on meeting a funeral, to turn back and walk at least three steps with the funeral: these were known as the three steps of mercy.]

676. **Three things** a man should not be without—a cat, a chimney, and a woman-of-the-house.

677. **Three things** that cannot be taught—a singing voice, generosity, and poetry.

678. **Three things** that pertain to age—greed, hair, and finger-nails.

679. The **threshold** is the dog's patrimony. (*Armagh.*)

680. The blackest **thorn** bears the whitest blossom.

681. Every **thorn** is sharp.

682. There's another **tide** in the sea.

683. However great the **tide,** it ebbs.

684. There is no **tide** that does not ebb, but the tide of grace. (*Cork.*)

685. **Time** is a good story-teller. (*Cork.*)

686. The man that's up is **toasted**; the man that's down is trampled on.

687. One's **tongue** has often broken his nose. (*Munster.*)

688. A slip of the **tongue** is no fault of the mind. (*Munster.*)

689. The **tongue** often tied a knot that the tongue could not loosen.

690. Tie up your **tongue** or she will tie you up.

691. Do not keep your **tongue** under your belt. (*Ulster.*)

692. He did not put a **tooth** in it.

[i.e. he told the story without softening or euphemizing it.]

693. A bad **trade** is better than idleness.

694. A **trade** not learned is an enemy. (*Galway.*)

695. Without **treasure** repute is cold. (*Cork.*)

696. Do not go between the **tree** and its bark.

[i.e. man and wife.]

697. It is not the **tree** that is a long time shaking that is the first to fall. (*Farney.*)

698. Buy the **trickster,** and you need have no fear of the honest man.

699. The man is *that* " classical " [**tricky**] and *that* plausible, that he would put feet under flies (*Meath*)—or wooden legs under the hens (*Galway*).

700. List to the flow of the river and you'll get a **trout.** (*Satirical saying. Farney—Co. Monaghan.*)

701. **Truth** is bitter, but never shamed.

702. **Twenty years** a child, twenty years going mad [in the wildness of youth], twenty years a [sane] person, and after that offering up your prayers. (*Armagh.*)

703. **Two-thirds** of sickness belong to the night, two-thirds of folly belong to youth, two-thirds of covetousness belong to the old people, two-thirds of talk belong to the drinking folk.

704. Every unfortunate person is **ugly.**

705. Often was **ugly** amiable and handsome unfortunate.

706. It is the children of the fortunate who make the **unfortunate** people. (*Farney, Armagh, and Donegal.*)

707. Nothing [lit. not even Ireland] is better [worth more] than its **value.** (*West Clare.*)

708. A **vessel** holds only its fill. (*Ulster.*)

709. Eight **views,** eight recollections.

710. The man who **walked** the world said the big road was the short cut. (*Farney.*)

711. Speak easy, **walls** have ears. (*West Connaught.*)

712. **Want** is a good guide.

713. The greatest **war** had peace at last.

714. It's a lonesome **washing** that there's not a man's shirt in. (*Farney.*)

715. All **wealth** is consumed by small spending. (*West Cork.*)

716. A **wedge** of the elm splits itself.

717. Two stormy days—two holidays and two rainy days—or two holidays fine—two days wind and rain and two days for work—an ideal lazy one's **week.**

718. Be compliant that you may be **well loved.**

719. The warmest thing without is the full of a thimble of the **west wind.** (*Farney.*)

720. Inches doesn't break squares in a load of **whins.** (*Ulster.*)

721. What butter or **whiskey** will not cure, there is no cure for. (*Donegal.*)

722. The pillow-**whispering** is never good.

723. A man cannot grow rich without his **wife's** leave.

724. The **wind** is wide. (*Farney.*)

725. The **wind** that withers; the sun that dries; the action that proves [a man]. (*Farney.*)

726. Let every man break a **window** for himself.

727. **Wisdom** is [often] hard.

728. Nobody is **wise** till something goes against him.

729. If you are too **wise,** [too much] will be expected of you.

730. Bought **wit** is the best.

731. Cold walls make dissatisfied **wives.**

732. If you want to advertise a thing tell it as a secret to a **woman.** (*West Connaught.*)

733. Till the duck parts with the practice of swimming on the pool,
Till the swan parts with her white plumage,
Till the dog parts with his faith in the bone,
Guile will not part with the mind of a **woman.**

734. There are three without rule: a mule, a pig, and a **woman.** (*Donegal.*)

735. A whistling **woman** and a crowing hen are two things that are unlucky about a house.

736. Where you find a cow you find a **woman**; and where you find a woman you find bother.

737. Wherever you go have a **woman** friend. (*Derry.*)

738. A **woman** has an excuse readier than an apron.

739. The fair-haired **woman**—in and out with you like the tide.
The black-haired woman—will change as the strand when the tide is gone.
The brown-haired woman—is like a ship on clear water.

740. While a **woman** lives she will have an eye for colour.

741. A **woman** never looked over her shoulder but she found an excuse.

742. A **woman** overcomes the devil. (*Armagh.*)

743. A pig is more impudent than a goat, but a **woman** surpasses all. (*Galway.*)

744. Ask a **woman** once or twice, and if she does not accept your view, take you hers.

745. A **woman** without a baby has no excuse [for sitting down].

746. Everything dear is a **woman's** fancy.

747. The wind is not swifter than a **woman's** mind [choice] between two men.

748. The **women** are the better after scolding [or cursing].

749. Where there's **women** there's talk, and where there's geese there's cackling.

750. Three kinds of men fail to understand **women**—young men, old men, and middle-aged men.

751. There was never yet a **wood** but contained its own burning.

752. Be first in a **wood,** but last in a bog; be behind the smith, but before the miller.

753. The greenest **wood** is fated to lose its bloom.

754. The **wood** will renew the foliage it sheds.
[i.e. after rain, sunshine.]

755. Every **word** has three explanations and three interpretations.

756. Say a **word** or two, and if you are not listened to come away.

757. **Words** do not support. (*South Galway.*)

758. It is the food that does **work.**

759. He who will not **work** for himself will work for others.

760. Change of **work** is equivalent to rest.

761. The **work** praises the man. (*Farney—Co. Monaghan.*)

762. Take the **world** as it comes to you.

763. Why **worry?**—it is coming off a broad board. (*Ulster.*)
[i.e. someone else pays.]

764. The size is more than the **worth.**

765. There is a slender head on **youth.**

766. A pious **youth,** an old-age devil.

767. Praise **youth** and it will prosper.

768. **Youth** cannot believe. (*Farney.*)

769. Many a skin does **youth** cast off. (*Cork.*)

770. **Youth** has a small head. (*Cork.*)

771. **Youth** often sheds its skin.

MANX

1. The crooked **bannock** straightens the body.
2. Eaten **bread** is forgotten.
3. A miserable **bush** is better than the open field.
4. If **custom** is not indulged with custom, custom will weep.
5. He who lies down with **dogs** will rise up with fleas.
6. A slow **fire** makes sweet malt.
7. Life to men and death to **fish.** (*Manx toast.*)
8. Thou wouldst fain be numbered with the flock, but thy bleat is the bleat of the **goat.**
9. **A green hill** when far from me; bare, bare when it is near.
10. The little **hemlock** is sister to the great hemlock.
11. No **herring,** no wedding.
12. Live, **horse,** and you'll get grass.
13. Hit him again, for he is **Irish.**
14. **Learning** is fine clothes for the rich man, and riches for the poor man.
15. Thou canst not sell thy **loss.**
16. There's much **lost** between the hand and mouth.
17. **Poor** once, poor for ever.
18. When one **poor man** helps another poor man, God Himself laughs.
19. Black as is the **raven,** he'll get a partner.
20. Give a piece to the **raven** and he'll come again.
21. Thy **recompense** is in thine own hand.
22. Soon **ripe**, soon rotten.
23. Near is my **shirt,** but nearer is my skin.
24. Cold **soup** warms quickly.
    [Reference to lovers' quarrel.]
25. When the **sport** is merriest it is best to leave off.
26. After **spring-tide,** neap.
27. You must summer and winter a **stranger** before you can form an opinion of him.
28. What comes with the **wind** goes with the water.
29. Change of **work** is rest.

SCOTTISH

(Including Gaelic, Orkney and Shetland)

1. Hand in use is father of **afflu-ence.**
2. **All's** no part.
3. He that seeks **alms** for God's sake begs for two.
4. **Amends** is worth misdeeds.
5. Take wit with your **anger.**
6. All things **anger** you, and the cat breaks your heart.
    [i.e. you are annoyed by trifles.]
7. Never put your **arm** out farther than you can draw it easily back again.
8. Devil speed them that **ask** and know full well.
9. Folk should never **ask** for more than they can make good use of.
10. **At once** is two hours and a half.
11. Once **away,** always away.
    [Said of people who frequently leave their homes.]
12. Never trust your **back** to a slap.
13. The **bait** must be gathered when the tide's out.
14. A broken **bannock** is as good as eaten.
15. Dry **bargains** bode ill.
16. Better the **barn** filled than the bed.
    [i.e. rather have the corn than the chaff with which mattresses are stuffed.]

17. When the **barn's** full you may thresh before the door.
18. Ilka [i.e. every] **bean** has its black, and ilka path its puddle.
19. The crumbs in thy neighbour's **beard** are his own. (*Gaelic.*)
20. He that tholes [i.e. **bears**] overcomes.
21. Get the word of early rising and you may lie in **bed** all day.
22. The three Fernian **bed stuffs**: fresh tree-tops, moss, and fresh rushes. (*Gaelic.*)
23. There belongs more to a **bed** than four bare legs. (*Marriage proverb.*)
24. **Bees** that have honey in their mouths have stings in their tails.
25. The devil is always good to **beginners.**
26. You will **beguile** none but them that trust in you.
27. Far **behind** must follow the faster.
28. Far **behind** that may not follow, and far before that cannot look back.
29. A hungry **belly** has no ears.
30. Every man buckles his **belt** his own way.
31. **Bide** well, betide well.
32. He's awful **big** behind the door.
33. The **bird** must flutter that flies with one wing.
34. All **bite** the bitten dog.
35. Never **bite** unless you make your teeth meet.
36. **Black** will take no other hue.

    [i.e. evil has no colour.]
37. The **blade** wears out the scabbard.
38. There are many things too bad for **blessing** and too good for cursing.
39. You know not where a **blessing** may light.
40. Men are **blind** in their own cause.
41. In the country of the **blind** the one-eyed is king.
42. There may be **blue** and better blue.

    [i.e. there may be difference between things of the same kind, and persons of the same station.]
43. If you don't see the **bottom,** don't wade.
44. A **bow** o'er-bent will weaken.
45. He must **bow** that has a low door.
46. **Bread** is the staff of life, but the pudding makes a good crutch.
47. Your **bread's** baked, you may hang up your girdle.

    [Said of a lucky man.]
48. A new pair of **breeks** [trousers] will cast down an old coat.

    [i.e. a new friend may tend to lower one's esteem for an old one.]
49. He sits full still that has a riven **breik** [trousers].
50. A bonnie **bride** is soon busked [dressed]; a short horse is soon whisked [curried].
51. All's lost that's put in a **broken dish.**

    [Said of favours to ungrateful people.]
52. It's not the **burden,** but the overburden that kills the beast.
53. When the **burn** does not babble it is either over-empty or overfull.
54. We must not wish the **burn** dry because it wets our feet.
55. Every man bows to the **bush** that he gets shelter from.
56. Scorn not the **bush** that shields you.
57. **Butter** to butter's no kitchen.

    [i.e. like to like is no relish. Used when women kiss each other.]
58. **Buy** in the market and sell at home.
59. All the winning's in the first **buying.**
60. He that **buys** land buys stones, he that buys beef buys bones; he that buys nuts buys shells; he that buys good ale buys nothing else.

61. Peace to his soul, and a stone to thy **cairn.** (*Gaelic.*)

    [A cairn of stones was always raised where the coffin rested by the way.]

62. Be the same thing that you would be **called.**
63. "**Can do**" is easily carried about.
64. "**Cannot**" has no craft.
65. "**Care not**" would have more.
66. Let them **care** that come ahint [i.e. behind].
67. An unhappy man's **cart** is easy to overturn.
68. It's not the rumbling **cart** that falls first over the brae.
69. They push at the **cart** that is always going.
70. Who dare bell the **cat**?
71. I am too old a **cat** to draw that straw in front of.

    [Old woman's reply to offer of marriage.]

72. **Chalk** is no shears.

    [Taken from tailors marking out their cloth before they cut it; signifying that a thing may be proposed that will never be executed.]

73. **Charity** begins at home, but should not end there.
74. He that **cheats** me once, shame fall him; he that cheats me twice, shame fall me.
75. King's **cheese** goes half-away in parings.

    [i.e. greater part of income absorbed in the expenses of collecting it.]

76. After **cheese** nothing.
77. You are no **chicken** for all your chirping.
78. A beltless **child** cannot lie.
79. Many a one kisses the **child** for love of the nurse.
80. The bairn [**child**] speaks in the fields what he heard by the fireside.
81. When **children** are young they make their parents' heads ache; when they are old they make their hearts ache.
82. Serve yourself till your **children** grow up.
83. Long may your lum [**chimney**] reek [smoke].
84. It is easier to build lums [**chimneys**] than keep them reeking [smoking].
85. It's long ere "likely to die" fills the **churchyard.**
86. Where they **clip** there needs no comb.
87. **Clout** [i.e. patch] upon a hole is good gentry; clout upon clout is good yeomanry; but clout upon clouted clout is downright beggary.
88. A **collie** has the brains of a man and the ways of a woman.
89. Kythe [i.e. appear] in your own **colours** that folk may know you.
90. One hour's **cold** will drive out seven years' heat.
91. A young **colt** will canter, be it uphill or down.
92. **Comb** seldom, comb sore.
93. The blow that falls to one who tries to part **combatants** is always the worst of the battle.
94. Such a man as thou would be, draw thee to such **company.**
95. Known folk's no **company.**
96. **Condition** makes, condition breaks.
97. **Confess** and be hanged.
98. **Content** is no child of wealth.
99. Let him **cool** in the skin he heated in.
100. **Corbies** [ravens] do not pick out corbies' eyes.
101. **Corbies** [ravens] do not gather unless they smell carrion.
102. Half-acres bear always good **corn.**

     [i.e. little property is well looked after.]

103. **Count** again is not forbidden.
104. Full of **courtesy,** full of craft.
105. "Home's homely," quoth the devil, when he found himself in the **Court-of-Session.**
106. It is idle to swallow the **cow** and choke on the tail.

107. Drive a **cow** to the hall, she'll run to the byre.
108. A fleyer [**coward**] would always have a follower.
109. **Craft** must have clothes, but truth goes naked.
110. **Credit** keeps the crown of the causeway.
111. Those that have most need of **credit** seldom get much.
112. Put your hand in the **creel,** take out an adder or an eel. (*Marriage proverb.*)
113. If you go a year with a **cripple** you'll limp at the end of it.
114. **Cripples** are always great doers —break your leg and try.
115. Things must always be someway, even if they're **crooked.**
116. We must take the **crop** as it grows.
117. He that has a good **crop** may endure some thistles.
118. If you had not been among the **crows**, you would not have been shot.
119. A full **cup** is ill to carry.
120. Give you a use, and you'll call it a **custom.**
121. Many a one loses the sixpenny **dagger** for the halfpenny thong.
122. A long-gathered **dam** soon runs out.
123. Choose a good mother's **daughter,** though her father were the devil.
124. **Daughters** and dead fish are no keeping ware.
125. Come **day,** go day, God send Sunday.
  [Spoken to lazy unconscionable servants who only mind to serve out their time and get their wages.]
126. The **day** has eyes, the night has ears.
127. It is a good **day** that puts off the night. (*Shetland.*)
128. A **day** to come seems longer than a year that's gone.
129. **Daylight** has many eyes.
130. **Daylight** will peep through a small hole.
131. There's a cure for everything but stark **dead.**
132. He goes long bare-foot that waits for **dead men's shoes.**
133. **Deal** small and serve all.
134. He should wear iron shoes that bides his neighbour's **death.**
135. **Death** at one door, and heirship at the other.
136. There is no going through the world without a wee bit of **deceit.**
137. **Deed** shows proof.
138. If the **devil** were dead, folk would do little for God's sake.
139. The **devil's** boots don't creak.
  [i.e. temptations are insidious.]
140. Raise no more **devils** than you can lay.
141. Every blade of grass gets its own drop of **dew.**
142. If we **did** as we should, we might have as we would.
143. Never draw your **dirk** [dagger] when a blow will do't.
144. He that eats but one dish seldom needs the **doctor.**
145. A drunken **doctor** is always clever.
146. A bark from a toothless **dog** is as good as a bite.
147. Howling is natural to **dogs.**
148. He that sleeps with **dogs** must rise with fleas.
149. The thing that's **done** is not to do.
150. He must stoop that has a low **door.**
151. When one **door** shuts, another opens.
152. It is a true **dream** that is seen waking.
153. As you brew, so must you **drink.**
154. A dry **drink** is better than a dry sermon.
155. A **drink** is shorter than a tale.
156. They that **drink** longest live longest.
157. They speak of my **drinking,** but never think of my thirst.

158. Double **drinks** are good for thirst.

159. A **dumb man** holds all.
[i.e. makes no disclosures.]

160. You spoiled a **dwarf** and did not make a man.

161. Everyone leaps the **dyke** where it's lowest.

162. **Eagles** catch not fleas.

163. They who are **early** up; and have no business, have either an ill wife, an ill bed, or an ill conscience.

164. Farther **east,** the shorter west.

165. A given piece is soon **eaten.**

166. **Eaten meat** is ill to pay.

167. **Eating,** drinking, and cleaning need but a beginning.

168. An **empty hand** is no lure for a hawk.

169. An **empty pocket** goes quickly through the market.

170. More than **enough** is over-much.

171. Of **enough** men leave.

172. Many a one would have been worse had their **estates** been better.

173. The **evening** brings all home.

174. All's but lip-wit that wants **experience.**

175. Trouble follows all **extremes.**

176. Happy for the son when the **father** goes to the devil.

177. You may lose the **father** looking for the son.

178. Trot **father,** trot mother, how can the foal amble?

179. A **father's blessing** bigs [builds] the town [house or village]; a mother's curse can ding [overthrow] it down.

180. Wink at small **faults,** for you have great ones yourself.

181. A man's **faults** will be as large as a mountain ere he himself sees them. (*Gaelic.*)

182. **Favours** unused are favours abused.

183. **Fear** has long legs.

184. Little odds between a **feast** and a full belly.

185. Fiddlers, dogs, and flesh-flies come always to **feasts** uncalled.

186. Always take the **fee** when the tear's in the eye.

187. **Feeling** has no fellow.

188. When you can suit your **feet** to my shoes you may speak.

189. Make your **feet** your friend.

190. Please your kimmer [**female gossip**] and you'll easy guide your gossip.

191. Two to **fight** and one to settle the dispute.
[Three children ideal number for family.]

192. One **fine thing** needs two to set it off.

193. Better a **finger** off as always wagging.

194. Let him that's cold blow the **fire.**

195. Longest at the **fire** soonest finds cold.

196. Who steals the **fire** steals the blessing.
[Gaelic proverb which has its origin in Druidical days. The " wee folk " (fairies) go off with the fire if it goes out.]

197. Better a wee **fire** to warm you than a big fire to burn you.

198. Do not light a wisp [a **fire**] you cannot yourself put out. (*Gaelic.*)

199. Fanned **fires** and forced love never did well.

200. We must give our **fish-guts** to our own sea-maws [sea-gulls].

201. One at a time is good **fishing.**

202. **Fish** must swim thrice.
[First in water, then in sauce, and lastly in wine.]

203. All's **fish** that comes to the net.

204. Don't gut your **fish** till you get them.

205. There never was a **five-pound note** but there was a ten-pound road for it!

206. It's hard to keep **flax** from the flame.

207. Nothing to be done in haste but catching **fleas.**

208. The **flesh** is always fairest that's farthest from the bone.

[This is the opposite of the English saying, "The nearer the bone, the sweeter the meat".]

209. It's a poor **flock** where the ewe bears the bell.

210. Evening orts are good morning's **fodder.**

["Orts"—rejected provender.]

211. Do not tell your **foe** when your foot sleeps.

212. There's nought as queer as **folk.**

213. A nod from a lord is a breakfast for a **fool.**

214. A **fool** is happier thinking well of himself than a wise man is in others thinking well of him.

215. None can play the **fool** so well as a wise man.

216. Dogs and children are fond of **fools.**

217. **Fools** and children should not see half-done work.

218. For fault of wise men **fools** sit on benches.

219. Even a young **foot** finds ease in an old slipper.

220. A going **foot** is always getting.

221. Ride the **ford** as you find it.

222. Flee as fast as you will, your **fortune** will be at your tail.

223. Woe to the father of the **foster-son** who is unfaithful to his trust. (*Gaelic.*)

224. Long **foul,** long fair.

225. As long as you serve the **fox** you must carry his tail.

226. Tods [**foxes**] keep their own holes clean.

227. **Friday** rules Sunday.

228. Before you choose a **friend,** eat a peck of salt with him.

229. It's no loss what a **friend** gets.

230. No man can be happy without a **friend,** nor be sure of him till he's unhappy.

231. Be slow in choosing a **friend,** slower in changing him.

232. Be a **friend** to yourself, and others will.

233. Giff gaff [give and take] makes good **friends.**

234. Love your **friends** and look to yourself.

235. **Friends** are lost by calling often and calling seldom.

236. Oft counting keeps **friends** long together.

237. Make **friends** of fremit [strange] folk.

[Generally used to dissuade from marriage with near kinswomen.]

238. Fresh fish and unwelcome **friends** stink before they are three days old.

239. Old **fruit** has little savour.

[i.e. many forget past favours and old friends.]

240. Ripe **fruit** is soonest rotten.

[i.e. prodigies and precocious children are generally not lasting.]

241. When all **fruits** fail, welcome haws.

242. The **full** and the empty go all one way.

243. It's ill speaking between a **full man** and a fasting.

244. If you be not **galled** you needn't fling.

245. God forgive you for **galloping** when trotting's not a sin.

246. A given **game** was never won.

247. Eat your fill, but pocket none, is **gardener's** law.

248. Liked **gear** is half bought.

249. Little **gear,** little care.

250. Send your **gentle blood** to the market and see what it will buy.

251. He that **gets** forgets, but he that wants thinks on.

252. They that come with a **gift** don't need to stand long at the door.

253. He doubles his **gift** that gives in time.

254. She that takes **gifts,** herself she sells, and she that gives them does nothing else.

255. **Give** a thing, take a thing, old man's [devil's] gold ring.

[Said in reproach to those who ask back a gift.]

256. **Give** is a good fellow, but he soon wearies.

257. What you **give** shines always; what you get smells ill next day.

258. Give your heart to **God,** and your alms to the poor.

259. I am going out on Thy path—**God** be behind me, God be before me, God be in my footsteps. (*Gaelic.*)

[Ancient frith to avert evil.]

260. Danger past, **God** forgotten.

261. Have **God,** have all.

262. The grace of **God** is gear enough.

263. **God** never measures men by inches.

264. There must be no patience when **God** says haste.

265. **God** shapes the back for the burden.

266. Do the likeliest and **God** will do the best.

267. Spend and **God** will send; spare and ever bare.

268. Get your rock [distaff used in spinning] ready, **God** will send the tow.

269. Out of **God's** blessing into the warm sun.

270. Decency is a debt; **godliness** a duty. (*Shetland.*)

271. If a body be **going down** the hill each one will give him a push.

272. Give a **going man** a drink, and a rising man a knock.

273. He's worth **gold** that can win it.

274. Thanks to **Goll,** he has killed his mother.

[A Gaelic proverb of immense antiquity, of cave life, which may still be heard repeated when a nuisance is got rid of by the action of the individual responsible for it. Goll was a one-eyed hero who killed his mother by mistake with a bone.]

275. There's a **good** and bad side to everything; all the art is to find it out.

276. They had never an ill day that had a **good evening.**

277. All **good** has an end save the goodness of God.

278. When the **goodman** drinks to the goodwife all would be well; when the goodwife drinks to the goodman all is well.

279. No tear should ever fall on the face of a **good man** dying. (*Gaelic.*)

280. A **good name** is sooner lost than won.

281. Many "**good nights**" is loath away.

282. A man has no more **goods** than he gets good of.

283. He's worth no **good** that can bide no sorrow.

284. Do a man a **good turn** and he'll never forgive you. (*Shetland.*)

285. The **grandsire** buys, the father builds, the son sells, and the grandson begs.

286. Nearer the rock, the sweeter the **grass.**

287. There grows no **grass** at the market cross.

288. **Gratitude** is a heavy burden.

289. **Grief** pays no debts.

290. **Grin** when ye bind, and laugh when ye lose.

291. Show me the **guest** the house is the worse of.

292. A **hairy man's** a geary [rich] man, a hairy wife's a witch.

[It would appear that when this proverb originated only rich men allowed their beards to grow.]

293. Nothing enters into a closed **hand.**

294. You know not what's behind your **hand.**

295. **Hand** in use is father of lear.

296. One **hand** is no hand.

297. A dirty **hand** makes a clean hearth-stone.

298. Put your **hand** no further out than your sleeve will reach.

299. It's a feeble **hand** that cannot do good when the heart is willing.

300. One **hand** will not wash the other for nothing.

301. A man was once **hanged** for leaving his drink.

302. A wee house well filled, a wee piece of land well tilled, a wee wife well willed, will make a **happy man.**

303. The **happy man** cannot be ruined.

304. God send you readier meat than running **hares.**
[Spoken to those who have unlikely expectations.]

305. **Hasty** was hanged, but speed of foot went away.

306. **Hatching** time's a happy time.

307. A man's **hat** in his hand never did him any harm.

308. **Have** is half full.

309. A scabbed **head** is easy to bleed.
[i.e. a questionable reputation is easily lost.]

310. He has need of a clean pow [**head**] that calls his neighbour "nitty-now" [lousy-head].

311. Much must a good **heart** bear.

312. When the **heart** is full the tongue will speak.

313. Nearest the **heart,** nearest the mouth.

314. A full **heart** never lied.

315. A sorrowful **heart's** always dry.

316. One's own **hearth** is gold's worth.

317. It's not what we have, but what we do with what we have, that counts in **heaven.**

318. There's nobody can prevent you getting into **heaven,** but there's many always ready to give you a shove into hell.

319. Take **help** at your elbows.
[i.e. God helps those who help themselves.]

320. All's not **help** that's at hand.

321. It is no the **hen** that cackles the loudest that lays the biggest egg.

322. A **hen** that lays away should have a white nest-egg.

323. **Hens** are free of horse corn.
[Said to those who are free of what is not their own.]

324. He that comes of **hens** must scrape.

325. It is not common for **hens** to have pillows. (*Gaelic.*)

326. It's but kindly that the bag savour of the **herring.**

327. Let every **herring** hang by its own tail.

328. Nothing comes fairer to light than what's been long **hidden.**

329. The **highway** is wide and may be trod.

330. Do on **hill** as in hall.

331. He who stands on a **hillock** is sure to be noticed.

332. Better to **hold** than draw.

333. They are not all saints that get **holy water.**

334. **Honesty** holds long the way.

335. It's dear cost **honey** that's licked off a thorn.

336. **Honour** won't patch.

337. Were it not for **hope** the heart would break.

338. Let **horns** go with the hide.

339. In a frost a nail is worth a **horse.**
[i.e. a trifle is sometimes of the highest importance.]

340. In some man's possession must the old **horse** die.

341. An eating **horse** never foundered.

342. A gift **horse** should not be looked in the mouth.

343. He's a proud **horse** that won't carry his own oats.

344. He will go mad on a **horse** who's proud on a pony.

345. Empty stalls make biting **horses.**

346. A wee **house** has a wide throat.

347. He whose **house** is burnt must become a soldier. (*Gaelic.*)

348. A man may love his **house** well without riding on the ridge.

349. The **hurt man** writes with steel on a marble stone.

350. To feed the land before it gets hungry; to give it rest before it grows weary; to weed it well

before it gets dirty—the marks of a good **husbandman.** (*Gaelic.*)

351. An **idle brain** is the devil's workshop.
352. A man is well or **ill** as he thinks himself so.
353. If you be not **ill,** be not ill-like.
354. It's a good tongue that says no **ill,** but a better one that thinks none.
355. **Ill** comes upon worse's back.

    [i.e. misfortunes seldom come singly.]
356. All's not **ill** that's ill-like.
357. **Ill-doers** are always ill-dreaders.
358. **Ill hearing** makes wrong rehearsing.
359. He that does you an **ill turn** will never forgive you.
360. All **ills** are good untried.
361. Your worst **ill-wisher** is he who once has done you a wrong. (*Gaelic.*)
362. **Ill workers** are always good onlookers.
363. An **inch** breaks no squares.

    [i.e. a little difference ought not to occasion any contests among good neighbours.]
364. Dree [endure] out the **inch** when you have tholed [borne] the span.
365. Men are not to be measured by **inches.**
366. Love-less as an **Irishman.** (*Gaelic.*)
367. A true **jest** is no jest.
368. Count like **Jews** and agree like brethren.
369. **Judge** warily; you know not who blames yourself.
370. He has good **judgment** that doesn't trust to his own.
371. To **ken** [know] a' folk you must winter 'em and summer 'em.
372. **Kindness** comes of will, it cannot be bought.
373. **Kindness** creeps where it cannot go.
374. **Kindred** to twenty degrees, fosterage to a hundred. (*Gaelic.*)
375. Nearest the **king,** nearest the widdy [gallows].
376. A **king's face** should give grace.
377. A **kiss** and a drink of water is but a tasteless breakfast.

    [Said to those who marry for love regardless of means.]
378. Many a daft kitlin [**kitten**] makes a douce [wise] cat.
379. Set your **knee** to it and right it.
380. Better thin **kneading** than to be empty. (*Hebridean.*)
381. It's better not to slip one **knot** till another be tied.
382. They **know** as well that do not ask.
383. Better hear the **lark** sing than the mouse squeak.

    [Saying of the Douglas family—meaning it was better to keep to the forest than to shut themselves up in fortified castles.]
384. **Laugh** and lay it down again.
385. A body lives long after they're **laughed** at.
386. He that **laughs** alone will make sport in company.
387. Show me the man and I'll show you the **law.**

    [i.e. to show the want of impartiality in Scotch judges at that time.]
388. Abundance of **law** breaks no law.

    [i.e. those who know the law best are least likely to break it.]
389. All **law** is not justice.
390. **Law** licks up all.
391. In a thousand pounds of **law** there's not an ounce of love.
392. **Law's** costly; take a pint and agree.
393. One **lawsuit** breeds twenty.
394. **Laziness** is worth much when it is well guided.
395. It's easy cutting whangs off other folks' **leather.**
396. Raw **leather** stretches well.
397. Work **legs** and win legs, have legs and lose legs.
398. It's long before four bare **legs** gather heat in a bed.

    [Used to dissuade people who have no stock from marrying.]

399. He that **lends** you hinders you to buy.
400. " Almost " and " nearly " have always been great **liars.**
401. Never **lie** for want of news.
402. There is always **life** for a living man.
403. **Lifeless,** faultless.
404. Don't **lift** me before I fall.
405. " **Likely** " lies in the mire, and " unlikely " gets over.
406. A man is a **lion** for his own cause.
407. Of a **little,** take a little ; when there's nothing, take all.
408. Better long **little** than soon nothing.
409. A slice off a new-cut **loaf's** never missed.
410. A borrowed **loan** should go laughing home.
411. Some folk **look** up and others look down.
412. Give **losing** gamesters leave to talk.
413. A man cannot tell his **loss.**
414. For a **lost thing** care not.
415. A hungry **louse** bites sore.
416. See for **love** and buy for money.
417. Follow **love** and it will flee thee ; flee love and it will follow thee.
418. Everything will perish save **love** and music. (*Gaelic.*)
419. If you **love** me, let it appear.
420. They that **love** most speak least.
421. None gave **love** quickly but gave sudden hate.
422. True **love's** the weft of life, but it sometimes comes through a sorrowful shuttle.
423. Much meat, many **maladies.**
424. The well of Kildenguie and the dulce [sea-weed] of Guiodin will cure all **maladies** save black death. (*Orkney.*)
425. **Malice** is always mindful.
426. A slow fire makes sweet **malt.**
427. The **malt's** above the meal.
    [i.e. he has had too much to drink.]
428. A **man of straw** is worth a woman of gold.
429. He that lacks [belittles] my **mare** may buy my mare.
430. **Marriage** o'er the midden, sponsorship o'er the sea.
431. Man is April when he makes love and December when he is **married.**
432. **Married** folk are like rats in a trap—fain to get others in, but fain to get out themselves.
433. **Marry** for love and work for siller. (*Gaelic.*)
434. Never **marry** for money, ye'll borrow it cheaper.
435. If you wish to be blamed, **marry** ; if you wish to be praised, die ! (*Gaelic.*)
436. They that **marry** in green, their sorrow is soon seen.
437. Better **marry** over the midden than over the muir [moor].
438. Honest men **marry** soon, wise men never.
439. **Marry** your son when you will, but your daughter when you can.
440. Early **master,** long servant.
441. A falling **master** makes a standing man.
442. What **may** be may not be.
443. Folks sometimes get a good **meal** out of a dirty dish.
    [i.e. a good article from a tainted source.]
444. Eats **meat,** and is never fed ; wears clothes, and is never clad.
445. **Meat** and mass never hindered work.
446. To take **meat** before grace.
    [i.e. to be married and not " churched ".]
447. Quick at **meat,** quick at work.
448. It's ill **meddling** between the bark and the rind.
    [i.e. don't meddle in quarrels of near relations.]
449. Of little **meddling** comes much ease.
450. The muck **midden** is the mother of the meal-chest.

451. They that like the **midden** see no motes in it.

452. It's by the mouth of the cow that the **milk** comes.

453. A man's **mind** is a dark mirror.

454. The mother of **mischief** is no bigger than a midge's wing.

455. He who can't do better must be a **monk.** (*Gaelic.*)

456. The bonny **moon** is on her back —mend your shoes and sort your thack.

457. It's a bare **moor** that you go through and not get a heather cow.

[i.e. a tuft of heather.]

458. Mickle [much] would always have **more.**

459. Let the **morn** come and the meat with it.

460. A light-heeled **mother** makes a heavy-heeled daughter.

461. An ounce of **mother-wit** is worth a pound of clergy.

462. A close **mouth** catches no flies.

463. Make not meikle **[much]** of little.

464. Where there is **muck** there is luck.

465. Little may an old **nag** do that must not neigh.

466. Nothing got without pains but an ill name and long **nails.**

467. **Nature** passes nurture.

468. No man can live longer in peace than his **neighbour** pleases.

469. Know yourself, and your **neighbour** will not mistake you.

470. He's very full in his own house that cannot pick a bone in his **neighbour's.**

471. We can live without our kin, but not without our **neighbours.**

472. He sits with little ease who sits on his **neighbour's** coat-tail.

473. My **neighbour's** harm's my own peril.

474. Lock your door and keep your **neighbours** honest.

475. Better learn by your **neighbour's** injury than by your own.

476. The testimony of **neighbours** is everybody's test. (*Gaelic.*)

477. Bring down the **nests** and the rooks will fly away.

[i.e. destroy the place where villains shelter and they will disperse.]

478. The proudest **nettle** grows on a midden.

479. They that get the **next best** are not ill off.

480. **Night** is a good herdsman, she brings all creatures home.

481. The more **noble,** the more humble.

482. He that has a great **nose** thinks everybody speaks of it.

483. "**Not well**" is worse than "sick in bed".

484. He that would eat the kernel must crack the **nut.**

485. There's no sport where there's neither **old folk** nor children.

486. It's the life of an **old hat** to be set jauntily.

487. An **old man's** a bedful of bones.

488. There's shelter beneath an **old man's** beard.

489. It's lost what's done to **old men** and bairns.

490. The three dearest of things: hen's eggs, pork, and **old woman's** praise. (*Gaelic.*)

491. Never open your **pack** and sell no wares.

[i.e. never proffer your service where it is not likely to be accepted.]

492. No penny—no **paternoster.**

493. The best **payment** is on the peck bottom.

[When you have measured out your grain to receive your payment on the peck that measured it.]

494. Ell and tell [i.e. good measure and prompt payment] is ne'er forgotten, and the best **pay's** on the peck bottom.

495. Better **peace** in a bush than peace in fetters. (*Gaelic.*)

496. Put two **pennies** in a purse and they'll creep together.

497. No friend like the **penny.**

498. Old wives and bairns make fools of **physicians.**

499. **Pigeons** and dominies leave always a foul house.

500. He that **pities** another remembers himself.

501. The less **play** the better.

502. Give over while the **play's** good.

503. He knows not the pleasures of **plenty** who never felt the pains of poverty.

504. Let not the **plough** stand to kill a mouse.

505. Standing **ponds** gather dirt.

506. The **poor** must pay for all.

507. **Poor folk** are fain of little.

508. The best that can happen a **poor man** is that one child die and the rest follow.

509. A **poor man's debt** makes much din.

510. The **poor man's** shilling is but a penny.

511. Begin on **porridge** that you may end with chicken.

512. Never **pot** boiled but the scum was cast uppermost.

513. When the **pot's** full it will boil over.

514. **Preach** according to your stipend.

515. If we cannot **preach** in the church we can sing Mass in the choir.

516. You cannot **preach** out of your own pulpit.

517. **Pride** and laziness need much upholding.

518. **Pride** never left his master without a fall.

519. **Pride** without profit wears shoes and goes barefoot.

520. When **pride's** in the van begging's in the rear.

521. The **priest** christens his own child first.

522. Common **proverb** seldom lies.

523. Wise men make **proverbs** and fools repeat them.

524. There's a **puddle** at every door, and before some doors there are two.

525. Be ready with your bonnet, but slow with your **purse.**

526. Ask your **purse** what you should buy.

527. Who burns **rags** will want a winding-sheet.

528. There is little for the **rake** after the besom.

529. Many a one brings the **rake,** but few the shovel.

530. **Ravens** and clergy are ticklish shot.

531. A **red nose** makes a ragged back.

532. **Rice** and thyme grow both in one garden.

533. **Ride** fair and bespatter none.

534. He does not always **ride** when he saddles his horse.

535. He that **rides** behind another doesn't saddle when he pleases.
[i.e. a dependent man must do as he is told.]

536. He **rides** slowly who observes. (*Gaelic.*)

537. The shortest **road's** where the company's good.

538. He who never **rode** never fell.

539. Don't speak of a **rope** to a child whose father was hanged.

540. **Rue** and thyme grow both in one garden.

541. Going to **ruin** is silent work. (*Gaelic.*)

542. One may bind a **sack** before it is full.

543. A full **sack** can bear a clout in the side.

544. He's a causeway **saint** and a house devil.

545. One **saint** makes twenty sinners.

546. Young **saints**—old sinners.

547. Old **saws** speak truth.

548. " My own property ", " my own wife ", and " come home ", the three sweetest **sayings** there are. (*Gaelic.*)

549. Seek your **salve** where you got your hurt, and beg your barm [yeast] where you buy your ale.

550. The wrinkled skin easily conceals a **scar.**

551. The **scholar** may be better than the master.

552. The **Scot** will not fight till he sees his own blood.

553. A **Scotsman** is always wise behind the hand.

554. The **Scotsman** is never at home but when he's abroad.

555. Three failures and a fire make a **Scotsman's fortune.**

556. **Scotsmen** always reckon from an ill hour.

557. **Seeing's** believing, but feeling's the naked truth.

558. If it will not **sell** it will not sour.

559. The **selvedge** is aye the worst part o' the web.

560. **Send** and fetch.

561. It that lies not in your way breaks not your **shin.**

562. Near's my **shirt,** but nearer's my skin.

563. Walk as your **shoes** will let you.

564. A **shroud** has no pockets.

565. Be long **sick** that you may be soon well.

566. The purse of the **sick person** prolongs his cure.

567. The **sigh** goes further than the shout. (*Gaelic.*)

568. Count **silver** after all your kindred.

569. He reads his **sin** in his punishment.

570. Old **sins** breed new sores.

571. Poorly **sits,** richly warms.

[i.e. a mean condition is both more safe and more comfortable than a high estate.]

572. He's the **slave** of a slave who serves none but himself.

573. The torn **sleeve** keeps the hand back. (*Shetland.*)

574. **Smoke** follows the fairest.

[i.e. envy follows excellence.]

575. The **snail** is as soon at its rest as the swallow.

576. Under **snow,** bread; under water, dearth.

577. Do not fling **snowballs** if you cannot take one.

578. My **son's** my son till he's got him a wife; my daughter's my daughter all the days of her life.

579. Keep something for a **sore foot.**

580. He's well worthy of **sorrow** that buys it with his own silver.

581. From the **sow** comes but a little pig. (*Gaelic.*)

582. **Sow** thin—shear thin [or mow thin].

583. To **spare** is to have.

584. When all men **speak,** no man hears.

585. A man may **spit** in his palm and do little.

586. Black is the stone that a man **spits** on. (*Shetland.*)

587. A man must **spoil** ere he spin.

588. It's the loose **spoke** in the wheel that rattles most.

589. A horn **spoon** holds no poison.

[i.e. they who cannot procure better spoons are not worth poisoning.]

590. You have put an empty **spoon** in my mouth.

591. A **spur** in the head's worth two in the heel.

592. All the speed is not in the **spurs.**

[Exactly opposite to the English version.]

593. There is a time to **squint,** and a time to look straight.

594. The crook in an old **stick** is hard to take out.

595. A crooked **stick** will throw a crooked shadow.

596. As good may hold the **stirrup** as he who leaps on.

597. There is always a slippery **stone** in front of everybody's door.

598. He that sits upon a **stone** is twice glad.

[i.e. glad to sit down because he is weary, and glad to rise because the stone is hard.]

599. Boil **stones** in butter and the broth will be good. (*Shetland.*)

[i.e. good ingredients will make even impossible things savoury.]

600. Nothing to do but draw in your **stool** and sit down.

601. **Stoop** and let the wave go by.
602. It is not easy to **straighten** in the oak the crook that grew in the sapling.
603. He starts at **straws,** and lets windlins [bottles of straw] go.
604. When the burn [**stream**] doesn't babble it's either too full or too empty.
605. If **strokes** be good to give they'll be good to take.
606. All **Stuarts** are not related to the King.
607. A dry **summer** never made a dear peck.
608. It's better to **sup** with a cutty than want a spoon.
   [" Cutty " is a small horn spoon.]
609. Nobody's **sweetheart's** ugly.
610. Every man's **tale** is good till another's be told.
611. It's a dry **tale** that does not end in a drink.
612. Long **tarrying** takes all the thanks away.
613. Blame your **teeth** if your tail be small.
614. A fish from the river, a tree from the forest, a deer from the mountain, are **thefts** no man was ever ashamed of. (*Gaelic.*)
615. He that shows his purse bribes the **thief.**
616. Buy a **thief** from the gallows and he'll help to hang you.
617. **Thrift's** good revenue.
618. What may be done at any **time** will be done at no time.
619. Keep your **tongue** a prisoner and your body will go free.
620. A long **tongue** has a short hand.
621. Give your **tongue** more holidays than your head.
622. Never tie a knot with your **tongue** that you cannot loose with your teeth.
623. Handle your **tools** without mittens.
624. You will not boast **trade.**
625. Dip in thine own **treacle.**
626. Remove an old **tree** and it will wither.
627. He that plants **trees** loves others besides himself.
628. It may be **true** what some men say ; it must be true what all men say.
629. No luck till the second **tumbler,** and no peace after the fourth.
630. A **turn** well done is soon done.
631. Come **uncalled,** sits unserved.
632. **Unseen,** unrued.
633. As much **upwards,** as much downwards.
634. Young cows' calves are dear **veal.**
635. A **wager** is a fool's argument.
636. What won't **wash** won't wring. (*Shetland.*)
637. Good **watch** hinders harm.
638. **Water** will be where water has been. (*Shetland.*)
639. We must all go one **way.**
640. A man may ask the **way** he knows full well.
641. When you're going and coming the **way's** not empty.
642. **Wealth** breeds a pleurisy, ambition a fever, liberty a vertigo, and poverty is a dead palsy. (*Gaelic.*)
643. Bear **wealth** well, and poverty will bear itself.
644. **Weapons** offer peace.
645. All the wealth of the world is in the **weather.**
646. No **weather's** ill if the wind be still.
647. He's no good **weaver** that leaves long threads.
648. A man may woo where he will, but must **wed** where his fate is.
649. Leave **welcome** always behind you.
650. When I did **well,** I heard it never ; when I did ill, I heard it ever.
651. When the **well** is full it will run over.
   [i.e. when people are much wronged they show their resentment.]
652. He's worth no **well** that can bide no woe.

653. God send water to that **well** that folk think will never be dry.

654. Sow **wheat** in dirt and rye in dust.

655. He that marries a **widow** with two daughters has three back doors to his house.

656. He who tells his **wife** all is but newly married.

657. Who speaks ill of his **wife** dishonours himself.

658. He that has a **wife** has a master.

659. A **wife** is wise enough when she knows her husband's breeks from her own kirtle [petticoat].

660. No man can thrive unless his **wife** will let him.

661. Choose your **wife** with her night-cap on. (*Gaelic.*)

662. The **wife's** always welcome that comes with a crooked arm.

663. Come with the **wind,** and go with the water.

664. As the **wind** blows seek your shelter.

665. When the **wind's** still the shower falls softly.

666. Good **wine** needs not a wispe [bush].

[A wisp of straw stuck upon the top of a country house was a sign that ale was sold there, but if the ale was good, people would haunt the house, though there be none. The association of the "bush" with wine is seen in the "Bush-house". A bough was used as a "bush" as a sign for a tavern, and a bunch of ivy was the sign of a vintner's shop. "Bush" was also a term for a spray of rosemary or other herb, which was laid in the bottom of a drinking-cup by publicans. A "bush" was hung out at the top of mines to show that they were at work.]

667. A **winter day** and a wintry way is the life of man.

668. A **wise man** gets learning from them that have none of their own.

669. A **wise man** wavers, a fool is fixed.

670. Fools look to to-morrow, and **wise men** use to-night.

671. **Wit** bought makes folk wise.

672. Bought **wit** is best. (*Gaelic.*)

673. He that makes friends afraid of his **wit** should be afraid of their memories.

674. **Wives** and wind are necessary evils.

675. All one **wool.**

[i.e. all to the same pattern.]

676. He that goes for **wool** may chance to come home shorn.

677. **Wool-sellers** always know wool-buyers.

[i.e. roguish people know their own consorts.]

678. Take a man by his **word,** and a cow by her horn.

679. You're master of your own **words,** but once spoken, your words may master you.

680. The **worst** may be tholed [borne] when it's known.

681. **Years** bring fears.

682. **Yellow's** forsaken, and green's forsworn, but blue and red ought to be worn.

683. A **Yule** feast may be relinquished at Easter.

WELSH

An Introduction to this collection by J. J. Jones, M.A., will be found on p. cv.

1. Better a free meal of **acorns** than a honey feast on trust.

2. **Adversity** comes with instruction in its hand.

3. Preparation for **adversity** is the best way to prosperity.

4. **Afflictions** are the staves of the ladder that ascends to heaven.

5. The **aged** knows; the young supposes.
6. An **agreement** will break a custom.
7. Good **ale** is a key to the heart.
8. The trap to the high-born is **ambition.**
9. An **angel** on the highway, a devil on the hearth.
10. The **apple** will not fall far from the apple-tree.
11. He who would be the top of a **bag,** let him not commit what suits the bottom of the bag.
12. A person waiting for hair is not **bald.**
13. Half the **banquet** is pride.
14. Burnished be thy **beads,** rusty thy weapons.
15. The origin of **bees** is from paradise, and it was because of man's sin they came, and God gave his blessing to them.
16. Everything is small in its **beginning.**
17. The **belly** will strip the back.
18. Seldom is there a **benefit** unbegrudged.
19. The **best** of all is the best that can be done.
20. Long will the **bitter morsel** be chewed.
21. There is nothing brave but a **black cock.**
22. Who has the hilt has the **blade.**
23. There will not be anything smooth without its **blemish.**
24. **Blood** shows on a grey horse.
25. It is when old that the **blows** received in youth are felt.
26. I was wise once, that was in crying when I was **born.**
27. A **boy** [child] knows who fondles him; he knows not who loves him.
28. A **boy's face** when he finds a nest!
29. Two **brands** burn better than one.
30. That which is too tight will **break;** that which is too full will spill; that which is too high will fall.
31. Let everybody praise the **bridge** that carries him across.
32. There is no **bridge** without a place the other side of it.
33. Sip by sip the **broth** ended.
34. The **brown hair** is not heavier than the white.
35. The **butter** is in the cow's horns.
36. **Butterflies** are the gems of the leaves.
37. **Buy** what is old and you must buy again.
38. Let a **camp** be green.
39. **Carrion** will make known where it is.
40. An old **cat** knows fresh milk.
41. The **cat** knows whose beard she licks.
42. He who will not feed his **cat,** let him feed mice.
43. There is a measure for everything, but there is no measure for **charity.**
44. A **child** in the house is a hundred enjoyments.
45. A naked **child** laughs, a hungry one never.
46. Better an old **claim** than an old feud.
47. He who **climbeth** late soon descends.
48. The qualities of a **cock** are singing and treading.
49. A **coin** is the best friend.
50. He who complains of a small **complaint** foretells a great complaint.
51. **Conscience** is the nest where every good is hatched.
52. A little is the mother of **contention.**
53. Shame on the **cook** who licks not his hand.
54. A man's load is his **coracle.**
55. A full ear of **corn** will bend its head; an empty ear will stand upright.
56. A dry **cough** ends all ills.
57. A sad **countenance** awaits mischief.
58. The forlorn one is common in **court.**

59. The **cow** is milked from her head.
60. Let him who owns the **cow** take to her tail.
61. Wider will the **cow-dung** be for trampling on it.
62. Better a **craft** than wealth.
63. **Craftsmen** are brothers.
64. **Customs,** then law.
65. Two parts of a town are its **customs.**
66. The **day** will reveal the work of the night.
67. No one is well but he who is **dead.**
68. The trumpet of **death** is a dry cough.
69. Not less will a man seek his **death** than his reward.
70. From a long **debt** nothing is due.
71. **Deceit** will kill deceit.
72. To **deceive** another greatly is to deceive thyself more.
73. In three things a man may be **deceived:** in a man till known, in a tree till down, in the day till done.
74. He whose mind is on **departing** will do no good before starting.
75. It is necessary to have a long spoon to eat with the **devil.**
76. What is obtained on the **devil's** back is spent under his belly.
77. No income but **diligence.**
78. The **diligent** is seldom an exile.
79. A **dimple** in the chin, your living comes in; a dimple in the cheek, your living to seek.
80. After **drinking** there is thirst.
81. Send thy **dog,** don't run with it.
82. Better a **dog** that roams than one that sits down.
83. When thou wishest to kill thy **dog,** thou callest it a mad dog.
84. The **dog** will lick the weapon with which he is wounded.
85. Stroke a surly **dog.**
86. With the **dog** walks his tail.
87. A **dog's** protection of a bag of salt!
88. Pat the **dog's head** in passing.
89. The **door** is opened quickly to a loved one.
90. He who gathers a **dunghill** will have one faithful friend.
91. Trust the **ear** less than the eye.
92. The **elbow** is nearer than the wrist.
93. Before starting, see the **end.**
94. **Evening** will come although the day be long.
95. Incomplete is every **event.**
96. No **evil** comes to one without good coming to another.
97. Seek the nest of **evil** in the bosom of a good word.
98. He who complains of **excess** does not grieve at all.
99. **Failures** are the pillars of success.
100. Two-thirds of **fame** is in the skull.
101. **Fame** is longer than life.
102. He who would win **fame,** let him die.
103. The husbandman's chamber is his **farmyard.**
104. Better the share of **fear** than the share of love.
105. It is not what a man sees that **feeds** him.
106. There never was evil without a **female** at some end.
107. A **finger** is sweet when burnt.
108. A slow **fire** makes sweet malt.
109. It is easy to light a **fire** on an old hearth.
110. The greater the **flood,** the greater will be the ebb.
111. **Folly** does not see its magnitude.
112. A mess of **food** lasts long if your knife is blunt.
113. Another man's **food** tastes sweeter.
114. Only the rich **fool** is said to speak sense.
115. If thou play the **fool,** stay for a fellow.
116. Let everybody praise the **ford** as he finds it.
117. A **fox** does not smell his own stench.

118. Through lack of a lion the **fox** will ascend to the throne.
119. A road **friend** is unreliable.
120. Better a chamber **friend** than a song friend.
121. He who is a **friend** to himself will have the friendship of others.
122. A servant's **friendship** is froth.
123. No dew will rest upon a **gander.**
124. A **gentle word** will make the argument strong.
125. If tall, you're a **giant**; if small, you're a dwarf.
126. Accept a **gift** from a frog's mouth.
127. He who will not **give** what he loves will not obtain what he wishes.
128. **God** arms the harmless.
129. It is better to have **God** as one's friend than the host of the world.
130. Not the praying at morn, at noon, and at night is the service of **God,** but the doing aright.
131. **God** can; man talks.
132. That which **God** does man will judge.
133. **God** sleeps not when He delivers.
134. Pass sentence on thyself equitably and **God** will become thy surety.
135. It is not a host that conquers, but **God.**
136. When the more straitened it is with [for] man, the more open it is for **God.**
137. **God's** eye is on a pledge.
138. A man knows when he **goes** but does not know when he comes.
139. Nothing is **good** while better is possible.
140. Daily **good fortune** is hourly misfortune.
141. A **gossip's mouth** is the devil's mail-bag.
142. It was through reaching for the green blade of **grass** that the mare was drowned.
143. Sweetest the **grass** next to the ground.
144. Small is the seed of every **greatness.**
145. The genius of a **grinding-stone.**
146. Better one **guard** than two pursuers.
147. To be in the **habit** of no habit is the worst habit in the world.
148. A **hag** dreams what she wills.
149. A skilful **hand** is not laborious.
150. The **hand** reaches not what the heart does not wish to give.
151. Cast with thy one **hand,** seek with thy two hands.
152. The **hand** which gives, gathers.
153. The **hand** will not reach for what the heart does not long for.
154. The **happy** wants only to be born.
155. It is the flattering **harp** which never lacked golden strings.
156. Where the **harrow** goes the thorn hurdle will go.
157. The first with his **harrow** is the first with his sickle.
158. While the **harrow** moves let the mill move.
159. It is hair by hair the **head** grows bald.
160. A **head** is higher than two shoulders.
161. Let the **healthy** be happy.
162. He who would be **healthy** let him drink mead.
163. Let the **heart** that will not glow, slumber.
164. He who has distributed has had [known] **heaven.**
165. Better the shelter of a **hedge** than its place.
166. Let the **hen** prepare a nest before laying.
167. **Hens** flourish not where cows do not prosper.
168. There is no **hill** without a slope.
169. Sweet is **honey,** bitter when paid for.
170. **Hope** without exertion is like a voyage without a ship.
171. It is hair by hair that the **horse** grows bob-tailed.
172. Have a **horse** of thine own, and thou mayest borrow another's.

173. An old **horse** recognises chaff.
174. Where the **horse** rolls itself it leaves some of its hair.
175. Better the **horse** that is on its way than the one in its stall.
176. A **horse** will see the corn but not the fence.
177. Seek for a good rider under his **horse's** feet.
178. A **host** in flight takes no gift.
179. Three things that will drive a man from his **house:** a leaking roof, a smoky chimney, and a quarrelsome wife.
180. There is nothing worse always about the **house** than what a man is.
181. Woe to the **house** where the voice of reproof is not heard.
182. A **hundred pounds** a year is the difference between "go" and "come".
183. Better **"I fled"** than "He was slain".
184. As good an **inch** wide as an inch long.
185. No one is **informed** but he who inquires.
186. The best protection is **innocence.**
187. Let the **iron** respect the life of man.
188. **Jealousy** does not grow old.
189. A step over the threshold is half the **journey.**
190. Three pillars of **judgment:** bold purpose, frequent usage, and frequent erring.
191. There will be no **judgment** without its contradiction.
192. One can too often do that which is **just.**
193. It is easier to **keep** than to trace.
194. The shell must be cracked to get the **kernel.**
195. Better a **knuckle** of a man than a mountain of a woman.
196. Bad **land** will not conceal its vegetation.
197. It is a strong man's job to hold **land.**
198. The houses of **lawyers** are roofed with the skins of litigants.
199. **A lazy man** is the devil's walking-stick.
200. He who is **leader,** let him be the bridge.
201. The best walker is a **lie.**
202. Three seats [abodes] of **life:** head, stomach, and lap.
203. **Life,** however long its stay, will end in a day and a night.
204. If you desire to see my **light** you must minister oil to my lamp.
205. **Lightly** it came, lightly it went.
206. Every **like** strives.
207. A **little** frequently will make a lot.
208. A **loan** is a denial.
209. Reconciliation is easy where **love** is.
210. Faults are thick where **love** is thin.
211. In every pardon there is **love.**
212. He who is **loved** or hated is seen from afar.
213. It is easy to persuade one that is **loved.**
214. He who **loves** is remembered by all.
215. Everyone's eyes are on that which he **loves.**
216. There will be no **loving** completely until the grandchild comes.
217. Everyone is **lord** over his own.
218. Everyone's **luck** is on his brow.
219. A rope is strong, a **maid** draws stronger.
220. A **man** is better than his lot.
221. No **man** is good unless others are made better by him.
222. It is not an enemy that will dispose of **man's life.**
223. The way will not be more obstructed by hearing a **Mass.**
224. **Mead** will pull off the mask.
225. A slice to wait for a **meal.**
226. **Milk** and grain are the best things in the world.

227. **Milk** for a child; meat for a man; beer for the aged.
228. The **mill** that grinds must have water.
229. There is work for the **mill** when the harrow works.
230. Good is the **mill** which has been worn out.
231. The **mind** does not grow old.
232. **Misfortunes** come by forties.
233. No **mistletoe**—no luck.
234. **Money** is like an eel in the hand.
235. The end of the song is **money.**
236. **Necessity** breaks law.
237. **Necessity** will buy and will sell.
238. **Necessity** will not thank being fed.
239. **Necessity** will teach the old to run.
240. That which is kept will be found in **need.**
241. What is not often seen is **neglected.**
242. A mirror to everyone is his **neighbour.**
243. The **new** alone is honoured.
244. Give no credit to **news** unless they be old.
245. Because of the **nurse** the child is kissed.
246. The empty **nut** is the hardest.
247. Sooner will the **oak** fall before the wind than a bramble.
248. A hundred disorders has **old age.**
249. It is better to **open** than to contain.
250. The three **opportunities** of all things: time, place, and kind.
251. The thinner the **ox** the better it will work.
252. Bare is the hired **ox.**
253. Do not lose your old **path** for the sake of the new one.
254. Every **path** in a gorge leads to the same place.
255. Everyone is bold towards his **patron saint.**
256. He who would have **peace** let him ask leave of his tongue.
257. Better a **penny** than a brother.
258. One **penny** will bring a hundred.
259. There is a lesson in every **perplexity.**
260. Three remedies of the **physicians** of Myddfai: water, honey, and labour.
261. It is good to place a ring in the nose of a **pig** that turns up the ground.
262. He who got up has lost his **place.**
263. He who goes to **play,** let him leave his skin at home.
264. Not by running is **ploughing** done.
265. What is given to the **poor** will be paid on the day of doom.
266. An enemy to a man are his **possessions.**
267. **Poverty** will not prevent liberality.
268. **Pride** must pinch.
269. There will be no **profit** from a little.
270. **Profit** prevents fatigue.
271. There is no enemy like too much **prosperity.**
272. True is every **proverb,** false every superstition.
273. Old **proverbs** are the children of truth.
274. A **puddle** will not grow dirty.
275. It is easy to **reap** a poor acre.
276. **Religion** destroys evil, morality merely hides it.
277. Small is his **religion** who seeks daily for it.
278. Two parts of **respect** is custom.
279. Where there is no fear there is no **respect.**
280. Two parts of a **road** is to know it.
281. Better the **rod** that bends than the one that breaks.
282. It is customary where there is water to have **rushes.**
283. The greatest feat is to keep **safe.**
284. The common **sayings** of the multitude, too true to be laughed at.

285. There is no **sea** without a place beyond it.
286. The **seas** will do nothing worse than drown.
287. It is no **secret** except it be between two.
288. The **secret** of three, a hundred will hear it.
289. Every **shelter** is a hall.
290. The end of the aged is keeping **sheep.**
291. The deeper the sea, the more secure it will be for the **ship.**
292. He who is **sick** will lie down.
293. Better the work of the **sickle** than the bow.
294. There will be no **sigh** without its tear.
295. He who is **silent** admits.
296. Avoid the first **sin,** for a legion is close at its heel.
297. One **sin** will draw a hundred after it.
298. The **skilful** will always have two tasks.
299. One must have a clean mouth to **slander.**
300. Better is my own **small beer** than the wine of charity.
301. He who avoids not the **smoke** avoids not its evils.
302. The **snail** deserves the end of its journey.
303. Easier is the evening **song** than the morning.
304. Everyone's hand on his **sore.**
305. The **sow** which is silent will eat the draff.
306. He who will **steal** an egg will steal something more.
307. The best **step,** the first step.
308. A third foot to the aged is his **stick.**
309. It is better to **stint** than to lavish.
310. It is easier to fill the **stomach** than the eye.
311. A **stone** runs until it reaches the level.
312. A **stone** will swim to the bottom.
313. A **stoppage** is usual after a run.
314. If thou be a **stranger,** be merry and give the first "good morrow".
315. Woe to him who will trust a **stranger.**
316. Where the **strawberries** abound snakes abound.
317. The tighter the **string** the sooner it will break.
318. He thou didst bring up will **substitute** thee.
319. **Suffering** is better than care.
320. Who **suffers** much is silent.
321. There is no **sufficiency** without a remainder.
322. Look for the beauty of the **sun** in its heat and not in its face.
323. There is nothing warm but the **sun ;** there is nothing cold but the moon.
324. Two parts of a **task** is to start it.
325. **Tears** wear cheeks.
326. The first to be a **thief** is the first to be king.
327. He **thinks** not who reflects not.
328. That which will not pierce when a **thorn,** will not pierce when a raw stump.
329. He who sows **thorns** let him not walk bare-footed.
330. **Thrift** begins at the mouth of the sack.
331. The **tongue** can break a bone.
332. The **tongue** will relate ; living will show.
333. A tooth is good to check the **tongue.**
334. **Too much** is no better than too little.
335. A long dam will collect a **torrent.**
336. What everyone says is **true.**
337. **A trumpet** is heard before it is seen.
338. **Truth** is despised where it is not loved.
339. Extremely offensive is every naked **truth.**
340. He **understands** badly who listens badly.
341. The **ungenerous** heart counts giving a fault in the generous.

342. The **unlucky** will have a thorn in his gruel.
343. There will not be contained in a **vessel** more than its full.
344. **A vessel** that is not full will not break.
345. Though the **waggon** creaks it will bear its load.
346. Long is every **waiting.**
347. It was better for the man who **wandered** than for the man who died of hunger.
348. He who excels in **war** will excel in peace.
349. Much **water** flows by unknown to the miller.
350. Let everyone seek **water** for his own ship.
351. The **water** is shallowest where it babbles.
352. To the hollow will the **water** run.
353. There is no obstruction but **water.**
354. The **way** is bad which is walked but once.
355. There's nothing **weak** without its strength.
356. The **weapon** of the brave is in his heart.
357. Rain and fair **weather** repay justly one another.
358. Little by little the **wedge** goes into the wood.
359. There is refuse among **wheat.**
360. A **whisper** is shy.
361. Let not thy **wife** be thy confidant.
362. If you refuse a **wife** with one fault, you will take one with two.
363. To meet every kind of unwisdom, **wisdom** is best.
364. The father of **wisdom** is memory; his mother reflection.
365. **Wisdom,** like the best of the honey, will be at the bottom.
366. A **wish** hides between the hand and the sleeve.
367. The **wolf** will die in the skin in which he was born.
368. Let a **woman** go after her reproach.
369. It is common for a **woman** to prefer that which is worse for her.
370. A **woman** will not lack an excuse.
371. There is no disappointment but a **woman.**
372. A **woman's** advice is of little value, but woe to the man who will not take it.
373. **A woman's** word starts off like the wind.
374. Better one **word** before than two after.
375. The easiest **work** is to fail.
376. He loves not **work** who is not accustomed to it.
377. Where the **wound** is there will the hand be.
378. For every **wound** the ointment of time.
379. There is seldom a **wound** without blood.
380. The dregs of **wrath** are surly words.
381. One **year** will be a mother to a man, another a stepmother.
382. He who wishes to be **young** long let him soon become old.
383. There is no allurement but **youth.**
384. A **youth's promise** is like the froth of water.
385. Choose either the **yoke** or the axe.

BULGARIAN

1. He is good who is **absent.**
2. If you like **accepting,** start by giving.
3. Even an **ant** casts a shadow.
4. Eat the **apple** peeled, the pear unpeeled.
5. Thrash the **apprentice** while he has not yet broken the water-jug.
6. Whip the saddle, that the **ass** may meditate.
7. **Ass** to Vienna—ass from Vienna.
8. If you wish to know a man, give him **authority.**
9. **Awls** are not carried in a sack.
10. A handless **axe** does not scare the forest.
11. If you have a **back,** there are three hundred saddles for it.
12. An empty **bag** is heavier than a full one.
13. He who has a **beard** buys himself a comb.
14. Make every **bed** as if you were to rest on it.
15. If you are a **bee,** there is always a hive for you.
16. There is no picking out in a **bee-hive.**
17. When you **begin**—consider the end.
18. Edible **birds** do not live long.
19. At **birth** we cry—at death we see why.
20. A good **bishop** does not deem himself a saint.
21. Everyone draws the **blanket** towards himself.
22. **Blessing** is the father of cursing.
23. If you go to sleep with the **blind** you will awake squinting.
24. **Blow** before you have been scalded.
25. He who knows **books** has four eyes.
26. Hunger sees nothing but **bread.**
27. He who gives me a chance to earn my daily **bread** is at once my father and my brother.
28. If you have **bread** there are plenty of dogs.
29. Good or bad, it matters not—they are all **Bulgarian.**
30. Bottomless **bushel,** empty granary.
31. Even **butter** and honey make you sick in time.
32. He who has overmuch **butter** greases his boots.
33. Spank small **buttock** that large buttock may not be flogged.
34. Whip his **buttocks** lest he beat his head with his fists.
35. Your own **calamity** is more useful to you than another's triumph.
36. The **camel** is expensive at a penny, cheap at a thousand.
37. If you make friends with the **camel driver,** build your gates high.
38. If you burn one **candle** in veneration of God, burn two to the devil.
39. When the **cart** is broken there are many straight roads in sight.
40. If you do not rear **cats** you will raise mice.
41. **Chicken** are counted in autumn.
42. A father suffers through his **children** and through his children fares well.
43. If your **children** are bad they should not inherit any property ; if they are good they need none.
44. The **chip** does not fly far from the block.
45. In every village is the grave of **Christ.**
46. No snow at **Christmas,** no green at Easter.
47. The **clean** gets dirty more easily.
48. The **clergyman's** son is the devil's grandson.

49. He wove his **cloth,** then kicked the loom.
50. Man is received according to his **clothes,** but sent away according to his mind.
51. Tail-less **cock,** eternal chicken.
52. A **cock** has never too many hens.
53. A scalded **cock** runs away from the rain.
54. White **coins** for black days.
55. One must look for the truly faithful [people] far away from the **convents** and monasteries.
56. Keep the **cross** and keep yourself from those who cross themselves.
57. The **crow** does not louse the buffalo to clean him, but to feed itself.
58. Feed the **crow** to pick out your eyes.
59. One does not get **crucified,** one crucifies oneself.
60. **Custom** is not a law, but it has the vigour of one.
61. If the **day** is too short, the year is not.
62. New **day**—new fate.
63. Two happy **days** are seldom brothers.
64. **Death** speaks the truth.
65. If your house is burning, its **debts** are escaping through the chimney.
66. Do a good **deed** and throw it into the sea.
67. From word to **deed** as from leaf to root.
68. The **devil** is the devil, but a woman can out-devil him.
69. The **devil** knows everything except the place where women sharpen their knives.
70. I commanded the **dog** and it commanded its tail.
71. White **dog,** black dog—always a dog.
72. When they wish to kill a **dog** they say it is mad.
73. Feed a **dog** to bark at you.
74. Should God hearken to the **dogs,** loaves of bread would rain.
75. A **dog's** viciousness, the pepper's hotness, and man's goodness are valuable.
76. When the **donkey** is invited to the wedding it is because there is either no wood or no water.
77. Scabby **donkeys** scent each other over nine hills.
78. Touch not a **door** that grates.
79. He who believes in **dreams** pastures the winds.
80. He who likes to **drink** will sleep without a wife.
81. He who **drinks** on credit gets doubly drunk.
82. When ready to fall a **drop** is biggest.
83. **Drops** excavate rocks.
84. If you wish to **drown,** do not torture yourself with shallow waters.
85. As long as a man pushes or pulls, he is not **dying.**
86. The **eagle** neither hunts for flies nor feeds on flies.
87. The **earth** is man's only friend.
88. Were it **eatable** it would not be hanging.
89. Better an **egg** to-day than a hen to-morrow.
90. Other people's **eggs** have two yolks.
91. The **elder** gives no winter supplies, nor does the poplar give shade.
92. Consider not thyself the man of the house if thou enter thy house **empty handed.**
93. For the fleeing **enemy** build a golden bridge.
94. To **enquire** is neither a disaster nor a disgrace.
95. **Evil** seldom goes alone.
96. If you do not see **evil** you cannot appreciate good.
97. **Evil people** have no pattern.
98. His **eyes** are on his feet.
99. Hungry **eyes** do not sleep.
100. The **eyes** have no boundaries.

101. Not before night covers the **eyes** of one, will the day dawn for the other.
102. **Eyes** see everything except themselves.
103. He who breaks **faith** will be broken by distrust.
104. He who **falls** by himself does not complain.
105. He **falls** low who flies high.
106. **Fear** has magnifying eyes.
107. **Fear** sees much.
108. If the head does not direct the **feet,** heaven help both !
109. The **fields** have eyes, the woods have ears.
110. He who broils not in the **fields,** struts not at the dance.
111. Not before one has swallowed enough smoke will one enjoy a good **fire.**
112. **Fire** and water are good servants but cruel masters.
113. Dry pants eat no **fish.**
114. Should you have a pound of **flour,** ask an expert to knead it for you.
115. Preserve the **flower**—to eat the fruit.
116. If you have no **foe,** your own mother has given him birth.
117. **Forests** have eyes ; meadows ears.
118. You cannot consider the **for-gotten** as found.
119. Time builds a **fortress** and also destroys it.
120. A **fortress** surrenders from within.
121. Do not disturb the **fountain** from which you are about to drink.
122. If a **fox** has a tooth left he won't be pious.
123. The **frog** saw that they were shoeing the ox and lifted up his leg too.
124. An unfenced **garden** is a fenced desert.
125. For a bad **girl** put in a good word ; of a good one you may speak as you like.
126. First **glass** for health ; second for joy ; third for good cheer ; fourth for folly.
127. If the **goat** lies, his horns do not.

    [His age is marked by yearly rings on his horns.]
128. Yellow **goat,** yellow kid.
129. Where there is love there is **God.**
130. If you respect the aged you respect **God.**
131. Without **God** and concord no-thing can be done.
132. Fear **God** and him who fears **God.**
133. **God** can be held by ten fingers.
134. **God** does not pay every Satur-day.
135. **God** gave a herb for every ill.
136. **God** gave, God took.
137. **God** gives, but does not lock the gate of the fold.
138. **God** gives, but leads not into the sheep-fold.
139. **God** helps him who early rises.
140. **God** is not sinless, He created the world.
141. **God** lives with gods, man lives with men.
142. Whom **God** means to punish, He first deprives of his reason.
143. Where there is concord, there **God** sends His blessing.
144. **God** shuts one door, but opens ten.
145. Before **God** you can say " I cannot ", but not before men.
146. **God's** feet are wool ; His hands are iron.
147. Go **God's** way, remembering Satan.
148. An empty **gourd** always rattles.
149. If the **grass** is mown it is not uprooted.
150. After shaking hands with a **Greek** always count your fingers.
151. One **guest** hates the other, and the host both.
152. The father is the **guest** in the house.

153. An untimely **guest** is worse than a Turk.
154. The **guilty** flees even when not pursued.
155. The **gullet** has no bottom.
156. Two men are frightened of an unloaded **gun.**
157. A loaded **gun** frightens one; an unloaded two.
158. The **gun** may err, but not the cudgel.
159. As long as the **gypsy** has tongs, he will not burn his fingers.
160. What's in the **hand** is real.
161. One **hand** washes the other, both the face.
162. There are a hundred **hands** in a wise head.
163. White **hands**—others' work.
164. The **hands** sanctify, the hands defile.
165. As long as there are heads there will be **hats.**
166. A big **head**, a big headache.
167. A **head** without cares is like a gourd in the garden.
168. As many **heads,** so many opinions.
169. If you would live long, open your **heart.**
170. Stronger even than stone is man's **heart.**
171. If the **heart** will not speak, the eyes will.
172. An **heir's** sobbing is laughing in disguise.
173. One does not go to **hell** to light a cigarette.
174. Where the **hen** crows the house goes to ruin.
175. A hungry **hen** dreams of millet.
176. Old **hen**—good soup.
177. A feather-legged **hen** is not a cock.
178. The **hen** that cackles much lays small eggs.
179. The true **hermit** retires from himself.
180. Do not chase the little one, for you will make him a **hero.**
181. Don't be a **hero** out in the cold.
182. No **hero** without a wound.
183. Where there is no woman there is no **home.**
184. A **home** is deserted through a father's curse, but uprooted through a mother's.
185. A **home** is like the sea.
186. Wherever you go, come back **home** to be happy.
187. Your **home**—your kingdom.
188. He who deals in **honey** must lick his fingers.
189. Soft grass for an old **horse!**
190. The old **horse** does not bite the bit.
191. The **house** is always spacious enough if the inmates live in concord.
192. In winter **hunger** awaits him who in summer sits in the shade.
193. A **hurricane,** like all winds, will pass away.
194. An **idle man** makes a good prophet.
195. **Ignorance**—slaves.
196. Where you see a church, there you will find two **inns.**
197. **Invited**—as good as bequested.
198. Where the **itch,** there the scratch.
199. Many an ass has entered **Jerusalem.**
200. **Justice** is always hungry.
201. A good word is a golden **key.**
202. Live, but do not deal with your **kin.**
203. The greater the **labour** the less the loss.
204. A gentle **lamb** sucks two mothers.
205. Test the **lamb's** fatness by touching its tail, and that of a kid by touching its breasts.
    [Meekness and forwardness.]
206. There are more **lamb's** skins on the market than those of wolves.
207. If you walk with the **lame** you will soon learn to limp.
208. To **learn** costs you one effort, to unlearn, two.

209. Stretch your **legs** no further than your coverlet.

210. You should never **lend** your horse, your watch, or your wife.

211. Do not **lie** for want of news.

212. A **lie** is a curse of God.

213. To have **life** one must buy the days.

214. **Life** would be splendid were it not for death.

215. **A lion** lurks in everyone's heart; awake him not.

216. Grain by grain—a **loaf;** stone upon stone—a palace.

217. Lend if you are prepared to lose your **loan** or acquire a new enemy.

218. **Long-haired,** shallow-minded. [Said of women.]

219. Tangled threads are not put on to the **loom.**

220. By enquiring your way you will come to the **Lord's tomb.**

221. **Love** alone does not tolerate partners.

222. Give me, mother, **luck** at birth, then throw me if you will on to the rubbish heap.

223. Wheresoever the **magpie** goes she manures her nest.

224. Shoot a **maiden** rather than slander her.

225. Should you lose your hold on the **mane,** do not grip the tail.

226. He never regrets who dines early and **marries** early.

227. Either **marry** young or take orders young.

228. **Marry** your son when you wish; your daughter as soon as you can.

229. He who wants to attain water and earth at the same time will wade in a **marsh.**

230. Consider the servants and you will know the **master.**

231. The **master's eye** fattens the horse.

232. **Measure** nine times, cut once.

233. If a man is doomed to live, **medicine** will be found always.

234. **Mending** keeps the house.

235. Better an ounce of **mercy** than a pound of gold to the church.

236. **Might** never prays.

237. Covered **milk** is not lapped by cats.

238. Everybody drives the stream to his own [water] **mill.**

239. He who has been to the **mill** has flour on his cap.

240. **Mind** is as the sea, reason as the razor.

241. The **mind** reigns, the mind slaves, the mind pastures geese.

242. If **misfortune** has not found you, wait a moment, you will find it.

243. Ready **money** is the safest medicine.

244. Ready **money**—ready business.

245. Milk the **mosquito** to serve your king.

246. Consider the **mother,** woo the daughter.

247. The **mountain** made a great effort and brought forth a mouse.

248. **Mountains** cannot meet, men can.

249. He who takes **much** takes but little.

250. Patience transforms the **mulberry leaf** into silk.

251. Our business is like a **mule's tail**—it grows not and grows not smaller.

252. One **nail** drives out another.

253. **Necessity** changes all laws.

254. He is threading an eyeless **needle.**

255. Rather quarrel with your key than with your **neighbour.**

256. May God think of you as your **neighbours** think.

257. The **nigger's devil** is white.

258. **Nightfall** is the best shepherd, it drives all to the fold.

259. Only the **nightingale** can understand the rose.

260. A growth on a man's **nose** conceals the man behind **it.**

261. Never a willow tree bore any **olives.**

262. Seize the **opportunity** by the beard, for it is bald behind.
263. Many an **opportunity** has been lost for want of knocking [on the door].
264. " **Our Father** " is not enough.
265. It is not enough to say " **Our Father** "; one must also say " Amen ".
266. **Over-work** is hard; no work harder still.
267. The **ox** is tied by the horns, man by the tongue.
268. **Padlocks** are for good folks, walls are useless for bad people.
269. Every **pain** for a time.
270. One's own **pain** is better than another's happiness.
271. Neither above nor below the ground can **paradise** or hell be found.
272. Even dogs refuse to eat meat belonging to **partners.**
273. **Patient**—saved.
274. Where will the **pear** fall, if not under the pear-tree?
275. Every **pear** has its stem.
276. Who sits under a **pear-tree** will eat pears.
277. If you do what **people** tell you, you will be fishing hares in the sea and hunting fish in the woods.
278. He who mixes himself with bran will be eaten by **pigs.**
279. If there is in the **plate** there will be in the spoon.
280. For one moment of **pleasure,** a thousand days of sorrow.
281. The **plough** and the hoe feed the world.
282. Whatsoever is given to the **poor** is not lost.
283. When the sea turned into honey, the **poor man** lost his spoon.
284. An old **pot** boils tasty broth.
285. The **pot** rolled and found its lid. (*Marriage proverb.*)
286. **Poverty** and scheming are twin sisters.
287. If **power** is violent it is not long-lasting.
288. If you are looking for the **priest,** enquire from the innkeeper, not the sexton.
289. **Profit** gives no headache.
290. From the **promise** to the deed is a day's journey.
291. If we are brothers, our **purses** are not sisters.
292. The wider you prick out the **radishes** the larger they grow.
293. If **rats** have enough food, the boat will sail safely into the harbour.
294. The **raven** does not croak in vain.
295. **A raven** does not pluck the eyes out of a brother raven.
296. **Riches** do not buy health, yet they take health away.
297. No **riches** without health.
298. The less **riches** you accumulate the less sorrow you inflict on others.
299. **Righteousness** wears out but never wears through.
300. A small **river** comes sooner to the sea than a great one.
301. Who comes out of a **river** fears no rain.
302. He who flees keeps to one **road**; the pursuers one hundred.
303. There is more **sailing** along the coast than on the high sea.
304. The oversaintly **saint** is not pleasing even unto God.
305. The smaller **saints** will be the ruin of God.
306. Do not **salt** other people's food.
307. Make a bond with **Satan** too, while the bridge is under you.
308. The **satiated** does not believe the hungry.
309. To the **sea** for a brother; through the sea for a sweetheart.
310. 'Tis better to **see** than to hear.
311. Man is ever **self-forgiving.**
312. He who cannot **serve** cannot rule.
313. If you **serve** you will be served.
314. God does not **shave**—why should I?

315. Become a **sheep** and you will see the wolf.
316. The **sick** are asked, the healthy are offered.
317. With **silence** one irritates the devil.
318. Who lives in **sin** is buried alive.
319. Call him "**sir**" and please him.
320. You may **sit** crookedly, but judge rightly.
321. The **slaughter-house** kills the city man, the law-courts the peasant.
322. The **snake** is always cold; alive or dead.
323. The **snake** is tortuous only while creeping to her hole, but straight when inside.
324. A married **son** is but a neighbour.
325. A **son-in-law** is as honey, a son as wormwood.
326. **Song** has no master.
327. The **song** has no owner.
328. He who fears **sparrows** never sows millet.
329. Whatsoever the mother **spins,** the daughter weaves.
330. **Spinsterhood** is far worse than life in bad wedlock.
331. When the **stallions** kick each other, the donkeys feed on better hay.
332. **Steeds** kick; asses pull.
333. A **stick** is not felt after a cudgel.
334. One **stick** is sufficient for a cart of pottery.
335. A **stone** cannot shelter.
336. Do not throw **stones** into thin mud.
337. **Strangers** forgive—parents forget.
338. Consider a **stranger's** head your relative's feet.
339. Do not go with a large basket for overpraised **strawberries.**
340. If a man be **struck** once, people say he was thrashed.
341. Who knows much will **suffer** much.
342. Ask the **sufferer,** not the wanderer.
343. If the **summer** gave nothing, neither will the autumn.
344. Short **supper**—long life.
345. The best **swimmers** are drowned.
346. Where there are many **tails** there are few heads.
347. Where it is **thinnest,** there it tears.

    [Said mostly when a poor man loses his last coin.]

348. **Thrash** your fur coat, and it will keep you warmer; your wife, and you will love her more dearly.
349. The **tongue** always goes to the aching tooth.
350. A head with a **tongue** is more costly.
351. Without **tools** there is no handicraft.
352. Even the king's **treasury** comes to an end.
353. How can there be a forest without a crooked **tree?**
354. While a **tree** is young you may bend it at will.
355. First look at the **tree,** then sit beneath it.
356. Only young **trees** may be bent.
357. One **trouble** bears another.
358. **Trouble** is not trouble when it brings no other troubles.
359. Children, imbeciles, and drunkards speak the **truth.**
360. Where there is **union** a bullet can swim.
361. The **victor** feels no fatigue.
362. A **village** is known by its roads.
363. When you see a **village** with nine houses and ten inns, flee from it.
364. Sharp **vinegar** corrodes its own container.
365. Fear keeps the **vineyard.**
366. The **vineyard** needs no prayer, but a hoe.
367. From **walking** — something; from sitting—nothing.

368. He who **walks** slowly goes far.
369. If you saw gipsies you would admit that the **Wallachs** are men.
370. The **ware** speaks for itself.
371. **Wares** do not make a rubbish-heap.
372. **Water** may slumber, but not the enemy.
373. Clear **water,** peaceful mind.
374. As long as a man is healthy, even **water** will be a tasty beverage.
375. **Water** will run where it ran before.
376. Still **waters** sap the banks.
377. The **weak man** gets strong, the strong man dies.
378. As the **weaving** is begun, so will it end.
379. To a **wedding** wait to be invited ; to a funeral go uninvited.
380. The **whetstone** does not cut, but makes the knife cut.
381. He who takes the **whistler's** hint needs not a drum.
382. Even the skirt of a **widow** is her enemy.
383. Trust your bitch sooner than your pretty **wife.**
384. He who beats his oxen beats his purse, but he who beats his **wife** beats his head.
385. You may show your gun, your horse and your **wife,** but do not lend either.
386. The **wife** carries her husband on her face ; the husband carries his wife on his linen.
387. An aproned **wife** has no time to be bad.
388. Pretty **wife,** old wine—many friends.
389. My first **wife** was my wife ; the second—my ruler ; the third—my ikon.
390. Thrash the **wild,** he will be wilder.
391. From whatever side the **wind** blows, from that side the " Yapand jack " is lifted.

   [" Yapand jack " is a heavy hooded cape in white and brown stripes that the peasants wear in winter and cold weather.]
392. If you wish to know where there is good **wine,** enquire where the priests and monks go.
393. If **winter** does not bite you with its mouth it will whip you with its tail.

   [March and April may be very cold in the Balkans.]
394. Everybody has a pennyworth of **wisdom.**
395. Dip your tongue in **wisdom,** then give counsel.
396. Do not measure the tail of a live **wolf.**
397. The gorged **wolf** does more mischief.
398. Toothless **wolf**—dog's laughing-stock.
399. Who calls one **wolf** invites a pack.
400. Consider your opponent a **wolf,** not a lamb.
401. He who sees the **wolf,** shouts ; he who sees him not, shouts twice.
402. The **wolf** will eat even counted and ear-marked sheep.
403. No bones stay in a **wolf's** lair.
404. When with **wolves,** howl and devour !
405. A petted **woman** does not spin.
406. A house without a **woman** is a well without a pail.
407. A **woman** keeps secret only her age and what she does not know.
408. **Woman** opens up a home but does not close it down.
409. Beat a **woman** to drive the seven devils out of her.
410. The pretty **woman** wants three husbands : one rich, to support her ; one handsome, to love her ; one brigand, to beat her.
411. A **woman** without a husband is a horse without a bit.
412. Do not trust the winter sun or a **woman's** heart.
413. If **women** did not sin, there would be no priests to confess them.

414. Water and **women** go as you direct them.

415. If Mr. "**Won't**" will not, Mr. "Will" will.

416. Out of one piece of **wood**: a fan and an ikon.

417. With dry **wood,** the green also burns.

[i.e. the righteous pay for sinners.]

418. When a **wool merchant** speaks of sheep he means cloth.

419. A **word** is no arrow, but it can pierce the heart.

420. A gentle **word** opens an iron gate.

421. A good **word** travels far, a bad one farther.

422. He who breaks his **word** will by it be broken.

423. **Words** have no boundaries.

424. Do not enquire about a man, look at his **work.**

425. **Work** as though you will live a hundred years; think as though you will die to-morrow.

426. Hasty **work,** double work.

427. Every **work** dreads its master.

428. **Work** for the living and please the dead.

429. **Work** without a man is lightning without rain.

430. Everyone cuts out with his own **yard-stick.**

431. A long dark night—the **year.**

432. With whom **you are**—such you are.

433. **Youth** has no boundaries—age has the grave.

434. There would be miracles if **youth** could know and age could do.

CHANNEL ISLANDS

GUERNSEY

1. Little by little the **bird** builds her nest.

2. When the **bushel** measure is full it runs over.

3. One must not make the crib before the **calf** is born.

4. There is always a spike of **corn** lacking in the sheaf.

5. There is no **faggot** but at last finds a band.

6. He is making a streak of **fat.**

[Said of a man prospering in his affairs. The allusion is to a pig being fattened.]

7. All that comes with the **flood** will return with the ebb.

8. The devil's **flour** turns to bran.

9. No one goes to cut **furze** without gloves.

10. He who **itches** scratches himself.

[i.e. the cap fits.]

11. An old **magpie** has more than one hole in her nest.

12. **Need** will make an old woman trot.

13. Precious **ointments** are in small boxes.

14. The little **pig** gets the big parsnip.

15. It is not they who **plough** nearest the hedge who are the richest.

16. Where you see their droppings you may expect to find **rabbits.**

17. To bind up two **sheaves** with one wisp.

18. A man who has not the sense to **speak** is still a wise man if he has the sense to hold his tongue.

19. It is the **tail** that is the hardest to flay.

20. If there were an "**un-marryer**" he would have more work to do than all the "marryers".

JERSEY

1. Better stretch the **arm** than the neck.
2. We call each other "**cousin**", for all Jersey people are cousins.
3. One can tell when a man has **drunk,** but one cannot tell when he is thirsty.
4. Who has **drunk,** will drink.
5. Fisherman **farmer,** lazy farmer; last beginner, poor harvester.
6. If one were young twice, one would be a **fool** but once.
7. When **girls** whistle the devil laughs outright.
8. Everyone knows his own home and the good **God** knows them all.
9. Many beasts eat **hay** and many more eat bread.
10. A good **housewife's skirt** is longer than her petticoat.
11. "Nearly" prevents a **lie.**
12. "Too **little**" is worth nothing, and that little is too much.
13. Old **loves** and dead embers are soon rekindled.
14. The **market** is not worth the candle.
15. The **mob's rage** does not last.
16. **Money** which circulates, accumulates.
17. What one has never seen and never will see, is a **mouse's nest** in a cat's ear. (*Common also in Guernsey and Brittany.*)
18. Mind your **pullets,** my cocks are abroad.
19. He is about to furl his **sails.** [Refers to a dying man.]
20. Hot **smoke** is better than cold wind.

CORSICAN

1. He who serves the **community** serves no one.
2. There is no worse **dog** than the one that won't bite.
3. There are two presents to be made to an **enemy**—hot shot or cold steel.
4. Every **fountain** goes down to the sea.
5. Beware of those crossed by **God.**
6. **Hunger** is one of the greatest enemies of man.
7. He who does **ill** thinks ill.
8. He who takes a step longer than his leg only accomplishes half his **journey.**
9. The **night** is the mother of advice.
10. **Rifle,** dagger, or flight.
11. He who goes to **sea** without biscuits returns without teeth.
12. It is better to be head of a **village** than the tail of a city.
13. Heaven has scattered on the earth twelve ounces of honesty and **woman** has picked up eleven.

CROATIAN

(Including Dalmatian)

1. Whatever you do not understand you **admire.**
2. Following God's commandments, he was reduced to **begging** in His name.
3. Even a **dog** refuses a dry bone. (*Dalmatian.*)
4. Children talk about what they are **doing**: old people about what they used to do; fools about what they ought to be doing; courageous people about what they want to do; the wise about what is meet to do.
5. One does not **eat** in front of fine houses.
6. **Flies** never alight on a boiling pot. (*Dalmatian.*)
7. **Four things** are more numerous than we think: our years, our debts, our enemies, and our faults.
8. God knows which **goat** has grown its horns.
9. Without **health** no one is rich.
10. **Hunger** has no eyes.
11. **Hunger,** labour, and sweat are the best herbs.
12. He who **kills** an innocent person is a hero; he who kills a knave is an assassin.
13. Grain by grain a **loaf**: stone by stone a castle. (*Dalmatian.*)
14. Without **money** one cannot go anywhere, not even to church.
15. Where **right** has no force, force becomes right willingly.
16. Two **soldiers,** nine captains.
17. **Speaking** much and doing little willingly inhabit the same house.
18. Whilst the **wise** philosophise fools live.

CURWALSH

1. The **apple** doesn't roll far from the tree.

   [i.e. as the father, so the son.]
2. He who goes with a **cripple** learns how to limp.
3. One **enemy** is too much, and a hundred friends too little.
4. The **eye** is bigger than the stomach.
5. **Mountains** stand still, but men meet.
6. **Stretch** yourself according to your coverlet.

CZECH, OR CHEH

(Including Bohemian)

1. You have either to **annoy** other people or suffer to be annoyed by them.
2. He who eats **apples** every day takes the doctor's bread away.
3. Since Adam, grey is the colour of the **ass.** (*Bohemian.*)
4. Confide in an **aunt** and the world will know.
5. If you catch hold of both **bank** sides, both will give way under your grip.
6. Do not blow into a **bear's** ear.
7. **Beer** is to be drunk, speech to be spoken.
8. The little **bees**—poverty's little cows.

   [Bees are to the poor what cows are to the rich.]
9. When a **beggar** gets on horseback the devil will not catch him up.
10. It is better not to **begin** than, having begun, to leave unfinished.
11. I **believe** in what I hold in my hand.
12. He who **believes** easily is easily deceived.
13. If a man desires another man's **belongings,** surely he is tired of his own.
14. An early **bird** hops far.
15. When the **bird** is being caught, nice songs are being sung for him.
16. Amongst the **blind** the one-eyed is a king.
17. A sackful of **boasting**—two of lies.
18. Cherish the **body,** harm the soul. (*Bohemian.*)
19. One does not know where his neighbour's **boot** pinches.
20. He who has not been given **brains** from above will not buy them at the apothecary's.
21. He who cannot cut the **bread** evenly cannot get on well with people.

    [Bread is highly prized and much eaten by the Slavs. A man's character is judged according to the way in which he treats and respects bread.]
22. He who goes for a day into the forest should take **bread** for a week. (*Bohemian.*)
23. **Bread** has everywhere two crusts.
24. There were three **brothers :** liar, thief, hanging.
25. He who **builds** by the wayside will have many critics.
26. **Buy** what you do not need—soon you will sell what you need.
27. One has never been filled with **cakes** which were sent by messengers.
28. He who has **cakes** will easily find a best man. (*Marriage proverb.*)
29. **A calf** went out and an **ox** came back.
30. It is easier to throw the load off the **cart** than to put it on.
31. Where there is a **Catherine** [a shrew] ten houses round about do not need a watchdog.

    [Catherines are supposed to be clever but difficult, just as Charleses.]
32. The **cat** makes sure whose chin it may lick.
33. The **cat** which does not catch mice, and the man who does not like to talk will both go hungry.
34. What is born of a **cat** will catch mice.
35. Accept even **chaff** and a sterile goat from him who pays badly.
36. It is a fine **chapel,** but without Saints. (*Bohemian.*)

37. The **chemist's shop** is an expensive kitchen.
38. First **chew** and then spit.
39. Not even a **chicken** digs for nothing.
40. Peculiar people's **children** are usually failures.
41. Small **children** eat porridge, big ones eat their parents' hearts.
42. Small **children** stamp on your lap, big ones on your heart.
43. **Children**—steps to heaven.
44. If there were no **children,** there would be no tears. (*Bohemian.*)
45. There is no **church** in which there is no sermon.

    [Said about husband and wife scolding each other.]
46. Who does not know the **church,** worships an oven [any common object].
47. It is an unhappy house where the **cock** is silent and the hen crows.
48. When the **cook** dies of hunger he should be buried under the hearthstone. (*Bohemian.*)
49. Two, **counsel** ; three, treason.
50. Even a **coward** pursues him who runs away.
51. Nothing seems expensive on **credit.**
52. He who participates is called to account with the actual **criminal.** (*Bohemian.*)
53. **Cry** or not, it is all the same.
54. Even the coat trembles on the **culprit.**
55. **Custom** is rust that mocks at every file. (*Bohemian.*)
56. It is easy to play a tune for him who feels like **dancing.**
57. Comb your **daughter's** hair until she is twelve, safeguard her until she is sixteen, after sixteen say " thank you " to whomsoever will wed her [take her off your hands].
58. He who has **daughters** has a family, and he who has sons has strangers.
59. **Death** alone measures equally.
60. Better go to bed without supper than to live with **debts.**
61. Unpaid **debts** are unforgiven sins. (*Bohemian.*)
62. Our **debts** eat with us from one dish.
63. The **devil** took the offerings, but the altar remains.
64. He who draws a **devil** upon a wall, draws his own likeness.
65. He who **dies** from fears is not worth a place in the churchyard.
66. Where the sun never comes, the **doctor** comes often.
67. Woe to the sick person when the **doctor** has to collect his fees from the tomb. (*Bohemian.*)
68. Many **doctors**—death accomplished.
69. It is enough to show a whip to a beaten **dog.**
70. He who goes to sleep with **dogs** will get up with fleas.
71. When a **donkey** is well off he goes dancing on ice.
72. **Doubts** mean losing half of one's case beforehand.
73. If you do not **drive** in sleet to the woods, singing, you have to drive crying.
74. Drink yourself **drunk,** and within one night you will commit all the sins there are.
75. At a strange table, **eat** what they give you ; at home, what you have.
76. The way one **eats,** in that way one works.
77. He who **economises** has as much as three others.
78. Everyone rakes the **embers** under his own pipkin. (*Bohemian.*)
79. **Example** is a great orator.
80. **Experience**—master-man.
81. He who cannot see with his **eyes** will have to see with his purse.
82. A clean **face** needs no water. (*Bohemian.*)
83. The **farmer's** footprints make the field fertile.

84. The first **fault** prepares the bench for the second.

85. Don't praise the **feast** until you are going home.

86. **Fencing** and tricks are no use against a pommel.

87. The lords are going to have a **fight** : farmers, lend your hair !

88. The **fish** does not go after the hook, but after the bait.

89. Who sits on the **floor,** is not afraid of a fall.

90. The **fly** stings most when dying.

91. If the **fool** knew how to be silent he could sit amongst the wise.

92. The **fool** never undertakes little.

93. **Foolishness** grows by itself—no need to sow it.

94. A brazen **forehead** is better than a small estate.

95. The strong wipes his **forehead** ; the wily his mouth.

96. Correct your **friend** secretly and praise him publicly.

97. **Friend** to everybody, true to nobody.

98. Many a **friend** was lost through a joke, but none has ever been gained so.

99. Select your **friend** with a silk-gloved hand and hold him with an iron gauntlet.

100. Frequent reckoning makes good **friends.**

101. Do not protect yourself by a fence, but rather by **friends.**

102. Blessed is the man who has **friends,** but woe to him who needs them.

103. May God rid me of my **friends,** I can rid myself of my enemies.

104. Compliance brings **friends** ; truthfulness, hatred.

105. The first **gain** is the bait that hides the hook. (*Bohemian.*)

106. He who eats **garlic** and butter need fear no poison. (*Bohemian.*)

107. I am a **gentleman,** you are a gentleman ; who is going to mind the swine ?

108. Gentlemen do not want to **give** too much, and are ashamed to give little.

109. **Give** with discretion, accept with memory.

110. If the **goat** had a longer tail it would sweep stars with it.

111. It is enough to have one **God,** but not only one friend.

112. **God** did not give us a tongue only for tasting. (*Bohemian.*)

113. Everything in time, and **God** for ever.

114. **God** gave us teeth, He will also give us bread.

115. **God** gives, but not a letter and seal. (*Bohemian.*)

116. **God** gives the grain, but we must make the furrow. (*Bohemian.*)

117. **God** has more than He has given away.

118. He to whom **God** has shown a treasure must dig it out. (*Bohemian.*)

119. **God** helps the navigator, but on condition that he rows. (*Bohemian.*)

120. **God** is high up above, the king far away—there is but little truth and righteousness in the world : one has only to wrap up one's head and wait for death.

121. **God** repays for thankless people.

122. He who throws away **gold** is often compelled to pick up copper. (*Bohemian.*)

123. Oats make the horse, beer makes the hero, and **gold** makes the gentleman. (*Bohemian.*)

124. A good man grows **grey,** a rascal grows bald.

125. Hold the **grosh** [shilling] lest the ducat runs away.

126. A **guest** in the house—God in the house.

127. After three days, fish and a **guest** who tarries become odious.

128. **Habit** has an iron shirt.

129. **Habit** is a suit of iron and he who takes it off hurts himself. (*Bohemian.*)

130. Even a **hair** has a shadow.
131. One **hand** washes another.
132. One does not need to show the way to an old **hare.** (*Bohemian.*)
133. A live head will gain a **hat.**
134. What we **hate,** clings to us; what we like, does not want us.
135. One should listen to people more with one's **head** than with one's ears. (*Bohemian.*)
136. Suffer, my **head**; that is why thou art made of bones!
137. **Health** comes from the heart and illness goes to the heart.
138. He who only looks at **heaven** may easily break his nose on the earth. (*Bohemian.*)
139. The **he-goat** is hard to milk.
140. Do not set a fool over the **herrings.**

 [Herrings were the only sea fish that used to be imported.]
141. **Hope** is a good breakfast but a poor supper.
142. Praise a **horse** after a month and a woman after a year.
143. A good **horse** finds a buyer even if it stops in the stable; a bad one has to be taken to fairs.
144. A weary **horse** finds even his own tail a burden.
145. The **horse** has four feet and yet it falters.
146. The **horse** is once a foal; man is a child twice in his lifetime.
147. The **horse** which earns the oats eats the least of it.
148. Do not buy a **horse** with your ears, but with your eyes.
149. One's own **house** is both heaven and hell.
150. Do not trust a **Hungarian** unless he has a third eye on his forehead.
151. **Hunger** is a creditor from whom one cannot escape. (*Bohemian.*)
152. **Idleness**—the devil's pet cushion.
153. **Ignorance** is an ungrateful guest. (*Bohemian.*)
154. **Illness** comes by many roads but always uninvited. (*Bohemian.*)
155. The lord's **illness** is the poor people's health.
156. A **joke** ought to have sheep's teeth, not a dog's.
157. One often goes to the **judge** in the right and comes away in the wrong. (*Bohemian.*)
158. Do not **jump** high under a low ceiling.
159. Even **kings** bow at the threshold.
160. The warm **kitchen** never lacks flies. (*Bohemian.*)
161. Warm **kitchen,** warm friends.
162. He who places his **ladder** too steeply will easily fall backwards.
163. As long as the **language** lives the nation is not dead. (*Bohemian.*)
164. The **law** has a nose of wax.
165. The **law** is like a cobweb; a beetle breaks through, but a fly is caught.
166. **Laws** without penalties are bells without clappers. (*Bohemian.*)
167. **Learning** is a bitter root, but it bears sweet fruit. (*Bohemian.*)
168. It is easy to beat the drum covered with another's **leather.**
169. It is a good thing to cut a wide kuze [strap] off someone else's **leather.**

 [Kuze means not only leather, hide, fur, etc., but also the skin of the human body.]
170. **Leisure** is the mother of sins and the stepmother of virtues.
171. **A liar** ought to lie with memory.
172. It is easy to **lie** if you have come from afar.
173. You can go all through the country with a **lie,** but if you are found out, how are you going to travel back?
174. Better a **lie** that heals than a truth that wounds. (*Bohemian.*)
175. There are three roads in **life;** ingress, egress, and progress. (*Bohemian.*)
176. Don't be a **lion** in your own home. (*Bohemian.*)

177. Where the **lion's skin** cannot go through, put on a foxskin.
178. **A loan** often comes home crying.
179. He who wants to become quickly a **lord** will be a valet for a long time.
180. An old **love** does not grow rusty, but a new one strangles the devil.
181. **Love** drives out fear. (*Bohemian.*)
182. When **love** grows cold the legs grow old. (*Bohemian.*)
183. The **magpie** cannot leave off jumping.
184. Beware of **marked** people.
[Said of the squint-eyed, those with a hare lip, lameness, etc., who are considered unreliable in character or temperament.]
185. To the **market** without money, home without salt.
186. A timely **marriage** is like getting up at the right time.
187. He who **marries** might be sorry ; he who does not will be sorry.
188. He who would **marry** should make more use of his ears than his eyes. (*Bohemian.*)
189. **Marry** your son when you wish, your daughter when you can.
190. The house does not make the **master,** but the master makes the house. (*Bohemian.*)
191. Two are **master** for one ; three, a whole army.
192. The roof, the gutter, and the ridge know when a new **master** has come.
193. A **master** ought to be a buckle for the good and a hammer for the bad.
194. **Measure** twice, cut once.
195. **Meat** twice cooked and a friend twice reconciled are hardly ever good.
196. When we are **merriest,** it is best to leave and drive home.
197. Better to have a handful of **might** than a bag of justice.
198. As many **millers,** so many bushels—as many parsons, so many creeds.
199. A **miser** is like a sow, useful only when dead.
200. Happy is he who repents by another's **misfortune.**
201. **Misfortunes** always come in at the door that is left open for them. (*Bohemian.*)
202. **Misfortunes** find their way even on the darkest night. (*Bohemian.*)
203. **Money** is a master everywhere.
204. Promise for your **neighbour** and pay out of your own pocket.
205. If you do not know what your birth and life are worth, make your **neighbour** angry, he will soon tell you.
206. He who has **a good neighbour** can sell his house a hundred pounds dearer.
207. Our own sacred—**neighbour's** more sacred.
208. He who has **nothing** wants something, and he who has something wants everything.
209. Be an **old man** when you are young, so that you can be a young boy in your old age.
210. Sheltered by a wall, even an **old woman** becomes courageous.
211. The **ox** is caught by its horns, man by his tongue.
212. You must sometimes **pass by** and sometimes roll up.
213. The inexperienced **physician** makes a humpy churchyard.
214. Live with reason and you will live without **physicians.**
215. Tell it to the **pig,** and the pig will tell it to the boar, and the boar will tell it to the forest. (*Bohemian.*)
216. It is easy to make **pipes** sitting amongst bulrushes.
217. **Politeness** pleases even a cat.
218. The **poor** are heaven's messengers. (*Bohemian.*)
219. Rarely a man is **poor** for nothing.
220. The **poor man** has only one sickness, the rich man a hundred. (*Bohemian.*)

221. One cannot possibly be a **poor man** if one's wife is dying and one's horses standing in the stable.
222. He who scalded his lips with **porridge** blows upon whey.
223. He who **postpones** is worse than the lazy.
224. **Poverty** is safe, and therefore happy.
225. Do not **praise** a day before sunset, a horse before a year, and a wife before she is dead.
226. **Praise** is a spur to the good, a thorn to the evil. (*Bohemian.*)
227. If you **pull,** they will goad you.
228. Who is unable to pay with his **purse** has to pay with his back.
    [i.e. work or get beaten.]
229. Hi! all common things, step aside—the **rag** is driving hither!
230. Morning **rain** and an evening contract are both unstable.
231. Not even God is sorry for him who gets drenched by **rain** sitting at home.
232. A good **remembrance** lasts long, a bad one still longer.
233. Do not wait for a **reward** for good, the reward for ill will not miss you.
234. A pocketful of **right** needs a pocketful of gold. (*Bohemian.*)
235. All the **rivers** do what they can for the sea. (*Bohemian.*)
236. Not even a hundred **robbers** can rob him who is naked.
237. Not all whose heels tread round the church are **saints.**
238. It is easy for the **satiated** man to fast.
239. He who licks the **saucepans** at home will not be killed in battle.
240. He who goes seeking other people's **sausages** often loses his own ham. (*Bohemian.*)
241. " Mr. Oh-dear " put his **savings** aside, and " Mr. Hurrah " spent them.
242. Do not **scratch** where it does not itch, and do not pull a dog's tail when he is asleep.
243. The **seats** in heaven which are prepared for good guardians are still vacant.
244. Who praises would like to **sell**; who disparages would like to buy.
245. Who wishes to be as poor as a dog, let him rely upon his **servants.**
246. **Service** is no heritage. (*Bohemian.*)
247. Thick **service**—thin shirt.
248. Where **sheep** are lacking, the goats are honoured. (*Bohemian.*)
249. With **silence** you can turn whichever way you wish.
250. Each **sin** has its own excuse.
251. For others' **sins** we have the eyes of a lynx, for our own the eyes of a mole. (*Bohemian.*)
252. Our neighbour's **sins** we keep in front of our nose, but our own behind our back.
253. He tucks up other people's **skirts** but trails his own.
254. The net of him who **sleeps** catches. (*Bohemian.*)
255. Better one's own **slice** than a strange loaf.
256. A good roast **smells** far, and a nasty one still farther.
257. You have to suffer **smoke** in order to keep warm.
258. When a **snake** gets warm on ice, then a German will wish well to a Czech.
259. A good **song** may be sung three times. (*Bohemian.*)
260. The **soup** at the Court is very good, but you have to jump high for it.
261. The **sow,** when washed, returns to the muck.
262. Father and mother have taught us how to **speak,** and the world how to keep quiet.
263. The **spendthrift** becomes a beggar, but the miser is always one. (*Bohemian.*)
264. When I have had enough I will lend you my **spoon.**

265. The **spoon** is prized when the soup is being eaten. (*Bohemian.*)

266. Not he who **steals** is hanged, but he who is caught stealing. (*Bohemian.*)

267. Good **stick**—a good cause.

268. An empty **stomach** is shameless, a full one still more so.

269. The **swallow** carries spring on its wings. (*Bohemian.*)

270. It is difficult to catch by the **tail** if you have let the horns go.

271. Where the **tail's** advice is taken, the head loses its way.

272. **Temperance** does not show in need, but at a banquet.

273. A **thief** catches most in crowds, and the devil in solitary places.

274. When a **thief** is ripe for punishment, even a lame beadle will catch him.

275. Three scores of millers, three scores of weavers, and three scores of tailors makes three three-scores of **thieves.**

276. Big **thieves** hang little ones.

277. It is **time,** not the comb, that makes men bald. (*Bohemian.*)

278. A whipped **tom-cat** is good.

279. The **tongue** is boneless, but it breaks bones.

[An allusion to mediæval times when wheels were used for breaking bones of criminals.]

280. Long **tongue**—short hands.

281. I do not want to be one **too many** where I am not missed when absent.

282. **Trade** has a golden bottom.

283. Nine **trades**—misery the tenth.

284. Suffer **tribulation** willingly when you are young and you will not have to suffer misery against your will when you are old.

285. Not every opinion is **truth.** (*Bohemian.*)

286. **Truth** breaks the head, prayer breaks heaven.

287. If a person is not good-looking at **twenty,** strong at thirty, rich at forty and wise at fifty, he will never become so.

288. **Violets** and lilies do not blossom always.

289. There have been few **wars** which did not originate through priests or women.

290. A **wedding** lasts a day or two, but the misery for ever.

291. One's **welcome** is measured by one's coat; one's farewell by one's merits.

292. Do not spit into a **well,** you do not know when you will drink out of it yourself.

293. Do not choose your **wife** at a dance, but on the field amongst the harvesters.

294. Take a **wife** from near, but steal from afar.

295. Young **wife,** old husband—children a certainty; old wife, young husband—beating a certainty.

296. Smoke, a leaking roof, and a nagging **wife**—these three drive the farmer away from his house.

297. The time will come when **winter** will ask us: "What were you doing all the summer?" (*Bohemian.*)

298. Too much **wisdom** does not produce courage.

299. **Wisdom** is easy to carry but difficult to load. (*Bohemian.*)

300. You may christen a **wolf** and he will ask "Which way to the wood?"

301. You cannot out-bark a dog, out-crow a crow, or out-quarrel a **woman.**

302. A house without a **woman** is a meadow without dew. (*Bohemian.*)

303. When a **woman** is lazy in her house, the servants work with their mouths. (*Bohemian.*)

304. Where a **woman** whistles, seven churches tremble.

305. Heaven save us from a **woman** who is already good.

306. Early rain and a **woman's tears** are soon over.

307. A **word** which flew out of the mouth like a sparrow cannot be drawn back, even by four **horses.**

308. He who is busy with **work** cares little for news.

309. The **world** does not lead to Hell nor the convent to Paradise. (*Bohemian.*)

310. As the thing is cut and sewn, so it must be **worn.**

311. **Young people** and dogs take many useless steps in an hour. (*Bohemian.*)

DANISH

1. **Adam** took a spade and Eve a distaff, and from them come all our nobility.

2. Good **advice** is no better than bad advice unless it is taken at the right time.

3. **Age** is a sorry travelling companion.

4. Give **alms** that thy children may not ask them.

5. **Ambition** and revenge always die of hunger.

6. No **answer** is also an answer.

7. When the **arm** bends the mouth opens.

8. **Asses** only come to court to carry sacks.

9. **Authority** compels not to do good, but prevents from doing ill.

10. If **authority** has no ears to listen it has no head to govern.

11. It often feels heavy on one's **back** what one takes lightly on one's conscience.

12. Being a **baker** is poor work if your head is made of butter.

13. If the **beard** were all, goats might preach.

14. He who will not tend his own **beasts** comes to clearing away the dung from under another's.

15. Better thin **beer** than an empty jug.

16. He who knows how to **beg** may leave his money at home.

17. There is no order so numerous as that of a **beggar.**

18. When it rains porridge the **beggar** has no spoon.

19. A good example is like a **bell** that calls many to Church.

20. The **belly** gives no credit.

21. If a **bird** knew how poor it was it would not sing so sweetly.

22. Every **bird** needs its own feathers.

23. **Blame** is the lazy man's wages.

24. The nobler the **blood,** the less the pride.

25. The **branch** is seldom better than the stem.

26. **Bread** eaten in advance makes lazy workers and bad payers.

27. The child gives away little who eats the **bread** he has used as a plate.

[Old custom to use a square of bread for a plate.]

28. When the **bread** is eaten the kindness is not forgotten.

29. **Bridals** for young, barrows for old.

30. One must **build** with the stones one has.

31. There would be no **calumny** if it were not listened to.

32. You may light another's **candle** at your own without loss.

33. Many have good **cards** in their hands if they only knew how to play them.

34. It is better to be in an old **carriage** than in a new ship.

35. If all drive in the **cart** who will sit on the box [seat] ?

36. He who eats **cherries** with his superiors will have the pips thrown in his face.
37. He who takes the **child** by the hand takes the mother by the heart.
38. A scurfy **child** must needs be combed.
39. Little **children,** little sorrows; big children, big sorrows.
40. A long **cloak** and one's own house can cover much.
41. Many people are like **clocks,** they show one hour and strike another.
42. **Clothes** do not damn, neither do they sanctify.
43. The **cock** often crows without a victory.
44. A clear **conscience** is the best guest of the house.
45. Alone in **counsel,** alone in sorrow.
46. One should take one's own **cow** by the tail [when it has to be pulled out of the mud.]
47. **Credit** helps many up but also many down.
48. That which is to be **crooked** must be bent early.
49. Even **crumbs** are bread.
50. Follow the **customs** or fly the country.
51. A good **day** and a bad day are equally long when they are over, but it is not equally easy to get to the end.
52. Don't judge the **day** from its coat.
53. One **day** teaches another.
54. The **day** that passes with joy doesn't return with sorrow.
55. **Death** does not blow a trumpet.
56. **Death** is a dying man's friend.
57. Where the **debtor** sits is a dear place.
58. Of bad **debtors** you may take spoilt herrings.
59. That which is **desired** by many is owned by few.
60. Where something good blooms the **Devil** puts a worm underneath.
61. He who would eat from another man's **dish** rarely gets anything on his own.
62. Fresh air impoverishes the **doctor.**
63. A house closed to the poor will open to the **doctor.**
64. He who makes himself a **dog** must gnaw bones.
65. The **door** has the hardest job of the house.
66. Shut your **door** in such a way that you can open it again.
67. When one **door** shuts another opens.
68. As the man goes to the **door** so he is indoors.
69. A man does not look behind the **door** unless he has been there himself.
70. Better **drink** from a beaker than from bent palms.

    [i.e. Men weary from wayfaring found it easier to take up the water in a goblet than in the palms.]
71. A **drunken man** is either a lamb or a pig, a monkey or a lion.
72. You cannot distinguish between a **drunken man** and a mad man until they have slept.
73. One must walk a long time behind a wild **duck** before one picks up an ostrich feather.
74. Something is sometimes whispered in the **ear** and heard all over the town.
75. One learns more with one's **ears** than with one's eyes.
76. Don't lend your **ears** to him who would lend you his tongue.
77. We have to walk the **earth** even if it is red-hot.
78. The better the **earth,** the worse the road; the better the land, the worse the people.
79. What you **eat** out of the pot you won't get in the spoon.
80. He who **eats** when he should fast shall fast when he should eat.
81. He cannot lay **eggs,** but he can cackle.

82. If you lay **eggs** in nettles you must take them out yourself.
83. One's own **embers** are sweet, therefore many little houses smoke.
84. Though the **enemy** be only like an ant, yet regard him like an elephant.
85. For the beaten **enemy** build a golden bridge.
86. The **envious** thinks that he can walk better when his neighbour has broken his leg.
87. **Envy** is an early riser.
88. An old **error** has more friends than a new truth.
89. It is only when **evil** is outside that good can come into the house.
90. He who feeds on **expectation** risks dying of hunger.
91. He who does not open his **eyes** when he buys must open his purse when he pays.
92. It is not hard for a person [a monk] to **fast** when he finds fish on his plate.
93. Long **fasting** is not bread saving.
94. If everyone understood his own **faults** he would not notice another's.
95. Things never go so well that one should have no **fear,** and never so ill that one should have no hope.
96. He who **fears** finds a way out.
97. He that can sit upon a stone and **feed** himself should not move.
98. Every little **fish** expects to become a whale.
99. It is easy to poke another man's **fire.**
100. **Fire** and water are good servants but bad masters.
101. Many kindle the **fire** at which others warm themselves.
102. **Fire** often comes into the mocker's house.
103. One should not light a **fire** unless one wants to cook.
104. The **flame** is not far from the smoke.
105. No one has greater liberty than the **fly,** which settles even on the nose of the king.
106. **Food** tastes best when one eats it with one's own spoon.
107. A **fool** always wins the first game.
108. Praise a **fool** and you make him useful.
109. Everyone wants to find a **fool** but not to feed him.
110. If you praise the **fool** he will grow ass's ears.
111. A **fool** is like other folk when he is silent.
112. If a **fool** lay hold of you, cut off a piece [of your coat] and let him go.
113. He who would make a **fool** of himself finds many to help him.
114. When **fools** come in the village is rich.
115. **Fools** need no passport.
116. Never let **fools** see half-finished work.
117. The **forge** that does not send its smoke away soon turns black.
118. If you would catch a **fox** you must hunt with geese.
119. Keep your mouth and keep your **friend.**
120. Lend to your **friend** and ask payment of your enemy.
121. Everybody's **friend** is everybody's fool.
122. Tell nothing to thy **friend** that thine enemy may not know.
123. To a **friend's** house the road is never long.
124. If you would warm your **friends** you must rake up the fire.
125. Diffidence is the poison of **friendship.**
126. Where gifts are paid for **friendship** has feet of clay.
127. In the division of the inheritance **friendship** standeth still.
128. He who clothes himself in another's **garments** is soon undressed.
129. **Gifts** make women condescending, priests indulgent, and the law crooked.

130. **Gifts** should be handed, not hurled.

131. He who returns to **give** loses the thanks.

132. So **give** to-day, that thou shalt be able to give to-morrow.

133. So **give** to one, that thou shalt have to give to another.

134. He who **gives** to me teaches me to give.

135. Move hand and foot so helps you **God.**

136. It is better to be given up by the doctor than to be given up by **God.**

137. It is good to lend to **God** and to the soil—they pay good interest.

138. **God** gives every bird its food, but does not throw it into the nest.

139. **God** knows who is the most pious pilgrim.

140. One limps towards **God**; one leaps towards the Devil.

141. Next to **God** 'tis best to rely on oneself.

142. He is nearest to **God** who needs the least.

143. **Good** becomes ill when it comes not at the right time.

144. A little **good** shall one set high.

145. A **goose** drinks as much as a gander.

146. Often comes a **guest** to the house and makes himself the master.

147. Fish and **guests** smell at three days old.

148. Badly cut **hair** is two men's shame.

149. Put your **hand** quickly to your hat and slowly in your purse, and you will take no harm.

150. It is not well to buy of those to whom you must take off your **hat.**

151. **Hate** and wealth are more easily hidden than love and poverty.

152. Let no one see what is in your **heart** and your purse.

153. One should have one's **heart** in the right place, neither in one's neck nor in one's trousers.

154. When there is room in the **heart** there is room in the house.

155. The curse on the **hearth** wounds the deepest.

156. The greatest **hero** is he who can overcome himself.

157. One often cuts broad straps from another's **hide.**

158. He who **holds** owns.

159. He who would stop up all **holes** stops up the useful as well as the harmful.

160. An **honest man** does not make himself a dog for the sake of a bone.

161. When our days run down hill **hope** becomes a memory and hopes become less.

162. **Hope** is the dream of the waking.

163. The **horse** one cannot have has always a fault.

164. Where the **horse** treads, the lobster wants to crawl too.

165. The morning **hour** has gold in its mouth.

166. He who builds according to every man's advice will have a crooked **house.**

167. An old **house** has dark windows.

168. Many build a **house** who are the first to leave it.

169. **Hunger** is a sharp sword in a healthy stomach.

170. He is nearest his **hurt** who sits farthest away from the dish.

171. He is nearest his **hurt** who sits longest amongst the few.

172. Shared **joy** is doubled joy.

173. When **joy** is in the parlour, sorrow is in the entry [hall].

174. **Joy** is like the ague, has one good day between two bad ones.

175. Nothing **kills** like doing nothing.

176. An impudent **knife** is always the first in the butter.

177. If one will climb a **ladder** one must begin at the lowest rung.

178. **Land** is ruled by lip, sea by hand.

179. Where **law** lacks, honour should eke it out.

180. With **law** must the land be built.

181. One goes to **law** with one case and returns home with two.

182. When a horse which has four **legs** may fall, how much more can a man who has only two.

183. It hurts one's **legs** to ride a wooden horse.

184. Don't snuff the **light** too close, otherwise you will burn your fingers.

185. Too **little** and too much spoils everything.

186. **Little folk** can have big hearts.

187. It is not easy to keep the **lock** fastened to which everyone has the key.

188. Better a wooden **lock** than an open door.

189. What is outwardly **lost** may be inwardly won.

190. Old **love** never rusts.

191. **Love** prefers the middle path.

192. **Luck** and ill luck are like buckets in a well, the one goes up and the other goes down.

193. **Luck** may carry a man across the brook if he will leap.

194. **Luck** stops at the door, and asks whether Prudence is in.

195. You must judge a **maiden** at the kneading-trough, not at the dance.

196. Many **marry** for money who only get the purse.

197. In **marrying** and sleighing one should look out whilst there is still time.

198. Don't throw small stones at your **master** for he will throw big ones at you.

199. Young **master**—old beggar.

200. A hungry **meal** drags another by the hair.

201. One would always **measure** folk with one's own ell.

202. Dull edge and point should only carve soft **meat.**

203. One can make **mid-day** when one will, the evening comes of itself.

204. The nether **millstone** also grinds.

205. **Misfortune** easily gets a little brother or sister.

206. To a poor man **mocking** is worse than injury.

207. All water hastens to the shore, and **money** to the rich man.

208. The longest road is from the **mother** to the front door.

209. Every man works only for his **mouth.**

210. It is no use to stand with an open **mouth** in front of an oven.

211. The **mouth** is the healer and executioner of the body.

212. If one would bind another's **mouth** one should first bind one's own.

213. " **Nearly** " and " next to " pull no man off his horse.

214. **Necessity** makes one inventive.

215. No one is rich enough to do without his **neighbour.**

216. Love your **neighbour,** but don't pull down the fence.

217. You cannot have peace longer than your **neighbour** chooses.

218. He who has a good **neighbour** has a good morning.

219. A good **neighbour** is better than a brother in the next village.

220. Diffidence and enmity are **neighbours.**

221. He shall praise himself who has bad **neighbours.**

222. There are three bad **neighbours :** great rivers, great lords, and great roads.

223. Two " **no's** " are better than one lie.

224. He must have clean fingers who would blow another's **nose.**

225. " **Nothing** " is good in the eye and ill in the stomach.

226. Let him stay at the **oar** who has learnt to row.

227. **Old** at home, old at the court.

228. **Old** at home, young in the cloister.

229. **Old age** is a bad travelling companion.

230. An **old man** laments a barren month's greenness.

231. An **old man's** sayings are seldom untrue.

232. **Opinion** leads the world by the nose.

233. You may always find an **opportunity** in your sleeve if you like.

234. One must plough with the **ox** one has.

235. The earthen **pan** gains nothing by contact with the copper pot.

236. **Paper** is patient.

237. He who sows **peas** on the highway doesn't get all the pods into the barn.

238. He who is minted a **penny** never becomes a shilling.

239. The ground is always frozen for lazy **pigs.**

240. He who mixes with clover is eaten by **pigs.**

241. **A pilgrimage** does not make a man a saint.

242. The best advice is found on the **pillow.**

243. Those who are farthest from the **plate** eat the most.

244. He who is too **pleasing** to himself is equally displeasing to others.

245. Between two **points** one cannot draw more than one straight line.

246. The **poor man** needs much, the miser needs everything.

247. Little **pots** soon boil over.

248. To always save is to always live in **poverty.**

249. **Poverty,** lice, and fleas come from oneself.

250. If you can keep yourself with **poverty** you have no need of riches.

251. From **praise,** as from a shadow, a man is neither bigger nor smaller.

252. **Praise** makes a good man better and a bad man worse.

253. It is good to be **priest** at Easter, child in Lent, peasant at Christmas, and fool in harvest-time.

254. If you leave your **property** to your children, let your good name be the chief part.

255. The heaviest burden on the road is an empty **purse.**

256. The **purse** is empty in which another man's gold lies.

257. Where the **purse** gapes the kitchen smokes.

258. A greedy **quern** mills all manner of corn.

259. **Rancour** chafes others but wounds itself.

260. One must have good fingers to pull up old **rancour** with the roots.

261. A **rat** is more devouring than time.

262. **Repentance** is a pill unwillingly swallowed.

263. **Riches** are often blamed but never rejected.

264. **Riches** breed care, poverty is safe.

265. It is better to **ride** than to drag.

266. When a man is in a **sack** he must either get out through the mouth or the bottom.

267. He who would **save** should begin with the mouth.

268. He who **saves** for to-morrow saves for the cat.

269. He who **says** all he knows doesn't know himself.

270. Not everything can be weighed in **scales.**

271. Often nine **secrets** should be kept to oneself and the tenth not revealed.

272. One often **seeks** that which one does not want.

273. **Shears** make a child blind, and a knife one-eyed.

274. One should not judge the **ship** before it has experienced the sea.

275. He who would make the hole under his nose bigger must wear patched **shoes.**
276. One's own **shoes** are the ones that pinch the most.
277. He that you seat upon your **shoulder** will often try to get upon your head.
278. A sincere **sigh** is better than a hypocritical prayer.
279. **Silence** is a beautiful jewel for a woman, but she wears it so seldom.
280. Nature gives speech, but **silence** teaches understanding.
281. **Slander** expires at a good woman's door.
282. **Slanderers** have the devil in their tongues, but listeners have him in their ears.
283. The man who does not know how hard his bed is **sleeps** best.
284. He who **sleeps** the red from the sun sleeps the fat from the cabbage.
285. One can see a patched **sleeve** but not a hungry gut.
286. **Sloth** gives nothing but lice and long nails.
287. He who is **small** for the big is big for the small.
288. **Smoke** and reputation follow a man to the door.
289. The **snail** carries its house with it because it distrusts its neighbour.
290. That which falls in the **snow** comes to light in the thaw.
291. Shared **sorrow** is only half sorrow.
292. **Sparrows'** food and horses' work go ill together.
293. One should **speak** little with others and much with oneself.
294. It is better to use **spectacles** yourself than for others to put them on for you.
295. Chop, and you will have **splinters.**
296. From a fat **steak** drop fat drops.
297. The biggest **step** is that through the door.
298. The **stomach** has enough sooner than the eye.
299. A child's **stomach** is blind.
300. A full **stomach** never thinks it can be empty again.
301. He who sits on a **stone** is twice rested.
302. One must build with the **stones** one has.
303. There is no one so long that he must not **stretch** himself, and no one so short he must not bend.
304. We must **suffer** much, or die young.
305. He who would not **sweat** in the summer must learn to freeze in the winter.
306. He is worthy of **sweet** who has tasted of bitter.
307. When the **sword** is in the mouth one must caress the scabbard.
308. A worn-out **sword** is two men's fear.
309. One **sword** keeps another in its scabbard.
310. No one can see in others further than the **teeth.**
311. The most difficult mountain to cross is the **threshold.**
312. **To-morrow** is another day.
313. There is nothing to choose between bad **tongues** and wicked ears.
314. He who would **travel** should shut his mouth and open his purse.
315. It is a good **trunk** where an axe grows at the end.
316. **Trust** helps many both up and down.
317. When **truth** and falsehood meet, falsehood suffers damage.
318. To tell the **truth** is dangerous, to listen to it is annoying.
319. A **truthteller** finds the doors closed against him.
320. He who would take **uncertainty** home loses certainty out of his cart.
321. Where a man is **unnamed** he is unknown.

322. Always to be sparing is always to be in **want.**
323. **Want** teaches naked women spinning.
324. Good **wares** sell themselves.
325. After an earner comes a **waster.**
326. If you will wade through all **waters** you will drown in the end.
327. He who **weeps** to-day because he has no bread, weeps to-morrow because he has no appetite.
328. The cross-roads are wide; blessed is **well-doing.**
329. Deep **wells** may likewise be emptied.
330. A comb and a razor deceive many a **wife.**
331. He who beats his **wife** beats his left hand with his right.
332. Have no greater desire to **win** than you have patience to lose.
333. **Wisdom** is the least burdensome travelling pack.
334. He who goes with **wolves** must know how to howl.
335. One would rather be bitten by **wolves** than by sheep.
336. If a bad man is like a devil, a bad **woman** is like an entire hell.
337. In a house the **woman** should be the left eye and you yourself the right.
338. The **woman** should wear the short knife and leave the long one to the man.
339. She is a foolish **woman** who blames her own cabbage.
340. He who would hide his money should not place it under a **woman's** tongue.
341. Three **women** and a goose make a market.
342. All **women** are good Lutherans, for they would rather preach than listen to Mass.
343. One should **work** as though one were going to live for ever, and be pious as though one might die any day.
344. **Work** half done should be neither praised nor blamed.
345. The **worm** consumes the nut, and the usurer the inhabitants of a town.
346. If you can't heal the **wound,** don't tear it open.
347. An old **wound** soon bleeds.
348. One should not heal one's own **wound** with other people's blood.
349. The **year** has a wide mouth and a big belly.

DUTCH

(Including Friesian, East Indian and Boer)

1. **Ability** and necessity dwell in the same cabin.
2. We are all sons of **Adam** excepting those who go in rags, and those who go in silk.
3. **Advisers** are not givers.
4. Street-**angel**—house-devil.
5. He bites through the sour **apple.**
6. Stretch your **arm** no further than your sleeve will reach.
7. By **asking** one learns.
8. Seven things oppress the **ass** and eight the driver.
9. Many call their neighbours **asses** and carry sacks themselves.
10. At the bottom of the **bag** one finds the bill.
11. When I go to **bed** I leave my troubles in my clothes.

12. A **bee** without a sting makes no honey.
13. The **Bible** is the book with golden letters.
14. **Blood** creeps where it cannot flow. (*Boer.*)
15. **Blossoms** are not fruits.
16. Other men's **books** are difficult to read.
17. Who plays at **bowls** must expect the ball returned.
18. Long fasting is no sparing of **bread.**
19. The nurse's **bread** is sweeter than the mother's cake. (*Friesian.*)
20. For want of **bread** one eats the crumbs of pastry.
21. One often eats so much white **bread** that one desires black.
22. She hangs out the **broom.**
    [i.e. waits a husband.]
23. To go slowly and to live a long time are two **brothers.**
24. He who **burns** himself must sit on the blisters.
25. Of what use is wisdom when the **butter** won't stick to the bread.
26. The third strand makes the **cable.**
27. Who wants the last drop out of the **can** gets the lid on his nose.
28. For the sake of the grease the **cat** licks the candlestick.
29. A **cat** that is locked up may change into a lion.
30. A **cat** which meweth loudly catcheth few mice.
    [Blowing your own trumpet.]
31. **Chats** don't fill gaps.
32. The world likes to be **cheated.**
33. Through diligence one sees the **chimney** smoke.
34. One should not ask the time of a rusty **clock.**
35. He has heard the **clock** chime but does not know where the pendulum is.
36. The **clock** ticks nowhere as it ticks at home.
37. Those that **complain** are not in need.
38. A bad **conscience** is accuser, judge, witness and hangman.
39. The Dutch hold the **cow**; the Chinese and Arabs milk it. (*East Indian.*)
40. If all **crosses** were put into a bundle everyone would seize his own.
41. He that bringeth himself into needless **dangers** dieth the devil's martyr.
42. **Darkness** and night are mothers of thought.
43. A diamond **daughter** turns to glass as a wife.
44. A house full of **daughters** is a cellar full of sour beer.
45. He who has **daughters** is always a shepherd.
46. Men can bear all things except good **days.**
47. Stone **dead** hath no fellow.
48. The thirteenth man brings **death.**
49. At the bottom of the **devil's** bag one always finds his bill.
50. He who shakes every man by the hand may be glad to fee the **doctor.**
51. A young **doctor** requires a big cemetery.
52. A good **doctor** should have a falcon's eye, a girl's hand, and a lion's heart.
53. A **door** must be open or closed.
54. Many open a **door** to shut a window.
55. He who would become a big **dragon** must first of all eat many little snakes.
56. One is easier run over by a **dung-cart** than a coach.
57. He who cannot build the **dyke** should hand over the land.
58. Fortunate is the man who has two **ears** that can open and shut.
59. Of little meddling comes great **ease.**
60. One may support anything better than too much **ease.**
61. Too far **east** is west.

62. Better be **embarrassed** by a thing than by the want of it.
63. The later in the **evening** the nicer the people.
64. " Nothing " is good in the **eyes** but bad in the stomach [purse, mouth].
65. To make a **family,** more is required than four legs under a table.
66. He who keeps a **fancy** must pay a tax for it.
67. By the end of market-day one learns to know the **farmer.**
68. A long **fast** saves no bread. (*Friesian.*)
69. Nothing in haste but catching **fleas.**
70. Much too good is half-way to **folly.**
71. **Folly** has the wings of an eagle and the eyes of an owl.
72. A white wall is a **fool's** writing-paper.
73. The **forbidden** is the motto of the wise man.
74. Must is **force.**
75. The usual end of a **fox** is the furrier's shop.
76. He who cannot do you good as a **friend** can do you harm as an enemy.
77. Your **friend** lends and your enemy asks payment.
78. When one **friend** washes another both become clean.
79. He who looks at people through his fingers has many **friends.**
80. One should keep old roads and old **friends.**
81. **Friends** are the nearest relations.
82. The **frog** jumps back to its puddle even when seated on a golden chair.
83. **Froth** is no beer.
84. He who has the **frying-pan** in his hand turns it at will.
85. First a turnip, then a sheep ; next a cow, and then the **gallows.**
86. Cultivate your own **garden.**
87. **Geese** are plucked as long as the feathers last.
88. There are only two things a **girl** chooses for herself—her potatoes and her lover.
89. Who **gives** to me teaches me to give.
90. **God** does not pay weekly, He pays at the end.
91. **God** gives birds their food, but they must fly for it.
92. **God** gives every bird its food but does not throw it into the nest.
93. **God** made the earth but the Dutch made Holland.
94. **God** made the sea but the Hollander made the land.
95. **God** sells knowledge for labour, honour for risk.
96. **God's** service hath sure walls.
97. Words of **gold** are often followed by deeds of lead.
98. He who looks fixedly at **gold** loses his sight.
99. He who would make a **golden-gate** must bring a nail daily.
100. Do **good** and don't look back.
101. He who dies not in his twenty-third year, drowns not in his twenty-fourth, and is not slain in his twenty-fifth, may boast of **good days.**
102. **Good things** need time.
103. With the **good** we become good.
104. A daily **guest** is a thief in the kitchen.
105. A **guest,** like a fish, stinks the third day.
106. God, what things a man sees when he goes out without a **gun !** (*Boer.*)
107. **Habit** hardens the feet.
108. 'Tis easier to throw away old shoes than old **habits.**
109. When " **had** " comes " have " is too late.
110. Thin **hands** make fat feet.
111. With the **hat** in the hand one can travel throughout the land.
112. If **hay** follows the horse it will be eaten.

113. The **heart** does not lie.
114. What is **heaviest** should weigh heaviest.
115. When it rains and the sun shines, then there is a fair in **hell.**
116. When the **hen** loses her feathers one knows out of which nest she has flown.
117. A **hen** will never crow. (*Boer.*)
118. During the cats' harvest **hens** are deaf.
119. **Hens** are free of horse corn.
120. There is no **heretic** who has not his belief.
121. **Herring** in the land, the doctor at a stand.
122. Where there is no fish **herring** is fish.
123. As the sun disperses fog, so **herrings** disperse maladies.
124. Whom you frequent you **honour.**
125. After **honour** and state follow envy and hate.
126. One cannot shoe a running **horse.**
127. The morning **hour** has gold in its mouth.
128. When one builds a new **house** friends give the window-frames.
129. He who builds a **house** is given the glass for the windows by his friends.
130. A new **house** should be lived in the first year by an enemy, the second by a friend, and the third by yourself.
131. **Hunger** shows itself at the door of the hard-working man, but dare not enter in.
132. What one does not know cannot **hurt.**
133. Who is too well off dances on **ice.**
134. An ounce of **illness** is felt more than an hundredweight of health.
135. The **impossible** requires no excuse.
136. The more naked the **jackal** the larger the tail. (*Boer.*)
137. He who is outside the door has already a good part of his **journey** behind him.
138. **June** walks with shoes of wool.
139. **Justice** looks no one in the face.
140. **Justice** often helps ill.
141. The **labour** we delight in physics pain.
142. He who has the like **ladders** reaches to the like windows.
143. After the **land's** manner is mannerly.
144. Need breaks **laws.**
145. A lean compromise is better than a fat **lawsuit.**
146. " Mine " and " thine " is the source of all **lawsuits.**
147. The better **lawyer,** the worse Christian.
148. **Laziness** goes so slowly that poverty overtakes it.
149. He who **learns** from others learns easily.
150. That which is good for the **legs** is bad for the boots.
151. A **lie** has short legs, truth overtakes it.
152. He does not **live** in this world who can skin a grindstone.
153. He who puts carelessly into the oven has a crooked **loaf.**
154. He has put by his last **loaf.**
    [i.e. is dead.]
155. Many toil hard to earn a **loaf** when a slice is sufficient.
156. He bakes little **loaves.**
157. Calf **love,** half love ; old love, cold love. (*Friesian.*)
158. Who writes **love-letters** grows thin ; who carries them fat.
159. Even if it were to rain gold a **lover** would never become rich.
160. Often he who afflicts **loves.**
161. It needs strong legs to carry **luxury.**
162. **A man,** a man ; a word, a word.
163. When the **market** breaks up one gets to know the merchants.
164. To **marry** once is a duty, twice is folly, and the third time madness.
165. One should not think about it too much when **marrying** and taking pills.

166. **Meal** clings to a new sack.
167. Long **meals,** like short prayers, are much beloved.
168. He is no **merchant** who always gains.
169. Where the **minute-hand** suffices the hour-hand is not required.
170. The end of **mirth** is the beginning of sorrow.
171. One **misfortune** carries another on its back. (*Friesian.*)
172. Who does not know how to squander his **money**—buy some porcelain and drop it.
173. Little **money,** little law.
174. When the **moon** is full she shines over all.
175. The **morsel** not toiled for makes the neck white.
176. Idle curiosity sometimes fills the **mousetrap.**
177. The **nail** suffers as much as the hole.
178. Damage your **nose,** damage your face.
179. He who will eat the **nut** must crack it. (*Friesian.*)
180. Row with the **oars** you have.
181. **Oil** is best at the beginning, honey at the end, and wine in the middle.
182. One should not board a ship without an **onion.**
183. **Owls** fly as much in the church as over it.
184. The hindermost **ox** also reaches the kraal. (*Boer.*)
185. **Painting** and white washing cost nothing.
186. He who **pays** well may borrow again.
187. There is no art in becoming a **peasant,** the art is to remain one.
188. He who pulls a **pig** out of the river gets dirt for thanks.
189. If the **pill** had an agreeable taste it would not be gilded.
190. The prick of a **pin** is enough to make an empire joyless for a time.
191. The man on the wall is the best **player.**
192. A **poor man** is never believed.
193. There are no better masters than **poverty** and want.
194. **Poverty** claims many things, plenty more.
195. **Pray** to the saint till you have passed the slough.
196. " Would to God " is the mother of all **prayers.**
197. Everyone is a **preacher** under the gallows.
198. Twelve **professions**—thirteen failures.
199. In the land of **promise** a man may die of hunger.
200. **Property** which travels goes up and down.
201. In **prosperity** caution; in adversity patience.
202. **Proverbs** are the daughters of daily experience.
203. **Prudence** is mother of the china cupboard.
204. He who serves the **public** hath but a scurvy master.
205. He who pays well is master of another's purse.
206. Quick to the hat is slow to the **purse.**
207. A full **purse** is a good thing providing it does not empty itself.
208. Heavy **purses** and light hearts bear many things.
209. Old **purses** shut badly.
210. When it **rains** on one it only drips on another.
211. There is often also a **rock** between the nose and the lips.
212. Pull gently at a weak **rope.**
213. Rest—**rust.**
214. Nothing comes out of a **sack** but what was put in.
215. 'Tis better to begin with an empty **sack** than to end with one.
216. He that is at **sea** has not the wind in his hands.
217. **Self's** the man.

218. Coupled **sheep** drown one another.
219. A **ship** on the shore is a lighthouse at sea.
220. Better an old cart on the heath than a new **ship** on the sea.
221. He who sees the port from afar often **shipwrecks** when close to.
222. Even a new **shoe** becomes one day a cast-off.
223. Between saying and doing one often wears out a pair of **shoes.**
224. **Sickness** comes on horseback and departs on foot.
225. 'Tis a good word that can better a good **silence.**
226. With a good name one may easily **sin.**
227. **Soup** is not eaten as hot as it is served.
228. It is difficult to **steal** where the landlord is a thief.
229. One may just as well sit with two legs in the **stock** as with one.
230. He who jumps over a big **stone** often stumbles over a pebble.
231. Two hard **stones** seldom grind well.
232. One sprinkles the most **sugar** where the tart is burnt.
233. He who goes to **table** without a knife loses many a bite.
234. Those who have the fewest **teeth** chew the most.
235. Everyone is a **thief** in his own craft.
236. See that you **tie** so that you can untie.
237. Seven **trades** instead of one make eight beggars.
238. He who plants the **tree** rarely tastes its fruit.
239. Honour the **tree** which gives one shade.
240. **Truth** has all the benefits of appearances without the disadvantages.
241. No one is more **unhappy** than the man who is always happy.
242. **Unknown** makes unloved.
243. In the course of time small defects become **vices.**
244. Creaking **waggons** are long in passing. (*Friesian.*)
245. He who drinks **water** need not pay for wine.
246. Whoso is tired of happy days let him take a **wife.**
247. Cent-**wisdom** and dollar-folly.
248. A person's **wish** is a person's life.
249. A **woman** can take away more from a house in her apron than a man can bring into it in a hay-cart.
250. A **woman** eats bitterness.
251. When there is a good **woman** in the house joy laughs from the window.
252. When **women** make the bread and do the washing they have the devil in their body.
253. He who does his own **work** soils not his hands.
254. He who wants a new **world** must first buy the old.
255. What one **writes** remains.

ESTONIAN

An Introduction to this collection by Professor Osker Loorits will be found on page xliii

1. When nothing is **accepted,** nothing is brought.
2. What you are **afraid** of overtakes you.
3. **Anger** takes the grain from the fields ; envy takes the fish from the sea.
4. An **apple** does not fall far from the tree.
5. Sour **apples** must also be eaten.
6. First **ask,** then do.
7. **Autumn** feeds ; Spring enfeebles.
8. A night in **autumn** has seven sons.

   [i.e. a night in Autumn changes seven times.]
9. All **autumns** do not fill granaries.
10. How long will an **awl** stay in a bag ?
11. A sharp **axe** always finds a stone.
12. The blunt **axe** of the landlord cuts more than those of three labourers.
13. A **bachelor** costs a bushel of coal ; a spinster a ton of wheat.

    [Said in praise of the spinster.]
14. An old **bachelor** is a cudgel of Hell ; a spinster a dove of Heaven.
15. A **bachelor** is the crows' meat, the loaf of the blackbirds, the nose-bag of the daws.
16. **Bachelors** grow foolish.
17. The **basin** must hold what the cauldron cooks.
18. A **bast-shoe** with a bast-shoe ; a weaver's reed with a weaver's reed.

    [i.e. like goes with like.]
19. Let a beggar come into your **bath-house** and he will want a bath-tuft ; give him a bath-tuft and he will want to get on the sweating-bench ; let him get on to the sweating-bench and he will want to be scrubbed too.

    [The bath-tuft is a small broom of leafed birch twigs, used by bathers to beat themselves with. The sweating-bench is a raised platform in the Finnish bath where bathers sit and sweat before washing themselves.]
20. If you chase a **bear,** make your bed ready ; if you chase a deer, provide yourself with a coffin.
21. A **beard** is a man's honour, his wife his tool.
22. It is better under an old man's **beard** than under a young man's whip.
23. He who eats, **beats.**

    [i.e. a full man hits hard with the flail when threshing.]
24. One cannot make soup out of **beauty.**
25. One can neither put **beauty** into the pot, nor loveliness into the kettle.
26. **Beauty** is not bad, if it only would not bury so much money.
27. When is a cook's ladle hungry or a **beer jug** thirsty ?
28. Because of a **beetle's hum** the evening does not come.

    [i.e. the sun does not set.]
29. **Beg** with the cap, receive without it.
30. A **beggar** is grateful as long as his mouth is wet.
31. Church for **beggars,** chapel for sinners.
32. A **beggar's bag** is light.
33. Where there is smoke there is a **beggar's debt.**
34. A **beggar's staff** is the heaviest burden.
35. Every **beginning** is difficult.
36. The **beginning** difficult, the middle easy, the end pleasant.
37. **Beginning** is more precious than money.

38. He who **begins** must finish.
39. He who rings the **bell** hears the sound.
40. The **bell** of the world is very mighty.
41. Distress takes away all [false shame],—an empty **belly** does not sound.
42. An empty **belly** has no ears.
43. The **belly** is an exacting bailiff.
44. An empty **belly** is the best cook.
45. An empty **belly** knows no law.
46. What does not **bend,** breaks.
47. Too much **bending** brings breaking.
48. He who roams through all heaths tastes all **berries.**
49. The late **bird** shakes its wings ; the early one wipes its bill.
50. There is no **bird** that cannot wear its own feathers.
51. An early **bird** wipes its beak ; a late one wipes its buttocks.
52. **Birds** are lean as long as their young ones are small.
53. The **bird's path** under the sky and the boy's [bridegroom's] path to the maid are trace-less.
54. **Black** is the enemy of white.
55. **Black** soils white.
56. The **blind man's eyes** are on his ears [or finger-tips].
57. Water is thinner than **blood.**
    [i.e. difference between relations and strangers.]
58. **Blood** is always thicker [or warmer] than water.
59. What **blossoms** beautifully, withers fast.
60. A man deals **blows ;** a man bears blows.
61. One **blows** not only on hot things.
62. In whichever **boat** one finds oneself, one must row.
63. Never fear, the new **boat** will find the old stones.
    [i.e. history will repeat itself. (The new boat and the old one will be wrecked alike.)]
64. Round the **bone** the flesh is good ; round the bush the grass is good.
65. He who looks for meat finds **bones.**
66. Heat does not break the **bones.**
    [i.e. grumbling does not harm the skin.]
67. Forget the dream, mind the **bonnet,** remember the young man.
68. The man in **boots** does not know the needs of the man in moccasins.
69. **Boots** for the messenger, shoes for the quarreller.
70. The longer the year, the bigger the **booty.**
71. The cork is always bigger than the mouth of the **bottle.**
72. Dense **branches** chafe against each other.
73. The dirtier the hands the whiter the **bread.**
74. If a farmer sells his straw he sells his **bread.**
75. Where there are children there is **bread.**
76. It is not in one place only they make **bread** and drink home-brewed ale.
77. If one has eaten enough, **bread** becomes tasteless.
78. Slices of **bread** do not grow together.
79. A poor man's addition to his **bread** is an empty stomach.
80. When the **bread** is consumed, hang your teeth on the hanger.
81. **Bread** is older than man.
82. Bought **bread** is thin.
83. To an empty stomach white **bread** tastes like brown.
84. **Bread** that has been left is afterwards sweet.
85. Don't give away the piece of **bread** till you have the loaf in your hand.
86. Offered **bread** will find an eater, white bread a kneader.
87. The bran-shed is the **bread-chest** in Spring.

88. When was a **bread shovel** hungry ; when was an ale-tap thirsty ?

89. For the **bride,** music and beauty ; for the wife, hunger and thirst.

90. An old **broom** still sweeps the room.

91. Where you get a **broom** you also get a wisp.

92. **Broth** is never eaten as hot as it is cooked.

93. The cauldron cooks a thick **broth,** the kettle bubbles a thin one.

94. Lick the **broth** while the soup is warming.

[Said to a person who asks for a story to be repeated.]

95. **Brown bread** will find an eater, white bread a kneader.

96. The **bucket** whines ; the swab weeps.

[Said about wash-day. Even the very tools you use cry out against so much work to do.]

97. Every **bush** is female.

[i.e. it keeps breeding.]

98. The treasure does not spoil the **bushel.**

[i.e. whatever kind of treasure, ill or well got, you put in a bushel, it will not spoil it.]

99. A good **buttock** finds a bench for itself.

100. One missing **button** strikes the eye more than one missing day.

101. The **buyer** has reins on his neck.

[i.e. the buyer is as much tied to the bargain he has struck as a horse is to its driver who holds the reins in his hands—he cannot break away.]

102. Put out the eye of him who recalls a **bygone thing.**

103. **Calamity** does not shout [when coming].

104. **Calamity** will teach.

105. **A calling** does not ask for bread.

106. Nine **callings**—the tenth starvation.

107. When in motion a **cart load** is not heavy.

108. A greased **cart wheel** does not squeak.

109. A **cat** always eats fish from the tail.

110. He who is a little **cat** outside is a little dog at home.

111. The more you stroke a **cat,** the more it lifts its tail.

112. Deed as big as a **chicken,** shame as big as an ox.

113. Bitter rod, dear **child.**

114. A **child** from sleep to sleep ; a maiden from work to work.

115. A good **child** has several names.

116. When God gives a **child** He also gives clothing for it.

117. Whose the **child** is, his is the name.

[i.e. whose goods it is, his is the price.]

118. A **child** is more than a chip.

119. Baked bread is eaten ; a **child** out of wedlock is found.

120. Remain a **child** so that your children may always love you.

121. A **child** that grows up without fear dies without honour.

122. A **child** that has a word in its mouth has a leg under its body.

123. The summer comes and kisses the **child ;** the winter comes and kills it.

124. Man is a **child** twice.

125. A **child** until there is another child.

126. A little **child** weighs on your knee, a big one on your heart.

127. The **child's** finger-tips hurt the mother's heart.

128. Many **children,** wide ears.

129. **Children's** bread is sandy.

130. One who **climbs** high falls low.

131. An old **cloth**—a new hole.

132. The **cloth** woven in winter is a little lamb ; in summer a wolf-cub.

[i.e. easy in winter when there is little other work to do ; hard in summer when you have your hands full.]

133. He who laughs at another's **clothes,** laughs at his **tailor.**

134. The silken **coat** also has fleas.
[i.e. the rich are plagued by many cares and anxieties which prevent rest.]

135. He who does not wear his old **coat** has no new one.

136. An old **coat,** new crumples.

137. A **cock** of straw may get a golden hen.

138. The **cold** drives a man from the sledge and sits there itself.

139. A clean **conscience** is a soft pillow.

140. **Copper,** the gold of the poor,—lead, the silver of the needy.

141. No mill will grind wet **corn.**

142. The length of the **corn** in summer depends on the thickness of the snow in winter.

143. Even the **cow** raises her tail when she walks through the water.

144. A **crab** has eyes, a forest has ears.

145. It is better to give from the **cradle** than from the bed.
[i.e. it is better that man should die a child.]

146. The **crane** doesn't look at a low bush.

147. He who drinks the **cream** must also drink the milk from the bottom of the butt.

148. **Cruelty** takes from the spoon; evil from the pot.

149. With a **cry** you come into the world, but so live that you leave it with a laugh.

150. A full stomach **dances,** not a clean shirt.

151. The new coat **dances,** not the empty stomach.

152. An only **daughter** becomes a bitch; an only son a dog.

153. A **daughter** carries out of the house, but a son brings into the house.

154. When the **daughter** is the height of your knee, let her dowry chest come up to her breast.

155. It is better to live at a **daughter's** foot-end than at a son's head-end.

156. The **daughters** of the house are nothing but ornaments of the front garden and articles for sale.

157. It is better to die on a wicked **daughter's** bed-foot than a good daughter-in-law's bed-head.

158. A **daughter-in-law** is the mother-in-law's medicine.

159. The **dead** teach the living.

160. You offspring of **death.**
[i.e. girls must die the death of getting married.]

161. There is no medicine against **death.**

162. Man learns till his **death.**

163. Nobody's hand can be put before **death.**

164. Like life, like **death.**

165. The old man has his **death** before his eyes; the young man behind his back.

166. When **death** comes, the rich man has no money, the poor man no debt.

167. **Death** does not take the offered child.

168. He who is afraid of **death** has lost his life.

169. Everyone carries **death** in his bosom.

170. Before **death** nobody can be esteemed happy.

171. What does **death** take from an empty room?

172. Man is **death's** child.

173. There are ninety-nine **deaths** in the world.

174. A **debt** is always new.

175. **Debt** makes a man a stranger's servant.

176. **Desire** leads [you] on, the wish pushes [you] from behind.

177. The **dew** is but a little shepherd boy to the rain.

178. The young may **die,** the old must die.

179. Every **disease** has its physician, every sickness its doctor.

180. Man grows older, but the **disease** grows younger.

181. **Diseases** come on courier's horses, but go away on tired oxen.

182. **Do** and sweat ; look and suffer.

183. He who has something to **do** has something to get.

184. Time helps even the **doctor.**

185. He who is lazy is sleepy ; for the invalid a **doctor,** for the healthy a sausage.

186. The **dog** barks, the wind carries.

187. An old **dog** does not bark a lie.

188. Who does not feed the **dog** feeds the thief.

189. The **dog** grows, the tooth too.

190. The small **dog** is for a long while a puppy.

191. What else makes a **dog** old if not empty footfalls ?

192. Strike a **dog** or stroke him.

193. A **dog** out of two yards never gets anything to eat.

194. If you have stepped over the **dog**, step over its tail too.

195. The **dog** that is dragged along on a chain will never become a herd dog.

196. The **dog** will come home.

[Said to one who wishes another evil or accuses him.]

197. A **dog** will know another dog.

198. Live with **dogs**—suffer fleas.

199. A **dog's tongue** has nine healings ; a cat's claw has snake's poison.

200. High is the threshold of the **door** of home when one returns.

[Refers to a recently married woman.]

201. To him who knocks, the **door** will be opened.

202. All **doors** are opened by a golden key.

203. **Doors** creak until the cock wakes up ; gates bang until daylight.

[This proverb originated in the time of slavery, when our forefathers had to work for the manor all night—doors and gates moving until daylight.]

204. He who **drinks** the dregs fetches the full [cup].

205. The **dung-cart** feeds the coach.

206. He who works in the **dust** cannot stay clean.

207. Where there are **dying** people there are heirs.

208. A grainless [empty] **ear** stands erect.

209. The **early** one never regrets.

210. The **early hour** has gold in its mouth.

211. **Earth** buries all.

212. **Earth** is dearer than gold. (*Farmers' proverb.*)

213. To **eat** standing is seven sins, to eat lying on one side is ten sins, to eat kneeling is numberless sins.

214. **Eat** what is ripe. speak what is true.

215. It is better to feed those who have **eaten,** and better to doctor those who are healthy.

216. Never regret having **eaten** too little.

217. As one calls in the wood, so comes the **echo** back again.

218. A rotten **egg** must likewise be in the nest.

219. The **egg** teaches the hen.

220. First lay the **egg,** then cackle.

221. **Eggs** that roll far from the nest often perish.

222. Don't boil **eggs** until the hen has laid them.

223. **Enough** is everybody's master.

224. **Envy** plucks its own hen.

225. In an empty room even an **epidemic** finds nothing.

226. Man **errs** as long as he strives.

227. Where a mountain, there an **estate ;** where a hill, there a tavern ; farms among the marsh and moor.

228. Even the longest day comes to an **evening.**

229. Do not rejoice before the **evening.**

230. One's own **eye** does not deceive.

231. Your own **eye** is king.

[Said by a good householder who wants to supervise everything himself.]

232. The **eye** is king, the hand executor.

233. The **eye** is the richest of all.

234. Where the **eye** is, there it is cold; where the knot is, there it is warm.

[" Eye " is the mesh in a worsted material.]

235. The **eye** of the stranger is the witch of the house.

236. If you do not keep your **eyes** open, keep your purse open.

237. A **fallow field** needs a sharp harrow.

238. **Falsehood** is the beginning of theft.

239. **Falsehood** is the support of truth.

240. One **family** always sings one song.

241. The daughter and the buckwheat, the frying-pan and the small cauldron are the ruin of the **farm.**

242. Another **farm,** another cottage.

243. Different **farm**—different drink. (*Tailors' saying.*)

244. In spring the **farmer** carries a bag of ignorance; in autumn a bag of wisdom.

245. The **farmer's daughter** a bulrush; the orphan a little blossom of the meadow.

246. A **farmer's wife** has a dollar name and a cent life, but a cottager's wife has a cent name and a dollar life.

247. Put the **farrow** [young pig] into the sack while his head is towards it.

248. **Fast** while the kettle boils. (*An old saying of the Estonian Russians.*)

249. Nine children find room enough in a **father's bosom,** but for one father there is not room enough in the courtyard of nine sons.

250. Where you find **fault** come and help.

251. **Fear** has big eyes.

252. Who takes part in all **feasts** has to suffer all hungers.

253. He who has thirst has **feet;** he who has scabs has nails.

254. Anyone will jump on a low **fence.**

255. Without the master the **field** is an orphan.

256. A poor [woman's] **field** is under her apron, her meadow under her breasts.

257. If one deceives the **field** once, one is deceived nine times by the field.

258. One's **field,** one's farrow.

259. When a **fir** falls down, the top end is broken.

[Said of a grown-up daughter of the family; the youngest is most easily married.]

260. A **fir cone** does not fall far from the tree.

261. Silk and velvet put out the kitchen **fire.**

262. **Fire** has a broad hand.

263. It is easy to kindle a **fire** on the embers of an old one.

264. If you have **fire-tongs,** why use your hands?

265. The **fish** comes to the rod of him who waits.

266. He who has hands has **fish;** he who has thirst has feet.

267. When the **fish** is in the net it wants to get out; when it is out it wants to get in. (*Marriage proverb.*)

268. One gets the **fish** one fishes for.

269. Cheap **fish**—thin glue.

[" Kaliim " is isinglass.]

270. **Flax** makes no farmer rich.

271. He who has many **fleas** doesn't notice them biting.

272. One scratches one's own **flea bites.**

273. The **floor** is the woman's whetstone and the hen's handkerchief.

274. Lend your **food** to others, hang your own teeth on the peg.

275. If God creates a **fool** He gives him also a trough.
276. A real man who deceives—a **fool** who is being deceived.
277. The **fool's** windows are always dirty.
278. Big **foot**—big shoe.
279. The earthy **foot** has a white-bready mouth.
280. A smooth way makes the **foot** slip.
281. **A forest** and a sleeper are not to be believed.
282. The **forest** is the poor man's fur coat.
283. **Forgive** others everything, yourself nothing.
284. Everyone is the smith of his own **fortune.**
285. **Fortune** is blind ; it knows not into whose lap it will fall.
286. An old road—an old **friend.**
287. Keep an old **friend** and an old way.
288. If you want to lose your **friend,** grant him a loan.
289. An old **friend** is like a peg in the wall.
290. A **friend** spits into a friend's pocket.
291. Good **friends** in need are like feathers in the wind.
292. The **friendship** of a lord makes you a beggar.
293. Where it **fries,** there it drips.
294. You do not become a man till you drive a **furrow** across the field.
295. Darkness out of doors—whip in hand ; daylight out of doors—a **furrow** drawn ; dawn out of doors—the bag shouldered.
    [i.e. an overworked peasant must take his whip when it is still dark ; when daylight begins he must already have drawn a furrow ; when dawn has come he has well started his day's work with his bread bag shouldered.]
296. A low **gap** everyone steps over.
297. The poorer, the more **generous.**
298. A **gentleman** does not die in silk, nor is a king buried in gold.
299. I a **gentleman,** you a gentleman, who then is the carrier of the sack ?
300. You cannot know a **girl** before she has become the wearer of a bonnet.
    [in old times married women used to wear bonnets.]
301. A **girl** without a needle is like a cat without a claw.
302. Young **girls** and wheaten bread quickly grow old.
303. He to whom you **give** much will want more.
304. **Give** of what has been given [to you] ; break off what has been broken [to you].
    [i.e. share the bread that has fallen to your lot.]
305. He who **gives,** has.
306. He who **gives** is king.
307. He who **gives,** tires ; he who receives never wearies.
308. Where the **goat** is tethered, there he is always pulling.
309. Better a milking **goat** than a sterile cow.
310. Even the **goat's horns** turn towards his back.
    [i.e. everyone is for himself.]
311. He who helps the poor lends to **God.**
312. To live is to serve **God.**
313. **God** does not hold you by the hand.
314. **God** has time ; the farmer bread.
315. Be faithful, then **God** will keep you.
316. The field is **God's** table.
317. A good conscience is **God's** voice.
318. The **god of sand** has never received thanks.
319. Man strives after **gold,** and gold strives after the soul.
320. What is **gold** to-day may be earth to-morrow.
321. Even a **golden bed** does not help a sick person.
322. Give **good** and get good.
323. Do **good** or evil, you will always find it ahead [of you].

324. The **good** praises the beautiful.
325. The **good** teaches the better.
326. Who seeks **good** will find better.
327. You will meet your **good deed** again.
328. A **good deed** bears interest.
329. A **good deed** is forgotten, a bad one remembered.
330. A **good deed** is written on snow.
331. Carve **good deeds** in stone, bad ones in sand.
332. There are two **good people**; one of them is dead, the other one was not born.
333. **Good things** are sought after, bad things are found.
334. There is always plenty of room for a **good word.**
335. A **good word** always falls on a friendly spot.
336. A **good word** finds a place in everybody's heart.
337. Empty **gossip** jumps with one leg.
338. Eat what you can with your **grandfather's fork.**
339. There is time enough to yawn in the **grave.**
340. Where the **great** are put, the small are thrust.
341. **Grey hair** is to be honoured; a bald head deserves a bow.
342. **Guests** and fish will get old on the third day.
343. Long **hair**—short brain.
344. The **hand** goes in and out of the sleeve.

    [The Estonian equivalent of "How are you?" is "How goes (your) hand?"]
345. Unshakeable **happiness** does not want a string.
346. No one is as **happy** or as unhappy as he thinks.
347. A **hard** [thing] lasts long.
348. The **harness** will stand what the horse can draw.
349. He who **hates** another loves himself but little.
350. **Hatred** blasts the crop on the land; envy the fish in the sea.
351. One of a brood must always remain a **hawk.**
352. Grey **head**—a child's reason.
353. The **head** bent, the harness limp.
354. Empty **heads** are always erect.
355. The mouth is the interpreter of the **heart.**
356. The **heart** also has ears.
357. Of what the **heart** is full the mouth will speak.
358. The road from one's **heart** is more than long prayers from one's head.
359. Hen's singing, cow's crooning, and female's sighing are heard in **hell.**
360. A blind **hen** also finds a grain of barley, and a drunkard a wife.
361. A **hen** gets from between the two measures.

    [Said when grain falls on the floor at the time of measuring.]
362. If you duck your head before a **hen** it will spring on your neck.
363. **Hens** that cackle much lay few eggs.
364. What is **high,** pass by; what is low, leap over.
365. The **hind wheels** got ahead.

    [Said when a girl has a baby without a wedded husband.]
366. Big **hole**—big stopper.
367. **Holidays** come like kings and go like beggars.
368. The **home** is the wife's world; the world is the man's home.
369. Late to church, early to the mill, thus one returns **home** sooner.
370. A **honey seller** sometimes licks his fingers.
371. One's **honour,** one's stench.
372. A **hook** will find a hole for itself.
373. The load is as the **horse.**
374. There are many who will say "Good **horse,** fine horse," but no one will put on the bridle.

    [Said about a girl who has many suitors.]
375. To be without a **horse** is to be without care; to be without a boat is to be without bad weather.

376. What a colt learns, an old **horse** keeps.

377. Buy a **horse** praised; take a wife blamed.

378. A whip does not seek the **horse**; the horse seeks the whip.

379. The buttock knows a good **horse**; the mouth knows a good meal.

380. If you have a good **horse** you must have a better whip.

381. He who has not built a **house** thinks the walls grow out of the earth.

382. When has the **housewife** an appetite?

383. The **housewife** is the lock of the house.

384. Hairy **husband**—smooth happiness.

385. The nimble get **husbands**—the wise get bonnets.

[i.e. bonnets were always worn by married women.]

386. The **idler** is the greatest thief.

387. The **idler** will always find company.

388. He who is **ill** must groan.

389. He is not **ill** who always eats.

390. A dead man's **inheritance**, the fire of the birch bark, a wife's riches, and a wet nurse's wages do not last long.

391. **Injustice** has no price.

392. An **inn keeper** must be everyone's tongs.

393. Where there is an **invalid** there is a hand [to help]; where there is a scar there is an eye.

394. Haggle like a **Jew**; pay like a brother.

395. None die of **joy**.

396. The **jug** goes to the well until it gets broken; the wolf goes to the herd until he gets killed.

397. Like **jug**, like lid.

398. **Justice** knows no friendship.

399. **Justice** with a cudgel on the shoulder.

400. The prettier the shell, the bitterer the **kernel**.

401. Little **kettles** soon boil over.

402. He who **kills**, buries.

403. The tip of the nose is to be seen, but not the end of **kindness**.

404. **Kindness** is ashamed more than cruelty is feared.

405. The **king's eyes** are covered by gold.

406. Before birth—**kinsfolk**; in childhood separated; in grown-up life they do not know one another; while alive they keep apart; dying they are kinsfolk again.

407. A dark room—a blunt **knife**.

408. **Know** yourself; afterwards know your fellow-man.

409. **Knowledge** does not want bread.

410. The given **kopeck** is cheap, the earned one dear.

411. A motherless **lamb** is always butted by others.

412. Where the **lamb** is sheared there is the wool.

413. The **lark** brings midday warmth, the swallow warmth all day; the nightingale warmth at night.

414. If you **laugh** at my face you laugh at God; if you laugh at my clothes you laugh at my tailor; if you laugh at my actions you laugh at me.

415 **Laughter** does not spoil the skin; empty talk does not take a piece. [off you]

416. **Law** is three days older than the world.

417. The **law** on the table, justice under the table.

418. A **lawyer's ink** writes nothing until you have thrown silver into it.

419. As you **leave** it, so it remains.

420. A little **leaven** leavens the whole dough.

421. What hits you is a **lesson** to you; what misses you is wasted.

422. The **liar** and the murderer are children of the same village.

423. A **lie** has short legs.

424. One who **lies** a little and steals a little is getting on all right.

425. He who **lies,** steals.
426. **Light** always laughs at the work of darkness.
427. To **live** is to fight.
428. What **lives,** moves.
429. The **living-room** is man's general school.
430. If you try to get a **loaf** you lose the slice; if you try to catch a partridge you lose the hen.
431. A **lock** is a security against animals; nothing holds against man.
432. Better put a cockroach in the corner of your house than a **lodger.**
433. Better a stone in a corner than a **lodger** in the family circle.
434. What a man **looks** for he finds.
435. A servant has a **louse** on his forehead, a lazy beggar on the top of his head, and a walker on the edge of his ear.
436. Old **love** does not rust.
437. **Love** is caught with a silken thread, but driven away with a ship's cable.
438. The father's **love** lasts to the grave; the mother's love eternally.
439. **Love** makes cottages manors; straw, silken ribbons.
440. It is better to **love** than to be loved.
441. **Love** yourself, then you will have no rivals.
442. If you wish to be **loved,** love.
443. He who **loves** mankind can more easily do without people than he who hates them.
444. Do not despise the first **luck.**
445. **Luck** and misfortune walk together.
446. **Lying** a little, stealing a little, is as good as half an acre of land.
447. **Lying** a little, stealing a little, you get nicely through the world.
448. **Manure** is master of the field.
449. **Manure** is the farmer's gold.
450. If the bread-making goes wrong it means a week's loss; if the harvest goes wrong, a year's loss; if **marriage** goes wrong, a lifetime's loss.
451. Early rising and early **marriage** no one has repented of.
452. Happy the **marriage** where the husband is the head and the wife the heart.
453. Before a young couple gets **married** the devil wears out seven pairs of moccasins.
454. Some **marry** from out of the wood; some jump off a tree-stump.
455. Without the **master** the field is an orphan.
456. The **master's eye** does more than the hands of two servants.
457. The **master's eye** fattens the horse.
458. The **master's footprints** make the field fertile.
459. A curved swath in the **meadow** —a straight furrow in the field.
460. The **meadow** is the master of the field.
461. Full man, full **measure.**
462. Small **measure,** frequent throw.

    [i.e. if the sower takes a small measure of corn, he will have to throw more frequently than if he took a larger one.]
463. Full **measure,** full money.
464. What **measure** you measure with, that measure you will be measured by.
465. **Midsummer** [St. John's Day] takes a vat; St. James's Day, two; St. Lawrence's Day laps the bottom.

    [Said about the lessening of the milk of cows in the course of the year.]
466. **Misfortune** does not walk ringing a bell, and misery does not whistle.
467. **Misfortune** does not come with a bell on its neck.
468. **Misfortune** prolongs life; happiness shortens it.
469. The **mistakes** of others are good teachers.
470. **Money** begets robbers.

471. **Money** cries in one's pocket.

472. He who has **money** has a friend.

473. If **money** is being counted, go out; if work is being done, come near to it.

474. He who has **money** is lifted into the coach; he who has a bag, on top of the load.

475. **Money** is round.

476. **Money** is the thief of the soul.

477. Light **money**—light wares.

478. When **money** speaks the world is silent.

479. During the old **moon** trees with leaves are hewn.

480. **Morning** is wiser than evening.

481. **Morning** time—golden time.

482. A **mosquito** evacuates during its lifetime as much as an ox once.

483. When the **mother** dies the father becomes blind.

484. A **mother** has a mother's love.

485. He who flatters the **mother** will hug the daughter.

486. A **mother's bosom** holds six children, but the courtyard of nine children does not hold one mother.

487. It is safer in **mother's lap** than in a lord's bed.

488. She took her **mother's toboggan** down from the loft.

[i.e. said when the mother has had a child born out of wedlock, and the daughter likewise.]

489. Trust the **mountain** [the stove] to dry the wet.

490. Man always strives to get a bigger bit than will go into his **mouth.**

491. When two are together, the third is in the **mouth.**

492. A clean **mouth** and a clean hand go all the world over.

493. The **mouth** is the measure of the heart.

494. He who has a wide **mouth** must also have a broad back.

495. He who gets **much,** eats much.

496. He who gets **much,** uses much.

497. Neither is the **mug of ale** thirsty, nor the cook's ladle hungry.

498. A **nail** helps a nail.

499. A **name** doesn't harm a man if a man doesn't harm the name.

500. The **neck** uses up more than the hands earn.

501. The **new** drives out the old.

502. A long **night** and hard work; a crying child and a broken cradle. (*The best man's wish at a wedding.*)

503. Where **night** falls there is a night's lodging.

504. The **night** has nine sons.

505. **Oak** is the farmer's iron.

506. With the **old** one must serve the new.

507. It is a gain what the **old one** does; a loss what the old one eats.

508. Learn your way from **old people.**

509. An **old woman** is the cradle's prop and the baby's prisoner.

510. **Ornaments** exalt a man.

511. A fatherless child is half an **orphan**; a motherless child is a whole one.

512. An **orphan** grows a span and shrinks two.

513. [Food] is given to an **orphan** with a spoon and taken away with a ladle.

514. Seldom are an **orphan's** cheeks red when her eyes are full of tears.

515. The **oven** is greedy, the cauldron a witch.

516. Where the **ox** is slaughtered, there the blood is sprinkled.

517. Where an **ox,** there a hoof.

518. One's own **pain** is in one's own body; the pain of others is on the tree.

519. Blisters on your **palm** are more useful than a gold ring on your finger.

520. A **patch** kills a rag.

521. **Patience** makes all hardships light.

522. Let the **pauper** be silent.

523. He who asks, **pays.**

524. The ache looks for a **physician.**

525. Every pain has its **physician** ; every disease its doctor.

526. A **pie** is also eaten under the bench.

527. The **pig** that does not whine while being carried does not generate.

528. Salt is **pig's** death.

529. He who smokes a **pipe** has a smell of pitch.

530. The **pipe** is nearer than the wife.

531. He who digs a **pit** for another should take his own measure.

532. Where there is no fear there is no **pity.**

533. The hidden stone finds the **plough.**

534. Cheat a little, steal a little, is half the servitude of the **plough.**

535. The **plough** goes after the sickle.

536. He who begins to **plough** must draw the edge furrow.

537. A much used **plough** shines ; stagnant waters stink.

538. **Pomp** does not fear cold.

539. **Poor** and yet rich.

540. The **poor** feed the rich.

541. He who shows mercy to the **poor** lends to God.

542. Church-going does not waste time ; the **poor man's** gift does not make poor.

543. If the hunter goes into the forest, put the **pot** aside ; if the fisherman goes to fish, put the pot on the fire.

544. Like **pot,** like lid.

545. The slave of riches is **poverty.**

546. The **praise** of self stinks.

547. Diligent **precaution** slits the eyes of misfortune.

548. **Pride** is the clearest hall-mark of stupidity.

549. **Pride** [lodges] in a new coat and on the stem of an old pipe.

550. You sin for the **priest** and do wrong for the parish clerk.

551. The **priest's bag** and the pit of hell never get full.

552. **Profit** and loss are twin brothers.

553. Even a **promise** is a good man.

554. A **proverb** does not tell a lie ; an empty pipe does not burn.

555. A **proverb** is the key of the thought.

556. The **proverb** makes the thief wise.

557. **Public house** hours are short.

558. Learnt as a **puppy,** kept as an old dog.

559. How you **push,** so it goes ; how you pull, so it comes.

560. Emptiness brings a **quarrel** into the house ; envy takes the fish out of the sea ; hatred the corn from the field.

561. A **quarter** seeks a quarter.

562. As you are yourself, so are your **rags.**

563. **Rags** laugh, tatters weep.

564. **Rain** doesn't remain in the sky.

565. A **raven** does not pick out the eye of a raven.

566. Where the carrion is, there the **ravens** gather together.

567. Don't use the horse or the wife without **reins.**

568. A man is held by the word, a horse by the **reins.**

569. What is soft and warm is long **remembered.**

570. Once you get half-rich it is easy to get quite **rich.**

571. An officer is sometimes **rich** ; a merchant is often rich ; a farmer is constantly rich.

572. The **rich** have money ; the poor children.

573. The **rich** have money ; the poor peace.

574. It is difficult for a poor [man] to become a small **rich** [man], but easy for a small rich [man] to become a big rich [man].

575. A **rich man's** disease and a poor man's beer are heard far.

576. What is **right** for one man is right for another.

577. **Right** is older than the law.

578. **Right** must remain right.

579. **Right** will set itself right.

580. **Righteous** mind, righteous tongue.

581. Even **righteousness** may sometimes have a waxen nose.

582. Your **ring** will not drop off your finger.

[Said to those who think they are too good for some humble work.]

583. An old **road** is known.

584. A crooked **road** leads into crooked ways.

585. One's own **rods**—bitter rods.

586. It is your own **rods** that flog ; it is yourself who brings up your own coffin-nail.

[i.e. if you spare the rod you spoil the child, who becomes the nail to your coffin.]

587. If you go only once round the **room,** you are wiser than he who sits still.

588. **Russian friendship** does not get sour.

589. The cold is **Russia's** cholera.

590. An empty **sack** does not stand erect.

[Said of a hungry man.]

591. He who lives close to a town dies of **salt hunger.**

592. Old **salty food** does not make thirsty.

593. **Satan** does not always come in boots, but often in stockings.

594. The **satiated** breathe, the sick groan.

595. Old **saw**—old silver.

596. Old **saws**—wise saws.

597. That which you would **say** to another, say to yourself first.

598. Who has **scabies** has nails too.

599. What falls over the **scissors** belongs to the tailor.

600. The **sea** gives, the sea takes, the sea buries a man.

601. The **seaman** is right, so is the landsman.

602. Wind and storm are a **seaman's holiday.**

603. What you **see,** appear not to see ; what you hear, appear not to hear.

604. That is **seen** that is done.

605. In standing water lives the **serpent.**

606. Beware of a **servant** become master, or a goat become gardener.

607. A **servant** sighs in the morning ; an orphan when it is daylight.

608. He who has no **shame** has no honour.

609. One fold will hold many quiet **sheep.**

610. A bleating **sheep** gets hay.

611. Wash your **sheepskin** but do not soak it.

[Said if someone is told something about a third person whose name is not mentioned.]

612. Rough **shell**—sweet kernel.

613. As the **shepherd,** so the herd ; as the light, so the shade.

614. The **shirt** is near, death nearer still.

615. In the beginning they fit into one **shirt ;** later not into one cottage.

[Refers to marriage.]

616. Every **shoe** fits a bare foot.

617. Better a crease in the **shoe** than a blister on the toe.

618. All who are cruel get married ; all who are miserable are carried away, but none takes the **sick** one.

619. One always hangs up a new **sieve.**

620. **Silence** is sometimes an answer.

621. He who acts has one **sin ;** he who speaks has nine.

622. He who **sinks** disappears.

623. The **sled** and the wheel die on the road.

624. In summer make a **sledge ;** in winter a carriage.

[Then you can drive at any time.]

625. A **sledge** must be loaded behind ; a cart in front.

626. The proud one will perish, the haughty one will be furious, the hot-headed will get scabies, the **slow one** goes on.

627. Drive **slowly,** you will get farther.
628. As it **smokes,** so it tastes.
629. Write a bad thing in **snow,** but a good thing in rock.
630. Wet **soil** needs no rain.
631. A son is a **son** until he takes a wife.
632. Better nine **sons** than one daughter.
633. Better in a **son's courtyard** than on a daughter's breast.
634. A good **song** can be sung twice.
635. Large household—thin **soup.**
636. The **sourer,** the better.
637. What you **sow** you reap.
638. The **sower** has never been wise.
639. What was not **sown** in spring cannot be reaped in autumn.
640. **Sparrows** clean their beaks against the branch on which they sit.
641. **Speak** little with others, much with yourself.
642. He who **speaks** is right.
643. If the **spear-head** missed, the shaft missed still more.
644. Everyone must spin on their own **spinning wheel.**
645. A **spinster** gets to heaven, a gold chain round her neck; a bachelor gets to hell with a harrow-clog [or wooden leg in his claws].
646. Earth in **spring** is more than grass in autumn.
647. It is better for animals to gnaw a twig in **spring** than a lapful of hay in autumn.
648. **Stars** shine always in a clear sky.
649. One who **steals** a little is hanged; one who steals much goes by carriage.
650. He who wants to **step upwards** must begin below.
651. **Stitch** slowly, sew sparingly, and every man will get his own. (*Tailor's consolation.*)
652. The **stocking** wide—the foot warm; the glove wide—the hand cold.
653. The **stomach** never becomes full with licking.
654. He who is not strong enough to lift the **stone** must roll it.
655. On a level road a small **stone** upsets the cart-load.
656. New boots are bought by the **stork** in spring.
657. The **stork** looks over a low fence.
658. A short man gets a **strawberry** from the earth quicker than a tall man a star from the sky.
659. **Strawberries** ripen sooner in a low wood than in a high one.
660. The **stump** also is proud when an ornament is put round it.
661. Who **suffers** lives long.
662. **Suffering** is bitter, but its fruits are sweet.
663. **Summer** and winter are always at loggerheads.
664. **Summer** has eyes, winter teeth.
665. You will never taste **sweetness** if you do not like bitterness.
666. The **table** of the stranger is high.
667. Who counts a **tailor** a man, or a goat for cattle?
668. He who is worth anything is **talked** about.
669. He who is in the fore is the man; he who is in the middle is the emperor; he who is in the rear is a **Tartar's** navel. (*Herdboy's saying.*)
670. Whom father and mother do not **teach,** the world teaches.
671. Who does not **thank** for little will not thank for much.
672. He who chews the **thick** [end] has the thin [end] in his mouth.
673. A **thief** always robs himself.
674. A **thief** has long fingers.
675. The **thief** has nine ways, the pursuer one.
676. The **thief** has one way, the pursuer nine.
677. A **thief** leaves a peg in the wall; a fire leaves but ashes.
678. Sledge and wheel die at the roadside; the **thief** on the gallows.

679. Where there is no receiver there is no bringer; where there is no **thief** there is no fence.
680. A **thin** thing has a long end.
681. He who has **thirst** has feet.
682. A **thirsty** one has feet; a hungry one has fingers.
683. That which is created a **thorn** is sharp from youth.
684. A long **time** consumes much.
685. **Time** enough to live, time enough to die.
686. Take **time** in front, not behind.
687. Wasting **time** is robbing oneself.
688. **Time** is the grave-digger of happiness.
689. It is better to be without a wife for a bit than without **tobacco** for an hour.
690. With **tobacco** the wife is fed; with the pipe the family is supported.
691. The work of **to-day,** do not leave for to-morrow.
692. What has the smith got his **tongs** for if he must needs put his fingers into the fire?
693. What is in the mind is on the **tongue.**
694. A fleshy **tongue** cuts off the bony neck.
695. The **tongue** guides one to Kiev.
696. He who has a long **tongue** has a long road.
697. Keep your **tongue** on a string.
698. An enterprising man finds a **tool** everywhere.
699. The **town** is new every day.
700. **Trade** has a golden bottom.
701. A **trade** is never so bad that it cannot feed a man.
702. What the **trap** catches, the owner keeps.
703. Much **treasure,** many moths.
704. Like **tree,** like growth; like stump, like sapling.
705. A green **tree** must be felled; a rotten one falls by itself.
706. One mouth says, ten ears listen, one hand makes, a hundred mouths bring to **trial.**
707. If you have a **trouble,** complain of it to yourself.
708. The bigger the **trouble** the nearer the help.
709. What a pleasure to sit in the fire having on strange **trousers!**
710. A friend peels his neighbour's **trousers.**
711. He who has **trousers** on will always get a wife.
712. The wider the **trousers,** the finer the boy; the shorter the skirt, the prettier the girl.
713. Give your wife your **trousers** to wear and go without trousers yourself.
714. **Truth** pricks the eye.
715. Bend the **twig** when pliant, not when a tree.
716. **Two** will not remain without a third.
717. God is on high, the **Tzar** far away.
718. What is **unheard** is unanswered.
719. What has not come is **unknown.**
720. What is **unknown** is unseen.
721. When a **vessel** is full it runs over.
722. A half-empty **vessel** will not cry after the brim.
723. Where there are **vessels** there are gifts.
724. The **village** praises, the manor blames; the manor praises, the parish blames.

    [This proverb refers to the manorial bailiffs of former times.]
725. **Wares** are always new.
726. Still **water**—deep bottom.
727. What moves, **wears.**
728. Do not trust the **weather** in the evening, nor yesterday's bride.
729. If you go to the **wedding** you cover up the sledge.

    [Using a beautiful carpet to make a good impression.]
730. The **wedge** must go where the axe drives.
731. When the **well** is empty, water is dear.
732. The tiny **wheel** always rolls in first.

733. The ungreased **wheel** has always noise behind.

734. A **widow** is a low fence over which everyone walks.

735. A **widow** [or widower] is a roofless building.

736. Take from the rich farm a horse; from the poor farm a **wife.**

737. A man always gets a **wife.**

738. If you want all the world to know, tell your **wife.**

739. A dove when a girl; a club when a **wife.**

740. He who knocks his **wife** about properly will be forgiven a hundred sins.

741. A man is allowed to beat his **wife** as long as a cauldron of porridge goes on boiling on the floor.

742. A **wife** can carry away in her apron more than her husband carries in on wheels and horses.

743. Do not take your **wife** from on the way to church.

744. Never trust a ship, a horse, or a **wife** in the hands of others.

745. The **wife** is a man's lock.

746. A **wife** is not to be chosen with the eyes but with the ears.

747. A man is free when his **wife** is three handles of a spoon away.

748. Hold a **wife** like a bottle.

749. A **wife** spoils a man's life.

750. Fool your **wife,** use your bride, teach your children to eat coal.

751. Do not govern your **wife** with your eyes but with your ears.

752. All girls are good; where do the bad **wives** come from?

753. Do not fight empty **wind.**

754. Do not talk to [or tell] the **wind.**

755. He grows up supported by the **wind** and refreshed by the dew.
[Said of an orphan.]

756. A north-easterly **wind** is heaven's broom.

757. The **wind** is sown, storm is reaped.

758. **Winnow** your corn when the wind blows; marry your daughter when a man wants her.

759. If you want to travel in **winter,** make wheels in summer.

760. **Winter** pulls the mittens out of your pocket.

761. **Wisdom** is the slave of stupidity.

762. Even a **wolf** does not eat the offered meat.

763. A **wolf** does not step on the tail of a wolf.

764. The **wolf** forgets, the dog remembers.

765. The **wolf** has the wolf's luck.

766. Live with a **wolf,** howl like a wolf.

767. The **wolf** is in the swamp with stockings on; the sheep is in the market with pearls on [the neck].
[i.e. misfortune walks without (a) sound in stockings (silently), but the poor man wanders with bells on.]

768. The master goes on a rainy day; the **wolf** roams on a foggy one.

769. In the **wolf's** mouth, in the wolf's throat.

770. The work of a **woman** and the food of an old horse are not to be seen.

771. Who thinks of a **woman** as a human being, a man inhabiting the moon, a goat as an animal, or a juniper as a tree?

772. A **woman** has long hair but short brain.

773. A **woman** is attractive only as long as you have not yet had her.

774. A **woman** is like an earthen pot; take it out of the oven, it hisses more than ever. (*Old popular saying about women.*)

775. A beautiful **woman** is paradise for the eye, the soul's hell, and purgatory for the purse.

776. A **woman** is wiser in autumn than a man in spring.

777. Like **woman,** like petticoat.

778. One **woman** never praises another.

779. When an old **woman** sits in the carriage, the wheel is in a hurry.

780. An old **woman,** the children's shadow ; a rotten log, the keeper of the fire.

781. Have a **woman** young and liver warm.

782. A **woman's finger** and a mare's jaw are always in motion.

783. A **woman's head** and a hen's head are alike.

784. A sieve will hold water better than a **woman's mouth** a secret.

785. **Woman's sense** is like a ragged shirt.

786. The **woman's whet-stone** and the hen's handkerchief are unknown to the devil.

787. From where the wind, from there the mind : **woman's wisdom** is—to keep indoors from wolves.

788. One **woman's woof**—nine women's warp.

789. **Women** do not understand what men see in a man.

790. The **wood** has eyes, the wall has ears.

791. You had rather look into the eyes of a thief than complain of your need to a **wood-cutter.**

792. Begin a **wood-pile** at the top, not in the middle.

[Said by old women when the younger daughters get married and the older ones left.]

793. A busy one has **wool,** a lazy one has sheep.

794. A man is held by his **word,** an ox by his horns.

795. The happiness of the unhappy is **work.**

796. **Work,** and fasten your belt.

797. **Work** does not end until your two hands are laid on your breast.

798. Hurried **work** has no tail.

799. **Work** in the morning—gold ; work in the evening—dross.

800. Self-done **work** is a master's work.

801. **Work** is in awe of the master-craftsman.

802. **Work,** knowing that work is life.

803. **Work,** not beauty, is put into the pot ; labour, not the white hand, is put into the dish.

804. The **work** praises the master.

805. Every **work** stands in awe of the master.

806. Do your **work** to the root ; push a thing to the branches.

807. The harder the **work,** the quieter the night.

808. The **work** will teach you.

[Said when somebody is asked to do some work and says he does not know how to do it.]

809. Do not **work** yawning ; do not hurry blindfold.

810. He who **works** before dawn will soon be his own master.

811. The hard **worker** and good health are always friends.

812. A slender pitchfork and a sharp scythe are the **worker's** health.

813. Idling tires ; **working** never does.

814. Believing the **world,** one gets something into the eye.

815. The **world** taught [him] ; the saw of the world broke [him].

816. The **worry** of the betrothed is half-worry ; the worry of the bonnet lasting.

[In the old times married women wore bonnets.]

817. "**Would be**" is a poor man.

818. Time heals a **wound,** but leaves a scar.

819. You cannot tie up another one's **wound** while your own is still bleeding.

820. Not all **years** are brothers.

821. Every day has its **yoke** ; every hour its work.

822. If you did [it] **yourself,** suffer [for it] yourself.

FINNISH

(Including Lap)

An Introduction to this collection by Mrs. Aino Tuomikoski, M.A., will be found on page xlvi.

1. Where the **ache,** there the hand ; where the eye, there the sweetheart.
2. Be always a little **afraid** so that you never have need of being much afraid.
3. **Age** does not give sense, it only makes one go slowly.
4. **Anger** beats the shoulders with its own rod until they bleed, and love tints the face with its own rouge.
5. He who gets **angry** without reason is conciliated without a gift.
6. The night of **autumn** travels with seven horses.
7. He is a man who keeps his word on an **autumn day.**
8. All friends have not room at the same **banquet.**
9. All know the **bear,** but the bear knows nobody.
10. A good **bell** is heard far, a bad one still farther.
11. It will not do to go **berrying** with the gentry : they take both berries and baskets.
12. The **bird** is leanest when the nestlings are smallest.
13. Even the **blind** gets by chance a bit of fat into his spoon.
14. In the country of the **blind** the one-eyed lives at ease.
15. Under one's own skin runs **blood ;** under the skin of others, water.
16. The **bone** is left in the hand of the distributor.
17. Even a crust is **bread.**
18. Do not eat **bread** which is still growing.
19. Happy the **brother-in-law** of the housewife : he parades at the head of the table ; miserable brother-in-law of the host ; he slinks at the door.
20. Sense is required for **business,** music for dancing.
21. Keep still, **calf,** and let the grown-up cow low.
22. He needs a long **candle** who awaits the death of another.
23. The more one strokes the **cat,** the higher she lifts her tail.
24. No one will lift the **cat's** tail unless the cat itself does.
25. Fault in **charcoal,** fault in smith.
26. Once a man, twice a **child.**
27. The **child** also is a help, it cleans one fish and eats two.
28. From sleep to sleep the **child ;** from work to work the bride.
29. The motherless **child** is in the way when the stepmother bakes.
30. He who does not go to **church** in bad weather goes in fair weather to hell.
31. Do not lift the **club** too high, it may fall on your head.
32. The **cock** which crows early in the morning is in the evening in the hawk's mouth.
33. **Concord** has a spacious dwelling, discord a narrow.
34. One reaps the same **corn** one sows.
35. An old **cow** does not remember having been a calf.
36. One has to **creep** before one can go.
37. It is not better **crying,** nor easier yelling.
38. The **days** are not one upon another but one after another.
39. Who did not escape birth cannot escape **death.**
40. If the bath-house and brandy cannot help a man, **death** is near at hand.
41. **Delicacies** mangle the body ; praise spoils even the best.

42. The **devil** always paints himself black, but we always see him rose-coloured.
43. Where is the **dirt** if not on the wheel ?
44. A biting **dog** does not bark.
45. A **dog** does not take it ill when he is hit with bread.
46. If you fawn on the master, feed also his **dogs.**
47. It is home in the **dog's** mind where it has been three nights.
48. He who **dresses** with a needle undresses with a knife.
49. It is none of the **driver's** business if those behind him talk.
50. The heart of the **drunkard** is in his mouth.
51. Who does not hear with his **ears** comes to know with his back.
52. In the **east** there are many days and they all pass away in the west.
53. The **echo** knows all languages.
54. Kill the **elk** in your youth if you would lie on its skin in your old age.
55. The **evil** is soon done ; the sore is aching long.
56. One sees with nothing so well as with the **eyes.**
57. If a man knew where he would **fall,** he would spread straw first.
58. On the earth are even the **feet** of the small, nor do the heads of the tall reach to heaven.
59. Everybody jumps over a low **fence.**
60. The steps of the master enrich the **field.**
61. The meadow is the mother of the **field.**
62. The ditch is the master of the **field.**
63. Deceive your **field,** the field pays the deceit.
64. The child puts the **finery** in his mouth ; the young puts it on ; the old woman puts it in her box.
65. Go into the **fire** when another commands.
66. It is easy to sit down in the **fire** with another's trousers.
67. The south-east takes the **fish** from the sea, east-south-east from the kettle, north-west even from the spoon.
68. That's a **fish** which is brought from afar.
69. Better to stem the ditch than the **flood.**
70. Two hard stones do not make good **flour.**
71. To the merry man every weed is a **flower ;** to the afflicted man every flower is a weed.
72. More show the way than give **food.**
73. **Food** does not end by eating, but by lack of enterprise.
74. The **fool** praises his horse, the madman his daughter-in-law, the ignorant his daughter.
75. The **fool** tells his cares to another who lives in comfort.
76. It is better to be a **fool** than to make a fool of another.
77. **Fools** are not sown nor ploughed, they grow of themselves.
78. The **form** is as God creates, the clothes according to one's resources, the manners at will.
79. **Foxes** are caught with foxes.
80. In youth **frailties** are got, in old age they are felt.
81. The first night is worst on the **gallows.**
82. The **gift** of the poor does not last long ; he gives it in the cottage and takes it away in the passage.
83. All **girls** are good, but whence come the naughty old women ?
84. The voice of the **gnat** does not carry to heaven.
85. The **goat** eats where it is tied.
86. Even the masters have their master—**God.**
87. Some have luck, most have summer, all have **God.**
88. **God** gives sense but hope takes it away.

89. It is best to do business with **God,** He has two hands and both of like warmth.

90. **God** is not yet going on crutches.

91. He who does not know his **God** may go to sea.

92. He whom **God** takes by the forelock is easily dragged up to heaven.

93. A spot in **gold** and a fault in a wise man are soon visible.

94. There is **good** where we are not.

95. One must even remain after a **good one,** and live with a bad one.

96. Don't become enraptured with one **good thing** nor scared at two bad ones.

97. Hunting a **grouse** in the woods one loses a hen from one's home.

98. Blessed the **guest** of the hostess, wretched the guest of the host.

99. Sore are the **hands** of the idle, blistery is the palm of the lazy man.

100. No one is **hanged** with his purse around his neck.

101. The **hare** has victory in his feet, the vile woman in her tongue, man in a noble mind.

102. The faultless **head** seldom bleeds.

103. Walking through doubts the way to **heaven** is long.

104. Even a blind **hen** sometimes finds a grain.

105. He who holds all **holidays** suffers all hungers.

106. Who curries a strange **horse** gets the hairs for his labour.

107. Where the **horse** wallows the hair remains behind.

108. It is hard to water a **horse** which does not hold down his head.

109. The satisfied man knows nothing of **hunger,** and the laughing man nothing of tears.

110. God did not create **hurry.**

111. He who has a broad **jaw** must have a broad back.

112. One cannot **jump** higher than one's head.

113. Everybody collects coals under his own **kettle.**

114. The **kettle** is good on the fire, even if boiling with nothing but water ; the housewife is good in the house, even if she sit idle.

115. A **king** is blamed before he does wrong, and praised before he does good.

116. Memory does not forget the promised **kiss,** but the remembrance of the kiss received is soon lost.

117. Even in the sheath the **knife** must be sharp.

118. What can a man understand about a **ladle ?**

119. Begun with **ladle,** ended with spoon.

120. The stomach teaches the **Laplander** to shoot.

121. Gifts cripple the **law,** and grease makes the wheels go round.

122. The **law** is as it is read.

[i.e. it is read in nine ways and always right.]

123. Businesses are as they are done, **laws** are as they are read.

124. When can the **lazy** work ? In the autumn there is much mud, in the spring much water, in the winter biting cold, in the summer burning heat.

125. There's always a **listener** where there's a speaker.

126. He who cannot kindle a fire cannot **love.**

127. When my **luck** is harder my mouth is bolder.

128. The **lung** is not thirsty nor the ladle hungry.

129. A **man** is a man, even a ruined one.

130. Love is a flower which turns into fruit at **marriage.**

131. Love is a fair garden and **marriage** a field of nettles.

132. The **married** man has many cares, the unmarried one many more.

133. A man is often too young to **marry,** but a man is never too old to love.

134. I am a **master,** you are a master, which of us shall carry the wallet?
135. He gets first milled who comes first to the **mill.**
136. Early to the **mill** and late to church, one comes soon back.
137. When one is in the **mill** one gets dusty.
138. The **milling** goes according to the man; according to the wife the milking.
139. Wise from the **misfortune** but not rich.
140. He is not a man who gets **money,** but who holds it.
141. He who has a little mound of **money** has a mountain of friends.
142. When **money** is gone many ways are left.
143. Even the **moon** does not shine before it rises.
144. It is not hard to be **naughty,** but to be good—that costs something.
145. When your **neighbour's** corner burns, then your own is in danger.
146. No **night** so long that a day will not follow it.
147. Called with **oats,** driven with spurs.
148. What else is there on the **old footing** save the old women and the north wind?
149. Half **orphan** is the fatherless child, whole orphan the motherless.
150. The **ox** lives safely as long as the knife is being sharpened.
151. He who drives **oxen** speaks of oxen.
152. He who gives his **oxen** to others may harrow with his fingers.
153. The hours of **parting** are the warmest.
154. He that praises the **past** blames the present.
155. The **perch** has the choice to take the bait or leave it.
156. The **pig** dreams of his trough.
157. The frost brings the **pig** home.
158. The **pig** which is once seen in the crevice of the fence is accused of all faults.
159. The **pike** knows the bottom of the lake, and God the bottom of the sea.
160. As the man gets older the **plantation** gets smaller.
161. The axe and the shovel of the church pay the debt of the **poor.**
162. The **poor** does not fall from a great height, only from the besom on the floor.
163. The **poor** does not lose in anything except in his hope to become rich.
164. Hope keeps alive the **poor**; fear kills the rich.
165. The **poor** has patience to boil, but not to let cool.
166. The **poor** lives as the wet burns.
167. No one is too **poor** to help another and no one too rich to need help.
168. Who is the **poorest** of the poorest, the most miserable of the miserable? The greedy dissatisfied, he has an everlasting poverty.
169. **Praise** the weather in the evening, your son when grey-headed.
170. **Praise** your horse to-morrow, your son when he is bearded, your daughter when she is married, yourself never.
171. **Praise** your new horse in the morning, your wife in the second year, only in the third year your brother-in-law, and yourself never in your life.
172. The **proud** always punishes himself.
173. Do not examine the **reindeer** given you by the rich man lest you find it to be without horns.
174. Do not disregard a poor **relative** nor a slight wound.
175. Everything one may **repent** except the early rising and the early beginning.
176. One does not get **rich** gaining but saving.

177. The illness of the **rich** is known to all, but not even the death of the poor.
178. When the **rich** quarrel the poor get peace.
179. He is not **rich** who has not anything old.
180. Who is engaged with **rivalry** is not married with rivalry.
181. A narrow **river** is soon rowed, a shallow sea measured, a small mind stirred.
182. He who mocks at a **rivulet** should be a deep sea.
183. The **road** gives comrades.
184. The woollen **rod** of the mother may whip half a day ; the rod of the stranger draws blood though he touch only once.
185. He who lives beneath the **roses** seeks his friend beneath the thorns.
186. An empty **sack** does not stand upright.
187. Who **saves** when he gets, has when he needs.
188. Don't believe in the tears of the **sea,** for its eyes are always full of water.
189. He who has slipped into the **sea** goes cautiously alongside the brook.
190. One **sheep** bleats, the whole pen is thirsty.
191. That **ship** which sails by every wind comes never in the harbour.
192. A **shirt,** though linen, is warm when sewn by one's own mother, but when sewn by a stranger, even a woollen cloak is cold.
193. The **short one** takes sooner a bit of dirt from the earth than the tall one a star from the sky.
194. Take a **silver sickle** and you will reap golden ears.
195. The yard is one step longer, the threshold one timber higher, when there's a strange **sister-in-law** in the place of the old mother.
196. One cannot **ski** so softly that the traces cannot be seen.
197. One cannot go to heaven with tallow-greased **skis.**
198. The **skin** of the young is elastic.
199. A low stump upsets the **sledge.**
200. Drive slowly on the slope, the **sledge** holds better.
201. There is nothing as it was [in olden days] except **sleep** and hunger.
202. **Sleep** does not end with sleep nor work with work.
203. A **sleigh** demands a colt, a house needs a man.
204. The **sleigh** does not keep long on the road which is drawn by one shaft.
205. It is better to be once in the church **sleigh** than always in the back runners.
206. On whose water I row his **song** I sing.
207. **Sorrows** are our reins, bad days our bridle.
208. Don't **spit** to-day on the shore of the sea that you want to furrow to-morrow.
209. Even a small **star** shines in the darkness.
210. Poverty does not bid **stealing,** and wealth does not forbid it.
211. Who **steals** a needle steals also a nail.
212. What can the wind do to the **stone ?**
213. There is always a **straw** left where the load turns over.
214. My country is wild **strawberries,** a foreign land is bilberries.
215. Better a little **stupid** than too wise.
216. Courage vanquishes some **sufferings** and patience the others.
217. **Summer** comes jumping and winter yawning.
218. Even the **sun** does not shine long from one side.
219. It is easy to **swim** when one's head is held up.
220. The **tailor** of three shillings makes a damage of six shillings.

221. When two **thieves** quarrel the farmer gets back his cow.
222. He is not in the way who is on the **threshold.**
223. **Time** is always before us.
224. The smith has **tongs** that the hands may not burn.
225. A nasty **tongue** cuts a bony neck.
226. A foaming **torrent** does not freeze.
227. One climbs up the **tree** from the root, not from the top.
228. A rotting **tree** leans long before it falls.
229. He who confesses the **truth** fails to get a night's lodging.
230. Better a finger-tip of **virtue** than a firkin of learning.
231. The frightened man has many **voices.**
232. **Walking** one gets into the village, leaping one is left on the way.
233. The more one **walks** the more hills one sees.
234. He who does not help others was never in **want.**
235. What is gained in **war** is eaten in war.
236. The **water** is the same on both sides of the boat.
237. What the **waterfall** brings the stream carries away.
238. **Wealth** can be concealed, but not poverty.
239. The striking man easily finds his **weapon.**
240. The **wet** is not afraid of becoming moist.
241. What you will drop, lay it in your bosom ; what you will reveal, say it to your **wife.**
242. A man has plenty of time to choose a **wife.**
243. From a rich house buy a horse, from a poor house take a **wife.**
244. It is well to seek a **wife** in the village, but not in the street.
245. A man without a **wife** is a man without thoughts.
246. The goat's butter, the **wife's property**—these things are not needed in the house.
247. The **wind** ceased to blow when the rain came from the clouds.

    [i.e. the angry woman ceased to scold when the tears came from her eyes.]
248. Who lies when the **wind** is fair must row when the wind is against him.
249. The **wind** is my refuge, the opposite shore my support.
250. Warm days in **winter** are also cold, and cold days in summer are also warm.
251. The **winter** does not go without looking backward.
252. The **wise man** is cheated only once.
253. The mill goes with the current and **woman** against it.
254. A man is needed for a day, a dog for a week, a **woman** always.
255. The stony earth grows the corn, the angry **woman** does the work.
256. A poor **woman** has many troubles : weeping children, wet firewood, leaking kettle, and a cross man.
257. A man goes out of his house for business, a **woman** to be looked at.
258. His tongue is not burnt with porridge who quarrels with old **women.**
259. With old **women** and wolves the Lord spoiled the world.
260. Who does not understand half a **word** will not be wiser for a whole word.
261. The **world** is a sure teacher, but it takes a big payment.
262. One stick of **wood** does not burn even in the fire of the poor.
263. Throw a crooked stick of **wood** into the stove, the less room there is for other wood.
264. The **years** are grave-diggers of our joys and sorrows.
265. The **years** are not brethren.
266. Before us stands **yesterday.**

267. The mind of the **young** is like the water in the trough: it splashes out from both sides.

268. The thoughts of **youth** are long, long thoughts. (*Lap.*)

FRENCH

(Including Alsatian, Gascon, Languedoc and Provençal)

An Introduction to this collection by Professor Denis Saurat, D.ès.L., will be found on page xlvii

1. In all **abstention** is some good.
2. Old **accounts** make new disputes.
3. **Adam's rib** has more aloes than honey.
4. **Admiration** is the daughter of ignorance.
5. If **adversity** finds you always on foot prosperity will not make you go faster.
6. **Adversity** is the touchstone of friendship.
7. **Adversity** makes men, but prosperity makes monsters.
8. It is good to give **advice,** but better to give the remedy.
9. There is no good **advice** unless it is followed.
10. **Age** is only made for horses.
11. **All** passes, all breaks, all wearies.
12. **Allegory** dwells in a transparent place.
13. The little **alms** are the best alms.
14. He who serves the **altar** must live by the altar.
15. To ask in **anger** is to go to sea in a storm.
16. That's a vicious **animal,** when one attacks him, he defends himself.
17. We drink without being thirsty, and make love at any time; that is the only distinction between us and the other **animals.**
18. The **apple** never falls far from the tree.
19. A beautiful disorder is an effect of **art.**
20. An **art** requires a whole man.
21. Do not buy the muleteer's **ass,** nor marry the innkeeper's daughter.
22. There are many **asses** at the fair that resemble each other. (*Old French. Before XVth Cent.*)
23. It takes a **bad heart** to say a good thing.
24. A **bad man** is never comical.

    [i.e. a really amusing man cannot be a bad man.]
25. Be not a **baker** if your head be of butter.
26. When one **bakes,** some dough remains on the fingers.
27. Take the **ball** as it bounces.
28. After a great **banquet,** little bread.
29. It is better to go back from one's word than to make a bad **bargain.** (*Gascon.*)
30. It is only good **bargains** that ruin.
31. None but the **bashful** lose.
32. Every hooked **beak** is maintained by prey.
33. He has found the **bean** in the cake.

    [i.e. ancient custom of the king of the bean was known in most European countries.]
34. It is the **beaten man** who clamours for more fighting.
35. Without grace **beauty** is an unbaited hook.

36. **Beauty** is eloquent even when silent.
37. There is nothing so proud as the rich man who has been a **beggar.** (*Gascon.*)
38. There is no pride like the **beggar** grown rich.
39. Nothing is dearer than the **begged** and the expected.
40. He has not done who is **beginning.**
41. Who hears only one **bell** hears only one sound.
    [i.e. one story is good till another is told.]
42. He is like a **bell** that says, " Come in, come in," but itself remains outside.
43. A hungry **belly** has no ears.
44. To make oneself **beloved** is after all the best way to be useful.
45. " **Better** " is the enemy of " good ".
46. He who doesn't know of whom to **beware** bewares of everyone. (*Old French. Before XVth Cent.*)
47. Golden **bishop,** wooden crosier ; wooden bishop, golden crosier.
48. He that shows his teeth has no skill in **biting.**
49. By force of striking one becomes a **blacksmith.** (*Gascon.*)
50. He who thinks to do well should not be **blamed.** (*Old French. Before XVth Cent.*)
51. **Boldness,** and again boldness, and always boldness.
52. For the last the **bones.**
53. One must learn to be **bored.**
54. He who finds **boredom** everywhere doesn't know which way to escape. (*Old French. Before XVth Cent.*)
55. He who **borrows** most pays the most.
56. Unstringing the **bow** does not cure the wound.
57. Who comes from afar may **brag** without fear.
58. He thinks of everything who wants **bread.**
59. Failing fowl, **bread** and onion.
60. To be like **bread** and knife.
    [i.e. familiar.]
61. Forbidden **bread** creates an appetite.
62. He eats his **bread** from his pocket.
    [i.e. selfish person.]
63. Cut **bread** has no master.
64. Hot **bread** has only three quarters and dry bread has four.
65. Egg of an hour, **bread** of a day, wine of a year, drink of ten, woman of fifteen, and friend of thirty.
66. Of smells, **bread** ; of tastes, salt.
67. To strike **bread** with both hands.
    [i.e. to eat much.]
68. A mouth busy with song is not busy with the **bunch.** (*Vineyard proverb.*)
69. He who takes a **bundle** in the morning carries it all day.
70. A useful **burden** becomes light.
71. **Burgundy** for kings, champagne for duchesses, claret for gentlemen, and port for citizens.
72. Push your **business,** but don't let your business push you.
73. Those who have no **business** make one.
74. You should not promise more **butter** than cheese.
75. There are more foolish **buyers** than foolish sellers.
76. **Cabbage** for cabbage.
77. There are **calumnies** against which even innocence loses courage.
78. **Capon** comes to him who eats capon.
79. There is nothing so well done but may be **carped at.**
80. He defends a fair **castle** who defends his own heart.
81. The **cat** knows well whose beard it licks.
82. Who is born a **cat** will run after mice.
83. The man is not escaped who still drags his **chain** after him.

84. The more things **change** the more they remain the same.
85. He who does not eat **cheese** will go mad.
86. To one dove alone **cherries** are bitter.
87. In **chess** the fools are nearest the kings.
88. At the bottom of the sack are found the broken **chestnuts.** (*Languedoc.*)
89. He that eats **chicken** gets chicken.
90. The man is always the **child,** and the child is always the man.
91. It is easier to build many **chimneys** than to keep one warm.
92. In all things a man's **choice** lies not between the good and the bad, but between the bad and the worse.
93. The worst **clothed** are still put to the windward.
94. The **coat** remakes many a man.
95. A **colt** is worth nothing unless he breaks his halter.
96. Beware of that man the day he receives **communion.**
97. He who has a **companion** has a master.
98. He who lives **complains.** (*Old French. Before XVth Cent.*)
99. Never enter into a **compromise** where you will leave your coat.
100. There is no debt pains so quickly as **contempt.**
101. To **contradict** sometimes means to knock at the door to know whether there is anyone in the house.
102. Every **cook** makes his sauce. (*Gascon.*)
103. He has eaten his **corn** in the blade.
104. The night brings **counsel.**
105. **Count** after your father.
106. He who takes and doesn't **count** doesn't know what he spends. (*Old French. Before XVth Cent.*)
107. If you have a good case, try to compromise; if a bad one, take it into **court.**
108. In descending, the **cow** pulls as hard as the ox. (*Gascon.*)
109. The old **cow** thinks that she was never a calf. (*Old French. Before XVth Cent.*)
110. He does the **crime** who profits by it.
111. The **crown** of France never fell to the distaff.
112. The **crust** is squeezed so hard that the crumb jumps out. (*Old French. Before XVth Cent.*)
113. One may press the **crust** so much that the crumb is worth nothing. (*Old French. Before XVth Cent.*)
114. He who would be **cured** must tell his ill. (*Gascon.*)
115. A **dainty morsel** is only good as long as it remains in the mouth.
116. After good cheer comes **dancing.**
117. He who has **daughters** is always a shepherd.
118. Every **day** which we do not time to the full is a day wasted.
119. The **dead** are always wrong.
120. Those whom we pronounce **dead** are doing wondrously well.
121. If you give before you are **dead** prepare yourself for suffering.
122. A thing too much seen is not held **dear.**
123. **Dearness** gluts.
124. **Death** is deaf to our wailings.
125. Those who are ready to advise you will not pay your **debts.**
126. He who only sees with other people's eyes is **deceived.**
127. **Desire** promises more than enjoyment holds.
128. He who **desires,** goes; he who does not desire, sends.
129. The **devil** goes away from a closed door.
130. The **devil** is not always at the poor man's door.
131. Having sold her skin to the **devil,** she bequeaths her bones to God.
132. The **devil** was good-looking when he was young.

133. One can't comb a **devil** who has no hair.
134. Half the **devil's flour** is chaff.
135. To part is to **die** a little.
136. Go where you will ; **die** when you must.
137. He endures much who doesn't **die** young.
138. He **dies** every day who lives a lingering life.
139. It is mustard after **dinner.**
140. Order, counter-order, **disorder.**
141. All **disputes** arise out of " yes " and " no "
142. To **do,** one must be doing.
143. He is a fool who makes his **doctor** his heir.
144. The **doctor** is often more to be feared than the disease.
145. The presence of the **doctor** is the beginning of the cure.
146. The gentle-handed **doctor** makes a stinking wound.
147. Young **doctors** make humpy cemeteries.
148. It is only **doctors** who are allowed to lie.
149. Only a **dog** and a Frenchman walks after he has eaten.
150. He who would drown his **dog** first calls him mad.
151. A well-bred **dog** hunts by nature.
152. When in doubt one beats the **dog** in front of the lion.
153. One must flatter the **dog** till one has reached the stones.
154. There are good **dogs** of all sizes.
155. The braying of a **donkey** never reaches heaven. (*Gascon.*)
156. A **door** must be either open or shut.

    [Said on any occasion where there is only one alternative.]
157. The open **door** tempts the saint.
158. Through big **doors** blow great gusts [of wind]. (*Languedoc.*)
159. To seek to know is to seek occasion to **doubt.**
160. **Doubt,** and you'll not be deceived.
161. The **dough** of poor people freezes in the oven.
162. Beware of the anger of the **dove.**
163. **Dress** slowly when you are in a hurry.
164. It is better to **drink** from the fountain than from the stream. (*Old French. Before XVth Cent.*)
165. Who **drinks** will drink again.
166. There is no god for **drunkards.**
167. One sees more old **drunkards** than old doctors.
168. A **dumb wife** has never been hit by her husband.
169. He who **earns** easily spends easily. (*Old French. Before XVth Cent.*)
170. The **ears** often believe others, but the eyes only themselves.
171. He who thinks he has an **egg** on the fire has only the shell.
172. A bad **ember** smokes every **day.**
173. He who **embraces** much collects little.
174. One should not **employ** those one suspects, nor suspect those one employs.
175. The **enemies** of my enemies are my friends.
176. The best is always the **enemy** of good.
177. The **English** have one hundred religions, but only one sauce.
178. One **enjoys** without care only that which one can lose without pain.
179. What is **enough** was never little.
180. **Envy** surpasses avarice.
181. Many people are **esteemed** merely because they are not known.
182. One **evening** is worth two mornings. (*Old French. Before XVth Cent.*)
183. There is somebody who knows better than anybody, and that is **everybody.**
184. **Everything** comes to the man who does not need it.
185. **Everything** has belonged to others and returns to others.

186. Precept begins ; **example** perfects.
187. The **eyes** are always children.
188. To sore **eyes** light is dark.
189. Joy and courage make a handsome **face.**
190. One **faith,** one tongue, one heart.
191. One never **falls** but on the side towards which one leans.
192. A **father** is a banker given by nature.
193. A **fault** which is denied is committed twice over.
194. People count up the **faults** of those who keep them waiting.
195. **Fear** is a great inventor.
196. **February** which gives snow pledges a fine summer.
197. No **female,** save woman, seeks the male except in the spring. (*Gascon.*)
198. The beaten pay the **fine.**
199. Any water puts out **fire.**
200. A crooked log makes a good **fire.**
    [i.e. don't judge from personal appearances.]
201. The most covered **fire** is the strongest.
202. He who is nearest the **fire** warms himself the soonest.
203. He who needs **fire** will seek it with his fingers. (*Provençal.*)
204. Catching one **fish** is always fishing.
205. He **fishes** on who catches one.
206. The **flag** protects the cargo.
207. Every **flatterer** lives at the expense of him who listens.
208. He who **flees** finds someone to pursue him.
209. Everyone takes his **flogging** in his own way.
210. What is earned by the **flute** goes with the drum.
    [i.e. light come, light go.]
211. Best **fly** low on account of the branches.
212. The shortest **follies** are the best.
213. He who is never guilty of **folly** is not as wise as he fancies.
214. He who speaks **folly** of others forgets himself. (*Old French. Before XVth Cent.*)
215. He who chases **folly** soon catches it. (*Old French. Before XVth Cent.*)
216. He who **fondles** you more than usual has either deceived you or wishes to do so.
217. The **fool** who is silent passes for wise.
218. God only can understand **fools.**
219. **Fools** are more useful to the wise than the wise to fools.
220. A **fool's** head never whitens.
221. To want to **forget** something is to think of it.
222. To understand everything is to **forgive** everything.
223. A **fortress** that is not attacked has no need of defence.
224. **Fortune** sells what we think she gives.
225. In a house it is better to have a **fountain** than a cistern.
226. The **fox** believes that everyone eats hens like himself.
227. A time will come when **foxes** will need their tails.
228. He who is not too cruel to his enemy will be too harsh to his **friend.**
229. The interested **friend** is a swallow on the roof.
230. A table **friend** is a variable friend.
231. If your **friend** is one-eyed, look at him in profile.
232. A good **friend** is worth a hundred relations.
233. He who would keep a **friend** should do no business with him.
234. He cannot be a **friend** to anyone who is his own enemy.
235. He never was a **friend** who ceased to be one.
236. One has always enough strength to bear the misfortunes of one's **friends.**
237. One is never betrayed except by one's own **friends.**

238. My **friends'** friends are my friends.
239. **Friendship** is love without wings.
240. **Friendship** makes more happy households than love.
241. After the **fruit,** wine or the priest.
242. Leave off playing when the **game** is at its best.
243. He who leaves the **game** loses it. (*Gascon.*)
244. Of two lookers-on at a **game,** one will become a player. (*Gascon.*)
245. Knocking over a **game-keeper** is not knocking over a man—it is crushing a principle.
246. There is no one so **generous** as the man who has nothing to give.
247. **Genius** means patience.
248. No purchase is as good as a **gift.**
249. A pretty **girl** and a tattered gown always meet something to catch them.
250. It is **giving** nothing to men not to give oneself.
251. There is still something more to be **gleaned.**
252. He who resists the **goad** is pricked twice. (*Old French. Before XVth Cent.*)
253. Where the **goat** is tethered she must browse.
254. A little and peace with it is the gift of **God.**
255. He who has the grace of the world has the grace of **God.**
256. Nothing without **God.**
257. The good **God** does not allow little trees to grow up to heaven.
258. **God** guards the moon from the wolves.
[i.e. dread of remote danger.]
259. **God** hath often a great share in a little house.
260. **God,** our parents, and our master can never be requited.
261. **God** puts a good root in the little pig's way.
262. To the washed hand **God** sends a good meal.
263. For a web begun **God** sends the thread.
264. **God** works in moments.
265. He whom **God** would help loses his wife.
266. The hour is in **God's** hands. Hope is in the reach of all.
267. One may buy **gold** too dear.
268. That is **gold** which is worth gold.
269. Many a one is **good** because he can do no mischief.
270. In order to be **good** enough, one must [often] be too good.
271. When doing **good** we never know all the good that we do.
272. There is no **good deed** for which you will not be punished one day.
273. They will be hushed by a **good deed** who laugh at a wise speech.
274. **Good fortune** comes to us in our sleep. (*Gascon.*)
275. Ill-gotten **goods** consume the rest. (*Languedoc.*)
276. One has always more **goods** than life.
277. **Good things** come to some people while they sleep.
278. **Good words** make us laugh ; good deeds make us silent.
279. Who eats of the king's **goose** will void a feather forty years after. (*Gascon.*)
280. Pluck the **goose** without making it scream.
281. **Gratitude** is the memory of the heart.
282. **Green wood** and warm bread bring ruin to a house. (*Languedoc.*)
283. A **guest** and a fish after three days are poison.
284. There's nothing like being bespattered for making a man defy the **gutter.**
285. Once is not **habit.**
286. She does her **hair** well and is fond of her Mamma.
[Said of an ugly girl.]

287. It is better to stretch out one's **hand** than one's neck.
288. To fold your **hands** is well; to open them is better.
[i.e. prayer is good; alms are better.]
289. The only **happy man** is he who thinks he is.
290. A **hatchet** is a key for any lock.
291. There is no lack of **hats** for the man who has a good head. (*Gascon.*)
292. A **head wind** makes a man wise.
293. He who is careful of his **health** is at death's door. (*Old French. Before XVth Cent.*)
294. Good **health** or bad makes our philosophy.
295. One is as old as one's **heart.**
296. The greatest thoughts are from the **heart.**
297. The **heart** has no secret which our conduct does not reveal.
298. The **heart** has its reasons that reason wots not of.
299. A satisfied **heart** will often sigh.
300. There is nothing so cold as the **hearth.**
301. It is a sorry house in which the cock is silent and the **hen** crows.
302. The **hen** ought not to cackle when the cock is by.
303. He pays too dear a price for **honey** who licks it off thorns.
304. **Honours** change manners.
305. **Hope** is the bread of the unlucky.
306. **Hope** is the dream of the man awake.
307. It is **hope** that makes the future.
308. Bright harness to an old **horse.**
309. It is easy to go afoot when one leads one's **horse** by the bridle.
310. To bridle the **horse** by the tail.
[i.e. to begin at the wrong end.]
311. A good **horse** goes alone to the trough.
312. The **horse** which draws most is most whipped.
313. One whips always the **horse** who draws.
314. He who would have a **horse** without a fault must go on foot. (*Gascon.*)
315. One **hour** is worse than a hundred.
316. We only count the **hours** when they are lost.
317. One is never so rich as when one moves **house.**
318. **A hundred years** a banner, a hundred years a barrow.
319. All are not **hunters** who blow the horn.
320. To live happily together the **husband** must be deaf and the wife blind.
321. With an old **husband's** goods one buys a young one.
322. The **ideal** is but the truth at a distance.
323. It is profound **ignorance** that inspires the dogmatic tone.
324. **Ignorance** and incuriosity are two very soft pillows.
325. By dint of going **ill** all will be well.
326. One sometimes forgives the **ill** one has suffered, but never the ill one has done.
327. The **ill clad** are put against the wind.
328. He who does not grow tired, tires out his **ill-luck** at last.
329. For all **ills** there are two remedies—time and silence.
330. To believe a thing **impossible** is to make it so.
331. It is always the **impossible** that happens.
332. According to the man, the **incense.** (*Gascon.*)
333. A little **incense** burned sets most things right.
334. **Indolence** is often taken for patience.
335. One finds but little **ingratitude** so long as one is in a position to do good.
336. An **innkeeper's daughter** and a fig-tree in a corner are ripe before their time. (*Languedoc.*)
337. Never did **innocence** and mystery long together dwell.

338. Even **iron** may be chafed into a heat.

339. Without **jealousy** there is no love.

340. Trust a snake before a **Jew,** a Jew before a Greek, but never trust an Armenian.

341. The sword of **justice** has no scabbard.

342. Excessive **justice** is often excessive wrong.

343. The love of **justice** is in most men nothing more than the fear of suffering injustice.

344. Nothing grows old more quickly than a **kindness.**

345. Much **kindred,** much trouble.

346. The **king** never leaves hold until the people pull too hard for him.

347. The silence of the people is the lesson of **kings.**

348. A **kiss** is nought when the heart is silent.

349. Nothing more closely resembles an honest man than a **knave.**

350. You must **knot** both ends.

351. There is no use in looking for **knots** in a bulrush.

352. To wish to **know** is to wish to doubt.

353. He who **knows** better should say best.

354. He who **knows** himself the most esteems himself the least. (*Old French. Before XVth Cent.*)

355. Don't rely on the **label** of the bag.

356. Where the **lamb** comes from there returns the skin.

357. Who has but one **lamb** makes it fat.

358. We must wait for the **lame.**

359. He who has a little and loses a little **laments** a lot.

360. A **lame man** won't walk with one who is more lame.

361. A man who knows two **languages** is worth two men.

362. We must **laugh** before we are happy, lest we should die without having laughed.

363. The most wasted of all days is the day when we have not **laughed.**

364. **Laughter** does not prove a man at ease.

365. Who goes to **law** should have three bags : one of papers, one of money, and one of patience.

366. He who does what he can fulfils all the **laws.**

367. Nothing is so damaging to **laws** as their number.

368. **Laws** have wax noses.

369. A good **lawyer** is a bad neighbour.

370. One may steal nothing save a **lawyer's** purse.

371. **Lazy people** are always anxious to be doing something.

372. He who trembles to hear a **leaf** fall should keep out of the wood.

373. One must draw back in order to **leap** further.

374. He who sees **leather** cut asks for a strap.

375. A little bit of **leaven** sours a big bit of paste. (*Old French. Before XVth Cent.*)

376. "They say" is often a great **liar.**

377. **Liberty** is the right to do whatever the law permits.

378. He who can **lick** can bite.

379. **Licking** is better than biting. (*Languedoc.*)

380. Eyes and brow often **lie** and the mouth still more often.

381. **Life** is an onion which one peels crying.

382. **Life** is half spent before we know what life is.

383. The first half of **life** is spent in longing for the second ; the second in regretting the first.

384. We come and cry, and that is **life** ; we cry and go, and that is death.

385. He only recites the **litany** during a storm. (*Gasçon.*)

386. To a **loaf** fifteen days old, hunger of three weeks.

387. To borrow a **loaf** from the batch.
[i.e. to have intercourse before marriage.]
388. A hard **loaf** needs a sharp tooth.
389. To make little **loaves.**
[i.e. to say little in an important manner. To pay court to a woman.]
390. At the other door one gives two **loaves.**
391. He who **loses,** sins.
392. After **losing** at first one becomes a good loser.
393. When you are **losing,** wear a winning face.
394. After a **loss** one loses all the more.
395. **Love,** a cough, smoke, and money cannot long be hid.
396. **Love** and ambition suffer no rival.
397. **Love** and gout, no one knows where they put themselves. (*Gascon.*)
398. **Love** and the itch never look to see where they will attach themselves. (*Languedoc.*)
399. One grows used to **love** and to fire.
400. **Love** can do much ; money everything. (*Old French. Before XVth Cent.*)
401. In hawks, hounds, arms, and **love,** for one pleasure a thousand pains.
402. He who forbids **love** gives it spurs.
403. **Love** lasts as long as money, but money goes in search of adventure.
404. **Love** rarely dies a sudden death.
405. Those who do not **love** seldom feel great joy ; those who do love are liable to great sorrow.
406. **Love** teaches even asses to dance.
407. If we cannot have what we **love,** we must love what we have.
408. A good hater makes a good **lover.**
409. We always return to our first **loves.**
410. Old **loves** and old embers soon catch alight.
411. Who **loves** most, chastises most.
412. One only **loves** well when it is no longer necessary to tell each other so.
413. He who **loves** without being loved is charmed with love. (*Gascon.*)
414. The biggest piece of **luck** is oft a stumbling-block.
415. Better be **mad** with the crowd than wise by yourself.
416. A **mansion** pulled down is half built up again.
417. To eat and drink, and sleep together, is **marriage,** methinks.
418. All will go well save the **marriage** of an old woman. (*Old French. Before XVth Cent.*)
419. **Marry** your son when you will and your daughter when you can.
420. It is hunger **marrying** thirst.
421. The last to come is often the **master.**
422. Bolt thy fine **meal,** and eat good paste, without report or trumpets' blast.
423. Bread and cheese is **medicine** for the well.
424. Most men die of their **medicines** and not of their maladies.
425. Every man complains of his **memory,** but no man complains of his judgment.
426. **Men** are rare.
427. **Men** are taken by their words and beasts by their horns.
428. Between **merchant** and merchant there is only the hand.
429. With **merchants** as with pigs, one can only know if they were fat when they are dead. (*Languedoc.*)
430. Everyone must go to the **mill** with his own sack.
431. **Misfortune** comes on horseback and gces away on foot.
432. One has always enough strength to bear the **misfortunes** of one's friends.

433. There is something in the **misfortunes** of our best friends which is not altogether displeasing to us.

434. **Mistrust** is the mother of security.

435. **Miracles** come to those who believe in them.

436. He who is in the **mire** himself would push another in.

437. The **miser** and the pig are useless until they are dead.

438. Only he who does nothing makes a **mistake.** (*Gascon.*)

439. Nothing is more eloquent than ready **money.**

440. It is better to waste one's steps than one's **money.**

441. Peace makes **money** and money makes war. (*Languedoc.*)

442. He who has **money** has capers.

443. The poor man's **money** disappears like dew in the sun. (*Languedoc.*)

444. **Money** is a good passport.

445. A man without **money** is like a wolf without teeth.

446. **Money** makes play.

447. No **money,** no Swiss.

[Originally meant as a hit at the Swiss guards, signifying if you want a thing, you must pay for it.]

448. **Money** serves wise men and governs fools.

449. He who lends **money** to a friend loses both.

450. You must have **money** to commence the game.

451. If you would know the value of **money,** try to borrow some.

452. One never gets more than one's **money's worth** of anything.

453. There is only the **morning** in all things.

454. He shames his **mother** who does not resemble his father. (*Old French. Before XVth Cent.*)

455. **Mother's love** is ever in its spring.

456. When the **mountains** are white the valleys are cold. (*Languedoc.*)

457. He who puts a good morsel in his **mouth** sends good news to his heart. (*Old French. Before XVth Cent.*)

458. The clearest water can make **mud.**

459. Were you as black as a **mulberry,** you are white [fair] for him who loves you.

460. The **mule** long keeps a kick in reserve for its master.

461. One often has **need** of a lesser than oneself.

462. There is no such thing as a **necessary man.**

463. Bread and wine to your **neighbour.**

464. A good **neighbour,** a good morrow.

465. He who can give has many good **neighbours.**

466. Stroke a **nettle** and it will sting you ; grasp it and it is as soft as silk.

467. At the bakehouse and the mill one hears all the **news.**

468. **Night** has no friend.

469. He who puts up for the **night** late goes to bed angry. (*Old French. Before XVth Cent.*)

470. He whose own **nose** runs always wants to blow other people's.

471. A big **nose** never spoiled a pretty face.

472. **Nothing** happens for nothing.

473. To **offer** much to him who asks little is to flatly refuse his request.

474. Few persons know how to be **old.**

475. A dealer in **onions** is a good judge of leeks.

476. Form your **opinion** of a man from his questions rather than from his answers.

477. For **over-buying** there is no remedy but selling again.

478. People **paid** in advance have broken arms.

479. You may put anything on **paper.**

480. **Paper** suffers everything.

481. Where **paper** speaks beards are silent. (*Languedoc.*)

482. **Paper** speaks when men are silent.

483. Take men by their **passions,** and you may carry them whither you please.

484. With the trowel of **patience** we dig out the roots of truth.

485. The securest wall of a town is **peace.** (*Languedoc.*)

486. A stick is a good **peacemaker.**

487. Between the **pear** and the cheese.
[i.e. over the walnuts and wine.]

488. A mess of broth hath lost the **physician** his fee.

489. To the satiated **pigeon** the cherries are sour.

490. **Pills** are to be swallowed, not chewed.
[i.e. discontent.]

491. **Play** with the hands is boorish play.

492. Every age wants its **playthings.**

493. At twenty-one devours **pleasure,** at thirty-one enjoys it, at forty and fifty-one seeks it, at sixty-one regrets it.

494. He who has little is not **poor,** but he who desires much. (*Gascon.*)

495. If it is **possible,** it is done ; if it is not possible, it shall be done.

496. I can tell by my own **pot** how the others are boiling.

497. **Praise** is generally given only that it may be returned.

498. We make large promises to avoid making small **presents.**

499. When **pride** rides before, misfortune follows fast behind.

500. No **priest** blames his relics. (*Old French. Before XVth Cent.*)

501. He who values a clean house should not let into it either a **priest** or a pigeon.

502. It is fair that the **priest** should live by the altar.

503. It is human ignorance alone which causes the pot to boil for **priests.**

504. Things **promised** are things due.

505. **Property** is theft. (*Socialistic proverb.*)

506. Children and fools are **prophets.**

507. **Prosperity** makes few friends.

508. A good **proverb** is made to remember. (*Old French. Before XVth Cent.*)

509. He who has his **purse** full preaches to the poor man.

510. Tired folk are **quarrelsome.**

511. **Rain** always falls on those who are wet. (*Gascon.*)

512. It is a little **rain** that wets.

513. A man is **rated** by others as he rates himself.

514. Feed a **raven** and it will pick out your eyes.

515. Great **realms** have never been conquered by other people's arms.

516. When a man begins to **reason** he ceases to feel.

517. He who **refuses** a little must not take a lot. (*Old French. Before XVth Cent.*)

518. The man that knows how to dissemble knows how to **reign.**

519. On the **removal** of one, another is not wanting.

520. He who sees well and takes badly rightly **repents.** (*Old French. Before XVth Cent.*)

521. There are some **reproaches** which commend, and some praises which slander.

522. **Repute** hangs a man.

523. If one became **rich** through hard work, a donkey would have a packsaddle of gold. (*Languedoc.*)

524. The **rich man** does not know who are his friends. (*Old French. Before XVth Cent.*)

525. **Right** needs aid.

526. A good country, a bad **road.**

527. Save a **rogue** from the rope and he will hang you with it.

528. One must leave a **room** by door or window.

529. It is by believing in **roses** that brings them to bloom.

530. Green wood, new bread and new cider **ruin** a house. (*Normandy.*)

531. It is not enough to **run,** one must set out in time.

532. **Rust** wears more than use.

533. At the bottom of the **sack** is found the worst corn. (*Gascon.*)

534. Two that are proud can't sit on the same **saddle.**

535. Everyone preaches for his **saint.**

536. For love of the **saint** one kisses the relics. (*Old French. Before XVth Cent.*)

537. All **saints** help in the descents. (*Gascon.*)

538. Between two **Saturdays** happen many marvels. (*Old French. Before XVth Cent.*)

539. The **sauce** is better than the fish.

540. No one is more hindered than he who holds the handle of the **saucepan.**

541. **Saying well** causes a laugh; doing well produces silence.

542. One must **scratch** people where they itch. (*Gascon.*)

543. He who **scratches** where it itches does wrong to no one. (*Gascon.*)

544. There is no need for a **sculptor** to be himself made of marble.

545. The stronger the **seam** the worse the rent.

546. The only **secret** a woman can keep is that of her age.

547. The **secret** of two is God's secret.

548. Offended **self-esteem** will never forgive.

549. Some **sell** who cannot deliver.

550. One is never so well **served** as by oneself.

551. The best **served** is not he who puts other people's arms at the ends of his arms.

552. There are three **sexes,** men, women, and clergy.

553. He **shakes hands** often who is loathe to go.

554. He does not suffer **shame** who turns back half-way. (*Old French. Before XVth Cent.*)

555. He who isn't there hasn't his **share.** (*Old French. Before XVth Cent.*)

556. He who seeks the **sheep** finds the wolf. (*Gascon.*)

557. The **shepherd's** hour.

[i.e. propitious time for wooers—lucky moment.]

558. If you would make a pair of good **shoes** take for the sole the tongue of a woman—it never wears out. (*Alsatian.*)

559. **A short mass** and a long dinner is the joy of the cavalier. (*Old French. Before XVth Cent.*)

560. He who is **shut outside** is forgotten inside. (*Old French. Before XVth Cent.*)

561. All **sicknesses** arrive on wings and depart limpingly.

562. The **sign-board** brings the custom.

563. **Silence** makes no mistakes.

564. One is **silent** more through judgment than stupidity.

565. A **sin** concealed is half pardoned.

[When care is taken to conceal the scandal.]

566. An old **sin** makes a new shame. (*Old French. Before XVth Cent.*)

567. When all other **sins** are old avarice is young.

568. An old **skin** doesn't bear stitching. (*Old French. Before XVth Cent.*)

569. The **skin** is nearer than the shirt.

570. One half of the world take delight in uttering **slander,** and the other half in believing it.

571. A **slate** that falls in the present weighs heavier than a tower that falls in the past.

572. To **sleep** is to eat.

573. He who **sleeps** dines.

574. **Smoke** goes to the beautiful.

575. An old **soldier,** an old fool.

576. The man who has got a good **son-in-law** has found a son, but he who has met with a bad one has lost a daughter.

577. He who only has nineteen **sous** can't count in francs.

578. You must spoil before you **spin.**

579. If you would drink pure water go to the **spring.**

580. That which doesn't **sprout** into grass, doesn't sprout into an ear. (*Old French. Before XVth Cent.*)

581. The **stable** wears out a horse more than a road.

582. No one knows the **stars** who has not slept.

583. The first **step** binds one to the second.

584. The **sting** lies in the tail.

585. **A stingy man** is always poor.

586. He who moves **stones** breaks his fingers. (*Old French. Before XVth Cent.*)

587. **Stones** go to the heap. (*Languedoc.*)

588. People throw **stones** only at the tree which is loaded with fruit.

589. He who works has the **straw ;** he who idles has the hay.

590. **Strike** high and speak low.

591. He who fears to **suffer,** suffers from fear.

592. What you can't get is just what **suits** you.

593. When the **sun** shines the moon has nothing to do. (*Languedoc.*)

594. Nowadays, whatever is not worth saying is **sung.**

595. He who buys the **superfluous** will soon sell the needful.

596. When one finds oneself among **swine** the best thing to do is to dispense with a plate.

597. He who bears the **sword,** he bears peace.

598. A brave arm makes a short **sword** long.

599. A bottle of Chambertin, a ragout sardanapalus, and a lady to talk to are the three best **table companions** in France.

600. There is nothing so difficult to skin as the **tail.**

601. That which is worth **taking** is worth returning. (*Gascon.*)

602. The cost takes away the **taste.**

603. He is in a **tavern** for nothing who doesn't drink. (*Old French. Before XVth Cent.*)

604. Everything tempts the man who fears **temptation.**

605. The greatest **thief** is not on the road.

606. He who is master of his **thirst** is master of his health.

607. They that are **thirsty** drink silently.

608. He is not **thirsty** who doesn't drink water. (*Old French. Before XVth Cent.*)

609. A **thorn** comes forth point foremost.

610. The **thought** is worthless if the counter-thought be not there. (*Old French. Before XVth Cent.*)

611. He who holds the **thread** holds the ball.

612. He who **threatens** is always afraid.

613. It is too late to put one's hand to one's **throat** when the word has come out. (*Old French. Before XVth Cent.*)

614. **Time** carries away, brings, but never brings back.

615. No **time** is wasted, for some have the good and others have the bad.

616. If no one lost **time,** no one would gain time.

617. One **time** [or once] is the first. (*Old French. Before XVth Cent.*)

618. **Time** strengthens that which it does not shake.

619. Why kill **time** when one can employ it ?

620. One may go a long way after one is **tired.**

621. The three animals that spend the most time over their **toilet** are cats, flies and women.

622. **Too much** and too little spoil the game. (*Alsatian.*)

623. No " **too much** " is good. (*Old French. Before XVth Cent.*)

624. There are **toys** for all ages.

625. On a beaten **track** no grass grows. (*Old French. Before XVth Cent.*)

626. The **true** is not always most like truth.
627. To the villages a **trumpet** of wood.
628. Nothing is beautiful but the **truth.**
629. Love **truth,** but pardon error.
630. **Truth** is the club that knocks down and kills everybody.
631. When one has one's hand full of **truth** it is not always wise to open it.
632. **Truth** lies hidden at the bottom of the well.
633. **Truth** lies in a hogshead, not in a well.
634. It is only the **truth** that offends.
635. When **ugly** comes on to ugly it loses its ugliness. (*Old French. Before XVth Cent.*)
636. The **unfortunate** are easily wounded.
637. He who obliges creates **ungrateful** folk. (*Gascon.*)
638. A man whom nobody pleases is much more **unhappy** than a man who pleases nobody.
639. **Vanity** has no greater foe than vanity.
640. **Variety** is life.
641. When **vices** forsake us we flatter ourselves that it is we who forsake them.
642. Anoint a **villain** and he will prick you ; prick a villain and he will anoint you.
643. Warm a **viper** in your bosom and he will sting you.
644. A fifth wheel in the **waggon** hinders more than helps.
645. Bad **wares** are never cheap.
646. **Water** is the eye of the land.
647. It takes little trouble to amass great **wealth,** but much to amass a little.
648. The secret of being **wearisome** is to tell everything.
649. If the **weather** is fine take your cloak ; if it rains do as you please.
650. **Weathercocks** turn more easily when placed very high.
651. The ass invited to a **wedding** ought to bring wood or water.
652. A **weed** always grows.
653. The worst **wheel** always creaks most.

    [i.e. complaint.]
654. He has eaten his **white bread** first.

    [i.e. he had the best of his life first.]
655. Beware of a good cook and a young **wife.**

    [Advice to men of sixty.]
656. A **wife** and a broken leg are best kept at home.
657. One should be the companion of one's **wife** and the master of one's hope.
658. **Wind** in the face makes a man wise.
659. **Wind** never goes in if it cannot see where to get out.
660. For a restive morsel a spur of **wine.**
661. There are dregs in the best bottle of **wine.**
662. **Wine** and confession reveal everything. (*Old French. Before XVth Cent.*)
663. One pardons the **wine** but hangs the bottle.
664. Cloudy **wine** doesn't destroy the teeth. (*Old French. Before XVth Cent.*)
665. The **wine** is drawn ; it must be drunk.
666. Bad **wine** [is] given to drive away poor relations.
667. **Wine** poured out is not wine swallowed.
668. White meat, white **wine** ; red meat, red wine.
669. In **winter** it rains everywhere ; in summer where God wills.
670. Who **wishes** the end, wishes the means.
671. Great **wits** jump.
672. For **wolf's** flesh dog sauce.
673. You must howl if you are among the **wolves.**
674. When **wolves** get into the sheepfold, should the shepherd be blamed for using his dogs ?

675. There is nothing so virtuous as the ear of an abandoned **woman.**

676. A **woman** and a melon are hard to select.

677. A **woman** and a ship always need trimming. (*Provençal.*)

678. That which **woman** desires, God desires.

679. A **woman** is an animal who dresses, chatters, and besmears herself.

680. **Woman** is an invalid.

681. An ugly **woman** is a true remedy for love.

682. A **woman** is a very perfect devil.

683. **Woman** is made for man's purse.

684. **Woman** is man's soap.

685. The most praised **woman** is the one who is never spoken of.

686. If a **woman** knew how much an apple is worth she would never give any to a man.

687. In her first passion **woman** loves her lover, but in the others what she loves is love.

688. Without **woman** men were but ill-licked cubs. (*Provençal.*)

689. A man of straw is worth a **woman** of gold.

690. If a **woman** were as small as she is good one could make her a whole dress and a crown out of a parsley leaf.

691. A **woman** who accepts, sells herself; a woman who gives, surrenders. (*Gascon.*)

692. Mistrust a **woman** who talks of her virtue.

693. A **woman's** lips have cured many ills.

694. A **woman's tongue** does no dishonesty.

695. If you would understand men, study **women.**

696. Of **women** and horses there are none without defects.

697. With **women** and ships there is always the fear that they may capsize. (*Provençal.*)

698. **Women** can effect everything, because they govern those who govern everything.

699. Men are the reason for **women** disliking one another.

700. All the talent of **women** is abortive happiness.

701. In **women,** money, and wine lurks both profit and poison.

702. There are few honest **women** who are not tired of their trade.

703. He who has **wood** can make shavings.

704. If a **wood** hasn't eyes it has ears. (*Old French. Before XVth Cent.*)

705. A tiny little **word** can be a clap of thunder.

706. The escaped **word** is your master, the kept one your servant.

707. The **world** always ends by condemning those whom it accuses.

708. The **world** is woman's book.

709. Things are only **worth** what we make them worth.

710. **Write** like clever people and talk like everybody.

711. When everyone is **wrong,** then everyone is right.

712. Out of "**yes and no**" comes all disputes.

713. **Yesterday,** to-day, and to-morrow are the three days of man.

714. Such as **you are** we were, and such as we are you will be. (*Old French. Before XVth Cent.*)

715. **Young folks** tell what they do, old folks what they have done, and fools what they intend to do.

716. Ask the **young people**; they know everything.

717. Forty is the old age of **youth**; fifty is the youth of old age.

718. **Youth** lives on hope, old age on remembrance.

719. If **youth** only knew! If age only could!

720. **Youth** returns from afar.

BRETON

1. To know people, it is necessary to divide **beans** with them.
   [No longer the "salt" of Aristotle.]
2. The ugliest things are a poor **braggart** and a rich thief.
3. There is no difference between **bread-and-milk** and milk-and-bread.
   [i.e. don't split hairs.]
4. To put the **calf's** tail into his mouth.
   [i.e. cleverly imposing on a man.]
5. Do not shake **chestnuts** when there are children under [the tree].
   [i.e. do not tell secrets before children.]
6. A **child's affection** [is] water in a sieve.
7. When the **cock** crows at eleven, it is within an hour of midday.
   [Said to people who quote the obvious.]
8. Take the **colt** over its dam's mane.
   [i.e. flatter the mother if you want her daughter in marriage.]
9. Our Lady of Pity and Mr. Saint Peter give bad **cows** short horns.
10. The old **customs** are the good customs.
11. Seek a place easy [suitable] to **die** in.
12. A **dog** limps when it likes.
    [Said to one who makes pretexts.]
13. There is no such thing as a little **enemy.**
14. To pass by the **eyes** what is given to others.
    [i.e. to be envious of what others have.]
15. To remain between the world's **feet.**
    [i.e. to be alone without relations or support.]
16. Drive the **furrow** to the end.
17. After **giving** one must take.
18. Why deny to **God** what the saints know?
    [Said to would-be keepers of open secrets.]
19. Man goes further with his **hat** in his hand than with a stick.
20. The **horse** that resists spurs does much injustice to its flanks.
21. He that is **ignorant** can learn.
22. A **kick** is better than a tongue-blow.
23. The Sunday **labourer** gains but nine deniers the year, labour he never so hard.
24. After **laughter,** tears; after play, pain.
25. Were you as black as a mulberry, you are white [fair] for him who **loves** you.
26. To go from **meadow** to common.
    [Said of servants who go farther and fare worse.]
27. Good is sweet **milk,** good is sour milk, and good is it for everyone to remain in his rank [of life].
28. **Poverty** is not a sin; still it is best to keep it in.
29. To fry **poverty,** you want no butter.
30. From whatever quarter **rain** comes, it always wets.
31. The worst **shoe** will find its match.
32. There will be discord in the house if the **spindle** rules.
33. Good **swimmer,** good drowner.
    [Used in the passive sense.]
34. One does not untie with the nails what one has done [tied] with the **tongue.**
35. Between **too much** and too little is the exact measure.
36. The **vessel** that will not obey her helm will have to obey the rocks.
37. Winds, winds, all is but **wind!**
38. To keep a **wolf** quiet, marry him.
    [i.e. if you would keep a stubborn son quiet, get him a wife.]
39. A red sky in the morning and a **woman's advice** turn, now to good, now to bad.
40. **Work** should guide the man.

GEORGIA SEE GROUZIA, PAGE 193

GERMAN

(Including Swabian)

An Introduction to this collection by Professor Otto Höfler will be found on page lv

1. He who says " **A** " at last comes to " **Z** ".
2. When one has said " **A** ", one must also say " B ".
3. **Absolution** is a divine deception.
4. Nobody lives on **abundance.**
5. **Abundance** kills more than hunger.
6. **Abuse** is written into iron, kindness into sand.
7. Not every **abyss** has a parapet.
8. A thing that is easily **acquired** is often ill kept.
9. **Adam** and Eve ate the apple and I who didn't taste it have to pay for it.
10. **Adam** ate the apple and we still have the fever.
11. **Affection** is a bad counsellor, and in judging as in advising it should be relegated to a corner.
12. He who listens to **affection** is deaf to truth.
13. Rejoiced in youth, repented in **age.**
14. **Age** writes in sand, youth in stone.
15. Give **alms** so that your children need none.
16. In our **alphabet** " B " comes after " A ".
17. To **alter** and to make better are two different things ; much has been altered but little has been made better in the world.
18. **Ambition** and fleas jump high.
19. With a golden **anchor** one can moor in every bay.
20. **Animals** are taken by their horns, men by their word.
21. No **answer** is likewise an answer.
22. One must be either **anvil** or hammer.
23. With nice **appearance** people want to be deceived.
24. He who would not lose his **appetite** should not go into the kitchen.
25. Who has tasted a sour **apple** will have the more relish for a sweet one.
26. Even red **apples** are wormy.
27. **April** and May are the keys to the whole year.
28. **Argument** is often a sieve with which one sifts the truth.
29. Long **arms** often do less harm than short ones.
30. **Arms,** women, and locks should be looked at daily.
31. To scorn an **art** is the same as not to know it.
32. You can see by the **ashes** where the pot has stood.
33. Better **ask** twice than go wrong once.
34. He who is timorous in **asking** gives courage to refuse.
35. The loaded **ass** brays.
36. An **ass** in Germany is a professor in Rome.
37. An **axe** in the house spares the carpenter.
38. **Bacon** and rind are of the same kind.
39. A **bad cause** requires many words.
40. One remembers **bad days** longer than good ones.
41. All **bad luck** is good when one has bread with it.
42. **Bad times** make good men.
43. An empty **bag** does not stand upright.
44. When you have **ball** and bat you soon find players.
45. To go **barefoot** does not make the saint.
46. **Barefoot** travels uncomfortably but travels sure.
47. Two words to a **bargain.** (*Legal proverb.*)

48. One must also **bark** with the dogs with which one runs.
49. An empty **barrel** makes more noise than a full one.
50. The full **barrel** must be spared, the empty one spares itself.
51. No **battle** was ever lost on account of the small people.
52. Everyone likes to bore a **beam** where it is thinnest.
53. **A beautiful maid** carries her dowry on her face.
54. **Beauty** is woman's best dowry.
55. He who serves **beauty** soon becomes its servant.
56. Who lies in a silver **bed** has golden dreams.
57. **Bed** is the lazy man's prison.
58. When one goes to **bed** one should leave one's troubles in one's shoes.
59. Shared **bed**—severed hearts.
60. Many have **bees** and buy wax.
61. A **beggar** never goes astray.
62. An empty **beggar's wallet** is heavier than a full one.
63. The **beginning** and the end stretch out their hands to each other.
64. **Beginning** is always difficult.
65. Whatever the **beginning** may be 'tis the end that earns the praise.
66. He who **begins** much ends little.
67. That which one cannot grasp one must **believe.**
68. He who **believes** easily is easily deceived.
69. An empty **belly** dares more than a full head.
70. The **belly** has no conscience.
71. One must be able to sit under the **bench** as well as on it.
72. One must go to the **benches** before one comes to the chairs.
73. When **berries** are ripe they fall more often in the mire than on to a rose-leaf.
74. The **best** is often-times the enemy of the good.
75. The **best** is said, the worst thought.
76. The **best** is thoughtful, the worst talkative.
77. **Better** is better.
78. What the Big Bear is for navigators, the **Bible** is for Christians.
79. The **birch** one makes for oneself hits always the hardest.
80. If one is a **bird** one is plucked, if a fish one is scaled.
81. The older the **bird** the harder he is to pluck.
82. He who is born **black** saves the washing.
83. Don't **blame** a thing which you would not know how to praise.
84. He who wants to **blame** sometimes finds the sugar sour.
85. To remain young and yet grow old is the highest **blessing.**
86. He who is born **blind** never believes in the light.
87. Amongst the **blind** one forgets how to see.
88. **A blind man** falls less often than he with eyes.
89. Many a man asks for **blows** like a horse for its fodder.
90. God protect us from him who has read but one **book.**
91. He who raises a **boor** out of the mud has as many thanks as he who throws him in.
92. The **boot** must put up with the dirt.
93. **Boots** make the soldier.
94. When man is **born,** he cries and others laugh; when he dies he smiles and others cry.
95. **Borrowing** does well only once.
96. He who has only one **bow** should be content with one fiddle.
97. He who teaches a **boy** teaches three, a youth, a young man, and an old one.
98. Small **brain** and big heart may achieve great things.
99. **A brave man** needs but a short dagger.

100. Whose **bread** I eat, his song I sing.
101. **Bread** in a stranger's house has seven crusts.
102. Eaten **bread** is soon forgotten.
103. He who has no **bread** must eat his butter dry.
104. When the **broom** is worn out one sees what purpose it has served.
105. An old **broom** knows the corners of the house.
106. He who makes himself a **broom** should not complain of the dust.
107. When it rains **broth** the bowls are turned upside down.
108. Though they are **brothers,** yet their pockets are not sisters.
109. What can't be **brushed** must be stroked.
110. He who **builds** behind me must dwell behind me.
111. Man **builds** castles—time ruins.
112. He who **builds** on the favour of the great, advances towards fortune mounted on a crab.
113. He who **builds** on the public way must let the people have their say.
114. He who **builds** under the ground is not far from Hell.
115. He who aims at an iron target gets the **bullet** in his face.
116. If you can't get it in **bushels** take it in spoonfuls.
117. **Business** kills friendship.
118. In **business** the beginning and the end are rarely alike—if the beginning is sweet the end is bitter; and if the beginning hurts, the end heals.
119. There is no man without a " **but** ".
120. " **But** " is a fence over which few venture.
121. **Buying** is cheaper than asking.
122. The narrower the **cage,** the sweeter liberty.
123. Always **cake** spoils the appetite.
124. **Calumny** is like snowballs ; the longer one rolls them, the bigger they become.
125. He who would have the last drop out of the **can** has the lid fall on his nose.
126. He who puts out another's **candle** likewise remains in the dark.
127. The **candle** throws the light upwards.
128. As the **cap** is put on so must it be worn.
129. Each one of us must play his own **cards.**
130. **Cards** are not always played as they are dealt.
131. **Care** runs after possessions.
132. Small **cares** make many words, great ones are mute.
133. A greased **carriage** saves a horse.
134. A small heap overturns a big **cart.**
135. Fill an empty **cask** and you will see where it leaks.
136. The beginning of the **cask,** however good, always ends in dregs.
137. Many build **castles** in the air who are not capable of building a hut on the earth.
138. Even mice may bite dead **cats.**
139. **Caution** is the mother of the porcelain chest.
140. To **change** and to better are two different things.
141. **Change** brings life.
142. **Charity** gives itself rich ; covetousness hoards itself poor.
143. He who boasts with **charity** has paid himself.
144. **Charity** is a stately plant, its very rare flower is gratitude.
145. **Charity** looks at the need and not at the cause.
146. Very **cheap** is very dear.
147. With a pennyworth of **cheerfulness** one drives away a pound's worth of care.
148. To know how **cherries** and berries taste, ask children and sparrows.
149. He who likes **cherries** soon learns climbing.

150. Everybody dips into an open **chest.**
151. An open **chest** corrupts a Saint.
152. He who **chews** well will feel it in his heels.
153. Many a man **chides** himself by praising another.
154. Every **child** brings its luck with it.
155. A **child** brought up at home is an animal in other people's houses.
156. When a **child** gets its teeth the mother should sell her skirt to buy it wine.
157. Better the **child** weep than the father.
158. To be afraid of throwing away the **child** with the bath-water.
159. **Children** are like snow on the hedge.
160. If you send **children,** children come back.
161. He who teaches **children** learns more than they.
162. He who wipes the **child's** nose means to kiss the mother's cheek.
163. From a low **chimney** smoke soon gets into the air.
164. From profit the **chimney** smokes.
165. **Christ** is crucified every day.
166. In the visible church the true **Christians** are invisible.
167. **Christians** have no neighbours.
168. Everyone has a **church** in his breast.
169. What is not taken by the **Church** is taken by the Exchequer.
170. He who serves the **Church** lives on the Church.
171. The **Church** only blesses those who bless it.
172. A rich **church**—poor peasants.
173. In the primitive **Church** there were chalices of wood and priests of gold ; in the modern Church there are chalices of gold and priests of wood.
174. The best **climber** falls the most often.
175. He who **climbs** up is easily seized by the feet.
176. No **cloak** was ever made for only one shower.
177. He who would understand the hands of a **clock** must get inside the works.
178. No **clock** strikes for the happy.
179. One makes of a thing what it is ; out of coarse **cloth** a coarse garment.
180. Clean and whole gives the poorest **cloth** lustre.
181. Old **clothes** laugh at a soft brush.
182. **Clothes** make the man and rags make lice.
183. It is not so easy to avoid a hot **coal** as a flame.
184. A silken **coat** in the kitchen puts out the fire in the grate.
185. When the **cock** collects and the hen scatters a heap is never made.
186. An old **cock** makes strong soup.
187. The **cock** shuts his eyes when he crows, because he knows it by heart.
188. Empty **coffers** need not be locked.
189. The **coffin** is the brother of the cradle.
190. The **comforter's head** never aches.
191. Where one can **command** one need not request.
192. **Conscience** for many people lives in the middle of the street.
193. He who **consumes** more than he gains must afterwards eat with the mice.
194. That which is neither useful to God nor man belongs to the **convents.**
195. Don't **cook** in the pot in which others have already cooked.
196. The **cook** must have the tongue of his master.
197. What is **cooked** at home should be eaten at home.
198. When one re-knots a broken **cord** it holds, but one feels the knot.
199. One stone alone cannot grind **corn.**

200. Those who pay in advance have their **corn** coarsely ground.

201. Empty ears of **corn** stand erect, full ones bow.

202. He who has **corns** on his toes is easily overtaken.

203. A pillow is the best **councillor.**

204. He who keeps his own **counsel** must weep alone.

205. Great things are done more through **courage** than through wisdom.

206. The **cow** is milked through its mouth.

207. Favour, women, and money make a knight and a hero out of a **cow boy.**

208. He who goes with **crabs** learns to walk backwards.

209. He who makes **cream** with his mouth must make butter with his nose.

210. Caught with [a **criminal**], hanged with [a criminal].

211. An old **crust** helps the house [to save].

212. Where there is no hope of a **cure** one saves the medicine.

213. **Curses** operate quickly, they are not to be turned aside.

214. **Custom** takes the taste from the most savoury dishes.

215. Men fear **danger ;** women only the sight thereof.

216. Another **day,** another market.

217. The **day** has eyes, the night ears.

218. One **day** teaches the other, one day judges by the other, but the last one by all.

219. A **day** wants its night.

220. The **day** we fear comes quickly, the hour we long for, slowly.

221. One can see **daylight** even through the smallest hole.

222. The **days** are brothers, yet they are seldom alike.

223. The **dead** are always wrong.

224. The real **dead** one must not seek in graves.

225. When the **deaf** gives the blind a lamp he receives bagpipes.

226. The **deaf** hears with his eyes.

227. **Death** and the cloister give back nothing.

228. **Death** and women are of the same mind ; they seek those who flee from them, and flee from those who seek them.

229. He who thinks of **death** begins to live.

230. **Death** for one is bread for another.

231. **Death** is the poor man's physician.

232. **Death** makes us equal in the grave, but unequal in eternity.

233. He who pays his **debt** adds to his capital.

234. Take a straw for an old **debt,** otherwise you fatten the lawyer.

235. One does not pay old **debts,** and new ones are allowed to get old.

236. **Debts** are the real heirs.

237. **Deceivers** have full mouths and empty hands.

238. If a man **deceives** me may God forgive him ; if he deceives me again may God forgive me.

239. One talks of good **deeds,** but does not do them ; one does bad ones, but does not talk of them.

240. He who can shoot a **deer** lets the hare run away.

241. Other people's **defects** are good teachers.

242. **Destiny** leads the willing but drives the unwilling.

243. When the **devil** knocks at your door, work.

244. The **devil** likes to pour water where it is already damp.

245. Before the deed the **devil** makes it small, but afterwards he makes it big.

246. Where the abbot provides the **dice,** the monastery may play.

247. Man has only to **die** to be praised.

248. For the **diligent** the week has seven to-days, for the slothful seven to-morrows.

249. If everyone swept the **dirt** from his own door the town would be clean.

250. Where **disaster** batters the door in, fresh air also gets into the room.
251. **Disaster** only enters that door which one has left open for it.
252. Let no **discouragement** pass your knees to reach your heart.
253. There is no **discretion** below the girdle.
254. **Disease** itself is a physician.
255. Those who sit furthest from the **dish** eat the most.
256. So long as people are still singing, **divine service** is not over.
257. **Do** what thou doest.
258. If God helps you—thank the **doctor.**
259. Do not ask the **doctor,** ask the patient.
260. A young **doctor** is a new graveyard.
261. No **doctor** is better than three.
262. New **doctor**—new churchyard.
263. Good **doctors** don't like big bottles.
264. The **doctor's** errors are covered with earth, our own mistakes with love.
265. Mirth, temperance, and tranquillity shut the door in the **doctor's** face.
266. Healthy folk make sick **doctors.**
267. When there are three **doctors** to one patient the cemetery can return thanks.
268. A **dog** does not eat sausages very easily, for he has to steal them first.
269. A **dog** does not long remain tied to a sausage.
270. Even the king's **dog** has fleas.
271. He who puts up at a **dog** kennel must also gnaw bones.
272. **Dogs** and gentlemen leave the doors open.
273. Where **dogs** are, dogs bark.
274. Everybody does what he can; **dogs** bark, wolves howl, and monks lie.
275. All **dogs** bite the bitten dog.
276. With **dogs** one catches hares, with praise fools, with money women.
277. **Doing nothing** belongs to him who puts on a coat of green grass.
278. A lost **dollar** has no higher value than a lost penny.
279. He who finds a **dollar** has two dollars' worth of friends.
280. Where there is a **dollar** there is a devil, where there is none, two.
281. One first knows the value of a **dollar** when one tries to borrow one.
282. He who is in a hurry rides on a **donkey.**
283. The trot of a **donkey** does not last long.
284. He who owns the **donkey** holds him by his tail.
285. The sack carries the **donkey** to the mill.
286. Hat in hand will open any **door.**
287. No one looks for another behind a **door** if he has not hidden himself there first.
288. **Doubt** has many mantles with which to cloak itself.
289. When a **dove** flies with a raven its feathers remain white but its heart gets black.
290. Roast **doves** fly into no one's mouth.
291. **A dream** grants what one covets when awake.
292. **Drink** or run.
293. If you wish to follow people **drink** wine; if you wish to follow ducks, drink water.
294. He who **drinks** a little too much drinks much too much.
295. Even the **drop** requires time to fall.
296. What was born a **drum** is beaten till death.
297. He who sighs at his own **duties** makes of a pound a hundredweight.
298. **A dwarf** sees giants everywhere.
299. Going in at one **ear** and out at the other makes no noise.
300. Listen to him who has four **ears.**

301. He who has the **earth** for a bed must have the sky for a coverlet.
302. That which the **earth** gives she takes back again.
303. **Eat** like a healthy man and drink like a sick one.
304. Take no heed of that which is said between **eating** and drinking.
305. A man is what he **eats.**
306. As a man **eats** so he works.
307. To the **echo** belongs the last word.
308. Many will swallow an **egg** and give away the shell in alms.
309. They dispute about an **egg** and let the hens fly away.
310. "An **egg** is an egg," said the sexton, but he took the goose-egg.
311. The best **enemies** are those who threaten before.
312. Many **enemies,** much honour.
313. A beaten **enemy** is not always defeated.
314. One should respect the **enemy** through whose mistakes one learns to avoid one's own.
315. The **enemy** who fears himself is soon beaten.
316. He who seeks the **entrance** should also think of the exit.
317. One has too much, another has too little, but nobody has **enough.**
318. He who is not **envied** has not yet done anything great.
319. **Envy** eats nothing but its own heart.
320. **Envy** envies itself.
321. **Envy** is born at court, brought up in a monastery, and buried in a hospital.
322. If all were **equal,** if all were rich, and if all were at table, who would lay the cloth?
323. He who seeks **equality** should go to the cemetery.
324. **Erring** is not cheating and [a mistake is no fraud].
325. An old **error** has more friends than a new truth.
326. An **error** no wider than a hair will lead a hundred miles away from the goal.
327. He who **errs** himself can lead others.
328. The **evening** praises the day, death the life.
329. Well served, rewarded with **evil.**
330. All **evil** comes from what youth does not know and age cannot do.
331. One does **evil** enough when one does nothing good.
332. He who never does **evil** never does good.
333. **Evil** that does no harm is no worse than good that does not benefit.
334. Teaching is a long way, **example** a short one.
335. **Example** is a mute admonition.
336. **Experience** is a good medicine, but it does not come until the illness has passed.
337. Many look with one **eye** at what they give and with seven at what they receive.
338. One **eye** is a necessity, two is a luxury.
339. The **eye** should be no bigger than the stomach.
340. An **eye** that is accustomed to dust will soon bear sand.
341. He who has only one **eye** wipes it well.
342. He who looks at others over his shoulder damages his own **eyes.**
343. **Eyes** and ears have also their tongues.
344. **Eyes** are windows through which one looks into the heart.
345. The **eyes** believe themselves, the ears other people.
346. Nothing is good in the **eyes,** but bad in the stomach [also purse or mouth].
347. He who buys requires a hundred **eyes**; he who sells but one.
348. He who knows sees with his own **eyes**; he who believes, through spectacles.

349. He who does not open his **eyes** must open his purse.

350. Big **eyes** see no more than little eyes.

351. **Faithfulness** is a sister of love.

352. **Faithfulness** is found in the dog's kennel.

353. Seek **faithfulness** where you left it.

354. In a **fall** the depth is always equal to the height.

355. When **fame** comes, memory vanishes.

356. " A lot "—the **farmer** carries on his cart.

[Said to greedy children who ask for more.]

357. He who inherits a **farthing** is expected to disburse a dollar.

358. It is in vain to mistake the present **fashion.**

359. He who has nothing can **fast** easily.

360. **Fasting** to-day cooks the food sweet to-morrow.

361. The **father's** words help more than the mother's smacks.

362. The first **favour** is a favour, the second becomes a duty.

363. A hair of **favour** pulls better than a hundred oxen.

364. **Fear** has created more gods than piety.

365. A thing often brings more **fear** than damage.

366. It is better to be on one's own **feet** than on another person's stilts.

367. A **fence** lasts three years, a dog lasts three fences, a horse three dogs, and a man three horses.

368. The **fiddle** makes the feast.

369. Nothing manures a **field** so well as the shoes of the master.

370. The **fig** distributed by the rich is sourer than the crab-apple offered by the poor.

371. The **file** blunts in polishing other people's iron.

372. When the **fire** goes out in the kitchen it goes out in the heart.

373. He who has **fire** in his heart gets smoke in his head.

374. When you light a **fire** under an empty pot a soul is being burnt in it.

375. He who blows in the **fire** will get sparks in his eyes.

376. She is not the **first.**

377. **Fish** begin to stink at the head.

378. Sometimes one must allow that **five** is an equal number.

379. At twelve childhood is buried, at eighteen youth, at twenty the first love, at thirty faith in men, at forty hope, at fifty desire, and from sixty onwards little by little the **five senses.**

380. A tattered **flag** brings more honour than a whole one.

381. What **flatterers** say try to make true.

382. **Flattery** is sweet poison.

383. Nothing in haste but catching **fleas.**

384. A **florin** well used is worth ten.

385. It is folly to put **flour** into a bag facing the wind.

386. To have been, to be, and will be, are three faded **flowers.**

387. On a bog a **fly** is an admiral.

388. No one has more freedom than the **fly** that sits on any man's forehead.

389. Trotting stallion, trotting mare, how can the **foal** go slow ?

390. There is no art in beating **foam.**

391. One **foe** is too many, and a hundred friends too few.

392. The mountain brews the **fog** and the plain must drink it.

393. A whole nation often pays for the **folly** of one man.

394. Let the **folly** of others be your wisdom.

395. He is not wise who cannot sometimes be a **fool.**

396. The man who is always lucky becomes a **fool.**

397. Even a **fool** can govern if nothing happens.

398. Every **fool** likes his cap.

399. Nothing looks so like a man of sense as a **fool** who holds his tongue.

400. Everybody has his **fool** with him, only one can hide him better than the other.

401. Fortune and women are partial to **fools.**

402. Wise men want **fools.**

403. Old **fools** are the best.

404. Only **fools** are modest.

405. The biggest **fools** are those who are paid to be wise.

406. Three speak the truth, **fools,** children and drunkards.

407. In the book of **fools** one must write with a stick.

408. Everyone must wear out a pair of **fool's shoes.**

409. **Force** is life's beginning, continuation and finish.

410. One cannot always avoid **foreign countries.**

411. **Fore-talk** spares after-talk.

412. **Forgetfulness** is the mother of ingratitude.

413. What one does not do willingly one soon **forgets.**

414. He is lucky who **forgets** what cannot be mended.

415. **Forgive** thyself nothing, others much.

416. **Fortune** has weak hands, for he whom she raises up she soon lets fall.

417. In bad **fortune** hold out ; in good, hold in.

418. **Fortune** is like women ; loves youth and is fickle.

419. **Fortune** weighs heavy on him whom misfortune has spared.

420. He who eats his **fowl** himself must saddle his horse himself.

421. **Free man**—free goods.

422. The friendship of the **French** is like their wine, exquisite but of short duration.

423. Water does not help **fried fish.**

424. My friend's enemy is often my best **friend.**

425. Deal with your **friend** as though he might become your enemy, and with your enemy as though he might become your friend.

426. He who wants to get to know a **friend** must share an inheritance with him.

427. What one lends to a **friend** one must demand back from an enemy.

428. Be a **friend** to thyself and others will be so too.

429. To tolerate a **friend's** faults is to commit them oneself.

430. A **friend's** wound festers longest.

431. When you require nothing go to your **friends.**

432. **Friends** are made in wine and proved in tears.

433. Good **friends** in rain are also good friends in sunshine, but not the reverse.

434. There are three kinds of **friends** in the world: friends who love you, friends who hate you, and friends who don't trouble about you.

435. Being without **friends** is worse than having enemies.

436. One loses more **friends** through kindness than one gains through gratitude.

437. They are not all **friends** who laugh with you.

438. Warm soup, warm **friendship.**

439. One may mend a torn **friendship** but it soon falls in tatters.

440. In trade and commerce **friendship** ceases.

441. Real **friendship** does not freeze in winter.

442. **Friendship** is a bread that tastes good as long as it is new.

443. **Friendship** is a plant which must be often watered.

444. **Friendship** is love coupled with reason.

445. **Friendship** lasts as long as the kitchen smokes.

446. A **friendship** lost is an enmity refound.

447. **Friendship** must be sought but enmity is found without a lantern.

448. The **friendship** of a son-in-law and the sun in winter have the same warmth.

449. Put a **frog** on a chair of gold and it will jump back into the swamp.

450. On the shady side of the street the **funeral coach** turns twice as often as on the sunny side.

451. **Gain** without your neighbour's loss is gain.

452. We must eat and drink though every tree were the **gallows.**

453. Rich **gamblers** and old trumpets are rare.

454. Young **gamblers,** old beggars.

455. The **garden** is the poor man's apothecary.

456. **Generosity** is a wall that should not be built higher than the materials allow.

457. **Gentry** and dogs leave doors open.

458. A **gift** is sold dearly.

459. What you **give** is written in sand ; what you take with an iron hand.

460. That which you would **give** no one, you should ask of no one.

461. **Give** with closed eyes and take with open eyes.

462. When the **giver** comes, the gate opens by itself.

463. The **giver** is dead, the donor has broken a leg.

464. To whom one **gives** is written in sand, from whom one takes in granite.

465. The first **glass** bites, the second kisses, and the third embraces.

466. Give **glass** to friends of glass.

467. **Glory** is a circle in water which grows wider and then disappears.

468. Hungry **gnats** sting deep.

469. Slow also gets to the **goal.**

470. God doesn't let the **goat's tail** grow longer than he can use it.

471. First get rich, then serve **God.**

472. What the world does not want is sacrificed to **God.**

473. Men are the pack of cards of **God.**

474. To believe against hope is a gift of **God.**

475. Before **God** and the bus-conductor we are all equal.

476. Take the glass into your hand with caution, since **God** and the devil are inside.

477. **God** and the doctor are acknowledged in need.

478. The wisdom of **God** and the folly of man govern the world.

479. **God** blesses the seeking, not the finding.

480. **God** cuts down all trees before they reach the sky.

481. **God** does not give to all alike ; to one He gives the goose and to another the egg.

482. If **God** does not give us what we want He gives us what we need.

483. Where **God** does not help, no saint avails.

484. **God** does not let any shoe fit so well that it doesn't pinch somewhere.

485. **God** does not look down upon him who does not look up to Him.

486. **God** does not pay according to the hours but according to the heartbeats.

487. Where **God** dwells, the devil also has his nest.

488. He who keeps **God** for his friend has the world for his enemy.

489. **God** forgives sins, otherwise heaven would be empty.

490. **God** gives, but man must open his hand.

491. When **God** gives daily hunger He likewise gives daily bread.

492. Where **God** gives hard bread He gives sharp teeth.

493. **God** gives no linen, but flax to spin.

494. Where **God** gives nothing, no candle can be lighted to Him.

495. **God** gives the drinker the vine but not the goblet.

496. **God** gives the milk but not the pail.
497. **God** gives the rich cattle and the poor children.
498. **God** gives us nuts, but He does not crack them.
499. **God** greets all, but few return His greeting.
500. When the apple falls, **God** has broken the stalk.
501. Where there is a belfry [campanile] **God** has planted His finger in the ground.
502. **God** helps the poor, the rich help themselves.
503. **God** helps the seaman in time of need, but he must steer himself.
504. That which is not to be worshipped **God** Himself should bury.
505. One is no nearer **God** in a bedroom than in a cellar.
506. The friend of **God** is the enemy of the priest.
507. When **God** lets it rain the poor man's nettles thrive even as the rich man's roses.
508. **God** makes chaff for him who wants to make gold out of corn.
509. For the weary, **God** makes of a stone a pillow.
510. To **God** one limps, to the devil one jumps.
511. **God** reigns in heaven and money on earth.
512. From whom **God** takes the light, to him he gives deft fingers.
513. He is nearest to **God** who requires the least.
514. One must worship the **gods** under which one lives.
515. The design is in our own hands, the colouring of it is in **God's**.
516. What is only half **God's** is wholly the devil's.
517. **God's** ways are always shortest.
518. A dish of **God's blessings** will never be empty, even if thousands eat from it.
519. At **God's table** all eat from one dish.
520. Faithful to the old, kind to the new, mix both and you make **gold.**
521. One does not find **gold** in every purse that is shut.
522. When everything is dear **gold** is cheap.
523. Rich in **gold,** rich in care.
524. One may buy **gold** too dear.
525. Some are thought **good** and some bad, and both are wronged.
526. **Good** is good but too good is every man's fool.
527. For what is **good** one does not pay too much.
528. Of the **good** one readily deducts, to the bad one adds something.
529. Do nobody any **good,** that you may not receive evil in exchange.
530. It is as hard to follow **good advice** as to give it.
531. One must open the door to a **good day** and expect a bad one.
532. Let in the **good day,** the bad one enters without knocking.
533. Nothing in the world is so hard to bear as a series of **good days.**
534. **Good days** make torn boots and holes in your purse.
535. On **good days** mornings and evenings are close together.
536. **Good news** remains even in a fool's mouth.
537. **Goods** held in common mostly get lost.
538. All **goods** must have two persons, one who makes them, one who destroys them.
539. Other folks' **goods,** other folks' cares.
540. Plenty of **goods,** poor in heart.
541. **Good times** make bad people.
542. A **gosling** flew over the Rhine and came back a goose.
543. For the last **gown** one needs no pockets.
544. In a small **grate** one requires little wood.
545. **Gratitude** and wheat only grow on good ground.

546. He who goes often for a walk shortens the way to his **grave.**

547. In the cradle lies the **grave.**

548. He who is **great** need not inflate himself.

549. Hearty **greetings** are half the food.

550. **Grief** shared is half grief; joy shared is double joy.

551. When your goods **grow,** courage grows.

552. What **grows** makes no noise.

553. It is better to **grumble** into the beard than into the air.

554. In the morning one knows the **guest,** at noon the host.

555. Poor folks' **guests** return home early.

556. Let everybody look into his own **gutter!**

557. **Habit** is the intelligence of the multitude.

558. Even a **hair** has its shadow.

559. The longer the **hair** the smaller the brain.

560. A slice of **ham** is better than a fat pig in a dream.

561. Big **hammers** don't play with little nails.

562. What the **hand** acquires must die in the mouth.

563. Where the **hand** cannot grasp, thought begins.

564. A thrifty **hand** doesn't plunge into an empty pocket.

565. A clean **hand** goes throughout the land.

566. Better the **hand** hit than the tongue sting.

567. Only that which is in the **hand** is no lie.

568. That which is built with the **hand** is often destroyed with the feet.

569. A full **hand** opens itself the door.

570. From the **hand** to the mouth is further than from the mouth to the stomach.

571. What the **hand** wounds the heart heals.

572. No nail polish helps old **hands.**

573. When the **hands** and the feet are bound the tongue runs faster.

574. Where **hands** are required words and letters are useless.

575. He who bathes his **hands** in blood must wash them in tears.

576. Thin **hands** make fat feet.

577. He who throws away with the **hands** must seek again with the feet.

578. He who spares his **hands** rusts his teeth.

579. He who cannot control his **hands** should control his eyes.

580. One cannot fall into worse **hands** than one's own.

581. A golden **handshake** is better than ten witnesses.

582. No one is as **happy** as the man who thinks he is.

583. When a man is **happy** he does not hear the clock strike.

584. When one is **happy** one wants to know no one, when one is unhappy no one wants to know you.

585. The **hare** says, "I can run fast," but the field says, "I am long."

586. **Hares** are caught with hands, fools with praise, and women with gold.

587. A bad thing that does no **harm** is the same as a good one that does no good.

588. A little too much does more **harm** than a little too little.

589. He who doesn't **harness** himself can't be harnessed.

590. A heaven full of **harps** hangs round him.

[i.e. a fool's paradise.]

591. One goes further with one's **hat** in one's hand than on one's head.

592. From the midst of the wood the **hatchet** gets its handle.

593. He who cannot **hate** cannot love.

594. When **hay** follows the horse, it wants to be eaten.

595. The biggest drops rain on a bald **head.**
596. He never lets his **head** save his heels.
597. If you would live a long **healthy life,** eat like a cat and drink like a dog.
598. A poor man is a **healthy man ;** a healthy man is a rich man.
599. He who will not **hear** must feel.
600. There are nowhere more hiding places than in the human **heart.**
601. No theatre stage is so changeable as man's **heart.**
602. Heaven and hell is in your **heart.**
603. There is no better witness than one's own **heart.**
604. Nothing is as hard and as soft as the **heart.**
605. **Heart** and snow first get hard before they thaw.
606. The **heart** and the tongue are small but they show the greatness of the man.
607. What comes straight from the **heart** goes straight to the heart.
608. The **heart** is a child, it hopes what it wishes.
609. The **heart** is the fountain, the tongue the river.
610. A fire in the **heart** makes smoke in the head.
611. He who has a short **heart** must have long legs.
612. A hungry **heart** often has a full stomach as a neighbour.
613. Everyone can read in the **heart** of the man whose chest is of glass.
614. He who has his **heart** on his tongue, soon gets it between his teeth.
615. He who opens his **heart** surrenders himself a prisoner.
616. In a golden swing one may fly to **heaven.**
617. The way to **heaven** is by Weeping Cross.
618. **Heaven** is the poor man's money box.
619. More people go to **heaven** from the gallows than from the cemetery.
620. He is nearest **heaven** who troubles the least about the earth.
621. **Hell** and chancery are always open.
622. He who has done one step towards **hell** has half the way behind him.
623. It is a greater toil to get to **hell** than to heaven.
624. No **help** is also help.
625. When one is **helping** another both are strong.
626. When a **hen** carries a cock's comb she is often afraid of herself.
627. A **hen** has right over nine hedges.
628. The **hen** lays in the nest where there are eggs already.
629. An old **hen** makes a fat brew.
630. There is no dearer **hen** than the one received as a gift.
631. In the eyes of the **hen** the worm is always in the wrong.
632. Even prudent **hens** sometimes lay their eggs amongst nettles.
633. There was never a **hermit,** however pious, who did not sometimes poke his head out of his cell.
634. He who cannot pay for **herrings** should not want trout.
635. One may **hide** himself behind a leaf, and another is not hidden by a tree.
636. With one's own stick one often gets the soundest **hiding.**
637. He who rides no **hobby-horse** is ridden by the devil.
638. At **home** everything is easy.
639. **Honey** on his tongue—guard your purse.
640. When **honour** gets a rent in it, it stands open to all.
641. He who falls with **honour** soon gets on to his feet again.
642. **Honour** walks on stilts of glass.
643. Whatever is to be a **hook** bends early.

644. **Hope** is an egg of which one has the shell, another the white, and few the yolk.

645. **Hope** is the dream of the man awake.

646. **Hope** is the poor man's riches.

647. **Hope** is the rope at which we all pull with all our might.

648. What you **hope** to get already belongs to someone else.

649. When one blows into a silvery **horn** it is heard far away.

650. He to whom nature hasn't given **horns** shouldn't butt.

651. A stranger's **horse** and your own spurs will soon leave the wind behind.

652. Who will sell a blind **horse** praises the feet.

653. One requires a spur for good and bad **horses.**

654. He who shows **hospitality** to another makes two days out of one.

655. Where the **host** is a thief it is difficult to steal.

656. A fair **hostess** can sell stale beer.

657. Every **hour** wounds and the last one kills.

658. The **hours** of the day are twelve, that which one gives not, the other gives.

659. When one builds a **house** another looks out of the window.

660. If you build a **house** build it to the roof.

661. The empty **house** is full of noise.

662. Half a **house** is half a hell.

663. He who lives in the middle of a **house** is overlooked from above and smoked from below.

664. An old **house** is used to smoke.

665. The **house** in which there are two women will not be swept clean.

666. A **house** of gold has hours of lead.

667. To change **house** three times equals a fire.

668. **House-devil ;** street-angel.

669. When **hunger** is abroad even the saints are aware of it.

670. **Hunger** is a creditor whom one cannot escape.

671. **Hunger** is stronger than love.

672. To suffer **hunger** is to save no bread.

673. **Hunger** makes raw beans into almonds.

674. **Hunger** teaches many arts.

675. For the **hungry man** every hour is midday.

676. The **hunt** is a masculine ball and the ball is a feminine hunt.

677. All are not **hunters** that blow the horn.

678. If the **husband** gathers like the bees, and the wife dispenses like the hour-glass, they will both get rich.

679. The **husband's** love, the woman's life.

680. The **husband's** mother is the wife's devil.

681. The **hypocrite** goes on the way to Paradise into Purgatory.

682. Never be **idle,** for the year has a big mouth.

683. **Idleness** is hard labour.

684. The **ignorant** do not sin.

685. **Ignorant heads** read the past in history, wise ones read the future.

686. **Illness** always enters where it is well nursed.

687. **Illness** comes on horseback and leaves on foot.

688. When two invalids meet, the **illness** remains in the middle.

689. He who does good to others a hundred times, but misses once, is rewarded with **ingratitude.**

690. He who seeks **injustice** needs no lamp.

691. We all arrive in the end at the same **inn.**

692. **Insolence** is a kingdom without a crown.

693. He who keeps silent over the first **insult,** breaks the bones of the second.

694. **Insults** and pills must not be chewed.

695. **Intemperance** is the doctor's wet-nurse.

696. **Invalids** live longest.

697. Better an order of **iron** than an anarchy of gold.

698. **Jealousy** is a pain which eagerly seeks what causes pain.

699. We knock in **jest,** and it is opened in earnest.

700. **Jests** must have sheep's, not dog's teeth.

701. One can never paint the **Jesuit** as black as he is.

702. He that would cheat a **Jew** must be a Jew.

703. Trade has spoilt the **Jews** and the Jews have spoilt trade.

704. He who turns the **joint** doesn't eat it.

705. A sinewy **joint** doesn't fear a sharp knife.

706. He who comes in and goes out makes a good **journey.**

707. **Joy** and sorrow are next-door neighbours.

708. Every **joy** bears a sorrow on its back.

709. **Joy** is hung on thorns.

710. **Judges** should have big ears and small hands.

711. **Judges** should have two ears both alike.

712. He who has tasted the **juice** doesn't want the skins.

713. He who wants to **jump** far must step back.

714. **Justice** has a waxen nose.

715. Where **justice** only shows one finger, wrong has the game in his hands.

716. **Justice** would be quite good if one did not bend it crooked.

717. When one finds the old **key** again, one throws the new one away.

718. Where no **key** fits, patience opens.

719. A golden **key** opens the gates to hell.

720. Many have a **key** to everybody's back door, but none to their own.

721. Nothing ages so quickly as a **kindness.**

722. Refused with **kindness** is half promised.

723. He who is grateful for a **kindness** unlocks the door for another.

724. One should be born either a **king** or a fool.

725. Even under a round hat a **kiss** has its savour.

726. A fat **kitchen**—a lean legacy.

727. Silk and velvet put out the **kitchen fire.**

728. He who is nearest the **knee** is nearest the inheritance.

729. Up to the **knee** is permitted.

730. A **knife** that is used does not rust.

731. One learns to **know** oneself best behind one's back.

732. Men should set **knowledge** before virtue, women virtue before knowledge.

733. The store of **knowledge** has no bargain sales.

734. **Labour** makes bread out of a stone.

735. **Labourers** are never paid.

736. Folks say there is a **lack** of four sorts of people on the earth : of priests, else one would not have six or seven benefices ; of gentlemen, else every boor would not want to be a squire ; of whores, else married women and nuns would not carry on the trade ; of Jews, else Christians would not practise usury.

737. He who holds the **ladder** is as guilty as he who mounts the wall.

738. The **ladder** starts with the first rung.

739. Where God holds the **ladder** there is luck in climbing.

740. The **lame** is always ready for a dance.

741. A foreign **language** is more easily learnt in the kitchen than at school.

742. A little too **late** is much too late.

743. The man who tickles himself can **laugh** when he chooses.

744. Bad customs make a good **law.**

745. He that goes to **law** for a sheep loses his cow.

746. The **law** has a nose of wax, one may turn it as one pleases.

747. **Law** separates, compromise conciliates.

748. **Laws** are like spider's webs, bumble-bees fly through them but flies are caught.

749. A lean compromise is better than a fat **lawsuit.**

750. Who will win in a **lawsuit** must have three sacks—one with briefs, one with gold, and one with luck.

751. A **lawyer** and a cart-wheel must be well greased.

752. **Lawyers** are bad Christians.

753. One must not knock on the **lawyer's** door with an iron hammer.

754. The **lawyers** purge the purse, the doctors the stomach, the parsons the soul.

755. Ambition and the belly are the two worst **law-givers.**

756. **Laziness** is the stupidity of the body, and stupidity is the laziness of the brain.

757. **Learn,** so that you may have something to forget.

758. **Learn** something that you may do something.

759. **Leases** and interests never sleep.

760. No more **leaves** can fall in autumn than were grown in spring.

761. **Leaves** don't spring straight from the tree, they come from the buds.

762. Not all **leaves** wait for the autumn.

763. Better sound **legs** than golden crutches.

764. They must be strong **legs** that can support prosperous days.

765. The man who **lends** not loses his friends, and the man who lends gains enemies.

766. The wise read a **letter** backwards.

767. A hasty "yes" makes ready **liars.**

768. **Liars** are good priests but bad prophets.

769. A **lie** becomes true when one believes it.

770. A **lie,** in order to live, requires ten others for food.

771. If one would believe a **lie** it must be patched with truths.

772. It's best to tell **lies** alone.

773. Who **lies,** steals.

774. All men have the same entrance into **life** but not the same exit.

775. **Life** is lent, not given.

776. Three things belong to a happy **life**—to sink the past, to guide the present, and to reflect on the future.

777. **Light** comes from the same source as shadow.

778. A **light** high up is put out by the wind and one low down by the children.

779. A **light** is more easily put out than kindled.

780. When all **limp** everybody thinks he is walking straight.

781. Where all **limp** one laughs at sound feet.

782. Be in time at the hedge if you would dry your **linen.**

783. Any hare may pull a dead **lion's** mane.

784. Thin **lips,** pointed noses, and witty heads go together.

785. Too **little** can bear an addition, but too much has no recipe.

786. Often a **little** makes a lot.

787. **A little man** often casts a big shadow.

788. One should build as if one had to **live** for ever, and live as if one had to die to-morrow.

789. He who **lives** everywhere is at home nowhere.

790. **Living** means striving.

791. The hotter the oven, the harder the **loaf.**

792. Keep the **loaf,** eggs will come.

793. **Lock** and key are not made for faithful fingers.

794. Of two **lookers-on** one is sure to become a player.

795. In the **looking-glass** we see our form, in wine the heart.

796. Our **Lord** is more willing to give than we are to ask and to take.

797. Those who love in the **Lord** never see each other for the last time.

798. With great **lords** one must let five be even.

799. Many **lose** when they win, and others win when they lose.

800. What is learnt through **loss** is long remembered.

801. He who has suffered **loss** need not trouble about scorn.

802. Buried treasure and hidden sense is **loss** without profit.

803. A wall between preserves **love.**

804. Nothing is so dead as yesterday's **love.**

805. Do not trust three counsellors—wine, night, and **love.**

806. Those in **love** always know the time.

807. **Love** and hate are blood relations.

808. **Love** and intoxication look out of the window.

809. **Love,** and you will have an occupation.

810. Coffee and **love** are best when they are hot.

811. **Love** as if one day you will hate, and hate as if one day you will love.

812. **Love** at a distance keeps warm longest.

813. **Love,** but distrust.

814. Only **love** can overcome love.

815. **Love** consists of three things, a long hoping, a sweet impoverishing, and a quick hating.

816. **Love** ends where pay begins.

817. Eternal **Love**—Eternal Lie.

818. **Love,** fire, the itch, a cough, and gout are not to be concealed.

819. One buys and sells **love** for love.

820. Straw in the shoes and **love** in the heart always poke out at every rent.

821. **Love** is a bitter weed.

822. **Love** is a mole, marriage a lynx.

823. When the fire of **love** is extinguished one finds cinders but not gold.

824. When **love** is greatest, words are fewest.

825. Unrequited **love** is like a question without an answer.

826. **Love** is like holes in the stockings.

827. **Love** is love's reward.

828. **Love** is not blind, it merely doesn't see.

829. **Love** is one-eyed, but hatred is blind.

830. **Love** is venison.

831. Where the first **love** is written time does not cancel a single line.

832. **Love** knows neither winter nor summer.

833. **Love** leads to acts of folly, but money to marriages.

834. To those in **love** miles are only paces.

835. Three things make no difference in social standing : **love,** need, and death.

836. Never rely on **love** or the weather.

837. **Love** penetrates the glove.

838. **Love** sees only roses without thorns.

839. **Love** sought out is good, but love discovered is better.

840. **Love** speaks, even when the lips are closed.

841. **Love** spread on the bread is a long way from bread and butter.

842. **Love** takes away the sight and matrimony restores it.

843. Not what is beautiful is **loved ;** rather what is loved is beautiful.

844. **Love letters** do not need to be dated.

845. He who writes **love letters** should have damp hands.

846. In hunting and in **love-making** one knows where one begins, but not where one ends.
847. **Lovers** have much to relate—but it is always the same thing.
848. **Lovers** measure time with desire.
849. For him who **loves,** every ink-stain is a Venus.
850. He who **loves** has every pocket filled with hope.
851. Man only **loves** once.
852. He who **loves** without pleasure, drinks without thirst, and eats without hunger, only lives a short time.
853. **Luck** and glass soon break.
854. Never despair of your **luck,** for it needs only a minute to bring it. (*Swabian.*)
855. **Luck** is luck's mother.
856. Good **luck** makes one happy, bad luck great.
857. Who has got **luck** need only sit at home with his mouth open. (*Swabian.*)
858. There is no one **luckier** than he who thinks himself so.
859. He who is **lucky** gets piglets from his dog.
860. **Maidenhood** is peace, chastity salvation, matrimony imprisonment.
861. **Maidenhood** is sun, chastity moon, matrimony night.
862. To **maintain** is not to prove.
863. Who **makes** others make himself, makes too.
864. When God wants to castigate a man He gives him thoughts of **marriage.**
865. Near **marriage** and distant service are the best.
866. **Marriage** is a covered dish which one has to chew till death.
867. **Marriage** is the first step to penitence.
868. Early **marriage,** long love.
869. The single man is a peacock, the engaged man a lion, the **married** man an ass.
870. One joins **married** people with their hands, and with their feet they run asunder.
871. An impudent face never **marries.**
872. He who **marries,** changes.
873. He who **marries** for beauty has good nights but sorry days.
874. He who **marries** has half the loaf.
875. Many **marry** for money who only get the purse.
876. If you want a good year, **marry ;** if you want two, do not marry.
877. He who wants to be master of his house must not **marry** money.
878. Not all those should **marry** who yawn once together.
879. No one will repent getting up early and **marrying** early.
880. A copper coin—a copper **mass.**
881. He who cannot see the **master** flatters the servant.
882. Better be a little **master** than a big servant.
883. I **master,** you master, who shall clean the boots ?
884. **Matrimony** is a reversed fever, it starts with heat and ends with cold.
885. **Matrimony** is a school in which one learns too late.
886. **Matrimony** is the hospital for love.
887. When you enjoy your **meal** most, stop eating.
888. He who wants to take part in the **meal** must take part in the threshing.
889. There is no better **memory** than that which forgets offences soon.
890. **Men** count for more than people.
891. A **merry man** has paid half his expenses.
892. A handful of **might** is better than a sackful of right.
893. He who has to go ten **miles** must regard nine as only half-way.

894. No **milk** comes from court that has not had a mouse drowned in it.

895. The best of the **mill** is that the sacks can't speak.

896. A **mill** without wheat grinds itself.

897. What is bolder than a **miller's** neckcloth, which takes a thief by the throat every morning?

898. A **mirror** eats up asses and spits out fools.

899. **Mirth** is the sugar of life.

900. **Misfortune** does not wrap its pills in coloured paper.

901. All **misfortunes** begin in the name of God.

902. He who is spared **misfortunes** is hit by prosperity.

903. **Mistrust** carries one further than trust.

904. **Mistrust** is the mother of security.

905. **Mistrust** leads further than confidence.

906. An ornament is **modesty,** but you go further without her.

907. When **modesty** goes to the ball it dances in shoes of glass.

908. He who despises **money** at the right time often gains greatly.

909. **Money** is acquired with the hands and dispersed with the feet.

910. He who has no **money** is known by no one, and he who has knows not himself.

911. Where there is no **money** there is no forgiveness of sins.

912. Do not lend **money** to those to whom you have to take off your hat.

913. Offend one **monk,** and the lappets of all cowls will flutter as far as Rome.

914. The **moon** is safe from the wolves.

915. The **morning hour** has gold in its mouth.

916. That which goes to the **mother's** heart only goes to the father's knees.

917. A **mother's** love never ages.

918. Even if you cannot climb the **mountain** do not remain in the valley.

919. One should not wish to level all **mountains** and make all that is crooked straight.

920. The greatest **mountains** have the greatest valleys, and the greatest understanding often makes the greatest mistakes.

921. Behind the **mountains** there are people to be found.

922. One cannot help a silent **mouth.**

923. Bitter in the **mouth,** health in the body.

924. The **mouth** is the executioner and the doctor of the body.

925. That which one takes from the **mouth** is worth the rent of a field.

926. What the **mouth** likes, the heart enjoys.

927. He who gets once into people's **mouths,** seldom comes out of them.

928. When **moving,** one is always richer than one thinks.

929. **Much** also becomes exhausted.

930. He who brings in **much** takes much out.

[i.e. gossip.]

931. It is no disgrace to fall into **mud,** but it is a disgrace to remain there.

932. **Mules** boast much that their ancestors were horses.

933. One need not take the **mustard** with one, one will find it.

934. Everyone should be allowed to keep his **natural colour,** his natural food, and his natural religion.

935. **Nature** and the sin of Adam can ill be concealed by fig-leaves.

936. That which **Nature** paints never fades.

937. He who follows **Nature's** lantern never loses his way.

938. When **necessity** knocks, love opens the door and goes away.

939. **Necessity** makes feet.

940. Even the smallest thing deserves its honour; the **needle** maintains the tailor.

941. He who notices a **needle** stuck in a barn door stumbles easily over a broom in front of his feet.

942. Love your **neighbour,** but don't tear down the fence.

943. The **neighbour** gives the house its value.

944. **Neighbour** once over the hedge, neighbour over it again.

945. Lock up your door so that your **neighbour** remains honest.

946. He who has a good **neighbour** requires no fence.

947. He who wants to know himself should offend two or three of his **neighbours.**

948. I want as my **neighbours** neither fools nor saints.

949. It is not as thy mother says, but as thy **neighbours** say.

950. Look into your **neighbour's kitchen,** but most into your own pot.

951. The plant that grows by the wayside, let it stay, for it is often a **nettle.**

952. Whatever is to be a **nettle** stings early.

953. The more you squeeze a **nettle** the less it stings.

954. He who throws **nettles** across his neighbour's fence will find them grow again in his own garden.

955. The **nettles** in the king's garden prick also.

956. **Neutrals** are soused from above and singed from below.

957. He who does not know the **new** loves the old.

958. All those who are to have a bad **night** have not yet gone to bed.

959. The **night** is no man's friend.

960. **Night** rinses what the day has soaped.

961. The world will have **night-owls,** to have something to wonder at.

962. Where there are **nits** there also are lice.

963. **Nobility** doesn't make the cabbage fat.

964. When **nobility** sins the peasantry do penance.

965. A "**No**" comes out of the mouth as quickly as a "Yes".

966. A short **nose** is soon blown.

967. Every sore-eyed person is an **oculist.**

968. He must become **old** young who would be old a long time.

969. If the **old** don't serve as a floor they serve as a ceiling.

970. The **old** may be left behind in the race but not in the council.

971. What one is accustomed to in youth one does in **old age.**

972. Where **old age** comes in it never goes out.

973. Three things enter a house without being announced, **old age,** debts, and death.

974. **Old age** doesn't protect from folly.

975. **Old age** is a hospital that takes in all diseases.

976. **Old age** writes in sand, youth carves in stone.

977. One does an **old man** no wrong when one steals his supper.

978. An **old man** sees better behind him[self] than a young man in front of him[self].

979. The **old man's** shadow is better than the young man's gun.

980. An **old woman** and a new plough are nowhere better than in the earth.

981. **Once** is never.

982. **Once** is not often and twice is not always.

983. He who deals in **onions** no longer smells them.

984. A good **opinion** covers all faults.

985. **Opinions** govern the world.

986. When you miss an **opportunity** it shows you its back.

987. What is overdone in giving **orders** is underdone in carrying them out.

988. He who speaks much of **others** burns his tongue.

989. Follow the **owl** and he will lead you amongst the ruins.

990. It is better to sit with an **owl** than to hop with a blackbird.

991. God comfort him who has to plough with **oxen.**

992. Small **pain** is eloquent.

993. One often speaks of the **palm** and means the date.

994. **Paper** is patient.

995. He who only leaves a pen and ink to his heirs is sure of **paradise.**

996. Every **paradise** has its serpent.

997. **Parasites** never come late.

998. Not all those who gird their loins eat the lamb of the **Passover.**

999. He who carries his head between his ears needs no **passport.**

1000. It is in the garden of **patience** that strength grows best.

1001. The purse of the **patient** protracts his cure.

1002. One often does a thing that ten **pay** for.

1003. He who does what he is obliged to do makes only a **payment** and no present.

1004. Take nothing in and nothing out and there is always **peace** in the house.

1005. One **peace** is better than ten victories.

1006. When the **pear** is ripe it soon falls into the mud.

1007. The **pearl** weeps on the wrinkled neck.

1008. The nearer the convent the poorer the **peasant.**

1009. When the **peasant** becomes a nobleman he looks at the plough through spectacles.

1010. No shears cut closer than when a **peasant** becomes a nobleman.

1011. What the **peasant** does not know he won't eat.

1012. He who looks only above has seldom picked up a **penny.**

1013. The unrighteous **penny** corrupts the righteous pound.

1014. He who finds a **penny** has a crown's worth of joy.

1015. Three sorts of **people** are always to be found, soldiers, professors, and women.

1016. He who depends on the **people** hangs from a tree.

1017. Great **people,** little weaknesses.

1018. It matters not how many **people** one pleases, but the kind of people.

1019. There is always a **Pharaoh** who does not know Joseph.

1020. Where **philosophy** ends, medicine begins.

1021. When all the **physic** has been taken the spoon tastes of it long after.

1022. When you call the **physician,** call the judge to make your will.

1023. Who has a **physician** has an executioner.

1024. A lucky **physician** is better than a learned one.

1025. No **physician** is better than three.

1026. Three things a good **physician** must have : a lion's heart, a maiden's hand, and an eagle's eye.

1027. A young **physician** should have three graveyards.

1028. Where the **pie** is burnt one sprinkles sugar on.

1029. To the **pig** a carrot is a present.

1030. A borrowed **pig** grunts all the year.

1031. **Pilgrims** seldom come home saints.

1032. The **pitcher** carries water until its time arrives.

1033. Every **plaintiff** is right.

1034. The **plaintiff** should be heard once, the defendant twice.

1035. **Pleasure** in virtue is itself a virtue.

1036. He who begins with **pleasure** is half-way through his task.

1037. No **pleasure,** no profit.

1038. A **Polish** bridge, a Bohemian monk, a Swabian nun, an Austrian soldier, Italian reverence, and German fasting, are worth a bean.

1039. **Politeness** is an air cushion ; though there is little in it, yet it softens the blows of life.

1040. No one knows the **poor,** and the rich don't know themselves.

1041. When the **poor** are sick their pills are not gilded.

1042. That which is given to the **poor** grows again in the furrow.

1043. The **poor** sit on the front benches in Paradise.

1044. " I have had it " is a **poor man.**

1045. The liberty of the **poor man** is to be allowed to beg.

1046. A **poor man** who sings is rich.

1047. The **poor man's** roast and the rich man's sickness can be smelt a long way off.

1048. The **Pope** is a human invention of which God knows nothing.

1049. Each one should look into his own **pot.**

1050. An empty **pot** cracks on the fire.

1051. One can see from the fragment [splinter] what the **pot** has been.

1052. He who weighs with a **pound** doesn't need the ounce.

1053. Everyone is ready to wipe his boots on **poverty.**

1054. He who puts his hands in the sack fills it with **poverty.**

1055. Abundance causes **poverty.**

1056. **Poverty** does not hurt him who has not been rich before.

1057. When **poverty** darns the jerkin no friend threads the needle.

1058. **Poverty** is a sixth sense.

1059. **Poverty** is the cow of the rich man.

1060. **Poverty** is the hands and feet of wealth.

1061. If there were no **poverty** there would be no art.

1062. Two things make one either greater or smaller, **praise** and shadows.

1063. He who doesn't strive for **praise** is not hurt by abuse.

1064. Nothing grows old so soon as **praise,** matrimony, and kindness.

1065. **Pray** as though no work could help, and work as though no prayer could help.

1066. When you go to war **pray** once, when you go to sea pray twice, when you take a wife pray three times.

1067. When in **prayer** you clasp your hands, God opens His.

1068. With **prayers** one unlocks heaven.

1069. When one is near the coast **prayers** stop.

1070. A **preacher** should be like a hen who always has an egg in reserve.

1071. There are many **preachers** who don't hear themselves.

1072. **Pride** begs more than poverty.

1073. A **priest** and a woman may be found at the bottom of all mischief.

1074. **Priests** and signposts, though they show the way, do not accompany one.

1075. **Priests** and women never forget.

1076. Like the bites of wolves, those of **priests** are hard to heal.

1077. **Priests** bless themselves first.

1078. It is not necessary for **priests** to marry as long as the peasants have wives.

1079. If the **prince** has no ears to hear his subjects he has no head to govern them.

1080. There is only one first **prize** in a lucky bag.

1081. **Proffered ware** has lame feet.

1082. A **promise** has legs, only the gift has hands.

1083. **Promise** is a bridge of words, unsafe to walk across.

1084. It is inadvisable to lend to people who are entering the **promised land.**

1085. **Promises** are like the full moon, if they are not kept at once they diminish day by day.

1086. A **proverb** deceives not; the heavens fall not.

1087. A **proverb** never lies, it is only its meaning which deceives.

1088. As the country, so the morals; as the morals, so the **proverbs.**

1089. **Proverbs** are like butterflies, some are caught, others fly away.

1090. **Proverbs** are the wisdom of the streets.

1091. There are many blunt **proverbs,** but they have good meanings.

1092. Death and **proverbs** love brevity.

1093. **Punishment** ought to be like salad—more oil than vinegar.

1094. The **pup** I have brought up bites me when it has become a dog.

1095. He who is ready to raise his hat is slow to untie his **purse.**

1096. A full **purse** and a countryman's shoe tread roughly.

1097. Never show the bottom of two things, your **purse** and your mouth.

1098. He who lies in his **purse** deceives no one but himself.

1099. On a journey an empty **purse** is a heavier burden than a full one.

1100. The **purse** of our covetousness is fastened with the leaves of a leek.

1101. Old **purses** fasten badly.

1102. What one is **pushing** one need not pull.

1103. A little **quarrel** refreshes love.

1104. " Mine " and " thine " is the origin of all **quarrels.**

1105. He who **quarrels** about a penny has a crown's worth of loss.

1106. Old **rags** burn more easily than new linen.

1107. Where **rags** govern, people make clothes.

1108. Everyone sells his **rags** in the market.

1109. He who does not stay at home does not know where the **rain** comes in.

1110. When it **rains** the trees become wet.

1111. A **rascal** without is also a rascal within.

1112. One can catch **rats** for others but not even a mouse for oneself.

1113. Three things cannot be **recalled,** a stone that has been thrown, an arrow that has been shot, and a word that has been spoken.

1114. A man is **received** according to his coat, and takes his leave according to his intelligence.

1115. A **red-beard** was never good.

1116. He who seeks the **reel** must follow the thread.

1117. A **reel** runs till the thread is finished.

1118. He who would **reform** everything, overturns everything.

1119. **Rejected** pieces often come back again into the dish.

1120. With **relations** one may drink and eat, but never count and measure.

1121. He who serves with **relations** need not fear hell any longer.

1122. " I have learned **religion**—I believe what I like."

1123. **Remorse** is lust's dessert.

1124. **Repentance** is a halting messenger, but it comes surely.

1125. **Repentance** is the virtue of fools.

1126. A bad **reputation** has better legs than a good one.

1127. **Reputation** precedes, fame follows a man.

1128. **Requests** are warm—thanks cold.

1129. If I **rest,** I rust.

1130. **Rest** is half the food.

1131. Continuous **rest** makes tired feet.

1132. **Revenge** is a dish that should be eaten cold.

1133. **Rhubarb** and patience work wonders.

1134. We give to the **rich** and take from the poor.

1135. The **rich** find, the poor invent.

1136. The **rich** impoverish, the poor enrich.

1137. Who would be **rich** must keep his conscience in his cash-box.

1138. No one is either **rich** or poor who has not helped himself to be so.

1139. The **rich** pardon their dogs, the poor their children.

1140. He who gets **rich** quickly never grows old.

1141. To the **rich** the poor are like rocks in the sea.

1142. He who wants to get **rich** within one year, gets to the gallows within six months.

1143. **Rich people** use only one eye, they have the other in their pocket.

1144. **Riches** are as a baker's shirt, not too long and not too short.

1145. **Rider** and pedestrian come in the evening to the same inn.

1146. **Right** has not always success, but success is always right.

1147. He who has a sackful of **rights** often loses a purse full of gold.

1148. The nearer the inn, the longer the **road.**

1149. One finds everywhere a mile of bad **road.**

1150. Nice **road**—short road.

1151. A fat **roast** need not be larded.

1152. A **rogue** at games is a rogue everywhere.

1153. He who is apprenticed to a **rogue** may easily become master.

1154. Beware of **Rome** if you would remain pious.

1155. There is no greater sin in **Rome** than to be poor.

1156. **Rome** unlocks heaven only to him who can pay.

1157. There is no **roof** without broken tiles.

1158. He who gives his son the **rope** must not complain when his hands are tied.

1159. Those who draw a **rope** too tight, keep the ends in their hands.

1160. One does not remember the hip was once a **rose.**

1161. In the **rose** garden the rose is no rare flower.

1162. Will he who slanders the **rose** honour the nettle?

1163. He who wants the **rose** must also take the thorns.

1164. The last **rose** that falls off makes the rose-bush a bush.

1165. One must not dream of **roses** and tulips in autumn.

1166. **Roses** for a brief space and thorns for eternity is folly.

1167. Hail beats down more fresh **roses** than withered.

1168. **Roses** wither, but thorns remain.

1169. Ten must get **ruined** before one gets rich.

1170. When God sends a **ruler** the fever, the subjects shiver.

1171. It is not enough to **run,** one must also arrive.

1172. **Running** and buying don't go together, but running and selling.

1173. One rides safest in one's own **saddle.**

1174. A **saddle** does not suit an ass.

1175. If you would climb into the **saddle** don't despise the stirrup.

1176. When the **saddle** is empty you can mount.

1177. **Saddled** early, ridden late.

1178. **Safety** is nowhere safe.

1179. Nothing is **said** so well but something can be said against it.

1180. **Saintly people** are bad neighbours.

1181. **Saintly people** easily weep.

1182. **Saintly people** sit far apart.

1183. Keep your eyes open; a **sale** is a sale.

1184. A gift is a gift and a purchase is a purchase, but no one thanks you for a cheap **sale.**

1185. Whoever spills **salt** arouses enmity.

1186. **Salt** only serves for salting.

1187. There is a **salve** for every sore.

1188. What you **save** on the hay you must add to the whip.

1189. To be warned is halfway to being **saved.**

1190. Everyone **says** it, no one knows it.
[i.e. calumny.]

1191. He laughs at **scars** who never felt a wound.

1192. Where the **scissors** cut the thread a new beginning begins.

1193. Every **scoundrel** has his bad morning.

1194. **Scratch** people where they itch.

1195. The **sea** is a bad inn.

1196. **Seaman**—no man.

1197. Your **secret** is your prisoner so long as you do not reveal it ; when revealed, you are its prisoner.

1198. Men keep other people's **secrets** and women their own.

1199. Of ten **secrets** keep nine to yourself and don't let out the tenth.

1200. **Security** is the first cause of misfortune.

1201. What one likes to **see,** one likes to believe.

1202. There is no **seed** for a famous name.

1203. One only knows half of him whom one **sees,** but the whole of him whom one hears.

1204. **Seldom** is always welcome.

1205. **Self** is the man.

1206. **Separation** reveals love.

1207. **Separation** unites.

1208. The best **sermon** is to listen to oneself.

1209. Funeral **sermon**—lying sermon.

1210. If the **servant** becomes rich and the master poor, they are both worthless.

1211. He who serves ten years well, but one badly, has been a bad **servant** for ten years.

1212. The people's **servant** has a bad master.

1213. He who has one **servant** has him wholly, who has two servants has half a one, who has three has none.

1214. There is only one **servant** in the house and he is [called] the master.

1215. What one gives to a faithful **servant** is always too little, and what one gives to an unfaithful one always too much.

1216. Praise and payment make good **servants.**

1217. That which is given to him who faithfully **serves** is too little, and to him who unfaithfully serves too much.

1218. He **serves** well who serves time.

1219. **Service** is the road to mastery, like the ladder to the roof.

1220. One must not trust one's own **shadow,** no matter how far it stretches.

1221. **Shadows** follow those who walk in the sun.

1222. Those who snatch at **shadows** have nothing in their pockets.

1223. Where there is **shame** there is virtue.

1224. One wrangles more about **shell** and husk than kernel and fruit.

1225. There is more disputing about the **shell** than the kernel.

1226. Even counted **sheep** are eaten by the wolf.

1227. Never give the **sheep** when you can pay with the wool.

1228. Even the finest **shoe** becomes in the end a slipper.

1229. He who goes barefoot isn't pinched by his **shoes.**

1230. He who is often **shooting** hits the mark at last.

1231. A **shroud** is made without pockets.

1232. For the **sick** and the well the hours do not strike alike.

1233. A **sickle** in a bag, a straw in a shoe, and a maid at the window always show forth.

1234. He who speaks out of season loses a good **silence.**

1235. **Silence** is a fence round wisdom.

1236. Even a **silk shirt** only clothes a naked body.

1237. When **silver** talks all fools listen; when gold talks even the wise listen.

1238. **Simplicity** is old.

1239. **Simplicity** was at the beginning of the world and will be at the end of the world.

1240. **Sin** and punishment are tied on one chain.

1241. To **sin** one rushes, to virtue one crawls.

1242. Contempt of **sin** is praise of virtue.

1243. Not to **sin** is the best penance.

1244. Men, like larks, **sing** in the open; women, like nightingales, sing in the dark.

1245. He who cannot **sing** will be always singing.

1246. Small **sins** are chewed, big ones swallowed.

1247. Old **sins** often make new shame.

1248. All **skins** are tough.

1249. He who cannot **sleep** goes to church.

1250. **Sleep** is the greatest thief, for it steals half one's life.

1251. One does not **sleep** to sleep, but to act.

1252. **Small people** are soon in harness.

1253. What **smarts,** teaches.

1254. A paid-for **smock** is warmer than a borrowed fur coat.

1255. One suffers the **smoke** because of the fire.

1256. **Snow** is the earth's fur coat.

1257. Far from the combat makes old **soldiers.**

1258. **Soldiers,** fire and water quickly make room.

1259. When one starts the **song** too high it isn't finished.

1260. He who lives without **sons** knows not trouble, he who dies without sons knows not joy.

1261. One may chatter long before the **soup** boils.

1262. The **soup** is never swallowed as hot as it is cooked.

1263. Those who **sow** have the right to reap.

1264. No **sow** is so dirty but finds a boar to kiss her.

1265. He who talks, **sows,** and does not know what; he who listens, reaps, and has the choice.

1266. A busy **spade** is always bright.

1267. Better a **sparrow** in the hand than a crane on the roof.

1268. One may **speak** a long time without saying anything.

1269. He who can **speak** is at home everywhere.

1270. **Speak** little with others, much with yourself.

1271. **Speak** that I may see thee.

1272. He who **speaks** much must either know a lot or lie a lot.

1273. He who **speaks** well has a shield against every blow.

1274. Those who won't see have always mislaid their **spectacles.**

1275. The **spectacles** through which one would look at the world should be of gold.

1276. One man's **speech** is only half a speech.
[i.e. hear both sides.]

1277. **Splinters** bring luck.

1278. A **sponge** sucks itself full, but when it has to yield anything one has to squeeze it.

1279. He who is always fed with a **spoon,** never learns to eat by himself.

1280. **Spoons** are generally judged by the soup.

1281. Better no **spoons** than no broth.

1282. The **spring** that doesn't send its water to the valley never becomes a river.

1283. One often uses the **spurs** instead of the bridle.

1284. The first **step** is the most difficult one.

1285. When one washes the **steps** one must begin at the top.

1286. In youth one must get ready a **stick** on which to lean in old age.

1287. Many a man carries the **stick** with which he is beaten.

1288. No high-road leads through the **stomach.**

1289. The **stomach** is an inn where there is coming and going.

1290. Whatever the **stomach** is full of, with that the mouth runs over. (*Swabian.*)

1291. The **stomach** is life's misfortune.

1292. A fat **stomach** makes a lean brain.

1293. When the **stone** has left the hand it belongs to the devil.

1294. Before every house lies a **stone,** if not a big one, a little one.

1295. He who invites **storks** must have frogs.

1296. Beware of old **streets** and new inns.

1297. **Stupidity** is a hardy perennial.

1298. A quick answer is often the birthplace of **success.**

1299. **Suffer** much or die early.

1300. A **sufferer** soon becomes a great talker.

1301. **Summer** is a slave, winter a master.

1302. What stands in the **sun** ripens or withers.

1303. **Suspicion** makes cables out of spider's webs.

1304. Downstream **swims** he who counsels others, upstream he who knows himself.

1305. One **sword** keeps the other in its scabbard.

1306. A broken **sword** must be left in its scabbard.

1307. What one has **sworn** that must one do, both the less and the most.

1308. At a round **table** every seat is first.

1309. He who does not **take** need not give.

1310. One "**take this**" is better than ten "God help you."

1311. Everybody ought to be what he wants to be **taken for.**

1312. The old man's staff is his **teeth.**

1313. He who breaks his **teeth** with the shell seldom gets the kernel.

1314. Better an end with **terror** than a terror without end.

1315. To **thank** too much is to secretly ask for more.

1316. He who requires **thanks** makes the gift cheap.

1317. The **thief** cannot find any tree that suits him for a gallows.

1318. Office without salary breeds **thieves.**

1319. We hang little **thieves** and take off our hats to great ones.

1320. Do not **think** what all may not know, do not speak what all may not hear, and do not do what all may not see.

1321. He who **thinks** that he does too much certainly does too little.

1322. He who **thinks** well need not think much.

1323. **Thistles** that have been lopped in their youth don't prick in their old age.

1324. One may live where one likes, but one finds a **thorn-bush** near one's door.

1325. No one deceives us as much as our own **thoughts.**

1326. From a full head and stomach seldom come fine **thoughts.**

1327. Bound hands make free **thoughts.**

1328. Good **thoughts** and lame horses come in last.

1329. **Thoughts** are like bullets, few hit the mark.

1330. **Thoughts** are toll-free, but not hell-free.

1331. Who knows what slumbers in the background of **time.**

1332. There is nothing dearer than **time** and nothing more squandered.

1333. The best doctor is **time,** and the most solid wall is eternity.

1334. **Time** brings roses, but not the rose tree.

1335. **Time** covers and uncovers everything.

1336. **Time** destroys everything that has been done, the tongue everything that has yet to be done.

1337. **Time** is a robber and thief, it eats up youth and love.

1338. **Time** is anger's medicine.

1339. There are more old **tipplers** than old doctors.

1340. Go **together,** be hanged together.

1341. He who always thinks it is too soon always comes **too late.**

1342. He who is afraid of doing **too much** always does too little.

1343. " **Too much** " tears the bag.

1344. The shadow of a **tower** is often larger than the tower.

1345. In a small **town** one knows the other by his nose.

1346. The heaviest weight for a **traveller** is an empty purse.

1347. Nobody raises his hat to a hidden **treasure.**

1348. Big **treasures** spoil the heart.

1349. Where a big **tree** has fallen grass does not grow at once.

1350. The **tree** is respected for its shadow.

1351. One should not cut down a **tree** on account of the caterpillars.

1352. It is a bad **tree** that falls at the first stroke of the axe.

1353. Don't cut down the **tree** which gives you shade.

1354. Many love the **tree of life** for the sake of the tree of wisdom.

1355. God prevents the **trees** from growing into heaven.

1356. The oldest **trees** have often the sweetest fruit.

1357. There is always something to be cut off young **trees** if they are to grow well.

1358. Nobody is **trodden** on unless he lies down first.

1359. Where **trouble** looks out of the window, friends do not look in.

1360. To **trust** once is necessary, to trust twice is foolish, to trust three times madness.

1361. A limping messenger brings the **truth.**

1362. He who tells the **truth** can never find a lodging.

1363. He who dies for the **truth** finds holy ground everywhere for his grave.

1364. He who fiddles **truth** gets the bow thrown at his head.

1365. **Truth** is a spectre that scares many.

1366. **Truth** is the daughter of time.

1367. He that speaks the **truth** must have one foot in the stirrup.

1368. Would you seek the **truth,** return again up the road of doubt.

1369. What smoke is to the eyes, and vinegar is to the teeth, is **truth** to the ears.

1370. Sometimes one must let **turnips** be pears.

1371. **Two** are an army for one.

1372. He who dares not say that he is **uncomfortable** must remain so.

1373. One should not **undress** before one goes to bed.
[i.e. one should not divide one's fortune before one dies.]

1374. What you do three times out of charity, the **ungrateful** asks the fourth time as a duty.

1375. **Unhappy people** make the saints rich.

1376. In necessary things **unity,** in doubtful things liberty, but in everything charity.

1377. In **unity** little things increase, in discord big things decrease.

1378. He who comes masked goes away **unthanked.**

1379. There must be a **valley** between two hills.

1380. **Venturing** wins, venturing loses.

1381. **Victory** never replaces what war has lost.

1382. Where the **vine** grows best one drinks the worst wine.

1383. A **virgin** should neither take nor give.

1384. **Virtue** crucified rises in three days.

1385. God blesses him who pays short **visits.**

1386. He who lets one **wait,** counts by seconds ; he who has to wait, by hours.

1387. He who goes for a **walk** does not pick up dry sticks.

1388. Those who always **walk** in Sunday clothes are either rich or short of money.

1389. A word has caused more than one **war.**

1390. One should wage **war** in such a manner that one can tie one's horse to the enemy's fence.

1391. The advantage of **war** is to make of a secret enemy an open one.

1392. After the **war** there is no lack of brave men.

1393. The deeper **water** falls, the higher it springs.

1394. Old **water** flows willingly.

1395. **Water** has a small head.

1396. Until the **water** has entered your mouth you will not learn to swim.

1397. A little drop of **water** silences a boiling pot.

1398. A good **way** round is not crooked.

1399. He who does not forget his **weakness** is the strongest amongst the weak.

1400. If you want to be strong, know your **weaknesses.**

1401. **Weak people** have also fists.

1402. **Wealth** is a master, poverty a servant.

1403. All signs fail in dry **weather.**

1404. **Weeds** never die.

1405. If you would not **weep** over your edifice build only with your own stones.

1406. One must not throw a stone into a **well** out of which one has drunk.

1407. **Wheat** makes cake, but bread satisfies hunger.

1408. **Whores** and rogues always speak of their honour.

1409. He who becomes **wicked** without motive becomes good without merit.

1410. A **widow** is a low hedge over which everyone jumps.

1411. A **widow's** dress reminds of the past, her tears of the present, and her heart seeks the future.

1412. Happy the man who has a bee as his **wife.**

1413. One God, one coat, one **wife.**

1414. Spinning, crying, and talking about her husband is often all a **wife** can do.

1415. Would you take a **wife,** consult your ears rather than your eyes.

1416. When an old man takes a young **wife,** death laughs.

1417. He who has had a **wife** deserves a crown of patience ; he who takes a second, a fool's cap.

1418. He who has taken a rich **wife** has sold his freedom.

1419. He that truly loves his **wife** leaves her at home.

1420. If a man beats his **wife** once, he beats her often ; if the man kisses the nun once, he kisses her still more often.

1421. The loved one is milk, the fiancée is butter, and the **wife** seasoned cheese.

1422. To whom God gives a **wife,** to him He gives also patience.

1423. Praise the day at even, a **wife** when dead, a weapon when tried, a maid when married, ice when 'tis crossed, and ale when 'tis drunk.

1424. A **wife** who must be guarded is not worth the guard.

1425. To always **win** brings suspicion, to always lose brings contempt.

1426. The **winds** are the world's broom.

1427. There is **wine** at any price in the tavern.

1428. Three glasses of **wine** drive away the evil spirits, but with the fourth they return.

1429. He who drinks **wine** early gets rich late.

1430. When cook and waiter quarrel one gets to know where the **wine** has gone.

1431. **Wine** invents nothing.

1432. In water you may see your own face, in **wine** the heart of another.

1433. There is an art in keeping **winnings.**

1434. **Winter** asks what summer has earned.

1435. He who has **winter** on his head must not have spring in his legs.

1436. In **winter** one requires two cooks and one cellar, in summer two cellars and one cook.

1437. The wise seek **wisdom,** a fool has found it.

1438. Hidden **wisdom** is a buried treasure.

1439. To know oneself is **wisdom,** to forget oneself is folly.

1440. The **wise** make more use of their enemies than fools of their friends.

1441. Where one is **wise** two are lucky.

1442. It is the main business of **wise men** to correct the mistakes of fools.

1443. The king of **wishes** has died in hospital.

1444. One **witness** is no witness. (*Legal proverb.*)

1445. Venturing **wives,** venturing woes.

1446. The **wolf** eats the last man.

1447. Even a **wolf** has tears in his eyes when he has fallen into a pit.

1448. When a **wolf** howls he turns his mouth towards heaven.

1449. The sleeping **wolf** is lean, the running one fat.

1450. Where a **wolf** lives no bird starves.

1451. If the **wolf** stayed in the forest and the monk in the monastery they would not get such a bad name.

1452. Arrange matters so that the **wolf** remains satisfied and the lamb still lives.

1453. He who stands godfather to a **wolf** should have a dog under his coat.

1454. One need not show a **wolf** the way.

1455. Do not trust a lame **wolf** unless you have yourself broken his leg.

1456. **Wolf's** meat requires dog's teeth.

1457. **Wolf's** sauce and dog's meat belong to one course.

1458. To spin, to cry, to wash, to lie, and to cheat her best friend is the manner of many a **woman.**

1459. A sackful of fleas is easier to watch than a **woman.**

1460. A **woman,** a mill, and an old house always require something repairing.

1461. A **woman** and a fish speak like two men.

1462. He who does not love wine, **woman,** and song remains a fool his life long.

1463. What the devil cannot do a **woman** can.

1464. When a **woman** dies, there is one quarrel less on earth.

1465. A cock masters twelve hens, a **woman** half as many men.

1466. A **woman** has the form of an angel, the heart of a serpent, and the sense of an ass.

1467. Man without **woman** is head without body; woman without man is body without head.

1468. **Woman** is like an onion, nice and white to look at, but when cut into, there is no kernel, no heart, and one must cry.

1469. **Woman** is man's Satan.

1470. A **woman** is not a fiddle to be hung on the wall after being played on.

1471. A **woman** keeps secret only what she does not know.

1472. Every **woman** may be caught as surely by gold as a hare by dogs or a gentleman by flattery.

1473. Wood and **woman** never remain the same.

1474. Between " Yes " and " No " of a **woman** one cannot put a needle-point.

1475. The devil requires ten hours to deceive one man, a **woman** one hour to deceive ten men.

1476. Where **woman** only weds the kitchen, love soon dies of hunger.

1477. Where a **woman** rules, the devil is chief servant.

1478. Never has a **woman** spoilt a thing with silence.

1479. A **woman** who is unaccompanied is all accompanied.

1480. A **woman** who accepts, sells herself ; a woman who gives, surrenders.

1481. A **woman** without a man is like a garden without a hedge.

1482. Every **woman** would rather be beautiful than good.

1483. **Woman's** crying is furtive laughing.

1484. It is difficult to believe in **woman's** faithfulness and miracles.

1485. Many a **woman's virtue** has hung itself with a chain of diamonds.

1486. **Women** and death have the same way, they seek those who flee from them and flee from those who seek them.

1487. **Women** and fish are best in the middle.

1488. **Women** and goats want a long rope.

1489. **Women** and projectiles no one must trust.

1490. **Women** and watches seldom go right.

1491. Bad legs and virtuous **women** are found at home.

1492. Cats and **women** are said to have been made on the same day.

1493. Cross **women** can light fires well.

1494. **Women** carry their swords in their mouths.

1495. Good **women** have no ears.

1496. One should praise beautiful days in the evening, beautiful **women** in the morning.

1497. There are only two good **women** in the world ; the one is dead, the other not to be found.

1498. **Women** laugh when they can and cry when they want.

1499. When men meet they listen to each other ; when **women** meet they look at each other.

1500. Summer-sown corn and **women's** advice turn out well once in seven years.

1501. Beauty, gold and youth are **women's virtue.**

1502. In a **wood** it rains twice.

1503. One must carve one's life out of the **wood** one has.

1504. There is more crooked than straight **wood** in the forest.

1505. Remember well three things ; **woods** have ears, fields have eyes, and borrowed money has feet.

1506. No man is better than his **word.**

1507. A man, a **word.**

1508. A **word** flies away like a sparrow and returns to the house like a crow.

1509. A **word** goes further than a man.

1510. A **word** has a hundred heads.

1511. One **word,** no word.

1512. He who will not listen to one **word** is often compelled to listen to many.

1513. Many speak a **word** which if it were a florin they would put back in their purse.

1514. **Words** are good, but fowls lay eggs.
1515. " Yes " and " No " are small **words** but produce great things.
1516. To kill with **words** is also murder.
1517. Use **words** like money.
1518. Good **words** sell bad wares.
1519. Often the best **words** stumble on the smooth threshold of the lips.
1520. The fewer the **words,** the better the prayer.
1521. **Work** and rest closes the physician's door.
1522. **Work** has bitter roots but sweet fruit.
1523. Prepaid **work** has lead on its feet.
1524. One may **work** like a slave, but to the one who looks on it is always little.
1525. Every **work** revenges itself on its master.
1526. Leave the **world** before the world leaves you.
1527. Accommodate yourself in the **world,** for your head is far too small for the world to accommodate itself therein.
1528. The **world** is like a Turkish bath, the higher one sits, the more one sweats.
1529. The history of the **world** is the judgment of the world.
1530. Three things support the **world**; paper, pens, and money.
1531. He who would not gamble with the **world** should not sit at its table.
1532. Many would understand the **world** who have only seen it through the keyhole.
1533. Eat dirt and give gold, and the **world** will be kind to you.
1534. He who wishes to ascend the ladder of the **world** will find at the same time the staircase of heaven.
1535. Without " mine " and " thine " the **world** would be heaven.
1536. For the sake of the **world's** thanks begin nothing, and because of its thanklessness leave nothing undone.
1537. **Wrath** is vain in the absence of power.
1538. **Wrath** wounds others with a needle, itself with a dagger.
1539. A man wears his **years** in his bones, a woman wears hers on her face.
1540. Lack of **years** is a fault that is corrected every day.
1541. **" Yes and no "** are not too small for honest folk.
1542. **" Yes and no "** divide people.
1543. He who would be **young** in his old age must be old in his youth.
1544. **Young maids** are grapes, old ones raisins.
1545. From a **young man** who prays and an old man who fasts, Good Lord deliver us.
1546. **Youth** and rabbits should be caught by the ears.
1547. **Youth** is a brief intoxication, old age a long fast.
1548. Sense in a **youth** is ice in spring.
1549. **Youth** is intoxication without wine, old age wine without intoxication.
1550. If **youth** knew how much old age needed, it would often shut its purse.
1551. **Youth** plays its best cards first, old age keeps its trumps till the last.
1552. **Youth** should be sent early to the carpenter to have the rough bits planed off.
1553. In our **youth** we believe many things that are wrong, in old age we doubt many things that are true.
1554. He who hardens his skin in his **youth** will not be pricked by thorns in his old age.
1555. That which is twisted in **youth** won't become straight in old age.
1556. **Youth's** clothes are always short.

GREEK

1. Everything **ancient** is to be respected.
2. Master **anger.**
3. Always **appear** what you are and a little below it.
4. Every land fosters its own **art.**
5. Fortune lifts up **art,** but not art fortune.
6. An **artist** lives everywhere.
7. **Barley bread** is good after wheat.
8. When a **bear** is at your heels do not look for his footprints.
9. What is **beautiful** is dear to us ; what is not beautiful is not dear to us.
10. The **beautiful** is difficult.
11. What is **beautiful** is hard.
12. **Beautiful** things harass.
13. What is not good for the hive is not good for the **bee.**
14. The **beginning** is half of the whole.
15. The **best** is always arduous.
16. Keep away from a **bigger man.**
17. A great **book** is a great evil.
18. A seat in the **bows** is dangerous.
19. A dry **bramble** is most unyielding.
20. What finds me **bread** is God to me.
21. He who puts on **breeches** for the first time stops at every step to admire them.
22. **Business** to-morrow.
23. **Cabbage** cooked twice is death.

    [i.e. a tale told twice, or too much of a good thing.]
24. The **camel,** even when mangy, bears the burden of many asses.

    [Applied to one who has lost much but is not ruined.]
25. One **cherry-tree** sufficeth not two jays.
26. Who praises his father better than the unfortunate **child ?**
27. It is the men who make a **city.**
28. You are wearing out your **cloak** in the summer.
29. A comb for a bald man, a **concubine** for a eunuch, a flute-player for a deaf man, a mirror for a blind man, an oar for a landsman, a plough for a steersman.
30. Nothing will **content** him who is not content with a little.
31. When your own **courtyard** thirsts do not pour the water abroad.
32. A lame man **copulates** best. (*Proverb quoted by the Queen of the Amazons with reference to a conquered tribe who had been hamstrung.*)
33. Many things find place between the **cup** and lip.
34. He who is out of the **dance** knows many songs.
35. **A day** is sometimes a mother, sometimes a stepmother.
36. **Deeds** for young men ; advice for older ones.
37. The **dice** of the gods always fall well.
38. **Dionysius** dances best with three nymphs.

    [When celebrating the cult of Dionysius in springtime at Athens, many of the worshippers became hysterical. Later they emigrated to Rome and became followers of Bacchus.]
39. Remember to **distrust.**
40. Don't consult the **doctor,** but the one who has been ill.
41. **Dog** does not attack dog.
42. The **dog** is worth its food.
43. By mixing clear water with mud you will never find a **drink.**
44. **Drink** or begone.
45. The thirsty **drink** silently.
46. I hate a man with a memory at a **drinking bout.**
47. **Drive** on your own track.
48. I have taught thee to dive and thou seekest to **drown** me.

49. When they tell you that you are **drunk,** hold by the wall and go on.
50. The old age of an **eagle ;** the youth of a lark.
51. May the **earth** be light upon him. (*A common inscription on tombstones.*)
52. As you have ground, so **eat.**
53. He who **eats** and drinks with the great risks rising from the table with hunger.
54. **Economy** is useless at the bottom.
55. A bad **egg** comes from a bad crow.
56. **Eggs,** but not wings.

    [i.e. mere promises, but no performance.]
57. **Empty people** consider empty things.
58. Remember the **end.**
59. If an **enemy** does good things, they are evil.
60. From something shared in common there is most **enjoyment,** and least expense.
61. **Envy** is better worth having than pity.
62. Flee **evil ;** find better.
63. A small **evil** is a great good.
64. The bearer of an **excuse** does not admit it.
65. Drink to me only with thine **eyes.**
66. The **eyes** believe themselves ; the ears believe other people.
67. **Fame** is the perfume of heroic deeds.
68. A **favour** becomes old sooner than anything else.
69. Not **feeding** yourself, you feed dogs.
70. Extend not your **feet** beyond your blanket.
71. The man who runs away will **fight** again.
72. He who would **fight** well should not take a lance thicker than his hand.
73. **Fight** with silver spears and you will conquer everywhere.
74. Birds love **figs,** but they will not plant them.
75. An old **fig-tree** delights the neighbours.

    [Said of an old married man.]
76. **Fire** is not put out by fire.
77. Stir not the **fire** with a sword.
78. A **fish** begins to stink at its head.

    [i.e. corruption of a state begins first in the higher classes.]
79. He who eats **flax seed** eats his own shirt.

    [i.e. the future sacrificed to the present.]
80. A sound from the tongue is possible even among **flute players.**
81. Where a **fly** can alight there is room for Satan.

    [Saying alluding to the necessity of covering every inch of skin.]
82. Your **foal** is always small.
83. The first stage of **folly** is to think oneself wise.
84. A man may learn and learn and yet remain a **fool.**
85. Everyone is kinsman to the **fortunate.**
86. The wise carries his **fortune** with him.
87. **A fox** knows much ; a hedgehog one great thing.
88. He that has friends has no **friend.**
89. Distant **friends** are a trouble.
90. Where **friends** are, there is also wealth.
91. **Friends** burst in on friends unbidden.
92. Know the habits of your **friends,** but do not imitate them.
93. Go slowly to the entertainment of your **friends,** but quickly to their misfortunes.
94. The pot boils, **friendship** boils.
95. **Gain** does not delight as much as loss grieves.
96. **Gifts** appease the gods.
97. **Gifts** mislead even the wise.
98. **Goats** are free from the plough.
99. Free **goats** run away.

100. **God** can raise to Abraham children of stones. (*Motto of Paviours' Company.*)
101. **God** lets loose the good things without control.
102. The **gods** have placed sweat in front of virtue.
103. The **gods** sell all things at a fair price.
104. Who spares the wicked does an injury to the **good.**
105. The **good** are always prone to tears.
106. A heap of **good people**—an ant-hill of good people.
107. There is **grace** in small things.
108. The [three] **graces** are nude.

    [i.e. lovingkindness should be open and unniggardly.]
109. A **grasshopper** does not always come when one breaks a string.
110. Each man rears his own **gravestone** [obelisk].
111. The **greedy** fight till death for a needle.
112. No **Greek** was ever an old man.
113. Let the **guests** at table be three or four—at the most five.
114. **Hand** washes hand, and finger finger.
115. Everything has two **handles.**
116. Man has nothing to fear so much as the loss of **happiness.**
117. The really **happy man** must stay at home.
118. He who enlarges his **heart** restricts his tongue.
119. Take the **highest** and you will keep the middle.
120. **History** is philosophy derived from examples.
121. Who has eaten the **honey ?** He who has a fly on his umbrella.
122. Exiles subsist on **hope.**
123. If it were not for **hope** the heart would break.
124. There is nothing so bold as a blind **horse.**
125. Nothing fattens the **horse** so well as the master's eye.
126. Put smaller wheels for the **horse** which is growing old.
127. **Hunger** teaches a man many things.
128. Beware the **husband** who talks.
129. My **husband** does not love me because he does not beat me.
130. The cranes of **Ibycus.**

    [The Grecian poet Ibycus, when assailed by robbers, called on a flock of cranes soaring overhead to avenge his blood. His murderers betrayed themselves a little time later at Corinth when this flight of cranes appeared again above them, and one said scoffingly, "Lo, there the avengers of Ibycus." This led to their discovery and doom.]
131. **Iron** of itself draws a man thereto.
132. **Jackdaw** with jackdaw.
133. The **jaws** are the support of an old man.
134. A bankrupt **Jew** searches his old accounts.
135. **Judge,** hear both justly and unjustly.
136. A good **judge** of cattle, a good judge of character.
137. Don't hear one and **judge** two.
138. **Justice** begets justice, and hurt begets hurt.
139. If it suffered the things it accomplished **justice** would become just.
140. Unfading are the gardens of **kindness.**
141. Ill-tuned **kindness** differs not from enmity.
142. The **knee** is nearer than the shin.
143. Whatever is good to **know** is difficult to learn.
144. **Know** thyself. (*Inscription on the walls of Delphic Apollo.*)
145. The **label** is bigger than the package.
146. Do not stir up **Lake Camarina.**

    [i.e. the Lake which caused pestilency through futile attempts to drain it.]
147. Those that require a **lamp** pour oil in it.
148. **Last year's** things are always better.

149. Sit askew when you sit in the **law courts,** provided your judgment is straight.

150. **Laws** are like cobwebs; the small flies are caught and the great ones break through.

151. A **lawsuit** does not accept an excuse, nor does friendship.

152. You must drink up the **lees** also.

153. What you have not **let down** do not draw up.

154. Regard the end of **life.**

155. Better **life,** better living.

156. **Like** pleases like.

157. If the **lion's skin** is not available, put on the fox-skin.

158. We do not **live,** we wear ourselves out one against the other.

159. For **living creatures,** not as we wish but as we can.

160. Likeness is the mother of **love.**

161. **Love** as though you might have to hate; hate as though you might have to love.

162. **Love** cures the very wound it makes.

163. **Love** thy friend with his foibles.

164. One man **loves** the priest, another his wife.

165. From seeing comes **loving.**

166. For him who is **lucky** even the cock lays eggs.

167. There is no **lyric poetry** if you drink water.

168. **Madness** is not the same for all men.

169. **Man** is a god to man.

170. One **man,** no man.

171. **Marriage** is an evil that men pray for.

172. It is a matter of indifference whether a man **marries** or does not marry, for in either case he will regret it.

173. Either do not **marry** at all, or if you marry, be the master.

174. **Marry,** in preference to all other women, one who dwells near thee.

175. He who is about to **marry** is on the way to repentance.

176. Either **marry** very young or turn monk very young.

177. Everything has its **measure.**

178. The land where **mice** eat iron.
[i.e. great poverty.]

179. Who shirks the **mill** has no meal.

180. The **millstones** of the gods grind for a long time, but they grind very small.

181. Man is **money.**

182. Every land is a **Motherland** [Fatherland].

183. The **mountain** was in labour and then brought forth a mouse.

184. To be a **mouse** in a glue-pot.
[i.e. to be embarrassed.]

185. **Music** unheard has no value.

186. Nothing is greater than dread **necessity.**

187. **Neighbours** watch more closely than foxes.

188. **Nemesis** goes on foot.

189. The **net** of the sleeping [fisherman] takes.

190. When the **oak** falls every man gathers wood.

191. Go and shake another **oak** for acorns.
[Said to beggars.]

192. The **oak** is tamed by many blows.

193. Enough of the **oak-tree.**
[i.e. of acorns, now that we have corn and wine.]

194. How **office** proves the man!

195. Fear **old age,** for it does not come alone.

196. An **old man** pleases an old man.

197. **Old men** are boys twice.

198. Know your **opportunity.**

199. If you cannot drive **oxen** drive asses.

200. Where the **pain** is there is the hand.

201. The fruit of the **papyrus** does not surpass an ear of corn.

202. **Paradise** is certain and hell not less so.

203. When the **path** is before you, do not look for a road.

204. A moment's **patience** is a ten-years' comfort.
205. The disorder is a **physician.**
206. Consult not the **physician** but the disorder.
207. Hang your **plough-beam** o'er the hearth.
208. To be **poor** on land is better than to be rich at sea.
209. His **poppy** grows among the corn.
  [i.e. sleep.]
210. A **potter** envies a potter.
211. **Poverty** is the teacher of manners.
212. **Prosperity** is never friendless.
213. A beggar's **purse** is never full.
214. Men are neither suddenly **rich** nor suddenly good.
215. He is truly **rich** who desires nothing ; he is truly poor who covets all.
216. You have got a **rope,** coil it.
217. A stretched **rope** will snap.
218. The **rose** that has bloomed do not seek again.
219. Neither promise wax to the **saint** nor cakes to the child.
220. Do not overstep the **salt** and the table.
  [i.e. hospitality.]
221. **Say** what you like, hear in return what you do not like.
222. Under every stone a **scorpion** sleeps.
223. **Second things** are best.
224. **Shamelessness** is a god.
225. Let not the **shoe** be too large for the foot.
226. Any wood will do to make a **sign-post.**
227. Either say what is better than **silence** or keep silent.
228. Springs of **silver** chatter.
  [i.e. money talks.]
229. An old man's **skull** is a raisin.
  [i.e. very weak.]
230. **Slander** sits on the high-road and mocks at all the passers-by.
231. There is even a city of **slaves.**
232. There is **smoke** from all wood.
233. A great city—a great **solitude.**
234. **Sow** with the hand and not with the whole sack.
  [i.e. the seed corn must be providently dispersed with the hand, not prodigally shaken from the sack's mouth—so it is with benefits.]
235. Among the unmusical the **sparrow** is reckoned a fine singer.
236. He wants the **spring** since he has an old cloak.
237. If you sit with one who **squints,** before evening you will become cat-eyed.
238. A full **stomach** breeds an empty mind.
239. It is disgraceful to **stumble** twice against the same stone.
240. **Success** is befriended by many people.
241. **Suffering** brings understanding.
242. **Sufferings** are lessons.
243. I will do everything in the **summer.**
244. More people worship the rising than the setting **sun.**
245. That which is **sweet,** if it be often repeated, is no longer sweet.
246. Be more cunning than the **tempter.**
247. **Time** judges everything.
248. Give me **to-day** and take to-morrow.
249. The **tongue** has no bones, yet it breaks bones.
250. Nothing **too much.**
251. **Truth** hardens itself to the hammer.
252. Speaking the **truth** in love. (*St. Paul.*)
253. **Truth** in wine.
254. **Truth** is quarrelsome.
255. The story of the **truth** is simple.
256. **Truth** lies at the bottom of a well.
257. The stake has cheated the **vine.**
258. **Water** is best. (*Inscription over the Pump Room at Bath.*)
259. Drawn **wells** have sweetest water.
260. **Wickedness** alone lacks excuse.

261. **Wisdom** falls to the lot of poverty.
262. Nourish a **wolf** in the winter and he will devour you in the summer.
263. A **wolf** is accused whether he is guilty or not guilty.
264. A **wolf** runs away from noise.
265. A **wolf** shepherds the sheep.
266. The **wolf** unites with the lion when it is fenced in.
267. A **woman** either commands or serves.
268. Nothing is worse than a **woman,** even than the best of them.
269. Believe no **woman,** even when she is dead.
270. When the candle is taken away, every **woman** is alike.
271. Neither an old father, nor a **woman,** nor a spiteful child, nor anyone's dog, nor a sleeping helmsman, nor a chattering rower.
272. The sea, fire, **woman** ; three evils.
273. **Wonder** at nothing.
274. The deeds of the **young,** the counsels of the middle-aged, the prayers of the old.
275. The **young** do not know how much greater the half is than the whole.

GROUZIAN (GEORGIAN OR SAK'ART'VELO)

An Introduction to this Collection by A. Gugushvili will be found on page xlix.

1. One **blames** one's friend to his face and one's enemy to his back.
2. If two people tell you you are **blind,** shut one eye.
3. One should beware of the front of a **bull,** the back of a horse, and all sides of a blind man.
4. The **bull** without a tail drives away the flies from the other bulls.
5. The **cart** is heavy but it makes the load light.
6. On the top of the **cherry-tree** the cherry is sour.
7. For a good **cloth,** good lining.
8. The **cock** cannot profit by the friendship of the fox.
9. **Dew** is not rain, but just as useful.
10. First the **doctor,** then God.
11. Open your **door** and the door of others will be opened to you.
12. If the **ear** did not hear astonishing things it would become as big as a donkey's.
13. A **field** held in common is always ravaged by the bears.
14. The **fish** said, "I have much to say, but my mouth is full of water."
15. The **fool** scatters and the wise man picks up.
16. The **ford** is good, but one drowns oneself at the edge.
17. He who has not known ill **fortune** cannot enjoy good fortune.
18. If you forgive the **fox** for stealing your hen he will carry off your sheep.
19. He who does not seek **friends** is his own enemy.
20. To him to whom **God** gives He gives with both hands ; from him from whom He takes away He takes with both hands likewise.
21. The **hand** discovers what is heavy and the throat what is fat.
22. God created evil so that **hell** should not be empty.
23. **Hunger** doesn't say, "Stale bread," and cold doesn't say, "Old coat."
24. The man who is in a **hurry** is always late.

25. An **indispensable** thing has never much value.
26. That which one loses by **laughing** one does not find again by crying.
27. The **lazy man** thinks his hands and feet were lent him.
28. Let a **liar** tell you lies until he tells the truth.
29. One must follow the **liar** to the door of the lie.
30. Great **love** is followed by great hate.
31. **Low places** are considered high when high places are lacking.
32. He who loses **Monday** loses all the week.
33. Your **neighbour** is your mirror.
34. The **night** is pregnant and no one knows what the morning will bring forth.
35. The laugh of the rose makes the **nightingale** lose its head.
36. The **nightingale** sings as beautifully on thorns as on roses.
37. If you put your **nose** into water you will also wet your cheeks.
38. If the **nose** was not between the eyes they would eat each other.
39. When you give a child a **nut,** give it also something to break it with.
40. Put your **ox** with another and he will change either his colour or his character.
41. If you admit your **pig** to table he will put his feet on your head.
42. When the barley is on the **pig's** neck he can't reach it.
43. If everyone gave a needleful of thread to the **poor man,** he would soon have a shirt.
44. The **prudent man** bewares of stumbling, but when he stumbles he breaks his neck.
45. The **robber** has committed one crime, and the robbed a thousand.
46. Don't **sit** down from where they will make you get up.
47. Don't **spit** into a well ; one day it may serve to quench your thirst.
48. There is always a dirty **spoon** in every family.
49. It is better to drink warm water from a small **spring** than salt water from a great sea.
50. Click the teeth and the **stomach** will open the door.
51. The **summer** works for the winter.
52. Picking one's **teeth** doesn't satisfy the stomach.
53. He who doesn't know how to keep his property is the confederate of the **thief.**
54. He who is born on **thorns** prefers to **die** on them.
55. In a thorny place grow **thorns.**
56. One always deceives the man who tells the **truth.**
57. Even if **water** flows in all directions, the sand will remain at the bottom.
58. Man prefers another man's **wife,** but his own son.
59. The lucky man loses his **wife,** the unlucky one his horse.
60. That which was brought by the **wind** will be carried away by the wind.
61. Whilst the month of March is in front of you neither praise nor blame the **winter.**
62. If **wives** were good, God would have had one.
63. A **woman's** weapons are her tears.

HUNGARIAN

(Including Austrian and Galician)

An Introduction to this Collection by Professor Vilmos Tolnai will be found on page lvii.

1. An **angel** on the street, a devil in the house.
2. He who slowly gets **angry** keeps his anger longer.
3. Adam has eaten the **apple,** and our teeth ache from it.
4. The **apple** doesn't fall far from its tree.
5. He who **asks** much gives unwillingly.
6. An empty **bag** is often heavier than a full one.
7. **Bargain** like a gipsy, pay like a gentleman.
8. A bashful **beggar** has an empty wallet.
9. He who has not tasted **bitter** doesn't know what is sweet.
10. Shut your eyes if you are among the **blind.**
11. **Blushing** is the paint of good morals.
12. It is best to begin at the **bottom** and end at the top.
13. When the **bridge** is gone the narrowest plank becomes precious.
14. The damaged **cask** is not easily broken.
15. A lovely **child** has many names.
16. No **cloak** is big enough to cover poverty and drunkenness.
17. Good **coffee** should be black like the devil, hot like hell, and sweet like a kiss.
18. The **copse** does not rustle if the wind does not blow.
19. The owner's eye makes the **crop** grow.
20. One does not raise one's hat before a fallen **crucifix.**
21. The willing **dancer** is easily played to.
22. Sometimes a quick **death** is better than a long life.
23. The interest of the uncertain **debt** is straw.
24. A **debtor** must often lie.
25. Two things are difficult to **deceive**—the eye and the ear.
26. The **devil** tempts every man except the idle man, and he tempts the devil.
27. A man, if he is only a little bit prettier than the **devil,** is already sufficiently good-looking.
28. Only a **doctor** can kill you without punishment.
29. When everybody is doing well, the **doctor** is miserable.
30. After a time even a **dog** makes a compromise with the cat.
31. **Dog's** fur is the medicine against a dog's bite.
32. People must have something to say ; **dogs** something to bark at. (*Austrian.*)
33. Give him to **drink** and you will learn whose son he is.
34. **Eagles** do not catch flies.
35. One **eats** the roast and the other licks the spit.
36. At the **end** the thing is praised.
37. If an **envier** is sad, either he is in trouble, or somebody else had luck.
38. One bad **example** destroys more than twenty good ones build up.
39. We keep **fast days** when there is neither bread nor bacon in the cupboard.
40. It is a fine thing to die for one's **fatherland,** but a still finer to live for it.
41. It's better to **fear** than to be frightened.
42. From its head starts the **fish** rotting.
43. He who is **flattering** either has, or wants to cheat you.

44. A **fool** makes his doctor his heir.
45. Everybody thinks himself wise ; that is why there are so many **fools.**
46. A foolish **friend** is more harmful than a sensible enemy.
47. One **friend** is the god of the other.
48. Bargain like an enemy ; pay like a **friend.**
49. Luck brings, misery tries the **friend.**
50. God save me from my **friends,** I will manage to deal with my enemies.
51. Did you **give,** forget it ; did you accept, mention it.
52. If you **give,** give easily ; if you accept, accept cheerily.
53. Not he who has, **gives,** but he who wants to.
54. Full **glass,** empty advice.
55. **God** has legs of wool but hands of lead.
56. The hand of **God** is always open and always full.
57. Even **God** keeps the strong.
58. **God** lets us be born small, but lets us grow big.
59. The hands of the **God** of Hungary never become too short.
60. When **God** so wills, the broom loses its handle.
61. With **God's** protection even a cobweb is a castle.
62. **Gold** clarifies, dirt burns in fire.
63. A **great man** falls heavily.
64. Honest men **grow white,** the shrewd bald.
65. A bad **habit** is first a pilgrim, then a guest, and finally the host.
66. It's better to return from **halfway** than to lose your way.
67. Nobody is **hanged** for thinking.
68. **Happiness** begins where ambition ends.
69. No one is **happy** before his death.
70. He who believes is **happy,** who doesn't is wise.
71. One often greets the **hedge** for love of the nettle.
72. There is no such place in the world from where a path would not lead to **hell.**
73. A long **hope** is sweeter than a short surprise.
74. Outside **Hungary** there is no life ; if there is any it is not the same.

    [This proverb was originally used in Latin : " Extra Hungariam non est vita, si est vita, non est ita."]
75. It is better to always **hurry** than to be late once.
76. **Illness** gives you the taste of health.
77. In a severe **illness** God is the doctor.
78. It is easier to **inherit** than to learn.
79. Of what use to the **invalid** is a golden bed ?
80. Even amongst the Apostles there was a **Judas.**
81. The **jug** goes to the well till it breaks.
82. A golden **key** fits in every lock.
83. Frequent **kisses** end in a baby.
84. **Law** is a spider's web ; big flies break through but the little ones are caught.
85. The **law** moves on golden wheels.
86. Not always the pen, often the weapon writes the **law.**
87. New king, new **laws.**
88. Even rest will make the **lazy** tired.
89. He who is struck by the **lightning** doesn't hear the thunder.
90. **Lightning** doesn't strike the nettle.
91. The **lightning** strikes the running man.
92. Even a white **lily** casts a black shadow.
93. A dead **lion** is kicked even by an ass.
94. **Love** and foolishness differ from each other only in name.
95. **Love** is a dark pit.

96. In dreams and in **love** nothing is impossible.
97. Let nothing on earth sadden you so long as you can still **love.**
98. Look at the mother, **marry** the daughter.
99. Everywhere is a **master** ; if he is not at home, he may yet come home. (*Austrian.*)
100. **Men** are carried by horses, fed by cattle, clothed by sheep, defended by dogs, imitated by monkeys, and eaten up by worms.
101. **Men** stand and wait, life brings and goes, death comes and takes.
102. **Money** speaks ; dogs bark.
103. If you want to get rid of your friend, lend him **money.**
104. He has **much** who doesn't want more.
105. There is no man so rich that he needs not his **neighbour.**
106. Who cannot **obey** cannot order.
107. **One child** is God's punishment. (*Austrian.*)
108. Don't ask the **origin** of men and of good wine.
109. The **owl,** too, thinks his son a hawk.
110. If you like **peace** don't contradict anybody.
111. From a **peasant** you may earn a stick for a good word, but a cake for a hard one.
112. Better a frequent **penny** than a rare shilling.
113. He who sells **poison** uses a flowery signboard.
114. Great **pomp** is the coffin of the purse.
115. **Porridge** is no meal ; stick is no weapon.
116. When there is grass in the yard there is **poverty** in the house.
117. Accept a **present** and you have sold your freedom.
118. The most over-populated **professions :** doctors, fools, advisers.
119. A **promise** makes you debtor.
120. **Proverbs** are common sayings.
121. He who goes **quickly** is quickly tired.
122. When God made the **rabbit** He made bushes too.
123. He is **rich** enough who owes nothing.
124. One **road** leads to heaven but many lead to hell.
125. Divide and **rule.** (*Austrian.*)
126. Nobody can rest in his own **shadow.**
127. A little **sin** at home is a big one abroad.
128. A **sin,** even if committed by many, remains a sin.
129. Many people would not be mentioned if they had not **sinned.**
130. Better a friend with seven **sins** than a stranger with one.
131. The **skinflint** spends more money, the idler works more, than other people.
132. **Sparks** fly, even from a small forge.
133. Better a **sparrow** to-day than a buzzard to-morrow.
134. Who **speaks** much, either knows or lies much.
135. An old **spinster** is not worth more than an unposted letter.
136. Give shelter to a **Slovak** and he will turn you out of your house.
137. The wise, if he **stumbles,** falls heavily.
138. Even in the **sun** there are spots.
139. Out of a hundred **suspicions** ninety-nine are incorrect.
140. He who falls into bran will be eaten by **swine.**
141. If your **sword** is short, lengthen it by a step.
142. He who **toils** the most for the cow gets the least enjoyment from it.
143. Thirty-two teeth can often not bridle the **tongue.**
144. Don't lop the **tree** which gives you shade.
145. A good man never hurts a **tree.** (*Galician.*)

146. Time brings out the **truth** better than the judge.
147. Don't deny the **truth** even for the sake of your friend.
148. A child, a drunkard, and a fool tell the **truth.**
149. Slow **water** washes a bank.
150. Don't choose a **wife** and linen by candlelight.
151. The first **wife** comes from God, the second from men, but the third from the devil.
152. For a young man a **wife** is a support and his walking-stick a luxury ; for an old man his wife is the luxury and the stick the support.
153. A bone for my dog ; a stick for my **wife.** (*Galician.*)
154. The **wind** will fell an oak, but cannot destroy the reed.
155. He drinks **wine** and preaches water.
156. In **wine** there is happiness.
157. What you **wish** you readily believe.
158. It is much easier to take care of a sackful of fleas than a **woman.**
159. Two **women** are a party, three a crowd.
160. From **women,** evil, and cucumbers, the smaller is the better.
161. Nothing is **worse** than a poor Jew, lean pork, or a drunken woman.

ICELANDIC

(Including Eskimoan)

1. **Ale** is the man himself.
2. Two are an **army** against one.
3. Bare is **back** without a brother.
4. The **beard** is related to the chin, and the nose is nearest the eyes.
5. A **bend** [or crook] seeks its fellow.
6. To be **better** one must first be worse.
7. Better is a little with **blessings** than the double with grief.
8. Light **burdens** in the end are heavy.
9. It is a lazy man who flees from a **calm.**
10. **Character** is always corrupted by prosperity.
11. It is a short distance between the **chin** and the beard.
12. Only important things should be made the subject of general **conversation.**
13. A sitting **crow** starves.
14. More belongs to **dancing** than a pair of fine shoes.
15. **Desire** bears [carries] man half the road [way].
16. He who lives without **discipline** dies without honour.
17. A man's best friend is his **dog,** better even than his wife. (*Eskimoan.*)
18. A **dog** knows what it has eaten.
19. It is difficult to teach an old **dog** to sit down.
20. There are many **eatables** in the buttery that can't be placed on the table.
21. Some imagine that their **eggs** are better than other people's fowls.
22. One **enemy** is too much, and a hundred friends too little.
23. That man is to be pitied who is never **envied.**
24. Insignificant is he who is not threatened by **envy.**

25. **Errands** are small on a spring day.
26. **Everyone** is nearest to himself.
27. **Evil** is before good in nothing.
28. **Eyesight** is more powerful than hearsay.
29. Few things are better than to **fare well.**
30. The dishing up compensates for the scarcity of the **food.**
31. It is ill to be the **friend** of both and true to both.
32. Man works and **God** blesses.
33. **God** is in heaven and grass is on the earth.
34. He who **guesses** often takes the wrong turning.
35. A **guest's eye** is sharp sighted.
36. A good **hand** repairs.
37. **Hand** washes hand and stone polishes stone.
38. Better a **hawk** in the hand than two in flight.
39. Old **hides** need much grease.
40. It goes backwards for all when they have reached the **highest point.**
41. A little **hill** has often power over a heavy burden.
42. Every man is master at **home.**
43. An **honest man** seldom sits on his doorstep.
44. **Honour** is poor capital.
45. The **horse** is the most willing when he is the most tormented.
46. You do not know who is your friend or who is your enemy until the **ice** breaks. (*Eskimoan.*)
47. Not all **journeys** are for profit.
48. **Kinsmen** are worst to kinsmen.
49. He who has a **lazy hand** has an empty mouth.
50. Strong **legs** are needed to carry good days.
51. **A little** can be kept a long time.
52. Many a man stretches right round the door to get at the **lock.**
53. **Love** comes after marriage. (*Eskimoan.*)
54. **Love** ends when the can is empty.
55. **Luck** is better than long legs.
56. **Mediocrity** is climbing mole-hills without sweating.
57. Need is no **merchant.**
58. He who once gets into another man's **mouth** gets out again with difficulty.
59. Don't open your **mouth** until a goose has flown in.
60. **Much** always desires more.
61. In time of trouble a near **neighbour** is better than a distant brother.
62. When your **neighbour's wall** breaks, your own is in danger.
63. One must honour the **oak** beneath which one dwells.
64. Everyone would live long, but no one wants to be called **old.**
65. No one should forget old roads and **old friends.**
66. An **old man** is a child for a long time.
67. The will of man is his **paradise,** but it often becomes his hell.
68. **Penny-less** is better than honour-less.
69. The **piglings** squeal, the old swine are the cause.
70. The **pigs** would grunt now if they knew what the old one suffers.
71. No one is another's brother in **play.**
72. It is better to **postpone** than to forget.
73. **Praise** a maid in the morning and weather in the evening.
74. Many get **praise** for little and burdens for nothing.
75. He must get up early who would have another's **property** together with his life.
76. All old **proverbs** are spread abroad.
77. The **purse** is empty in which another man's gold lies.
78. The **revenge** that is postponed is not forgotten.
79. **Riches** are not the only wealth.
80. That which oneself thinks true is **right.**

81. He should fear the wicked who looks upon himself as **righteous.**
82. Folk who consider themselves **righteous** have much in common.
83. 'Tis a lean **roast** from which no fat drops.
84. All **sails** do not suit every ship.
85. One does not know for whom one **saves.**
86. All old **sayings** have something in them.
87. He goes forward who goes **slowly.**
88. If many **spit** on a stone it becomes wet at last.
89. It is not easy to **steal** when the landlord is a thief.
90. The **story** is only half told when one side tells it.
91. Often little comes of the **stroke** for which a man heaved his arm up high.
92. When **sweet** is blended together it prefers to remain sour.
93. It is all one when men have risen from **table.**
94. Keep your **teeth** in front of your tongue.
95. That which leaves no **trace** has done no harm.
96. Often must **truth** lie quiet.
97. The **twigs** are rarely better than the trunk.
98. It's good to have **two mouths** and to speak to oneself with each.
99. It is best to drive home in a whole **waggon.**
100. Little **wit,** little fear.
101. **Women's counsels** are often fatal.
102. It is better to keep back one **word** than to speak two.
103. **Wrath** often consumes what goodness husbands.
104. " **Yes and no** " make a long quarrel.
105. He who would soon be a man remains long a **youth.**

ITALIAN

(Including Abruzzi, Bergamo, Ligurian, Lombardy, Neapolitan, Piedmontese, Roccaraso, Sicilian, Tuscan, Tyrolese and Venetian)

An Introduction to this collection by Professor Emilio Bodrero, Ph.D., will be found on page lxv.

1. **Abundance** creates daintiness.
2. What you can't have, **abuse.**
3. **Affection** is a bad judge.
4. Don't go **a-fishing** to a famous stream.
5. Every ditch is full of **after-wits.**
6. Better a lean **agreement** than a fat judgment [lawsuit].
7. No one ever became poor through giving **alms.**
8. **Ambassadors** suffer no penalty.
9. It is a good **answer** which knows when to stop.
10. An iron **anvil** should have a hammer of feathers.
11. An **argus** at home, a mole abroad.
12. With **art** and knavery men may live through half the year, and with knavery and art through the other half.
13. An **ass's** trot does not last long.
14. If a **baby** laughs in its sleep [he laughs with the angels]. (*Abruzzi.*)
15. Old **bacon** seasons the pot.
16. Fraud squats under a good **bargain.** (*Tuscan.*)

17. Great **bargains** empty the purse.
18. He who is meant to be a **basket-carrier** is born with the handle in his hand.
19. The **beauty** of heaven is the stars; the beauty of women is their hair. (*Abruzzi.*)
20. He who doesn't think at the **beginning,** sighs at the end. (*Abruzzi.*)
21. He who never **begins** never ends. (*Abruzzi.*)
22. One **bell** serves a parish.
23. " **Better** " is the enemy of good.
24. The older the **bird** the more unwillingly it parts with its feathers.
25. He who has **bitter** in his mouth can't spit out sweet. (*Venetian.*)
26. Light pursues the **blind.** (*Abruzzi.*)
27. When the **body** wears out, the soul readjusts itself.
28. A good **book,** a good friend.
29. There is no worse robber than a bad **book.**
30. **Border-folk** are either thieves or murderers.
31. Where one was **born,** every blade of grass pleases.
32. Sharp teeth for hard **bread.**
33. They are **bread** and cheese. [i.e. sworn friends.]
34. He that has his teeth has not **bread;** he that has bread has not teeth.
35. Eaten **bread** is soon forgotten.
36. Dry **bread,** long life. (*Abruzzi.*)
37. The **bread** of servants has seven crusts.
38. To hunt for better **bread** than is made of corn.
39. He who wins at the outset returns with his **breeches** in his hands.
40. He who buys the **broom** can also buy the handle.
41. The animal with long ears, after having drunk, gives a kick to the **bucket.**
42. He who **builds** on other people's land loses both lime and stones.
43. From the window it is easy to frighten the **bull.**
44. A **burden** which one chooses is not felt.
45. He who manages other people's **business** doesn't go to bed without supper.
46. The would-be **buyer** always depreciates.
47. Others have eaten the **candle** and you digest the wick.
48. One no longer lights **candles** to old saints.
49. A **cat** pent up becomes a lion.
50. Old **cattle** die in the stall of the foolish peasant.
51. The man who is always in his **cell** belongs to heaven or else to hell.
52. Sincere **charity** goes through the door and comes through the window. (*Tyrolese.*)
53. Through practising **charity** one finds enemies.
54. The **chestnut** is for the man who takes its shell off.
55. The " why " of a **child** is the key of philosophy.
56. When **children** are little they make our heads ache; when grown, our hearts.
57. He who has no **children** does not understand love.
58. A new **chimney** is soon smoked.
59. Every **chimney** makes its own smoke. (*Abruzzi.*)
60. Give the **church** a hand and it will demand an arm.
61. When there is nothing the **church** loses.
62. Sometimes **clemency** is cruelty and cruelty clemency.
63. Those who have fine **clothes** in their chests can wear rags. (*Venetian.*)
64. He was born with his **clothes** on.
65. It is a sorry house in which the **cock** is silent and the hen crows.
66. Where many **cocks** crow the day never breaks.

67. **Coffee** from the top (of the **cup**) and chocolate from the bottom. (*Venetian.*)
68. Where the **cold** doesn't enter, the heat doesn't enter. (*Abruzzi.*)
69. It is easier to **comfort** than to be comforted.
70. The consolation of the **condemned** is to be in a numerous company.
71. **Conscience** is like tickling, some fear it and some don't.
72. **Consideration** is a constant scource of error.
73. **Copper** produces a short mass.
74. When **corn** is in the fields, it belongs to God and to the saints. (*Abruzzi.*)
75. Give neither **counsel** nor salt till you are asked for it.
76. He who lives at **court** dies on straw.
77. A **courtesy** is a flower.
78. He who has not his **cross** at the door has it at the window.
79. The love of the wood-worm eats away **crucifixes.**
80. That which is **customary** requires no excuse.
81. The **dead** open the eyes of the living.
82. It takes four to move a **dead man,** and many more to move a live one. (*Abruzzi.*)
83. That which comes naturally continues till **death.**
84. **Death** pardons no one. (*Tuscan.*)
85. Water and **death** stand behind the door. (*Abruzzi.*)
86. A hundred years of melancholy will not pay one farthing of **debt.**
87. Who thinks to **deceive** God has already deceived himself.
88. The **deceiver** is ever at the foot of the deceived.
89. **Deception** finds deception.
90. He who **denies** all, admits all.
91. When one stands with one hand over the other the **devil** dances in one's apron. (*Venetian.*)
92. He who labours is tempted by one **devil ;** he who is idle is tempted by a thousand.
93. The **devil** tempts everybody, but the idle man tempts even the devil.
94. One cannot **die** hidden from God. (*Abruzzi.*)
95. To wait for what never comes, to lie a-bed and not sleep, to serve well and not be advanced, are three things to **die** of.
96. When one is satisfied one **dies.**
97. **Dirty water** does not wash clean.
98. **Discord** often makes concord.
99. **Discretion** is the mother of asses.
100. He who doesn't know a trade becomes a **doctor.**
101. Where the sun does not go, the **doctor** goes.
102. While the **doctor** is reflecting the patient dies. (*Venetian.*)
103. A **doctor's** error, the will of God. (*Tuscan.*)
104. An eating **dog** and a sleeping man, let them be. (*Venetian.*)
105. When a mad **dog** dies it has tasted hen-bane. (*Piedmontese.*)
106. Even the **dog** gets bread by wagging his tail!
107. Every **dog** is a lion at home.
108. Pelt a **dog** with a bone and you will not offend him.
109. Bark with the **dogs** and howl with the wolves.
110. Once the most is **done** it is better to do the least. (*Ligurean.*)
111. The **donkey** doesn't know his tail until he has lost it. (*Ligurean.*)
112. Let him who remains behind, lock the **door.**
113. Every **door** has its knocker. (*Venetian.*)
114. Knock on the threshold that the **door** may hear you. (*Ligurean.*)
115. Sometimes it is wise to **drink** in order not to be drowned.
116. When everybody says you are **drunk,** go to sleep.

117. If you want to know how much a **ducat** is worth, borrow one.

118. Go slowly to raise no **dust.**

119. The more you think of **dying** the better you live.

120. One pair of **ears** would exhaust a hundred tongues.

121. **Earth** to begin with, and earth to end with.

[i.e. man's history.]

122. **Eat** after your own fashion, dress as others do.

123. Who **eats** of but one dish never needs a physician.

124. The last one **eats** with those who are painted on the wall.

125. Better an **egg** to-day than a hen to-morrow.

126. The **elephant** cannot feel the biting of the flea.

127. That is pleasant to remember which was hard to **endure.**

128. That which was bitter to **endure** is sweet to recall.

129. Man's great **enemy** is his own opinion.

130. War with all the world but peace with **England.**

131. **England** is a prison for men, a paradise for women, purgatory for servants, a hell for horses. (*Tuscan.*)

132. An **Englishman** Italianized is the devil incarnate.

133. Only **Englishmen** and dogs walk in the sun.

134. With little one **enjoys** much, with much one enjoys little. (*Bergamese.*)

135. Beware of a reconciled **enemy.**

136. There is never **enmity** between the cook and the butler.

137. All feasts come and go; **Epiphany** tarries. (*Roccaraso.*)

138. **Everything** is of every year.

139. **Evil** does not always come to do harm.

140. He who does **evil** never lacks for an excuse.

141. An unasked-for **excuse** infers transgression.

142. Any **excuse** is good if it hold good.

143. He who **excuses** himself without being accused makes his guilt clear.

144. The most jealous thing is the **eye.** (*Abruzzi.*)

145. He that sees with the **eye** believes with the heart.

146. He who paints my **face** soils my back.

147. When a man is **falling,** every saint pushes him.

148. **Falsehood** has beauty if it works for good.

149. Under water, **famine**; under snow, bread.

150. When the **feast** is over the saint is neglected.

151. An old **feud** is soon renewed.

152. Pull a **fig** for your friend, and a peach for your enemy.

153. He who remains the last puts out the **fire.** (*Abruzzi.*)

[i.e. the last of a family.]

154. The coldest corner is near the **fire.** (*Abruzzi.*)

155. He who needs **fire** carries a shovel.

156. **Fire** is not extinguished by fire.

157. Go to the sea if you would **fish** well.

158. The **flame** is not far from the smoke.

159. One **flea** does not hinder sleep.

160. Let every one keep off the **flies** with his own tail.

161. Even a **fly** has a cough. (*Abruzzi.*)

162. Words do not make **flour.**

[This is probably the most used proverb in Italy.]

163. Who has little **flour** in the sack adds the water little by little.

[i.e. a poor man goes along little by little.]

164. He who buys his **flour** is blind of one eye; he who buys his bread is blind of both.

165. Little **flour** makes few loaves and little money makes few friends. (*Sicilian.*)

166. Every **flower** loses its perfume in the end.
167. Every **flower** wishes to be one of the nosegay.
168. The shadow of a lord is a cap for a **fool.**
169. The wise man is a **fool** in other people's houses, and the fool is a wise man in his own.
170. The **fool** learns to live at his own expense ; the wise man at the expense of others.
171. He who governs himself as a **fool** suffers as a wise man.
172. **Fortune** is a cow who shows her head to some and her tail to others. (*Venetian.*)
173. In the **fray** the weak are strong.
174. Everyone's **friend** is no one's friend.
175. Take a **friend** for what he does, a wife for what she has, and goods for what they are worth.
176. The **friend** of the priest loses his religion, the friend of the doctor loses his health, the friend of the lawyer loses his substance. (*Venetian.*)
177. Speak well of your **friend,** of your enemy neither well nor ill.
178. Love your **friend** with his faults.
179. If you have three **friends** it is not enough ; if you have one enemy it is too much.
180. **Friends** tie their purses with a spider's thread.
181. In order to preserve **friendship** one must set up walls.
182. **Friendship** should be unpicked, not rent.
183. Even the **frog** would bite if it had teeth.
184. There is no worse **fruit** than that which never ripens.
185. Where there is nothing to **gain** there is something to lose. (*Venetian.*)
186. The **gardener's** foot doesn't spoil the garden.
187. Your last **garment** has no pockets.
188. Who arrays himself in other men's **garments** is stripped in the middle of the street.
189. A **gift** long awaited is sold, not donated.
190. **Gifts** are often losses.
191. **Give** time, time.
192. **God** does not pay on a Saturday.
193. Who has **God** for his friend has all the saints in his pocket.
194. **God** helps him who is in possession.
195. **God** listens to short prayers.
196. To the good spender **God** is treasurer. (*Tuscan.*)
197. **God** is treasurer to the charitable man.
198. **God** puts food into clean hands. (*Tuscan.*)
199. When one can do no more **God** sends death. (*Venetian.*)
200. That which **God** sends is better than that which man asks for. (*Tuscan.*)
201. He who **goes** himself means it ; he who sends another does not care.
202. Gold's worth is **gold.**
203. One may buy **gold** too dear.
204. That is **gold** which buys gold.
205. **Good** is recognised when it goes, and evil when it comes.
206. Keep company with **good men,** and you will increase their number.
207. With the **gospel** men may become heretics.
208. Everyone hath enough to do to **govern** himself well.
209. A **guest** and a fish smell in three days.
210. A **guest** is received according to his coat and speeded according to his disccurse.
211. He who digs a **grave** is the first to fall into it. (*Sicilian.*)
212. He who has had enough, **grumbles.**
213. Some look for **hair** in a new-laid egg.
214. Dogs and rude people have no **hands.**

215. Cold **hands** live long. (*Abruzzi.*)
216. Everyone has his **hanged man** on his threshold.
217. He who has not seen a **hare** run, must not speak of fear. (*Abruzzi.*)
218. Who **has,** is.
219. That which is done has a **head.**
    [i.e. a thing is never done until it is perfectly completed.]
220. No comforter's **head** ever aches.
221. Let not him whose **head** is of wax walk in the sun.
222. He who has no **head** must have legs. (*Venetian.*)
223. Any **head-dress** is good enough for the night.
224. **Health** without wealth is half a sickness.
225. **Hear** the other side—believe little.
226. Every thorn makes a **hedge.** (*Abruzzi.*)
227. The **hedge** has no eyes, but it has ears.
228. There is no **hen** nor capon that lays no eggs in January. (*Abruzzi.*)
229. The **hen** which doesn't peck, has pecked.
230. **Hens** make eggs by their beaks. (*Abruzzi.*)
231. Four things are necessary for a **home**; grain, a cock, a cat, and a wife.
232. The last thing lost is **hope.**
233. Death alone can kill **hope.**
234. The last thing one loses is **hope.** (*Venetian.*)
235. **Hope** is the poor man's bread.
236. He who has a good **horse** in his stable is not ashamed to go on foot.
237. To the lean **horse** God sends flies. (*Neapolitan.*)
238. Every **horse** scares the flies away with its own tail.
239. One does not beat the **horse** that trots.
240. He who goes on **horseback** in his youth, goes on foot in his old age.
241. He who has good **horses** in his stables can go on foot. (*Venetian.*)
242. He who stays much in other folks' **houses** becomes a stranger in his own.
243. **Hunger** changes beans into almonds.
244. When **hunger** mounts, pride descends. (*Ligurean.*)
245. Good **husbandry** is good divinity.
246. To a covered **ill** an open razor.
247. There are ninety-nine ways of being **ill,** and a hundred ways of curing. (*Abruzzi.*)
248. He who is well does everything to make himself **ill,** and he who is ill does everything to make himself well.
249. **Ill** comes in hundredweights and goes away in ounces.
250. **Illnesses** tell us what we are.
251. By asking for the **impossible** we obtain the best possible.
252. Who doth not burn doth not **inflame.**
253. The **invalid** is at liberty to say anything.
254. He who goes on horseback is **invited** three times, and he who goes on foot, once. (*Abruzzi.*)
255. He who speaks **Italian** goes to Rome.
256. The **Italians** are wise before the deed; the Germans in the deed; the French after the deed.
257. If **January** stay in his shirt-sleeves [is mild], March will explode with laughing [will mock you with rough weather].
258. If **January's** shirts are white, March bursts into laughter light. (*Abruzzi.*)
259. It takes nine **Jews** to make one Genoese.
260. Don't worry about the **joint** being browned if it has not to come to table.
261. **Justice** is made like the nose which goes whichever way you pull it.

262. A broken **kettle** never falls from its hook.
263. **A kind action** should close the mouth of him who does it and open the mouth of him who receives it.
264. After the game the **king** goes into the sack like the pawn.
265. There are three things a **king** shouldn't do : eat the spiced bread of appetite, see the sun rise, and hear the truth.
266. Oft heart is missed where mouth is **kissed.**
267. Blessed is the house that has only one **knocker.**
268. To know everything is to **know** nothing.
269. Who **knows** most knows least.
270. The more a man **knows,** the more he forgives.
271. He who **knows** the most believes the least.
272. Where one can reach with the hands one doesn't need a **ladder.**
273. The more you care for **land** and animals the better results you get. (*Abruzzi.*)
274. Every time one **laughs** a nail is removed from one's coffin.
275. A **lawsuit** is a fair tree in a lawyer's garden, that takes root and never dies.
276. The robes of **lawyers** are lined with the obstinacy of suitors.
277. Who hath no courage must have **legs.**
278. There is usually **less** money, less wisdom, and less good faith than men do count upon.
279. The **liar** is sooner caught than a cripple.
280. A **liar's** punishment is not being believed when he speaks the truth.
281. **Liberty** and hard crusts. (*Sicilian.*)
282. A little bit of truth makes the whole **lie** believed.
283. A **lie** well told is worth more than a stupid fact. (*Abruzzi.*)
284. **Lies** have short legs.
285. He who catches **lions** in their absence is afraid of mice in their presence.
286. He who would **live** long must sometimes change his way of living.
287. It is better to **live** small than to die big. (*Ligurean.*)
288. A man has **lived** to no purpose unless he has either built a house, begotten a son, or written a book.
289. One **lives** with little and dies with nothing.
290. The trough is dirtied by ten **loaves** as much as by twenty.
291. He who has **loaves** has dogs.
292. Beware of him who has nothing to **lose.**
293. Anger increases **love.**
294. It is all one whether you die of sickness or of **love.**
295. Find as much **love** as was given by thy father and mother many times. (*Abruzzi.*)
296. **Love** can accomplish all, death conquers all, time consumes all, and death ends all.
297. One **love** expels another.
298. **Love** is a forger of suspicions.
299. **Love** is like tears, it is born in the eyes and falls on the breast.
300. The anger of those in **love** is like the spider's web. (*Venetian.*)
301. The feet of those we **love** make a bare path green. (*Sicilian.*)
302. Old **love** never rusts.
303. In the war of **love** who flies conquers.
304. With song and music **love** will start, but in a sea of weeping part. (*Abruzzi.*)
305. **Lovers,** like bees, spend a honeyed life.
306. He who **loves,** believes.
307. The more one **loves** the other the less one knows the other.
308. He saith little that **loveth** much.
309. A **maid** that taketh yieldeth.
310. Three women and a goose make a **market.**

311. Words make the **market** and gold pays.

312. There is no **marriage** where there is no weeping, and no funeral where there is no laughing. (*Abruzzi.*)

313. Praise **married** life but remain single.

314. The girl who is going to be **married** must have her dowry in her hands. (*Abruzzi.*)
[i.e. must work.]

315. Who **marries** for love without money hath good nights and sorry days.

316. In high society one **marries** one woman, lives with another, but loves only oneself. (*Piedmontese.*)

317. He who eats the **marrow** with his teeth eats the crust with his gums.

318. To an unjust government a **martyr** is more dangerous than a rebel.

319. A **mass** is as good whether it be sung or said.

320. No one is born a **master.**

321. The eye of the **master** fattens the horse.

322. When there is much **meat** boiling someone must watch the pot. (*Neapolitan.*)

323. Too much **meat** in the pot won't cook.

324. Old **meat** makes good broth. (*Venetian.*)
[i.e. elderly women make good wives.]

325. Bed is a **medicine.** (*Venetian.*)

326. A **merchant** and a pig are only weighed when dead. (*Venetian.*)

327. Oil **merchant**; gold merchant. (*Abruzzi.*)

328. One changes one's **mind** oftener than one's shirt.

329. The **miser** is like the donkey which carries wine and drinks water.

330. The **mission** and the galleys leave a man as he was.

331. Does your neighbour's presence annoy you?—Lend him **money.**

332. **Money** and friendship break the arms of justice.

333. **Money** is money's brother.

334. Who would make **money** must begin by spending.

335. Whatever the **monk** gets, he gets for the monastery.

336. The **morning** is the eye of the day. (*Lombardy.*)

337. The **morning** is the mother of trades and the evening the mother of thoughts.

338. One good **morsel** and a hundred vexations.

339. If you are a **mouse** don't follow frogs.

340. The **mouth** carries the legs.

341. The virtue of the **mouth** healeth all it touches.

342. Who is always looking for **mud** generally finds it.

343. He who is born a **mule** is bound to kick.

344. A bad **mule** needs a good stick.

345. Year of **mushrooms,** year of trouble. (*Abruzzi.*)

346. The **Neapolitan** is wide-mouthed [i.e. irascible] and narrow-handed [i.e. close-fisted].

347. He who is to break his **neck,** finds the stairs in the dark.

348. Once in every ten years, every man needs his **neighbour.**

349. A good **neighbour,** a good morrow.

350. He who has a bad **neighbour** has a bad morning.

351. A near **neighbour** is better than distant relatives. (*Sicilian.*)

352. When your **neighbour's** house is on fire, carry water to your own.

353. **Night** is the mother of thoughts.

354. **Night** strengthens hand and foot and sharpens the understanding.

355. He cuts his **nose** and covers his own mouth with blood. (*Venetian.*)
[Said of one who speaks ill of his relations.]

356. "**Nothing**" is good for the eyes but not for the teeth. (*Abruzzi.*)

357. He who knows **nothing,** doubts nothing.

358. He who does **nothing** makes no blunder.

359. He who **offends** writes on sand ; he who is offended, on marble. (*Sicilian.*)

360. He who **offends** you never forgives you.

361. What **old age** spoils no master can make good. (*Sicilian.*)

362. He who feels his body too much never makes **old bones.**

363. An **old man** hath the almanac in his body.

364. A man's own **opinion** is never in the wrong.

365. Keep yourself from **opportunities** and God will keep you from sins.

366. An **ox** is bound with ropes and a man with words. (*Bergamo.*)

367. **Paper** does not blush.

368. One would not be alone in **paradise.**

369. To **part** is to die a little.

370. **Patch** and long sit, build and soon flit.

371. They put on **patches** to hide their wealth. (*Piedmontese.*)

372. If the **patient** dies, it is the doctor who has killed him, and if he gets well, it is the saints who have cured him. (*Abruzzi.*)

373. **Paying** and dying come both in good time. (*Venetian.*)

374. It is better to keep **peace** than to make peace.

375. **Peace** would be universal if there were neither "mine" nor "thine".

376. To be content to let twelve **pennies** pass for a shilling.

377. At a good **pennyworth** pause awhile.

378. 'Tis a mark of great **perfection** to bear with the imperfections of others.

379. He who kills a **pig** eats a year, and he who kills an ox eats a week.

380. He that takes not up a **pin** slights his wife.

381. The **pitcher** that goes often to the fountain leaves there either its handle or its spout.

382. Any **place** is bad which is not susceptible of change.

383. It is not an art to **play,** but it is very good art to leave off play.

384. **Pleasure** has no family, but sorrow has wife and children.

385. He who **ploughs** from West to East loses a loaf in every furrow.

[i.e. the sun cannot shine on both sides of the furrow.]

386. **Poets** and pigs are appreciated only after their death.

387. What does not **poison,** fattens.

388. You may read **Pompeii** in some men's faces.

389. A broken **pot** never falls from the rail.

390. No one knows the sorrows of the **pot** save the ladle. (*Neapolitan.*)

391. No **pot** so ugly as not to find a cover. (*Marriage proverb.*)

392. He who has made the **pots** may break them. (*Venetian.*)

393. **Poverty** doesn't spoil grace. (*Venetian.*)

394. **Poverty** has no kin.

395. **Poverty** is a blessing hated by all men.

396. **Poverty** is the mother of health.

397. **Poverty** is the worst guard for chastity.

398. Good **preachers** give fruits, not flowers.

399. Scanty people, scanty **preaching.**

400. If **pride** were an art, how many graduates we should have.

401. There are those who despise **pride** with a greater pride.

402. Go in front of mules, but go behind **priests.** (*Abruzzi.*)

403. The **printing press** is the mother of errors.

404. No man goes to **prison** without a reason.

405. He who **promises** for others pays for himself.

406. In **prosperity** no altars smoke.

407. **Proverbs** are so called because they are proved.

408. He that serves the **public** obliges nobody.

409. **Public money** is like holy water, everybody helps himself to it.

410. Only a **pumpkin** is a head without cares. (*Abruzzi.*)

411. Moderate profits fill the **purse.**

412. He who errs with his mouth pays with his **purse.** (*Venetian.*)

413. The lover's **purse** is closed with a spider's web.

414. The **purse** pays for the eye's mistake.

415. Every **rag** wants to be sent to the wash.

416. **Rain** which does not fall remains in the sky. (*Sicilian.*)

417. A **red flag** is a sign of war. (*Abruzzi.*)
[Said of consumption.]

418. He who would live and be happy must live far from **relations.**

419. There is a **remedy** for everything except for the bone of the neck. (*Piedmontese and Venetian.*)

420. Get a **reputation** and go to bed. (*Sicilian.*)

421. **Respect,** disrespect and suspect spoil the world.

422. **Respect** should not be taken either to table or to bed.

423. **Revenge** a hundred years old has still its milk teeth.

424. **Revenge** is a morsel for God.

425. The **rich** and ignorant are sheep with golden wool.

426. A **river** does not swell with clear water.

427. Who leaves the old **road** to take the new knows what he leaves but not what he shall find. (*Sicilian.*)

428. Our last **robe** is made without pockets.

429. Long **robe,** little science.

430. All men **row** galley way.
[Draweth towards himself.]

431. A full **sack** cocks its ears.

432. One closes the mouths of **sacks.** (*Venetian.*)

433. Love, alms, devotion, and patience are the four elements which make a layman a **saint.**

434. A young **saint,** an old devil.

435. The **saints** of the home work no miracles. (*Venetian.*)

436. **Sandal-shod** vegetable diet, well-covered head and nothing to worry it.

437. Who **saves,** saves for the cat.

438. It requires a **scamp** and a half to recognise another scamp. (*Venetian.*)

439. He who falls into the **sea** without getting wet has to pay the penalty.

440. No one knows less about his **servants** than their master.

441. Even counted **sheep** are eaten by the wolf.

442. He who makes himself a **sheep** is devoured by the wolves.

443. We generally need someone to **shew** us things that should be apparent to all.

444. You cannot damage a wrecked **ship.**

445. All **ships** leak.

446. That **ship** which will have no rudder, must have a rock.

447. He who works has one **shirt,** and he who doesn't work has two. (*Venetian.*)

448. There never was a **shoe** however handsome that did not become an ugly slipper.

449. It is the first **shower** that wets.

450. Wise **silence** has never been written down.

451. No one repents for having remained **silent,** but many for having spoken.

452. A **sin** concealed is half pardoned.

453. In men every mortal **sin** is venial; in women every venial sin is mortal.

454. If I **sleep,** I sleep for myself; if I work, I know not for whom.

455. A **solitary man** is either a brute or an angel.

456. Angels gave the gift of **song,** and while one sings one thinks no wrong. (*Abruzzi.*)

457. The **soul** to God, the body to the soil, and property to whom it belongs. (*Venetian.*)

458. He who waits for another's **soup** eats it cold. (*Sicilian.*)

459. Warmed-up **soup** tastes of smoke.

460. Neither **soup** that has been warmed up, nor a serving maid who has come back. (*Venetian.*)

461. The **sour** falls before the ripe. (*Abruzzi.*)

462. The **spade** has a point of gold, the hoe a point of silver, and the plough a point of iron.

463. He who would **speak** of others should behold himself and remain silent.

464. Who **speaks** of it commits it not.

465. Where God's help is, the **spider's** web becomes a wall; where it is not, the wall becomes a spider's web.

466. She who **spins** has one shift; she who does not spin has two.

467. To drink pure water go to the **spring.**

468. He who **steals** for others is hanged for himself.

469. Crooked **sticks** are straightened in fire. (*Abruzzi.*)

470. The difficult thing is to get foot in the **stirrup.**

471. As many **strokes** by destiny I give so many steps towards when thou'lt cease to live. (*Abruzzi.*)
[Motto on the clock of the church at Santa Maria in Valle Porclareta.]

472. **Succour** never comes too late.

473. **Summer** is the mother of the poor.

474. The **sun** sets, the moon rises.

475. When the **sun** shines on thee thou needest not care for the moon.

476. There is no **Sunday** without sun, there is no woman who does not make love. (*Abruzzi.*)

477. **Suspicion** releases faith.

478. It is better to **sweat** than to cough. (*Venetian.*)

479. Only the **sweep** knows what is up the chimney.

480. The **table,** a secret thief, sends its master to the hospital.

481. That which is said at **table** should be wrapped up in the tablecloth.

482. Who **teaches** often learns himself.

483. Nothing dries quicker than **tears.**

484. There are two sorts of **tears** in a woman's eyes, one for sorrow and the other for deception.

485. The **tears** of the congregation are the praises of the minister.

486. **Tell** not all you know, believe not all you hear, do not all you are able.

487. **Things** are not as they are, but as they are regarded.

488. The **thistle** which is to prick soon grows thorns.

489. **Threats** are arms for the threatened.

490. The hardest step is that over the **threshold.**

491. **Tie** me hand and foot, and throw me among my own.

492. There is nothing that revenges itself more than **time.**

493. **Time** is a file that emits no noise.

494. The pen of the **tongue** should be dipped in the ink of the heart.

495. The fly that bites the **tortoise** breaks its beak.

496. **Translators,** traitors.

497. To **travel** safely through the world, a man must have a falcon's eye, an ass's ears, an ape's face, a merchant's words, a camel's back, a hog's mouth, and a hart's legs.

498. I know no difference between buried **treasure** and concealed knowledge.

499. To the fallen **tree,** hatchets! hatchets!

500. **Trees** struck by lightning should not be extinguished. (*Abruzzi.*)

501. **Troubles** are ever ready like tables at an inn. (*Ligurean.*)

502. From him I **trust** may God keep me; from him I do not trust I will keep myself.

503. Tell someone the **truth** and make him your enemy.

504. **Truth** can be bent, but not broken.

505. **Truth** is often punished.

506. **Truth** is the daughter of time.

507. **Truth** stings and falsehood heals.

508. The weak man always has his **tyrant.**

509. He who is born **unlucky** has the rain on his seat even when he is sitting. (*Venetian.*)

510. Leave behind the **vices** of your house and take those where you go. (*Abruzzi.*)

511. Take a **vine** of a good soil and a daughter of a good mother.

512. **Vine** in stones—kitchen garden in fat land. (*Abruzzi.*)

513. Beware of **vinegar** that is made of sweet wine.

514. There are no **violets** after the Ascension, for the Lord hath taken them all to heaven.

515. Even old **violins** provide themselves with new strings.

516. Great without small makes a bad **wall.**

517. When **want** knocks at the door everything is good.

518. He who buys land buys **war.**

519. One **washes** the body in vain if one does not wash the soul.

520. No **washing** is done at night that is not hung out in the daytime.

521. **Water** breaks out where it is not expected.

522. **Water** for the skin, but wine for the vitals.

523. Under **water,** hunger; under snow, bread.

524. A glass of **water** is sometimes worth a tun of wine.

525. Of **wealth** and saintliness [only believe] the half of the half. (*Venetian.*)

526. Every man has a good **wife** and a bad trade.

527. A **wife** and oxen choose from your own country.

528. Your **wife** and your nag get from a neighbour.

529. He who has had a **wife** deserves a crown of patience, but he who has had two deserves a strait-waistcoat.

530. Water, smoke and a bad **wife** drive men out of the house.

531. Your **wife** is a calf of your own country.

532. The first **wife** is matrimony, the second company, the third heresy.

533. In buying horses and in taking a **wife,** shut your eyes tight and commend yourself to God.

534. If the **wife** sins, the husband is not innocent.

535. Better shut the **window** than the door. (*Abruzzi.*)

[i.e. it is better to lose one's sight than to die.]

536. Drink **wine** and let water go to the mill.

537. A cask of **wine** works more miracle than a church full of saints. (*Abruzzi.*)

538. **Wives,** horses and books should never be lent.

539. When you see the **wolf,** do not look for his track.

540. The **wolf** is always left out of the reckoning.

541. As both a good horse and a bad horse need the spur, so both a good **woman** and a bad woman need the stick.

542. A mill and a **woman** are always in want of something.

543. The smiles of a pretty **woman** are the tears of the purse.

544. An angry **woman** is a sea without a shore.

545. A man of straw needs a **woman** of gold.

546. A **woman** of good family always bears a girl as her first child.

547. Never run after a **woman** or an omnibus, another one is sure to be round soon.

548. When **woman** reigns the devil governs.

549. Where **woman** reigns war rages. (*Sicilian.*)

550. Who says **woman** says loss, who says man says misfortune.

551. Tell a **woman** she is beautiful and the devil will repeat it to her ten times.

552. A beautiful **woman** smiling means a purse weeping.

553. A **woman** that loves to be at the window is like a bunch of grapes on the highway.

554. Everything comes from God except **women.**

555. In every house there should be two **women**—a wife and a statue of the virgin over the door.

556. Leave **women** alone, and go and study mathematics.

[This exclamation, which has passed into a proverb, was made by the beautiful Venetian courtesan Guilietta to J. J. Rousseau.]

557. **Women** are wise impromptu, fools on reflection.

558. **Women,** asses, and nuts require strong hands.

559. **Women** in love always speak the truth, but not the whole truth.

560. **Women,** priests, and poultry never have enough.

561. **Women** resist in order to be conquered.

562. A **word** has a hundred heads.

563. **Words** and deeds are not weighed in the same balance.

564. **Words** are feminine; deeds are masculine.

565. **Words** are like cherries, pick one and ten come.

566. Unspoken **words** cannot be recorded. (*Sicilian.*)

567. **Words** need but little space.

568. Evening **words** the wind carries away.

569. **Working** in your calling is half praying.

570. We found the **world** already made. (*Abruzzi.*)

571. The **world** belongs to him who takes it.

572. The **world** belongs to the patient man.

573. The **world** is a fine book but of little use to him who knows not how to read.

574. All the **world** is one country.

575. The **world** persecutes him who follows it, and follows him who persecutes it.

576. A **wound** is not cured by the unbending of the bow.

577. The **year** is long and one eats every day.

578. One's **years** and sins are always more than one says.

579. Cursed is the **young man** of a hundred, and blessed is the old man of twenty.

580. Do not look in front of **yourself,** but behind yourself.

GENOESE

1. The **ass's** trot doesn't last long.
2. The **beautiful** are looked at, the ugly are taken.
3. **Beauty** does not make the pot boil.
4. The **cask** gives of the wine it contains.
5. **Children** and glasses are never too many.
6. Whoever has one has none ; whoever has two has one ; and whoever has three has the **devil.**
   [Refers to children.]
7. He who wants **figs** should lower the branches, and he who wants the daughter should kiss the mother.
8. Where there are more steps than mouthfuls is a **fool's** journey.
9. Sleight of hand is a loser's **game.**
10. **God** shuts a door and opens a balcony.
11. A grey **head** is never believed.
12. The **horse** that is sworn at has a shiny coat.
13. An ounce of " **I am** " is worth more than a hundredweight of " I was ".
14. With hot water and a clyster one cures all **ill.**
15. All **knots** come to the comb.
16. **Laughter** makes good blood.
17. You give the **lettuce** into the keeping of the geese.
18. **Lies** are like cherries, after one come ten.
19. **Light** is half a companion.
20. Who suffers for **love** feels no pain.
21. A **married** man is a caged bird.
22. Bread and nuts is the food of the newly **married** ; nuts and bread is the food of the peasant.
23. **Matrimony** and macaroni, if they are not hot, are not good.
24. Blessed is the house where **old age** is known.
25. One does not go to **paradise** in a carriage.
26. A **purse** without money is called leather.
27. He who pays his **rent** can speak his mind.
28. It is not enough to be **right,** one should know how to profit by it.
29. A live **serpent** never lacks a nest.
30. It is better to wear out one's **shoes** than one's sheets.
31. All **soup** is soaked bread.
32. **Saint Catherine** says, " Whoever has created them must rock them."
   [i.e. children.]
33. Let him whose **tooth** aches pull it out.
34. A **woman,** a horse and a ship belong to him who masters them.
35. A little **woman** always seems newly married.
36. **Women** always attach themselves to the worst.

SARDINIAN

1. If an **ass** kicks you, don't kick him back.
2. If you return an **ass's kicks,** most of the pain is yours.
3. **Conscience** is as good as a thousand witnesses.
4. **Curses,** like processions, come back to their starting-point.
5. The **devil** makes pots, but not always lids.
6. When the **disease** is a fatal one, the doctor is blind.

7. When the sun enters, the **doctor** remains outside.
8. A good **dog** never lacks a master, and he who has bread never lacks a dog.
9. If you work like a **donkey** you will feed like a noble, but if you work like a noble you will feed like a donkey.
10. A man who cannot **flatter** knows not how to talk.
11. He who makes a good **friend** acquires good capital.
12. It is well to have **friends,** even in the house of the devil.
13. **Goats** go from summit to summit, and yawns from mouth to mouth.
14. Everything may be born but **good fortune.**
15. Each one has his **hanged man** in his doorway.
16. It is better to have a pain in the purse than an ache in the **heart.**
17. A hundred years cannot repair a moment's loss of **honour.**
18. With a **horse,** either stand very close to it, or very far away.
19. He who has fallen from a **horse** says to the donkey that he wants to dismount.
20. All the world is like our own **house.**
21. Every mouthful is the enemy of **hunger.**
22. He who goes and returns makes a good **journey.**
23. Don't make a stitch without making a **knot.**
24. When two are in a **lawsuit,** one remains in his shirt and the other naked.
25. He who causes his own **misfortune** must weep himself.
26. **Money** is in the eyes of many, but in the hands of few.
27. He who has his **nail** torn off his finger looks at it often.
28. He who has no house has no **neighbour.**
29. If the **oaks** don't die, the acorns return.
30. A short **road** ages the donkey.
31. The **salt** is worth more than the fish.
32. He who **steals** for others is hanged for himself.
33. The **sun** at a distance warms us, but close to it burns us.
34. It is better to **take** and repent than to leave and repent.
35. One cannot know the **truth** from the nose to the mouth.
36. Each one **weeps** with his own eyes.
37. The **wise man** forgives, the fool forgets.
38. The **world** is for him who wishes it ; heaven for him who attains it.

LATIN

(Including Roman)

1. The **absent** will not be heir.

   [i.e. out of sight, out of mind.]
2. The **abuse** of a thing is no argument against its use.
3. There are three **accursed things** in a house : dripping, an evil woman, smoke.
4. No one is bound to **accuse** himself, except before God.
5. **Acorns** were good till corn was discovered.
6. Things **adjudicated** are considered true.
7. Man **adorns** the place, not the place the man.

8. He who does not **advance,** recedes.
9. In **adversity** hope, in prosperity apprehend.
10. **Adversity** is a good preacher.
11. **Adversity** is the touchstone of virtue.
12. That is neglected by **all** which is possessed by all.
13. He who takes it to himself makes the **allusion.**
14. Never less **alone** than when alone.
15. It is safe riding at ten **anchors.**
16. Do not take the **antidote** before the poison.
17. Not even **Apollo** keeps his bow always at full stretch.
18. **Art** is the concealment of art.
19. Where **art** is too conspicuous, truth seems to be wanting.
20. He who cannot touch the **ass** beats the housings.
21. He who is once **bad** is presumed always to be so.
22. No one becomes **bad** suddenly.
23. Seven's a **banquet,** nine's a brawl.
24. Abstain from **beans.**

    [Anciently men cast in a bean when they gave their suffrages in public elections.]
25. No **bees,** no honey.
26. The **beginning** is always difficult.
27. The principal part of everything is the **beginning.**
28. Resist the **beginnings.**
29. We soon **believe** what we desire.
30. **Believe** you have it, and you have it.
31. He can who **believes** he can.
32. The **belly** has no ears.
33. **Benefits** received are soon forgotten, but the memory of an injury endureth for ever.
34. Fly even from what seems pleasant but may turn out to be **bitter** in the end.
35. Do not **blame** what you permit.
36. May the **blessed** one bless.
37. A **blind man** may hit a crow.
38. **Borrow** from oneself.
39. Man is a leather **bottle** filled with wind.
40. To saw off the **bough** on which one is sitting.
41. No one is **bound** beyond his power.
42. Better to **bow** than to break.
43. He who has not had **breakfast** will not be able to distinguish a citizen from a stranger.
44. When the tale of **bricks** is doubled, then comes Moses. (*Mediæval.*)
45. The rain falls in the lap of the happy **bride.**
46. Assist him who is carrying his **burden,** but by no means him who is laying it aside.
47. Rougher than **butcher's-broom ;** cheaper than the seaweed on the shore.
48. **Buy** on credit and sell for cash.
49. Let the **buyer** beware.
50. **Cabbage** twice cooked, or served.

    [i.e. to harp on the same string.]
51. A **cask** is easily moved.

    [i.e. a weak man is easily turned.]
52. The **cask** savours of the first fill.
53. We [**censors**] read books to prevent their being read by others.
54. We lose the **certain things** while we seek the uncertain ones.
55. Out of much **chaff** I have gathered but little grain.
56. Are they to be marked with **chalk** or with charcoal ?

    [Wise men or fools.]
57. In things necessary, unity ; in things doubtful, liberty ; in all things, **charity.**
58. Not your good words but your **charity.**
59. If you can't be good, be **chaste.**
60. It is well worth while letting oneself be **cheated** sometimes.
61. A great **city** is a great solitude.

62. You may mould soft **clay** into any shape you please.
63. Hold on carefully to the **cloak** your mother gave you.
[i.e. your mother's apron strings.]
64. My **coat** is nearer than my cloak.
65. **Cobbler** do not judge above the shoe.
66. Much **coin,** much care ; much meat, much malady.
67. He who **commits** an act by another's agency commits the act himself.
68. The **companion** of my companion is not my companion.
69. Let [your **compositions**] be kept in your desk for nine years.
70. **Concealment** is one thing, silence is another. (*Law maxim.*)
71. He who may **condemn** may acquit.
72. **Confession** is as medicine to him who has gone astray.
73. To **conquer** by yielding.
74. He **conquers** a second time who controls himself in victory.
75. **Contentment** is true riches.
76. The **cook** should have his master's palate.
77. **Corruption** of the best is the worst.
78. Take **counsel** in the night.
79. In the night is **counsel.**
80. Where one is well off there is his **country.**
81. **Crime** to veil crime.
82. All **crimes** committed openly are considered lighter.
83. When the **criminal** is acquitted the judge is found guilty.
84. A ripe **crop** must not wait for to-morrow.
85. The **cross** is the touchstone of faith.
86. A **crow** does not peck out the eyes of a crow.
87. **Custom** is a second law.
88. Men do more from **custom** than from reason.
89. Laugh at **danger,** and it comes all the sooner.
90. Without **danger,** danger canno be surmounted.
91. A common **danger** produce concord.
92. Without **danger** the game grow cold.
93. The **dawn** is a friend to th Muses.
94. The **day** is praised in the even ing, the host in the morning.
95. One **day** teaches the other.
96. No **day** without its trace.
97. The **dead** are the best advisers
98. He who is not present is **dead**
99. **Death** levels all.
100. Of ill **debtors** men take oats.
[i.e. take what you can in settle ments of bad debts.]
101. We never find our own **deficiencies.**
102. Every **definition** is dangerous
103. The feet of the [avenging **deities** are shod with wool.
104. No **desire** is felt for a thing unknown.
105. He will **die** before he is old who is wise before his time.
106. By **discord** concord become dearer.
107. Treat the **disease** at the beginning.
108. Unknown **diseases** are the worst.
109. He who knows not how to **dissemble** knows not how to live
110. **Do** what you are doing.
111. **Dog** won't eat dog.
112. Do not do what is **done.**
[i.e. let well alone.]
113. When you **doubt** do not act.
114. Morning **dreams** come true.
115. Either **drink** or depart.
116. The **eagle** does not catch flies
117. Nothing is so **easy** that it wil not become difficult when you do it against your will.
118. You must **eat** what you have spoilt.
119. **Economy** is itself a great income.

120. He who holds an **eel** by the tail does not have it.

121. From the **egg** to the apples.

[Old Roman custom of commencing a feast with an egg and ending with an apple. This proverb is used when a speaker monopolizes the conversation from soup to dessert.]

122. **Emulation** begets emulation.

123. **Emulation** is the whetstone of wits.

124. Look to the **end.**

125. The nearer the summit the nearer the **end.**

126. No one has precisely **enough.**

127. He who **envies** admits his inferiority.

128. **Envy** always makes for the highest point.

129. **Envy** is honour's foe.

130. He who reads many **epitaphs,** loses his memory.

131. Always, **everywhere,** and by everybody.

[i.e. views which have been universally held by all mankind in all times.]

132. **Everywhere** is nowhere.

133. You can't drive out **evil** by evil.

134. A slight **evil** must be endured. (*Maxim of ecclesiastical lawyers in reference to a quarrelsome wife.*)

135. By doing nothing men learn to do **evil.**

136. The sea, fire and a woman are three **evils.**

137. We live more by **example** than by reason.

138. All **excess** turns into vice.

139. **Experience** is the mistress of fools.

140. **Extremity** of right is wrong.

141. He who lies on the ground has no place from which to **fall.**

142. A full stomach praises **fast-days.**

143. A **fault** finds its own authors.

144. To receive a **favour** is to sell your liberty.

145. He who awes others is more in **fear** himself.

146. **Fear** is an impediment of every virtue.

147. He must **fear** many whom many fear.

148. Injured **females** are generally implacable.

149. Praise a large **field** but cultivate a small one.

150. Every man reaps his own **field.**

151. Woe to that city in which a **fish** costs more than an ox.

152. The net of the sleeping [**fisherman**] takes.

153. To snatch at a garland and gain a **flower.**

154. When Fortune caresses a man too much, she makes him a **fool.**

155. He who teaches himself has a **fool** for a master.

156. He who stumbles twice over the same stone is a **fool.**

157. **Fools** use chalk to write with, and walls for paper.

158. The result is the schoolmaster of **fools.**

159. Small **foot,** big gulf.

160. There are no backward **footsteps.**

161. **Force** finds a way.

162. What has no **force** in the beginning can gain no strength from the lapse of time.

163. **Fortune** is glass ; just when it is bright it is broken.

164. **Fortune** takes from us nothing but what she has given us.

165. Even the **fountains** complain of being thirsty.

166. **Fraud** lurks in generalities.

167. Unless you bear with the faults of a **friend** you betray your own.

168. Better spare your wit than lose your **friend.**

169. Where there are **friends** there are riches.

170. Compliance makes **friends,** truth hatred. (*Roman.*)

171. All things are common property amongst **friends.**

172. **Friendship** is more necessary than fire or water.

[The German adds " or bread ".]

173. While the pot boils **friendship** lasts.
174. Community of purpose makes **friendship.**
175. **Froth** quickly evaporates.
176. **Fungus** grows where soil is rich.
177. **Fury** provides arms.
178. The giver adds value to the **gift.**
179. Let him who exhorts others to give, **give** of his own.
180. You still possess what you have **given.**
181. He **gives** twice who gives promptly.
182. **Giving** has no bottom.
183. A **gladiator** only takes counsel in the arena.
184. Other people's **goats** have always the biggest udders.
185. The act of **God** does wrong to none. (*Law maxim.*)
186. He whom **God** favours becomes rich in his sleep.
187. Man plants and waters, but **God** gives the increase.
188. Nothing without **God.**
189. The true **goddess** was recognized by her walk.
190. Many meet the **gods,** but few salute them.
191. The **gods** have feet of wool.
192. The **gods** sell all things to hard labour.
193. When **gold** talks, speech is useless.
194. Even doors of adamant are broken through by **gold.**
195. It is only the **golden hours** that count.
196. Private yields to public **good.**
197. He hurts the **good** who spares the bad.
198. A **good thing** is appreciated more by its absence than by its enjoyment.
199. Every **good thing** is three-fold.
200. Offered **goods** stink.
201. Divide and **govern.**
202. **Grasp** all, lose all.
203. **Grass** must turn to hay.
204. Fear the **Greeks** even when they bring gifts.
205. **Grief** borders on the extremes of gladness.
206. It is difficult to **guard** what many are in love with.
207. After three days, a woman, a **guest,** and the rain become very tiresome.
208. **Guilt** is always timid.
209. How nearly a man may approach to **guilt** without being guilty.
210. Pursuits grow into **habits.**
211. Even a single **hair** casts a shadow.
212. A **hairy man,** either strong or lustful.
213. **Hand** washes hand.
214. **Happiness** has many friends.
215. Who eats a **hare** is beautiful for seven days.
216. Even **hares** insult a dead lion.
217. With winter dust and spring mud you will reap big **harvests.**
218. **Haste** is slow.
219. Let them **hate** so long as they fear.
220. Many will **hate** you if you love yourself.
221. Man **hates** those he fears.
222. To **have** and to give.
223. Not what you **have,** but what you are.
224. An empty hand is no lure for a **hawk.**
225. **Hawks** do not pick out hawks' eyes.
226. He has **hay** on his horn, keep at a safe distance.
    [The Romans, to warn passers-by, fastened a wisp of hay on the horn of a dangerous bull.]
227. **Hear** the other side. (*Law maxim.*)
228. A bold **heart** is half the battle.
229. The sound of the mouth is derived from the habit of the **heart.**
230. What escapes the eyes is no longer in the heart.
231. **Heaven** is equally distant from all places.

232. The weeping of an **heir** is laughter under a mask.
233. The **heir** of my heir is my heir.
234. The road to **hell** is everywhere alike.
235. No **hemlock** is drunk out of earthenware.
[i.e. suspect poison only in golden vessels.]
236. Bad **hen,** bad eggs.
237. **Honesty** is praised and starves.
238. Too much **honey** is bitter.
239. **Honours** are a burden.
240. **Honours** change manners.
241. Do not foster animals with **hooked claws.**
242. **Hope** tells a flattering tale.
243. The master's eye makes the **horse** fat.
244. To come from a **horse** to an ass.
245. Behind the **horseman** sits black care.
246. **Hunger** sweetens beans.
247. **Hunger** teaches much.
248. A **hungry man** does not distinguish.
249. Don't get in the way of a **hungry man.**
250. No man is **hurt** but by himself.
251. He **hurts** the good who spares the bad.
252. No deity assists the **idle.**
253. **Ill** got, ill spent.
254. He lives too well who has no **ill.**
255. **Ill luck** is good for nothing.
256. Private **inconvenience** is made up for by public benefit.
257. Forgetfulness is the remedy for **injuries.**
258. No **injury** is done to one who is willing.
259. It is easy to add to **inventions.**
260. **Jealousy** is the fox of honour.
261. If you **judge,** understand.
262. Far from **Jupiter,** far from lightning. (*Roman.*)
263. One ought to be born either a **king** or a fool.
[To have unlimited licence allowed one.]
264. Goose, bee and calf rule the **kingdoms** of the world.
[Pen, wax and parchment.]
265. **Kings** have long hands.
266. All wish to **know ;** no one to pay the price.
267. **Knowledge** has bitter roots but sweet fruits.
268. **Knowledge** too hastily acquired is not on guard.
269. The mountains are in **labour,** a ridiculous mouse will be born.
270. **Labour** gives the best relish.
271. No poor reward for **labour.**
272. If you live with a **lame man** you will learn to limp.
273. **Laugh** if you are wise.
274. The **laughter** in cottages is the most genuine.
275. Consent makes **law.**
276. The **law** does not concern itself about trifles. (*Law maxim.*)
277. Extreme **law** is extreme injustice.
278. Where the **law** is uncertain there is no law.
279. When the reason for the **law** no longer exists, the law ceases to exist.
280. Bad custom makes good **law.**
281. Good **laws** spring from bad morals.
282. From one **learn** all.
283. **Learn** by teaching.
284. **Learn,** or leave.
285. **Learn** young or not at all.
286. **Learning** untold is of no use.
287. He who distinguishes well, **learns** well.
288. To cut large thongs from another man's **leather.**
289. The written **letter** remains, the spoken word perishes.
290. Memory in a **liar** is no more than needs.
291. A sudden **lie** has best luck.
292. Ask no questions and I'll tell you no **lies.**
293. **Like** will to like.
294. He often is a **lion** with words who has a hare's heart in his breast.

295. By his claw one knows the **lion.**
296. Puppies will bite a dead **lion.**
297. If the **lion's** skin is not enough, sew the fox's to it.
298. **Lions** in peace are often deer in war.
299. Life without **literature** is death.
300. He who **lives** after nature shall never be poor; after opinion shall never be rich.
301. He **lives** unworthily through whom no other person lives.
302. Generally one **loses** less by being known too little than by being known too much.
303. **Love** and a cough cannot be hidden.
304. To **love** and be wise is scarcely granted even to a god.
305. **Love** and lordship never like fellowship.
306. In **love** anger is always lying.
307. **Love** as though you might hate; hate as though you might love.
308. When in **love** even Jupiter is an ass.
309. Without corn and wine **love** grows cold.
310. **Love,** if you would be loved.
311. An old **love** is a prison.
312. If many are better led by **love,** more are corrected by fear.
313. **Love,** the best master.
314. Eyes are the ambassadors of **love.**
315. Let him who does not wish to become indolent fall in **love.**
316. Nothing is difficult to one in **love.**
317. The same hand gives and cures the wounds of **love.**
318. There is no remedy for old **love.**
319. The anger of **lovers** is the renewal of love.
320. **Lovers,** lunatics.
321. **Luxury,** more terrible in its ravages than war.
322. We have all once been **mad.**
323. Every **man** is nearest to himself.
324. One **man** is no man.
325. What a **man does** through another he does through himself.
326. Fortunate people have children three months after **marriage.**
327. So much **meal** cannot all have come from your own sack.
328. A **mercury** is not made out of any block of wood.
329. The **middle way** is golden.
330. **Mine,** thine, his.
[The cause of all trouble.]
331. The poor man needs much; the **miser** desires everything.
332. The **miser** is ever in want.
333. Be a **miser** with the miser.
334. **Misery** loves company.
335. **Misfortune** is a second master.
336. 'Tis easy to bear other people's **misfortunes.**
337. **Moderate things** endure.
338. **Modesty** is useless to a man in want.
339. Who cannot pay with **money** must pay with his body.
340. Where there is most mind there is least **money.**
341. A **mouse** never trusts to one hole.
342. I am always nearest to **myself.**
343. What is **natural** is not vile.
344. Offences against **nature** are the heaviest.
345. **Nature** is content with little.
346. You may drive **nature** out with a pitchfork but she will inevitably return.
347. Nothing is becoming to man that is contrary to **nature.**
348. Nothing is grievous which **necessity** enjoins.
349. **Need** [necessity] is the last and greatest weapon. (*Roman.*)
350. Gross **negligence** is a fault; gross fault is a fraud.
351. A bad **neighbour,** daily misfortune.
352. What everybody does himself, he does not blame his **neighbour** for.
353. He wrongfully accuses **Neptune** who makes shipwreck a second time.

354. To stretch one's wings over one's **nest.**

355. The real **nettle** stings early.

356. **Nothing** comes of nothing.
[The dictum of Lucretius.]

357. The things which are above us [or below us] are **nothing** to us.

358. He who would eat the **nut** must crack the shell.

359. Go and shake some other **oak.**
[i.e. try someone else.]

360. He that cannot **obey** cannot command.

361. The act is the daughter of the **obligation.**

362. The impossible is no **obligation.**

363. **Old** young and old long.

364. **Old age** is a disease.

365. An **old man** is twice a child.

366. **Opportunity** has hair on her forehead but is bald behind.

367. Know your **opportunity.**

368. To the fierce **ox** God gives short horns.

369. Tired **oxen** tread hard.

370. **Pardon** another often, thyself never.

371. **Parsimony** is a revenue.

372. A wise man will not let **past blessings** fade from memory, and it is his duty to forget past misfortunes.

373. The beaten **path** is the safest way.

374. The **pearl** is found in mud.

375. Of what avail are **pedigrees**?

376. He that has plenty of **pepper** can season his cabbage well.

377. We **perish** by permitted things.

378. Make much of a **physician** through necessity.

379. Where there are three **physicians** there are two atheists.

380. Every idiot, priest, Jew, monk, actor, barber, and old woman fancy themselves **physicians.**

381. A **plant,** often transplanted, never prospers.

382. Things that others have **please** us more; things that we have please others more.

383. **Poets** are fathers of lies.

384. **Poison** is drunk from golden vessels.

385. His plenty made him **poor.**

386. The **pot** chooses its own vegetables.

387. Every **pot** has its lid.

388. Honest **poverty** is better than brocaded dishonour.

389. **Poverty** obstructs the road to virtue.

390. **Poverty** wants many things; avarice everything.

391. **Poverty's** bitterest drop is that it makes men a laughing stock.

392. **Pray** and work.
[Old maxim of Benedictine monks was "Laborare est orare"—"To work is to pray."]

393. To have **prayed** well is to have studied well.

394. A **precipice** ahead, wolves behind.

395. He sends his **presents** with a hook attached.

396. As the people, so the **priest.**

397. For copper, **priests** chant masses of copper.

398. A **privilege** is not valued when it has been obtained.

399. It is best to **profit** by the madness of others.

400. The best **prophet** is he who guesses best.

401. The **rabble** sometimes see rightly.

402. The hatred of the nearest **relations** is most intense.

403. A man without **religion** is like a horse without bridle.

404. Where there is a right there is a **remedy.**

405. On the **removal** of one another is not wanting.

406. Great men's **requests** are orders.

407. A wise man alone is **rich.**

408. **Riches** will bear out folly.

409. A **rich man** is either himself an unjust one, or the heir of one.

410. **Rights** are forfeited by disuse. (*Law maxim.*)

411. You a **river** and contending with the ocean.
412. Wherever he treads **roses** grow.
413. When you lay down a **rule,** be short.
414. **Rumour** acquires strength in her progress.
415. Small **sacrileges** are punished ; great ones are celebrated by triumphs.
416. **Salt** and bread maketh cheeks red.
417. **Salt** seasons all things.
418. A **satiated man** treads on honey-combs.
419. What suffices, **satisfies.**
420. Take to **satisfy.**
421. But the **sea** is not ruffled except by the winds.

 [i.e. no cause without effect, and vice versa.]
422. The highest **seat** will not admit of two.
423. Men keep secret others' **secrets,** women only their own.
424. Unless a **serpent** devours a serpent it will not become a dragon.

 [i.e. a wise man avails himself of the wisdom of another.]
425. **Servants** should know when not to know.
426. So many **servants,** so many enemies.
427. Shear the **sheep,** don't skin it.
428. **Shoes** too large trip one up.
429. A **sieve** should have a new handle.
430. The reward of **silence** is sure.
431. He that cannot speak cannot keep **silence.**
432. No **simile** ever yet ran on all fours.
433. If a man has it in his power to commit a **sin,** he is less inclined to do so.
434. I do not **sleep** for all.
435. One is not **smelt** where all stink.
436. To be a **smith** you must work at the forge.
437. Every **soil** is the country of the fortunate.
438. He who owns the **soil** owns up to the sky.
439. Man in **solitude** is either a god or a devil.
440. Where they make a **solitude** they call it peace.
441. After a bad crop, **sow.**
442. **Sowing** early oft deceives, sowing late, never.
443. Perchance some little **spark** may lie unseen.

 [Motto of Royal Humane Society.]
444. **Sparks** become flame.
445. While the **sparrow** remains under the eaves, the swallow departs.
446. Do not **speak** against the sun.
447. An army of **stags** led by a lion would be more formidable than an army of lions led by a stag.
448. To the **stars** through difficulties.

 [i.e. to win eternal renown.]
449. We are by nature as hard as **steel.**
450. An empty **stomach** does not willingly listen.
451. A full **stomach** does not work willingly.
452. From a clear **stream,** clear water flows.
453. He who **suffers,** remembers.
454. The **sun** of all days has not yet gone down.
455. There is no disputing about **tastes.**
456. Whom the gods hate, they make a **teacher.**
457. He who **teaches,** learns.
458. Nothing dries sooner than a **tear.**
459. **Tears** sometimes have the weight of words.
460. With **tears** you will melt adamant.
461. Unless **the Lord** is with us, our efforts are vain.
462. I **think,** therefore I am.
463. **Three** is the most perfect number.

464. The **tongue** plays round the aching tooth. (*Roman.*)
465. **Too much** is worse than too little.
466. To stand by things decided, and not to disturb those that are **tranquil.**
467. A twig in time becomes a **tree.**
468. First the leaves fall, then the **trees.**
469. So many branches, so many **trees.**
[Motto of Royal Asiatic Society.]
470. **Truth** begets hatred.
471. **Truth** breeds hate, prosperity pride, safety danger, familiarity contempt.
472. **Truth** has but one colour, falsehood many.
473. **Truth** is afraid of nothing but concealment.
474. It is as well to **try.**
475. Whatever is first poured into the **tub,** flavours it ever afterwards.
476. **Two** are an army against one.
477. To do good to the **ungrateful** is to throw rose-water into the sea.
478. If you say he is **ungrateful,** you say everything.
479. The **unknown** is ever magnified.
480. What is **useful** is sweet.
481. What used to be **vices** are now common manners.
482. **Vices** are neighbours of virtues.
483. **Vices** are virtues carried to excess.
484. What is **violent** is not lasting.
485. Even with the bad **virtue** has authority. (*Roman.*)
486. **Virtue** is the only necessary thing.
487. **Virtue** increases under a burden.
488. **Virtue** is always green.
489. **Virtue** is praised and starves.
490. There must always be room for **virtue.**
491. The **voice** of the people is the voice of God.
492. It is solved by **walking.**
493. A severer **war** lies hidden under peace.
494. Who watches the **watchman ?**
495. He drinks **water** by measure.
[i.e. penny wise and pound foolish.]
496. **Water** tastes better at the source.
497. Infamy is nothing when one has **wealth.**
498. There is a certain pleasure in **weeping.**
499. **Well done** is quick enough.
500. Drawn **wells** have sweetest water.
501. Not who, but **what.**
502. The use of a **whetstone** is to sharpen.
503. The man who has a quiet house has no **wife.**
504. **Winds** carry one's words to the ocean.
505. No one is **wise** alone.
506. Think no place without a **witness.**
507. **Woe** succeeds woe.
508. The **wolf** eats counted sheep.
509. One man is a **wolf** to another.
510. When you have seen the **wolf's** ears you will soon see his tail.
511. A **woman** either loves or hates.
512. **Woman** is an evil, but a necessary one.
513. When a **woman** is openly bad, then at least she is honest.
514. When a **woman** thinks by herself, she thinks of mischief.
515. Anyone may take the **wood** from a fallen tree.
516. The written **word** remains.
517. The **world** wishes to be deceived.
518. Things are **worth** what they will sell for.
519. Give the right hand to the **wretched.**

LETTISH (LATVIA)

An introduction to this collection by Marguerite Grosvald will be found on page lxx.

1. Don't call a morsel fat before you've skinned the **animal.**
2. As the dressing, so the **appetite.**
3. You won't hide an **awl** in a sack.
4. A sharp **axe** grows blunt quickly.
5. The ready **back** gets all the loads.
6. The **back** gets what the mouth deserves.
7. One is as good as the other, in the **bag** they go !
8. A man without a **beard** is like a loaf that has no crust.
9. Better under an old man's **beard** than under a young man's whip.
10. It is better to go to **bed** on an empty stomach than to rise with debts.
11. One's **belly** isn't a book.
12. A **big man,** a big pie.
13. Don't shout before the **birch-rod** falls.
14. Steal up to him on his **blind side.**
    [i.e. discover his weak point.]
15. As the **blow,** so the pain.
16. The **book** of our life is bulky.
17. Folded hands gain no **bread.**
18. Cut **bread** cannot be put together again.
19. **Bread** doesn't get stuck in one's throat.
20. **Bread** doesn't run after the eater.
21. He who heeds his parents kneads a whole troughful of **bread** for himself.
22. Children's **bread** lies on a high shelf.
23. Don't let your **bread** pass your door !
24. **Bread** that's been eaten up is hard to earn.
25. A **brute** does a brute's job.
26. An old **buck** has stiff horns.
27. You can't **carry** what you can't lift.
28. A small stump upsets a big **cart.**
29. **Charity** is always shabbily dressed.
30. Small **children** weigh heavily on our knees ; grown-up children weigh on our hearts.
31. Where there's a **church** there's an inn not far away.
32. As the job, so the **clothes.**
33. As the **coat,** so the lining.
34. Not until a **cow** has no tail left does one know what it was good for.
35. As in the **cradle,** so in the grave.
36. That which **creaks** must be oiled.
37. **Death** doesn't look at our teeth.
38. **Death** is nearer at hand than my shirt.
39. Marshes and woods may rot away, but not a **debt.**
40. A **debt** isn't a brother.
41. It's not as **deep** as it's dark.
42. Let the **devil** into a church and he will climb into the pulpit.
43. No one will help a **dog** to lift his tail unless he does it himself.
44. He who comes last is barked at by the **dogs.**
45. The **donor** profits by the gift he makes.
46. So much **dough,** so many buns.
47. More people are **drowned** in the glass than in the sea.
48. What you've **eaten** at home lasts till you reach your friend's gate ; what you've eaten when visiting lasts till you reach your own gate.
49. Whatever you're doing, bear the **end** in mind ; whatever you're sewing, make a knot first.
50. The more **enemies,** the more honour.
51. **Envy** has smarting eyes.

52. The **eye** wonders, the hand performs.
53. If you can't use your **eyes,** follow your nose.
54. Use your **eyes** in the field and your ears in the forest.
55. Stealing with your **eyes** is no sin.
56. He who doesn't keep his **eyes** open has to open his purse.
57. There are many **eyes** to see you in the open, but none at home.
58. A smiling **face** is half the meal.
59. Where the **fence** is down everyone can get over.
60. Where there's a high **fence** there's a snowdrift.
61. I wouldn't douse a **fire** that doesn't burn me.
62. Sit on your **fist,** lean on your thumb.
    [i.e. in order not to get into trouble.]
63. Who can prevent the master from catching **fleas** with his gloves on?
64. **Flour** isn't showered upon anyone for nothing—as you grind it, it drops.
65. He who swallows his **food** hot burns his lips.
66. To a **fool** the ice seems slippery.
67. Where there's a strong current there need not be a **ford.**
68. The **forest** will soon teach him!
    [i.e. meaning the birch-rod.]
69. Where there is **frying** there's a smell.
70. Any **gift** morsel tastes sweet.
71. The longer a **girl** remains single, the better place Fortune prepares for her.
72. He who **gives** to me is my God; he who takes from me is my devil.
73. He sleeps as if he lay in the very ear of **God.**
74. May your lips speak into the ears of **God.**
75. **God** and I go halves.
76. **God** has days in plenty.
77. A nobleman drives six horses and a beggar leans on two sticks, but he overtakes the nobleman at the **grave.**
78. May the earth be light on his **grave** and the sunshine bright!
79. Mountains of gold remain in the **grave** as well as the beggar's pouch.
80. Fold your **hands** in your lap; hang your teeth on the nail.
81. Many **hares** hang on one nail.
82. It's from stalks that you pile up a **hay-stack.**
83. One **head,** one worry.
84. My eyes want some more, my mouth wants some more, but there's no more room in my **heart.**
85. His **heart** seems to creep out at his very heels.
86. **Honour** makes way for honour.
87. The master's **horse** and one's own whip make fast driving.
88. Everyone knows how to drive a **horse** that is harnessed.
89. Where there's a **horse** there's a cart-load; where there's a woman there's gossip.
90. He who is **ill** has the soul of a lamb.
91. A master's **illness** is a poor man's health.
92. No one buys **illness** with money.
93. **Immodesty** never starves.
94. If you undertake nine **jobs,** starvation will be the tenth.
95. One **kinsman** is another's devil.
96. **Labour** teaches the labourer.
97. **Labour** uses a heavy whip.
98. Black **labour**—white bread.
99. **Lies** are patches on truth.
100. You **lift** it, I'll do the groaning!
101. **Love** can be stretched like treacle.
102. Put your **lucky days** in your pocket, so they should not drop out.
103. By the time one couple gets **married,** the devil has worn out nine pairs of shoes.

104. **Money** doesn't tear one's pockets.
105. **Money** is clever—in the hands of a man.
106. **Money** is waiting to be counted.
107. It's we who earn **money**—we are not earned by it.
108. Her heart takes after the **mugwort.**

    [This is a plant that always grows in company.]
109. If you're **naked** it's cold everywhere; if you're lazy it's hard everywhere.
110. A **naked man** can be seen from afar, a rude one close at hand.
111. It's your **neighbour's** chimney-smoke that makes your eyes smart.
112. **Old things** earn new ones.
113. We grow **older,** our ills grow younger.
114. An **orphan's** tears soar to God.
115. There's no more than beef to be had from an **ox.**
116. One **ox** can't be sold to two butchers.
117. He who doesn't heed his **parents** bakes his loaf in ashes.
118. An overloaded **peg** gets broken.
119. Where a **pig** burrows there are roots.
120. He who **ploughs** with a colt makes crooked furrows.
121. **Poor** in goods, rich in joys.
122. A **promise** made at an inn never leaves it.
123. The first litter of **puppies** had better be drowned.

    [i.e. one's first effort is seldom any good.]
124. A meagre peace is better than a fat **quarrel.**
125. A wife's **relations** are in greater favour than those of a husband.
126. In **Riga** [meaning far away] in words, under the table in deeds.
127. He who is the last to be put in the **sack** is the first to get out of it.
128. A bright **saucepan** means a tasty morsel.
129. However much you eat, leave some **seed** for sowing.
130. Men make for the **shallows,** fish for the deep.
131. If one **sheep** bleats, the whole flock is fed.
132. Counting your **sheep** won't keep the wolf away.
133. Cut as deep as you have **sinned** [and make a fresh start].
134. He carries a sackful of **sins** on his own back and sees the small bag on that of another.
135. **Sleep** is the poor man's treasure.
136. If you're **slow-witted,** be light-footed.
137. Where there's a lot of **smoke** there's little heat.
138. If you take care of the **soil,** the soil will take care of you.
139. What's the good of a **spoon** after the meal is over?
140. A bad **start** means a good end.
141. He who doesn't make a bad **start** never makes a good one.
142. Grudge one **step,** lose ten.
143. Never wrestle with a **strong man** nor bring a rich man into court.
144. **Stumps** wide apart have deep roots.
145. Where you wade into the **swamp,** there you have to gather your berries.
146. He who **talks**—sows; he who listens—reaps.
147. Not every **tear** drops to the ground.
148. There's but one road open to a **thief,** but every road will do for his captors.
149. It's the tall **tree** that is stirred by every wind.
150. In a dense forest the **trees** grow straight.
151. He who speaks the **truth** doesn't find a night's shelter.
152. A collar of **velvet,** a couch of chaff.
153. **Want** makes you find your legs.
154. Black bread doesn't mean **want,** nor coarse cloth nakedness.

155. **Water** cannot lie on fat.
156. It isn't every kind of wood that a **whistle** can be made from.
157. What is **white** is quickly soiled.
158. A husband is the head of his **wife**; a wife is her husband's key.
159. One's **wife** and one's stove stay at home.
160. A white mare needs washing; a pretty **wife**—watching.
161. The **winter** asks you what you have done during the summer.
162. Manage things so that the **wolf** gets his fill while the goat remains alive.
163. A **wolf** never bites while his jaw is wide open.
164. A **wolf** thrives by his legs.
165. He who is in the middle is picked out first by the **wolves.**
166. The mind of a **woman** is like the wind and the water.
167. By the time a **woman's whim** passes, four fathoms of green ash wood are burnt up.
168. The devil himself doesn't know where **women** sharpen their knives.
169. When they're in company, men listen to each other—**women** watch each other.
170. The life of man is as spotted as a **woodpecker's** coat.
171. One log of **wood** won't burn by itself, even if it be the master's.
172. He who possesses **wool** must be shorn.
173. It's a long way from **words** to deeds.
174. The roots of **work** are bitter, but its fruit is sweet.
175. **Work** is not a hare, it won't run away.
176. There's **work** that isn't woodcutting; there's food that isn't meat.
177. Your **work** won't be delayed while you're sharpening your scythe.
178. Cover yourself according to the size of your **wrap.**
179. No **year** is the next year's brother.
180. **Yeast** added once will go on fermenting.

LITHUANIAN

1. An **age** to an age is not a brother.
2. One does not live two **ages.**
3. They live like an **axe** with a stone.

   [i.e. cat and dog life.]
4. Upon all flowers the **bee** alights, but not from all of them it gathers the nectar.
5. Give **beer** to a feared man and to a beloved one.
6. To a starving man **bread** is sweeter than honey.
7. There are many crosses upon a **cemetery,** but no cares.
8. It is good to **complain** when there is one who consoles.
9. I shall hold the horns and you will milk the **cow.**
10. The **dawn** grants a day.
11. One **day** teaches the other.
12. **Death** will come uninvited.
13. To a **drunkard** even a drop is dear.
14. Everything has its **end.**
15. Ask the **eyes** and you will find.
16. **Fear** and love do not walk together.

17. Rely upon **God,** but have bread in a bag.
18. He thinks he has grasped **God** by the beard.
19. **God** has given teeth, God will give bread.
20. You have not measured your fingers with **God's,** therefore you cannot know what is in store.
21. **Gold** shines even in the mire.
22. Without **gold** even the light fades.
23. Come expected, leave loved, so you will be a true **guest.**
24. A small **home,** but his own.
25. A common **horse** is always lean.
26. A **house** is blind without a dog, dumb without a cock.
27. **Hunger** increases the understanding.
28. There is **justice** in the world, but it is blind.
29. Without **learning,** without eyes.
30. **Listen** much and speak little.
31. With eyes you will not win **love.**
32. The **needle's** age is a short age.
33. **Ploughing,** we learn to plough ; mowing, we learn to mow.
34. From a large cloud comes little **rain.**
35. A man without **shame** is always filled.
36. He who wears no **shirt** himself, mostly calls the naked.
37. From expecting I have lost my **sight.**
38. In **sight** one is like silk ; out of sight one is like a wolf.
39. A cut **slice** will not stick on.
40. Good eyes are not afraid of **smoke.**
41. Even the severest winter is afraid of the **spring.**
42. A stationary **stone** grows round with moss, but when thrown is bare.
43. The **stone** that remains in one spot becomes covered with moss.
44. The end of the way is upon the **tongue.**
45. Other **trees,** other woodcutters.
46. There is in the world one **truth,** but it seems as if there were a hundred.
47. The hungry **wolf** goes for food even into the village.
48. She wept, as if she had lost the **wreath.**

    [To lose a wreath means in Lithuanian folk-songs to lose virginity.]

LIVONIAN

1. An **apple** does not fall far from the tree.
2. A sharp **axe** quickly finds a stone.
3. The **back** receives what the mouth earns.
4. An empty **barrel** sounds far.
5. The more one heats the **bathroom,** the more one gets the steam.
6. He who sleeps on a **bed** of silver has dreams of gold.
7. Every **beginning** is difficult.
8. **Belief** can never be poured into anyone with a spoon.
9. Every **bird** has a beak.
10. A **bird** who wakes up early wipes its beak early.
11. One cannot get **bread** from sleep.
12. One who does not obey his parents bakes **bread** in the ashes.
13. Strange **bread** lasts only until the gate of home.
14. Everyone carries his own **burden.**

15. The more you stroke a **cat,** the more it lifts its tail.
16. Who can forbid to a **cat** the top of the oven, or a boy to a girl?
17. One who **chatters** much, lies much.
18. The **cheat** has short legs.
19. When the **child** is small it tramples the knees; when it grows big, it tramples the heart.
20. One father feeds five **children,** but five children do not feed one father.
21. **Children** scatter with a fork what parents have scraped together with a rake.
22. Time changes the oak-tree into a **coffin.**
23. The place is known where the mother has hung the **cradle,** but it is unknown where the place for the coffin will be.
24. One who smarts **cries.**
25. A **crow** does not scratch the eyes of another crow.
26. A washed **crow** is like an unwashed one: it has been black and will remain black.
27. A **crust** at home is better than the bread of a stranger.
28. **Death** does not look at the years, it takes one who is in the way.
29. Give the **devil** a finger, and he will take the whole hand.
30. The **dew** cools the heat; good words cool anger.
31. The **dog** grows, and the teeth of the dog grow too.
32. Pull the **dog** out of the water, and it will bite your legs.
33. Landlady's talking and **dog's** barking are the same.
34. Many **dogs** do not watch the home.
35. Many **dogs,** thin broth.
36. It goes as it is **driven.**
37. **Drugs** which do good are bitter.
38. One learns to eat **earth** before dying of hunger.
39. He who **eats** [hungry] has a long hand.
    [i.e. can reach everything.]
40. The more one **eats,** the more one wants.
41. The **egg** wants to be wiser than the hen.
42. Whatever you do, always think of the **end.**
43. **Evening** is wiser than morning.
44. The child names the **father,** the mother knows him.
45. A much-played **fiddle** sounds better.
    [Said about women.]
46. A generous person has long **fingers,** the hands of a miser are short.
47. A **fisherman** is wise in the morning, a shepherd is wise in the evening.
48. One **foe** does more evil than ninety-nine friends do good.
49. **Fraudulence** cuts rods for itself.
50. A good **friend** is like a vessel with a hole.
51. At a full bowl there are plenty of **friends;** at an empty bowl there are none.
52. If you want to reach the **goal** quickly, do not sit on the roadside.
53. An old **goat** has hard horns.
54. Man thinks, but **God** does.
55. **God** gives with a seed-bag, the devil takes with a bushel.
56. **God** has many days.
57. The fear of **God** is the beginning of wisdom.
58. **God** loves one who gives with joy.
59. **Gold** melts in the fire, man melts in sorrow.
60. **Good** comes with waiting, evil comes hurrying.
61. A full head of **grain** droops, an empty one stands erect.
62. Bitter **grass** grows fast.
63. To the **grave** sinks a mountain of gold, as well as a poor insect.
64. **Great men** have little strength and little shame.

65. The bald pate talks most of **hair.**
66. One **hand** washes the other; both will get white.
67. One who is **handy** gets.
68. You may freely give a rope to him who talks of **hanging.**
69. **Happiness** and glass are delicate things.
70. Do not be **happy** about what you have not yet got.
71. Many **heads,** many minds.
72. An **hireling** has a difficult life: the master took the bride, the wolf killed the colt, he himself dies because of the loss.
73. The man who strikes his **horse** strikes his wife too.
74. **Hunger** teaches to live, cold teaches to run.
75. One whose skin **itches** should scratch.
76. A **Jew** does not give anything for "perhaps", because a hare does not have a tail.
77. Nine **jobs** and the tenth is hunger.
78. The **key** turns in the lock, the idler turns in the bed.
79. **Know** a lot, talk a little.
80. One who does not save **kopecks** does not get roubles.
81. One sees the end of one's nose, but doesn't see the end of **life.**
82. **Light** finds, darkness loses.
83. One must **live** so that others can live too.
84. A **log** does not burn alone.
85. Old **love** does not rust.
86. One who has **money** is right.
87. There is gold in the mouth of the **morning** hour.
88. **A mother's heart** is a blossom which never fades.
89. When the **mouse** has eaten its stomach full, then the flour is bitter.
90. The **mouth** speaks of what the heart is full.
91. Everyone is **nearest** to himself.
92. It rolls as it is **oiled.**
93. The **old** earns the new.
94. Mother does not bake **pancakes** every day.
95. "**Perhaps**", "almost" and "if"—these three are brothers.
96. A slow **pig** digs deep roots.
97. The **plain** has eyes, the bush has ears.
98. When you have put the hand to the **plough,** do not look back.
99. The first **puppy** must always be drowned.

    [i.e. first efforts are hardly ever successful.]
100. **Relations** are only for visits and not for living with.
101. The disease of a **rich man** and the beer of a poor man sound far.
102. The slower one **rides,** the farther one goes.
103. With the mouth to **Riga,** with the deed behind the oven.
104. The honest walks on the **road** the dishonest walks on the side of the road.
105. One who **runs** fast, tires fast.
106. A happy one does not have a **shirt.**

    [This proverb is based on a national fairy tale. The king sent to seek the happiest person in his country, who was found to be one living in a cabin and without even a shirt.]
107. It is better to endure the mistake of another than to **sin.**
108. **Smoke** is always bigger than fire.
109. Where the **smoke** is, there is the heat.
110. **Sorrow** has short legs.
111. Hot **soup** burns the mouth.
112. One does not care for the **spoon** after the meal.
113. If our child **squints,** our neighbour's child has a cast in both eyes.
114. One who **steps** high falls low.
115. The full **stomach** does not know what the empty stomach does.
116. Two hard **stones** do not grind well.

117. A little **stump** overthrows a big load.
118. One does not look at the **teeth** of a presented horse.
119. There are **three** of all good things.
120. Where there is no sense of modesty, there is a rude **tongue.**
121. Honey on the **tongue,** ice under the tongue.
122. **A tree** does not fall with one blow.
123. **Trouble** never comes crying.
124. Wherever the **wedge** is hammered, there the wood splits.
125. The skin of the **wolf** does not grow on the lamb.
126. A **woman** can carry out in her lap more than a man can carry in in a cart-load.
127. A **woman** has long hair and short reason.
128. **Work** does not finish with work, nor sleep with sleeping.
129. **Work** shows what the master is like.
130. **Work** teaches the worker.
131. Dirty **work,** white bread.
132. He who does not sow in **youth** does not reap in old age.

MALTESE

1. Don't put your **affairs** into the hands of him who has failed to manage his own.
2. The good **ass** is sold in his own country.
3. All that is said behind my **back** I shall leave behind my footsteps.
4. **Beauty** is loved without knowing anything, and ugliness is hated without being to blame.
5. He who **believes** all that is told him doesn't believe in himself.
6. Always seek the **best** so that the good does not escape you.
7. **Blame** blames and shame shames.
8. A piece of **bread** eaten in harmony is enough to feed a hundred persons.
9. Give **bread** to him who knows how to eat it.
10. He who **buys** dear eats cheap.
11. He who fears wild **cranes** should not sow beans.
12. The **crow,** by thinking of the others, has become black.

    [i.e. you bring trouble to yourself by meddling with other people's.]
13. **Discourse** is a distaff for spinning.
14. **Doors** are not opened without keys.
15. He who steals the **egg** will also steal the hen.
16. Every **ember** has its smoke.
17. Each **eye** demands its own portion.
18. Where your **eye** looks there are others.
19. A pert **face** never dies wrinkled.
20. **Flies** always go to the used ass.
21. A **flight** is better than a sigh.
22. **Give** if you can before they give to you.
23. Do **good** and forget it ; do ill and remember it.
24. When the **heart** is full the mouth vomits.
25. **Justice** flees the world because no one will give it shelter in his house.
26. To the place where the heart **loves** the feet will carry you.
27. **Man** will never know till he has tried it.
28. When a **miser** opens his hand you can't guess the quantity.
29. **Misfortune** and discord travel by sea.

30. Let **money** see the dark that it may let you see the light.
31. According to the **music** you make for me I will dance.
32. Everyone continues to hammer his **nail** into the wall.
33. When you go into a country whose people have **one eye,** blind one of yours.
34. The words of the **poor man** are lost.
35. The **pot** and the spoon that stirs know what the pot contains.
36. Malta would be a delightful place if every **priest** were a tree.
37. He who **promises** much will give nothing.
38. To get out a **rusty nail** you must take away a piece of the wall.
39. Let the **ship** go forward since it has its wind.
40. All that we have **spun** has returned again to wool.
41. **Sweet**; and you will be eaten, bitter; and you will be spat out.
42. The **tortoise,** after taking ninety-nine years to climb a stairway, falls and says that haste is accursed.
43. Each little splinter holds up a **wall.**
44. To drink pure **water** go to the source.
45. All **water** quenches thirst.
46. No one is born knowing how to do more than **whimper.**
47. Never walk against the **wind.**
48. All **wood** has its worm.
49. Pass at a distance from him who chops **wood.**
50. We all leave the **world** as we found it.

MONTENEGRIN

An introduction to this collection by the late Woislav M. Petrovitch, M.A., will be found on page lxxiii.

1. **Advice** is like medicine; the better it is, the nastier to take.
2. Universal **affliction** is easy to bear.
3. If you wish to be **angry,** pay for something in advance.
4. Even an **ant** casts a shadow.
5. Where will the **apple** fall if not under the tree?
6. Better an **apple** pie than apple blossom.
7. When three wise men tell you you are an **ass,** bray!
8. Whip the saddle that the **ass** may see and ponder.
9. An **ass** to Jerusalem—an ass from Jerusalem.
10. "Surely you are getting short of wood and water!" [thought the **ass** when invited to the wedding feast].
11. Who is proud on an **ass** will run mad on a horse.
12. If you want to know a man, give him **authority.**
13. Who **bargains**—buys.
14. Good **bargains** empty the purse.
15. Where the **bee** finds honey the spider finds poison.
16. There is always a **bee** to sting a weeping face.
17. There is no picking out in a **bee's hive.**
18. **Belief** is better than investigation.
19. The **belly** has no windows.
20. Better **bent** than broken.
21. God gives food to every **bird,** but does not throw it into the nest.
22. The **blade** cuts its own scabbard.

23. Amongst the **blind** the one-eyed is king.
24. Spank small **bottoms** that large bottoms may not be flogged.
25. Without rakiya [**brandy**] there is no conversation.
26. There is no **bravery** without a brave company.
27. Married **brother**—two neighbours.
28. As long as you **build** you live.
29. Better your own **calf** than a bull in partnership.
30. He is the fifth wheel to the **carriage.**
31. In whose **carriage** you are riding, his song you should sing.
32. When the **cart** is broken there are many straight roads in sight.
33. Time builds a **castle** and demolishes it.
34. The **chip** does not fall far from the block.
35. Still waters sap the **cliffs.**
36. A tail-less **cock**—eternal chick.
37. 'Tis better to be a **cock** for a day than a hen for a year.
38. White **coins** for black days.
39. Written **contracts** are unnecessary for honest men and rogues.
40. Without **conversation** there is no agreement.
41. **Counting** twice has defeated counting once.
42. First the shed—then the **cow.**
43. Where the **cow** goes, let the halter go too.
44. **Custom** and law are neighbours.
45. No **day** but has its evening.
46. If the **day** is short, the year is not.
47. Without **death** there is no resurrection.
48. Better ten **deaths** on the road than to die at home.
49. If the **debtor** has died his debt has not.
50. If the house burns, its **debts** fly up the chimney.
51. If the **devil** breaks not the cradle, he will break the tomb.
52. Where the **devil** cannot succeed, there he sends the old woman.
53. When the **devil** catches you by the tail of your coat, cut it off.
54. The **devil** tempts all—the pretty woman tempts the devil.
55. Where the **dike** is lowest, there the water runs over.
56. No one can **dishonour** you, but you yourself.
57. If the old **dog** barks, look for the reason.
58. Where the **dog** laps, there also he barks.
59. Feed the **dog** to bark at you.
60. Bang the **door** so that the window may hear.
61. Better to **drink** and be unwell than not to drink and be unwell.
62. If all tell you that you are **drunk,** go to bed, even if you have drunk only water.
63. Where the **eagle** dines many crows may sup.
64. Evil times forced the **eagle** to winter amongst hens.

    [One of the most quoted proverbs in the Serbian language.]
65. Your **egg** is more valuable than your neighbour's hen.
66. Consider the **end** more than the beginning.
67. If your **enemy** be as small as an ant, beware of him as if he were a lion.
68. Say " No " and avert a hundred **evils.**
69. Who **excuses** himself without cause accuses himself.
70. The master's **eye** fattens the steed.
71. Who can read and write has four **eyes.**
72. Far from the **eyes**—far from the heart.
73. Where the **eyes** look, there is the heart.
74. Forests have **eyes**—meadows ears.
75. Not before darkness covers one man's **eyes** will there be sunshine for another.

76. There is but little flesh on a **falcon.**
77. **Fate** sells what we think she gives.
78. He is a great man whose **faults** can be counted.
79. **Fear** and jealousy have big eyes.
80. When a **fence** is falling, every passer-by kicks it.
81. Who does not wet his pants will not eat **fish.**
82. Even a **flea** has its gall.
83. A **fool** is always beginning.
84. **Fools** build houses, the wise buy them.
85. The **foot** is slow in unknown lands.
86. No **forest** fears a handless axe.
87. Even his own brush is a burden to a weary **fox.**
88. If the **fox** preaches the gospel, double your watch in the poultry yard.
89. Give me a co-weeping **friend** ; co-drinkers I can find for myself.
90. God save me from my **friends** ; from my enemies I can save myself.
91. While the pot boils **friendship** lasts.
92. **Gain** gives no headache.
93. More grows in the **garden** than we have sown there.
94. Do not look into the mouth of a **gift-horse.**
95. Say a good word for a bad **girl ;** of a good one you may speak as you like.
96. He **gives** twice who quickly gives.
97. A nannie **goat** fawns two kids ; the skin of one goes to the big drum, the other for the Bible.
98. If the **goat** lies, his horns do not.
99. No one makes contracts with **God.**
100. Where there is concord there is **God.**
101. Who gives to the poor lends to **God.**
102. Who has never suffered is not dear to **God.**
103. **God** always helps fools, children, and the drunken.
104. Pray to **God** but keep to the shore.
105. **God** closes one door and opens one hundred.
106. **God** comes everywhere on every eighth day.

    [Probably a Jewish superstition and an allusion to the Biblical story of six days' creation and one day's rest.]
107. **God** does not pay every Saturday.
108. **God** gives a curst cow only short horns or none at all.
109. Even **God** has His Mother.
110. If **God** has smitten everything, He has spared patience and kind words.
111. **God** never smites with both ends of the stick.
112. **God** often gives nuts to toothless people.
113. **God** preserve me from everybody too sober !
114. **God** remains debtor to no one.
115. **God** tempers the wind to the shorn lamb.
116. Whom **God** wishes to punish He first deprives of his reason.
117. **God's** friend—the priest's foe.
118. **God's** mill goes slowly but it grinds well.
119. When **gold** speaks everyone is silent.
120. A good **guest** departs on the first day.
121. One **guest** hates the other, and the host both.
122. **Guests** and fish stink on the third day.
123. Make your **guest's** bed better than your own.
124. **Guest-ship** for three days.
125. Do not fear a bright **gun** but a sooty one.
126. A loaded **gun** frightens one ; an unloaded one two.
127. If I have given you my **gun** I have not given you my right eye.
128. Long **hair**—short brains.

129. One **hand** washes the other—both the face.

130. White **hands** caress others' work.

131. Do not speak of ropes in the house of a man who was **hanged.**

132. **Happiness** has horns, misery feet.

133. If in **haste,** go round.

134. Do not come near the fire if your **head** is made of bees'-wax.

135. As many **heads,** so many opinions.

136. As your **heart**—so the world.

137. Where there is least **heart** there is most speech.

138. Better once in **heaven** than ten times at its gates.

139. Unless **hell** be full, no judge will ever be saved.

140. A hungry **hen** dreams of millet.

141. A **hen** which cackles overnight lays no egg in the morning.

142. Better make a short circuit than never arrive **home.**

143. Do not make yourself **honey,** for they will eat you, nor rubbish, for they will spit at you.

144. Depend upon thyself and thy **horse.**

145. Who blames the **horse** buys it.

146. If you do not catch the **horse** by the mane, vainly will you try to catch him by the tail.

147. Where **horses** play, asses die.

148. Mending and doing without keep the **house.**

149. The **house** does not rest upon the ground, but upon a woman.

150. **Hunger** has no eyes.

151. The **hungry** never overbakes his loaf.

152. Who **hurries** much remains on the road.

153. If there were no " **ifs** " and " buts " we would all be happy.

154. **Ignorance** earns slavery.

155. Out of the same tree the fan and the **ikon** are made.

156. When one is **ill** one's mind is also ill.

157. When a **Jew** shakes you by the hand, count your fingers.
[Also said of Greeks.]

158. **Joy** and sadness are a wheel in motion.

159. The **just man** always goes about with a bruised head.

160. Without **knowledge**—without sin.

161. There is no **ladyship** without knighthood.

162. A gentle **lamb** sucks two mothers.

163. To **learn**—one effort ; to unlearn—two.

164. Where the **lie** has dined there will she not breakfast.

165. The **lioness** bears but one cub—but it is a lion.

166. Blessed is he who **lives** for ever—he had reason to be born.

167. Not even the **Lord's tomb** is guarded for no wages.

168. Better **lose** and forget than lose more by lamenting.

169. Brotherly **love** for brotherly love, but cheese for money.

170. **Love** for love, but flour for prunes.

171. The despised **love** most.

172. Where there is **love** there is God.

173. Where there is **love** there is no sin.

174. The heart that **loves** is always young.

175. Give me, mother, **luck** at birth, and throw me on the dung-hill.

176. Wheresoever a **magpie** goes she manures her nest.

177. " What is **marriage,** mother ? "—" Kneading, spinning, bearing children, and crying, my daughter."

178. Who dines and **marries** early will not repent.

179. **Marry** with your ears and not with your eyes.

180. To **marry** young is too early ; to marry old is too late.

181. **Measure** twice, cut once.

182. Eat the **meat** from the skin, and the flesh from the water.
[i.e. fresh.]

183. Everyone drives the water to his own **mill.**

184. Do not follow **misfortune** lest she turn.

185. Without **money**—not even to the church.

186. There is no freedom outside **Montenegro.**

187. Consider the **mother**—woo the daughter.

188. Men may meet, but **mountains** never.

189. Better be the head of a **mouse** than the tail of a lion.

190. When the **oak** falls, everyone runs to cut branches.

191. If you do not know what is **over-salted** you know what is over-heated.

192. Where can an **ox** go but he must plough?

193. **Patience**—salvation.

194. The **peace-maker** gets two-thirds of the blows.

195. When the **pear** is ripe it falls.

196. Where the **pig** gets its fat there it leaves it.

197. Mix yourself with bran and the **pigs** will eat you.

198. **Pleasure** is the germ of sorrow.

199. An empty **pocket** passes quickly through the market.

200. Why use **poison** since you can kill with honey?

201. The **Pope** and the peasant know more than the Pope alone.

202. Be not the lid to every **pot.**

203. An empty **pot** sings.

204. The shorter the **prayer,** the dearer to God.

205. **Priests** and flies can enter any house at any time.

206. If there are parishes **priests** will not be lacking.

207. From **promise** to fulfilment—a day's journey.

208. If we are brothers our **purses** are not sisters.

209. When it is fine, take your **rain-coat** with you; when it rains, do as you please.

210. As the **religion**—so the supper.
[i.e. food offered to a guest depends upon the religion of the host.]

211. A good **reputation** goes far—a bad one farther.

212. In the hands of a good shot every **rifle** is deadly.

213. Do not laugh at a fallen man, slippery is the **road** before you.

214. The fugitive keeps to one **road,** the pursuers to one hundred.

215. If it does not **run,** at least it drops.

216. When the **sack** is full it pricks up its ears.

217. Better shake out the **sack** than start a full bag.

218. Not before you have eaten a sackful of **salt** with a man can you say, "I know him."

219. The **satiated** does not believe the hungry.

220. Beware of him to whom you have rendered the greatest **service.**

221. Better a meagre **settlement** than full justice in the court.

222. Every time the **sheep** bleats she loses a mouthful.

223. When on the high sea the **ship** belongs to the pilot.

224. The **shirt** is closer than the coat.

225. **Sit** crooked but speak straight.

226. More lambs' **skins** than sheep-skins are on the market.

227. Not before you have endured enough **smoke** will you enjoy a good fire.

228. **Solitude** belongs only to God.

229. Neither save for your industrious **son** nor bequeath anything to your lazy one.

230. Nobody **sows** but what he hopes to sell.

231. Better **spare** at the brim than at the bottom.

232. If the word is **spoken** it belongs to those who heard it.

233. When it rains honey and milk the poor man has no **spoon.**
234. When God made the earth and was distributing the **stones,** the bag that held them burst and they fell on Montenegro.
235. Where **strawberries** are most abundant take a small basket.
236. Throw the good down the **stream** and it will come back to you up the stream.
237. The more you know the more will you **suffer.**
238. Not all **sunshine** warms.
239. In a good hand every **sword** cuts well.
240. A good **swordsman** is seldom quarrelsome.
241. Where there are too many **tails** there are few heads.
242. Even water has **teeth.**
243. The **thunderbolt** will not strike the nettles.
244. **Time** covers and reveals everything.
245. **Time** is sometimes a mother and sometimes a stepmother.
246. **Time** is the best and infallible consoler.
247. The **tongue** always goes to the aching tooth.
248. Without **tools** there is no handicraft.
249. Better to win **trading** in bran than to lose trading in gold.
250. One man leans upon another as **trees** in a forest.
251. Tell the **truth** and flee.
252. **Truth** is mostly bitter.
253. The more you plunder a **Turk** the richer he is.
254. The **vendor** barks, goods speak.
255. The **victor** feels no fatigue.
256. The **vineyard** does not require prayers, but a hoe.
257. When a **vixen** crosses over a frozen river, you can cross it with siege-guns.
258. The **voice** of the people—the voice of God.
259. Who does not gather up **walks** more easily.
260. Two hazel nuts are the **walnut's** army.
261. Bad **wares** need advertising—good ones sell themselves.
262. There is no stronger drink than **water.**
263. **Water** and fire are good servants but cruel masters.
264. Where **water** has once flowed it will flow again.
265. The more **water** you draw from a well, the more will come back to it.
266. If you would acquire **wealth** and fame, let not the sun shine on you in bed.
267. What you cannot avoid—**welcome.**
268. A man is twice happy, when he marries and when he buries his **wife.**
269. The first **wife** is from God, the second from men, the third from the devil.
270. My **wife** is my mule.
271. You may carry your **wife** on your back all your life, but if you once set her down she will say, " I am tired."
272. If the **wife** sins, the husband is seldom innocent.
273. Who dines on **wine** breakfasts on water.
274. Good **wine** drives out bad intentions.
275. If **winter** bites not with its teeth, it will whip with its tail.
276. Toothless **wolf**—dogs' laughing-stock.
277. The **wolf** eats even counted sheep.
278. Who calls one **wolf** invites a pack.
279. The **wolf** never ate any ordered meat.
280. It is easier to keep guard over a bush full of hares than over one **woman.**
281. Wherever trouble—there is a **woman.**
282. Trust not a weeping man, still less a **woman** who speaks of her chastity.

283. A **woman** will change one hundred religions to obtain her heart's desires.

284. Two **women** and two geese make a fair.

285. Water and **women** will run as men direct them.

286. Quick **work**—double work.

287. The whole **world** lives on credit and trust.

288. The summer and winter make the **year.**

289. **Youth** is not a virtue [nor old age a sin].

290. If **youth** knew how, and if old age could!

NORWEGIAN

1. One sits best on one's own **bench.**
2. He who owns the **boat** should give it a name.
3. Many become **brave** when brought to bay.
4. First think of bread and then of the **bride.**
5. As one **calls** out to the rock so it answers.
6. A sip at a time empties the **cask.**
7. One must **chew** according to one's teeth.
8. A **child** learns quicker to talk than to be silent.
9. He cannot **climb** up who cannot climb down.
10. Good **counsel** is like bad counsel if not followed in time.
11. **Death** and life may fight for long.
12. He who would have a bone from a **dog** must give the meat instead.
13. No town is unenterable if there is a hole in the wall big enough for a **donkey** to go through.
14. **Envy** impedes its owner more than anyone else.
15. **Evil thoughts** should be met at the door-post.
16. He is wise who learns at another's **expense.**
17. "Nothing" is good in the **eyes,** but bad in the stomach [purse, mouth].
18. A good word does much, but doesn't fill the **fasting.**
19. A **fish** bites best on a silver hook.
20. He who lies on the **floor** doesn't fall down.
21. He who recognizes his **folly** is on the road to wisdom.
22. Too much wisdom is akin to **foolishness.**
23. If there were no **fools'** how could one recognize the wise?
24. Know this, if thou hast a **friend** whom thou trustest well, go often to see him—for with brushwood and with high grass will be overgrown the path on which no one walks.
25. To whom **God** gives an office He likewise gives understanding.
26. Bad is called **good** when worse happens.
27. No **grass** grows on every man's road.
28. Old **habits** have deep roots.
29. A little **hand** can often give great help.
30. There is many a good head under an old **hat.**
31. The word that lies nearest the **heart** comes first in the mouth.
32. All that mortals undertake requires the **helping hand.**
33. **Heroism** consists in hanging on one minute longer.
34. He who has never gone along any road has never met a **hill.**
35. You don't know what there is in a man till you have **hit him** on the nose.

36. The higher the **house,** the worse the storm.
37. He is ill **housed** who is housed everywhere.
38. Not all **keys** hang from one girdle.
39. When **knowledge** is least the will is strongest.
40. He who comes **last** sees least.
41. " Virtue in the middle," said the devil as he sat between two **lawyers.**
42. He who has the **least** misses the least.
43. He who knows **little** forgets little.
44. It is better to **live** in a good neighbourhood than to be known afar.
45. **Live** thy life well and get thee workmen and live with men.
46. Poverty and **love** are hard to conceal.
47. That which is **loved** is always beautiful.
48. **Luck** and ill-luck are neighbours.
49. **Luck** is loaned and not owned.
50. **Luck** is like women who like fools best.
51. **Man** is the joy of man.
52. He who buys **meat** has to take the bone with it.
53. One does not look at the **moon** when the sun is up.
54. Each one is **nearest** to himself.
55. **Necessity** makes sour sweet.
56. **Necessity** teaches new arts.
57. No one has peace longer than his **neighbour** will.
58. One may go where one will, but one can't go from **oneself.**
59. The **pardon** may be severer than the penalty.
60. A **peasant** on his feet is taller than a nobleman on his knees.
61. He who sows pennies reaps **poverty.**
62. **Reproach** is the world's salary.
63. When **right** is bent it breaks.
64. He who follows the **river** comes at last to the sea.
65. He cannot speak who cannot be **silent.**
66. He who loses the **skin** may also give the tail in.
67. The full and the fasting sing the same **song.**
68. It is a little **stick** on which no one can lean.
69. When everyone spits on a **stone** it is always wet.
70. When a big **stone** rolls it carries many with it.
71. It isn't easy to sit on a borrowed **stool.**
72. Little **straws** stand the stones best.
73. There is no one so tall that he has not to **stretch** himself, and no one so small that he has not to bend.
74. Everyone finds his **superior** once in a lifetime.
75. One says at one's **table** what one would not listen to outside one's parlour door.
76. He who would **taste** everything gets both sour and salt.
77. They are not all **thieves** at whom the dog barks.
78. He who sits in the middle of the **threshold** is in every man's way.
79. **Time** and opportunity one never has in one's hand.
80. Pawning to-morrow to enjoy **to-day.**
81. One should spare the **tree** that gives one shade.
82. None sigh deeper than those who have no **troubles.**
83. Better **unlearned** than ill-learned.
84. He who has waded knows the **water.**
85. He knows the **way** best who went there last.
86. Let those who know the **way** go before.
87. I expect the **wolf** where I see his ears.
88. A **wooer** should open his ears more than his eyes.
89. The **word** that has departed grows on the way.
90. He is **worth** much who has learnt much.

POLISH

An introduction to this collection by A. Przybyzewski will be found on page lxxxvii.

1. Who said **'A'** must also say 'B'.
   [i.e. to read between the lines.]
2. He went embraced to **Abraham's** bosom.
3. He who speaks ill of an **absent person** ill treats a dead one.
4. The **absent** is always to blame.
5. Every **Adam** can find his Eve.
6. **Adam** has been expelled from the garden of Eden.
   [News known to all.]
7. What could **Adam** have done if God had not put Eve in the garden of Eden?
8. **Adam's** rib does not bring so much usefulness as damage.
9. A good **advocate** is a bad neighbour.
10. **Age** is a sorry travelling companion.
11. Nowadays you must go to heaven to meet an **angel.**
12. Even a sour **apple** is gnawed by maggots.
13. If you wish to enjoy leisure, join the **army.**
14. He who **asks** diffidently asks to be refused.
15. A **bachelor** and a dog may do everything.
16. **Bacon** is not for dogs.
17. A straw **bailiff** will overcome an oaken peasant.
18. The **bald** need no comb.
19. Short **banquets,** long life.
20. He who goes **barefoot** cannot do others harm.
21. Hold tight to the first **bargain.**
22. **Bargain** like a Jew but pay like a Christian.
23. **Bargaining** teaches us how to buy.
24. Do not put your hand between the **bark** and the tree. (*Man and wife marriage proverb.*)
25. No grass grows on the **battlefield.**
26. When going to hunt a **bear** prepare a bed; when going to hunt a boar prepare a bier.
27. Every **beast** knows its time.
28. **Beauty** is the seasoning of virtue.
29. **Beauty** will not season your soup.
30. If you can afford **beer,** drink water; if you can afford wine, drink beer.
31. Young **beer** is frothy.
32. The best **beer** is where the coachmen and the priests go for their drink.
33. The spendthrift is a future **beggar,** but the mean man is an eternal beggar.
34. The **bell** is loud because it is empty.
35. He who buys a cage will want a **bird.**
36. Even **bird's** milk is not lacking.
37. Don't be **bitter** and you won't be spat out; don't be sweet and you won't be swallowed.
38. He that **blames** himself praises himself.
39. Where the **body** wants to rest, there the legs must carry it.
40. Rich and poor alike say: "It is better to wear out the feet than the **boots.**"
41. He that is waiting for someone else's **boots** will have to walk about barefoot a long time.
42. With a **bottle** and a girl one does not count the hours.
43. Through **bravery** you win and through bravery you lose.
44. Stop up the peasant's mouth with **bread.**
45. Don't jeer at poverty unless you have **bread.**
46. Without **bread**—a poor banquet.

47. He lost his **bread** and has not found his cake.
48. Find the **bread** and the teeth will be there.
49. **Bread** cries when eaten unearned.
50. When you have **bread,** do not look for cake.
51. Without **bread** even game is tasteless.
52. Eaten **bread** is difficult to earn.
53. **Bread** makes his teeth ache.

    [i.e. an expression used to describe someone who has become rich and haughty.]
54. He who is without **bread** should be without children.
55. There were two **brothers** who had brains and a third who was married.
56. Every **bubble** bursts.
57. Nobody is without a " **but** ".
58. Where there is **butter** there are flies.
59. Every **calf** will find its slaughterer.
60. If you are born for the **cap,** do not covet the crown.
61. He who is on the **cart** is often under it.
62. From someone else's **cart** you must get off half-way.
63. He who **cheats** at cards should not complain of peaches on his face.
64. **Cheese** in the morning is gold ; at midday silver ; at night lead.
65. A **child** is caressed by its mother, but an orphan is caressed by God.
66. The **children** of the peasant are his assets ; of the gentleman his liabilities ; and of the nobleman thieves.
67. Teach your **children** to bite stones.
68. Who hasn't seen a **church** bows before a fireplace.
69. If it were not for the hands the **clock** would be useless.
70. From a big **cloud** little rain.
71. **Cock**—the village clock.
72. The master has got a **cold** in the head, and all the servants sneeze.
73. He that is **content** with little is not so poor as he that never has enough.
74. Even if a **cook** were to cook a fly, he would still keep a wing for himself.
75. That which is **cooked** in the house must be eaten in the house.
76. The upright ear of **corn** is empty.
77. In one's own **cottage** even smoke is pleasant.
78. The **cottage** gives freely whatever it has.
79. A strange **cottage** is worse than the executioner.
80. He that **cries** in his lifetime, dies smiling.
81. Both the **cross** and the gallows are made of wood.
82. Every **Czech** a musician.
83. As the **dance** so the music.
84. To a bad **dancer** even the hem of her skirt will be in the way.
85. When a **daughter** is born it is as though seven thieves had got into the larder.
86. When **death** is on the tongue, repentance is not difficult.
87. One man is another's **devil.**
88. The Pole is deceived by the German, the German by the Italian, the Italian by the Spaniard, the Spaniard by the Jew, the Jew by the **devil.**
89. He is damned who gives the flower of his youth to the **devil** and to God the dregs of his old age.
90. Where the **devil** cannot succeed he sends an old woman.
91. Even the **devil** comes to grief attacking the shrine.
92. If you are going to sup with the **devil,** find a long spoon.
93. The worst **devil** is the one who prays.
94. The **devil** often sits at the foot of the cross.

95. The young may **die,** the old must.
96. **Dirt** will not stain unless you touch it.
97. One who attains **distinction** is immediately changed.
98. The mistakes of the **doctor** are covered by earth.
99. Better no **doctor** at all than three.
100. Before a **doctor** can cure one he will kill ten.
101. Wait with your pains till the **doctor** comes.
102. The **doctor** cures when he can smell money.
103. The **doctor** demands his fees whether he has killed the illness or the patient.
104. A beggar does not hate another beggar as much as one **doctor** hates another.
105. Ask the patient, not the **doctor,** where the pain is.
106. In Padua there are more **doctors** than patients.
107. The fatter the flea, the leaner the **dog.**
108. The lean **dog** lives longest.
109. Who yaps like a **dog** will be beaten like a dog.
110. Only what I **drink** is mine.
111. No one can **drink** out of a gallon measure.
    [Literally: one-eighth of a barrel.]
112. It is easier to **drink** two glasses than to excuse yourself from one.
113. Where you have got **drunk,** there go to sleep.
114. He who lends to a friend makes an **enemy.**
115. In church, in an inn, and in a coffin, all men are **equal.**
116. Every **error** has its excuse.
117. Watch the **face** of him who bows low.
118. He who says **farewell** with tears will greet with joy.
119. The **farm** is of more use to the bailiff than to the owner.
120. To accept a **favour** is to lose your liberty.
121. If you are **feared** by many, be afraid of many.
122. Let him who is **feared** be well armed.
123. Everyone will get in where the **fence** is low.
124. Where two are **fighting** there is a stick for the third.
125. Where there is **fire** a wind will soon be blowing.
126. **Fish** to be tasty must swim three times: in water, in butter and in wine.
127. There is more honour in the belly bursting than in **food** going to waste.
    [i.e. lavish hospitality expressed in the over-generous treating to food which is considered bad manners for the guest not to eat up.]
128. A **fool** is always in the rain.
129. Everyone is free to make a **fool** of himself.
130. Hope is the mother of **fools.**
131. **Fools** need not be sown; they grow by themselves.
132. **Forgive** others easily but yourself never.
133. There is a Sunday in the week, but also a **Friday.**
    [i.e. Friday is a fast day.]
134. An old boot and an old **friend** are the most dear.
135. What you give to a good **friend** is not lost.
136. **Friends** are thieves of your time.
137. **Friendship** is like wine—the older the better.
138. His Lordship has promised me a **fur coat** and already I feel warm.
139. He who has no **fur coat** keeps warm even in a shirt.
140. Like **fur,** like moth.
141. He who has been shut out at the main **gate** must knock at the side entrance.
142. It is easier to watch over one hundred fleas than one young **girl.**
143. Select a groom on horseback and a **girl** at a dance.

144. Put in a good word for a bad **girl**; for a good one say what you like.
145. The dog that intends to bite growls; the bee that intends to sting hums; but a **girl** only makes her eyes sparkle.
146. What you cannot refuse, **give** before you are asked.
147. He who first asks does not **give** very willingly.
148. He who **gives** ought to forget; he who takes ought to remember for ever.
149. Lower the sword and raise the **glass.**
150. Any **goat** can jump over a low fence.
151. You will not buy much with a "**God bless you**".
152. Fear **God,** and next to God, him that has no fear of God.
153. Trust in **God** and put your shoulder to the wheel.
154. Offer the candle to **God,** and to the devil the butt.
155. Hold **God** by the feet and the devil by the horns.
156. **God** can shave without soap.
157. **God** did not join brains with beauty.
158. When praising **God** do not bow to the devil.
159. To him whom **God** favours, a bitch will bear a litter of pigs.
160. To him who rises early **God** gives.
161. **God** gives the wideness of the mouth according to the bigness of the spoon.
162. Man shoots, but **God** guides the bullet.
163. **God** has given all to all and not all to one.
164. **God** has given; God has taken.
165. What **God** has given will not be taken away by envy; what God has not given will fall out of your hands.
166. When it pleases **God,** He likewise gives behind the hearth.
167. Thou wouldest do little for **God** if the devil were dead.
168. He who swims with **God** never goes to the bottom.
169. Where **God** puts one finger the devil puts his whole hand.
170. **God** saves the moon from the wolves.
171. Man carries the powder and **God** the bullets.
172. **God** will afflict; God will console.
173. **God** will help a ploughing man.
174. If **God** wills, even a cock will lay an egg.
175. Whom **God** wishes to punish He will deprive of his reason.
176. The news of a **good deed** travels far, but that of a bad one farther.
177. **Good deeds** are written on sand; bad deeds are graven upon rock.
178. The **good** are easily deceived.
179. The **good** have died out.
180. **Gratitude** has gone to heaven and has taken the ladder.
181. A poor **groom** can manage without work in Poland if he can play cards; in Italy if he can steal; and in Moscow if he can flirt.
182. That which is **guarded** by everybody will soon disappear.
183. A **guest** plants a nail in the wall, even if he only stays a night.
184. Everyone has his **hands** turned towards himself.
185. What will **hang** will never drown.
186. Many **hares** are hunted who haven't eaten cabbages.
187. When God blesses the **harvest,** there is enough for the thief as well as for the farmer.
188. Four things are difficult to **hide:** fire, the itch, a cough and love.
189. **Hops** without a support will not rise from the ground.

190. He whose coach is drawn by **hope** has poverty for a coachman.
191. It is easy enough to walk when you are holding a **horse** by the bridle.
192. A good **horse** is bought in the stable.
193. A handsome **horse** should have a head like a maiden, a chest like a widow, and a foot like a baby.
194. He who buys a **horse** takes the bridle with it.
195. They pat the **horse** until they have saddled him.
196. Where there is a **Hungarian** there is anger ; where there is a Slovak there is a song.
197. The **infirm** live longest.
198. **Ink,** if not used, will dry up.
199. The **inn** cannot pollute the virtuous, nor the church improve the wicked.
200. In time of need one first turns to God and then to the **Jew.**
201. In misfortune even a **Jew** can be looked upon as a brother.
202. In want, to the **Jew ;** in distress, to the priest ; in fear, to God.
203. Two cheeses and one **Jew** make three smells.
204. Punish the **Jew** with a whip and the peasant with money.
205. He who sleeps in a **kennel** will get up flea-ridden.
206. A golden **key** fits every door.
207. If they do not open after three **knocks,** do not wait.
208. Praise to the sorceress who adds to your **larder.**
209. He who goes to **law** over a hen will have to be content with an egg.
210. One ducat before the **lawsuit** is better than three afterwards.
211. The roots of **learning** are bitter but the fruit is sweet.
212. The lawyer's **legacy** is a pen ; the priest's a breviary ; the coachman's a whip ; the merchant's nothing.
213. The **lemon,** after being squeezed, is thrown away.
214. A **liar** can go round the world but cannot come back.
215. The lean **lice** bite most.
216. Better to be killing your own **lice** than counting someone else's money.
217. **Life** is like the moon ; now dark, now full.
218. A good **listener** makes a good teacher.
219. The **Lithuanian** is stupid like a pig but cunning like a serpent.
220. In Spain, the lawyer ; in Italy, the doctor ; in France, the flirt ; in Germany, the artisan ; in England, the merchant ; in the Balkans, the thief ; in Turkey, the soldier ; in Poland, a Treasury official ; in Moscow, the liar—can always make a **living.**
221. Where you have **lost** a thing, there you look for it.
222. Everyone has his **louse.**
223. Without bread and salt **love** cannot exist.
224. **Love** enters man through his eyes ; woman through her ears.
225. The greatest **love** is mother-love ; after that comes a dog's love ; and after that the love of a sweetheart.
226. He who **loves** much beats hard.
227. If you **love** you are the slave ; if you are loved you are the master.
228. **Love** yourself, and be hated by multitudes.
229. With a **maiden** as you will ; with a widow as she wills.
230. A **mare** that is born piebald will die piebald.
231. Two women and one goose—a **market.**
232. Three women, three geese, and three frogs, make a **market.**
233. He that **marries** acts well ; he that doesn't acts better.
234. **Marry** and you will be all right for a week ; kill a pig and you will be all right for a month ; become a priest and you will be all right for life.

235. Before **marrying** live wildly for three years.

236. Neither advise nor dissuade from **marrying**; neither prevent nor force into it.

237. Man cannot be **measured** by an ell.

238. Without measure **medicine** will become poison.

239. Two hard **millstones** do not grind fine.

240. He who likes to stay in the **mire** must ask the devil to be his partner.

241. Let him who has deliberately walked into the **mire** walk out by himself.

242. **Misfortune** arrives on horseback but departs on foot.

243. Common **misfortune** extinguishes private dissension.

244. He of whom **misfortune** has taken hold will sprain his thumb, even when wiping his nose.

245. When **misfortune** knocks at the door, friends are asleep.

246. When I had **money** everybody called me brother.

247. When **money** talks everyone is silent.

248. Find the **mud,** and the devil will not take long to find you.

249. You cannot drive out one **nail** with another.

250. The **naked** will always meet those who have no clothes.

251. Where the **needle** goes the thread must follow.

252. One who hates his **neighbour** can see blemishes even in the sun.

253. The house of one who does not help to put out his **neighbour's fire** will soon be in danger.

254. He who is always **nice** is not always nice.

255. The **night** has its own code [of morals].

256. The rich man has only two holes to his **nose,** the same as the poor man.

257. "**Nothing**" is good for the eyes.

258. He that wishes to eat the **nut,** does not mind cracking the shell.

259. Everyone will come and chop a fallen **oak.**

260. Let him who wants to be **old** a long time not be young long.

261. Do not ask the **old,** "How are you?" but "What ails you?"

262. Where one **owl** comes out two others will soon follow.

263. It hurts more if no one knows about our **pain.**

264. A good **painter** need not give a name to his picture; a bad one must.

265. The doorstep of the **palace** is very slippery.

266. The **parson's** eyes and the wolf's jaw will eat all they see.

267. **Partnership** was invented by the devil.

268. He who holds a sword will maintain **peace.**

269. There is **peace** in a home where the husband is deaf and the wife blind.

270. There is no lasting **peace** without battle.

271. If the **peasant** does not beat his wife, her liver rots, but if he beats her now and again, her liver improves.

[Literally: grows larger.]

272. The **peasant** earns, the aristocrat spends, and the **Jew** profits.

273. Where the **peasant** is poor the whole country is poor.

274 The peasant is born a **philosopher**; the aristocrat has to learn to be one.

275. The woman had no troubles, so she bought a **piglet.**

276. Even a **pin** is worth bending down for.

277. It is not clever to **play** but to stop playing.

278. Learn in Italy; clothe yourself in Germany; flirt in France; banquet in **Poland.**

279. In Russia as one must; in **Poland** as one wishes.

280. Eat in **Poland,** drink in Hungary, sleep in Germany, flirt in Italy.

281. **Poland** is the peasant's hell, the Jew's paradise, the citizen's purgatory, the noble's heaven and the grave of the stranger's gold.

282. We are not in **Poland,** where the women are stronger than the men.

283. Every Czech is a musician ; every Italian, a doctor ; every German, a merchant ; every **Pole,** a nobleman.

284. What an Englishman cares to invent, a Frenchman to design, or a German to patch together, the stupid **Pole** will buy.

285. When God made the world He sent to the **Poles** some reason and the feet of a gnat, but even this little was taken away by a woman.

286. God save us from a **Polish bridge !**

287. You can be rich though **poor,** and poor though rich.

288. No one knows the **poor,** and the rich don't know themselves.

289. The **poor** are cured by work ; the rich by the doctor.

290. To the **poor** even the wedding night is short.

291. For the **poor** it is always dark and always winter.

292. The **poor** have always the wind in their faces.

293. The wind blows always against the **poor man's** eyes.

294. In the **poor man's** house it is always after dinner.

295. It is only the **poor** who pay dearly.

296. Where the **Pope** is, there is Rome.

297. In a small **pot** the broth runs over the brim exactly as in a large pot.

298. Where the inn-keeper is mayor, the baker town-councillor, and the butcher and grocer the aldermen, there is **poverty** among the townsfolk.

299. Do not look for **poverty ;** it will find you.

300. Do not wake **poverty** when it sleeps.

301. Walk slowly and **poverty** will overtake you ; walk quickly and you will catch up with it.

302. **Praise** and cabbage have a nice taste, but they inflate.

303. If you want to be **praised,** die ; if you want to be blamed, get married.

304. **Praise** is a spur to the good, a thorn to the evil.

305. Do not **praise** the day in the morning, nor a son-in-law till he is dead.

306. Before going to war say one **prayer ;** before going to sea, two ; before getting married, three.

307. He who says his **prayers** lying down is listened to by God sleeping.

308. He who wants enough for a day should cook a goose ; for a week a pig ; for a month an ox ; for a lifetime he should become a **priest.**

309. Do not put paper into water, a feather near the fire, nor a **priest** near your wife.

310. A **priest's** property and a Jew's are always safe.

311. A **priest's servant** perspires at meals and freezes at work.

312. As the **priest,** so the blessing.

313. A **proof** too many will not spoil the case.

314. **Proverbs** are not vain words.

315. Words will not fill your **purse.**

316. If you are feeling nice, keep **quiet.**

317. The wet are not afraid of **rain.**

318. A **reed** need not be afraid when the winds uproot the oak.

319. A **relative** on Adam's side.

[i.e. an answer to someone boasting of relationship to a notability.]

320. May our **relatives** be prosperous, and may we never find the way to them !

321. Three **removals** are worse than a fire.

322. It is better to cling to the door-handle of a **rich man** than to the whole door of a poor one.

323. You can smell the **rich man's** illness and the poor man's beer from a distance.

324. He who wishes to become **rich** must become a swine.

325. Do not push the **river**: it will flow by itself.

326. If there is no wind, **row.**

327. He that comes to terms with humanity must be a **saint.**

328. The bread of **St. Agatha** saves the home from fire.

[This proverb springs from the belief held by the peasants in the immunifying ritual of carrying bread round the house on St. Agatha's day, 5th February.]

329. **Saints** are not struck off the calendar.

330. Even the **saints** are troubled with warts.

331. Even a **saint** sins seven times a day.

332. You add **salt** to bread, not bread to salt.

333. Better a **sausage** in hand than a ham at the butcher's.

334. Bang the table and the **scissors** will answer you.

335. The Rabbi is dead, but the **scripture** remains.

336. To the garrulous a **secret** is a burden.

337. One can often **see** better from afar than close to.

338. One **servant** is a servant; two servants are half a servant; three servants are no servant at all.

339. He that lives in complete integrity will have no **shirt** to wear.

340. Only the **shoe** knows of the hole in the stocking.

341. One day the **sickle** will cut down the nettle.

342. **Silence** goes better with shrewdness than with a kind heart.

343. He who would **sleep** well should fasten his thoughts to the door-bell.

344. The more one **sleeps** the less one lives.

345. The **smile** on a hungry man's face is a lie.

346. From someone else's **snuff** you will get nose-ache; from your own headache.

347. In **sorrow** nothing is tasty.

348. Cherish the body, harm the **soul.**

349. You cannot season **soup** with noble birth.

350. He that **sows** in his shirt sleeves will reap in a fur coat; he that sows in a fur coat will reap in a bare shirt.

351. The **spark** will destroy, and itself become extinct.

352. If you **spit** in his eye he says, "It is raining."

[Said of one who is difficult to insult.]

353. **Spring** is a maiden; summer a mother; autumn a widow; and winter a stepmother.

354. The **stag** does not feel the weight of his antlers.

355. The **stars** will twinkle at one who is shone on by the moon.

356. If you will not **steal** you will not eat. (*Thieves' proverb.*)

357. An empty **stomach** has no pity.

358. Man is not a **stork,** he need not cleanse the world.

359. Where there is a **stork** there is peace.

[i.e. the stork is considered a symbol of friendship and peace. Therefore the farmer on whose land the stork nests must by inference be a good man.]

360. He who is without work in **summer** is without boots in winter.

361. If everyone **swept** in front of his house, the whole town would be clean.

362. One **swine** recognizes another.

363. God grant me a good **sword** and no need to use it.

364. He who lies under the **table** gets kicked.

365. One must let people **talk,** since fish can't.

366. He who laughs at **tears** will cry.

367. Horses, bread, beer and candles are the nobleman's **testimonials.**

368. The **thief** only takes something, but flames take everything.

369. On the **thief's** head the cap burns.

370. A **thunderbolt** strikes a tall house most often.

371. He who **tickles** himself laughs when he pleases.

372. **Time** is bald behind.

373. The **timid man,** like wood, is chopped by everybody.

374. **Timidity** and hope go hand in hand.

375. Tuck your shirt in between your legs, and your **tongue** behind your teeth.

376. Cut down the sound **tree** and the unsound will fall by itself.

377. The new year follows upon the old one; those who were in **trouble** will be in trouble.

378. With **truth** one goes everywhere, even in prison.

379. **Truth** will not fill you, and a lie will not choke you.

380. Old **truths,** old laws, old friends, an old book and old wine are best.

381. Anoint the **ungrateful** with balsam and he will still smell of dung.

382. That which is **useful** can also be harmful.

383. The world is like a **vapour bath,** the higher up one is the more one sweats.

384. When **Venus** is ruler of the farm, Mars must sit with the chickens in the coop.

[i.e. when the hen crows the house goes to ruin.]

385. Every **village** has its inn.

386. In **Vilna** there are seven roads for the Jew and three for the Pole.

387. He who wants to find a **virgin** must go to Cologne.

[This is an allusion to the story of the eleven thousand virgins buried with St. Ursula at Cologne.]

388. The **virtuous,** fallen, make the worst evil-doers.

389. **Want** is harder after prosperity.

390. The fear of **want** is worse than want itself.

391. In **want** we learn to pray.

392. Without cake there is no **wedding.**

393. The woman cries before the **wedding** and the man after.

394. There is no corn without **weeds.**

395. It is the ear, not the eye, that should choose a **wife.**

396. A **wife,** a razor and a horse are things not to be lent.

397. The first **wife** from God; the second from men; the third from the devil.

398. The first **wife** is a slave; the second a companion; the third a master.

399. A **wife** is like mint; the more you chop it the sweeter it smells.

400. A young **wife** is to an old man the horse on which he rides to hell.

401. He that drinks will get fat; he that loves will be healthy; and he that beats his **wife** will be saved.

402. He who often **witnesses** earns little.

403. It is easier to reconcile a hundred husbands than two **wives.**

404. A dead man's **will** is the mirror of his life.

405. It is safer to tease a dog than a **woman.**

406. You have to get up early to be able to deceive a **woman.**

407. When the devil is at his wits' end he sends a **woman.**

408. Selling your soul to the devil is the same as selling it to a **woman.**

409. The devil is no match for a **woman.**

410. Approach a **woman** and a horse from the front.

411. A grey-haired man is to a **woman** as a hedgehog to a dog.

412. **Woman**—as small as your finger and as evil as a viper.

413. What a **woman** brings up and a monk educates, is fit for the devil.

414. The devil swallowed a **woman,** but he could not digest her.

415. The devil cannot go as far as a **woman** can.

416. In partnership with a **woman** even the devil has been the loser.

417. A fire scorches from near; a beautiful **woman** from near and from afar.

418. A **woman** goes mad twice: when she loves and when she begins to go grey.

419. One **woman** in a town makes more noise than two hundred men.

420. When a **woman** is marrying she holds seven devils under her arm.

421. The peasant wants land; the nobleman honours; the soldier war; the merchant money; the farmer peace; the artisan work; the painter beauty; and **woman** the whole world.

422. Do not trust the dog that sleeps, the Jew who swears, the drunken man who prays, and the **woman** who weeps.

423. No fish without bones; no **woman** without a temper.

424. A **woman's** knees, a peasant's chest, an aristocrat's ears and a Jew's heels are never cold.

425. It is easier to make a hundred watches agree than ten **women.**

426. A hundred **women**—a hundred counsels.

427. There are only two good **women** in the world—one is lost and the other cannot be found.

428. Children, chickens, priests and **women** never have enough.

429. The fewer **women,** the less trouble.

430. Water, fire and **women** will never say "Enough".

431. There is no key to the **woods** and the fields.

432. **Words** must be weighed, not counted.

433. "Mine" and "thine" divide the **world.**

434. The **world** is wide, yet there is little room in it.

435. Wealth — **worry**; poverty — worry.

436. There are a thousand roads to every **wrong.**

437. It took the hedgehog ten years to fetch the **yeast,** and then on the doorstep he stumbled.
[Yeast in former times was only obtainable in liquid form.]

438. Wherever you go you can never get rid of **yourself.**

PORTUGUESE

1. He brooks no **advice** whose mind is made up.

2. Never say **all** that you know; never believe all that you hear; never do all that you can.

3. The **ass** embraced the thistle, and they found themselves relations.

4. The wolves eat the **ass** which many folk own.

5. It is the sickness of our **asses** that makes us veterinaries.

6. Never go to a **baptism** or a wedding uninvited.

7. The **basket-maker** who makes one basket makes a hundred.

8. At a sale keep the **beard** still.
9. There was never **beauty** without aid.
10. The king of the **bees** has no sting.
11. Put the **beggar** in your straw rick and he will become your heir.
12. He buys very dear who **begs.**
13. There was never a **blind man** who saw himself, or a man in the wrong who knew it.
14. Better a **blush** in the face than a spot in the heart.
15. Hard to **boil,** hard to eat.
16. What is **bought** is cheaper than a gift.
17. A sharp tooth for hard **bread.**
18. When there is no **bread** at home everyone grumbles and no one is right.
19. Another's **bread** costs dear.
20. May the stomach suffer that forgets the **bread** it has eaten.
21. Three **brothers,** three fortresses.
22. Bleed him, purge him, and if he dies, **bury** him.
23. Too big a wax **candle** burns the church.
24. The **candle** that goes in front lights twice.
25. A singing **cart** goes towards its master.
26. **Chairs** sink and stools rise.
27. Dear is **cheap,** and cheap is dear.
28. A collector of **cinders,** and scatterer of flour.

    [i.e. penny-wise and pound-foolish.]
29. He who **clothes** himself in bad cloth clothes himself twice.
30. Be not too brief in **conversation** lest you be not understood, nor too diffuse lest you be troublesome.
31. To every country its **customs,** and to every distaff its spindle.
32. It is not for **dawning** that the day breaks earlier.
33. Take the fine **day** into thine house.
34. **Death** makes us equal in the grave and unequal in Eternity.
35. He who lives well **dies** well.
36. He who **divides** and re-divides takes the best part.
37. The more **doctors,** the more diseases.
38. All bite the bitten **dog.**
39. A house which has neither a **dog** nor cat is the house of a rogue.
40. If you wish to know the value of a **dollar,** seek the loan of one.
41. Lock your **door** and you will make your neighbour honest.
42. Beware of a **door** that has many keys.
43. He who comes late **eats** what he finds.
44. However soon it may dawn the **evening** doesn't come any earlier.
45. **Experience** is the teacher of life.
46. A blue **eye** in a Portuguese woman is a mistake of nature.
47. The **eye** sees everything except itself.
48. **Eyes** which never see anything are eyes which never sin.
49. Each one speaks of the **fair** as he finds it.
50. **Faith** has no eyes; he has no faith who wishes to see.
51. Win good **fame** and go to sleep.
52. From **far off** one makes close to.
53. **Feet** accustomed to go cannot be still.
54. The **feet** go where the heart wills.
55. **Fire** is never put out with straw.
56. The **fish** dies by its mouth.

    [i.e. silence is golden.]
57. One cannot **fish** for trout with dry trousers.
58. Everyone takes his **flogging** in his own way.
59. A **fly** does not enter a closed mouth.
60. When the **food** is fat the will is lean.

61. On the **fool's** beard all learn to shave.
62. He who eats his **fowl** alone, alone must saddle his nag.
63. It is better to give to an enemy than to ask of a **friend.**
64. A false **friend** is worse than an avowed enemy.
65. He's my **friend** that grindeth at my mill.
66. A **friend** to be besought is an enemy to be paid.
67. He never was a **friend** who ceases to be so for a slight cause.
68. **Friends** and mules fail on the roughest ground.
69. Where **friends,** there riches.
70. A broken **friendship** may be mended but it always sounds cracked.
71. If you would know the **future** behold the past.
72. With **God** before, the sea is solid ground.
73. **God** gives nuts to him who has no teeth.
74. Leave it to **God** who is an old Saint.
75. When **gold** speaks all else keeps silence.
76. **Good** comes to good and evil to him who has it.
77. It is after we have departed that the **good** is better known.
78. Give a **grateful** man more than he asks.
79. A **guest** and a fish stink in three days.
80. To change one's **habits** smacks of death.
81. **Happy** is he who only desires what he may and does what he ought.
82. The **happy** man ought always to fear ; the unhappy ought always to hope.
83. Old **hate** never wearies.
84. Be not a baker if your **head** be of butter.
85. Long of sight, long of **heart.**
86. Prepare a nest for the **hen** and she will lay eggs for you.
87. Where the cock is, the **hen** does not crow.
88. Of presumption and **holy water** each one takes what he will.
89. **Honour** and profit will not stay in one sack.
90. Those who live on **hope** die of disillusion.
91. Who does not **hope** does not work.
92. **Hunger** is a bad counsellor.
93. He who never uses **ill** bears not ill in mind.
94. The **ill** of many is a joy.
95. Keep **illness** for Fridays, and don't fast.
96. **Inclination** is the first step to knowledge.
97. **Ingratitude** is the sepulchre of love.
98. Those loaded with **iron** go loaded with fear.
99. Where the **iron** goes, there goes also rust.
100. The **key** at the girdle keeps me good and my neighbour too.
101. You will never be a **knight** where you were a page.
102. Tell your friend a **lie** and if he keep it secret tell him the truth.
103. He who never takes an oath tells no **lies.**
104. In **little** much is said.
105. **Love,** anger, and a cough betray their owner.
106. **Love** is like the moon, when it doesn't increase it decreases.
107. An old man in **love** is like a flower in winter.
108. **Love,** love, the beginning is bad and the end worse.
109. Of soup and **love,** the first is the best.
110. **Love** them who love you, and answer those who call you.
111. **Lovers'** squabbles are redoubled love.
112. He who **loves** much suffers much.
113. He **loves** well who never forgets.
114. The **lucky** man has a daughter for his first child.

115. What is **marriage,** mother? Daughter, it is spinning, bearing children, and weeping.

116. **Marry** and grow tame.

117. What is another's always sighs for its **master.**

118. When the **master** is out it is a holy day [holiday] in the shop.

119. He who serves two **masters** has to lie to one.

120. Water that has passed doesn't turn the **mill.**

121. **Misers'** money goes twice to market.

122. Work done expects **money.**

123. If you would make an enemy, lend a man **money,** and ask it of him again.

124. The poor man's **money** goes twice to market.

125. Never put **money** into a sack without seeing if it has a hole.

126. The **money** you lent has gained you an enemy.

127. A busy **mother** makes an idle daughter.

128. The **mouthful** is kept for him who has to eat it.

129. The bad **neighbour** gives a needle without thread.

130. He who has a good **nest** finds good friends.

131. It is better to begin **nothing** than to end nothing.

132. He can never **obey** who cannot command.

133. To catch the **occasions** for the hairs.

134. Give **orders,** and do it, and you will be free from anxiety.

135. The **oven** is heated through its mouth.

136. The hand to the **pain**; the eye towards love.

137. If you have a friend who is a **physician,** send him to the house of your enemy.

138. Every **pig** has its Martinmas.

[i.e. every dog its day.]

139. A **pig** on credit makes a good winter and a bad spring.

140. The **pitcher** that goes often to the fountain either leaves its handle or its spout.

141. An hour of **play** discovers more than a year of conversation.

142. Beware of a **pledge** that eats.

143. For **poor** people small coin.

144. Don't make yourself **poor** to one who won't make you rich.

145. It is **prohibition** which makes temptation.

146. **Promising** is not giving, but it contents fools.

147. A stolen **rabbit** has its ears outside.

148. That which has no **remedy** is remedied.

149. What was hard to bear is sweet to **remember.**

150. Where there is no might **right** loses itself.

151. The **righteous** pays for the sinner.

152. A tortuous **river** is crossed ten times.

153. Follow the **road** and you will come to an inn.

154. Time brings **roses.**

155. The **saints** of the house never perform miracles.

156. **Seat** yourself in your place, and they will not make you rise.

157. He who fears no **shame,** all the world is his.

158. The greater the **ship,** the greater the tempest.

159. Good **silence** is called saintliness.

160. The wise gets a **sledge** in summer and a carriage in winter.

161. When the **snake** is dead its poison is dead.

162. Alas for the **son** whose father goes to heaven.

163. Lay your hand on your bosom and you will not **speak ill** of another.

164. Black and white **speaks** like folk.

[Refers to writing.]

165. He who **speaks** with closed eyes wishes to see others deceived.

166. Never take a **stitch** without a knot.

167. Don't make out the **stomach** to be the heart.

168. Who holds his peace and gathers **stones,** will find a time to throw them.

169. **Stumbling** is not falling.

170. Who does not tire, **succeeds.**

171. We must **suffer** much or die young.

172. When the **sun** rises it rises for all.

173. The **task** that pleases is soon ended.

174. **Think** of many things ; do one.

175. He **threatens** many who affronts one.

176. Never cut what you can **untie.**

177. **Visits** always give pleasure, if not the arriving, the departing.

178. The **voice** of the people is the voice of God.

179. What **water** gives, water takes away.

180. Too much **wax** burns the church.

181. He does more who **will** than he who is able.

182. He who sows **wind** reaps tempests.

183. Good **wine** excuses commendation.

184. All **wine** would be Port if it could.

185. A pen and ink are the best **witnesses.**

186. **Wives** and sheep should be brought home early.

187. Buy flesh of a **wolf.**

188. To **wolf's** flesh dog's teeth.

189. The **woman** who loves two, deceives both.

190. **Women** are supernumerary when present and missed when absent.

191. The wind collects the **wood** for him whom God wants to help.

192. There are many ways of going out of the **world** but only one way of coming into it.

193. Better **wrong** with the many than right with the few.

ROUMANIAN

(Including Dacian, Istrian, Transylvanian, Vlach and Wallachian)

1. If you are the **anvil,** suffer ; if hammer, strike.

2. **Bacon** makes bold.

3. You should write **bad things** on running water. (*Dacian.*)

4. The **billy-goat** leaps the table, but the nanny-goat leaps the house. (*Dacian.*)

5. In vain you show light to the **blind.**

6. Beware of a new **boyar** and an old beggar. (*Dacian.*)
   [Boyar = nobleman.]

7. **A child** is a blessing for any man's roof.

8. The blessing of having many **children** has never broken a man's roof.

9. Borrowed **clothes** do not keep one warm. (*Dacian.*)

10. Save some white **coins** for black days.

11. One **crow** never pecks out another's eyes.

12. He who drinks of the water of the **Dambovika** comes to drink again.

13. Only the **deaf** and blind are obliged to believe.

14. Better an **egg** to-day than an ox to-morrow. (*Dacian.*)

15. A wise **enemy** is better than a foolish friend.
16. Who **flatters** you has either cheated you or hopes to do so.
17. A change of rulers is the joy of **fools.** (*Dacian.*)
18. A **foreigner** scratches you where you do not itch. (*Vlach.*)
19. There is no bitterer fruit than **foreigners** in one's land. (*Dacian.*)
20. A **foreigner's** pity is like a thorn's shadow. (*Dacian.*)
21. Don't sell the **fox skin** in the wood.
22. Protect me, Lord, from my **friends**; my enemies I shall take care of myself. (*Dacian.*)
23. A **girl's** honesty is like snow; when it melts, the whiteness is no longer seen. (*Dacian.*)
24. Before you find **God** you are eaten by the saints. (*Dacian.*)
25. Whom the **gods** love die young.
26. In whose mouth **God's** name dwells overmuch, in his heart dwells the devil.
27. Do **good** and throw it on the road. (*Dacian.*)
28. Where you cannot catch anything, it is useless to stretch out your **hand.**
29. Kiss the **hand** you cannot bite. (*Dacian.*)
30. Only what is in your **hands** is no lie.
31. When the **head** does not work, the legs suffer.
32. Heaven is far, but we are only separated from **hell** by a hedge. (*Wallachian.*)
33. Woe to the house where the **hen** crows and the cock keeps silent. (*Dacian.*)
34. One's **home** is both paradise and hell. (*Dacian.*)
35. The **husband** doesn't know what all the village knows. (*Dacian.*)
36. Sit not **idle,** for your luck sits with you. (*Dacian.*)
37. **Illness** comes in a coach and goes away through the eye of a needle. (*Wallachian.*)
38. **Justice** is as the rulers make it.
39. Trust not **knaves,** lest, trusting them, you revile them.
40. A mild **lamb** sucks two mothers. (*Dacian.*)
41. Our **language** is one great salad. (*Vlach.*)
42. The man who goes to **law** often loses an ox to win a cat. (*Dacian.*)
43. **A lie** is a bone which you throw into the mouth of another, but it chokes you.
44. Man's **life** is like an egg in the hands of a child. (*Dacian.*)
45. Five Vlachs make a **market.** (*Vlach.*)
46. When the **master** is away the mice play on the table. (*Wallachian.*)
47. Men always **meet** but mountains never.
48. **Money** is round and rolls easily.
49. With **money** one can even buy rabbit-cheese. (*Dacian.*)
50. **Nakedness** turns round; hunger goes straight. (*Dacian.*)
51. **Names** are not the pledge for things, but things for names.
52. When the **nuns** dance the devil does not weep.
53. **Old maids** and young dogs should be drowned.
54. **Oxen** are tied by their horns, men by their words.
55. Men are all made of the same **paste.** (*Dacian.*)
56. If you wish to die soon, make your **physician** your heir. (*Istrian.*)
57. If your **pint** is full, your sentence is also good. (*Dacian.*)
58. Do not put your spoon into the **pot** which does not boil for you.
59. Better a crooked **reconcilement** than a straight judgment. (*Dacian.*)
60. **Right** goes with a broken head. (*Dacian.*)
61. The **stairs** are swept downwards, not upwards. (*Dacian.*)

62. Who **talks,** sells ; who listens, buys. (*Vlach.*)

63. **Thieves** increase with the making of new laws.

64. **Thieves** nowadays are not in the forests, but in the offices.

65. **Thistle** doesn't catch in smooth cloth. (*Vlach.*)

66. The **tongue** is boneless, but can break bones.

67. No one throws stones at a fruitless **tree.** (*Dacian.*)

68. Wine and children speak the **truth.**

69. Who beats his **wife** beats his own head ; who beats his mule beats his purse. (*Vlach.*)

70. A tent without a **wife** is like a fiddle without a string.

71. You may carry your **wife** on your back all your life, but put her down once and she will turn round and say " I am tired."

72. Drink the **wine,** do not be drunk by it. (*Dacian.*)

73. In **wine** there is truth.

74. You will never find father and mother again, but **wives** as many as you like.

75. It is easier to guard a bush full of hares than one **woman.** (*Wallachian.*)

76. A **woman** cuts her wisdom teeth when she is dead. (*Dacian.*)

77. When God made the **woman,** He put beside her the distaff to distinguish her from man.

78. **Woman's** eyes are at one's purse. (*Dacian.*)

79. A **woman's** petticoat is the devil's binder. (*Dacian.*)

80. It is not good to be the driver of white horses or the servant of **women.** (*Dacian.*)

81. Even the best of **women** has still a devil's rib in her. (*Dacian.*)

82. **Women** learn how to weep in order to lie.

83. Spoken **words** are like winds, neither caught in a net nor overtaken with greyhounds.

84. **Work** is a golden bracelet. (*Transylvanian.*)

GREAT RUSSIAN (ALSO CERTAIN UKRAINIAN AND WHITE RUSSIAN)

An Introduction to this collection by Andrew Ivanovich Guershoon, LL.B., will be found on page xcv.

1. He was good as a " two ", but no good as an **ace.**

2. **All** for one and one for all. (*Community proverb.*)

3. The **angry** and the weak are their own enemies.

4. The **apple** does not fall far from the apple-tree.

5. Beside the rotten **apple** the good one also spoils.

6. Don't pluck the **apple** while it is green ; when it is ripe it will fall of itself.

7. No **apple-tree** is immune from worms.

8. An **army** stands until peace, and a lie does so till the truth is out.

9. **Asia** is more honest than Africa, and August is warmer than March.

10. When an **ass** bears too light a load he wants to lie down.

11. It is with men as with **asses ;** whoever would keep them fast must find a very good hold at their ears.

12. The **Ataman** gets the first whipping, but he gets the first drink also.

 [Cossack Ataman = a Cossack Chief.]

13. It is a sin to allow a **baby** to die in its cradle ; it is the same as on the gallows. (*Sectarian superstition.*)

14. A **bachelor** is a goose sans water.

15. A **bachelor** is never sent as a " go-between ".

16. He who offers his **back** should not complain if it is beaten.

17. Why should two **bald men** fight over a comb ?

18. There is plenty of sound in an empty **barrel.**

19. Whatever has been taken in **battle** is sacred. (*Military.*)

20. The **bear** dances, but the gipsy takes the money.

21. A **bear** which is not tied up won't dance.

22. Without a **beard** no admission to Paradise. (*Sectarian.*)

23. To live is either to **beat** or to be beaten.

24. **Beat** your own, the others will fear you.

25. **Beauty** of the chaste is a virtue ; that of a whore a quality.

26. **Beauty's** sister is vanity, and its daughter lust.

27. When you have made your **bed** everybody wants to lie on it.

28. Better a **bed** of wood than a bier of gold.

29. As you make your **bed** so will you lie on it.

30. Who fell from the tree ? The **bee-keeper ;** Who got drowned? The fisherman ; Who lies in the field ? The soldier.

31. In the steppe even a **beetle** is meat.

32. **Beginning** and ending take each other by the hand.

33. It is easier to fill twenty **bellies** than one pair of eyes.

34. On an empty **belly** every burden is heavy.

35. The **belly** is a scamp, it remembers not the good done to it.

36. The **belly** is like a judge who keeps silent but asks for it.

 [Pre-Reformal judges, before 1863, open to bribery.]

37. You didn't teach him while he was lying across the **bench ;** when he is lying along the bench you cannot teach him any more.

 [Russian peasantry used to sleep on benches along the walls, beds not being in use. Children when small slept across the bench ; when grown up they slept along the bench.]

38. He has been sent to count the **birches.**

 [Said of a man sentenced to Siberia, whither he had to walk, the road being in some parts flanked by birches.]

39. If you give **birth,** pay—if you bury, pay again.

40. That which is born **blind** is not fit for food.

41. Don't **boast** when you depart, but when you arrive.

42. He who builds in a **bog** must not be sparing with the stakes.

43. The **bones** grow flesh.

44. A narrow **boot** will stretch ; a broad one will shrink.

45. Two **boots** make a pair.

46. They were bowing to you when **borrowing,** but you are bowing to them when collecting.

47. Limits and **boundaries**—arguments and fights.

48. The broken **bow** frightens two.

 [i.e. the shooter and the one shot at.]

49. Even a **boyar** [old Russian nobleman] is held in captivity by his own whims.

50. Whoever buys straw sells **bread.**

51. Where there was grass there will be **bread.**

52. One can get sick of cake, but never of **bread.**

53. Whoever owns the ground owns the **bread.**

54. Necessity teaches to eat white **bread.**

[Peasants unable to earn a livelihood in the Northern districts had to go South where wheaten bread was eaten—a luxury to a man from the North.]

55. You can think as much as you like but you will invent nothing better than **bread** and salt.

56. Throw **bread** and salt behind you, you get them before you.

57. **Bread** and salt never quarrel.

58. **Bread** and salt together, but each his own tobacco.

59. If you would eat **bread** don't remain sitting on the oven.

60. If you have no **bread,** drink wine.

61. **Bread** is a father; water is a mother.

62. **Bread** on a journey is no burden.

63. **Bread** sleeps in man.

[i.e. when a man is well fed he sleeps well.]

64. It is the **bread** that keeps one warm, not the fur.

65. He who eats old **bread** will swim easily.

66. Better **bread** with water than cake with trouble.

67. Without **bread,** without salt—bad company.

68. **Bridal candles** must be blown out at the same time, so as to live together and die together.

[Two candles lit at wedding ceremony and blown out together.]

69. When the **bride** is in the cradle, the bridegroom ought to be old enough to start riding.

70. Weeping **bride,** laughing wife; laughing bride, weeping wife.

71. She who sews for the **bride** will get younger.

72. More expensive than a stone **bridge.**

[According to the plans of one Christler summoned to Moscow by Mihail Federovich in 1643, a remarkable bridge was built, but at an exorbitant cost. Robbers were called " uncles from the ninth span " which also referred to that bridge because they used to gather under it.]

73. " Perhaps " and " Never mind " are born **brothers.**

74. Two **brothers** against a bear, and two brothers-in-law at a milk pudding.

75. **Business** for a poltina and gratuities for a rouble.

[Poltina is equivalent to a shilling and a rouble equivalent to two shillings.]

76. Never let the first **buyer** go. (*Superstition.*)

77. Forbidden goods find many **buyers.**

78. It isn't the **buying** that teaches, it is the selling.

79. Even **cabbage** enters into favour.

[During Lent.]

80. One must not despise even a **calamity.**

81. Someone else's **calamity** doesn't add to your own wisdom.

82. Moscow was burnt by a kopek **candle.**

[In 1443 Moscow was burnt down from a candle in the church of St. Nicholas on the Sands, and in 1537 from a candle in Miloslavsky's house.]

83. Offer a **candle** to God and a sack of money to the judge.

84. **Carpenters** and joiners are cursed by God.

[Because they spoil so much timber.]

85. What is fallen off the **cart** is gone.

86. If you are sitting on his **cart** you must sing his song.

87. The higher the **castle** the nearer to the lightning.

88. Man builds **castles,** time ruins them.

89. He that denies the **cat** skimmed milk must give the mouse cream.

90. Do not **catch** everything that swims.

91. One passes by the **cemetery** so often that in the end one falls into it.

92. A **charred place** smells a long time.

93. Even a good **chemist** will shorten your life.

94. A **chemist's** white bill is like a dark autumn night.

95. **Chickens** are counted in the autumn.

96. It is easier to bear a **child** once a year than to shave every day.
[Said by soldiers to their wives.]

97. The daughter's **children** are dearer than one's own.

98. You cannot bear sufficient **children** to satisfy Death.
[Refers to infantile mortality.]

99. People's opinion has crucified **Christ.**

100. The face of **Christ** is like all men's faces.

101. A stranger in a house is a **church bell.**

102. **Clemency** is the support of justice.

103. Seek the brave in prison and the stupid among the **clergy.**

104. **Cloth** shrinks, words still more,

105. Measure your **cloth** seven times, you can cut it but once.

106. One is received according to one's **coat** ; one is dismissed according to one's brain.

107. A fighting **cockerel** does not get fat.

108. A dead body has its **coffin,** and a live man his hut.

109. Even a **coffin** is made to measure.

110. What does a **coffin** of silver help him who has to lie in it?

111. Nobody dare differ from the **community.**
[If there were a few dissenters they were usually quietened down by force. In Great Novgorod those who disobeyed were drowned and their houses looted.]

112. One man cannot eat the **community.** (*Community proverb.*)

113. **Community** is as strong as water, and as stupid as a pig. (*Community proverb.*)

114. Blame the **community,** it will stand everything. (*Community proverb.*)

115. If the whole **community** sigh, then a rumour will reach even the Tsar. (*Community proverb.*)

116. The **community** will stand for itself.
[The total populace of a Russian village was treated as a unit, and was called " Mir " or Community —which was responsible for all its individual members.]

117. The **confectioner** likes bread best.

118. One does not beat the **corn** on account of the chaff.

119. **Corn** rustles less than straw.

120. When there is **corn** the measure will be found.

121. One sees from one's own **corn** when the neighbour's rye is ripe.

122. Man is a walking **corpse.**

123. Without horse, no **Cossack.**

124. A **Cossack** himself will starve, but his horse has to be fed.

125. When a **Cossack** is on horseback only God is above him.

126. Have patience, **Cossack,** one day you will be the Ataman. (*Cossack.*)

127. Set foot into **court** and your hand goes into your pocket.
[Bribes.]

128. The **court** is straight but the judge is crooked.
[Before Courts were reformed.]

129. To a vicious **cow** God doesn't give horns.

130. As soon as a **cow** has an udder of silver she will quickly get golden nipples.

131. The job fears the **craftsman.**

132. A very good **crop** is worse than a very bad one.
[Through fall in prices.]

133. A good **crop,** sell early ; a bad crop, sell late.

134. If you are not a brother to me, give me back my **cross.**
[The custom to exchange crosses on the occasion of becoming sworn brothers when strangers promised each other help and support.]

135. A hungry Frenchman welcomes a **crow.**

[In Napoleon's retreat from Moscow in 1812, French soldiers were compelled to make soup from crows.]

136. He is caught like a **crow** in the soup.

[Explanation as above.]

137. In its own nest even the **crow** will pick the vulture's eyes.

138. When wrath and vengeance marry, **cruelty** is born.

139. Where there are **crumbs** there will be mice.

140. A husband's **cuffs** leave no marks.

141. **Curly hair,** curly thoughts.

142. Potatoes are **cursed,** tea is twice cursed, tobacco and coffee are thrice cursed. (*Sectarian.*)

143. **Custom** is stronger than law.

144. Clever father, clever **daughter ;** clever mother, clever son.

145. A **daughter** is a bad asset when the mother is to be wed.

146. People sometimes sin like **David,** but do not sorrow like him.

147. Praise the **day** in the evening.

148. Every **day** learns from the one that went before, but no day teaches the one that follows.

149. **Death** answers before it is asked.

150. **Death** carries a fat Tsar on his shoulders as easily as a lean beggar.

151. **Death** for a common cause is beautiful.

152. We do not even get **death** free of charge, for it costs us our life.

153. **Death** has no almanack.

154. **Death** is a brother to the Russian soldier.

155. **Death** is concise like a good proverb.

156. When **death** is there, dying is over.

157. **Death** regards spring as winter.

158. There are not as many **deaths** as there are sorrows.

[The pestilence in Moscow in 1771—a field was allotted near the Andronius Monastery for people afflicted with the pestilence. The dying and the convalescent were moaning so dreadfully that they were inflicting more terror than the corpses.]

159. Do not **decry** anything human.

160. Every **devil** can hunt his own swamp.

161. The **devil** is poor, he has no God.

162. Until the sun rises the **dew** will eat your eyes out.

163. One cannot **die** before one's death.

164. The soldier will **die** in the field and the sailor in the sea.

165. Who hastens to live soon **dies.**

166. A **dog** can only dream of bones.

167. A **dog** is wiser than a woman, he does not bark at his master.

168. Your **dog** wishes you a long life.

169. Leave something for the **dogs.**

170. One **door** is locked, but another is wide open.

171. If everyone washed his own **doorstep** how clean the town would be!

172. He who finds a **doorway** too low must stoop.

173. **Drink** at table, not behind a pillar.

174. Eat until you are half satisfied, and **drink** until you are half drunk.

175. If you **drink** you die, if you don't drink you die, so it is better to drink.

176. Don't disdain **drinking** out of a ladle ; you may have to drink lying down [from a stream].

177. If the husband **drinks,** half the house is burning ; if the wife drinks, the whole house is ablaze.

178. One cannot **drive** straight ahead when one is on a bend.

[When dealing with crooked people.]

179. The slower you **drive,** the further you get.

180. It is a sin to have been present at a wedding without being **drunk.**

181. If two people tell you you are **drunk,** go to sleep.

182. To a **drunken man** the sea is only knee-deep.

183. **Eagles** do not catch flies.

184. **Ears** do not grow higher than the head.

185. **Eat** or not eat, it will be counted to you as a meal.

186. One must not **eat** round hoofs.

[i.e. the flesh of animals with a single hoof.]

187. He who **eats** quickly works quickly.

188. A gift **egg** is dear on Easter Day.

[An irony on account of costly bribes given on Easter Day to Court officials.]

189. **Eggs** don't teach the hen.

190. One cannot sit **embraced** all one's life.

191. An **enemy** will give in, but a friend will argue.

192. The **Englishman** has his intelligence at the end of his fingers, the Frenchman at the end of his tongue.

193. This is **English workmanship.**

[i.e. the highest praise.]

194. **Envy** hatches swans from rotten duck eggs.

195. **Envy** sees the sea but not the rocks.

196. **Eternity** gives place to a salted cucumber.

197. Only the **evening** will show what the day has been.

198. In every **evil** there is something good.

199. Pay the **executioner** his due.

[Fee collected on market day from visitors to market, as late as 1814.]

200. Our **eyes** are our enemies.

201. There are no replete **eyes** in the world.

202. Nowhere in the world do **eyes** look satisfied.

203. If a man knew where he would **fall** he would spread straw first.

204. To **fall** is allowed ; to get up is commanded.

205. Do not put your head into the noose before your **father.**

[Head of the family first. When whole families were hanged, the father was the first victim.]

206. If you live without being a **father** you will die without having been a human being.

207. **Fear** has very large eyes.

208. **Fear** life not death.

209. Two are less to **fear** than one.

210. Whichever **finger** you bite, every one hurts.

211. **Finland** is the devil's country.

[i.e. unfertile, rocky country.]

212. Between two **fires.**

[Russian princes and envoys were made to pass between two fires in the Tartar Horde, as a sign of abasement.]

213. Where there is no **fish,** even the cray-fish is deemed to be fish.

214. You catch **fish** in troubled waters.

215. One **fisherman** sees another fisherman from afar.

216. Only **fleas** are to be caught quickly.

217. Where the **flower** is the honey is also.

218. One gathers the **flowers,** one does not choose them.

219. A **fool** and his goods are soon parted ; a wise man and his poverty always remain united.

220. When the **fool** drops his bread it falls into the honey-pot.

221. If a **fool** has a hump nobody notices it ; if the wise man has a pimple everybody talks about it.

222. When a **fool** has too many roses he plants thorns amongst them.

223. A **fool** hopes to get honey, even from wasps.

224. A **fool's** country is where his family is.

225. If it were not for **fools** in this world there would be no reason.

226. In a **foreign land** even a child is an enemy.

227. As long as there is a **forest** an axe will be found.

228. He who is a friend of the **forest** cannot be an enemy of the tree.

229. **Fraud** is often the mother of gain, but gain is not always the son of fraud.

230. **Free will** is worse than constraint.

231. He who seeks a constant **friend** goes to the cemetery.

232. If you have had enough of your **friend,** grant him a loan.

233. For a **friend** seven versts do not make a detour.

234. As you pour out for your **friend** so must you drink.

235. As to taste and colour there are no **friends.**

236. When **friendship** has a rent there is no reel of cotton that can mend it.

237. Were it not for the **frost** the hops would overgrow the hedge.

238. One cannot make a **fur coat** from a "Thank you"

239. Do not rejoice over the first **gain.**

240. The **game** is a traitor, but the bludgeon is a friend.

[i.e. robbery surer than gaming.]

241. He who plants a hedge round his **garden** invites it to be jumped.

242. In the **garden** of time grows the flower of consolation.

243. **Garlic** heals seven illnesses.

244. The poorer, the more **generous.**

245. Even in the other world we shall have to serve the **gentry,** for they will be in the cauldrons and we shall have to stoke the fires.

[Before serfdom was abolished.

246. Hang a **German** even if he is a good man.

247. Some think they are **giants** when they sit on the hump of a camel.

248. It is not the **gift** which is precious, it is the love.

249. **Gipsy truth** is worse than an Orthodox lie.

[Greek Orthodox religion.]

250. That which a **girl** does not know adorns her.

251. When a **girl** is born all four walls weep.

252. A **girl** is like a shadow; follow her, she runs; flee from her, she follows you.

253. A **girl** may be allowed to sin, otherwise she would have nothing to repent. (*Sectarian.*)

254. A **girl** is only born when she is fit to get married.

255. A **girl's shame** only reaches the threshold, directly she steps over she forgets it.

256. Where there is love there is **God.**

257. Every day is a messenger of **God.**

258. Who is pleased with little is not forgotten by **God.**

259. Praise **God** and love men.

260. Prayers to **God** and service to the Tsar are not lost.

[From a speech of Peter the Great.]

261. Pray to **God** but continue to row to the shore.

262. You can earn your reward from **God** but never from man.

263. Heaven has many cracks through which **God** can see.

264. When **God** denies a field rain He increases its dew.

265. **God** does not give more beard than soap.

266. Where **God** does not make the key the lock is not secure.

267. You cannot deceive **God** even by getting up early.

268. **God** gave—God took.

[Usually said when an infant dies.]

269. When **God** gives a pebble to be masticated He first softens it.

270. **God** gives potatoes, but with the peel.

271. **God** gives the day and provides the food for it.

272. **God** gives man a cross according to his strength.

273. **God** gives to the rich man biscuit without appetite ; to the poor man bread with hunger.

274. **God** goes to him who comes to Him.

275. With **God** go over the sea ; without Him do not go over the threshold.

276. Fish cooked by **God** has no bones.

277. Man has the bow, **God** has the arrows.

278. **God** help us, but don't lie on your back.

279. **God** is an old worker of miracles.

280. Dreams are dreadful but **God** is merciful.

281. **God** is the judge of your crutches.

[i.e. man can be deceived but not God.]

282. Cheer up ; **God** is where He was.

283. **God** never lets both the ears and the straw turn out badly.

284. To get near to **God** one need not climb the mountain.

285. **God** spreads the moss as a carpet for the poor.

286. If **God** were listening to a bad shepherd all the flock would die.

[Shepherds' habit of invoking death on cattle by cursing.]

287. The **God** who soaks will make dry.

288. **God** will cook the soup for him who has water, herbs and wood.

289. The beginning of wisdom is **God's** fear.

290. A good conscience is **God's eye.**

291. Go **Godward :** thou wilt find a good road.

292. Many who have **gold** in the house are looking for copper outside.

293. Only that is **good** which other people praise.

294. Of all **good things,** only a little.

295. **Gossip** needs no carriage.

296. When I get **grandchildren** I get to know fairy tales. (*Western Russia.*)

297. If you can't get **grapes** get an apple.

298. The **Greeks** only tell the truth once a year.

299. What has been reaped **green** will be eaten raw.

300. The **ground** is like a dish : whatever you put on you take off.

301. **Ground** without a master is an orphan.

302. One cannot **grow** higher than oneself.

303. **Gruel** cannot be spoilt by butter.

[i.e. things can always be improved.]

304. If a **guest** gets up early he intends to stay for the night.

305. **Habit** is a shirt that we wear till death.

306. It is better to be the **hammer** than the anvil.

307. A **hand** that takes never gets tired.

308. White **hands** like someone else's labours.

309. The **hands** soon forget what the mouth promises.

310. Who will **hang** will never drown.

311. **Happiness** is a step-mother.

312. **Happiness** is not a horse, it does not drive along a straight road.

313. **Happiness** is not a horse, you cannot harness it.

314. The **harm** we do others we easily forget.

315. **Harsh law** creates guilt.

316. Even good seeds can give a poor **harvest.**

317. The matter is inside the **hat.**

[Lots were usually drawn out of a hat.]

318. Old **hats** don't like being raised.

319. **Health** goes in puds and comes back in zolotniks.

[Pud = 40 Russian lb. Zolotnik = 1/96th of a lb.]

320. Who is not **healthy** at twenty, wise at thirty, or rich at forty, will never be either.

321. One can always be **healthy** so long as one is not ill.

322. To a **healthy man** everything is healthy.

323. One closes one's house better than one's **heart.**

324. The **heart** has no window.

325. He whose **heart** is a rose, his mouth will speak fragrant words.

326. The book of the **heart** is read from the eyes; the book of the head is read from the hands.

327. **Heaven** created me and earth supports me.

328. It never goes well when the **hen** crows.

329. The **high-road** is recognized by poles, and the Volga by the steep banks.

330. Who drives straight ahead does not get **home.**

331. **Honour** trusts honour.

332. The horses of **hope** gallop, but the asses of experience go slowly.

333. **Hope** has noble relations.

334. In the kingdom of **hope** there is no winter.

335. It is not the **horse** but the oats that draw the cart.

336. If the **horse** did not blow on its oats it would swallow a lot of dust.

337. Don't buy a **horse** from a parson, and don't marry a widow's daughter.

338. Don't look a given **horse** in the teeth.

339. Don't drive the **horse** with a whip, but with oats.

340. Don't stroke the **horse** with your hand, but with the sack.

341. **Hospitality** was a boon, as the guest served as a walking newspaper.

342. Where the **hostess** is beautiful the wine is good.

343. After visiting another man's **house** one notices rotten beams in one's own.

344. The **house-bell** considers itself the daughter of the church-bell.

345. You must **howl** if others yell.

346. One is more likely to get **hunchbacked** than rich through work.

347. In time of repletion remember **hunger**; in the time of riches remember poverty.

348. **Hunger** is a finger which points out the fruit on the tree to the blind man.

349. To a **hungry man** it is always noon.

350. A **husband** is father of his wife.

351. A miserable **idol** cannot even stop calves licking it. (*Very old proverb.*)

352. **Illness** and poverty are not known under the hat.

353. **Illness** is galloping home post-haste, but is leaving the house on slow horses.

354. For every **illness** there is a herb growing.

355. An **ikon** and a spade are made from the same tree.

356. **Ikons** are not bought but exchanged.

[Ikons are pictures of the saints. To apply the terms of buying or selling these was considered an outrage to religious feeling.]

357. In the eyes of the **jealous** a mushroom grows into a palm-tree.

358. Do not **jest** beyond one rouble.

[i.e. within small limits.]

359. Deceive a **Jew** and he will kiss you; kiss a Jew and he will deceive you.

360. If a **Jew** can have the rope free of charge he will let himself be hanged.

361. A baptized **Jew** is an unbaptized Christian.

362. When you baptize a **Jew** keep him under water.

363. The weight of the load lies at the end of the **journey.**

364. One gets to know people during games and on **journeys.**

365. **A judge** is like a carpenter, what he wants he carves.

366. A mended **jug** lasts two hundred years.

367. The lining is dearer than the **kaftan** [man's dress].

[From the custom to sew money into the lining.]

368. A word of **kindness** is better than a fat pie.

369. A **kind word** is like a spring day.

370. The **kitchen** first eats the house and then itself.

371. With one hand I do not even tie a **knot.**

372. Do not promise the Kingdom of God and do not whip with the **knout.**

[This proverb remains from the time when the sectarians were fiercely persecuted by Peter the Great.]

373. The first **knout** [whip] is for the denouncer.

374. You cannot always use the **knout,** sometimes the whistle will do.

[Boatswain's whistle. Naval proverb.]

375. The **knout** isn't God, but it will find the truth.

376. **Knowledge** is not always a water that washes away vices.

377. A **kopek** [about ¼*d.*] at home is better than a rouble [about two shillings] abroad.

378. A **kopek** into the till and a grosh in the cheek.

[Dishonest cashier.]

379. **Kurilka** is alive, not dead.

[Kurilka is a game with a lighted match. The word is also used by the people to depict drunkards and wastrels.]

380. Two hands upon the breast and **labour** is past.

381. It is better to be **lame** than always seated.

382. Some **laughter** savours of tears.

383. Necessity alters the **law.**

384. Where the power, there the **law.**

385. Fear not the **law,** but the judge.

386. **Law** is a flag, and gold is the wind that makes it wave.

387. The **law** is like the shaft of a carriage—you can turn it wherever you please.

388. **Laws** are spiders' webs; hornets pass through them, but flies are caught.

389. God wanted to chastize mankind so He sent **lawyers.**

390. The fall of a **leaf** is a whisper to the living.

391. One **leg** is the other leg's friend, but one arm is the other arm's enemy.

392. If you don't **lend,** enmity; if you do lend, an interminable lawsuit.

393. When one erects a throne to **lies** one erects a gallows to truth.

394. In the pond of **lies** only dead fish swim.

395. There is more **light** than can be seen through the window.

396. The **lightning** more often strikes the peasant's tree than the noble's forest.

397. A **lion** doesn't catch mice.

398. **Live** as you can, but die as you wish.

399. We do not **live** uphill but downhill.

400. The **loaf** of one house and the loaf of another are brothers.

[Hospitality.]

401. The beauty of a **loan** is repayment.

402. The **loan** is the first heir.

403. No joy emanates from a **lonely** person.

404. Without **losing** you cannot win.

405. Without skill you cannot even catch a **louse.**

406. Copper money makes rusty **love.**

407. Mistrust is an axe at the tree of **love.**

408. **Love** and eggs should be fresh to be enjoyed.

409. **Love** and hunger are the foundation stones of all things.

410. **Love** has wings on its shoulders; matrimony has crutches under its arms.

411. Whom I **love** I beat.

412. **Love** is a ring, and a ring has no end.

413. He whom we **love** is white even when unwashed.

414. Do **love** me when I'm black, everyone likes me when I'm white.

415. **Love** starts from the eyes.

416. **Lovers** seek willingly new roads; the married seek the old.

417. **Luck** and bad luck are driving in the same sledge.

418. Once bad **luck** has come, open your gates.
[Uselessness of resisting more trouble.]

419. Good **luck** is an eel in the pond of fools.

420. Too much **luck** is dangerous.

421. Bad **luck** is fertile.

422. **Luck** without wisdom is like a knapsack with holes.
[i.e. you lose what you find.]

423. If you are afraid of bad **luck** you will never get good luck. (*Saying of Peter the Great.*)

424. A **maiden's** heart is a dark forest.

425. Once you have sold the **mare** you may burn the saddle.

426. Once you have gone to **market** you have told the whole world.

427. One doesn't go to **market** with his own price.

428. There is no such fiery love that would not be cooled down by **marriage.**

429. There is **marriage** but there is no "dis-marriage".

430. Even a good **marriage** is a time of trial.

431. **Marriage** is not a race, you can always get there in time.

432. **Marriage** is the tomb of love.

433. If you go to war, pray; if you go on a sea journey, pray twice, but pray three times when you are going to be **married.**

434. They were **married** round a pine-tree and the devils sang.
[Heathen marriage.]

435. Don't choose the bride, but choose the **match-maker.**

436. He who has let his **meadow** must buy his grass.

437. When the **mere** freezes, the people thaw.

438. That which is taken in with the mother's **milk** only goes out with the soul.

439. An empty **mill** grinds, even without wind.

440. A thread from each member of the **mir** [community] becomes a shirt for the naked. (*Community proverb.*)

441. What the **mir** has arranged is God's decision. (*Community proverb.*)

442. The **mir** sighs and the rock is rent asunder. (*Community proverb.*)

443. Over the **mir** there is no judge but God. (*Community proverb.*)

444. Walk fast and you catch **misfortune;** walk slowly and it catches you.

445. Some people are masters of **money,** and some are slaves.

446. **Money** does not smell.
[i.e. it does not matter whence the money comes.]

447. **Money** goes where money is.

448. Another's **money** has very sharp teeth.

449. **Money** is iron; clothing is futility.

450. **Money** loves to be counted.

451. When **money** speaks the truth keeps silent.

452. You give **money** with your hand, but you go after it with your feet.

453. The **moon** is the Cossack's sun.
[Night raids.]

454. The **morning** is wiser than the evening.

455. Beat the board, sound the alarm and remember **Moscow.**
[An incendiary fire.]

456. To some people **Moscow** is a mother, and to others a stepmother.

457. You cannot get pity from **Moscow.**
[Too large.]

458. In **Moscow** there is never a scarcity of bread.

459. No bones are broken by a **mother's** fist.

460. The **mouth** is more often enticed by the stomach than the stomach by the mouth.

461. To fall into **mud** is not a virtue, but it is a disgrace to remain there.

462. A good **name** replaces a shirt that is missing.

463. **Napoleon** was an animal, taking what his stomach whispered to him.

[Current after 1812 and still quoted.]

464. Where **necessity** speaks it demands.

465. Where there is a **neck** there will be a yoke.

466. The **need** knows no price.

467. When the **needle** sees the dagger it calls out " My brother ".

468. Where goes the **needle**, there goes the thread.

469. Buy not the house, buy the **neighbour.**

470. Love your **neighbour,** but put up a fence.

471. A near **neighbour** is better than a distant relative.

472. He who throws nettles over his **neighbour's** fence has them growing again in his own garden.

473. In our **neighbour's** hands the morsel always appears big.

474. You cannot sew buttons on your **neighbour's** mouth.

475. Where **nettles** thrive roses cannot grow.

476. In the field, **Nicholas** is the common God. (*Military proverb.*)

[St. Nicholas is the patron saint of soldiers.]

477. The darkness of **night** is surer than the light of day.

478. " **No** " lives by " Yes ".

479. Ten flowers together will make a **nosegay.**

480. With seven **nurses** the child loses its eye.

481. An empty **nut** is worthy of a hollow tooth.

482. They perished like the **Obry** [Avari].

[This proverb was quoted in Nestor's *History in the 13th Century* and is often used to-day. Slavonic tribes living in South Russia were constantly attacked and defeated by non-Slavonic people, called in Slavonic " Obry " (in Latin " Avari "). The Slavs invoked their gods' wrath on the aggressors, and it so happened that once the Obry were smitten with a pestilence which caused them to die one and all. Since then the proverb is quoted in Russia when a number of people die at the same time.]

483. One should not kiss the **occasion** that has a dirty mouth.

484. Who has not been to **Odessa** has not seen dust.

485. If you talk to an **official** you must talk roubles.

486. Do not know too much or you will grow **old.**

487. The cure for **old age** is the grave.

488. **Onion** and garlic are born brothers.

489. He who has an **order,** would like to hang it on his forehead ; he who has ten, buttons his coat over them.

490. Be fathers to **orphans.**

491. The road to the **other world** is the same from everywhere.

492. When the geese arrive from the south the peasant descends from the **oven,** and when the geese go south the peasant climbs up to the oven.

[i.e. spring and autumn.]

493. If you get into the **pack** you need not bark, but wag your tail you must.

494. If you give the **pain** freedom you will have to lie down and die.

495. When the old Adam is turned out, an angel must guard **paradise.**

496. Even under a single fir-tree with a crust of bread is **paradise.**

497. They did not live like people, nor die as **parents.**

[The dead were generally called parents and were remembered on the Parents' Saturdays, and the sense of the proverb is that whoever leads a bad life will not be remembered after his death.]

498. Console the **parson** and die.

499. The **parson's** eyes and the wolf's jaw will eat what they see.

500. The last is only the **parson's** wife.

[Russian clergyman is not allowed to remarry.]

501. A life like that of the **parson's** wife.

[The Russian clergyman has to treasure his wife, since he must not remarry.]

502. Eternal **peace** only lasts till the first fight.

503. Make **peace** with men, and quarrel with your sins.

504. The **peasant** carries the sack, whatever you put in it.

505. Every **peasant** is proud of the pond in his village, because from it he measures the sea.

506. The noblemen's quarrels can be read on the backs of the **peasants.**

507. One hears **pedestrians** sing most of the riding songs.

508. The **pie** is the dinner's enemy.

[i.e. heavy pie served at beginning of dinner.]

509. Give the trough and the **pigs** will appear.

510. You have the **pleasures,** but the pleasures have got you.

511. One with the **plough** and seven with the spoon.

512. You cannot hide between the **plough** and the harrow.

[i.e. the peasant cannot make both ends meet by means of his husbandry alone without recurring to outside pursuits.]

513. In the next world every **pockmark** turns into a pearl. (*Sectarian.*)

[Bigoted hatred of vaccination.]

514. When God made the world He sent to the **Poles** some reason and the feet of a gnat, but even this little was taken away by a woman.

515. The devils live in a quiet **pool.**

516. In a still **pool** swarm devils.

[The reference is to Vodyany, or water sprite.]

517. **Poverty** is no crime.

518. **Poverty** is not a sin, it is something worse.

519. What you cannot **praise** do not disparage.

520. The **prayer** " Our Father " is short but it saves.

521. Whatever a man **prays** for, he prays for a miracle.

522. A **present** looks for a present.

523. One loves the **priest** and another his wife.

524. The **priest** and the cock sing on an empty stomach.

525. To be a complete man one should have spent three years at a public school, one at a University, and two in **prison.**

526. Never be sure that you will be free from a knapsack or **prison.**

[Knapsack carried by beggars.]

527. Don't be afraid of a loss, then you will get **profit.**

528. **Profits** and losses walk in the same shoes.

529. **Profits** don't live without losses.

530. You would not know where to put all the **profits** if there were no losses.

531. The word of the Tsar is a **proverb.**

532. There is no disputing a **proverb,** a fool, and the truth.

533. For the sake of a **proverb** a peasant walked to Moscow.

534. The **proverb** comes from the intellect, and the intellect from the proverb.

535. A good **proverb** does not strike one in the brow, but full in the eye.

536. There is no **proverb** without a grain of truth.

537. **Proverbs** are butterflies, some are caught, others escape.

538. **Proverbs** are the coins of the people.

539. A **purse** cries before leaving the pocket.

540. There is no market for empty **purses.**

541. **Ready money** is a wizard.

542. Who gives many **reasons** tells many lies.

543. A man's **reception** is according to his coat ; his dismissal according to his sense.

544. The **reckoning** does not spoil friendship.

545. From the front entrance, a **refusal ;** from the back entrance, a welcome. (*Corruption.*)

546. **Relatives** are friends from necessity.

547. We are **relatives,** we have dried our rags in the same sun.

548. **Religion** has two children, love and hatred.

549. A good **reputation** sits still ; a bad one runs about.

550. He will be **rich** for whom the rouble prays.

551. Even the doorway of the **rich** is ashamed of the poor.

552. Whoever is **rich** is my brother.

553. One must pluck the **rich ;** the poor are bare.

554. If heaven rained milk, only the **rich** would have pitchers to catch it in.

555. Climbed into **riches** and forgot his kinsmen.

556. Anything can happen—even the **rich man** can knock at the poor man's door.

557. The **rich man** gets calves ; the poor man children.

558. The **rich man** wonders how the poor man lives, but God helps him.

559. **Right** is a piece of gold which may be cut into strips.

560. Trust the **river** but do not trust the brook.

561. Even a great **river's** glory ends at the sea.

562. One **road** for the fugitive and a hundred for the pursuer.

563. Where the **road** is straight don't look for a short cut.

564. For **rotten goods** a blind buyer.

565. A word spoken by him is like a present of a **rouble.**

566. The **rouble** in the lake is cheaper than the kopek in the meadow.

567. The strength of the **rouble** is in the kopek.

568. He is happy for whom the **rouble** prays.

569. When **roubles** fall from heaven there is no sack ; when there is a sack roubles do not fall.

570. There are no ties between **Russia** and the summer.

[Snow-bound more than half the year.]

571. In **Russia** as one must ; in Poland as one wants to.

[This proverb no doubt refers to the fact that there was no serfdom in Poland when it still existed in Russia.]

572. **Russia's** joy is drink. (*Saying of Prince Vladimir, The Holy, Xth Cent.*)

573. If you beat a **Russian** he can even make you a watch.

574. A **Russian month** can wait.

[Because the calendar was thirteen days behind.]

575. **Rust** eats iron.

576. Mother **rye** feeds all the fools alike, but wheat chosen people only.

577. An empty **sack** cannot stand up.

578. One's own **sadness** is dearer than another's gladness.

579. Among the **saints** there was not a single one with auburn hair.

580. In order to know a man you must eat a pud of **salt** with him.

[A pud is 40 Russian lb.]

581. The language of the **sand-hills** does not know the name " Granite ".

582. He who scratches a **scar** is wounded twice.

583. Not he is a good **scribe** who writes well, but he who erases well.

584. Put your **secret** in the mouth of the Bosphorus and it will tell it to the Black Sea.

585. **Self-interest** is a fire which first consumes others and then self.

586. Without praise you cannot **sell**; without disparagement you cannot buy.

587. He who buys the **serf's** arms buys also his feet.

588. You may **serve** a hundred years, but you will not earn a hundred turnips. (*Military proverb.*)

589. **Seven** don't wait for one. (*Community proverb.*)

590. To **shave** destroys the image of God.

[The beard held in veneration.]

591. Make thyself a **sheep**, and the wolf is ready.

592. The **shell** is needed till the bird is hatched.

593. The **shepherd's** boy is a shepherd.

594. He was born in a **shirt.**

595. The **shore** likewise belongs to the sea.

596. Who owns the **shore** owns the fish.

597. The road from Piter [St. Petersburg] to **Siberia** is shorter than from Siberia to Moscow.

[Banishment to Siberia and the unlikely return.]

598. To a **sick man** even honey tastes bitter.

599. It is not the **sick man** who is moody, it is his illness.

600. The **sighs** of the happy are only featherweight.

601. Out of **sight,** out of heart.

602. A good **silence** is better than a bad dispute.

603. Every wise man has a measure of **simplicity.**

604. **Sin** has no master.

605. A **sin** of gold is followed by a punishment of lead.

606. The husband's **sin** remains on the threshold; the wife's enters the house.

607. A repentant **sinner** is more worthy than ten saints who never succumb to temptation.

608. If thou lovest **sledging,** love to pull thine own sledge too.

609. The **smoker** is brother to the dog. (*Sectarian.*)

610. After much **snow,** much bread; after much water, much grass.

611. One drowns more in **soil** than in water.

612. A **soldier's** span is twenty-five years.

[Length of military service in Russia, first half of XIXth Cent.]

613. A **soldier's wife** is neither a wife nor a widow.

[Compulsory service 25 years.]

614. He who gives his **son** a rope should not complain if he binds his hands.

615. One **son** is no son; two sons is no son; but three sons is a son.

[i.e. sure of one living.]

616. With one **son** you can walk, with two you can ride, but with three you must stop at home.

617. If you have no devil in the house, take in a **son-in-law.**

618. With us it is **sorrow,** but it is our own.

619. **Sorrow** follows in gaiety's footsteps.

620. Whoever **sows** by the calendar winnows very little.

621. Seven axes are together, but two **spinning-wheels** are apart.

[i.e. men and women.]

622. Two scythes can lie together, but two **spinning-wheels** never.

[Discord among women.]

623. A dry **spoon** scratches the mouth.

624. **Spring** and autumn are riding on a piebald mare.

[i.e. changeable weather.]

625. The swallow starts the **spring** and the nightingale finishes it.

626. In a strange place even **spring** has no charm.
627. The **spring** will show everything.
628. Either **squire** or lost.
629. There are seven **squires** to every peasant.
    [i.e. oppressed by everyone.]
630. The **squirrel** climbs up the painted fir and dies of hunger.
631. It is hard for a man who **stands** to talk to one who is seated.
632. Where can we get it unless we **steal** it? (*Military proverb.*)
633. A stationary **stone** gathers moss.
634. Bury it as a **stone** in water, only bubbles at the top.
635. In a **storm** grass fares better than trees.
636. "What are you **suffering** from?"—"Just as you wish, sir."
    [Reply to a doctor.]
637. He who avoids the **sun** will always be cold.
638. Men carry their **superiority** inside; animals outside.
639. The breast of a **swan,** the walk of a peacock, the eyes of a falcon, and the eyebrows of a sable.
640. Perished like a **Swede** at Poltava. (*Historic Russian proverb.*)
    [Charles XII of Sweden led his army in battle, and lost at Poltava to the Russians, 1709.]
641. A **sword** does not bend and gold does not rust.
642. The worst bit is always last on the **table.**
643. One **talks** of what hurts one.
644. A **tar dealer** smells of tar.
645. **Tea** is the Chinese arrow which has pierced the Russian heart. (*Sectarian proverb.*)
646. **Tears** come more often from the eyes than from the heart.
647. Are there **tears**—there is conscience.
648. The **tenth** man is guilty.
    [When the actually guilty man is unknown.]
649. One does not put "**Thank you**" in one's pocket.
650. For timber, even a parson is a **thief.**
651. The altin [about $\frac{3}{4}$*d.*] **thief** is hanged, and the poltina [about one shilling] thief is honoured.
652. The **thief** is no thief, the fence is the thief.
653. There is no greater **thief** than a master tailor.
654. Take thy **thoughts** to bed with thee, for the morning is wiser than the evening.
655. If the **thunder** does not break, the peasant does not cross himself.
656. If you **tickle** yourself you can laugh when you like.
657. Stolen **timber** also burns.
658. With **time** an ear of barley becomes a jug of beer.
659. **To-day** is not without its tomorrow.
660. **To-morrow** has no end.
661. When the wise man makes an arm of his **tongue,** he makes it a shield and not a sword.
662. My **tongue** is my enemy.
663. The licking **tongue** may make a wound.
664. Your **tongue** will get you to Kiev [city in S.W. Russia].
665. The air has a sharp **tooth** which has already devoured many palaces.
666. Where it is thin, there it gets **torn.**
667. A **trade** does not ask for bread, it feeds you.
668. Whoever **trades** grieves.
669. A man can hang himself from his own **tree** as well as from his neighbour's.
670. Whichever way the **tree** is bending, it will fall.
671. The **tree** is felled in the forest and the splinters fly to the village.
672. Everybody loves the **tree** which gives him shelter.
673. A **tree** which gives too much or too little shade should be cut down.

674. Even **truth** gets drowned when gold comes to the surface.

675. **Truth** may be harsh, but pleasing to God.

676. Russia cannot exist without a **Tsar.**
[Before 1917.]

677. The **Tsar** cannot see for the hedge.

678. A drop of water in the eyes of the **Tsar** costs the country many handkerchiefs.

679. When the **Tsar** has a cold all Russia coughs.

680. When the **Tsar** has smallpox the Empire is pock-marked.

681. The **Tsar** has three hands but only one ear.

682. God is very high and the **Tsar** is a long way off.

683. The **Tsar** is gracious, but not so his kennel-keeper.

684. If the **Tsar** makes you a present of an egg he takes from you a hen.

685. One's body belongs to the **Tsar,** one's soul to God, and one's back to the squire.
[Conditions before 1861.]

686. When a **Tsar** reigns who has only one leg he issues an ukase ordering limping.

687. When the **Tsar** sins the Empire must do penance.

688. Without the **Tsar** the earth is a widow.

689. The day is the **Tsar's,** but the night is ours. (*Military proverb.*)

690. The **Tsar's** rouble is worth more than one hundred kopeks.

691. " **Under-salting** " is on the table ; " over-salting " is on the cook's back.

692. In the next world **usurers** have to count red-hot coins with bare hands.

693. **Vaccination** is the seal of anti-Christ. (*Sectarian.*)

694. The **veil** that covers the face seldom covers beauty.

695. Every Russian place is a " **village** ".

696. The **village** stands by the needle and by the harrow.

697. In **vinegar** sharpness is a virtue.

698. Many would be regarded **virgins** if it were not for their looks.

699. You cannot drink water, it is not **vodka.**

700. **Vodka** is aunt to wine.

701. The **Volga** is a good horse, it will drive anything.

702. Don't **vouch** for three things—a watch, a horse, and a wife.

703. He who **walks** is not a comrade to him who rides.

704. Who has not experienced **want** cannot appreciate happiness.

705. Good **wares** praise themselves.

706. If not by **washing,** then by mangling.

707. The ends into the **water.**
[The throwing of vanquished people into the water with stones tied to them. Shemyaka in Norgorod : John IV in Norgorod.]

708. Into the sack and then into the **water.**
[The Court of the Mordvins—a tribe living in east of European Russia.]

709. Downstream the **water** carries ; upstream necessity.
[Volga boatman. Timber carried downstream ; upstream grain which required a team of men.]

710. Within a Russian hour much **water** flows.
[Ancient calculation of time according to the quantity of water flowing out of a container.]

711. Wherever **water** flows it will find a way.

712. The more abundantly **water** gushes from its source, the less is the source esteemed.

713. Where **water** has been, there it will be ; where money once went, there will it go again.

714. You must drink the **water** of the river you are travelling on.

715. The ninth **wave** is fateful. (*Naval superstition.*)

716. Where **wealth** is established it is difficult for friendship to find a place.

717. Those who **wed** once wail always.

718. The **wedge** must fit the hole.

719. One **weeps** more rarely with one's heart than with one's eyes.

720. Do not spit into the **well**—you may have to drink out of it.

721. He who has **wheat** also wants rice.

722. There is no **whip** for those that deceive themselves.

723. Wear your **whiskers** round your shoulders.
[i.e. look back.]

724. He has not known misfortune who has not married a young **widow.**

725. A **widow** is spared by God but not by men.

726. To be a **widow** is to be ducked in water.

727. **Widow,** thou shouldst sew thy sleeves wide to have somewhere to put calumnies.

728. Into a **widow's** house even shavings are thrown.

729. Freedom spoils [even] a good **wife.**

730. Having a good **wife** and rich cabbage soup, other seek not.

731. Do not wish for any other blessing than a good **wife** and rich soup.

732. Beat your **wife** before dinner and again before supper.

733. If your **wife** flatters you she has ill designs.

734. The **wife** is dear twice: when led into the house and when led out of the house [in a coffin].

735. A **wife** is not a balalaika, you cannot hang her on the wall.
[Balalaika, Russian musical instrument.]

736. A **wife** is not a pot, she will not break so easily.
[Wife beating.]

737. A **wife** is twice kind—on her wedding day and at her funeral.

738. Love your **wife** like your soul, and shake her like a pear-tree.

739. The more you beat your **wife,** the better will be the soup.

740. Beat your **wife** with the butt end of an axe; if she falls down, sniffs and gasps, she is deceiving, give her some more.

741. Choose your **wife** with your ears rather than with your eyes.

742. If your **wife's relations** arrive, open the gate; if your own arrive, shut the gate.

743. It is better to give through the **window** than to stand beneath the window.
[Beggars and alms. Alms were given by the rich through the window to the poor standing underneath.]

744. He is happy who doesn't drink **wine.**

745. Bread puts one on his feet; **wine** throws one off.

746. For him who stands on top of the tower there is no other season than **winter.**

747. Learn to go naked in summer that you may do without a fur in **winter.**

748. No union between **winter** and summer.

749. It is easy to be **wise** for yesterday.

750. To every **wish** there is a patience.

751. Lord, there are so many nasty things in the world, and Thou hast still created **wives.**

752. Whatever is grey is a **wolf.**

753. The **wolf** eats even the counted sheep.

754. If you live with **wolves** you must howl as a wolf.

755. It is better to put out to sea in a leaking boat than to entrust a secret to a **woman.**

756. When the devil cannot get he sends a **woman.**

757. A man and a dog are always out of doors, but a **woman** and a cat are always indoors.

758. Where the devil is powerless he sends a **woman** as his messenger.

759. Do not love a **woman** because she is young, nor cast her off because she is old.

760. Like a **woman** dug into the ground.
[Punishment of wives for the murder of their husbands by being buried neck-deep in the ground and left to starve.]

761. A **woman** has got seven Fridays in the week.

762. The flattery of a **woman** has no teeth, but it would eat the flesh off your bones.

763. A **woman** has seventy-seven thoughts at once.

764. A **woman** is a pot, everything put in will boil.

765. A chicken is not a bird; a **woman** is not a human being.

766. A **woman** is no witness against her husband. (*Tsar Alexei Mihailovich's code, Ch. X.*)

767. **Woman** most often complains without reason, lies deliberately, weeps visibly, and laughs secretly.

768. There is nothing sincere in the weeping of a **woman,** or the limping of a dog.

769. Beat a **woman** with a hammer and you'll make gold.

770. The wise man only sees in **woman's** tears water in the eyes.

771. Every man is a **woman's** son.

772. **Woman's** span of life is forty years.
[Russian peasant women lose their youth early.]

773. **Woman's journey** is from the oven to the threshold.

774. Do what you like with **women** and cattle.

775. When hens cackle eggs are laid; when **women** cackle none are there.

776. **Women** have long hair but short brain.

777. A live **word** is more precious than a dead letter.

778. Golden **words** often come from a heart of copper.

779. If we eat seeds there will be no need to **work.**
[During a hard winter seeds are often ground for flour.]

780. Mix **work** with leisure and you will never go mad.

781. One never tires **working** for himself.

782. The **world** doesn't end in a wedge.
[i.e. room for all.]

783. The **world** is a child and love its father.

784. The **world** stands on concord and love.

785. You cannot kill a beast without a **wound.**

786. The **years** have raced by like spring waters.

787. Between a woman's **"Yes" and "No"** you cannot insert the point of a needle.

788. What the **young one** begs for the grown up throws away.

789. **Youth** has the almanack in his heart; old age in his head.

790. A **zolotnik** is small but dear.
[Zolotnik = 1/96th of a lb.]

UKRAINIAN (RUTHENIAN OR MALO-RUSSIAN OR LITTLE RUSSIAN)

1. Do not ask the old people for **advice,** but those who have suffered.

2. Ask people's **advice,** but decide yourself.

3. Yellow **apples** keep longer than red ones.
[Said of pale-looking but healthy people.]

4. **Bacon** is not for dogs.

5. **Baptize** only what is born.
6. As the **block,** so the chip.
7. **Blood** is no water.
8. Man began to learn when he became short of **bread.**
9. Men, not Tartars, will give you a piece of **bread.**
10. Without "Our Father" there is no **bread.**
11. The generous will want **bread** himself.
12. They gave me **bread** when I had no teeth.
13. Light a **candle** even for the devil's sake.
14. Good **cattle** find every pasture good.
15. The **chastising** cane came from heaven.
16. Although he chirps, he is no **chick.**
17. Small **children** give you headache; big children—heartache.
18. What small **children** wear out and pigs eat no one sees.
19. Love your **children** with your heart, but train them with your hands.
20. The **child's** finger-ache gives its mother heartache.
21. Nobody can betray you so completely as your favourite **concubine.**
22. **Courteous** asking breaks even city walls.
23. First the shed, then the **cow.**
24. A married **daughter** is only a neighbour.
25. One **day** before you is better than ten years behind you.
26. Praise the **day** in the evening.
27. Do not count the **days** of the year which may never be yours.
28. There is no repentance after **death.**
29. Good **deeds** travel far; bad ones further.
30. The **destitute** does not live, but dies by inches.
31. He is not **destitute** who has little, but he who thirsts after riches.
32. What the **devil** brings he also takes away.
33. Where the **devil** could not reach he sent the old woman.
34. Black **devil,** white devil—always devil.
35. It is in the still muddy waters that the **devils** dwell.
36. Niggers paint their **devils** white.
37. It is not the old who **die,** but the inactive.
38. The **dog** does not know how to swim until the water reaches his ears.
39. The **dog** is a lion in his own home.
40. Better a **dog** to-day than a horse yesterday.
41. A **dog** will never pass another.
42. Dread silent **dogs.**
43. Even **dogs** hear when it suits them.
44. He who associates with **dogs** learns to pant.
45. He who goes to bed with **dogs** wakes up with fleas.
46. Only what is seen is **envied.**
47. There is no **evil** without some good in it.
48. What the **eyes** do not see the heart does not desire.
49. Doubt even your **eyes,** still less trust other people's words.
50. **Failure** teaches you more than success.
51. Who dies for his **faith** [religion] gains a kingdom.
52. Mock not the **fallen,** for slippery is the road ahead of you.
53. Through one action—**famous;** through another—infamous.
54. There is no salvation through excessive **fasting.**
55. Of ready-cut logs it is easy to make a **fire.**
56. Who owns the bank owns the **fish.**
57. Caution is no cowardice, even **fleas** are armed.
58. He who **flies** high falls low.
59. **Flies** never alight on boiling **pots.**

60. Who is not strong at twenty, married at thirty, and rich at forty, is a complete **fool.**
61. The **fool** carries his heart on his tongue; the wise carries his tongue in his heart.
62. To a **fool** the ocean is knee-deep.
63. **Fools** rejoice at promises.
64. If there is a marsh there will be **frogs.**
65. Another's **fur coat** does not warm you as your own.
66. Who is doomed to the **gallows** will never be drowned.
67. Do not look into the mouth of a **gift horse.**
68. Who **gives** at once gives twice.
69. Who **gives** in necessity doubles his gift.
70. The **goat** sued the wolf, and all that was left of him was his beard and horns.
71. No one makes contracts with **God.**
72. Only the living can praise **God.**
73. **God** gave the mouth; He will give bread also.
74. Whatever **God** gives throw gratefully into your bag.
75. **God** in heaven; father on earth.
76. **God** sells wisdom for labour and suffering.
77. Allied with one **God** thou wilt conquer one hundred enemies.
78. When **God** wishes, even water can burn.
79. Whom **God** wishes to punish He first deprives of his reason.
80. A man is **good** if he makes others better men.
81. For a big man a big **grave.**
82. He is **guilty** who is not at home.
83. **Happiness** has horns; misery feet.
84. Who looks for **happiness** outside his own home is chasing after his own shadow.
85. There is no **happiness** without jealousy.
86. Do not become too **hard,** lest you get broken.
87. Do not enter where your **head** cannot pass through comfortably.
88. The **head** is God-like; the flesh swine-like.
89. As your **heart,** so is your word.
90. Another's **hearth** does not spread the same warmth as your own.
91. In your own **home** even the walls help you.
92. Your own **home**—your own jurisdiction.
93. Suffer, Kossak! you will drink **honey** above.
94. Who becomes **honey** shall be eaten by flies.
95. You ride as you like on your own **horse.**
96. On a borrowed **horse** you cannot travel far.
97. The **hump-backed** is straightened only in his grave.
98. The **husband** is the law to his wife.
99. The maker of **idols** does not worship them.
100. **Ignorance** does not commit sins.
101. To murder a **Jew** is to remove forty sins from off one's soul.
102. Sit as crookedly as you like, but **judge** justly.
103. As we **judge** men, so men judge us.
104. **Justice,** like oil, will come to the surface, however deeply you have sunk it.
105. **Justice** never sinks nor burns.
106. With **justice** you can make a tour around the world; with injustice you cannot cross the threshold.
107. Where three men are **Kossaks,** two of them become judges to the third.
108. Not until old age, but until death we **learn.**
109. If there is **life** there will be a cure.
110. Walk with a **lord,** but keep a stone under your arm.

111. **Love** and blindness are twin sisters.
112. **Love** and fear cannot be hidden.
113. **Love** tells us things which are not.
114. Say a good word for a bad **maiden**; of a good one you may say what you please.
115. Two women—a **market**; three—a fair.
116. Preserve me, O God, from a second **marriage** and from a third removal.
117. He will never regret who rises early and **marries** early.
118. Even the walls of a house weep when the **master** is away.
119. Three times **measure,** cut once.
120. When the **mill** grinds—flour; when tongues grind—trouble.
121. The **miser** pays twice.
122. Wherever there are men there is also **misfortune.**
123. When **misfortune** is asleep, do not wake her.
124. The road to **misfortune** is short.
125. Without **money**—without hands.
126. The **moon** also shines, but does not warm.
127. Two cannot dine off one **mouse.**
128. Flay a **muzhik's** [peasant's] skin off to-day and he will grow a new skin during the night.
129. One **nail** is driven out by another.
130. It is easy to undress the **naked.**
131. Wisdom adorns **old age.**
132. **Opportunity** brings success.
133. An **owlet** is a beauty in the eyes of its mother.
134. Master **passion** cannot be hidden.
135. **Physicians** and judges murder with impunity.
136. The **pig** knows no meal-hours.
137. Grant, O God, no horns to the **pig,** nor any riches to the muzhik [peasant].
138. The **ploughman** has no time for mischief.
139. He who **ploughs** will sing.
140. He perished like the Swede at **Poltava.** (*Historic proverb*).
    [Charles XII of Sweden led his army in battle and lost at Poltava (1709) to the Russians.]
141. Too long **pondering** brings no resolution.
142. **Poverty** is no vice but something far worse.
143. Whose **power,** his will.
144. Amongst **priests** be a priest; amongst deacons, a deacon; amongst wolves, howl; amongst pigs, devour.
145. Flies and **priests** can enter any house.
146. The **rich** and pigs are appreciated after their death.
147. May you be as **rich** as the earth.
148. To the **rich** even devils lay eggs.
149. After the **rich** even devils run with trays of cakes.
150. He is **rich** who does not know either what he has or what he has not.
151. Every **road** has two directions.
152. Every **rouble** bears a sin.
153. One **rouble**—one genius; two roubles—two geniuses.
154. If there are backs, **saddles** will not be lacking.
155. You must be a **saint** to judge and condemn others.
156. Only **saints** may censure others.
157. The **satiated** does not believe the hungry.
158. Who has been **scalded** with hot soup blows on cold water.
159. **A secret** is a friend; an enemy if you confide it.
160. In **service** no companionship.
161. To a good **sheep** good pasture.
162. Do not kill the **sheep** to take her wool.
163. If you do not live you do not **sin.**
164. No **sin**—no salvation.
165. As many steps a man has paced, so many **sins** has he committed.
166. The more you know the less will you **sleep.**

167. Who has been bitten by a **snake** dreads even earthworms.

168. The **soil-tiller's** hands are muddy and black, but his loaves are sweet and white.

169. Do not ask me whose **son** I am, but who I am.

170. Better a **sparrow** in the granary than an eagle in heaven.

171. It is easier to **speak** than to say something.

172. Defile not the **spring** from which you may drink.

173. **Sufferers** are saved.

174. Not the old, but the one who **suffers** much is wise.

175. Not all **sunshine** warms.

176. Respect thy **teachers** more than thy parents.

177. Bite your **tongue.** [Lest you offend.]

178. He whose **tongue** is arrested by his front teeth will never offend

179. You can never tie up people's **tongues.**

180. Bend the **tree** only while it is young.

181. Tell the **truth** and try to escape.

182. There is no freedom outside **Ukrainia.**

[Current throughout Ukrainia.]

183. Praise the **uplands,** but sow in the lowlands.

184. Who does not gather up, **walks** more easily.

185. Even **walls** have ears.

186. Still **waters** sap the cliffs.

187. Do not praise your **wife** before seven years.

188. Your first **wife** is sent to you by God; the second by man; the third by the devil.

189. If a husband does not beat his pretty **wife** three times a day, she trains her feet to jump over the house.

190. If a man is too old, it is his **wife's** fault.

191. Sow **winds** and you will harvest tempests.

192. Who sells **winds** will be paid in smoke.

193. The **winter sun** is like a step-mother; it shines, but does not warm.

194. **Wives,** razors, and horses should never be lent.

195. The **wolf** does not fear the sheep-dog, but his collar of nails.

196. Trust not the laughing **woman** and the weeping man.

197. If a **woman** is cold, it is her husband's fault.

198. Mistrust the **woman** who speaks only of her virtue.

199. **Work** as if you were to live for ever; pray as if you were to die to-night.

200. Half the **world** leaps, the other half weeps.

201. Who **wrongs** his people wrongs his children.

202. **Youth**—folly; old age—illness.

SERBIAN

(Including Serbo-Croatian)

1. In **affluence** do not be proud; in penury do not humiliate yourself.

2. You ask for the **age** of houses and property, but a wise man is always young. (*S.-Croatian.*)

3. Don't let your **age** ask "Where was your youth?" (*S.-Croatian.*)
4. When an **ant** gets wings it perishes. (*S.-Croatian.*)
5. Even an **ant** is six feet tall when measured by its own foot.
6. Even **ant** talks to ant. (*S. Croatian.*)
7. An **apple** that ripens late keeps longest.
8. The **ass** carries wine but drinks water. (*S.-Croatian.*)
9. The **ass** does not know how to swim till the water reaches his ears.
10. A small **ass** everyone mounts.
11. What **autumn** carries in, winter carries out.
12. It is the **back door** that harms the house. (*S.-Croatian.*)
13. It is not God that saves the **bag** but the string. (*S.-Croatian.*)
14. **Bargain** like a gypsy but pay like a gentleman. (*S.-Croatian.*)
15. When the **bear** dances at your neighbour's, prepare your house to receive him. (*S.-Croatian.*)
16. He who has a **beard** will find a comb.
17. Whose **bed** is warm his dinner is cold. (*S.-Croatian.*)
18. Even **beech leaves** are good when they are fried in butter. (*S.-Croatian.*)
19. Better to **beg** from house to house than from son to son.
20. A shy **beggar**—an empty pocket.
21. Only a **beggar** can count his wealth.
22. A **beginner** is worse than a sinner. (*S.-Croatian.*)
23. **Belief** is easier than investigation.
24. It is easier to **believe** than to ask.
25. Not even a **bell** always rings the same way.
26. Don't touch the **bell** or it will ring. (*S.-Croatian.*)
27. The **belly** has no windows.
28. "**Better**" does most harm to "good". (*S.-Croatian.*)
29. Don't **bite** if you don't know whether it is bread or stone. (*S.-Croatian.*)
30. **Blame** a man where he can hear you and praise him where he cannot.
31. In the land of the **blind** the one-eyed sees much.
32. If it doesn't give out in the **bottle** it won't in the glass. (*S.-Croatian.*)
33. Better gain on **bran** than lose on gold. (*S.-Croatian.*)
34. Alas for him who sits on one **branch.** (*S.-Croatian.*)
35. **Brandy** doesn't know the judge.
36. Blessed are the hands that knead the **bread.**
37. Cut **bread** is easy to eat.
38. Whose **bread** you eat, his song you sing. (*S.-Croatian.*)
39. **Brothers** are brothers, nevertheless cheese costs money.
40. **Business** is sometimes a mother and sometimes a stepmother.
41. A man with no **business** of his own collects other people's business. (*S.-Croatian.*)
42. **Cabbage** is the best invalid, it needs only a little water. (*S.-Croatian.*)
43. Where the **calf** has gone let also the lead go.
44. No one's **candle** ever burnt till daybreak.
45. Light one **candle** to God and two to the devil.
46. It is not bad occasionally to light a **candle** to the devil.
47. Short **candles,** near sparks. (*S.-Croatian.*)
48. The ointment of the **cane** is miraculous. (*S.-Croatian.*)
49. Other people's **cares** sleep beside your feet. (*S.-Croatian.*)
50. Oats pull the **cart** out of the mud.
51. Don't make a credit out of **cash.**
52. Who doesn't feed the **cat** feeds the mice.

53. If the **cattle** are quiet the pen isn't small. (*S.-Croatian.*)
54. **Cattle** die without witness. (*S.-Croatian.*)
55. Who **cheats** me once is a rascal; who cheats me twice is a deserving man.
56. A **cheese** that weeps and a whisky that warms are worth something.
57. Who takes the **child** by the hand takes the mother by the heart. (*S.-Croatian.*)
58. In a strange home **children** grow fast. (*S.-Croatian.*)
59. Every house has a black **chimney.** (*S.-Croatian.*)
60. You may seek your own, even on a **church altar.** (*S.-Croatian.*)
61. The moonlight accentuates the silence of the **churchyard,** the sunshine the clamour of the market-place.
62. Dirty **clothes** are washed at home.
63. If a **coal** doesn't scorch it will blacken.
64. Hidden **coals** scorch worst. (*S.-Croatian.*)
65. The **coals** under the slack burn you most.
66. In every house there are always **cobwebs.** (*S.-Croatian.*)
67. Day can dawn even without the **cock.** (*S.-Croatian.*)
68. Whatever has to **come** comes soon.
69. Who dresses first will **command** the rest.
70. Give me a **comrade** who will weep with me—one who laughs with me I can easily find myself.
71. You can get to **Constantinople** by asking the way.
72. Don't **cook** more than your vessel will hold.
73. Even the **copper** has ears. (*S.-Croatian.*)
74. **Covetousness** is the world's peace-breaker.
75. First the stall, then the **cow.** (*S.-Croatian.*)
76. The **cow** runs as far as its rope goes. (*S.-Croatian.*)
77. A **crow** doesn't peck out a crow's eyes.
78. Pet the **crow** till you get a hawk. (*S. Croatian.*)
79. A married **daughter** is but a neighbour.
80. Who does not beat his **daughter** will beat his breast [lit. knee]. (*S.-Croatian.*)
81. Do not praise the **day** before the nightfall.
82. If the **day** is short the year is long. (*S.-Croatian.*)
83. What is **dearer** is sweeter. (*S.-Croatian.*)
84. When the house burns down, the **debt** flies up on top of the chimney.
85. **Debts** are bad companions.
86. Who **decries** wants to buy. (*S.-Croatian.*)
87. **Devil** and old woman are always together. (*S.-Croatian.*)
88. What the **devil** brings the cross will take away. (*S.-Croatian.*)
89. The **devil** can make a pot but not the lid. (*S.-Croatian.*)
90. When the **devil** catches your coat-tails, rip them off.
91. Even the **devil** waits for a soul. (*S.-Croatian.*)
92. There is only one way to be born and a thousand ways to **die.**
93. I **die,** the world dies. (*S.-Croatian.*)
94. **Dirt** is dirt but takes a part in work.
95. What one can **do** all can do. (*S.-Croatian.*)
96. The bone binds the **dog.**
97. Give a **dog** a bone not to bark at you.
98. Never did a **dog** bite but he healed it with his coat. (*S.-Croatian.*)
99. The **dog** is brother to the dog. (*S.-Croatian.*)
100. A **dog** last year is a dog this year.
101. When they want to **kill a dog** they say it is mad.

102. The **dog** which has swum the Danube once will swim it again. (*S.-Croatian.*)

103. A **donkey** must not die before his grass grows.

104. To the **donkey** the sea is only knee deep.

105. When the **door** is wide even a blind man can enter easily.

106. Wherever you go leave the **door** open behind you.

107. Only great gentlemen and dogs leave the **doors** open behind them.

108. What starts **downstream** doesn't return upstream.

109. Who **drinks** on credit gets twice drunk.

110. If everyone tells you you are **drunk,** go to bed—even if you are perfectly sober.

111. The more **eggs,** the thicker the soup.

112. Preserve me, God, from what a man can **endure.**

113. Though your **enemy** be like an ant, beware of him as of a lion. (*S.-Croatian.*)

114. Man never has **enough.**

115. **Eve** is nearer to us than Adam. (*S.-Croatian.*)

116. It is bad enough with **evil** but worse without it.

117. No **evil** comes alone without a great dowry. (*S.-Croatian.*)

118. Even **evil** seems good when you are used to it. (*S.-Croatian.*)

119. Words shake but **examples** attract. (*S.-Croatian.*)

120. Who has large **eyes** doesn't see well.

121. A shining **face** needs little water.

122. Three women and a goose make a **fair.**

123. Who bows to both east and west is of no **faith** at all.

124. Save me from my **family** ; I will protect myself from my enemies.

125. A large **family**—quick help.

126. Do a man a hundred **favours,** but neglect him once, and he'll forget them all.

127. Who is born with **feathers** flies early. (*S.-Croatian.*)

128. Who gives a **finger** will give a hand.

129. Just two ends and the middle and all will be **finished.**

130. If your neighbour's house is on **fire,** look to your own.

131. He who warms himself by the **fire** must first put up with the smoke.

132. A **fisherman's mother** seldom dines, a hunter's never.

133. The **flood** goes but the sand remains.

134. You can't say **florin** till you've said farthing.

135. Who **follows** everyone does wrong ; who follows no one does worse.

136. Cast thy **food** down the stream, it will come back to thee up the stream.

137. Avoid both the **fool** and the saint.

138. Heaven help the legs governed by a **foolish head.**

139. What is taken by **force** is cursed.

140. Neither cut down all the **forest** nor go home without any wood.

141. **Fortune** at first gives you a glass brimming over with blossoms ; woo her again and she hands you a glass full of wine ; marry a third wife and the glass is filled with poison.

142. If **fortune** does not come to meet you, you will not be able to catch her even when riding.

143. When the **fox** crosses the ice, then you can take a cannon over.

144. A foolish **fox** is caught by one leg, but a wise one by all four.

145. Look at the eye of a **friend** and the foot of an enemy.

146. It is a good thing to have a **friend** even in hell.

147. Don't believe in **friends** at table, but at the prison door.

148. Flies and **friends** come in the summer. (*S.-Croatian.*)

149. Preserve me, O Lord, from my **friends ;** from my enemies I can defend myself.

150. If you like to get **friendship** from a man, say only a good word about him in his absence. If you like to pacify a dog, say a good word to his face.

151. **Friendship** rides after luck. (*S.-Croatian.*)

152. It is easy to drive a **frog** into the water.

153. When the **frog** sees how the horse is shod it takes its own feet to the blacksmith.

154. What matter what blossom it is if there is no **fruit ?**

155. Ripe **fruit** falls of itself. (*S.-Croatian.*)

156. There is no worse **fruit** than that which does not ripen. (*S.-Croatian.*)

157. Even a good **game** palls.

158. It is a lesser sin to burn a church than to speak evil of a **girl.**

159. Speak good of a bad **girl** and what you like of a good one.

160. **Give** with your hands and get back with your feet.

161. He need not wait his turn who holds the **glass.**

162. Before an empty **glass** no need of grace.

163. A **goat** has two kids ; the skin of one covers a drum, the other a Bible.

164. If the **goat** lies his horn doesn't.

165. It is the fate of the **goat** to wear horns. (*S.-Croatian.*)

166. Solitude is full of **God.**

167. **God** and poverty make us wise.

168. Pray to **God** and row towards the shore.

169. **God** closes one door but opens a score.

170. When **God** deals out fortune He doesn't ask whose son you are.

171. **God** does not love a man who never suffered.

172. **God** does not pay every Saturday.

173. **God** gave the rudder but the devil the sails. (*S.-Croatian.*)

174. Even **God** has a mother.

175. **God** has feet of wool but hands of iron.

176. **God** is with the worker.

177. **God** knows whose oil burned in the ikon lamp.

178. **God** made a beard for Himself first.

179. **God** save you from butting with the horned, and hair-pulling with the bald. (*S.-Croatian.*)

180. Better what **God** sends than man asks. (*S.-Croatian.*)

181. If you love **God** you cannot fear Him ; if you fear Him you cannot love Him.

182. In **God's** pen there are all kinds of cattle. (*S.-Croatian.*)

183. There is no more powerful enemy than **gold.**

184. A **golden aim** gilds even an ungolden beginning.

185. Do a **good deed** and throw it in the sea, it won't sink.

186. Send a **good deed** down the stream, and if the fish don't recognize it, God will. (*S.-Croatian.*)

187. **Goods** speak—vendor barks.

188. An empty **gourd** sings in the wind. (*S.-Croatian.*)

189. **Gratis** is both cheapest and dearest.

190. The **grave - digger** buries exactly what the cradle lulled to sleep.

191. A **guest** and a fish stink on the third day. (*S.-Croatian.*)

192. Even our favourite **guest** is a bore after three days.

193. A **guest** knows no fast. (*S.-Croatian.*)

194. " Work a little, steal a little," said the **gypsy** to his son when he taught him maxims of life. (*S.-Croatian.*)

195. A **gypsy** was made king and the first man he hanged was his own father.

196. Tangled **hair** wants a wide comb. (*S.-Croatian.*)

197. When you cannot catch anything, do not stretch out your **hand.**

198. What is dear may come to be **hated** ; what is hated may come to be dear. (*S.-Croatian.*)

199. Above every bird there is a **hawk.** (*S.-Croatian.*)

200. Two **hazel nuts** make an army for the walnut.

201. If the **head** begins to stink there is no doubt about the tail. (*S.-Croatian.*)

202. The bigger the **head,** the worse the headache.

203. If you don't like **headaches,** have less to do with other people. (*S.-Croatian.*)

204. The **healthy man** doesn't count his years. (*S.-Croatian.*)

205. There cannot be a pool on a **heap.**

206. No devil will miss his **hell.** (*S.-Croatian.*)

207. A **hen** that cackles much lays little.

208. Some can **hide** behind a leaf, and for others not even an oak-tree is enough.

209. A little **hole** waits for a big one. (*S.-Croatian.*)

210. You can't live on the **Holy Ghost.**

211. There is most room at **home.** (*S.-Croatian.*)

212. Don't be **honey** for others to lick, nor bile to poison them. (*S.-Croatian.*)

213. If you are **honey** people will lick you ; if you are poison they will spit you out.

214. Those who take **honey** together lick fingers together. (*S.-Croatian.*)

215. **Hope** is a bad woman. (*S.-Croatian.*)

216. Who can't beat the **horse** beats the saddle. (*S.-Croatian.*)

217. A good **horse** has many faults, a bad horse only one.

218. Tend your **horse** like a brother but ride him like an enemy.

219. It is easy to curse the pedestrian when you are on **horseback.** (*S.-Croatian.*)

220. Who grudges the nail will lose the **horseshoe.**

221. What is play to **horses** is death to donkeys.

222. Where **horses** play asses die. (*S.-Croatian.*)

223. Everyone may not know what is sweet or rich, but everyone knows what is **hot.** (*S.-Croatian.*)

224. **Hounds** hunt best hungry.

225. In a poor **house** even cobwebs are of use. (*S.-Croatian.*)

226. A **house** is not built on earth, but on a woman.

227. Our **house** is the Lord's.

228. Of other **households** little, of your own less, of yourself nothing. (*S.-Croatian.*)

229. **Hunger** has no eyes.

230. Send the **hungry** at dinner-time and the timid at nightfall and they'll soon come back. (*S.-Croatian.*)

231. "**I haven't**" and "I can't" are the same thing.

232. Who was never **ill** isn't dear to God. (*S.-Croatian.*)

233. **Illness** comes by litres and goes by grams. (*S.-Croatian.*)

234. Though it rained **ink** I could not be any blacker. (*S.-Croatian.*)

235. A real **Jew** will never pause to eat till he has cheated you.

236. When I'm on a **journey,** grant me, God, what is in the mind, not of my mother, but of my wife. (*S.-Croatian.*)

237. **Judas** never sleeps. (*S.-Croatian.*)

238. If **justice** doesn't die injustice never will.

239. Exaggerated **justice** is great injustice.

240. To eat the **kernel,** first break the shell. (*S.-Croatian.*)

241. Loved by a **king** is not loved. (*S.-Croatian.*)

242. The **king's beard** is worth as much as three summer rains.

243. A **king's loaf** has nine crusts. (*S.-Croatian.*)
244. Who doesn't want to **kiss** finds he has a sore mouth. (*S.-Croatian.*)
245. An empty **knapsack** is heavier to carry than a full one.
246. Have me and you don't **know** me ; lose me and you know me.
247. You a **lady,** and I a lady, who will milk the cow?
248. A gentle **lamb** sucks two mothers.
249. Travel with the **lame** and you are sure to stumble.
250. Oh! that I was as wise when going to **law** as I was when coming away.
251. The more **laws,** the less justice.
252. Better a lean agreement than a fat **lawsuit.**
253. After the **lawsuit** one party is naked and the other in his shirt. (*S.-Croatian.*)
254. **Learn** in tears, rejoice in song.
255. A good **lie** is a poor man's treasure.
256. When you **lie,** lie so that you yourself believe it is the truth. (*S.-Croatian.*)
257. He **lies** boldly who comes from afar.
258. **Lies** dine well, but sup badly.
259. **Lightning** strikes no nettles.
260. Where the **lion** lunches he won't sup.
261. The **lioness** has but one cub, but it is a lion.
262. The first **litre** pays for the rest.
263. A **loan** is given in order to be repaid.
264. **Loans** don't die but repayments do.
265. Do not count the **loaves** as they go into the oven.
266. When an old **log** takes fire you can't put it out. (*S.-Croatian.*)
267. Even the **Lord's tomb** isn't guarded for nothing.
268. **Love** and wealth don't want company. (*S.-Croatian.*)
269. **Love** for love, but cheese for money. (*S.-Croatian.*)
270. The greatest **luck** is a good husband, and the next a loyal servant. (*S.-Croatian.*)
271. If you don't meet **luck** you will never overtake it. (*S.-Croatian.*)
272. **A man** is hard to find but easy to recognize.
273. **A man** likes to be better than everyone else but worse than his son.
274. **A man** may be your brother but he should pay for his cheese.
275. The man who lunches and **marries** early will never regret either.
276. To **marry** young is early ; to marry old is late.
277. **Marry** with your ears, not your eyes. (*S.-Croatian.*)
278. The eyes of the **master** fatten the horse.
279. Woe to the **master** of the house whom the servant teaches.
280. Where **meat** is eaten bones are gnawed.
281. Cheap **meat**—soup on the dust-heap. (*S.-Croatian.*)
282. **Men** are thickly sown but grow sparsely. (*S.-Croatian.*)
283. **Mending** keeps the home together. (*S.-Croatian.*)
284. If a **merchant** were always to profit he wouldn't be called a merchant, but a profiteer.
285. Enter the **mill** and you come out floury.
286. In a **mill** you have to speak twice.
287. The **miser** ends by giving more, and the lazy man by going further.
288. **Misfortune** has a long tail. (*S.-Croatian.*)
289. Welcome, **misfortune,** if you come alone! (*S.-Croatian.*)
290. Advice after **misfortune** is like medicine after death.
291. **Money** and the devil cannot be quiet.

292. Save white **money** for black days. (*S.-Croatian.*)

293. **Money** has a hundred legs when it goes and only two when it comes.

294. **Money** stands twice counting.

295. In company even **monks** marry.

296. **Morning** is cleverer than evening.

297. It is better to suffer the satiated **mosquitoes** to stay than to admit the hungry ones.

298. Look at the **mother** before affiancing the daughter.

299. **Mountain** to mountain never; man to man ever. (*S.-Croatian.*)

300. Two **moves** and one fire come to the same thing. (*S.-Croatian.*)

301. **Mud** doesn't settle in flowing water.

302. When **nail** drives nail the truth is driven out.

303. The **nation** is a strong mare.

304. A **needle** may pass through gold and silver, but will still come out naked.

305. A **needle** pricks young skin sooner than old. (*S.-Croatian.*)

306. Three hundred things at **night** and nothing in the morning.

307. Who sells **night** buys day.

308. **Night** has ears; day eyes.

309. With whom before **noon,** like him after noon. (*S.-Croatian.*)

310. Every face agrees with its own **nose.**

311. When the **oak** falls everyone steals its wood. (*S.-Croatian.*)

312. He who **offends** writes in the sand; he who is offended writes in marble.

313. Sew the **old** and waste your thread; kiss the old and waste your days. (*S.-Croatian.*)

314. Who does not mend the **old** will never wear the new.

315. Two things are bad for an **old man,** a young wife and a good cook.

316. Where all are **one-eyed** you had better close one eye.

317. A man may go when he pleases to his own **orchard.**

318. An **owlet** is a beauty in the eyes of its mother.

319. Be as patient as an **ox,** as brave as a lion, as industrious as a bee, and as cheerful as a bird.

320. True **pain** cannot be concealed.

321. Who **pays** not with his hands pays with his soul. (*S.-Croatian.*)

322. Where the **pence** jingle philosophers are silent.

323. Beware of the man who swallows his **phlegm.** (*S.-Croatian.*)

324. Everything comes, even **pie.** (*S.-Croatian.*)

325. **Pierce** with a gimlet where you can't pierce with an awl. (*S.-Croatian.*)

326. What fills the **pig** fattens it.

327. Where the **pig** gets his fat he leaves it. (*S.-Croatian.*)

328. When the **pig** is full he overturns the trough.

329. A clean **pig** is never fat.

330. **Play,** but then put your pipe away.

331. Don't **play** if you don't want to lose. (*S.-Croatian.*)

332. Though we are brothers our **pockets** are not sisters.

333. A forked **pole** won't go into the ground.

334. He is not **poor** who never had, but he who had and lost.

335. There is no stronger castle than a **poor man.**

336. Who eats **porridge** has no toothache. (*S.-Croatian.*)

337. The fly doesn't settle on a boiling **pot.** (*S.-Croatian.*)

338. Little **pot**—little handle.

339. Call me a black **pot** providing you don't break me.

340. Well-ordered **poverty** is great wealth.

341. If you want to know a man, put **power** in his hands.

342. Alas for him whom all **praise.**

343. There is no need to **pray** for rain and death.

344. Good deeds are the best **prayer.** (*S.-Croatian.*)

345. Heaven **preserve** you from whiskered women, horned sheep and beardless men. (*S.-Croatian.*)

346. First **prick** yourself with a needle, then another with an awl.

347. Let a goat into a wood or a **priest** into a village and neither will go hungry.

348. **A priest** is no man. (*S.-Croatian.*)

349. Give the **priest** the priest's, and the lord the lord's, then leave them alone. (*S.-Croatian.*)

350. An idle **priest** will baptize even goats.

351. He who drowns in a **puddle** needs no other sea.

352. **Quarrel** and repentance are brother and sister. (*S.-Croatian.*)

353. Where there is no **quarrel** there is no peace.

354. As the **question,** so the answer.

355. When it is going to **rain** it begins with a few drops. (*S.-Croatian.*)

356. To the poor even a **relative** is an enemy; to the rich even an enemy is a relative.

357. He is **rich** who asks nothing of others.

358. Go to the **rich** with empty honours and to the poor for hospitality.

359. Don't fear the shiny but the grimy **rifle.** (*S.-Croatian.*)

360. Of a loaded **rifle** one man is afraid; of an empty one two.

361. If you come with a **right** you will not come off well; if you come and are in the wrong you will not come off alive.

362. When the **river Pliva** falls into the river Vrbas it loses its voice.

363. Back foot foremost all the time and you get to **Rome.**

364. When a bird sleeps with a **rook** it will caw like a rook.

365. **Rust** does not affect gold.

366. In fair weather all are **sailors.** (*S.-Croatian.*)

367. If you have the Lord for your uncle it is easy to become a **saint.** (*S.-Croatian.*)

368. **Save** while your sack is full. (*S.-Croatian.*)

369. There is no better judge than the **scales.**

370. Who is **scorched** smells. (*S.-Croatian.*)

371. Earth swore to heaven that all **secrets** will be known. (*S.-Croatian.*)

372. To **serve** the old is a duty, one's equals a kindness, and the young a humiliation. (*S.-Croatian.*)

373. A **servant** come back is like warmed-up soup. (*S.-Croatian.*)

374. He who has not **served** cannot command.

375. Better reaped in the **sheaf** than praised in the ear. (*S.-Croatian.*)

376. To a wrecked **ship** every wind is contrary.

377. What is the use of a wide world if your **shoes** are narrow? (*S.-Croatian.*)

378. Who possesses the **shore** possesses the sea; and the castle is his who holds the plain.

379. Don't take your **sickle** into another man's crop.

380. **A sick man** eats little but spends much.

381. You can fathom everything but **silence.**

382. He who preserves a wise **silence** speaks well.

383. Time and patience turn the mulberry leaf into **silk.** (*S.-Croatian.*)

384. Worn **silk** doesn't rot. (*S.-Croatian.*)

385. Kissing the young and giving short measure to the rich are no **sin.**

386. The greatest **sin** is not to know sin.

387. One **sin** is much, but a thousand good deeds are little.

388. Who **sings** plans no evil. (*S.-Croatian.*)
389. Who boasts his **sins**, sins twice. (*S.-Croatian.*)
390. When the head **sins** the tail pays. (*S.-Croatian.*)
391. One **sister** marries another and one barrel sells another.
392. Who **sleeps,** his dinner sleeps. (*S.-Croatian.*)
393. A **smith** has tongs to save his hands.
394. **Smoke** and perfume from the censer are inseparable.
395. Till the **snake** swallows the snake it cannot become a dragon.
396. Late **snow** is white manure. (*S.-Croatian.*)
397. Wet **soil** needs little rain.
398. The **soldier** in peace time is to us what the stove is in summer.
399. Every village sings its own **song.**
400. Where it is **sore** a man always rubs. (*S.-Croatian.*)
401. If **sorrow** could not talk it would die. (*S.-Croatian.*)
402. It was a **spark** that burned down Moscow. (*S.-Croatian.*)
403. For empty **speech** there is plenty of room.
404. **Speed** broke its neck. (*S.-Croatian.*)
405. What a man doesn't **spend** he gains. (*S.-Croatian.*)
406. If it weren't for the wind the **spiders** would web the sky.
407. Whatever is **spoken** either has been or will be.
408. Beware of him who **squints** or has red hair.
409. A **stick** has two ends.
410. You can't deceive the **stomach.** (*S.-Croatian.*)
411. Better put tired hands on a full **stomach** than fresh ones on an empty stomach. (*S.-Croatian.*)
412. He is a **stranger** whom nobody knows. (*S.-Croatian.*)
413. Who wants to straighten a crooked **street** will have to pull down many houses.
414. Who knows much **suffers** much.
415. The **sugar** didn't fall into the water in order to melt.
416. **Summer** is most loved in winter, and winter in summer.
417. Who is warmed by the **sun** cares little for the moon. (*S.-Croatian.*)
418. It is the same **sun** that is born and dies on the same day. (*S.-Croatian.*)
419. What **Sunday** buys, Monday does not return.
420. Short **supper**—long life.
421. Let each **sweep** before his own door.
422. If everyone **swept** before his own door all the streets would be clean. (*S.-Croatian.*)
423. With **swine** one must speak like swine.
424. Alas for the house where the **sword** obeys and the hemp commands. (*S.-Croatian.*)
425. He who **thanks** thinks not of repayment.
426. A **thief** goes from needle to bullock and from bullock to gallows. (*S.-Croatian.*)
427. A mean father has **thieves** for children.
428. The **thin place** tears first.
429. Save **three** and the fourth will fall by itself into your hands. (*S.-Croatian.*)
430. The home **threshold** is the highest hill to cross.
431. Who **ties** tightly will untie easily.
432. **Time** builds a castle and also demolishes it.
433. What isn't **to-day** will be to-morrow. (*S.-Croatian.*)
434. The **tongue** has no bones.
435. The **tongue** speaks best moistened. (*S.-Croatian.*)
436. The price of a **trade** is more than gold.
437. No **trade** without tools.
438. Better to gain **trading** in straw than to lose by dealing in gold.
439. No one throws stones at a barren **tree.**

440. A bent **tree** even goats can climb.

441. In the forest **tree** leans on tree, so why not man on man?

442. Few **trees** by the roadside are not lopped. (*S.-Croatian.*)

443. The skilful man fells **trees**; the unskilful is felled by them.

444. Who hasn't wrestled with **trouble** doesn't know what is good.

445. Speak the **truth** and look which way to run.

446. Glass after glass and **truth** at last.

447. People always chastise the fiddler of **truth** with his own bow.

448. Better that a **Turk** drive you with a sword than a German with a pen. (*S.-Croatian.*)

449. **Ugliness** moves slowly, but beauty is in great haste.

450. By **using** our hands we become strong; by using our brains, wiser; by using our hearts, merciful.

451. Who goes round the **village** long enough will get either a dog-bite or a dinner.

452. The **vineyard** needs no prayers, but a hoe.

453. Don't **walk** in the mud when there is a dry path. (*S.-Croatian.*)

454. **War** is brother to no one.

455. **Warriors** in times of peace are like fires in summer.

456. The cane fetches the **water.** (*S.-Croatian.*)

457. If you want to drink **water** don't foul it.

458. Where **water** has flowed it will flow again.

459. Everyone has his own **way**; the donkey the old way.

460. Small **wealth**—small worry.

461. There is no **wealth** without pouring out one purse into another.

462. When the **weather** is good take your coat; when it is bad do what you like.

463. **White hands** like other people's work.

464. A **widow** is no maid and liver no meat. (*S.-Croatian.*)

465. A **widow's** wine is best. (*S.-Croatian.*)

466. When God wants to punish a man He gives him an only daughter for his **wife.**

467. It is sometimes right even to obey a sensible **wife.**

468. Twice only man rejoices, when he marries a **wife,** and when he buries her.

469. Who has no **wife** beats her every day.

470. The first **wife** fears her husband, the husband fears the second.

471. A **wife** is an evil that you can't do without.

472. Don't trust your crop till you put it in the granary, nor your **wife** till you put her in the grave. (*S.-Croatian.*)

473. When **wine** comes to an end, so does conversation; when money comes to an end, so do friends.

474. **Wine** says not "Come in", but "Sit down". (*S.-Croatian.*)

475. When it is **winter,** it is winter everywhere.

476. No **winter** till the frost, no spring till the sunshine, no gladness till it is shared. (*S.-Croatian.*)

477. He is a **wise man** who can be both foolish and sensible.

478. If you have nothing to do, be a **witness.** (*S.-Croatian.*)

479. A lucky man's **wives** die; an unlucky one's marry.

480. **Woe** to me without me. (*S.-Croatian.*)

481. Alas for the **wolf** after whom the dogs do not bark.

482. You can baptize the **wolf,** but he'll go back to the forest.

483. The **wolf** kills even numbered sheep.

484. Where the **wolf** lunches the fox easily sups.

485. Where a **wolf** once finds a sheep he will look again.

486. **Wolves** need no larder.

487. Where the devil fails he sends an old **woman.**

488. Fire, **woman,** and the sea, who can tell the worst of the three?

489. The only secret a **woman** can keep is the one she doesn't know.

490. **Woman** has long hair but short brains.

491. **A woman** reflects her husband in her face, and a man's wife is known by his shirt.

492. **Woman's** love is a devil's net. (*S.-Croatian.*)

493. With dry **wood** even green wood burns. (*S.-Croatian.*)

494. Dry **wood** gives no sap. (*S.-Croatian.*)

495. He who goes out to plunder the **wool** of others often comes back shorn himself.

496. From **word** to deed as from leaf to root.

497. Fair **words** butter no cabbage. (*S.-Croatian.*)

498. **Work** as if **thou** art to live a hundred years, and pray to God as if thou art to die to-morrow.

499. A man sees another's **work** better than his own. (*S.-Croatian.*)

500. Every **work** fears its own master.

501. The **world** lives on faith and tradition.

502. On a bitter **wound** bitter herbs. (*S.-Croatian.*)

503. A **wound** still in bandage easily opens.

504. The **year** has a large mouth. (*S.-Croatian.*)

SILESIAN

1. He who spits into an **ants' nest** gets swollen lips.

2. Years have no respect for **beauty.**

3. Those who think of every feather will never make the **bed.**

4. He who wears the thinnest **coat** must sit nearest the door.

5. One good **day** often costs several months of bad nights.

6. All **days** are brothers, but one seldom resembles the other.

7. No one **deceives** us more than our own thoughts.

8. The **donkey** that belongs to many is the first to be eaten by wolves.

9. The **eel** escapes quickest when it is held the fastest.

10. The longest day has also its **evening.**

11. Old **flesh** makes fat soup.

12. **Flies** settle most on thin horses.

13. **Friendship** is like bread, which only tastes good whilst it is fresh.

14. With time and leisure the **frog** hops a mile.

15. The **glasses** through which one beholds the world should be of gold.

16. Some folks' **grass** costs them more than other folks' flowers.

17. Thin **hands** make fat feet.

18. Under water is **hunger,** under snow bread.

19. The best **incense** comes from old trees.

20. A **kiss** without a beard is like broth without salt.

21. He who climbs a **ladder** must have his understanding in his feet.

22. The first night of **marriage** is generally the last night of love.

23. **Money** lost, little lost; time lost, everything lost.

24. So it goes in the world the one has the **money,** the other the purse.
25. So long as the **monkey** sits it isn't noticed that it has no tail.
26. That which reaches to the father's knees reaches to the **mother's heart.**
27. The world doesn't let itself be governed by the **pater-noster.**
28. He who feeds himself with a **quill** must stick it behind his ear.
29. The **rose** knows in whose hands it is—and the fire knows whose cap is burning.
30. When the **roses** are over one thinks no more of the thorns.
31. A little body can't make a big **shadow.**
32. Every day a thread, in the year makes a **shirt.**
33. It is better to tear one's **shoes** than the sheets.
34. One cannot request anything more from **snow** than water.
35. He who speaks **sows** and he who listens harvests.
36. **Sparing** comes too late when the butter is already on the bread.
37. One first realizes the value of a **thaler** when one has to borrow it from another.
38. **Three-quarters** is neither half nor all.
39. One must take what **time** brings.
40. **Time** wins and time loses.
41. The smaller the heart the bigger the **tongue.**
42. He who thinks it is always too soon comes always **too late.**
43. He who stirs up **water** everywhere will never get a pure drink.
44. Water teaches how to weep, **wine** how to sing.
45. In buying **wives** and melons there is always danger.
46. The best **women** are those of which one speaks the least.
47. A hard **word** is not always a hard heart.
48. A **word** spoken at the right moment is like a golden apple on a silver dish.
49. He who doesn't see the **world** doesn't know it.
50. The **years** know more than books.

SLOVAKIAN

1. **Abuse** is no argument against the use of a thing.
2. Kill your **anger** while it's small.
3. **Apples** do not fall far from the apple-tree.
4. Do not look for **apples** under a poplar.
5. You cannot pack **awls** in a sack.
6. A full **bag** is heavy, an empty one is heavier.
7. **Bellies** have no windows.
8. To the absent the **bones.**
9. Big **book,** great evil.
10. In whose **carriage** you ride, his song you sing.
11. If a **child** cuts its finger it has cut its mother's heart.
12. The **chip** does not fall far from the block.
13. Soft **clay** may be moulded at will.
14. The best-fitting **clothes** wear out fastest.
15. Why should the **cow** trouble to think if she has plenty of hay?
16. Amongst **cows** the bull is judge.
17. What the **cradle** has rocked the spade will bury.
18. Whom have not full **cups** made eloquent?

19. **Custom** and law are sisters.
20. A common **danger** produces unity.
21. Consider each **day** as your best day.
22. If the **day** is short, the year is not.
23. The young may **die** ; the old must.
24. I taught you to **dive** and you wish to drown me.
25. **Divide** and govern.
26. Feed the **dog** to bite you.
27. Bacon is not for **dogs.**
28. **Dogs** are wiser than many women, they do not bark at their masters.
29. An **eagle** does not catch flies.
30. What you like **eat.**
31. Who **eats** much knows little.
32. **Exiles** subsist on hopes.
33. Who sits on the ground fears no **fall.**
34. Nobody died from **fasting.**
35. He who accepts a **favour** sells his liberty.
36. **Fields** have eyes, forests ears.
37. Who blows into the **fire** will have smoke in his eyes.
38. When the **food** tastes best, stop eating.
39. **Force** finds many ways.
40. **Forgive** others, yourself never.
41. Deal with your **friends** as though they might become your enemies.
42. The giver adds value to the **gift.**
43. Who wishes to possess must **give.**
44. Who **gives** to me teaches me to give.
45. Only the living can praise **God.**
46. **God** does not pay every Saturday.
47. **God** gave, God took.
48. **God** gave the mouth—He will give bread also.
49. **God** remains debtor to no one.
50. **God** strikes us with one hand and caresses us with the other.
51. **God** wets you with His rain, but He also dries you with His sun.
52. He whom **God** wishes to punish He first deprives of his reason.
53. Do not expect **good,** but let evil not surprise you.
54. For **good** do not expect good.
55. Great **griefs** are mute.
56. **Guests** and fish stink on the third day.
57. Clean **hands**—free speech.
58. Everybody is the forger of his own **happiness.**
59. Good **health** will endure anything.
60. As your **heart**—so your word.
61. Such **heart**—such tongue.
62. Who **helps** quickly helps doubly.
63. The gates to **hell** are always open—even at midnight.
64. The walking **hen's** crop is always full.
65. Your **honour** is on the tip of your tongue.
66. The fast **horse** soon gets tired.
67. The **horse** wished for the yoke ; the ox for the saddle.
68. Three corners of the **house** rest upon the wife ; the fourth upon the husband.
69. The **husband** is the head ; the wife the crown on it.
70. The pretty woman wants three **husbands :** one to pay her debts, one to love her, and one to beat her.
71. **Illness** comes on a racehorse but departs on foot.
72. Painful **illnesses** are less dangerous than the painless ones.
73. Others' hands cannot scratch your **itch.**
74. What you cannot **jump** over bend under.
75. **Justice** is power.
76. The **language** of the true is always simple.
77. With each newly learned **language** you acquire a new soul.
78. Draw back and take a better **leap.**

79. What little John has **learned,** old John cannot unlearn.
80. Wherever there is some whispering of **leaves** there must be some wind.
81. **Little things** have their value.
82. He has **lived** twice who has lived unknown.
83. **Love** is sweet captivity.
84. Whom you **love** most from him will you suffer the worst.
85. The **master** of the house is the greatest servant.
86. I am the **master,** you are the master, but who will tend the pigs?
87. When you **master** yourself you will be a man.
88. **Measure** twice, cut once.
89. If you hurry you will catch **misfortune ;** if you go slowly she will catch you.
90. Count your **money ;** beat your wife.
91. Who has **money** has a devil ; who has none has two devils.
92. You cannot sew up people's **mouths.**
93. The mountains shook—a **mouse** was born!
94. A good **neighbour** over the wall is better than a brother over the sea.
95. Every stone you throw at your **neighbour's** roof will fall upon your own.
96. **Old men** are twice boys.
97. **Old people** have their teeth in their stomach.
98. As many heads, so many **opinions.**
99. Who runs too fast jumps over his **opportunity.**
100. An **owlet** is a beauty in the eyes of its mother.
101. The more the **path** is beaten the safer it is.
102. Who wishes to live in **peace** must carry fire in one hand and water in the other.
103. Who mixes himself with bran shall be eaten by **pigs.**
104. Be not the lid to every **pot.**
105. Every **pot** will have its lid.
106. **Poverty** is the mother of the arts.
107. Who is first silent in a **quarrel** belongs to a good family.
108. The **rich** and pigs are appreciated only after their death.
109. The **rich** need no brains.
110. Soon **ripe**—soon rotten.
111. Take rough **roads** and get to the stars.
112. Time and patience bring **roses.**
113. To every **saint** his candle.
114. Young **saint**—old devil.
115. What **satiates** also feeds.
116. Faithful **servants** — master's wealth.
117. The **shirt** is nearer to the body than the coat.
118. One **sin** begets another.
119. There are more **skins** of young animals on the market than those of the old.
120. Too much **sleep** becomes a pain.
121. **Sleep** is Death's brother.
122. Who **suffers** shall rule.
123. Hard against hard—a **spark.**
124. Who **speaks** much either knows much or lies much.
125. From a clear **spring**—limpid water.
126. As you put it so it will **stand.**
127. Not the hands feed the **stomach,** but the stomach the hands.
128. Everybody shuts out the setting **sun.**
129. Short **supper**—long life.
130. Only in water can you learn to **swim.**
131. Do not try to catch by the **tail** what you can catch by the horns.
132. By **teaching** we learn.
133. The good are always prone to **tears.**
134. Let your **teeth** bridle your tongue.
135. **Time** builds and destroys everything.

136. When nothing can help, **time** will.
137. Without **tools** no handicraft.
138. **Truth** begets hatred.
139. The **unknown** is always magnificent.
140. The **unwilling** alone is unable.
141. An ass to **Vienna**—an ass from Vienna.
142. Do not lean against a falling **wall.**
143. Pure **water** is the world's first and foremost medicine.
144. Everybody drives the **watercourse** to his own mill.
145. Great **wealth,** great slavery.
146. The worst **wheel** makes the biggest noise.
147. First **wife** from God, second from men, third from the devil.
148. Everything for a time, but a **wife** till death, and God for ever.
149. Praise water, but drink **wine.**
150. **Wine** and children speak the truth.
151. Pure **wine** unties the tongue.
152. The **wise man** counts only golden days.
153. He whose **wives** die and bees swarm will assuredly become rich.
154. Where the devil fails he sends an old **woman.**
155. Two old **women** and a goose—a market.
156. **Women** will keep silent only those things which they do not know.
157. Where there is **wood** there are chips.
158. **Work** is the mother of life.
159. Where the **wound** is there the hand will go.
160. The world remains for the **young.**
161. **Youth** is no virtue.
162. If **youth** knew and old age could!

SLOVENIAN

1. The **absent** get farther and farther away every day.
2. **Adversity** breathes virtue.
3. An **ant** is over six feet tall when measured by its own foot-rule.
4. The **apple** does not fall far from the apple-tree.
5. The ripe **apple** falls of itself.
6. An **ass** to Zagreb—an ass from Zagreb.
7. It is with men as with **asses,** whoever would keep them fast must find a good hold at their ears.
8. The **bargainer** buys, not the praiser.
9. Cheap things and good **bargains** empty your purse.
10. Who **bargains** much is the real buyer.
11. **Begin** well and do not fear the end.
12. Every **beginning** is difficult.
13. **Belief** is simpler than investigation.
14. Everybody thinks that every **bell** echoes his own thoughts.
15. What you **build** easily will fall quickly.
16. As it **came,** so will it go.
17. He is the fifth wheel to the **carriage.**
18. Time builds a **castle** and demolishes it.
19. Ten healthy [happy] **children**—eleven blessings!

20. Who is forced to go to **church** will not pray.
21. Let the **cock** over the doorstep and you will soon have him at the dresser.
22. One false **coin** spoils ten good ones.
23. The **contented** needs the least.
24. Who stops half-way has committed only half a **crime.**
25. In **darkness** all things are black.
26. Every **day** has its own fate.
27. Neither whisper to the **deaf** nor wink at the blind.
28. When the house burns its **debts** fly up the chimney.
29. **Despair** and hope are sisters.
30. Where the **devil** was unsuccessful he sent the old woman.
31. Man's life is like a drop of **dew** on a leaf.
32. Who sleeps with **dogs** will wake up with fleas.
33. If a **donkey** bide for a wedding, surely there will be either wood wanting or water scarce.
34. You cannot **enjoy** in peace what everybody likes.
35. **Enough** is better than much.
36. Three women and one goose make a **fair.**
37. Never laugh at others' **falls,** for the road ahead is slippery.
38. **Fate** sells what we think she gives.
39. **Fear** is hollow in its centre and around it there is nothing.
40. A falling **fence** is kicked by every passer-by.
41. When your neighbour's house is on **fire,** bring water to your own.
42. The wise warms himself at the **fire** ; the fool burns himself by it.
43. **Fish** begins to stink from its head.

    [i.e. corruption comes from the upper classes.]
44. Even a **flea** has its gall.
45. **Fortune** is accumulated by drops and is poured out by pails.
46. Small presents keep **friendship** warm.
47. The **frog** saw how horses were shod, so she also lifted up her foot.
48. **Fruit** is but wood if there be no bread with it.
49. Throw no stones at a **fruit tree** from which fruit falls of itself.
50. Your smallest **gift** may alleviate a great suffering.
51. Who gives to the poor lends to **God.**
52. **God** closes one door but opens ten.
53. If **God** drenches you with His rain, He will dry you with His sun.
54. Pray to **God** for a good harvest, but continue to hoe!
55. **God** gathers the clouds and disperses them also.
56. **God** knows why He shortens some people's wings.
57. **God** provides food for every bird, but does not throw it into the nest.
58. There is no **good fortune** which is not shadowed by misfortune.
59. Who **grasps** at everything holds fast nothing.
60. Who digs a **grave** for another falls into it himself.
61. Such **guest**—such feast.
62. For the uninvited **guest** the place is behind the door.
63. **Habit** is a shirt of iron.
64. One **hand** washes the other—both the face.
65. Bless the **hands** that plough and those that knead the bread.
66. In the house of the **hanged** speak not of ropes.
67. Whose **head** is made of bees'-wax must not come out in the sun.
68. Who has a good **head** will never lack hats.
69. Your own **head**—your own success or failure.
70. What does not come from the **heart** does not reach the heart.

71. Go everywhere but return **home** to live.
72. You cannot handle **honey** without licking your fingers.
73. The path of **honour** is made of snow—it soon melts away.
74. The lead goes with the **horse.** [i.e. when you sell him.]
75. Where **horses** play asses fall.
76. Build your **house** far from your relatives and close to a watercourse.
77. To a long **illness** the spade is the end.
78. For the **industrious** there is a loaf behind every tree and a penny under every stone.
79. The **inevitable** must be welcomed.
80. The **insulter** forgets but not the insulted.
81. Forget the **irreparable** and be less miserable.
82. When a **Jew** shakes you by the hand, count your fingers!
83. **Joy** and sorrow are next-door neighbours.
84. Rigorous **justice** is often injustice.
85. If you wish for the **kernel** you must break the shell.
86. The **lame** gets further than the sitter.
87. One is shielded by a **leaf**; another is not covered by the whole tree.
88. **Lend** sitting and you will run to collect.
89. **Lend** to a friend what you can afford to lose.
90. **Lend** with the hands, collect with the feet.
91. **Lies** may dine but never sup.
92. **Life** is ascending, descending, and running in the valley with an invisible hole [in it].
93. The **loaf** in another's hand is always bigger.
94. Grain by grain—a **loaf**; stone upon stone—a palace.
95. If **loans** were of any use, even wives would be lent.
96. If there are **loaves** there will be plenty of teeth.
97. **Love** is full of honey and gall.
98. A wise woman will **marry** the man who loves her rather than the one she loves.
99. **Marry** your son when you will —your daughter as soon as you can.
100. All **men** alone know all.
101. Everybody leads the water to his own **mill.**
102. Sudden **misfortune**—double misfortune.
103. **Misfortune** neither ploughs nor sows, yet she lives well.
104. **Mistrust** a man who speaks of his honesty more than a woman who speaks of her chastity.
105. Who **mistrusts** is mistrusted.
106. If you run away from a **mosquito** the sharper will its sting be.
107. As the **music,** so the dance.
108. **Necessity** breaks iron.
109. **Nettles** are never frost-bitten.
110. A sapling becomes an **oak.**
111. As many heads, so many **opinions.**
112. Seize **opportunity** by its beard, for it is bald behind.
113. Who **pays** back turns his back.
114. Only **physicians** may murder with impunity.
115. A bad **piastre** knows many people.
116. Who mixes himself with the bran will be eaten by **pigs.**
117. On a calm sea everybody is a good **pilot.**
118. When the **play** favours you most, turn your back on it.
119. The more a **plough** is used the brighter it becomes.
120. A small **pot** boils quickly.
121. Flies and **priests** can enter everywhere.
122. From **promise** to fulfilment as from flower to fruit.
123. Things **promised** are things due.

124. The experienced man is a small **prophet.**
125. Behind a **proud man's** ear a star rises, and it sets behind his heel.
126. Who comes out of a river fears no **rain.**
127. Where the carcass is, there will the **ravens** gather together.
128. He is **rich** who knows how to mend and do without.
129. He is **rich** who neither borrows nor flatters.
130. If there were no **riches** there would be no poverty.
131. There is no midway between **right** and wrong.
132. What **ripens** fast rots fast.
133. Slow **rivers** sap the banks.
134. Every **road** does not lead to Rome.
135. If it does not **run,** it drops.
136. An open **safe** will tempt even a bishop.
137. A small **saint** is big in a small church.
138. Who cannot **serve** cannot command.
139. Better even a crooked **settlement** than the straightest judgment.
140. Everyone knows best where his **shoe** pinches him.
141. There is no headache from **silence.**
142. Who is afraid of **smoke** will not enjoy the warmth of the fire.
143. Every **song** has its end.
144. Who **speaks** much either knows much or lies much.
145. The **spider** does not weave his web for one fly.
146. Who **spits** against the wind spits in his own face.
147. Overfill your **stomach** and load your feet.
148. **Stones** are thrown only at a fruit-bearing branch.
149. **Strangers** forgive—friends forget.
150. Who has **suffered** much remembers much.
151. Where there is **sunshine** there are loaves baked.
152. The **sun** shines nowhere as it shines at home.
153. The **sun** will come to shine also at our door.
154. Short **supper**—long life.
155. The hand that holds a **sword** should be kissed.
156. The **tear** of the pious does not fall to the ground.
157. **Tears** of purity and innocence never dry; they evaporate to heaven.
158. **Thieves** are only those who are not caught.
159. Big **thieves** hang little thieves.
160. The **threshold** is the tallest mountain.
161. **Time** saps everything.
162. Man is tied by his **tongue,** the bull by his horns.
163. Without **tools** there is no handicraft.
164. Who greases his way **travels** easily.
165. A rotten **tree** falls of itself.
166. One **tree** leans upon another, and man upon man.
167. A young **tree** you can bend at will.
168. The shadows of tall **trees** are long.
169. Tell the **truth** and flee!
170. The **victor** feels no fatigue.
171. You will know a **village** by its roads, and the master by his servants.
172. A **viper** is a viper, whether big or small.
173. Who **waits** sees and receives.
174. The hardest **walnut** has the smallest kernel.
175. Two hazelnuts are the **walnut's** army.
176. **Wares** which cannot sell themselves need advertising.
177. **Water** will run again where it once ran.

178. There is no great **wealth** without pouring out from one purse into another.
179. Who brings is **welcome.**
180. No **wheat** without chaff.
181. The **wife** is three walls, the husband one.
182. Good **wine** damages your purse —bad wine your stomach.
183. **Wives,** horses and razors should never be lent.
184. Who befriends a **wolf** must learn to howl.
185. The **wolf** will eat even counted sheep.
186. When you are chased by a **wolf** you call the boar your uncle.
187. **Woman** is a necessary evil.
188. Prosperity and beautiful **women** are the most treacherous things in the world.
189. **Women** have long hair, but short brains and faith.
190. Out of the same piece of **wood** both ikons and fans are made.
191. Who picks up all the **wood** soon finds his cart full.
192. By the side of dry **wood** the green will also burn.
193. **Youth** is not virtue.

SPANISH

(Including Castilian Galician, and Iberian)

An Introduction to this collection by Professor Aurelio M. Espinosa, Ph.D., Litt.D., LL.D., will be found on page xcviii.

1. The **abbot** dines off his singing.
2. There is no worse **abbot** than the one who has been a monk.
3. **Absence** is the mother of disillusion.
4. An affront, or **abusive word** from a master, and a husband, is never thrown in one's dish.
5. **Admiration** is the daughter of ignorance.
6. There is no price for good **advice.**
7. Beware of risking much if .he who gives **advice** is a poor man.
8. **Affliction** blinds reason.
9. That which from equal to equal is called an **affront,** from greater to lesser is called force.
10. He who does not look **ahead** remains behind.
11. God gives **almonds** to the man without teeth.
12. Since you have made the Church, make the **altar.**
13. That which is **another's** always yearns for its lord.
14. There is no **answer** to " Get you out of my house ", and " What have you to do with my wife ? "
15. The **ant** has wings to its own hurt.
16. I will give you the whole world, if you will give me **April and May.**
17. An orchard, a man that has but one eye, a servant, a colt, and a squinting woman, require **art** to manage them.
18. Don't **ask** of him who asked, and don't serve him who served.
19. It is other people's burdens that kill the **ass.**
20. Other people's worries kill the **ass.**
21. The son of an **ass** brays twice a day.
22. When the **ass** is dead, barley at his tail.
23. When all men say you are an **ass,** it is time to bray.
24. The **ass** knows well in whose face he brays.

25. An **ass** laden with gold overtakes everything.
26. The golden **ass** passes everywhere.
27. If a single man says that one is an **ass** then one must look behind one, but if two men say so, one must pray to God.
28. A bad **ass** trots near the house.
29. There is nothing for an **ass** which is better than a packsaddle.
30. **Avarice** is the only passion that never ages.
31. We were already twenty in family, so my grandmother had a **baby.**
32. **Bachelor,** a peacock; betrothed, a lion; wedded, an ass.
33. Many think to find **bacon** where there are not even hooks [to hang it on].
34. A **bad** thing never dies.
35. **Bad fortune** comes by arrobes, and goes by drams.

    [An arrobe is a Spanish measure of 25 lb. weight.]
36. It is the **bait** that tempts, not the fisher or the rod.
37. That which goes in with the **baptismal** cap goes out with the shroud.
38. He who does not intend to pay is not troubled in making his **bargain.**
39. A man that is prepared has half won the **battle.**
40. Little **beard,** little shame.
41. Men see **beauty** as a quality, women see quality as a beauty.
42. A man possesses **beauty** in his quality, and a woman possesses quality in her beauty.
43. He who makes his **bed** badly will work hard in the night.
44. When the **bed** is small lie in the centre.
45. No one goes to **bed** without learning something new.
46. When the **bee** sucks, it turns to honey; when the spider sucks, it turns to poison.
47. Help the **beetle** and it will carry your load.
48. Neither **beg** of him who has been a beggar, nor serve him who has been a servant.
49. The **beggar** has the right to ask the king for a light.
50. Never stand **begging** for what you have the power to take.
51. Don't **believe** him who comes from afar, but him who returns from it.
52. To **believe** is a courtesy from the tiles downwards.
53. He who **believes** too easily collects water in a sieve.
54. He who rings the **bell** is quite safe.
55. That is **best** which is near to very good.
56. **Bleed** him and purge him; if he dies, bury him.
57. Among the **blind,** squint-eyes was king.
58. Better an ounce of **blood** than a pound of friendship.
59. He who gives you a **bone** does not wish to see you dead.
60. By ever taking out and never putting in, one soon reaches the **bottom.**
61. A **bow** always bent gets either limp or breaks.
62. A **boy's love** is water in a sieve.
63. A sharp tooth for hard **bread.**
64. Griefs with **bread** are bearable.
65. Others' **bread** costs dearly.
66. **Bread** eaten is companionship dissolved.
67. **Bread** is relief for all kinds of grief.
68. She wanted better **bread** than can be made with wheat.
69. He who does not **breed** is always craving.
70. The pearls a **bride** wears on her wedding-day are the tears that she will shed.
71. When the enemy is fleeing, build him a silver **bridge.**

72. For him who does not like **broth** there are three cups of it waiting.
73. Between **brother** and brother, two witnesses and a notary.
74. The **brother** for a bad day.
75. A half **brother** is like a patch on a sack.
76. He who **builds** makes dirt with his silver and gold.
77. He who finds fault wants to **buy.**
78. Do you want to **buy** cheap? Buy of a needy fool.
79. Let him who does not know you **buy** you.
80. He who underrates a thing **buys** it.
81. By the street of "**Bye-and-bye**" one arrives at the house of "Never".
82. Buy a **capon** and a judge when you require them.
83. When there is mud on the road, oil the **cart.**
84. The **cat** always leaves its friend marked [scratched].
85. The scalded **cat** dreads cold water.
86. He who denies the **cat** skimmed milk, must give the mice the cream.
87. She alone is **chaste** who has never been sought.
88. He who does not **chastize** the small backside will chastize the big one.
89. He who **chastizes** one threatens a hundred.
90. Beauty and **chastity** have always a mortal quarrel between them.
91. A **chicken** is not hatched for itself alone.
92. Embraces and kisses don't make **children** but they ring for vespers [are the forerunners].
93. Beware of the man with a long **chin.**
94. On going into a **church** leave the world behind the door.
95. What the **Church** leaves, the Exchequer takes.
96. A **church** stone drops gold. (*Galician.*)
97. The **Church,** the sea, or the Court.

    [The three professions open to a man of birth in mediæval times.]
98. Fresh pork and new wine send a Christian to the **churchyard.**
99. The fortunes of the **clergy** come in by the door and go out by the chimney.
100. The spot always falls on the best **cloth.**
101. The best **cloth** has uneven thread.
102. Good **cloth** is sold in a chest.
103. Needle and thread are half **clothing.**
104. In the house where there are **cobwebs** the girls don't marry.
105. He who eats his **cock** alone saddles his horse alone.
106. Every **cock** crows on his own dunghill, and the hen all about the town.
107. It is a fine thing to **command,** though it is but a herd of cattle.
108. He who **covers** thee discovers thee.
109. He who eats the king's **cow,** in a hundred years pays for its bones.
110. He who takes away the occasion takes away the **crime.**
111. He who does not mix with the **crowd** knows nothing.
112. We breed **crows** to peck our eyes out. (*Spanish-American.*)
113. He that **cuts** does not deal.
114. A lucky man's first child is a **daughter.**
115. When a good offer comes for your **daughter** don't wait until her father returns from market.
116. Three **daughters** and a mother are four devils for the father.
117. He who has **daughters** to marry, let him give them silk to spin.
118. When God sends the **dawn** He sends it for all.
119. Take hold of a good **day.**

120. The **day** after is the pupil of the day before.

121. **Dead** men open the eyes of the living.

122. **Death** is as certain as life is uncertain.

123. **Death** is deaf.

124. Better to go to bed supperless than to get up in **debt.**

125. A man in **debt** is stoned every year.

126. He that sleeps too long in the morning let him borrow the pillow of a **debtor.**

127. **Debts** are like children, the smaller they are the more they scream.

128. When a master has **debts** he has thieving servants.

129. At the end of the year the **deceased** eats more than the living.

[i.e. fees paid for lawyers, etc.]

130. It is in the best cloth that one is the most **deceived.**

131. There is nothing like **deprivation** to excite content and gratitude for small mercies.

132. **Desire** and inclination combined find everything exquisite.

133. What is much **desired** is not believed when it comes.

134. **Desperation** is the mistress of the impossible.

135. Renounce the **devil,** and thou shalt wear a shabby cloak.

136. By the vicar's skirts the **devil** climbs up into the belfry.

137. The **devil** is not always behind the door.

138. Since the **devil** takes us may it be in a nice coach.

139. All things are **difficult** before they are easy.

140. The beginning of the cure is knowing the **disease.**

141. He that has a **disease** must open his purse and have patience.

142. God grant that **disputes** may arise that I may live. (*Legal proverb.*)

143. He who knows not how to **dissemble** knows not how to command.

144. The house where the **distaff** rules the sword is in a bad way.

145. Six men give a **doctor** less to do than one woman.

146. A draught of water on a salad deprives the **doctor** of a ducat; a draught of water on an egg deprives him of two.

147. Don't take every ill to the **doctor,** or every quarrel to the lawyer, or every thirst to the pitcher.

148. When **doctors** fast it is bad for the curés.

149. The lean **dog** is all fleas.

150. The **dog** is the same, he has only changed his collar.

151. Whoever gives a crust to another's **dog** loses both crust and dog.

152. From a silent man and from a **dog** that does not bark deliver us.

153. The **dog** that has a brother in the town is never a good barker.

154. The **dog** with the open eye.

[i.e. the waiter as he sleeps at inns.]

155. There is no better hunting than with old **dogs.**

156. The **dogs** bark, but the caravan passes.

157. A **dog's** faithfulness lasts all its life; a woman's till the first opportunity.

158. When one **door** closes, a hundred are barred.

159. When one **door** is shut, a hundred are opened.

160. An open **door** tempts a saint.

161. At an open **door** the just man sins.

162. It is no easy thing to guard a house that has two **doors.**

163. New **doors** for old houses.

164. Among the safest courses, the safest of all is to **doubt.**

165. In case of **doubt,** to abstain is the best.

166. **Dreams** are themselves nothing but dreams.
167. No one gets **drunk** with his own wine.
168. The pinnacles of high walls fall down, and the **dung-heaps** rise.
169. To **eat** and to scratch one has but to begin.
170. A little [to **eat**] in the morning is too little ; a little at dinner is enough ; a little at night is too much.
171. What you are not to **eat,** leave it to boil.
172. What you **eat** yourself never gains you a friend.
173. **Eating** a lot leads to eating a little.
174. In the house of an **enemy** have his wife for a friend.
175. If the **enemy** be in the water to the girdle, lend him thy hand to help him out ; if he be in to the shoulders, set hold on him and keep him down.
176. He is your **enemy** who is of your trade.
177. War with all the world, and peace with **England.**
178. That which we **enjoyed** for many days we pay for in one.
179. If **evil** were not blamed, good would not be praised.
180. The **evil** which issues from thy mouth falls into thy bosom.
181. He that **expects** despairs.
182. For him who sees much one **eye** is sufficient.
183. With the **eyes** a woman asks, takes, despises, and kills.
184. They who have only **eyes** are blind in the dark.
185. He that hath **eyes** in his head shall learn as long as he lives, and shall see what he shall see.
186. **Eyes** that see do not grow old.
    [Plea of curious people.]
187. You wash my **face.**
    [i.e. flatter me.]
188. The **face** without shame possesses the whole world.
189. There are but two **families** in the world, the " haves " and the " have-nots ".
190. In a **fan** of quality even if the paper tears the cane remains.
191. A **fast day** is the eve of a feast day.
192. **Fate** carries some on her wings and drags others on the ground.
193. Tho' the man commit a hundred **faults,** the woman must not let the wind blow upon her.
194. A drachm of **favour** weighs more than a hundred pounds of justice.
195. Do not ask as a **favour** what you can obtain by force.
196. He who is **feared** by many should fear many.
197. Leave the **feast** when most it pleases you. (*Castilian.*)
198. Not with whom thou art bred but with whom thou art **fed.**
199. The crop of the **fields** is always rich in hope.
200. He who watches over the **fig** tree eats its fruit.
201. Never show your wounded **finger** to the world.
202. Absence is the wind that puts out a little **fire** and fans a big one.
203. She is good who is close to the **fire** and does not burn.
204. A **fire** is easily kindled on a warm hearth.
205. A **fish** dies by an open mouth.
206. Our **flag** is blood and gold.
207. When thou seest thine house in **flames,** approach and warm thyself by it.
208. When **flatterers** assemble, the devil goes to dinner.
209. Everyone his own way of killing **fleas.**
210. April and May make **flour** for the whole year.
211. No **fly** dares approach a boiling pot.
212. The busy **fly** is in every man's dish.

213. **Fond** of lawyer, little wealth; fond of doctor, little health; fond of friar, little honour.
214. One must give way to a **fool** and a bull.
215. If every **fool** carried a stick, firewood would be scarce.
216. Every **fool** is in love with his own bauble.
217. Wise people say **foolish** things, and foolish people do them.
218. The Mother of God appears to **fools.**
219. The event is master of **fools.**
220. The sorrows of others are the consolation of **fools.**
221. If **fools** did not go to markets, the rubbish would never be sold.
222. Where your **foot** is, beware of my ear.
223. Until the end no one is **fortunate.**
224. **Fortune** has only one hair on her head, you must seize it if you want her to stay.
225. We have most to fear from **fortune** when we have the largest handful from her.
226. He who doesn't look **forward** falls backwards.
227. **Four things** put a man beside himself: a woman, snuff, cards, and wine.
228. It is not much to give the leg to him that gave you the **fowl.**
229. One turn of the lock is better than the conscience of a **friar.**
230. It is best neither to have a good **friar** for a friend nor a bad one for an enemy.
231. In a small house and on a wide road one recognizes a good **friend.**
232. There is no better mirror than an old **friend.**
233. When a **friend** asks there is no morrow.
234. There is no **friend** for a friend.
235. To a **friend** his faults.
236. Only one who was formerly a **friend** is an enemy.
237. A conciliated **friend** is a two-fold enemy.
238. It is a bad **friend** that covers with his wings and pecks with his beak.
239. Misfortunes and roads make **friends.**
240. In bad times false **friends** and flies disappear.
241. Amongst soldiers and **friends** compliments are superfluous.
242. With **friends** we must do until we can do no more, and pay until nothing is left us.
243. **Friends** who know one another salute from afar.
244. A blow from the **frying-pan,** if it doesn't hurt, blackens.
245. No one will meddle with a piece of **furniture** that has a mouth.
246. The **gallows** were made for the unlucky.
247. One may as well lose the **game** by a card too much as a card too little.
248. Where they **give,** they take.
249. He who is **given** [something] does not choose.
250. To no one what he **gives** seems little, nor what he has, much.
251. At the end the **Gloria** is chanted.
252. The lame **goat** has no siesta.
253. He that commits a fault and mends, recommends himself to **God.**
254. I am alone; I go with **God.**
255. Let that which is lost be for **God.**

    [A father making his will ordained that a cow which had strayed, if found should be for his children, if not, for God.]

256. The voice of the people is the voice of **God.**
257. **God** aids him who changes.
258. When **God** corrects He greatly afflicts.
259. **God** cures, and the doctor takes the fee.
260. When **God** gives the wound He gives the medicine.
261. **God** is always opening His hand.

262. He who is punished by **God** is deprived of justice.
263. **God** may love a poor man, but not a dirty one.
264. **God** never wounds with both hands.
265. **God** puts food into clean hands.
266. **God** sends us walnuts when we have no teeth.
267. Trust in **God** upon good security.
268. **God** works in a little hour.
269. Out of **God's** blessing into the warm sun.
270. Those whom the **gods** forsake, they blind.
271. It avails nothing to be **good,** but rather to look good.
272. When **good** comes, put it in your house.
273. To him who does not expect **good,** no ill can do harm.
274. The **good** that is done to-day constitutes the happiness of to-morrow.
275. In **good** the deed is more than the power [intention] and in evil the power [intention] is more than the deed.
276. He who is not **good** to himself, how can he be good to others?
277. Open your door to a **good day** and prepare yourself for a bad one.
278. If you would have a **good day** trim yourself; if a good month kill a hog; if a good year marry; if a good [life] turn clergyman.
279. Get a **good name** and go to sleep.
280. Who **gossips** to you will gossip of you. (*Spanish-American.*)
281. So **got,** so gone.
282. **Gout** is cured by walling up the mouth.
283. You may believe any good of a **grateful** man.
284. The sun, sorrows, and suppers fill the **graves.**
285. **Graves** are full of sufferings and suppers.
286. Of the **great** speak neither well nor ill, for if you speak well, you lie, and if ill, you place yourself in danger.
287. The **green** burns for the dry, and the righteous pay for sinners.
288. A **guest** and a fish stink in three days.
289. A **guest** is beautiful at his back.
290. Who repairs not his **gutter** repairs his whole house.
291. Break the leg of an ill **habit.**
292. **Half-way** is twelve miles when you have fourteen miles to go.
293. I don't want it, but drop it into my **hand.**
294. A garden, a squinter, a manservant, a colt, and an ogling woman, all need careful **handling.**
295. White **hands** cannot hurt.
296. Not all **haste** is the daughter of imprudence, nor all delay that of cowardice.
297. The edifice of **hate** is built up on the stone of affronts.
298. When your **head** aches, anoint your knee-pans.
299. Be not a baker if your **head** be of butter.
300. **Health** is a precious gift that God takes from the slothful man.
301. If thou wilt be **healthful,** make thyself old betimes.
302. He that would be **healthy** must wear the same clothes in summer as in winter.
303. The **heart** bears up the body.
304. The **heart** is no traitor.
305. Every way, or at every end, there are three leagues of **heart-breaking.**
306. Much on earth; and little in **heaven.**
307. When they give you a **heifer** be ready with the rope.
308. The **hen** lays upon an egg, that is the nest-egg.
309. It goes ill with the house where the **hen** sings and the cock is silent.

310. The **hen's** eyes are where her eggs are. (*Galician.*)
311. **High walls** sink, and dunghills rise.
   [i.e. humility is the mark of the truly great.]
312. He whose work is on the **high-way** will have many advisers.
313. His **home** is savoury whom God loves.
314. There is no **home** without a hush.
315. If you make yourself **honey** the flies will eat you.
316. **Honour** and profit are not found in the same sack.
317. The **horseshoe** that clatters needs a nail.
   [i.e. men boast of that quality which they really lack.]
318. Beware of a **host** who laughs and a priest who weeps.
319. A beautiful **hostess** or landlady is bad for the purse.
320. A **hot iron,** though black, can blister.
321. Every **hour** that passes wounds us, and the last kills us.
322. Every **house** is a world.
323. Sour wine, old bacon, and rye bread keep a **house** rich.
324. The greatest **humiliation** for a man is to give proofs that he is a man.
325. Love your **husband** as a friend, and fear him as an enemy.
326. A **husband** by the fireside is as bad as a pain in the side.
327. No man can be a good **husband** who can't eat a big breakfast.
328. He has already gained something who recognizes his **ignorance.**
329. Nothing has dared so much as **ignorance.**
330. Another man's **ill** hangs on a hair.
331. There is no worse **ill** than everyone's discontent.
332. There is no **ill** that does not come for good.
333. For the **ill** that occurs to-day that of to-morrow is no remedy.
334. Only God helps the **ill-dressed.**
335. **Ill luck** enters by fathoms and departs by inches.
336. There is nothing **ill-said** that is not ill-taken.
337. He whom it touches nearest always learns his **injury** last.
338. He leaves nothing in his **ink-stand.**
339. It is much better to do **in vain** than to be in vain.
340. Everyone should scratch his own **itch.**
341. A **jade** trots near home.
342. **Jealousy** bites deeper than fleas.
343. **Jesting** costs money.
344. The **Jew** ruins himself with Passovers, the Moor with wedding feasts, and the Christian with lawsuits.
345. To the **judges** of Galicia go with feet in hand.
   [i.e. poultry held by legs as a bribe.]
346. With an old **kettle** one can buy a new one.
   [Marriage and money.]
347. **Kings'** swords cut and priests' fires burn, but street songs kill quickest.
348. Do not make me **kiss** and you will not make me sin.
349. Some say what they **know** and some know what they say.
350. You, a **lady**—I, a lady—who is to bed the sow? (*Galician.*)
351. The **land** a man knows is his mother.
352. **Laws** follow the roads that kings wish them to take.
353. A bad compromise is better than a good **lawsuit.**
354. A pennyworth of **lawsuit** costs half-a-crown's worth of paper.
355. May you have a **lawsuit** in which you know that you are in the right. (*Gipsy curse.*)
356. A good **lawyer** is a bad neighbour.

357. A **leap** from a hedge is better than a prayer of a bishop.

358. **Lend** everything to your friend except your horse, your gun, or your wife.

359. Who **lends** recovers not ; or if he recovers, recovers not all ; or if all, not much ; or if much, a mortal enemy.

360. Treat the **lesser** as you would have the greater treat you.

361. The **liar** is more quickly caught than the lame man.

362. **Liberty** has no price.

363. A **lie** has short legs.

364. Even a **lie** is a lady of birth.

365. Although a **lie** is armed it is always defeated.

366. He who always tells me a **lie** never cheats me.

367. Tell a **lie** to find the truth.

368. Where they **like** you do not go often.

369. To **limp** on the same foot with someone.

[i.e. to share the same fault or failing.]

370. The **lion** does not hunt meat for the jackal. (*Iberian.*)

371. When you cannot clothe yourself in the **lion's** skin, put on that of the fox.

372. If you wish to **live** long, make yourself old young.

373. Not the **load,** but the overload kills.

374. A **loaf** fifteen days old and hunger of three weeks.

375. A slight **loss** alarms, a heavy loss quiets.

376. May the sun set for me where I keep my **love.**

377. To **love** and be wise is impossible.

378. Deeds are **love,** and not fine phrases.

379. If **love** be timid, it is not true.

380. One **love** drives out another.

381. He who finds not **love** finds nothing.

382. A piece of bread with **love** is better than a hen with suffering.

383. The remedy for **love** is land between.

384. **Love** is like a sprain, a second time it arrives more easily.

385. **Love** is like soup, the first mouthful is very hot, and the ones that follow become gradually cooler.

386. **Love** is like the eye of a needle.

[A small thing, but without it one could make nothing to keep us warm against the chills of sorrow.]

387. A girl's **love** is water in a basket.

388. **Love** looks through spectacles which make copper appear gold, poverty riches, and weak eyes distil pearls.

389. Of soup and **love,** the first is the best.

390. Where there is much **love,** there are usually but few freedoms.

391. In **love** there is no choosing.

392. Where there is much **love,** there is seldom great boldness.

393. Absence is to **love** what air is to fire—it puts out a little one and fans a big one.

394. There are eyes that fall in **love** with bleared ones.

395. In hunting and in **love** you begin when you like, and leave off when you can.

396. The **lover** lives on iron.

[Because his sweetheart speaks to him through iron window bars on the ground floor.]

397. **Lovers** always think that other people have had their eyes put out.

398. He who **loves** God without suffering will have little to do

399. He who **loves** much, fears much.

400. He **loves** thee well who makes thee weep.

401. Who **loves** truly forgets slowly.

402. He who **loves** ugly things thinks them beautiful.

403. He who **loves** well sees from afar.

404. Good **luck** comes by elbowing.

405. Good **luck** enters by dint of cuffs.

406. Who has no ill **luck** grows tired of good.

407. **Madness** must necessarily have more followers than discretion.

408. The virtuous **maid** and the broken leg must stay at home.

409. Of the **malady** a man fears he dies.

410. Think more of not missing once, than of hitting the **mark** a hundred times.

411. Tell your affairs in the **market-place,** and one will call them black and another white.

412. **Marriage** is like thrusting your hand into a bag of serpents on the chance of snatching an eel.

413. **Marriage** is a sack in which are found ninety-nine vipers and an eel.

414. The bacon of paradise is for that **married** man who has not repented.

415. He who **marries** badly becomes a widower late.

416. Who **marries** for love must live in sorrow.

417. **Marry** and grow tame.

418. He who goes a distance to **marry,** either goes to be deceived, or to deceive.

419. The day you **marry,** it is either kill or cure.

420. He who is determined to **marry** ought to look at his neighbours.

421. He who goes to **Mass** with brothers-in-law comes out alone.

422. He who eats the **meat,** let him pick the bone.

423. **Melons** and women are hard to know.

424. **Memory,** like woman, is wont to be unfaithful.

425. The art of being a **merchant** consists more in getting paid than in making sales.

426. A stopped **mill** is better than a friendly miller.

427. The door to **misery** is patience.

428. Welcome, **misfortune,** if thou comest alone.

429. The **misfortune** that involves many is a pleasure.

430. **Misfortunes** of many console.

431. He is always right who suspects that he is always making **mistakes.**

432. Love and suffering slay **modesty.**

433. The best foundation in the world is **money.**

434. **Money** finds soldiers.

435. When the **money** is paid, the arms are broken.

[i.e. idle.]

436. When **money** speaks the rest are silent.

437. With **money** you would not know yourself; without money nobody would know you.

438. In Spain it is enough to be a **mother.**

439. An ounce of **mother** is worth a ton of priest.

440. My home, my **mother's** breast.

441. That which you should give to the **mouse** give to the cat and it will get you out of the difficulty.

442. Those whom you wound with the **mouth** you must heal with the mouth.

443. Have patience, and the **mulberry** leaf will become satin.

444. Better a late **mulberry** than an almond-tree in flower.

445. A good **mule** should be like a widow.

[i.e. fat and a good walker.]

446. Where there is **music,** there can be no harm.

447. The **needle** knows what it sews, and the thimble what it pushes.

448. Keep a good opinion of your **neighbour** and lock the door.

449. The bad **neighbour** gives a needle without thread. (*Galician.*)

450. If you have a good **neighbour,** you'll marry your daughter and sell your wine.

451. Every **neighbour's son** has his actions for godfather.

452. It is better to be stung by a **nettle** than pricked by a rose.

453. The street of "soon" leads to the square of **"never."**

454. A **niggard** with the ashes and a spendthrift with the flour.

[i.e. penny wise, pound foolish.

455. Never say **"no"** from pride, or "yes" from weakness.

456. Wipe your neighbour's son's **nose,** and take him into your house.

457. That man who has **nothing** is afraid of nothing.

458. To **offer** much is a kind of denial.

459. Grease yourself with **oil,** and if it doesn't make you well it will make you shine.

460. He wrongs not an **old man** who steals his supper from him.

461. One and none is all **one.**

462. Every **owl** to its olive-tree.

463. Do not seek shelter for an old **ox.**

464. To the old **ox** a new bell.

465. He who has lost his **oxen** is always hearing bells.

466. Patience, and shuffle the **pack.**

467. **Paid** first never grieves.

468. An orchard with a pigeon-house is an earthly **paradise.**

469. You would never stop the **parrot's** chocolate.

470. There is no better **patch** than that of the same cloth.

471. The **patient** who is not destined to die will need no other medicine than water.

472. Do not look for a good man's **pedigree.**

473. Every man is a **people.** (*Andalusian.*)

474. Better lose a supper than have a hundred **physicians.**

475. To steal the **pig,** and give away the feet for God's sake.

476. A **pilgrimage** close at hand—much wine and little wax.

477. One **pin** for your purse and two for your mouth.

478. He that **pitieth** another remembereth himself.

479. Where wilt thou go that thou wilt not have to **plough ?**

480. Even if your **pockets** are empty, see that your hat is straight.

481. Prison and Lent were made for the **poor.**

482. From the **poor** to the rich two palms; from the rich to the poor two fingers.

483. He is not **poor** who has little, but he who desires much.

484. Nobody lives as **poorly** as he was born.

485. To a **poor man** a goblet of silver, a pan of copper, and a table of oak.

486. A **poor man** is all schemes.

487. The body of the **Pope** does not occupy more feet of ground than that of the sacristan.

488. Don't humble yourself through **poverty,** and don't exalt yourself through riches.

489. He who **praises** himself overmuch blames himself.

490. There is nothing so dear as that which is bought by **prayer.**

491. Before the door of a man who is always **praying,** never leave your corn to dry.

492. In **praying** to God you must use your hammer.

493. He who **preaches** in the desert loses his sermon.

494. Ask but enough, and you may lower the **price** as you list.

495. **Prosperity** forgets father and mother.

496. A **proverb** is the voice of God.

497. **Proverbs** are little gospels.

498. **Punishment** is a cripple, but it arrives.

499. Honour and money are not found in the same **purse.**

500. If you have an empty **purse,** keep honey in your mouth.

501. Where there are two friends to one **purse,** one sings, the other weeps.

502. **Quarrels** and the sea are best viewed from afar.

503. When the **rabbit** has gone advice has come.

504. He who **rails** is not far from forgiving.

505. A **raven** can't be blacker than its wings.

506. He who sets up as a **redeemer** is apt to get crucified.

507. A poor **relation** has no existence.

508. With the **repique** in hand the game is sure.

509. The idle remarks of the **rich** are taken as maxims of wisdom.

510. He who would be **rich** has not to pile up money, but to diminish his wants.

511. He who wishes to be **rich** in a year is hanged in six months.

512. Always take away one half in **riches** and sanctity.

513. **Riches** are the baggage of fortune.

514. He who **rides** behind another does not saddle when he pleases.

515. There is no **right** side without a wrong side.

516. The **righteous** man sins before an open chest.

517. It is of no importance to lose the **rings** if your fingers remain.

518. Soon **ripe,** soon rotten.

[i.e. women who marry early, more quickly become barren.]

519. The **river** doesn't grow [bigger] with clean water.

520. What runs into the **river,** the river carries away.

521. Whatever way you take there is a league of bad **road.**

522. In every direction there are three leagues of bad **road.**

523. On a long **road** a short step.

524. Take the middle of the **road** and you won't fall.

525. On the bad **road** go at once.

526. The **rose** that is smelt by many loses its fragrance.

527. To wise silence men give the name of **saint.**

528. The absent **saint** gets no candle.

529. Let the **salad-maker** be a spendthrift for oil, a miser for vinegar, a statesman for salt, and a madman for mixing.

530. All good **salt** stings.

531. Long live the **salt-cellar !**

[The salt-cellar typifies the wit, grace and imagination of Spain.]

532. He who eats a **sardine** in his youth carries the backbone in his old age.

533. No **Saturday** without sun, no girl without love.

534. **Science** is madness if good sense does not cure it.

535. He who has been stung by a **scorpion** fears a shadow.

536. The **sea** divided becomes brooks.

537. In taking a **seat** and putting on his hat a man shows much of his skill.

538. The tepid water of incredulity acts as an emetic on **secrets.**

539. **Sell** publicly and buy privately.

540. At the end of the year a **servant** has the habits of the master.

541. Past **services** are like old debts, very few are ever paid.

542. He who **shares** has the worst share.

543. That **sheep** has his belly full which butts his companions.

544. Between the **shortening** comes the lengthening.

545. Time cures the **sick man,** not the ointment.

546. **Silence** was never written down.

547. He who is **silent** does not say nothing.

548. **Silk** and velvet put out the kitchen fire.

549. We are all children of Adam, it's the **silk** makes the difference.

550. Do away with the motive, and you do away with the **sin.**

551. Take away the opportunity and you take away the **sin.**

552. For a fresh **sin,** a fresh penance.

553. Let **sin** be deaf.

554. If a Spaniard **sing,** he is either mad or penniless.

555. He who **sings** frightens away his ills.

[Idea common in the East that singing drives away evil spirits. The origin of ringing church bells was to frighten the devil.]

556. Who **sings** in grief procures relief.

557. Green burns for dry, and the righteous pay for **sinners.**

558. Give where I may **sit down,** and I will make where I may lie down.

559. There is not the thickness of a **sixpence** betwixt good and evil.

560. The night is short for him who would **sleep.**

561. **Sleep** high and live long.

562. To **sleep** in the inn of the stars.

[i.e. out of doors.]

563. There is no **slope** above without a slope below.

[i.e. everything has its compensations.]

564. If there is a bad **smell** you'll have no nose in a hundred years.

565. The **smoke** in a man's own house is better than the fire in another's.

566. Draw the **snake** from its hole by another man's hand.

567. It is a wise **son** that knows his own father.

568. Blessed is the **son** whose father went to the devil.

569. A **soul** alone neither sings nor weeps. (*Castilian.*)

570. The **Spaniard** is a judge of two things—fine women and fine sherry.

571. **Spain** makes men and wastes them. (*Castilian.*)

572. Italy to be born in, France to live in, and **Spain** to die in.

573. Though the **speaker** may be foolish, the listener may be wise.

574. He who **speaks** ill hears worse.

575. Through not **spending** enough we spend too much.

576. He who buys and sells does not feel what he **spends.**

577. He who doesn't kill the **spider** doesn't destroy the web.

578. Alas for the **spindle** when the beard is not over it!

579. I gave it you to drink with a silver **spoon.**

580. With the **spoon** that you choose you will eat.

581. An old straw **stack** soon catches fire.

582. Do not fear a **stain** that disappears with water.

583. He who **steals** once is always a thief.

584. There is no argument equal to that of a **stick.**

585. There is no arguing with an empty **stomach.**

586. A full **stomach** can neither flee well nor fight well.

587. **Stones** are like wine, the older they are the better they are.

588. Come, but come **stooping.**

589. He who **stumbles** over a straw may easily break his neck.

590. **Success** is the master of the ignorant.

591. For those who do not know how to **suffer,** any life is death.

592. The **sun** comes out for all.

593. The **sun** plays before it is born.

594. Seek the **sun** that warms the most.

595. He who does not **swallow** a matter hangs himself with thirst.

596. It is better to **sweat** than to sneeze.

597. There is no ugly **sweetheart.**

598. The best art of the **swimmer** is to know how to secure his clothes.

599. He who never draws the **sword** without cause never lays it down without honour.

600. Beware of a man who doesn't **talk,** and a dog that doesn't bark.

601. **Talk** if you wish to be known.

602. A **talkative man** soon consoles himself.

603. Sometimes **talking** loses what silence has gained.

604. We should attack a difficult **task** as though it were easy, and an easy one as though it were difficult.
605. There is no disputing about **taste.**
606. Only by **taste** can we account for taste.
607. The honest man enjoys the **theft.**
608. The soul of a **thief** and water from a well won't rise without a rope.
609. He who sows **thistles** should not go barefoot.
610. By the **thread** we unwind the skein.
611. **Three,** helping each other, will bear the burden of six.
612. The **threshold** says nothing but what it hears of the hinge.
613. The **thorn** comes into the world point foremost.
614. Who **ties** well, unties well.
615. He who has **time** and waits, time will come when he repents.
616. God gives "**to-day**", but the devil tempts with "to-morrow".
617. **To-morrow** is often the busiest day of the week.
618. The remedy of **to-morrow** is too late for the evil of to-day.
619. This **to-morrow** of yours lasts for ever.
620. A long **tongue** is the sign of a short hand.
621. That which the **tongue** says is paid for by the throat.
622. The **tongue** should not say what the head has to pay for.
623. It is not safe for **tow** to jest with embers.
624. He who has a **trade** may travel everywhere.
625. One can't catch **trout** with dry breeches.
626. How can those be **trusted** who know not how to blush?
627. He who **trusts** to himself errs every day.
628. Fools and children speak the **truth.**
629. The **truth** is always green.
630. **Truth** is God's daughter.
631. Desire beautifies what is **ugly.**
632. The most **unfortunate** is not the man who has no friends, but the man who has no enemies.
633. What is much **valued** costs much.
634. Houses as much as will hold you, **vineyards** as much as you can drink, lands as many as you can see, olive gardens on mountains and valleys.
635. What a pity that the **Virgin** only condescends to appear to fools and children.
636. Poverty does not destroy **virtue,** nor does wealth bestow it.
637. **Virtuous** of the virtuous through lack of followers.
638. When **wages** are paid, work is over.
639. Every **war** ends where it should begin.
640. In crossing **water** and giving money, never be the first.
641. **Water** causes neither illness, nor intoxication, nor debts.
642. **Water** causes neither sickness, debt, nor widowhood.
643. One should not stir up the **water** one has to drink.
644. At the end of a thousand years, the **water** returns to its cask.

    [i.e. we always return to our old loves.]
645. Of **water** that has been poured out, collect what you can.
646. There is no **wax** that does not melt.
647. Begin in other people's **way** so as to end by having your own way.
648. He who would bring home the **wealth** of the Indies must carry the wealth of the Indies with him.
649. The **wedding** feast is not made of mushrooms only.
650. There is no worse **wedge** than that of the same wood.
651. Ill **weeds** both grow and get old quickly.

652. We can offer you a dish of **welcome.**
653. There is no stranger who isn't **well born,** nor old man who wasn't brave.
654. A **well-wisher** sees from afar.
655. I **wept** when I was born, and every day shows why.
656. A buxom **widow** must be either married, buried, or shut up in a convent.
657. A man's best or worst fortune is his **wife.**
658. Hast thou a mind to quarrel with thy **wife,** bid her bring water to thee in the sunshine.
659. If you want a fine **wife** don't pick her on Sunday.
660. Who hath a **wife** hath also an enemy.
661. The first **wife** is a broom, the second a lady.
662. When your **wife** tells you to jump off a roof, pray God that it is a low one.
663. Wring a **wife's** and a hen's neck, if you want them good.
664. Where there is **will** there is skill.
665. Where there is no want of **will** there will be no want of opportunity.
666. " **Will pay** " is a fine bird, but " cash down " sings.
667. Drink water like an ox, and **wine** like a king.
    [i.e. drink water freely, wine sparingly.]
668. **Wine** wears no breeches.
669. The **wise man** never says " I did not think ".
670. The **wolf** commits no mischief at home.
671. A hungry **wolf** is fixed to no place.
672. To buy flesh of a **wolf** is to buy dear.
673. For **wolf's** flesh a dog's tooth.
674. It is useless to watch a bad **woman.**
675. A **woman** and a hen as far as my neighbour's house.
676. Confide to a **woman** and a magpie what you want spreading in the market-place.
677. A **woman** and a mule must be made handsome by the mouth.
678. The **woman** and the pear, the one that falls is good.
679. Take heed of an ill **woman,** and trust a good one with nothing.
680. Beware of the wicked **woman** and trust not at all in the good one.
681. A mule and a **woman** do that which is expected of them.
682. To tell a **woman** everything she may not do is to tell her what she can do.
683. For the chaste **woman** God suffices.
684. **Woman** is a pill and must be gilded when she is taken.
685. **Woman** is as hard to know as a melon.
686. **Woman** is as little to be trusted as a magpie.
687. A nightingale will cease to sing before a **woman** is in want of words.
688. **Woman** is like your shadow : follow her, she flies ; fly from her, she follows.
689. The counsel of a **woman** is not worth much, but he who does not take it is worth nothing.
690. The more a **woman** looks at herself the more she destroys the home.
691. Of glass is **woman** made.
692. From the sea, salt ; and from **woman** much evil.
693. Don't trust a silent **woman,** nor a dog without a bark.
694. Tell a **woman** she's handsome and she'll run mad.
695. One **woman** spoils the wisest man.
696. Man is fire, and **woman** tow ; the devil comes and sets them in a blaze.
697. A hen that crows and a **woman** who knows Latin never come to a good end.

698. A **woman** with a beard salute from a distance.

699. A **woman's** advice is never worth having, but no one but a fool refuses to follow it.

700. A **woman's** honour is a ship at sea without a rudder.

701. A **woman's** honour consists in the good opinion the world has of her.

702. Between a **woman's** " yes " and " no " I would not venture to stick the point of a pin.

703. **Women** and an orchard don't want more than one master.

704. **Women** and cherries adorn themselves to their own undoing.

705. **Women** and glass are always in danger.

706. They that are bold with **women** are never bold with men.

707. **Women** ever like to cover their foolishness by ingratitude.

708. Only he is fortunate with **women** of whom they take no notice.

709. It is the nature of **women** to disdain those who love them, and to love those who abhor them.

710. **Women** undervalue what is given to them, and die for what is denied them.

711. Whilst the ones acquire the fame, the others card the **wool.**

712. Just as a **word** appears so light to him who throws it, so it appears heavy to him who receives it.

713. The best **word** is the word that remains to be spoken.

714. **Words** should be weighed, not counted.

715. **Words** will pay for most things.

716. He who flees from **work** flees from rest.

717. That **work** is not hard that suffices to release us from it.

718. A **workman's** day-wages come in at the door, and go out at the chimney.

719. Everyone is the son of his own **works.**

720. He who **works** begins well ; he who economizes ends better.

721. With Latin, a nag, and money, you can traverse the **world.**

722. All things of this **world** are nothing unless they have reference to the next.

723. So much thou art **worth** as thou hast, and so much thou hast as thou art worth.

724. Let **writings** speak and mouths be silent.

725. We cannot catch up with our **yesterdays.**

726. If you wish to arrive **like a young man,** go like an old one.

CATALONIAN

1. **Abundance** kills hunger.

2. He can ill judge of an **art** who has no part in it.

3. There are many **asses** in the market that resemble each other.

4. **Bad news** is carried by the wind.

5. It is better to **blame** justly than to praise unjustly.

6. Nothing is so dearly **bought** as that which is bought in praying.

7. However securely you may **climb,** never say you cannot fall.

8. He who **consoles** himself alone will lament his grief alone.

9. Do not speak ill of the **day** until it is passed.

10. The **dead** and the absent have neither friends nor relations.

11. The **deceiver,** like the bee, has honey in his mouth and gall in his tail.

12. From the bitterness of **disease** man learns the sweetness of health.
13. The poor man's **dog** barks without profit.
14. I prefer a **donkey** that carries me to a horse that unsaddles me.
15. He who goes badly makes a bad **end.**
16. The **example** of the big ones makes good or bad the little ones.
17. He who **falls** gathers stones.
18. **Fear** is the prison of the heart.
19. The **fish** dies through its mouth.
20. Many **flies** kill an ass.
21. A **friend** is a heart in two bodies.
22. If you would know a man ask whom he has for **friends.**
23. He who **gives** what he has is not obliged to [give] more.
24. A **head** without a brain has no need of a hat.
25. He who flies from **home** to home returns.
26. He who loses **hope** loses many things.
27. He who makes a **hostel** of another's house makes a yard of his own.
28. To know **ill** is not to ill know.
29. Hidden **joy** is an extinguished candle.
30. It is better to conceal one's **knowledge** than to reveal one's ignorance.
31. He who cannot have what he would **like** should like what he can have.
32. In **love** and in death it is of no avail to be strong.
33. He who **loves** fears, and he who fears loves not.
34. The love of a **maid** is water in a basket.
35. He who goes far to **marry** is either deceived or is deceiving.
36. The **miser,** like the pig, is of no profit until he is dead.
37. If you would have enemies, lend **money** to your friends.
38. Govern your **mouth** according to your purse.
39. The **neighbour** calls on the day when I have not done my hair.
40. **Obedience** is more than sacrifice.
41. Do not share **pears** with your superior, for he will eat the ripe and you the green.
42. Every gilded **pill** has its hidden bitterness.
43. The **privilege** of the few does not make the law of the many.
44. He who **punishes** one gives advice [counsel] to a hundred.
45. From a great **quarrel** comes a great friendship.
46. The poor man has great hopes of becoming **rich,** and the rich man has great fear of becoming poor.
47. Wherever you taste the **sea** you will always find it salt.
48. **Shame** lasts longer than fear.
49. He who **speaks** ill of you in your absence fears you in your presence.
50. There is a time for picking up **stones** and a time for throwing them.
51. He is a good **surgeon** who has been well cut.
52. That which the **tongue** owes the throat pays for.
53. He who draws near to a good **tree** enjoys both its fruit and its shade.
54. Running **water** is not harmful to man.
55. Beware of **water** that doesn't run and a cat that doesn't mew.
56. Everyone draws **water** to his own mill and leaves his neighbour's dry.
57. Man has to take the **weather** as it comes, and folk as they are.
58. There is no **wedding** without flowers, and no burial without tears.
59. A fair **wind** is better than strength of oars.
60. Too sweet **wine** makes the heart acid.
61. **A woman's beauty** is her own perdition and the perdition of others.
62. The best **word** is that which remains to be spoken.
63. Few **years**—few cares.

SWEDISH

An Introduction to this collection by Lieut.-Col. Carl A. Bäckström will be found on page c.

1. **Advice** should be viewed from behind and not from in front.
2. The **afternoon** knows what the morning never suspected.
3. **Appetite** comes with eating.
4. The **apple** falls not far from the tree.
5. When a prince wants an **apple,** his servant gathers them all from the tree.
6. He who has taken the **bear** into the boat must cross over with him.
7. No one can live on **beauty,** but they can die for it.
8. One should choose one's **bed-fellow** whilst it is daylight.
9. Everything has had a **beginning** except God.
10. All **beginnings** are difficult.
11. One often binds the **birch** for one's own rump.
12. When the **blind man** carries the lame man, both go forward.
13. He who eats his **bread** alone saddles his horse alone.
14. A piece of **bread** in one's pocket is better than a feather in one's hat.
15. Eaten **bread** is soon forgotten.
16. Better **breadless** than witless.
17. What the moment **broke** may take years to mend.
18. Don't throw away the old **bucket** until you know whether the new one holds water.
19. He who has **burnt** himself once blows on his soup.
20. The **butterfly** often forgets it was a caterpillar.
21. He who **chases** another has himself no rest.
22. A **child** is a certain worry and an uncertain joy.
23. A **child's** hand is soon filled and a child's anger soon emptied.
24. **Chips** don't fall without being hacked from the tree.
25. There is a **church** in every man's heart, but it is not always God who preaches the sermon.
26. The **clock** must be the master in the house.
27. When one wheel in the **clock** stands still, all stand still.
28. Silken **clothes** put out the fire in the stove.
29. A roomy **conscience** has a narrow dwelling place.
30. Midsummer night is not long, but it sets many **cradles** rocking.
31. One should **cultivate** one's acres so that one does not forget to cultivate one's soul.
32. **Day** follows even on the winter night.
33. **Day** gives and night takes.
34. The **day** we fear hastens towards us, the day we long for creeps.
35. **Death** combs us all with the same comb.
36. **Death** helps out of difficulties, but demands high payment.
37. **Death** is the last doctor.
38. He who would have all his **desire** weeps when others laugh.
39. Everyone has his own **devil,** and some have two.
40. All must **die** for sake of an apple.
41. **Diffidence** separates hearts and shirts.
42. No one becomes a good **doctor** before he has filled a churchyard.
43. The **doctor** who would heal another's hurt should not show his own.
44. With a young lawyer you lose your inheritance ; with a young **doctor** your health.

45. Many make themselves a **dog** for the sake of a bone.
46. The rich man rides and the poor man goes on foot, but they both reach **doomsday** equally fast.
47. When one **door** slams to another often bursts open.
48. **Dust** is always dust, however near to heaven it may be blown.
49. The art of **dying** can never be studied too much.
50. Black **earth** gives white bread.
51. **Envy** shoots at others and wounds herself.
52. The **evening** crowns the day.
53. The **evening** of every day has not yet come.
54. **Experience** is a long road.
55. The **eye** that sees not need not weep.
56. Open **eyes** are the best sign-post.
57. The **eyes** believe their own evidence, the ears that of others.
58. Strange **eyes** see more than one's own.
59. To **fall** is easy ; to get up is difficult.
60. To **fall** is no shame, but to remain fallen is.
61. When a man **falls** the whole world rides over him.
62. **Fear** is greater than danger.
63. Slender **fingers** are lazy hands.
64. He who has long **fingers** should have long legs.
65. The **fir** by the harbour stretches its arms towards the land.
66. **Five fingers** are wiser than the point of a knife.
67. Fair **flowers** don't remain long by the wayside.
68. He who does not commit **follies** in his youth commits them in his old age.
69. Eating is half one's **food,** sleeping the other half.
70. If a **fool** could keep silent he would not be a fool.
71. The **fool** has his heart in his mouth, the wise man has his mouth in his heart.
72. We all have a **fool** under our cloaks, but some can hide it better than others.
73. The **fool's** knife is first in the butter.
74. Each one thinks much of his own wisdom, therefore the world is full of **fools.**
75. Unnecessary wisdom is twofold **foolishness.**
76. **Fortune** follows him who flees from it, and flees from him who seeks it.
77. One should go invited to a **friend** in good fortune and uninvited in misfortune.
78. Everyman's **friend** is often everyman's fool.
79. He is a **friend** to none who is a friend to all.
80. Too close spoils the **friendship.**
81. The most **frightened** strikes the first.
82. To **give** of what has been given is no sin.
83. The hand that **gives** gathers.
84. Against the vice of asking there is the virtue of not **giving.**
85. Don't throw gravel at **God,** for He will throw stones at you.
86. **God** gives every bird its food but does not cast it into the nest.
87. In a little house **God** has a corner, but in a big house He has to stand in the hall.
88. **God** makes no wreck without cause.
89. **God** often goes about in worn-out shoes.
90. The calendar is made by man ; the weather by **God.**
91. The greater the need the nearer is **God.**
92. One **good day** often costs a hundred bad nights.
93. He who thinks of the **good days** makes the bad days worse.
94. **Good luck** is the guardian of the stupid.
95. No **grass** grows under the stone that is often moved.

96. **Guests** should not forget to go home.
97. He who spares his **hands** spares his teeth.
98. The comforter's **head** never aches.
99. One can never see through another's **head,** still less through his heart.
100. Neither hat nor crown help against **headache.**
101. It is hard to put many **heads** under one hat.
102. Everybody's wish is his kingdom of **heaven.**
103. He who thinks of buying an estate in **hell** does not need a forest attached.
104. A hare and a gipsy make two **heroes.**
105. He who has acquired **honour** early commits many follies.
106. **Honour** has a big shadow.
107. **Honour** [meaning reputation] lives on wind.
108. **Honour** the house in which you were born, the tree that gave you shade, and the village in which you grew up.
109. He who travels with **hope** has poverty for a driver.
110. A loaned **horse** and one's own spurs make the miles short.
111. In war it is better to fasten one's **horse** to someone else's manger.
112. An **hour** lost is often a year lost.
113. Those you let stand in the **house** easily come into the rooms.
114. A dark **house** has eyes that see ; a lighted-up house has eyes that are seen.
115. A tall **house** is empty under the rafters.
116. The **house** that is built after every man's advice seldom gets a roof.
117. By doing nothing we learn to do **ill.**
118. You should look out for yourself in front with an ox, behind with an ass, and on both sides with a **Jesuit.**
119. Everyone prizes **justice** but shuts the door when it comes.
120. Keep measure in your **kindness.**
121. What one **knows** no one knows ; what two know everyone knows.
122. No one walks **lame** on another man's foot.
123. What one hasn't in one's head one should have in one's **legs.**
124. Spare the **lid** and the bottom will look after itself.
125. A well-tinted **lie** counts as the truth.
126. A **lie** in time of need is as good as the truth.
127. If every **lie** were to knock out a tooth many would be toothless.
128. If **lies** were as heavy as stones to carry many would prefer the truth.
129. What **life** gives death takes.
130. As **life** sings so death plays.
131. The **light** laughs at the dark's work.
132. The **light** shines for others and not for itself.
133. If you set a **light** too high it is blown out by the wind ; if you set it too low, it is blown out by the child.
134. Every **likeness** limps.
135. A life without **love,** a year without summer.
136. No thief steals **love,** but love often makes thieves.
137. **Love** creeps where it cannot go.
138. **Love** goes downhill.
139. **Love** has made heroes of many and fools of many more.
140. **Love** is like dew that falls on both nettles and lilies.
141. **Love** or fire in your trousers is not easy to conceal.
142. **Luck** never gives, it only lends.
143. When **luck** offers a finger one must take the whole hand.
144. The best **manure** falls from the master's boot.
145. The best **manure** falls from the peasant's boots.

146. When the eyes go to **market** with the purse, the stomach must prepare itself for a fast.
147. He who builds and he who **marries** is never safe.
148. Money-bags **marries** ugliness.
149. A forbidden **meal** is quickly eaten.
150. One man is another man's **mirror.**
151. **Misfortune** rides into the villages, but leaves them on foot.
152. One **misfortune** shakes hands with another.
153. All **misfortunes** begin in God's name.
154. **Money** follows the high road.
155. A man without **money** is like a ship without sails.
156. **Money** is round and rolls easily.
157. One hand full of **money** is stronger than two full of truth.
158. When **money** speaks the world keeps silent.
159. He who guards his **mouth** often guards his life.
160. Better a good **neighbour** than a sister in the next village.
161. No one has peace longer than his **neighbour** wishes.
162. No one has so big a house that he does not need a good **neighbour.**
163. Many sweep before their **neighbour's door** and pass their own by.
164. That which is to become a good **nettle** must sting early.
165. He who makes a long **nose** makes a short meal.
166. The **old man** shows what the young man was.
167. The **old man's** counsel is the young man's staff.
168. **Old people** have always new pains.
169. **Old shoes** need much wax.
170. A **peacock** has too little in its head and too much in its tail.
171. The **peasant's** eyes do more than his hands.
172. A **peasant's foot** and a lord's shoe won't go together.
173. A **pen** often reaches further than a sword.
174. A good **pig** finds its way home in the evening.
175. To lazy **pigs** the ground is always frozen.
176. The little **pigs** would grunt if they knew what the boar was suffering.
177. He who **ploughs** at night loses a loaf at every furrow.
178. The **poor** are not those who have little, but those who need much.
179. When it rains soup the **poor man** has no spoon.
180. Small sores and **poor relations** must never be scorned.
181. It is a bad **porter** who opens to all.
182. The most stupid peasants get the largest **potatoes.**
183. Small **pots** soon run over.
184. **Praise** not the sun till the day is out ; praise counsel when you have followed it, and ale when you have drunk it.
185. I **proud,** and thou proud, who shall carry the dirt out ?
186. A **proverb** says what man thinks.
187. Words make the **purchase** but the pence pay.
188. Empty is the **purse** that holds other folk's money.
189. He who does not look up with his eyes must look up with his **purse.**
190. He who owes and pays is master of another's **purse.**
191. **Quick** in tooth, quick in hand.
192. **Relations** and friends should be visited but not lived with.
193. **Repentance** is a bitter physic.
194. The **rope** has never been made that binds thoughts.
195. Not all who turn their backs are **running** away.
196. That which goes last into the **sack** comes first out.

197. **Saddle** early and ride late.
198. **Satan** comes where money is, and where it isn't he comes twice.
199. One's own days are another's **school teacher.**
200. **Seeing** once is better than hearing twice.
201. The rich man has five **senses,** the poor man six.
202. Give the **servant** good food, and the cow will yield more milk and the cat drink less.
203. A **shadow** is a feeble thing but no sun can drive it away.
204. That which fate makes a **shilling** never becomes a dollar.
205. In calm water every **ship** has a good captain.
206. He who cannot keep **silence** cannot speak.
207. Where **sin** drives, shame sits in the back seat.
208. **Small people** often live in big houses.
209. No one thinks of the **snow** that fell last year.
210. Don't let your **sorrow** come higher than your knees.
211. It is better to **spare** [save] at the brim than at the bottom [of the sack].
212. **Spite** is an early riser.
213. One must take the **spoon** in the right hand if one would not spill the soup.
214. He who buys what he doesn't need **steals** from himself.
215. The **stomach** is the workshop of the body.
216. He who cannot carry the **stone** must roll it.
217. No one is so tall that he has not sometimes **stretched** himself.
218. He on whom the **sun** shines doesn't ask about the moon.
219. The **sun** shines even into a little room.
220. The **thief** finds the chalice quicker than the sacristan.
221. A lazy **thief** is better than a lazy servant.
222. A wise **thief** keeps his neighbour honest.
223. Big **thieves** hang little thieves.
224. A **tree** bears fruit even if stones are thrown at it.
225. A tall **tree** lets itself sooner be bent than broken.
226. A **tree** that cannot serve for a statue can serve for a pig-trough.
227. Better to suffer for the **truth** than be rewarded for a lie.
228. **Vices** willingly bear the names of virtues.
229. Age's **virtues** are dearly bought.
230. He who has nothing but **virtues** is not much better than he who has nothing but faults.
231. In **war** all suffer defeat, even the victors.
232. **Water** comes where water has been.
233. He who throws **water** over his head can easily get it in his ears.
234. Amongst the **weak** the strongest is the one who doesn't forget his weakness.
235. **Wedlock** is like an eel-basket, those who are out of it want to get in, and those who are in want to get out.
236. **Weeds** grow best in good ground.
237. What one **whispers** in the ear is heard throughout the town.
238. The sweetest **wine** makes the sharpest vinegar.
239. Where **wisdom** doesn't go in it doesn't come out.
240. **Wisdom** is in the head and not in the beard.
241. **Wisdom** without use is fire without warmth.
242. He is wise who can use his **wisdom.**
243. A **wise man** has his tongue in his heart.
244. One finds many grey hairs but few **wise men.**
245. All the **wit** of the world is not in one head.
246. It is better to let oneself be bitten by a **wolf** than by a sheep.

247. He who wants to wrestle with **wolves** must have a bear's claws.

248. Taking an eel by its tail and a **woman** at her word leaves little in the hand.

249. **Woman** has long hair and short sense.

250. Man is the head and **woman** is the hat.

251. A **woman's** heart sees more than ten men's eyes.

252. **Women** are like shadows, follow them and they fly from you, fly from them and they follow you.

253. Soft **words** hurt not the mouth.

254. Young men's **work** is old men's ease.

255. The indirect road to **work** is the direct road to want.

256. **Worry** often gives a small thing a big shadow.

257. The **worth** of a thing is best known by the want.

258. " **Yes** " binds ; " no " unbinds.

259. Between **" yes " and " no "** stand the gallows.

260. Being **young** is a fault which improves daily.

261. **Youth** goes in a flock, manhood in pairs, and old age alone.

262. **Youth** has a beautiful face and old age a beautiful soul.

SWISS

(Including Swiss-German)

An Introduction to this collection by Herr J. Schnyder will be found on page cii.

1. When the purchase has been made it is too late to **bargain.** (*Swiss-German.*)

2. You lie nowhere better than in your own **bed.**

3. It doesn't matter to the **bed** who celebrates his marriage in it. (*Swiss-German.*)

4. If the devil has the **bird,** let him also take the cage.

5. One cannot prevent **birds** flying over our heads, but we can prevent them from nesting in our hair.

6. One is caught with the same **birds** with which one flies.

7. **A bonnet** does not always hide a dove.

8. Strange **bread** makes the cheeks red. (*Swiss-German.*)

9. Keep at least two paces from him who loves not **bread** or the voice of a child.

10. First eat the black **bread,** then the white.

11. The **bull** is held by the horns, man by his word, and woman by the skirt.

12. He who would **buy** what he sees must soon sell what he has. (*Swiss-German.*)

13. Don't **buy** what you need, but what you can't do without. (*Swiss-German.*)

14. One finds more foolish **buyers** than sellers. (*Swiss-German.*)

15. **Buying** is cheaper than begging. (*Swiss-German.*)

16. He who **buys** dearly can't give cheaply. (*Swiss-German.*)

17. When you have trodden on the **cat,** what help is it to stroke her back ? (*Swiss-German.*)

18. It is possible to talk to **cattle** if you have common sense.

19. The **careful** man has also tumbled downstairs.

20. The hand of a **child** and the mouth of a fool are always open.
21. Small **children**—small sorrows; big children—big sorrows; while small they trample on one's feet, when big they trample on one's heart.
22. A **child's** hand and a pig's trough must always be full.
23. By saying and **contradicting** a thing is carried through the town.
24. Where it is customary the **cow** is put to bed.
25. The day comes when the **cow** needs her tail. (*Swiss-German.*)
26. What seems **dark** in the evening is made light by the morning. (*Swiss-German.*)
27. No **day** can be compared with the day that has gone by. (*Swiss-German.*)
28. Grass bedewed, a horse harnessed, and a woman clothed are three **deceiving** things.
29. It is easier to beat two **devils** into a child than one out of it.
30. You mustn't try to take away **dirt** with filth.
31. As every **drop** increases every drop decreases.
32. The first and the last to go on the lake are **drowned.**
33. One may keep midday when one will, but the **evening** sets in on its own account. (*Swiss-German.*)
34. **Experience** is not bound to years, for years may be lived in a single hour. (*Swiss-German.*)
35. When the **eye** is sufficient one should not use the hand. (*Swiss-German.*)
36. When one shuts one **eye** one does not hear everything. (*Swiss-German.*)
37. When the **eye** will not see light spectacles are of no avail. (*Swiss-German.*)
38. **Eyes** and ears have also got a tongue.
39. The **eyes** believe themselves, the ears other people. (*Swiss-German.*)
40. The **eyes** devour much, but they don't fill the stomach. (*Swiss-German.*)
41. Take your **eyes** in your hand and the cat on your knee, what you don't see she does. (*Swiss-German.*)
42. Keep watch over your **eyes** openly and in secret that they may behold only that which is good and overlook that which is evil.
43. Sore **eyes** see nothing good.
44. One can only see one's own **faults** with other people's eyes. (*Swiss-German.*)
45. He who **finds** before it is lost dies before he is ill.
46. **Fire** burns near to, and beauty far off. (*Swiss-German.*)
47. He who has no **fire** in himself cannot warm others. (*Swiss-German.*)
48. A **fire** in the heart brings smoke in the head. (*Swiss-German.*)
49. What one has lost in the **fire** one finds again in the ashes. (*Swiss-German.*)
50. He who rakes another's **fire** puts out his own. (*Swiss-German.*)
51. To be a **fool** at the right moment is also an art.
52. The **fox** slinks readily into a ready-made hole. (*Swiss-German.*)
53. To have **friends** is good, but not to have to use them is better.
54. The shorter the bill, the longer the **friendship.**
55. A tree with ripe **fruit** needs little shaking. (*Swiss-German.*)
56. Old houses and young **girls** soon burn.
57. No **goat** can butt alone.
58. Even **goats** climb on to trees that bend. (*Swiss-German.*)
59. **God** has no sympathy with him who lets it rain through his roof.

60. When **God** makes things wet, He makes them dry again.
61. Not easily would **God** wound a man without giving him an ointment at the same time.
62. Empty **greetings** go barefoot.
63. He who would have a **grey day** must make it himself. (*Swiss-German.*)
64. The first day a **guest,** the second a burden, the third a dirty mess.
65. Words are good, but **hens** lay eggs. (*Swiss-German.*)
66. An old **horse** doesn't fear the whip.
67. On a young **horse** one soon reaches the cemetery.
68. Speedy **horses** cast the most shoes.
69. **Horses** kick each other only at an empty trough.
70. If you build a **house** another looks out of the windows.
71. A low **house** is also shone upon by the sun.
72. An empty **house** is full of noise.
73. Everyone gives a push to the **house** that is about to fall.
74. In a rich **house** the table is soon laid.
75. In a golden **house** there are at times leaden hours.
76. There is no **house** through which some smoke does not drift.
77. High **houses** are often empty under the roof.
78. Everybody has got a **kink,** and he who does not believe it has two.
79. A **lawyer** devours a horse for breakfast.
80. To the timorous all **leaves** seem to rustle.
81. A word is useful, **lies** are for adornment. (*Swiss-German.*)
82. Many buyers make the **loaves** dear. (*Swiss-German.*)
83. The value of **lost goods** is always weighed with double **weights.**
84. **Love** presses through the gloves.
85. Not every day is **market-day.** (*Swiss-German.*)
86. **Marriage** is a covered dish.
87. The first day of **marriage** is often the last day of love. (*Swiss-German.*)
88. **Marry** across the manure-heap and you know who she is.
89. Buy your neighbour's cattle and **marry** your neighbour's child and you know what you have.
90. **Men,** like birds, always allow themselves to be caught in the same net.
91. A **merchant** and a pig are only valued when they are dead. (*Swiss-German.*)
92. To be a **merchant** is easy, to remain one an art. (*Swiss-German.*)
93. A merchant without **money** is a peasant without a field. (*Swiss-German.*)
94. **Money** makes the market, not the people. (*Swiss-German.*)
95. One goes wrong chiefly with the **mouth.**
96. **Necessity** compels the saying of many things.
97. It is wise to pay one guilder more for a house that has a good **neighbour.**
98. Many a man calls his **neighbour** an ass who himself carries sacks.
99. One can trust one's **neighbour,** but a good hedge more.
100. Love your **neighbour** but don't pull down the hedge.
101. When one's **neighbour** has a divorce suit, one thinks of one's own wife.
102. Our **neighbour** is a glass that easily breaks if we take it into our hands too often.
103. He who shakes his **neighbour's** house, his own falls soon on his head.
104. It also concerns you if your **neighbour's** house is on fire.
105. **Night** is the mother of thought. (*Swiss-German.*)

106. The **night** washes what the day has soaped. (*Swiss-German.*)

107. Where one has lost **nothing** one should seek nothing.

108. There is no **office** without sloth.

109. The **peasants** are our walls. (*Swiss-German.*)

110. You must look at the **pig** and not at the trough. (*Swiss-German.*)

111. God preserve us from **pitch-forks,** for they make three holes. (*Swiss-German.*)

112. A **proverb** characterises nations but must first dwell amongst them. (*Swiss-German.*)

113. A beautiful **proverb** in the memory is like a golden piece in the money chest. (*Swiss-German.*)

114. A **proverb** is shorter than a bird's beak. (*Swiss-German.*)

115. A **proverb** places the words in one's mouth. (*Swiss-German.*)

116. In a **proverb** you buy with your ears a good lesson at the cheapest price. (*Swiss-German.*)

117. **Proverbs** are constantly warring against each other. (*Swiss-German.*)

118. **Proverbs** are like butterflies, some are caught and others fly away. (*Swiss-German.*)

119. **Proverbs** are often in themselves beautiful little allegories. (*Swiss-German.*)

120. **Proverbs** are the echoes of experience. (*Swiss-German.*)

121. **Proverbs** are the wisdom of the alley. (*Swiss-German.*)

122. We have many coarse **proverbs,** but their meaning is good. (*Swiss-German.*)

123. In **proverbs** the conscience of the people sits in judgment. (*Swiss-German.*)

124. They make a good **purchase** who bring nothing home. (*Swiss-German.*)

125. When the peasants become gentlemen and the gentlemen become peasants there are **rags.** (*Swiss-German.*)

126. Beware of a **red beard,** for a red beard was never good.

127. He who is born **red-haired** is in purgatory already in this world.

128. Time brings **roses**—but first of all buds.

129. Great consolation may grow out of the smallest **saying.** (*Swiss-German.*)

130. A **saying** of the people is often a salutary warning. (*Swiss-German.*)

131. Better to **sell** with regret than to keep with regret. (*Swiss-German.*)

132. A house and a cloak cover much **shame.**

133. When a merchant speaks of **sheep** he means the cloth [or hide]. (*Swiss-German.*)

134. Stick to those **sheep** which have got wool.

135. What doesn't **shine** in the day shines at night. (*Swiss-German.*)

136. **Sign-posts** only show the road, they don't go along it. (*Swiss-German.*)

137. **Silence** may often say sufficient.

138. One may say what one has kept **silent,** but not keep silent what one has said.

139. It has often **snowed** on the mountains but the valley has remained green. (*Swiss-German.*)
 [i.e. grey hair does not make one old.]

140. He who has **sold** everything in the morning can run lighter in the evening. (*Swiss-German.*)

141. In velvet and silk are hidden the greatest **sorrows.**

142. A good **spectator** also creates. (*Swiss-German.*)

143. A man **stands** as high as he places himself. (*Swiss-German.*)

144. If you have once taken an egg you can't stop **stealing.**

145. The roughest **stone** becomes smooth when it is much rolled. (*Swiss-German.*)

146. When a big **stone** falls from the mountain many small stones fall after it. (*Swiss-German.*)

147. When the **stone** has left the hand it belongs to the devil. (*Swiss-German.*)
148. Before every house a **stone,** if not big, then small.
149. There is no **stone** so small that it cannot fill a hole. (*Swiss-German.*)
150. One stumbles against a **stone** that another doesn't see. (*Swiss-German.*)
151. Everything may be bought except **time.** (*Swiss-German.*)
152. **Time** seems long to him who longs. (*Swiss-German.*)
153. An upset stomach and an upset humour are recognized by the **tongue.**
154. The head is recognized by the **tongue.**
155. A tame **tongue** is a rare bird.
156. The **tongue** is the worst piece of meat in the world.
157. The **tongue** often spots the whole body.
158. He who bridles his **tongue** protects his head.
159. When the **tongue** slips it speaks the truth.
160. The **tree** doesn't enjoy its own apples. (*Swiss-German.*)
161. The **tree** of knowledge is watered with tears. (*Swiss-German.*)
162. The **tree** that bears fruit has much to put up with. (*Swiss-German.*)
163. One sees best the direction of the wind from tall **trees.** (*Swiss-German.*)
164. Under **trees** it rains twice. (*Swiss-German.*)
165. **Trousers** help trousers ; skirts help skirts.
166. In a large family there are easily some dry **twigs.**
167. Three-day-old fish and **visitors,** though they may keep, start to stink.
168. With good words one sells bad **wares.** (*Swiss-German.*)
169. The woman who likes **washing** can always find water. (*Swiss-German.*)
170. There is no **way** so long as the one from the heart and head to the hand. (*Swiss-German.*)
171. **Ways** separate and ways meet each other again. (*Swiss-German.*)
172. He who beats his **wife** gives three holidays to her and three fasting days to himself.
173. You should not take one **wife** if you cannot keep two.
174. He who wants a **wife** must look for the bride's looking-glass in the kitchen.
175. A fire, a **woman,** and a game never say " It is too much "
176. Best a pint of wine and keep away from **women.**
177. Old houses and old **women** always need repairing.
178. He who has to do with **women** and pigs finds himself in a great turmoil. (*Swiss-German.*)
179. He to whom **women** are unkind and bees are kind, will be rich.
180. Night, love, and **women** give wrong ideas.
181. If there are more **women** in the house than hearths, there is no peace in it.
182. Fear guards the **wood** better than the hunter.
183. A bitter **word** comes from a bitter heart. (*Swiss-German.*)
184. **Words** are like the bees, they have honey and a sting. (*Swiss-German.*)
185. **Words** are dwarfs, but examples are giants. (*Swiss-German.*)
186. Behind big **words** dwells a little soul. (*Swiss-German.*)
187. Better dabble with **work** than not work at all.
188. Only seven refusals produce the right " **yes** ".

VOYVODINA

(Including The Banat and Syrmia)

1. Better to **drink** and be ill than not to drink and be ill. (*The Banat.*)
2. If God deprives a **horse** of his legs, He does not rob him of his neigh. (*The Banat.*)

   [Said to the type of old men who still speak and boast like youths.]
3. The **inn-keeper** makes one account and the drunkard another. (*The Banat.*)
4. The **master's eye** fattens the horse. (*The Banat.*)
5. Even **pencil notes** are better than the best memory. (*Syrmia.*)
6. It is the inexpensive goods that empty one's **purse.** (*The Banat.*)
7. He who drinks **wine** after his soup should never be asked for advice. (*Syrmia.*)

YIDDISH

1. Not that which is **beautiful** is dear, but that which is dear is beautiful.
2. Better the **best** of the worst than the worst of the best. (*Yiddish*)
3. You can't have even a **boil** for nothing. (*Russian.*)
4. When a Jew has a **boil** he has no onion, and when he has an onion he has no boil.
5. The **bowel** has no windows.

   [i.e. one cannot see what has been put into one's stomach.]
6. He who has **butter** on his bread should not go into the sun.
7. **Children** and fools speak the truth.
8. Of **children** and glasses, one never has too much.

   [i.e. they are both fragile.]
9. Little **children,** small pleasures ; big children, great troubles.
10. When one has a new **coat** hanging on the wall, the old one doesn't shame.
11. On black earth grows the best **corn.**

    [i.e. simple folk have often the best hearts.]
12. He who can **cringe** well creeps forward.
13. It will not be any lighter until it is first quite **dark.**
14. Since **death** has come along, one is not sure of life.
15. The angel of **death** slays and remains justified. (*Russian.*)
16. It is better to **die** young at home than to die old in hospital.
17. If you invest a fever you will realize a **disease.** (*Russian.*)
18. Time is the best **doctor.**
19. In through a wide **doorway** and out of a narrow one.

    [Said of a business that seems to be good to start with.]
20. If two say " **drunk** " the third must go to sleep. (*Russian.*)
21. Everyone has his **dung-heap** before his door.
22. A box on the **ears** passes, but a word stays.
23. Pray that you may never have to **endure** all that you can learn to bear. (*Russian.*)

24. Do not ask the wise man, ask the **experienced** one. *(Russian.)*
25. What you don't see with your **eyes,** don't assume with your mouth.
26. A **fool** has a fine world.
27. One's best **friend** is in the mirror.
28. A **friend** remains a friend up to his pocket. *(Russian.)*
29. He who doesn't eat **garlic** hasn't a stinking mouth.
30. The topmost **garment** hides the undermost grief.
31. He who has no shame before the world has no fear before **God.**
32. The best trading is with **God.**
33. Man drives and **God** holds the bridle.
34. **God** sends the remedy before the disease. *(Russian.)*
35. When **goods** lie a long time the price is forgotten.
36. He who has a **guardian angel** in heaven has also one on earth.
37. What one hasn't in one's **head** one must have in one's feet.
38. When it is bitter in the **heart,** no sugar in the mouth helps.
39. To fall from a good **horse** is at least worth while.
40. Too much **humility** is half pride.
41. If you won't give to **Jacob** you will have to give to Esau.

    [i.e. if you are too mean to give money in a good cause your money will be taken from you by your enemies.]
42. On the gravestone all **Jews** are beautiful.
43. The smaller the gathering the greater the **joy.**
44. A golden **key** opens every door.
45. One shouldn't dare **kiss** an ugly maiden.

    [She will talk about it.]
46. To **kiss** the child is as good as kissing the mother.
47. It is easier to know ten **lands** than one man.
48. When you **laugh** everyone sees; when you weep no one sees.
49. A good **lie** is sometimes worth gold.
50. With a **lie** one goes far, but not back again.
51. A **lock** is only made for an honest man.

    [It is no protection against thieves.]
52. **Luck** never grows old.
53. A **man** is what he is, but not what he was.
54. It is never too late to die or get **married.** *(Russian.)*
55. **Marriage** is like a ladder; the more you slant it the easier it is to climb.

    [i.e. marriages that appear unlikely to turn out well, because the parties concerned don't seem to be suited to each other, often are the happiest.]
56. The more **merchant,** the more luck; the more thief, the more rope.
57. The **mirror** seeks out the truth.
58. There is no better messenger than **money.**
59. Where there is no **money** there is no kinship.
60. A **mother-in-law** and a daughter-in-law in one house are like two cats in a bag.
61. The **mother** must have a big apron to cover the faults of her children.
62. **Mountains** cannot meet, but men can. *(Russian.)*
63. There may be **mud** before my door, too, some day. *(Russian.)*
64. He who has a wide mouth has a **narrow heart.**

    [i.e. promises much that he cannot carry out.]
65. A **neighbour** in the room is like a bell on the door.

    [i.e. makes everything heard outside.]
66. He who praises himself must have bad **neighbours.**

67. Ask about your **neighbours,** then buy the house.
68. When you go to your **neighbour's** you find out what is happening in your home. (*Russian*)
69. That which is **new** is true ; that which is old is cold.
    [Said specially of servants.]
70. An **old vessel** lives longer than a new pot.
71. Ask the **patient,** not the physician. (*Russian*)
72. When the **pea-hen** looks at her feathers she puffs herself out ; when she looks at her feet she weeps.
73. **Pleasure** for an ell and suffering for a mile.
74. The **prayer** goes up and the blessing comes down.
75. A **proverb** is a true word.
76. A **rabbi's wife** has long hands and short ears.
77. From a few drops comes a whole **rain** [fall].
78. A **red-haired** man must write down his name [in a book] in his youth.
    [So that in his old age he cannot deny having had red hair, a sign of cunning according to Jews.]
79. **Respect** is a shadow ; the faster one runs after it, the farther it runs away.
80. **Revenge** is half consolation.
81. A **rich man** carries his God in his pocket ; a poor man in his heart.
82. A **room** without a window is no good dwelling-place, and a coat without a button-hole is no good garment.
    [i.e. grave and shroud.]
83. **Sabbath stitches** don't hold.
    [Refers to the work done by a tailor in order to finish before the beginning of a Jewish Sabbath.]
84. The **sea** has no bottom, and the suffering of the Jews no bank.
85. A **secret** only goes in trousers.
    [Women can't keep one.]
86. Where it isn't to be found, one doesn't **seek.**
87. Before one is **seventy** everything comes before one's eyes.
88. No one knows where the **shoe** pinches save the one who walks in it.
89. The sole of a **shoe** that has trodden in money is likewise sweet.
90. **Silence** is often more rewarded than speech.
91. **Silence** may also be eloquent.
92. A **slattern** rides horseback on her apron. (*Russian*)
    [i.e. always in a hurry.]
93. In **sleep** all passes away.
    [i.e. one forgets everything.]
94. Little **speech** and much meant.
95. For the good **stepmother** there is a golden chair in the garden of Eden.
96. A **stick** in the hand helps more than a tongue in the mouth.
97. When one strikes a cold **stone** a hot spark leaps from it.
    [i.e. the most gentle person becomes heated when provoked.]
98. A **stone** lying in one place becomes overgrown with grass.
99. The same **sun** makes linen white and the gipsy black.
100. If each one **sweeps** before his own door the whole street is cleaned.
101. Don't be too **sweet** and you won't be eaten ; don't be too sour and you won't be spat out.
102. He who likes **taking** doesn't like giving.
103. If one doesn't pay the **tailor** he doesn't pull out the basting threads.
104. He who **tears** much must darn much.
105. One can't put " **thank you** " in his pocket. (*Russian*)
106. A little **town** is like a lantern.
    [i.e. everything is transparent.]
107. A young **tree** bends ; an old tree breaks. (*Russian*)

108. The bitterest thing in the world is **truth.**

109. She crawls on the **walls.** (*Russian*)

[Said of a very particular housekeeper.]

110. Look behind at the back **wheel.**

[i.e. remember your past.]

111. A bad **wheel** creaks the worst.

[i.e. the least deserving make the most noise.]

112. " **Why ?** " is no question, and " Therefore " is no answer.

113. If a man is too good for the world he is bad for his **wife.**

114. When an old man takes a young **wife,** the man becomes young and the woman old.

115. **Wisdom** has no bottom.

116. A **wise man** builds two words out of one. (*Russian*)

117. Don't cast words amongst **women.**

118. Pray to God to preserve you from bad **women,** and preserve yourself from the good ones.

119. **Women** have nine measures of talk. (*Russian*)

120. One cannot measure the whole **world** with one's own ell.

121. If all men were to pull on one side, the **world** would be overturned.

ASIA

ARABIC

(Including Bedouin, Druse, Iraq, Mesopotamian and Syrian)

An Introduction to this collection by Professor H. A. R. Gibb, M.A., will be found on page xxxvii.

1. An **adulteress** passed by a dog at a well, and he was a-dying of thirst and could not reach the water; she took off her boot and tied it to her garment and drew water for him and for that she was forgiven.
2. If I listen I have the **advantage,** if I speak the others have it.
3. The **afflicted** cannot console the afflicted.
4. He that hath drunk of **Africa's fountains** will drink again.
5. A man is safe when **alone.**
6. Every **ambitious man** is a captive and every covetous one a pauper.
7. One night of **anarchy** does more harm than a hundred years of tyranny.
8. His **anger** is on the edge of his nose.
9. If God proposes the destruction of an **ant** He gives her wings.
10. He was once **anvil,** but is now hammer.
11. If you are an **anvil** you will suffer like an anvil, if you are a hammer you will hit like a hammer.
12. The understanding of an **Arab** is in his eyes.
13. The Yemen is the cradle of the **Arab race**; the Iraq is its grave.
14. To **ask** well is to know much.
15. If the **ass** is summoned to the wedding it is to carry wood.
16. He who drives an **ass** must of necessity smell its wind.
17. Tie the **ass** where the owner wants.
18. If I am master, and you are master, who shall drive the **asses**?
19. The lazy man becomes an **astrologer.**
20. If a mother loves her **baby** she is happy. (*Mesopotamian.*)
21. If you are no listener you will be no **backbiter.**
22. More just than a **balance.**
23. First at the **banquet** and last at the brawl.
24. The **barber** learns his art on the orphan's face.
25. Every **bean** finds its blind measurer.
26. No worm-eaten **bean** remains without finding a half-blind measurer.
27. Each man is master of his own **beard.**
28. When your son's **beard** has grown, shave your own.
    [i.e. the father must make way for his son when he is grown up.]
29. Every **beard** has its comb.
    [i.e. honour a person according to his dignity.]
30. The **beard** of the guest is in the hands of the owner of the tent.
31. All is soap to **Bedouins.**
32. The **Beduwy's** mind is in his eyes. (*Bedouin.*)
33. A handful of **bees** is worth more than a sackful of flies.
34. Ride on a **beetle,** rather than walk on a carpet.
35. They came to shoe the Pasha's horse and the **beetle** stretched out his leg.
36. Defend me from the **beggar** become wealthy, and from the slave become a freeman.
37. **Begging** is a philosopher's stone, but standing at the door is hard.
38. **Begging** is an easy trade, only the standing at the door is tiresome.

39. The merit belongs to the **beginner** [originator] should even the successor do better.
40. Thy **beloved** is the object thou lovest, were it even a monkey.
41. Man is the slave of **beneficence.**
42. Whatever you bring up will **benefit** you, except man; if you bring him up, he will uproot you.
43. He that **betrays** one that betrays him not, Allah shall betray him.
44. **Birth** is the messenger of death. (*Syrian.*)
45. This is not the **bishop's square.**
46. He who compels you to **blame** him has made up his mind to forsake you.
47. **Blame** not, nor boast, until a year and a half shall have passed away.
48. A person sat demanding from God the rise of morn—when morn rose he became **blind.**
49. Kohl is better than **blindness.** (*Syrian.*)

    [i.e. better to have a little than lose all.—Kohl, if used for a month, may save the eye.]
50. A **book** is like a garden carried in the pocket.
51. One kisses the **book** out of consideration for its contents.
52. When one gives **bread** [gifts or an entertainment] to honourable men it is a loan, but to contemptible or dishonourable men it is charity.
53. His **bread** is baked, and his jar is full.

    [Said of a prosperous and contented man.]
54. Send your **bread** to the oven of the baker, though he should eat the half of it.
55. The man of good **breeding** eats beans, and returns to his breeding. (*Syrian.*)
56. Me and my **brother** against my cousin; me and my cousin against the foreigner.
57. A **brother** of girls is one to whom God has given a pure heart to love all women as his sisters and a strong arm to fight in their defence.
58. Be **brothers,** but keep accounts.
59. When a **business** seizes thee by the head, take it thou by the tail.
60. Everyone rakes the embers to his own **cake.**
61. The **camel-driver** has his plans, and the camel has his.
62. A **camel** going to seek horns lost his ears.
63. The **camel** is an open shop.

    [i.e. it is always accessible.]
64. The **camel** is satisfied only with the milk-thistle.
65. The **camel** kneels on the place of the camel. (*Syrian.*)

    [Spoken when dismissing a servant; another can soon be found.]
66. A **camel** knows not God until he splits. (*Mesopotamian.*)

    [i.e. dies.]
67. The **camel** laughed till he split his lip. (*Bedouin.*)

    [Said of extremists.]
68. He who houses a **camel** must make his door higher.
69. The **camel** never sees its own hump, but that of its brothers is always before its eyes.
70. Rather endure the flatulencies of the **camel** than the prayers of the fishes.
71. Eat like **camels** eat, and rise thou before men.
72. The dogs bark, but the **caravan** passes.
73. The ultimate remedy is a **cautery.**
74. He who sows **charity** reaps friendship.
75. He who is not **chastised** by his parents is chastised by his ill-wisher.
76. The **cheerfulness** of the countenance does more [better] than the generosity of the hand.

77. That which is in the **chest** is spread out upon the body.
78. Men are like closed **chests.**
79. When the **chickens'** feathers are of gold it is foolishness to make broth of the hen. (*Syrian.*)
80. That **child** is loved most who is young until he is grown up, or sick until he recovers, or absent until he returns home.
81. The **child** which is not thine, the more of a fool it is, the greater is thy joy.
82. In the house where there are no **children** they have no light.
83. The **church** which is near does not cure. (*Syrian.*)
84. Live in **cities** even if they oppress you.
85. The holier the **city,** the wickeder its citizens.
86. The borrowed **cloak** never warms. (*Syrian.*)
87. The [live] **coal** burns only its place. (*Syrian.*)
    [i.e. the heart knoweth its own bitterness.]
88. The clever **cock** crows from the egg. (*Syrian.*)
89. The lively **cock** crows from under its mother.
90. He who takes a **cock** for his guide has a hen-coop for refuge.
91. Eating little drives away many **complaints.**
92. **Consideration** may take the place of experience.
93. Be **constant** ; if you say " one ", do not say " two ".
94. **Correspondence** is half a presence.
95. Seek **counsel** of him who makes you weep and not of him who makes you laugh.
96. The greedy mouth of **covetousness** is not filled except by the earth of the grave.
97. He who makes **a crack** can also fill it in.
98. Give **credit** and thou wilt dispose of thy merchandise, claim thy debts and thou wilt have quarrels.
99. A **crow** exclaimed, " God is the truth," then quoth one, " The dirt-scraper has become a preacher."
100. When the **crow** is your guide he will lead you to the corpses of dogs.
101. The **crown** weighs heavy and beneath a diadem there often flow at night more tears than pearls.
102. **Cruelty** is the strength of the wicked.
103. When the **cure** is effected avarice sets in.
104. **Custom** is from Allah.
105. **Custom** is the fifth element in the universe. (*Syrian.*)
106. The habitation of **danger** is on the borders of security.
107. The **date-palm** must have its feet in water and its head in fire.
108. A small **date-stone** props up the water-jar.
109. Bless the **date-trees,** for they are your aunts.
110. Better a handful of dry **dates** and content therewith than to own the Gate of Peacocks and be kicked in the eye by a broody camel.
111. An unmarried **daughter** has a broken wing.
112. Mother a weed, father a weed, do you expect the **daughter** to be a saffron root?
113. The **dawn** does not come twice to awaken a man.
114. The **day** effaces the promise of the night.
115. Do not count the **days** of a month which may never belong to thee.
116. The **dead** is a dog, and yet the funeral procession is numerous.
117. **Death** sends his challenge in a grey hair.
118. He who does not let himself be **deceived** does not let himself be accompanied.
119. The shadow of the **deformed** is deformed also.

120. He who leaves [has] **descendants** is not dead.

121. Always sunshine makes the **desert.**

122. In the **desert** one forgets everything, one remembers nothing any more.

123. There is relief in **despair.**

124. In **despair** are many hopes.

125. The life of man is a **diary** in which he should only write down the good actions.

126. He who puts aside his **dinner** for to-morrow's breakfast will be smiled upon by fortune.

127. He has an incurable **disease** who believes all he hears.

128. Big **dishes** can contain little ones.

129. Every **dog** barks at its door.

130. By all means make friends with the **dog,** but do not lay aside the stick.

131. A leashed **dog** doesn't hunt well.

132. A **dog** travelling with good men becomes a rational being.

133. The spilt blood of a **dog** will soon avenge itself.

134. Don't drive away a **dog** without knowing who is his master.

135. The hunting **dogs** have scratched faces.

136. Only **donkeys** that have sore backs walk haughtily. (*Syrian.*)

[Said of a proud man who is, and has, nothing, and wishes to be thought much of.]

137. Whoso knocks at the **door** hears the reply. (*Syrian.*)

138. If thou knock at the **door** which is not opened to thee, consult thine honour and go. (*Syrian.*)

[Sail when a favour is asked of one who makes excuses.]

139. The **dunghill** must make itself smelt in the field before we can breathe the perfume of the flowers.

140. Nothing but a handful of **dust** will fill the eye of man.

141. Change your **dwelling-place** often, for the sweetness of life consists in variety.

142. **Eat** the present and break the dish.

[Otherwise the dish will remind you of the obligation.]

143. **Eat** whatsoever thou likest, but dress as others do.

144. He who **eats** alone, coughs alone.

145. **Ecclesiastical money** pulls the roof down.

146. Better a thousand **enemies** outside the house than one inside.

147. The **English** are uncles of the Sultan on the mother's side. (*Bedouin.*)

148. He lingers like **English** colonization. (*Iraq.*)

[i.e. a guest who has outstayed his welcome.]

149. The **enmity** of a wise man is worth more than the friendship of a fool.

150. Man is the child of **error.**

151. Universal **errors** are correct.

152. **Escape** from self is better than escape from a lion. (*Syrian.*)

153. One cannot praise the **evening** before it is dawn.

154. The blessings of the **evil genii** are curses.

155. **Experience** is the looking-glass of the intellect.

156. The **eye** does not rise above the eyebrow. (*Syrian.*)

[Said when a person wishes to put himself lower than his friends.]

157. The **eye** of a good horse serves for a tooth. (*Bedouin.*)

158. The dust that is in thine **eye** thou seest it not, but thou canst see the straw that is in the eye of another.

159. Dim **eyes** do not injure when the mind's eye is bright.

160. The **eyes** weep not there where the hands are never fatigued.

161. A **fable** is a bridge which leads to truth.

162. Look first at the **face** before you give a box on the ears.

163. His **face** cuts off all gain.

164. Every man is justified in his own **faith.**

165. Have **faith,** though it be only in a stone, and you will recover.
166. The date of **faithfulness** grows only on the palm of confidence.
167. **False coin** is passed on none but the over-shrewd money-lender.
168. He that leaves **fame** behind him does not die.
169. When **fate** arrives the physician becomes a fool.
170. There are no **faults** in the thing we want badly.
171. He who sees his own **faults** is too much occupied to see the faults of others.
172. **Fear** teaches how to run.
173. **Fear** the attack of the generous man when he is hungry and the mean man when he is satisfied.
174. **February** has no rules.
175. Though **February** storms and blusters, it has the smell of summer in it.
176. If thou **feedest** satisfy, and if thou beatest hurt. (*Syrian.*)
177. To the measure of your bed stretch your **feet.** (*Syrian.*)
178. The **female** is of all animals the better save only in mankind. (*Bedouin.*)
179. There is none in the **ferry-boat** for God's sake.
180. The hope of the **field** is not the heap of the threshing-floor. (*Syrian.*)
181. The best **fighting** is against yourself.
182. **A fig-tree,** looking upon another fig-tree, becometh fruitful.
183. There are four **fingers** between truth and lies. (*Mesopotamian.*)

    [i.e. four fingers fit in between the eye and the ear.]
184. Thou kindlest the **fire** and criest, " Fire."
185. He who warms himself at a **fire** should know that it burns.
186. He who lights a **fire** should not ask to be protected from the flames.
187. Every man thinks his own **fleas** gazelles.
188. Eat the **flesh** of thy wrist and thou shalt have no need of a butcher.
189. A **fly** cannot enter a mouth that knows how to keep silence.
190. Pass by thy **foe** hungry ; but pass him not naked [so that he can see you]. (*Syrian.*)

    [i.e. if you ask a favour of an enemy, do not let him see you want it.]
191. A thousand " Come-to-dinner's " are not equal to setting the **food** before us at once.
192. Pretend to be a **fool** and all will respect you.
193. The most wonderful thing in the world is the success of a **fool** and the failure of a wise man.
194. The doorkeeper of a **fool** can always say there is no one in his master's house.
195. The **fool** has his understanding in his mouth ; but the wise man has his mouth filled with understanding.
196. He who knows not that he knows not is a **fool**—shun him. He who knows that he knows not is wise—teach him.
197. The **fool** who falleth into the fire, rarely falleth out of it.
198. The **foot** only strikes the place it goes to.
199. Everything **forbidden** is sweet.
200. The **forest** is only burnt through its own wood.
201. **Forgiveness** is perfect when the sin is not remembered.
202. He who **forgiveth** others, God forgiveth him.
203. Follow the tracks of the **fortunate man** and you will come to fortune.
204. He who intimately frequents people for **forty days** becomes one of their number.
205. If you live **forty days** with people, you will then either leave them or become like them. (*Syrian.*)

206. He who has gone for **forty days** with the enemy belongs to them.

207. Never start, never arrive on a **Friday** or a Tuesday.

208. If your **friend** be honey, do not eat him.

209. Prove your **friend** before you have need of him.

210. Pray not for the prosperity of thy **friend** lest thou destroy him. (*Syrian.*)

[i.e. when he prospers he will forget you.]

211. The hill you climb to go to a **friend** should be for you a road that goes downhill.

212. The **friend** who makes us lose is a declared enemy.

213. He who has the hands empty has no **friends.**

214. A **friend's dinner** is soon dressed.

215. One of the laws of **friendship** is not to be importunate.

216. **Friendship** of the lips, absent heart.

217. Don't wash the cup of **friendship** with vinegar.

218. **Fruit's** scarce where leaves most abound. (*Mesopotamian.*)

219. The crooked **furrow** is [the work] of the big bull. (*Syrian.*)

[i.e. the fault is from the great man.]

220. The twisted **furrow** proceeds from the great bull.

221. If you would **gain,** send away shame.

222. **Gain** on dirt rather than loss on musk.

223. The **garment** in which you clothe another will last longer than that in which you clothe yourself.

224. The **garment** of salvation never grows old.

225. In proportion to the length of thy **garment,** stretch out thy legs.

226. Remove the **gates** of thy stable to another side [when thy house is in danger from the evil eye].

227. Broad is the shadow of **generosity.**

228. **Generosity** is to do a kindness before it is asked.

229. The bane of a **generous** action is to mention it.

230. A **generous** man is nigh unto God, nigh unto men, nigh unto paradise, far from hell.

231. When someone brings a **gift** on an ass, he receives a gift on a camel.

232. The threshold weeps forty days when a **girl** is born.

233. Do not be ashamed to **give little,** for it is less than that if you give nothing.

234. The thing that has been **given** by the hand is pursued by the foot.

[i.e. a lent thing has to be gone for often.]

235. Every **goat** is tethered by the foot.

[i.e. everyone is answerable for his actions.]

236. The mangy **goat** will drink only from the head of the spring.

237. He who knows himself knows his **God.**

238. No one but **God** and I know what is in my heart.

239. When **God** denies the cultivated date, He gives the wild one.

240. Since **God** has not bent the top of the palm-tree, He has given a long neck to the giraffe.

241. **God** helps everyone in his own religion.

242. **God** lets the coconut fall when there is no one under the palm-tree.

243. **God** may work much mercy before the morning.

244. If you want to disobey **God,** seek a place where He cannot see you.

245. **God** sells knowledge for labour, honour for risk.

246. The man is the shadow of **God,** the slave is the shadow of man, the king is like God.

247. Towards **God's** Gate.
[An Arab saying when one knows not whither he goes.]
248. Think of the **going out** before you enter.
249. **Gold** wants bran [to clean it]—[dependence].
250. Do **good,** and throw it into the sea.
251. Only expect **good** from the good.
252. Do no **good**—thou shalt not find evil.
253. If minds were alike **goods** would age in the shops [bazaars].
254. He who sows kindness reaps **gratitude.**
255. **Gratitude** makes the good turn last.
256. **Gratitude** takes three forms—a feeling in the heart, an expression in words, and a giving in return.
257. Only the **grave clothes** change the physical nature.
258. Honour the **guest** although he be an infidel. (*Mesopotamian.*)
259. The evening **guest** gets no supper.
260. Entertain a **guest** three days before you ask any questions. (*Bedouin.*)
261. Don't lend your **gutter pipe** on a rainy day.
262. **Habit** is a sixth sense that overcomes all the others.
263. May her envier stumble over her **hair.**
264. The **hand** of a man attentive to his work is a balance.
265. Kiss the **hand** that thou canst not bite and pray that it be broken to pieces [utterly broken].
266. **Handicraft** is a spout which sends down gold.
267. Withdraw from **harm** and sing to it.
268. A well-populated **head** is a sign of a generous mind. (*Bedouin.*)
269. He whose **head** is light soon tires his feet. (*Syrian.*)
270. If thou canst not take things by the **head,** then take them by the tail.
271. Two things are only appreciated when we no longer have them, **health** and youth.
272. One day in perfect **health** is much.
273. **Hearsay** is half lies.
274. How many are the roads that lead not to the **heart.**
275. Let not the eye discover what pains the **heart.** (*Syrian.*)
276. What comes out of the mouth comes also out of the **heart.**
277. **Hearts** are the depositories of secrets, lips their locks, and tongues their keys.
278. **Hearts** are witnesses.
279. Keep your tents separate and bring your **hearts** together.
280. There are no fans in **hell.**
281. He who eats the **hen** of the Sultan will return her to him a cow.
282. Even the worm inside a stone eats **herbs.**
283. **Honey** in the bee-hive of fortune turns easily sour.
284. He who touches **honey** is compelled to lick his fingers.
285. The hand of **honour** is a balance. (*Syrian.*)
286. The more you **hope,** the more you suffer.
287. To every noble **horse** a stumble, and to every learned man an error.
288. Honour dwells in the manes of **horses.**
[This is taken from the saying of Mohammed and is often quoted to show the superior distinction which a horseman claims above him who rides upon an ass.]
289. The air of heaven is that which blows between the **horse's ears.**
290. The **host** is the prisoner of his guests. (*Druse.*)
291. The owner of a **house** knows what is in it. (*Syrian.*)
292. O my **house,** my dear little house, hider of my little failings.

293. **Hunger** is an infidel. (*Syrian.*)
[i.e. has no moral scruples.]

294. **Hurry** belongs to the Evil One.

295. My **husband** is not jealous, though my lover came seeking me with a lighted candle in his hand.

296. A **husband** of wood is better than to remain seated in the paternal home.

297. She who has her **husband** with her shall turn the moon with her finger. (*Syrian.*)

298. In bad company the good seem **hypocrites.**

299. I sowed an "**if**" in the valley of "it has been", and there grew up an "I would it were". (*Syrian.*)

300. **Ignorance** that supports me is better than wisdom which I must support.

301. He who treats you as he treats himself does you no **injustice.**

302. Strike the **innocent** that the guilty may confess.

303. The opinion of the **intelligent** is worth more than the certitude of the ignorant.

304. Sup with the **Jew,** but sleep in the house of the Christian.

305. **Judge** not, in order that ye be not judged.

306. When the **judge's** mule dies; everybody goes to the funeral, when the judge himself dies, nobody goes.

307. He who has done **justice** in the night has built himself a house for the next day.

308. The noise of the **kettledrum** goes far. (*Syrian.*)
[i.e. report goes abroad.]

309. He who helps is **kin.**

310. Is the reward of **kindness** anything but kindness?

311. If you wish to be a **king,** become a wild ass. (*Syrian.*)

312. In social matters act as **kinsmen;** in business matters be strangers.

313. Angels bend down their wings to a seeker of **knowledge.**

314. He who gives **knowledge** to those who are not fit for it is a fool; he who withholds knowledge from those who are fit for it is an evil-doer.

315. Light your **lamp** before it becomes dark.

316. Every **land** drinks its water.

317. The **land** of Fear [the Arabs call the desert].

318. Each **language** requires a man.

319. Men **laugh** with their hearts; women only with their mouths.

320. The man who is **lean,** not from hunger, is harder than brass.

321. **Learning** in one's youth is engraving in stone.

322. That which one has **let go,** one must later bring in.

323. Follow the **liar** to the door of his home.

324. The **liberality** of the poor is the best.

325. A learned assembly is a living **library.**

326. One **lie** in the Sultan's head will keep out twenty truths.

327. To **lie** is the salt of a man, but shame to him who believes.

328. A **lie** may be wise, but truth is wisdom itself.

329. Every day in thy **life** is a leaf in thy history.

330. **Life** is a quarantine for Paradise.

331. **Life** is composed of two parts: that which is passed—a dream; and that which is to come—a wish.

332. **Life,** like fire, begins with smoke and ends with ashes.

333. **Light** comes from light, and both lights come from God.

334. If the **light** serves to see it also serves to be seen.

335. Ye that are **like** unto us, come unto us. (*Syrian.*)

336. He who **limps** should visit him who has broken his leg.
[Help those weaker than yourself.]

337. It is more useful to fly from yourself than from a **lion.**

338. The **lion's den** is never empty of bones.

339. **Live**, thou ass, until the clover springs up.

340. **Live** with him who prays and thou prayest, live with the singer and thou singest.

341. Where you get a **living,** remain.

342. Too much tying **loosens.** (*Syrian.*)

343. Who remarks your patience, oh! **louse** that wanders on the head?

344. They wooed her and she resisted; they neglected her and she fell in **love.**

345. **Love** and pregnancy and riding upon a camel cannot be hid. (*Syrian.*)

346. **Love** covers blemishes.

347. Sometimes **love** has been planted by one glance alone.

348. **Love** is the companion of blindness.

349. **Love** lasts seven seconds, the fantasia seven minutes, and the unhappiness lasts all one's life.

350. The **love** of a man for a woman waxes and wanes as the moon, but the love of brother for brother is as steadfast as the stars and endureth as the word of a Prophet.

351. One hour for thy **love,** one hour for thy Lord.

352. If thou wert to see my **luck,** thou wouldst trample it underfoot.

353. Pitch the **lucky man** into the Nile and he will come up with a fish in his mouth.

354. **Lunch** and rest, dine and walk. (*Bedouin.*)

355. The **maggot** is from the cheese itself.

[Said when something disagreeable happens in a family, caused by one of its members.]

356. There is no good in a **man** who is not ashamed of men.

357. **Man's heart** is known only in the fray, and man's head is known only on the way.

358. Accompany a funeral procession, but do not mix thyself up with a **marriage.**

359. He who does not invite me to his **marriage** will not have me at his funeral.

360. Take the high road, though it turn; and **marry** a woman of good birth though she may have been passed by.

361. A good **master** makes a good servant.

362. You are **master** of the unspoken word, the spoken word is master of you.

363. If you buy **meat** cheap, when it boils you will smell what you have saved.

364. If your neighbour has made a pilgrimage to **Mecca** once, watch him; if twice, avoid his society; if three times, move into another street.

365. The mouth isn't cooled by the cutting of the **melon.**

366. Go a **mile** to see a sick man, go two miles to make peace between two men, and go three miles to call on a friend.

367. Every village has a road to the **mill.**

368. When the **mind** becomes large speech becomes little.

369. Where the **mind** inclines, the feet lead.

370. Do not stand in a place of danger trusting in **miracles.**

371. Gold does not belong to the **miser** but the miser to gold.

372. A rich **miser** is poorer than a poor man.

373. A **misfortune** is one, but it becomes two to the impatient.

374. He who is a **mocker** dances without a tambourine.

375. He who earns **money** earns tears.

376. The **moon** is with thee, thou needest not to care about the stars.

377. The **moon** only shines in the absence of the sun—do not strike a nail with your fist, nor mistake the sun for the puff of a candle.

378. The dog howls at the **moon**—the moon heeds it not; therefore be as the moon.

379. **Moonshine** and oil, these are the ruin of a house.

380. There be none less **Moslems** than the Moslemin.

381. When the **mosque** falls in, its prayer niches come into view.

382. If you hear that a **mountain** has moved from its place believe it, but if you hear that a man has changed his character believe it not.

383. The **mouse** that has but one hole is soon caught.

384. Feed the **mouth** and the eye will be bashful.

385. **A mouth** that prays, a hand that kills.

386. A solitary **mule** denies its origin.

387. **Music** is nothing if love is gone.

388. Unhappy is the man who has no **nails** with which to scratch his head.

[i.e. one can only count on oneself.]

389. He has written his **name** in water.

[Said of one whose fame has spread.]

390. At the **narrow passage** there is no brother and no friend.

391. Every creature does according to its **nature.**

392. The **needy** are always listening.

393. The land on which rain has fallen tells it to its **neighbour.**

[i.e. one beggar tells another where alms are given.]

394. Keep thy door closed and so have confidence in thy **neighbour.**

395. Before thou askest about the house, ask about the **neighbour.**

396. Seek the good of thy **neighbour** and thou wilt find good at home. (*Syrian.*)

397. Choose your **neighbour** before your house and your companion before [taking] the road.

398. Thy **neighbour** is thy teacher.

399. Your **neighbour** is your neighbour though he should act otherwise.

400. A loaf more or less, but never let your **neighbour** want.

401. He who cropped your **neighbour** will crop you.

402. God grant us not any **neighbour** with two eyes.

403. Be friends, but do not become **neighbours.**

404. If fat sticks to your own hand, wipe it off on your **neighbour's.**

405. Don't ride on your **neighbour's saddle.**

406. Every **new thing** [novelty] has its delight [sweetness]; the old on the contrary is bitter.

407. If the king at noon-day says it is **night,** behold the stars.

408. The end of **night** is the beginning of day.

409. What is said at **night** the day blots out.

410. He that once drinks of the waters of the **Nile** returns to the Nile.

411. Take the **noble,** though [sleeping] upon a mat. (*Syrian.*)

[i.e. in marriage or hiring servants, prefer blood to money.]

412. The biggest **nuts** are those which are empty.

413. **Obey** him whom thou servest; sell right out rather than pledge or pawn anything.

414. **Oil** comes not but by pressure.

415. He that is **older** than you by a day is wiser than you by a year. (*Syrian.*)

416. An **old man** continues to be young in two things—love of money and love of life.

417. Thou art like **olives:** it is needful to beat thee.

418. "The **one-eyed.**"
[i.e. a face dark on one side and bright on the other. Relates to February showers and sunshine rapidly alternating.]

419. Between the **onion** and its skin one gets nothing but a stink.

420. If the father be **onion** and the mother garlic, how can there be any sweet perfume?

421. Ask the **opinion** of an older one and a younger one than thyself, and return to thine own opinion. (*Syrian.*)

422. He is the best **orator** who can turn men's ears into eyes.

423. Never teach an **orphan** how to weep.

424. Follow the **owl** and he will lead you into a ruined place.

425. In the land of **palm-trees** they feed donkeys on dates.

426. **Paradise** is only to be found on the back of a horse or in the arms of one's beloved.

427. **Paradise** lies under the feet of mothers.

428. To enter through the door of the **passions** is easy, to go out is difficult.

429. Things **past** should not be mentioned.

430. Put on the garment of **patience.**

431. The device of a man who hath no device is **patience.**

432. **Patience** is the key of joy, but haste is the key of sorrow.

433. **Patience** is the key to solace.

434. **Patience** is the medicine of the world.

435. After **patience** there remains only the shovel and the grave.

436. Grease the **paw** and thou mayest take thy ease.

437. The garment of **peace** never fades. (*Syrian.*)

438. Better to have bread and an onion with **peace** than stuffed fowl with strife.

439. There is no **peace** until after enmity.

440. A **peace-maker** gets two-thirds of the blows.

441. Consult the patient, not the **physician.**

442. No man is a good **physician** who has never been sick.

443. That which you **plant** in your garden will bring you profit, but if you plant a man there he will drive you out.

444. Strike thy **platter** ; thou wilt receive a hundred lickers.
[i.e. plenty of parasites when the meal is ready.]

445. **Play** alone, thou wilt win. (*Syrian.*)

446. Live with one who **plays** and thou playest.

447. **Pleasure** is the son of love, but it is an unnatural son who slays his father.

448. Do not drink **poison,** relying upon the antidote you may possess.

449. He that stirs **poison** will taste it. (*Syrian.*)

450. He who sleeps in a **pond** wakes up cousin to the frogs.

451. A **poor man** went to enjoy himself, but found no room. (*Syrian.*)

452. You can only take out of a **pot** what you put into it.

453. What you put into the **pot** you will take out in the ladle.

454. Were it not for fractures there would be no **pottery.**

455. **Poverty** with freedom from debt is great wealth.

456. His business is soon dispatched who sends a **present** before him.
[Said of people who visit officials of the government.]

457. The **promise** of the night is rubbed with butter, which melts away when the day shines on it.

458. **Promises** made in the night-time be not binding by day-light.

459. Consider thy **property** nothing else than a trust in thy hands.

460. There is something wise in every **proverb.**

461. That a **proverb** is to speech what salt is to food.

462. **Proverbs** are the lamps to words.

463. **Prudence** appears in two things: in moderation when we are angry, and in forgiveness when we have the power to punish.

464. **Punishment** does not right a wrong, but it prevents a hundred others.

465. **Punishment** is lame, but it comes.

466. Tear off the curtain of doubt by **questions.**

467. He fled from the **rain** and sat down under the waterspout.

468. He who comes with **rain** comes with a blessing.

469. Summer **rain** is like a guest.

[i.e. the latter should not stay too long.]

470. A thousand **raps,** but no welcome.

471. Beware of **rashness,** for it has been well called the Mother of Regrets.

472. The young **ravens** are beaked like the old.

473. If they call thee **reaper,** whet thy scythe.

474. No **religion** without courage.

475. There is a **remedy** for everything in patience, but for lack of patience there is no remedy.

476. The best part of **repentance** is little sinning.

477. **Reproaches** are the soap of the heart.

478. He who **resembles** his own kind wrongs no one.

479. Who does not take his just **revenge** has an ass for uncle.

480. To abstain from desires is **riches.**

481. There is no **rising up** without a falling down before it. (*Syrian.*)

482. Take the **road** to salvation even though it goes a roundabout way.

483. All **roads** lead to the flour mill. (*Syrian.*)

484. A **rose** sometimes falls to the lot of a monkey.

485. How can a man die who has **sage** in his garden?

[The aromatic scent of sage carried to the herbalist of the past a sense of life over death.]

486. The morning **salutation** to the bean-seller and not to the druggist.

487. There is **salve** in nature for every sore. (*Bedouin.*)

488. The **sand** blows in the face of him who prays.

489. Walk with **sandals** till God procures you shoes.

490. There are two that are never **satisfied**—the seeker of knowledge and the seeker of wealth. (*Syrian.*)

491. The ink of **science** is more precious than the blood of martyrs.

492. You must **scratch** your own head with your own nails.

493. A stream doesn't trouble the **sea.**

494. If you would keep your **secret** from your enemies, keep it also from your friends.

495. One who puts a **secret** in a sling.

[i.e. the habitual tale-bearer.]

496. He that tells a **secret** is another's servant.

497. He who hides his **secret** obtains his desire.

498. [Son of man] If you have no **self-respect,** do what you will.

499. If a **serpent** love thee, wear him as a necklace.

500. **Seven** thou shalt not neglect: thy wife as long as she lives in peace with thee; thy livelihood as long as it provides for thee; thy ornament as long as it adorns thee; thy friend as long as he is just to thee; thy table com-

panion as long as he understands thee; thy son as long as he cannot take care of himself; and thy guest as long as he does not molest thee.

501. When a **Sheikh** dies his friendships die with him. (*Druse.*)

[i.e. the tribe is free to make new alliances.]

502. The captain of the **ship** loves thee; wipe thy hand on the sail.

503. I had no **shoes,** and I murmured, till I met the man who had no feet.

504. When the **shopkeeper** has nothing to do he changes the weights.

505. An enemy's visit to a **sick person** is worse than the disease.

506. The **sight** is more truthful than the voice.

507. **Silence** is the best answer to the stupid.

508. **Silence** is the sweet medicine of the heart.

509. Pass near to that which makes a noise, but beware of that which is **silent.**

510. A man should not sleep on **silk** till he has walked on sand.

511. No **sin** in which one persists is venial and no fault for which one asks pardon is mortal.

512. Never **sit** in the place of the man who can say to you, "Rise."

513. **Sleep** comes not to him who is cold, nor to him who is hungry, nor to him who is in fear.

514. To **sleep** on the mountain peaks.

[i.e. dream.]

515. The **snake** when he is in straits wounds himself in the belly.

516. If you are too **soft** you will be squeezed, and if you are too dry you will be broken.

517. Thy **son** is as thou art.

518. My heart is on my **son,** my son's is on a stone.

519. The **son** of fifty dieth not at thirty.

520. There is no **sorrow** of which one finds not one day the end; there is no position in life which gives not place to another.

521. The Almighty laughed when He made the **Soudan.**

522. **Sparks** fly on to him who goes with the smith.

523. **Spend** that which will not remain with you; purchase that which will remain.

524. A **sponge** to wipe out the past; a rose to make the present sweet; and a kiss to salute the future.

525. He who has no **spoon** burns his hand.

[i.e. he who has no friends has much difficulty in getting on in life.]

526. Wait [for grass], O donkey, until **spring** comes. (*Syrian.*)

527. Never **stand** when you can sit, never sit when you can lie.

[Applied to men only.]

528 A **strainer** is none the worse for having another hole.

529. The **stranger** is for the wolf. (*Bedouin.*)

530. All **strangers** are relatives to each other.

531. Dwell not upon thy weariness, thy **strength** shall be according to the measure of thy desire.

532. He who **strikes** himself with his own hand weeps not.

533. He who receives the **strokes** is not like him who counts them.

534. The **strong man** and the waterfall channel out their own path.

535. When another man **suffers,** a piece of wood suffers.

536. He who visits the **Sultan** should enter the palace blind, and come out dumb.

537. Every man is a **Sultan** to himself, and the tail of a dog is never straight.

538. The **sun** cannot withdraw from the bleacher.

539. You cannot **surprise** the protected.

540. He who inhabits a promontory is a **swimmer.**

541. It is better to hear "**Take**" a thousand times than once the word "Give."

542. As hills of sand to the feet of the traveller, so is the voice of the incessant **talker** to the ears of the wise.

543. He **talks** a stick from every valley. (*Syrian.*)

[Said of one who talks much nonsense.]

544. The **teaching** of children is like engraving in stone, the teaching of adults like waves on the sea.

545. In bad times all the old have **teeth.**

546. Man is hidden under the **teeth.**

547. Who gives not **thanks** to men gives not thanks to God.

548. One cannot watch the **thief** of [in] one's own house.

549. If a man **think well** of you, make his thought true.

550. Most **thoughts** are wishes.

551. There are **three classes** of people in the world: the first learn from their own experience—these are wise; the second learn from the experience of others—these are the happy; the third learn neither from their own experience nor the experience of others—these are fools.

552. **Three things** cannot hide themselves: love, a mountain, and a man on a camel.

553. **Time** consists of two days—one for thee, the other against thee.

554. The thing that did not come **to-day** is prepared for to-morrow.

555. The egg of **to-day,** not the hen of to-morrow. (*Syrian.*)

556. With **to-day** there is to-morrow.

557. The ills of man come to him from his **tongue.**

558. Man is hidden behind his **tongue.**

559. The saving of man is the holding of his **tongue.**

560. Nothing on earth is so deserving of a long imprisonment as the **tongue.**

561. Let not your **tongue** cut your throat.

562. The **tongue** is the neck's enemy.

563. The **tongue** of the wise is in his heart, the heart of the fool is in his mouth.

564. The **tongues** of men are the pens of truth.

565. All that is **too much** is too little.

566. When one has too many **trades** one dies of hunger.

567. From the tree of silence hangs its fruit, **tranquillity.**

568. Judge a **tree** by its bark and not by its fruit.

569. Do not order the **tree** to be cut down which gives thee shade.

570. When you shoot the arrow of **truth,** first dip its point in honey.

571. **Truth** is armed with horns.

572. It is a good thing to hear the **truth,** it is a good thing to speak the truth, and—to talk about date-stones!

573. **Truth** may walk through the world unarmed. (*Bedouin.*)

574. He who speaks the **truth** must have one foot in the stirrup.

575. Tie a **turban** of straw round thy head, but do not forget thy engagements.

576. The tyranny of the **Turk** is better than the justice of the Arab.

577. Better the cruelty of the **Turks** than the justice of the Bedouins.

578. There are **two classes** of men: those who have the means to enjoy themselves but are not happy; and those who seek happiness and find it not.

579. If the **unlucky man** were to trade in winding sheets, no one would die.

580. Nothing can ooze from a **vase** but drops of the liquid it contains.

581. He wears a **veil** upon a veil.

582. The contemplation of **vice** is a vice.

583. On the day of **victory** no fatigue is felt.

584. **Vinegar** given is better than honey bought.

585. One **vinegar seller** does not like another vinegar seller.

586. God bless him who pays **visits** —and short visits.

587. The month in which thou hast no **wages**—do not count its days.

588. Remain afar and await what you **want.**

589. [To carry on] **war** with spy-glasses is easy.

590. Beat the **water,** and [still] it is water. (*Syrian.*)

[Said of a pig-headed person.]

591. The lowland drinks its own **water** and the water of the other [upland]. (*Syrian.*)

[i.e. he keeps friendly with all.]

592. If the **water** comes like a deluge, place thy son under thy feet.

593. He who gives his **weapon** is himself struck with it.

594. Those who give the **wedding feast** sigh for the broth.

[i.e. customary to put best portions before the guests.]

595. **Wedlock** is like a besieged fortress ; those who are outside wish to get in, and those who are inside wish to get out.

596. Dew fills not an empty **well.** (*Syrian.*)

597. **Well-being** and tranquillity are found in the moderation of the desires.

598. A **well** is not to be filled with dew.

599. Reserve the **white coin** for the black day.

600. The most **wicked** of men is he who accepts no apology, covers no sin, and forgives no fault.

601. Alas for the man whose affliction is his **wife.**

602. Each one must manage his **wife** according to his experience.

603. **Wisdom** is made up of ten parts, nine of which are silence, and the tenth is brevity of language.

604. **A wise man's** day is worth a fool's life.

605. Good for the **wolf** and good for the sheep.

[i.e. a fair price.]

606. Speak of the **wolf** and prepare the stick.

607. Who can act so as to please a **woman ?**

608. What manner of man is he who is less than a **woman ?**

609. When a **woman** goes on a journey it is because a man opens the door for her.

610. If a **woman** has sworn your undoing, pass the night awake ; if a man has sworn your undoing, pass the night sleeping.

611. The disgrace of a **woman** is abiding.

612. The scald - headed **woman** prides herself on the hair of her [maternal] aunt's daughter. (*Syrian.*)

[Said about a small or a bad man who boasts the greatness of his relations.]

613. It is better for a **woman** to marry the man who loves her than to mate with the man she loves.

614. Drink from the hand of the **woman** you love, but do not let her drink from yours.

615. He who wishes to excel in wisdom should not allow himself to be ruled by **women.**

616. Where **women** are honoured there the gods are pleased.

617. **Women** are part cut out of men.

618. **Women** are the snares of Satan.

619. When you get near **women** you get near trouble.

620. Give me **wool** to-day and take sheep to-morrow.

621. The **word** which you keep between your lips is your slave, the word spoken out of season is your master.

622. He who is impatient to hear one **word** will have to listen to many.

623. Be content with **work** for moderate wages—do not throw thyself out of work [for a shadow].

624. All the world replenishes the basket of him who **works.**

625. The **world** is a scratching of donkeys.

626. Purchase the next **world** with this ; so shalt thou win both.

627. The most **worthless things** on earth are these four : rain on a barren soil, a lamp in sunshine, a beautiful woman given in marriage to a blind man, and a good deed to one who is ungrateful.

628. Who rises with **wrath** sits down with loss.

629. There are three states of **wretchedness**—sickness, fasting, and travel.

630. What you **write** is the truest thing that can be said of you.

631. With whom **you are** such one you are. (*Syrian.*)

632. The remembrance of **youth** is a sigh.

ARMENIAN

1. Although you know very much, nevertheless take **advice** from your hat.

2. It is better to be **ashamed** below the mountain than on its top.

3. The **ass** can swim in seven ways, but when he sees water he forgets them all.

4. The **ass** does not bray under its load.

5. My **bread** has no salt.
   [i.e. my good acts are not known.]

6. Eat the **bread** of the friend as that of the enemy.

7. He that mounts a **camel** would not become hunch-backed.

8. If you send your **child** on an errand, go with him.

9. The **cock** that crows at an untimely hour must lose its head.

10. Choose your **consort** with the eyes of an old man, and your horse with the eyes of a young man.

11. The **day** can dawn without the cock's crowing.

12. To fill a **ditch** a mound must come down.

13. Our **dog** is so good that the fox has pupped in our poultry house.

14. As much as the **dog** runs, it comes to the village with its master.

15. **Dogs** which fight each other unite against the wolf.

16. Stand far from **dwarfs,** for God has stricken them on the head.

17. He whose **eyes** move in their orbit has the devil in the belly.

18. The **eyes** of him who buys are in the hands of him who sells.

19. Can one **fast** with the cake in his hand ?

20. One cannot give a **fist cuff** on the point of a needle.

21. Be learned, but be taken for a **fool.**

22. Having called a man a **fool** for forty days, he became one.

23. The **fool** is never unhappy ; the wise is not always happy.

24. **Foot-ache** is forgotten, headache not.

25. When one's **fortune** augments, the column of his house appears to him crooked.

26. The **fox** sits but once on the thorns.
27. The **fox's** last hole is the furrier's shop.
28. At first sight **friend**; at second meeting brother.
29. Dine with thy **friend**, but do no business with him.
30. The **friend** looks at the head, the enemy at the feet.
31. The **friend** who does not help me, the enemy who does not injure me, are both a pair of ear-rings.
32. Nobody casts stones at a **fruitless tree.**
33. A good **girl** is worth more than seven boys.
34. **God** helps the careless man.
35. **God** turns the mill of the fool.
36. If **God** wishes to rejoice the heart of a poor man He makes him lose his donkey and find it.
37. **Gold** shines in obscurity.
38. Everyone's **grain** grows straight, mine grows crooked.
39. To a bald **head** a golden comb.
40. Every man has in his **heart** a lion that sleeps.
41. He who is nearer to your **heart** is he who is farther from you.
42. Dark **heart**—white teeth.
43. He feeds the **hen** with one hand and takes her egg with the other.
44. When he rides a **horse** he forgets God; when he comes down from the horse he forgets the horse.
45. The kick of a quiet **horse** strikes strong.
46. The new **house**, like the new consort, fails every day, on one side.
47. Who **knows** much, mistakes much.
48. If you are favoured by the sky, the **lamb** of the feast will come of itself to your door.
49. There is a **life** of iron and a life of silver.
50. A **light** abroad—a fire at home.
51. If everyone becomes **lord**, who will turn our mill?
52. **Love** has got grown garlic.
53. **Love** without clamour, hatred can come; hate without rancour, love can return it.
54. The **miser** is one-eyed, the ambitious is blind.
55. The **miser** is the real poor.
56. **Misfortune** and fortune are sisters.
57. The **mother** who has a daughter always has a hand in her purse.
58. When you open the **mouth**, open also the eyes.
59. Everyone places wood under his own **pot**.
60. He who takes the **raven** for companion must not come off the dung-hill.
61. The eyes of the **rich** are dim.
62. If you cannot become **rich**, become the neighbour of a rich man.
63. **Riches** give beauty to the ugly, feet to the cripple, eyes to the blind, and interest to tears.
64. The **robber** has only committed one crime, the robbed one hundred.
65. What can the **rose** do in the sea, and the violet before the fire?
66. Will you know a **secret?** Ask a child, a madman, a drunkard, and a wife.
67. Warm a frozen **serpent**, and it will sting you first.
68. The **serpent** goes everywhere crooked, but enters straight into its hole.
69. He who asks has one **shame**, but he who refuses has two.
70. He who mounts an ass has one **shame**; he who falls from it has two.
71. Before the **stout one** has become thin, the thin one is already dead.
72. Every **stream** does not carry joists.
73. **Tears** are a language; he who weeps only understands them.
74. Thick and **thin** fetch the same price; alas for her who spins thin.

75. The **tree** says to the axe, "You could not **cut** me if I had not given you the handle."

76. Give a horse to him who tells the **truth.**

[i.e. that he may escape after telling it.]

77. I do not **want** it ; put it in my pocket.

78. The **water** in which I drown I call an ocean.

79. Mistrust the **water** that does not warble, and the stream that does not chirp.

80. Do not spit into the **well** from which you have drunk.

81. The **wife** makes herself known at the cradle.

82. What the **wind** brings the wind carries away.

83. The **winter** be bathkeeper, the summer vinekeeper.

84. The **wolf** knows no reckoning.

85. The **wolf** with education becomes no lamb.

86. **Words** draw the nails from the heart.

87. The **world** is a pot ; man a spoon in it.

88. The **world** is a whet-stone and man a knife.

89. **Youth** carves on stone ; old age on ice.

BURMESE

1. **Affliction** is the touchstone of friendship.

2. If you do not know, **ask ;** if it is not clean, wash.

3. If the **beginning** is good, the end must be perfect.

4. There is no one on earth who is not **blamed.**

5. One's **blood** kills one.

6. A short **boat** is hard to steer.

[i.e. a dwarf is quick in temper.]

7. Even **Buddha** cannot become enlightened unless he has something to lean on.

8. A **centipede** doesn't stop for a game leg.

9. If a **cock** ruffles up his feathers it is easy to pluck him.

[i.e. if a man gets angry he is done for.]

10. A **cow** that can give no milk will kick.

[i.e. an ignorant man is to be feared for his ignorance.]

11. When a person has once **died** he understands the price of boards.

12. The **doctor** should be old, the lawyer should be young.

13. Men pay no heed to a **dog** that is always barking.

14. One **dreams** though one is awake.

15. **Eating** while seated makes one stout, eating standing increases strength, walking augments life, running wards off sickness.

16. If it is a real tusk of the **elephant** it will never be eaten up by insects.

17. There is no **enemy** like sickness ; no love is equal to self-love ; no power equal to moral merit.

18. If you want to go **fast,** go the old road.

19. **Fire,** water, a woman, a fool, a snake, royal families—these should be zealously avoided, knowing that they protect life like Death himself.

20. One throws away the baked **fish** when one sees the fresh fish.

21. Where these **five**—a man of wealth, an astrologer, a king, a river, and likewise a doctor—are not to be found, there one should not remain for even a day.

22. With **fowls** it is hereditary strain, with men it is lineage.

23. People are their own **friends** or their own enemies ; one is always a friend to himself, or always an enemy.

24. The **good,** like clouds, receive only to give away.

25. Desire for **haste** is delay.

26. The thoughts of his **heart,** these are the wealth of a man.

27. A man from **hell** is not afraid of hot ashes.

28. Those who **help** others will not be poor even when they become old.

29. Day does not dawn because the **hen** crows. [Applied to interfering, officious women.]

30. **Iron** destroys and rusts itself.

[i.e. a man is often his own worst enemy.]

31. In **journeying** at an improper time, one step ; in eating improper food, one mouthful (is sufficient to cause mishap).

32. Basking in the rising sun, inhaling the smoke from the bodies of the dead, maintaining an aged wife, and eating a curd meal at night, always destroy **life.**

33. Wishing for **long life,** one should eat facing east ; wishing for wealth he should face the south ; if he desire prosperity he should eat facing the west ; one should not eat facing the north.

34. One life, one **love.**

35. Great **love,** great resentment.

36. The more you know, the more **luck** you have.

37. If the **medicine** is good, it is as big as the head of a louse.

38. It cannot be later than **midnight.**

[i.e. a man cannot suffer greater misery than he has already undergone.]

39. More **money** always wins the case.

40. Don't speak like the **mountain,** it is so easy to fall off.

41. The **mouth** of man knows only how to find fault.

42. Where the **needle** goes, the cotton must follow.

43. A thing floats when it gets rotten ; the **news,** if not true, will not spread.

44. Among wonderful things is a sore-eyed person who is an **oculist.**

45. One **part** should be used in enjoyment, two parts in business, a fourth should be put by ; it will answer for emergencies.

46. **Property** is guarded by luck.

47. If there is a **question,** there is also an answer.

48. If you trust the **servants** you will be only one eye blind ; you will be two eyes blind if you trust your sons and daughters.

49. Beware of a man's **shadow** [i.e. his relations], and a bee's sting.

50. It is only when there is elevation that a **shadow** is cast.

51. **Shame,** not fright, kills one.

52. The stick falls on the **sore.**

53. Don't help a **sound man,** or salve an official's boat.

54. The five **spirits** which remain in the body—calmness, ability, wisdom, modesty, and honour—are taken away from the portals of request [one who loses these qualities].

55. One can be **straightforward** only when one is well fed.

56. What is there that can justify **tears** and lamentations ?

57. One should not open the mouth of a presentation cow and look at the **teeth.**

58. If unskilful in picking up, it is **theft ;** if skilful in theft, it is picking up.

[i.e. one may steal a horse while another may not look over the hedge.]

59. **Three things** on the earth are accounted precious—knowledge, grain, and friendship.

60. **Thrift** makes one a slave.

61. Taking shelter under the shade of a **tree** and breaking off its branches [ingratitude].

62. Better a **woman** blind than too beautiful.

63. **Women's** appetite is twice that of a man, their intelligence four times, and their desires eight times.

KHYAUNGTHA OR CHAUNGTHA

(SEE INDIA AND CEYLON, PAGE 418)

PALAUNG

(Shan States, Burma)

1. If thou art not skilful at **dancing,** then thou canst strike the gong [so that others may dance].
2. Water does not enter the heart of a **fish.**

   [i.e. a little brother cannot enter into the thoughts of an older one.]
3. To hear and to see is good for the **heart ;** when the heart is sweet it lives in the mouth.
4. People who come from **hell** are not afraid of hot ashes ; people with curly hair have been in hell.

   [i.e. previous existence.]
5. Step on the blade of a **hoe,** and the handle may hit thy forehead.

   [i.e. if one of a family is injured, the others will avenge him.]
6. When a **knife** is broken, it has been too sharp.
7. It is as difficult to win **love** as to wrap salt in pine-needles.
8. **Money** is like a flea ; it skips away, here a moment, then where it has gone, who can say ?
9. People who never have had **money,** speak like the flowers of the pumpkin ; people who never have been poor, have words as sweet as jaggery.

   [Palaungs say pumpkin flowers gape with open mouths ; poor people are often boastful. Jaggery is a coarse sugar.]
10. **Silver** hoarded is only worth copper.
11. Whoever **speaks** sweetly, eats out of a bowl of red lacquer, but he who speaks ill, eats from the chipped cover of a pot of earthenware.
12. Cattle, **tigers ;** slaves, masters.

    [i.e. servile people always have masters.]
13. Go quickly and return quickly, for thou hast still many roads to **travel.**
14. If **water** is noisy, there are no fish in it.
15. **Widows** [and widowers] are very brave ; they look to right, they look to left, and are not afraid to try again.

    [i.e. flirt.]
16. Do not look at the edge of a **winnowing-basket,** rather look at the edge of the horizon.

    [i.e. do not be narrow-minded.]
17. One **word** spoken may last for a lifetime.
18. **Work** little, eat little.

SHAN

1. Don't **bathe** if there is no water.

   [i.e. don't undertake impossible tasks.]

2. If your arm **breaks,** let it break in your sleeve; if your head breaks, let it break in your hat.

   [i.e. keep your troubles to yourself.]

3. If you **eat** slowly you will not have stomach-ache.

   [i.e. take time for deliberation.]

4. Do not lift your **jacket** to show your back.

   [i.e. if you have done anything disgraceful, hide it.]

5. Every **pond** has its fish; every dog has its owner.

   [i.e. no one is so poor as to be without possessions.]

6. **Thunder** without rain is like words without deeds.

7. What is difficult to **understand,** place before you; what is easy to understand, place behind you.

   [i.e. be not afraid to tackle difficult problems.]

CHINESE

(Including Buddhism, Confucianism and Taoism)

An Introduction to this collection by Lionel Giles, M.A., D.Litt., will be found on page xl.

1. Three-tenths according to a man's **abilities;** seven-tenths according to his costume.
2. Behind the **able man** there are able men.
3. In **accommodating** others you accommodate yourself.
4. The best kind of **acquaintance** is acquaintance with each other's hearts.
5. **Act** as if you were watching over an infant.
6. He who grasps at a small **advantage** incurs a great loss.
7. Thinking of others' **advantage** will turn out to one's own.
8. When the bitters of **adversity** are exhausted, then come the sweets of happiness.
9. **Adversity** is sometimes the rain of spring.
10. If you are old, give **advice;** if you are young, take it.
11. All human **affairs** are my affairs.
12. To plan **affairs** rests with man; to complete affairs rests with heaven.
13. There are only **affectionate** fathers and mothers, but no affectionate sons and daughters.
14. **Age** lacks kindness as dry weather dew.
15. **Almonds** come to those who have no teeth.
16. **Alms** done openly will be repaid secretly.
17. The poor give **alms** modestly, the rich fling them contemptuously and the great accompany them with reproofs.
18. Only imbeciles want credit for the achievements of their **ancestors.**
19. Bad descendants involve **ancestors** in disgrace.

    [The sins of descendants are charged upon ancestors—a purely Chinese notion. They must have committed some enormous crime to cause their descendants thus to sin.]

20. When you are very **angry,** don't go to law; when you are very hungry, don't make verses.
21. When a man is **angry** he cannot be in the right.

22. An eating-house keeper doesn't care how big your **appetite** is.
23. Man's **arithmetic** is small; heaven deals in large figures.
24. Keep your broken **arm** inside your sleeve.
25. A man may be **arrested** by mistake, but not released.
26. When the **arrow** is on the string it must go.
27. Just so long as you **ask** nothing, man's nature is bland; for wine, abstainers care little what price you demand.
28. One does not lose by **asking** the way.
29. **Authorities** are to be weighed, not counted.
30. The **autumn chill** is first felt by the thin man.
31. Three things cross the road to **avoid**: a falling tree, your chief and second wives whispering in agreement, and a goat wearing a leopard's tail.
32. When aroused, become **awake**; when awake, reach understanding.
33. The **axe** strikes the chisel, and the chisel enters the wood.
34. In hewing an **axe-handle** the pattern is not far off.
35. Your "**B.A.**" comes by struggling, your "M.A." is heaven-given.
36. An old **bachelor** compares life to a shirt-button, because it so often hangs by a thread.
37. A **Bachelor of Arts'** kindness is but half a sheet of paper.
38. **Bald-headed men** are ready-made Buddhist priests.
39. Of ten **bald men**, nine are deceitful and the tenth is dumb.
40. Better meals without meat, than a home without **bamboo**.
41. The **bamboo** but creaks because the wind bends it.
42. The hollow **bamboo** has drooping leaves.
43. He who lacks a single tael sees many **bargains**.
44. Men and **beasts** are all alike.

    [i.e. all life the same. This proverb is used by the Buddhists to dissuade people from cruelty or killing animals.]
45. A **beast's spots** are on the outside, a man's on the inside.
46. In **bed**—husband and wife; out of bed—guests.
47. The flower attracts the **bee**, but when he departs it is to his lips that the honey clings.
48. The good **bee** will not sip from the faded flower.
49. The **beggar** cannot carry what he has begged himself.
50. The **beginning** and the end reach out their hands to each other.
51. **Behave** towards everyone as if receiving a great guest. (*Confucianism.*)
52. He that does not **believe** in others finds they do not believe in him.
53. A motionless **bell** never chimes.
54. A great **bend** must have a great straightening.

    [Grievous wrong necessitates signal redress.]
55. There are also **better** men to be found even than the best.
56. Compare yourself with the **better off**, and you are dissatisfied; but compare yourself with the worse off and you have more than enough.
57. To go **beyond** is as bad as to fall short. (*Confucianism.*)
58. If a chattering **bird** be not placed in the mouth, vexation will not sit between the eyebrows.
59. A **bird** can roost only on one branch; a mouse can drink no more than its fill from a river.
60. A **bird** in the soup is better than an eagle's nest in the desert.
61. When the wild **bird** lacks food, all the earth is before him.
62. It is the beautiful **bird** which gets caged.

63. Full-fledged **birds** fly away.

64. You cannot prevent the **birds** of sadness from flying over your head, but you can prevent them from nesting in your hair.

65. Man brings nothing at **birth** and at death takes nothing away.

66. **Birth** and death are decreed, wealth and honour rest with God.

67. Without tasting the **bitterest** we never reach the highest.

[No cross, no crown.]

68. If you want to see **black-hearted** people, look among those who pray to Buddha.

69. **Blame** yourself as you would blame others ; excuse others as you would excuse yourself.

70. However stupid a man may be, he grows clever enough when **blaming** others ; however wise, he becomes a dolt when blaming himself.

71. **Blessings** do not come in pairs ; misfortunes never come singly.

72. Guide the **blind** over the bridge.

73. Men do not calculate when the **blossom** is out.

74. He who knows not how to **boast** knows not how to succeed.

75. Never be **boastful ;** someone may come along who knew you as a child.

76. The front **boat** is eyes for the boat behind.

77. A worn-out **boat** still has three thousand nails in it.

78. A **boat** straightens its course when it gets to a bridge.

79. If you ply a large **boat** you will have large debts.

80. Many **boats** do not obstruct a channel ; many vehicles do not block up the road.

[i.e. there is room for all sorts of traders.]

81. The **body** is born whole by the mother ; it is for the son to return it again whole.

82. Pouring in water to stop the **boiling** is not so good as pulling out the firewood from under the oven.

83. To read a **book** for the first time is to make the acquaintance of a new friend ; to read it a second time is to meet an old one.

84. To open a **book** there is profit.

85. If one wishes to be acquainted with the past and the present, he must read five cartloads of **books.**

86. A Bachelor of Arts discusses **books ;** a pork-butcher pigs.

87. One is happy when one has **books,** but happier still when one has no need of them.

88. **Books** do not exhaust words, nor words thoughts.

89. **Books** speak to the mind, friends to the heart, heaven to the soul, and all the rest to the ears.

90. There is a day to be **born** and a time to die.

91. To be **born** is to come out ; to die is to return. (*Taoism.*)

92. Stand and **borrow,** kneel and beg the return.

[The borrower stands, but the creditor has to kneel.]

93. If you **bow** at all, bow low.

94. Draw your **bow,** but do not discharge the arrow ; it is better to frighten a man than to strike him.

95. A hair's breadth at the **bow** is a mile beside the butt.

96. To hand over the **bow** is to hand over the arrow.

[i.e. you are responsible for any injury.]

97. A **bow** long bent waxes weak.

98. **Bowing** in the dark is according to every man's own fancy.

[i.e. to do good secretly is optional.]

99. A **boy** is born facing in ; a girl is born facing out.

[i.e. a boy will remain in the house, a girl will leave it and go to her husband.]

100. If one **branch** does not move, none of the other branches will be swayed.

101. Better establish a **branch** than cut off a line.

[i.e. you must perpetuate yourself in some way or other, either through your own or an adopted child.]

102. The **bread** is gnawed to the flavouring.

[i.e. don't leave off studying just when you are beginning to taste its sweet flavour.]

103. He that builds **bridges** and repairs roads will become blind in both eyes ; he that commits murder and arson will enjoy long life.

104. All within the four seas are **brothers.** (*Confucianism.*)

105. **Brothers** resemble hands and feet.

106. When **brothers** work together mountains are turned into gold.

107. One man will carry two **buckets** of water for his own use ; two will carry one for their joint use ; three will carry none for anybody's use.

[The fewer servants the better served.]

108. You may offer mud loaves to **Buddha.**

[i.e. if only you first settle with the priest.]

109. The sea of **Buddha** has no shore.

110. **Buddha** lives in one's heart.

111. If you pray to **Buddha,** pray to one only.

112. Destroy all passion while you light **Buddha's lamp.**

113. A **bully** does not owe debts.

114. The most important thing in life is to get **buried** well.

115. Any soil will do to **bury** in.

116. There are only two **busy people** in the world.

[i.e. fame and gain.]

117. When the **butcher** dies, do you suppose we shall eat our pork with the bristles on ?

118 Able to **buy,** don't so buy as to frighten the seller ; able to sell, don't so sell as to frighten the buyer.

119. Before you think of **buying,** calculate on selling.

120. The **cabbage** grub in the end dies in the cabbage.

[i.e. the wicked die in their sins.]

121. He is equal to any task who can live on **cabbage-stalks.**

122. The only way to keep a family in existence for generations is to think **cabbage-stalks** nice.

[i.e. to be economical in food.]

123. Prepare for **calamity** while not yet in bud.

124. **Calamities** [do] not single walk.

125. New-born **calves** don't fear tigers.

126. At the **camping-place** where there's water there's no grazing ; where there's grazing there's no water ; where there are no mosquitoes the wind is bitter ; when you've got your father your mother isn't there.

127. When the **canals** are full the wells are full.

128. A **candle** as big as a cup cannot illuminate to-morrow.

129. One should be able to eat in **Canton,** to live in Soochow, and to die in Hangchow.

[Canton has the best food, Soochow is noted for its beautiful women, and Hangchow for its coffins.]

130. Union of **capital** is like union of fate.

131. A man without distant **care** must have near sorrow.

132. When the leading **carriage** is upset the next one is more careful.

133. **Carrying-poles** which bend easily do not break.

[Inculcating forbearance.]

134. When there is a **cart** ahead there is a track behind.

[i.e. follow the precedent.]

135. You may make a **cart** indoors, but if you go out with it, it must follow the ordinary ruts.

136. A string of **cash** can but reach to the back of one's heel.

137. The want of a single **cash** may drag a hero to the ground.

138. When a **cat** and a rat sleep together, death is well in sight.

139. I gave an order to the **cat,** and the cat gave it to its tail.

[Oriental servants pass on orders to one another and nothing is done.]

140. A blind **cat** catches only a dead rat.

141. A lame **cat** is better than a swift horse when rats infest the palace.

142. What **cat** will not worry rats?

[i.e. who does not desire riches?]

143. It is not the fear of dogs that will make **cats** mew.

144. Better an earth-lined **cave** from which the stars are visible than a golden pagoda roofed over with iniquity.

145. Every **century** repeats it to the other; all false gods produce real ills.

146. There are three hundred rules of **ceremony** and three thousand of behaviour.

147. **Certainty** eats more midday rice than hope.

148. He who sits in the **chair** is a man; he who carries a chair is a man also.

149. He who sends **charcoal** in a snowstorm is the true superior man.

150. To drive the fairy **chariot** on a long journey.

[i.e. to die.]

151. If you are **charitable** you cannot become rich; if you are rich you cannot be charitable.

152. The door of **charity** is hard to open and hard to shut.

153. If you would not be **cheated,** ask the price at three shops.

154. He is truly a superior man who can look upon a game of **chess** in silence.

155. Better be the beak of a **chicken** than the rump of an ox.

[i.e. better to reign in hell than serve in heaven.]

156. One needn't devour a whole **chicken** to know the flavour of the bird.

157. The gem of the sky is the sun; the gem of the house is the **child.** (*Buddhism.*)

158. A **child** but a foot long requires three feet of cloth.

159. When a **child** goes abroad he takes with him his mother's hand.

[i.e. handiwork shows kind of mother.]

160. If one has plenty of money but no **child,** he cannot be reckoned rich; if one has children but no money, he cannot be considered poor.

161. The heart of a little **child** is like the heart of Buddha.

162. A poor family rearing a **child** is oppressed by poverty for three years.

163. If you wish your **children** to have a quiet life, let them always be a little hungry and cold.

164. In **China** are more tutors than scholars, and more physicians than patients.

165. **Chinese rulers** do not concern themselves with barbarians outside the Wall.

166. You can't **chop** a thing as round as you can pare it.

167. The **cicada** knows nothing of snow [it dies in the autumn].

168. Where there is no **cinnabar,** red earth is in high esteem—among the blind, a one-eyed man is king.

169. A clever man builds **cities,** a clever woman throws them down.

[Said to refer to the spoilt favourite Pao Ssŭ.]

170. Be inwardly **clever** but outwardly clownish.

171. **Cleverness** and stupidity betray themselves.

172. A man is estimated by his **clothes,** and a horse by his saddle.

173. To wear embroidered **clothes** and travel by night.

[Hide one's light under a bushel.]

174. He who wears [more] **clothes** is colder; he who wears no [i.e. fewer] clothes is less cold.

175. There is nothing like newness in **clothes**; nothing like age in man.

176. The autumn **cloud** is thin, but the well-wishing of man is thinner.

177. Marry a **cock,** follow a cock.

[i.e. the bed you make you must lie on.]

178. In cold weather **cocks** crow at midnight.

179. He who sits with his back to a draught looks straight into his **coffin.**

180. See always your **coffin** at the end of your cart.

181. Even a bad **coin** must have two sides.

182. Don't let the place get **cold.**

[i.e. strike while the iron is hot.]

183. **Collect** at leisure to use in haste.

184. The **competent** execute, the incompetent enjoy the advantage; the competent toil, the incompetent rest.

185. If you **compliment** everybody, who is there who would be your enemy?

186. The **conceited** man stinks.

187. You expect condiments with vegetables, and a pretty face with a **concubine.**

188. Of all important things, the first is not to cheat **conscience.**

189. Talk of **conscience** and you will have nothing to eat.

190. A good **conscience** pays badly.

191. He who sacrifices his **conscience** to ambition burns a picture to obtain the ashes.

192. A man without **constancy** cannot be either a wizard or a doctor. (*Confucianism.*)

193. To the **contented** even poverty and obscurity bring happiness; to the discontented even riches and honours bring misery.

194. Our **convenience** is the convenience of others.

195. There are three hundred and forty-six subjects for elegant **conversation.**

196. A three years' drought will not starve a **cook.**

197. Beware of helping yourself to **corn** from the manger of the blind mule.

198. When you enter a **country,** enquire what is forbidden there. (*Confucianism.*)

199. Much **courtesy** forestalls offence.

200. He who does not **covet** and who can control his words will be comfortable wherever he goes.

201. **Credit** cuts off customers.

202. Although there exist many thousand subjects for elegant conversation there are persons who cannot meet a **cripple** without talking about feet.

203. Studying in the solitude of the mountains is not equal to sitting at the **cross-roads** and listening to the talk of men.

204. They all say they are good, but who can tell the sex of a **crow?**

205. Call out a name in a **crowd** and somebody is sure to answer.

206. To meet in a **crowd** is to do your business in secret.

207. **Crows** are black all the world over.

208. Better to be a **crystal** and be broken than to remain perfect like a tile upon the house-top.

209. The **culprit** talks small when he sees the bamboo.

210. Of the myriad pleasures none is as the **cup** in the hand; in man's life how often does he see the moon exactly over his head?

211. A **cup** in the hand is worth all besides.

212. The fuller the **cup** the sooner the spill.

213. To **curse** a man every day only adds to his happiness and long life.

214. If there is a **custom,** do not seek to diminish it; if there is no custom, do not seek to add one.

215. **Customers** are to be valued; goods are mere grass.

216. There are **customers** for all sorts of goods.

217. Every time the **cymbals** clash there go three taels of silver.

[This illustrates the expensiveness of idol worship.]

218. If Heaven drops a **date,** you must open your mouth.

219. You can't swallow **dates** whole.

[i.e. you must assimilate what you learn.]

220. A **date stone** cannot stop a waggon.

221. When a **daughter** has grown up she is like smuggled salt.

[Only security to see her disposed of as early as possible.]

222. The elder **daughter-in-law's** shoes are a pattern for the younger.

223. Eighteen goddess-like **daughters** are not equal to one son with a hump.

[Alludes to the eighteen personal disciples of Buddha, the images of which are to be seen in Chinese temples.]

224. The upper classes endow their **daughters** on marriage; the middle classes do nothing, but rear and marry them; the lower classes make money by marrying them.

225. A chance **day** is better than a chosen day.

226. Let the **dead** care for the dead, and the living for the living.

227. A **dead man** is more fortunate than a poor man.

228. **Deaf people** like to pry into other people's affairs; dumb people love to gossip.

229. The fear of **death** is the beginning of discipline.

230. When **decay** has reached its acme, vigour sets in.

[i.e. when things get to the worst, they begin to mend.]

231. Enlightened men perform no dark **deeds.**

232. Teach your **descendants** the two proper roads—literature and farming.

233. Few **desires**—buoyant spirits; many cares—feeble health.

234. **Desires** empty the heart and not to desire refills it.

235. Do not **despair;** even Yen Yüan once cast a missile at the Tablets.

236. When marked out by **destiny,** a person will assuredly be drowned, even though he passes the whole of his existence among the highest branches of a date-tree.

237. **Destiny** has four feet, eight hands, and sixteen eyes; how then shall the ill-doer with only two of each hope to escape?

238. **Deviate** an inch and lose a thousand miles.

239. The poorer one is, the more **devils** he meets.

240. There is **dew** for every blade of grass.

241. He that is afraid to shake the **dice** will never throw a six.

242. Whichever side wins, the **dice-man** doesn't suffer.

243. Man will **die** for money, birds for food.

244. To be born is in the course of nature, but to **die** is according to the decree of destiny.

245. When a bird is about to **die,** its notes are mournful; when a man is about to die his words are good. *(Confucianism.)*

246. **Die** of anger, but don't go to law; die of hunger, but don't be a thief.

247. It is better to **die** two years too soon than to live one year too long.

248. Man **dies** and leaves a name—the tiger dies and leaves a skin.

249. He who **dies** ceases to live, but ceasing to live does not always mean dying.

250. A man at whom everybody points **dies** without being ill.

[Give a dog a bad name and hang him.]

251. He that takes medicine and neglects to **diet** himself, wastes the skill of the physician.

252. When men come face to face their **differences** vanish.

253. In **difficulties** men are easily tested and easily saved.

254. Before **dinner** let us explore the Southern plains and climb the Northern mountains ; after dinner there are snakes in the Southern plains, and there are tigers in the Northern mountains.

255. There is no **dipper** which never strikes the edge of the cooking-pot.

256. Murder may be condoned, but **discourtesy** never.

257. **Discretion** is the handmaiden of truth.

258. An immoderate use of dainties generally ends in **disease ;** and pleasure when past is converted into pain.

259. If there is no **disease** in the abdomen the patient won't die.

260. When a **disease** returns, no medicine can cure it.

261. **Divided** in heart, divided in practice.

262. When you are ill, call in any **doctor.**

263. Nature is better than a middling **doctor.**

264. To take no medicine is as good as a middling **doctor.**

265. When you shut out the sun from coming through the window, the **doctor** comes in at the door.

266. The unlucky **doctor** treats the head of a disease ; the lucky doctor its tail.

267. The son of a great **doctor** usually dies of disease.

268. If you do not pay the **doctor** who has cured you, beware of falling ill again.

269. You should **doctor** your teeth as you govern the military—with severity ; you should doctor your eyes as you govern the people—with gentleness.

270. **Doctors** have a run of ten years' luck.

271. **Doctors** knock at no doors ; they only come when invited.

272. Every **doctrine** has its gate, every gate has its god.

273. If you hear the **doctrine** in the morning you may die in peace at night. (*Confucianism.*)

274. The **doctrine** that enters only into the eye and ear is like the repast one takes in a dream.

275. Give a **dog** an appetizing name and eat him.

276. One **dog** barks at nothing, the rest bark at him.

277. If the **dog** goes when the cat comes there will be no quarrelling.

278. The **dog** guards the night ; the cock rules the morn.

279. A **dog** has no aversion to a poor family.

280. In beating a **dog** have regard to its master.

[i.e. look before you leap.]

281. The **dog** in the kennel barks at his fleas ; the dog that hunts does not feel them.

282. A **dog** is not the only creature that barks.

283. A lean **dog** shames his master.

284. There is no **dog** so thin that you cannot scrape a little fat off him.

285. Never feed a **dog** with corn, nor attempt to pick your teeth with a pair of scissors.

286. **Dogs** have more good in them than men think they have.

287. Spoilt **dogs** steal their master's dinner.

288. If something is **done** for you, it must always be reckoned as good.

[i.e. don't look a gift horse in the mouth.]

289. Other people's **donkey** best turns the mill; the priest from a distance best reads the ritual.

[No man is a prophet in his own country.]

290. When a man who has never been on a **donkey** gets one to ride, he kills it.

291. If he is not of your sort he should not enter your **door.**

292. Who can go out but by the **door?** (*Confucianism.*)

293. To him who waits, time opens every **door.**

294. There is always a way to the open **door.**

295. Only govern your own **door,** and don't talk about other men's daughters and wives.

296. The good **door** is hard to open.

[i.e. it is difficult to begin doing good deeds.]

297. The most securely shut **door** is the one that could be left open.

298. One whose **door** opens on the top of his house.

[i.e. inhospitable man.]

299. Before everyone's **door** there is a part of Heaven.

300. The **dove** recognizes only its own ridge-pole.

301. The **dragon** in shallow water becomes the butt of shrimps.

302. Content with only a kind word is like a **dragon-fly** sipping water.

303. Once scale the **dragon gate,** and your reputation is increased tenfold.

[To "scale the dragon gate" means to take the B.A. degree.]

304. To believe in one's **dreams** is to spend all one's life asleep.

305. In the second and eighth months there is no rule for **dress.**

306. In **dress** and food do not break rules.

307. Friends are at fault when a man is allowed to wear his **dress** awry.

308. At court one sings to **drink;** at the inn one drinks to sing.

309. Ask no favours and everywhere men are affable; if you don't **drink** it doesn't matter what price wine is.

310. After three years of **drought,** all who go out for a day hope for fine weather.

311. **Drunkenness** does not produce faults; it discovers them.

312. The best cure for **drunkenness** is while sober to see a drunken man.

313. It is the sick **duck** that is worried by the weasel.

314. The quiet **duck** puts his foot on the unobservant worm.

315. The lame **duck** should avoid the ploughed field.

316. It is as difficult to gauge a man's heart as it is to chop a **duck's gizzard.**

317. The energy of the **dung-beetle** is put into rolling its ball of dung.

[Every man to his trade.]

318. The **dust** is stirred up by one and flees into the eyes of another.

319. Don't talk small to a **dwarf.**

[i.e. don't talk of ropes in the family of a man who was hanged.]

320. What is told in the **ear** of a man is often heard a hundred miles away.

321. When the **ear** will not listen the heart escapes sorrow.

322. Your **ears** won't go deaf if you don't have them examined; your eyes won't go blind if you refuse to use washes.

323. If two men are of one mind, yellow **earth** can be changed into gold [by their energy].

324. Better linger on **earth** than lie in it.

325. The more you **eat,** the less flavour; the less you eat, the more flavour.

326. What needs warming up may just as well be **eaten** cold.

327. Work may be hastened, but not **eating.**

328. In **eating** other people's food, one eats until the perspiration flows ; in eating one's own, one eats and the tears come.

329. When going to an **eating-house,** go to one which is full of customers [because there everything is fresh, and you can always get what you want] ; when about to take a bath, go to a bath-house that has lost its custom [because there alone will you find clean water].

330. When the face is strong, one **eats** long.

331. There is no **economy** in going to bed early to save candles if the result be twins.

332. The young won't make **efforts** and the old make them in vain.

333. The **eggs** which are laid will be like the fly.

334. There is no **elbow** that bends outward.

335. Even a big **elephant** is caught by a woman's hair.

336. The road to **eminence** lies through the cheap and exceedingly uninviting eating-house.

337. It is a mark of insincerity of purpose to spend one's time in looking for the sacred **emperor** in the low-class tea-shops.

338. If you suspect a man, don't **employ** him, and if you employ him, don't suspect him.

339. Everything is **emptiness,** and emptiness is everything.

[Used in exhorting men not to be anxious.]

340. The more we approach an **enemy,** the more the tigers of the heart become lambs.

341. **Enlightened men** pronounce sentence on themselves.

342. **Enough** is always something more than a man possesses—to obtain one, leads to wishing for two.

343. Always leave some way of escape for the **erring.**

344. The **error** of one moment becomes the sorrow of a whole life.

345. Without **error** there can be no such thing as truth.

346. That from which we can **escape** is not an ill.

347. He who considers **everything** decides nothing.

348. Deal with **evil** as if it were a sickness in your person.

349. **Evil** never travels alone.

350. What the **eye** does not see is regarded as clean.

351. What the **eye** doesn't see, the heart doesn't grieve for.

352. There is no **eye** like the understanding, no blindness like ignorance, no enemy like sickness, nothing so dreaded as death. (*Buddhism.*)

353. Present to the **eye,** present to the mind.

[Out of sight, out of mind.]

354. **Eyebrows** like the leaf of the willow ; eyes like the kernel of the apricot ; a mouth like a cherry ; a face shaped like a melon-seed ; a waist like the poplar and the willow.

355. Nowadays men's **eyelids** are thin.

[i.e. they can see everything and want everything they see.]

356. Matter in the **eyes** gets nothing between the teeth.

357. With **eyes,** life is the road to heaven ; without them, the gate to hell.

358. Never take away a man's **face.**

[i.e. never correct a man in public.]

359. To know a man is not to know his **face,** but to know his heart.

360. To see a person's **face** is better than hearing of his reputation.

361. A man's " **face** " is worth a thousand taels.

362. All men have **faces** as all trees have bark.

363. **Fair maidens** are mostly unlucky ; clever young men are seldom good looking.

364. Don't loose the **falcon** till you see the hare.

[i.e. ask for ready money.]

365. **Falling** hurts least those who fly low.

366. When one **falls** it is not one's foot that is to blame.

367. **False humility** is genuine arrogance.

[i.e. the pride that apes humility.]

368. For **fame** and profit man rushes to a land which even wild geese do not visit.

369. Half a lifetime's **fame** provokes the resentment of a hundred generations.

370. Nobody's **family** can hang up the sign, " Nothing the matter here."

371. Every **family** has a Goddess of Mercy, every place has Amita Buddha.

372. Three years after a **family** has been divided its members become as neighbours.

373. In the **family,** leave the family ; in the world, separate from the world.

[Used of priests.]

374. You can't be the head of a **family** unless you show yourself both stupid and deaf.

[Able to ignore a great deal that goes on.]

375. The woman who sells **fans** often shades her eyes with her hands.

376. To carry out a **fast** is from within ; to break a fast is from without.

377. In a **fast** there must necessarily be a change in food.

378. If a **father** will not be a father, a daughter must still be a daughter.

379. He who tells me of my **faults** is my teacher ; he who tells me of my virtues does me harm.

380. Deal with the **faults** of others as gently as with your own.

381. The first part of the night, think of your own **faults ;** the latter, think of the faults of others.

[When you are asleep.]

382. The **faults** which a man condemns when out of office he commits when in.

383. One can only see one's own **faults** with other people's eyes.

384. To row with the stream in doing a **favour.**

[i.e. to give wine or books to those who are fond of them.]

385. When no **favour** is sought, men are equal ; where water does not flow, it remains at the same level.

386. The first time it is a **favour,** the second time a rule.

387. There are none so fortunate as never to be obliged to ask **favours.**

388. Be forgetful of **favours** given ; be mindful of blessings received.

389. **Feast,** and your halls are crowded ; fast and the world goes by.

390. Earth has no **feasts** which don't break up.

391. It is homely fare that **feeds** and coarse cloth that warms.

392. Big **feet,** great luck ; we all suppose felicity hangs from the tips of the toes.

393. Blessed man who says and does —his **feet** I hold close to my heart.

394. Hurrying along on both one's **feet,** is all for clothes and something to eat.

395. Everyone pushes a falling **fence.**

396. There is no **fence** that does not let the wind through.

397. If you **ferry** at all, ferry right over.

398. Be the first to the **field** and the last to the couch.

399. Among the ten **fingers** there are long and short.

[We must take the short with the long.]

400. More fuel, more **fire.**

401. Once the **fire** is lighted, can you command what it will burn and what it will leave untouched?

402. To escape from **fire** men will plunge into boiling water.

403. Strike a flint, and you'll get **fire;** strike it not and you'll not get even smoke.

404. Swiftly running water is a good place to catch **fish.**

[i.e. have your business on a busy street.]

405. There is often a space between the **fish** and the fish-plate.

406. A **fish** on a wall, like cash, has but one eye.

[i.e. there is another eye but it cannot be seen.]

407. **Fish** see the bait but not the hook, men see the profit but not the peril.

408. The **fish** that gets away is always a large one.

[i.e. things that have been stolen are always the best.]

409. Near putrid **fish** you'll stink; near epidendrum you'll be fragrant.

410. They are not good **fists** which fight, nor good words which curse.

411. **Flattery** is sickness, reproof is medicine.

412. All bad **flesh** smells alike.

413. When the **flight** is not high the fall is not heavy.

414. Do not seek to escape from a **flood** by clinging to a tiger's tail.

415. Cooks never make up for the **flour** which they spoil.

416. When the new-born infant slips into a **flour-jar,** he remains white all his life.

[i.e. of one who never prospers, and who appears to have come into the world in vain.]

417. If the **flower** is good, the fruit will be good.

418. To add **flowers** to embroidery.

[i.e. to send presents to the rich.]

419. **A flushing face** carries its own conviction.

420. Do not remove a **fly** from your friend's forehead with a hatchet.

421. One year borrows another year's **food.**

422. One has never so much need of his wit as when he has to deal with a **fool.**

423. The **fool** hopes that the heavens will fall; the pauper longs for a riot.

424. He who knows he is a **fool** is not a big fool.

425. A **fool** never admires himself so much as when he has committed some folly.

426. Whom Heaven at his birth has endowed as a **fool,** 'tis a waste of instruction to teach.

427. **Fools** never know how to be merciful.

428. **Fools,** only fools, try to turn a somersault in an oyster shell.

429. In every small **foot** there is a jar full of tears.

[Old custom of binding up young girls' feet.]

430. The very word "**forbearance**" is precious in a house. (*Confucianism.*)

431. He who is a good **forgetter** should seek for the remembering-pearl.

432. To **forgive** is considered man's duty; to win is considered man's ingenuity.

433. **Forethought** is easy, repentance is hard.

434. Those who make a **fortune** by being miserly, will not enjoy it long.

435. If **fortune** comes, who does not come? If it comes not, who comes?

436. When the waggon of **fortune** goes well, spite and envy hang on to the wheels.

437. When good **fortune** is exhausted, then follows evil fortune.

438. He who knows his good **fortune** is happy.

439. He lightly esteems the domestic **fowl,** but loves the wild pheasant.

[i.e. he detests his own wife but loves other men's.]

440. **Free sitters** grumble most at the play.

441. A humble **friend** in the same village is better than sixteen influential brothers in the Royal Palace.

442. When men are **friendly** even water is sweet.

443. New clothes but old **friends** are best.

444. Even **friends** should be separated by a high wall.

445. Cooked at one stirring makes **friends** too easily.

446. Be **friends** with a man's goodness and not with his wealth.

447. Ceremonial is the smoke of **friendship.**

448. To a **frog** in a well, heaven is only a sieve in size.

449. The **frost** only destroys the solitary blades of grass.

[i.e. mutual help will avert evil.]

450. It is easier to slip from **frugality** to extravagance than to pass from extravagance to frugality.

451. Ripe **fruit** falls of itself; water makes its own channel.

452. Do not eat the **fruit** of the stricken branch.

453. When a neighbour is in your **fruit-garden** inattention is the truest politeness.

454. There is sure to be **fuel** near a big tree.

455. Take away **fuel,** take away flame.

456. The chase of **gain** is rich in hate. (*Confucianism.*)

457. To persuade men not to **gamble** is to win money for them.

458. If the **gambler** can change, then there is medicine for leprosy.

459. He who believes in **gambling** will live to sell his sandals.

460. Men in the **game** are blind to what men looking on see clearly.

461. **Garlic** may be pounded in an earthenware saucepan, but it can be done only once.

462. At the front **gate** do not plant the mulberry-tree, and at the back gate do not plant the willow.

[The word "sang" for mulberry is similar to "sang" for funeral. The willow belongs to the "yin" and so would lead in demons at the back gate.]

463. A **gem** is not polished without rubbing, nor a man perfected without trials. (*Inscription in the Temple of Everlasting Harmony.*)

464. **Gems** unwrought form nothing useful.

465. Under a good **general** there are no bad soldiers.

[Good officers make good men.]

466. A single **general's reputation** is made of ten thousand corpses.

467. Even **genii** sometimes drop their swords.

[Even the best are liable to occasional mistakes.]

468. Old **ginger** is the sharpest.

469. Oriental-place **ginger** not pungent.

[i.e. a prophet is not without honour except in his own country.]

470. A **girl** is worth one-tenth of a boy.

471. A young **girl** must be kept like a tiger in the house.

472. Without clouds in the sky it cannot rain, so without a **go-between** a match can never be made.

473. When an earthen **god** crosses the river it can't take care of itself.

474. Three feet from the ground; if not a **god,** he is at least a fairy.

[Refers to one who can afford to ride on horseback, in a cart, or sedan chair.]

475. If you are upright and without guile, what **god** need you pray to for pardon?

476. He who resolves to amend has **God** [T'ien] on his side.

477. T'ien [**God**] responds to man as quickly as shadow to form or echo to voice.

478. Three feet over your head is [**God**] T'ien.

479. Imperial T'ien [**God**] will never slight men of sorrow.

480. **Gods** and fairies also make blunders.

481. The **gods** of the door are one good [pleasant] and one bad [severe].

482. Though you don't believe in other **gods** you believe in the God of Thunder ; though you don't believe in medicine generally, you believe in purgatives.

483. Without **going** there is no returning.

484. An inch of **gold** cannot buy an inch of time.

485. **Gold** is tested by fire, men by gold.

486. **Gold** sinks deeper than dross.

487. It is easier to obtain thousands of **gold** pieces than kind words.

488. Though you have much **gold** you cannot buy that which is not for sale.

489. Beat your **gong** and sell your candies.

[i.e. every man to his own trade.]

490. An unbeaten **gong** gives no sound.

491. There is a reward for **good,** and a punishment for evil.

492. The pleasure of doing **good** is the only one that will not wear out.

493. The **good** you do, to be seen of men, is not true goodness ; the evil that you are afraid to have men know is real evil.

494. To see a man do a **good deed** is to forget all his other faults.

495. It is difficult to do **good deeds,** there are so many evil ones.

496. Three-tenths of **good looks** are due to nature, seven-tenths to dress.

497. One more **good man** on earth is better than an extra man in heaven.

498. Keep company with **good men** and good men you'll imitate.

499. There are two **good men :** one dead, the other unborn.

500. In **good works** don't yield place to others.

501. Listen to all, plucking a feather from every passing **goose,** but, follow no one absolutely.

502. What one hears by **gossip** is empty ; what one beholds with the eye is solid.

503. **Govern** a great nation as you would cook a small fish. (*Taoism.*)

[i.e. don't **overdo** it.]

504. Ten years a **graduate** [without studying] and one is a nobody.

505. One root of **grass** has one root of grass's dew to nourish it.

506. **Grave-yard** plot is not so good as a heart-plot ; the house of the dead is not so good as concealed merit.

507. He who has split firewood for three years, is fit to inspect **graveyards.**

508. A truly **great man** never puts away the simplicity of a child. (*Confucianism.*)

509. A **great man** will not see a little man's faults.

510. All **great men** have this in common, that beneath their wisdom and their courage there lies the heart of a little child.

511. The **great way** is very smooth, but all love the by-paths. (*Taoism.*)

512. **Grief or poverty** is ten times bitterer than gentian.

513. No **grief** so great as for a dead heart.

514. Men do not live a hundred years, yet harbour the **griefs** of a thousand.

515. The **guest** who outstays his fellow-guests loses his overcoat.

516. He only is genuine who treats his **guests** with wine.

517. **Guilt** is always jealous.

518. Man combs his **hair** every morning, why not his heart?

519. Whose black **hair** will not change colour?

520. The **hairless lip** in managing affairs is apt to slip.

521. **Half-an-hour** is worth a thousand ounces of silver.

[Half-an-hour refers to the sun-dial.]

522. There is no one to sweep a common **hall.**

523. Fowls in a hencoop and fishes in a net, can all be caught with the **hand.**

524. Though the left **hand** conquer the right, no advantage is gained.

[i.e. the importance of harmony among brothers.]

525. To stop the **hand** is the way to stop the mouth.

526. If you lift your **hand** to strike, you are three-tenths lower than your opponent.

527. You can't clap **hands** with one palm.

[i.e. it takes two to make a quarrel.]

528. For one ounce of gold you must have four ounces of **happiness.**

[i.e. to enable you to avail yourself of the possession of the gold.]

529. Peace in a thatched hut—that is **happiness.**

530. **Happiness** and misery are not fated but self-sought.

531. Be very careful of **happiness,** and provoke not calamity.

532. Possessed of **happiness,** don't exhaust it.

533. **Happiness** has its foundation, and misery its womb.

534. Whatever **happiness** is in the world has arisen from a wish for the welfare of others; whatever misery there is has arisen from indulging selfishness. (*Buddhism.*)

535. **Happiness** is near to the ugly.

536. With coarse food to eat, water to drink, and the bended arm as a pillow, **happiness** may still exist. (*Confucianism.*)

537. Peace is **happiness**; merit is long life; contentment is wealth; and the obtaining of one's desires is honour.

538. He who goes out of his house in search of **happiness** runs after a shadow.

539. The three secrets of **happiness:** to see no evil, to hear no evil, to do no evil.

540. He who enters an asylum for the aged at twenty enjoys **happiness** too soon.

541. If you would extend the fields of your **happiness** you must level the soil of your heart.

542. Man is never **happy** for a thousand days, a flower never blooms for a hundred.

543. Make **happy** those who are near, and those who are far will come. (*Confucianism.*)

544. Do not in this life ask for the three **hard things:** good sons, old age, and a long beard.

545. When three men are perfectly **harmonious** even earth may be turned into gold.

546. **Haste** comes of the evil one; leisure from God.

547. A **hasty man** drinks his tea with a fork.

548. With one's **hat** in one's hand one goes throughout the land.

549. **Hats** don't differ by a foot.

550. Bend your **head** if the eaves are low.

551. Who won't bow his **head** when he knocks it against the eaves?

[i.e. submit to circumstances.]

552. After being struck on the **head** with an axe it is a positive pleasure to be beaten about the body with a wooden club.

553. **Hearing** is Paradise, and seeing is Hell.

554. A hundred **hearings** are not equal to one seeing.

555. Under heaven there is no thing impossible; all you need is a man with a **heart.**

556. Glory and hell are within the **heart.**

557. When you casually meet a man, say three short words; by no means show him all your **heart.**

558. Looks are born in the **heart.**

559. After many days we see a man's **heart.**

560. A good **heart** always does a little extra.

561. The mouth wounds the **heart,** as when a mosquito provokes a rap from a fan.

562. Cleanse your **heart** as you would cleanse a dish.

563. A man's kindness of **heart** cannot be measured by the amount he gives.

564. He who expands his **heart** contracts his mouth.

565. The people's **heart** is heaven's will.

566. Man's **heart** is iron; the laws of the land are the furnace.

567. Man's **heart** is never satisfied, the snake would swallow the elephant.

568. Man's **heart** is naturally just. (*Confucianism.*)

569. To know a man's **heart,** listen to his words.

570. He who knows his **heart** mistrusts his eyes.

571. Vast chasms can be filled, but the **heart** of man never.

572. The **heart** of man, to what lengths will it not go?

573. It is the emptiness of a **heart** that makes it spiritually receptive. It is the emptiness of a valley that makes it yield an echo.

574. If you use the **heart** with which you reprove others to reprove self, there will be fewer faults; if you use the heart with which you forgive self to forgive others, there will be perfect friendship.

575. Though conversing face to face, their **hearts** have a thousand miles between them.

576. The **hearts** that are the nearest are not those that touch.

577. A thousand or ten thousand reckonings of men are not equal to one reckoning of **heaven.**

578. Each interprets in his own way the music of **heaven.**

579. **Heaven** does not grudge truth, nor earth it's gems.

580. **Heaven** for a compass if conscience is not at the helm.

581. If I can attain **heaven** for a cash, why should you be envious?

582. **Heaven** has a road, but no one travels it; Hell has no gate, but men will bore through to get there.

583. **Heaven** never cuts off a man's way.

584. **Hell** and Heaven both have their Quiet Land.

[i.e. a place of rest and peace.]

585. He who sows **hemp** will reap hemp; he who sows beans will reap beans.

586. A **hen** does not usually announce the break of day.

587. The wise **hen** is never too old to dread the spring.

588. Go you along your great **highway,** and I'll get across my one-pole bridge.

589. If you never go up a **hill** you will never know what a plain is like.

590. One docile **hind** in the barn is worth six spitting cats on the hearth.

591. At a distance from **home** a man is judged by what he seems; near home, by what he is.

592. If you have nothing to do, go **home** early.

593. For every foot of **honour** shown me, I show ten.

594. The **hornet** comes too to the sugar-pot.

595. The trotting **horse** hears not the story-teller's yarn.

[Busy people are too occupied to listen.]

596. A good **horse** is to be ridden.

597. If two men keep a **horse,** it is thin ; if two families keep a boat, it leaks.

598. It's no use starving the **horse** to fatten the mule.

599. It is not the **horse** which costs money, it is the saddle.

600. The **horse's back** is not so safe as the buffalo's.

[i.e. a politician is not so secure as a husbandman.]

601. To disclose the **horse's foot.**

[i.e. to divulge a secret. The " horse's foot " is the popular name for the process of exorcising demons in sickness.]

602. **Hospitality** is the virtue of the son and the wisdom of the ancestor.

603. The **host** is happy when the guest is gone.

604. A **host** who escorts a guest no farther than the door is not a real host.

605. In **hot weather** there is no superior man.

[Nobody stands on ceremony in hot weather.]

606. It is better to get one's clothes wet than to **hurry.**

607. A girl receives—a widow takes, her **husband.**

608. A **hut** of reeds with mirth therein is better than a palace with grief therein.

609. **Ice** is not frozen three feet thick with one day's cold.

[i.e. Rome was not built in a day.]

610. He who removes an **idol** to bathe it, puts the gods to needless inconvenience.

611. A maker of **idols** is never an idolator.

612. **Ignorance** acquits of guilt.

613. **Ignorance** is the night of the mind, a night without moon and stars.

614. He who speaks **ill** of me fears me, he who praises me to my face despises me.

615. Whoever suffered for not speaking **ill** of others ?

616. An extra **immortal** in the heavens is not equal to having an extra saint or sage on earth.

[i.e. immortals are of no help to man.]

617. A little **impatience** will spoil great plans.

618. He who laughs at an **impertinence** makes himself its accomplice.

619. There is nothing **impossible** in this world ; the only fear is that men of determination are wanting.

620. First **impressions** rule the mind.

621. If the domestic duties be duly performed, where is the necessity of going afar to burn **incense ?**

622. Do not burn false **incense** before a true god.

623. Though you neglect to offer **incense** when all is well, you will have to fall at Buddha's feet in times of sorrow.

624. An extra **incense burner** attracts an extra demon.

[i.e. wealth provokes trouble.]

625. An **indictment** cannot be got up without lies.

626. Affect a little **indistinctness** rather than insist upon absolute correctness.

627. The less **indulgence** one has for oneself, the more one may have for others. (*Inscription in Examination Hall of Canton.*)

628. Only **inferiors** flatter superiors.

629. **Injure** others, injure yourself.

630. The palest **ink** is better than the most retentive memory.

631. Enter the **inn** [turn in] before nightfall, and arise at cockcrow in the morning.

[Early to bed and early to rise.]

632. Superior men are good without **instruction ;** medium men are good with it ; but low fellows are bad, despite it.

633. A man must **insult** himself before others will.

634. He who **insults** me to my face can yet be an honest man and my friend.

635. One fit of **intoxication** dispels three anxieties.

636. Good **iron** is not used for nails, and good men do not become soldiers.

637. You can't get **ivory** out of a dog's mouth.

[i.e. you can't make a silk purse out of a sow's ear.]

638. In years of plenty, **jade**; in years of dearth, grain.

639. If **jade** is not polished, it cannot become a thing of use.

640. **Jade** unpolished does not make a gem.

641. The crocodile opens his **jaws**; the rat-trap closes his; keep yours shut.

642. A small man commits a sin when he is tempted by a **jewel.**

643. **Jewels** and coral are but stones.

644. A **journey** of a thousand miles began with a single step. (*Taoism.*)

645. If you set out on a **journey** of ten miles, remember that nine miles is only half-way.

646. In the midst of great **joy** do not promise to give a man anything; in the midst of great anger do not answer a man's letter.

647. When **joy** is extreme it is the forerunner to grief.

648. One **key** doesn't rattle.

[i.e. there is peace with one wife.]

649. One day husband and wife implies a hundred days' **kindness.**

650. It is only **kindness** and not severity that can impress at the distance of a thousand miles.

651. For a **kindness** as small as a drop of water one should give in return a whole spring.

652. **Kindness** is more binding than a loan.

653. Better do a **kindness** near home than go far away to burn incense.

654. Better not do a **kindness** than do it with the hope of reward.

655. Do not forget little **kindnesses,** and do not remember small faults.

656. A **kind word** warms for three winters.

657. If the string is long the **kite** will fly high.

658. Those who **know** how to do a thing do not find it difficult; those who find it difficult know not how to do it.

659. It is easier to **know** how to do a thing, than to do it.

660. Would you **know** what you were, see what you are; would you know what you will be, see what you do?

661. To know and to know you know, not to know and to know you do not know, this is **knowledge.**

662. A little **knowledge** is a dangerous thing.

663. I am not concerned that I am not **known**; I seek to be worthy to be known.

664. Who **knows** himself knows others, for heart can be compared with heart.

665. It costs no strength to watch other men **labour.**

666. There is no **ladle** which never strikes the edge of the cooking-pot.

[i.e. there are little unpleasantnesses in the best of families.]

667. The new-born **lamb** does not fear a tiger, but before he becomes a sheep he will flee from a wolf.

668. Lo, even **lambs** have the grace to suck kneeling.

669. Do the **lame** offer to carry the footsore; the blind to protect the one-eyed?

670. You but waste time on an oil-less **lamp.**

671. When the oil is exhausted the **lamp** goes out.

672. The foot of the **lamp** is the worst lighted.

673. Don't thrust your fingers through your own paper **lantern.**

[i.e. don't give the situation away.]

674. To light one's **lantern** for another man.

675. Death, a woman, and a dumb mute always have the **last word.**

676. Whether rich or poor, be pleased with your lot, for he is a fool who can't **laugh** [under all circumstances].

677. A piece of paper blown by the wind into the **law-court** may in the end only be drawn out again by two oxen.

678. Win your **law-suit** and lose your money.

679. A **law-suit,** however protracted, can never go beyond the original documents.

680. The **lazy** use a long thread, the clumsy a bent needle.

681. When one **leaf** moves, a hundred branches shake.

682. **Learn** as if you could not reach your object and were always fearing also lest you should lose it. (*Confucianism.*)

683. Most things are easy to **learn,** but hard to master.

684. **Learn** the past and you will know the future.

685. **To learn** the Way at daybreak and die at eve were enough. (*Confucianism.*)

686. A thousand **learnings** are not worth one seeing.

687. To be entirely at **leisure** for one day is to be for one day an Immortal.

688. Done **leisurely,** done well.

689. **Lending** is like throwing away; receiving payment is like finding something.

690. **Lending** to a spendthrift is like pelting a trespassing dog with meat dumplings.

691. A dying **leopard** leaves his skin; a dying man his name.

692. **Lice** do not bite busy men.

[i.e. they have no flies on them.]

693. He who tells a **lie** in praising himself will not tell the truth when blaming himself.

694. Who saves another's **life** adds ten years to his own.

695. Through **life** do nothing to make men knit their brows, then the world should not contain a man to grind his teeth at you.

696. **Life** springs from sorrow and calamity, and death from ease and pleasures. (*Confucianism.*)

697. Those who have not tasted the bitterest of **life's bitters** can never appreciate the sweetest of life's sweets.

698. If there be no **light** in the east there will be in the west.

[i.e. if you won't employ me another will.]

699. The **lightning** discovers objects which the paper lantern fails to reveal.

700. If you have two loaves of bread, sell one and buy a **lily.**

701. When the **lips** are gone the teeth are cold.

[An historic saying often applied to the seizure of key territories on the Chinese frontier.]

702. He who has seen **little** marvels much.

703. Use the **little** to get the big.

704. **Little** will grow to much.

705. Cease to struggle and you cease to **live.**

706. Who will give back the years that the **locusts** have eaten?

707. **Lookers-on** are clear-sighted.

[Onlookers see most of the game.]

708. Everything has its **lord.**

709. He that grasps, **loses.** (*Taoism.*)

710. The **lotus** springs from the mud.

711. One **louse** cannot raise a coverlet.

712. To rank the effort above the prize may be called **love** [virtue]. (*Confucianism.*)

713. **Love** and leprosy few escape.

714. There is mutual **love** between men of the same creed ; mutual jealousy between men of the same trade.

715. Those who possess the same virtue **love** each other, and those who exercise the same trade hate each other.

716. It is only the truly virtuous man who can **love,** or who can hate, others. (*Confucianism.*)

717. Never the time and the place and the **loved** one all together.

718. If your **luck** is good you need not practise deceit ; if your heart is good you need not resort to asceticism.

719. A man may be more vigorous than his **luck ;** or he may be more unbending than his goods.

720. The **lucky man** meets a friend ; the unlucky man a fair lady.

721. When the **lucky time** comes flowers will be added to the embroidery.

[i.e. if you are lifted up by fortune, others will add gifts to your wealth.]

722. Of the myriad vices **lust** is the worst.

723. Before you arrest a **magistrate,** arrest his domestic.

724. An honest **magistrate** has lean clerks ; a powerful god has fat priests.

725. On the **magistrate's** table a sheet of paper ; at his feet a pair of lips.

726. A **maid's virtue** is unlimited, a wife's resentment without end.

727. Asthma, consumption, wind, worms, and obstruction are **maladies** that neither gods nor fairies can cure.

728. To be a **man** is easy, to play the man is hard.

729. **Man** is Heaven and Earth in miniature.

730. Nobody on earth is difficult to **manage,** all that is necessary is three times to examine oneself.

731. Every **mandarin** has three hands, and every soldier a like number of feet.

732. Men's hearts are like iron and the rule of **mandarins** like a furnace.

733. From life to death is **man's reach.** (*Confucianism.*)

734. The **mark** must be made in youth.

735. Don't trouble yourself over the absence of a good go-between to negotiate a **marriage** for you—study will provide you with a lady as beautiful as jade.

736. Early **marriage** is the duty of the adults of both sexes.

737. When doorways match and houses pair, a **marriage** may be settled there.

738. When there is no north wind the sky isn't clear, and he who hasn't **married** the second time isn't poor.

739. **Marry** a wife for her virtue, a concubine for her beauty.

740. If heaven wants to rain or your mother to **marry** again, nothing can prevent them.

741. The **mean man** is always dejected.

742. Better add a **measure** than add a mouth.

743. One piece of bad **meat** makes the whole pot smell.

744. **Meat** on a block can be chopped any way you like.

[i.e. you can treat an inferior any way you please.]

745. A bitter mouth is good **medicine.**

746. **Medicine** cures curable sickness.

747. **Medicine** cures the man who is fated not to die.

748. When **medicine** cures, the patient is under providential care.

749. **Medicine** does not kill, the physician kills.

750. Those who purchase drugs and **medicines** ought to have two eyes ; only one is required in those that administer them ; none at all in those that take them.

751. When the **melon** is ripe it will drop of itself.

752. Do not adjust your sandals in a **melon field,** or arrange your hat under a plum tree.

[Lest you be thought stealing.]

753. If you have to use force in picking **melons** and fruit, they will not be sweet.

754. A clever **memory** is not equal to a clumsy brush.

755. Serve but a day and you are a slave; carry four ounces of silver on the shoulder and you are a **merchant.**

756. If you cannot get any **mercury,** red earth becomes valuable.

[i.e. if boys are not to be had, still, girls are better than nothing.]

757. If two men are of one mind, their sharpness will cut through **metal.**

758. At **midnight** one seems to have a thousand devices; by daylight not a move can be made.

759. **Milk,** by repeated agitation, turns to butter.

760. The body may be healed, but not the **mind.**

761. Do not darken your own **mind,** and all things will be clear to you.

762. Although the **mind** covers more ground than the heart it doesn't go so far.

763. Do not fill—fullness makes **mischief.**

764. If a man is a **miser** he will certainly have a prodigal son.

765. **Misfortune** comes to all men and most women.

766. In **misfortune** gold is dull; in happiness iron is bright.

767. **Misfortune** is not that which can be avoided, but that which cannot.

768. One casts a net of golden meshes with both hands and one draws in a hundred **misfortunes.**

769. The three great **misfortunes** in life are: in youth to bury one's father; at middle age to lose one's wife; and being old to have no sons.

770. One may buy by **mistake,** but one never sells by mistake.

771. Do not be ashamed of **mistakes** and thus make them crimes.

772. One **Mohammedan** is no Mohammedan; two Mohammedans make half a Mohammedan; three Mohammedans make one Mohammedan.

773. Which of these are first broken? —the tired truce, the vulture's fast, or the **Moi's** promise.

774. Even a **mole** may instruct a philosopher in the art of digging.

775. The **monastery** faces the nunnery.

[Used to express doubt when one is claiming everything to be all right.]

776. Losing comes of winning **money.**

777. Even the blind open their eyes at **money.**

778. A bellyful of learning is not as good as a purse full of **money.**

779. With **money** a man can appear in public.

780. If you have **money,** all you say is gospel truth.

781. Underlings see **money** as a fly sees blood.

782. He who has **money** can get the devil to turn his mill.

783. **Money** cannot buy things that are not for sale.

784. **Money** covers a hundred uglinesses.

785. Without **money** do not enter a crowd; in adversity do not seek your relatives.

786. Where no **money** goes before, no road is open.

787. All **money** is evil.

788. **Money** is hundred-footed.

789. Spending **money** is like water soaking into sand.

790. Where no **money** is spent, there no grace is gained.

791. When the **money** is stolen there remains but the watch-dog to beat.

792. To have **money** is to add on thirty years' dignity.

793. Without **money** it is no use calling—no one will come.

794. Those who make **money** make little exertion ; those who make much exertion make no money.

795. **Money** makes the blind see, and the priest sell his holy books.

796. **Money** makes the man.

797. He that is without **money** may as well be buried in a rice tub with his mouth sewed up.

798. When a man has **money** outsiders have money scales.

799. The sight of **money** to a law officer is like the sight of blood to a fly.

800. **Money** will not buy a son of your own begetting.

801. With **money** you are a dragon, without it a worm.

802. It doesn't matter whether you are right or not, if you have no **money** you are wrong.

803. With **money** you can move the gods ; without it you cannot move a man.

804. All your lifetime you fear you will not be able to make enough ; just as you come to the time when you are making a great deal [of **money**] you close your eyes in death.

805. **Moneyed** men are always listened to.

806. None will carry on a **money-losing** business, but some will engage in a head-losing occupation.

807. The **money-maker** is never weary ; the weary man never makes money.

808. Though you set a **monkey** on horseback, yet will his hands and feet remain hairy.

809. What in a contesting **mood** cannot be yielded, in a yielding mood will be granted several times over.

810. A broken drum saves the **moon**.

[This refers to the custom of using drums and gongs on the occasion of an eclipse of the moon].

811. By the middle of the tenth **moon** combing one's hair and washing one's face is all the work to be expected.

[i.e. the days are at their shortest.]

812. When the **moon** is full, it begins to wane ; when the waters are high, they must overflow.

813. How seldom in life is the **moon** overhead.

814. He who confounds **morals** must confound manners.

815. The fairest **morrow** doesn't restore yesterday.

816. One **Moslem** travelling will grow fat ; two on a journey will grow thin.

[i.e. one will eat pork being unobserved, while two dare not.]

817. One can surrender his own **mother,** but not give up sauce made from the So fish.

[The daintiest fish in the sea.]

818. One may give up a father though he be a magistrate, but not a **mother** though she be a beggar.

819. He who thinks that he is raising a **mound** may only in reality be digging a pit.

820. There are many paths to the top of the **mountain**—but the view is always the same.

821. If you do not scale the **mountain** you cannot view the plain.

822. The man who removed the **mountain** was he who began carrying away the small stones. (*Taoism.*)

823. The wise find pleasure in waters ; the virtuous in **mountains** (*Confucianism.*)

824. The **mountains** of to-day are not so lofty as the mountains of yore.

825. If a **mourner,** you cannot sing ; if you sing you cannot mourn.

826. Keep the **mouth** as you would keep a bottle [cork it] ; guard your thoughts as you would a city.

827. When your **mouth** eats, let it consult with your stomach.

828. That which goes out of your **mouth** enters other people's ears.

829. He who never opens his **mouth** in strife can always close his eyes in peace.

830. The **mouth** is [but] wind; the pen is a mark [a proof].

831. When you stir up the **mud** in the river water you can catch fish.

832. With patience, the **mulberry leaf** becomes a silk gown.

833. Where there is **musk** there will of course be perfume; it will not be necessary to stand in the wind.

834. The **musk-deer** carries its own perfume.

835. **Naked** we come, and naked we go.

[Intended to act as a check on covetousness.]

836. By **nature** men are all alike, but their habits carry them far apart. (*Confucianism.*)

837. No **needle** is sharp at both ends.

[i.e. no man is talented in every direction.]

838. You need a **needle** to draw the thread.

839. A relative at a distance is not so good as a near **neighbour.**

840. Would you discover the truth about a man, enquire only of his **neighbours.**

841. The real art of divination lies in the choice of **neighbours,** not of houses.

842. When the **nest** falls there are no whole eggs.

843. You had better return home and make a **net** than go down to the river and desire to get fishes.

844. If a man has no **nickname** he will never become wealthy.

845. It is the **nobody** who has great muscular strength.

846. **Notoriety** is not distinction.

847. **Oblige** and you will be obliged.

848. That which we are eager to **obtain** may be that which we have striven to avoid.

849. To **obtain** one leads to wishing for two.

850. Keep your **offence** in your bosom and you may meet as before.

851. An honest **official** has no fat subordinates.

852. If you wish to eat the food of an **official,** you must be born with the teeth of an official.

853. There are three classes of people one must not provoke: **officials,** customers and widows.

854. If you wish to succeed, consult three **old people.**

855. A family that has an **old person** in it, has a jewel.

856. **Once,** an event; twice, a precedent.

857. **Once** is enough—you must not do it again.

858. The **one-legged** never stumble.

859. The gods cannot help a man who loses **opportunities.**

860. A year's **opportunities** depend on the spring; a day's on the dawn; a family's on harmony; and a life's on industry.

861. He who can grasp **opportunity** as she slips by does not need a lucky dream.

862. Half an **orange** tastes as sweet as a whole one.

863. One can give up his old father and mother [as he does not make anything out of them] but not a fruit **orchard.**

864. If you **owe** a man anything, there is nothing like seeing him often.

865. The hand that feeds the **ox** grasps the knife when it is fattened.

866. When persons meet, they greet each other; when **oxen** see each other, they low.

867. **Parents** are never in the wrong.

868. If men's **passions** are deep, their divinity is shallow. (*Taoism.*)

869. Everything in the **past** died yesterday; everything in the future was born to-day.

870. Cease to mention **past** matters.
[Let bygones be bygones.]

871. Without the **past** we never could have had the present.

872. Nothing so full of victory as **patience.**

873. **Patience**—in time the grass becomes milk.

874. **Patience** is the knot which secures the seam of victory.

875. Red tassels [of office] with glory are not as good as sleeping in **peace.**

876. The two words **peace** and Rest are worth a thousand taels of gold.

877. Rather take one bite of the **peach** giving immortality, than eat a basketful of apricots.
[i.e. rather get a little of the best, than a great deal of a poorer article.]

878. The sweeter the **perfume,** the uglier the flies which gather round the bottle.

879. The disease does not kill, the **physician** kills.

880. The boastful **physician** never has good medicine.

881. There are **pictures** in poems and poems in pictures.
[Said of the painter-poet Wang Wei of the T'ang Dynasty.]

882. The **pig's head** was so offensive that it knocked over the idol that couldn't smell.

883. Take no notice of what you hear said on the **pillow.**

884. Each gains his own **place.**

885. He who has nothing in his **plate** looks at the dish.

886. If you neither **play** nor laugh, no one will want you.

887. Vice poisons **pleasure,** passion falsifies it, temperance sharpens it, innocence purifies it, beneficence doubles it, and friendship multiplies it.

888. Our **pleasures** are shallow, our troubles deep.

889. **Pleasures** were cheap before money became dear.

890. A man is better than a **pledge.**

891. To look at a **plum** is not to quench one's thirst.

892. To defame the **plum-perfume** is to defame the host.
[Plum-perfume is the common name for a singing girl.]

893. On earth there are four **poisonous** things: the Sun, in the clouds; the Wind, coming through an opening; a scorpion's tail; and a stepmother's heart.

894. A weighing **pole** without stars [a scale of dots], weighs nothing with certainty.
[i.e. of one who has no fixed purpose, who cannot decide, etc.]

895. No one blames you for being too **polite.**

896. Being **polite** means taking nothing amiss.

897. Everything can be got by **politeness.**

898. Let the **politeness** of first acquaintance characterize all after intercourse, and in the longest friendship nothing disagreeable will arise.

899. He whose steps resound like the beating of a drum will be always **poor.**

900. **Poor** by condition, rich by ambition.

901. If **poor,** don't cheat; if rich, don't presume.

902. If you are **poor,** keep out of the crowd; if unfortunate, don't seek a relation.

903. The **poor** never leave the fortune-teller's shop; the rich are never distant from the medicine cup.

904. If you are **poor,** stand on one side; if unfortunate, keep away from the fortunate.

905. It is harder to be **poor** without murmuring than to be rich without arrogance. (*Confucianism.*)

906. If the **poor man** associates with the rich, he will soon have no trousers to wear.
[i.e. he will spend beyond his means.]

907. A healthy **poor man** is half a rich one.

908. He who has tasted of the **poppy cup** has nothing to ask of love.

909. Once taste **porpoise,** and all other food will be insipid.

910. Who hasn't got a **pot** at home that leaks?

911. **Poverty** and an ugly face cannot be hid.

912. A magistrate will not consider your **poverty,** nor the devil your leanness.

913. **Poverty** springs not from roots, wealth and riches have no shoots.

914. He who can endure in **poverty** will keep his position when wealthy.

915. **Power** has no friends, envy has no rest, and crime has no satisfaction.

916. If your heart is in your **prayer,** the deity will know [he will take the will for the deed].

917. **Pretence** may become reality.

918. **Pretty face,** poor fate.

["Beauty and anguish walking hand in hand, the downward slope to death."]

919. When one cheats up to heaven in the **price** he asks, you come down to earth in the price you offer.

920. If one son becomes a **priest**—nine generations are sure of heaven.

921. He who is first is **prince;** he who comes after is minister only.

922. **Princes** and fair women—the less they speak the more they say.

923. The **prison** is shut night and day, yet it is always full; the temples are always open, and yet find no one in them.

924. **Probity** is the only coin that has value everywhere.

925. A **prodigal's** repentance is a priceless treasure.

926. Husbandry and letters are the two chief **professions.**

927. Small **profits** on large capital are after all great; big profits on small capital are after all only small.

928. Stable in **property,** stable in mind.

929. Cherish the false **prophet** who predicts disaster, and the true one who foresees health.

930. In the **prosperity** and decay of the State a common man has his share.

931. If you really wish for **prosperity,** let great become little.

932. In **prosperity,** man defies demons, but in adversity, the demons make mock of him.

933. In **prosperity,** strangers claim kin; in adversity, kindred become strangers.

934. Men have more sympathy with other people's **prosperity;** women with their adversity.

935. **Proverbs** are common talk or common sayings.

936. Man ponders upon **punishment,** but not on virtue.

937. A **pure** man seeing it calls it pure.

[To the pure all things are pure.]

938. **Purity** and impurity cannot co-exist.

939. A well-filled **purse** is a trusty earth-anchor.

940. A **purse** is sure to have cash inside.

941. A good **question** is like one beating a bell.

942. For the persistent **questioner** there will emerge at last a golden colt.

943. **Rain** and dew are mercies, so are ice and frost.

944. **Rain** in spring is as precious as oil.

945. If you are worried by the **rain** you can always plunge into the sea.

946. When it is dark the sun no longer shines, but who shall forget the colours of the **rainbow?**

947. It is madness to apply the **ram's head** to the unlocked door.

948. Everybody is obliged to help **rascals.**

949. **Rats** know the ways of rats.
[i.e. set a thief to catch a thief.]

950. The boat **rats** seek their food in the boat's compartments.
[i.e. living on one's own business.]

951. First time **raw,** second time ripe.
[Practice makes perfect.]

952. **Reason** will not act in vain.

953. **Rebuke** yourself as you rebuke others ; love others as you love yourself.

954. There is one word which may serve as a rule of practice for all one's life—**reciprocity** [charity]. (*Confucianism.*)

955. **Recite** according to the book.

956. A thousand or ten thousand **reckonings** of man are not equal to one reckoning of Heaven.

957. You can **reflect** what is another's ; you can radiate only what is your own.

958. **Relations** must be seldom visited ; kitchen gardens often.

959. The three **religions** are but one.

960. A thousand **remembrances** don't give one thought.

961. If you can **renovate** yourself one day, do so every day for ever. (*Inscription on the bathing-tub of the Emperor T'ang.*)

962. **Repentance** is the loveliest of the virtues.

963. Don't consider your **reputation** and you may do anything you like.

964. There is sure **requital** for both good and evil ; if nothing happens it is only because the hour has not yet come.

965. **Resolution** has nothing to do with length of years.

966. If a man has **resolution** he can live by it, if not, he must live by the toil of his hands.

967. **Retreat** and [merely] think about it, and everything will prove difficult.

968. A man need never **revenge** himself, the body of his enemy will be brought to his own door.

969. In **reviling,** it is not necessary to prepare a preliminary draft.

970. In China we have only three religions, but we have a hundred dishes we can make from **rice.**

971. Thunder will not strike one when eating **rice.**

972. It is the crust which sticks to the **rice,** not the rice that sticks to the crust.
[i.e. the poor cling to the rich, not the rich to the poor.]

973. You cannot buy honourable **rice** from a dead uncle.

974. I have gathered my **rice,** I have mended my roof. Blow now winds and let the cold rain fall.

975. You must have a couple of grains of **rice** in order to catch fowls.
[i.e. you cannot trade without capital.]

976. The sorrows of the **rich** are not great sorrows ; the comforts of the poor are not real comforts.

977. Whoever can foresee the affairs of three days, will be **rich** for several thousand years.

978. The **rich** man thinks of the future, the poor man of the present.

979. **Rich** men speak loud, strong men insult others.

980. The **rich** stand by the rich as the stream seeks the desert.

981. The colossal **rich** takes no man's gold.

982. A really **rich man** is careless of his dress.

983. If **rich men** are not sick they are living genii.
[i.e. there is no greater happiness than to be rich without being sick.]

984. **Riches** take away more pleasures than they give.

985. The best **riders** have the hardest falls.

986. **Right** makes one bold.

987. When gain is in view, think of **righteousness.**

988. By **river** come, by water go.

[i.e. easily earned, easily spent ; lightly come, lightly go.]

989. The **river** does not overflow the well.

[Alluding to the barrier that separates men of different trades.]

990. The great **river** does not reject the small streams.

991. Although the **river** is broad there are times when boats collide.

992. As the mountains rise, so the **river** winds.

993. **Rivers** have sources ; trees have roots.

[i.e. every effect has its cause.]

994. As the **rivers** pour their waters back again into the sea, so what a man has lent is returned to him again.

995. All the **rivers** run into the sea, yet the sea is not full.

996. There is no light burden on a long **road.**

997. Where the **road** bends abruptly, take short steps.

998. Whether the pedestrian walks fast or slowly the **road** is always the same.

999. When a **road** is uneven, those who are on each side level it.

[Said when bystanders take up an ill-used man's quarrel and punish his oppressor.]

1000. Every **road** leads in two directions.

1001. Of three **roads** take the middle one.

1002. There is always a **rogue** to rob a rogue.

1003. When the **root** is deep, there is no need to fear the wind ; when the tree is straight, why trouble if the moon gives slanting shadows.

[i.e. don't heed slander.]

1004. Every **rope** has two ends, and to-morrow is yet to come.

1005. The **rose** has thorns only for those who would gather it.

1006. **Rotten wood** cannot be carved, and mud walls cannot be plastered. (*Confucianism.*)

1007. Without **rules** there can be no perfection.

1008. Seeing a **rush,** don't pursue.

1009. A broken **rush-fan** shakes in each direction.

1010. To **sacrifice** to a spirit with which you have nothing to do is mere servility. (*Confucianism.*)

1011. One **saddle,** one horse.

[i.e. no second husband.]

1012. A thousand strokes with the oar, and ten thousand pushes with the pole, are not equal to a fully-set ragged **sail.**

1013. Raise your **sail** one foot and you get ten feet of wind.

1014. Without sorrow none become **saints.**

1015. Even the **saints** and sages of old had at least three parts out of ten bad.

1016. A dry finger cannot pick up **salt.**

[This is specially applicable to cases of bribery or gifts with a purpose.]

1017. When in their lives are men **satisfied ;** seeking leisure in old age, when are they at leisure ?

1018. To **say** is easy ; when you try to do, you find how hard it is.

1019. **Scabbed-heads** get flowery boughs.

[i.e. ugly men marry pretty wives.]

1020. Just **scales** and full measures injure no man.

1021. All **scholars** are brethren.

1022. **Scholars** discuss reason ; workmen what they are to eat.

1023. When youth takes the **scorpion** for a bed-fellow the aged go out on the roof.

1024. The vast bitter **sea.**
[i.e. the world.]

1025. The **sea** is not worn by ships, nor is a road ruined by travel.

1026. A boundless, bitter **sea,** turn your head and there is the shore.

1027. Any **seat** after a long tramp.

1028. Let the pools of fate hold their own **secrets.**

1029. Every **sect** has its doctrine and every doctrine its sect.

1030. If what we **see** is doubtful, how can we believe what is spoken behind the back? (*Inscription in the Celestial Influence Temple.*) (*Confucianism.*)

1031. One "**see**" is worth a hundred "tells"

1032. To **see** oneself is to be clear of sight. (*Taoism.*)

1033. There is no **seed** to a great man.

1034. A man may tell what he has **seen.**

1035. One man **sees** short; two men see long.
[i.e. two heads are better than one.]

1036. Putting aside virtuous deeds and not doing them may be styled **self-robbery.**

1037. A thief has as much talent as a **senior wrangler.**

1038. There is a **senior wrangler** in every calling.

1039. It is better to be **separated** by a thousand ranges of hills than by the thickness of one board.
[i.e. a living relative widely separated is better than one in the coffin.]

1040. The **serpent** knows his own hole.

1041. Where no handsome **servant** is kept the family must be virtuous.

1042. Do not employ handsome **servants.**

1043. The fewer **servants,** the better served.

1044. Distrust an inordinate appearance of **servility.**

1045. People of **seventy** you should not keep overnight, and do not invite a person of eighty to sit down.

1046. The **shadow** moves as the sun directs.

1047. **Shame** fades in the morning; debts remain from day to day.

1048. **Shoes** for the same foot must be worn by different people.

1049. I was angered for I had no **shoes,** then I met a man who had no feet.

1050. A man without a smiling face must not open a **shop.**

1051. It is easy to open a **shop,** but hard to keep it open.

1052. A good customer won't change his **shop,** nor a good shop lose its customer, once in three years.

1053. When there is no fish in the river, **shrimps** are valued.

1054. Allow the **sick man** to furnish his own perspiration.

1055. **Silence** is of the gods; only monkeys chatter.

1056. If one has three ounces of **silver,** he is a tiger; with five ounces of silver he is a dragon.

1057. In passing over the day in the usual way there are four ounces of **sin.**

1058. If you **sin** against heaven, there is no place for prayer. (*Confucianism.*)

1059. Merits and **sins,** the two are balanced.

1060. He who does nothing but **sit** and eat will wear away a mountain of wealth.

1061. There are few **situations** in life that cannot be honestly settled and without loss of time, either by suicide, a bag of gold, or by thrusting a despised antagonist over the edge of a precipice on a dark night.

1062. He who sees the **sky** in water sees fishes on the trees.

1063. What is said to a man's face is not **slander.**

1064. Do not let **slander** enter in by the ears and go down to the heart.

1065. **Slander** is of daily occurrence, but if nobody would listen to it, it would soon cease.

1066. A man of few words escapes **slander,** a man of few desires preserves his health.

1067. Don't wait for **slander** to enter into your ears, lest it turn former love into hatred.

1068. If **slander** were to examine itself it would hold its tongue.

1069. **Slander** slits pantaloons.

1070. The **slanderer** kills a thousand times; the assassin but once.

1071. **Slanders** cluster round a widow's door.

1072. The meaner the **slave,** the greater the lord.

1073. Be not afraid of going **slowly;** be only afraid of standing still.

1074. When the silver trail soils the floor, why visit the **snail** in his shell to ask why he left it there.

1075. One year bitten by a **snake,** three years afraid of grass ropes.

[Once bitten, twice shy.]

1076. Sweep the **snow** from your own door before you complain of the frost on your neighbour's tiles.

1077. The **softest** things in the world override the hardest. (*Taoism.*)

1078. If you love your **son,** give him plenty of cudgel; if you hate him, cram him with dainties.

1079. When the **son** has offended his father, he can do no more than carry to him the instrument of his own punishment.

1080. Many **sons** and many daughters, many family foes; no sons and no daughters, a living Bodhisattra.

1081. He who has **sons** cannot long remain poor; he who has none cannot long remain rich.

1082. **Sorrow** is born of excessive joy.

1083. Barley and beans make **soup.**

1084. Do not buy **soy** with money intended for vinegar.

1085. One who can **speak,** speaks of the city; one who can't, speaks merely of household affairs.

1086. Those who know do not **speak;** those who speak do not know. (*Taoism.*)

1087. Those who can **speak** well have not always the best things to say.

1088. He who **speaks** within walls is listened to outside.

1089. It is easy to avoid a naked **spear,** but not a hidden sword.

1090. What man, behind his back, is not **spoken** against; and who, before others, does not speak against men?

1091. When you drink the water, think of the **spring.**

1092. Plan the whole year in the **spring.**

1093. In **spring** keep well covered, in autumn delay putting on thick garments, and you will never be sick.

1094. Reserve the **square-inch plot** for your descendants to till.

[i.e. the "square-inch plot" is the heart, and the meaning is that parents must leave a good example to be followed by their children.]

1095. Kindness to the **starfish** is as wind in the desert.

1096. You cannot walk and look at the **stars** if you have a stone in your shoe.

1097. May the three **stars** illuminate here.

[According to popular belief there are three powers which control Happiness, Official Emoluments, and Old Age, and these powers are called "Stars." Hence the felicitous phrase over doorways.]

1098. To the **starving** a blow from a skewer of meat is more acceptable than a caress from the hand of a maiden.

1099. **Steal** needles when young, you'll steal money when old.

1100. Better ten **steps** around than one step in the mire.

1101. A **stick's** a stick, whether long or short; a man's a man, whether great or small.

1102. He who only thinks of feeding his **stomach** leaves his head to fast.

1103. If one has a mind to beat the **stone,** the stone will have a hole in it.

1104. You can stop a **stream** at its source by a twig, but let it run unchecked and it will swamp an elephant.

1105. When you drink from the **stream,** remember the spring.

1106. **Strong men** have strong men to curb them, and able men have able men at their heels.

1107. They are mere cattle in clothes who do not **study.**

1108. Three days' neglect of **study** leaves one's conversation flavourless.

1109. Some **study** shows the need for more.

1110. The more **stupid,** the more happy.

1111. A **successful** man is not easy-going, and an easy-going man is not successful.

1112. To **sue** a flea and catch a bite.

[i.e. the results of litigation.]

1113. Good men **suffer** much.

1114. **Suffering** does not manifest itself.

1115. There is always one who **suffers.**

1116. Those who are unmoved by the threat of a vat of flaming **sulphur** in the Beyond, rend the air if they chance to step on a burning cinder here on earth.

1117. The **summer** insect does not foresee the winter.

1118. The **sun** cannot shine into an inverted bowl.

1119. When the **sun** sets, the moon rises; when the moon sets, the sun rises. *(Confucianism)*

1120. When the gods veil the **sun** the wise put out their rushlight.

1121. Compared with **superiors,** I have less; compared with inferiors, I have more.

1122. **Surety** for the bow, surety for the arrow.

1123. The sharp **sword** is given to the brave soldier.

1124. Gods and genii sometimes lose their **swords.**

[i.e. the best will err.]

1125. A man worth a thousand **taels** does not sit with one leg of his chair overhanging the dais; a man with one hundred taels does not bestride the rail of a balcony.

1126. Ten **taels** will move the gods; one hundred will move Heaven itself.

1127. Leave a little of the **tail** to whisk off flies.

[i.e. don't be too economical.]

1128. Out of ten **tailors** nine are consumptive.

1129. A **tale** half told is the father of many lies.

1130. When you meet men or devils, **talk** as they do.

1131. One acrid **taste** relieves three longings of the stomach.

1132. Sour, sweet, bitter, pungent, all must be **tasted.**

1133. After **tautness,** slackness [of a bow].

[Work first, play after.]

1134. With plenty of food and a cup of **tea,** one is equal to the living immortals.

1135. He who is one day my **teacher** is my father for life.

1136. A rain of **tears** is necessary for the harvest of learning.

1137. Man reaches scarce a hundred years, yet his **tears** would fill a life-time of a thousand.

1138. When the **teeth** fall out, the tongue wags loose.

1139. A red-nosed man may be a **teetotaller,** but no one will believe it.

1140. Those near the **temple** deride the gods.

1141. **Temptation** wrings integrity even as the thumb-screw twists a man's fingers.

1142. A **thief** from a distance must have feet that are near.

1143. The coolie **thief** is caught by the roadside ; when the mandarin robs, the curtains are drawn across his door.

1144. There is no **thief** like a family of five daughters.

1145. Why should there be any anxious **thought** and care in the world ?

1146. Wishing to know the heart's **thoughts,** listen to the mouth.

1147. **Thoughts** should be welcomed as guests, and wishes as children.

1148 She who has spun the **thread** knows the weakness of the net.

1149. The " **throw-in** " is more thought of than the bought.

1150. If one is struck by a **thunderbolt** it is superfluous to consult the Book of Dates as to the exact meaning of the omen.

1151. A dead man is terrible as a **tiger** ; a dead tiger harmless as a lamb.

1152. Should you miss the **tiger,** be assured that he will not miss you.

1153. He who rides on a **tiger** can never dismount.

1154. A **tiger** doesn't eat stale meat.

[i.e. one should not seek a position he has left.]

1155. Even a **tiger** has his naps.

1156. He who kills **tigers** does not wear rat-skin sleeves.

1157. If one will not enter a **tiger's** lair, how can he obtain her whelps ?

1158. Even a **tile** will turn some day.

1159. A thousand taels will not buy an inch of **time.**

1160. You must make **time** and time go together.

1161. An inch of **time** is an inch of gold.

1162. **Time** is like an arrow ; days and months like a weaver's shuttle.

1163. Make every inch of **time** your own.

1164. With plenty of food and a pipe of **tobacco,** one is equal to the living immortals.

1165. Until **to-day** becomes to-morrow, men will be blind to the good fortune of the present.

1166. He who **toils** with pain will eat with pleasure.

1167. Four horses cannot overtake the **tongue.** (*Confucianism.*)

1168. A woman's sword is her **tongue** and she does not let it rust.

1169. The **tongue** is soft and constantly remains in ; the teeth are hard and fall out.

1170. Under the **tongue** men are crushed to death.

1171. In the **tongue** there lurks a dragon's den—no blood is seen and yet it murders men.

1172. The **tongue** weaves for clothes ; the pen tills for food.

1173. No ease for the mouth when one **tooth** is aching.

1174. The wise **tortoise** keeps his pain inside.

1175. **Towers** are measured by their shadows, and great men by their calumniators.

1176. The highest **towers** begin from the ground.

1177. Those who can do a good **trade** don't wrangle over taxes.

1178. To do a good **trade** wants nothing but resolution, and to do a large one nothing but application.

1179. Since life has nothing in it like **tranquillity,** can it be a thing obtained by chance ?

1180. Whilst **travelling**, don't reckon the distance; whilst eating, don't reckon the quantity.

1181. A great **tree** attracts the wind.

[i.e. a rich man is likely to tempt the cupidity of others.]

1182. Though a **tree** be a thousand chang in height its leaves must return to the earth at last.

[Chang is ten Chinese feet.]

1183. A **tree** blown down by the the wind has more branches than roots.

1184. The **tree** exists for its fruit, and man for righteousness and self-control.

1185. The **tree** for shade; the man for reputation.

1186. When the **tree** has fallen it no longer casts a shadow.

1187. When the **tree** has grown large it will straighten itself.

1188. When the **tree** is full the doubtful fruit remains upon the branch.

1189. If a **tree** is straight, why be concerned that in the moonlight it casts a slanting shadow?

1190. He who is near to a big **tree** lacks not wood for his fire.

1191. However high the **tree**, the shortest axe can reach its trunk.

1192. Only from the **tree** which is sound cometh sound fruit.

1193. Straight **trees** are first felled, and sweet wells first drained.

[i.e. able men are first employed.] *(Taoism.)*

1194. **Trees** are for shade, and children for old age.

1195. More **trees** are upright than men.

1196. Old **trees** have withered tops.

1197. He who has an iron mouth and bean-curd feet will not be able to escape **trouble**.

[Said of one whose words are not supported by his actions.]

1198. **Trouble** travels swiftly.

1199. When **troubles** are few, dreams are few; when words are scarce, faults are scarce.

1200. A clever man turns great **troubles** into little ones, and little ones into none at all.

1201. Small pairs of **trousers** never come singly.

1202. Even a silver **trumpet** may not prevail above a score of brazen horns.

1203. If one does not **trust** enough, one does not meet with trust.

1204. Words cannot change the **truth.**

1205. **Truth** often hides in an ugly pool.

1206. He only is wise who knows the **truth** when he hears it, and hearing gives heed.

1207. As the **twig** is bent, the tree is inclined.

1208. After a **typhoon** there are pears to gather up.

1209. He who hoards to-day and to-morrow, and by constant hoarding has bought a new **umbrella,** finds that suddenly a strong wind arises and leaves him nothing but a bare bamboo stick.

1210. Carry your **umbrella** when the weather is fine; carry food when you are not hungry.

1211. There are three things which are **unfilial,** and to have no posterity is the greatest of them.

1212. The wise forget insults, like the **ungrateful** a kindness.

1213. The **unicorn,** the phœnix, the tortoise, and the dragon are the four spiritually endowed creatures.

1214. Be **upright** without being punctilious.

1215. Away from their home men lose in **value,** but goods gain in value.

1216. Fields and lands are all **vanity,** they are constantly changing hands; gold and silver are all vanity, after death they cannot be retained; wives and children are all vanity, you never meet them in Hades.

1217. In the choicest **vase** are found the ugliest cracks.

1218. The one who constantly eats **vegetable** roots can do anything.

1219. If you become a **vegetarian** you separate from your ancestors and cut off posterity.

1220. The old villager having never seen a gauze **veil,** does not mind about his face.

[i.e. of one who has no self-respect.]

1221. Near **vermilion** one is stained pink ; near ink one is stained black.

1222. Leaning **vessels** are easily upset.

1223. Do not consider any **vice** trivial, and so practise it ; do not consider any virtue trivial, and so neglect it.

1224. Tighten the cord of your helmet after **victory.**

1225. A **village mouth** is good physic.

1226. **Virtue** bought is always too dear.

1227. **Virtue** cannot live in solitude ; neighbours are sure to grow up round it. (*Confucianism.*)

1228. In a man whom we know we respect nothing but **virtue ;** in a man we do not know we respect nothing but the coat.

1229. A man's **virtue** is considered an endowment ; a woman's want of endowment is considered a virtue.

1230. The gate of **virtue** is difficult to open, but not easily closed.

1231. **Virtue** practised to be seen is not real virtue ; vice which fears to be seen is real vice.

1232. First of **virtues,** as all books confess, filial piety and righteousness.

1233. Speak of men's **virtues** as though they were your own, and of their vices as if you were liable to their punishment.

1234. Men will no more be **virtuous** without exhortation than a bell will sound without being struck.

1235. If at home a man receives no **visitors,** when abroad he will have no host.

1236. Long **visits** bring short compliments.

1237. Being in the right does not depend on having a loud **voice.**

1238. **Wade** the deep places, lift thy robe through the shallows. (*Confucianism.*)

1239. It is the small wheels of the **waggon** that come in first.

1240. When the **waggon** comes a way is found for it.

1241. Everyone gives a push to a tumbling **wall.**

1242. If you raise a mud **wall,** let both sides be smooth.

1243. **Walls** have ears.

1244. We never **wander** so far as when we think we know the way.

1245. **Want** a thing long enough, and you don't.

1246. In plenty, think of **want ;** in want, do not presume on plenty.

1247. If one generation has been **war-like,** the ten following will be timid.

1248. Of opposing **warriors,** he who has pity conquers. (*Taoism.*)

1249. **Water** always flows downhill.

[i.e. love always descends from parent to child.]

1250. To drink **water** and forget him who dug the well.

1251. **Water** can both sustain and upset a ship.

1252. Level **water** does not run, nor a contented man grumble.

1253. Cold **water** entering the mouth drops into the heart.

1254. Man is naturally ambitious, but **water** flows downwards.

1255. Well **water** is not opposed to river water.

[i.e. our interests do not clash.]

1256. As the **water** recedes, the stones appear.

1257. When the **waters** rise, the boats rise also.

1258. Before one **wave** has passed, another wave rises.

[i.e. it never rains but it pours.]

1259. Don't raise **waves** in the world and you'll keep ice and cold out of your bosom.

1260. Bar the **way** and folk strive to walk upon it. Throw wide the gates and they pass by to find something to break down.

1261. There is a highway for the production of **wealth.**

1262. Open the door of **wealth,** and go out.

1263. Covet **wealth,** and want it; don't, and luck will grant it.

1264. **Wealth** is but dung; a face is worth thousands of gold.

1265. Great **wealth** is from Heaven; little wealth is from diligence.

1266. With **wealth** one can command demons; without it one cannot summon even a slave.

1267. **Wealth** rules the world; clothes make the age.

1268. If you share a man's **wealth,** try to lessen his misfortune.

1269. Much **wealth** will not come if a little does not go.

1270. He who is not stingy is not **wealthy,** and he who is not wealthy is not stingy.

1271. When one is past thirty, he can about half comprehend the **weather.**

1272. One day of **wedded life** deserves a hundred days of kindness.

1273. The **wedding** present arrives before the wedding.

1274. Cutting down a **weed** is not so good as uprooting it.

1275. When there is mud at the bottom of the **well,** stirring it will not make the water clear.

1276. To the desert traveller all **wells** are sparkling.

1277. The **whip** that's lost always had a golden handle.

1278. **Whispered words** are heard afar.

1279. A **widow** is a rudderless boat.

1280. What is worn is clothing, what dies is a **wife.**

[or, worn out it is clothing, when old 'tis a wife.]

1281. A whole house-full of sons and daughters is not after all equal to a second **wife.**

1282. An ugly **wife** and a lean piece of ground protect the house.

1283. You may beat your **wife** as much as you like providing the stick is no bigger than your thumb.

1284. A man can have a **wife** for five dollars, for a donkey he must give fifteen.

1285. Husband and **wife** have no enmities that can survive a night.

1286. A **wife** is like a wall of mud bricks, take off one row and there is another below it.

[i.e. a wife no sooner dead than the husband plans to secure another.]

1287. If a man is unfaithful to his **wife,** it is like spitting from a house into the street, but if a woman is unfaithful to her husband, it is like spitting from the street into the house.

1288. Teach your son in the hall and your **wife** on the pillow.

1289. The **wife** should sing and the husband accompany.

1290. **Wife,** wealth, children, pay, are all predestined.

1291. A **wife's** long tongue is the flight of steps by which misfortune comes [to the house].

1292. Do not burn down your house in order to inconvenience even your chief **wife's mother.**

1293. The chance-planted **willow** twig grows into shade.

1294. When the **wind** blows, the grass bends. (*Confucianism.*)

[i.e. those who are below imitate those who are above.]

1295. The **wind** has the Wind Goddess to govern it.

[i.e. everything has its manager.]

1296. A raging **wind** only strikes those who are in it.

1297. A fair **wind** raises no storm.

1298. He has no dissimulation who treats his guests with **wine.**

1299. Three glasses of **wine** can set everything to rights.

1300. **Wine** does not intoxicate men : men intoxicate themselves.

1301. He who gives bad **wine** to his guests will only drink tea in their houses.

1302. When the **wine cellar** is empty, then will man climb to the pure stream on the mountain-side.

1303. **Windlass** stopped—bed dry.

1304. Even if you stick on **wings** it is difficult to fly.

1305. If one does not store up vital force in **winter**, one will be sure to suffer from an epidemic in the spring.

1306. He who puts on **winter dress** and uses a summer fan, doesn't know the difference between hot and cold.

1307. **Wisdom** is oft-time nearer when we stoop than when we soar.

1308. To boast of one's **wisdom** makes the way more obscure ; to proclaim oneself a fool only adds to one's trouble.

1309. The **wise man** doesn't tell what he does, but never does what cannot be told.

1310. The **wise man** is great in small things ; the vicious man is small in great things.

1311. The views of **wise men** are pretty much the same.

1312. **Wise men** care not for what they cannot have.

1313. Mill-makers lead the water whither they will, fletchers bend the arrows, carpenters shape the log, but **wise men** fashion themselves. (*Buddhism.*)

1314. What is truly **within** will be manifested without.

[i.e. what's bred in the bone will come out in the flesh.]

1315. Men love their own compositions and other men's **wives.**

1316. Ugly **wives** and stupid maids are priceless treasures.

1317. Other people's **wives** are best ; one's own children are the best ; vegetables in one's own garden are not relished, those from other gardens are the best.

1318. When one cuts down the long grass the **wolf** appears.

1319. When you are with the **wolf** you must howl like the wolves.

1320. It is impossible to be more malevolent than a **woman.**

1321. Rouge is bestowed upon the beautiful **woman.**

1322. It is easier for one dishonest **woman** clad in furs to gain admittance to the Temple than for ten honest females in rags to enter a good man's house.

1323. Though a **woman** has given you ten sons, do not trust her.

1324. A secret revealed to a **woman** is as a bubble that is blown.

1325. A man thinks he knows, but a **woman** knows better.

1326. Such is the stupidity of **woman** that it is incumbent on her, in every particular, to distrust herself and obey her husband.

1327. A hundred men can make an encampment, but it takes a **woman** to make a home.

1328. When a man is mad on a **woman**—wait—only she herself can cure him.

1329. No **woman** was ever egotistic without becoming envious, nor envious without becoming malignant.

1330. A gracious **woman** will cause more strife than twelve armed men can quell.

1331. The advice of a clever **woman** will ruin a walled city.

1332. The ingenuity of a guileless **woman** will undermine nine mountains.

1333. A **woman** with a long tongue is a ladder of woe.

1334. Like a **woman's benevolence** and a mean man's courage.

1335. There is no such poison in the green snake's mouth, or the hornet's sting, as in a **woman's heart.**

1336. When a **woman's lips** say, "It is enough," she looks at you with her eyes and they say, "Again."

1337. Men fear a slip of their pens; **women** a slip of their morals.

1338. **Women** and sparrows twitter in company.

1339. **Women** can appreciate what is immediately before their eyes.

[i.e. they can appreciate nothing else.]

1340. **Women** can share one's adversity, but not one's prosperity.

1341. The first counsel [deliberation] of **women** is the wisest, and their last resolution the most dangerous.

1342. The palaces of the great are full of **women**; the cottages of the poor full of children.

1343. Good **women** will not drink the tea of two families.

[Will not remarry.]

1344. If you don't **wonder** at the wonderful it ceases to be a wonder.

1345. Use men as you would use **wood**; because one inch is worm-eaten, you would never throw away the whole trunk.

1346. Who keeps the hills burns the **wood**; who keeps the stream drinks the water.

1347. For one **word** a man is often deemed wise; for one word he is often deemed foolish.

1348. One kind **word** will keep you warm for three winters.

1349. If one **word** misses the mark a thousand will do the same.

1350. Light **words** are easily spoken behind barred doors.

1351. Fine **words** are incredible; credible words are not fine. (*Taoism.*)

1352. Bitter **words** are medicine; sweet words an epidemic.

1353. **Words** are mere bubbles of water, but deeds are drops of gold.

1354. If your **words** are not pleasing, hold in half of them.

1355. **Words** are sounds of the heart.

1356. The **words** of a man are like a dart, they go straight to the target; those of a woman resemble a broken fan.

1357. **Work** fears a resolute man.

1358. He who will not **work** shall not eat.

1359. One can **work** well with many and eat well with few.

1360. **Work** with the rising, rest with the setting sun.

1361. He who sleeps over his **workshop** brings four eyes into the business.

1362. When **wrath** speaks wisdom veils her face.

1363. The skilful **writer** does not choose his brush.

1364. Those who have three acres of land never leave the door of the **yamen.**

[i.e. those who have substance can afford to go to Law.]

1365. When the **Yellow River** is in flood, even the strongest junk is dragged from its anchor.

1366. Even the **Yellow River** is sometimes clear.

1367. The eyebrows of **youth** cannot compare with the beard of age.

1368. **Youth** pursues the butterfly; old age knows that it began as a worm and will end in a hole in the wall.

DYAK, OR DAYAK (BORNEO)

1. He who enters as a whirlwind will depart as an **ant.**
2. Does the **ant** ask favours of the hornbill ?
3. The **betel leaf** is returned to its stalk. (*Malay.*)
4. The **bird's** strength is in its wings, the crabs in its claws, and the strength of a ruler in his ministers.
5. Let the **bones** whiten, but not the eyes.
6. Men hold the **buffalo** by its rope, a ruler by his word.
7. The lot of the **coconut shell** is to float and the lot of the stone is to sink.
8. It is hard to raise a **coconut-tree** from a green seed nut, but once the tree grows it will become a pillar of the state.
9. If you wash a **crow** in rose-water, will its feathers become white ?
10. You may plant bitter **cucumber** on a bed of sago, and manure it with honey, water it with treacle, and train it to grow over sugar-cane, yet when cooked it will still be bitter to the taste.
11. **Custom** is a mother whom all must obey.
12. Do not hope for **dew-drops** when the sun is high.
13. Will a **dog** not return to a place where there are bones ?
14. In the land where there are no **eagles** the sparrow pretends he is an eagle.
15. The **egg** which is laid by a duck is sometimes hatched by a hen.
16. The **eyes** may be closed, yet the hand will be open.
17. To low with the cattle and bleat with the **goats.**
18. Where the **heart** is willing it will find a thousand ways, but where it is unwilling it will find a thousand excuses.
19. When a city is in flames there is smoke to be seen, but a **heart** may be on fire and no one knows it.
20. Your mouth brings **honey** while your tail carries a sting.
21. **Hornbills** with hornbills and sparrows with sparrows.
22. When the staff is broken the **lame** must go on all fours.
23. To go to the **monkey** for justice.

    [This proverb originated in the story of two men who disputed over the ownership of some bananas and took their case to a monkey for judgment, who ordered the fruit to be divided. When one suitor cried that the other had received too large a share the monkey, to make matters even, ate some of the bananas himself. Then the second suitor complained, so the monkey took a few more. Thus the case went on until there was not one banana to wrangle about.]

24. By the **mouth** the body is ruined.
25. That **plough** bites deep only where the soil is soft.
26. When the **pulley** is broken the tackle falls.
27. Those who take their harvest from the **sea** must market it on the land.
28. Why should a man who has no burden carry a **stone**?
29. **A tiger** will not eat its own cubs.
30. The teeth will sometimes bite the **tongue.**
31. If a **tree** is firm, why should it fear the storm ?
32. Who can tell the value of what is **unseen**?
33. **Vermin** devours the purest corn and moths eat into the finest cloth.
34. Calm counsel is a faithful **wife,** hastiness is a harlot.

HEBREW

(Including Aramaic and Talmud)

1. Rather any **ache** than heart-ache.
2. He who performs a single good **action** gains for himself an advocate; he who commits a single sin, procures for himself an accuser. (*Talmud.*)
3. If you ask the **advice** of a wise man you have the half of his wisdom.
4. Old **age** is a crown of nettles; youth is a crown of roses.
5. **Alms** are the salt of riches.
6. When the wise is **angry** he is wise no longer. (*Talmud.*)
7. If one person tell thee thou hast **ass's** ears, take no notice; should two tell thee so, procure a saddle for thyself.
8. The handle of the **axe** goes back to the wood from which it came. (*Aramaic.*)
9. When the **barley** is consumed from the pitcher, strife knocks and enters the house.
10. He who hangs up his provision **basket** hangs up his sustenance.

    [There existed a superstition in ancient times that it was unlucky to hang up the basket which was used for storing provisions.]
11. He who goes not to **bed,** will be early up.
12. The **birds** of the air despise a miser. (*Talmud.*)
13. Do not place a **blemish** on thine own flesh. (*Talmud.*)
14. Mention not a **blemish** which is thine own, in detraction of thy neighbour. (*Talmud.*)
15. **Blood** is the originating cause of all men's diseases. (*Talmud.*)
16. Gnaw the **bone** which is fallen to thy lot.
17. Hast **bought,** thou hast gained; sell, and thou wilt lose.
18. A **branch** brings forth a fig.

    [Chip of the old block.]
19. Buttered **bread** falls on its face.
20. He who has some **bread** in his basket and says, "What shall I eat to-morrow?" belongs to those of little faith. (*Talmud.*)
21. Scatter your **bread** in the land and in the end your hand will find it.
22. The pulling down of the old is **building**; the building of youth is destruction. (*Talmud.*)
23. The weakness of thy walls invites the **burglar.** (*Talmud.*)
24. The **camel** desired horns, and his ears were taken from him. (*Talmud.*)
25. The **camel** went to look for horns and the ears he had were cut off. (*Aramaic.*)
26. In three things a man's **character** is recognized; in the wine cup, in his purse, and in his anger. (*Talmud.*)
27. **Charity** is the salt of riches. (*Talmud.*)
28. **Charity,** that which is given in health, is gold; in sickness, silver; after death, lead.
29. Take care of the **children** of the poor, for from them will knowledge arise. (*Talmud.*)
30. Two pieces of **coin** in one bag make more noise than a hundred. (*Talmud.*)
31. With two **cooks** the cooking-pot is neither hot nor cold.
32. One loose **cord** loosens many. (*Talmud.*)
33. No **cow** [is considered] a gorer until her calf is a **kicker.**

    [i.e. the mother is judged by the character of her daughter.]
34. No man is impatient with his **creditors.** (*Talmud.*)
35. In two kabs of **dates** there is one kab of stones.

    [i.e. no corn without chaff. "Kab" is a dry measure.]
36. Hast seen the **dawn,** thou hast not yet seen the dusk.

37. Be with a man **deaf** and hearing, silent and speaking.

38. If you have taken of a man his plough or his pillow for **debt,** return his plough in the morning and his pillow at night. (*Talmud.*)

39. Greater is he who causes good **deeds** than he who does them. (*Talmud.*)

40. Room can always be found for a **delicacy.**

41. No man **dies** and has the half of his wishes realized. (*Talmud.*)

42. Whatever thou hast to thy **discredit** be the first to tell it.

43. A **doctor** from a distance is like a blind eye. (*Aramaic.*)

44. The **doctor** who prescribes gratuitously gives a worthless prescription. (*Talmud.*)

45. If the **dog** bark at thee, go in; if the bitch bark at thee, go out.

    [i.e. you can endure a quarrelsome son-in-law, but not a quarrelsome daughter-in-law.]

46. **Dreams** give wings to fools.

47. Let the **drunkard** alone and he will fall of himself.

48. The path of **duty** in this world is the road to salvation in the next.

49. Hadst got up **early,** thou needest not have stayed up late.

50. Sixty aches has the tooth of the man who hears his neighbour **eating** and himself eats none. (*Aramaic.*)

51. One **eats,** another says grace. (*Talmud.*)

52. The **educator** deserves the name of father more than the parent. (*Talmud.*)

53. **Eight things** are difficult to enjoy in abundance, but in moderation are good; labour, sleep, riches, journeyings, love, warm water, bleeding and wine. (*Talmud.*)

54. He who can **endure** barley bread shall eat no wheaten bread. (*Talmud.*)

55. A man can conceal himself from his **enemies** rather than from his friends. (*Talmud.*)

56. To **expect** is worth four hundred drachmas.

57. What is **expensive** for thy back, what is reasonable for thy stomach.

58. He is great whose **failings** can be numbered.

59. When one acquires **fame,** one soon ceases to merit it.

60. The **famine** lasted seven years, but it passed by the door of the worker. (*Talmud.*)

61. The way man wishes to go, thither his **feet** will carry him. (*Talmud.*)

62. A **fence** is fenced in, and a breach is broken.

63. Make a **fence** round the law.

64. For the lack of wood the **fire** goes out, and where there is no whisperer, contention ceaseth.

65. Look not at the **flask** but at its contents. (*Talmud.*)

66. Deal with those who are **fortunate.** (*Talmud.*)

67. If the **fox** is king, bow before him. (*Talmud.*)

68. **Foxes** sons of foxes.

69. Thy **friend** has a friend and thy friend's friend has a friend, be discreet. (*Talmud.*)

70. What is in thy heart concerning thy **friend** is in his heart concerning thee.

71. **Friendship** confides the secret, love divulges it.

72. **Friendship** draws men together, self-interest separates them.

73. A **friendship** that can grow old should never die.

74. As is the **garden,** such is the gardener.

75. He who rents one **garden** will eat birds; who rents gardens, the birds will eat him.

76. If one does not eat **garlic** one does not stink.

77. He **gives** little who gives much with a frown; he gives much who gives even little with a smile. (*Talmud.*)

78. He that **gives** should never remember, he that receives should never forget. (*Talmud.*)

79. At the first **glass**—a lamb; at the second glass—a lion; at the third glass—a swine. (*Talmud.*)

80. Man has been created on the last day; even the **gnat** is of a more ancient lineage. (*Talmud.*)

81. The voice of the people is as the voice of **God.** (*Talmud.*)

82. Before **God** a good intention is as the deed. (*Talmud.*)

83. Men should be careful lest they cause women to weep, for **God** counts their tears. (*Talmud.*)

84. **God** did not make woman from man's head, that she should not rule over him; nor from his feet, that she should not be his slave; but from his side that she should be near his heart. (*Talmud.*)

85. **God** is more delighted in adverbs than in nouns.

86. Whosoever walks towards **God** one cubit, God runs towards him twain.

87. Everything is in the hands of **God** save the fear of God. (*Talmud.*)

88. In the name of **God** we do all manner of wrong.

89. Beat the **gods,** and the priest will tremble. (*Talmud.*)

90. If thou hast taken up **God's** trade, put on His livery also [charity]. (*Talmud.*)

91. The **governor** took us and the scent came into the hand.

92. Let the **grapes** pray for the welfare of the branches. (*Talmud.*)

[i.e. without branches there would be no grapes.]

93. **Grass** dreads the scythe. (*Talmud.*)

94. It is better to dwell in **grief** than in widowhood.

95. He who denies his **guilt** doubles his guilt. (*Talmud.*)

96. **Habit** strips sin of its enormity. (*Talmud.*)

97. The **happiness** of the impious and the unhappiness of the righteous are incomprehensible things.

98. The **heart** carries the feet. (*Talmud.*)

99. He who hath a narrow **heart** hath a broad tongue.

100. To put them in thy **heart** is good.

101. The **heart** that loves is always young. (*Talmud.*)

102. The best preacher is the **heart;** the best teacher is time; the best book is the world; the best friend is God. (*Talmud.*)

103. Even when the gates of **heaven** are shut to prayer, they are open to those of tears. (*Talmud.*)

104. **Honest** for a penny [peruta], honest for a pound [dinar]. (*Talmud.*)

105. Hast thou found **honey**? Eat so much as is convenient for thee.

106. The **horse** fed too liberally with oats becomes unruly. (*Talmud.*)

107. Who practises **hospitality** entertains God Himself. (*Talmud.*)

108. **Hospitality** is an expression of Divine worship. (*Talmud.*)

109. From one **house** to another a shirt; from one land to another a life.

[i.e. three removals are as bad as a fire, the household goods are completely ruined.]

110. Be very **humble,** the hopes of men are worms.

111. Be the **husband** only as big as an ant, yet the wife seats herself among the great. (*Talmud.*)

112. **Impurity** in the beginning like a spider's web, in the end like a cart rope.

113. A wicked **inclination** is at first a guest. If thou grant it hospitality it will soon make itself master of the house. (*Talmud.*)

114. The man who deserted thee will teach thee **knowledge.** (*Talmud.*)

115. He alone possesses **knowledge** who knows that he knows nothing. (*Talmud.*)

116. The **labourer's** appetite laboureth for him, for his mouth constrains him to toil.

117. There is no occasion to light thy **lamp** at noontide. (*Talmud.*)

118. He who possesses no **land** is no man. (*Talmud.*)

119. First **learn,** then form opinions.

120. First **learn,** then think independently. (*Talmud.*)

121. Much have I **learned** from my masters, more from my colleagues, most from my disciples.

122. Stretch your **leg** according to the length of your coverlet.

123. The punishment of a **liar** is that he is not believed even when he tells the truth.

124. **A lie** has no feet. (*Talmud.*)

125. He who wishes to **lie** should take care that the testimony is afar off.

126. A **lie** stands upon one leg, but truth upon two.

127. **Life** is but a loan to a man; death is the creditor who will one day claim it. (*Talmud.*)

128. A slain **lion** hast thou slain; ground flour hast thou ground; a burnt house hast thou burnt.

129. One would **live** and cannot, another can and will not.

130. How little does he whom the **Lord** aideth need to grieve or worry.

131. Time strengthens friendship and weakens **love.**

132. To **love** a thing makes the eye blind, the ear deaf. (*Talmud.*)

133. **Love** without rebuke is no love. (*Talmud.*)

134. **Loving-kindness** is greater than laws; and the charities of life are more than all ceremonies. (*Talmud.*)

135. My **lowliness** is my exaltation and my exaltation is my lowliness.

136. If a **man of Naresh** has kissed thee, count thy teeth.

[The town of Naresh in Babylonia had a bad reputation.]

137. Where there is no **man,** be thou the man. (*Talmud.*)

138. Where there is a **man,** there do not thou show thyself a man.

139. He from whom a **mantle** has been confiscated by the court should go on his way singing.

[i.e. one should not resent the penalty inflicted by lawful judges.]

140. Buy at **market,** but sell at home.

[i.e. better is a small profit derived from the place where you dwell than a larger from afar off.]

141. In the **measure** in which a man measures is he measured.

142. He that buys and sells is called a **merchant.**

143. Make but one sale, and thou art called a **merchant.** (*Talmud.*)

144. There is even some **merit** in a resolution to repent. (*Talmud.*)

145. Each of our **miseries** is a piece of golden calf.

146. Attend no auctions if thou hast no **money.** (*Talmud.*)

147. The salt of **money** is diminution.

148. If a word spoken in its time is worth one piece of **money,** silence in its time is worth two. (*Talmud.*)

149. When the tale of bricks is doubled, **Moses** comes!

150. It is not as thy **mother** says, but as thy neighbours say.

151. Keep shut the doors of thy **mouth** even from the wife of thy bosom. (*Talmud.*)

152. **A myrtle** among nettles is still a myrtle. (*Talmud.*)

153. If I am not for **myself,** who is for me? and if I am for myself [only], what am I? (*Talmud.*)

154. The **nail** of the former generations is better than the stomach of the later generations.

[i.e. the good old times.]

155. In your own country your **name,** in other countries your appearance.

156. In the city, my **name,** out of the city, my garment. (*Talmud.*)

157. He who prays for his **neighbour** will be heard for himself. (*Talmud.*)

158. What is intended for thy **neighbour** will never be thine. (*Talmud.*)

159. To him who is dependent upon his **neighbour's** table, the world looks dark. (*Talmud.*)

160. An **old man** in a house is a good sign in a house.

161. An **old man** in the house is a scarecrow, an old woman a pearl.

162. In **old men** there is no taste, in young no insight.

163. When the **ox** is down, many are the butchers. (*Talmud.*)

164. Sixty **pains** afflict the teeth of him who hears the sound of his neighbour [eating] but himself hath nothing to eat.

165. As the **pains,** so the gains. (*Talmud.*)

166. A pot belonging to **partners** is neither hot nor cold.

167. **Passion** is at first as slender as a spider's web; but in the end it becomes like a thick cable. (*Talmud.*)

168. The **pauper** hungers without noticing it.

169. From **peddlers,** news; from rags, vermin.

170. Go out and see how the **people** act.

171. The house that does not open to the poor shall open to the **physician.** (*Talmud.*)

172. He that sinneth before his Maker will behave himself proudly before a **physician.**

173. Do not dwell in a town where the chief man in it is a **physician.**

174. A **physician** afar off is a blind eye.

175. Honour a **physician** before thou hast need of him.

176. Wait not to honour the **physician** until thou fallest sick. (*Talmud.*)

177. The **physician** who accepts no fee is worth no fee.

178. A **physician** whose services are obtained gratis is worth nothing. (*Talmud.*)

179. The best of **physicians** is worthy of Gehenna.

180. The best of **physicians** will go to Hades. (*Talmud.*)

181. Sooner than remain **poor,** sell.

182. Hast given [the **poor**] to eat and drink, accompany them on their way.

183. Healthy **poverty** is opulence, compared with ailing wealth. (*Talmud.*)

184. **Poverty** runs after the poor and riches after the rich. (*Talmud.*)

185. **Poverty** sits as gracefully on some people as a red saddle upon a white horse.

186. When the gates of **prayer** are closed, the gates of repentance are yet open. (*Talmud.*)

187. If our **predecessors** were angels we are human; if they were human we are asses.

188. **Pride** is the mask of one's own faults.

189. He who **promises** runs in debt. (*Talmud.*)

190. The man who is **proud** is a man with a blemish. (*Talmud.*)

191. A man's life is often builded on a **proverb.**

192. What flowers are to gardens, spices to food, gems to a garment, and stars to heaven, such are **proverbs** interwoven in speech.

193. Every **pumpkin** is known by its stem.

[i.e. the child is father of the man.]

194. Loosen thy **purse-strings**, [then] open thy sack.

195. Who is first silent in a **quarrel** springs from a good family. (*Talmud.*)

196. **Rain** is the consort of the earth.

197. He who has issued from thee teacheth thee **reason.**

198. Be as flexible as a **reed** and not as hard as a cedar. (*Talmud.*)

199. **Remorse** and good deeds are a shield from the wrath of heaven.

200. Who is rich? He who enjoys his **riches.**

201. Be not **righteous** overmuch.

202. When a **rogue** kisses you, count your teeth.

203. Sixty **runners** may run, but they will not overtake the man who has breakfasted early.

204. If thou art **satisfied** [with] false munchings, they are a diversion in thy saliva.

205. The **scholar** is greater than the prophet.

206. Thy **secret** is thy slave. If thou let it loose, thou becomest its slave. (*Talmud.*)

207. Do not speak of **secret** matters in a field that is full of little hills.

208. If thou tellest thy **secret** to three persons, ten know of it. (*Talmud.*)

209. The **servant** of a king is a king.

210. Hast spoiled thy work, take a needle and **sew.**

211. **Sheep** follow sheep. (*Talmud.*)

212. While thy **shoe** is on thy foot tread upon the thorns.

213. I do not want a **shoe** larger than my foot.

[i.e. I do not want a husband from a rank higher than my own.]

214. If thy **sieve** be stopped up, knock on it.

[i.e. in prosperity one tends to become forgetful of promises and duties, and it requires strenuous measures to bring them to one's mind.]

215. **Silence** is a healing for all [ailments].

216. **Silence** is the fence round wisdom. (*Talmud.*)

217. If a word be worth one shekel, **silence** is worth a pair.

218. Eye and heart are the brokers of **sin.** (*Talmud.*)

219. He who has committed a **sin** twice considers it no longer a sin.

220. Of the ten measures of **sleep** that came down into the world, slaves received nine and the rest of the world only one. (*Palestine.*)

221. **Smell** at [or strike on] his flask.

[i.e. test his intelligence.]

222. He who does no good in his own **soul** will do no good to other's.

223. **Speech** is the messenger of the heart. (*Talmud.*)

224. **Spend** according to thy means on eating, less on clothing, and more on dwelling.

225. Throw no stone into the **spring** from which you have drunk. (*Aramaic.*)

226. Two dry **sticks** will set on fire one green.

227. The **stomach** carries the feet.

228. He whose **stomach** is full increaseth deeds of evil.

229. If I had not lifted up the **stone,** you had not found the jewel.

[Said of pioneers.]

230. May thy **strength** be firm.

[Used by the Jews as the equivalent of "Thank you."]

231. When the **sun** rises the malady ceases.

232. The **sun** sets of itself.

233. The **sun** will set without thy assistance. (*Talmud.*)

234. Your **surety** wants a surety.

235. He who is **suspicious** should be suspected. (*Talmud.*)

236. Spread the **table,** and contention will cease.

237. The **table** at which strangers eat becomes an altar. (*Talmud.*)

238. Rather be the **tail** among lions, than the head among foxes. (*Talmud.*)

239. On account of the **teacher** the pupil has eaten.

240. He who **teaches** not his son a trade teaches him to be a thief. (*Talmud.*)

241. There are four kinds of **tempers;** he whom it is easy to provoke and easy to pacify—his loss disappears in his gain ; he whom it is hard to provoke and hard to pacify—his gain disappears in his loss ; he whom it is hard to provoke and easy to pacify is a saint ; he whom it is easy to provoke and hard to pacify is a wicked man. (*Palestine.*)

242. Not the mouse is the **thief** but the hole. (*Aramaic.*)

243. The **thief** who finds no opportunity to steal thinks himself an honest man. (*Talmud.*)

244. A man's **thigh** becomes diseased through itself. (*Talmud.*)

245. From the **thorn-bush** comes the rose.

246. Don't say, " I will do it when I have time," for who tells you that you will have **time**?

247. The third **tongue** slays three : the speaker, the spoken to, and the spoken of.

[The " third tongue " means slander.]

248. Accustom thy **tongue** to say, " I know not." (*Talmud.*)

249. It is well to add a **trade** to your studies if you would be free from sin. (*Talmud.*)

250. **Tradition** is a fence to the law. (*Talmud.*)

251. One **transgression** draws another in its train.

252. What everyone says must be **true.**

253. **Truth** is heavy, therefore few care to carry it. (*Talmud.*)

254. **Truth** is the seal of God. (*Talmud.*)

255. **Vinegar,** the son of wine.

[i.e. the bad son of a good father.]

256. There are three **voices** in the world—that of running water, of the Jewish Law, and of money.

257. In the hour of distress—a **vow** ; in the hour of release—forgetfulness.

258. He that **walks** daily over his estates finds a little coin each time.

259. Thou hast added **water,** add flour also.

[Said of a person who is constantly asking questions, but rarely ventures to add anything more substantial to the conversation.]

260. Into the **well** out of which one has drunk one should not cast a stone. (*Talmud.*)

261. Drain not the waters of thy **well** while other people may desire them. (*Talmud.*)

262. If the **wheat** of the city be rye-grass, sow of it.

263. Jump when you want to buy a field, walk slowly when you want to take a **wife.** (*Talmud.*)

264. He among the full-grown pumpkins and his **wife** among the young ones.

[i.e. unfaithfulness on the part of the husband leads to his wife's unchastity.]

265. Descend a step in taking a **wife** ; ascend a step in choosing a friend.

266. If your **wife** is small, stoop down and whisper in her ear. (*Talmud.*)

267. **A wife** speaks and spins.

268. Before **wine-drinkers** [set] wine ; before a ploughman a measure of roots.

269. **Wisdom** is a crown for the head, modesty sandals for the feet.

270. Lackest thou **wisdom,** what hast thou acquired? Hast acquired wisdom, what lackest thou?

271. He is not called **wise** who knows good and ill, but he who can recognize of two ills the lesser.

272. A **woman** is only envious of her companion's thigh.

[i.e. one can control a wife more readily by working on her feeling of jealousy, than by using violence.]

273. A **woman** spins even while she talks.

274. Ten measures of garrulity came down from heaven says the Talmud and the **woman** took nine of them. (*Talmud.*)

275. When an ass climbs a ladder, we may find wisdom in **women.**

276. Carry **wood** after a man of treasures. (*Talmud.*)

277. Carry **wood** behind the owner of property.

278. My **words** may occasion regret, but my silence will avoid it.

279. The value of **words** uttered with the lips, is determined by the devotion of the heart. (*Talmud.*)

280. At the door of the fold, **words**; within the fold, an account.

281. Love thy **work.** (*Talmud.*)

282. The day is short and the **work** is much.

283. It is not incumbent on thee to finish thy **work**; thou shalt not, therefore, cease from it. (*Talmud.*)

284. The **world** is a wedding. (*Talmud.*)

285. This **world** is a world of work, the next, a world of recompense. (*Talmud.*)

286. The **world** is like the wheel of the well, with its two buckets, the full one is ever emptied, and the empty one is ever filled. (*Talmud.*)

287. Every man carries his **worth** in his basket.

288. Let thy **yea** be yea, and thy nay, nay. (*Talmud.*)

289. A **year** of scarcity will change a weaver [for the better] if he be not proud.

290. **Youth** is a garland of roses, old age a garland of willows. (*Aramaic.*)

291. **Youth** is a wreath of roses. (*Talmud.*)

INDIA AND CEYLON

An Introduction to this collection by H. N. Randle Ph.D., M.A., will be found on page lx.

BENGALI

1. The boat of **affection** ascends even mountains.

2. With **affection** two can lie on the leaves of a tamarind; without it, not even on arum leaves.

3. The **ant** gets wings to his destruction.

[i.e. the crows then devour him.]

4. The **blacksmith** knows what he will make of the iron.

5. A known **Brahman** needs no sacred thread [on his body for recognition].

6. A hunting **cat** is known by his whiskers.

[Cats in Bengal that hunt have their whiskers high. This proverb is applied to a man whose incompetency is shown by his deeds.]

7. **Cheap** things are thrice accursed.

8. Even a holy **cow,** if found in company with a stolen one, may be impounded.
9. **Death** and absence are the same.
10. Notice a **dog** and he will leap on your neck.
11. Even though there be a stream of water, the **dog** has to lap.
12. A **dog's** bite is below the knees.
13. **Droppings** from his own thatch drown him, yet he would cross the ocean.
14. Pull the **ear,** the head follows.
15. To obtain **employment,** be willing even to wash dogs' feet.
16. Ten **flowers** will make a nosegay.
17. The **fool,** not knowing how to walk, cries out the road is rough.
18. I will **go** where ten go.

    [According to the early policy of the Anglo-Saxons, each village was divided into ten wards or petty districts.]
19. If ten persons are gathered together, **God** is in the midst of them.

    [Explanation as above.]
20. In order to be **great,** be first little.
21. The sight of a **horse** makes the traveller lame.
22. All shake the **kul-tree.**

    [Applied to a person at the service of all.]
23. Using a **looking-glass** to look at one's bracelets.
24. He who gives blows is a **master**; he who gives none is a dog.
25. With men of one **mind** even the sea might be dried up.
26. **Money** makes iron float.
27. Going in, a **needle**; coming out, a ploughshare.
28. **Oil** your own wheel first.
29. The eater of **pancakes** counts not the holes in them.

    [i.e. when occupied with great pleasure, we do not mind a little inconvenience.]
30. One's own **pedal** proves a crocodile.

    [i.e. one's own kith and kin are the most hostile.]
31. Even if taken up to heaven, the **pedal** would continue to husk the rice.
32. The death of a thousand patients makes a man a **physician.**
33. The destruction of a bushel of eyes makes an oculist; the destruction of one hundred patients makes a doctor; the destruction of a thousand a **physician.**
34. Once a patient, and a **physician** ever after.
35. When the **poor man** grows rich he beholds the stars at noonday.
36. [The water of] the **river** does not ripple unless there is wind.
37. Who sleeps on the **sea,** is he afraid of dew?
38. The **sieve** says to the needle, "You have a hole in your tail."
39. The **soup** increases by work.
40. If the **stomach** be empty, blushing is of no consequence.
41. [Whenever] the **tiger** and the buffalo fight [with each other], the reeds and bulrushes die.

    [i.e. suffer most.]
42. In talk a **tiger**; in fighting, a lizard.
43. There is no hand to catch **time.**
44. Cutting the root and watering the top of the **tree.**

    [i.e. locking the stable door when the horse is gone.]
45. **Truth** has not branches.

    [i.e. supports itself.]
46. **Vice** and virtue arise from our associations.
47. Quiet **water** splits a stone.
48. For sweetness, honey; for love, a **wife.**
49. The **work** done, the broom is a rascal.

BHOJPURĪ

1. As **action,** so fulfilment.
2. **Agriculture** is the best of all professions; trade is middling good; service is to be despised; begging is the last resort.
3. Among men the **barber,** among birds the crow.

   [i.e. both great talkers and gossips.]
4. Don't go into **Bhojpur;** if you go, don't stay; if you stay, don't eat; if you eat, don't go to sleep; if you sleep, don't feel for your purse; if you should feel for your purse, don't weep!

   [You will not find it.]
5. Give a **Brahman** clarified butter and he wriggles with delight.
6. If a **Brahman** should swear by the sacred fossil ammonite, his sacred thread and his bible, standing the while in the water of the Ganges, even then place no trust in what he says.

   [For a Hindu it is regarded as sufficient to take an oath in any one of these ways.]
7. **Brahmans,** dogs and bards are always quarrelling among themselves.
8. He who carries the bludgeon owns the **buffalo.**
9. Does anyone inspect the teeth of a **bullock** borrowed from a neighbour to plough one's field?
10. Clarified **butter** cannot be extracted [from a jar or pitcher] by a straight finger.

    [Proverb counselling subtlety, diplomacy and avoidance of doing things the wrong way.]
11. Where there are no trees the **castor-oil plant** is chief.
12. One can stand being kicked by both hind legs at once if the **cow** be a good milker.
13. The **crow** has cawed, the day has dawned.
14. How can a **crow** sleep soundly when the figs are ripe?
15. Where there is no **crow** will there be no dawn?
16. He gives neither offerings to **crows** nor alms to beggars.

    [i.e. though crows be of such doubtful omen, offerings must be made to them in the ceremonies after death, known as " crow-offerings ".]
17. The egg of the **cuckoo** will hatch into a cuckoo; the crow will be ashamed of itself.

    [i.e. in India the cuckoo often lays eggs in a crow's nest.]
18. A washerman uses no animal but a **donkey,** and a donkey has no other master but a washerman.

    [i.e. no orthodox Hindu in these parts will touch a donkey; it is only the washerman caste (one of the untouchable castes) that will use them.]
19. He does not notice the hard swelling of the cornea [i.e. " beam "] in his own **eye,** but he glares at the leucoma [i.e. a white opacity of the cornea—" mote "] in another's eye.
20. The **fish** that has to live in the water should not make an enemy of the alligator.
21. [If the] mind [be] pure, the [water in the] kneading-trough [is as good as] **Ganges** [water].
22. If you accept it as such it is a **god,** otherwise it is only a lump of earth smeared over.

    [The reference is to village godlings which are usually represented by small round mounds of earth.]
23. A **heron** a saint!

    [Said of anyone affecting piety; a hypocrite. A " bhagat " is a devotee, generally a worshipper of Vishnu, who abstains from eating any kind of flesh, whereas the heron spends the day catching and eating fish.]
24. If **hit,** hit back and don't stop to consider whether you be committing a sin or a virtue.
25. Without a **housewife** a house is but an abode of evil spirits.

26. Can the **lapwing** support the sky on its feet?

    [i.e. you cannot expect an incompetent person to perform a difficult task. The belief is widely current in Bihar that the lapwing sleeps on its back with its long thin legs sticking up in the air.

27. The **marrying** of a daughter is like the digging of a well.

    [i.e. equally essential and expensive.]

28. A **meal** consisting of fowl, fish and meat, with vegetables well pounded, preceded by clarified butter and finishing with curds —that is rightly called a meal.

29. A **meal** without flesh is like feeding on grass.

30. Both an **oath** and vegetables are for eating.

    [In the vernacular the English expression "to take an oath" is rendered "to eat an oath".]

31. All that is in the **priest-astrologer's** almanac is in the hem of his wife's garment.

    [i.e. she really knows more than he does.]

32. He cannot get **prosperity** and quarrels with adversity.

33. The **snake** even turns and bites its charmer.

34. What reliance can be placed on a **sneeze?**

    [i.e. a sneeze is usually considered unlucky, but it depends on the circumstances, the point of the compass from whence it is heard, and various other conditions.]

35. If you **sneeze,** bathe; if you sneeze, go and have a sleep; if you sneeze, don't go into your house though it be all made of gold.

36. A **son** born after three daughters is destined to become a beggar; a daughter born after three sons will rule a kingdom.

37. What dread has **truth** for fire?

38. When **wheat** is cheap, then worship is performed in every house.

39. For the weak, forty-nine **winds.**

    [Said of either the physically weak or infirm, or of the morally weak.]

40. She who wields a big **wooden ladle** rules all.

41. It is the fellow who dances and jumps and strikes up a tune that the **world** pays attention to.

BIHARI

1. He who gives away in **alms** what he has received in charity, conquers the three worlds.

2. Suit your **appearance** to the country.

3. The **barber** and boatman are the only people who recognize their caste fellows [i.e. who help them]. The high caste are only good at fine talks!

4. If you **believe,** it is a deity; otherwise, a stone.

5. There are three **careless people:** the washerman, the tailor, and the barber.

6. After eating nine hundred rats, the **cat** is now going on a pilgrimage.

   [i.e. pretending to turn over a new leaf.]

7. He is dependent on another, what does he know of **comfort?**

8. A blind **cow** requires a separate house [cattle-yard].

9. First **eat** four mouthfuls, then think of deities and ancestral heroes.

10. The **fallen** are cudgelled repeatedly.

11. He who keeps a horse at home and yet goes about on foot; he who is wealthy and yet borrows; and he who keeps anything on trust with a son-in-law, are the three greatest **fools** in the whole world.

12. Before a **gale,** the breeze from a fan has no effect.

13. A Musalman, a parrot, and a hare, these three are never **grateful.**
14. A **horse** when loose is sure to stand near the chaff-house.
15. The root of quarrels is practical **jokes,** just as the root of all sickness is cough.
16. A **Kayath** does what you want on payment, a Brahman on being fed, paddy and betel on being watered, but a low-caste man on being kicked.
17. Three people dance in the houses of others : **Kayeth,** the physician, and the broker.
18. He who holds the **ladle** commands everybody.
19. **Love** knows no lowly caste ; hunger minds not stale repast ; thirst knows not the "ghāt" [where the dead are burned] ; sleep objects not to a broken cot.
20. Even two kicks from a good **milker** are to be valued.
21. Four days of **moonshine,** and then comes again dark night !
22. Rarely do you meet with a **one-eyed man** who is a gentleman [a good man].
23. The **rope** will burn but not the twist.
24. The man who becomes blind in the month of **Sāwan** [July–August], fancies that he sees everything fresh and green.
25. When a **snake** turns he bites the snake-charmer [its keeper].
26. A widow weeps because she is a widow, and perhaps a woman with a husband living [has also cause to weep] ; but in their company a **spinster** also weeps !
27. The son of a **tailor** ; he will sew as long as he lives.
28. The man who mixes **tobacco** with lime [for chewing] and offers it without being asked, conquers [by his virtuous action] heaven, earth, and the lower regions.
29. No soap ever touches clothes unless many **washermen** live together.
30. A new **washerwoman** applies soap to rags even.

    [Rags are seldom washed in India.]
31. In the **wedding** of the sickle, the song of the hoe !

    [Refers to a time when it was the custom to hold marriage ceremonies of agricultural implements ; this custom of wedding inanimate objects is still extant in regard to groves, wells, tanks, etc., which are formally married on being opened.]
32. Either have a handful of bangles or at once be a **widow.**

    [i.e. come to the point. A woman who becomes a widow has to break her lac bangles at once.]
33. When you see a cloud speckled like the wing of the partridge, and a **widow** applying scented oil to her hair, the former will rain and the latter will elope.
34. The trees in the orchard have not yet been planted, but the **wood-worms** have settled down there beforehand.

CHITTAGONG (DIALECT OF)

1. If you pick the fluff from a **blanket** it comes to pieces.

   [i.e. leave well alone.]
2. To the **blind man's** eye, waking and sleeping are the same.
3. The **boat** sinks at the landing-stage.

   [Expresses disgust when a nearly finished work is spoiled.]
4. In a treeless land the **castor-oil plant** is a tree.
5. The **cheat** carries a double load.
6. You can put up with its kicks if a **cow** gives milk.
7. **Cows** don't graze in their own farmyard.

   [i.e. a prophet has no honour in his own country.]

8. When rice is sprinkled there is no lack of **crows.**
9. Thin **dogs** bark loudest.
   [i.e. empty vessels sound loudest.]
10. When the **eyes** are closed the world is dark.
11. The **house** that is laughed at stands.
   [i.e. do not judge hastily.]
12. **Mat-makers** do not lie on mats.
   [i.e. the miser will not use his wealth—the confectioner does not eat his sweets.]
13. Are **ornaments** ever burdensome?
   [i.e. can you have too much of a good thing?]
14. One **straw** [in the river] draws another.
   [i.e. money breeds money.]
15. Use a **thorn** to extract a thorn.
   [i.e. set a thief to catch a thief.]
16. Big **tree**—big breeze.
17. The victory of **virtue** is the decline of vice.
18. **Virtue's** drum gets sounded by the wind.
   [i.e. the fame of a good action spreads far afield.]

HINDI

1. Eighty years of **age** and named "Mr. Infant".
2. He who will not open the door to give **alms** will open it for the doctor.
3. **Anger** has no eyes.
4. **Anger** injures itself; wisdom injures another.
5. In the **ant's** house there is ever mourning.
6. It will not always be **August** with green fields.
7. Without cash, why go **a-wooing?**
8. The **axe** attacks the forest, from whence it got its own handle.
9. What need have you of a **bag** if you have four and spend five?
10. He **barks**; so he will not bite.
11. If our name has risen, then we can lie in **bed.**
12. The **beggar's** appearance is a demand.
13. What is **begun** is ended.
14. The raft of the **benevolent** gets across.
15. It is a brave **bird** that makes its nest in the cat's ear.
16. Accept the **bitter**; fear the sweet.
17. He who **blames** himself need not expect praise from others.
18. **Blind** from his birth, and named "Bright Eyes".
19. The August **blind man** sees everything green.
20. Who has ferried across in a paper **boat?**
21. The paper **boat** will sink some day.
22. The **bountiful** and the miser come out even at the end of the year.
23. The **bow** always bent becomes slack.
24. Send the **boy** to travel that you love the best.
25. Woe to that **boy** whose father has gone to Heaven.
26. The **brains** are not in the beard.
27. If you go on the **branches** I will go on the leaves.
28. Begged **bread** is best.
29. Wheaten **bread** needs a stomach of steel.
30. The **bread** that is eaten is soon forgotten.
31. God who gives teeth gives **bread** too.
32. Labour is bitter, but sweet is the **bread** which it buys.
33. One **breath**; a thousand hopes.
34. No friend like a **brother**; no enemy like a brother.

35. A **buffalo** does not feel the weight of his own horns.

36. Even when **butter** is plentiful it comes in little drops.

37. **Buy** in the market ; sell in the house.

38. If you bring things to the **buyer** you sell them at half-price.

39. Leave a **calamity** alone for three years, and it will become a blessing.

40. A **cat** is a lion in a jungle of small bushes.

41. The **cat** went on a pilgrimage, having eaten nine hundred rats.

42. Call the fan a saint, who drives away the **chaff ;** call the sieve a sinner, who collects the chaff.

43. You cannot **cheat** in daily wages.

44. **Cherish** him, but he will be thy death.

45. Open **chests** tempt even the righteous.

46. He whose **clothes** are most torn shall sleep next the wind.

47. He came as a September **cloud**, rained and went away.

48. He who has **come,** will go.

49. Little to give ; much **comfort.**

50. **Company** will influence.

51. **Contentment** is great gain.

52. High house, tasteless **cookery.**

53. Where the **cow** is, there is her calf.

54. March and April are the key to **credit.**

55. The **cure** of one is two.

56. If you **curse** anyone, first prepare two graves.

57. Three **dance** in the houses of others : the clerk, the doctor, the go-between.

58. Under the lamp, **darkness.**

59. Many can sin like **David,** but few can repent like him.

60. There never came a **day** without an evening.

61. Sometimes the **days** are long, sometimes the night.

62. The **dead** are all right on the third day.

63. The **deaf** are deep pools.

64. The hair of a tiger, the gem of a snake, the breast of a chaste woman, the tusk of an elephant, the sword of a brave man, the riches of a Brahman, are got only after their **death.**

65. Put him in danger of **death,** then he will be content with a fever.

66. **Death** to you ; amusement to the world.

67. Kine are of divers colours, but all milk is alike ; the kinds of flowers vary, yet all worship is one ; systems of faith are different, but the **Deity** is one.

68. **Depression** first maims the mind and then kills the body.

69. Never **despise** anyone, consider him who is above you as your father, your equal as your brother, and your inferior as your son.

70. Man is his own **devil.**

71. He will soon **die** who sleeps on straw in September, on a cot in January, and who travels in May.

72. Cared for, **dies ;** uncared for, lives.

73. Are there delightful **diseases,** and luscious medicines ?

74. The new **doctor** gives opium.

75. The **doctor** said, "I have lanced many boils, but none pained like my own."

76. Woe to the city whose **doctors** have gouty feet.

77. You should water the **doctor's** trees with tears.

78. Shall I keep a **dog** and bark myself?

79. Go like the **dog ;** come like the cat.

80. Take a **dog** into the midst of the sea and he will only drink by lapping.

81. The strolling **dog** is beaten everywhere.

82. If one **door** be shut, a thousand are open.
83. Beware of the **door** which has several keys.
84. He reigned in **dreams,** but day brought the old poverty.
85. To each one his own **drum,** and his own tune.
86. Read everything; remained a **dunce,**
87. What will not the **dying** do?
88. The **eagle** will not pursue flies.
89. First **earn,** then eat.
90. The **elder** was just the elder, but save us from the younger.
91. The **elephant** walks and the curs bark.
92. **Enjoyment** is the grace of God.
93. Where is your **enemy?** In your bosom.
94. Every one keeps his **enemy** under his armpit.
95. There is **enmity** between digging and causing to dig.
96. **Evening** is the mother of patience.
97. **Excuse** is worse than the offence.
98. Fields have **eyes,** and the wilderness has ears.
99. What the **eyes** can see, the hands will do.
100. **Eyes** concealed mean a wound to the heart.
101. What hides the **eyes** equals a mountain.
102. The buyer needs a hundred **eyes;** the shopkeeper has need of none.
103. **Fasting** is the best medicine.
104. One or two **faults** may pass, the third is hereditary.
105. **Fear** the well-fed clown and the hungry gentleman.
106. It is in vain to look for yesterday's **fish** in the house of the otter.
107. The closed **fist** locks up heaven, and the open hand is the key of mercy.
108. Catching **fleas** is the only work to hasten.
109. The more water you put in the more **flour** you must put in.
110. It is in the silence that follows the storm, and not the silence before it, that we should search for the budding **flower.**
111. The **fly** will never quit the confectioner's shop.
112. **Fools** and babes speak the truth.
113. Shaving **fools** the barber learned his trade.
114. The strong find a **footing** everywhere.
115. **Forgotten** music and pleasure, forgotten service; three things will not be forgotten, salt, oil, and wood.
116. The **fox's** last run is to the tanner's shop.
117. **Friend** and mule, fail in the time of need.
118. What is unwatched goes to your **friends.**
119. One enemy is too many; a hundred **friends** are not enough.
120. He feeds his **friends** doubly in the dark.
121. It is not a far road to a **friend's** house.
122. Go to thy rich **friend's** house when called; go uncalled to thy poor friend's house.
123. Close for meals; far from **friendship.**
124. Tell me what **fruit** is bitter when ripe, delightful when green, and sweet when half-ripe?
125. It will be a **furlong** if you stand, two miles if you sit, and six if you eat.
126. **Give** in this world, to get back in the next.
127. **Give** of your own, and buy a fight.
128. What you have **given** will be a shield.
129. The **giver** sails uphill in a ship.
130. Beware of a religious teacher who is a **glutton.**
131. Eaters in fast-time rob **God.**

132. It is good to lend to **God,** and to the land; they both give good interest.
133. If **God** be merciful, He breaks the roof in giving.
134. **God** builds the nest of the blind bird.
135. Call on **God,** but row away from the rocks.
136. While we meditate one thing, **God** determines another.
137. Even **God** forgives three sins.
138. **God** gives food to every bird, but does not throw it into the nest.
139. He whom **God** has marked, the market-man cheats.
140. If you believe, it is a **god**; if not, it is a stone.
141. Let no one inquire about caste; who worships **God** is His.
142. When **God** is pleased He will again fill up.
143. A little child cannot take God's name, but **God** loves him.
144. We have not seen **God**: reason recognizes Him.
145. If **God** says, "Pull," He will give you a rope. If He says, "Ride," He will furnish a horse.
146. We give to **God** the flower that is out of reach.
147. **God,** who has soaked you, will dry you again.
148. It is **God's** doing; sometimes sunshine, sometimes shadow.
149. Morning sales, and trust in **God's** friendship.
150. Taste is **God's** gift.
151. Steel is softer than **gold.**
152. **Gold** and sweet smell!
153. **Gold** can come in all doors but Heaven's.
154. Where you find both **good** and evil, there you find a city.
155. What **good** thing have I done this day? The setting sun will carry with it a portion of my life.
156. The **good** we do to-day becomes the happiness of to-morrow.
157. To dig one's **grave** with one's own hands.
158. First day a **guest**; next a bore.
159. The first day a **guest,** the second a guest, the third day a calamity.
160. It is not the stones that build the house—it is the **guests.**
161. Fish and **guests** become unpleasant after three days.
162. **Hair** long; wisdom little.
163. Scatter with one **hand,** collect with both.
164. Are the lines of the **hand** ever rubbed out?
165. Take with one **hand,** give with the other.
166. **Hand** knows hand.
167. If the **hand** would do what the tongue says there would be no poverty.
168. Man comes into the world with his **hands** shut, and goes out of it with his hands open.
169. True **happiness** consists in making happy.
170. The nearest approach to **happiness** for man in the course of his life is to possess liberty, health and a peaceful mind.
171. **Happiness** is guarded by bold warriors.
172. Do not adjust your **hat** under a pear-tree, nor tie your shoes in a melon patch.
173. You **hear** by paying; the poor hear by luck.
174. To walk on someone's **heart.**
175. **Heart** accepts; head rejects.
176. The pure in **heart** has the Ganges in his tub.
177. If there be no **heart,** let there at least be feet.
178. If there be a place in the **heart,** there will be a place in the home.
179. The hand to the nail and the **heart** to the beloved.
180. An earthen **hearth** is in every house.
181. Look at the **heel.**
182. A needle wound is enough for a **hen.**

183. If you are a **hen,** lay eggs ; if a cock, crow.

184. The **hide** that is stretched is a dead one.

185. The **high** mix with the high ; the low with the low ; water mingles with water ; mire with mire.

186. One can see one's own **home** afar off.

187. Eat and drink at **home,** and dwell with an enemy.

188. To make a **home** in one's heart.

189. To build one's **home** in the eyes.

190. Make a **home,** make a home, and bring seventy calamities on your head.

191. Through laughing **homes,** are founded.

192. Where the **honey** is spread there will the flies gather.

193. **Honour** and profit are not found in the same dish.

194. The master's eye fattens his **horse.**

195. It is well to walk, when you have a **horse** at hand.

196. **Horse** at home ; price in market.

197. The **horse** broke his halter, but could not escape.

198. Live not in that city where no **horse** neighs, nor dog barks.

199. He who is on **horseback** will not spare his own father alive.

200. Climb up and see ; all **houses** look alike.

201. Become **humble** before you become dust.

202. What is tasteless to the **hungry ?** and the sleepy need no pillow.

203. All are not **hunters** who blow the horn.

204. **Hunting,** fighting, wantonness ; one pleasure, a hundred pains.

205. Until man has been wet he will not build a **hut,** nor learn to stoop until his head has been bumped.

206. Who is more **industrious** than the man with work ?

207. In August was the **jackal** born and in September saw he a flood and said, " Never in my life have I seen such a flood."

208. At home a **jogi ;** elsewhere a saint.

209. **A joint pot** breaks at the cross-road.

210. No one will do strict **justice** in his own case.

211. If the **king** be angry, he can take away your livelihood, but not your good luck.

212. One **laugh :** one pain.

213. A meagre agreement is better than a fat **lawsuit.**

214. They **learn** by losing.

215. The new and withered **leaves** are everywhere to be found.

216. Is it necessary to add acid to the **lemon ?**

217. Sometimes to sink, sometimes to rise : this is **life.**

218. What you **loan** out, you will never see again ; or if you see it again, then it will be decreased ; or if not decreased then it will be different ; or if not different, then you will have found an enemy.

219. No **loss** nor gain, but just so ; neither good nor bad, but just so.

220. There are **losses** from which we get great gain.

221. I went in search of **love** and lost myself.

222. **Love** as the cotton does, which in life shields thee and goes with thee in death.

223. When four eyes met, then **love** came in the heart.

224. Who are **loved** in this world are loved in heaven.

225. Any **lure** is good that brings the bird to the net.

226. **Lust,** fire, cough, these three are not concealed.

227. **Lust** is bottomless.

228. She who is born beautiful is born **married.**

229. One **meal** a day : constant happiness.

230. He who has eaten tender **meat,** let him also eat tough.

231. Take **medicine** for your understanding.

232. There is **medicine** in the house : alas! we must die.

233. The **milk** of the sixth day is still sensible.

234. In a time of **misfortune** a dog will bite him who rides a camel.

235. Either **money** in your pocket or a sweet tongue in your mouth.

236. Even a **monkey** falls from a tree.

237. **A mother's love** is best of all.

238. No one **murders** with a golden dagger.

239. Do not force on thy **neighbour** a hat that hurts thine own head.

240. Love your **neighbour,** but do not throw down the dividing wall.

241. You may live in peace when your **neighbours** permit.

242. The truth is not as mother tells it, but as the **neighbours** tell it.

243. The man with **nostrils** is " Mr. Nose " among the noseless.

244. Three will **not understand :** the beggar, the debtor, the child.

245. **Old age,** and a thousand faults.

246. An **old man's** teaching sets the world straight.

247. Butting **ox** is better than empty stall.

248. Who will pay for the shoe of a **partnership horse ?**

249. **Patience** is the greatest prayer. (*Saying of Buddha.*)

250. **Patience,** rectitude, friend, and wife, all four are tested by calamity.

251. Live not in that city whose master is a **physician.**

252. Who will put you out, if you sit in your own **place ?**

253. A promising **plant** has shining leaves.

254. **Pleasure** is the seed of trouble.

255. The **poor** seek food, the rich seek an appetite.

256. Only know that **posterity** is thine when a grandson plays at thy gate.

257. The **pot** cooks best on its own stove.

258. A **pot** of wood will not cook twice.

259. The little **pot** soon boils.

260. That which is in the **pot,** will come up in the ladle.

261. The **potter's donkey** follows anyone with muddy trousers.

262. **Poverty** is a garment of fire.

263. Little **praise** is dispraise.

264. What do the great know of **prices ?**

265. **Pride** has three curtains before it.

266. You have not met **prosperity ;** why quarrel with adversity ?

267. Eat **pulse** and keep well ; eat vetches and break towers.

268. Eat **pulse,** or play the bagpipe.

269. The **punishment** of being born.

270. He ought to be **pure** who goes about blaming others.

271. To lend, is to buy a **quarrel.**

272. **Quarrels** come of laughter, and disease of coughing.

273. Why should he fear the **rain** who is very wet ?

274. In harvest time the **rat** has four wives.

275. **Reconcile** the offended, sew up the torn.

276. General **report** is generally true.

277. **Reputation** will feed you, and will grieve you.

278. Your own doing ; your own **reward.**

279. **riches** are a Hindu's beard.

[Hindus shave on all occasions of mourning, which often occur.]

280. The **rich man** gets a seat on a chair.

281. Do what is **right** and lawful, and do it a thousand times a day.

282. As far as the **river** flows, it carries mud.

283. One **road,** two objects.

284. Plant **roses** for him who plants thorns for you. For you they are roses, for him a trident.

285. Charity done in secret, eager courtesy to the visitor of his house, silence after doing kindness and public mention after receiving it ; modesty in fortune, conversation without spice of insolence, who taught good men this **rule of life,** hard as a sword's edge to tread ?

286. The **saint** has ever a feast, if there be wheat in the house.

287. Only a **saint** knows a saint.

288. Many turn **saints** for their stomach's sake.

289. The **science** of duty.

290. If one knows, it is a **secret ;** if two, it is public.

291. Thy **secret** is thy prisoner, but if thou tellest it, thou becomest its prisoner, for thy friend has a friend, who also has a friend, therefore keep thy mouth shut.

292. Do **service,** and eat fruit.

293. He who first bathes, then eats, then sleeps, will never get **sick.**

294. Always **sick,** but named " Mr. Healthy ".

295. He who spends his life without **sickness** will die without honour.

296. Who **sins** finds a master.

297. **Sleep** may come even at the stake.

298. He **sleeps,** having sold his mare.

299. He never **slept** on straw, but dreamed of a bed.

300. The **snake-bitten** fears a rope.

301. **Soil** that is fertile is unfit for the road.

302. Why save if your **son** is a good son ? Why save if your son is a bad son ?

303. Who **speaks** first must open the door.

[Native custom to call inmates to open the door.]

304. If **speech** be one rupee, then silence is two.

305. Do not defile the **spring** which has once quenched your thirst.

306. He who owns the **stick** also has the bullock.

307. A single **stick** will neither burn, nor light, nor shine.

308. The **stomach** has feet.

309. The **stomach** has no ear ; the hungry cannot hear.

310. Fill the **stomach ;** load the back.

311. Can a falling drop mark a hard **stone ?**

312. **A stream** is pure at its rising, but, like gossip, it becomes muddy.

313. One does, all **suffer.**

314. The **sugar** eater gets sugar.

315. In a fight **sweetmeats** are not distributed.

316. From fear of one **sword** another sword stays in its sheath.

317. What dries quicker than a **tear ?**

318. As the **temper,** so the world will be.

319. **Temperance** and fasting cure most diseases.

320. A **tenant** has come.

[i.e. she is in the family way.]

321. The cash **tenant** needs no sponsor.

322. The **thief** has a hundred days ; the merchant has one.

323. The unseen **thief** is equal to a king.

324. The **thief** is king over others' wealth.

325. Though the **thorn** in your foot be very little, stop and take it out.

326. Erstwhile we twain deemed that **thou** was I and I was thou, how comes it now that thou art thou and I am I ?

327. If you want to know what a **tiger** is like, look at a cat.

328. **Time** passes away, but sayings remain.

329. Who has seen **to-morrow ?**

330. From the bow in the hand of **to-morrow,** neither aged nor young shall escape.

331. Keep your **tongue,** and keep your friend.

332. The **tongue** can mount you on an elephant; the tongue can behead you.

333. Upon what **tree** does the wind not strike?

334. When the **tree** is about to perish, it brings forth blasted fruit.

335. It is the fruitful **tree** that is pelted with stones.

336. Will not he who has planted the **tree** water it?

337. Where there are no **trees,** the castor plant is a tree.

338. Always in **trouble,** but named "Mr. Happy".

339. **Troubled** from his birth, and named "Mr. Blissful".

340. A "No" averts seventy **troubles.**

341. That is **true** which stands the flame.

342. Who **trusts** in others, always fasts.

343. He who speaks the **truth** should have one foot in the stirrup.

344. The **twig** unbent within five years, will it be bent at fifty?

345. The **unattainable** is great.

346. **Virtue** is spotlessness of mind; all else is mere noise.

347. There is no disputing daily **wages.**

348. The first **watch** all watch, in the second the jogi watches, in the third the thief, and in the fourth the sick man.

349. First **water,** afterwards mire.

350. Where **water** is running, wash your hands.

351. Every man must dip in his own **waters.**

352. **Weak** and soon angry.

353. **Wealth** is the poison of pleasure, and the root of sorrows.

354. Where **wealth** is, there sorrow is.

355. That is **wealth,** which comes of use.

356. **Weep** once when things are dear; weep often when they are cheap.

357. The **weevil** gets ground with the wheat.

358. **Wheat** has chaff on every grain.

359. The **whisperer** is a liar.

360. Has no **wife** nor daughter; only related to Heaven.

361. Happy **wife,** whose husband does not speak to her!

362. **Winnow** while there is wind.

363. **Wisdom** has not vanished; the wise have vanished.

364. The home of **wisdom** is far away.

365. After **wisdom** the club.

366. It takes great **wisdom** to laugh at one's own misfortunes.

367. **Wisdom's** dogs smelled the threshold, and ran away.

368. The **wise man** does at first what the fool does at last.

369. If you live with **wolves,** you must howl like them.

370. The hearth is a **woman.**

371. A king, **woman,** and a creeping plant, alike twine round him who stands by their side.

372. To educate a **woman** is like placing a knife in the hands of a monkey.

373. **Woman** is the chief gate to hell.

374. A **woman** should be brought home in the evening, and a sheep in the morning.

375. Oil and the pure **woman** will both rise.

376. Three are inconstant: **woman,** wind, and wealth.

377. A **woman's** first counsel is good.

378. A **woman's** word is a bundle of water.

379. Regard not a **woman's** words.

380. **Women** and chickens get lost by wandering from house to house.

381. If **women** manage a village it will become a desert.

382. Where there are **women** there is trouble.

383. His **words** are sweet, but his hands empty.

384. Lack of **work** brings a thousand diseases.

385. The **world** will not conquer him who is always rubbing his beard.

386. **Write** like the learned; speak like the masses.

387. Wash off **yesterday's** plaster, and look to to-day's.

388. That is your **yoke** which is used by you.

389. To be healthy is **youth**; freedom from debt is wealth.

HINDUSTANI OR URDU

1. The miser's and the liberal man's **accounts** balance at the end of the year.
2. The **adult** looks to deeds, the child to love.
3. Like an **ant** on a fire-stick lit at both ends.
4. Give an **apple** where there is an orchard.
5. **Arrows** from one quiver.

   [i.e. chip of the old block.]
6. Man has one **beauty**, apparel a thousand, jewels a hundred thousand, and love a million.
7. The **beauty** [which arise from dress] is in the portmanteau, and that of the person is in the platter.
8. Only a **beggar** or a rich man can eat opium.
9. The **benedict** hath but one house, the bachelor a score.
10. **A blind man** loses his staff only once.
11. You throw a **bridge** before there is any water.
12. The **buffalo** belongs to the man with the big stick.

    [i.e. might is right.]
13. Who drinks boiled **buffalo's milk** will keep his strength through life.
14. Come **bull**, gore me.

    [Said of one who willingly brings misfortune on himself.]
15. **Charity** protects you.
16. **Charity's** a plant whose roots are ever green.
17. **Cheapness** moves to laughter, dearness to tears.
18. **A child** will judge the heart, a woman reads the eyes and lips, a man requires deeds.
19. There is a **choice** of but two things, loss or gain.
20. **Contention's** roots are three: women, land and gold.
21. To a **co-wife** a fairy is uglier than a goblin.
22. You cannot live in the river and be at enmity with the **crocodile**!
23. The **cup** fell into the hands of one who never saw one and she drank till she died.
24. He who has no **daughters** considers his threshold as one.
25. It is still the first **day**.
26. Sloth, sleep and yawning are the three brothers of **death.**
27. Who knows when **death** or a customer will come?
28. **Distrust** the man who hates the taste of curds, the scent of clover, and the song of birds.
29. Lost by a **drop** can't be recovered by a pond-full.
30. After twelve years, even a **dunghill** begins to prosper.
31. An uncle's **dwelling** is a place of rest, if one remain not more than seven days.
32. **Earth** laughs at him who calls a place his own.
33. When **ease** comes, corpulence comes.

34. An **elephant,** however lean, is valuable.

35. It comes through an **elephant's** mouth, and goes through an ant's.
[Said of illness.]

36. Out of **employment,** out of health.

37. The **evening** is the mother of all.

38. Wash your **face** with the water of a stagnant pool.
[Used contemptuously in refusing to grant a request.]

39. **Faith** keeps the world going.

40. The **feet grow** from the stomach.
[i.e. no work, no food.]

41. To **feet** that wear sandals the whole earth is leather.

42. Go to the wilderness, you cannot escape **fleas.**

43. When coming its name is "**forbearance**", when going its name is "relief".

44. A cartload of **friendship** is not worth a barley corn of kin.

45. O Samman, what **fruits** are those which become bitter by ripening, are pleasant when green, and sweet when half-ripe?
[Human life in three stages—youth, manhood, old age.]

46. **Gaiety** is the support of the body, but sadness makes it to grow old.

47. The **gardener** wants rain, the washerman sunshine, a banker a talk, and a thief quietude.

48. Tulsī, in this world are five chief **gems**: communion with saints, worship of God, mercy, faith, and kindliness of heart.

49. What thou **givest** shall be thy shield.

50. The voice of the people is the drum of **God.**

51. Shut your eyes, your nose and your mouth, and then call on **God.** Your inner doors will open when your outer doors are shut.
[Contemplation on Atheism leads to salvation.]

52. My friend, love **God** as the husbandman loves his fields; he suffers losses and pays tribute, and still he loves his fields.

53. If **God** be our friend we have already succeeded.

54. **God** dwells in music.

55. **God** fills the full.

56. **God** grant no nails to the bald.

57. Let none trouble about caste and creed; who calleth on **God** is called of God.

58. There is a **God,** so why do you grieve?

59. As I can conceal nothing from **God,** why should I stand in awe of man?

60. The **good** are two, and one is dead and one unborn.

61. A new **government** and a drum on a hen's back.

62. Who sells **grain** is a merchant, who hoards grain is a murderer of men.

63. For one or two days a **guest,** on the third, the misfortune of one's life.

64. One day a **guest,** the second day a sponge.

65. One **hand** cannot clap.

66. Empty **hands** don't go to the mouth.

67. The **harvest** of dregs is very great.

68. The **heart** at rest sees a feast in everything.

69. There is a way from **heart** to heart.

70. The crowing of a **hen** is no rule.

71. Keep your **honour,** but count your life as cast-off hair.

72. The **horse** is in the stable and you declare his price in the market.

73. The empty **house** is the wasp's estate.

74. For a **house** your own house, for company a man.

75. The **idol-carrier** worships not.

76. Grind the jaws and keep off seventy **ills.**

77. A mustard-seed of **kinship** is better than a gourd-full of love.
78. Better a dram of **kinship** than a cart-load of friendship.
79. **Knowledge**—know each other. Goodness—love thy brother.
80. **Labour** is the key to rest.
81. He who holds the **ladle** has everybody his friends.
82. Light your **lamp** first at home and afterwards at the mosque.
83. The **lamp** of a dark house—a son.
84. If a man **laughs,** it is at others; if he weeps, it is for himself.
85. A **leafless tree** is the husband [paramour] of the wind.

    [i.e. a poor man has no cause to fear misfortune.]
86. **Liars** died in days of old; now they never catch a cold!
87. When **life** is woe, and hope is dumb, the world says "Go," the grave says "Come."
88. Meet all, and play with all, and love all, and chime in with all, if you would **live** [peacefully] in your own village.
89. Give a **loan** and make an enemy.
90. Who **love** are fools, who love and break are fine fellows. Who but an ox will live on with a rope around his neck?
91. **Love** of men leads to love of God.
92. Eyes meet eyes, and **love** slips out between.
93. The **lover** is shaved clean in the lane of his love.
94. Young **lovers** wish, and married men regret.
95. All pretty **maids** are poisonous pests; an enemy kills by hiding, these by smiles and jests.
96. The **market** is his who pays.
97. Regularity is the best **medicine.**
98. No pleasure like **misery,** when it does not last long.
99. What the hand has given will be a bar to **misfortune.**
100. **Money,** land, and women are the roots of quarrel.
101. Toil and hoard in sweat and fear—**money's** good,—but much too dear!
102. "**No**" for an hour, brings peace for a whole day.
103. Who thrive are **nobles,** who fail are holy ascetics, who die are saints.
104. We get the **note** by striking the string.
105. **Opinion** slays and opinion keeps alive.
106. A butting **ox** is better than a lonely bed.
107. The **partnership** pot breaks where four roads meet.
108. Our **past** is ourselves, what we are, and will be.
109. Amongst men some are **pebbles,** but others are jewels.
110. **Philanthropy** is true religion.
111. Take it for **pleasure** and it is pleasure; take it for pain and it is pain.
112. Learn, my son, what will keep the **pot** boiling.
113. Who has the **pot** has the sword.
114. In one cooking **pot** two hands.
115. The **potter** makes, the world fills.
116. Use both **prayer** and medicine.
117. If **prayers** were not in vain, the world would be undone.
118. The **present** for the present; the future for the future.
119. The irregular **priest** makes a noise.

    [Dissenters are generally noisy.]
120. What comes with the stream is a lawful **prize.**
121. Make as much **profit** as there is salt in flour.
122. In **prosperity,** a father; in adversity, a mother.
123. Eat **pulse** and keep your health.
124. I a **queen,** you a queen, who is to fetch the water?
125. The **red spot** becomes coverture, and water becomes a well, learning becomes a teacher; remember this, my brother.

    [Red spot on forehead is sign of coverture among Hindu women.]

126. You may eat and **regret**, but not bathe and regret.
127. A mustard-seed of **relationship** is worth a cartload of friendship.
128. The **reputation** of a man is the shadow of a tree.
129. A following commands **respect**.
130. Nourish him, nourish him, [but] he will be your **ruin.**
131. He that **runs** will obtain.
132. What falls into **salt** becomes salt.
133. He knows not the charm, even for a **scorpion**, and yet he puts his hand into a snake's hole.
134. He that **searcheth** shall find, though he seek deep water. But what can that poor sinner obtain who sits inactive on the shore ?
135. A new **servant** will catch a deer.
136. Bathe early every day and **sickness** will avoid you.
137. A **sin** will guide you to a grave.
138. There is a thick mist, so **sing** as you please.
139. **Smile** and be entangled.
140. There are but two things [of value in the world], a **son** and a daughter.
141. He who has the **spoon** has all under his hand.
142. All hanker after a **stranger's** love : but there are two drawbacks ; he'll neither stay, nor take you with him.
143. If you can't give **sugar**, talk sugar.
144. If you **suspect** him, reject him ; if you select him, don't suspect him.
145. **Tears** have language, clear alone to him whose eyes have wept.
146. I own no **tears** wherewith to cry ; I have no leisure e'en to die.
147. Whoever has never seen a **tiger**, let him look at a cat, and whoever has never seen a robber, let him look at a butcher.
148. Men **trip** not on mountains, they stumble over stones.
149. Between **truth** and falsehood there is four fingers' breadth.

    [Four fingers fill up the facial angle between the eye and ear.]
150. The pincers of **truth** are the severest of their kind.
151. The **truth** is half a quarrel.
152. If you have a head you can get eighty-five **turbans.**
153. While the **wall** stands it receives lots of whitewash.
154. **Want** too much dies, want nothing lives.
155. **Wealth** is not caste.
156. In the loss of **wealth** life's safety lives.
157. Never make known one's **wealth,** one's remedies, one's lover, where one has hidden money, the good works one does, the insults one has received, or the debts one has contracted.
158. " Dear," O Sahib, **weeps** but once ; " Cheap " is always weeping.
159. Better catch a serpent and suck its poison, than have dealings with another's **wife.**
160. Without a **wife** a house is the abode of a devil.
161. The arrival of a **wife** is the beginning of posterity.
162. Cotton, oil, and a fire will conquer **winter.**
163. A hare and a **woman** are yours while in your power.
164. **Woman** is a poisonous creeper ; avoid her company ; her love destroys faith, caste, wealth and money.
165. The man thinks he knows, but the **woman** knows better.
166. **Woman,** thou hast three good qualities and four hundred thousand bad : to sing, to burn [as satī], and to produce sons.
167. A **woman** weeps without a husband, and a field without rain.

168. Tulsī, pleasant **words** please the whole world ; the charm for success is giving up harsh words.

169. The **world** befriends the elephant and tramples on the ant.

170. If you look at the **world** every moment, whom will you congratulate, and with whom condole ?

171. Flatter the **world** if you would eat sugar with your bread.

INDIAN

(General collection, partly unclassified)
(Including Assamese, Baluchi, Gujarati, Gurkhali, Kanarese, Manipuri, Marwari, Sikh and Tulu)

1. Let no man fix his **abode** where there is no wealth, no divine teacher, no magistrate, no river, and no physician.
2. Things not understood are **admired.**
3. **Alms** are food prepared for a journey. (*Kanarese.*)
4. The **altar fire** is born of the rubbed stick.
5. A coco-nut shell full of water is an ocean to an **ant.**
6. Even an **ant** is eight spans long as measured by its own hand.
7. Two **arrows** in the quiver are better than one ; and three are better still.
8. When a man cannot get a wife he turns **ascetic.**
9. An **ascetic's** friendship spells ruin to his friends.
10. An **ass** and a pack-saddle and no anxieties.
11. Trust a tiger, a scorpion, a snake, but a **Baniya's** word you can never take.
12. A **barber,** a dog, and a hawk are useless when full ; a Baniya [moneylender], a bullock, and a king are useless when empty.
13. Among men most deceitful is the **barber,** among birds the crow, among creatures of the water the tortoise.
14. **Barbers,** doctors, pleaders, prostitutes, all must have cash down.
15. It is too late to give **barley** when you are at the top of the hill.
16. The **bat** had a guest and said, " I'm hanging, you hang too."
17. A **bear** is an unsafe bed-fellow. (*Gurkhali.*)
18. There are three **blood-suckers** [butchers] in this world—the bug, the flea, and the Brahman.
19. A **book** is a good friend which reveals the mistakes of the past.
20. The **bow** always bent becomes slack.
21. Trust a **Brahman** before a snake, and a snake before a harlot, and a harlot before an Afghan.
22. Vishnu gets the barren prayers, while the **Brahman** devours the offerings.
23. Before the **Brahman** is in want the king's larder will be empty.
24. A slow fire, sweet **bread.**
25. Flatter the world if you would eat sugar with your **bread.**
26. Make your head into a cart and your feet into wheels and you'll get **bread.**
27. I don't eat my **bread,** but my bread eats me.
    [Anxiety of earning a living.]
28. The guest likes the **bread** which his host likes.
29. Be the slave of him whose **bread** you eat.

30. **Breath** is the music of life.
31. A man who wants to wash gains his end when the **bridge** breaks. (*Manipuri.*)
    [i.e. a man may sometimes get what he wants by an accident.]
32. I met a hundred men on the road to Delhi and they were all my **brothers.**
33. A burnt **cake** is any man's bread. (*Sikh.*)
34. Who eats the last **cake** will be a fool.
    [i.e. it is unlucky to eat it and it is given to a dog.]
35. The girl whose mother makes **cakes** must cry for them.
36. The life of a **camel** is but forty days. (*Baluchi.*)
37. Death is the black **camel** that kneels before every door.
38. Pay **cash** and keep your credit.
39. In a treeless country the **castor-oil plant** is a banyan. (*Assamese.*)
40. The **cat** does not catch mice for God.
41. Once **cheated,** ever watchful. (*Marwari.*)
42. Where **cheetal** are plentiful there is no tiger, where tigers are plentiful there is no cheetal. (*Gurkhali.*)
43. The **chick** does not die from a hen's kick.
44. A **child** that can walk is a god to the child in the cradle.
45. The day the **chuddar weaver** sings at his work he makes a perfect shawl.
46. He who does not **climb** will not fall.
47. Lift carefully the **cloth** which has fallen on the thorns.
48. Can you have no daylight without **cock's crow ?**
49. **Conceal** thy tenets, thy treasure, and thy travelling.
50. The **corpse** of an enemy is silent. (*Gurkhali.*)
51. He sleeps well who has neither **cow** nor calf.
52. **Crave** for nothing, grasp at nothing.
53. For the sick cow a **crow ;** for the sick man a Brahmin.
54. The country that has no **crows** has no Musalmans.
55. A **crust** for declining years.
    [i.e. money put away for a rainy day.]
56. It is still the first **day.**
57. The **deaf man** is fit for Heaven.
58. There is no medicine for **death** (*Gurkhali.*)
59. A man's **deed** is the touchstone of his greatness or littleness.
60. Ten **Dervishes** may sit on one carpet, but two kings may not exist in one country.
61. Don't **die** till death comes.
62. Who **disgraces** himself will not hesitate to disgrace others.
63. The **doctor** has ringworm on his nose. (*Assamese.*)
64. Half a **doctor** is a danger to life ; half a Mullah is a danger to faith.
65. The world exists through the sagacity of the **dog.**
66. The **dog** below the cart thinks he is carrying the whole burden. (*Gujarati.*)
67. One **door** is shut, but a thousand are open.
68. When I am **drowned** the world is drowned.
69. Many men are the **dupes** of these two favours, health and leisure.
70. A **duty** is that which is discharged.
71. He only knows the price of **ease** who once experiences difficulty.
72. **Eat** little if you would eat much, eat much if you would eat little.
73. There are many footsteps in the footprints of the **elephant.**
74. All are weak to the **elephant.** (*Gurkhali.*)
75. Keep seven cables' distance from an **elephant,** five from a horned beast, twenty from a woman, and thirty from a drunken man.

76. If you **engrave** it too much it will become a hole.
77. One " no " averts seventy **evils.**
78. I will change my **faith** and my bedding, but thou must pay for it.
79. It is impossible to darn the rent made by **fate,** even if you darn with the needle of wisdom.
80. Throw grain into the mill and you will get your **flour.**
81. The **fly** of the dinner-table.
82. From **four things** God preserve us: a painted woman, a conceited valet, salt beef without mustard, and a little late dinner. (*Assamese.*)
83. You may turn to the East to the Prophet, but all the **four winds** are God's. (*Suni.*)
84. Do not be any blinder to the defects of a **friend** than to the virtues of an enemy.
85. Seek a **friend** thou canst not lose, and find him only in God.
86. You should consider the society of **friends** as a momentary flash of lightning.
87. Nothing to bother you, eh? Then go and buy a **goat.**
88. Call on **God,** but row away from the rocks.
89. Victory is from **God,** but strike with all your might.
90. When **God** gives, He gives through the roof.
91. **God** is an enemy to excess.
92. **God** looks out of the window of heaven and keeps accounts.
93. **God** made the Hare and the Bengali. What shame?
94. If **God** orders you to pull, He will give you a rope; if He wants you to ride, He will give you a horse.
95. **God** takes all at once.

    [Even one short fortnight of drought may spell calamity.]
96. We give to **God** the flower beyond our reach.
97. As I can conceal nothing from **God,** why should I stand in awe of man?
98. Your **gods** and my gods—do you or I know which are the stronger?
99. Do **good** and cast it into water.
100. **Good** travels at a snail's pace—but evil has wings.
101. Of uncut **grass** there are nine hundred bundles. (*Assamese.*)
102. Two days a **guest,** but the third day a fool.
103. One day a **guest,** two days a guest, the third day a nuisance.
104. A farthing **hag** got her head shaved for a penny.
105. Let thy **hair** grow long and talk Punjabi.
106. It takes two **hands** to clap.
107. What is perfect **happiness?**—staying at home.
108. No one is all **happy** from his beak to his tail.
109. **Haste** is of the devil; only bad people run.
110. You train your **hawk** on another man's fist.
111. If you don't vex your own **heart** you will never make another's happy.
112. The **hearth** is not a stone, but a woman.
113. What trust is there in a crowing **hen?**
114. When the **hen** scratches the chickens learn.
115. He who goes to the **hills** goes to his mother.
116. Amongst the **honourable** a man becomes honourable; amongst the base, base.
117. **Hope** and courage are two bright diamonds in the crown of success.
118. The **hypocrite** asks always for the bird, but the valorous man asks only for the bow and arrows.
119. What **is** has been.
120. **Kill** many men with many weapons for a murderer's tool becomes known. (*Gurkhali.*)
121. **Kill** one, a murderer; kill thousands, a hero.

122. When do you find meat in a **kite's** nest?
123. He that **knows** not and knows not that he knows not. Shun him.
He that knows not and knows that he knows not. Teach him.
He that knows and knows not that he knows. Enlighten him.
He that knows and knows that he knows. Follow him.
124. Oil and bribes soften most things, but not a **kupa** [leather bottle used for carrying ghi], a Kaltai [liquor seller] or a Musalman.
125. **A lame man** commits an offence at every step. (*Assamese.*)
126. Don't **laugh** at me, you will catch the contagion. (*Assamese.*)
127. The new and withered **leaves** are everywhere to be found.
128. If thou hast lied, **lie** twice, lie thrice, but all must be the same lies. (*Gurkhali.*)
129. Give a **loan** and make an enemy.
130. To **lose** is to learn.
131. Be it a grain of pea-seed, let it be given with **love.**
132. **Love** can't be hid by hiding.
133. **Love** laughs at caste distinctions. Let your love be as a Hindu wife; with you in life and with you in death.
134. If you **love** your love, you should love her thoughts too.
135. To know the thing to be **measured** you must know the measure.
136. **Mercy** is the cotton; patience the thread; chastity is the pivot, and truth is the twisting. (*Sikh.*)
137. **Milk** and children are from fortune.
138. It is the turning of the **mill** that makes the flour heap.
139. Do not be **miserable** for the sake of pleasure.
140. Give your body and get **money.**
141. Slow, slow catch **monkey.**
142. What goes wrong in the stable falls on the **monkey's** head.
143. Whom will he help who does not help his **mother?**
144. A **mouse** found a piece of turmeric and set up a druggist's shop.
145. A **Musalman,** a wasp, and a parrot are no man's friends; in time of difficulty they will turn and sting or bite.
146. When you are getting **old,** look old, then people will do what you ask them.
147. There is no answer to an **order.** (*Gurkhali.*)
148. I live upon **others,** I go with the tide. (*Assamese.*)
149. Only an **owl** knows the worth of an owl.
150. The housewife keeps the **parrot,** the lover keeps the avadavat, and the thief keeps pigeons.
151. On a green tree there are many **parrots.** (*Gujarati.*)
[i.e. a full purse never lacks friends.]
152. The Hindu bows down to stones [idols], the Musalman worships saints; but **Parsi's** religion is pure as Ganges water.
[Parsi proverb of the freedom of their religion from the stain of idolatry.]
153. Every European who comes to India acquires **patience** if he has none, and loses it if he has.
154. Be **patient** in your mind, that you may find ease for your body.
155. **A poor man** getting rich regards the world as straw.
156. A wooden **pot** cannot be often put on the fire.
[i.e. deceit cannot be frequently repeated.]
157. The mother-in-law is great; the daughter-in-law is also great; the **pot** is burning, who will take it off the fire?
158. To the **potter** a year, to the cudgel a minute.
[The making and breaking of pots.]
159. The **potter** eats from broken pots.
160. Old **priest**—young tiger.

161. Give out of your **purse**, but not out of your intellect.

162. Another's **purse** has a tight mouth.

163. **Quietness** is worth thousands of gold.

164. There is fruit on the trees; there is sweet water in the pure river; there are soft beds on leaves—yet wretched people suffer pain at the door of the **rich.**

165. Don't use **ridicule,** some of it is sure to fall on your own head and feet.

166. After crossing the **river** the boatman gets a cuff.

167. In the centre of a great **river** the water is pure; it is a strong man that can taste its purity. (*Gurkhali.*)

168. No one was ever lost on a straight **road.**

169. There are many **rosaries,** the beads of which are not told in devotion. (*Assamese.*)

170. It is better to follow no **saint** than six.

171. He who ate **salt** will drink water. (*Tulu.*)

172. In the **sandal-tree** are serpents.

173. The **sandal-tree** perfumes the axe that fells it.

174. **Scandal** is the pastime of babes, the right of man, the weapon of women, and the privilege of old age. (*Gurkhali.*)

175. He knows no charm even for a **scorpion,** yet he puts his hand into a snake's hole.

176. Before the smith can make a **screw** he must learn to make a nail.

177. To steal **sesumum** or sugar is a sin.

178. Even a **she-ass** is pretty when she is young.

179. Those who beg in **silence** starve in silence.

180. It is better to **sit** than to walk, to lie down than to sit, to sleep than to wake, and death is the best of all.

181. Walking and wandering does not kill, but **sitting** does.

182. The **snake-bite** goes in like a needle, but comes out like a ploughshare.

183. After **snake-bite** sleep, after scorpion weep.

184. Kill the **snake** but do not break the stick.

185. Like a **snake** in a monkey's hand.

186. A **spoon** for every pot.

187. Don't drive everyone with the same **stick.**

188. A **stranger** who is kind is a kinsman.

189. There is no remedy for **superstition.** (*Gujarati.*)

190. What caste has the **sweeper?** What credit has the liar?

191. There are more ways of getting to a **sweetheart** than butting down a wall.

192. **Sweetmeats** are not distributed during a battle.

193. The husbands of the **talkative** have a great reward hereafter.

194. Drink even water at a **tavern** and you are suspected of having drunk spirits.

195. In a **temporary residence** there is no rule. (*Assamese.*)

196. Blessed is he that **thirsteth** for nothing, for he shall be at peace.

197. He who lays **thorns** for others, dies amongst them himself. (*Assamese.*)

198. **Three things** ease the heart from sorrow: water, green grass, and the beauty of women.

199. Learn the value of **time.**

200. **To hold** is to let go.

201. The **tongue** because it has no bone says various things. (*Assamese.*)

202. A fruit-bearing **tree** bends.

203. When the **tree** is about to perish it brings forth blasted fruit.

204. A **Turk,** a parrot and a hare; these three are never grateful.

205. He that calls a man **ungrateful,** sums up all the evil that a man can be guilty of. (*Gujarati.*)

206. It is not our professed religion, still less the colour of our skin, that produces **virtue.**
207. **Voyaging** is victory.
208. What **war** is to man, child-birth is to woman. (*Assamese.*)
209. Every man must dip in his own **waters.**
210. Never speak to a **white man** till he is fed.
211. You buy a **wife,** and you buy oxen.
212. What **will be**—will be.
213. He who is intoxicated with **wine** will be sober by dawn, but he who has lost his senses to the cup-bearer will not recover until the day of judgment.
214. Where a **woman** is not honoured, vain is sacrificial rite.
215. He who trusts a **woman** will walk on duckweed in a pool.
216. A thousand men may live together in harmony; two **women** cannot, even though they be sister.
217. To a **wooden god** give a slipper as an offering. (*Gujarati.*)
218. We are masters of the unspoken **word,** but the spoken word masters us.
219. **Words** are the daughters of Earth, and things are the sons of Heaven.
220. If you are in the **world,** be rightly of it.

KASHMIRI

1. The world is **Allah's,** the land is the Pasha's, but the company [Old John Company] rules.
2. The dew to the **ant** is a flood.
3. To bite on the red side [of an **apple**].

   [i.e. to take a giant share in the partnership.]
4. An **apple** gets colour from seeing an apple.
5. In the moment of **birth** my head was squeezed.

   [i.e. a man commences his troublous career as soon as he is born.]
6. What **bloomed,** bloomed when it was in the bud.
7. There is a darkness under the **candle.**

   [i e. a good king, but bad ministers; a good master, but bad servants.]
8. **Cheap** is dear, and dear is cheap.
9. O God, preserve me from him whom I **cherished.**
10. **Chickens** do not die from the hen's kick.
11. A **child's pain** is a hundred thousand pains.
12. There is an account between the **corpse** and the grave.
13. One must take the **cow's kick** as well as her milk and butter.
14. What shall a **crooked man** do to a straight man?
15. If a paisá [coin] be placed upon a **dead man** he will rise up.

    [i.e. money will bring people back from the dead. The Hindus place a paisá inside the mouth of the corpse wherewith to pay the ferry. A similar custom obtained in Grecian mythology when a small piece of money was placed in the mouth of the dead to pay the Stygian ferryman to row the corpse across the river Styx, Acheron, or Cocytus.]
16. More than enough is as **dirt.**

    [i.e. no use to a man.]
17. The **disease** will go by the doctor's shop, but the habit will never go.
18. O God, deliver me from the **doctor** and the ruler.

19. The **dogs** bark, but the caravan goes on.
20. Don't give me anything, but let me have your **ear.**
21. A handful of grass for an **elephant's** stomach.
22. No share in the good, but in the **evil.**

    [i.e. a real friend].
23. **Expect** and live ; seek and find.
24. There is no light like that of the **eyes ;** there is no pilgrimage like that of the knees ; there is no relation like one's pocket ; there is no ease like that of the mendicant's cloak.
25. A **fat man** has no religion.
26. A man loves his own **fault.**
27. A man should stretch out his **feet** after looking at the bed-clothes.
28. Where the **finger-nail** will enter, there is no necessity for iron.
29. The **flour** must come out either by the lower or by the upper stone.

    [i.e. by hook or by crook.]
30. Now, while it is early morning, seek out your **friend.**
31. **Friends** are rice-stores.
32. A little for you and a little for me, this is **friendship.**
33. He who is gentle is a **gentleman.**
34. If you won't **get up** and sit down, then eat your own flesh.

    [i.e. work is health and life.]
35. Broken hearted, yet called " **gladness** ".
36. The water of **God** for the pines of the wood.

    [The pine is very common on the Himalayas.]
37. Whom **God** has given a mouth, to him will not He, the same God, give a little pot for his dinner ?
38. If **God** intends to give, He will give at the door ; but if God will not give, then what is the good of going a thousand kos [about two thousand English miles] for it ?
39. **God** is a giver.
40. **God** makes the egg to live.
41. Be up and doing and **God** will bless you.
42. If you pick up earth, may it become **gold** to you.

    [i.e. a Kashmiri's blessing.]
43. " **Good day** " to the rich or honourable man.
44. If the breakfast is bad, all the day will **go wrong ;** if the dress is bad, then all the year will go wrong ; if the wife is bad, then all the life-time will go wrong.
45. There must be blossoming of the **heart,** and then the flower blossom will not be needed.
46. **Honour** is inside your mouth.
47. The **horse** will go according as he is held by the bridle.
48. **Ignorance** is the peace of life.
49. If the **ignorant man** knows that he is ignorant, then he is not ignorant.
50. **Justice** is better than worship.
51. A **knife** with honey.

    [Said of an arrangement which looks fair at first, but is yet unjust.]
52. **Land** is like beaten gold.
53. If I **laugh** not, how can I live ?
54. A **lean man** is clever.
55. The world is a theatre of **love.**
56. **Love** is as dust.

    [i.e. must show itself.]
57. The **master** is great in three hours ; the servant is great in a year.
58. Bring a **maund** and spend it.

    [i.e. it is a great sin to store. Jogis sometimes quote these words.]
59. What answer will the **meat** give to the knife ?
60. A company of men is as good as a **miracle.**

    [i.e. difficult matters are easily accomplished by mutual and united help.]
61. From a speck of dust **misfortune** flies.

    [i.e. a word, and the thing is done.]

62. Your own **money** is flowers and wine, but another's money is but weed [nothing].

63. Gathering **money** is like gathering a heap of stones—it is as the king's property.

[i.e. it is appropriated by the State after death.]

64. One man's pocketful of **money** [is more than] another man's work.

65. **Mud** comes from a fall of rain.

[i.e. punishment follows sin.]

66. I brought the **nettle,** I sowed the nettle, and then the nettle stung me.

[The stinging-nettle is a plant sacred to the Hindu god Shiva, who is said to have first planted it. A famous fakir in Kashmir punished himself by planting a nettle in some mud in the palm of his hand. As the plant grew he became famous. A disciple whom the fakir had befriended from infancy was jealous of the honour which his master received, and one day hit the nettle out of his master's hand. The fakir then used this proverb.]

67. A harvest of **peace** is produced from a seed of contentment.

68. Until the **physician** has killed one or two he is not a physician.

69. There is fruit to the **plough** and rice for the raking.

70. **Politeness** is required in man ; scent is required in a flower.

71. The **poor man** sleeps upon a bed [without a care], but the rich man sleeps upon the stairs [for fear of thieves].

72. Where the flame, there the **pot.**

73. The mother-in-law is great, the daughter-in-law is also great ; the **pot** is burnt, who will take it off the fire ?

74. **Prayer** is a duty and plunder is a debt. (*Pathan saying.*)

75. A **prophet** is not accepted by his own people.

76. For **quarrelling,** a heap of money, plenty of friends, and abundance of food are required.

[i.e. money to bribe and pay Court fees, friends to swear falsely and to back you up, and food to nourish and strengthen in these troublous times.]

77. From the **radish,** radish leaves.

78. Better to follow no **saint** than [to try] to follow six.

79. Half the people are burnt with wishing, and half with **scandal.**

[i.e. the struggle for popularity and place.]

80. As many as cherish a **scorpion,** so many will it sting.

81. **Service** is greatness.

82. To the **shameless,** shame is distant.

83. Where the **shepherd's flock,** there the shepherd's lair.

84. As much profit from **silence** as there is profit to the dinner from cooking.

85. As **snow** dissolves snow, so one sin another.

86. A **son-in-law** is a giver of reproach and curses.

87. As I earn, so will I **sow.**

[i.e. dress according to position.]

88. If the **spit** is right, then the meat is right.

89. A single **stick** upon the hearth does not burn.

[i.e. a man is no good alone.]

90. Better to fill your house with **stones** than to have a stranger in it.

91. Where **sunshine,** there shade.

92. **Ten** in the pocket ; ten in the heart ; ten in the pillow.

[i.e. secretiveness.]

93. Whence the **timber,** thence the wedge.

[i.e. set a thief to catch a thief.]

94. What you can do with your **tongue** you can do with your legs.

95. **Too much** is despised.

96. A man may as well take out his eyes as tell the **truth.**

97. Men bind on their **turbans** for honour's sake, not for warmth.
98. **Understanding** is butler to success.
99. A horse, a wife, and a sword, these three are **unfaithful.**
100. He is an **unintelligent man** whose business is with an unintelligent man.
101. Empty **vessels** sound.
102. First he asks for your **walking-stick,** and then he wants your pet daughter.
103. Where there is **water,** there is a god.

    [Rivers and springs are invested with a sacred character by the Hindus, and they have a great number of water gods.]
104. If it has come then it is like **wool,** but if it has gone, then it is as grass.

    [i.e. indifference.]
105. A **word** stirs up anger or love.
106. One must **work** like an ass, but eat his dinner like a man.
107. Reputation is the **world.**
108. If you **worry** it will bring you to the grave, but if you do not worry you will never die.
109. "**Yes**" is worth fifty rupees, and "no" is worth a lakh.

KHYAUNGTHA OR CHAUNGTHA (COUNTRY HILL TRACTS OF CHITTAGONG)

1. In **age,** talk; in childhood, tears.
2. **Beasts** die eating; we die thinking.
3. In man lean sides; in a **buffalo** curved horns.

    [i.e. signs of excellence.]
4. A **child** is weaned from its mother by rice; a woman is weaned from her mother by a husband.
5. In your own village **crow** and be cock, but when you're in another you must be a hen.
6. Home **counsel** is better; you will get honey enough outside.
7. Do not be **dirty** because the water is cold; do not be wilful because you are a favourite.
8. He who does **evil** to a benefactor is like a dog which eats up the piece of leather on which he sleeps.
9. If you **give,** give quickly; if you trade, ready money.
10. Prop up an old **house**; cherish an old wife.
11. **Look** and you may; touch and you pay.
12. It is only the **pupils** who become masters.
13. **Thorn** on leaf, pierced leaf; leaf on thorn, pierced leaf.

    [i.e. you cannot please any way.]
14. Use a **thorn** to extract a thorn.
15. Mixed **vegetables** are tasty; a child of mixed parentage [adulterous] is handsome.
16. For sweetness, honey; for love, a **wife.**
17. If a man runs after a **woman** he falls into marriage; if a woman runs after a man she falls into ruin.
18. A **woman** with one child talks for two.
19. Man's life is ambition; **woman's** life is man.

KUMAUNI AND GARHWALI

1. **Alms** once given is as phlegm which has been expectorated, not worth taking back.
2. A small-minded man shows **anger** in his nose.
   [i.e. a little pot is soon hot.]
3. The **boat** will fill before it sinks.
4. After eating nine hundred rats the **cat** has gone on a pilgrimage.
   [Refers to hypocrisy or repentance.]
5. Only what one has given [in **charity**] or eaten is one's own.
6. A shameless man's **coat** is very loose in the arms.
   [i.e. when one's coat is very tight his movements are restricted. A shameless man is not restricted from doing whatever he wishes.]
7. The **crime** is the father of the sinner.
8. **Day** another's, but night one's own.
   [i.e. leisure comes to all when day's work is over.]
9. **Death** flies away when the jaws work [literally " sound "].
   [i.e. sick persons are thus induced to eat as much as they can, so that they may get well soon.]
10. A poor man's **debt** makes much noise.
    [i.e. to borrow from a man of small capital is dangerous, as he will give much trouble over the debt.]
11. One **ear** or two ears, but if three ears, then the open plain.
    [i.e. secrets should be confined at most to two persons.]
12. The **East** for disease, the West for sorrow, the North for penance, and the South for pleasure.
13. The **frog** croaks by the aid of the water.
    [i.e. a poor and weak person can only achieve anything by the patronage of a greater man.]
14. A straight finger cannot bring any **ghi** [clarified butter] out of a narrow vessel.
    [i.e. simplicity cannot thrive in this world; trickiness is needed.]
15. **God** gives even through the roof of one's house.
16. The **grain** has teeth.
    [i.e. if you eat too much it will kill you.]
17. The sickle cuts [**grass**] to its own side [inwards].
    [Refers to clannishness.]
18. Clapping cannot be done with one **hand** only.
19. The right **hand** washes the left.
20. No one can see **Heaven** without dying.
    [i.e. if a man wishes to accomplish some good work he must do it himself.]
21. **Interest** runs, even at night.
    [Some animals move about in the daytime and others at night, but interest never ceases to accumulate.]
22. Naked men sleep in the **jungle.**
    [i.e. no fear of being robbed.]
23. The **kettle-drum** sounds well when its mouth is smeared with flour.
    [i.e. alms and bribes solicit praise.]
24. Where there is **kinship** there is enmity.
25. Darkness under the **lamp.**
26. **Love,** musk, and a cough cannot be suppressed or concealed.
27. If you put your head in a **mortar,** why should you fear the pestle?
    [This proverb is used to encourage one to cope with the difficulties and dangers of a business already started by him.]
28. If you bring **much** you will get much.
29. Drive in a silver **nail** and see wonders wrought.
30. A man in **need** is a man insane.
    [i.e. he will go to any length to obtain what he wants.]
31. The point of a **needle** is sharpened by a blacksmith, but who sharpens the point of a thorn?
    [Applied to a clever person who needs no tutor.]

32. The world is [like] a leaf of **nettle** [pricking on both sides].
    [i.e. no one can escape criticism.]
33. One ought to look at the country of **one-eyed men** with only one eye.
34. One cup of **poison** should be accepted at the hands of the man who has already given one hundred of nectar.
35. You are a **queen,** and I am a queen, but who will husk the millet?
36. The **reward** is his who gives [the flour], not of the one who receives.
37. You can catch the hand of one who is about to strike you, but who can seize the tongue of the **slanderer?**
38. Throw a **stone** into the mud and you splash your own face.
39. He who stands **surety** will have to give up his own house.
40. Eating **sweet-meats** of fancy.
41. Two **swords** cannot be kept in one sheath.
42. A thing that has slipped from one's **teeth** cannot be held by the lips.
    [Refers to lost opportunities.]
43. One who is **tempted** to-day by a cucumber will be tempted to-morrow by a goat.
    [i.e. beginnings of bad habits.]
44. Whoever has a **tongue** has everything.
45. The **tongue** is cleverer than the teeth.
    [i.e. it remains unhurt, though close to sharp teeth. Advice to deal wisely with dangerous people.]
46. A new [unused] **vessel** [soon] gets black.
    [i.e. a small fault tarnishes a good reputation which would not be noticed did a scoundrel commit it.]
47. **Work** teaches work.

MALAYALAM (MALABAR)

1. When you have crossed a river in a **boat,** the oar has paid the passage money.
2. To break **eggs** and staff is quite unnecessary.
3. While you sit on an **elephant** you will be able to break through your neighbour's hedge.
4. The **feet** of the one who runs and the one who pursues the runner get equally tired.
5. **Feet** that jump and tongues that sing are similar.
6. He who has a good **friend** has no need of a mirror.
7. He who does not **know** himself is subsequently compelled to know much.
8. He who advances by **leaps and bounds,** by leaps and bounds falls into the ditch.
9. There is always in **misery** more of anger [than anything else].
10. **Money** is the hatchet to separate pleasant friends.
11. If there is falsity in a **proverb,** then milk can be sour.
12. No treasure is equal to **rice.**
    [Their daily bread.]
13. In **sin** the real sin is the malicious sin.
14. When anyone has learnt to **steal** he must also learn hanging.
15. In running **water** there is no filth.

MARATHI

1. The **animal** that moves about will find pasture.
2. In the hot season an **ascetic**; in the rainy season ill, and in the cold season enjoyment.
3. **Asceticism** is better than life's cares.
4. There is no **austerity** like forgiveness.
5. A **blanket** becomes heavier as it becomes wetter.

   [i.e. an evil neglected becomes worse.]
6. If you invite a **blind man** you will have two guests.
7. No **branch** to hold, no shade to sit under.

   [i.e. a widow.]
8. The **bread** is hungry.

   [i.e. dinner is waiting.]
9. **Bubbles** do not rise to the surface unless the bottom is reached.

   [i.e. no smoke without fire.]
10. Beat a **bullock** every other furrow, and a wife every other day.
11. If **butter** be taken near the fire it melts.

   [A caution against the influence of female society.]
12. To break off one's horns and go among the **calves.**
13. Why impede a moving **cart**?
14. Anyone will grease the wheels of a **cart** in use.
15. Even one's own **cart** will not go without grease.
16. A **child's** run extends to its mother.
17. A lame **cow** is prime minister among blind cows.
18. A gift **cow**—why has it no teeth?
19. He who is guilty of sin easily begets **daughters.**
20. The **dead child** of a married woman is but gone to play.
21. There is no **disease** like hope [suspense].
22. First farming, next trade, last service, or at least begging; if you cannot obtain alms, learn to be a **doctor.**
23. Fomentation is half a **doctor.**
24. When the need is ended, then a fig for the **doctor.**
25. Sārada [October–November] is the mother of the **doctors.**

   [i.e. unhealthy season after the rains.]
26. It is more difficult to cross the **door-sill** than to walk about the house.
27. The **earth** laughs at one who calls a place in it his own.
28. A small **eater** is happy.
29. Myriads of ants feed with the **elephant.**
30. If you kill, kill an **elephant**; if you rob, rob a treasury.
31. In an army, an **elephant**; in a garden, a cypress.
32. When the **elephant** went his tail remained.

   [Said when a great undertaking is completed all but a trifle.]
33. The **English** rule—salary at an appointed time.
34. Take the pestle out of your own **eye,** then take the mote out of another's.
35. Ashes of **failure.**
36. In **famine** the husbandman; in plenty the weaver.
37. **Fate** began to give and [they had] no lap in which to receive.
38. **Fate** is lame without effort.
39. By remembering our own **faults** we forget another's.
40. The virtue of your **feet.**

   [i.e. the foot brings good or bad fortune.]

41. A **fireplace** has only three stones.

[Native fireplace is formed by three stones.]

42. He who has good **food** has heaps of difficulties.

43. **Food** saves, food destroys; there is no enemy like food.

44. The **fool** vomits, the wise man swallows.

[i.e. the first tells all his thoughts, the latter keeps them to himself.]

45. Who is able to wipe off what is written on the **forehead?**

46. There is a difference of **four fingers'** breadth between truth and falsehood.

[Four fingers fit in between the eye and ear.]

47. Our **friend** is friendly while our hand is full.

48. He who wants the **fruit** should not nip off the flower.

49. Someone or other will throw a stone at a ripe **fruit-tree.**

[i.e. a good man.]

50. At the end of effort is **God.**

51. First endeavour, then **God.**

52. We give to **God** by grains and take by bushels.

53. **God** came to give, but he had no lap in which to receive.

54. Do not stab yourself because you have a **golden knife.**

55. If the **grocer** will give, the man will eat.

56. **A guest** for one or two days, but on the third day he should be ashamed.

57. The **guest** of two houses dies of hunger.

58. He has made four **hands** out of two.

[i.e. added to himself a wife.]

59. If you bear trouble you will see **happiness.**

60. One can see one's **home** twelve miles away.

61. To come with the legs of a **horse;** to go with the legs of an ant.

62. The **horse** which belonged to partners died of sores.

63. He who is **hungry** is always happy.

64. When **hunting** a hare take the weapons used in hunting a tiger.

65. **A husband's** beating is like a fall in the mud.

66. So many **idols,** so much health.

67. When a severe **illness** comes, eat bread and onions.

68. Wear torn things but be **independent.**

69. If there be a **lamp** at home there will be one in the temple.

70. Under the **lamp** it is dark.

[i.e. a good man has some blemish.]

71. A royal store-house, dairy, and stable are places where a **living** can be made.

72. If we have it we **loathe** it; if we have it not we long for it even in our dreams.

73. There's no taste where there's liking; there's no defilement where there's **love.**

74. **Marriage** says, "Try me and see"; a house says, "Build me and see"; the sugar-cane mill says, "Start me and see."

75. **Merit** diminishes by happiness, sin by pain.

76. The **naked** have no shame.

[i.e. when a man's character has gone he loses self-respect.]

77. Only the **nightingale** understands the rose.

78. If you have a **nose** you can wear a nose-ring.

79. The household god does not want an **offering.**

[i.e. if not given no one will be the wiser. Denotes inattention to a member of the family.]

80. "Mr. Immortal" is dead; "Mr. Possessor-of-wealth" is begging; "Mrs. Riches" is gathering cow-dung cakes, so "**Mr. Owner-of-nothing**" is best of all.

81. Where there is a [husband of] stone there will be a **paramour.**

82. If once a man be disgraced, **reform** is hard.

83. He who falls in with one's habits is a **relative;** he who notices one's failings is an enemy.
84. A **relative** is a cutthroat.
85. The field is good, but a **relative** lives in the village.
86. [Live] far from **relatives** and near water.
87. We boil our **rice** only once.
    [i.e. cannot repeat the story.]
88. The proper place for **sandals** is on the feet.
89. If insects and ants have food the **ship** will go safely.
90. A **shoe** of silver makes iron soft.
    [i.e. bribery.]
91. In **sickness** a wife, in adversity a relative.
92. A father for the profitable **son,** a mother for the unprofitable.
93. Sixteen years a **son,** then a friend.
94. The gods give everything to the eater of **sugar.**
95. His **talking** is like mixed vegetables.
    [i.e. he speaks softly but not strongly.]
96. He who minds the **tank** will taste the water.
97. Among **trees** there is only one, the teak; the rest are old women.
98. To tie one's **troubles** to the village-gate.
    [i.e. to make them public.]
99. Tell your **troubles** to your own mind, your happiness to the world.
100. He who makes **trousers** will leave a hole in them [for the legs].
101. "**Uncle**" as long as he can be of use to us; "Aunt" as long as there is butter-milk.
102. As the **wages,** so the washing.
103. The **water** of the water-course will go in that very course.
104. Tie up and carry with you your **wife** and your money.
105. A good-looking **wife** is the world's, an ugly one your own.
106. The field's border shows the man, the door the **woman.**
107. A **woman's talk** [is like] heat from grass.
    [i.e. it is useless.]
108. **Write** a nibful more, eat a mouthful less.
109. No one abstains from **writing** for fear of falling into the ink-pot.

PUNJABI

(Including Multani and Shahpuri)

1. To an **ant** a cup is the sea.
2. A **banker** without debtors is only one for four days; a farmer without debt is his own banker.
3. If a **Bengali** is a man, what is a devil?
4. Do not have **business** transactions where there is friendship; if you have business transactions, do not lend; if you do lend, forget it.
5. A poor man near the head of a **camel** is [as good as] a rich man at its tail.
6. When the house is built the **carpenter** is forgotten.
7. The more **clothes** you wear, the more you feel the cold; the larger the family, the more disgrace you are likely to have.
8. In a ruined village a **corn bin** is a palace.

9. If you live in the river you should make friends with the **crocodile.**
10. Who knows when **death** or a customer will come?
11. **Debt** is accursed, have cash transactions; this one asks, the other does not give, the face of both are blackened.
12. In thirty-six dishes are seventy-two **diseases.**
13. A demon took a monkey to wife—the result, by the Grace of God, was the **English.**
14. The **fish** is still in the river, and the woman is pounding chillies [to eat it with]. (*Multani.*)
    [i.e. counting her chickens before they are hatched.]
15. A sick man's **food** and a debtor's earnings [are like each other].
16. Eat simple **food** [lit. pulse and bread] and follow your nose.
17. All wise men think the same; every **fool** has his own opinion.
18. **Friends'** accounts are kept in the heart.
19. So many cannot be true **friends**—hope, dice, a courtesan, a robber, a cheat, a goldsmith, a monkey, a doctor, and a distiller. (*Shahpuri.*)
20. If **frost** has come, then manure has come.
21. Whatever is eaten and drunk is **gained;** what remains goes to the moneylender.
22. Even Satan prays for protection from **girls.**
23. The voice of the people is the drum of **God.**
24. What Moses wrote, **God** alone can read.
25. When **God** gives, He gives through the roof.
26. I met neither **God** nor my love; I have failed in this world and the next.
27. The **gods** live in town, the devils in the country.
28. One day a **guest,** two days a guest, three days a nuisance.
29. Evening **guests** and evening clouds don't go away empty.
30. Who does not **hoard** what he has, or eat by himself, his perfume will pervade three worlds.
31. **Horses** and men take after their mother's family. (*Shahpuri.*)
32. Best is **husbandry,** middling is trade, bad is service, beggary a fool's part.
33. If you cultivate manured **land** you may have weddings perpetually.
34. Give a **loan** and buy a quarrel.
35. Has the mother of **loan** died?
36. There are a thousand miseries in one **love.**
37. Let your **love** be as a cotton sheet round you in life, and round you in death.
38. Winter frost is a sack of **manure.**
39. **Manure** is the land's king.
40. Old grain, new butter, a well-bred wife, and the back of a horse; these are the four **marks of Heaven.**
41. Fine rice, buffalo's milk, a good wife, white clothes; these are the four **marks of Heaven.**
42. Try **medicine** as well as prayer.
43. Only the ground benefits from the **miser's** earnings. (*Multani.*)
44. A **moneylender** is superior to a king.
45. A butting **ox** is better than a lonely bed.
46. Form a **partnership** and have your hair pulled.
47. **Partnership** is hair-pulling. (*Multani.*)
48. A **partridge's wing** appeared, why go to consult the astrologer [about the weather, as there is a certainty of rain]?
49. **Payment** in kind is easy; payment in cash is difficult.
50. The cat ate up seven rats and then went on a **pilgrimage.**
    [i.e. hypocrisy.]
51. The heap you will gather will depend on the number of times you **plough.**
52. The **plough** is at the bottom of all arts.

53. The **plough** is king, the shop is queen; every other business has the mark of hell.
54. Fortune comes at random, but **ploughing** cannot fail.
55. He who **ploughs** gives manure.
56. He gets all the fruits of husbandry who **ploughs** his own land; he gets half who provides seed and bullocks; he gets neither whole nor half who sits at home and asks where his ploughs were being worked.
57. If I be **queen** and thou be queen, who will bang the butter?
58. **Rain** falls where it has rained before. (*Shahpuri.*)

    [i.e. a thief goes to steal at the place he has seen.]
59. **Rain** is the land's husband.
60. Mother and father both weeds, and the **son** a plant of saffron. (*Shahpuri.*)
61. Reap what you **sow.**
62. **Starving** is a friend; borrowing an enemy.
63. The **summer** always dies of drowning. (*Multani.*)
64. To **tear** is easy, and to sew is difficult. (*Multani.*)

    [i.e. it is easy to quarrel, but hard to make it up again.]
65. **Test** a friend in trouble, a cow in February [grass is scarcest then], and a housewife when there is nothing left in the house.
66. One man **travels,** two enjoy it, three fight over it, four make a funeral procession of it.
67. The lame and the one-eyed have one **vein** more than other people. (*Multani.*)
68. A **village** should live in a valley.
69. Talk is good, but not too much; silence is good, but not too much; rain is good, but not too much; sun is good, but not too much; but we cannot have too much rain in August, sun in May, talk in our story-tellers or silence in our **wives.**
70. A fat **woman** is a quilt for the winter. (*Multani.*)
71. The husband of the **woman** is man; the man's husband is his business.
72. Clouds like partridge feathers, a **woman** that eats cream; one will rain, the other will elope.

    [This saying never fails.]
73. Soil and **woman** yield to power; when powers fail they become another's.
74. The man who **works** like a slave eats like a king.
75. Farming, letter-writing, worship, and the tightening of your horse's girth; these things should be done by **yourself,** though you have a hundred thousand attendants.

SANSKRIT

1. Great warmth, at first, is the certain ruin of every great **achievement.**
2. Failing to obtain a lovely woman, affection is lavished on **animals.**
3. **Anxiety** is the fever of life.
4. One's own **body** does not hinder one.
5. The **bride** is not married for the destruction of the bridegroom.
6. **Butter** is life.
7. The house without **children** is a cemetery.
8. The **counsel** which has been told in six ears is destroyed.
9. There is not a better **counsellor** than a competitor for the overthrow of an enemy.
10. Better a doubtful condition of things than a crushing **defeat.**

11. Who knows the limit of **desire ?**
12. Day and night, evening and morning, winter and spring come again and again ; time sports, life goes, but nevertheless the chain of **desire** loosens not.
13. Those who eat but to support life, who wed but for the sake of progeny, and who speak the truth, surmount **difficulties.**
14. Although the garlic has been eaten the **disease** is not cured.
15. Water in a bed of reeds is **disease** of the feet.
16. A ruined alchymist [makes] a capital **doctor.**
17. He who causes a thing to be done by another is himself the real **doer** of it.
18. One should abandon an individual for the sake of a whole **family.**
19. **Fasting** is the best medicine.
20. He who brought you forth ; he who invested you with the sacred thread ; he from whom you received instruction ; the giver of food ; he who saved you from danger—these five are to be remembered as **fathers.**
21. He who is dear to me is dear even in the very commission of a **fault.**
22. Stay with **five,** walk along with five, eat along with five ; with five there is no sorrow.

    [Indian jury is five in number.]
23. As long as there is **food** in the mouth, so long will the words be sweet.
24. A **fool** is always discovered if he stayeth too long.
25. A **fool** shineth no longer than he holdeth his tongue.
26. A **fool's** refuge is a fool.
27. You cannot take one part of a **fowl** for cooking and leave the other part to lay eggs.
28. A **friend** may be known in adversity, a hero in battle, an honest man in a loan, a wife when riches are spent, and a relation in trouble.
29. Where there is **friendship** the friend is never far off.
30. That which is **given** once is received back a thousand times.
31. **God** destroys nothing.
32. The **heart** of the wise is as soft as a lotus flower in prosperity, but in adversity it is as firm as a mountain rock.
33. When **honey** is wanting, give treacle.
34. The empty **kettle** sings, not the full one.
35. **Laughing,** a thing is done ; weeping, the fruit of it is suffered.
36. That only is **lost** which is not given.
37. **Marriage** is ruin to learning, and the consummation of marriage is ruin to everything.
38. To know the thing to be **measured** you must know the measure.
39. Without **merit** and demerit nobody can enter into existence.
40. " **More** " is the fruit of " much ".
41. Even a **mountain** may be crossed by degrees.
42. Anything that has been made is **non-eternal.**
43. He who regardeth another's wife as his mother, another's goods as clods of earth, and all mankind as himself, is a **philosopher.**
44. A **plough** is existence.
45. **Poison** is the remedy for poison.
46. **Popular usage** overpowers etymological meaning.
47. **Poverty** destroys every virtue.
48. **Praise** food when it is digested ; the wife when her youth is past ; the hero when he has returned from battle ; the grain when it is harvested.
49. When the **ritual** is at an end, up comes a goblin !
50. **Rivers** flow with sweet water, but having joined the ocean become undrinkable.
51. That is the **road** which is **trodden** by the great.

52. A face shaped like the petals of the lotus ; a voice as cool [pleasing] as sandal ; a heart like a pair of scissors, and excessive humility—these are the signs of a **rogue.**
53. Wishing to grow, you have destroyed your **root.**
54. Everything is one, but the **sages** call it variously.
55. When there is **sense-perception,** what is the use of inference ?
56. In sandal-trees there are **serpents,** in the waters with lotuses there are also alligators.
    [i.e. there are no unobstructed pleasures.]
57. In the time of **sickness** there is no rule.
58. The **skull,** the skull, the skull is the root of all.
59. **Sorrow** ceases when it is shared with five.
60. **Sorrow** is the fever of men.
61. Who is poor in **speech** ?
62. When his **stomach** is full his coffers are full.
63. Who is a **stranger** to those who have the habit of speaking kindly ?
64. Not to injure is the first of **virtues.**
65. There is pain in acquiring **wealth,** pain in preserving what has been acquired, pain in its loss, and pain in its expenditure. Why have such a receptacle of sorrow ?
66. A **weapon** is silenced by a weapon.
67. The **wind** purifies the road.
68. A **wise man** moveth one foot and standeth fast with the other.
69. Infidelity, violence, deceit, envy, extreme avariciousness, a total want of good qualities, with impurity, are the innate faults of **womankind.**
70. The flowers of the fig-tree, a white-coloured crow, a fish's foot in the water one may see, but not what is in a **woman's** mind.
71. Honey dwelleth upon a **woman's** speech, but in her breast there is nothing but poison.
72. In the absence of men all **women** are chaste.
73. What **women** eat, we are told, is twofold ; their cunning fourfold ; their perseverance sixfold, and their passions eightfold.
74. Unto **women** no man is to be found disagreeable, no one agreeable.

SINDHI

1. A different **bell** each hour.
2. If a **diamond** is in the stomach, it shines forth in the face.
3. **Diseases** come swift as horses and go back slow as lice.
4. Man possesses thirty-two **faculties,** while a shoe thirty-six.
    [Blows or punishment given with a shoe.]
5. **God** always gives horns discreetly.
6. Do **good,** have good.
7. The dirt of home should be measured at **home.**
8. **Laugh,** thou father of victory.
9. The mother of " **lending** " is not dead.
10. **Money** lies in a lion's ear.
11. " **Paid up** " is the son of " free ".
12. The mouth is a half-**physician.**
13. **Plenty** and discontent go hand in hand.
14. There is no **tree** which has not been shaken by the wind.
15. **Woman,** land and money are all three homes of death.
16. **Women** are the food of women.
    [Require their company.]

SINGHALESE (SINHALESE) (CEYLON)

1. Even a fifty-tongued man cannot equal a single-tongued woman at **abusing.**
2. The **bat** that has come to the house of another bat must remain suspended.
3. What you do to others will **bear fruit** in you.
4. He who breaks a **beehive** will lick his hand.
5. Every kind of **bird** will resort to a fruit-tree.
6. A **blow** with a pestle will make no impression on one to whom a wink is of no effect.
7. Pity and compassion spoil **business.**
8. Like the **chastity** of an ugly woman.
9. The gem of the house is the **child.**
10. Eat **coconuts** while you have your teeth.
11. The possessor of five **coins** puts on twice as many airs.
12. **Conversation** is a ladder for a journey.
13. The white of the **crane** will be seen when it flies.
14. For those who **cried** standing, we should cry standing, and for those who cried sitting, we should cry sitting.
15. Even the fall of a **dancer** is a somersault.
16. If the **Devil** becomes your godfather you can go to hell easily.
17. The soles of one's feet only will know where he is to **die.**
18. A tailless **dog** cannot show his love.
19. Though the **dog** has no work, yet he never walks slowly.
20. If **fathers** cultivate, the children will have a chance of gleaning.
21. You see the **faults** of the servant girl through seven covers; those of the mistress are hidden by one.
22. The **fruit** on a creeper is no burden to it.
23. A stab with a **golden weapon** is just as painful as that with any other.
24. **Grief** leads to comfort; suffering to patience.
25. If you have **hair** you can tie it in all four directions.
26. The **hare** that escaped had eight legs.
27. The circumstances of a man will appear from the condition of his **hat.**
28. If you want to touch the **head,** first touch the foot.
29. Even **headache** is good which can be obtained gratis.
30. If you cannot become a king, then take to the **healing art.**
31. If you **jump up** you will also fall down.
32. To those who can walk, even the **jungle** is a royal road.
33. A **line** inscribed in water.
34. There is no **monkey** but is mischievous, no woman but is a tatler, and no silversmith but is a thief.
35. One's own **mother** and the sky are never well spoken of.
36. **Old people** crawl about in the house where there are no infants.
37. If we are of **one mind,** let us live even on herbs; if not, let us separate.
38. **Patience** begets comfort.
39. Every difficulty is to the **poor.**
40. **A pot** filled to the brim does not shake.
41. The water in a half-filled **pot** shakes.
42. The **poverty** of the poor shall end when they regard the want of each other.
43. **Ripeness** renders only man unsightly.
44. It is better to be one's victim than his **security.**
45. **Self-control** will place a man among the gods.

46. Even the **shadow** of a disagreeable man is deformed.
47. Even the **shadow** of a disagreeable wife looks deformed to her husband.
48. Even the **shadow** of the wife to be divorced is deformed.
49. A **shower** is doubled underneath a tree.
50. There is the curse that is not the consequence of **sin.**
51. Excessive fondness for a **spouse** betokens approaching widowhood.
52. It is rain that fills up **streams** and not dew.
53. If the **swing** goes forward it will come backward too.
54. Wipe off the **tears** of him who comes weeping.
55. Without practice one cannot even clean his **teeth.**
56. The **tongue** is safe, though in the midst of thirty teeth.
57. The **truthful man** has no room even in the tavern.
58. Never a straight palm or a straight **woman.**
59. If you want to go to the gallows without the aid of a ladder, you can go by the aid of a **woman.**
60. **Woman** is the way to prison.
61. A master who gives **work** is the friend who gives happiness.

TAMIL

1. **Abstinence** is the best medicine.
2. Each has his own **abundance.**
3. The condition of the man who keeps no **accounts** is like the place in which an ass has rolled itself.
4. Even bundles of grass may be of use in **adversity.**
5. Give **alms** only when you know the begging-bowl.
6. What you give to another is **alms ;** what you gain for yourself by that alms is bliss.
7. **Anger** ends in cruelty.
8. **Anger** is sin ; sleep is an enemy.
9. A coconut-shell full of water is an ocean to an **ant.**
10. Each has his own **anxiety.**
11. There is no **artificer** who does not praise himself.
12. **Ashes** are medicine for the sores of a bull.
13. If an **ass** goes astray, it may be found near a ruinous wall.
14. The handle of the **axe** is the enemy of its kind.
15. Touching one's own comfort, a **bald head ;** in respect to others, luxuriant hair is preferable.
16. If the rubbish heap of the **barber** is stirred, nothing but hair turns up.
17. There are some who take up the **battle-axe,** and there are others who stop tigers, but givers are scarce.
18. A clean **beast** will join a clean beast.
19. **Beauty** and ugliness are in the face.
20. **Beauty** will sit and weep ; fortune will sit and eat.
21. **Behave** as though seeing, you see not, and hearing, you hear not.
22. The need of a **blind man** is a staff.
23. That which exists in the **bottom** is likewise in the middle and top.
24. Why should a man without a **bow** seek arrows ?
25. It is the bent **bow** that will shoot.
26. The **box** that has a mouth has no bottom.

27. Bring up a **boy** with blows and a girl with praise.
28. Six **Brahmins** have [only] two eyes.
29. One must come down on the **branch** by which one ascends.
30. That which was not nipped in the **bud** will have to be felled with an axe when matured.
31. For the **building** completed critics abound.
32. Where the **bull** goes, there goes its rope.
33. Why feed a **bullock** after it is sold ?
34. If the **bullock** and the cart keep together, what does it matter how many ups and downs there are ?
   [i.e. marriage.]
35. What matters the ruggedness of the road, if the **bullocks** and bandy [a country cart] hold together ?
   [Marriage.]
36. A **calf** that goes with a pig will eat excrement.
37. If the right man enters, **castor seed** will turn into lamp-oil.
38. Do not fill up an old **channel** ; do not cut a new one.
39. At fifty discrimination ; at sixty moderation ; after sixty no distinguishing **characteristic.**
40. Nothing will be diminished by **charity.**
41. That which is left belongs to **charity.**
42. **Charity** guards the head.
43. The future prosperity of a person may be known when he is playing as a **child.**
44. The drink of which one never tires is water ; the fruit of which one never wearies is a **child.**
45. If the **child** have a mouth it will live.
46. A **child** in the grave is a child in the womb.
47. The roof that has not seen rain is like the **child** that has not seen its mother.
48. The harvest of little **children** will never be housed.
49. A **coin** not current is always so.
50. No **cold** to them that are completely wet.
51. He who has **commanded** will protect.
52. It is always term-time in the Court of **conscience.**
53. If fresh-drawn milk unboiled be drunk, **consumption** may be cured.
54. He who **counsels** us to weep does so to favour life ; he who counsels mirth seeks our ruin.
55. A **cow** eats moving ; a house eats standing.
56. A **crazy man** thinks his behaviour straighter than a straight line.
57. The homestead says go, the place of **cremation** says come.
58. **Cupid** has no eyes.
59. **Danger** slumbers on a mat.
60. No matter what may be eaten, if four **dates** be taken afterwards, the whole will be digested.
61. A woman who gives her **daughter** for a wife is like God who gives a pair of eyes.
62. All the **days** before the age of discretion are as the days before birth.
63. Length of **days** is in the hands of Him who gave prosperity.
64. The **dead** is the pilot of the living.
65. The day of birth leads to **death.**
66. Except imaginary **devils** there are no others.
67. Someone **died** ; someone cried.
68. He who has an old sore is half a **doctor.**
69. He who kills a thousand people is half a **doctor.**
70. One must fear a **doctor** as well as a traitor.
71. The friendship of the **doctor** ends at the threshold.
72. A loquacious **doctor** is successful.

73. The **doctor's** child dies not from disease but from medicine.
74. If we see a **dog** there is no stone; and if we see a stone there is no dog.
75. Why seek the key of an open **door?**
76. When **drought** prevails, charity fails.
77. The world is **drowned** to him who is drowned.
78. The ocean is knee deep to him who is **dying.**
79. A listening **ear** is worse than a seeing eye.
80. The family of an **enemy** must be destroyed by friendliness.
81. What the **eye** has seen, the hand may do.
82. If the mother dies, the **father** becomes an uncle.
83. The value of a **father** is known after his decease, that of salt when exhausted.
84. If every **fault** be noticed, all intercourse must cease.
85. Think of those who have done you even one **favour** as long as you live.
86. **Fearing**—do valiantly.
87. The knife should be applied where there is **flesh.**
88. They who live on **flesh** are acquainted with the medicine for toothache.
89. **Flies** do not swarm on a new pot.
90. Are you to crush a **flower** to smell it?
91. **Flowers** beyond reach are sacred to God, but those within reach are for themselves.
92. That which one eats as the fruit of his own labour, is properly called **food.**
93. Those who masticate their **food** live a hundred years.
94. **Food** without hospitality is medicine.
95. He who has no ties is like a **foreigner.**
96. **Forget** at once what cannot be obtained.
97. The goddess of **fortune** is in the mouth of the prosperous.
98. A **fowl** brought up with a **pig** will eat dirt.
99. If distant, even enemies are **friends.**
100. If you look at men's faults you will have no **friends.**
101. They who advise weeping are one's **friends**; they who advise laughing are strangers.
102. No feast, no **friendship.**
103. Separation secures manifest **friendship.**
104. When apart, even enmity becomes **friendship.**
105. Stunted grain—**friendship** at sight.
106. If apart, long **friendship**; if together, the least touch will provoke hatred.
107. For the **friendship** of two the patience of one is necessary.
108. **Friendship** so close that a hair cannot be introduced between the parties, will be destroyed if money matters interpose.
109. It is the beauty of **friendship** to be surrounded by friends.
110. On forming **friendship** try it, and on being convinced of its sincerity rely on it.
111. Ripe **fruit** falls of itself.
112. Premature **genius** fortokens a short life.
113. At the ankled feet of the **Giver of all Good** is found the refuge of the world.
114. Let things take their course; there is a **God.**
115. **God** dements him who is to be destroyed.
116. **God,** who deprived him of sight, gave him a staff.
117. Why weep for **gold** when you have the tulip-tree?
118. He who knows not the price of **grain,** knows not sorrow.
119. Where he treads **grass** will not die.
120. What flows to the paddy flows also to the **grass.**

121. Even falls are feats in the **great.**
122. **Greatness** is always humble.
123. **Grief** and joy are a revolving wheel.
124. **Grief** leads to comfort, suffering to patience.
125. Though it be medicine, share it with a **guest.**
126. Fear **guilt.**
127. **Habit** is the rule of the stomach and the hair.
128. A man of luxurious **habits** is an ass.
129. Freedom from sickness is true **happiness,** and competence is true riches.
130. We must either enjoy **happiness** or practise austerities.
131. A thousand men may live together in **harmony,** whereas two women are unable to do so, although they be sisters.
132. Why should a man meddle with a **hatchet** lying on the road, and hurt his foot?
133. Though you may dissolve a rock, you may fail in melting the **heart.**
134. He wounds the **heart** which is as tender as the eye.
135. Can a **hen** flap her wings and crow like a cock?
136. To the real **hero** life is a mere straw.
137. At **home** an elephant, abroad a cat.
138. Win your enemy by **hospitality.**
139. **Hospitality** and medicine must be confined to three days.
140. One step as an entrance to the **house,** and one key to a lock.
141. Before building a **house,** dig a well.
142. If one becomes a **householder** he must expect both good and evil.
143. The sense of **hunger** ends on the mat.
144. **Hunger** knows no taste nor sleep comfort.
145. All are **huntsmen** who take up sticks.
146. **Husbands** are in heaven whose wives chide not.
147. The goddess of **ill-luck** lives in his face.
148. Oneself is the remedy for one's **illness.**
149. When a severe **illness** comes, eat bread and onions.
150. Make a pitfall for **imprudence.**
151. **Indolence** changes nectar into poison.
152. The body is an **inscription** on water.
153. Conversation on a **journey** is equal to a conveyance.
154. The hole in a mortar is paradise to a **jungle-fowl.**
155. Popular agitation leads to **justice.**
156. The sin arising from **killing** is expiated by eating the flesh so killed.
157. It will be clear if you loose the third **knot.**
158. He that increaseth **knowledge** increaseth sorrow.
159. What! remove the **ladder** after allowing one to mount.
160. **A lame man** is a hero before a cripple.
161. **A lamp** lit in a house for the inmates may answer for a feast.
162. Feigned **laughter** ruins the teeth.
163. Desire **learning.**
164. The rain of tears is necessary to the harvest of **learning.**
165. **Learning** can suffer no damage.
166. He who cut off the **leaves** to-day may possibly cut off the bunch to-morrow.
167. The **leg** that has stumbled, stumbles.
168. That of which no part is taken out will not **lessen**; that which is not uttered will not get out.
169. Half a **letter** is equal to a thousand words.
170. The **liberal** have all things, the niggardly nothing.
171. **Litigation** is a pole planted in mud.

172. If you wish to **live** long, eat iron.

173. When only one is born there is **loneliness** ; when two, enmity.

174. **Look** before, look behind, look at yourself, look at me.

175. Hard dealing ends in **loss.**

176. **Love** alone will abide.

177. If there be **love,** impossibilities will become possible.

178. **Love** is all important, and is its own reward.

179. If a **low-bred** man obtain wealth, he will carry an umbrella at midnight.

180. Renounce **lust.**

181. **Lust** is a burning block of wood in a house not on fire.

182. He who ties on a rag in a country where all go naked will be considered a **madman.**

183. It is better to throw oneself into a well than to **marry** an old man.

184. Three days for testing **medicine** and for a feast.

185. Take **medicine** at sunset.

186. Dust is **medicine** for the sores of an ass.

187. Domestic **medicine** is preferable to that of a physician.

188. **Medicine** one-fourth, common sense three-fourths.

189. Do not make **merchandise** of your tongue for a livelihood.

190. Know the efficacy of **mercury** by the glow of health on the cheeks.

191. **Merriment** is the poison of friendship.

192. He who has drunk **milk** belches with milk, and he who has drunk toddy belches with toddy.

193. If you constantly drink **milk** it will become sour to you.

194. A **miser** has double expenses.

195. **Money** is called a man-slayer.

196. He who sits down to lend **money** will have to walk to get it back again.

197. The kernel of a coconut is a feast to a **monkey.**

198. No temple is more beautiful than one's **mother.**

199. One may buy everything except a **mother** and a father.

200. Who are related to each other? The **mother** and her child.

201. Look at the **mother** before affiancing the daughter.

202. The whole village is mother to the **motherless.**

203. The way is in one's **mouth.**

204. The **mouth** is sugar-cane, the hand is iron.

205. One's **mouth** makes one great or small.

206. What is not pinched with a **nail** must be split with an axe.

207. If in excess even **nectar** is poison.

208. The **one-eyed man** mocks the man who squints.

209. Having placed the thing on the **palm,** why lick the back of the hand?

210. Well being does not last, and **penance** does not last.

211. Be the eleventh **person** among ten.

212. Every medical practitioner is a **physician.**

213. The whole town is friendly to a **physician.**

214. A **physician** and a schoolmaster never disagree.

215. The malady of a **physician** cleaves to him till death.

216. A **physician** does not attain to heaven ; a teacher may.

217. A **physician** is common to all.

218. A **physician** is like a father.

219. Whatever a **physician** prescribes is a remedy.

220. Better to **plough** deep than wide.

221. **Poison** is the medicine for poison.

222. Even a beast without horns will attack the **poor.**

223. If in the **pot,** it will come into the spoon.

224. Undeserved **punishment** is better than deserved punishment.

225. A **quarrel** in a neighbouring house is refreshing.
226. **Quietness** is worth thousands of gold.
227. In harvest time even a **rat** has five wives.
228. Live close to your **relations.**
229. Even a **remedy** has its conditions.
230. Cultivate **rice.**
231. Why examine spoiled **rice?**
232. One grain suffices to test a whole pot of boiled **rice.**
233. While on earth the things that do not cloy are **rice** and water.
234. Give **rice** to the aged and add mud to a ruinous wall.
235. After the **river** is crossed, who are you and who am I?
236. A **river** never flows straight.
237. When a neighbour's **roof** is in flames one's own is in danger.
238. It matters little with whom a **ruined woman** sins.
239. Mere **rumours** have neither head nor foot.
240. The **sacred** and the secular are both indispensable.
241. Remember through life those who have given you **salt.**
242. **Sandalwood,** even when rubbed down to a stick, will not lose its fragrance.
243. The **scorpion** stings him who helps it out of the fire.
244. Excessive **sharpness** is perfect bluntness.
245. A useless **shrub** growing on a rubbish heap of ostentation.
246. He who does not give place to **sin** will conquer it.
247. One's **sins** will be expiated by giving cloth to the destitute.
248. The **sleepless** is the abiding one.
249 A bamboo stick is king to a **snake.**
250. A **snake** will bite him who removes a fence.
251. There is no distinction between big and little when you are talking about **snakes.**
252. A **sore** on a monkey never heals.
253. Even in a healed **sore** there will be some matter left.
254. One ought to **speak** as evenly as a rape-pod splits.
255. Do not **speak** in a studied way.
256. An *ex parte* **statement** is straighter than a line.
257. **Sugar-cane** tasting bitter is the fault of the mouth.
258. Halting where the **sun** sets.
259. The man who tried to walk like a **swan** lost his own way of walking.
260. If the **tank** be full its bank will be moist.
261. Wipe off the **tears** of him who comes weeping.
262. All that is seen is **temporary.**
263. He who has nothing in hand is a **thief.**
264. A pliant **thorn** will not penetrate.
265. **Thorns** are extracted by thorns.
266. Why **throw,** why scratch?
267. A double **tongue** will slip.
268. A **top** that spins no longer.
269. The stream of grace is the source of all **treasures.**
270. Parts of the same **tree** are alike.
    [i.e. family traits.]
271. He who planted the **tree** will water it.
272. Constant **trouble,** long life.
273. Who is really **true** to another?
274. There is only four fingers' breadth between **truth** and falsehood.
275. He who is **truthful** may be the enemy of many.
276. Bend the **twig** and you bend the tree.
277. It is time to fear when **tyrants** seem to kiss.
278. He speaks like one gathering mixed **vegetables.**
    [i.e. softly and indistinctly.]
279. You can stop a boiling **pot,** but not the mouth of the **village.**

280. When the mouth is good, the **village** is good.

281. If you **walk** gently, the earth will bear you.

282. Why put your hand on a tottering **wall**?

283. The **washerwoman** knows the defects of the village.

284. **Water** will stand in a hollow.

285. Go by the **way** and return by the way.

286. Although the **way** go round, go by it.

287. If a low-bred man obtain **wealth**, he will carry an umbrella at midnight.

288. A man of **wealth** is the slave of his possessions.

289. Mere **weapons** are ineffective.

290. When all occupations are duly weighed, that of **weaving** will appear unequalled.

291. Do not believe a **weeping man** or a laughing woman.

292. A house without a **wife** is a burning-ground.

293. A stubborn **wife** is a mat rolled up.

294. A **wife** is her own dowry.

295. The husband is like an ear of corn; the **wife** is like a rice-bin or grain receptacle.

296. Another name for the **wife** is the mistress of the house.

297. A **wife** is the ornament of the house.

298. **Winnow** while the wind blows.

299. Even the devil will pity a **woman.**

300. Rather give room to a devil than a **woman.**

301. Who can act so as to please a **woman**?

302. If a **woman** be chaste she may live in the street of the harlots.

303. **Woman** is a chain round the feet, and a child a bit in the mouth.

304. Though you see a **woman** sin with your own eyes, cover it over with earth.

305. A **woman's** thoughts are afterthoughts.

306. Is one veil sufficient to cover a **woman's wickedness**?

307. Is anyone ever tired of **women** and wealth?

308. He who listens to the advice of **women** is a fool.

309. The pleasure of the **wood-apple** ceases with the shell.

310. **Words** will endure; ways will fall into disuse.

311. If the **world** agree, there is no question about the matter.

312. To the **world** wisdom is folly; to wisdom the world is folly.

313. **Written bonds** are not needed for honest men or rogues.

TELUGU

1. **Acquaintance** is a handful of money.

2. One must be a master of **alms** or a master of lakhs.

3. **Avarice** knows not shame; sleep knows not comfort.

   [i.e. when sleep overpowers comfort is not thought of.]

4. An old **barber** and a new washerman.

5. The **beggar** of crumbs gets more than the beggar of loaves.

6. The old **bough** will not bend.

7. The **bullock** pulls towards the sun and the buffalo towards the shade.

   [i.e. every couple is not a pair.]

8. **A child** brought up by a widow is like a bullock without a nose-rope.

9. A motherless **child** is like a curry without onions.
10. There are **comforters** but no real helpers.
11. After **conception** there's nothing for it but to bring forth.
    [i.e. a work undertaken must be completed.]
12. Pretend to **condole** when you cauterize.
13. No man has ever died from **cursing** or lived from blessing.
14. Remains of a **debt,** of an ulcer, or of fire, should not be left.
15. There is no limit to **desire.**
16. **Desire** incites, [the fear of] shame prevents.
17. Count the **disadvantages** first, then the advantages.
18. One cold in the head is as bad as ten **diseases.**
19. Are there sweet **diseases** and delicious medicines?
20. When a **dog** comes a stone cannot be found; when a stone is found the dog does not come.
21. If you can afford it, [your **dress**] should cover your feet; if not, it should cover your knees.
22. In **eating** and in business you should not be modest.
23. The man who has mounted an **elephant** will not be afraid at the bark of a dog.
24. In your **evil hour** your own stick will become a snake.
25. If the members of your **family** point their fingers at you, the outsiders will point their legs.
26. She is not his mate but his **fate.**
27. Put the **faultless man** into the salt.
28. The **feet** which are wont to wander and the mouth which is accustomed to abuse will never be quiet.
29. Every home has an earthen **fire-place.**
    [i.e. fallibility.]
30. The **fireplace** takes the crookedness out of the stick.
    [i.e. a bad man's evil qualities only disappear in the funeral pile.]
31. An offering to the deity of the **flowers** which cannot be reached.
32. One sixty-fourth part of **folly** will bring ten millions of sorrows.
33. Ten million arts are only for [getting] **food.**
34. Every garb [i.e. occupation] is for **food.**
35. **Food** without a feast is medicine.
    [i.e. to dine alone is disagreeable.]
36. His words leap over **forts;** his feet do not cross the threshold.
37. **Garlic** is as good as ten mothers.
38. Unless you had touched **garlic** your fingers would not have smelt.
39. You must cut a **gem** with a gem.
40. The **grief** of the neck [lasts] six months; the grief of the womb for ever.
    [i.e. "grief of the neck" signifies widowhood, when the marriage cord is broken. "Grief of the womb" signifies the loss of a child.]
41. To **grow** is but to be broken.
42. The **hand** which has a bit of iron, the itch, or a bit of cane in it never remains quiet.
43. The **hand** which touches a pice will touch a pagoda.
44. If you clap with one **hand** will there be any sound?
45. **Happiness** is half [a man's] strength.
46. Make the **hedge** when you have sowed the seed.
47. Give **honour,** get honour.
48. **Hunger** knows not taste, sleep knows not comfort, lust knows not shame.
49. A man will not build a **hut** until he has been drenched, nor stoop until he has hit his head.
50. **Lame** in the village, an antelope in the jungle.
51. It is always dark underneath a **lamp.**
    [i.e. roguery hides under the judgment-seat.]
52. A **lamp** under a torch.
    [i.e. one insignificant before the other.]

53. A **laughing woman** and a crying man should never be trusted.

54. If given with **love,** a handful is sufficient.

55. Try building a house, try making a **marriage.**

56. The tree in the back yard won't do for **medicine.**

[i.e. that which is near is not valued.]

57. [The benefit derived from] the **medicine** is to be deducted from [the harm done by] carelessness in diet, and the balance remaining is an increase of the disease.

58. What matters it whether we drink **milk** in a dream out of bell-metal or gold ?

59. If you exceed the bounds of **moderation,** nectar even is poison.

60. In the place where there is **molasses** flies swarm.

61. The hand which touches bran will touch **money.**

62. **Money** left in the hands of a woman won't last ; a child left in the hands of a man won't live.

63. Look at the **mother** before you take the daughter ; see how much milk the buffalo gives before you buy her.

64. When the **mother** dies the father is equal to an uncle.

65. A **mother** is a divinity, a father a treasure.

66. The **mother** will look at his belly, the wife at his back.

[i.e. the mother will look to see how her son fares, the wife to see what her husband has brought home for her.]

67. Even a river will forgive three **offences.**

68. Every man must dip in his **own waters.**

69. If all get into the **palankin,** who will be the bearers ?

70. **Partiality** belongs to a mother and to the earth.

71. A full **pot** will not spill.

72. If you are content with a girdle no **poverty** will distress you.

73. There is no limit to **purity** nor any beginning to impurity.

74. Your wife's people are your own **relations ;** your mother's people are distant relations ; your father's people are enemies [because they are co-heirs].

75. The **rich man** will feed the rich man and the poor man will feed the rich man.

76. A rap with **ringed fingers** will cause no pain.

77. When you are **ruined** you may go to your friend's house, but not to your sister's.

78. To a man who wears **sandals** the whole earth seems to be covered with leather.

79. [Where] the **servant** [is] without pay, the master [must be] without anger.

80. A man's **shadow** remains with himself.

[i.e. the fruits of a man's action remain with him.]

81. The **sheep** only trusts him who cuts its throat.

82. At home he is a **spider,** abroad he is a tiger.

83. A **squint eye** is better than a blind eye.

84. An unjust word is the throwing of a **stone.**

85. You should look what you can **swallow** and what can swallow you.

86. **Sycophants** scratch pimples for a livelihood.

87. If you drink milk under a date-tree they will say it is **toddy.**

88. Is there a day called **to-morrow ?**

89. The straw **torch** has burnt to the knob.

90. An old **tree** has a firm core.

91. When the **tree** is about to perish it brings forth blasted fruit.

[Applied to the first signs of the coming ruin of a bad man.]

92. Will he who plants a **tree** not water it ?

93. You should not **trust** a man who writes, cuts or pares.

[i.e. a village accountant, a butcher or a toddy-drawer.]

94. **Water** runs towards water.
[i.e. men help their own caste.]

95. If a **woman** lies it is like building a wall; if a man lies it is like putting up a mat [easily seen through].

96. A **woman's** sense is wrong sense.

97. A **woman's** word—a bundle of water.

98. When three **women** join together the stars come out in broad daylight.

99. A **word** is medicine to the wise.

JAPANESE

(Including Korean and Shinto)

An Introduction to this collection by Professor Kochi Doi will be found on page lxviii.

1. Give sail to **ability.**
[i.e. to assist talent.]

2. The **absent** get farther off every day.

3. **Accomplishments** remain with oneself.

4. Where there is an **advantage** there is also a disadvantage.

5. The laden **almond-tree** by the wayside is sure to be bitter.

6. Let men know by your own deeds who were your **ancestors.**

7. To the **ant,** a few drops of rain is a flood.

8. Even the wishes of an **ant** reach to heaven.

9. No purse so fat as to buy back a lost **appetite.**

10. **Applause** is the beginning of abuse.

11. Beware of a returning **arrow.**

12. Nothing is too hard for the **arrow** to pierce when the bow is drawn with full force.

13. The putting-off man sharpens his **arrows** when he sees the boar.

14. Rather than study [an **art,**] get accustomed to it.

15. A borrowed **axe** is just the same as one's own. (*Korean.*)
[i.e. a newly engaged servant is just as bad as an old one.]

16. The **back** and the belly can't change places.
[i.e. food is better than reputation.]

17. The **back** has no eyes.

18. The man who makes the first **bad move** always loses the game.

19. Bad **beans,** when put to sprout, grow only roots. (*Korean.*)
[Said of anything which has cost money and yet turned out badly.]

20. To be **beaten** is to win.

21. **Beauty** is only one layer.

22. Get rid of your own **bees** (or flies).
[i.e. sweep before your own door.]

23. Even **beggars** can make a crowd.

24. A **blind man's** mirror and a priest's comb.

25. **Blood** is but blood.

26. Fallen **blossoms** leave their perfume behind.

27. Too many boatmen carry the **boat** up the mountain.

28. A **bow** long bent waxeth weak.

29. If you grasp it tightly it **breaks,** and if you loosen it, it flies away. (*Korean.*)
[i.e. if children are brought up too severely it is bad, and if brought up too lax they are spoilt.]

30. A man's own **breast** is the best wallet to carry his troubles in.

31. Better **breeding,** than birth.

32. **Brothers** and sisters are the forerunners of strangers.
[i.e. blood relationship gradually wanes.]

33. He who never suffers persecution will never become a **Buddha.**

34. [It is] preaching before **Buddha.**

35. Not to know is to be a **Buddha**; not to see is Paradise.

36. If you pray to a **Buddha,** pray to one only.

37. Strike even the face of a **Buddha** three times, and his anger will be roused.

38. Don't make a **Buddha** without putting in a soul.

39. Any soil will do to **bury** in.

40. Having both hands full of **cakes.** (*Korean.*)

[i.e. unable to do anything.]

41. If you throw **cakes** at a man he will throw cakes at you. (*Korean.*)

42. A **candle,** by consuming itself, gives light to others.

43. Even a **castle** ten thousand feet high collapses from an ant-hill.

44. Even a dead **cherry-tree** can bring picturesqueness to a barren hill.

45. In the hum of the market there is money, but under the **cherry-tree** there is rest.

46. A **child** brought up by its grandmother is three hundred farthings cheaper.

47. A **child** is a shackle that ties its parents for the three worlds. (*A Buddhist saying.*)

48. Send abroad the **child** you love most.

49. When old, obey your **children.**

50. Moral people beget many **children.**

51. **Children** are poor men's treasures.

52. Scolded **children** fear not reproof.

53. Hated **children** fear not the world.

54. He keeps his **child's** heart.

55. The great man is he who does not lose his **child's** love.

56. Ten men—ten **colours.**

57. That which one would **conceal,** easily comes to light.

58. A truthful **courtesan** is as great a miracle as a square egg.

59. Too much **courtesy** is discourtesy.

60. One **crane's** voice is better than the chirping of a thousand sparrows.

61. Good **critic**—bad worker. (*Korean.*)

62. Better to be a **crystal** and to be broken than to be a tile upon the house-top.

63. A **cur** barks bravely before his own gate.

64. Awaiting brings a good **day.**

65. **Day and night** wait for no man.

66. **Daylight** will peep through a very small hole.

67. The **dead** have no tongue.

68. **Death** is both larger than a mountain and smaller than a hair.

69. In wandering about the world one nowhere finds the **Devil.**

70. While the **Devil** is away [let us] wash [our] clothes.

[i.e. cat's away, mice play.]

71. Even the **Devil** was comely at eighteen, and coarse tea has its fragrant first cup.

72. Those who **die** are poor.

73. When it is cold there are no **dirty clothes.**

74. He holds **disease** in his arms. (*Korean.*)

[i.e. a very sick person.]

75. He is a bag of **diseases.** (*Korean.*)

[i.e. a chronic patient.]

76. **Diseases** enter by the mouth.

77. No **dispute** is possible without an adversary.

78. The **doctor** cures the sick man who does not die.

79. Good **doctrine** needs no miracle.

80. What one **does,** one becomes.

81. If you would be a **dog,** at least be the dog of a great house.

82. Even the street **dog** has his lucky days.

83. A roving **dog** runs against a stick.
84. A lean **dog** shames its master.
85. A **dog** will remember a three days' kindness, three years, while a cat will forget a three years' kindness in three days.
86. The stupid man leaves the **door** an inch open ; the lazy man three inches, and the fool wide open.
87. There is no **door** for the buying that will shut out the world of men.
88. **Drink** and sing : an inch before us is black night.
89. First the man takes a **drink,** then the drink takes a drink, then the drink takes the man.
90. **Drums** sound as they are beaten.
91. Better the **dumplings** than the cherry blossom.
92. When **dust** accumulates it will make a mountain.
93. The path of **duty** is near at hand, men seek it in what is remote.
94. **Early rising** has three virtues.
95. Walls have **ears,** bottles have mouths.
96. From the **east** the root—from the west the fruit.
97. That which is **eaten** in the parents' house lasts three days.
98. One who is carrying a load of bad **eggs,** yet fears to go near a stone wall. (*Korean.*)

    [Said of one who is a great coward.]
99. Even the **Emperor** has straw-sandled relations.
100. To **employ** a man is to be employed.

    [i.e. masters are mostly the greatest servants in the house.]
101. Do not despise the **enemy** who looks small.
102. The **evil action** speeds a thousand Ri away ; the good action goes not through the door.
103. After three years an **evil** becomes a necessity.
104. In the house where **evil** has been piled up, unhappiness remains behind [for the descendants].
105. An **evil deed** remains with the evil-doer.
106. The **eye** is harder to please than the stomach.
107. What's an inch in the **eye** of a man is a foot in the eye of his master.
108. It is no use applying **eye-medicine** from a two-storey window.
109. Lookers-on have eight **eyes.**
110. A wise **falcon** hides its claws.
111. The **fallen blossom** never returns to the branch ; the shattered mirror never again reflects.
112. Seven **falls**—eight rises.
113. If **falsehood** takes the road ; truth hides.
114. What has been the **fashion** will come into fashion again.
115. The **fate** of every man is bound about his neck.
116. A **father's** goodness is higher than the mountain ; a mother's goodness is deeper than the sea.
117. Riches after the **fire.**
118. Where there is no **fire** there is no smoke.
119. Small **fish** flock where big ones are.
120. No **fish** in clear water.
121. A **fish** is larger for being lost.
122. The **fish** that is golden shall swim in the sun.
123. Scare away the **flies** from off your own head.
124. When the **floor** is raised too much the ceiling is too low.
125. A **flower** that is in bloom in the morning withers by noon. (*Korean.*)

    [Said of a precocious child who shows great promise but poor fulfilment.]
126. The **fly** finds the diseased spot.
127. A **fog** cannot be dispelled with a fan.
128. Those who swallow their **food** whole, choke. (*Korean.*)

129. Even the **fool** has his art.

130. Because there are **fools,** wise men look well.

131. When **fortune** comes to a house the devil accompanies it to the door.

132. **Fortune** will call at the smiling gate.

133. Even the **fortune-teller** does not know his own destiny.

134. The second word makes the **fray.**

135. When the character of a man is not clear to you, look at his **friends.**

136. **Frogs** breed frogs.

137. When thou crossest a **frontier,** inquire what is forbidden within it.

138. Ripe **fruit** on a dead tree. (*Korean.*)

[Said of a posthumous child.]

139. **Game** is cheaper in the market, but sweeter in the field.

140. The road of time has no **gatekeeper.**

141. The **general** has no child.

142. A man lives a **generation**; a name to the end of all generations.

143. If you want to **get on** in the world, first help others to get on.

144. Look the other way when the **girl** in the tea-house smiles.

145. Practise the art of **giving up.**

146. The **gods** sit on the brow of the just.

147. There are some **gods** who abandon men; they are those gods who know men.

148. What **goes out** of you comes back to you.

149. In the gleam of **gold** even a fool looks wise.

150. One **good deed** is better than three days of fasting at a shrine.

151. When food and clothing are present in plenty, **good manners** arise.

152. **Good people** walk on, whatever befall.

153. One **good word** can warm three winter months.

154. **Gossip** lasts but seventy-five days.

155. **Government** law lasts three days.

[Early proverb of Nipon.]

156. Through **green spectacles** the world is green.

157. Even a welcome **guest** becomes a bore on the third day.

158. Fish and **guests** are wearisome on the third day.

159. The **guests** change, but the host remains the same.

160. A **gummed thing** soon ungums.

161. Every man has a **habit.**

162. Everybody has seven **habits.**

[Faults, vices.]

163. He has a big **hand.** (*Korean.*)

[i.e. to be liberal.]

164. A good **handwriter** never loses his pen.

165. The **hare-lip** is taken for a dimple.

[i.e. to indicate the blindness of love.]

166. If in **haste,** go round.

167. Live under your own **hat.**

[Correct version probably " Live in your own hut ".]

168. If you **hate** a man, let him live.

169. If one thing is **heard,** ten will be understood.

170. **Hearing** is Paradise, seeing is Hell.

171. Be the master of your **heart,** but do not make it your master.

172. Even the **heart** has its boundaries.

173. Thine own **heart** makes the world.

174. The **heart** of a child of three years remains until he is sixty.

175. **Hearts** are as unlike as faces.

176. It is better to go to **Heaven** in rags than to Hell in embroidery.

177. The climbing of a **height** begins from the base.

178. Instead of praying to Paradise don't make yourself a **Hell.**

179. **Hell** is full of dirty housewives.
180. In evil times the **hen** appears.
181. When the **hen** crows the house goes to ruin.
182. It is better to be the beak of a **hen** than the tail of an ox.
183. It is the **hen** that tells the cock to crow.
184. Where **honour** is, there is no need of bolts.
185. There is more delight in **hope** than in enjoyment.
186. He who sells a **house** gets the price of the nails.
187. Don't stay long when the **husband** is not at home.
188. **Idlers** have no spare time.
189. The man who confesses his **ignorance** shows it once; the man who tries to conceal it shows it many times.
190. **Impossibility** is a good reason.
191. **Indolence** is a powerful enemy.
192. To others be **indulgent,** but not to yourself.
193. An **insect** an inch long has half an inch of soul.
194. He receives **instruction** into a cow's ear. (*Korean.*)
    [Said of one who is heedless or obstinate.]
195. An **invalid** lives long.
196. One cannot reach the place that **itches.**
197. The hand goes to the **itching** spot.
198. Unpolished **jewels** do not shine.
199. Requite evil with **kindness.**
200. There is no sword against **kindness.**
201. Consult, even with your own **knee.**
202. Thankless **labour** gains fatigue.
203. The **lamb** drinks its milk kneeling.
204. Human life is like a revolving **lantern.**
205. The **lantern carrier** should go ahead.
206. Dark as the **lantern's** base [while light streams far abroad].
207. **Laughter** cannot bring back what anger has driven away.
208. A falling **leaf** foretells the approach of autumn.
209. **Learn** well, play well.
210. It is better to **lie** a little than to be unhappy much.
211. A **lie** has no legs, but scandalous wings.
212. The little that one has **lost** is at the end of one's **life.**
213. **Life** is a light in the wind.
214. **Life** is but death.
215. **Life** is love and wife.
216. At the foot of the **lighthouse** it is dark.
217. Where **light** is, there is shadow.
218. Where anyone **listens,** the ground becomes three inches lower.
219. **Lookers-on** see eight pieces ahead of the players.
    [i.e. of go games.]
220. **Lose** and gain.
221. The **lotus** springs from the mud.
222. **Love** flies with the red petticoat.
    [i.e. only unmarried girls wear this garment.]
223. He who falls in **love** has come to the end of happiness.
224. **Love** reaches even to a crow on a roof.
225. To be **loved** is to be hindered.
226. The **loves** of youth are as a cluster of silver buds, but the love of maturity is like unto golden flowers.
227. Wait in bed for **luck.**
228. To wait for **luck** is the same thing as waiting for death.
229. Though driven away, the " Dog of **Lust** " cannot be kept from coming back again.
230. **Lust** has no bottom.
231. All **lust** is grief.
232. When there is truth in a **maid** a round egg becomes square.
233. A **man** is good when he is old, a thing is good when it is new. (*Korean.*)
234. **Man** is the soul of all things.

235. All **married women** are not wives.

236. Even when one sleeps on a thousand **mats** one only needs one.

237. Rest after a **meal** even if your parents are dead.

238. **Meeting** is the beginning of parting.

239. It is the **melancholy face** that gets stung by the bee.

240. Ripe **melons** drop without plucking.

241. He who would go a hundred **miles** should consider ninety-nine as half-way.

242. There is a piece of fortune in **misfortune.**

243. **Misfortune** also becomes a bridge to happiness.

244. Keep **misfortune** for three years, it may turn out to be useful.

245. To save one **Mon,** one loses a thousand Mon.

[i.e. penny wise, pound foolish. Mon is the smallest coin of old Japan.]

246. Even hell's torments are measured by **money.**

[Said of the Buddhist priesthood.]

247. **Money** is earless, but it hears.

248. **Money** is legless, yet it runs.

249. A man without **money** is like a ship without sails.

250. Getting **money** is like digging with a needle, spending it like water soaking into sand.

251. Lend **money** to a city, but never to a man.

252. A **monkey** only lacks three hairs of being a man.

253. Even **monkeys** fall from trees.

254. Never rely on the glory of the morning nor the smiles of your **mother-in-law.**

255. Be civil to your **mother-in-law** and she will come to your house three times a day.

256. The noble-minded loves **mountains ;** and the wise delights in water.

257. No door can be **made** for the **mouth.**

258. The **mouth** is the front **gate** of all misfortune.

259. A satiated **mouth** soon forgets the benefactor.

260. A collector of **mummies** will be one.

261. A **nail** that sticks out is struck.

262. Curse a **neighbour** and dig two graves.

263. The end of snow is **Nirvana.**

264. Even drops from the **nose** fall in turn.

265. Doing **nothing** is doing ill.

266. Going downhill no one is **old.**

267. By searching the **old,** learn the new.

268. **Old age** is a medicine.

269. Treat every **old man** as thy father.

270. " **Once** " is the beginning of all things.

271. Three persons have good **opinion.**

272. When the **oranges** are golden, physicians' faces grow pale.

273. A fruitful **paddy-field** lowers its head.

274. Where there is comfort there is **pain.**

275. One can stand others' **pains** even for three years.

276. When something falls in the hands of the **painter** or the lawyer, white becomes black.

277. The interval of sleep is **Paradise.**

278. Every man carries a **parasite** somewhere.

279. The string of a man's sack of **patience** is generally tied with a slip knot.

280. Even in a village of eight there's generally a **patriot** to be found.

281. If you would climb to the top of the **peaks** that seem to pierce the sky, there is a way.

282. Eating **pears** also cleans one's teeth. (*Korean.*)

[i.e. to kill two birds with one stone.]

283. It's the **physician** that breaks the rules of health.

284. It is only half a **pilgrimage** without visiting the girls.

285. **Pinch** yourself and know how others feel.

286. When the snow oppresses [the branches] one recognizes the loyalty of the **pine-tree** [by remaining green].

287. **Pleasure** is the germ of sorrow.

288. In **plenty,** think of want; in want, do not presume on plenty.

289. In the eyes of the lover, **pock-marks** are dimples.

290. The **poet** at home sees the whole world.

291. The **poor** eat little, but are at ease.

292. It's the **poor** who give alms to the poor.

293. A **poor family** cannot always remain poor.

294. A **poor horse** has always a thick tail. (*Korean.*)

[i.e. talent and capacity badly located.]

295. A projecting **post** is [often] knocked against.

296. If a **post** is smeared with the mud of the river-bed, it is little use its head aspiring to the heavens.

297. For a broken **pot** a mended lid.

[i.e. every Jack has his Jill.]

298. Be a head, though only the head of a **potato.**

299. **Poverty** is more painful than disease.

300. **Poverty** is worse than four hundred and four [all] diseases.

301. From **poverty** to profusion is a hard journey, but the way back is easy.

302. **Praise** is the origin of blame.

303. If that which is within is not bright, it is useless to **pray** for that which is without. (*Shinto.*)

304. Clever **preacher,** short sermon.

305. To rouse the village you must first rouse the **priest.**

306. Where **profit** is, loss is hidden near by.

307. **Proof** is better than discussion.

308. A day old **puppy** fears not a tiger. (*Korean.*)

[i.e. the rustic violates the law through ignorance, not knowing the danger.]

309. After **rain** the earth gets firm.

310. The old **raven** laughs at the blackness of the pig and knows nothing of his own ugliness.

311. **Reason** and plasters will stick together.

312. **Recreation** first, medicine next.

313. All **religions** start from Asia.

314. The **reputation** of a thousand years may be determined by the conduct of one hour.

315. The **reverse** side has its reverse side.

[Or everything has its front and back.]

316. Do not allow yourself to be **reviled** more than you are praised.

317. Two things never pall—a moonlight night and well-cooked **rice.**

318. One meal without **rice** mars domestic happiness for a week.

319. Sunshine and **rice** may be found everywhere.

320. It becomes neither **rice** nor soup.

[Said of anything which turns out to be an absolute failure.]

321. Even with ten million " kokus " of **rice** one can only eat one's fill.

[" Koku " is 4,196 bushels.]

322. The very **rich** cannot remain very rich for more than three generations.

323. **Riches** are a treasure for a lifetime.

324. The **rich man** and the ash-tray become dirtier as they heap up.

325. The **rich man** thinks of next year; the poor man of the present moment.

326. A shallow **river** should always be crossed as if it were **deep.**

327. If you look for the source of the **River Yoshino** you will find it to be the drops of water beneath the moss and the drops of dew that fall from the reeds.

328. A **road** of a thousand miles begins with one step.

329. No branch is better than the **root.**

330. **Rubbish** accumulates, mountains arise.

331. **Sables** feel proud in the absence of ermines.

[Correct version probably is, "Bats feel proud in the absence of birds".]

332. If another offers **sacrifices,** what matters it whether they are persimmons or pears? (*Korean.*)

333. He who hath eaten **salt** drinketh water.

334. If I peddle **salt** it rains, and if I peddle flour, the wind blows. (*Korean.*)

[i.e. unlucky.]

335. If you pray even to a **sardine's head,** with faith [it will grant you what you wish].

[In Japan the head of a fish is sometimes hung upon a tree to keep off evil spirits.]

336. What you want to **say,** say it to-morrow.

337. After the swallowing the **scalding** is forgotten.

[i.e. past dangers are laughed at.]

338. **A sea voyage** is an inch of hell.

339. Hearing a hundred times is not so good as **seeing** once.

340. That which you would **sell,** deck with flowers.

341. If a few **sen** do not go, many sen will not come.

[Sen—coin.]

342. A new **servant** works hard but twenty days.

343. Of whom we speak, his is the **shadow.**

[i.e. he of whom we speak throws his shadow upon us.]

344. If a **shadow** falls across your path, look about.

345. If there is a channel the **ship** can go. (*Korean.*)

[i.e. if you do a man a kindness you will make a way to his heart.]

346. The **shop** that has a few customers is dear.

347. A family that has no **sickness** for ten years must be rich. (*Korean.*)

348. The **silent man** is often worth listening to.

349. To put on a **silk dress** to travel at night. (*Korean.*)

[i.e. to do a good action and not have it known.]

350. The **sinner** is never beautiful.

351. Long **sleeves** dance well; much money buys well.

352. Offensively **smelling** people do not notice their own smell.

353. He who cannot look at others with a **smiling face** should not open a shop.

354. Bitten by a **snake,** one fears a rotten rope.

355. By poking a bush [lit. a bamboo thicket] you make **snakes** crawl out.

356. All good movements in **social life** begin at the top.

357. Where exorcisms are, there are the **sorceresses;** where masses are said, there are the monks.

358. Don't rub salt on a **sore.**

359. A knowledge of the sacred books is the beginning of **sorrow.**

360. A **sorrow** is an itching place that is made worse by scratching.

361. Never follow on the heels of a **sorrow** or it may turn back.

362. Fear not to **sow** because of the birds.

363. A year's opportunity depends on the **spring,** a day's on the dawn.

364. Even a gushing **spring** sometimes dries up.

365. No **standing** in the world without stooping.

366. He who **steals** money is executed; he who steals land becomes king.

367. Use the **stick** and save a fall.

368. It is easy to hurt yourself on a **stone** that has sharp corners. (*Korean.*)

[Said of a bad-tempered man.]

369. When **stones** swim the leaves sink.

370. If the source of the **stream** is muddy the whole course will be muddy. (*Korean.*)

371. It is difficult to be **strong** and not to be rash.

372. We can never see the **sun** rise by looking into the west.

373. **Suspicion** breeds phantoms.

374. **Sweet things** remain in the stomach.

375. Good **swimmers** die in water and good riders in shooting.

376. He who can **talk** well can also lie well.

377. Though **tears** fall they do not help to pay the debt.

378. Open lips make cold **teeth.**

379. A man's **teeth** often bite his own tongue.

380. Excessive **tenderness** is followed by a hundredfold dislike.

381. From one to know **ten thousand** [all].

382. When even **three persons** come together, there is a world of bitterness.

383. One can paint the fur of a **tiger** but not his joints. (*Korean.*)

384. The **tiger** leaves behind his skin; and man his name.

385. The result of **toleration** is pleasure.

386. Don't say, " There is **to-morrow.**"

387. **To-morrow** blows the wind of to-morrow.

388. A bridled **tongue** is a guarantee of a care-free heart.

389. Take rather **too little** than too much.

390. **Too much** done is nothing done.

391. A strong man can spin his **top** in the sand.

392. It's the **tortoise** that discounts the value of a pair of fast legs.

393. For **travelling,** a companion; for the world, kindness.

394. " The **treasure** which always circulates without an obstacle " is " cash " or sapeks. (*Korean.*)

395. Seek shelter under a big **tree.**

396. The dead **tree** blossoms. (*Korean.*)

[i.e. from failure to success.]

397. A tall **tree** is easily broken by the wind.

398. A **tree** that bears fruit is known by its flowers.

399. Be like the **tree** which covers with flowers the hand that shakes it.

400. No branch is better than the **trunk.**

401. An **ugly woman** shuns the mirror.

402. An **ulcer** and a boil do not choose where to appear.

403. An **unskilled** man's attempt is sure to be a failure.

404. There is no limit to looking **upward.**

405. To submit is **victory.**

406. A man learns little from **victory**—much from defeat.

407. After **victory,** tighten your helmet cord.

408. **Virtue** carries a lean purse.

409. **Virtue** is not alone, it certainly has a neighbour.

410. The ignorant have **virtues,** just as well as the wise faults.

411. Everybody's **voice** is God's voice.

412. A man who stands behind a **wall** can see nothing else. (*Korean.*)

[Said of a man who is obsessed with one thing to the exclusion of everything else.]

413. Having waxed, **wanes.**

414. **Warm** an object for ten days and it will cool in a day.

415. One night stop the flowing **water,** but the things which never return are the days and months.

416. **Water** does not flow out of an old river.

417. Things never change since the time of the gods, the flowing of **water,** the way of love.

418. Go back while you can see your **way.**

419. There's always a wasp to sting a **weeping face.**

420. If you dig a **well**, dig only in one place. (*Korean.*)

421. At least I have learned that the **whirlpool** of Diva is a calm without wind or wave compared to human life.

422. Peach and chestnut trees take three years to bear fruit ; but a **widow** remains a widow for a year only.

423. Flowers will bloom on **widows ;** maggots will be hatched on widowers.

424. A good **wife** is a good householder.

425. A bad **wife** is sixty years bad harvest.

426. A young **wife** should be but a shadow and an echo in her house.

427. A [**wife's**] tongue three inches long can kill a man six feet high.

428. Branches of **willow-trees** are never broken by snow.

429. **Willow twigs** dig no snow.

430. No **wind** collects in the meshes of a net.

431. A **wind** is as good as a thousand doses of medicine.

432. **Wine** is the best broom for troubles.

433. **Winnow** while the wind is blowing.

434. Not to speak is the flower of **wisdom.**

435. **Wisdom** and virtue are like the two wheels of a cart.

436. **Wisdom** is a treasure for all time.

437. One **wishes** for nothing so much as that which one has seen from the outside.

438. **Wives** and mats are best when new.

439. Never trust a **woman,** even if she has borne you seven children.

440. The tongue of a **woman** is her sword which never rusts.

441. A wise **woman** seldom crosses her husband's threshold.

442. Saying " No," a **woman** shakes her head lengthwise.

443. Trust a **woman** so long as thy mother's eyes are on her.

444. For a **woman** to rule is as for a hen to crow in the mornings.

445. A cat's nose and a **woman's hips** are cold.

446. A **woman's thoughts** are afterthoughts.

447. A **woman's wisdom** is under her nose.

448. Beware of beautiful **women** as you would of red pepper.

449. At ten years a **wonder child ;** at fifteen a talented youth ; at twenty a common man.

450. A true **word** is not beautiful and a beautiful word is not true.

451. Where **words** are excessive, the quality is deficient.

452. Many **words,** little sense.

453. The **world** is dark an inch ahead.

454. Silent **worms** bore holes in the wall.

455. One finds a **wound** by blowing hairs.

456. **Wounds** afflicted by a sword may be healed, but not wounds afflicted by words.

457. When **wrong** passes on the road, right disappears.

458. **Yesterday** is the " once " of to-day.

KALMYK (KALMUK)

1. A **bad man** discusses what he ate and drank; a good one, what he saw and heard.
2. A **bad shot** blames his sleeves.
3. A great **barker** sees nothing.
4. The **child** that has fallen by itself does not cry.
5. No horns are given to the goring **cow.**
6. A good man indicted for a **crime** is like a white horse fallen into the mud.
7. A **dog** only starts to swim when the water reaches its chin.
8. The **dog** runs under the cart and says, " I am drawing it."
9. As long as both feet do not reach the ground one is **driving.** As long as something has passed through the throat, one is eating.
10. **Ears** are deceitful, but eyes are truthful.
11. Where there is a head there is **food.**
12. Jump the **frog** as it may, it still remains in its puddle.
13. During the big man's **fun** the common man loses his life.
14. Though a girl's **hair** be long, her brain is short.
15. One **hand** washes the other.
16. A man accidentally met is better than one **invited.**
17. Do not ask the **knave,** he will tell himself.
18. A **lie** will come out later, but the truth is known beforehand.
19. One does not unsheath the sword against a **louse.**
20. A bad **physician** and a bad bull spread the disease.
21. The **pig** does not see the sky.
22. The **sea** is made bigger even by one drop.
23. A man's own **smell** is unknown to him.
24. What they have **sown** they are reaping.
25. Every **stick** has two ends.
26. **Sugar** is sweet from all four corners.

    [i.e. wherever you eat it.]
27. The **tongue** has no bones.
28. The clever man hides his **virtues** within, the fool keeps them on his tongue.
29. He who has no **wishes** has no eyes.
30. All men know the **wolf,** but the wolf knows no one.
31. So long as the hands **work,** the mouth works.

KURDISH

1. Do not throw the **arrow** which will return against you.
2. The skin of cattle is the burden of the **ass.**
3. With an **ass** you possess a son; with a son-in-law only an ass.
4. An **assassin** is perhaps less guilty than a debtor.
5. When the **bear** ages, he becomes the plaything of the cubs.
6. " You give your juice," said the **bee** to the flowers, " but it is I who make the honey."
7. In the most gilded cage, the **bird** sighs, " O my country, O my country."
8. For you the rock; for me the **booty.**
9. If thou canst not offer wheaten **bread,** at least offer gentle words.

10. Everything **breaks** by becoming too thin; man breaks by becoming too strong.
11. When the great man becomes a **bridge,** avoid passing over him.
12. A **brother** is a brother—but business is business.
13. **Buying** too cheaply is like putting water into a pierced waterskin.
14. **Children** are the fruits of the house.
15. In a house full of **children,** the devil rules not.
16. The **cloak** came to him after the rain.
17. Not every **cloud** falls in rain.
18. It is better to be a **cock** for one day than a hen for a year.
19. When the house is full of **cocks** the morning is tardy.
20. He who **confides** to another the care of his affairs, puts gall in his wounds.
21. Thou who **confidest** to a passer-by, the flesh of thy soul will repent it.
22. **Courage** overcomes numbers.
23. When the **cup** is broken by the mistress of the house, one hears no noise.
24. **Death** is our host.
25. Our **dog** will take our blows, but he flies from the stick of a stranger.
26. The **dogs** bark, the caravan passes on.
27. Out of a **dog's tail** you cannot get fat.
28. **Eat** little and often.
29. He who **eats** for two must work for three.
30. Sleep, suffering and hunger, are our most cruel **enemies.**
31. The nights sleep—the **enemies** watch.
32. If thine **enemy** falls beneath thy foot, crush him.
33. An intelligent **enemy** is better than a foolish friend.
34. The **enemy** of the father does not become the friend of the son.
35. If one of your **eyes** repulses me, both mine will turn from you.
36. The **fatigue** of the body comes from the ignorance of the brain.
37. It is the **feet** which carry the burden of an empty brain.
38. **Fire** and water are merciless.
39. One does not discuss the price of **fish** that is still in the sea.
40. A thousand **friends** are little; one enemy too many.
41. One does not throw stones at a barren **fruit-tree.**
42. The **glass** says to the stone, "Break me, but silently."
    [i.e. without scandal.]
43. The **goat** without horns bears not for long the injustice of the goat with horns.
44. The nest of the blind partridge is made by **God.**
45. Search yourself and you will find **God.**
46. **Grass** grows quickly over blood shed in fair fight.
47. One **hand** washes the other, and both wash the face.
48. Every **head** has its own opinion.
49. You need three children to make a **home.**
50. When **honesty** fails, it is like a drop of water, it is lost.
51. For you the **honour,** for me the profit.
52. The **jar** does not always return intact from the mountains.
53. **Kissing** girls in their fathers' houses is a custom; kissing them in your own house is a crime.
54. Put off thy repast until to-morrow, but not thy **labour.**
55. He who comes **late** must be satisfied with that which his host offers him.
56. The **liar** profits but once.
57. Each of us is free to keep silence—a **lie** is then without excuse.
58. At a distance all is **light.**
59. The **lion's** den is never without bones.
60. The best **luxury** is simplicity.

61. It is better to be a **male** for one day than a female for ten.

62. **Man** is a river—woman a lake.

63. **A marriage** between the poor—naked children.

64. **Marry** young, that you may have big children while you are still young.

65. It is the **mediator** who receives the blows.

66. Glorify not him who is without **merit,** and make not an ass's saddle with silk.

67. White **money** for black days.

68. The **mouth** is not a hole in the wall that can be stopped with mud.

69. Distrust **mud**—it becomes dust.

70. Leave the **needle** to those who know how to sew.

71. If you do not knock at your **neighbour's** door, he will not knock at yours.

72. When the **ox** is slain the knives are numerous.

73. If the **pole** sinks not into the ground, take a hammer.

74. Have no faith in the words of a **priest,** even though his turban be covered with precious stones.

75. Each **prophet** prays for his own soul.

76. If you receive a **reed,** give a horse in exchange.

77. A good **reputation** is worth every sacrifice. Keep your own intact at all costs.

78. The **riches** of the rich make wag incessantly the tongues of the poor.

79. All **roads** where the ox has passed lead to the village.

80. The **root** may become a palm, but our enemy will never be our friend.

81. He who loves the **rose,** loves the thorn.

82. Come **seldom,** leave often.

83. If the mistress breaks, it is an accident ; if the **servant** breaks, it is a fault.

84. The **sheep** thinks only of the knife, the butcher only of the meat.

85. When one has been bitten by a **snake,** one fears the sound of a rope.

86. To be **solitary** is alone worthy of God.

87. **Solitude** is the nest of thought.

88. Be **sufficient** unto thyself and thou wilt be considered.

89. **Summer** is the father of the poor.

90. The **stick** learns the truth.

91. Big **stones** are held up by little ones.

92. One may forecast a black night by the colour of the **sunset.**

93. The **thief's** mother shivers twice, with joy and with fear.

94. The **tongue** is the head's misfortune.

95. Only the worm which comes from the marrow of the **tree** makes the tree fall.

96. Every gold **tress** is followed by a fair moustache.

97. The **ungrateful** man is the first victim of ingratitude.

98. Fear still **waters ;** they are more dangerous than **running** water.

99. **Wealth** covers all faults.

100. Rather frequent him who makes you **weep,** and avoid him who makes you laugh.

101. Disquiet not thyself about the **wife** thou wilt take, but know her family.

102. Do not pursue the **wind** that carries away your hat.

103. The man who has two **wives** is a porter.

104. When the **wolf** is advised to walk in front of the sheep, he says his foot hurts him.

105. **Woman** and man—spade and bucket.

106. **Woman** is a fortress—man her prisoner.

107. A **woman** never belongs entirely to him who takes her.

108. We like the man who is like us. The **woman** who is like us is nothing.

109. All a **woman's** intelligence is in her home; if she leaves it she will be worthless.

110. The **word** is one.

111. There are **words** which kill.

MALAYAN

(Including Besisi and Belandas)

An Introduction to this collection by E. S. Hose, C.M.G., will be found on page lxxii.

1. It is in sugar that you see the dead **ant.**

2. Where is it that **ants** die if not in sugar?

   [i.e. ruin results if all is abandoned for pleasure.]

3. **Ants** die in sugar.

   [i.e. evil passions are killed by kindness.]

4. If you **bathe,** get thoroughly wet.

5. The **bean** forgets its pod.

6. There is not only one **bee,** nor but a single flower.

   [As good fish in the sea as ever came out.]

7. There is not only one **beetle** and but a single flower.

8. The **betrothed** of good is evil, the betrothed of life is death, the betrothed of love is separation.

   [A polite expression of resignation when the details of a divorce are being arranged.]

9. Better all **black** than just ink splashed all around.

10. To trust one's child is **blindness** in one eye, to trust a stranger is blindness in both.

11. A **boat** steered from the bow.

    [Said of a house where the wife rules.]

12. Hug your **body** and lecture yourself.

13. Better white **bones** than white eyes.

    [Death is better than disgrace.]

14. That which is **broken off** shoots afresh; that which is lost is replaced.

15. One **buffalo** brings mud and all the herd are smeared with it.

16. Men hold a **buffalo** by a cord, a man by his word.

    [i.e. different people treated in different ways.]

17. The **bug** was the death of the louse.

18. The **buttress** leads to the fall.

    [Trusting to a friend who betrays you.]

19. Think not because the **cane** is bent the sugar is crooked too.

20. When insulted, men who lack **cannon** never answer back.

21. Where a **carcase** is, there will vultures also be.

22. While small, **children**; grown big, thorns.

    [Too late to train after childhood.]

23. When you enter a company of **cocks,** crow.

24. The lot of **coconut fibre** is to float, and the lot of a stone is to sink.

    [i.e. it is useless to strive against Fate.]

25. What you lose on the **cost** you will gain in the wear.

26. On his own **couch** a man may sing.

27. The **crack** awaits the fissure.

    [Ready to part company at any moment and only waiting a decent excuse.]

28. What is **cracked** must break.

29. The **crocodile** is not averse to a corpse.

30. Will the **crocodile** reject the carcase?

[Is it likely that a good offer will be refused?]

31. Don't think there are no **crocodiles** because the water's calm.

[When things are calm, do not imagine there is no danger.]

32. To pole down the stream makes the **crocodiles** laugh.

[No Malay believes in undue exertion.]

33. Let our children die rather than our **customs.**

34. The less we sever by **cutting,** the more we break by pulling and twisting.

35 In **death** a tiger leaves his skin behind him—a warrior his fame.

36. 'Tis **death** to follow one's will, 'tis destruction to give way to desire.

37. A single word creates a **debt,** a single word releases it.

38. If you must **die,** it is nobler to be taken by a big crocodile than to be nibbled to pieces by little fishes.

39. We **die,** not for curses; we live, not for prayers.

[Fatalistic attitude.]

40. However much **dogs** may bark, will the hill fall to pieces?

[i.e. does the man of assured position regard the slander of his inferiors?]

41. Shut one **door,** you will find ten others open.

[A thing you cannot keep secret.]

42. **Dough** meets yeast.

[Things are taking the most promising turn.]

43. Be content to lose a **drop,** so long as you do not lose the whole.

44. As the **drum** beats, so goes the dance.

45. A man with soft **ears** is sure to get them pulled.

46. An **elephant** dies, but no one finds his trunk; a tiger dies, but no one finds stripes.

[i.e. crime often goes undiscovered.]

47. **Entering,** look forward; departing, look backward.

48. A lax **eye** spells a broken head.

49. The **eye** that looks on does not suffer; the shoulder that bears the burden gets to know its weight.

50. A spotted Malay **father** has a speckled son.

51. The **fence** devours the crop.

52. The **field** for a ship is the ocean, the field for the heart is reflection.

53. Never mind being beaten in the **fight,** if you win in crowing over it.

[i.e. if you reap the consequence of victory.]

54. Between **fire** and water there is but little difference.

55. **Fire** when small is a friend, but when large is an enemy.

56. What is **firm** is propped up, what is fallen is pressed down.

[Money begets money and poverty pauperism.]

57. Anything with scales counts as a **fish.**

[The absence of selection; the acceptance of what comes first to hand.]

58. Different holes have different **fish.**

[Different men have different ways.]

59. Let the **fish** be caught, but let not the fish-spear be bent.

[i.e. act with discretion.]

60. The custom of anglers, if a **fish** escape it was a big one.

61. **Fish** perish through bait.

[Men are tempted by women to ruin.]

62. The **flowers** fall, and so must all things fair, the old drop off and the fully ripe.

63. The **fortune** of a garden is a fence, of a house an inmate, of a girl a husband.
   [Said in self-depreciation by (Naning) parents, the hand of whose daughter is sought.]
64. Cut a **fowl's** throat with a knife and a man's with cotton.
   [i.e. men are deceived with soft words.]
65. **Friends** and acquaintances are as leaves that the wind of misfortune blows away; blood relations are as the fruit of the tree which always falls near the parent stem.
66. A **frog** beneath a coconut-shell believes that there is no other world.
67. When the lower **frond** falls, let not the upper frond be amused.
68. **Gentle words** lead to bones being broken.
   [Men are ruined by flattery.]
69. If you have, **give**; if you have not, seek. (*Besisi.*)
70. To bleat when you enter the company of **goats.**
71. **God** gives every man his day of sainthood, and every woman her day of devilry.
72. Wherever there is a field, there are **grasshoppers.**
   [Wherever there is a settlement there is population.]
73. Where is the **gravy** to be poured if not on the rice?
   [A child follows his father's example and teaching.]
74. What the **hand** plucks the shoulder bears.
75. If there is a **handle** it can be held, if there is a cord it can be pulled.
   [i.e. given a clue it can be followed.]
76. **Haste** loses.
77. Play the **hen** for once for the sake of peace.
78. If you are **hidden,** do not go creeping farther back into your hiding-place.
79. Everyone bastes the fat **hog** while the lean one is burning.
80. Golden rain afar, hailstones at **home**—yet home is best.
81. What is one **hornbill** to another?
   [What does it matter what happens to strangers.]
82. They are **hornbills,** we are sparrows; how can we possibly fly in the same flock?
83. **Hornbills** with hornbills, sparrows with sparrows.
84. The empty **house** is a roost of ghosts; the unmarried a roost of slanders.
   [Marry to avoid the calumnies that attend a single life.]
85. A looking-glass **husband**—or—a shield husband.
   [Expression commonly used by widows on their re-marriage. A marriage for purposes of protection or convenience.]
86. The **junk** capsizes and the shark has his bellyful.
87. The **key** is bad, the box turns traitor.
   [If the husband is bad, the wife is unfaithful.]
88. When among the **kine** I have striven to low; when among the goats I have joined in the bleating; when among the fowls I have crowed with the cocks.
89. If you meet a snake and a **Kling** [a Tamil], never mind the snake, but first kill the Kling.
   [Klings are imported and breed snakes for pay, and are much despised by Malays.]
90. Why light a **lamp** if it has no wick in it?
   [Why cast amorous glances if you mean nothing by them.]
91. Give the **leg** and the thigh is wanted.
92. A rose fell to the lot of a **monkey.**
93. The **mortar** seeks the pestle.
   [Said of a woman who makes love to a man, or any similar reversion of the usual order of things.]
94. As the **mould** is, so will the cake be.
   [As the parent so the children.]
95. A sweet **mouth** breaks bones.

96. A stone **mouth** is needed to exhort the tongue to keep peace.

97. It is by the **mouth** the body is ruined.

98. If there is **nourishment** one can eat.

[Faith in God's Providence.]

99. What **ocean** is waveless ?

[Who is blameless ?]

100. **One man's** boat, another man's rollers ; one man's swellings, another man's runnings ; one man's loins, another man's clouts

[i.e. one man sins, another suffers.]

101. When the lower **palm leaf** falls let not the upper palm leaves laugh.

[Don't be amused at a man's death, your turn will come.]

102. From the endless **past** to the endless future.

103. If the **pestle** be broken, the mortar will be lost.

[i.e. if the husband be impotent, the wife will prove unfaithful.]

104. When the **pestles** fall together into the mortar the fowls have their bellies full.

[When men of rank quarrel, the common people reap the benefit.]

105. Whosoever digs a **pit,** he shall fall into it himself.

106. Only once does a **plantain** bear.

[i.e. lost chances never recur.]

107. A **plant** must sprout before it climbs ; if it were not true people would not say it.

[i.e. no smoke without fire.]

108. The **plated ware** which shows its nature when scratched.

109. Where the **plates** are broken, there the broken segments remain.

110. The **plough** bites only where the soil is soft.

[The fool who submits to extortion has only himself to thank.]

111. The less **porridge,** the more spoons.

[The more trifling it is, the more fuss made about it.]

112. The larger the **pot,** the more rice adheres.

113. Who has the **pot** has the sword.

114. The lower the **price,** the more you cheapen it.

[Give an inch and you take an ell.]

115. What does scraping matter to the **rasp ?**

[It is the coconut that is ruined by it. What does a man really care for the sufferings he inflicts on others.]

116. Seven changes of **residence** make one a pauper.

117. A dig in the **ribs** should cause an ache.

[If a bribe is offered, let it be considerable.]

118. If you have **rice,** put it away among the unhusked grain.

[Injunction to secrecy.]

119. **Rice** that enters the spoon does not always enter the mouth.

120. **Rocks** need no protection from the rain.

121. Like the fragrance of the **rose** when it is struck all wet with dew by the rays of the rising sun.

122. Let what is once **said** be as reliable as a fort.

123. Let us heat our **saucepans** separately.

[A suggestion of divorce.]

124. The **scum** always finds its way to the side.

[The poor always get the worst place.]

125. What **sea** is waveless ? Where is the land where rain never falls ?

[A long lane that has no turning.]

126. The existence of **sea** [means] the existence of pirates.

127. If you make holes in the ground **seeds** will be forthcoming.

[i.e. if an offence is committed retaliation will follow.]

128. You may bale out a sinking **ship,** but in a shipwreck of the affections the vessel founders.

129. The more **shoots,** the more leaves.

[i.e. the more you do for a man the more he will do for you.]

130. Many **shrimps,** many flavours ; many men, many whims.

131. The eyes close in **sleep,** but the pillow remains awake.

132. A man is a prince on his own **sleeping platform.**

133. The **slumberers** are the prey of the wakeful.

134. When you kill a **snake,** do not break your stick.

135. If it **snaps** you can bind it ; if it spills you can dig it up. (*Besisi.*)

136. As a man **sows,** so shall he reap.

137. A **stone** even would be softened, much more than the heart of a man.

138. The length of your **stretch** is the length of your sheet.

139. If we must be **struck,** let it be with a hand that weareth a ring ; if we must be kicked, let it be by a foot that weareth a sandal.

140. Where there is **sugar** there are ants.

[i.e. man will always be attracted by food and money.]

141. Who can plaster over the rays of the **sun ?**

142. As is the cadence of the **tabor,** so must the measure of the dance be.

[A man should regulate his conduct according to the orders he gets from his superiors.]

143. Skilful **thefts** appear like earnings ; unskilful earnings appear like thefts.

144. Does one sharpen **thorns ?**

[You cannot make the vicious man worse.]

145. **Thought** is the lamp of the mind.

146. A broken **thread** may be joined again ; a broken piece of charcoal is broken for ever.

[There are quarrels which can be settled, others rankle for ever.]

147. He who ventures to **threaten** should be bold enough to fight.

148. While the **thunder** only is heard in the sky, and the rain has not yet come, don't empty the water out of the jars.

149. The **tiger** roars at the end of the cape. (*Bĕlandas.*)

150. To carry a light when the moon shines makes the **tigers** laugh.

151. The teeth sometimes bite the **tongue.**

152. **Tongues** are boneless.

153. When the **tree** falls, the woodpecker that lives on it must also perish.

154. The **turtle** lays eggs by the thousand and no man knows of it ; the fowl lays a single egg and the whole town is acquainted with the fact.

155. When the **village** burns there is smoke to be seen, but a man's heart may be in flames and no one know it.

156. A **wallet** new take to the jungle. (*Besisi.*)

157 A **wallet** old leave at home. (*Besisi.*)

158. For **washing** one's hands and feet.

[i.e. for one's absolute use.]

159. Can muddy **water** come from a clear well ?

160. Even **water** has its high and low tides.

[If the sea-level changes, how much more must a man's circumstances change ?]

161. Where is **water** on the ridge of a roof to descend to if it does not run to the eaves ?

[i.e. natural laws and tendencies are naturally followed.]

162. Wherever there is **water** there is fish.

[There is no smoke without fire.]

163. Will **water** which fills a bucket shake about ? It is the half-filled bucket which is unsteady.

[Only half-educated men make a noise.]

164. **Wealth** is a harlot, wisdom is faithful.

165. **Wealth** ruins courtliness and poverty ruins discretion.

166. A year's fine **weather** is wiped out by a day's rain.

167. A **widow** is as frisky as a horse that has thrown its rider.

168. If there is no **wind** the trees do not quiver.

169. A travelled **woman** is like a garden trespassed by cattle.

170. When God shut up Satan in Hell He created **woman** to replace Satan on earth.

171. "**Won't**" in time will conquer pain.

172. The **worms** get at last to the eyes.

[Allow one thing after another and you are ruined in the end.]

173. If there are **worms** in the earth, need one dig them up?

174. The **yam** remains still and increases in bulk; iron lies quiet and wastes away the more.

MONGOLIAN

(Including Yakut)

1. If an elder **brother** should [go] seven feet, then the younger brother may be expected to traverse three feet and a half.

[This proverb shows the relative positions of brothers; the younger one's share being half that of his elder brother.]

2. He who washes off the **dirt** washes off the luck.

3. When you take a cudgel to call a **dog** he doesn't come.

4. When one shuts one's **door** one is emperor of one's own kingdom.

5. The **goat** with his little tail ventures everywhere.

6. **Good deeds** remain unknown; evil deeds run through all the streets.

7. Great **happiness** comes from heaven; small joys from men.

8. When one falls **ill** one thinks of one's life; when one gets well one thinks of one's money.

9. When the mother of **lightning** has lost her shoe, she knows not whether it be in the clouds or in the fog.

10. To the **living** one denies a table; to the dead one gives a whole box. (*Yakut.*)

11. To say a few words is not difficult, but giving **money** is a reality.

12. When one has read the book of **Proverbs**, no effort is needed to speak well.

13. If one wishes to be compassionate one cannot remain **rich**, and if one desires to become wealthy one cannot remain sympathetic.

14. If the body holds itself erect, what matter if the **shadow** be crooked?

15. If you **strike** someone, strike him dead; if you save someone, save him alive.

16. If you leave for one day take provisions for two, and if you **travel** in summer take your clothes for winter.

17. **Vanquishers** are kings; the vanquished thieves.

18. If one generation has been **warlike** the ten following will be timid.

ORIENTAL (GENERAL COLLECTION)

(Including Mohammedan)

1. The **air** is playing upon his face.
2. Prayer carries us half-way to **Allah**; fasting brings us to the door of his palace; alms gains us admission. (*Mohammedan.*)
3. It is easier to take poison than **alms.**
4. Who will not give **alms** into a golden cup?
5. That which you have given in **alms,** will be your safety at the last day.
6. Even an **ass** promises well whilst young.
7. The **beard** is the light of God. (*Mohammedan.*)
8. Allah pity him who must **beg** of a beggar. (*Mohammedan.*)
9. It is unlawful to beg from a **beggar.**
10. A **beggar's** son struts like a peer.
11. A **blanket** is a shawl to a beggar.
12. An hour's **blessing** is worth a year's labour.
13. Weep before a **blind man** and lose both your eyes.
14. The sinner's **boat** must necessarily sink.
15. To wipe one's **bread.**

    [i.e. to flatter.]
16. Give **bread** and buy life.
17. One eats more **bread** by dipping it in honey than in vinegar.
18. Cast thy **bread** upon the waters; God will know of it if the fishes do not.
19. **Brother** to a king and fellow to a beggar if he be found worthy.
20. Only a **Buddha** can fully comprehend a Buddha.
21. Suffer me first to **bury** my father.

    [Idiom expressing a polite refusal to a request.]
22. Everyone rakes the embers to his own **cake.**
23. The wise man sits on the hole in his **carpet.**
24. Dine upon **charity** and call out for sauce.
25. A **closed fist** is equal to a plum.
26. He **closeth,** and uncloseth, and doeth well. (*Mohammedan.*)
27. A black **cloud** threatens, but a white cloud gives rain.
28. He who sees a straight **coconut** or a crooked areca shall never see death.
29. Even two kicks from a milch **cow** are acceptable.
30. Better the **crow** of one's own country than the phœnix of a strange land.
31. In the inn of **decision** men sleep well.
32. **Destiny** of everyone is with everyone.
33. **Deviation** from right is deviation from peace.
34. The proper **devil** of mankind is man.
35. A **dog** on the run can safely be kicked.
36. It is easy to mount a little **donkey.**
37. **Earn** and dine, or else fast. (*Mohammedan.*)
38. Man wants but seven feet of **earth.** (*Mohammedan.*)
39. Even the **earth** does not commit breach of trust.
40. An **enemy** neither sleeps nor allows his foe to sleep.
41. **Enjoyment** is the grace of God.
42. **Eyes** that are not seen are soon forgotten.
43. The eyes of a dead **father** are large.
44. Who spreads his table hath a hundred **faults**; who spreads it not hath only one. (*Mohammedan.*)

45. In the city where you wish to sell **flowers,** do not kick up the dust.
46. A live **fly** cannot be swallowed.
47. If you have to do with a **fool,** you must use club argument.
48. In the dreams of a **fowl,** barley is barley.
49. If you go **fox-hunting,** prepare to meet with a lion.
50. The best **friends** we have in the world are the spies of our actions, who publish our faults.
51. To **go** is at one's own option, but to return depends on another.
52. There is no house possessing a **goat** but a blessing abides therein. (*Mohammedan.*)
53. Call upon the name of **God,** and ask for what is good for you.
54. **God** does not kill everyone with a club, but takes away his understanding.
55. **God** has never spoken except to an Arab.
56. If **God** is our friend, our business is accomplished.
57. Where **God** is, there is everything.
58. **God** loves good accounts.
59. There are no two together but **God** makes a third.
60. Hold all the skirts of thy mantle extended, when heaven is raining **gold.**
61. The **grief** of the morrow is not to be eaten to-day.
62. One day a **guest,** two days a guest, the third day a nuisance. (*Mohammedan.*)
63. The house that receives no **guests** never receives angels. (*Mohammedan.*)
64. May her enemies stumble over her **hair.**
65. One **hand** is a mirror of the other.
66. **Health** alone is equal to a thousand blessings.
67. If two **hearts** are one, a straw-bin becomes a palace.
68. What trust is there in a crowing **hen?** (*Mohammedan.*)
69. The **hen** of our neighbours appears to us as a goose.
70. The loose **horse** makes for his stall.
71. A man's **house** is seen far off.
72. **Hurry** is of the devil, but slow advancing comes from God.
73. One hour in doing **justice** is worth a hundred in prayer. (*Mohammedan.*)
74. If fate throws a **knife** at you, there are two ways of catching it—by the blade and by the handle.
75. **A liberal disposition** is always poor.
76. The **lizard** runs no farther than the heap of cow-dung.
77. If a man hath two **loaves,** let him sell one and buy some flowers of narcissus. (*Mohammedan.*)
78. There are a thousand miseries in one falling in **love.**
79. **Love** is like a caravanserai where one only finds what one brings.
80. Wake and be **merry,** sleep and weep.
81. The **miser** who refuses at once, is preferable to the liberal man who gives slowly.
82. He is **miserable** once who feels it, but twice who fears it before it comes.
83. **Money** is the fuel of the soul.
84. I have put my head into the **mortar,** it is useless to dread the sound of the pestle.
85. If thou hearest that a **mountain** has moved, believe it; but if thou hearest that a man has changed his character, believe it not. (*Mohammedan.*)
86. Remove thy foot from thy **neighbour's** house, lest he grow weary of thee and so hate thee.
87. The **nose** of one who has it cut off, grows an ell and a quarter.
88. A good **old man** is like old wine which has deposited its lees.

89. **Patience** opens the door of rest.
90. The **plaintiff** and defendant are in a boat, the witnesses are obliged to swim.
91. **Play** with the hands is boorish play.
92. The **poor man's** wisdom is as useless as a palace in a wilderness.
93. Righteous gains make the **pot** boil.
94. My son, learn those things that will keep the **pot** boiling.
95. The **pot** has rolled and found its cover.
    [i.e. a good match.]
96. That which is in the **pot,** will come on the plate.
97. Hast thou mounted the pulpit, thou art not therefore a **preacher.**
98. He never met with **prosperity** yet quarrels with adversity.
99. The passage of a **rat** is nothing, but it soon becomes a thoroughfare.
100. He that takes the **raven** for a guide, shall light upon carrion.
101. One **refusal** prevents a hundred reproaches.
102. The door of **repentance** is open. (*Mohammedan.*)
103. **Reward** is for work, reaping is to the sower.
104. Do the **right** and lawful, and do it a hundred times a day. (*Mohammedan.*)
105. Every **rogue** is at length outrogued.
106. I was common earth until some **roses** were planted in me.
107. He that **runs** shall find what is written.
108. Open not your **sail** to every wind.
109. What he cooks in the **saucepan,** he eats in its cover.
    [A miser.]
110. **Say** what is true and what is pleasant. Do not say what is pleasant and not true, nor what is true and not pleasant.
111. **Servitude** is ever new.
112. Good luck to **simplicity.** May simplicity prosper!
113. There are many who can **sing,** but know no songs.
114. Even God forgives three **sins.** (*Mohammedan.*)
115. In Golgotha are **skulls** of all sizes.
116. Distrust the **smiles** of thine adversary.
117. By patience and perseverance and a bottle of sweet oil the **snail** at length reaches Jerusalem.
118. Bad company is friendship with a **snake,** fencing with a sword.
119. As the sands of the desert are to the weary traveller, so is over-much **speech** to him who loveth silence.
120. A **spider** dances by means of a stick.
121. Once in forty years I set out to **steal,** and then the moon shone all night.
122. A **stone** does not rot in water.
123. The father of **sugar** is the cane-press.
124. The teacher remained raw **sugar;** the disciple became refined sugar.
125. God gives **sugar** to him who eats sugar.
126. If he dies from **sugar,** why should you give him poison?
127. The **sweet** is swallowed; the bitter spat out.
128. **Sweetmeats** do not come without sweat.
129. The language of thirty-two **teeth** is never uttered in vain.
130. The **teeth** of one's own calf are visible from a distance.
131. There are some **teeth** to eat with, some to exhibit.
132. It is no use calling the **tiger** to chase away the dog.
133. Give God **time.**
134. **Tithe** and be rich.
135. There is no ditch before one's **tongue.**

136. A beggar, a borrower, and a child, are all three destitute of **understanding.**

137. From **water** we have made all things live.

[In Palestine, so great is the appreciation of all moisture, that this tenet is still sometimes seen in ornamental relief over city fountains.]

138. **Water-jars** are broken on the way to the fountain.

139. The **wealth** of sinners goes in expiation.

140. He that goes out **weeping,** brings intelligence of the dead.

141. Keep the dog near when thou suppest with the **wolf.**

142. When the **wolf** is alone he is a lion.

143. There is no calamity more hurtful to man than **woman.** (*Mohammedan.*)

144. A wise **woman** is one who has a great deal to say and remains silent.

145. A **woman's** talk—heat from grass.

146. **Women** are defective in understanding and religion. (*Mohammedan.*)

147. **Women** have been omitted by God from his mercy. (*Mohammedan.*)

148. Speak one **word** while you listen to one thousand.

149. The **work** is dearer than the gold.

150. He that **works** shall eat.

151. Neither speak well nor ill of **yourself.** If well, men will not believe you; if ill, they will believe a great deal more than you say.

152. **Youth** is madness.

PASHTO (AFGHANISTAN)

1. A very little water is a sea to an **ant.**

2. If the night be dark, the **apples** will be counted.

[i.e. folk take precautions when there is likely to be danger.]

3. When the **arm** is broken the hand goes to the shoulder.

[i.e. when down in the world one turns to one's friends.]

4. I have one **ass** and one pack-saddle; I have no anxieties above or below.

5. When necessary, an **ass** even is called "father".

6. To say "**Bismillah**" [in God's name] brings a blessing, but not in jackal hunting.

7. The first man is the last man's **bridge.**

8. Along with the dry also **burns** up the wet.

9. A small **calamity** says "Boo" to a big one.

10. There is always a **calf** behind a cow, sometimes her own and sometimes another's.

11. See on which side the **camel** will lie down.

[i.e. see on whom the blame will be laid.]

12. If you deal in **camels,** make the doors high.

13. If there were no **cock** to crow, night would never become morning.

14. I know nothing of your **coming and going.**

[A mosquito lived for a hundred years in an elephant's ear. When he was about to leave he said to the elephant, "I'm off now"; the elephant replied as above. This saying has become proverbial and is very common as a snub to a bumptious nonentity.]

15. First look out for a **companion,** then a road.
16. One can't get **currants** without stalks.
17. It is always **dark** round the candle.
18. A **deaf man** laughs twice.
    [i.e. once when he sees others laughing and again when he realizes what has been said.]
19. The **dust** of one country is the gunpowder of another.
20. If a man said to you, "A dog has carried away your **ear,**" would you go after the dog or search first for your ear?
21. Some ask what they will **eat ;** some ask what they will eat with.
    [i.e. rich and poor each have their troubles.]
22. Go with many, **eat** with many.
23. Though your **enemy** be a rope of reeds, call him a serpent.
24. **Eyes** feel shame from eyes.
    [i.e. better to reprimand a man verbally than in writing.]
25. The career of **falsehood** is short.
26. A **feather** does not stick without gum.
27. The **feet** go to that place that the heart goes.
28. Stretch your **feet** only as far as your covering goes.
29. Don't walk towards the light of a **fire** or the barking of a dog.
    [i.e. advice to those travelling at night. Everyone knows how close these things seem at night, and how far they often are.]
30. When a **fir-tree** gets old its sap goes to the bottom.
    [Said of old people who are in their dotage.]
31. Strange **food** is on loan.
    [i.e. you must invite your host to dinner in return.]
32. **Fortune** is like unto a potter ; it fashioneth and breaketh.
33. Is life best, or a **friend ?**
34. An old **friend** is like a saddled horse.
35. From whom did you **gain ?** From my brother—that is no gain.
36. A **gardener's** flirtations take place outside the garden.
37. A **girl** is of no account in her own house.
38. **Give** a little and you gain a lot.
39. What you **give** may become a rose ; what you eat, excrement.
40. The medicine for asking is **giving.**
41. When the knife is over a man's head, he remembers **God.**
42. Some marvel at the treasures of **God,** and others at the sewing of a garment.
43. **God** knows on which knee the camel will squat down.
    [i.e. native illustration of their idea of the glorious uncertainty of the laws.]
44. When **God** makes a man poor, he [the poor man] cooks twice in the daytime.
45. **God** will remain—friends will not.
46. When **God** wills the destruction of an ant He supplies it with wings.
47. Open-handed, **God-befriended.**
48. Bear witness for **God's** sake, use a stick for a friend's.
49. If **gold** is pure, why should it fear fire?
50. The **great** have ears, not eyes.
    [i.e. must trust others.]
51. If there is food in the house, a **guest** is no worry. If a man is religious, death is no worry.
52. If you do not vex your own **heart,** you will not make another's happy.
53. From **hearts** to hearts are ways.
54. Even if the **hill** be high, there will be a road at the top.
55. Either go to high **hills** or great houses.
    [i.e. don't bury yourself at the back of beyond.]
56. Amongst the **honourable** a man becomes honourable ; amongst the base, base.

57. He who placeth any **hope** upon the fabric of this world, embarketh on a tour of the ocean in a paper boat.
58. The **horse** can stand the horse's kick.
59. The **horses** were shoeing themselves, the frogs held up their legs.
60. To speak **ill** [of anyone] is to speak ill of oneself.
61. If your **informer** belongs to the house, his home must be a poor one.
 [i.e. no one will give his own people away.]
62. **Invited** is entertained.
63. The **jackal's** messenger is the jackal, the lion's the lion.
64. If you are not a good **judge,** choose a young animal.
65. The **jungle** will not be without a tiger.
66. Ploughed **land** is all clods of earth.
 [i.e. "There are many more at home like you."]
67. If you and I agree, what is the **lawyer** wanted for?
68. Is a **legacy** best, or what is left? Curses on them both!
 [i.e. the most frequent causes of litigation amongst Pathans.]
69. Sooner may you stop the sea's mouth with wax than stifle the prayer which proceeds out of the heart of **love.**
70. When the heart is in **love,** beauty is of no account. When one is asleep, a pillow is unnecessary.
71. **Love** never weeps as blood weeps.
 [i.e. blood is thicker than water.]
72. Who **loves,** labours.
73. **Lying** is an honest man's wings.
74. Scalded by **milk,** he blows on curds.
75. The **mill-stone** is still a bit blunt, and the wheat a little damp.
 [i.e. you are still your old self. Said to one who has bettered himself and is ashamed of his former position.]
76. The road is open for the **moneyed man.**
77. The **moon** can be seen on the first of the month.
 [The Mohammedans have a lunar calendar. This proverb has the significance of "All in good time".]
78. See the **mother,** comprehend the daughter.
79. The **mouth** is a castle as well as a misfortune.
80. When **night** comes, fear is at the door; when day comes, fear is on the hills.
81. Don't lay yourself out over **old men,** they die and young ones forget.
82. Be it an **onion,** let it be given graciously.
83. The **parrot** has the lion's share of God's treasury.
 [i.e. beautiful plumage, the ability to talk, long life, etc.]
84. The **past** is underneath the stone.
85. **Pathans** die by taking the short cut.
86. **Pinch** yourself to find out how much it hurts others.
87. Every **plate** that is made breaks.
88. Though the country become **porridge,** the poor man's [share] is a spoonful.
89. Do every one a good turn except your own **relatives.**
90. Do not go on the **road** which neither your father nor your mother goes.
91. The **rose** from rose is born, the thorn from thorn.
92. Every **rose** has a thorn as its friend.
93. Cultivate **roses** and your land will become a rose garden. Don't plant thorns, they will stick into your feet.
94. Though the **sea** be large, you have your own spoon.
95. One **slap** hurts twenty faces.
 [i.e. the slapped one complains.]
96. The **sleep** of kings is on an ant-hill.

97. Until he gets over **small-pox,** parents do not count their child their own.

98. Throw a stone at anything that has the head of a **snake,** even though it be only a lizard.

99. The ungrateful **son** is a wart on his father's face ; to leave it is a blemish, to cut it a pain.

100. A dead **son's eyes** are always bigger.

[i.e. praising a thing which no longer exists.]

101. The **spectator** is a great hero.

102. What you **spit** out will not come back into your mouth.

[i.e. you cannot retract what has once been said.]

103. The **spoon** is always in the pot, but let the pot be sometimes in the spoon.

[i.e. the pot a powerful man, the spoon a dependant.]

104. A **spoon** proud because porridge has been poured on it.

105. With the arrival of the **stepmother** the father becomes a stepfather.

106. A crooked **stick** will be straightened by fire.

107. Physical **strength** tears open the stomach of common sense.

108. Either a **strong man** or a fool tells the truth.

109. If he will die from **sugar,** why kill him with poison ?

110. The **sword's** fellowship is sweet.

111. The first cup of **tea** is nothing, the second is enough, and the third is senseless.

112. The **thorn** which is sharp is so from its youth.

113. On the stake in the middle depends the **threshing.**

[i.e. bullocks yoked to a pole which turns on a central stake, treading out corn. This saying is used with reference to one who relies for success on a powerful friend.]

114. There is no **tree** which has not felt the force of the wind.

115. Put not your **trust** in a sword, woman, mare or water.

116. If the **truth** comes out, the land of lies will be burnt up.

117. **Water** falls on water.

118. A strong man's **water** flows uphill.

119. A little **water** is medicine for moist clay.

[i.e. a very little turns the scale.]

120. However high the **water** may rise, it will go under the bridge.

121. **Wealth** is a Hindu's beard.

[The Hindu shaves when in mourning, which is often.]

122. The way of the **wheat** is through the mill.

123. I have seen with my own eyes ripe **wheat** standing and the green crops reaped.

[i.e. a young man's death, etc.]

124. A **widow** dreams a double dream on her lonely cot.

[i.e. first of the late-lamented and again of her next love.]

125. A **widow** is good to love, for a calf won't go into the yoke of its own accord.

126. Where there is no **wind,** bushes don't shake.

127. Borrow a hundred rupees even, but spend a **winter's night** in your own home. (*A Turi saying.*)

[The winter in Kurram is very severe.]

128. A **wise man** once stumbles over a peg.

129. A **woman** is well either in the house or in the grave.

[The " Purdah " concealment is good for women.]

130. A **woman** without a veil is like food without salt—unattractive.

131. A **woman's** wisdom is under her heel, and she is well only in the house or in the grave.

132. A hen's crow and a **woman's** word no one trusts.

133. Men are mountains and **women** are levers which move them.

134. Ill-starred **women** have two babies a year.

135. The **world** is a traveller's serai [inn].

136. Why look for the **yoke** which is upon your own neck?

[Said to one who is his own worst enemy.]

PERSIAN

An Introduction to this collection by Sir E. Denison Ross, C.I.E., D.Litt., Ph.D., will be found on page lxxxiii.

1. **Adam and Eve** spoke of their love in Persian, and the angel who drove them out of Paradise spoke Turkish.
2. Giving **alms** prevents misfortunes.
3. The wife of the **amber-turner** wears pearls of glass.
4. When God wills the destruction of an **ant,** He gives it wings.
5. In the **ant's** house dew is a deluge.
6. Everyone who learned **archery** from me, in the end made me his butt.
7. If you can deal with an **Armenian** you can deal with the Devil.
8. The **ass's colt,** through its asininity, keeps ahead of its mother.
9. No man can **bathe** in the same river twice.
10. The wrath of a **beggar** is on his own head.
11. Man is a slave to his **benefactor.**
12. Shall the **birds** sing God's praise and I keep silent?
13. Beyond **black** there is no colour.

    [i.e. the limit has been reached.]
14. Help thou thy brother's **boat** across, and lo, thine own has touched the shore.
15. **A broken arm** can toil, but not a broken heart.
16. He that hath no **brother** has no strength in his legs.
17. If the **builder** sets the first brick awry, the wall will be crooked, although it reach to the Pleiades.
18. This **camel** lies at your door.

    [i.e. your sin has found you out.]
19. The flow of **cash** is better than the sweetmeats of credit.
20. One who pays **cash** is treated like a partner.
21. The winter is past, but the **charcoal-seller's** face is as black as ever.
22. He puts his **cheese** in a bottle and rubs his bread on the outside.

    [i.e. a miser.]
23. He that has no **child** has no light in his eyes.
24. **Children** are a bridge to heaven.
25. Be **civil** that you may become great.
26. **Class** with the same class, hand in hand flies. The pigeon with the pigeon—the kite with the kite.
27. **A closed fist** [miser] is the lock of heaven; an open hand [liberal] is the key of mercy.
28. If you be a **cock,** crow; if a hen, lay eggs.
29. **Conceit** is a jealous republican who only sees a tyrant in the superior man.
30. **Contemn** no one. Regard him who is above thee as thy father; him who is thine equal as thy brother; and him who is below thee as thy son.
31. He who sows **corn** sows holiness.
32. Every man loves his own **country,** even if it be hell.
33. Don't throw away the **coverlet** for fear of the bugs.

34. The **dead** are at the mercy of the living.
35. If you wish to make yourself **dear** [valuable] you must either die or go on a journey.
36. Ten **dervishes** can sleep on one carpet, but a whole empire cannot hold two kings.
37. To **die** with friends is a nuptial.
38. New sleeves get a good **dinner.**
39. If you wish to avoid **disgrace,** do as men do.
40. Beat your **dog** and he will not desert you, but cease a moment to do good to your neighbour and he will turn his back upon you.
41. Each glass of **dogh** [curdled milk] contains an extra year of life.
42. A **dog's tail** never became straight.
43. To the **donkey** one thistle is better than two hundred ass-loads of jewels.
44. For an object men kiss the **donkey's** tail.
45. Take the cotton out of thine **ear** and distribute justice to mankind.
46. Others planted what I should **eat**—I plant what others may eat.
47. **Eat** it, give it away, and leave some behind you.

    [Disposal of money during life-time.]
48. An **egg-stealer** will at last develop into a camel-stealer.
49. A wise **enemy** is better than a foolish friend.
50. Look at his **face** and don't ask about his circumstances.
51. He can walk who has **feet.**
52. In winter **fire** is better than a musk-rose.
53. If the **fire-worshipper** keeps the sacred fire burning even a hundred years, he will be consumed should he happen to fall into it.
54. The **fish** is rotten from the head.
55. To **flatter** is worse than to abuse.
56. What is it to the **fool** if his father was vizier to the Sultan?
57. To put one's **foot** outside the coverlet.

    [i.e. to live beyond one's means].
58. Of **four things** every man has more than he knows: of sins, of debts, of years, and of foes.
59. It is rest to take trouble for a **friend.**
60. One is never a **friend** by force.
61. The accounts of **friends** are kept in the heart.
62. It is better to be in chains with **friends** than in the garden with strangers.
63. A needle's eye is wide enough for two **friends**; the whole world is too narrow for two foes.
64. Absence and **friendship.**
65. I break the tie of my **friendship** that perchance when the knot is tied I may become closer to you.
66. Good juice from **fruit** comes without squeezing.
67. A town's **gate** can be shut; a foe's mouth never.
68. Things **given free** make the heart hard.
69. He who gives little **gives** from his heart, but he who gives much gives from his fortune.
70. The liberal man is the friend of **God.**
71. What can your enemies do if you enjoy the favour of **God**?
72. You can't have both **God** and dates.
73. If you have **God** as your protector, what affliction have you?
74. **God** gives much cold to the well clad, but little to those who lack clothing.
75. **God** has in store many hidden mercies.
76. Your saviour is your deeds and **God** Himself.
77. **God** is a tray of plunder.
78. **God** provides the dervish's kitchen.

79. **God** rights him that keeps silence.
80. **God** will not seek thy race, nor will He ask thy birth: alone He will demand of thee what hast thou done on earth?
81. **God's** club makes no noise; when it strikes there is no cure for the blow.
82. The legs of those who require proofs of **God's** existence are made of wood.
83. One **grape** and a hundred wasps.
84. **Grapes** derive their colour from grapes.
85. The **grave** is on the road of him who digs it.
86. The master of the house is the servant of the **guest.**
87. A loaded **gun** frightens one man; an unloaded one, two.
88. A **hair** separates the false from the true.
89. You must show **haste** over three things only—to bury your dead; to marry your daughter; and to set meat before a stranger.
90. **Heaven** is at the feet of mothers.
    [i.e. lies in dutiful obedience.]
91. That which comes from **heaven** is received by the earth.
92. The more property one leaves one's **heirs,** the fewer regrets.
93. If the **hen** wants to sing like the cock one must cut her throat.
94. No good comes from the house where the **hens** crow like the cocks.
95. A Persian thinks that a **hen's egg,** if it belongs to him, has been produced by a swan.
96. As thou yieldest no **honey,** wound not with thy sting.
97. If you possess a good **horse** it always becomes a gift.
98. A **house** that has two mistresses is unswept.
99. The owner has one **house,** the renter a thousand.
100. One stone is enough to destroy a **house** which is made of glass.
101. "**If**" was married to "but" and the offspring of the union was named "Oh, would that."
102. "**I have,** I have" is of use; "I had, I had"—what good is that?
103. If you do not wish to be **insulted,** behave like the rest of the company.
104. The **jackal** that lives in the wilds of Mazanderan can only be caught by the hounds of Mazanderan.
105. Except the thread of Mary there was none fit for the needle of **Jesus.**
106. Hast thou a **jewel**—take it to the jeweller.
107. A halt on the **journey,** a rest, a drink from the well, and the caravan moves on at the setting of the stars.
108. Brotherhood is brotherhood, but a **kid** is always worth half a crown.
109. Rely not on **kindred** or good ancestry.
110. For the righteous **king** the whole people is an army.
111. The **knife** has reached the bone.
112. Doubt is the key of **knowledge.**
113. **Knowledge** is a wild thing and must be hunted before it can be tamed.
114. Often the best way of giving oneself what one **lacks** is to take from oneself what one has.
115. The more your **lament** the more is your loss.
116. The foot of the **lamp** is dark.
117. The candle is put into the **lantern** and the moth is left outside fluttering.
118. What comes **late** lasts long.
119. There is **laughter** that follows every weeping.
120. There is no luck in **laziness.**
121. Practise **liberality,** but lay no stress on the obligation.
122. Whoso seeth the world telleth many a **lie.**

123. A word is useful, a **lie** is an ornament.

124. **A lie** that results in good is better than a truth that brings misfortune.

125. **Life** is a perpetual drunkenness—the pleasure passes, but the headache remains.

126. Do not raise **lion** cubs in a city.
[An ancient zoological collection saying.]

127. Distress gives to a **lion** the disposition of a fox.

128. Do well the **little things** now; so shall great things come to thee by and by asking to be done.

129. **Live** contented, you will be a king.

130. **Live** within your harvest.

131. Each time a man argues he loses a drop of blood from his **liver.**

132. A thousand leagues divide **love** and patience.

133. **Love** is born of satiety, and oblivion buries it.

134. Good **luck** is not sold in the market.

135. One can find out all about a **man** in two days, and about a beast in four.

136. **Man** returns to man, but the stone does not return to the mountain.

137. One learns **manners** from the mannerless.

138. One cannot hold two water **melons** in one hand.

139. The feet of **mendicants** drive away ill luck.

140. If thou wilt make **merit,** grow some recompenses.

141. When there are two **midwives,** the baby's head is crooked.

142. She went to **milk** with a sieve—can Fate be blamed?

143. The **miser** has locked up the gate of heaven.

144. When the **miser** is interred his silver is disinterred.

145. He who hath **money** hath fear, and he who hath none hath sorrow.

146. The **moon** looks on many flowers—the flowers see but one moon.

147. A wise man sews up his **mouth**; the candle is burned by means of its wick.

148. In time the **mulberry leaf** becomes satin.

149. The **neighbour's cup** has two feet.
[i.e. favours are reciprocal.]

150. May your **nose** be fat. (*A common greeting.*)

151. Everything that is round is not a **nut.**

152. All **pains** can be forgotten in forty days, but the pain of having been defrauded of food lasts for forty years.

153. A poor man waited a thousand years before the gate of **Paradise,** then while he snatched one little nap, it opened and shut.

154. If there exists a man without **passion,** that man is not a son of Adam.

155. **Patience** is a tree of which the roots are bitter and the fruits not sweet.

156. Get a **patron** and eat dainties.

157. Fill the eyes of a **Persian.**

158. Arabic is a language, **Persian** a sweetmeat, Turkish an art.

159. Arabic is good for flattering men, Turkish for reproving them, and **Persian** for convincing them.

160. His **place** is very green.
[Said of a person whose absence is much regretted.]

161. Why use **poison** when you can kill with honey?

162. A new **pot** keeps the water cold for a few days.

163. To boil the **pot** of our well-wishers let us turn our furniture into firewood.

164. The **potter** drinks water from a broken vessel.

165. Thou shalt sooner detect an ant moving in the dark night on the black earth than all the motions of **pride** in thine heart.

166. A **proverb** is an ornament to language.
167. **Proverbs** are the adornment of speech.
168. The **rat** could not enter his hole and he tied a broom to his tail.
169. A **religious man** is to be found at the door of the mosque; a drunkard at the tavern.
170. Swift is the dart, swifter vengeance, and swiftest **repentance.**
171. A man must cut out his own garments of **reputation.**
172. Men may hurt your **reputation** but not your character.
173. Nothing is better than **resignation.**
174. If you want to be **respected,** don't play with children and slaves.
175. Those who are **richest** have the greatest wants.
176. If you are in a **room,** be of the same colour as the people in it.
177. A snapped **rope** may be tied, but the knot remains.
178. He needs no other **rosary** whose thread of life is strung with the beads of love and thought.
179. Whatever goes into a **salt-mine** becomes salt.
180. To do things quickly is of **Satan,** because God works slowly.
181. Whoever pats **scorpions** with the hand of compassion receives punishment.
182. He's from good **seed.**
183. Fill the mouth of a **servant.**
184. A man's **servant** may live a year, a woman's slave dies in six months.
185. The dust of a flock of **sheep** is "Surmah" to the eye of a hungry wolf.

 ["Surmah" is the soot produced by the flame of wicks steeped in castor oil or goat's fat, and is used by Persian women to beautify the eyes and prevent ophthalmia.]
186. The **shell** was not filled with pearls until it was contented.

 [i.e. ceased from unrest.]
187. Take care, the **sleep** of non-existence will overtake you at last; for the coming and going of the breath is but the rocking of the cradle.
188. Who **sleeps,** dines.
189. To **speak** is to sow; to listen is to reap.
190. Picking up a large **stone** is a sign that it will not be thrown.
191. A **stone** that is fit for the wall is not left in the way.
192. I have taught no one the art of the bow who did not in the end make me his **target.**
193. He who has not **tasted** has a desire to do so, but he who has tasted has his desires increased an hundredfold.
194. The severity of a **teacher** is better than the fondness of a father.
195. To break one's **teeth** when eating jam.

 [Said of an unfortunate or unlucky man.]
196. No foal in India, no tabby cat in China, nor lion's cub in **Teheran.**

 [For hundreds of years lions never bred in Persia.]
197. The **thief** is safest under the castle wall.
198. There are **three things** I have never seen—the eye of an ant, the foot of a snake, and the charity of a mullah [priest].
199. Two **tigresses** in a house are better than two mistresses.
200. **Time** which strengthens friendship weakens love.
201. The **titmouse** holds up its feet that the sky may not fall upon it.
202. Who has seen **to-morrow?**
203. A **torrent** will be stopped by a twig at its source, but if unchecked, it will overthrow an elephant.
204. Much **travel** is needed to ripen a man's rawness.
205. The **traveller** is like a madman.
206. Fell not the **tree** which thou hast planted.
207. The man who speaks **truth** is always at ease.

208. The reply to a **Turkish** question should be in Turkish.
209. Thy **virtues** are in the palm of thy hand, thy vices under thy armpit.
210. The **walls** have mice and the mice have ears.
211. Nothing can be amiss with running **water.**
212. Enjoy thyself—that is **wisdom** ; make enjoyment—that is virtue.
213. A man can bear anything but the mention of his **wives.**
214. To be kind to the **wolf** is to be cruel to the lamb.
215. Trust neither a king, a horse, nor a **woman.**
216. There is danger for whoso snatches a delusion from a **woman.**
217. **Woman** is a calamity, but no house ought to be without this evil.
218. What man ever saw a horse, a **woman,** or a sword faithful!
219. What has a **woman** to do with the councils of a nation?
220. Obedience to a **woman** will have to be repented of.
221. Both **women** and dragons are best out of the world.
222. **Women** are the whips of Satan.
223. To consult **women** brings ruin to a man.
224. The god of **women** is a man, therefore all women must obey man.
225. All kinds of **wood** burn silently except thorns: they are constantly crying, " we also are wood."
226. Be not all sugar, or the **world** will swallow thee up; nor yet all wormwood, or the world will spit thee out.

ROMANY

Gipsy tribes of " the weary feet and wandering eye " have been nomads for over three thousand years. They were originally Hindu. The last emigrants from India, they arrived in Constantinople in the beginning of the fifteenth century; settled mainly in Wallachia and then spread over Europe, arriving in Scotland in 1514, and have inhabited England ever since.

A " Romany " is a true Gipsy. " Tacho " means Romany. " Rye " means gentleman. A " Gorgio " is a house-dwelling Gipsy.

1. You can count the number of **apples** on one tree, but you can never count the number of trees in one apple. (*English.*)
2. **Bad luck** sends a poor man further down, but it causes a great man to rise still more. (*English.*)
3. The **best** is soonest gone. (*English.*)
4. **Bold men** have generous hearts. (*English.*)
5. It is better for a real Gipsy to be killed by a Gipsy **brother** than to be hung by Gorgios. (*English.*)
6. The Gipsies' **church** was made of pork and the dogs ate it. (*German.*)
7. Cut your **coat** according to your fancy. (*English.*)
8. **Credit** is better than money. (*English.*)
9. For good or for ill you must dig deep to bury your **daddy.** (*English.*)

   [A Romany epitome of the " Play Boy of the western world ".]
10. Always go by the **day.** (*English.*)
11. The **dog** that trots about finds a bone. (*English.*)
12. When you have brandy [spirits], and keep yourself half **drunk,** you can go through the winter like a horse. (*English.*)

13. Do we keep the **fast days?** Yes, when there is neither bread nor bacon in the cupboard. (*Roumanian.*)

14. True [or good] like my **father.** (*English.*)

15. The poor **fool** who closeth his mouth never winneth a dollar. (*Spanish.*)

16. When you cut a **Gipsy** in ten pieces you have not killed him, you have only made ten Gipsies. (*English.*)

17. Go to the **Gipsy children** and choose the whitest. (*Greek.*)

    [i.e. when all is bad, whatever you choose must be equally bad.]

18. A true thing often looks like a false one; and the same is true [and that's same] of a true man, but a **girl** often looks right when she is not. (*English.*)

19. That which **God** kills is better than that which man kills.

    [The Gipsies sometimes eat carrion, justifying the practice by this proverb.]

20. **Great men** and small men sometimes like [agree in liking things] that which other people do not understand. (*English.*)

21. **Half-breeds** call themselves Gorgio among the Gorgios, and Gipsy among the Gipsies. (*English.*)

    [A Gorgio is a house-dwelling Gipsy, much despised by the true Romany.]

22. A man must always put the grain in the ground before he can cut the **harvest.** (*English.*)

23. When they are young they are arm-achy, and when they are old they are **heart-achy.** (*English.*)

    [Refers to children.]

24. The **horse** leaves his track on the road, and the snake makes his trail in the dust. (*English.*)

25. Where a **Jew** could not go, the Gipsy crept. (*Russian.*)

26. It is like a **kiss,** good for nothing until it is divided. (*Roumanian.*)

27. If people do not **know** much, do not laugh at them, for every one of them knows something that you do not. (*English.*)

28. May you have a **law-suit** in which you know that you are in the right. (*Spanish Gipsy curse.*)

29. Free of her **lips,** free of her hips. (*English.*)

30. **Luck** that is paid for is always somewhere [lit. " there "]. (*English.*)

31. I've two **masters,** God is the one, and the devil is the other. I work for the devil till I have got my dinner [one-o'clock food], and after that follow the Lord. (*English.*)

32. It is worth more to be the head of a **mouse** than the tail of a lion. (*Spanish.*)

33. Despise those who risk their **neck** for their bellies.

34. There are always two sides to a **prediction.** (*English.*)

35. What's luck to a **rabbit** is poison to a fox. (*English.*)

36. Where **rich men** can make money honestly, poor men have to steal. (*English.*)

37. The **river** which runneth with sound bears along with it stones and water. (*Spanish.*)

38. Don't throw stones at the **rooks,** because they are dark, and dark blood is Gipsy blood. (*English.*)

39. I wash my own **shirt.** (*English.*)

    [A saying indicating celibacy or independence.]

40. When **smugglers** lose and Gipsies find, nobody is the worse for it. (*English.*)

41. Every **stick** that breaks a window does not kill a dog. (*English.*)

42. A **stone** with a hole in it brings luck. (*English.*)

43. We **tattoo** and circumcise. (*Egyptian.*)

    [The street-cry of the Gipsy woman in Cairo.]

44. All men are not like **trees;** some must travel and cannot keep still. (*English.*)

45. A Gipsy once in his life tells the **truth,** but then he repents of it. (*Russian.*)
46. There are false **truths** and true lies. (*English.*)
47. If you cheat old **women** you will catch the devil. (*English.*)
48. **Work** a little, steal a little. (*Serbo-Croatian.*)

SIĀMESE (T'HAI OR THAI)

(Including Mon)

1. Let your fellow-man allow you to get a view of his **back** before he puts his coat on.

   [He may have a striped back as the result of some previous severe flogging—an index to his having committed something wrong, in which you are warned to be on your guard against him. In past days the back was, in this and neighbouring countries, a man's judiciary certificate of repute. Singlets and coats were sedulously donned by those who could not boast of a clean back, just as after footwear came into use socks and shoes were eagerly resorted to by certain individuals of the lowest classes in order to mask a yet more ominous certificate, viz. the marks of the iron chains on their ankles.]

2. Not having requited the **benefits** received, its feathers were plucked off with the aid of ashes. (*Mon.*)

   [Said of ungrateful people. This saying refers to a popular story in which an adjutant bird having proved ungrateful to its master was turned out from its master's house and on reaching the market street the people there pulled out its feathers, having first rubbed their hands in ashes in order to obtain a better grip on the slippery plumage.]

3. It is because of there being **birds** that there are nooses and snares.
4. A **blind man** comes into possession of eyeglasses.
5. In the land of **blinkards** endeavour to wink like them.
6. Preferring the **bones** to the flesh.

   [i.e. preferring flatterers to true friends.]

7. When **breed** comes in at one door, fortune often goes out at the other.
8. Having killed the **buffalo** [for food], don't begrudge the spices or seasoning.

   [i.e. don't regret the outlay entailed in carrying an enterprise to completion.]

9. Do not **cherish** what is aloof more than what is near thee.
10. When new-born **children** have been bathed and purified by their relatives, the celestials descend to impress characteristic marks on their foreheads. (*Mon.*)

    [This saying refers to a superstition which is apparently of Chinese origin. The Chinese appear to believe that when one is born the deities impress on his forehead and palms of the hands certain characteristic marks and lines by which the inner nature and destiny of the new-born may be judged.]

11. If **clear** thyself thou must, do it until full light is made.
12. A bald-headed man finds a **comb.**
13. What pleaseth thy sight do not **covet.**
14. Ten **cowries** are within hand's reach, but twenty are too far removed.
15. **Diseases** come by mountains and leave by driblets [lit. in bits of the size of a louse].
16. **A dog** when barking does not bite.
17. When **downfallen** all hate thee.
18. Don't prefer the [picturesque] grotto to thy own **dwelling.**

19. Don't meddle in assisting the **elephant** in carrying his tusks.

    [i.e. don't court danger or destruction.]

20. The mahout dies [killed] by **elephants,** the crocodile tamer by crocodiles and the snake charmer by snake-bites.

21. Aim at a definite **end.**

22. Let the wise destroy a stinging **enemy** by means of a pungent enemy; a harassing thorn by means of a thorn, for his welfare.

23. One's own **entrails** prove worms to oneself.

24. We look at others with our front **eyes,** but we see ourselves with those behind.

25. Stroke the **face** and thou wilt fall in with the nose; stroke the knee and thou wilt fall in with the leg.

    [i.e. to be confronted with obstacles in every direction; unable to deal with matters with a strong hand for fear of offending someone; having his hands tied by considerations of an opportunistic or sectarian nature.]

26. When thou art in **favour** they are ready to assist thee.

27. The **female heart** is as unstable as water rolling on a lotus leaf.

    [i.e. a drop of water falling on a lotus leaf invariably rolls off.]

28. A slow **fire,** a smouldering fire.

    [i.e. unceasing activity; long-nurtured resentment.]

29. The sun should not feel wroth at a **firefly.** (*Mon.*)

30. If **firefly** don't vie with fire.

31. Don't strike at **fish** in front of the trap.

32. To partake of **food** in the evening.

    [i.e. to behave dishonestly in secret. To take food after midday is forbidden to devotees who have taken the religious vows.]

33. To know a **girl** thou shouldst examine her mother; to know her more intimately thou shouldst push the inquiry back to her maternal grandmother.

34. On getting as much as can be **grasped** with both hands together do not relinquish the simple handful.

35. When **grasping,** grasp firmly; when squeezing, squeeze to death; when aiming, aim unswervingly.

36. Don't pull out the **guts** [i.e. intimate sorrows and troubles] for crows to feast upon.

37. Win other people's **hearts.**

38. Like having gone up to **heaven** in life. (*Also Mon.*)

    [i.e. to be the recipient of an unexpected boon.]

39. To gain **heaven** or hell lies within our breast and heart.

40. Don't soil the tree-shade that has been **hospitable** to thee.

41. If thou lovest **kine,** tie them; if thou lovest children, beat them [when at fault].

42. [The courtier should understand that] a **king** is like fire. (*Mon.*)

43. **Kissing** the baby touches the mother. (*Mon.*)

44. If **laying** anything, lay [or bury] it deep down.

45. Being a plain man thou must **learn** far more than those who are talented.

46. It is because of there being crystalline ponds that there are **lotus blossoms.**

47. Don't love the **louse** more than the hair.

48. **Love** thyself, guard thyself, and fondle thyself more than wealth.

49. **Love** thyself more than treasures.

50. **Males** are paddy and females hulled rice.

    [i.e. men can take root and settle by themselves in life, whereas women are not self-supporting.]

51. Don't love the **moon** more than the sun.

52. **A needle** with a small eye should be threaded slowly.

    [i.e. the little (or lowly) ones should be taught gently and patiently.]

53. Without **parsimony** thou wilt lose also thy coat.

54. To negotiate the **porridge** without [burning one's palate by] broaching its centre.

[i.e. tact and patience win where brutal rashness fails.]

55. **Praise** teachers while they are present ; subordinates when their work is done, and friends when absent.

56. Talk with the **priest** and you will [find you have sinned enough wherewith to] die a thousand times a day.

57. Keep the common **road** and you are safe.

58. Do not long for more than thy own **share** [in transactions].

59. Being a freeman, don't associate with **slaves.**

60. Little is **spent** with difficulty, much with ease.

61. He who **spits** towards the sky gets it back into his own face.

62. When one goes to a town inhabited by **squint-eyed** people one must squint one's eyes.

63. Beware of **squint-eyed** persons and of buffaloes with outspread horns.

64. If you don't hear the **story** clearly, don't carry it off with you under your arm.

65. When you are among the **swans** you become a swan.

66. Getting one's **tail** wet when about to reach the shore. (*Mon.*)

[i.e. to give up when the end is in sight.]

67. Extract a **thorn** from your skin with a thorn.

68. If a **thorn** sticks into the flesh, a sharp thorn must be used to draw it out. (*Mon.*)

69. To conceal the end of the **thread.**

[i.e. to conceal one's game or hand.]

70. Boneless **tongue.**

[i.e. not keeping one's word.]

71. Don't undermine others with thy **tongue** nor hurt them with thy glances.

72. Ten **tongues** [lit. mouths] asserting are not worth one eye seeing, nor are ten eyes seeing equal to a single hand feeling [one thing].

73. A birdless **tree,** a barren tree.

74. Wait until a **tree** has fallen to skip it.

75. Tuskers, poisonous snakes, old servants, beloved **wife,** do not trust too much.

76. Don't love **wind** more than water.

[i.e. the less useful more than the indispensable.]

77. By mere shunting it may be **wings** [i.e. the wings may be caught in the trap], but by withdrawing altogether it will be only tail [i.e. the tail only will be caught].

78. If the mother be a **witch,** when on the point of death she must spit [in the mouth] of her child, so that it may thereby receive in heirship the power of witchcraft possessed by her.

[It is commonly believed in this country that such is the way by which witches transmit their occult powers to their descendants, and it is held that unless they do so at their life's end they would be doomed to die a slow excruciating death.]

79. Nourish no **worms** that eat timber.

[i.e. be cautious in the selection of your friends.]

TAI (THAI) (ANNAM, INDO-CHINA AND BURMA)

1. The **bird** leaves no trace of its flight.
2. To be **born** is to come out ; to die is to return.
3. A **cock** is fine by reason of its feathers and a man by reason of his wealth.
4. To be born is in the course of nature, but to **die** is according to the decree of destiny.
5. He who **eats** too much feels discomfort, and he who speaks too much cannot be at peace with his neighbour.
6. The **elephant,** after his death, leaves his track, and the shellfish leaves its shell.
7. One **hen** that bursts makes the whole pen stink.

   [i.e. one evil man corrupts his whole surroundings.]
8. If you suffer **misfortune,** do not curse Heaven, but bow your head and quarrel with your soul [your shadow].
9. Where there are many people there are many **mouths,** and where there are many mouths there are many sounds.
10. One cannot breathe through another's **nose.**
11. If one pierces the **nose** the tears come out of the eyes.
12. The **road** is in the mouth of the traveller.

    [i.e. he must use his mouth to ask the way.]
13. When one goes the **road** is rough ; when one returns the road is smooth.
14. To **speak** well one must reflect, and to hit the mark one must aim.
15. One cannot stop the water from a **spring** or tie up the smoke from a fire.
16. The **tree** becomes moss-grown and man becomes bearded.
17. In a man whom we know, we respect nothing but **virtue ;** in a man whom we do not know, we respect nothing but the coat.

TARTAR

1. The master has promised me a **fur coat,** but his word also warms.
2. God will spoil the **sowing** of the man who leaves not a part of his harvest for the birds.
3. The **torch** is dark at its foot.

   [Alludes to the evil in the holy city of Mecca.]
4. Ask the neighbouring **village** what is happening in your own, and the house next door what is happening in yours.

TIBETAN

1. If the **animal's flesh** be eaten by one of merciful mind, it will be led on the road of perfect mercy.
2. Let us drink **beer** and be happy!
3. Beat a **Chinaman** enough and he will speak Tibetan.
4. **Credulity** is better than unbelief.
5. **Eat** according to the height of your meal-bag, and walk according to the width of your track.
6. The scabbard of my blue steel [spear] is the liver of my **enemy.**
7. If the **father's** qualities do not come up to the son, how does the hare get his lip split?
8. There is no hope of **fruit** from a tree which has been robbed of its flowers by the frost.
9. It is no use trying to tug the **glacier** backwards.
10. The **goal** will not be reached if the right distance be not travelled.
11. **Gods,** devils and men are alike in actions and thoughts.
12. **Gossip** is the scum of water, action is the drop of gold.
13. A long **head** is a mark of high birth.
14. If the **heart** be stout a mouse can lift an elephant.
15. If the **house** be rebuilt, then the pillar will fall [one of the family will die].
16. To hold the land of the **king** is even worse than to take the property of the priest.
17. Without a **Lama** in front there is no [approach to] God.
18. Religion's **laws** are soft as silken thread, but strong; the King's laws are heavy like a golden yoke; but the country's laws stand hard as iron pillars, and are inflexible.
19. Despise your own **life,** and you are master of the lives of others.
20. To get **milk** and eggs you must not frighten the cow and hen.
21. What handling will do for other weeds will not do for the **nettle.**
22. Unless words are spoken a son even will not understand his own father; unless a **proclamation** is hoisted in the market-place every man will do as he listeth.
23. The roots of **quarrels** are three, namely: Yes! [assertion], what! [doubting sarcasm], and You! [abuse].
24. Even the nibbling **rabbit** can gorge itself to death.
25. Though they are the country's ornaments, the **rich** die first by hunger's knife when famine comes.
    [i.e. robbed by the poor.]
26. The meek **sheep** should not try to imitate a furious bull.
27. There is no **sin** so great as killing.
28. When the time draws near for a **sinner** to go to hell, his good fortune bursts forth like a flaming fire.
29. You know the depth of the **snow** in the pass by the cry of the snow-cock below.
30. **Speech** must be bold as a lion, soft as a gentle hare, impressive as a serpent, pointed as an arrow, and evenly balanced like a sceptre held in the middle.
31. **Speech** should float forth freely like a bird in the sky, and be clothed in charming dress like a goddess.
32. The **stick** is greater than the King's command.
33. **Summer** comes gently like a mother, Winter comes fiercely like a foe.
34. If you have no debts become **surety** for a friend, if you have no trouble buy an old horse.

35. If your mind is free from care, stand **surety** for a loan! if your body is free from pain, stamp on a dog's tail!
36. India will be ruined by false scruples, **Tibet** by false hopes.
37. Teach ethics to a **wolf.**
38. Keep a **wolf,** but he is no watch-dog.

    [Unreliable servant not worth his keep.]
39. **Words** are mere bubbles of water, but deeds are drops of gold.

TURKI (TURKESTAN)

(Including Turfan)

1. If a **beggar** loses his temper, it is his pouch that suffers. (*Turfan.*)
2. Having mounted the **camel,** don't hide yourself behind the saddle trappings. (*Turfan.*)

    [i.e. people in high positions should not neglect their duties because they feel protected by the place they occupy.]
3. Who does not snatch at a **chance,** will worry himself about it till old age.
4. A **Chinaman** is ill only once in his life, and that is when he is dying.
5. When one beats a **cow** on its horns, the horns of forty cows hurt. (*Turfan.*)
6. He who has been near to **death** knows the worth of life.
7. Ten **dervishes** can sleep under one blanket, but two kings cannot find room in one clime.
8. The one who goes looks towards the **door;** the one who doesn't go looks towards the hole. (*Turfan.*)
9. He who **eats** sparingly eats ten times; he who eats too much eats once. (*Turfan.*)
10. His **excuse** is worse than his fault.
11. When there is **fat** on your hand, smear it on your side. (*Turfan.*)
12. To be a **father** isn't difficult. (*Turfan.*)
13. Who loses the **foe** in his grip?
14. What will a **foe** not say? What enters not into a dream?
15. Distrust your **friend,** he'll stuff your hide with straw.
16. Of my fur coats the new, and of my **friends** the old one is good. (*Turfan.*)
17. When you strike a stone against a rock your **hand** pains. (*Turfan.*)

    [i.e. don't attack anyone stronger than yourself.]
18. Never say, "My **horse** doesn't kick." (*Turfan.*)
19. What you have put into your **kettle** comes afterwards into your spoon. (*Turfan.*)
20. Be **kind** to the horse that carries you, to the cow that feeds you, and to the dog that guards your possessions.
21. A **narrow place** is large to the narrow-minded.
22. Even if a man becomes **old** his heart is not old. (*Turfan.*)
23. The food of the **poor** is medicine for the teeth. (*Turfan.*)
24. The **red tongue** gives the green hand to the wind. (*Proverb of menace.*)
25. A **river,** like a king, obeys no law.
26. Much spotting [dropping] makes a **sea.** (*Turfan.*)

27. He who has **seen** does what he has seen; what does he do who has seen nothing? (*Turfan.*)
28. A **smiling man** is like an open pistachio.
29. Cheap **soup** has no taste. (*Turfan.*)
30. **Travel** is a foretaste of hell.
31. Arabic is science, Persian is sugar, Hindustani is salt, but **Turki** is art.
32. Rather **work** without an object than sit without an object. (*Turfan.*)
33. The **young man** comes to work, the old man comes to food. (*Turfan.*)

TURKISH

(Including Allagish, Illirian, Oezbegish)

An Introduction to this collection by S. Topalian will be found on page ciii.

1. One **accident** teaches us more than a thousand good counsels.
2. A wrong **account** returns even from Bagdad.
3. When **Allah** gives, He does not ask "Whose son art thou?"
4. Who gives **alms,** sows one and reaps one thousand.
5. There is no fall for an **ambassador.**
6. If you get up in **anger,** you will sit down with loss.
7. God made serpents and rabbits and **Armenians.**
8. He who **asks** has one black face; he who refuses has two.
9. The saddle is not counted in the **ass's** burden.
10. **Bachelorhood** is sovereignty.
11. If your [companion] is a good one, **Bagdad** becomes quite near.
12. The **bazaar** knows neither father nor mother.
13. The **bear** knew nine songs; all were on wild pears [or honey].
14. The **bear** that is hungry never dances.
15. Call the **bear** uncle until you have crossed the bridge.
16. When a hungry man goes to bed with a hungry woman, a **beggar** comes into the world.
17. The **beggar's** bag never gets full.
18. Don't look at the **beginning** but at the end of a thing.
19. He who washes a **black-a-moor,** loses his soap.
20. Among the **blind** close your eyes.
21. One does not speak of colour to a **blind man.**
22. You cannot repress the **blood** destined to come out.
23. He who asks to be given, **blushes** once; he who doesn't give, blushes twice.
24. If **bravery** is ten, nine is strategy.
25. He who eats his **bread** alone raises his burden with his teeth alone.
26. No **bread**—no authority.
27. Everything **breaks** because it is weak, only man because he thinks himself too strong.
28. That which is **broken,** keeps not its place.
29. As long as a man **builds,** he lives.
30. The damp **burns** with the dry.
31. **Business** by the ounce, friendship by the pound.
32. One **calamity** is better than a thousand counsels.
33. A public **calamity** is festivity to that which befalls individually.

34. He who is on visiting terms with a **camel-driver** must open his door wide.

35. He who joins a **camel-rider** needs a big gate.

36. The **candle** does not give light to itself.

37. Even if the woman's **candle-stick** be made of gold, it is the man who puts the candle in.

38. Well-doing is the best **capital.**

39. Everyone has **cares** in his head, and the miller water.

40. Time sells the **chaff.**

41. He sprang from a **chestnut shell** and he does not admire his husk.

42. The **chimney** never takes fire except from within.

43. A torn **coat** should not have golden buttons.

44. Where there are many **cocks,** the morning comes early.

[i.e. when too many people have a voice in the matter, no good comes of it.]

45. **Coffee** and tobacco are complete repose.

46. One is always free to **come,** but not always to come back.

47. A man who expects **comfort** must be deaf, blind and dumb.

48. At **Constantinople** fire devours your goods, plague takes your life, and women your wit.

49. The courteous learns his **courtesy** from the discourteous.

50. A **crow** does not pick out the eyes of a crow.

51. A poor man refused a **cucumber** because it was crooked.

52. Close your eyes if there be **darkness** in the place where you have gone.

53. Observe the edge and take the linen, observe the mother and take the **daughter.**

54. Whoever does not beat his **daughters** will one day strike his knees in vain.

55. The **dawn** shows a fine and a bad day.

[Said of people.]

56. **Death** came and headache is only a pretext.

57. **Death** is a black camel which kneels at every man's gate.

[i.e. to take up the burden of a coffin—death is universal, common for everyone.]

58. A thousand cares don't pay one penny of your **debt.**

59. **Debt** is finished by paying and the journey by travelling.

60. A man **deceives** a man only once.

61. Running water takes no **defilement.**

62. For every **descent,** there is an ascent.

63. Few **desires**—happy life.

64. Oh **destiny !** It pleases you to caress a few, and to molest others.

65. The **devil** mixes himself with hasty work.

66. The **devil** tempts the busy man, but the idle man tempts the devil.

67. We **die** as we live.

68. **Disjoining,** it joins.

69. God keep me from judge and **doctor.**

70. To the place where the sun doesn't come, comes the **doctor.**

71. Ask not [advice] from a **doctor ;** ask from a sufferer.

72. Half a **doctor** loses your health ; half a priest your faith.

73. A biting **dog** does not show his teeth.

74. When a **dog** is destined to die, he pollutes the wall of the mosque.

75. He who has killed the **dog** must remove it out of the way.

[i.e. as we make our bed, so we must lie on it.]

76. If the prayers of **dogs** were accepted, bones would rain from the sky.

77. Golden words open an iron **door.**
78. If you cannot shut the **door** again, do not raise the latch.
79. Who does not come in at the **door,** must go out of the window.
80. Were it not for **dreams** and illusions, the poor man's soul would quit [his body].
81. If it does not run, it **drops.**
82. Let your **ear** hear what comes out of your mouth.
83. Man does not **eat** what he desires, but what he finds.
84. He who **eats** when he is full, digs his grave with his teeth.
85. **Economy,** not work, profits.
86. The **egg** of to-day is better than the hen of to-morrow.
87. Yesterday he came out of his **egg,** to-day he does not admire his shell.
88. He who **embraces** much, collects little.
89. Whatever comes is **endured.**
90. Be thine **enemy** an ant, see in him an elephant.
91. He who knows much, **errs** much.
92. I am an **esquire,** you are an esquire, who will harness the horses ?
93. What day is there that we have not had its **evening ?**
94. An old **eye-ache**—an old heart-ache.

    [i.e. an old grief which caused pain.]
95. Far from the **eyes,** farther from the heart.
96. Leave a space, for **face** to look on face.
97. **Falcon** with falcon ; goose with goose ; the bald hen with the lame cock.
98. He that **falls** by himself never cries.
99. He that **falls** has no friends ; only tumble and see.
100. Where a man **falls,** he rises.

    [i.e. the same thing that brings ill luck brings good luck.]
101. **Fame** is not acquired on a feather bed.
102. Where you **fell,** get up.
103. There is no **festival** without a to-morrow.
104. With the smooth-tongued, it is proverbial that there is no **fidelity.**
105. Five **fingers** are not equal.

    [i.e. no equality in anything in the world.]
106. **Fire** is the fruit of a winter's day.

    [i.e. everything has its season.]
107. He who fears **fire,** protects himself from smoke.
108. One often throws oneself into the **fire** to escape the smoke.
109. The **fireside** is the tulip-bed of a winter day.
110. **Fish** begin to stink from the head.

    [i.e. corruption starts from the upper classes.]
111. Every **fish** that escapes, appears great.
112. The **flesh** separates not from the bone.

    [Said of two inseparable people or things.]
113. They divided the **flowers ;** the rose fell to the lot of the thorn.
114. One **fool** throws a stone into the sea, and forty wise men can't get it out.
115. He is a **fool** who speaks and listens to himself.
116. The suffering of an unreasonable head is borne by the **foot.**
117. He who slips with his **foot** shows many the way.
118. To bray in a **foreign land** is like singing in the bath.

    [i.e. useless.]
119. Better a **fox** roaming, than a lion sleeping.
120. An old **friend** is a mount for a black day.
121. The **friend** looks at the head, the enemy at the foot.
122. For the mill, two millstones ; for **friendship** two hearts.

123. Eat the **fruit**—don't enquire of the tree.
124. Ripe **fruit** falls to the ground.
125. The teeth of a **gift horse** are not to be inspected.
126. A small **gift** comes from the heart, a big gift from the purse.
127. Man is the slave of **gifts.**
128. What I **give** away is mine.
129. He that **gives** little gives from his heart.
130. He **gives** twice who gives quickly.
131. The nest of a blind bird is made by **God.**
132. **God** is the enemy of the proud.
133. **God** is with the patient.
134. **God** only gives man as much as his heart craves.
135. May **God** preserve us from too little food and too many words.
136. What **God** reserves for one no one else profits by.
137. When **God** wants to please a poor man He first makes him lose his ass and then find it again.
138. Don't make your **golden name** copper.
139. Who **gossips** to you will gossip of you.
140. The **grape,** observing the grape, becomes black.
141. He flings **grass** to the lion and flesh to the horse.
142. The eyes of the **great** are dim.
143. If **guilt** were even a sable fur, no one would wear it.
144. Long **hair**—little brain.
145. Don't move that which your own **hand** didn't put down.
146. The **hand** that gives is above the hand that takes.
147. Kiss the **hands** that you cannot cut off.
148. To find **happiness** one must walk till he be wearied.
149. He who seeks for **harm** finds it.
150. A big **head** has a big headache.
[i.e. a man of importance has many responsibilities.]
151. A bowed **head** is not cut off.
[i.e. humility in admitting a fault.]
152. The **head** that bleeds is seldom cut off.
153. To him who is in **health** every day is a wedding.
154. That which comes in a **heap** goes in a mountain.
155. It is only by sacrificing a head that one conquers a **heart.**
156. In every **heart** a lion sleeps.
157. The **heart** has its summer and its winter.
158. The **heart** is a child ; it hopes as it desires.
159. The **heart** is a glass castle ; when it is broken it cannot be set up.
160. There is a road from **heart** to heart.
161. The father's **heir** is like a burning candle.
162. Even a **hen,** when it drinks, looks towards heaven.
163. From a low [lying] place even a little **hill** appears a mountain.
164. He who lives on **hope** dies hungry.
165. **Hope** is half happiness. (*Oezbegish.*)
166. Everyone mounts a low **horse.**
[i.e. anyone can do an easy thing.]
167. The **horse** kicks out and the mule kicks out ; between the two the donkey dies.
[i.e. when the great quarrel, the small pay the penalty.]
168. The **horse** knows by the bridle who leads it.
169. Tend your **horse** like a friend but ride him as an enemy.
170. " **If** " and " when " were planted and " nothing " grew up.
171. **Ignorance** is always repentance.
172. From the house of the **Imam** comes no food ; from the eyes of the dead come no tears.
[i.e. the Imam is stingy.]
173. No matter how large the mosque is, the **Imam** [priest] preaches what he knows.

174. **Industry** is often concealed under a straw.
175. Buy the respect of the **insolent.**
176. While it rains fill the **jar.**
177. The water of a fresh **jar** is cold.
178. To him of good **judgment** the sound of a gnat suffices, but to him who lacks it, the noise of an orchestra availeth not.
179. A full **kettle** boils late.
[i.e. good things come about slowly.]
180. **Kill,** but make no laws.
181. The **knife** does not make the cork.
182. He who **knows** does not speak ; he who speaks does not know.
183. The **leaf** does not move unless the wind blows.
184. The **legs** bear the faults of the head.
185. **A letter** written after dinner is read in hell.
186. **A liar's candle** burns until the Yatsi [first watch] of the night.
187. At the near end of the market-square he told a **lie ;** at the far end he himself believed it.
188. He who says what he **likes** hears what he doesn't like.
189. Two **lions** cannot be on one skin.
190. **A listener** needs more intelligence than a speaker.
191. He who doesn't know the **little** will never see the much.
192. **A loan** goes smilingly, smilingly, [but] comes weepingly, weepingly.
193. Each **loss** is counsel.
194. For the **lover** Bagdad is not remote.
195. For a **madman** every day is a feast day [holiday].
196. He who **makes** waits.
197. He who **marries** early makes no mistake.
198. The **master** of the house is the guest of the servant.
199. **Measure** a thousand times and cut once.
200. For hard **meat** a sharp tooth.
201. The caprice of fate gives to the one a ripe, to the other an unripe **melon.**
202. **Memory** is a falcon, that if it be caught is not held ; affection is a sparrow's nest, that if it be crushed is not made [again].
203. Among ten **men,** nine are women.
204. The **mill** must have two stones. (*Marriage proverb.*)
205. He who steals a **minaret** must prepare a holder.
206. White **money** for a black day.
207. The face of **money** is warm.
208. If the **mosque** is destroyed, the Mihrab [prayer niche, or altar] remains.
209. What is necessary to a **mosque** is unlawful to a seminary.
210. His **mother** an onion, his father garlic, himself comes out conserve of rose.
211. The **mother** of a timid son never weeps.
212. He who climbs a **mountain** does not seek a plain.
[i.e. don't expect to find things the same as they are at home.]
213. He who has burnt his **mouth** with milk blows on ice-cream.
214. The flood goes but the **mud** remains.
215. A **nail** may save a horseshoe, a horseshoe a horse, a horse a rider, and a rider a country.
216. Two **naked** people only suit each other in the bath.
217. He who would have peace in his own house should not knock at his **neighbour's** door.
218. **Once,** for ever.
219. **Opportunity** makes of the honest and devout man a thief.
220. To the Greek wealth, to the Circassian beauty, to the Frank wealth, but to the **Osmanli** majesty.
221. A creaking **pack-saddle** gives the horse's ear no peace. (*Allagish.*)

222. He who hides his **pain** finds no cure.

223. The cheapest **passions** in the world are hope and love, and they exact the heaviest payment in the end.

224. The **past** is the past.

225. **Patience** is the key of Paradise.

226. Who enters without contract goes out without **paying.**

227. If your friend has made the **pilgrimage** once, distrust him ; if twice, cut him dead.

228. He that begins the **play** must continue it.

229. One doesn't **play** with wool and fire at the same time.

230. Though they are brothers their **pockets** are not sisters.

231. He who gives to the **poor** lends to God.

232. **Poverty** is a shirt of fire.

233. He lingered between two mosques and returned home without having **prayed.**

234. The **prayer** of the stranger is accepted.

235. **Promises** never exhaust the estate.

236. He who does not heed **proverbs** will not avoid mistakes.

237. Nourish a **raven** and it will pick out thine eyes.

238. The foundation of a late **repentance** does not abide.

239. It is your **reputation** that makes your work succeed, not yourself.

240. The wealth of the **rich** tires the chin of the poor.

241. Beware of the smooth currents of a **river** and a man's glances on the ground.

242. No matter how far you have gone on a wrong **road,** turn back.

243 Where one rides there is a **road** ; where one lives there is a people. (*Allagish.*)

244. All, even to his slippers, is thrown upon the **roof.**

245. For the sake of one **rose** the gardener becomes the servant of a thousand thorns.

246. He who loves the **rose** resigns himself to suffering from the thorns.

247. Do not open the mouth of the **sack.**

248. **Satan's** friendship reaches to the prison door.

249. Find the gate of **satisfaction.**

250. He who comes may also **see.**

251. He who **seeks,** finds either his God or his misfortune.

252. The end of **separation** is meeting again.

253. He that falls in the sea takes hold of the **serpent** to be saved.

254. He who has not learned to do **service** cannot do mastership.

255. To demand is a **shame** ; not to give is a two-fold shame.

256. A tethered **sheep** grazes where it is tied.

257. Every **sheep** is hung up by its own leg.

[i.e. everyone must bear the consequence of their own acts.]

258. It is well for the **shopkeeper** to be lame of one foot.

259. The grass that the **snake** hates grows just under its nose.

260. Who has the seal is the **Solomon.**

261. Until the **soup** boils over the ladle has no value.

262. Whatsoever a man **soweth,** that shall he also reap.

263. If you would be **spared,** spare others.

264. Sit crooked but **speak** straight.

265. A dry **spoon** doesn't please.

266. **Starve** together—eat together.

267. Man is harder than **stone** and more delicate than the rose.

268. A building **stone** never remains out of a building.

269. The **sufferer** becomes a chatterer.

270. The **sword** is for him who wears it, the bridge for him who crosses it, the horse for him who mounts it.

271. Let us sit bent but **talk** straight.

272. He who sheds **tears** for everyone in the end loses his eyes.

273. That is not necessary to a chapel which belongs to a **temple.**

274. An insolent **thief** accuses the owner.

275. If the **thief** lies, the theft doesn't. (*Illirian.*)

276. He who has exalted **thoughts** doesn't reach the evening, and he who takes long steps doesn't reach the door. (*Allagish.*)

277. Give to no one the end of the **thread.**

278. If **time** is not favourable to thee, render thyself favourable to it.

279. **To-morrow** is also a day.

280. All that one suffers from unhappiness comes from the **tongue.**

281. The **tongue** has no bone, yet it crushes.

282. The good man carries his heart on his **tongue** ; the prudent man carries his tongue in his heart.

283. The too-flattering **tongue** will soon have to lick wounds. (*Oezbegish.*)

284. The **tool** works but the hand gets the praise.

285. The **tooth,** not the hand, is the real saver.

286. A **trade** is an estate for life.

287. There is many an axe that strikes a fallen **tree.**

288. In the shelter of a single **tree** a thousand sheep will collect.

[i.e. many want to benefit from a rich man.]

289. He who tells the **truth** is turned out of nine cities.

290. He who speaks the **truth** must have one foot in the stirrup.

291. Don't be deceived by the whiteness of the **turban** ; soap is bought on credit.

292. Where the horse of the **Turk** goes grass ceases to grow.

293. Every " **up** " has its " down " and every " going " its " coming ".

294. The thicker the **veil,** the less worth lifting.

295. The **vessel** leans but the road is straight.

296. A **village** in sight does not require a guide.

297. **Vinegar** given is sweeter than honey.

298. A **vineyard** does not require prayers, but a hoe.

299. The **wagon** is broken in pieces, yet the signposts are many.

300. Damp casts down **walls** ; trouble casts down men.

301. Do not drink **water** from a free fountain.

[i.e. avoid freely given things.]

302. **Water** is clear only when it has first been muddy.

[i.e. good times follow bad.]

303. The **wealth** of those with means tires the chin of those without means.

304. A **weapon** is an enemy even to its owner.

305. One knows already on **Wednesday** that Thursday will come.

[i.e. when things are bad they are not likely to be better the next day.]

306. One cannot dig a **well** with a needle.

307. The quite stupid praises his **wife** ; the quite wise praises his dog. (*Allagish.*)

308. The **wise** man says not what he knows ; the fool knows not what he says.

309. Take a dog if you accept an invitation from a **wolf.**

310. It is a good thing to listen to the words of one **woman** in forty.

311. With dry **wood,** green wood also burns.

312. One **word** brings out another.

313. A fair **word** opens an iron door.

314. **Working** is half religion.

315. He whose wind is favourable laughs at the **world.**

316. The **world** a cauldron—man the ladle.

317. If my shoe is narrow, what matter if the **world** is wide?

318. The **wrong** side is dearer than the right.

319. The **wound** from a knife heals; the wound from a tongue never.

320. If one knew the value of **youth** there would be little to lament in old age.

RELIGIONS

(Buddhism, Christianity and Judaism [Bible: Old Testament, Proverbs of Solomon, New Testament and Apocrypha], Confucianism, Egyptian, Hinduism, Islam, Jainism, Shinto, Sikh, Súfiism, Taoism and Zoroastrianism)

An Introduction to this section by P. Macleod Yearsley, F.R.C.S., F.R.A.I., will be found on page lxxxviii.

All Religions start from Asia. (*Japanese Proverb.*)

Among cultured peoples there now exist only eleven distinct religious systems which have lived for more than one hundred years and which have maintained their own art, literature, social organization, and ecclesiastical worship. Considered chronologically, only two religions, Islamism and Sikhism, have originated later than the beginning of the Christian era. All the other eight living religions of the world, namely: Hinduism, Judaism, Shintoism, Zoroastrianism, Taoism, Jainism, Buddhism and Confucianism are more ancient than Christianity by at least five hundred years. Considered geographically, all of these eleven religions originated in the Continent of Asia. All the other Continents, Europe, Africa, North America, South America and Australia, have produced religions of a kind, but no religion with the power of survival. Southern Asia gave birth to four of the living religions, namely: Hinduism, Jainism, Buddhism and Sikhism—all born in India. China, Japan, and Eastern Asia produced three distinct religions: Confucianism, Taoism and Shintoism. From Western Asia there sprang four other living religions: Judaism, Zoroastrianism, Christianity and Islamism . . . the only religions which have managed to survive the devastations of time are the ones which possess a canon of sacred scriptures revered as authoritative depositories of saving truths.

Extract from the Preface to R. E. Hume's
Treasure House of the Living Religions.

BUDDHISM

1. He who is free from **affection** [greed or love] knows neither grief nor fear.

2. They **blame** him who sits silent, they blame him who speaks much, they also blame him who says little; there is no one on earth who is not blamed.

3. Destroy all passions when you light **Buddha's lamp.**

4. There is no **eye** like the understanding, no blindness like ignorance, no enemy like sickness, nothing so dreaded as death.

5. Those who love nothing, and hate nothing, have no **fetters.**

6. The **gem** of the sky is the sun; the gem of the house is the child; in the assembly the wise man.

7. Save thyself by **giving**; what's given is well saved.

8. **Good people** walk on, whatever befall.

9. Whatever **happiness** is in the world has arisen from a wish for the welfare of others; whatever misery there is has arisen from indulging selfishness.

10. There is no losing throw like **hatred.**

11. Let a man overcome anger by **kindness,** evil by good, the stingy by a gift, the liar by truth.

12. **Liberality,** courtesy, kindliness, and unselfishness—these are to the world what the linchpin is to the rolling chariot.

13. So long as the **love** of man towards women, even the smallest, is not destroyed, so long is his mind in bondage, as the calf that drinks milk is to its mother.

14. When thou hast cut off passion and hatred, thou wilt go to **Nirvâna.**

15. There is no fire like **passion,** there is no shark like hatred, there is no snare like folly, there is no torment like greed.

16. **Patience** is the greatest prayer.

17. Let a man make himself what he **preaches** to others.

18. To the virtuous all is **pure.**

19. Cut out the love of **self.**

20. As long as the **sin** bears no fruit, the fool thinks it honey.

21. **Speech** must be bold as a lion, gentle and soft as a hare, impressive as a serpent, pointed as an arrow, and evenly balanced as a waist held by its middle.

22. The **taint** of prayers is non-repetition; the taint of houses, non-repair; the taint of the body is sloth.

23. All that we are is the result of what we have **thought;** it is founded on our thoughts; it is made up of our thoughts.

24. Well-makers lead the water; fletchers bend the arrow; carpenters bend a log of wood; **wise people** fashion themselves,

CHRISTIANITY AND JUDAISM

BIBLE

OLD TESTAMENT

1. Doth the wild **ass** bray when he hath grass, or loweth the ox over his fodder? (*Job vi.*)

2. A time to be **born** and a time to die. (*Ecclesiastes iii.*)

3. Cast thy **bread** upon the waters; for thou shalt find it after many days. (*Ecclesiastes xi.*)

4. What is the **chaff** to the wheat? (*Jeremiah xxiii.*)

5. The race is not to the swift, nor the battle to the strong, neither yet bread to the wise, nor yet riches to men of understanding, nor yet favour to men of skill; but time and **chance** happeneth to them all. (*Ecclesiastes ix.*)

6. **Day** unto day uttereth speech, and night unto night sheweth knowledge. (*Psalm xix.*)

7. Yea, though I walk through the valley of the shadow of **death,** I will fear no evil: for thou art with me; thy rod and thy staff they comfort me. (*Psalm xxiii.*)

8. For the **ear** trieth words as the mouth tasteth meat. (*Job xxxiv.*)

9. Can an **Ethiopian** change his skin, or the leopard his spots? (*Jeremiah xiii.*)

10. Walk in the light of your **fire,** and in the sparks that ye have kindled. (*Isaiah iv.*)

11. The **fool** hath said in his heart, there is no God. (*Psalm liii.*)

12. The **fool** will speak folly. (*Isaiah xx.*)

13. Endless would be the fire-offerings required for our sins and numberless the sweet savours for our trespasses; but thou knowest that our latter end is death, and therefore hast thou multiplied the measures of our **forgiveness.** (*Jewish cry for forgiveness, Day of Atonement, 16th September.*) (*Talmud.*)

14. Or ever the silver cord be loosed, or the **golden bowl** broken, or the pitcher be broken at the fountain, or the wheel broken at the cistern, then shall the dust return to the earth as it was; and the spirit shall return unto God who gave it. (*Ecclesiastes xii.*)

15. The fathers have eaten a sour **grape** and the children's teeth are set on edge. (*Proverb concerning the Children of Israel.*) *Jeremiah xxxi.*)

16. When they shall be afraid of that which is high, and fears shall be in the way, and the almond-tree shall flourish, and the **grasshopper** shall be a burden, and desire shall fail, because man goeth to his long home, and the mourners go about the streets. (*Ecclesiastes xii.*)

17. Ye shall bring down my **grey hairs** with sorrow to the grave. (*Genesis xlii.*)

18. Whatsoever thy **hand** findeth to do, do it with thy might. (*Ecclesiastes ix.*)

19. Thou shalt open thy **hand** wide unto thy brother, to thy poor, and to thy needy, in thy land. (*Deuteronomy xv.*)

20. For he maketh sore, and bindeth up: he woundeth, and his **hands** make whole. (*Job v.*)

21. The **heart** is deceitful above all things, and desperately wicked; who can know it? (*Jeremiah xvii.*)

22. Take counsel, execute **judgment;** make thy shadow as the night in the midst of the noonday; hide the outcasts; betray not him that wandereth. (*Isaiah xvi.*)

23. Thy word is a **lamp** unto my feet. (*Psalm cxix.*)

24. **Learn** to do well; seek judgment, relieve the oppressed, plead for the widow. (*Isaiah i.*)

25. The **lines** are fallen unto me in pleasant places; yea, I have a goodly heritage. (*Psalm xvi.*)

26. Many waters cannot quench **love,** neither can the floods drown it. (*Song of Solomon viii.*)

27. A feast is made for laughter, and wine maketh merry; but **money** answereth all things. (*Ecclesiastes x.*)

28. Behold, to **obey** is better than sacrifice, and to hearken than the fat of rams. (*1 Samuel xv.*)

29. The **ox** knoweth his owner, and the ass his master's crib. (*Isaiah i.*)

30. And thou shalt become an astonishment, a **proverb,** and a byword among all nations. (*Deuteronomy xxviii.*)

31. Therefore it became a **proverb,** is Saul also among the prophets? (*1 Samuel x.*)

32. He gave good heed, and sought out, and set in order many **proverbs.** (*Ecclesiastes xii.*)

33. And he, Solomon, spake three thousand **proverbs,** and his songs were a thousand and five. (*1 Kings iv.*)

34. **Rest** in the Lord, and wait patiently for Him; fret not thyself because of him who prospereth in his way. (*Psalm xxxvii.*)

35. Be not **righteous** over much; neither make thyself over wise. (*Ecclesiastes vii.*)

36. **Skin** for skin. (*Job ii.*)

37. He that observeth the wind shall not **sow;** and he that regardeth the clouds shall not reap. (*Ecclesiastes xi.*)

38. Be **still** and know that I am God. (*Psalm xlvi.*)

39. My **times** are in Thy hand. (*Psalm xxxi.*)
40. Yet man is born unto **trouble,** as the sparks fly upward. (*Job v.*)
41. **Vanity** of vanities, saith the preacher; all is vanity. (*Ecclesiastes i.*)
42. They shall sit every man under his **vine** and under his fig-tree. (*Micah iv.*)
43. The **waters** wear the stones. (*Job xiv.*)
44. My days are swifter than a **weaver's shuttle.** (*Job vi.*)
45. There the **wicked** cease from troubling: and the weary be at rest. (*Job iii.*)
46. Out of the **wicked** cometh forth wickedness. (*1 Samuel xxiv.*)
47. For they have sown the **wind,** and they shall reap the whirlwind. (*Hosea viii.*)
48. Keep me as the apple of the eye, hide me under the shadow of Thy **wings.** (*Psalm xvii.*)
49. For in much **wisdom** is much grief: and he that increaseth knowledge increaseth sorrow. (*Ecclesiastes i.*)
50. Remember now thy Creator in the days of thy **youth,** while the evil days come not, nor the years draw nigh when thou shalt say I have no pleasure in them. (*Ecclesiastes xii.*)

PROVERBS OF SOLOMON

The Proverbs of Solomon, the Son of David, King of Israel

To know wisdom and instruction; to perceive the words of understanding. (*Ch. i.*)

To understand a proverb, and the interpretation, the words of the wise, and their dark sayings. (*Ch. i.*)

1. If thou faint in the day of **adversity,** thy strength is small. (*Ch. xxiv.*)
2. He that is slow to **anger** is better than the mighty; and he that ruleth his spirit than he that taketh a city. (*Ch. xvi.*)
3. A soft **answer** turneth away wrath. (*Ch. xxv.*)
4. Go to the **ant,** thou sluggard; consider her ways and be wise. (*Ch. vi.*)
5. **Children's** children are the crown of old men; and the glory of children are their fathers. (*Ch. xvii.*)
6. In the multitude of **counsellors** there is safety. (*Ch. xxiv.*)
7. The hand of the **diligent** maketh rich. (*Ch. x.*)
8. The hearing **ear,** and the seeing eye. (*Ch. xx.*)
9. If thine **enemy** be hungry, give him bread to eat; and if he be thirsty, give him water to drink. (*Ch. xxv.*)
10. As in water, **face** answereth face, so the heart of man to man. (*Ch. xxvii.*)
11. A **faithful man** who can find? (*Ch. xx.*)
12. Ponder the path of thy **feet.** (*Ch. iv.*)
13. Where no wood is, there the **fire** goeth out: so where there is no tale-bearer, the strife ceaseth. (*Ch. xxvi.*)
14. A reproof entereth more into a wise man than a hundred stripes into a **fool.** (*Ch. xvii.*)
15. Answer a **fool** according to his folly, lest he be wise in his own conceit. (*Ch. xxvi.*)
16. Answer not a **fool** according to his folly, lest thou also be like unto him. (*Ch. xxvi.*)
17. Though thou shouldest bray a **fool** in a mortar among wheat with a pestel, yet will not his foolishness depart from him. (*Ch. xxvii.*)
18. Let a bear robbed of her whelps meet a man rather than a **fool** in his folly. (*Ch. xvii.*)
19. Seeth thou a man that is hasty in his words? There is more hope of a **fool** than of him. (*Ch. xxix.*)

20. Seest thou a man wise in his own conceit? There is more hope of a **fool** than of him. (*Ch. xxvi.*)

21. Even a **fool,** when he holdeth his peace, is counted wise: and he that shutteth his lips is esteemed a man of understanding. (*Ch. xvii.*)

22. The legs of the lame are not equal: so is a parable in the mouth of **fools.** (*Ch. xxvi.*)

23. A whip for a horse, a bridle for the ass, and a rod for the **fool's** back. (*Ch. xxvi.*)

24. **Four things** say not, "It is enough"—the grave; and the barren womb; the earth that is not filled with water; and the fire that saith not, "It is enough." (*Ch. xxx.*)

25. There be **four things** which are too wonderful for me, which I know not—the way of an eagle in the air; the way of a serpent upon a rock; the way of a ship in the midst of the sea; and the way of a man with a maid. (*Ch. xxx.*)

26. **A friend** loveth at all times, and a brother is born for adversity. (*Ch. xvii.*)

27. A man that hath **friends** must show himself friendly. (*Ch. xviii.*)

28. A man's **gift** maketh room for him. (*Ch. xviii.*)

29. Most men will proclaim everyone his own **goodness**; but a faithful man who can find? (*Ch. xx.*)

30. The hoary **head** is a crown of glory. (*Ch. xvi.*)

31. The **heart** knoweth its own bitterness; and a stranger doth not intermeddle with his joy. (*Ch. xiv.*)

32. Keep thy **heart** with all diligence; for out of it are the issues of life. (*Ch. iv.*)

33. **Hope** deferred maketh the heart sick: but when the desire cometh, it is a tree of life. (*Ch. xiii.*)

34. Take fast hold of **instruction**; let her not go: keep her; for she is thy life. (*Ch. iv.*)

35. In all **labour** there is profit: but the talk of the lips tendeth only to penury. (*Ch. xiv.*)

36. The **lambs** are for thy clothing, and the goats are the price of the field. (*Ch. xxvii.*)

37. Remove not the old **landmark,** and enter not into the fields of the fatherless. (*Ch. xxiii.*)

38. The **liberal soul** shall be made fat. (*Ch. xi.*)

39. Better is a dinner of herbs where **love** is, than a stalled ox and hatred therewith. (*Ch. xv.*)

40. Let not **mercy** and truth forsake thee; bind them about thy neck; write them upon the table of thine heart. (*Ch. iii.*)

41. **A merry heart** doeth good like a medicine; but a broken spirit drieth the bones. (*Ch. xvii.*)

42. Far better is a **neighbour** that is near than a brother far off. (*Ch. xxvii.*)

43. Withdraw thy foot from thy **neighbour's** house; lest he be weary of thee, and so hate thee. (*Ch. xxv.*)

44. Surely in vain the **net** is spread in the sight of any bird. (*Ch. i.*)

45. Where no **oxen** are the crib is clean. (*Ch. xiv.*)

46. Whoso stoppeth his ears at the cry of the **poor,** he also shall cry himself, but shall not be heard. (*Ch. xxi.*)

47. He that hath pity upon the **poor** lendeth unto the Lord; and that which he hath given will He pay him again. (*Ch. xix.*)

48. Give me neither **poverty** nor riches. (*Ch. xxx.*)

49. Let another man **praise** thee, not thine own mouth; a stranger, and not thine own lips. (*Ch. xxvii.*)

50. **Pride** goeth before destruction, and a haughty spirit before a fall. (*Ch. xvi.*)

51. The wise in heart shall be called **prudent**; and the sweetness of the lips increaseth learning. (*Ch. xvi.*)

52. Better is a dry morsel and **quietness** therewith, than a house full of sacrifices with strife. (*Ch. xvii.*)
53. Open **rebuke** is better than secret love. (*Ch. xxvii.*)
54. **Righteousness** exalteth a nation. (*Ch. xiv.*)
55. There is that **scattereth,** and yet increaseth; and there is that withholdeth more than is meet, but it tendeth to poverty. (*Ch. xi.*)
56. The fining pot is for **silver,** and the furnace for gold. (*Ch. xvii.*)
57. Take away the dross from the **silver** and there shall come forth a vessel for the finer. (*Ch. xxv.*)
58. Yet a little **sleep,** a little slumber, a little folding of the hands to sleep. (*Ch. vi.*)
59. Love not **sleep** lest thou come to poverty: open thine eyes, and thou shalt be satisfied with bread. (*Ch. xx.*)
60. The **spirit** of a man will sustain his infirmity; but a wounded spirit who can bear? (*Ch. xviii.*)
61. It is an honour for a man to cease from **strife;** but every fool will be meddling. (*Ch. xx.*)
62. He that passeth by, and meddleth with **strife** belonging not to him, is like one that taketh a dog by the ears. (*Ch. xxvi.*)
63. Boast not thyself of **to-morrow;** for thou knowest not what a day may bring forth. (*Ch. xxvii.*)
64. He that covereth a **transgression** seeketh love; but he that repeateth a matter separateth very friends. (*Ch. xvii.*)
65. Buy the **truth,** and sell it not; also wisdom, and instruction, and understanding. (*Ch. xxiii.*)
66. Where there is no **vision** the people perish. (*Ch. xxix.*)
67. Stolen **waters** are sweet, and bread eaten in secret is pleasant. (*Ch. ix.*)
68. Drink **waters** out of thine own cistern, and running waters out of thine own well. (*Ch. v.*)
69. There is a **way** that seemeth right unto man, but the end thereof are the ways of death. (*Ch. xvi.*)
70. Who hath woe? Who hath sorrow? Who hath contentions? Who hath babbling? Who hath wounds without cause? Who hath redness of eyes? They that tarry long at the **wine.** (*Ch. xxiii.*)
71. Look not thou upon the **wine** when it is red . . . thine eyes shall behold strange women, and thine heart shall utter perverse things. (*Ch. xxiii.*)
72. **Wisdom** is the principal thing; therefore get wisdom; and with all thy getting, get understanding. (*Ch. iv.*)
73. **A word** fitly spoken is like apples of gold in pictures of silver. (*Ch. xxv.*)
74. The glory of **young men** is their strength; and the beauty of old men is the grey head. (*Ch. xx.*)

NEW TESTAMENT

1. When thou doest thine **alms** do not sound a trumpet before thee. (*St. Matthew vi.*)
2. Be not forgetful to entertain strangers; for thereby some have entertained **angels** unawares. (*Hebrews xiii.*)
3. **Ask,** and it shall be given you; seek, and ye shall find; knock, and it shall be opened unto you. (*St. Matthew vii.*)
4. If the **blind** guide the blind, both shall fall into a pit. (*St. Matthew xv.*)
5. It is written that man shall not live by **bread** alone. (*St. Matthew iv.*)
6. For every man shall bear his own **burden.** (*Galatians vi.*)
7. Bear ye one another's **burdens,** and so fulfil the law of Christ. (*Galatians vi.*)

8. It is easier for a **camel** to go through the eye of a needle than for a rich man to enter the Kingdom of God. (*St. Matthew xix.*)
9. Wheresoever the **carcass** is, there will the eagles be gathered together. (*St. Matthew xxiv.*)
10. And now abideth faith, hope, charity, these three; but the greatest of these is **charity.** (*1 Corinthians xiii.*)
11. Let all your things be done with **charity.** (*1 Corinthians xvi.*)
12. **Charity** beareth all things, believeth all things, hopeth all things, endureth all things, and never faileth. (*1 Corinthians xiii.*)
13. Though I speak with the tongues of men and of angels, and have not **charity,** I am become as sounding brass, or a tinkling cymbal. (*1 Corinthians xiii.*)
14. **Charity** shall cover the multitude of sins. (*1 Peter iv.*)
15. **Charity** suffereth long, and is kind; charity envieth not; charity vaunteth not itself, is not puffed up; doth not behave itself unseemly, seeketh not her own, is not easily provoked, thinketh no evil. (*1 Corinthians xiii.*)
16. Whosoever shall smite thee on the right **cheek,** turn to him the other also. (*St. Matthew v.*)
17. Suffer little **children** to come unto me, and forbid them not: for of such is the Kingdom of God. (*St. Mark x.*)
18. Be not wise in your own **conceits.** (*Romans xii.*)
19. Let us eat and drink, for tomorrow we **die.** (*1 Corinthians xv.*)
20. For scarcely for a righteous man will one **die**; yet peradventure for a good man some would even dare to die. (*Romans v.*)
21. The **dog** is turned to his own vomit again; and the sow that was washed, to her wallowing in the mire. (*2 Peter iii.*)
22. He that hath **ears** to hear, let him hear. (*St. Matthew xi.*)
23. Be not deceived: **evil** communications corrupt good manners. (*1 Corinthians xv.*)
24. Sufficient unto the day is the **evil** thereof. (*St. Matthew vi.*)
25. The light of the body is the **eye**; if therefore thy eye be single, thy whole body shall be full of light. (*St. Matthew vi.*)
26. **Faith** is the substance of things hoped for, the evidence of things not seen. (*Hebrews xi.*)
27. Let him that thinketh he standeth take heed lest he **fall.** (*1 Corinthians x.*)
28. When thou makest a **feast** call the poor, the maimed, the lame, the blind; and thou shalt be blessed; for they cannot recompense thee. (*St. Luke xiv.*)
29. Behold how great a matter a little **fire** kindleth. (*James iii.*)
30. A man's **foes** shall be they of his own household. (*St. Matthew x.*)
31. For ye suffer **fools** gladly, seeing ye yourselves are wise. (*2 Corinthians xi.*)
32. I will never leave thee nor **forsake** thee. (*Hebrews xiii.*)
33. Ye shall know them by their **fruits.** Do men gather grapes of thorns, or figs of thistles? (*St. Matthew vii.*)
34. **Give** and it shall be given unto you, good measure pressed down and shaken together and running over shall men give into your bosom. (*St. Luke vi.*)
35. For he that hath, to him shall be **given**; and he that hath not, from him shall be taken even that which he hath. (*St. Mark iv.*)
36. If **God** be for us, who can be against us? (*Romans viii.*)
37. Lift up the **hands** which hang down, and the feeble knees; make straight paths for your feet, lest that which is lame be turned out of the way. (*Hebrews xii.*)
38. Let not your **heart** be troubled, neither let it be afraid. (*St. John xiv.*)

39. Out of the abundance of the **heart** the mouth speaketh. (*St. Matthew xii.*)
40. Be clothed with **humility** (*1 Peter v.*)
41. **Judge** not that ye be not judged. (*St. Matthew vii.*)
42. It is hard for thee to **kick** against the pricks. (*Acts xxvi.*)
43. Come unto me all ye that **labour** and are heavy laden. (*St. Matthew ix.*)
44. A little **leaven** leaveneth the whole lump. (*1 Corinthians v.*)
45. And if ye **lend** to them of whom ye hope to receive, what thanks have ye? For sinners also lend to sinners to receive as much again . . . lend hoping for nothing again. (*St. Luke vi.*)
46. Whosoever will save his **life** shall lose it. (*St. Matthew xvi.*)
47. Let brotherly **love** continue. (*Hebrews xiii.*)
48. **Love** your enemies, do good to them that hate you, bless them that curse you, and pray for them which despitefully use you, and unto him that smiteth thee on the one cheek, offer also the other, and for him that taketh away thy cloak forbid not to take thy coat also. (*St. Luke vi.*)
49. In **malice** be ye children, but in understanding be men. (*1 Corinthians xiv.*)
50. No man can serve two **masters** . . . ye cannot serve God and mammon. (*St. Matthew vi.*)
51. With what **measure** ye meet, it shall be measured unto you. (*St. Matthew vii.*)
52. Is not the life more than **meat,** and the body than raiment? (*St. Matthew vi.*)
53. Whosoever shall compel thee to go a **mile,** go with him twain. (*St. Matthew v.*)
54. Let your **moderation** be known unto all men. (*Philippians iv.*)
55. For the love of **money** is the root of all evil. (*Timothy vi.*)
56. Take therefore no thought for the **morrow** . . . sufficient unto the day is the evil thereof. (*St. Matthew vii.*)
57. Thou shalt love thy **neighbour** as thyself. (*St. Matthew xix.*)
58. The **night** cometh when no man can work. (*St. John ix.*)
59. The **night** is far spent, the day is at hand. (*Romans xiii.*)
60. Thou shalt not muzzle the mouth of the **ox** that treadeth out the corn. (*1 Corinthians ix.*)
61. The **peace** of God, which passeth all understanding, shall keep your hearts and minds. (*Philippians iv.*)
62. They that be whole need not a **physician,** but they that are sick. (*St. Matthew ix.*)
63. **Physician** heal thyself. (*St. Luke iv.*)
64. No man, having put his hand to the **plough,** and looking back, is fit for the kingdom. (*St. Luke ix.*)
65. Watch and **pray,** that ye enter not into temptation; the spirit indeed is willing, but the flesh is weak. (*St. Matthew xxvi.*)
66. And all things whatsoever ye shall ask in **prayer,** believing, ye shall receive. (*St. Matthew xxi.*)
67. **A prophet** is not without honour, save in his own country, and in his own house. (*St. Matthew xiii.*)
68. These things have I [Jesus] spoken unto you in **proverbs,** but the time cometh, when I shall no more speak unto you in proverbs. (*St. John xvi.*)
69. Unto the **pure** all things are pure. (*Titus i.*)
70. **Reaping** where thou didst not sow and gathering where thou didst not scatter. (*St. Matthew xxv.*)
71. As sorrowful, yet always **rejoicing**; as poor, yet making many rich; as having nothing, and yet possessing all things. (*2 Corinthians vi.*)

72. Pure **religion** and undefiled before God and the Father is this, to visit the fatherless and widows in their affliction, and to keep himself unspotted from the world. (*James i.*)

73. He that is without **sin** among you, let him first cast a stone at her. (*St. John viii.*)

74. **Sin** no more. (*St. John v.*)

75. For what shall it profit a man if he shall gain the whole world and lose his own **soul.** (*St. Mark viii.*)

76. One **soweth** and another reapeth. (*St. John iv.*)

77. For whatsoever a man **soweth,** that shall he also reap. (*Galatians vi.*)

78. Into Thy hands I commend my **spirit.** (*St. Luke xxiii.*)

79. And they that take the **sword** shall perish with the sword. (*St. Matthew xxvi.*)

80. **Touch** not; taste not; handle not. (*Colossians ii.*)

81. Where your **treasure** is, there will your heart be also. (*St. Luke xii.*)

82. Lay not up for yourselves **treasures** upon earth. (*St. Matthew vi.*)

83. I am the **vine,** ye are the branches; he that abideth in me, and I in him, the same bringeth forth much fruit, for without me ye can do nothing. (*St. John xv.*)

84. But **wisdom** is justified of her children. (*St. Matthew xii.*)

85. If any would not **work,** neither should he eat. (*Thessalonians iii.*)

86. Let not the sun go down upon your **wrath.** (*Ephesians iv.*)

87. Let your **yea** be yea, and your nay, nay; lest ye fall into condemnation. (*James v.*)

APOCRYPHA

1. The **affliction** of an hour maketh a man forget pleasure. (*Ecclesiasticus xi.*)

2. Whatsoever thou takest in hand, remember the **end,** and thou shalt never do amiss. (*Ecclesiasticus vii.*)

3. Instead of a **friend** become not an enemy. (*Ecclesiasticus vi.*)

4. A **friend** cannot be known in prosperity: and an enemy cannot be hidden in adversity. (*Ecclesiasticus xii.*)

5. The heart of **fools** is in their mouth: but the mouth of the wise is in their heart. (*Ecclesiasticus xxi.*)

6. **Give** and take and sanctify thy soul: for there is no seeking of dainties in the grave. (*Ecclesiasticus xiv.*)

7. For **gold** is tried in fire, and acceptable men in the furnace of adversity. (*Ecclesiasticus ii.*)

8. For my danger is in my **hand.** (*Esther xiv.*)

9. Let not thy **hand** be stretched out to receive, and shut when thou shouldest repay. (*Ecclesiasticus iv.*)

10. If thou be among the **indiscreet,** observe the time. (*Ecclesiasticus xxvii.*)

11. For the ear of **jealousy** heareth all things: and the noise of murmuring is not hid. (*Wisdom of Solomon i.*)

12. Let us leave tokens of our **joyfulness** in every place. (*Wisdom of Solomon ii.*)

13. For how agree the **kettle** and earthen pot together? (*Ecclesiasticus xiii.*)

14. For all men have one entrance into **life,** and the like going out. (*Wisdom of Solomon vii.*)

15. The principal things for the whole use of **man's life** are water, fire, iron, and salt, flour of wheat, honey, milk, and the blood of the grape, and oil and clothing. (*Ecclesiasticus xxxix.*)

16. Lose thy **money** for thy brother and thy friend, and let it not rust under a stone to be lost. (*Ecclesiasticus xxix.*)

17. As near as thou canst guess at thy **neighbour,** and consult with the wise. (*Ecclesiasticus ix.*)

18. Remember the commandments, and bear no malice to thy **neighbour:** [remember] the covenant of the Highest, and wink at ignorance. (*Ecclesiasticus xxviii.*)

19. Honour a **physician** with the honour due unto him for the uses which ye may have of him: for the Lord hath created him. (*Ecclesiasticus xxxviii.*)

20. In the day of **prosperity** there is a forgetfulness of affliction: and in the day of affliction there is no more remembrance of prosperity. (*Ecclesiasticus xi.*)

21. Despise not the discourse of the wise, but acquaint thyself with their **proverbs:** for of them thou shalt learn instruction, and how to serve great men with ease. (*Ecclesiasticus viii.*)

22. As a nail sticketh fast between the joinings of the stones: so doth **sin** stick close between buying and selling. (*Ecclesiasticus xxvii.*)

23. Be not ashamed to confess thy **sins;** and force not the course of the river. (*Ecclesiasticus iv.*)

24. Learn before thou **speak,** and use physick or ever thou be sick. (*Ecclesiasticus xviii.*)

25. A **tale** out of season [is as] musick in mourning: but stripes and correction of wisdom are never out of time. (*Ecclesiasticus xxi.*)

26. Many have fallen by the edge of the sword: but not so many as have fallen by the **tongue.** (*Ecclesiasticus xxviii.*)

27. If thou seest a man of **understanding,** get thee betimes unto him, and let thy foot wear the steps of his door. (*Ecclesiasticus vi.*)

28. Do right to the **widow,** judge for the fatherless, give to the poor, defend the orphan, clothe the naked, heal the broken and the weak, laugh not a lame man to scorn, defend the maimed, and let the blind man come into the sight of thy clearness. (*2 Esdras ii.*)

29. Let us fill ourselves with costly **wine** and ointments: and let no flower of the spring pass by us. (*Wisdom of Solomon ii.*)

30. **Winnow** not with every wind, and go not into every way. (*Ecclesiasticus v.*)

31. Give me any plague, but the plague of the heart: and any wickedness, but the wickedness of a **woman.** (*Ecclesiasticus xxv.*)

32. There is no **word** so secret that shall go for nought. (*Wisdom of Solomon i.*)

33. Weigh thy **words** in a balance, and make a door and bar for thy mouth. (*Ecclesiasticus xxviii.*)

34. Use not many **words** in a multitude of elders, and make not much babbling when thou prayest. (*Ecclesiasticus vii.*)

CONFUCIANISM

1. Only the wise of the highest class, and the stupid of the lowest class, who cannot be **changed.**

2. If we could all be **courteous** for even a single day, the hatreds of humanity would turn to love.

3. Wade the **deep places**, lift thy robe through the shallows.
4. The **fault** is to cleave to a fault.
5. The very word "**forbearance**" is precious in a house.
6. The chase of **gain** is rich in hate.
7. For a **gentleman** there is no other name; he is always a gentleman.
8. Wheresoever you **go**, go with all your heart.
9. The tendency of man's nature to do **good** is like the tendency of water to flow downwards.
10. The small man thinks that small acts of **goodness** are of no benefit, and does not do them; and that small deeds of evil do no harm, and does not abstain from them.
11. The **great man** [or good man] is he who does not lose his child-heart. (*Mencius, 371–288* B.C.)
12. To keep old **knowledge** warm and get new, makes the teacher.
13. Do not think yourself so **large** as to deem others small.
14. **Learn** as though the time were short, as one who fears to lose.
15. **Learning** knows no rank.
16. To rank the effort above the prize may be called **love.**
17. **Love** alone can love others, or hate others.
18. Few men **love** and know the bad qualities of the object of their love, or who hate, and yet know the excellences of the object of their hatred.
19. **Love** is to conquer self and turn to courtesy.
20. What is **love?** To love mankind. What is wisdom? To know mankind.
21. **Loveless men** cannot bear need long, or fortune long.
22. From life to death is **man's reach.**
23. Do not be ashamed of **mistakes,** and thus make them crimes.
24. By **nature** men are nearly all alike; by practice they get to be wide apart.
25. The **path** is not far from man.
26. It is more difficult to bear **poverty** without murmuring, than to be rich without pride.
27. There is one word which may serve as a rule of practice for all one's life—**reciprocity.**
28. Better is one who knows what is **right,** is one who is fond of what is right; and better than one who is fond of what is right, is one who delights in what is right.
29. There is nothing more visible than what is **secret,** and nothing more manifest than what is minute.
30. **Sincerity** is the end and beginning of things.
31. If a man take no thought about what is distant, he will find **sorrow** near at hand.
32. The whole end of **speech** is to be understood.
33. If thy **strength** will serve, go forward in the ranks; if not, stand still.
34. To pierce through the **target** does not score in shooting.
35 Four horses cannot overtake the **tongue.**
36. What needs no display is **virtue.**
37. **Virtue** never dwells alone, it always has neighbours.
38. To learn the **way** at daybreak and die at eve were enough. [i.e. without regret.]
39. Keep thy will on the **way**; lean on the mind; rest in love; move in art.
40. A man does not know the **wickedness** of his son; or the richness of his growing corn.
41. The grass must bend when the **wind** blows
42. What truly is **within** will be manifested without.
43. I have never found anyone who loves goodness so much as he loves **women.**
44. What you do not want done to **yourself,** do not do to others.

EGYPTIAN

1. Seat thyself in the hands of **God.**
2. One doth not get **good things** when one saith evil things.
3. Let not thy **heart** be great because of thy knowledge, but converse with the ignorant as with the learned.
4. Let thy **heart** be overflowing, but let thy mouth be restrained.
5. Keep to thyself thine own **heart,** for friends exist not for a man on the day of troubles.
6. He that obeyeth his **heart** shall command.
7. Fill not thy **heart** with the things of another.
8. If the **hour** be passed, one seeks to save another.
9. Thy **mother** carried thee for months, she suckled thee for three years, when thou wast at school she brought thee bread and beer each day . . . cause not her to raise her hands to God in complaint of thee.
10. Let not thy mouth be filled at thy **neighbour's** table.
11. He that **obeyeth** becometh one obeyed. *(Ptah-Hôtep.)*
12. When thou **ploughest,** labour in the field God has given thee.
13. If thou art found good in the time of **prosperity,** when adversity comes thou wilt find thyself able to endure.
14. If thou goest in the straight **road,** thou shalt reach the intended place.
15. **Sin** is begotten even in our own dreams.
16. Guard thyself from **sinning** in words, that they may not wound.
17. If thou wouldst be a perfect man make thy **son** pleasing to God.
18. There is no **son** to the chief of the treasury, there is no heir to the chief of the seal.
19. Do not build up thy **tomb** above those who command thee.
20. The ruin of a man is in his **tongue** ; guard thyself that thou make no loss.
21. Thy entering into a **village** begins with acclamations ; at thy going out thou art saved by thy hand.
22. The **water-courses** shifted in past years and will yet again next year.
23. I have made no one to **weep.**

HINDUISM

1. All sorts of **crookedness** mean death ; all sorts of sincerity are called the eternal.
2. One satisfies the **debt** to his fellow-men by doing good to them.
3. Kine are of divers colours, but all milk is alike ; the kinds of flowers vary, yet all worship is one ; systems of faith are different, but the **deity** is one.
4. He who is **dishonest** with respect to speech is dishonest in everything.
5. This is the sum of **duty :** do naught to others which, if done to thee, would cause thee pain.
6. Let him not do **evil** to others, who desires not that sorrows should pursue himself. (*The Golden Rule.*)
7. He who has come through the **fire** will not fade in the sun.
8. From the unreal lead me to the **real**—from darkness lead me to light—from death lead me to immortality.

9. Charity done in secret, eager courtesy to the visitor of his house, silence after doing kindness, and public mention after receiving it, modesty in fortune, conversation without spice of insolence—who taught good men this **rule of life,** hard as a sword's edge to tread ?
10. When confessed the **sin** becomes less, since it becomes truth.
11. As fragrance is inherent in flowers, oil in sesame seed, fire in wood, Ghī in milk, sweetness in sugar-cane, so wise men should recognize the **soul** in a body.
12. O good man ! if thou shouldest **speak** falsely, all thy pure deeds would go to the dogs.
13. That art **thou.**
14. **Virtue** is spotlessness of mind, all else is mere noise.
15. Not with **wealth** is a man to be satisfied.

ISLAM

1. Be constant in prayer and give **alms.**
2. The **beard** is the light of God.
3. Allah pity him who must **beg** of a beggar.
4. Those who are **blind** in this world shall be blind in the next world.
5. He **closeth** and uncloseth, and doeth well.
6. **Earn** and dine or else fast.
7. Man wants but seven feet of **earth.**
8. Everyone finds **easy** that for which he was created.
9. Man prayeth for **evil** as he prayeth for good, for man is hasty.
10. " Commanding to **evil** " is the greatest of all veils between God and Man.
11. To **God** alone I make my plaint of sorrow and grief.
12. Call upon the name of **God,** and ask for what is good for you.
13. Even **God** forgives three sins.
14. **God** has always chosen a prophet from the sheep-fold.
15. If **God** is our friend, our business is accomplished.
16. There is no private discourse among three persons, but **God** is the fourth of them.
17. Where **God** is, there is everything.
18. Of those who serve **God,** only the savants fear Him.
19. Give **God** time.
20. In the name of **God,** the Compassionate, the Merciful.
21. Shall the reward of **good** be aught but good ?
22. If ye do **good** it is to yourselves ; and if ye do evil, it is to yourselves.
23. The house that receives no **guests,** never receives angels.
24. God will increase the **guidance** of the already guided.
25. Let not thy **hand** be tied up to thy neck ; nor yet open it with all openness, lest thou sit thee down in rebuke, in beggary.
26. The believer's **intention** is better than his performance.
27. One hour in doing **justice** is worth a hundred in prayer.
28. **Kings,** when they enter a city, ruin it.
29. Thou dost not practice what thou **knowest** ; why, then, dost thou seek what thou knowest not ?
30. Seek **knowledge** even in China.
31. To seek **knowledge** is obligatory on every Moslem man and woman.

32. If a man hath two **loaves,** let him sell one and buy some flowers of narcissus.
33. O God, make me live **lowly,** and die lowly, and rise from the dead amongst the lowly.
34. Did there not come over **man** a time when he was not anything worthy of mention?
35. If thou hearest that a **mountain** has moved, believe it: but if thou hearest that a man has changed his character, believe it not.
36. They say with their **mouths** what is not in their hearts.
37. **Paradise** lies under the feet of mothers.
38. God is with the **patient.**
39. On the day of Resurrection God will say to the angels "Bring ye My loved ones nigh unto me"—the **poor** and destitute.
40. [Give alms] unto the **poor** who are kept fighting in God's cause and cannot go to and fro on the earth; whom the ignorant deem rich forasmuch as they refrain [from begging].
41. **Poverty** is glorious to those who are worthy of it.
42. **Poverty** is near to unbelief.
43. **Prayer** carries us half-way to Allah; fasting brings us to the door of his palace; alms gains us admission.
44. Observe the **prayers,** and pay the legal alms, and lend God a liberal loan.
45. To you your **religion;** and to me my religion.
46. The door of **repentance** is open.
47. Do the **right** and lawful and do it a hundred times a day.
48. The **sword** is the key of Heaven and of Hell.
49. Most men refuse to be aught but **thankless.**
50. Verily, if ye return **thanks,** I will give you an increase.
51. The **wise** aspire to know, the foolish to relate.
52. I have not left any calamity more hurtful to man than **woman** . . . O! assembly of women, give alms though it be of your gold and silver ornaments; for verily you are mostly of hell on the day of Resurrection.
53. **Women** have been omitted by God from His mercy.

JAINISM (INDIA)

1. The **anger** which is kept overnight has grown deadly by the morning.
2. **Avarice** is the root of sin.
3. He who is **born** must die some day or other, and he who is dead must be born in some form or other.
4. He who **eats** much will sleep much.
5. Blessed are the **eunuchs** who have made themselves so for the Kingdom of Heaven.
6. **Fight** with yourself, why fight with external foes?
7. I **forgive** all souls; let all souls forgive me. I am on friendly terms with all; I have no enmity with anybody.
8. Man! Thou are thine own **friend,** why wishest thou for a friend beyond thyself?
9. **Happy** are we, happy live we who call nothing our own.
10. The sin incurred in destroying one **honeycomb** is as great as that accumulated by destroying twelve villages.
11. Blessed are ye if ye **hunger** now, for ye shall be filled.

12. A man sitting **idle** brings ruin to pass.
13. **Look** upon other beings as you would look upon yourself.
14. In one **potato** there are countless bodies, and in each body countless lives exist.
15. That which holds beings from falling into an evil state [after death] is called **religion.**
16. What avail **riches** for the practice of religion?
17. To hold the **truth** as truth, and untruth as untruth, this is true faith.
18. **Truth** is untruth if it is not pleasant and wholesome.
19. **Water** should be allowed to flow that it become not stagnant; Monks should be allowed to wander that they may be stainless.

SHINTO (JAPAN)

1. Every little yielding to **anxiety** is a step away from the natural heart of man.
2. When the sky is clear, and the wind hums in the fir-trees; 'tis the heart of **God** who has revealed Himself.
3. The **heart** is the chief of the gods, therefore do not injure it.
4. If that which is within is not bright, it is useless to **pray** for that which is without.
5. **Rectitude** is the bone which gives firmness and stature.

SIKH (INDIA)

1. Hearing the name is equal to **bathing** at the sixty-eight places of pilgrimages.
2. **Birth** and death do not cease.
3. Who has **come** will depart again.
4. Everyone desires **comfort,** no one desires pain.
5. Make **continence** thy matted hair, union with God thine ablutions, thy daily religious duties the growth of thy nails.
6. **Covetousness** is a dog, falsehood a sweeper, food obtained by cheating is carrion.
7. **Covetousness** is a well of error.
8. The **day** rises and sets again, the whole night passes.
9. The whole world is fettered by **death.**
10. It is according to **destiny** that one speaks, eats, hears, sees and takes breath.
11. Though a hundred nectars be sprinkled, yet the **dhau** [poisonous shrub] will bear poisonous fruit.
12. A **diamond,** having met with a diamond, is perforated.
13. Though sandalwood be applied to a **dog,** yet he runs after the bitch.
14. There is the **enjoyment** of gold, enjoyment of silver, enjoyment of a fascinating woman, [and] the scent of sandalwood.
15. Every one is subject to **error.**
16. The water of **existence** is difficult and terrible, it has no shore nor limit.

17. In **fear** man is born, in fear he dies.
18. Turn my **feet** in a direction in which God is not.
19. **Fire** dies if water is poured [upon it], as a child by the milk of the mother [is satiated].
20. What can the cold do to the **fire,** the night to the sun, the darkness to the moon?
21. Where there is **forgiveness** there is God himself.
22. The **gift** is in the hand of the giver.
23. He who knows himself will comprehend **God.**
24. They have understanding, they have honour, they have wealth in their lap in whose heart [**God**] is contained.
25. It is **God** who arrangeth marriages. . . . Those whom he hath once joined He joineth for ever.
26. **God's name** is wealth, which accompanieth and assisteth us.
27. Without **good works** no one can be saved.
28. Of what use are the **greatnesses** of the world?
29. How can **grief** affect him who looks upon pain and pleasure as the same?
30. Without the **guru** man is ruined by wandering.
31. Make discrimination, search [thy] **heart** and inquire well.
32. Many millions search for God and find Him in their **hearts.**
33. If I please **Him** [God] that is my place of pilgrimage to bathe in; if I please Him not, what ablutions shall I make?
34. The fruit of **humility** is tranquillity.
35. The desert is not satiated by rain; the fire [of] **hunger** does not cease.
36. **Ignorance** is darkness.
37. Mother, father, son, relative, all **kinsmen** are false.
38. Thou shalt not go to Heaven by **lip-service.**
39. The **lord** is the strength of the weak.
40. Always the **Lord** should be remembered; put Him and keep Him within thy breast.
41. Burn worldly **love.**
42. How often hath youth become dry and withered with **love.**
43. True **love** does not break.
44. Make **mercy** thy cotton, contentment thy thread, continence its knot, truth its twist.
45. Why sayest thou "**Mine,** mine"?
46. Not by wearing a wooden **necklace,** nor by twisting matted hair round the head that God is found.
47. Those who practise works of **poison** are absorbed in poison.
48. Wandering about, I ascend a **sand-hill;** having ascended a sand-hill I go to a mountain.
49. Wherever I go, there is thy **service.**
50. [Who] practises **sincerity** accomplishes [his] heart's purpose.
51. From **sins** sins spring up.
52. When dust is mingled with dust what will become of the **soul?**
53. What he **sows,** that he will reap.
54. The mouth is not satiated with **speaking,** the ear with hearing, nor the eye with seeing.
55. Why art thou conceited of a **trifle?**
56. To an inverted **vessel** nothing adheres.
57. By the fullness of **water** in the moat [there] is sap [in] the lotus.
58. Without **water** there is no lotus.
59. **Wealth** is a net of anxieties.
60. No one hath brought **wealth** with him; and no one shall take it away.
61. Make **wisdom** the mother, contentment the father, truth the brother.

62. Who reflects on himself becomes **wise.**
63. Those who do excellent **works** are called excellent at the gate [of God]; those who do low works sit outside and weep.
64. The **world** is a house of smoke.
65. All the **world** is coming and going.
66. How shall that which is **written** be blotted out?
67. The few days [of **youth**] are [soon] over, and the coat [i.e. body] has become old.

SÚFIISM (PERSIA)

1. Be constant in **ablution,** that thy two guardian angels may love thee.
2. Were there no **affliction,** there were no way to God.
3. Everything has its **alms,** and the alms of a house is the guest-room.
4. Ye shall never attain to righteousness until ye give in **alms** of that which ye love.
5. **Appear** as thou art, or be as thou appearest.
6. The way of the elect is to see only the **causer,** and not to see the cause.
7. Whosoever looketh with **complacency** on himself is lost.
8. Whoever desires to be living in his life, let him not admit **covetousness** to dwell in his heart.
9. The pen does not record [**evil actions**] against the sleeper until he awakes, or against the boy until he reached puberty, or against the madman until he recovers his wits.
10. I will go a thousand leagues in **falsehood,** that one step of the journey may be true.
11. **Fasting** is half of the Way.
12. When God wishes a man well, He gives him insight into his **faults.**
13. He who **fears** not God of his own free will, must fear mankind of necessity.
14. He who **finds** shall seek.
15. **Generosity** consists in doing justice and in not demanding justice.
16. There are three signs of **generosity**—to keep faith without resistance, to praise without being incited thereto by liberality, and to give without being asked.
17. Whoever **gives** and does not take, he is a man; whoever gives and takes, he is half a man; but he who takes and gives not is not a human being.
18. Take **God** as thy companion and leave mankind alone.
19. Union with **God** is separation from all else, and separation from all else is union with Him.
20. Since I have known **God,** neither truth nor falsehood has entered my heart.
21. I never saw anything without seeing **God** therein.
22. Those who regard things as determined by **God** turn to God in everything.
23. Whoever knows **God** turns his back on all else.
24. When his **heart** is empty of phenomena he is poor.
25. **Hunger** is a cloud which rains naught but wisdom.
26. Make your bellies **hungry** and your livers thirsty, and your bodies naked that perchance your hearts may see God in this world.
27. He who **knows** himself already knows his Lord.
28. A **lamp** is of no use when the dawn rises.
29. Everything wherein one forgets not God is **lawful.**
30. A man is with the object of his **love.**

31. **Love** is this—that thou shouldst account thyself very little and God very great.
32. Whoever **loveth** God will assuredly hate self.
33. God hath made the **pious** living in their death, and hath made the wicked dead during their lives.
34. The **poor man** does not rest content with anything except God.
35. The **poor man** is not he whose hand is empty of provisions, but he whose nature is empty of desires.
36. **Poverty** consists in never being independent of poverty.
37. **Poverty** is to dwell in the unseen.
38. **Poverty** is wealth in God.
39. See that ye wear woollen **raiment,** that ye may feel the sweetness of faith. (Súfis were known as "wool wearers". A hair cloth was worn by penitents).
40. A moment's **reflection** is better than sixty years of devotion.
41. None of you shall be **saved** by his works.
42. Oblivion of **self** is remembrance of God.
43. Anyone who is ignorant of the nature of **servantship** is yet more ignorant of the nature of lordship.
44. The first stage of **service** is emergence from self.
45. **Sleep** is the brother of death.
46. Safety lies in **solitude.**
47. The **súfi** is absent from himself and present with God.
48. The **súfi** is he that has nothing in his possession, nor is himself possessed by anything.
49. The **súfi** is he that sees nothing except God in the two worlds.
50. The **súfi** is he whose thought keeps pace with his foot.
51. **Súfiism** is the renunciation of all selfish pleasures.
52. Speaking **tongues** are the destruction of silent hearts.
53. Association with the **wicked** produces suspicion of the good.
54. If the first of the **wine-jar** is dregs, what will its last be?
55. I never saw anyone more just than the **world** ; if you serve her she will serve you, and if you leave her she will leave you.
56. None can **worship** rightly so he be not hungry.

TAOISM

1. When opposing warriors join in **battle,** he who has pity conquers.
2. Among mankind, the recognition of **beauty** as such implies the idea of ugliness, and the recognition of good implies the idea of evil.
3. To see small **beginnings** is clearness of sight ; to rest in weakness is strength.
4. Keep **behind,** and you shall be put in front ; keep out, and you shall be kept in.
5. Abandon ostentatious **benevolence** and conspicuous righteousness ; then people will return to the primal virtues of filial piety and parental affection.
6. That which is **brittle** is easily broken ; that which is minute is easily dissipated.
7. If you would **contract,** you must first expand ; if you would weaken, you must first strengthen ; if you would overthrow, you must first raise up ; if you would take, you must first give.
8. **Desire** not to desire, and you will not value things difficult to obtain.
9. He who always thinks things **easy** is sure to find them difficult.

10. **Failure** is the foundation of success, and the means by which it is attained.
11. He who has not **faith** in others shall find no faith in them.
12. **Goodness** strives not, and therefore it is not rebuked.
13. **Govern** a great nation as you would cook a little fish.
    [i.e. don't overdo it.]
14. Do **great things** while they are still small.
15. The **great way** is very smooth, but the people love the by-paths.
16. The **heavy** is the foundation of the light ; repose is the ruler of unrest.
17. He that **humbles** himself shall be preserved entire ; he that bends shall be made straight ; he that is empty shall be filled ; he that is worn out shall be renewed ; he who has little shall succeed ; he who has much shall go astray.
18. He who is great must make **humility** his base ; he who is high must make lowliness his foundation.
19. Recompense **injury** with virtue [kindness].
20. A **journey** of a thousand miles began with a single step.
21. Not to **know** and yet to affect knowledge is a vice.
22. To **know,** but to be as though not knowing is the height of wisdom.
23. He who **meddles** mars ; he who holds it by force loses it.
24. Take pity on **orphans,** assist widows, respect the old, be kind to children, assist those in need, and rescue those in danger.
25. He who lightly **promises** is sure to keep but little faith.
26. Among men **reject** none.
27. He is **rich** who knows when he has enough.
28. Abandon the show of **saintliness ;** the people will benefit a hundredfold.
29. The truest **sayings** are paradoxical.
30. To **see** oneself is to be clear of sight.
31. He who is **self-approving** is not held in esteem.
32. It is only **self-assertion** that one need fear.
33. He who is **self-displaying** does not shine.
34. He who is **self-exalting** does not rise high.
35. He who is **self-praising** has no merit.
36. The **softest things** in the world override the hardest.
37. Those who know do not **speak ;** those who speak do not know.
38. Extreme **straightness** is as bad as crookedness ; extreme cleverness is as bad as folly ; extreme fluency is as bad as stammering.
39. That which has no **substance** enters where there is no crevice.
40. **Success** is the lurking-place of failure ; but who can tell when the turning-point will come ?
41. Be **square** without being angular ; be honest without being mean ; be upright without being punctilious ; be brilliant without being showy.
42. **Temper** your sharpness, disentangle your ideas, moderate your brilliancy, live in harmony with your age.
43. The absence of desire gives **tranquillity.**
44. True **words** are not fine ; fine words are not true.

ZOROASTRIANISM, (OR MAZDEISM,) RELIGION OF THE PÂRSÎS

1. The **babe** is wise that weepeth, being born.
2. Of two **bed-fellows** who hear the cock crowing, the one who gets up first will first enter paradise.
3. As the **country** so is the speech; as is the prince so is the people; as is the mother so is the daughter; as is the seed so is the shoot.
4. **Drowning men** snatch at the foam.
5. Men do not gather **figs** of thorns; nor of a bramble bush gather they grapes; for every tree is known by its own fruit.
6. Though the Gabar may serve **fire** a hundred years, yet the moment he falls into it he will be burned.

   [Gabar is a Pârsî or Fireworshipper.]
7. If you place your reliance on **God,** you may break your own neck without harm.
8. **Good** will be the final goal of ill.
9. The mind in its own place and "Good Thought" is the home of the **good man** for ever.
10. The **law** is ever standing at thy door in the person of thy brethren.
11. Nothing in the world is better than **light,** both among small and great.
12. **Like** produces like.
13. Is it not a **man's self** which is to be his ultimate reward or retribution?
14. To nourish the **poor,** to give fodder to cattle, to bring firewood to the fire, to pour Hōm-juice into water.
15. The first object of man is **purity.**
16. A man has not only to fill his bag or purse with money, but has to fill it up with **righteousness.**
17. A muddy **stream** cannot send forth pure waters.
18. There is one thing that every man in the world may love, he may love **virtue.**

AFRICA

An Introduction to the African Proverbs by Robert R. Marett, D.Sc., LL.D., F.B.A., M.A., will be found on page xxxv.

AFRICAN LANGUAGE FAMILIES

BANTU

Bantu (Loosely classified collection)
Bemba (N. Rhodesia)
Bondei (Kenya Colony)
Chaga (Kilimanjaro)
Chuana or Sechuana (Bechuanaland and W. Transvaal)
Duala (Cameroons)
Ganda or Luganda (Uganda)
Giryama (Kenya Colony)
Gogo or Cigogo (Kenya Colony)
Haya (NW. Tanganyika)
Herero (Damaraland)
Ila (N. Rhodesia)
Kamba (Kenya Colony)
Kikuyu (Kenya Colony)
Kongo (Belgian Congo)
Kweli or Wakweli (Cameroons)
Lamba (N. Rhodesia)
Ndau or Vandau (Portuguese S. Africa)
Ndebele or Sindebele (Matabeleland)
Ndonga or Aandonga (Ovo-Mpo-land)
Ngoni (Nyasaland)
Nyanja or Chinyanja (Nyasaland)
Nyika (Zanzibar)
Nyoro (Uganda)
Pedi (Transvaal Sotho) N. Transvaal)
Pondo (Pondoland)
Ronga or Sikonga (Portuguese E. Africa—Lourenço Marques)
Ruanda or Kinyarwanda (Lake Kivu—Belgian Territory)
Shona (Mashonaland)
Sotho or Se-suto (Basutoland)
Swahili (Zanzibar)
Thonga (Portuguese E. Africa)
Tumbuka or Kamanga (N. Nyasaland)
Xhosa, Xosa or Kafir (Kaffraria)
Yao (Nyasaland)
Zulu (Zululand)

HAMITIC

Fulfulde or Ful (N. Cameroons, French Guinea and Upper Niger)
Galla (S. Abyssinia)
Hausa (N. Nigeria)
Masai (Kenya Colony)
Somali (Somaliland)
Tamashek or Taureg (Central Sahara)

MALAY

Malagasy (Madagascar)

NILO-HAMITIC

Nandi (Kenya Colony)

NILOTIC

Lango (Uganda)

SEMITIC

Algerian-Arabic (Algeria and Morocco)
Amharic (Abyssinia)
Egyptian-Arabic
Moorish
Sudanese-Arabic
Tunisian-Arabic

SUDANIC

Bambara (French W. Africa)
Basa (Liberia and Nigeria)
Efik (Southern Nigeria)
Ewe (Dahome—Slave Coast)
Fanti
Ga or Accra (Gold Coast)
Grebo (Liberia)
Ho (German Togoland)
Ibo (S. Nigeria)
Jabo (Liberia)
Jukun (Kenya Colony and N. Nigeria)
Kanuri (Bornu—N. Nigeria)
Kru (Liberia)
Liberian-Negro (Liberia)
Mandingo (Senegambia)
Nupe (N. Nigeria)
Nyang (Cameroons)
Nzima (Apollonia—Gold Coast)
Oji (Ashanti)
Tiv (Benue—Nigeria)
Vai (Liberia and Sierra Leone)
Wolof (Senegambia)
Yoruba (S. Nigeria)

ALGERIAN-ARABIC (ALGERIA AND MOROCCO)

[Language Family—Semitic]

1. The thinnest **bread** finds itself married to bread.
2. **Cold** teaches to steal coal.
3. The heart of a **fool** is in his mouth and the mouth of the wise man is in his heart.
4. **Lies** buzz like flies, but truth has the brilliance of the sun.
5. Each day brings its **loaf.**
6. A drop of **water** on a field is riches, a drop of water on a viper is poison [makes poison].
7. The other **world** is a dwelling-place of which this world is the vestibule.
8. The word " **yes** " brings trouble, the word " no " leads to no evil.

AMHARIC (ABYSSINIA)

(Including Ethiopic)

[Language Family—Semitic]

1. Beware of the man who cannot deal **blows.**
2. That which is consumed by the **brother-in-law** is as though it were destroyed by fire.

   [Brothers-in-law have a bad reputation in Abyssinia.]
3. To wear unwashed **clothes.**

   [To accuse someone without being sure of his faults.]
4. The man who is not hungry says the **coco-nut** has a hard shell.
5. When you travel in a country of **corn-ears,** take a sickle with you.
6. Men fear **danger,** women only its aspect.
7. When the **date-crop** is over everyone mocks at the palm-tree.
8. If you are a **date-tree,** suffer fools to throw stones at you.
9. The **egg** that stops with its master doesn't get broken.
10. Sore **eyes** are seen, but a sore head is hidden.
11. When a **fool** does not succeed in bleaching ebony he tries to blacken ivory.
12. A powerful **friend** becomes a powerful enemy.
13. The flower of **glory** only grows in the field of mint.
14. **God** gave you, to give to me.
15. He who travels with **gold shoes** may reach the world's end.
16. **Gratitude** is a lotus flower whose leaves soon wither.
17. Honour withdraws from those who **lie.**
18. When a **lion** allows himself to be put on a chain it is no disgrace for him to stay there.
19. The smaller the **lizard** the greater its hope of becoming a crocodile.
20. The **marvellous** and the astonishing only surprise for a week.
21. The death of a **mother** and a stone seat hurt with time.
22. When your **neighbour** is accused, listen and say to yourself, " I hear my own [accusation]."
23. If the **Nile** knows your secret it will soon be known in the desert.
24. On the **palm-tree** of glory the date of modesty withers.
25. Those who wear **pearls** do not know how often the shark bites the leg of the diver.

26. A man has come ; a **quarrel** will come.
27. The little **stars** always shine whilst the great sun is often eclipsed.
28. When one **suffers** in the entrails, the teeth smile.
    [Fatalism.]
29. Do not blame God for having created the **tiger**, but thank Him for not having given it wings.
30. One **travels** and travels and ends by returning home ; one lives and lives and ends by returning to the earth.
31. **Truth** and the morning become light with time.
32. An old **wife** at home and a slope in front of his house weary a man.
33. That which is **written** is binding, but that which is spoken is forgotten.
34. Against the goodness of **woman** the sadness of man is also good. (*Ethiopic.*)

BAMBARA (FRENCH WEST AFRICA)

[Language Family—Sudanic]

1. When the **ape** cannot reach the ripe banana with its hand, he says it is sour.
2. Fear is no obstacle to **death.**
3. One lump of **dough** whitens the whole river.
    [Said of the moon.]
4. The **frog** and its contents belong to the horn-bill [a bird which lives on frogs].
5. A **hare** is like an ass in the length of its ears, yet it is not its son.
6. You may ride a **horse** well, but don't try to sit on your horse's nose.
7. It is no use trying to sell a ring to a **leper.**
8. **Smoke** rises from beneath every roof.
    [i.e. everyone has his own cares.]
9. Each knows best the **worms** that nest in his head.
    [i.e. every man has his own sorrow which gnaws at him.]

BANTU

(Loosely classified collection, tribal origin unknown)

1. The **African** race is an india-rubber ball ; the harder you dash it to the ground, the higher it will rise.
2. Every **beast** roars in its own den.
3. A **brother** is born for adversity.
4. Where you have once set your **cooking-pot** throw no stones.
5. A **debt** is not a corpse.
6. **Debts** make slaves.
7. A good **deed** will make a good neighbour.
8. The **door** sees everything that is going on, both inside and out of the hut.
    [Said of a tale-bearer or busybody.]
9. The **earth** is a beehive ; we all enter by the same door but live in different cells.
10. The **egg** gives the hen instruction in brooding.

11. Where there is more than **enough**, more than enough is wasted.
12. True **friendship** outlives relationship.
13. He who gives to **God** does not go to bed hungry.
14. When you are happiest **God** sees you.
15. Of time and thought the **heart** is full.
16. A **hen** that is being fed on corn [i.e. a man who earns a good-living wage] is satisfied.
17. Do not expect to come into a **heritage** by coughing.

    [i.e. one must belong to the clan.]
18. **Law makers**—law breakers.
19. There are forty kinds of **lunacy**, but only one kind of common sense.
20. No **monkey** eats during the night.

    [i.e. ask favours in the daytime.]
21. A man with a **mouth** cannot go astray.
22. **Poison** should be tried out on a frog.
23. A **promise** is a debt.
24. Only the **speech** is criticized, not the man himself.

    [i.e. encouragement for a beginner to speak in council.]
25. He who would **sweep** the hut must not sit on the broom.
26. **To-day** is to-day!
27. A man who creates **trouble** seldom eats it himself.
28. **Want** and suffering never betray.
29. **Water** never loses its way.
30. Where the **water** rules, the land submits.

    [The rich are always on top.]
31. Marry a **wife** and buy clothes.
32. A **woman's** clothes are the price of her husband's peace.
33. The **woods** are full of trees.

    [i.e. women are plentiful; you need not tie yourself to the first one you meet.]
34. The **woods** are not heartless.

    [i.e. there is comfort in solitude.]
35. **Work** is good provided you do not forget to live.

BASA (LIBERIA AND NIGERIA)

[Language Family—Sudanic]

1. The **back** has its share behind and the belly in front.
2. He who ran about with **boys** was buried in two graves.
3. When the **crickets** come out into the road the wandering ants are at their heels.

    [i.e. all things have their forerunners.]
4. One **hand** can't tie a bundle.
5. When one **hen** broods, another can't sit on the eggs.
6. He who has eaten doesn't make a fire for the **hungry**.
7. The man who says he knows everything **marries** his mother.

    [i.e. he may be deceived in spite of his wisdom.]
8. That which brings **misfortune** is not big.
9. The "**palaver**" **drum** is not only beaten on one side.

    [i.e. both sides of a question must be heard.]
10. On the swollen **river** in the rainy season you row for your own head.

    [i.e. the danger is the same for him who ferries as for the others in the boat.]
11. When you have been bitten by a **snake** you flee from a worm.
12. **Superabundance** is not far from want.

BEMBA (NORTHERN RHODESIA)

[Language Family—Bantu]

1. If you are killing a **snake**, destroy its mouth also.

BONDEI (KENYA COLONY)

[Language Family—Bantu]

1. The **armed man** has no war.
2. **Beans** come from the place where the beans are.
3. A **brother** is milk, and milk does not like dirt!
4. A heavy **burden** does not kill on the day it is carried.
5. A **child** does not cry for meat unless it has seen it in the house.
6. **Conversation** is like dry meat; its savour abides.
7. The **dog's god** is the bit of food that falls to the ground.
8. If the **door** is wide open it is tantamount to sleeping in the open.
9. If you shut the **door** too tight you will sleep out of doors.
10. The man who is killed by " Please **eat** " needs no ordeal.
11. " Who has **eaten ?** " is not the same as " And what did you eat ? "
12. The journey of **folly** has to be travelled a second time.
13. One who **gains** to-day does not gain to-morrow.
14. A **gentleman** is abroad, his salt is soon put in the relish.
15. A **guest** is a fowl—he will have his neck wrung.
16. Being a **guest** is a matter of consent.
17. The man who refuses a house with a crack in it is the **heir.**
18. You who live in other people's houses, don't strain **hospitality.**
19. The sweetness of **hunger** has no " And how did you sleep ? "
20. The man who is homeward bound pays no heed to **ill-omens.**
21. The **komi** is never late—if he is, he is in leading strings.
22. Your friend's **loincloth** has no belly band.

    [Money is carried in the belly band.]
23. You cannot get your friend's good **luck** by going on a journey to get it.
24. To be too much **married** makes you say, " There's immorality about."
25. The child who has a **mother** eats a second time.
26. You may laugh at a friend's **roof ;** don't laugh at his sleeping accommodation.
27. To-day's **satiety** is to-morrow's hunger.
28. If you look after **sheep,** give over wrath.
29. The man who goes to the **spirit world** has no bribe or ordeal.
30. **Stand up,** stand up, that a light may shine.
31. **Sticks** in a bundle are unbreakable.
32. The man who goes ahead **stumbles** that the man who follows may have his wits about him.

33. If you think little of what you possess you are out for **theft.**

34. A **traveller** with a tongue does not lose his way.

35. **Two** are two, they don't miss the way.

36. One, one, drives away **war.**

37. The man ahead, does not drink the fouled **water.**

38. A hole here and there is not the same as a **window.**

39. The **wrongdoer** forgets, but not the wronged.

CHAGA (KILIMANJARO).

[Language Family—Bantu]

1. He who leaves a **child** lives eternally.

2. Do not **feast** on both sides like the knife.

3. **Fortune** is like unto the younger sister.

4. The blessing of **offspring** to herd and to tether be with you.

5. If the chief gives you a **ring,** hide it in your clothing.

6. He who cultivates in secret is betrayed by the **smoke.**

7. Your **wealth** is your destruction.

CHUANA (SECHUANA, TŠWANA) (BECHUANALAND AND WESTERN TRANSVAAL)

[Language Family—Bantu]

1. An **ant** once made an errand-boy of an elephant.

2. Forensic **arguments** are all acceptable.

3. The man who **ate** with him has killed him.

4. When the **bag** gets full, leave it alone.

5. Never follow a **beast** into its lair.

6. When a **bird** fans itself too much it hurts its eye with its wing.

7. A **bird** with sharp claws never gathers a crowd.

8. He pays with **bones** who pays once.

9. The **breast** is an intricate net [or mystery].

10. There are no **cattle** without a dung-heap.

11. **Chicanery** is not business.

12. The first **child** is the companion of its father.

13. **Children** born amid lightning flashes are fed during peals of thunder.

    [i.e. the devil's children have the devil's luck.]

14. **Children** talk with God.

15. **Clouds** do not always denote rain, but smoke is always a sign of fire.

16. **Comrades** in plunder know each other.

17. When an ear [of **corn**] breaks off, it is to fill another.

18. **Count** twice has defeated count once.
19. There is nothing without its **cousin.**
20. In the dark, the [**cow**] that lows gets milked.
21. A **crime** eateth its own child.
22. **Crippled** first does not mean die first.
23. In the **dark** people hold to one another's cloaks.
24. " Take this " does not hurt, only **darkness** [emptiness] does.

    [i.e. little is better than nothing.]
25. **Darkness** gossips about no one.
26. Happy is she who has borne a **daughter ;** a boy is the son of his mother-in-law.
27. There are many **dawns** [or daysprings].
28. He who wakes me before **day-break** I like him after daybreak.
29. A person is always thanked after **death.**
30. **Death** is at the end of the cloak.
31. When a man **dies** a man remains.
32. **Disease** is quick in coming, but slow in departing.
33. If you despise the **doctor,** despise the sickness also.
34. When the clever **doctor** fails, try one less clever.
35. **A doctor** who does not die goes on a journey.
36. You will go to the **doctor** with an ox.

    [i.e. if you are a bad payer the dealer will demand " cash on delivery ".]
37. If you are too smart to pay the **doctor,** you had better be too smart to get sick.
38. A **doctor's** bill is easier settled where he has some relatives.

    [He whose father is Judge goes safe to the trial.]
39. The **dog** I have brought up now bites me.
40. **Ears** usually witness a matter without invitation.
41. **Eating** won't hinder you ; to go on working will.

    [Equivalent to " Mass and meat hinder no man ".]
42. He who **eats** with you may be the same one to injure you.
43. The **evening** word does not kill on ox.
44. **Eyes** are never satisfied.
45. He has too many **eyes** [preferences].
46. It is not only those with thick necks that are **famous.**
47. Always build a **fence** round the king's word.
48. Long **fingers** go hardly to work.
49. The **fire** which is going out may yet flame up again.
50. Those who are fond of **flattery** are cheated out of their property.
51. The small piece [of **food**] is not so small that it will pass by the mouth.
52. A **fool** is a treasure to the wise.
53. It is difficult to recognize a **fool** who is also a proprietor.
54. The **fool** who owns an ox is seldom recognized [as a fool].
55. A man's **friends** are as many as his enemies.
56. To **gaze** long hinders.
57. To **give** away is to put away for yourself.
58. He who washes a beautiful **goat** seldom milks it.
59. **God** also loves veal.
60. When a man doesn't call, **God** does.
61. **God's** fire can never be quenched.
62. " **Goings out** " and " comings back " are among the things unknown.
63. The **hand** never loses its way to the mouth.
64. A **harbinger** is the lamp of his friends.
65. Only the **hawk** that carries something is looked up to.

66. The word within the **heart** does not satisfy.

67. The bitter **heart** eats its owner.

68. **Hill-tops** hide one another from view.

69. The real **home** is in the courtyard.

[i.e. the women's quarters.]

70. It is not necessary to grow **horns** to be convinced of a defect.

71. Adjoining **houses** always burn.

[i.e. the rotten apple injures its neighbour.]

72. **Houses** are covers [for a multitude of sins].

73. When you are sent to insult the **king,** do so.

74. The first **lame** is not the first to die.

75. Do not **laugh** at the fallen, there may be slippery places ahead.

76. The **lion** which kills is the one which does not roar.

77. A **lion's** inheritance is the skin.

[i.e. the lion's skin is never cheap.]

78. They who gather side by side do not **love** each other.

79. **Love** paralyses the joints.

80. He who laughs at a **maiden** is the one who will marry her.

81. In rainy weather dark [**maidens**] kick.

82. Even a **maidservant** has her relatives.

83. Visitors' footfalls are like **medicine ;** they heal the sick.

84. The **milker** drinks the milk of the second milking.

85. In winter time only the **milkman** can look into the pail.

86. The son-in-law of a **monkey** eats what a monkey eats.

87. The **mote** ever makes for the single eye.

88. The **mother** is she who catches the knife by the blade.

89. The **mourner** is not listened to.

90. A **multitude** will give you swollen cheeks.

[i.e. many servants result in ill service.]

91. **News** does not spend a night on the way.

92. The best **news** is in the eyes.

93. There is no **partnership** in luck.

94. **Polygamy** was boiled in the same pot as a stone : the stone got soft and polygamy remained.

[The literal translation of the word " lehufa " (polygamy) is jealousy.]

95. Even a **poor man** has a heart.

96. It is not the **pot**-put-on-first, but the pot-put-on-the-fire [that gets done].

97. In a large **pot** the food is cooked at the bottom.

98. Things hate being **praised** prematurely.

99. In the sweat of the forehead there is **profit ;** in the sweat of [the back of] the neck there is none.

100. **Reason** has no age.

101. The best **remedy** for a dispute is to discuss it.

102. The **rhinoceros** which has no calf takes itself to the muddy pool.

103. A roundabout **road** does not cause you to sleep abroad.

104. " What do I buy ? " will bring **ruins.**

105. The child of the **saviour** is not saved.

106. A man may be tripped by his own **shadow.**

107. Never fleece two **sheep** at a time ; the other one may bite you.

108. Men, unlike **sheep,** can never fill a place.

109. A veritable **sin** is empty-handedness.

110. If you are born with a **sin** you will grow lean when it waxes fat.

111. **Sleep,** the near relative of death.

112. O! **sleep,** the poor man's fat.
113. Do not cover a **snake** under your cloak; when it gets warm it will bite you.
114. Through others I am **somebody.**
115. **Starvation** does not teach, only cold does.
116. **Straws** foster other straws.
117. A **suppliant** knows no reason.
118. Men **surpass** one another while they are working together.
119. We pick each other's **teeth.**
    [i.e. on excellent terms.]
120. He is born with a full set of **teeth.**
    [Said of successful people.]
121. White **teeth** injure while they are laughing.
122. The one who is caught is the **thief.**
123. The **tree** is climbed by means of a notch.
124. Bend the **twig** while it is green.
    [Said in training the young.]
125. **Twin lambs** are known only to the shepherds.
126. A **visitor** should have no alternatives.
127. O! **visitors,** arrive so that we may eat.
128. **Vultures** eat with their blood relations.
129. The greatest **war** is the war of the mouth.
130. I smack the **wasp** that stings me on the back; the one on my front I fumble.
131. **Water** is never tired of flowing.
132. The **water pool** ahead is not to be trusted.
133. Where there is no **wealth** there is no poverty.
134. **Wealth** and poverty lie together.
135. **Whites** never fall out; only blacks do.
136. A **wife** never comes from the south, only winds do.
137. Men are just alike; Mrs. **Winter** found them out.
138. **Wisdom** has no dwelling of her own.
139. **Wisdom** killed the wise man.
140. A **woman** is like a dog which may even be enticed with a bone.
141. A **woman** is like a monkey, you can only eat her hands [labour].
142. A man's "Yes" is a "Yes"; a **woman's** "Yes" is often a "No."
143. A **wound** is best when it is scratched by its owner.
144. We **young folk** are the real old people.

DUALA (CAMEROONS)

[Language Family—Bantu]

1. **Begged** water doesn't bring the pot to the boil.
    [i.e. a beggar is never satisfied with what he receives.]
2. The way to the **beloved** is not thorny.
3. On the muddy bank there is always a white **bird.**
    [i.e. in a house with many daughters there are always young men.]
4. A chattering **bird** builds no nest.
5. On a slimy shore it is easy to push a **canoe.**
    [i.e. it is easy to rob a lazy man of his possessions.]
6. Many **complaints** have made the giant lizard deaf.
    [i.e. he who must listen to too many complaints doesn't know what to believe.]

7. The **cricket** digs its own grave.

   [i.e. a man brings ill-luck on himself by his own words.]

8. The breaking **day** is not without an event.
9. If you would entice a **dog** to you, don't hold a stick in your hand.
10. The hen and men go through the same **door.**
11. The **ear** is not hungry.

    [i.e. it always hears something.]

12. All noses look towards **earth.**

    [i.e. everyone must die.]

13. The **egg** shows the hen the place where to hatch [her eggs].

    [i.e. the advice of the young shouldn't be despised if good.]

14. Even if the **elephant** is thin he is still the lord of the forest.
15. The **eye** is not poor.

    [i.e. it always sees something.]

16. A single **eye** mustn't be played with.

    [i.e. an only child mustn't be beaten too often.]

17. When the **eye** weeps, the nose also becomes wet.

    [i.e. when my mother suffers I suffer.]

18. The soles of the **feet** feed the mouth.
19. Good **firewood** is not without ants.

    [i.e. a pretty wife is often stupid.]

20. If nothing has ever done you any harm, you will never have **foresight.**
21. **Foresight** spoils nothing.
22. When the **head** is off, dreams cease.
23. The house of the **heart** is never full.
24. The **heart's** case is hard to open.
25. Much standing has made the feet of the **hen** small.

    [i.e. those who are always beginning work and never going on with it achieve nothing.]

26. **Hunger** in the evening is in the knees.
27. The spear of **kinship** soon pierces the eye.
28. The **knife** eats away the whetstone and the whetstone the knife.
29. What **monkey** forgets its tail?
30. A little cause brings no **news** from afar.
31. One drop after another fills the **pot.**
32. The **pot** isn't tired of cooking.
33. The **rain** falls on every roof.
34. **Respect** concerns both parties [or sides].
35. The **shoulder** is not higher than the head.

    [i.e. the servant is not over his master.]

36. He who steps over the **spring** has some water remaining on his feet.
37. When you take a **squirrel** out of the water, it contrives a plot against you.
38. The **stomach** has done the head an injury.

    [i.e. the hungry stomach induces to steal.]

39. The **stream** won't be advised, therefore its course is crooked.
40. **Sweep** first before the door, you can sweep in the backyard afterwards.

    [i.e. bring order into your own house before you try to do so in another's.]

41. One **tooth** makes all the teeth foul.
42. When the trunk of the **tree** is not foul, no fungus comes out of it.
43. **Water** doesn't flow anywhere without carrying stones.

    [i.e. if anyone is conceited they must have a reason for it.]

44. **Words,** like teeth, are many in the mouth.

EFIK (OLD CALABAR) (SOUTHERN NIGERIA)

[Language Family—Sudanic]

1. God creates **dreams.**
2. You **drink** flood and ebb.
3. The **eye** is a thief.
4. He who **falls** by his foot shall rise again ; he who falls by his mouth shall not rise.
5. The asat [**fish**] gives laws to the fishes.
6. If the **goat** has anything, he eats it with the fowl ; if the fowl gets his portion, he goes up on the roof of the house.
7. **" If I had known "** stands behind, it does not come forward.
8. My **life** is set upon her.

   [Literally " my liver ". In many parts of Western Africa and Western Asia the liver is generally said to be the seat of the affections—the liver being looked upon as the intellectual viscus. The Efik speak of " a word from the liver " (sincere opinion) ; " no liver " (no courage). In danger " a man's liver never fails him ".
9. The tree-knot spoils the axe ; hunger spoils **love.**
10. The small tree-climbing **plant** adheres to the large one, and thus grows big.
11. A **poor man** makes market with his shoulders.

    [i.e. shrugs his shoulders.]
12. A straight **road** has no turning.
13. As an old torn basket on a farm road, so the world does not like a **sick man.**
14. By yourself **wisdom** destroys you ; with another you destroy wisdom.
15. The **world** speaks truth to a man as play.

EGYPTIAN-ARABIC

(Including Babylonian and Copt)

[Language Family—Semitic]

1. Who **abandons** a thing may live without it.
2. **Affability** rather than eating bread.
3. Thou hast eaten [or enjoyed] thy **age** for forty-four years ; wait then when it preys upon thee with its back teeth.
4. If God proposes the destruction of an **ant,** he allows wings to grow upon her.

   [i.e. the sudden elevation of persons to stations above their means or capacities may often cause their ruin.]
5. **Avarice** destroys what the avaricious gathers.
6. Expel **avidity** from thy heart ; the fetters will be loosened from thy feet.
7. The **basket** that has two handles can be carried by two.
8. The **beetle** in its hole is a Sultan.
9. The **beetle** is a beauty in the eyes of its mother.

   [Infatuation of parents.]
10. Riding, though upon a **beetle,** rather than walking upon carpets.

    [i.e. persons of high rank in Egypt hold walking in great horror ; and after childhood are rarely seen on foot beyond their own houses.]
11. The merit belongs to the **beginner,** should even the successor do better.
12. Thy **beloved** is the object that thou lovest, were it even a monkey.

13. Man is the slave of **beneficence.**
14. This is not the **bishop's square.**
    [i.e. this is not the proper place for a person—a saying derived from the chess-board, where the square is called " house ".]
15. Who wants a thing is **blind** [to its faults].
16. A **blow** on the purse of another is like a blow on a sand-hill.
17. A **blow** that is profitable does not hurt the neck.
18. A **borrowed cloak** does not keep one warm.
19. The **boy** is the mother's double.
20. He who **builds** on another's land brings up another's child.
21. If you see a town worshipping a **calf,** mow grass and feed him.
22. If thy **camel** break down, put on an **ass-load.**
    [i.e. suit thy business to thy circumstances.]
23. When the **camel** crouches down, put the ass's burden on his back.
24. When a slave mounts a **camel** he wants to ride on both humps.
25. Better the gurgling of the **camel** than the prayers of a fish.
26. He who **chatters** to you will chatter of you.
27. The clever **chicken** crows in the egg.
    [Precocious child.]
28. The **chicken** isn't wiser than the hen.
29. The **church** that is close at hand can work no cures.
30. Live, thou ass, until the **clover** sprouts up.
31. She who **conceives** on the oven will give birth in the " Gorn ".
    [The Egyptian peasant sleeps in winter on the oven ; the " Gorn " is the market-place where the corn is threshed.—What takes place secretly will become known openly.]
32. Avoid vain hopes—**content** is property.
33. Art thou a **corpse-washer,** and dost thou give security for Paradise ?
34. Put your **dates** in the honey-pot—but don't sink it afterwards in the mud of the Nile.
35. A small **date-stone** props up the water-jar.
    [i.e. great princes often owe their security to the meanest of their subjects.]
36. The **day** obliterates the word [or promise] of the night.
    [This means that, when passion has ceased, we forget the promise made while it influenced us.]
37. The **dead** is the best of his family.
38. The market of **debauch** is always open.
39. Always take from a bad **debtor** even if only a stone.
40. One must not shoot a glass arrow into a painted **deer**
41. He who **destroys** a thing should repair it.
42. Everyone has a **detractor** and an adulator.
43. **Dine** and recline if for two minutes ; sup and walk if for two paces.
44. If you owe a **dog** anything, call him " Sir ".
45. The prince's **dog** is a prince.
46. Teach your **dog** to snap and he'll soon bite you.
47. The barking of **dogs** doesn't hurt the clouds.
48. The hunting **dogs** have scratched faces.
49. A **dog's tail** is never straight.
    [Applied to one whose misconduct is invariable.]
50. Catch the halter-rope and it will lead you to the **donkey.**
51. Much goading will teach **donkeys** to rear.
52. Close the **door** from which comes the draught, and be tranquil.
53. He that knocks at the **door** hears an answer.
54. **Earth** is a blessing to those upon her.
55. He who **eats** alone coughs alone.

56. An **egg** cannot break a stone.
57. The riches of **Egypt** are for the foreigners therein.
58. Pass by your **enemy** hungry, but not naked.
59. An **enemy** will not go but at the cost of a friend.
60. You may overcome all **enmity** but that of a rival in trade.
61. **Equality** in injustice is justice.
62. **Evil** is of old date.
63. The master's **eye** is a second spring.
64. The dust alone can fill the **eye** of man.
65. The **eyes** believe themselves, the ears believe others.
66. **False coin** is passed upon none but the shrewd moneychanger.
67. [Treat] your elder as your **father,** your junior as your son, and your equal as your brother.
68. If there were no **fault,** there would be no pardon.
69. A **favour** with a good man is a debt, and with a bad man enmity.
70. **Feed** the mouth, the eye will be bashful.

    [i.e. give presents to great people and they will be ashamed not to look upon you with kindness.]
71. There is not in the **ferry-boat** any [gratis or] for God's sake.
72. Grass grows on his **fireplace.** (*Copt.*)

    [Lacks virtue of hospitality.]
73. Everything **forbidden** is sweet.
74. In crossing the **ford** one sees the defect of the leg.
75. What you can **ford** yourself may drown others.
76. Throw the **fortunate man** into the Nile and he will come out with a fish in his mouth.
77. The blows of a **friend** are like the eating of raisins.
78. Your **friend** chews gravel for you and your enemy counts your faults.
79. An onion with a **friend** is a [roast] lamb.
80. If there be grease on thy hand, rub it off at thy nearest **friends.**

    [Your own kindred share.]
81. A small house will hold a hundred **friends.**
82. No **friendship** except after enmity.
83. **Friendship** is of any day, but posterity is of eternity. (*Babylonian.*)
84. The image of **friendship** is truth.
85. **Gain** upon dirt rather than lose upon musk.
86. Green trees, sweet water, and a kind face make the **garden** [paradise].
87. **Generosity** covers all shame.
88. A **gift** goes on a donkey and returns on a camel.

    [i.e. a small kindness often results in a greater.]
89. A **gleed** will come to ashes.
90. Men depend on men, and all on **God.**
91. He who has no friend has **God.**
92. Every knot has an unraveller in **God.**
93. An hour for your heart and an hour for your **God.**
94. **God** could not be everywhere, so He sent Mother.
95. One can go without **God** into the desert, but not return into the valley of the Nile.
96. There are no two together, but **God** makes a third.
97. **God** provides for the insect between two stones.
98. Take what the **gods** give while their hands are open, for none know what they will withhold when they are shut.
99. The **gold** wants bran.

    [i.e. the great want the assistance of the lowly.—Gold is cleaned with bran.]
100. Do no **good**—thou shalt not find evil.

101. Conceal the **good** you do, take example from the Nile which hides its source.
102. The **hand** that you cannot bite, kiss.
103. If the **harlot** repent, she becomes a procuress.
104. **Haste** is of the devil.
105. One day in [perfect] **health** is much.
106. How many are the roads that lead not to the **heart.**
107. The **heart** cannot hold two.
108. What is in his **heart** is on the tip of his tongue.
109. **Hearts,** like bodies, become tired and should have recreation.
110. In **hell** there are no fans.
111. He commenced to trade in **hennah** and mourning became numerous.

    [Said of an unlucky man—Hennah used at rejoicings.]
112. **Hide** your principles, your money and your journey.
113. A bristle from the **hog's beard** is a gain.
114. Follow the **holy man** no farther than his threshold.
115. Honour [dwells] in the manes of **horses.**

    [This is taken from the saying of Mohammed, and is often quoted to show the superior distinction which a horseman claims above him who rides upon an ass.]
116. No darkness like **ignorance**.
117. Who has made you weep has **instructed** you ; who has made you laugh has ridiculed you.
118. Your **insulter** is he who brings you the report.
119. There are men who are **keys** to good and locks to evil.
120. From **knocking** till good-bye.
121. The griminess of **labour** is better than the saffron of sloth.
122. The dirt of **labour** rather than the saffron of indulgence.
123. He that is in the wrong has no **legs,** but he that is in the right has four.
124. Stretch your **legs** to the extent of your carpet [sleeping-rug].
125. If you are a **liar,** recollect.
126. A smooth **lie** is better than a distorted truth.
127. **Life** is a dancing girl.
128. Ye that are **like** unto us, come to us.
129. He who **likes** a thing will mention it often.
130. The **lion's den** is not free from bones.

    [Quoted to one who has money to spare though he denies it.]
131. A **loafer** [if he go to] another city becomes [its] head. (*Babylonian.*)

    [A prophet is not without honour save in his own country.]
132. The foot treads where you **love.**
133. **Love** and show, hate and hide.
134. Sometimes **love** has been implanted by one glance alone.
135. If you **love,** love a moon, and if you steal, steal a camel.
136. A blow from our **lover** is as [sweet as] the eating of raisins.
137. If you have no relatives, get **married.**
138. **Marry** from the sheepfold, and not from your relatives.
139. If **mendicity** should unfortunately be thy lot, knock at the large gates only.
140. The world is a **mirror** ; show thyself in it and it will reflect thy image.

    [People will be frank with you.]
141. **Misfortune** itself rather than suspense.
142. **Money** is sweet balm.
143. White **money** is useful in a black day.
144. A rose fell to the lot of a **monkey.**

    [Said of persons little deserving their good luck.]
145. If the **monkey** reigns, prostrate thyself before him.
146. If the **moon** be with thee, thou needest not to care about the stars.

147. Paradise is open at the command of **mothers.**

148. The **naked** in a caravan enjoys tranquiility.

149. At the **narrow-passage** there is no brother and no friend.

150. The **needle** carried but one thread, and the heart cannot carry two.

151. I speak to you, O daughter-in-law, that you may hear, O **neighbour.**

152. If your **neighbour** cannot endure you, change your house-door.

153. If thy **neighbour** dislike thee, change the gate of thy house.

154. Man can do without his friends, but not without his **neighbours.**

155. Take your **news** from the little ones.

156. The words of the **night** are coated with butter ; as soon as the sun shines they melt away.

157. Do not ask that that which you write in the **Nile** should be read in the desert.

158. When the **nut** laughs it is its death.

159. If you would be **obeyed,** ask what is feasible.

160. He that **obeyeth** becometh one obeyed.

(Ptah-Hotep.)

161. If there is no **oil** in the house one cannot very well give it to the mosque.

162. If thou seest a **one-eyed** person pass by, turn up a stone.

[The Arabs regard a one-eyed man as a bad omen and nobody wishes to meet him.]

163. If an **onion** causes his loud rejoicings, what then shall we say to sugar ?

164. Live in a place and eat of its **onions.**

165. Ask the **opinion** of an older one and a younger one than thyself, and return to thine own opinion.

166. Follow the **owl,** she will lead thee to a ruined place.

[On the consequences of bad company.]

167. The **ox** that ploughs is not to be muzzled.

[This was a precept of the Jewish law. See Deuteronomy xxv. 4. We must necessarily trust those we employ in any business. Oxen, camels and other cattle were muzzled to prevent their grazing in the fields of strangers in passing along the road ; for there are not in Egypt any enclosures.]

168. Without human companions **paradise** itself would be an undesirable place. (*Also Moslem.*)

169. **Partnership** is parting.

170. **Patience** opens the door of rest.

171. When the **patient** is cured he forgets the healing hand.

172. The marriage of **paupers** only increases beggars.

173. The **peace-maker** does not gain except by the tearing of his garments.

174. The **penniless** is the king's debtor.

175. Those are [esteemed] the best **people** through whom one gains.

176. Ask from the experienced rather than from the **physician.**

177. The **pilgrim's** back carries little to the fatherland.

178. **Pinching** is enmity even from a silver finger, and biting is affection even from a dog's mouth.

179. He that stirs **poison** will taste it.

180. Learn **politeness** from the impolite.

181. **Poverty** without debt is real wealth.

182. **Power** is sweet to nurse, bitter to wean.

183. Eat the **present** [sent to thee] and break the dish [in which it was brought]—the dish will otherwise remind you of the obligation.

184. If I am to be **prince**, and you are to be prince, who is to drive the donkey?

185. Everyone sells his **rags** in his own market.

[i.e. everyone displays his distinguishing qualities in his own circle of acquaintances.]

186. The **reed-player** of [your own] street does not charm.

187. Do not **rejoice** over him who goes, before you see him who comes.

188. Your **relations** are your scorpions.

189. The knife of **relatives** is blunt.

190. A **ring** does not give protection. (*Babylonian.*)

191. A long **road** brings out faults.

192. The **rose** left a thorn behind it, and the thorn a rose.

193. For the **rose** the thorn is watered.

194. Moonlight and oil [together] are the **ruin** of a house.

195. In every **ruin** we find a devil.

196. The **sad man** rose to enjoy himself, but found no room.

197. A thing that does not **satiate** creates hunger.

198. If thou feedest, **satisfy**; if thou beatest, hurt.

199. Half-naked, but carrying the **scales.**

[Miserable but still laying claim to the habits of the wealthy merchants, who carry a small balance in their wide sleeves to weigh the sequins and gold coins which they receive in payment.]

200. The **shadow** of a man and not the shadow of a wall.

[Expression used to induce a girl to marry.]

201. He teaches himself **shaving** on the heads of the orphans.

202. Thou hast the advantage of the angry, when thou keepest **silence.** (*From Ptah Hotep's collection.*)

203. Thou canst not **slap** with one hand.

204. He who is bitten by a **snake** is afraid of an end of rope.

205. The **something** is better than its want.

206. Every **soul** is monarch in its own body.

207. To him who is replete after **starvation,** pray God to give firmness of mind.

208. A **stone** turning is sure to be chipped.

209. The **strong man** lives from the price of his hire, but the weak lives from the price of his children. (*Babylonian.*)

210. If God make me **sultan** I would sow the earth with saffron.

211. He who is standing on the shore may as well be a spent **swimmer.**

212. Leave off ambiguous **talking,** should it even be true.

213. The impudent have their **tears** always ready.

214. Nothing wipes your **tears** away but your own hand.

215. He only loosed the **tent-peg.** (*Copt.*)

[Said of one who commits a trifling fault.]

216. **Three things** will make a man feel subdued; a woman if she were balm; a debt of even a drachm; a question, even if it be only to know the road.

217. **Tobacco** without coffee is like a prince without furs.

218. If I were to **trade** in winding-sheets, no one would die.

[Said of one unfortunate in commercial speculations.]

219. He who **treats** you as himself, does you no injustice.

220. A **tree** that affords thee shade, do not order it to be cut down.

221. **Truth** is the porter of God.

222. The **tyrant** is only the slave turned inside out.

223. If you are **ugly,** be winsome.

224. Everyone jumps a low **wall.**

225. Low-lying land drinks its own **water** and that of other places.

[i.e. humility.]

226. When **water** comes to hand, the washing with sand is abolished.
227. Rippling **water** will not drown anyone.
228. The man who carries a **water-skin** with holes in it, it leaks down his back.
229. He whose **wealth** perplexes him may buy pigeons and let them fly.
230. **Wealth** which comes in at the door unjustly, goes out at the windows.
231. I have made no man to **weep.**

    [A saying taken from " The Book of the Dead "—at least 4,000 years old.]
232. **Welcome** me rather than give me a meal.
233. In the **well** out of which you drink, throw no stone.
234. A **well** of sweet water is always empty.
235. The jealousy of a **wife** is the key to her divorce.
236. A **wife** will be doubly attached if her chain is pleasant.

    [Probably one of the oldest proverbs known—from Ptah Hotep's collection, over 3,000 years before the Christian era.]
237. What can the **wind** take from the stone paving?

    [Where there is nothing the King loses his rights.]
238. He built a **wine-shop** out of a raisin.

    [Shows how calumny makes a crime out of nothing.]
239. A house may hold a hundred men, but the heart of a **woman** has only room for one of them.
240. The gossip of two **women** will destroy two houses.
241. **Work** [were it only] for a single grain, and reckon up the profits of him who does nothing.
242. The **world** is like a dancing girl; it dances to everyone for a little while.
243. [That is] thy **world** wherein thou findest thyself.
244. He who has a **wound** on the head will touch it.
245. He who is **wrong** fights against himself. (*From Ptah Hotep's collection.*)

EWE (DAHOMÉ, SLAVE COAST)

[Language Family—Sudanic]

1. An **amiable person** is never good-for-nothing.
2. What encircles the **arm** is not enough for the loins.
3. **Birds** with long beaks eat far-off things.
4. It is easy to have a distant **brother** or relation.
5. **A child** that asks questions isn't stupid.
6. The **child** that has never been into a strange town, says its mother cooks best.
7. **Clothes** are men.
8. One **day** throws another day down.
9. That which one sees in the **day-time** one need not seek with torches.
10. **Distance** suppresses the unpleasant.
11. The hunting **dog** doesn't sleep over the leopard's den.
12. The little **dog** should cross the river first before it curses the crocodile's mouth.
13. The **dog** that is always running around gets dung on its ears.

14. Yesterday's **earth** isn't heavy for the neck.
 [i.e. work done no longer tires.]
15. What one does in the **field** is no better than what one does at home.
16. The ripe **fig** sends no message to the birds; they themselves observe that it is ripe.
17. **Firewood** from a distance is good wood.
18. The **fruit** falls under the tree.
19. He who has only one **garment** doesn't wash it on a rainy day.
20. When your **garment** is torn, you have nothing further to do with soap.
21. The **good stuff's** stripes are not wide.
22. Even if one lives a long life, one doesn't pass the **grave** by.
23. The **gums** understand best the teeth's affairs.
24. One can't clean with a bare **hand** [without sand, etc.].
25. That which one has in the **hand** doesn't deceive one.
26. The quickly moving **hand** gathers the mushroom.
27. So long as the **head** is alive the knee doesn't put on two hats.
 [i.e. while the King lives his son doesn't rule.]
28. A wandering **hunter** encounters a wandering beast.
29. **Joy** goes before, life's need follows after.
30. The dry **leaf** doesn't sink at once when it falls into the water.
31. **Maize** has no rights with the hen.
32. **Misfortune** doesn't bind a cloth round its head before it comes into the town.
 [i.e. misfortune comes unawares.]
33. When the **mouse** eats the stone pot, the pumpkin skin gets alarmed.
34. The **mouth** talks plenty that the heart does not say.
35. A [little] **needle** sews coarse cloth.
36. The broken **pitcher** doesn't go to the waterhole.
37. To the **potter** belong the broken pieces.
38. The **potter** eats off broken dishes.
39. The **rain** that is driven by the wind shows where the entrance to the house should be made.
40. He who stretches out his legs will never be **rich.**
41. Those who have gone before make the **road** dirty.
42. **Salt** is the earth's brother.
 [i.e. no separation of true friendship.]
43. One **scratches** where one is bitten.
44. The end of all roads is the **sleeping-chamber.**
 [i.e. death.]
45. Dry leaves make the importance of the **snake.**
 [Because even a small snake makes much noise moving through dry leaves.]
46. A crooked stick doesn't reach the **snake** in its hole.
47. When the **snake** is in the house one need not discuss the matter at length.
48. One finger alone cannot drink the **soup.**
49. Good **soup** draws the chair to it.
50. That which is in the **stomach** carries that which is on the head.
51. One **stomach** eats and another stomach is swelled up.
52. When the **stomach** sleeps, the man sleeps.
53. **A stone** in the water-hole does not feel the cold.
54. He who throws **stones** in the night kills his brother.
55. **Sweetness** goes before, and pain follows after.
56. The **thread** follows the needle.
57. One doesn't despise the **thumb** when one would bind the cord.
58. The **tongue** belongs to the disorderly woman.
59. When a single **tree** is exposed to the wind, it breaks.

60. The crooked **tree** says he has been bent to the earth.
61. One sits on a crooked **tree** to fell a straight one.
62. A **tree** without a crown [top] is not shaken by the wind.
63. A **trumpet** in the house hurts the ears.
    [i.e. self-praise.]
64. No one goes on foot into the **underworld.**
65. Dirty **water** also will wash dirt.
66. Those who have experienced nothing mistake the sound of **weeping** for singing.
67. It is better to have a disorderly **wife** than to remain a bachelor.
68. Crooked **wood** makes crooked ashes.
69. In crooked **wood** one recognizes the artist.
70. The **wood** that refuses a forest fire doesn't refuse a bonfire.

FANTI

[Language Family—Sudanic]

1. Cross the river before you abuse the **crocodile.**
2. **Day sleep** maketh the eyes sore.

FULFULDE (NORTH CAMEROONS, FRENCH GUINEA AND UPPER NIGER)

(Singular, " Ful " or " Pulo ". Called by the French " Peuls et Toucouleure ".)

[Language Family—Hamitic]

1. Every little **act** is an act in return.
2. A **being together** is good but also bad.
3. A single **bracelet** doesn't jingle.
    [There is peace with one wife.]
4. **Children** are the adornment of marriage.
5. He who has **children** is he who has blessings.
6. Against the illness of **death** there is no medicine.
7. All that has killed the foliage will **die** with it.
    [i.e. he who digs a grave for another will fall into it himself.]
8. Those who will weep for you on the day you **die,** you buy them whilst you are alive.
9. The best means against **dying** is giving birth.
10. If the word is ailing, may the **ears** be in good health.
11. That which prevents the **ears** from growing is that they have to hear every day something they haven't heard before.
    [i.e. rules and regulations are always being changed, so how can one get experience ?]
12. Gifted **ears** sprout on a gifted head.
    [i.e. an intelligent man makes use of all he hears.]
13. It is not in all pierced **ears** that gold is put.
    [i.e. not all realize their ambitions.]
14. Not all that which is white is **eaten.**
    [i.e. beware of appearances.]

15. The **eye** goes where it will not, but the foot never.

    [i.e. a proof of one's sincerity in visiting a friend.]

16. The **eyes** are truly equal in the head, but the hand goes to the one that has something in it.

    [i.e. help goes to those in distress although all men are equal.]

17. Three **fingers** cover the mouth of their master [so that it can't lie].

18. That which comes first is being **free,** and then ruling.

19. To-day and to-morrow ; only God sees the **future.**

20. The **gazelle** jumps, and should her child crawl ?

21. A bare **hand** doesn't grasp fire.

    [i.e. he who has no money cannot purchase anything.]

22. The keeping of one's **head** exceeds the keeping of one's hat.

23. That which is **hot** can become cold, and that which is cold can become hot.

24. "**It belongs to me**" is better than "it belongs to us"

25. Go your **journey** slowly and you sleep far.

26. When something is hot it is better to **kindle** it.

27. No one is without **knowledge** except him who asks no questions.

28. The hole of the **lie** is not deep.

29. **Love** is a donkey freed of all tethers.

30. **Love** is like seaweed, even if you have pushed it away, that will not prevent its coming [back].

31. When you see that your **neighbour's** beard is catching fire, bring water to your own.

32. To be **neighbours** of the heart, is better than being neighbours of the hearth.

    [i.e. to remain friends one should not live in the same house.]

33. The **one-eyed man** doesn't thank God until he sees a blind man.

34. The **patient man** becomes the victor.

35. Borrowing is the first-born of **poverty.**

36. A **priest** may also produce a thief.

37. The medicine for hate is **separation.**

38. **Silence** is also speech.

39. He who has not chosen a place to **sit down** will get up with bits of straw on his garment.

    [i.e. choose your companions.]

40. Going **slowly** doesn't stop one arriving.

41. He who has not consented to be **smelt** must consent to be bitten.

42. What each one **sows** he reaps.

43. That which the **stomach** can obtain could be all contained in the mouth.

    [i.e. one keeps for oneself many more things than one could say.]

44. He who has few **tears** must quickly make the face of one who is about to cry.

    [i.e. the weak must shout out soon for help.]

45. If someone has bitten you it reminds you that you have **teeth.**

46. To do **too much** to obtain a thing makes one miss it.

47. Mere **travelling** is better than mere sitting. Hitting the nail is better than shooting past.

48. Scattered **water** is better than a broken pitcher.

49. The **wind** drives into a cavity what it can no longer drive out.

    [i.e. a fault committed is difficult to repair.]

50. **Woman** is fire ; if you must take some, take a little.

51. Dry **wood** may not be bent, but fresh.

52. To the word of this **year** one replies next.

    [i.e. the offended party is wise to be patient.]

GA, OR ACCRA (GOLD COAST)

[Language Family—Sudanic]

1. Nobody is twice **ashamed.**
2. A **bad person** is better than an empty house.
3. An old **broom** is better than a new one.
4. Nobody shows heaven to a **child.**
5. A **child** builds a second storey and an old man dwells downstairs.

   [Relates to the changes and chances of life.]
6. A **crab** does not beget a bird.
7. If the **dedei** [fish] leaves the river and says the crocodile is sick, then it is truly sick.
8. It is the **ear** that troubles the mouth.
9. What is not **eaten** is not cooked.
10. Not with both **eyes** people look into a bottle.
11. Nobody measures the river with both of his **feet.**
12. About a sweet **fish** there is danger.
13. **Food** you will not eat you do not boil.

    [i.e. people will not work at any task unless they see their advantage in it.]
14. Nobody is twice a **fool.**
15. If thou huskest corn with the **fowl** it will not esteem thee.
16. The mother of the **goat** is looked at [if] the kid is bought.
17. The **hand** does not deceive one.
18. **Hate** has no medicine.
19. If thy **knife** cut thee, thou sheathest it.
20. He who makes a **knot,** knows how to loose it.
21. The **mouth** does not know that its master is afraid.
22. A hot **needle** burns the thread.
23. If thou pound **palm-nuts,** some will stain thy cloth.
24. The day when the **pig** will be caught, the wild boar will lead the way.
25. **A poor man's** pipe does not sound.
26. The **potter** eats out of a potsherd.
27. The days of **poverty** are more than the days of superfluity.
28. A **river** moves a river on.
29. No **sleep,** no dream.
30. A **stick** that goes into the fire begins to burn.
31. A **wife** is like a giant.
32. **Winds** have ears.

GALLA (SOUTHERN ABYSSINIA)

[Language Family—Hamitic]

1. The **Amara** who does not cultivate the earth spits upon five loaves.

   [The Amara despises agricultural work.]
2. What has been **blown away** is not found again.
3. That the **calf** has become a bull is known in the enclosure.

   [i.e. only the members of a family can appreciate the virtues of their relatives.]
4. A **calf** that is sucking does not bellow.

   [i.e. the vassal does not rebel so long as he has a rich country to exploit.]
5. The **calves** do not fear the horns of their mother.
6. A good **conversation** is better than a good bed.
7. When **cows** are about to go out they lick one another; when

men are about to die they love one another.

8. The way and the thought **divide** people.
9. The **dog** who likes soup does not quarrel.

   [He fears to lose his dinner.]
10. If thou hast not examined, do not burn thy **finger.**

    [i.e. do not undertake an enterprise without forethought.]
11. Upon **food** one does not grow fat ; upon thought one fattens.
12. O, **fool !** there is a precipice at thy back.

    [Said to one who is pleased with false flattery.]
13. What **God** has sent does not fail to reach the earth.
14. What one **hopes** for is better than what one finds.
15. One rises, one dies, the **land** increases.

    [The family property is increased as much by the birth of a son who can conquer new lands as by the death of an old man who leaves his heritage to the survivors.]
16. A **lie** cannot be overtaken.
17. The lower **lip** scorns the upper lip.

    [i.e. the pot calls the kettle black.]
18. If you wish to be blamed **marry ;** if you wish to be praised die.
19. Nothing sprouts in the enclosure [if] the **master** does not himself watch over it.
20. Move your **neck** according to the music.
21. One knows even when one's **neighbour's** bread is in the oven.
22. The **poor man** and the fire do not like to be poked.
23. If a man comes, a **quarrel** comes.
24. " [The other time] I was sweet ; lick me [now]," said the **salt.**
25. He who is **sated** spits out honey.
26. He who has nothing to do **scatters** and gathers.
27. Do not say, " I have heard him," do not say, " I have seen him," if thou hast not first **searched** his heart.
28. Wisely He [God] denied feet to the **serpent.**

    [With feet he would have destroyed the world.]
29. The **skin** creaks according to the country.

    [i.e. different countries, different customs.]
30. Thou hast not yet reached the warm **spring** and thou art already intoxicated with the water of the pool.
31. The **stick** only breaks earthenware utensils.
32. A single **stick** smokes but does not burn.
33. The **tail** and repentance go behind.
34. With one **wife** the heart is warmed ; with the other wife the kettle is warmed.

    [i.e. two wives are necessary, one beautiful and one rich.]

GANDA (LUGANDA) (UGANDA)

[Language Family—Bantu]

1. **Age** repeats youth like the red onion.

   [This fruit reddens when ripe, reproducing the colour of its blossom. A comparison between childhood and second childhood.]
2. **Beardlessness** is a cloudy day.

   [i.e. cannot tell age or time.]
3. If you suffer in order to be **beautiful,** don't blame anyone but yourself.

4. **Beer** isn't food ; don't be content with it.
   [i.e. sour grapes.]
5. He who **betrays** you is not one from afar.
6. Who seeks you to **borrow** doesn't seek you to repay.
7. The **canoes** may die at the landing-stage.
   [i.e. ingratitude.]
8. **Caution** is not cowardice ; even the ants march armed.
9. He who says they are **cheating** you does not lend to you.
10. If you look in a **chief's** bag you will always find something.
11. **Children** never have enough when they cater for themselves.
12. Who does not know the **cold** of the other world !
    [Local custom to cover grave with thatch of plantain leaves to keep off cold.]
13. The one who **confesses** will pay back a little.
14. **Death** is like a wild animal.
15. The **despised** person is ever present.
16. If **disgrace** falls on your mother, it falls on your father's wife.
    [i.e. one wife of a man gets implicated in the fault of her fellow-wife.]
17. The **dog** is wiser than his master.
    [When a man, accompanied by his dog, meets a friend in the street, the dog sits down, thus preserving his energies.]
18. They don't coax the **dog** with a stone in the hand.
19. Don't strain your **ears** where you lend your axe.
    [Listening for a return.]
20. **Eat** and put back.
21. The **eyes** are afraid.
22. Hungry **eyes** search the plantations.
23. Not knowing one's own [**failings**] makes one blame one better [than oneself].
24. **Familiarity** is like the sea which kills the fisherman.
25. You obtain many things when you do not see your **father** and mother.
26. No man **fears** what he has seen grow.
27. **Feet** are the life of men.
28. If a **fool** gives you his mother, take her away with you.
29. The man who is a **friend** doesn't think it necessary to tell you when he swallows his saliva.
30. My **friends** love me before I have had a bad fall.
31. **Friendship** costs much.
32. **Friendship** is like a tailor's seam, it is the unpicking that causes trouble.
33. **Friendship** slays many evils.
34. Even a little thing brings **friendship** to remembrance.
35. You can pray " **God help me** " when you have put forth all your speed.
36. The man who escorts you through the night wins your **gratitude** at daybreak.
37. He for whom you are **grieved** in your heart has only head sorrow for you.
38. The **grumbler** does not leave his job, but he discourages possible applicants.
39. The house does not die that welcomes a **guest.**
    [Said when a man stops beating his wife when a stranger arrives, or when a sick man is visited by the medicine-man.]
40. Empty **hands** are only pleasing to their owner.
41. Where the **heart** dwells the feet will early go.
42. The **heart** is a market-place.
43. That which does not kill the **herdsman** will not touch his cows.
44. Even a poor **hoe-handle** is remembered in the cultivating season.
45. He who takes **hold** slowly goes a long way.
46. The man of two **homes** dies of hunger.

47. Before the swelling comes the **illness** is only known to the sufferer.
48. The **iron** is lost without the wood.
    [Reference to hammer and handle.]
49. The **king** is like the sea.
    [i.e. the sea doesn't differentiate.]
50. **Laughter** kills the friendship of the young.
51. He who does not **lie** never grows up.
52. You may condemn the one you **love,** but you pay his fine for him.
53. Brethren **love** each other when they are equally rich.
54. Brotherly **love** is like thread in the needle, unless it projects beyond the eye it will not profit.
55. He who **loves** you makes you build on a rock.
56. Does the **monkey** pronounce judgment in the forest?
57. **Night** is the poor man's friend.
58. He who **passes** you in the morning, you pass him at night.
59. True **pity** for the sorrowful pays his debt.
60. The **poor man's** a fool, he lives on loss.
61. **Prudence** wasn't born yesterday; you're robbed when you sleep.
62. **Relationship** will die.
63. To **remain** in one place does not make you wise.
64. **Resting** isn't getting there.
65. **Reward** does not tie your feet.
66. That which is deadly does not lack a sweet **scent.**
67. The man who grows up by the **sea** is drowned at last.
68. The one who knows not **sorrow** makes you talk of yours in the doorway.
69. You can't dig with a **spade** handle, but it helps the spade to dig.
70. **Spirit** help me, having put my mind to it.
71. It is no good asking the **spirits** to help you run if you don't mean to sprint.
72. The **stick** that's in your neighbour's house is no use for the leopard [at your door].
73. He who has not **suffered** does not know how to pity.
74. Wait-till-it-passes pierces the **tail.**
75. Who makes you pay in **tears,** you make him pay in blood.
76. If you **wait** till [the whole animal] appears, you will only spear the tail.
77. You have no **wisdom** if you go to sleep before you make your bed.
78. Even a **wise man** makes a mistake; the ears do not perceive a smell.
79. The beautiful **woman** is the sister of many.
80. **Words** are easy, friendship hard.

GIRYAMA (KENYA COLONY)

[Language Family—Bantu]

1. **Advice** is the grandchild, it comes behind.
2. One's own **arrow** does not hurt.
3. He who refuses **beans** refuses the sauce.
4. In the house of **beer** no beer stays.
5. Chip, chip, finishes the **block.**
6. The **broth** from a distance grows cool on the road.
7. Where there is a **corpse,** there the vultures assemble.
8. The remedy for the **debtor** is to pay.
9. He who is not yet dead is not yet clear of **defects.**

10. **Desire** is above, gratification on the neck.

    [i.e. one desires things out of reach, but must be content with things at hand.]

11. That which thou hast **eaten** is thine own.

12. **Eating** and paying, that is [the way] to clear the road.

13. The **elephant** is not weighed down by his tusks.

    [i.e. the rich do not feel their wealth as a burden.]

14. **Endure,** and drink your medicine.

15. One **eye** does not finish the open country.

16. For the **eye** to see is not to eat.

17. The wound given by a **friend** does not heal.

18. He who has nothing of his own has **God.**

19. **Good words** bring out the lizard from his hole.

20. **Gossiping** and lying are brother and sister.

21. The **heart** has no fallow ground.

    [i.e. no spare ground which can be cultivated when the first is exhausted.]

22. To cultivate with an old worn-out **hoe** is to go without a new one.

23. When **hoes** are together they cannot fail to knock each other.

24. **Hot water** does not burn down the house.

    [i.e. hard words break no bones.]

25. **Human beings** do not love each other.

26. The **hyena** of your own country does not break your bone.

27. He who endures **ill** is not taught.

28. To rest [on the road] does not end the **journey.**

29. The **load** grows heavy near home.

30. The **load** without is wont to be carried by the load within.

31. That which is **loved** by the heart is a remedy.

32. He who gets drunk on **mead** gets sober, but he who gets drunk on wealth does not.

33. **Ordering** is not guarding.

34. The **poor man's** [beast] does not bring forth a heifer.

35. **Praise** is for the man who has gone to the grave.

    [i.e. it is considered unlucky to praise a man before his death.]

36. It is she who is **pregnant** who will bear the son.

    [i.e. the richer is the successful of two suitors.]

37. Those who **quarrel** are two.

38. A quarrel with a **relation** is a fall into water.

39. **Relationship** is not bought; what is bought is friendship.

40. An elder is a **rubbish heap** to carry everything to, good and evil.

41. A man **scratches** where he can reach.

42. The **sheep** is fat behind.

    [Said when a man has left his place on account of scarcity, and hears that plenty has prevailed since his departure.]

43. He who pegs out the **skin** of an animal draws it towards himself.

    [i.e. every man for himself.]

44. The child of a **snake** is not taught to bite.

45. If you burn the **soldier-ants** the [harmless] ants get scorched.

    [Fire seems to be the only check on the "tsalafu" which consume every living thing in their path.]

46. He who has one **soul** does not rejoice; let him make two hearts, one for laughing and the second for grieving.

47. **Speak,** lest to-morrow you be prevented.

48. A **stranger** is [like] rain, he strikes [you] and passes by.

49. If the **sun** shines it will warm.

50. **Tellers** there are ; listeners there are none.
51. The **toe** which has been wounded is the one which is stubbed.
52. **War** does not bring up a child.
53. **War** has no eyes.
54. The first-goer draws not muddy **water.**
55. [Things] of **water** are those which grow in water ; [things] of wood are those which grow in wood.

GOGO (CIGOGO) (KENYA COLONY)

[Language Family—Bantu]

1. Pay your **creditor** that he may not be following you.
2. If always in contact there is sure to be **friction.**
3. Leave a **good name** behind in case you return.
4. The **hand** giving out and the hand returning.
5. That which the **heart** likes you will eat.
6. **A liar** is in a hurry, take a seat and sit down.
7. Learn from the way your hair keeps from growing into your eyes to have **modesty.**
8. If you have no **mother** you won't neglect your work.
9. With the **mouth** one offends, and with the mouth one apologizes.
10. It is the custom of **relations** by marriage to help themselves to one another's things.
11. He who takes a light to find the whereabouts of a **snake** should commence at his feet.
12. The **world** is full of blanks.

GREBO (LIBERIA)

[Language Family—Sudanic]

1. We do not know the **child** of wealth by his size.
2. One should see with one's **eye,** never with one's hand.

   [Said to a Grebo when caught stealing.]
3. Do not measure your **house timbers** in the forest.
4. The **paddle** which you find in the canoe is the one that will take you across.

HAUSA (NORTHERN NIGERIA)

[Language Family—Hamitic]

1. There is no not-getting-a-thing if you seek it from **Allah.**
2. The truly contented man comes from **Allah.**
3. **Allah** does not give the expert in chewing any grain.
4. **Allah** has the portioning out [of blessings] ; if it was man who had the distribution of them, some would go without.
5. **Allah** is the cure for all [ills].
6. **Allah** preserve us from " Had I known ".

7. **Allah,** you have no evil, you make the rain to fall even on the wizard's garden.
8. He who **asks** does not go wrong, but his secret is dug up.
9. If a man says he is going to swallow his **axe,** hold the handle for him.
10. Better a poor **axe** than "cut and let me have yours".
11. **Axe,** there is the meat; meat, there is the fire.
12. If you see your brother's **beard** on fire, seek water to pour on your own.
13. A **bearded man** is a truthful one.

    [i.e. beard the hall-mark of respectability.]
14. The **blind man** says the eye has a bad smell.
15. Don't seek **blood** from a locust, God didn't put it there.
16. **Blood** has more dregs than water.
17. If the **bottle** is shaking it will not be filled.

    [i.e. a rolling stone gathers no moss.]
18. However cunning the **bride,** she will be smeared with oil.

    [Henna is now used instead of oil.]
19. When you eat a round **cake,** do you begin at the centre?
20. He who is **carried** does not realize that the town is far off.
21. Where there is **character,** ugliness is beauty; where no character, beauty is ugliness.
22. **Chattering** doesn't cook the rice.
23. The **chief** [or head of the family] is like a dust-heap, every one comes with his sweepings and deposits them.
24. You who **condemn** on hearsay evidence alone, your sins increase.
25. Quantity makes the **cotton** draw a stone.

    [i.e. unity is strength.]
26. They pat the **cow** before they begin to milk her.
27. The **dog** and his collar are both the booty of the hyena.
28. Does **dog** eat dog?
29. Bowing to a **dwarf** will not prevent your standing erect again.
30. The **dweller** in a room knows where the roof leaks.
31. If the **ear** hears, the body is saved.
32. An **egg** in the mouth is better than a hen in the coop.
33. **Eggs** and stones will not stay in the same place.
34. If a bad man has sown **evil, do** you set your sickle to it and cut it down.
35. **Evil** is a hill—everyone gets up on his own and proclaims that of another!
36. **Evil** knows where evil sleeps.
37. Dig the hole of **evil** shallow.
38. The **eye** which sees the smoke will look for fire.
39. It is not the **eye** which understands, but the mind.
40. Every **fault** is laid at the door of the hyena, but it does not steal a bale of cloth.
41. If you won't have a man in his shirt-sleeves on a **feast-day,** you must have him when mixing mud for building.
42. [If you have] a big log, you have a **fire** beside you all night; if a stick, then ashes only.
43. The only prevention against **fire** is to have two houses.
44. No, So-and-so is a **fish** from a well.

    [i.e. a shy man.]
45. It is not the obtaining of **food** which is hard, it is [the finding of] a place where you can go and eat it which is so difficult.
46. Two pieces of meat confuse the mind of the **fly.**
47. A **fool** is always a slave.
48. Returning [for a thing forgotten] is the cure for **forgetfulness.**
49. A ladder above a ladder, a friend's **friend.**

50. There are three **friends** in this world—courage, sense and insight.
51. **A frown** is not a slap.
    [i.e. it does not hurt.]
52. If you see a **goat** at the lion's sleeping-place, you fear her.
53. If the owner of a **goat** is not afraid to travel by night, the owner of a hyena certainly will not be.
54. The plant which **God** favours will grow, even lacking rain.
55. A grain of wheat on a rock, **God** must give it water.
56. If you are going to ask from **God,** take a big receptacle.
57. The man of the world, if you do him a **good turn,** will do you a bad one.
58. "**Had I known**" is like the back of a man's head, it is always left behind.
59. The prize for the race is given to the **hare** and the frog must accept the fact.
60. If you see a **hare** dancing on the dog's earth mound, you may be sure he is carrying a leopard on his back.
61. When the **heart** undertakes, the body is its slave.
62. **Henna** stains quickly.
63. "**He who has**" precedes "he who wants".
64. To have [a **horse**] is better than to be able [to ride].
65. Does **hunger** lick the hand of thirst?
66. **Hurry** is not strength.
67. It is the stinking bit of meat that catches the **hyena.**
68. The cry of the **hyena** and the loss of the goat are one.
    [i.e. they occur at the same time.]
69. While the **hyena** drinks, the dog can only look on.
70. Even when the **king** dances, the poor man says "good".
71. Lack of **knowledge** is darker than night.
72. **A lie** can give more pain than a spear.
73. If you dig a hole for a **lie,** don't dig deep.
74. **Live** patiently in the world; [know that] those who hate you are more numerous than those who love you.
75. **Love** yourself, others will hate you; hate yourself, others will love you.
76. The man with **meat** seeks fire.
77. We are **mice** of the same hole; if we do not meet when going in, we meet when going out.
78. Doing **mischief** is pleasanter than repairing it.
79. If one has not a **mother** of one's own, one makes one whom one calls one's "house-mother".
80. The **mouth** cuts through the neck.
    [i.e. can cause someone's destruction.]
81. Cease looking at its small size, the **needle** is steel.
82. The **nose** does not know the flavour of the salt.
83. **A one-eyed man** does not thank God until he sees a man wholly blind.
84. If you are not going to drink the **pap,** stop stirring it.
85. The small **pot** [the wife] goes to and fro, but the big pot [the husband] remains at home [does no work].
86. **Prayer** won't prevent you from dying.
87. **Relations** are like a coat of thorns, you put it on and it pricks you, you cannot [are not fit to] pull it off and throw it away.
88. **Relations** are like a part of your body; if anything touches it, however small, you feel it.
89. Who knows best? Who hates his own **relations** except a fool?
90. The value of **relationship** lies in the feet.
91. One pair of **shoulders,** ten gowns; one gown, ten pairs of shoulders.

92. Small **showers** fill the stream.
93. The hill of the **slanderer,** [when you take that way] follow it with the name of Allah [on your lips].
94. If you refuse to live with the **slanderer,** whom are you going to live with ?
95. Better **sleep** hungry than play with a boy.
96. Going **slowly** does not prevent arriving.
97. The **stone** which is in the water does not know that the hill is [parched] in the **sun.**
98. There are five of which a man should be **suspicious**—a horse, a woman, night, a river and the forest.
99. **Terror** is a thing of the wilds ; shame of the home [the abode of men].
100. It is because of **to-morrow** that one cleans up at night.

    [i.e. returning borrowed articles that they may be borrowed again.]
101. By **travelling** " softly, softly " you will sleep far away.
102. The share of the **turtle** is not found in the fire.
103. Since the **vulture** has brought me my heart's desire, the ostrich may go away with its beautiful feathers.
104. The **vulture's** foot spoils the soup.
105. At the same time as the **wall** itself is built the finger-marks on it are made.
106. **Wealth** is the cure for punishment.
107. If you hear " **welcome** " you will also hear " May you reach home in safety."

    [i.e. the guest will not stay for ever.]
108. With wealth one wins a **woman.**
109. **A woman** is more crafty than a king.
110. The wiles of a **woman** [which are known to men] are ninety-and-nine, but not even Satan has discovered the hundredth.
111. **A woman's** strength is a multitude of words.
112. To volunteer for **work** is worse than slavery.

HAYA (NORTH-WESTERN TANGANYIKA)

[Language Family—Bantu]

1. He who gnaws the **bones** knows how he will swallow them.
2. He who eats the **brain** must get through the hair.
3. He who has not carried your **burden** knows not what it weighs.
4. Two things agreeable to the taste burn the **cheeks.**

    [i.e. one cannot serve two masters.]
5. The **child** of others whom you send to the Capital to salute the king, pays court on his own account [forgets you].
6. The utility of the **cock** is shown at night.
7. Why criticize that which you have not **cooked ?**
8. If you have only one **cow** you don't say, " Which cow gave this milk ? "
9. The **crime** committed in the king's palace falls on the courtiers.
10. The **days** follow each other but one's fortunes remain.
11. He who finishes a **debt,** finishes a dispute.
12. Numerous calls confuse the **dog.**
13. Open, shut, use the **door.**

    [i.e. time passes and death arrives.]
14. Where you do not walk, your **ears** walk.
15. He who **eats** that which comes from thunder remains with his head in the air.

16. The days which follow each other make father and son **equal.**

17. He who knows how to bend the **fish-hook,** knows how to straighten it.

18. The hut that hides itself [not to be obliged to entertain] eats uncooked **food.**

19. Those who are buried in the same **grave,** don't insult each other.

20. That which will make you **hate,** you bear with you.

21. To where the **heart** has rejoiced at night, one returns in the morning.

22. That which gives is the **heart** ; the fingers only let go.

23. He who asks for a **hen** as a present, sees it scratching the soil.

24. The **hippopotamus** that shows itself doesn't upset the boat.

25. One small straw suffices to remove the **honey** from the hive.

26. That which will be beautiful [a song] commences with the **instrument.**

[i.e. one receives first little and then much.]

27. He who forgets the aim of his **journey** is still on the road.

28. Every hill has its **leopard.**

[i.e. each one has his vice.]

29. A spot warmed by the sun makes the **lizards** quarrel.

30. Two " **mambas** " [big fish] are not cooked on the same dish.

31. Little houses have fat **mice.**

[i.e. don't judge by appearances.]

32. One good thing leaves another ; **milk** leaves butter.

33. When you have no stick, the **mouse** passes close to you.

34. In the house of the **poor** one does not untie one's packet.

[i.e. so as not to be obliged to give.]

35. Many **presents** given with bad grace, are not worth a few given with good grace.

36. That which finds no **purchaser** returns to its master.

37. The **rain** does not always fall as it threatens.

38. The **ripeness** of the Ntongo [small pumpkin] is seen at the tip.

[This corresponds to the French proverb, " As one knows the king, one honours him."]

39. One **seeks** things where they are to be found.

40. When the **skin** is dry the flies return home.

[i.e. in time of prosperity one has many friends.]

41. He who learns to **steal** must learn to run.

42. He who is stronger than you, strikes you with the **stick** you carry.

43. He who says, " It is excellent," must have **tasted** it.

[i.e. one speaks of that of which one has knowledge.]

44. He who takes a **walk** has an object.

45. Tepid **water** doesn't forget the cold at home.

[i.e. chase away that which is natural and it returns at once.]

46. One does not bind the **wood** where one picks it up.

[i.e. one must work hard to obtain a result.]

47. The **wood** that will warm you—seek it yourself.

48. In order to go quickly and take a short cut the **worm** killed itself.

HERERO (DAMARALAND)

[Language Family—Bantu]

1. There is a **beaten** one who will beat the beater, there is the admonished who will admonish the admonisher.
2. Let them speak of [or about] us ; although they speak of us night and day, a **boil** [carbuncle] will not break out.
3. All they **say** will return to themselves.
4. A **weak person** goes where he is smiled at.

HO (GERMAN TOGOLAND)

(One of the dialects of the Ewe tribes)

[Language Family—Sudanic]

1. When the naked **bird** grows in the nest it gets feathers.

   [i.e. when a child grows up healthy it is capable of doing hard work.]
2. The **bird** that goes on living always gets new feathers.
3. One can't look into a **bottle** with both eyes.

   [i.e. two kings can't rule in one land.]
4. When the **calabash** falls to the ground the dish needn't laugh.

   [i.e. they both break.]
5. He who stays at home buries the dead **child.**

   [i.e. those who don't go out into the fields have always the most unpleasant work to do at home.]
6. The **child** who hasn't wandered [far] says, " Only my mother cooks well."
7. The **child** who takes a big piece from the food doesn't take a big piece from the word.

   [i.e. a full stomach learns unwillingly.]
8. **Death** brings the fish into the palace.

   [Luck and ill-luck.]
9. When one has made a promise one has a **debt.**
10. He who **dies** first has only gone before.
11. When a man **eats,** his own beard moves and not another's.
12. The **eye** and sleep have no quarrel with each other.

    [i.e. friends and neighbours should put up with one another.]
13. When the **fish** is killed his tail is stuck into his mouth.
14. The **fly** doesn't gird on a big sword.
15. The **fly** says, " The world is before and behind."

    [i.e. it is at home everywhere.]
16. He who would eat of **food** must take his hand to it.

    [i.e. without working, one gets nothing to eat.]
17. Three **friends** don't last long.
18. When you see a **frog** squatting in its home, don't ask for a chair.

    [i.e. when in Rome do as Rome does.]
19. Where there is a **head** one doesn't put the head-dress on the knee.

    [i.e. where there is an old man one doesn't ask advice of a young one.]
20. The word of the **home** slays no one.
21. With **patience** one achieves more than with anger.
22. Only he who knows the cause of a **quarrel** knows how to dispute.
23. When it **rains** on the hedge, the house will also be wet.

    [i.e. he who blames his son, blames also his father.]
24. An empty **river** doesn't roar.
25. The quarrel of the **sheep** doesn't concern the goats.

26. A good **soup** draws the chair to it.
27. The **spoon** does his job and the dish does his.
28. The **stranger** with the big eye doesn't know [the way] behind the house.

    [i.e. however wise one may be, there are always things one doesn't know.]
29. The man who **suffers** much knows much.
30. The **swimmer** doesn't see his own back.

    [People never see their own faults.]
31. On the face of the **thief** no grass grows.

    [i.e. he must first steal to be recognized. Only by his actions is a thief discovered. Outwardly he is the same as others.]
32. One doesn't despise the **thumb** when one would tie a rope.
33. When a single **tree** resists the wind it breaks.

    [i.e. strength is in union.]
34. Dirty **water** cannot be washed.
35. **Water** that carries away an entire house doesn't carry away the stone from its own bed.
36. The **water-carrier** drinks no slime.

    [i.e. those who exercise a trade get the best from it.]
37. The **well-doer** reaps hate.
38. A piece of **wood** that has already burned is soon rekindled.

    [i.e. an old experienced man easily answers questions.]
39. He who does **work** of his own making pulls no sour face.

IBO (SOUTHERN NIGERIA)

[Language Family—Sudanic]

1. **All** is never said.
2. A featherless **arrow** does not fly.
3. Wealth of **children** comes first, money second.
4. The **cock** lays nothing.
5. The **corpse** of a man is not carried as that of a woman.
6. The land is never void of **counsellors.**
7. Men are the wickedness of a **country.**
8. One who does what he says is not a **coward.**
9. **Death** does not recognize strength.
10. A man's **deeds** are his life.
11. The day one knows all, let him **die.**
12. If a **doctor** is mistaken he leaves by the back of the house.
13. The **doctor** is never killed because the patient dies.
14. Let not the rat wilfully tear the **doctor's** bag, and let not the doctor wilfully curse the rat.
15. The **dog's** nose is always cold.
16. " Come and I'll tell you " tickles the **ear.**
17. Who has much to do has much to **eat.**
18. A man who **eats** what he has, his desire is for what he has not.
19. Look to the **end.**
20. The **eye** cannot see the ear.
21. The **eyes** and the nose are kith and kin.
22. What one does is his **farm.**
23. **Fish** that do not feed upon other fish do not get proper nourishment.
24. The leaf that the big **goat** has eaten, its kids eat.
25. Who **hoes** a row never stands in one place.

    [Said of a woman who cannot stay in one man's house.]
26. Who **hoes** stands in the sun.
27. " **If I had known** " does not come first but last.

28. " Downcast " is king of **illness.**
29. What is sweet **kills.**
30. A **liar** is exposed to the heat of the sun.
31. One who is over-cautious of his **life** is always killed by the fall of a dry leaf.
32. **Life** is salt.
33. It is the place one **lives** in that one repairs.
34. **Money** has no end in giving satisfaction.
35. Put **money** in the bag, because one never knows.
36. **Money** is the source of right.
37. If you take the **mortar** take the pestle.

    [i.e. if a wife is taken by force, take the child too.]

38. Do not give a lame fowl to your **neighbour.**

    [i.e. cheat a stranger but not a friend.]

39. One man is another man's **obstacle.**
40. A **plantain-tree** always takes upon itself ground which does not belong to it.

    [Said to a stranger who attempts to meddle in matters that do not concern him.]

41. A **pond** is not a companion of a river.

    [Said if a young man tries to join his elders.]

42. " I am in a hurry " does not get a **present.**
43. **Prodigality** never lays hold of one who is little.
44. The **proverb** is the leaf that they use to eat a word.
45. **Proverb** or parable is the broth of speech.
46. When you play with a **puppy** he tears your clothes.
47. The **rain** cannot fall on the teeth so long as the lips cover them.
48. A **rich man** is seldom condemned, for the mouth which eats another man's property is benumbed.
49. You have your own **salt ;** if it pleases you, you may use it to fry flies.
50. Everything is with the **sick man.**

    [If he dies there will be much mourning, and if he lives there will be great thanksgiving.]

51. **Sitting** in one place makes one sleepy.

    [i.e. riches make a man forget his fellows.]

52. **Sneezing** is king.

    [i.e. it is considered lucky to sneeze ; everyone salutes the sneezer and he them.]

53. A **son** cannot first have a son before his father.

    [Parental snub administered to a son.]

54. A bad **son** enters his mother's womb by the back.
55. **Strangers** shall not be rulers.
56. A close observer knows the **street** that is swept by moonlight.
57. Taking thought is **strength.**
58. **Tales** are the food of the ear.
59. The son of a **tortoise** cannot confess to a crime of theft so long as there remains a chance of denial.
60. When you invite a **tortoise** to a meal it is no use giving him water to wash his paws with, because he will soon walk on the ground and dirty them.

    [i.e. ingratitude.]

61. A **traveller** does not buy raw fish.
62. **Truth** is greater than ten goats.
63. Take **water** out, other water runs in.
64. Bale out the **water** so that it reaches [only] to the ankles, lest it reach the knees.
65. **Wealth** makes the soup taste nice.
66. **Woman** is the house.

67. **Woman** never reigns.
68. **Word** never finishes in mouth.
69. He who waits patiently sees the back of the **world.**
    [i.e. lives long.]
70. Look at the **world.**
    [i.e. consolation for misfortune.]
71. **Yawning** is king.
    [i.e. it is considered lucky to yawn; everyone salutes the yawner and he them.]

ILA (NORTHERN RHODESIA)

[Language Family—Bantu]

1. An **axe-shaft** is made out of an ordinary piece of wood.
2. He who pulls a **branch** brings the leaves with it.
    [i.e. if you marry a woman you marry her family too.]
3. A **bull** does not enjoy fame in two herds.
4. **Buttocks** rubbing together do not lack sweat.
    [i.e. people cannot live long together without quarrelling.]
5. A **chicken** does not die of its mother's kicks.
6. A **chief** does not beget a chief.
    [i.e. not a chief merely by birth.]
7. A **chief** will not die with bracelets on his arms.
8. **Chiefdom** is serfdom.
9. Honour a **child** and it will honour you.
10. **Cruelty** is the mark of the chief.
11. **Death** has no heifer.
    [i.e. is inexorable.]
12. Annoy your **doctor** and sicknesses will come laughing.
13. When the **dog** barks, the fame belongs to the master of the village.
14. If you **eat** at night the night sees you; if you eat in the daytime the day sees you.
15. If you **eat** with one chief only, it is because you have no feet.
16. A man is an **elephant,** he is able to draw himself.
17. Much coming in and out finishes the **field.**
    [Inspiration to patience.]
18. Better help the **fighting man** than a hungry person, he [the latter] has no gratitude.
19. The **fly** that loves you is the one that sits on you.
20. They spurn the **frog** but drink the water.
21. To **give** is to hang up.
22. It is the prudent **hyena** that lives long.
23. **Land** owns men, not men land.
24. Though the **lion** growls it won't eat its child.
25. Give to your **mother,** a wife is a lion.
    [i.e. treat your mother better than your wife.]
26. A bad thing knows the **mouth.**
    [i.e. don't refuse without tasting; don't give up without trying.]
27. What is in the **path** belongs to all men.
28. Any old **pole** will find a hole in the fence.
29. A **river** that would not be straightened has bends in it.
30. The **scarecrow** may rest o' nights, but never the watcher of men.
31. A **small thing** is not noticed in a crowd.
32. The **speaker** may forget, but he who is spoken to does not.
33. A living **tortoise** is not worn as a charm.
    [i.e. one must not speak evil of living men.]
34. A **traveller** is not to be regarded as to his face but as to his stomach.

JABO (LIBERIA)

[Language Family—Sudanic]

1. A man does not perish **abroad.**
2. A **bald head** shines, but grey hair also shines.
3. There is no wealth where there are no **children.**
4. **Children** are the wisdom of the nation.
5. One does not embrace the **cotton-tree** [or hunger, or the leopard].
6. **Death** gives no answer.
7. A man is in his **deeds.**
8. Only in one's own country do his **deeds** become great.
9. A man **dies** before we appreciate him.
10. **Disappointment** is not difficult and happiness is not difficult.
11. The **dog's nose** is cold.
12. An untouched **drum** does not speak.
13. The **ear** has one hole.

    [i.e. the capacity of the listener is limited.]
14. " Come here, go there," **finishes** nothing.
15. The **foot** that travels the road is the one that is pricked by the thorn.
16. The **fruit** must have a stem before it grows.

    [Points to necessary order or sequence of events.]
17. It is not only **giants** that do great things.
18. We decide our affairs, then rest them with **God.**
19. Don't measure your **house timber** in the forest.
20. The **lame man** strikes once.

    [He will not have a chance to strike again.]
21. The one who **listens** is the one who understands.
22. If you **marry** a beautiful woman, you marry trouble.
23. When we count countries we count **men.**
24. Slowly, slowly, will catch the **monkey.**
25. Chicken says : If you scratch too hard, you come upon the bones of your **mother.**
26. **Paddle** advises paddle.
27. On the **palm-tree** that yields nuts the birds will tarry.

    [Said to an honoured chief on leaving his people, expressing the hope that he will return to his people again.]
28. **A patient man** has all the wealth that there is in this world.
29. When it **rains** the roof always drips the same way.
30. Whenever a **rat** teases a cat, he is leaning against a hole.
31. If you grind damp **rice,** it sticks to the mortar.

    [i.e. inadequate handling of a situation.]
32. What the **sea** has swallowed, it does not vomit out again.

    [Applied to anything overwhelming and final.]
33. Where a **small thing** comes from, there a big thing comes from.
34. Dead **tree** does not yield dew.
35. **War** does not look at the ground.
36. A man's **ways** are good in his own eyes.
37. **Weaver-bird** says : The mouth of the offender is not idle.

    [The weaver-bird is very talkative.]

JUKUN (BENUE PROVINCE, NORTHERN NIGERIA)

[Language Family—Sudanic]

1. An **arrow-head** in someone else's body is nothing but an arrow-shaft.

   [i.e. you don't appreciate another's difficulties until you have experienced them yourself.]

2. The **bow** breaks and becomes a walking-stick ; the hoe gets worn out and only the handle remains.

   [i.e. how are the mighty fallen.]

3. A single **bracelet** does not make a clatter.

   [i.e. two heads are better than one.]

4. You run away from a **crocodile** but eat crocodile stew.

   [i.e. you should act up to your principles.]

5. Don't abuse the **crocodile's** offspring until you are out of the river.

6. Even in time of **drought** one may still see dew.

   [i.e. half a loaf is better than no bread.]

7. It is when the **eye** falls on the mat that the owner begins to feel sleepy.

   [i.e. what the eye does not see, the heart does not desire.]

8. In the midst of your **illness** you will promise a goat, but when you have recovered, a chicken will seem sufficient.

9. You need not take someone else's hand to crush a **sand-fly.**

10. A man cannot get away from his own **shadow.**

    [i.e. you cannot avoid the inevitable.]

11. A **shrub** may grow into a tree.

    [i.e. despise no one.]

12. Good **soup** is always finished before the porridge.

    [i.e. whom the gods love die young.]

13. However broken down is the **spirit's shrine,** the spirit is there all the same.

    [i.e. appearances are deceitful.]

14. To exchange a full **stomach** for an empty one.

    [i.e. falling from the frying-pan into the fire.]

15. Let the child's **umbilical cord** fall into the hands of its mother.

    [i.e. stew in your own juice.]

16. What the bow has shot the **vulture** eats.

    [i.e. it is no use crying over spilt milk.]

17. It is the mouth of the **worm** that causes the worm's destruction.

    [i.e. dog eat dog.]

KAMBA (KENYA COLONY)

[Language Family—Bantu]

1. The wilderness has **ears.**

2. The **eye** usually deceives itself.

   [i.e. all is not gold that glitters.]

3. The **fence** of a simpleton is traversed by another simpleton.

4. If you refuse to be made straight when you are **green,** you will not be made straight when you are dry.

5. The **honey-pot** of the head is licked by [its] owner.

   [i.e. your thoughts are only known to yourself.]

6. A man who does not **know** another habitually calls him " That one."

7. The **partridge** sits with the one which has been caught.

   [The natives say that if a bird of

this species of partridge is caught in a trap, its mate will not desert it, but sits waiting alongside the trap.]

8. The thing that dies in **plenty** does not return in plenty.
9. The clans of the **wilderness** are two—the withered and fresh [trees].

   [i.e. there are two kinds of people, men (" withered trees "), and women (" fresh trees "). Men cannot bear children.]

KANURI (BORNU) (NORTHERN NIGERIA)

[Language Family—Sudanic]

1. I pay what I owe to **Allah.**
2. Verily, **beauty** is power.
3. Everything that has a **beginning** has an end.
4. A **blind man** goes straight forward ; the compelled man agrees to anything.
5. The **blind man** only knows that you have seen him when you hit him on the head.

   [Said of people who live in false security.]
6. Where you **climb** up you will climb down.
7. He who has a **dry eye** [no shame] is like a girl who has had an illegitimate child.
8. He who has put an **egg** into a bottle can easily take it out.
9. Don't dig the ditch of **evil** deep.

   [So that you won't fall into it yourself.]
10. However big an **eye** may be, two are better.
11. An **eye** that is quite white and not black in the centre is useless.

    [Said of those whose friendship is only in words and not in gifts.]
12. Foolish **falcon,** what have you gained by taking from the little bird its nest ?
13. All that comes into the stomach is **food.**
14. Hold a true **friend** with both your hands.
15. The **guest** who came in the morning welcomes the guest who comes in the evening.

    [i.e. he behaves as though he were at home.]
16. The **hand** above is better than the hand below.

    [i.e. giving is better than taking.]
17. To send someone rests the feet, but not the **heart.**
18. It is the **heart** which carries one to hell or Heaven.
19. Not where I was born, but where it goes well with me is my **home.**
20. **Hope** is the pillar of the world.
21. He who has a **house** knows the place where the water drops in.
22. One does not **love** another if one does not accept anything from him.
23. The world is like a **market,** the one does business and the other does none.
24. The days being finished there is no **medicine.**
25. **Memory** reaches further than the eyes.
26. An empty **mouth** is always hungry.
27. To bore in the **nose** is better than working in the field.

    [i.e. if the ruler of the town turns you out, the way to your nose remains yours.]
28. At the bottom of **patience** there is Heaven.
29. What a man **possesses** is not stronger than himself.

    [i.e. a ruler only has himself to blame if he cannot control those he rules.]
30. When the **pot** boils over it damages its surface.
31. **Poverty** comes from having nothing.

32. **Property** is the prop of life.
33. **Riches** are the pillar of the world.
34. Not to empty one's **stomach** doesn't help against hunger.
35. He who has deep-set eyes must begin to shed **tears** early.

    [The poor must start toiling soon to be able to pay the taxes.]
36. However long the way may be it leads to the **town.**
37. **Water** is the king of food.

    [i.e. where there is no water one can eat nothing.]
38. Whatever is thy intimacy, never give thy heart to a **woman.**
39. A **woman** is like a horse, he who can drive her is her master.
40. If thou givest thy heart to a **woman** she will kill thee.
41. If a **woman** speaks two words, take one and leave the other.

KIKUYU (KENYA COLONY)

[Language Family—Bantu]

1. **Anger** is misery.
2. The **beloved** one has no pimples.
3. A wet **bone** is better than a dry one.

    [i.e. a live enemy is better than a dead friend.]
4. When new **clothes** are sewn, where do the old ones go?
5. People do not **count** what they are given, they count what is withheld from them.
6. **Courage** has many things.
7. The **cup** frequently comes away from the lips [untasted].
8. The speed of "that I may not **die**" is great.
9. Strength does not prevent a man from **dying.**
10. The path of the **evil-doer** shall have dew all day.
11. The **fool** is killed by what belongs to himself.
12. **Friendship** is steps.
13. The eyes of the **frogs** do not prevent the cows drinking.
14. Though unpopular, a man will always find someone to cut his **hair.**
15. The **heart** eats what it wishes.
16. **A hero** does not necessarily rule the roost two seasons.
17. The **hunter's child** gets nothing that is shot.
18. Two smells of cooking meat break the **hyena's legs.**
19. It is the **hyenas** of the same den that hate one another.
20. By the side of "**I shall do**" was found "Not yet done."
21. **Lies** are not debts.
22. **Love** has no disputings.
23. When a **man** is not known, another calls him "You man."
24. The **medicine man** is not esteemed in his own village.
25. There is no medicine for **misfortune.**
26. The [**mouth**] which bewitches is the one that blesses. The [mouth] which cries "hurrah" is the one that cries "help".
27. He who has **necessity** has no shame.
28. He who has **need** is not shy.
29. The **ornament** of another tires the wearer's neck.
30. A **present** does not grow old.
31. The last little bit of the **root** breaks the digging stick.

    [i.e. it is the last little debt which costs so much to recover.]
32. The **seller** himself buys.
33. **Throwing** up is throwing away.
34. What's **too hard** for a man must be worth looking into.
35. **Tryings** are succeedings.

KONGO (BELGIAN CONGO)

(Including Mongo, Songe, Nkundu, Shongo)

[Language Family—Sudanic]

1. Where the **anvil** clanks the iron wears.
2. He who is in a position of **authority,** never coughs. (*Mongo.*)

    [i.e. need not remind others of his presence.]
3. You disposed of the **axe,** why listen for the sound of it chopping? (*Mongo.*)
4. **A bad thing** must have a bad effect.
5. In a field of bad **beans** there is bound to be some worth gleaning.
6. A **beautiful person** is not known to be an elder. (*Mongo.*)

    [i.e. does not show age.]
7. Drink **beer,** think beer.
8. **A bridge-pole** [over a river] held by an old man [whilst you cross over] never shakes or turns over.
9. High-water pools are left; the babbling **brook** obliterates them. (*Nkundu.*)

    [i.e. a wife prized and loved for some high quality, spoils all by talkativeness.]
10. It never does to have another burn the **brush-heap** for you. (*Nkundu.*)

    [i.e. if you want a thing well done, do it yourself.]
11. Everybody to his own **calling** and nobody to any other.
12. The **canoe** never again meets the stump of the tree from which it was cut. (*Mongo.*)
13. Do not show **caterpillars** leaves. (*Mongo.*)

    [i.e. do not tempt me to do evil.]
14. **A chicken** which has forgotten to scratch has forgotten the example of its parents.
15. Only lay hold of a **child,** and you will see its mother. (*Mongo.*)
16. The father loves the **child** only while the mother remains with him. (*Mongo.*)
17. A **child** regards his father's guest as a slave. (*Mongo.*)
18. The elders wear the **cloth** first, then the boys get the rags.
19. In a court of fowls the **cockroach** never wins his case.

    [i.e. the verdict of one race against another is to be received with caution.]
20. The **cocks** that crow have only come from eggs.
21. The river gives no **compensation;** earth receives no ransom. (*Mongo.*)
22. Man eats **corn,** but corn can eat man.

    [i.e. human beings sold for corn.]
23. Why **count?** When they are many you will feel their weight. (*Shongo.*)

    [Refers to age.]
24. I don't **criticize** others so that others may not criticize me. (*Songe.*)
25. Along the road on which you are to meet your **death** your legs will carry you, and you will go. (*Mongo.*)
26. For a running **deer,** a running shot.

    [Preacher's proverb on brevity.]
27. A new moon takes away **disease.**
28. **Distance** is not diminished by speed. (*Mongo.*)
29. **A doctor** bald to the nape of his neck is not likely to cure anybody of baldness.
30. A **dog** with four legs can't walk in two roads at the same time.
31. **Drink** first, die first.
32. Where the **drum** is burst is the place to mend it.
33. Give to the **earth** and the earth will give to you.
34. Things that crow come from **eggs.**
35. The partridge is your **enemy** and the cock is your enemy; who will tell you of the approach of dawn?

36. A full-grown man may **fall,** for his beard is not made of props.

    [i.e. young folk ought not to laugh at a man who slips.]

37. A man is never counted two because he is **fat,** or only half a man because he is lean.

38. A **Fawn** never forgets his own feeding-ground.

39. One **finger** gashed—all the fingers are covered with blood. (*Nkundu.*)

    [i.e. if one in a family does ill, all are smirched.]

40. **Foolishness** often precedes wisdom.

41. Those who inherit **fortunes** are often more troublesome than those who make them.

42. Here is a little **fowl** trying to lay a big egg.

43. Though a man has actually less wisdom than his **friend,** the friend treats him as though he had more.

44. **Friendship** never uses a peppercorn as an eyedrop.

45. Don't despise a **gift** because it is small.

46. **Give** to an old man before he asks you.

47. You continue to see **good,** don't forget evil. (*Mongo.*)

48. If you don't want the **gun** to go off, don't cock the trigger.

49. **Habit** is a full-grown mountain, hard to get over or to pull down.

50. A bald-headed man cannot grow **hair** by getting excited about it.

51. The **hearth** is the one which is filled with little packets of food. (*Mongo.*)

52. **Help** those who cannot help themselves.

53. The **home** is the place of affection.

54. **Hope** kills nobody.

55. **Hunger** does not know youth. (*Mongo.*)

56. One **inherits** from a dead man, not from a sick one. (*Songe.*)

57. **Justice** becomes injustice when it makes two wounds on a head which only deserves one.

58. Let the man who is cracking his **kernels** finish his nuts before you take his place or his nutcrackers [stones].

59. The **key** that opens is also the key that locks.

60. **Kindness** is like trees in a farm, they lean towards each other.

61. **Kindness** is never lost.

62. A **knife** does not know its master. (*Mongo.*)

63. Though a **leopard** give birth to a palm rat she does not eat it.

64. A **load** of salt on another man's head is easily carried.

65. No one should **look** behind himself. (*Songe.*)

66. If you **love** a hunter, love his dog.

67. If you **love** a man, do not take him along a dewy road [which will give him cause to quarrel].

68. Mutual **love** is often better than natural brotherhood.

69. Too much **luck** drives one mad.

70. A bullet fired in **malice,** if it does not draw blood where it starts, it will draw blood where it strikes.

71. **Miserliness** does not scatter your relatives; only evil deeds scatter them. (*Mongo.*)

72. The animal which can't climb a tree should not trust his money to a **monkey.**

73. **Moon-gazing** is never-ending. (*Mongo.*)

74. A **mosquito** feels no pity for an emaciated person. (*Mongo.*)

    [i.e. the oppressor has no pity for the poor.]

75. The source of [human] love is of the **mother.** (*Mongo.*)

76. A **mother** is not to be compared with another person—she is incomparable. (*Mongo.*)

77. Things **mourned** for will become things rejoiced over.

78. He possesses two **mouths.**

79. Rather a **negro** heart without words than negro words without heart.

80. Though the **night** tarry, the dawn will break.

81. It is best to let an **offence** repeat itself at least three times ; the first offence may be an accident ; the second a mistake, but the third is likely to be intentional.

82. An **old man,** when guilty, never argues.

83. The bunch of **palm-nuts** never falls without catching up some leaves. (*Nkundu.*)

84. **Partnership** in the trap, share of the meat.

85. The only one who feels pity for the **pot** [which someone has broken] is the one who bought it. (*Mongo.*)

86. **Pride** only goes the length one can spit.

87. **Proverbs** are the affairs of the nation.

88. When the **rabbit** was promised beans he produced a basket.

89. **Rats,** before they nibble you, blow upon the flesh in order to deaden the feeling. (*Songe.*)

90. There is something even in the worst for which one will always be kindly **remembered.**

91. To take **revenge** is often to sacrifice oneself.

92. If, O exasperated one, you are tied up in **ropes,** the more you tug, the tighter the knots become.

93. He who thinks of you in **sickness** will think of you in death.

94. You may drink out of a human **skull,** but you can never obliterate from your mind that it once had eyes in it.

[i.e. nothing can efface the happy memories of friendship once enjoyed.]

95. Where the **smoke** is, there are the fairies.

96. Chance **sparks** kindle chance tinder.

97. A **stone** is never uprooted by the wind.

98. If you destroy both the **sun** and the moon you leave yourself in utter darkness.

99. The **sun** does not rise once only. (*Mongo.*)

100. **Thirst** cannot be quenched by proxy.

101. If **thought** [or mind] does not pass on before [as forethought], it subsequently returns [as an afterthought]. (*Mongo.*)

102. **Thread** is made famous by the needle. (*Mongo.*)

103. Keep the **trail** white for us to return.

[i.e. traitor's catch-phrase. Make path white by paying extortionate tribute.]

104. All who **travel** in the rain get wet.

105. A sapless **tree** is a leafless tree. (*Mongo.*)

106. The little **tree** that saved you from the buffalo, you turn and cut it for a post. (*Nkundu.*)

107. **Walk** with a monkey and you will learn to jump ; walk with one in a fix and you will get in a fix.

108. **War** begets no good offspring. (*Mongo.*)

109. **Water** drawn by old men quenches thirst.

[i.e. old men relied upon.]

110. The man to whom you sell your **wine** is the man to go to for the bottle.

111. **Wisdom** is not a medicine to be swallowed.

KRU (LIBERIA)

[Language Family—Sudanic]

1. A man is in his **words.**
2. **Words** form a hard nut that never rots.

KWELI (KWIRI, WAKWELI OR BAKWIRI) (CAMEROONS)

[Language Family—Bantu]

1. The **back** brings the stomach into difficulties.

   [i.e. it prevents it from distending in more than one direction.]
2. The **back** greets no one.

   [i.e. who comes behind me is a matter of indifference.]
3. The **cock** does not crow for everybody in the village.
4. The **egg** teaches the hen how to hatch.
5. If you take a **fire-brand** you have also the smoke.

   [i.e. he who marries a wife has also her relations.]
6. The **forest** is not heartless.

   [i.e. he who is misunderstood by men finds comfort in solitude.]
7. **God** likes to take the young.
8. The **guest** who has broken the pot is not forgotten.

   [i.e. he who behaves badly.]
9. An **heir** doesn't inherit by coughing.

   [i.e. trying to call attention to himself.]
10. One stone doesn't break a **palm-nut.**
11. The **shoulder** isn't higher than the head.
12. When you **speak** of the oil-palm no wine-palm should be near.

    [i.e. don't speak of anyone in the hearing of their relatives.]
13. Borrowed **water** doesn't get a meal ready.
14. **Water** never loses the way.

    [i.e. it always reaches the sea.]

LAMBA (NORTHERN RHODESIA)

[Language Family—Bantu]

1. **Fire** doesn't pass over burnt ground.

   [i.e. don't start up again a dispute already settled.]
2. The leopard's **heir** inherits the spots as well.

   [i.e. debts as well as assets are taken over by the heir to an estate.]
3. **Seeing** one another is ill ; hearing one another is good.

   [i.e. less chance of quarrelling.]
4. Even if the **tree-snake** is long he can't sleep on two ant-hills at once.

   [i.e. limit to everything.]

LANGO (UGANDA)

[Language Family—Nilotic]

1. **Chickens** scratch on the midden.
2. **Fire** produces ashes.
3. Grown **grain** does not fear the sun.
4. A man's **grave** is in the bush.
5. A roaring **lion** kills no game.

LIBERIAN-NEGRO (LIBERIA)

[Language Family—Sudanic]

1. There are people who will help you get your **basket** on your head because they want to see what's in it.
2. The daughter of a **crab** does not give birth to a bird.
3. Hunt in every **jungle,** for there is wisdom and good hunting in all of them.
4. One man must not try to follow another man's **luck.**
5. He draws near the fire whose **meat** is raw.
6. If you want to keep your **milk** sweet, leave it in the cow.
7. A man does not run among thorns for nothing ; either he is chasing a **snake** or a snake is chasing him.
8. Leave all **women,** save your wife, alone.

MALAGASY (MADAGASCAR)

(Including Betsimisaraka)

[Language Family—Malay]

1. The little things and **acts** which preserve wealth fail, but those which preserve friendship fail not.
2. **Advice** is a stranger ; if welcome he stays for the night ; if not welcome he returns home the same day.
3. The **bad** is told that the good may appear.
4. Why are you glad to receive the **bad** like a mat?
5. Like an empty **bag,** no one remembers it again.
6. You went to the **barber** before us and of course you have the longer hair.
7. **Blame** is like the wind, felt but not seen.
8. Don't help a **bull** out of a ditch, for when he's out he'll butt.
9. To leave your own house fasting and do an injury to the **butterflies ;** whatever is poor dwells in the roots of the grass, and its wings don't clothe it when living or wrap it up when dead, so get your breakfast before leaving home and don't injure the butterflies.
10. Seven **children** won't hold a husband, but plenty of wisdom will.
11. Having **choked** you are able to chew ; having fallen you are able to walk.
12. Don't go up as a **cloud** and disappear as a mist.

13. Don't call me conquered when I go with the **conqueror.**

14. **A cow** is ill and a bull is the doctor's fee.

15. If you will neither milk [the **cow**] nor hold the calf, you ought not to skim off the cream.

    [i.e. the native cow gives no milk unless the calf is first allowed to suck a little, and then is held by the side of the cow.]

16. Cross in a crowd, the **crocodile** won't eat you.

17. Cheated **customers** and satisfied customers balance each other.

18. Don't think of the shortness of the **day,** but of the length of the year.

19. The **day** is declining, so the road is easy.

20. One **day** of meeting equals a hundred others [when there is no gathering of friends].

21. Don't you see the **dead ?** They lie together in their separate clothes ; they cover their heads to go nowhere ; they get not up in the morning ; they warm not themselves in the evening ; red earth is over their breasts and stone-work is at their sides.

22. Even the **dead** wish to be many.

    [The Malagasy are a very sociable people and their desire for the company of their fellows follows them to the grave, thus the occupants of the family tomb are said to be ever seeking additions to their numbers.]

23. Although the **dead** won't bless, shall not tears flow down, and although the living won't believe, shall not the proclamation be made ?

24. **Death** is the pursuer, disease the constant companion of man.

25. **Desire** doesn't equal destiny.

26. Don't **dislike** people, for they are wealth.

    [i.e. the means of getting it.]

27. The one fallen into the **ditch** should not wave his mantle in defiance.

    [i.e. should not make the challenge.]

28. Don't make a hundred **dollars** on the bed.

    [i.e. castles in the air.]

29. Don't look at a torn **dress.**

30. The song of the **dumb** is murmured to himself.

31. **Dying** is cleaning, like the broom.

32. The **earth** is God's chief wife, she maintains the living and guards the dead.

33. **Examine** long ; be in the right long.

34. **Eyes** seeing [yet] taking nothing home.

35. Don't be **faint-hearted,** for a man's fall is only on his hands and knees.

36. There are **faults** even in eating.

37. It is **fleas** that live on strangers.

38. The **foot** is in the canoe ; it can't draw back.

39. Don't pass by a place where there's a **friend.**

40. **Friends** are like those who have one father, lovers like those who have one mother.

41. Treat your **friends** as the kind herdsman does his oxen ; the foremost are stroked and the hindmost patted.

42. Getting **friends** is like gathering cow-dung ; the more you go about, the more you get.

    [Cow-dung is used for fuel.]

43. Don't forget your **friends,** like a bag from which the goods have been taken.

44. A **friend's** [or relative's] trouble reaches [you].

45. Better lose a little money than a little **friendship.**

46. Let your **friendship** be that of the mouth and the hand ; if the hand is hurt the mouth blows it, and if the mouth is hurt the hand strokes it.

47. **Friendship** is like a bad rope; if pulled tightly it breaks; if pulled lightly it comes undone.
48. **Friendship** is like a stiff cloth; when new it rustles [nicely], but when old it is full of rents.
49. **Friendship** is like the pond-weed; if you come near it goes away; if you go away it comes near.
50. Don't make it a dog's **friendship,** to be broken over a bone.
51. Having much of **God.**
52. May you be blessed of **God.**
53. **God** does not belong to only one; human beings are God's little dogs.
54. Go alone, you are judged by **God;** go with another, you are judged by men.
55. Think most of the silent valley, for the fragrant prince [**God**] is there.
56. Men are easily **good** and easily bad.
57. Don't do **good** by halves.
58. It is not the being rubbed with chillies that makes one smell bitter, nor the being smeared with honey that makes one smell sweet, but it is the thing done that makes **good** or bad.

    [i.e. a person is said to be of "bitter smell" when disliked by others, and of "sweet smell" when acceptable to them.]
59. Do **good** to a wall, there is something to lean against, and do good to a stone, there is something to sit on.
60. **Guilt** repented of becomes righteousness, but righteousness boasted of becomes the grandfather of guilt.
61. No **hair** grows on the forehead because of shame.
62. **Hair-knots** hold the men.
63. **Healing** without medicine is a good thing.
64. The **heart** isn't lame, so when I pass I give a look in.
65. Don't let your **heart** lean on riches.
66. The **heart** of man is not of stone but of rubber.
67. One does not like **heat** and the other does not like cold; make it tepid and still be friends.
68. Do not be a crowing **hen.**
69. Sweet **herbs** joined you and bitter herbs parted you.
70. Receiving **honour** won't make you a noble, and giving honour won't make you a slave, so it is well to honour one another.
71. If you know what **hurts** yourself you know what hurts others.
72. The last **husband** [a wife has] is a brother.
73. It's only the **idle** will be tired.
74. **Iron** doesn't rattle alone.
75. Begin in **jest** and end in earnest.
76. Love **law** and lose money.
77. Don't tell a shallow **lie** and get it scratched up by the hen with one chick.
78. A **lie** is plump in private but lean in public.
79. **Life** is a broken potsherd.
80. If the **liver** is poked, the gall-bladder feels it.

    [i.e. a friend's trouble reaches you.]
81. Too eager for more **love** and make light of what has already come.
82. Let your **love** be like misty rain; little in coming but flooding the river.
83. **Love** me as you do cotton; add to the thin and re-join the broken.
84. Don't **love** me as you do a door; liked but pushed to and fro.
85. Don't **love** me in prosperity and leave me in adversity.
86. Don't be so much in **love** that you can't tell when the rain is coming.
87. **Marriage** is like the giving out of beef; the hump falls to some, but the knee to others.

    [The hump is esteemed a great delicacy and the knee the reverse, being almost all bone.]

88. **Marriage** is not tied with a fast knot but with a slip-knot.

89. **Marry** the tall, and you've no need to borrow a ladder : marry the short, and you keep a little drum : marry a shrew, and you keep a thunderbolt in the house.

90. Let **matrimony** be like a fowl's clothing, not parted with until death.

91. When the **meat** is done, you come to the chopping-board.

92. Do not boil **meat** that has not a name.

93. The **medicine** for the weak is his doing what is right.

94. The **medicine** of the strong is to beg pardon ; the medicine of the weak is to beseech forgiveness.

95. A **mole** is wife to the skin.

96. The love of **money** is the tail of witchcraft.

97. Get into the **mud,** water will remove it ; get into dispute, the mouth will get you out of it ; be overtaken by sorrow, you can appeal to your friends.

98. Don't put an **ornament** over dirt.

99. The end of an **ox** is beef, and the end of a lie is exposure.

100. A lean **ox** is not licked by his companions.

101. Whoso points out a straight **path** gives life a new start.

102. A **patient** that can swallow food makes the nurse doubtful.

103. What gives **pleasure** when going to sleep is answered when waking.

104. **Powder** doesn't refuse fire, nor fire fuel.

105. Mr. Headshaker's **prediction**—if it's not a boy, it's a girl.

106. Don't **promise** much in sickness and little in health.

107. A **quarrel** about meat ; the one who gives it up is hungry.

108. Doing one's best drives away **regret.**

109. **Regret** is not first but last.

110. He is a near **relative** while there are shrimps [to be had], but when they are done he is only a distant relative.

111. The **residence** is not suitable because you can't agree with your neighbours.

112. How is it that the **rich** only are niggardly ?

113. He who has **riches** is a prince, but he who has not is a robber.

114. Man is the receiver, but **riches** the giver of blessings.

115. Men don't all go one **road.**

116. A **road** free from dew : it's trodden on by the weak.

117. There is nothing bigger than a **rock,** but as it doesn't speak, it is trodden on and soiled by the birds.

118. **Salute** those you meet, for you do not know who will be your last parents-in-law.

119. **Scandal** is like an egg ; when it is hatched it has wings.

120. Don't be like the **shadow :** a constant companion, but not a comrade.

121. The great are open to **shame,** and the small are open to fear.

122. The strong of voice to **shout ;** the tall to try the depth of water, and the sharp to cut.

123. He who is **sick** is a prince.

124. Don't lie down in **sickness.**

125. In **sickness** be good friends ; in health burn one another's houses.

126. Do like the **silkworm :** get into your house before you begin to improve it.

127. It is **sleep** that makes one like the wealthy.

128. **Sorrow** is like a cloud ; when it becomes heavy it falls.

129. **Sorrow** is like a precious treasure ; shown only to friends.

130. **Sorrow** is like rice in the store ; a basketful removed every day, it comes to an end at last.

131. A land abused becomes a burial-place: a **spouse** not desired you become old with.

132. The **spring** is like a dropped pearl.

[i.e. pick it up quickly or you'll lose it.]

133. The **stingy** spend much.

134. A rolling **stone,** it stops not till the bottom is reached.

135. No one gives up **suspicion,** though he be rewarded for it.

136. The **sweet** is in the bitter.

137. **Tears** hold not life.

138. Don't speak of **trees** in the forest.

[Said to people who talk platitudes.]

139. When **trouble** comes, one shrimp is too big for the mouth, and a fowl's dropping is a cause of stumbling.

140. Don't let your **uprightness** have any twistings.

141. To have one **want,** like the water-pot, and look for nothing but water.

142. **Water** doesn't refuse to go down, nor smoke to go up.

143. People are like the **water-lily** in a pond; they choose to turn about rather than be separated. (*Betsimisaraka.*)

144. **Wealth** is like hair in the nose; if much is pulled out, it is painful, if little, it is painful.

145. It will do no good to have **wealth** that you won't use.

146. " May you live and prosper " won't support the **wife** and family.

147. Young **wife**; bad cook.

148. What happens to your **wife** happens to yourself.

149. The **wife** is " Mistress Wished For ", and the husband is " Master Matchless ".

150. **A wife** to be divorced has many faults; a lass not married looks excellent; while a woman not yet made a mother-in-law seems easy to get on with.

151. Don't **winnow** the clean, or blow what's burning, or straighten wood already straight.

152. The **word** invites you to stay the night, but the countenance sends you home again the same day.

153. Soft **words** bring wealth.

154. You **work** when well in order to afford to stop when ill.

155. Don't shirk **work.**

156. People are like a **yam** growing on the rock; it certainly grows, but does not ripen. (*Betsimisaraka.*)

157. The **young** are overhanging rocks; the old are trees on the edge of a precipice; no one knows which will fall first.

MANDINGO (SENEGAMBIA)

[Language Family—Sudanic]

1. Take not the **fish** from your neighbour's net lest a bone stick in your throat.

2. Succour the **traveller** lest he return with his kindred and smite thee.

MASAI (KENYA COLONY)

[Language Family—Hamitic]

1. A **bargain** cannot be held in the palm of the hand.
2. **Coal** laughs at ashes.
3. Being **defeated** and dying are the same.
4. That which **eats** you is in your clothes.

   [i.e. those who harm you are in your own house.]
5. What the **eyes** of a man see, his heart desires.
6. The man who has heeded not his **father** eats earth.
7. **Fire** has no brother.
8. **Flies** have ears.
9. One **hand** can't take a louse from the head.
10. The **handle** knows the axe.
11. A **lie** cannot fill the palm.
12. **Mountains** do not meet.

    [i.e. a favourite saying when people part company. Equivalent to " We shall meet again."]
13. The **night** has ears.
14. The **night** sews no garment.
15. The **nose** doesn't always go in front.

    [i.e. one does not always know what one will meet in the place one goes to.]
16. He who separates the **paths,** or character, climate, or nature.

    [i.e. a common expression for the Almighty.]
17. Don't go to the **plain** without somebody to take the dust out of your eye.

    [i.e. necessity of joint action.]
18. It does not take as long to settle a **quarrel** as it takes a cow's udder to fill with milk after she has been covered.
19. When a **small one** comes out, a big one also comes out.

    [i.e. if someone has given you a small present he may also give you a big one.]
20. The bark of one **tree** will not adhere to another tree.

    [i.e. people of one tribe cannot assimilate the customs of another.]
21. He who **waits** drinks the milk of the cow-calf.

    [i.e. with time the mulberry leaf becomes silk.]
22. **Warriors** and cripples remain apart.

MOORISH (WESTERN ARABIC AND BERBER)

[Language Family—Semitic]

An Introduction to this collection by Professor Edward Westermarck, Ph.D., LL.D. will be found on page lxxvi.

1. **Abundance** in the world becomes great with good faith.
2. The cause of **abundance** in the world is pity and mercy and good faith.
3. **Abundance** is a friendly fellow, he is loved by big and small.
4. On the ground **affection** shows itself.

   [i.e. a man who has risen to a high position easily forgets a friend whom he had in those days when he, like other humble people, used to sit on the ground.]
5. The **affliction** does not last, nor will the enjoyment last.
6. An **agreement** is a kind of debt.
7. He who has no **alms** to give on Friday should give water in charity to his back.

   [i.e. ablutions on Friday are, according to Mohammedan tradition, obligatory on all persons who have attained the age of puberty.]

8. His **answer** is on his canine tooth.

   [Said of a person who answers well without delay.]

9. If you see **ants** on the staircase, know that there is semolina upstairs.

10. He who has a big **appetite** takes it all or leaves it all.

    [i.e. not worth while to engage in business unless a big profit is made.]

11. If she [i.e. wealth] **ascends,** she ascends by the aid of a hair, and if she descends, she cuts chains.

    [i.e. one person may become wealthy by owning a trifle ; another may suddenly become poor.]

12. If rest enters, **avarice** enters.

    [Said of a man who was once poor and afterwards became rich.]

13. When **August** sets in, give up fruit and eat food made of grain.

    [From the commencement of August many people abstain from all fruit except grapes and melons.]

14. The man who is a **bachelor** goes where he likes and is saved from running.

15. If someone dies a **bachelor** he will rise again with the evil spirits.

    [i.e. marriage is enjoined as a religious duty incumbent on all who possess the ability.]

16. On the heads of orphans **barbers** are learning.

    [i.e. an agricultural labourer should first learn his work in the least fertile part of the field.]

17. One eats **beans,** and for another they swell in his stomach.

    [i.e. innocent punished for the fault of the guilty.]

18. Don't say [I have] **beans** until they are in the measure.

19. **Bear** him unlucky, don't bear him lazy.

20. There is no **beauty** but the beauty of action.

    [Said by a man marrying a girl of good family who suffers from some bodily defect which is commented on by a friend.]

21. The **beauty** dies and its signs remain.

22. He who wants **beauty** in perfection should wait all night.

23. **Beauty** is on the oleander and the oleander is bitter.

24. The **beauty** you left behind you, where will you find it to-morrow ?

25. A handful of **bees** are better than a pannier of flies.

    [i.e. ordinary people.]

26. Every **beetle** is a gazelle in the eyes of its mother.

27. Propriety of **behaviour** is better than origin.

28. The true **believer** begins with himself.

29. Don't **belittle** him who is not small, don't magnify him who is not great.

30. He who is dressed in other people's **belongings** is naked, and he who is made satisfied by other people's belongings is hungry.

31. A **benefit** does not become old.

32. A **benefit** returns with stomach-ache.

    [Said by a creditor who has had much trouble in getting his money back.]

33. **Benefits** to [honest] men are loans and to rogues charity.

    [i.e. they will remember them.]

34. The **bird** in the sky says, " Livelihood is secured [by God] and why the toil ? "

35. Stretch your leg according to the size of your **blanket.**

36. A blear-eyed one is called black-eyed [a great compliment] in the country of the **blind.**

37. Blear-eyedness is better than **blindness.**

    [i.e. any work better than no work.]

38. Give to your brother the **bone** that you do not gnaw.

39. For the sake of the **book** [i.e. the "baraka" inside him] the binding is loved.

40. The sight of **books** removes sorrows from the heart.

41. The early **breakfast** is bought with gold.

42. **Brotherhood** is neither sold nor bought.

43. The **bullock** does not get tired of his horns [i.e. she is welcome back to his house].

[If a married man complain of his wife to her father and says that he is going to divorce her, this is the father's reply.]

44. He who blows upon **buttermilk** will [have to] long for it.

[Said of a person who has complained of his work, given it up, and then longs to go back to it.]

45. **Buy** and taste [instead of "taste and buy"] lest you be drowned to the neck.

[i.e. before buying a thing you should examine it carefully in order not to be cheated.]

46. O **buyer,** remember the day when you will sell.

47. What is in the head of the **camel** [i.e. himself] is not in the heads of the camel-drivers [i.e. the two would-be robbers].

[Said by a man when told that he is going to be robbed by two men. Also said if an apprentice pretends to know more than his master.]

48. He who riding on a **camel** is not afraid lest the dogs should bite him.

[i.e. a person belonging to a small, but good, family need not be afraid of low-bred people with a large family.]

49. The **candle** gives light and burns itself.

[Said of a man who is good to others and liked by them, and then commits some fault that ruins him.]

50. A naked one in a **caravan** is protected.

[i.e. a person owning nothing need not fear being robbed.]

51. He who is **careless** will be left to scratch himself [out of regrets].

[i.e. people should always be on guard against robbers.]

52. A herd of **cattle** should not be without a bull.

53. Don't let **charity** go out of your house until the children are satisfied.

[i.e. the first duty of parents is to support their children.]

54. If a rich man asks for **children** dollars come to him, and if a poor man asks for dollars children come to him.

55. Make a bed for the **children** of other people in the place where your own children sleep.

56. Male **children** should be found on the laps.

[i.e. grown-up sons have to take care of their parents ; they should not forget the time when they sat on the parents' lap.]

57. The **Christians** are infidels, they wish the Moslems nothing but loss.

58. Mend [your **clothes**] in a day, you will dress [in them] for a month.

59. Everyone sells his ragged old **clothes** in his market.

60. The **clouds** are not hurt by the barking of dogs.

[Said when a person denies the truth of a statement made by another.]

61. If you allow them to **comb** you, they will scratch you with the comb.

62. We made them **come in,** they made us go out.

[i.e. refers to a person who has been introduced to his work by another and afterwards has displaced him.]

63. **Compete,** don't envy.

64. From **contentment** with little comes satiation.

65. A **contract** in the field is better than a quarrel on the threshing floor.

66. Only **copper** returns and silver does not return.

[i.e. he who dies during the pilgrimage to Mecca is particularly blessed.]

67. The **country** where the stones know you is better than the country where the people know you.

68. When the **cow** falls down, the daggers are many.

69. **Cupidity** is a plague, and the plague kills.

70. A veil of rope is better than a breach of **custom.**

71. Every **day** has its fare.

72. One **day** is in favour of you and another against you.

73. The **dead** are dear to us, but as for the wounded, they will be cured.

[i.e. you should bestow charity on only those who are destitute.]

74. A **debt** [if left unpaid] demolishes religion.

75. Compliance with **destiny.**

76. [Even] a hut of spider-web is a loss for him who is going to **die.**

77. What they **do** we should do with them.

78. Ask the experienced one, don't ask the **doctor.**

[Reply of woman reproved of speaking badly about another woman.]

79. He who eats jackal's flesh is better than a hundred **doctors.**

[i.e. jackal's flesh is considered to contain much medicinal value.]

80. None but a **dog** bites in his own house.

[i.e. said of a person who quarrels with his guests.]

81. Kiss the **dog** on his mouth until you get what you want from him.

82. Not even a **dog** runs away from his tent.

83. Don't make your **dog** satisfied; leave him hungry, he will follow you.

84. Beat the **dog,** the other dogs will run away.

[i.e. punishment is a means of determent.]

85. We played with the **dogs,** in the morning they became our cousins.

86. I shall not tie the **donkey** at the place of the horse.

[The words in which the widow of a high-born one refuses the proposal of a low-born man.]

87. If you find them worshipping a **donkey,** bring him grass.

88. Beat the pack-saddle, the **donkey** will wake up.

[Said by a person who, when sitting in a company of people, hears bad talk about himself.]

89. He who knocks at the **door** will not be without an answer.

90. If you know his **dress** [i.e. origin] don't bother about his nakedness.

91. Carry away their **dung,** don't beg from them.

[i.e. any work better than none.]

92. He who clears away the **dunghill** of others should clear away his own, he will see no evil.

93. **Eat** and drink, and put what is left into a palmetto bag.

94. **Eat,** don't ask.

[Said in reply to one asking advice about marriage.]

95. If people have **eaten** [with you] they betray you, and if a dog has eaten [with you] he loves you.

96. **Endurance** pierces marble.

97. An intelligent **enemy** is better than an ignorant friend.

98. He who **envies** you has given you [something].

99. **Eye** does not see, heart does not suffer.

100. However high the **eye** may rise, it will find the eyebrow above it.

[Said to a low-born man who pretends to be higher than others.]

101. The day has its **eyes,** the night has its ears.

[Said to a liar.]

102. If the **face** disappears, no respect is left for the nape of the neck.

[i.e. if a high official is dismissed or dies, no notice is any longer taken of him or his children.]

103. He who becomes **fat** must become thin, and he who flies must come down.

104. He to whom his **father** left some hill should climb it.

[i.e. do not boast of being better than your family, or try to rise higher than your father.]

105. Do whatever you **find,** not what you want.

106. The **fire** leaves only ashes, and the rain leaves only roses.

[i.e. children will be like their parents.]

107. **Fire** underneath the straw.

[i.e. a show of friendship that hides enmity in the heart.]

108. Make the handful of **food** equal to your mouth before it chokes you.

[i.e. if a poor man wants to marry a girl whose parents are well off, he is warned by a friend.]

109. Only your own **foot** makes you go, and only your own nail scratches you, and only your own eyelash weeps for you.

110. The **forest** is only burnt by its own wood.

[i.e. said by a parent whose child does mischief.]

111. **Forgiveness** from the heart is better than a box of gold.

112. The brave man has two **fortunes.**

[One being his bravery and the other what he gains by it.]

113. He who eats the **fowls** of others should fatten his own.

[i.e. if a person has been entertained as a guest, he should in his turn entertain his host.]

114. Do as your **friend** does or leave him.

115. Pass by your **friend** hungry, don't pass by him naked.

116. A descent for the sake of a **friend** is an ascent.

117. A stone from the hand of a **friend** is an apple.

118. A **friend** is better than milk.

119. If your **friend** is honey don't eat it all.

120. The **friend** is known in the time of difficulty.

121. Where your **friend** is, there is your enemy.

122. Everyone afar is a great deceiver ; may he who makes a **friend** make a friend of his neighbour.

123. The **friend** of a little handful of food will not remain [a friend] for ever.

124. **A friend** says to his friend that he will find him in every difficulty.

125. If he increases the number of his **friends** he will remain without a friend.

126. To make **friends** with a wild beast is better than to make friends with an inquisitive person.

127. **Fright** is worse than a blow.

128. In everything [i.e. every kind of **fruit**] there is [both] sickness and medicine, with the exception of grapes and oranges when they are in their beginning [then there is no sickness in them].

129. A man only thinks of where he has **gained** or where he has lost.

130. Sell the new **garment** and don't give up the old one.

131. If they **get up,** get up with them, and if they sit, sit with them.

[i.e. accept any job whether it requires standing or sitting.]

132. If you have much **give** from your wealth, and if you have little give from your heart.

133. The houses of **girls** are soon empty.

[i.e. daughters leave the house as soon as they marry.]

134. He who does not know is excused by **God.**

135. A little for **God** and a little for my own heart.

[An employer replies thus when blamed for paying employees too high wages.]

136. Give it for the sake of **God,** and give it [even] to him who does not believe in God.

137. Slowness comes from **God** and quickness from the devil.

138. Repose trust [in **God**] and sleep with a snake.

139. Manage with bread and butter till **God** brings the jam.

140. **God** brings to all wheat its measurer.

[i.e. it is natural to marry a person of one's own class or position.]

141. May **God** close the door for him who has only one.

[i.e. a master who sends away his only servant may have the curse.]

142. He who eats before a hungry person, may **God** deprive him of his goods in the world.

143. **God** gives beans only to him who has no teeth.

[said by a man who has money but no children, to one who has children but no money.]

144. If **God** gives you and pays you, [even] the wind will cut wood for you.

145. If **God** has given you, what can a servant [of God] do [to you] ?

146. An innocent person's invocation to **God** has no curtains.

[It will be heard at once.]

147. [To commit] ten sins against **God** is better than [to commit] one against a servant [of God].

148. Every matter of importance which is begun without mention of **God** is maimed.

149. May **God** make us awake to our fault.

150. To every field of wheat **God** sends its reaper.

151. A hand for the sake of **God** that the load may be lifted [on to the pack-animal].

[i.e. if a young bachelor is too poor to marry and has no relations to assist him, someone in the village may suggest to others that each should give something to help him to get married.]

152. Give what there is in your pocket, **God** will bring you what is absent.

153. Be patient of little, **God** will give you much.

154. Give occasion and **God** will help you.

155. He who has **gold** is loved, even if he is a dog, son of dogs.

156. In everything offered there is **good.**

157. **Good** for good, and he who begins is more generous.

158. He who has done **good** will have colic in return.

[i.e. a good deed is often rewarded with evil.]

159. Do **good,** you will find good.

160. If [**good luck**] comes [to you] lead it [i.e. you may even lead it] with a hair, and if it goes down it breaks [even] chains.

161. An unjust **government** is better than corrupt subjects.

162. He who does not reach the bunch of **grapes** says, " Sour."

163. A strange **grave** is better than an empty bag.

[i.e. said to a man who does not get on well at home.]

164. There remains in the **grave** none but its master.

[Said by a man who has been well off and had many friends about him, but afterwards becomes poor and abandoned by them.]

165. To look at the **green** adorns the heart and the eye.

166. He who mixes with the **grocer** smells of his perfume.

167. The words of a **guest** are like rain in summer.

[An allusion to the fact that when it looks as if it were going to rain in summer nothing comes of it.]

168. The **guest** is a guest, even if he stays a winter or a summer.

[Used in reference to a person who comes to another, not as an ordinary guest, but as a refugee, appealing to him not by the phrase, "I am the guest of God," but by the exclamation, "I am with you"—then he cannot be told to go away when the three days have passed.]

169. Guard your **hand.**

170. May God not make the right **hand** beg of the left.

[Said to a man who refuses to lend money to another.]

171. He who has tied it with his **hand** has to open it with his teeth.

172. He who is beaten by his own **hand** must not weep.

[i.e. if a person steals from a member of his own family no complaint should be made.]

173. If men swear to do you **harm,** spend your night sleeping, but if women swear to do you harm, spend your night awake.

174. **Haste** is the sister of repentance.

175. He who **hates** you does not lack what to say about you.

176. The **heart** of the fool is in his mouth, and the mouth of the wise man is in his heart.

177. What makes you count a month for which you receive no **hire?**

178. He who has no **honey** in his place should put some on the tip of his tongue.

179. He who loves **honey** should be patient of the stinging of the bees.

[i.e. if a man is anxious to marry a certain woman and sends some persons to negotiate on his behalf, but the proposal is not accepted, somebody may give him this advice.]

180. He who **hopes** fares better than he who wishes, and he who wishes fares better than he who despairs.

181. The high-bred **horse** says, "Feed me as your brother and ride on me as your enemy."

[Said of a man who strictly pays his employees their wages, but shows them no kindness.]

182. My **house** covers my nakedness.

183. Shave your head in the **house** of your brother and cut your nails in the house of your enemy.

[Two of the various "taboos" to which a guest is subject.]

184. Everything you plant will be useful to you except a **human being,** and if you plant him he will root you up.

185. The camel does not see his own **hump,** he sees only the hump of his brother.

186. There is no **hunger** but the hunger of wheat.

187. **Hunger** is a slave and satiation is its mistress.

188. Ask of him who has been satisfied and is **hungry,** don't ask of him who has been hungry and become satisfied.

189. Be **insolent,** you will have rest.

190. The beauty of the man is in his **intelligence** and the intelligence of the woman is in her beauty.

191. The **iron** is struck only while it is hot.

[A man who sees that he is being robbed does not try to catch the robber, but when he meets him takes him to the sheikh. The robber denies the charge, no witness can be produced, and the sheikh dismisses the case with this saying.]

192. The **jackal** said, "Eat and measure."

[From the story of a hedgehog and jackal who went into a garden through a hole in the fence. After eating a large quantity of grapes the hedgehog went back to the opening to try if he still could get through, saying to the jackal, "Eat and measure," this the jackal failed to do, and was caught by the owner of the garden.]

193. Be a **jackal** so that the jackals may not eat you.

[i.e. a man who owns sheep is advised to watch them.]

194. Nobody is like his father except the **jackal** with his howl.

195. When the **Jew** is destitute he remembers his father's buttons.

[i.e. his father's old friends.]

196. Sleep in the beds of Christians [but] don't eat their food ; eat the food of **Jews** [but] don't sleep in their beds.

197. The **joy** [lasts] seven days and the sadness all the life.

198. One hundred and one **knocks** [at the door] are better than one " Peace be with you " [i.e. greeting].

199. **Laughing** without reasons comes from lack of good manners.

200. **Leave** the thing that leaves you.

201. There is nothing in **lies** to lie for, there is nothing in truth to repeat.

202. The **life** has its fixed limit, and why the fear ?

203. Be a **lion** and eat me, don't be a dog and worry me.

204. Every **lion** is roaring in his own country.

205. **Livelihood** is underneath the feet.

206. He who **loves** you wearies you ; he who hates you kills you.

207. If you are a **mallet,** beat, and if you are a peg, endure.

208. Nobody is really a **man** but he who is with other men.

209. One-half of **mankind** die from the evil eye.

210. He who is conquered by men at the **market** goes back to his wife in the house [to have his revenge on her].

211. The **market-place** has many little shops, buy to chew, hire to lodge.

[i.e. when a person leaves for another place he should have with him enough money to procure food and lodging, and not rely on hospitality.]

212. **Marriage** [takes] a night, the thinking of it a year.

213. **Marriage** with a strange woman is like drinking water from an earthenware bottle, but marriage with a cousin is like the drink from a dish.

[i.e. cousin marriages said to have many advantages.]

214. A **marriage** without children does not last long for men.

215. **Marriage** without good faith is like a teapot without a tray.

216. If he **marries** he embarks on a vessel, and if he gets a child he is wrecked.

217. The man who **marries** many wives marries trouble.

218. When a servant of God **marries,** verily he perfects half his religion.

[i.e. marriage is enjoined as a religious duty incumbent on all who possess the ability.]

219. **Marry** a woman of noble origin and sleep on a mat.

220. When you **marry,** marry a short one ; when you cut clothes for her you will have no trouble.

221. When you **marry,** surround [yourself] with a ditch of salt [i.e. salt water], you will be at rest.

[i.e. a married man should say " good " to anything his family ask of him, without thinking of doing it.]

222. He stayed the night in the **marshes,** in the morning he was one of the frogs.

[Said of a novice in a trade who pretends to be a master.]

223. Know how to **meet** and know how to part.

224. Soap makes a garment come out [clean], and mercy cleans the heart.

225. The **minaret** fell down, hang the barber.

[i.e. innocent punished for the fault of the guilty.]

226. **Misfortune** is misfortune's heir.

227. A hewer of trees and a burner of stones are never successful in making **money.**

228. Everything will satisfy you except **money,** as much as you have, so much [more] you want.

229. **Money** makes a road on the sea.

230. The **mouse** in its hole is a king.

231. The son of a **mouse** will only turn out to be a digger.

[Used in a good as well as in a bad sense.]

232. Into a closed **mouth** no fly can enter.

233. The **mouths** of gun-barrels are better than the mouths of dogs.

[i.e. it is better to be shot than slandered.]

234. A **mower** should not be a searcher.

235. None but a **mule** denies his origin.

[Said of a person who boasts of being better than his family.]

236. A **muzuna** in the palm is better than ten lost.

[A muzuna is an imaginary coin (Moorish) worth less than a farthing.]

237. He is like a **needle** that clothes the people and is himself naked.

[Said of a man who benefits others at the cost of himself and his family.]

238. The **negro** has a rib and a cup of blood more than the white man.

[i.e. a negro is stronger than a white man.]

239. He who has no house has no **neighbour.**

240. Choose the **neighbour** before the house and the companion before the road.

241. Do what your **neighbour** does or move away from him.

242. Your **neighbour** is your saw.

[Said of a bad neighbour.]

243. Good morning, O my **neighbour,** [may] you [stay] in your house and I in my house.

244. Your **neighbour** who is near is better than your brother who is far away.

245. The **niggard** [will go] to hell even though he worships God by night and day.

246. The work of the **night** is a wonder to the day.

247. To pass the **night** with iron is better than with pus.

[i.e. better to be stabbed than insulted.]

248. Whom you serve, **obey,** and what you are going to pawn, sell.

[A workman who disobeys his master is reprimanded with this.]

249. If you find a meal of fruit at the gate of the **orchard,** don't proceed into it.

250. The **oven** precedes the mosque.

251. We gave him milk to drink, he became a **partner** in the cow.

[Said of one who has been given something and then appropriates everything he is able to.]

252. In everything there is **partnership** with the exception of marriage and the blessed prayer.

253. What has **passed** has died, it will be repeated no more.

254. What is **past** is gone, and what is hoped for is absent, and for you is the hour in which you are.

255. **Patience** is the key of all well-being.

256. In the gate of **patience** there is no crowding.

257. Your **people** are your people, even though they hate you, you will find them in your evil.

258. **People** know people and horses know their riders.

[Said by a high-bred person when a low-bred person quarrels with him.]

259. Go with **people** without [doing them] harm ; he who opens a door will have to close it himself.

260. The **pillow** is the guarantee of sleep.

[i.e. where you have a friend you may sleep well.]

261. He who digs a **pit** for his brother will fall into it.

262. **Plant** him, he will pull you up.

263. Nobody knows the condition of a **poor man** but a poor man.

264. He who is afraid of a thing gives it **power** over him.

265. Don't **praise** nor blame him you have not mixed with.

266. Everybody who is **praised** [will be] despised.

267. **Prayer** at its [proper] time is better than the world and what is in it.

268. If the **prices** are equal, know that the best people no longer remain.

269. Everything is useful except that lies and slander bring no **profit.**

270. The **property** of the grandfathers will come to an end, but the craft of the hands will remain.

271. The cause of **quarrel** is bashfulness and food.

272. If you find **quietness** and joy don't proceed to toil and trouble

273. He became a **raisin** before he was a grape.

[Said of a student who pretends to be a scribe.]

274. **Repentance** for silence is better than repentance for speaking.

275. **Replace,** you will know.

[i.e. if you suspect an employee of dishonesty you should change him for another, then you will find if your suspicion was correct.]

276. Every absence increases the **respect.**

277. The tar of **respect** is better than the honey of quietness.

[Better to eat your own food than to sponge on others.]

278. Everybody who is **respected** will be despised.

279. Say " no " from the first, you will have **rest.**

280. There is no **rest** below the top of the hill.

[i.e. he who commences a task should go on with it until it is finished.]

281. If a person is away, his **right** is away.

282. The empty **river** will not take you away and the full one will not leave you.

283. [Choose] the **road** of safety even if it winds.

284. A **rose** comes from thorns, and a well-bred boy from your [instead of his] mother and father.

285. Everything is **rubbish** except wheat and wool.

[i.e. food and clothing.]

286. Catch him [and] he will make you **sad** ; release him [and] he will annoy you.

287. Never will **salt** become worm-eaten.

[Said of good people.]

288. Nothing will **scratch** you but your own nail or the son from your loins.

289. He who **seeks** a thing will find it, and he who hides a thing will find it.

290. **Settle** accounts with me as if I were your enemy and entertain me as your brother.

291. Every **sheep** hangs by its own leg.

292. He who **shelters** himself from you with a thread, shelter yourself from him with a wall.

[i.e. if you find that your friend no longer cares for you, you should have nothing more to do with him.]

293. Go on with the old **shoes** until God brings new ones.

294. **Silence** is in the door of consent.

295. O man, see and be **silent** ; if you eat meat say it is fish.

296. **Small** and spirited is better than big with money.

297. He remained fasting for a year and breakfasted on **snails.**

[Said of a bachelor who waits for an opportunity to get a beautiful wife and then marries an ugly one.]

298. He who has been bitten by a **snake** is afraid of a palmetto cord.

299. If you know his father and grandfather, don't worry about his **son.**

300. As you **sow** you will reap.

301. **Sow** wheat, don't sow thorns ; all the people will like you and love you.

302. He who has no **spoon** will burn his hand.

[Said of a person who has no family or friend.]

303. Go across the murmuring **stream,** don't go across the silent one.

[i.e. a rash and noisy person is more to be trusted than a quiet and silent one.]

304. In every **stumbling** there is good.

305. The **supposition** of the wise man is better than the certainty of the ignorant.

306. He who **swears** in good faith is like him who visits a shrine.

307. The **tables** were turned upside-down and the earthenware pots sat up.

[Said when good servants are dismissed to give place to bad ones.]

308. The **tail** of the greyhound will not be made straight even though it remains seven years in the melting-pot.

309. Greeting draws **talk.**

310. Eat according to your **taste,** and dress according to the taste of others.

311. **Teach** him, he will pull you up.

[Said of a person who has been taught by another and then takes his place.]

312. He who opposes his **tent** [i.e. his wife] empties it.

[Said as a reminder that a wife who has borne children should be treated with consideration.]

313. **Theft** is a worm, it does not die either by abuse or by a hatchet.

[i.e. a thief is incorrigible.]

314. He who sows **thorns** must walk on them barefoot.

315. **Toil** makes understanding.

316. Beautify your **tongue,** you will obtain what you desire.

317. The **tortoise** dies and does not scratch its back.

[i.e. a person should be patient in his work until it is completed.]

318. A **trade,** [even] if it does not make one rich, will cover one or even prolong one's life.

319. A comrade in your **trade** is your enemy.

320. **Travel** [and] you will see them, sit [and] they will come to you.

321. He who does not **travel** will not know the value of men.

322. There is no blessing in a woman who **travels,** and there is no blessing in a man who does not travel.

323. Don't **trust** [even] a country of safety.

324. Don't **trust** him whose grave is new, leave his head and come to his feet.

[i.e. don't trust a person whom you don't know.]

325. The owner of an **umbrella** goes as it pleases him, in the sun or in the shade.

[i.e. a person with money can do as he likes.]

326. When the **understanding** travels there is no courier like it.

327. May God bless him who pays a **visit** and makes it short.

328. Among the **walnuts** only the empty one speaks.

[Said of boasting and arrogance.]

329. Give **water** even though you are close to water.

[The best of all alms is water.]

330. To give **water** is better than to give bread.

[i.e. better to give water in charity than bread.]

331. The **water** of the well is better than the favour of the water-sellers.

[i.e. it is better to help oneself than to be helped by others.]

332. Boil the **water,** you will find the foam.

[i.e. said to one who makes a fuss about nothing.]

333. He who has **wheat** should lend flour.

334. The **wheat** turns round and round and comes back to the hole of the mill.

[i.e. home is best.]

335. A **wick** does not come out of a rag.

[Said to one of humble origin who pretends to come from a good family.]

336. Consult your **wife** and follow your own mind ; consult your wife and act contrary to her advice.

337. Don't take a widow for **wife,** she will have mercy on him whom God has had mercy upon [i.e. she will think of her late husband], and make you a dung-hill.

338. When you take a **wife,** take a poor one ; even though you bring her only a loaf of bread and a sardine, [she will be content].

339. **Wine** is the key of all evil.

340. For the **wise man** his look is sufficient.

341. When a **woman** becomes old, nothing remains in her but poison and the colour of sulphur.

342. What the devil does in a year an old **woman** does in an hour.

343. Don't marry an old **woman** even though you will eat with her young pigeons and lamb's meat [the most delicious food].

344. He who has an old **woman** [for wife] has a plague.

345. An old **woman** is worse than the devil.

346. Don't marry a tall **woman,** she will embarrass you in regard to clothes and drawers.

347. If you see an old **woman** with a rosary, know that she is truly a devil.

348. **Women** are a vessel of wood, and he who travels in it is lost.

[Advantages of bachelorhood.]

349. **Women** are the friends of the devil.

350. **Women** have been omitted by God from His mercy.

351. Obedience to **women** makes one enter hell.

352. He who cuts some **wood** gets warm over it.

353. With the piece of **wood** that I nursed I burned my skin.

[Said by a man who is robbed in his own house by his foster-son.]

354. He who fills his head with other people's **words** will find no place where he may put his own.

355. **Work** [and] you will be strong ; sit [and] you will stink.

356. **Work** at a feast is like the stabs of a dagger.

357. In **work** there is utility, it heals the wounds.

358. The **world** has not given promise to anybody.

359. Beat the **world,** the other world will caper. (*Proverb on alms-giving.*)

360. The **wound** caused by words is worse than the wound of bodies.

361. A barren **year,** [if] one eats and another looks on.

362. A **year** in which there are plenty of almonds and dates increases prosperity and life.

363. "**Yes**" and "**no**" are in the same position.

[i.e. a person should frankly speak the truth in the face of his friend, whether agreeable or not.]

364. Instruction in **youth** is like engraving in stones.

NANDI (KENYA COLONY)

[Language Family—Nilo-Hamitic]

1. If you take a knife away from a **child,** give him a piece of wood instead.

2. A man who is always **crying** is not listened to.

3. You cannot light a **fire** in water.

[Said to a liar.]

4. A **goat's** hide buys a goat's hide, and a gourd a gourd.

[i.e. an eye for an eye and a tooth for a tooth.]

5. Don't show a **hyena** how well you can bite.
6. There is no **saying** without a double meaning.
7. A **tree** is not twice struck by lightning.

   [If you have to punish a person or a tribe, do it so thoroughly that it will not require to be done a second time.]
8. If a dead **tree** falls, it carries with it a live one.

   [i.e. if a criminal is punished, his innocent relations suffer as well.]

NDAU (VANDAU) (PORTUGUESE SOUTH AFRICA)

[Language Family—Bantu]

1. The **boil** does not know its place.

   [i.e. misfortune comes to both rich and poor.]
2. **Chicks** that go into the chicken-house see their mother.
3. The strength of the **crocodile** is in the water.
4. The **elephant** does not feel the weight of its tusks.

   [i.e. the rich do not feel their wealth as a burden.]
5. **Fish** follow their river.

   [i.e. people will support their own family or tribe.]
6. By walking back, **game** is obtained.

   [i.e. it is often worth while to go back in order to get things which you own, rather than to seek something new at a distance.]
7. In the **home** is no darkness.

   [i.e. one is always happy at home.]
8. Nothing that enters the mouth of a **hyena** comes out again.
9. The **knife** does not know its owner.

   [i.e. it cuts everyone.]
10. **Poverty** is not laughed at.
11. Even a large **ship** may be wrecked in darkness.

    [i.e. small things may spoil great plans.]

NDEBELE (SINDEBELE) (MATABELELAND)

[Language Family—Bantu]

1. [What is] **behind** is in front.

   [i.e. one might some day have to return to what one has left, so it is well to take farewell properly.]
2. A **big thing** makes no noise.
3. A **cow** licks the one that licks it.
4. The **eagle** kills while wandering.

   [Opposite to our "Rolling stone gathers no moss".]
5. A **fire-brand** eats the owner.
6. A **foot** has no nose.
7. That which is made **forgets**—the maker forgets not.
8. One who **gives** to another is storing up for himself.
9. The breast of a man is a **granary**.

   [Used in defence of reticence.]
10. Wear out, body! Remain, O **heart**.
11. To stay in one place is to protect oneself through one's **neighbours**.

12. The wild **pig** caught by the dogs is the one which was the last to leave the lair.
13. **Pig melons** fall upon those who have no pot.
14. A **reflection** does not see itself.
15. To **see** once is to see twice.
    [i.e. once bitten, twice shy.]
16. To **stint** a person is to stint oneself.
17. **Water** does not forsake its road.

NDONGA (AANDONGA) (OVA-MPO-LAND)

[Language Family—Bantu]

1. One does not need to say " **Buy** " of a useful thing.
2. It doesn't **dawn** only on one day, to-morrow the sun will shine.
3. The breaking **day** has wisdom, the falling day experience.
4. It is better by the **door** than by the back wall.
    [i.e. one can escape more easily.]
5. The **doors** have let it in and the wharves have spread it about.
    [i.e. gossip.]
6. One **elephant** can't stir up much dust.
7. One **finger** alone can't rid itself of lice.
8. He who doesn't say it to you isn't your **friend.**
9. Practise with the left **hand** so long as the right is still there.
10. Even a small thing has its owner, and the **miser** his friends.
11. Fat isn't eaten out of your **neighbour's** hand.
    [i.e. don't expect good luck from others.]
12. Your **neighbour's** head is a little kingdom for itself, the heart of your neighbour a wood.
    [i.e. who can see into another's heart ?]
13. The **stomach** is like the eye, it is sensitive to little.
14. One cannot fence one's **stomach** round with a thorn-bush.
    [i.e. one cannot prevent hunger.]
15. He who has always **tasted** a little isn't dead.
    [i.e. in time of famine one must be sparing with food.]
16. Don't light the **wood** at both ends.

NGONI (NYASALAND)

[Language Family—Bantu]

1. The **chief** is like the rubbish heap, everything comes to him.
2. I saw with the **eyes,** the ears are liars.
3. **Laughing** finishes the teeth.
4. He dived into a **saucer** and his back showed up.
    [Said when a man tries to hide his fault by some shallow excuse.]
5. How can I **shoot** when the bird is on my bow-string ?
    [Said when the one to be charged is present or refuses to answer the charge.]

NUPE (NORTHERN NIGERIA)

[Language Family—Sudanic]

1. Oh! my **banjo** has no bells on it.

   [i.e. just because there is no outward show connected with your work, don't think it is useless.]

2. One **bee** is better than a handful of flies.
3. The **birch rod** doesn't reach the character, but the body will make the connection.
4. The **bird** that calls the rain will get wet itself.
5. **Black** will blacken people.
6. According to the size of the **blister,** so is the amount of water.
7. A **canoe** is never too small to carry the canoeman.
8. " **Catch me** " is close by; " save me " is far away.
9. With the right hand they thrash a **child,** and with the left draw it to them.

   [i.e. firm but loving.]

10. A **child** is like a camel's neck, it goes where it pleases.
11. The one who **converses** loudly is wanting witnesses.
12. If a grain of **corn** falls in the mud, the inside is still white.
13. Two hundred **cowries** will catch more guinea-fowls than bird-lime.

    [i.e. money is power.]

14. Among **dead** things will be found something with life; and among the living things are the dead.
15. The old man runs away from **death,** but the child stands and looks at it.
16. **Death** is the owner of the house and is no stranger, but when it comes it will be a stranger to us that day.
17. Always being in a hurry does not hinder **death,** neither does going slowly hinder living.
18. **Delay** does not spoil things, it makes them better.
19. The inexperienced man cured the **doctor.**
20. When an **elephant** kicks only an elephant can receive that kick.
21. The **eye** sees but cannot take away.
22. Don't rejoice over the finding of decayed **fish,** for what killed it would have eaten it if it had been good.
23. When the **fish** is fresh is the time to bend it.
24. **Force** will never be without a place to sit down.
25. If you enter a city carrying a **fowl** you will come out carrying a vulture.
26. If you loan a **garment** to a poor man, you may expect him to wear it out.
27. One may go around a ravine, or around a hill, but one cannot go around **God.**
28. **God** gives and does not remind us continually of it; the world gives and constantly reminds us.
29. No one who trusts in **God** will ever fall.
30. **God** will outlive eternity.
31. **God** who made the mouth will not close it up.

    [i.e. the Lord will provide.]

32. That which is extra **good** is a forerunner of something bad.
33. When they roast a **guinea-fowl,** the partridge has a headache.
34. When you have nothing more on the **hearth,** take your eyes away.
35. Even though you may enter the house, you don't always enter the **hearts.**
36. **Honour** is no play.
37. When they are sharpening a knife the **horse** has no fear.
38. The body prostrated on the ground does not make **humility.**
39. " I am going, I am going," that is what makes the **journey** so long.

40. While you are preparing to go on a **journey** you own the journey, but after you have started the journey owns you.

41. Little by little the **leper** pays his debt to the grave.

 [By losing his fingers.]

42. For one living in a **leper** town, it is better to close the fists [to appear to have no fingers].

43. **A lie** hurts more than a sore.

44. God knew how to hide the shame [nakedness] of the **maize** with the husks.

45. People do not hide away the seeds of **malice.**

46. If you intend to give a sick man **medicine,** let him get very ill first, so that he may see the benefit of your medicine.

47. **Medicine** that is mixed with food, even if it doesn't cure the disease, will cure hunger.

48. **Medicine** that is sweet is not medicine.

49. **Misfortune** is what keeps back the energetic man to make him wait for the feeble man.

50. **Money** is the witness.

51. **Money** kills more people than a club.

52. One comes to borrow **money** like a turtle " with his head on the ground ", but pays it back like a crocodile " with his head in the air ".

53. **Money** softens a dispute as water softens clay.

54. The red **monkey** still continues to have red young ones.

55. Whatever is sweet in the **mouth** will be bitter in the stomach, and whatever is bitter in the mouth will be sweet in the stomach.

56. A man is never so tall that he can be seen from here to the next town ; it is his **name** that goes.

57. An **old man** is a dumping ground, everybody throws sweepings on him.

58. If you see an **old man** running, either he is chasing something or something is chasing him.

59. Into the hearts of **old people** they tip rubbish.

60. An **onion** does not take the character of water.

 [i.e. a child is not always like its parents.]

61. **Pepper** is small, but it smarts.

62. You don't get a **pigeon** for nothing, so look at its wings.

63. When a man becomes **poor** he does not realize it, and it will take three years for him to find it out.

64. The **poor man's** chicken are his cattle.

 [Make the best of what you have.]

65. It is the water that doesn't fill the **pot** that makes the most noise.

66. To remain **quiet** is the same as being angry.

67. " Don't do it " is the best **remedy** for " Let it not be known ".

68. **Remorse** comes to warn us of after results, so it is really a forerunner, but we take it and place it behind.

69. If you **sit down** well you will rise up well.

 [i.e. do good in this world and you will not be ashamed in the next.]

70. **Sleep** is the younger brother of death.

71. **Smoke** cannot be confined to one place.

72. The man who carries a **stick** will not be bitten by a dog.

73. To bring a **stranger** in is to put the host in debt.

74. The **tale-bearer** does not leap over the wall, he comes in by the main road.

75. The friend of a **thief** is a thief.

76. A **timid person** does not enjoy the world.

77. **To-day** is this world, to-morrow is the next.

78. Do well **to-day** on account of to-morrow.

79. The big **toe** never does the ear any harm.

80. Even the **tongue** and the teeth quarrel now and then.

81. While waiting for a dried-up **tree** to fall, a green one falls instead.

82. To **trouble** me is better than to forget me.

83. **Truth** keeps the hands cleaner than soap.

84. There is always room for one who is **wanted.**

85. Running **water** never gets tired.

86. **Water** runs in ditches.

[i.e. there is a right way and a wrong way.]

87. **Water** standing in a pot will never rise.

88. It is **work** that puts one man ahead of another.

89. That which was used to make the **world** will also be used to destroy it.

NYANG (KENYANG) (CAMEROONS)

[Language Family—Sudanic]

1. He who has a **bundle,** looks for a rope.

2. It isn't hard to push a **canoe** on a muddy beach.

[i.e. a lazy man is soon brought to ruin.]

3. If the **crab** is small it associates with a smaller kind of crab.

4. When one is **dead,** is then everything dead?

5. The **death** of a man is only a day.

6. If a young **dog** doesn't know how to steal, the others teach him.

7. If you begin to call a **dog,** don't hold a stick in your hand.

8. A **dog** is proud of its teeth and yet eats dirt.

[i.e. don't judge by outward appearances.]

9. The hollow of the **ear** is never full.

[i.e. never tired of hearing.]

10. He who has **eaten** knows not that hunger torments another.

11. When an **elephant** follows you, you climb a prickly tree.

12. When the **eye** weeps, the nose is also wet.

[i.e. if my mother suffers, I also suffer.]

13. The **eyes** fear the eyelids.

[i.e. the inferiors are humble in presence of those placed in authority.]

14. **A father** can feed seven children, but seven children can't feed one father.

15. One **finger** can't catch a mother louse.

16. Good **firewood** is not without ants.

[i.e. a pretty woman has often faults.]

17. A man's **folly** is not made so public as a woman's.

18. Man leaves **food,** but food never leaves man.

19. **Foresight** spoils nothing.

20. **Freedom** is not in two yards.

[i.e. you cannot do in another's house as in your own.]

21. One can't tie up a bundle with one **hand.**

22. When the **head** is knocked off, it is all over with dreams.

23. The **heart's** house is never full.

24. A **hen** doesn't go without a reason into the Court when a market is being held.

[Said of a woman who wants a new husband.]

25. If you would give **hospitality** to a guest, stand behind the house.

    [i.e. don't let your left hand know what your right hand does.]

26. Hen and man go through the same **house door.**

    [i.e. said of two people living in the same house. When one has gone out and the other says he doesn't know where he has gone.]

27. For that which **interests** one, one has open eyes.

28. Always a **little** bit makes in the end something together.

29. The way to the **loved one** is not thorny.

30. He who is the first to make the **mistake** is the first to be laughed at.

31. Why did you go to the clearing in the bush without first making friends with the **monkeys ?**

32. He who has a **mouth** doesn't lose the way.

33. He whom **news** concerns soon hears it.

34. All **noses** look downwards.

    [i.e. men must die.]

35. An old **parcel** easily turns into tar.

    [i.e. if you don't fetch a packet you have been promised, when you say you will, you won't find it any longer.]

36. **Peace** has made the quarrel tired.

37. The eyes of a **poor man** let in the dirt.

    [i.e. nothing succeeds with him.]

38. The **pot** cooks, but the plate gets the name.

    [i.e. the slave has the trouble and the master gets the praise.]

39. **Rain** falls on every roof.

40. The **rat** that has no children builds her house by the river.

41. Don't throw **refuse** on to two rubbish heaps.

    [In case you want to look for something lost, you don't know on which to look.]

42. **Respect** depends on reciprocity.

43. That which is not yet **ripe** doesn't fall to the ground.

44. If you don't know what is at the source of a **river,** do you drink at its mouth ?

    [i.e. don't judge on a question of which you know nothing.]

45. When you have walked through a **river,** the traces remain.

46. If you have not remained long in the **river,** you will not be able to swim.

47. A mouth that has eaten **salt** can no longer eat unsalted.

48. If you know the **sea-wind,** can the land-wind deceive you ?

    [i.e. he can get out of small difficulties who can get out of great ones.]

49. One doesn't **sell** anything so long as it remains in the bag.

    [i.e. no one buys a pig in a poke.]

50. The **shoulder** is not higher than the head.

    [i.e. the servant is not greater than his master.]

51. **Sleep** begins in the feet.

    [i.e. illness begins with fever.]

52. When you have been bitten by a **snake** you fear the sight of a rain-worm.

53. Two **spoons** don't suit one mouth.

54. Much **standing** has made the hen's feet small.

    [i.e. he achieves nothing who begins work everywhere and never finishes it.]

55. The **stomach** has injured the head.

    [i.e. hunger leads to thoughts of theft.]

56. The **stomach** tells no tales.

    [i.e. when it has eaten well it doesn't proclaim.]

57. **Sweep** first in front of the door, and then inside the house.

58. The **teeth** encompass the tongue.

    [Said of someone who has many children.]

59. **Thinness** doesn't pierce the skin.
 [i.e. illness kills, but not thinness.]
60. The **toad** doesn't know that his skin is rough.
 [i.e. people who are nothing to look at themselves should not criticize others.]
61. If a **tree trunk** is not rotten, no fungus grows on it.
62. The **unfortunate man** doesn't only suffer from one thing.
63. When you come out twice by the same tree you have lost your **way.**

NYANJA (CHINYANJA) (NYASALAND)

[Language Family—Bantu]

1. **Cunning** does not kill the fish; the killer of the fish is the net.
2. The **ears** envy one another.
3. **Fear** has laughter with it; fierceness has mournings.
4. The eater of pods doesn't **forget**; the one who forgets is the eater of beans.
5. That which has seen your **friend** to-day has gone off; to-morrow it will pay you a visit.
6. Mr. " Laugh in the eyes "—in his **heart** there are other things.
7. Though it is an **ill thing,** take care of it; the day after to-morrow you will call it your guardian.
8. To go a **journey** is just like taking a partner at a dance.
9. If you pronounce " **lion** ", get up a tree.
10. You have cheated the **medicine-man,** heal your next sore if you can.
11. The one who circulates a lie doesn't **pay,** the payer is the one that laughs.
12. The mouth is not the place to **praise**; praise is right through the heart.
13. Indian corn comes in full measure to the **toothless man.**
14. To be **wealthy** is [like] the tail of the rat.

NYIKA (ZANZIBAR)

(Including Duruma)

[Language Family—Bantu]

1. The **arrows** that go waveringly are the ones that hit.
2. A good **bird** does not cry twice. (*Duruma.*)
 [i.e. a good omen is not repeated.]
3. Dipping, dipping, finishes the **corn sack.**
4. **Friendship** surpasses relationship.
5. Pray to **God,** He tires not.
6. All is in the **heart.** (*Duruma.*)
7. Where the **heart** desires, there it goes.
8. A licker of **honey** licks not once only.
9. **Knocking,** knocking, finishes the body.
10. " They say " is own brother to a **lie.**
11. A person who buys an **ox** by the footmark.
12. A man is **praised** in the grave. (*Duruma.*)

13. You do not wish to be **shaven,** you want to have the hairs plucked out.
14. The **snake** bites where he has reached.
15. **Thieves** have no smell.
16. A **thorn** of pricking one's own self does not pain.
17. When a **tree** falls it leans on its neighbour.

NYORO (UGANDA)

[Language Family—Bantu]

1. Hush your friend's **baby** when yours is asleep.
2. The sucking **child** says, "Mother is the best cook."

   [i.e. don't express preference without trying an alternative.]
3. That which will **eat** you, you abuse as it comes.

   [i.e. forewarned is forearmed.]
4. The **flute** of old age chafes the lips.

   [i.e. learn the flute in your youth or get sore lips.]
5. Save your **fowl** before it stops flapping.

   [i.e. while there is life there is hope.]
6. Too much confidence lost the **frog** his tail.

   [The origin of this proverb is a tale. The grandmother of all frogs was giving out tails, and one youngster said to himself, "It'll be alright, grannie is sure to keep me one, I'll go in the morning." When he went the tails were all gone; whence comes the race of tailless frogs we see to-day.]
7. "Mr. **Go-shares**" is after your bit.

   [lit. Come, let us eat together, he has seen your piece.]
8. Where the **heart** sleeps, there the legs get up early.
9. He who **hunts** two [rats] gets left.

   [i.e. between two stools you come to the ground.]
10. Messrs. **"I know you"** and "I know you" do not gobble up another's sauce.

    [i.e. mutual affection gives each his share.]
11. The **iron** has no power over the smith.
12. When the **master** is absent, the frogs climb up the house.
13. A bit of fresh **meat** livens up the dried.

    [i.e. a little leaven leavens the whole lump.]
14. He who hurries along at **night,** the darkness will rob him of a toenail.

    [i.e. night haste means morning pain.]
15. He who takes you by **night,** you thank him when morning breaks.
16. "Miss **obstinate**" sails in a china boat.
17. It is **pain** craves the pillow.
18. [The **stick**] that is to save you is found in your hand.
19. The "Help me" of the **stomach** never ends.
20. A **strawberry** blossom will not sweeten dry bread.
21. "I'll tie by myself" used all the **string** in tying.

    [i.e. two heads are better than one.]

NZIMA (APOLLONIA—GOLD COAST)

[Language Family—Sudanic]

1. If you play with **children** they call you their father's servant.
2. It is the **dog's** master who can take the bone from its mouth.
3. " Come near me " has an **enemy.**
4. The **fruit** you bear is what you will eat.
5. You need not tell a child that there is a **God.**
6. **Hand** go, hand come.
7. If you **have,** people know it.
8. Those who do not honour the **law** praise those who break it.
9. No man shall cut a **walking-stick** taller than himself.
10. Rebuke the **wise man** and he will like you.

OJI (ASHANTI)

[Language Family—Sudanic]

1. **Ancient things** remain in the ears.
2. **Bellies** mixed up, crocodiles mixed up ; we have between us only one belly, but if we get anything to eat, it passes down our respective gullets.
3. The **bird** caught in the trap is the one to sing sweetly.
4. When some really big **business** is on hand, no flag is flown.
5. A good **case** is not difficult to state.
6. A **chief's weights** are not the same as a poor man's weights.
7. It is not difficult to fill a **child's hand.**
8. No one says " good morning " before the **cock.**
9. When a person neglects to **congratulate** me, I congratulate myself.
10. The daughter of a **crab** does not give birth to a bird.
11. In consequence of banqueting with his friends, the **crab** has no head.
12. The straggling **creepers,** if you do not cut them, they entwine you ; if you cut them they entangle you.
13. **Death** has the key to open the miser's chest.
14. The **dog** has a proverb which runs : " A big thing does not get lost."
15. Even when a **dog's** mouth is watering he does not gnaw at the bells round his neck.
16. When a **donko** becomes rich he runs mad.
17. If you are an " **eat-by-myself** " person, you will often see a spirit.
18. When a man has **eaten** he will also drink.
19. When an **elder** portions out a dish it becomes cold.
    [i.e. arbitrates a quarrel.]
20. Once the **executioner** has cut off the head he is not afraid of anything again.
21. The **eye** envies, not the ear.
22. The **eye** knows nothing of grief.
23. **Food** which you will not eat, you do not boil.
24. When a **fool** is told a proverb, the meaning of it has to be explained to him.
25. A **forest** that has once sheltered you, never call a shrubbery.
    [i.e. ingratitude.]

26. When a **fowl** drinks water it [first] takes it and shows it to the Supreme Being.
27. When a **fowl** eats your neighbour's corn, drive it away; another time it will eat yours.
28. A **fowl** selects a single grain.
    [i.e. don't neglect small things.]
29. If you want to tell anything to **God,** tell it to the wind.
30. When **gold** is close to you it is pale.
31. If one could not make use of **gold dust,** then it would merely be called sand.
32. The **good thing** sells itself.
33. If you can pull out, pull out your own **grey hairs.**
34. No one who has seen "**Had I known,** I should not"; who has laid hold of "Had I known, I should not"; who has [ever] possessed "Had I known, I should not," would ever say [again], "Had I known, I should not."
35. **Hard words** are fit for the poor.
36. He who moulds your **head** like a water-pot, it is he who can break you.
    [i.e. your father.]
37. Pick up the **hen** and you can gather all her chickens. (*Ashanti warrior saying.*)
38. A poor man's **ivory** is a hog's tooth.
39. All power is in **land.**
    [Land tenure, upon which Ashanti confederacy is based.]
40. Who travels alone tells **lies.**
41. If you strike a **lion** your own head will pain you.
42. If anyone **loves** you he will beg of you.
43. If [spending] your **money** gives you pain, you will go hungry.
44. For a day like the present the **nails** are made.
45. If nothing touches the **palm leaves** they do not rustle.
46. A **path** has ears.
47. It is a **poor man** who has to go for firewood.
48. A man does not rub buttocks with a **porcupine.**
49. He who fetches water breaks the **pot.**
50. The monkey says there is nothing like **poverty** for taking the conceit out of a man.
51. When the occasion comes the **proverb** comes.
52. When a poor man makes a **proverb** it does not spread abroad.
53. He whom a **serpent** has bitten dreads a slow-worm.
54. When a **sick man** is drunk he is merely said to be unwell.
55. When a **slave** becomes a freeman he will drink rainwater.
56. If another **suffers** pain, [to you] a piece of wood suffers.
57. No one takes his **talking drums** and goes and beats them in the war camp to which he has fled.
58. No one knows the story of **to-morrow's dawn.**
59. When you place your **tongue** in pawn you cannot redeem it.
60. The **tongue** kills man and the tongue saves man.
61. One **tree** receiving [all] the wind, breaks.
62. There is not so much of **truth** that it should be cut off by falsehood.
63. Nocturnal **venison** is not fat.
64. If there had been no poverty in Europe, then the **white man** would not have come and spread his clothes in Africa.
65. A **wife** is like a blanket; when you cover yourself with it, it irritates you, and yet if you cast it aside you feel cold.
66. It is the path you do not fear that the **wild beast** catches you on.
67. A feast uncovers a European's **wooden leg.**
68. When your guns are few, your **words** are few.
69. In the **world** all things are two and two.

PEDI (TRANSVAAL—SOTHO) (NORTHERN TRANSVAAL)

[Language Family—Bantu]

1. Mother, when my **affairs** are discussed, I do not mind ; I clap my hands and let it all slide over my back.

   [" Mother " is used as an exclamation like " Oh well ".]

2. That which is near is reached by him who stretches out his **arm.**

   [i.e. even that which is easy can only be obtained by taking some trouble to acquire it.]

3. He who flees from **battle** is not mourned for at home.
4. A **bearded mouth** [an old man] speaks no untruth.
5. The sweat of a brave man is **blood.**
6. One man is **born** for another.
7. The mark on the **cow** is bigger on the calf.
8. In the house of the **coward** there is no weeping.

   [i.e. because he always turns up safe.]

9. An old **dog** kills by pouncing suddenly.
10. For the **elephant** his tusks are not too heavy.
11. An **elephant's kidneys** cannot be carried all at once.
12. The **fire** at which you don't warm yourself gives you no blisters.
13. To look for a fly in your **food** means that you have had enough.
14. Where the **fore hoof** of cattle has trodden there will also the hind hoof tread.
15. Don't ask me where I am **going,** but where I have come from.

    [i.e. don't always think of the future and forget the present.]

16. The wife of a **guest** is his stomach.

    [i.e. the thing he thinks most of.]

17. One does not wash one's **hands** for that which belongs to another.
18. The **heart** is like a goat that must be tied up.
19. Through the little **hole** of the small goes only " Mr. Small ".

    [i.e. only a master at his work can explain it.]

20. **Horns** fixed on don't remain firm on the head.

    [i.e. borrowed cunning is of no use.]

21. " Let us go " doesn't mean a **journey.**
22. He who learns how to **milk** learns it on his own cow.
23. He who waits for the **moon,** waits for darkness.
24. When a **mouse** has eaten enough it doesn't blow the flames.

    [i.e. a rich man is waited on.]

25. Even the hole of the **mouth** doesn't quite understand the spittle.

    [i.e. one cannot see whether a liar is telling the truth or not.]

26. A big **nose** cannot smell.

    [i.e. appearances deceive.]

27. He who clears a **place** is not the one who sits in it.
28. He who has accustomed himself to scrape out the **pot** has a crooked finger.
29. A poor **potter's clay** dries at once beneath his hand.

    [i.e. who cannot afford a helper has harder work.]

30. He who fears the **rain** runs into the mud puddles.
31. If you fear the **rain** you must fear the thunder ; if you fear the drops, they fall on you.
32. He who goes two **roads** at the same time splits his hip-joint.
33. He who makes the **shady spot** clean is not the one who will sit there.
34. Cure a **sick man** and when he is well he swears at the doctor.
35. Don't laugh at the man who has fallen when there are **slippery places** ahead.

36. The owner of a **soft head** takes good care of it.

37. When a man has found nothing he carries a **stone** home.

    [i.e. when you don't get what you want you must be satisfied with what you can get.]

38. It is the laughing **teeth** that bite each other.

39. The way to the **town** goes round a man's head.

    [i.e. he who goes a certain road has something definite in view.]

40. Only one digs the **well,** but many come to drink out of it.

PONDO (PONDOLAND)

[Language Family—Bantu]

1. A good **goat** does not bring forth in the midst of the flock.

   [i.e. matters best discussed in private.]

RONGA (BARONGA, SIKONGA) (PORTUGUESE EAST AFRICA, LOURENÇO MARQUES)

[Language Family—Bantu]

1. Pierce the **abscess.**

   [i.e. irrelevant talk—come to the point.]

2. You curse the **boatman** while you [or the boat] are [is] at the side [of the stream].

3. I will work when **chickens** have grown teeth.

4. The strength of the **crocodile** is water.

5. White people are only overcome by **death.**

6. **Eye's** fellowship.

   [i.e. false friend.]

7. To bid **farewell** causes people to be strangers.

8. A master of a **fool** does not laugh at him.

9. He who swallows **fruit-stones** trusts his throat.

10. A good **goat** does not bring forth in the midst of the flock.

11. The **heart** eats [even] bran.

12. The worker [of] to-morrow is **idleness.**

13. The man who has **oiled** himself never looks dull.

14. You praise the **rain** which has rained on you.

15. **Shame** has watchmen.

16. A **skeleton** has no flesh.

17. They who **sleep** in a house to-day sleep outside to-morrow.

18. The **speaker** forgets.

19. Sweet things never fill the **spoon.**

20. The **throat** has no pity.

    [i.e. bodily needs necessary even to those in grief.]

21. The **tongue** kills its owner.

RUANDA (KINYARWANDA) LAKE (KIVU, BELGIAN TERRITORY)

[Language Family—Bantu]

1. There is a "To be there **always**".
2. The **back** grows, but never outdistances the neck.

   [i.e. the poor can never overtake the rich.]
3. He who goes to another's house leaves his **bad habits** at the door.
4. Lend him your **coat** but not your tongue.
5. The little king over man is his **conscience.**
6. A **cracked utensil** is better than a grave.

   [i.e. a sick person is better than a dead one.]
7. The **crocodile** leaves the river to go and lick the dew.
8. He who has **diarrhœa** can't hold up him who vomits.
9. The **fire** goes where there is still grass.
10. He who has got his breath again **forgets** him who was pursuing him.
11. There is no one who, being clad in one **garment,** will refuse a second.
12. He who has received from **God** is not despoiled by the wind.

    [i.e. a weaker cannot take away what we have received from a stronger.]
13. He who is **greased** never lacks someone to finish polishing him.

    [i.e. the rich man never lacks flatterers.]
14. A new **handle** blisters the hands.

    [i.e. a new or young chief causes his inferiors to suffer through his ignorance.]
15. He who **has much** is he who has nothing.

    [i.e. he is never satisfied.]
16. That of which one's **heart** is full slips on to the tongue.
17. A single gust of wind suffices to expose the anus of a **hen.**

    [i.e. it requires very little to make one ridiculous.]
18. The preferred of the **hyena** is the one she devours first.

    [Said of a scoundrel who makes amiable advances.]
19. **Ill** attracts ill.
20. The height of **indulgence** is to be indulgent with those who slander us.
21. **Loving** one who doesn't love you is loving the rain that falls in the forest.
22. That which is **near** comes no more.

    [i.e. one doesn't expect that which one has already.]
23. Having left **nothing** you will find nothing.
24. A **proverb** comes not from nothing.
25. When the **rat** gnaws the handle it means it is going to attack the hoe.

    [i.e. one commences with small faults before committing big ones.]
26. The **road** says nothing to the traveller of that which awaits him at the end of his journey.
27. One has always something to **say** about others.
28. Words leave no **scar.**
29. Slowly, slowly, makes the **slug** arrive at the fountain.
30. In the **stomach** it is far.

    [Because it can't be reached.]
31. The **thorn** in another man's foot can always be pulled out.
32. Much **travelling** teaches how to see.
33. The drop of **water** one has drawn oneself tastes sweet.
34. He who draws **water** unwillingly draws bad water.
35. There is nothing one goes to meet with more pleasure than the **word.**

    [Because it satisfies one's curiosity.]

SHONA (MASHONALAND)

(Including Karanga)

[Language Family—Bantu]

1. **Comfort** does not last long.
2. **Dew** soon dries up.

   [i.e. so will chieftaincy rulers change.]
3. A **dog** returns to where he has been fed.
4. It is a poor **dog** that avoids an empty pot. (*Karanga.*)
5. When the **drum** [song] is at its loudest, that is when it bursts [ceases].
6. Only what you have **eaten** is yours—other things may not be.
7. Extreme **friendship** results in dissension.
8. Cursing follows **gossip.**
9. To wait long before you skin means that you will get no **meat.**
10. What were **pools** are now fords [drifts].

    [Said of a person of position after downfall.]
11. That which is on a **poor man** is on a slippery place.

    [i.e. there's many a slip, etc.]
12. A **river** is filled by its tributaries.
13. A **small matter** burns logs ahead.
14. A new thing does not come to him who sits, but to him who **travels.**
15. First **trouble,** then happiness.
16. You need double strength if you quarrel with a **woman** whose husband is absent.

SOMALI (SOMALILAND)

[Language Family—Hámitic]

1. **Length** is honourable, even in wood.

SOTHO (SE-SUTO) (BASUTOLAND)

[Language Family—Bantu]

1. "**Bind hard**" keeps things together.
2. Human **blood** is heavy, and hinders him who has shed it, from fleeing.
3. The old **bowl** always smells of its milk.
4. The duiker [**buck**] suckles its little one before dawn.

   [i.e. prudence is the mother of safety.]
5. The stem of the **calabash has** dried up.

   [i.e. fortune varies.]
6. It is yet an unborn **calf.**

   [Said of an unrealized ambition.]
7. Hit one ring and the whole **chain** will resound.
8. The **chicks** of man take long to fly.
9. The words of a **chief** are built in an enclosure [to keep them in].

   [i.e. the words of a chief are carefully remembered.]
10. The **child** that does not weep will die on its mother's back.

11. **Cleverness** eats its owner.
12. **Corn** is the daughter-in-law of all courtyards.
13. It is better to thresh the **corn** than to sharpen the spear.
14. All **countries** are frontiers.
15. He hit the **cow's horn.**
    [i.e. he went straight to the point.]
16. The child of a **crab** goes aslant.
17. The **cripple** is fair in its mother's eyes.
18. Drought draws the **crocodile** out of the pool.
19. **Cunning** devours its master.
20. **Death** is hiding in the corner of the blanket.
21. A **doctor** is taught his art but not his fees.
22. He bit my **ear.**
    [i.e. he gave me a hint.]
23. Did you sit on both your **ears ?**
    [i.e. how is it that when called you did not hear ?]
24. The one who **eats** first is like the one who eats later.
    [i.e. implying that the day will come when the hungry visitor will have the chance to serve the stingy one in his own fashion.]
25. **Embers** beget ashes.
26. **Eyes** embrace a wide perspective ; they can cross a river in full flood.
27. His **eyes** know no friends.
    [i.e. hunger has no ears (knows no friends).]
28. Man **falls** at the same time as his shadow.
29. **Famine** hides under the grain granary.
    [i.e. famine or poverty catches you unawares.]
30. The medicine of **far away** is dug from the ground when the big game drive takes place.
    [i.e. the thing you covet which is seemingly impossible to get, you may find by chance.]
31. **Fire** burns him who warms himself by it.
    [i.e. avoid intimacy with the powerful.]
32. A **fisherman** will die drowned.
33. A [good] man has his **flesh** cut into slices whilst alive.
    [i.e. too much kindness may bring you harm.]
34. He that did it **forgets ;** he who suffered it does not.
35. He who digs the **fountain** drinks none of its water.
36. To **give** away is to make provision for the future.
37. " **Give** me, give me " tires [people] my friend ; a man must be pleased with his own house.
38. He who **gives** to the gods shall partake of their food.
39. A scabby **goat** will spoil the whole herd.
40. Stolen **goods** do not make one grow.
41. To **grow** is to see.
42. **Guilt** never decays.
43. He disdains the flesh of the **guinea-fowl,** but he will drink of its gravy.
44. Our **hands** sow for our throats [mouths].
45. **Harness** is never tired.
46. When the herdboys hunt birds, the **hawk** will find food.
    [i.e. the king (chief) prospers through his people.]
47. The [edible] root is dug with the **heart.**
    [i.e. marrying without love is a bad thing.]
48. A man's **heart** is not to be picked up [and carried away].
    [i.e. the heart always longs for home.]
49. He has built his **house** with yellow stone [sandstone].
    [i.e. he has no firm foothold with us.]
50. **Hunger** brings the crocodile out of the water.
51. **Hunger** is hidden under the sacks.
52. The one that **hurts** [with its horns] is the silent one [that does not low before attacking].

53. The **jackal** that has plenty to eat is the one that carries mud on its paws.

[i.e. if you want to eat, do not shirk even dirty work.]

54. **Kindness** eats the kind one.
55. **Kindness** kills.
56. **A kind man** does not live long.
57. The **king's** messenger is the king himself.
58. To **kiss** [i.e. to love] the child is to kiss the mother.
59. A lent **knife** does not come back alone.
60. To **laugh** at an albino is to laugh at one's self.

[i.e. deformity may happen in one's own house.]

61. One **link** only sounds because of another.
62. Small **matters** breed important ones.
63. A [king's] **messenger** has no guilt.

[i.e. an envoy cannot be held responsible for the news he brings.]

64. A **mischief-maker** is a corn on the foot.
65. A **monkey** cannot see the protuberance on its forehead.
66. He entered my **mouth.**

[i.e. he interrupted me.]

67. The **mouth** that does not eat is an invitation to the mouth that does eat.

[i.e. idle riches are an invitation to robbers.]

68. **Mystery** is a witch-doctor.
69. A good **name** makes one sleep well.
70. The point of the **needle** must pass first.
71. An **ox** is caught by its horns, a man by his words.
72. We are **people** because of other people.
73. **Perseverance** always triumphs.
74. **Plenty** is like mist [that soon vanishes].
75. The first **pot** to boil is the one you pour flour into.

[i.e. first come, first served.]

76. People of the same blood **eat** from the same **pot.**
77. The **potter** cooks his food in broken earthenware.
78. The **poultry-yard** will be built up when the hyena has killed the fowls.
79. He who laughs at **poverty** attracts it to himself.
80. He sucked from the stem [of the **pumpkin**].

[i.e. he inherited his parents' qualities or defects.]

81. The **righteous** one is he who is dead.
82. The **road** is a chief.
83. A winding **road** may not cause the traveller to sleep in the open.
84. What is **seen** is seen by all.
85. He built the **shelter,** but had to remain outside.
86. He who builds a **shelter** does not live in it. (*Sesuto.*)
87. He raised **smoke** out of the ditch.

[i.e. he let the secret out.]

88. The **snare** catches him who laid it.
89. The **sorcerer** grows no hair on the body.

[i.e. evil has no colour.]

90. The **starlings** have hidden the pigeons.

[Starlings are allowed by natives to stay in the crops as they eat worms and insects only, whereas the pigeons are chased away, as they destroy crops. Sometimes you think there are starlings only in the field and you do not chase the birds, whereas you have left pigeons hidden in the field. The meaning of this proverb is that pretexts hide the true facts and it is used when a man in Court conceals the truth and leads his judges on the wrong track.]

91. **Swiftness** has an end, but the race-course remains.
92. The **thief** catches himself.
93. He stands on **tiptoe.**

[i.e. he is here only temporarily.]

94. The **tongue** knows no fastening.
95. The **tongue** will reach a point when skins of flies can be sewn together.
    [i.e. the tongue speaks on so many matters, that it would be impossible to put them all together.]
96. It [a **trap**] catches, even when covered with spiders' webs.
    [i.e. time will hide, but will not kill one's desire for revenge.]
97. To **travel** is to see.
98. An **ulcer** feels nice when rubbed by its owner.
99. **Want** dwells in the house of the wrangler.
100. **Water** is never weary of flowing.
    [Said of great talkers.]
101. Even deep **water-holes** may get dry.
102. **Wealth** is a fog which is soon dispersed.
103. **Woman** is a king.

SUDANESE-ARABIC

[Language Family—Semitic]

1. We taught them the trade of **beggary** and they reached the door before us.
2. The **blacksmith's sheep** dies by suffocation.
    [By Mohammedan custom every animal slaughtered for food must have its throat cut; blacksmiths in the Sudan are the manufacturers of slaughtering knives—the blacksmith is too busy making these knives to slaughter his own sheep, so leaves it to die a natural death.]
3. The one-eyed is king in the land of the **blind.**
4. [God] will give you peace, and fruitfulness in having **children** will fill the empty open places.
5. Tie the rope of **deliberation** and there will be plenty left over.
6. The **doctor** never forgets his old friends [old patients].
7. The **dog** barks, but the camel passes on.
8. Shut the **door** through which a draught is blowing.
9. For the sake of an **eye** a thousand eyes are honoured.
    [Doing favours to friends of a friend.]
10. **A favour** with a good man is a debt, and with a bad man enmity.
11. Not everyone is a **first-born.**
    [Used for people who expect something and don't get it.]
12. On account of the **flower** the root is watered, and on account of the river the bank is honoured.
13. The **grave** is the mother of all.
14. **Greed** loses what it has gained.
15. One **hand** won't wash the back, nor [one] finger cover the face.
16. **Heat** accepts cold, but not cold heat.
    [Can be said of painful dressings.]
17. **Hurry** bequeaths disappointment.
18. **Illness** comes in at the door and goes out through the needle's eye.
    [i.e. illness comes quickly and goes slowly.]
19. **Kindness** can pluck the hairs of a lion's moustache.
20. When **love** comes there is no need for blood relationship.
21. The greatness of **love** obliterates conventions.
22. We commit you to the care of the **Master of Farewells** [God].
    [A saying on departure, especially if going a long way or to war.]
23. He whose mother is **naked** is not likely to clothe his aunt.
24. The eye of the **needle** does not take two threads, and the heart does not contain two loves.
25. **A needle** won't hold two threads nor a mind two [thoughts].
26. The **oil,** if not sufficient for the house, is forbidden to the mosque.

27. In the village of the **one-eyed,** close one eye.
28. He gets nothing but an unpleasant smell who goes between an **onion** and its skin.

    [It is foolish to interfere between a man and his wife.]
29. He will not write down his soul wretched who has the **pencil** in his hand.

    [i.e. he who has the means will look after himself well—a wine merchant drinks the best wine.]
30. The **poor** are relieved from washing with soap.

    [Said if one has to do without a thing.]
31. Strike the onion before it becomes as large as a **python.**

    [This proverb is based on a legend that pythons originated as onions.]
32. He who does not take his **revenge**—the donkey is his uncle.
33. He who has been stung by a **serpent** fears a rope on the ground.
34. Three things cause **sorrow** to flee: water, green trees and a beautiful face.
35. Throw **stones** at him whom you cannot overtake.
36. Stripping a **tree's leaves** will not remove its roots.

    [Used almost entirely with reference to abortion of women or their children dying.]
37. Every **vessel** oozes what **is in it.**

    [i.e. innate characteristics are bound to show themselves. "Vessel" signifies the common Sudanese earthenware jar.]
38. The **visitor** is in the hands of the visited.
39. Those who **waste** are the brothers of devils.

SWAHILI (ZANZIBAR)

[Language Family—Bantu]

1. In the world there are only four "**aitches**", two [of which] have departed and two are left behind; Honour [lit. shame] and Humanity there are none; there remain Humbug and Hocus-Pocus.
2. An **amuser** is not amused.
3. A coco-nut shell full of water is a sea to an **ant.**
4. God does not forget the **ant** in its little hole.
5. A featherless **arrow** does not travel very far.
6. A **bad place** calls him who refuses a good one.
7. A **beam** has its successor.
8. **Bed** is your brother.
9. To **bend** in a place is to rise in that place.

    [i.e. where one falls one also rises.]
10. A little **bird** for a little cage.
11. What **bites** is in your own clothes.
12. There is no **bitterness** in what is past.
13. The first **blow** does not hurt like the second.
14. The **body** is carried by the ears.
15. Do not **borrow** off the world, for the world will require its own back with interest.
16. A **brother's war** [a quarrel with a relative] does not drive a man from the town.

    [Said by a dog when he is beaten or driven away.]
17. If you are a stayer, **build.**
18. The **camel** wanted horns and was deprived of her ears.
19. You could not burn the **candle** except by coming to an agreement with the wick.

20. The **cannon** of the European brings peace.
21. Fight a **cat** with the weapons you would use in fighting a lion.
22. If a **child** cries for a razor, give him a stick.
23. If a **child** cry for a knife, give it to him.
24. The evil **child** is [after all] the medicine of the family.
25. The love for a **child** is in the heart of its mother.

    [Said to mean the child won't be loved unless the mother is.]
26. The **chooser** over-much is wont to fall upon the rotten.
27. Borrowed **clothes** do not cover your nakedness.
28. The juice of the **coco-nut** needs an opening.
29. The **corpse-washer** gives no security for Paradise.
30. Unless you stop the **crack** you will build a wall.
31. He that fears lest his child **cry,** will cry himself.
32. The one who draws the **curtains** draws them in front of herself.

    [The word "Ukingo" in the original is the canopy in a wedding procession. A bride may draw its curtains so as to baffle curiosity.]
33. Who will **dance** to a lion's roaring?
34. The **dancer** at home is never given largesse.
35. **Dawn** is delayed [only] on the road.

    [i.e. present troubles will clear with time.]
36. **Death** and the doctor, their counsel is the same [lit. one].
37. **Deliverance** is twofold, meeting one's death and escaping.
38. One who chooses is never without **desire.**
39. **Desire** in front, death behind.
40. The **destroyer** of the country is a child of the country.
41. When thou seest a **disease** struggling with the medical treatment, fret not thyself, O doctor —there is something going to happen.
42. After **distress,** solace.
43. He who **dives** on dry land scarifies his face.
44. If a man can live up to the reputation of a **dog** he is a saint.
45. Every **door** with its key.
46. The palm-wine tapper eats the wealth of the **drunkard.**
47. **Dying** is a benefit.
48. The **ears** are not greater than the head.
49. The **ears** do not pass [before] the head.

    [i.e. do not come to conclusions on hearsay evidence.]
50. The man who has enough to **eat** does not know the man who has not.
51. What you **eat** you have; the rest belongs to the gravedigger.
52. The cultivator is one; the **eaters** are many.
53. If you are **eating** in secret, shut and bar the door.
54. That which **eats** a man is hungry.

    [i.e. used to express something which cannot be helped.]
55. The **elephant** is not weighed down by his tusks.
56. An **elephant's** death-scene is not so annoying as the life of a bug.
57. When two **elephants** struggle it is the grass that suffers.
58. The load of an **emmet** is one grain of rice.
59. That which has no **ender** ends itself.
60. He who has not is the **enemy** of him who has.
61. Better a clever **enemy** than a blundering friend.
62. You don't know what gets into your **eye.**

    [i.e. in a large group you cannot pick out your enemy.]

63. Two **eyes** are for ornament, one is enough for seeing.

64. It is better for the **eyes** to die than the heart.

65. If you are being carried you need not tire your **feet.**

66. That which **ferries** one across is rotten.

[Said to people who find fault with their benefactors.]

67. One day's **fever** takes away the health of the whole year.

68. The **finger** and the ring, the tongue and the saliva, the bow and the bow-string [are always together].

[Said of a man and his special friends.]

69. The ringless **finger** has a ring put on it.

70. **Fire** does not produce fire, it produces ashes.

71. The **fish** in the trap begin to think.

72. A man follows that which **floats,** he does not follow that which sinks.

73. It is better for **food** to be raw than burnt.

74. The prayer of the **fowl** does not reach the kite.

75. If you study what a **fowl** eats, you won't eat it.

76. He who eats his neighbour's **fowl,** the legs fall to his share.

[i.e. looking a gift horse in the mouth.]

77. Every day is not **Friday** ; there is also Thursday.

78. To give to thy **friend** is not to cast away, it is store for the future.

79. The man who is in **front** does not stay behind.

80. The **gadder-about** eats his feet.

81. The man who has two **garments** does not wear one only.

82. **Gentle birth** avails not, the important thing is—money.

83. If a **gentleman** hears himself abused he pours water in one ear and puts cotton in the other.

84. The tongue of him who receives a **gift** is short.

[i.e. ingratitude.]

85. The eater of a **goat** pays a cow.

86. Getting depends on [lit. has] **God.**

87. **God** and work.

88. " **God** give me ! God give me ! " He gives you a sore.

[i.e. too much importunity without your own exertion.]

89. **God** giveth him that sleepeth and him that sitteth still.

90. One who trusts **God** is not a lacker.

91. The fear of **God** is not a white turban.

[The white turban is the mark of a devotee and is affected by all the sects of the Ibâdhia.]

92. **God** made the sea, we make the ship ; He made the wind, we make a sail ; He made the calm, we make oars.

93. **Good** rots not.

94. Whither **good** [things] go, thence good [things] return.

95. A **good thing** sells itself ; a bad thing wants advertising.

96. If a man thatches with bad **grass,** give him good rushes.

97. The **gravedigger** is not buried, and the wailer [professional mourner] is not mourned for.

98. Where would the **gravy** be but for the water ?

[Don't despise humble people.]

99. It is better to be **green wood** than firewood.

[i.e. half a loaf is better than no bread.]

100. **Grey hairs** are the letter of death.

101. There is no **grief** without a companion.

102. The **grumbler** gets more given.

103. The **guinea-fowl** breeds not in captivity.

104. One **hand** does not cut the other.

105. An empty **hand** is not licked.

106. The **hand** of the homestead does not return empty.

[Slaves call their master's house "jumbe"; subjects their lord's palace.]

107. The **hand** which you cannot cut off you kiss.
108. **Health** is the chief thing.
109. **Hearing** is not seeing.
110. The will of the **heart** is medicine.
111. A cruel word is a wound of the **heart**; it does not heal, and even if it heals, the scar never departs.
112. The **heart** of your friend is a forest.

[i.e. unexplored.]

113. Three things refresh the **heart**: water, flowers, and a beautiful face.
114. The head of a **hen** cannot carry a turban.
115. He who is helped in cultivating breaks the handle of his **hoe.**
116. Better a **hole** than a plug.
117. He who licks **honey** will not lick it once only.
118. He wanted to have **horns** and was robbed of his ears.
119. The **hunger** of to-day is the repletion of to-morrow.
120. **Hunger** sleeps in the house of two fishermen.
121. The **hungry man** does not hear.
122. **Hurrying,** hurrying, has no blessing.
123. If the **hyena** eats the sick man he will eat the whole one.
124. **Idleness** is a house of hunger.
125. The **illegitimate child** was hidden in a bottle, and he put forth a finger.

[i.e. could not be quite suppressed.]

126. **Iron** is greater than silver, copper, and gold.
127. Whatever it **is** that is, be it [so].
128. He who fears the winds of the clouds will never start on a **journey.**
129. He who climbs a **ladder** has to come down.
130. The **lamp** consumes itself, but lights others.
131. **Laughter** is for him who has teeth; how shall he laugh who has none?
132. **Learning** is the light that leads into everything lovely.
133. A **letter** is half a meeting.
134. People who are far apart are wont to meet by **letters.**
135. He who **lights** you by day will set you on fire at night.
136. The leavings of the **lion** is welcome to the hyena.
137. Unity among the cattle makes the **lion** lie down hungry.
138. That which belongs to the **lion** the leopard cannot take.
139. There are three things which if a man does not know he cannot **live** long in the world: what is too much for him, what is too little for him, and what is just right for him.
140. A large **load** does not reach home.
141. A **log** and a chip.

[i.e. a log alone cannot burn.]

142. A cupful of water is the open sea for a **louse.**
143. The **louse** that bites is in the inner shirt.
144. How is one to **love** a person by being told [to] love [him]?
145. **Love** an enemy.
146. The disease of **love** has no physician.
147. A **lover** has no grudge.
148. If you roast **maize** you roast it for people who have teeth.

["Mbisi" means pop-corn in the original.]

149. A **man** is men.
150. A man **marries** beauty, he does not marry a wife.
151. When the **measure** is full it overflows.
152. **Meat** of the bow ends with the bow.

[i.e. that which comes by violence goes by violence.]

153. If you eat your **meat** on the tray, it is [because] your plate is broken.

154. There is **medicine** for madness but none for foolishness.

155. A **moth** has no best clothes.

156. A man's **mother** is his other [or second] God.

157. He who is not taught by his **mother** will be taught by the world.

158. A **needle** sews a mattress.

159. A **new thing** is good, though it be a sore place.

160. A far-off matter is a **night** of darkness.

161. The livelong **night** has many matters.

162. **Nine** is very near to ten.

[i.e. an exhortation to patience. It's a long lane that has no turning.]

163. Every [sort of] **nuisance** comes about through children and slaves.

164. Two hands can rub **oil** on each other.

165. Where there is an **old man** nothing need go wrong.

166. When thou goest to the [country of] the **one-eyed,** do thou also put out thine eye.

167. To buy an **ox** by the footmark.

[i.e. a pig in a poke.]

168. He who has nothing of his own is an **ox** ; he has to go where he is dragged.

169. **Patience** is wont to bear a fine child.

170. If you praise the man who taps the **palm-tree** he'll put water in the palm wine.

171. Silence produces **peace** and peace produces safety.

172. He who recognizes the disease is the **physician.**

173. He that **pleases** you not, do you please him.

174. The **poor man's** boat can't tack ; if it tacks it sinks.

[i.e. no one listens to a poor man's plaint ; if they do it means trouble for him.]

175. The matters that are of use to people are—those that go into the **pot.**

176. " Thank you " does not put the **pot** on the fire.

177. The **pot** that was unsound has become potsherds.

178. The **pot** will smell of that which is put into it.

179. The **potter** eats off a potsherd.

180. The man of birth **pouts** not with his cheeks, he pouts in his heart.

181. No one **praises** that which is alive.

182. The man who **prays** never tires.

183. **A promise** is a debt.

184. If your intention is **pure,** you can walk on the sea.

185. What is in your **purse** gets the praise.

186. The man without a **purse** is the destroyer of him who has one.

187. One who talks about the **rain** has been drenched by it.

188. The sign of **rain** is clouds.

189. [The **rain**] that pours has no cloud.

190. **Repentance** comes afterwards.

191. **Rest** comes not unless it be after hardship.

192. The **road** that winds brings you to the coast at last.

193. Have you neither vertical nor horizontal **roof-sticks** to spare ?

194. How shall a man cut the **roots** when he is leaning on the trunk ?

195. **Running** upon a flat roof will end at the brink.

196. He who asks for **salt** asks for the pot.

197. The man with the **scar** forgets not the sore.

198. The **scar** is a grandchild ; the wound is a child.

199. What is in the **sea** go and wait for on the beach.

200. Who comes in **secret** comes again.

[i.e. once a thief, always a thief.]

201. Never give up what you have **seen** for what you have heard.
202. When your neighbour is **shaving,** do you also pour water.
203. The **shepherd** has no anger.
204. He who is **sick** is visited.
205. The **sick man** is the garden of the physicians.
206. A **sick man's** [only] companion is his couch.
207. **Sickness** sleeps in the house of two old people.
208. Much **silence** has a mighty noise.
209. Fear a **silent man**; he has drums of the lips.
210. The stick which you have by you is the one with which you will kill the **snake.**
211. Don't be a **snake** in a lime-tree, and neither pick for yourself nor shake down for others.
212. The son of a **snake** is a snake.
213. The **sparks** cannot fail to reach him who goes close to the smith.
214. He who **speaks** alone cannot go wrong.
215. He who **speaks** without being answered, how great is his pain?
216. There is no [**spear**] so long but it has a point.
217. The **squirrel** is not heard in the forest.

 [i.e. too insignificant.]
218. Things are put **straight,** that is how they stay so.
219. When [the **sun**] comes out, bask in it.
220. You can't see what **swamps** you.

 [i.e. you can't tell where slander comes from.]
221. We ate the **sweet** together, then bear thou even with the bitter.
222. If **sweetness** is excessive it is no longer sweetness.
223. The poor man has a **tail**—if he goes ahead his tail draws him back.
224. Who hits you **teaches** you.
225. He that has a **thorn** pricking him will not be a walker.
226. Where [the **thorn**] went in, that is where it will come out.
227. There are **three things** [ever] alike, morning and evening.

 [i.e. marriage entails responsibilities. The word "Matatu" may be the meko, the three stones which form the native kitchen range. The tending and supplying of food to be cooked on these is a part of the bargain on either side. "Matatu" may refer to the chair and the dish-cover and the platter.]
228. He who is held by the **throat** cannot swallow.
229. There is no bad **tobacco** nor worthless betel mixture.

 [i.e. no gift is to be despised. Tobacco and betel are customarily offered to guests.]
230. **To-day** before to-morrow.
231. A man is betrayed by his own **tongue.**
232. Better to stumble with toe than to stumble with **tongue.**
233. The **tongue** has no bone.
234. The **tongue** has no medicine.
235. He who fears mud does not **travel.**
236. A **traveller** is poor, even if he be a sultan.
237. Do not climb the dry **tree**; do not swing on [the branches of] the green one.
238. He that is on one side does not have the **tree** fall on him.
239. A **tree** is brought into trouble by its [own] fruit.
240. The **tree** which has been too much for the baboon, the monkey cannot climb.
241. The wind uproots none but the largest **trees.**
242. Where the **trees** are there are no builders.
243. The **truth,** even though it be bitter.
244. **Truth teller** makes no mistake.
245. He who loves the **vase** loves also what is inside.
246. He who goes with a large [**vessel**] bathes not, nor does he see the billows.

247. **War** has no eyes.
248. The **war shield** is used in time of peace.
249. He that fixes his mind overmuch on **water** drinks it not.
250. The strength of **water** is stones.
251. **Water** [shallow enough] for the punting pole does not need a sail.
252. One doesn't forbid **water** to him who has dug the well.
253. To lose your **way** is one way of finding it.
254. To lose the **way**, that is to know the way.
255. Two **ways** hurt.
256. A **weak man**—press him.
257. **Wealth,** if you use it, comes to an end; learning, if you use it, increases.
258. [He] has eaten **wheat;** it has turned him out of Paradise.

  [The Mohammedans believe that the forbidden fruit was wheat.]
259. A **wife** means—clothes.
260. He that is drunk with **wine** gets sober; he that is drunk with wealth does not.
261. **Wits** are wealth.
262. Strife sleeps in the house of the man with two **wives.**
263. Two **wives** are vexation.
264. A **woman** is like the milk of the young coco-nut, it is not pleasant except in its shell.
265. **Women** carry two wallets; one for ill deeds in front, one for kindness behind.
266. The poison of a **word** is—a word.
267. **Words** are silver, the response is gold.
268. Is not poor **work** good play?
269. [Give me] bad **work** rather than good play.
270. The judgment of the **world** comes to us every day.
271. The **world** is a dry tree: mortal, rest not thy weight upon it.
272. The **world** is ashes.
273. In the **world** there are no two things that [really] like each other.
274. That which is **written** cannot be blotted out.

TAMASHEK

(Colloquial of "Tuareg". Singular, "Targui". "Tifineg." Modern form of ancient Numidian script)

(The wandering tribes inhabiting Central Sahara)

[Language Family—Hamitic]

1. It is better to spend the night in **anger** than in repentance.
2. It is whilst the old **bucket** is still in existence that one should make a new one.
3. When a noble spreads the rich material of his dress for thy **carpet,** sit not right in the middle.
4. Laugh at baked **clay.**

  [i.e. terra cotta.]
5. Reasoning is the shackle of the **coward.**
6. Hell itself holds **dishonour** in horror.
7. **Fear** the noble if thou make little of him; fear the base man if thou honour him.
8. If a man puts a cord round his neck, **God** will provide someone to pull it.
9. In doing **good** one does it to oneself; in doing evil one does it to oneself.
10. He who drinks out of a jug [the sedentary] is no **guide.**

11. Kiss the **hand** you cannot cut off.
12. Part your tents, bring your **hearts** together.
13. The **high road** even if it twists and turns; and the chief even if he is old.
14. Noise and **hunting** don't go together.
15. **Laughter** gives confidence; its absence causes dispute.
16. **Life** is but a turning and returning without repose.
17. The man who is not jealous in **love,** loves not.
18. Whoever **loves** thee, even a dog, thou wilt also love.
19. When you see a halo round the **moon,** a king is travelling by its light.
20. When one is **naked** it is better to sit down than to stand up.
21. In your **native land,** birth; in a foreign land, dress.
22. It is better to spend the night in the irritation of the **offence,** than in the repentance for the revenge.
23. The beaten **path** even if it winds; the king even if he is aged.
24. Living **people** often meet.
25. There cannot be two **stallions** in the same small troop of camels.
26. The palm of your hand does not eclipse the **sun.**
27. The **viper** takes the colour of the country it lives in.
28. A **woman** without modesty is like a stew without salt.
29. Men and **women** towards each other are for the eyes and for the heart, and not only for the bed.
30. A **wound** from a weapon may be cured, but not a wound from the tongue.

THONGA (PORTUGUESE EAST AFRICA)

(Including Chopi and Venda)

[Language Family—Bantu]

1. Pierce the **abscess.**

   [i.e. come to the point.]
2. An **abscess** heals when opened.

   [i.e. peace comes by sharing your troubles with another.]
3. **Authority** has no skin.

   [As leopards and lions always fight, their skins often have holes or scratches.—This proverb satirizes a chief who is afraid to give a decision in a case.]
4. **Authority** [Power] is the tail of the water-rat.

   [i.e. a chief's power slips away. If you try to catch a water-rat, its tail remains in your hand, while the rat escapes.]
5. Once a **baboon** has tasted honey, it does not touch earth again.

   [Once a man has been put in a position of authority, he does not accept an inferior one.]
6. A **banana-tree** [palm] is killed by its own fruit.
7. **Bangles** clang when they are many.

   [A man cannot be happy if he lives by himself.]
8. The heart of a man is a **bee.**

   [Finds its happiness in the company of those it loves.]
9. Sleepy **bees** do not gather honey.

   [A slow disease does not lead to health.]
10. Heavy **belly** does not weigh. (*Chopi.*)
11. A little **bird** is seen by its feathers.
12. One finger alone does not kill a **bug.**
13. **Care-taker,** it will take care of you.

    [If you take care of your child it will take care of you.]

14. The **chief** has no relative.

[When you have committed an offence, do not trust that the chief will acquit you because you are related to him.]

15. The **chief's trumpet** never refuses to blow.

[The chief's words are always orders to be obeyed.]

16. The **child** hurts itself inside and out.

[i.e. before it is born, and afterwards when grown up.]

17. Many **children,** many graves.

18. There are no **clothes** which do not wear out in travelling.

19. **Coal** gives birth to ashes.

[i.e. a clever man may beget a fool.]

20. **Cold's** remedy is the fire.

[In suffering the heart is warmed by sympathy.]

21. A **cow** does not calve in the herd.

[A secret is not shouted from the roof.]

22. A white **cow** has no milk.

[A beautiful woman will probably be either a fool or a witch.]

23. If a **cow** leads the herd, all the cattle will fall into the pool. (*Venda.*)

[Said when women rule.]

24. The **cricket** sings in its hole.

[A man is king in his home.]

25. The strength of the **crocodile** is water.

[A man is helpless without his own kin.]

26. **Days** are not counted with one finger.

[Days differ from the fingers, which are all alike.]

27. A man is only honoured after he is **dead.**

28. Eat the **dead man's** maize labouring.

[Don't trust in inherited wealth.]

29. You go with it, you come back with it [**death**].

30. **Death** comes from the stem.

[When the branches die, death has started in the trunk.]

31. **Death** is blind.

[Makes no distinction between people.]

32. **Death** is in the leg, we walk with it.

33. **Death** is sleep.

34. **Debt** [or sin] is dirt.

[i.e. it comes back like dirt.]

35. The evil man **dies** in the village ; the honourable man dies in the forest.

[The wicked prosper.]

36. Cut off the ear of the wild **dog.**

[Said of an ungrateful man who is likened to a wild dog which, once caught in the snare, will, they say, bark at you if you do not cut off its ear.]

37. Receive a **dog** and it will bite you.

[Ingratitude.]

38. A **dog** answers the call of a shell.

[Man responds to love, when a dog hears the sound of the snail-shell (used by natives to scrape the cooking-pots) it knows that some bits of food will be left for it. A proverb especially applied to a polygamist, whose favourite wife is the one who cooks best.]

39. When a **dog** cannot bark it has a bone in its mouth.

[i.e. when a man cannot reprove another it is because he has sinned in the same way.]

40. A wet **dog** has no master. (*Venda.*)

[If a member of your family does something wrong, you do not wish to admit that he is one of your kin —also when a man is struck by misfortune, he does not know where to go to, he becomes public property.]

41. A **dog's sweat** remains in its own hair.

[A dog is rewarded only with the bones of an animal he catches. The poor man's work does not profit him.]

42. A **dog's tail** cannot be made straight.

[When a man's heart is hard, no one can put it right.]

43. A **dog's tears** drop inside. (*Chopi.*)

[A poor man has no means of expressing his grief.]

44. **Ears** are a garden in a moist place.

[Never suffering from thirst of news.]

45. **Eat,** afterwards bones [only remain].

46. To **eat** is to go on eating.

47. **Eat-by-himself** is a thief.

48. By **eating** you appease the snake.

[The natives used to believe that we have a big snake inside which when hungry, bites and causes the pangs of hunger.]

49. An **elephant** does not die of one [broken] rib.

[A strong man does not lose heart through a single misfortune.]

50. The **elephant** does not forget its resting-place.

[A man of importance leaves no ruins. He will eventually come back and build up his old kraal.]

51. An **elephant** is not borne down by its own tusks [or belly].

[A man is not borne down by his responsibilities—family, money or troubles.]

52. The **elephant** is the trunk.

[Without its trunk the elephant cannot seize anything, without his subjects a chief cannot function. Without tools you cannot work.]

53. A single **eye** cannot see when it has a grain of dust in it.

[The disadvantage of having one child only, if you lose it, you will be like a man who has lost both eyes.]

54. The **family-in-law** [or relatives-in-law] is the hip of an elephant.

[One does not forget to help a father or mother-in-law, because they gave you your wife.]

55. He has **fat.**

[Magic medicine. " Fura " is the magic medicine mixed with fat to call the people round—according to native belief—the expression is applied to a man who has been lucky.]

56. **Feel** through your own body.

[One cannot suffer for others.]

57. A red **fig** does not lack worms inside.

[A beautiful girl is either lazy, a thief, ill-tempered or wicked.]

58. **Fire** begets ashes.

[A father's deeds are often contradicted by his son.]

59. The **fire** you sent for does not burn.

[Fires are lighted from the embers of previous fires. If the natives let their fires go out they must get fresh embers from a neighbour—i.e. what has been given you, you cannot choose—it may not always please you.]

60. The real **fish** is the first one.

[Be satisfied with the first wife you marry ; if you take another one it is another illusion.—Also said when a woman has lost her only child, and does not get any more children.]

61. **Fish** remain in the curves of the river.

[Men remain where there is peace.]

62. That which has pierced our mouths will give us **food.**

[Do not lose heart, when famine comes, because the thing that created them on earth will take care of them.]

63. One does not follow the **footprints** in the water.

[The way of a man following a woman.]

64. **Friendship** is a furrow in the sand.

[Take care of it.]

65. The **frog** has given orders to the elephant.

66. He who swallows a **fruit-stone** has a high opinion of [or trusts] his throat.

[One who undertakes a heavy job trusts in his strength.]

67. The wild **goat** does not give birth in the herd.

[A man does not disclose an important secret before a crowd of people.]

68. The **good man** is in the sea.

[Does not exist.]

69. Tell **good news** [lit. tell to grow fat].

[People's hearts "grow fat" when they are told good news.]

70. The **granary** of a man is [in] his hands.

[If you work you will obtain food or power.]

71. **Greatness** buys.

[A poor man has no right to dispute with or reprimand the chief.]

72. A man on the **ground** cannot fall.

[The philosophy of poverty.]

73. A **guinea-fowl** without chickens is nothing but colours only.

[A woman without children is useless.]

74. One **hand** cannot measure the clay [to mould a pot].

[One man alone cannot achieve anything.]

75. The **hand** gives, the hand receives.

76. He who puts up a **hare** chases it.

[He who raises a point of discussion must press it home.]

77. A **hare** gave orders to an elephant.

[A child gave orders to a grown-up person.]

78. The **heart** is a little baby.

[i.e. it cannot be comforted.]

79. The **heart** is like deep waters.

[It hides many things.]

80. The **heart** of a man is a sea.

[It is filled by rivers.]

81. To **help** is to store for oneself.

82. The **hen** comes from the egg and the egg comes from the hen.

[The man comes from the woman, and the woman comes from the man.]

83. Do not do like the **hen** which wipes its mouth while eating.

[Meaning that it does not enjoy its food much.—To eat and wipe one's mouth is to look for quarrels.]

84. Do not run after a **hen** with salt in your hand.

[Do not be over-hasty in the settlement of a matter which is not yet ripe for a solution.]

85. A **house** is made beautiful by its thatch.

[A woman is made beautiful by her clothes.]

86. **Houses** built close together burn together.

[People who live close to each other should help each other.]

87. It **hunts** for people.

[The blood (disease) hunts for the human body.]

88. **Hurry** with your legs, not with your tongue.

89. The crown of the **hut's** roof closes many things.

[Family secrets are not discussed outside.]

90. The **hyena** does not forget where it has hidden its kill.

[A boy often pays visits to his girl.]

91. To rest does not complete the **journey,** what brings it to an end is to walk.

92. **Joy** brings tears.

93. **Laugh,** for the sky [heaven] sees you.

94. One **leg** cannot dance alone.

[A solitary person does not get any joy out of life.]

95. The **leg** has no nose.

[Receive travellers hospitably because some day when travelling yourself, you may come to their village.]

96. He left his **leg** outside.

[He is not giving a full account of the matter. He wants only to delay it.]

97. Push on with your **legs** and not with your tongue.

98. When the chief **limps,** all his subjects limp also.

[When a chief is bad all his subjects go wrong.]

99. One **lion** is other lions.

[A man cannot live alone.]

100. The **lion** roars in the bush.

[A hero is seen on the battlefield.]

101. The **lion** sleeps with its teeth.

[A warrior asleep is not dangerous, his weapons sleep with him.

102. The great thing is to **live.**

103. To **live** is to see.

104. The **load** is tried on the shoulder.

[Do not shirk a task without trying it.]

105. One finger does not kill a **louse.**

[One man cannot do the work of many.]

106. **Love** enters even though it is forbidden [taboo].

107. The ties established between two families by a happy **marriage** are stronger than those of money.

108. A relative by **marriage** is the little knife on one's hip.

[A relative by marriage has given one one's wife ; one can have confidence in him and rely on his help.]

109. **Marriage** roasts [hardens].

110. To **marry** is to put a snake in one's handbag.

111. Men are **mealies.**

[Treat men with kindness as you do your mealies in the graneries.]

112. One finger cannot pick up one grain of **mealies.**

113. **Meat** forced into a pot breaks it. (*Venda.*)

[When you force a man it leads to a fight.]

114. One only digs for the **medicinal plant** which one knows.

115. Mr. "Seeing-for-himself" falls into **misfortune.**

116. **Misfortune** has a following [it sticks to one].

[Sorrows never come singly.]

117. The **monkeys** [baboons] laugh at each other's deep eye-sockets.

[i.e. the pot calls the kettle black.]

118. The drum does not make as much noise as the **mouth.**

119. The **mouth** is a switch to fan oneself.

[One defends oneself (usually) with untruths.]

120. The **mouth** is burnt.

[His words are valueless.]

121. His **mouth** is fat. The nape of the neck is only nerves [muscles].

[Applied to a man whose words are fine but whose deeds are bad.]

122. The burden of the **mouth** is not heavy.

[It is easy to talk about work.]

123. The **mouth** is the heart's shield.

[A man conceals his heart under the words of his mouth.]

124. The nape of the **neck** does not see.

[When the master of the village goes away, the people get out of control.]

125. **News** does not sleep on the way.

126. Who leads me in the **night** I will thank him when the day breaks.

127. They catch an **ox** by its horns, a man by his words.

128. The **palm-tree** which sweeps the ground far from the stem is bad.

[Said of a man who is generous or nice with outsiders or strangers, but is the reverse at home.]

129. The **partridge** pursues another partridge.

[A clever man gives birth to a clever child.]

130. The **partridge** who goes about seeking food will be caught in the snare.

131. Kinship of **partridges** is found in the chest [heart].

[Two clever people understand each other quickly.]

132. A fat **pig** scatters the bran.

[A well-fed person wastes food.]

133. A **pole** is strengthened by another pole.

134. A **polygamist** only ploughs one field.

[Said to a polygamist who has many wives, but really loves one only.]

135. **Poverty** [or grief] is bewitchment.

[A really poor man has no means of leading a tolerable life. He is like a bewitched person.]

136. The given **pumpkin** has no gravy.

[You cannot choose something you have been given. It may not always please you.]

137. A borrowed **pumpkin** has no taste.

138. Small **pumpkins** remain in the mealie stalks.

[After the crop has been reaped. Said of a girl who does not get married. The " Pindju " is a small pumpkin sown for pigs only, which remains in the field after everything else has been reaped.]

139. When you pull a **pumpkin** you also pull the small pumpkin attached to its stem.

[Said of a man who marries a widow with children.]

140. **Rain** is fat.

[When rain comes, people will eat.]

141. The **reed** finds the one who threw it.

[A matter comes back on the one who began it.]

142. The **rich** man cries every day.

143. The **river** is filled by the springs.

[When everybody gives something it will make a large sum—or a large quantity of food.]

144. An old **rooster** sleeps in the poultry-house.

[Applied to a bachelor—like an old cock sleeping alone.]

145. To **see** each other is to go on [seeing each other].

146. A **skeleton** has no flesh.

[You will not find meat on a skeleton nor wealth in a poor man.]

147. One rolls up a **skin** while it is still damp.

[i.e. a child must be chastised while still young ; also, let us go before the situation gets much worse ; or, a case must be settled at its own time.]

148. Where the **smoke** goes, the fire goes also.

[Where reprimand goes, punishment goes.]

149. The **snail** leaves its slime wherever it goes.

[Evidence of a wrongdoer's guilt.]

150. **Snake** and man fear each other.

[An adult and a child or a superior and his inferior must respect and fear each other.]

151. Do not laugh at the **snake** because it walks on its belly.

[Do not laugh at the infirmity of a person.]

152. Do not whirl a **snake** in the air when you have killed it ; the ones which remain in their holes see you.

[Said to a chief who deals very harshly with a poor person.]

153. The **snake** walks on its belly [lit. on its bowels].

[A man cannot work without tools or without money.]

154. A **snake** you see does not bite.

[To be forewarned is to be forearmed.]

155. The **soot** in the roof of the hut is known by the owner [of the hut].

[Quarrels between husband and wife are their own affair.]

156. **Sorrow** exceeds toothache.

157. **Sorrows** educate.

158. To hasten to **speak** is to hasten death.

159. If you hasten to **speak** you will hasten to die.

160. A man polishes his own **spear.**

[A man must look after his own village and family.]

161. Two **squirrels** do not remain in one hole.

[Two chiefs do not govern one country.]

162. My own **stick** which I myself have cut.

[This is my first wife (my first love).]

163. The second **stroke** hurts [more than the first].

[The stricken man will return your blows more severely.]

164. **Sweet things** never fill a spoon.

[You will never have enough of good things.]

165. **Tattoo marks** on the neck are known only by the one who made them.

[The girl who has them on her back cannot see them herself. Nobody knows what he leaves behind him, good or bad.]

166. **Thanks**-on-the-spot.

[i.e. true gratitude.]

167. The little spring ahead causes you much **thirst.**

[Don't rely upon the spring ahead.]

168. **A thorn** is pulled out the way it went in.

[To discuss a case one must begin at the beginning.]

169. A man's **thoughts** are [his] kingdom.

170. The **throat** has no sorrow.

[Though you feel sorry, you must eat.]

171. There is no burden for the **tongue.**

[i.e. the most difficult tasks do not weigh heavy on it. The natives have an extraordinary ability in dealing with all circumstances of life.]

172. If you travel with wisdom [lit. thoughts], you will find riches.

173. If you do not **travel** you will marry your own sister.

174. The wise **traveller** leaves his heart at home.

175. You destroy the shade [of a **tree**] and watch the cloudy sky.

[You chase your wife away and look at the woman passing by.]

176. Occupy yourself with your own **village.**

177. Where the **vultures** assemble there is a kill.

178. A man alone does not keep **warm.**

179. The **water** has drowned the swimmer.

[Said of a man who has committed an offence, thinking that he is clever and will not be caught.]

180. To pierce the **water** with an oar is to attract the waves.

[i.e. if you have a project, accomplish it at once, otherwise complications may arise.]

181. **Wealth** is bits of roasted meat, the great thing is one's kith and kin.

[Said especially on the day on which the " lobolo " cattle or money are given for a bride.]

182. **Wealth** is dew.

183. **Wealth** is salt, it just seasons, the important thing is kindness.

184. Ill **weeds** don't grow in the hand.

185. A **wife** is like a tick on one's body.

[Marriage brings trouble.]

186. **Wisdom** is found on the way.

[A man becomes wise when he travels.]

187. A **woman** does not lie fallow.

[A woman will not lack men to marry her.]

188. **Women** have no court.

[A woman's word has not much value.]

189. **Yesterday** does not pass away.

[The memory of those we love does not fade away.]

TIV (BENUE, NIGERIA)

(Called by the Hausas " Munshi ")

[Language Family—Sudanic]

1. **Bush cows** are not to be feared when they are moving in a herd.

[i.e. don't fear mere numbers.]

2. The **chicken** does not scrabble at night.

[i.e. everything at its right time.]

3. The **cow** does not bear calves in public.

[i.e. you have a secret you wish to impart in private.]

4. As long as life lasts, the **cow** never ceases to move its tail.

[i.e. while there's life there's hope.]

5. The **dog** makes his appearance as soon as gruel is spilled on the ground.
6. You have tied a bone round the **dog's** throat.

   [i.e. you are tempting providence.]
7. The **hippo** blocked up the ford, and no one could cross.

   [Typifies "the dog in the manger".]
8. A debt is like a **hippo's** foot-prints.

   [i.e. it takes much rain to obliterate the footprints of a hippopotamus.]
9. No **horse** bargains for itself.

   [i.e. if one is courting a woman, one must address oneself to her guardian, not to herself.]
10. A **horse** has four legs, yet it often falls.

    [Used to deny human infallibility.]
11. The **horse** that arrives early gets good drinking water.

    [cf. the English—"The early bird catches the worm".]
12. When the **leopard** moves away, it takes its tail with it.

    [i.e. a man does not migrate without his family.]
13. One will never lack a **mane** if one looks in a stable.

    [i.e. one can always find what one requires in the right quarter.]
14. I do not sow ground-nuts when the **monkey** is watching.

    [i.e. don't tempt providence.]
15. The **snake** feared the stick and the stick feared the snake.

    [Said when two persons stand in a mutual relationship to one another and their common welfare is interlinked.]

TUMBUKA (KAMANGA) (NORTHERN NYASALAND)

[Language Family—Bantu]

1. **Chieftainship** is a matter of the hand.

   [Give and you will get.]
2. The **child** of your neighbour is yours.
3. Is it the days you would count? The hairs of a **cow** are few.

   [It is no use attempting to forestall the future; you would have more chance to count correctly all the hairs on a cow.]
4. Little **dish** go—little dish come.

   [Giving means receiving.]
5. He has **dived** into a saucer, the back is seen.

   [Said of one attempting to take cover behind some excuse obviously inadequate.]
6. Should you see anything, **eat** of it; adversity has no day.

   [Take advantage of what the moment offers.]
7. That which is in the **eyes** is a [real] thing.
8. Before the **eyes** is to take notice, behind the back is to be unaware.
9. You **gave** to your companion, you have stored [hung] it up.
10. **Generosity** is chieftainship.
11. The world is **guile,** grass is a spy.

    [Don't imagine you can hide guilt, everything around you will find you out.]
12. You have wrapped **happiness** as it were a maize cob still in the sheath.

    [Don't count your chickens before they are hatched.]
13. **Little-by-little** is the one who tears the bag.

    [Many a mickle makes a muckle.]
14. A **lawsuit** is like the wax of the bees' hive.

    [No one can hope to escape trouble just as there is no honey without the waxcomb.]

15. The wild **pig** listens while digging.

[Warning against complete absorption in one occupation.]

16. A good day is that in which to lay by cold **porridge.**

[When things go well it is wise to remember it may not always be so.]

17. A sudden surprise such as **porridge** from one's " in-laws ".

18. Go and fry the **pumpkin-seed** and give to your companions.

[However little you have, share it.]

19. You have changed me into a little **reaping-knife.**

[i.e. I have lost all value to you.]

20. A full **stomach** is a snare, you go on and are in want.

[Don't let prosperity blind you to future possibilities.]

21. Make your defence very clear on the spot, at the **talking-place** it is slippery.

[Agree with your adversary quickly while you are in the way with him.]

22. **Travelling** is like dancing, the foot is a pumpkin, the buttock is sloth.

[The energetic man will prosper, the stay-at-home will not.]

23. **Wisdom** is mushrooms coming when the porridge is done.

[Referring to kind of person who begins to think when it is too late.]

TUNISIAN-ARABIC

[Language Family—Semitic]

1. To the **dog** that has money men say, " My lord dog."

2. When thou seest two people in constant converse, thou mayest know that the one is the **dupe** of the other.

3. The man who spends the night in a marsh wakes up a cousin to the **frogs.**

4. It is better to commit ten sins in the sight of **God** than one in the sight of man.

5. He who has **gold** is beloved, though he be a dog and the son of a dog.

6. He who desires to attain **great things** must pass through many nights.

7. The beauty of a man lies in his **intelligence ;** the intelligence of a woman is to be found in her beauty.

8. **Joy** lasts for seven days, but sadness endures for a lifetime.

9. He is a fool who **marries** a stranger when his cousin awaits him.

10. When the **moon** is with thee, of what account are the stars ?

11. Good morrow, **neighbour,** let us remain, I in my house and thou in thine.

12. Better a bad **prince** than protracted democracy.

13. **Shun** him who can be of no use to thee ; in this world he cannot serve thee and in that which is to come he cannot intercede on thy behalf.

14. Consult thy **wife** and do the reverse of what she advises.

15. Obedience to a **woman** is the avenue of hell.

VAI (LIBERIA AND SIERRA LEONE)

(Including Mende, Temne, Kuranko)

[Language Family—Sudanic]

1. To send a **bamboo-splint.**

   [When courting a widow, customary to send a piece of bamboo-rind in place of verbal application.]

2. Your **body** will hear better than your ear. (*Mende.*)

   [i.e. by a beating.]

3. **Bought wit** is best. (*Temne.*)

4. A **brother-in-law** [is] a fowl's feather; it sweeps the rubbish-pit. (*Mende.*)

   [i.e. I give you food, you give me none.]

5. A hill here, a hill there; the **bush-fowl** scratches between. (*Mende.*)

6. If you are under the **camwood-tree** your skin will become red. (*Mende.*)

7. A **child** with rice, an old man with tobacco. (*Temne.*)

8. Whatever you do you will **die.**

9. One takes the **elephant** for a friend on account of the way.

   [i.e. one makes a great man his friend.]

10. The **European** is like an unmarried woman.

    [The Vai permit an unmarried woman to keep company with anyone: similarly Europeans do not side with one faction, but are friends with anyone who serves them.]

11. There is no rust or fault in **God.**

12. If **green leaves** burn, what of dry ones? (*Temne.*)

13. The breeze that knocks down the **green trees** will not leave the dry. (*Temne.*)

14. One single **hair** only has fallen from my head; this will not spoil my head.

    [i.e. a trifling loss or injury, not worth speaking of.]

15. To put the **hand** into cold water.

    [i.e. to make peace from the ablution of the hands with cold water.]

16. To put both **hands** and both feet under anything.

    [i.e. to be exceedingly pleased with anything.]

17. The **heart** grows hard with someone.

    [i.e. becomes firm friends.]

18. Hang one **leg** of thine: leave thy leg hanging and give information.

    [i.e. thou art not to be longer in giving information than thou canst stand on one leg.]

19. We are **leopards**; we do not eat putrid meat.

    [i.e. we do not want the help of others to obtain our wishes.]

20. I **love** the man as a standing tree.

    [i.e. I love him just as he is.]

21. The **palm-nut** decays in its own bunch.

    [i.e. everyone wishes to die in his own home.]

22. The eye does not buy a **rag.**

    [One must first inspect a thing before buying it.]

23. There is a **rope** at one's neck.

    [i.e. he is in want of something.]

24. An empty **sack** will not stand by itself. (*Mende.*)

25. The **snake** that does not hide does not last long. (*Kuranko.*)

26. He who **spoils** [or disarranges] anything should know how to rearrange it. (*Temne.*)

WOLOF (SENEGAMBIA)

[Language Family—Sudanic]

1. If **Allah** gives reason to hate, He also gives reason to love.
2. If you know the **beginning** well, the end will not trouble you.
3. He who **betrays** one that betrays him not, Allah shall betray him.
4. He who wishes to blow out his **brains** need not fear their being blown out by others.
5. The **child** hates him who gives it all it wants.
6. If you love the **children** of others, you will love your own even better.
7. What the **convalescent** refuses would give pleasure to the dead.
8. Two **crocodiles** don't live in one pond.
9. The **cup** finds not out its master's death.
   [i.e. passes into other hands.]
10. Whoso knows one who will **die** with him, he [the known] will be his friend in this world.
11. The **diver-bird** cannot catch fish behind his companion.
12. If the **dog** is not at home, he barks not.
13. **Earth** is the queen of beds.
14. Were no **elephants** in the jungle the buffalo would be large.
15. His **eyes** are larger than his mouth.
16. What lowers itself, is ready to **fall.**
17. Without **fingers** the hand would be a spoon.
18. " I have **forgotten** thy name " is better than " I know thee not ".
19. If the fly flies, the **frog** goes not supperless to bed.
20. If the big finger be **greedy,** the heel is more so.
21. Many **guests** matter little to the ass of the inn.
22. **Horns** grow not before the head.
23. **Know** thyself better than he does who speaks of thee.
24. **Lies,** though many, will be caught by truth as soon as she rises up.
25. **Meat** eats not meat.
26. He who has no **mother** sucks his grandmother.
27. When the **mouse** laughs at the cat, there is a hole.
28. **Night** is the queen of shades.
29. When thou seest the **palm-tree,** the palm-tree has seen thee.
30. But for the wide trousers, **prayer** would be a scandal.
31. A **road** has no shadow.
32. Deny, but what thou **seest** believe!
33. He at whom Allah has discharged a **shaft,** cannot avoid it.
34. The **sky** is the king of sheds.
35. If you go to the **sparrows'** ball, take ears of corn for them.
36. Nothing can **suffice** a man except that which he has not.
37. If a man makes soup of his **tears** do not ask him for broth.
38. **Teeth** serve as a fence to the mouth.
39. Let man be bad if [only] his **tongue** be good.
40. The **tree** which is not taller than thou art cannot shade thee.
41. No good without **truth.**
42. The voice of **truth** is easily known.
43. Where are the cattle, there the **wolf** shall die.
44. A **woman** who has lost her rival has no sorrow.
45. The best **words** give no food.
    [i.e. " Fine words butter no parsnips."]

XHOSA (XOSA, KAFIR) (KAFFRARIA) (SOUTH OF ZULULAND)

[Language Family—Bantu]

1. **Abusing** does not leave a blemish.
2. A **bald head** enters [begins] at the temples.
   [i.e. a big result may issue from a small matter.]
3. Clever men do not **bargain** with one another.
4. There is no **beast** that does not roar in its own den.
5. A **bird** builds with another bird's feathers.
   [Said by one asking for assistance.]
6. Stop desiring a **bone** [to gnaw] when you are toothless.
7. A **brand** burns him who stirs it up.
8. The wayside **corn** does not grow.
9. All **countries** are frontiers.
   [i.e. wherever you are, you are exposed to danger.]
10. The **dance** is sweet by repetition.
11. **Dawn** does not come twice to awaken a person.
    [i.e. take advantage of the first opportunity.]
12. It matters little what kind of **death** one dies.
13. The wooden **dishes** go backwards and forwards.
    [i.e. give you "tit for tat".]
14. If a **dog** eats bones he will get to like them.
15. A **dog** of the wind.
    [i.e. no settled home.]
16. A **dog** that eats another never grows fat.
17. No **elephant** is over-burdened by its own trunk.
    [i.e. a man is capable of bearing his own troubles.]
18. You kindle a **fire** and leave it.
    [i.e. you are a tale-bearer.]
19. You are lighting a **fire** in the wind.
    [Said of one who favours strangers.]
20. The **fly** irritates the sore.
21. There is no **fly** that catches for others.
22. He has gone to the "**fold the feet's.**" place.
    [i.e. he has died—a euphemism for the grave.]
23. **Harness** is never tired.
    [i.e. travel has no ending.]
24. **Height** is not reached in a hurry.
25. **Hope** does not disappoint.
26. **Hunger** is hidden under the sacks of corn.
    [Said to people who are vain about their wealth.]
27. There can be no leaning against a **hungry man.**
    [i.e. do not trust in weak arguments to support a strong cause.]
28. The **knife** and the meat will never be friends.
    [A warning against adultery.]
29. The lent **knife** never returns alone.
    [i.e. one kind deed brings another.]
30. The **lion** which kills is not the one that roars.
31. The **messenger** who hungers not.
    [i.e. metaphoric name for a letter.]
32. The **miser** is a thief.
33. The **mouth** is a tail to switch away flies.
34. The **mouth** is not covered with a cloth.
35. The point of the **needle** goes through first.
    [i.e. attend to accuracy in small details.]
36. The **needy** man laughs.
37. No **partridge** scratches the ground for another.
38. The last **partridge** to rise gets the most sticks thrown at it.
    [i.e. the last man to run in war is most likely to be killed.]
39. The **potter** eats out of a broken dish.

40. A **repetition** will be by accident.
[i.e. once bitten, twice shy.]

41. There is no **rivulet** but makes a sound.
[i.e. everyone, however insignificant, has his own peculiar form of activity or natural expression.]

42. The **road** is king.
[i.e. do not hinder a traveller.]

43. He has drunk of the juice of the wild **sloe.**
[Said of a dull-witted person.]

44. No **stake** decays with [at the same time as] its bark on.
[i.e. the mind outlasts the body, or the body outlasts its clothing.]

45. **Stature** is not secured by violence.
[i.e. personal importance comes gradually.]

46. The **stick** has no kraal.
[i.e. abuse of authority destroys home life and breaks up the family. Said to wife-beaters.]

47. **Stolen goods** do not increase.

48. The **string** used as a snare need not be thick.
[i.e. a simple word is often sufficient to disconcert an antagonist in an argument.]

49. The **sun** does not set without some news.

50. A **thief** catches himself.
[i.e. murder will out.]

51. **To-morrow** will become the day after to-morrow.
[i.e. procrastination.]

52. **Water** is never tired of running.
[Said to a person who talks too much.]

53. There is no **wild animal** but will growl in its own burrow.

YAO (NYASALAND)

[Language Family—Bantu]

1. He who says, " I look at the sun," goes astray, but he who **asks** [the way] arrives at the village.

2. Being **bald,** you must not hide the razor.

3. What you won't **hear** you will hear when your head is boiling in the pot.
[The reference is to an insect sitting on a herb and gathered along with it.]

4. A thing that did not **listen** they cooked among the herbs.
[Explanation as above.]

5. In **moonlight** you cannot cut out a thorn.

6. " Mr. **Mouth** " hurt his master.

7. The **pig** was made a scapegoat on account of the gleanings.
[i.e. picking up what was left in the field after the robbers had stolen the crop.]

8. Having become **rich,** one must jump for joy in the dark corner.
[i.e. it is not wise to make a show of one's prosperity.]

9. " **Two-ness** " is good ; " oneness " cannot rub the back.
[i.e. to rub the back when bathing is a service performed for each other by friends.]

YORUBA (SOUTHERN NIGERIA)

[Language Family—Sudanic]

1. The distress of the **agriculturist** lasts no longer than a year.

2. Ask for help and you will see those who never oblige ; ask for **alms** and you will see the misers.

3. **Alms** are the father of [i.e. the best of] sacrifice.
[The word " sara ", which occurs in the original proverb, is the Moslem term for legal alms.]

4. **Ashes** always fly back in the face of him that throws them.

5. When the spear sees the **battle** it dances; when the lance sees the battle it rejoices.

6. Leave the **battle** to God and rest your head upon your hand.

7. The **belly** is the foremost of the gods.

[The Yoruba usually associates the mind with the stomach.]

8. In the land of the **blind** a one-eyed man is king.

9. He who is complete in all the members of his **body** cannot appreciate the value of that body.

10. "**I** will drag you through the **bush**" must needs clear the path with his own back.

11. The **butterfly** never attends the market in which there are thorns.

12. **A canoe** is paddled on both sides.

13. The **cap** usually fails to wear out the head.

14. No one can leave his **character** behind him when he goes on a journey.

15. **Charity** is easily first of all sacrifices.

16. That which a **child** likes never injured its stomach.

17. If with the right hand you flog the **child,** with the left draw him unto your breast.

[i.e. firm but loving.]

18. Too much hope should not be built on **children**. He who is buried by them is the man who has truly begotten children.

19. He on whose head we would break a **coco-nut** never stands still.

20. He who has no one to **comfort** him should never wear a tear-threatened face.

21. **Consideration** is the senior, calculation the junior, and wisdom the third-born.

22. There is a measure for **corn** in cases of dispute; in just the same way the world has a standard.

23. **Covetousness** is the father of disease.

24. **Covetousness** is the father of unsatisfied desires.

25. It takes three men of ripe years to know the significance of three **cowries.**

[The cowrie is a Yoruba coin worth about one-fifteenth of a penny.]

26. **A cripple** may serve the gods as a porter at the gate.

27. The **cross-road** ever confuses the stranger.

28. The **cross-roads** do not fear sacrifices.

[Ancients offered sacrifices at cross-roads.]

29. The distaff is the **death** of the cotton-wool; the needle the death of the cloth.

30. If **death** shuts the door, hunger will break it open.

31. The chronic invalid toys with **death,** the person in his death-throes is playing his final game preparatory to leaving for the other world.

32. When the old man was asked why he contracted so many **debts,** he replied in return, "Which of them am I likely to live to repay?"

33. Whenever I **die,** both I and you have to go and narrate it before God.

34. **Disease** does not go under any other name than "Conceal me and I cause your death."

35. The **disease** which affects the eye usually affects the nose as well.

36. **Disobedience** will drink water with his hands tied up.

37. An old **dog** must not be offered to Ogun [the god of iron, war and hunters].

38. It is not every kind of **dress** that is given an airing in the sun.

39. Do not live on **earth** and do not live in Heaven.
40. It is the **egg** that becomes the cock.
41. The **elegance** one displays in public has its beginning in the home.
42. The head of an **elephant** is no head for a child.
43. It is the hunter who wishes people to stand in dread of him who kills an **elephant** with his cap.
44. No one carrying **elephant's** flesh on his head should look for crickets underground.
45. The words of an **epileptic** are the utterances of a denizen of the other world.
46. Neither **evil** nor good will go unrequited.
47. The **eye** is the leader of the body.
48. When it [the missile] hits the **eye,** it will hit the nose as well.

    [Said to selfish people to remind them that what hurts them will hurt others.]
49. He who has only his **eyebrow** for a cross-bow never can kill an animal.
50. When the **face** is washed you finish at the chin.

    [i.e. last word in a dispute.]
51. Not until we have **fallen** do we know how to re-arrange our burden.
52. The **farm-house** will survive the farmer; the ridge of the roof will outlast the house.
53. When the person who has inherited his **father's god** prays to it that he may neither die nor suffer illness, the question might be asked, "What became of the person who first introduced the worship of the god into the family?"
54. **Fingers** are not equal.
55. When **fire** burns in the fields, the smuts fly to the town.
56. The **fire** which burns down a royal palace only adds to its magnificence.
57. When a **fish** is killed, its tail is put in its mouth.

    [Said of those who reap the fruits of their misdeeds.]
58. The acknowledged **foe** lives somewhere to the rear of our compound; but he who is responsible for our downfall has the door of his house facing ours.
59. The **foot** touches water before it touches sand.
60. He that **forgives** gains the victory.
61. It is the influence of the **fountain** which causes the stream to flow.
62. Long before the Indian corn was known, the **fowl** had been feeding on something.
63. The **fowl** has alighted on a cord; the cord is not at ease, neither is the fowl.
64. The **fowl** is the forerunner of the dead.

    [i.e. a fowl is beheaded at the death of a person, and the blood is sprinkled over the corpse as its passport to the invisible world.]
65. If thou huskest corn with the **fowl** it will not esteem thee.
66. **Friendship** that is kept up only while eyes see eyes, does not go to the heart.
67. The more intimate the **friendship** the deadlier the enmity.
68. Inordinate **gain** makes a hole in the pocket.
69. When the **game** is won it cannot be disputed.
70. The **glutton** liberally waters his soup.
71. Those whom we cannot catch we leave in the hands of **God.**
72. If **God** should compute our sins we should perish.
73. **Good health** is the recipe for wealth.
74. If a **great man** should wrong you, smile on him.

75. The absence of powder converts a **gun** into a stick.

76. It must grow **hairs** that is designated " head ".

77. There is no beauty in a **handkerchief** but in the tying.

78. They received me with **hands** and feet.

79. He who **harasses** me teaches me strength.

80. **Health** is the stepping-stone to wealth.

81. What an intricate maze of paths leading from the groves of the dead will there be in **Heaven.**

82. **A hog** that has wallowed in the mud seeks a clean person to rub against.

83. The **horse** never refuses a homeward gallop.

84. Who else could the **housefly** take sides with other than the person afflicted with sores?

85. We never build our **houses** facing the other way to those of our relations.

86. There is no such thing like **hustle** except him who hustles himself.

87. No matter how well an **idol** is made, it must have something to stand on.

[i.e. no smoke without fire.]

88. The **indolent man** reckons religious fasting a labour.

89. He who owns the **inner-square** of the house is the master of the outer.

90. **Joy** has a small body.

91. Not to aid one in distress is to **kill** him in your heart.

92. We do not carry a **king's load** and perspire.

93. If we hurl a stone into a market, it is usually our own **kith and kin** whom it hits in the eye.

94. He who **knows** us is not like him we know.

95. The **labourer** is always in the sun, the plantation-owner always in the shade.

96. **Laziness** lends a helping hand to fatigue; one must persevere because fatigue must be felt every day.

97. In turn comes round the **leadership.**

98. He who blockades a **leopard** will have trouble.

99. The **leper** declares that he is prepared to swear on behalf of his [uninfected] fellow-inmates that, should he go on a journey, none of them would ever dream of borrowing his bath-sponge during his absence.

100. **A lie** costs nothing to a liar.

101. He who tells a **lie** in the presence of intimates is indeed a master mind.

102. What is really a **load** should not be called an ornament.

103. If **lumps** [exaggerated weals] are easily raised on our flesh, we should never attend a meeting where cudgels will be drawn.

104. We never kill the **lunatic** of the family; in consideration of the day when another one from outside will come into the house.

105. He who has nobody to tie him up should never go **mad.**

106. One is usually at a loss to know how to sweep the ground in a **market-place.**

107. He who **marries** a beauty marries trouble.

108. He ought to be feared who sends you on a **message,** not he to whom you are sent.

109. Our **misfortunes** are never out of proportion to our capacity to bear them.

110. The **morning** of one's life foreshadows the eve.

111. There is no one who sympathizes with us as much as one's own **mother**; [for] who is it will show kindness to another person's child?

112. No one has ever had business relations with **Mother Earth** and come out a loser.

113. **Mouth** not keeping to mouth, and lip not keeping to lip, bring trouble to the jaws.

114. We should never be in a hurry to pluck the **mushroom** that will lead to bad feeling ; twenty thousand such mushrooms will never fill a gravy spoon.

115. " **Nearly** " is an individual we invariably meet on the way.

116. When **necessity** declares she will live with you, you reply, " There is no room." Have you forgotten that she can make room for herself even on the very tip of your nose ?

117. It is the path of the **needle** that the thread is accustomed to follow.

118. A near **neighbour** need not take a final leave till to-morrow.

119. The **news** has been heard right round, but the party it most concerns is deaf.

120. He will see his **nose** who lowers his eyes.

121. There is no medicine against **old age.**

122. The **palm** of the hand never deceives one.

[i.e. safety of a thing in hand.]

123. The **parasite** belongs to no class ; it claims kinship with every tree.

124. Who has **patience** has all things.

125. **Patience** is the elixir of life.

126. **Patience** is the father of virtues.

127. **Peace** is the father of friendship.

128. It is with its own face that the **plate** receives the soup.

[i.e. if you wish a thing done well, do it yourself.]

129. People think that the **poor** are not so wise as the rich, for if a man be wise, why is he poor ?

130. Nothing but a **potsherd** can endure fire.

131. **Poverty** destroys a man's reputation.

132. The **priest** will die ; the doctor will depart this life ; nor will the sorcerer be spared.

133. **Privation** has no voice, and suffering cannot speak.

134. A **proverb** is the horse of conversation ; when the conversation droops, a proverb revives it. Proverbs and conversation follow each other.

135. It is he who is as familiar with **proverbs** as he is with the matter in dispute who usually arbitrates.

136. A wise man who knows **proverbs** reconciles difficulties.

137. One cannot with decency complain of the action of another in excelling him : [as a result] those **quarrels** which have their origin in envy are not easily made up.

138. **Rags** make up a pad.

139. The **rain** does not recognize anyone as a friend ; whomsoever it sees it drenches.

140. One day of **rain** far surpasses a whole year of drought.

141. [In battle] the **sabre** does not know the head of the blacksmith [who made it].

[i.e. ingratitude.]

142. The **saucepan** that will taste of savoury food will have its bottom glow red with heat.

[i.e. all in search of distinction will have hardships.]

143. The very fact that we are **seeking** for a thing usually stands in the way of our finding it.

144. The dealer who **sells** cheap does not sell on credit ; he who sells on credit does not sell cheap.

145. With **shoes** one can get on in the midst of thorns.

146. Thanks are due to the **shoulders** which keep the shirt from slipping off.

147. A man does not run among thorns for nothing ; either he is chasing a **snake** or a snake is chasing him.

148. If a man lets fall his **stilts,** a hand will be stretched out to seize them.

149. When you see an illustrious man with a protruding **stomach,** you must know that it is full of plans.

[The Yoruba usually associates the mind with the stomach.]

150. An old **story** does not open the ear as a new one does.

151. The **stream** may dry up, but the watercourse retains its name.

152. **Strife** never begets a gentle child.

153. When we **sweep** the house, and sweep the streets, we usually end on the refuse heap.

154. It is the expert **swimmer** that the river carries away.

155. He runs away from the **sword** and hides in the scabbard.

[i.e. out of the frying-pan into the fire.]

156. What a **tale-bearer** gains is curses.

157. He who is pierced with a **thorn** must limp off to him who has a knife.

158. There is no god like the **throat ;** it accepts offerings every day.

159. The **thrower** of stone flings away the strength of his own arm.

160. **To-day** is the elder brother of to-morrow ; a copious dew is the elder brother of the rain.

161. The **tortoise** breathes ; it is only its shell which prevents our noticing it.

[i.e. the poor man has little opportunity for self-expression.]

162. The **town** is as a barren wilderness to him who is unhappy in his home life.

163. Whenever we fell **trees** in the forest we ought to imagine the situation reversed.

164. If borrowed **trousers** be not too slack towards the ankle, they make a tight fit around the calves.

165. What is there to put on in **trousers** of six pairs a penny?

166. The bird that imagines itself on a level with the **turkey-buzzard** will soon find itself on the grille.

[The turkey-buzzard is the scavenger of all food offered as sacrifice. Nobody is allowed to kill or molest it, and the general immunity renders it quite indifferent to the nearness of approach of human beings. For another bird to do this would be nothing short of suicide.]

167. **Venus** travels with the moon, and is supposed to be her dog.

[i.e. companionship is not necessarily dependence.]

168. When you are **warned,** warn yourself.

169. " I know it perfectly " prevents the **wasp** from learning to make honey.

170. Whatever we have a weakness for makes up the greater part of our **wealth ;** the master of two hundred slaves died leaving a single piece of cloth.

171. When the **white man** is about to leave a garden for good, he wrecks it.

172. The **white man** is the father of merchants, and want of money is the father of disgrace.

173. The man who puts down the seedling of **wickedness** has really planted it on the head of his own child.

174. There never is yet a stay-at-home wise man ; it is through one's own skin that **wisdom** is rubbed into one.

175. The **wisdom** of this year is the folly of the next.

176. **A witch** kills but never inherits.

177. Quick loving a **woman** means quick not loving a woman.

178. The man of mature years generally eats the heart ; **youth** the flesh.

[i.e. youth resents an insult to point of physical violence ; age nurses an injury.]

ZULU (ZULULAND)

[Language Family—Bantu]

1. The **body** is felt by its owner.

   [i.e. each heart knows its own bitterness.]

2. It is not known what **calf** the cow will have.

3. It [the **clay**] is moulded whilst it is still soft.

   [i.e. a stitch in time saves nine.]

4. The **corn's** second growth comes from the stump.

   [said of a son who takes after his father.]

5. The **creeper** binds [the tree] even though dried.

   [i.e. a feeble person is not to be despised, for he may do a deadly injury.]

6. Don't curse the **crocodile's** mother before you cross the river.

7. The pretty **cup** is not [long] used for drinking purposes.

   [i.e. whom the gods love die young.]

8. If we go forward we **die** ; if we go backward we die ; better go forward and die.

9. The **ear** tells the heart.

10. A beautiful vessel is not **eaten** out of.

11. No **elephant** is burdened by his own trunk.

    [i.e. a man won't admit a failure of his own idea.]

12. The **eye** can cross the river in flood.

    [i.e. desire will go far beyond what is possible.]

13. He has eaten **food** [but] it has eaten him.

    [Used of a drunken man.]

14. A **fool** is the wise man's ladder.

15. He that **forgives** gains the victory.

16. **Hand** and tongue never give alike.

17. The brave **hero** dies in his bravery, the swimmer in the water.

    [i.e. each should stick to his own proper work to the last.]

18. No **hillside** without its grave ; no valley without its shadow.

19. They [the bees] eat their own **honey.**

    [i.e. man must lie on the bed he has made for himself.]

20. **Hope** is the pillar of the world.

21. A **kettle** boils by keeping the fire going.

22. **A mother's love** is best of all.

23. The **mouth** is a man's tail for sweeping away flies.

24. He who lives longest has most **old clothes.**

25. There is no **partridge** that will scratch for another.

26. There is no **path** which won't go homeward.

27. **Plenty** sits still, hunger is a wanderer.

28. What the **poor man** says is not listened to.

29. We are like **saliva** and the tongue.

    [i.e. as thick as thieves.]

30. To **see** once is to see twice.

    [i.e. once bitten, twice shy.]

31. The **seed** waits for its garden where it will be sown.

32. The **seed** waits for its stalk.

    [i.e. the wrong will in due time propagate itself or produce its consequences.]

33. No **stake** ever grew old with its bark on.

    [i.e. years tell upon us all.]

34. The piece of **stick** burns him who pushes it to the fire.

35. The **sun** never sets without fresh news.

    [i.e. every day has its own events.]

36. A **traveller's** stomach is but small ; it is only in front, there's nothing behind but spine.

    [i.e. a form of request for food by a traveller, implying that he does not want much; he only asks for what is necessary for his stomach, not for his bones.]

37. **Travelling** begets sometimes a male, sometimes a female.

[i.e. you must not expect to have all things pleasant when you travel.]

38. The **tree** which is known is cut down.

[i.e. a man may be killed by his own friend.]

39. A **woman** who has lost her rival has no sorrow.

AMERICA

AMERICAN—U.S.A.

(Including New England)

1. Early to bed and early to rise ain't never no good if you don't **advertise.**
2. We hate those who will not take our **advice** and despise those who do.
3. Don't sell **America** short.
4. Man was made lower than the **angels,** and has been getting lower ever since.
5. A **babe** is a mother's anchor; she cannot swing from her moorings.
6. If it takes two to make a **bargain,** it should take two to break it.
7. It is better to get **beat** than to be in the wrong.
8. The **bigger** they come, the harder they fall.
9. One boy's a **boy,** two boys is half a boy, three boys is no boy at all.
10. All the world's a **camera**—look pleasant, please.
11. Paddle your own **canoe.**
12. To carry **care** to bed is to sleep with a pack on your back.
13. **Conscience** is only another name for Truth.
14. **Crows' feet** are always on the ground.
15. There is no leaping from **Delilah's lap** into Abraham's bosom.
16. The more you **eat,** the more you want.
17. You can't unscramble **eggs.**
18. There is no little **enemy.**
19. **Error** will creep through a crack, while truth will get stuck in a doorway.
20. **Fish** or cut bait.
21. Chated **food** is half digested.
22. Every time you **forgive** a man you weaken him and strengthen yourself.
23. Three faithful **friends:** an old wife, an old dog, and ready money.
24. Slog in! **genius** is one part inspiration and three parts perspiration.
25. In **God** we trust, all others pay cash.
26. Every man has a **goose** that lays golden eggs, if he only knew it.
27. If the **heart** is right, the head cannot be very far wrong.
28. A short **horse** is soon curried.
29. The thinner the **ice** is, the more anxious is everyone to see whether it will bear.
30. **Industry** need not wish.
31. **Lawyers** ain't like coachmen, they take their tip before they start.
32. **Life** is just one damned thing after another.
33. **Love** well; whip well.
34. Keep your eyes wide open before **marriage;** half-shut afterwards.
35. **Marrying** for love is risky, but God smiles on it.
36. **Matches** may be made in Heaven, but they are sold down here.
37. Any fool may make **money,** but it takes a wise man to keep it.
38. The **mother's heart** is the child's schoolroom.
39. A shady lane breeds **mud.**
    [i.e. secrecy creates wrongdoing.]
40. Wherever **Nature** does least, man does most.
41. **Necessity** never made a good bargain.

42. Don't take any wooden **nickels.**
43. **Opportunities,** like eggs, come one at a time.
44. There ain't much fun in **physic,** but there's a great deal of physic in fun.
45. When I eat with the children of **poverty** my heart sleeps.
46. It is not well for a man to **pray** cream and live skim milk.
47. The **proof** of gold is fire ; the proof of a woman, gold ; the proof of a man, a woman.
48. If you can't **push,** pull ; if you can't pull, please get out of the way.
49. There are two sides to every **question**—the wrong side and our side.
50. If a man is right, he cannot be too **radical ;** if wrong, he cannot be too conservative.
51. **Read** 'em and weep.
52. It is not often that a man's **reputation** outlasts his money.
53. Do **right,** and fear no man ; don't write, and fear no woman.
54. No man has a **right** to all his rights.
55. By the **road** called " Straight " we come to the house called " Beautiful." (*New England.*)
56. The road to **ruin** is kept in good repair, and the travellers pay the expense.
57. A **Scotchman** is one who keeps the Sabbath and every other darned thing he can lay hands on.
58. If a man is as wise as a **serpent,** he can afford to be as harmless as a dove.
59. Free **ships,** free goods.
60. A pot **shot** is a knave's shot.
61. Put up or **shut up.**
62. Every man must skin his own **skunk.**
63. Most men would rather say a **smart thing** than do a good one.
64. **Snow** is the poor man's manure.
65. If you **spit** on the floor at home, spit here, we want to make you feel at home.
66. **Sweat** and be saved. (*Said to be the favourite proverb of the late President Theodore Roosevelt.*)
67. **Thieves** hunt in couples, but a liar has no accomplice.
68. One-half the **troubles** in this world can be traced to saying " Yes " too quick, and " No " not soon enough.
69. Folks like the **truth** that hits their neighbour.
70. **Wild oats** are a sure crop, and a big yield for the seed.
71. The whole world is a market for a man's **wit.**
72. When a **woman** wears the breeches, she has a good right to them.
73. **Wool sellers** know wool buyers.

ARGENTINE

1. Clear **accounts** and thick chocolate.
2. Nothing is to be either all **bile** or all honey.
3. To the leaves [of **books**] go with limping legs.
4. The love of a **child** is like water in a basket.
5. The **child** weeps for its good and the old man for his ill.
6. To **cloth** with a rod and to silk with the hand.
7. For the young man and the **colt** a loose pack-saddle and a tight head-stall.
8. Three daughters and a mother are four **devils** for the father.

9. The **dog** is my friend, my wife is my enemy and my son my master.
10. A fertile **field,** if it doesn't rest, becomes sterile.
11. **God** sends the cold to each one according to his clothes.
12. He who has bad **habits** loses them late or never.
13. One **hen** will be as contented with one cock as another with eight.
14. A **learned man** is twice born.
15. He who **learns** well defends himself well.
16. Straps come from the same **leather.**
17. Many may be born, but how many will be **loved ?**
18. He who **loves** you will make you weep.
19. The threaded **needle** judges the girl.
20. He who **punishes** one chastises a hundred.
21. He bears a burning coal in his bosom who brings up another's **son.**
22. He weaves good cloth who brings up his **son.**
23. He who **speaks** sows and he who listens harvests.
24. He who flings **water** into a jar spills more than he collects.
25. The **wedge,** to be good, must be of the same wood.
26. **Wheat** is cleansed by the wind and vice by punishment.
27. A bad **woman** and a good woman both need the rod.

BOLIVIAN

1. The **morrow** is as good as to-day.

BRAZILIAN

1. The **bad action** remains with him who does it.
2. A **basket-maker** who makes one basket makes a hundred.
3. Where **blood** has been spilt the tree of forgetfulness cannot flourish.
4. A **card** which never appears neither wins nor loses.
5. By the roll of the **cart** one knows who is inside.
6. The **cheap** is dear.
7. A spot will fall on to the best **cloth.**
8. It is easier to tear **cloth** than to sew it.
9. He who **clothes himself** with bad cloth clothes himself twice in the year.
10. He who has a deep **eye** begins to weep soon.
11. A mouth full of water can't blow a **fire.**
12. The **fool** learns at his own cost, the wise man at the fool's cost.
13. He who never goes **forward** goes backward.
14. **God** loves cleanliness, but he who is cleanly He loves more.
15. **God** writes straight on crooked lines.

16. He who has no **godfather** dies a heathen.
17. If you would be of **good repute** never meet the sun in your bed.
18. **Goods** that are much on show lose their colour.
19. A **good will** makes the way short.
20. One grain doesn't fill a **granary,** but it helps its companion.
21. **Haste** is the mother of imperfection.
22. Of presumption and **holy water** each one takes what he wants.
23. There is no **ill** that lasts for ever and no good that does not end.
24. He who shoes with **iron** will be shod with iron.
25. If you would be a good **judge,** pay attention to what everyone says.
26. He who **kisses** my son sweetens my mouth.
27. He who **knows nothing** doubts nothing.
28. He who despises the **little** never likes the much.
29. He who doesn't **look ahead** remains behind.
30. Long sight, long **love.**
31. He who exposes himself to **love** exposes himself to suffering.
32. He who has no **malice** fears no malice.
33. A **man warned** is a man half saved.
34. Between the beginning and the end there is always a **middle.**
35. That which is done at **night** appears in the day.
36. A " **no** " in time is better than a late " yes ".
37. An **old father** and torn sleeves never dishonoured anyone.
38. The **oven** is warmed through its mouth.
39. Never promise a **poor man** and never owe a rich one.
40. **Poverty** is no vice, but it is better to hide it.
41. **Precious essences** are kept in small vessels.
42. When one doesn't want, two don' **quarrel.**
43. That which never has a **remed** is remedied.
44. That which does not reach a ma reaches his **reputation.**
45. For the sake of the **saint** on kisses the stones.
46. A **step** in the day is worth tw at night.
47. Each one knows with how man **threads** he sews.
48. **Time** never respects what is don with its aid.
49. The leafy **tree** does not alwa give savoury fruit.
50. He who goes before drinks pu **water.**
51. **Words** don't season soup.
52. He who seeks **work** has food the embers.

CANADIAN

1. Do not shout **dinner** till you have your knife in the loaf.
2. The devil places a pillow for a **drunken man** to fall on.
3. Three moves are as bad as a **fire.**
4. Look out for a sore **foot.**
   [i.e. lay by for a rainy day.]
5. A going **foot** always gets som thing, if it is only a thorn.
6. A green Christmas makes a f **graveyard.**
7. When all fruit fails, welco **haws.**

8. Half-past **kissing time,** and time to kiss again.

   [Reply to "What time is it?"]

9. You've drowned the **miller.**

   [Said when too much water is added to flour when bread-making.]

10. Don't have your **pants** laughing at your boots.

11. The ninth **wave** is always the strongest.

12. **A whistling maid** and a crowing hen is neither good nor canny about any poor man's house.

CHILIAN

1. If there was not **bad taste,** goods would not be sold.
2. That which **bears** a drop of dew bears a tempest.
3. Against the vice of **begging** there is the virtue of not giving.
4. He who **despises** the little will soon weep for the much.
5. One **devil** that is known is better than twenty to be known.
6. No one has done good who has not suffered **disillusionment.**
7. Of the **doctor,** the poet and the fool, we all have a small portion.
8. On a feeble **ewe** the ticks weigh heavy.
9. **Eyes** to see with, ears to hear with, and a mouth to keep silence.
10. There is no worse counsellor than **fear.**
11. **Friendship** to be strong must come to blows.
12. A little **frightens** and much softens.
13. He who saves for another day has no trust in **God.**
14. **God** punishes, but not with a rod.
15. When **God** wills it rains with every wind.
16. He who **goes away** without being turned out, comes back without being called.
17. If **good** pleases, evil entertains.
18. Why should a man without a head want a **hat?**
19. **Hide** mends itself, but cloth has to be mended.
20. It is better to preserve oneself from **ill** than to cure oneself of it.
21. He who becomes **irritated** burdens himself with a load of leaves, and he who becomes irritated a second time burdens himself with a load of salt.
22. He who becomes irritated has twofold work—to be irritated and to be quit of his **irritation.**
23. Scanty means are severe **judges.**
24. **A lie** runs until it is overtaken by truth.
25. Where distrust enters, **love** is no more than a page [boy].
26. He who **marries** prudence is the brother-in-law of peace.
27. The **poor man** stumbles on a flat road.
28. When an old **ranch** catches fire there is no fireman who can put it out.
29. With the **rod** with which you measure you will be measured.
30. Ten who **shout** obtain much more than ten who remain silent.
31. The **shrimp** that sleeps is carried away by the current.
32. That which cannot be remedied should be kept in **silence.**
33. That which is a **sin** in others is a virtue in ourselves.
34. **Taste** is in variety.
35. That which is left to **time** remains with time.
36. That which comes with **water** goes away with water.
37. If the **wise man** does not approve it is bad, but if the fool applauds it is worse.

COLUMBIAN

1. He who gives what he has teaches himself to **beg.**
2. A thieving **cow** doesn't miss the gap.
3. He who has to **die** dies in the dark, although he sells candles.
4. An old **dog** barks sitting down.
5. He who gives bread to a strange **dog** loses both his bread and the dog.
6. For every **dog** there is a leash.
7. In **eating** and scratching everything is in the beginning.
8. With patience and saliva the **elephant** swallows an ant.
9. He who has a tail of straw should not go near the **fire.**
10. There is no better **friend** than a burden.
11. He who **hopes,** despairs.
12. He who doesn't **know** is like him who doesn't see.
13. No one **knows** what anyone is.
14. The **monkey** knows on to which tree to climb.
15. The lazy **ox** drinks dirty water.
16. Better to be the **pot** than the lid.
17. When the **river** sounds it is carrying stones.
18. **See** and believe, and in order not to make a mistake, touch.
19. The sleeping **shrimp** is carried away by the tide.
20. Out of the leather come the **straps.**
21. No one knows for whom he **works.**

CUBAN

1. Whilst the **axe** goes and comes the log rests.
2. **Believe** only the half of what you see and nothing of what you are told.
3. Where he places his eye he places the **bullet.**
4. There is nothing so useful as one **day** for another.

   [i.e. what you cannot do to-day, do to-morrow.]
5. In **eating** and scratching, everything is in the beginning.
6. **Faults** never fall to the ground.
7. Each one bears his **friend** and his enemy with him.
8. Every **head** is a world.
9. Half the world **laughs** at the other half, and I laugh at the whole.
10. A **liar** falls sooner than a lame man.
11. **Listen** to what they say of others and you will know what they say of you.
12. In **lying** and eating fish, much care is needed.
13. A **mother-in-law,** like the Yucca tree, is useful underground.
14. The **new** pleases and the old satisfies.
15. Every **owl** to its olive-tree.
16. A **pain** in the bone is better than a pain in the heart.
17. **Rolling stones** meet each other.
18. Life is short, but a **smile** is only a second's effort.
19. Where the **sun** doesn't enter, the doctor does.
20. When the **sun** rises it rises for everyone.
21. He who is not of the water **swims** well.
22. That which goes not away in **tears,** goes away in sighs.

23. That which is of **water,** by water is carried away.
24. A **wife,** like a dog, is sought for her race-breed.
25. He who sows **wind** reaps a tempest.
26. **Women** and wine lead man on a bad road.

GEECHEE (NORTH AMERICAN INDIAN)

1. Burn up the **axe-helve** that can't hold up the blade.
2. Just hold up your end of the **beam** an' the world'll roll on.
3. " Stand further " better than " **beg pardon** ".
4. Trust no mistakes, when **bush** shakes, tear out.
5. One rain won't make a **crop.**
6. **Day's** short as ever, Time's long as it has been.
7. What goes over the **devil's** back has to come under his belly.
8. Let the **flat-iron** rust that puts cat's faces on the clothes.
9. Don't **fly** so high that you light on a candle.
10. A hard **head** makes a soft back.

    [i.e. if a child will not be admonished he will be beaten.]
11. **Mistakes** ain't haystacks or thar'd be more fat ponies than there is.
12. **Night's** a shadder, day's a shine, gone 'fore you catch it gwine [going].
13. If you dig a **pit** for me, you dig one for youtself.
14. **Pitcher** goes to the well every day ; one day more than all it will probably lose its handle.
15. Fire don't crack a full **pot.**
16. Seven years is not too long for a **rabbit** to wear a rough bosom shirt.

    [Said to a boasting person who pretends he needs no help.]
17. It **rains** and every man feels it some day.
18. **Trouble** follows sin as sure as fever follows chill.

INDIAN (NORTH AMERICAN)

(Including Tsimshian and Cree)

1. Don't get so **anxious** that you kill yourself.
2. A **deer,** although toothless, may accomplish something. (*Tsimshian.*)

    [i.e. don't judge a man by outward appearance.]
3. When the **devil** goes, Heaven comes in. (*Cree.*)
4. He wants to **die** with all his teeth in his head. (*Tsimshian.*)

    [i.e. he acts so foolishly that he will not live to be an old (toothless) man.]
5. **Heaven** looks down on him. (*Tsimshian.*)

    [Said of a poor man who is suddenly favoured by good fortune. Heaven is considered the Deity, and the man is successful upon whom He casts His eye.]
6. There is nothing so eloquent as a **rattlesnake's** tail.
7. No one gets out of bed to **sleep** on the floor.
8. Do not tell a story in the summer ; if you do, the **toads** will visit you.
9. He is just enjoying the **water-lilies** for a short time. (*Tsimshian.*)

    [i.e. the transientness of the pleasures of life.]
10. He who once drinks of the **waters** of the north will always return to them.

MEXICAN

1. In an old **allotment** there is never any lack of sweet potatoes.
2. Even if we are all of the same **clay,** the pot is not the same as the tavern.
3. The **coal** that has been an ember is easily rekindled.
4. A good **cock** will crow on any dung-heap.
5. He who is accustomed to **evil** is offended by good. (*New Mexican.*)
6. **Faces** we see, but not hearts. (*New Mexican.*)
7. He who **gives** what he has doesn't want what he sees. (*New Mexican.*)
8. He who does not speak is not heard by **God.**
9. **Hope** doesn't fatten but supports. (*New Mexican.*)
10. The **liar** tumbles much sooner than the lame man.
11. A jealous **lover** makes an indifferent husband.
12. With the **measure** you fear you will be feared. (*New Mexican.*)
13. A **miser's** money goes twice on the road. (*New Mexican.*)
14. There is no **pain** that lasts a hundred years, and no sick person who endures it. (*New Mexican.*)
15. One only goes to look at the **prickly pear-tree** when it is bearing fruit.
16. **Relations** and the sun, the further away the better.
17. It is not enough for a man to know how to **ride,** he must know how to fall.
18. He who has the most **saliva** can eat the most pinole.

    [Pinole is roasted maize flour.]
19. Each one **scratches** himself with his own nails.
20. He who takes one **step** takes two. (*New Mexican.*)
21. Amongst **tailors** work done is never paid for.
22. He who tells the **truth** doesn't sin, but he causes inconvenience.
23. **Vanity** and poverty are both of a piece. (*New Mexican.*)
24. There is no **wedge** like that of the same wood.

NEGRO

Including American, Bahama, British Guiana, Carribbean, Carolina (South), Creole, Demarara, Florida, Georgian, Haytian, Jamaican, Louisiana, Mauritius, Martinique, Plantation, Surinam, Trinidad, Tungo, West Indian)

An Introduction to this collection by Frank Cundall, O.B.E., F.S.A., F.R.Hist.S., will be found on page lxxx.

1. You want **all,** you lose all. (*Jamaican.*)
2. When turtle come out of pond and tells you **alligator** has sore eyes, believe him. (*Jamaican.*)
3. If the **alligator** says the ford is deep, believe him. (*Jamaican.*)
4. Before fording the river, do not curse the **alligator's** mother. (*Haytian.*)
5. **Ant** follow fat, fat-drowns ant. (*West Indian.*)
6. **Ant** follow fat, woman follow man. (*Jamaican.*)
7. First time **ant** tastes molasses, he washes skin in it. (*West Indian.*)
8. **Ants** follow fat. (*Creole.*)
9. Waiting on the table is a powerful way to get up an **appetite.** (*American.*)

10. **Appetite** don't regulate the time of day. (*American.*)

11. A mellow **apple** that drops on the ground without any shaking is most too willing. (*West Indian.*)

12. The best **apples** float on the top of the peck measure.

13. Be in a hurry to **ask,** no make people give. (*Jamaican.*)

14. Burn up the **axe-helve** that can't hold up the blade.

15. Gap in the **axe** show itself in the chip. (*American.*)

16. The morning glories aren't particularly lovely to a man with the **back-ache.** (*American.*)

17. It doesn't take a prophet to recollect **bad luck.** (*American.*)

18. Empty **bag** can't sit down, full one can't bend. (*Jamaican.*)

19. You never see empty **bag** stand up. (*Jamaican.*)

[i.e. if you are hungry you cannot work.]

20. When the **bait** is worth more than the fish 'tis time to stop fishing. (*American.*)

21. Cheap **bargain** take money. (*Jamaican.*)

22. **Barking** save a biting. (*Jamaican.*)

23. No put yourself in a **barrel** when match-box can hold you. (*Jamaican.*)

24. If nigger hate you, him give you **basket** fetch water; but if you clever, you put plantain leaf in bottom. (*Jamaican.*)

25. Don't hang your **basket** higher than you can reach 'em. (*Bahama.*)

26. Just hold up your end of the **beam** an' the world'll roll on.

27. Little billy-goat has **beard,** big bull has none. (*West Indian.*)

28. When you see your neighbour's **beard** catch fire, take water and wet yours. (*Martinique and Jamaican.*)

29. You make your **bed** soft, you lay down soft; you make your bed hard, you lay down hard. (*West Indian.*)

30. If **bee** didn't have sting, him would no keep him honey. (*Jamaican.*)

31. Mighty poor **bee** that doesn't make more honey than he wants. (*Jamaican.*)

32. Buy **beef** you buy bone; buy land you buy rock-stone. (*Jamaican.*)

33. **Beggar** beg from beggar him never get rich. (*West Indian.*)

34. "Stand further" better more than "**beg pardon**".

35. **Believe** half what you see—nothing what you hear. (*Jamaican.*)

36. Crack **bell** never mend.

37. Man **belly full,** him say anything. (*Jamaican.*)

38. When **belly full,** jaw must stop.

39. **Bellyfull** make potato have skin. (*Jamaican.*)

[i.e. if you are hungry you ignore trifles.]

40. Hungry **belly** no got ears. (*Jamaican.*)

41. Full **belly** tell empty belly no broken heart. (*West Indian.*)

42. Better for **belly** to burst than for good things to spoil. (*West Indian.*)

43. **Big word** no tear man's jawbone. (*Jamaican.*)

44. Satisfied **bird** and hungry bird can't fly together. (*British Guiana.*)

45. You can't prevent **bird** from flying over your head, but you can prevent him making nest in your head. (*Jamaican.*)

46. My grandmother say, the man that can crack a **biscuit** must work for it. (*West Indian.*)

47. **Bit** [i.e. 4½*d.*] old, it turn fippence [i.e. 3*d.*].

[i.e. when one is old one is liable to be less esteemed.]

48. Never depend too much on the **blackberry blossoms.** (*American.*)
49. Big **blanket** make man sleep late. (*Creole.*)
50. The **blind** has nothing but his stick. (*Jamaican.*)
51. **Blind eye** country, one-eyed man a governor. (*British Guiana.*)
52. If you won't stand **blow,** no play with stick. (*Jamaican.*)
53. **Blows** returned never hurt. (*Creole.*)
54. Coward man keep sound **bone.** (*Creole.*)
55. The **bones** before being thrown into the street were on the master's table. (*Surinam.*)
56. The best **bravery** is the sort that isn't skeered of the hot sun. (*American.*)
57. Hour may **break** what age never mend. (*Jamaican.*)
58. Never make goat trustee for **breadnut**-tree. (*West Indian.*)
59. You no done **breed,** so no laugh after your grannie. (*Jamaican.*)
60. Don't break down **bridge** you just crossed. (*Jamaican.*)
61. The **buggy whip** can't make up for light feed in the horse-trough. (*American.*)
62. When **bull** foot broke him eats with monkey. (*Jamaican.*)
63. **Bull** horn never too heavy for him head. (*Creole, Haytian and Mauritius.*)
64. When **bull** old him feed fence side. (*Jamaican.*)
65. **Bull** old, you take wis' wis' [straw] tie him. (*Creole.*)
66. **Bull** say, " Stand up no mean rest ". (*Jamaican*)
67. When trouble catch **bull-dog,** puppy breeches fit him. (*West Indian.*)
68. The **bull-frog** knows more about rain than the almanac. (*American.*)
69. A chosen **burden** never felt. (*Jamaican.*)
70. Trust no mistakes ; when **bush** shakes, tear out.
71. Little **bush** sometime grow better than big tree.
72. Any cry do for **buyin'** ! (*Jamaican.*)
73. All the **buzzards** in the settlement'll come to the grey mule's funeral. (*American.*)
74. " **Bye-and-bye** " very long rope. (*Jamaican.*)
75. See the **candle** light before you blow out the match. (*Jamaican.*)
76. **Cap** no fit you, you no take it up. (*Jamaican.*)
77. No **catch**—no have. (*Jamaican.*)
78. What no **catch** you, you no catch it. (*Jamaican.*)
79. A man that pets a live **cat-fish** ain't crowded with brains. (*American.*)
80. When the **cat's** away the rats give a ball. (*Creole.*)
81. **Chair** fall down, bench get up. (*Jamaican.*)
82. When man know him **chair-back** no strong, him shouldn't lean back. (*Jamaican.*)
83. House trash cover **character.** (*Jamaican.*)
84. There is no **cheese** but that can find brown bread. (*Mauritius and Creole.*)
85. Dead **chicken** bring dollar. (*British Guiana.*)
86. Bathe other people's **children,** but don't wash behind their ears. (*Creole.*)
87. **Children** suck their mother when them young, their father when them old. (*Jamaican.*)
88. Parson **christen** him own pickney first. (*Jamaican.*)
89. A fork in a strange road don't make a man any better **Christian.** (*American.*)
90. The people who stir up the most racket in the Meeting House ain't always the best **Christians.** (*West Indian.*)

91. **Christians** forgive freely and forget freely. (*Jamaican.*)

92. You in the right **church** but in the wrong pew. (*Jamaican.*)

[Partly right and partly wrong.]

93. No hang your **clothes** all upon one nail.

94. **Clothes** cover character. (*Jamaican.*)

95. He who has fine **clothes** should also have shabby ones. (*Surinam.*)

96. When **cloud** come, sun no set. (*Jamaican.*)

97. **Cloven foot** can't wear polish boot. (*Jamaican.*)

98. A good **cock** crows in any hen-house. (*Creole.*)

99. Bottle no have stopper belong to **cockroach.** (*Jamaican.*)

100. When **cockroach** give party he never ask fowl. (*Jamaican.*)

101. **Cockroach** have no right before fowl. (*West Indian.*)

102. A **cockroach** stands no show in a fowl country. (*Tungo.*)

103. When chicken is tied up, **cockroach** wants an explanation. (*West Indian.*)

104. **Cockroaches** never get justice when chicken judges. (*Jamaican.*)

105. When **cocoa** ripe, him must burst. (*West Indian.*)

106. Sometime standing **collar** stands top of empty belly. (*Jamaican.*)

107. A "**come in**" a nothing. (*Jamaican.*)

108. The bestest passion is **compassion.** (*Jamaican.*)

109. **Conversation** is the food of the ears. (*Creole.*)

110. Grass don't grow high round the **corn crib.** (*American.*)

111. Some **cornstalks** is like lots of folks, they fling all their power into the blades and tassels. (*American.*)

112. What **costs** nothing give good weight. (*Jamaican.*)

113. The **cotton patch** don't care which way you vote. (*West Indian.*)

114. Heaps of good **cotton stalks** get chopped up from association with the weeds. (*American.*)

115. "Hearsay" can't go to **court house.** (*Jamaican.*)

116. You catch **cow** by him horn, but man by him word. (*Jamaican.*)

117. A promised **cow** doesn't fatten. (*Surinam.*)

118. Man have **cow,** him look for milk. (*Jamaican.*)

119. You care for meagre **cow,** it is you she will butt. (*Jamaican.*)

120. **Cow** no know he lose his tail till cow-fly season. (*British Guiana.*)

121. 'Tis not for want of tongue what make **cow** not talk. (*West* Indian.)

122. You never see kicking **cow** without kicking calf. (*Jamaican.*)

123. When **cow-tail** cut off, God Almighty brush flies. (*Jamaican.*)

124. Only traveller learn that **crab** catch cold. (*Jamaican.*)

125. It is because of his good heart that the **crab** has no head. (*Creole.*)

126. The reason **crab** no have head is because him have too good a stomach. (*Jamaican.*)

127. When **crab** no have hole him never get fat. (*Jamaican*)

128. **Crab** say no trust shadder. (*Jamaican*)

129. **Crab** walk too much, him get in kutakoo. (*Creole.*)

[Kutakoo—a kind of crab soup.]

130. When **crab** walk too much him go a cutacoo. (*Jamaican.*)

[Cutacoo—a basket made of withies.]

131. Put me down softly, me a **cracked plate.** (*Jamaican.*)

132. Heap of folks is like **craw-fishes ;** they love to back water, but they won't stand no crowding for all that. (*American.*)

133. Pay to-day, **credit** to-morrow. (*Jamaican.*)

134. One rain won't make a **crop.**

135. **Cunnin'** better than strength. (*Creole.*)

136. Soon as **cup** full it flow over. (*Jamaican.*)

137. When **dainty lady** live well, she take pin to eat pea. (*Jamaican.*)

138. Man with half a foot always **dance** near his family. (*Jamaican.*)

139. When you go to a country where they all **dance** with one foot, then dance with one foot too. (*Caribbean.*)

140. Sun set, but **danger** never set. (*Jamaican.*)

141. One **day** no be all day.

142. **Day's** short as ever ; time's long as it has been.

143. When man **dead,** grass grow to him door. (*Bahama.*)

144. Nigger who finds **dead man** must be the man who kill him. (*Jamaican.*)

145. Man ever so hearty, **death day** watch him. (*Jamaican.*)

146. When poor man owe **debt,** even dog and puss know. (*Jamaican.*)

147. The man in **debt** is a swimmer with his boots on. (*American.*)

148. Eat with the **devil,** but give him long spoon. (*Jamaican.*)

149. I deal with the **devil,** but I use long spoon. (*Jamaican.*)

150. **Devil** tempt, but he no force. (*British Guiana.*)

151. What goes over the **devil's** back has to come under his belly. (*West Indian.*)

152. Nothin' ever done on the **devil's** back never buckle back under his belly. (*Florida.*)

[i.e. you will reap what you sow.]

153. The **dinner-bell's** always in tune. (*American.*)

154. It's a mighty deaf nigger that doesn't hear the **dinner horn.** (*American.*)

155. If you obliged to eat **dirt,** eat clean dirt. (*American.*)

156. **Dirt** no kill, but clean kill. (*Jamaican.*)

157. Every house have him **dirty corner.** (*Jamaican.*)

158. Give me to-day's meat, yesterday's bread, and last year's wine, and the **doctor** can go. (*Jamaican.*)

159. Pay the **doctor,** praise the Lord. (*Jamaican.*)

160. Dogs among **doctors**—matches. (*West Indian.*)

161. " Please " am a good **dog,** and him cost nothing. (*West Indian.*)

162. When **dog** foot broke him know master's door. (*Jamaican.*)

163. If **dog** have money him buy cheese. (*Jamaican.*)

164. Kick **dog,** him friend you ; feed him, him bite you. (*Jamaican.*)

165. If you sorry for meagre **dog,** him will turn round and bite you. (*Jamaican.*)

166. Man and **dog,** hog and pot water, brown man and rum. (*Jamaican.*)

[These are supposed to be affinities.]

167. The man who tie mad **dog** is the right somebody to loose him. (*Jamaican.*)

168. Behind **dog** it is " dog ", before dog it is " Mr. Dog ". (*Jamaican.*)

169. The howling **dog** knows what it sees. (*American.*)

170. Follow the fashion give **dog** mange. (*West Indian.*)

171. **Dog** never chaw razor.

172. **Dog** no eat dog. (*Louisiana and British Guiana.*)

173. The **dog** on three legs ain't always lame. (*American.*)

174. Mad **dogs** bite the hand that feed them.

175. **Dogs** don't bite at the front gate. (*American.*)

176. " Friend " a **dog's** name. (*Jamaican.*)

177. The man that always takes the shortest road to a **dollar** generally takes the longest road from it. (*American.*)

178. Every time **donkey** bray, him remember something. (*Jamaican.*)

179. **Donkey** gallop soon over.

180. When you go to a **donkey house** don't talk about ears. (*Jamaican.*)

181. "**Don't care**" keep big house. (*British Guiana.*)

182. Sweep your own **door** before you see mine. (*Jamaican.*)

183. Clean your **door** mouth first, then tell your neighbour about him own. (*Bahama.*)

184. **Dream** ain't good till you get it. (*American.*)

185. Dry **drink** better than sermon. (*Jamaican.*)

186. Always drink pure water ; many a man gets **drunk** from breaking this rule. (*American.*)

187. **Drunken** man talk the truth. (*Jamaican.*)

188. Hen agree for hatch **duck egg,** but him no agree for take duck-pickney for swim.

[i.e. even with a complacent person there is a limit.]

189. It is no sign of a **duck's** nest to see feathers on the fence. (*American.*)

190. Deaf **ear** gives story-carrier trouble. (*Jamaican.*)

191. The **ear** is nothing more than a door. (*Surinam.*)

192. **Ear** no hear, eye shall see. (*British Guiana.*)

193. **Ear** no hear, heart no leap. (*Jamaican.*)

194. Bad word and **ear-hole** never agree. (*Jamaican.*)

195. Stone walls have **ears.** (*Jamaican.*)

196. People who have their **ears** above their heads. (*Haytian.*)

197. One has two **ears** but one never hears the word twice. (*Surinam.*)

198. If **ears** grow ever so big, they can't pass the head. (*Creole.*)

199. Mouth **eat,** back pay. (*British Guiana.*)

200. No everything good to **eat** good for talk. (*Jamaican.*)

201. Assuming knowledge [bluffing] better than **education.**

202. **Education** don't come by bumping against the school-house. (*American.*)

203. If you eat **egg** you must break the shell. (*Jamaican.*)

204. There's reason in the roasting of **eggs.** (*West Indian.*)

205. Let him who wishes to hatch sit on his own **eggs.** (*Haytian.*)

206. Your worst **enemy** live in your house with you. (*Jamaican.*)

207. To defend the right does not offend the pupils of the **eye.**

208. When **eye** see, mouth talk. (*Jamaican.*)

209. **Eye** shame eye. (*Jamaican.*)

210. **Eyebrow** older than beard. (*Jamaican.*)

211. Bush have **eyes,** stump wear hat. (*Jamaican.*)

212. When six **eyes** meet story done. (*Jamaican.*)

213. **Eyes** must see and ears must hear, but mouth must shut. (*Jamaican.*)

214. The **face** came before the photograph.

215. To cover my **face** I don't take other people's hands.

216. Foller **fashion** broke neck. (*Creole.*)

217. **Fat** no feel. (*Jamaican.*)

218. Heap of people recollect **favours** by marking you down in the snow. (*American.*)

219. " Do little " better than " point **finger** ". (*Jamaican.*)

[i.e. little help better than mere criticism.]

220. **Finger** never say " look here ", him say " look yonder ". (*Jamaican.*)

[i.e. people do not usually point out their own faults.]

221. Man that carries straw mustn't fool with **fire.** (*Jamaican.*)

222. Where **fire** and water are, anyone can live. (*Jamaican.*)

223. You can hide the **fire,** but what you going to do with the smoke? (*Jamaican.*)

224. What you lose in the **fire** you will find in the ashes. (*Creole.*)

225. Old **fire-stick** no hard to catch. (*Jamaican.*)

[i.e. old habits are not hard to revive.]

226. He who goes with **fish** must eat worms. (*Surinam.*)

227. Fisherman never sees **fish** stink. (*Georgian.*)

[i.e. my own child is always good.]

228. The bigger the **fish,** the more butter him take. (*Jamaican.*)

229. Let the **flat-iron** rust that puts cat's faces on the clothes.

230. One finger can't catch **fleas.** (*Creole.*)

231. Don't **fly** so high that you light on a candle.

232. "Good boy" a nickname for **fool.** (*Jamaican.*)

233. One time no **fool,** but two time fool, him the fool. (*Jamaican.*)

234. If there was no **fool,** cunning man couldn't live. (*Jamaican.*)

235. If **fool** no go market, bad something never sell. (*Jamaican.*)

236. You follow **fool,** you fool yourself. (*Jamaican.*)

237. Every family have him broken **foot.** (*Jamaican.*)

238. It is when the wind is blowing that we see the skin of the **fowl.** (*Haytian.*)

[Exceptional circumstances reveal character.]

239. Black **fowl** can lay white egg.

[i.e. good may arise out of evil.]

240. When **fowl** drink water him say, "Thank God." When man drink water him say nothing. (*Jamaican.*)

241. If you follow what **fowl** eat, you never eat fowl meat. (*Jamaican.*)

242. Every time **fowl** lays eggs he tells the whole world. (*West Indian.*)

243. **Fowl** scratch up too much dirt, him run risk of finding him grandma's skeleton. (*Jamaican.*)

244. The mother of "**free-of-charge**" is dead. (*Surinam.*)

245. Pound worth of **fret** never pay quarter worth of debt. (*West Indian.*)

246. Man you can't beat you have to call him your **friend.** (*Jamaican.*)

247. When fire and water make **friend,** anybody can live. (*Jamaican.*)

248. Try your **friend** in small thing, use him in great. (*Jamaican.*)

249. If you want to know your **friend,** lie down by roadside, pretend to be drunk. (*Jamaican.*)

250. Promise get **friend**; perform keep him. (*British Guiana.*)

251. A long spell of rheumatism is apt to point out your best **friends.** (*American.*)

252. When you go to a **friend's** house, leave your stomach behind. (*British Guiana.*)

253. When you quarrel with your **friends,** then you know how much they know about you. (*Caribbean and Jamaican.*)

254. Make **friends** when you no need them. (*Jamaican.*)

255. They are not all **friends** who grin showing their teeth.

256. Tie a **frog** around a child's neck to make him teeth easy. (*Georgian.*)

257. If the **frog** tells you the alligator has sore eyes, believe him. (*Trinidad.*)

258. Idleness leaves the **frogs** without buttocks. (*Creole.*)

259. Many members of a family, many **ghosts.** (*Surinam.*)

260. Pretty **girl**; dirty tricks. (*West Indian.*)

261. Good nature make nanny **goat** carry short tail. (*West Indian.*)

262. Loose **goat** doesn't know what tied goat see. (*West Indian.*)

263. Nanny **goat** never scratch him back till him see wall. (*Jamaican.*)

[Await the proper opportunity.]

264. **God** Almighty never shut eye. (*West Indian.*)

265. After **God,** then the white people. (*West Indian.*)

266. Handsome face and **good luck** don't travel the same pass. (*Creole.*)

[It is not beauty which brings good fortune.]

267. Don't kill the old **goose** in sight of the feather-bed. (*American.*)

268. "**Go softly**" better than "beg pardon". (*British Guiana.*)

269. Those who eat can say **grace.** (*American.*)

270. Winter **grapes** sour whether you can reach him or not.

271. Man no done **grow,** no laugh at the long man. (*Creole.*)

272. Seven year no' enough to wash freckle off a **guinea-hen** back. (*Jamaican.*)

273. **Half-a-bit** [1½*d.*] make trouble, joe [$8.80 or £1 16*s.* 8*d.*] can't cure. (*British Guiana.*)

274. **Half-a-foot** is everywhere. (*Jamaican.*)

[i.e. the faults of people are to be found wherever you go.]

275. **Half-a-mouth** tell you "not hear"; whole-mouth tell you "too late". (*Jamaican.*)

276. **Hand** full, hand come. (*Jamaican.*)

277. When **hand** full, him have plenty company. (*West Indian.*)

278. Some man burn them **hand** when they only mean to warm them. (*Bahama.*)

279. Be ready with your **hat,** but slow with your money. (*Jamaican.*)

280. If a man **hate** you, give you fork to drink soup. (*Jamaican.*)

281. "**Have**" have "no want"; "no have" will die for it. (*Jamaican.*)

282. A hard **head** makes a soft back.

[i.e. if a child will not be admonished he will be beaten.]

283. You no **hear** with your ears, you will hear with your skin. (*Jamaican.*)

284. It is our **heart** that carries us either to Paradise or to Hell.

285. Going to **Heaven,** no child's play.

286. **Heel** never go before toe. (*Jamaican.*)

[i.e. important matters must be dealt with first.]

287. The **hen** that hatches out ducks is going to lose her children mighty quick. (*American.*)

288. Sitting **hens** don't hanker after fresh eggs. (*American.*)

289. The top of the **hill** is harder to find than the bottom. (*American.*)

290. Man no done climb **hill,** no throw away you stick. (*Creole.*)

291. **Hog** run for him life, dog run for him character. (*Creole.*)

[i.e. different causes produce the same effect.]

292. Watch out when you're getting all you want, fattening **hogs** ain't in luck. (*American.*)

293. Little **hole** in your pocket is worse than a big one at the knee. (*American.*)

294. Every man **honest** till the day they catch him. (*Caribbean and Jamaican.*)

295. **Hope** is the pillar of the world.

296. 'Tain't much difference between a **hornet** and a yellow jacket when they both get under your clothes. (*American.*)

297. When **horse** dead, cow get fat.

298. **Horse** has no business at cow fight. (*West Indian.*)

299. "**How do you do**" and "thank you" break no square. (*Jamaican.*)

300. If "**How do you do**" cost farthing, few men would get it. (*Jamaican.*)

301. " **How do you do** " come from door. (*Jamaican.*)

[i.e. social convention demands that a visitor give the first greeting.]

302. " **Hungry,** hungry " and " full, full " no travel same road. (*Jamaican.*)

303. Nigger that gets **hurt** working oughter show the scars.

304. Patience man drive **jackass.** (*West Indian.*)

305. When **jackass** fast they take him to draw cart. (*Jamaican.*)

306. **Jackass** say : The world no level. [Excuse.]

307. Every **jack-knife** found on the highway, on the highway will be lost. (*Haytian.*)

308. Some gravel walks may lead to the **jail.** (*American.*)

309. When you make the **jail** too nice, you better strengthen the hogpen. (*American.*)

310. Count like **Jew,** agree like brother. (*Jamaican.*)

311. If you fly with **John Crow** [vulture] you will eat dead meat. (*Jamaican.*)

312. A good **journey** is not the God of the pilgrim. (*Surinam.*)

313. Run from a **jumbie** [ghost] and you meet up with a coffin. (*West Indian.*)

314. All the **justice** in the world ain't fastened up in the court-house. (*American.*)

315. Lip **kiss** no touch the heart. (*Jamaican.*)

316. Hang your **knapsack** where you can reach it. (*Haytian.*)

317. It is only the **knife** that knows the heart of the yam. (*Haytian and Jamaican.*)

[Only those who investigate closely understand a subject.]

318. Occasionally, a man with right smart education can't find his **knife** when it gets in the wrong pocket. (*American.*)

319. What you don't **know** older than you. (*Jamaican.*)

320. The bridge between **laughing** and crying not long. (*Jamaican.*)

321. First word, go to **law.** (*Creole.*)

322. Good **lawyer,** bad neighbour. (*Jamaican.*)

323. **Lawyer** look upon nigger with one eye, but he look upon his pocket with two. (*Jamaican.*)

324. **Lawyer-house** built upon fool head. (*Jamaican.*)

325. **Lie** go upon foot, scandal have wing. (*Jamaican.*)

326. Man that no tell **lie,** hair grow on him hand middle. (*Jamaican.*)

327. In every **lie** there is an ounce of truth. (*Jamaican.*)

328. What is said over a dead **lion** is not said in the eyes of a living one. (*Jamaican.*)

329. **Liquor** talks mighty loud when it gets loose from the jug. (*American.*)

330. " **Live-well** " can't leave " very well " alone. (*Jamaican.*)

331. " **Live-well-man** " go tell governor "how-do-you-do". (*Jamaican.*)

332. Slice off cut **loaf** never missed. (*Jamaican.*)

333. Blind **louse** no judge a colour.

334. **Love** and cough never hide. (*Jamaican.*)

335. Tell me whom you **love,** I'll tell you who you are. (*Creole.*)

336. Faith dares everything, and **love** bears everything. (*Jamaican.*)

337. Them that want to **love** must love. (*Jamaican.*)

338. Never pass your first **luck.** (*Jamaican.*)

339. Your **luck** ain't always equal to the length of your fishing-pole. (*American.*)

340. Good **luck** says, " Open your mouth and shut your eyes." (*American.*)

341. In all nature except the human family the **male** is prettier than the female.

342. Me **mamma** dead, it no hurt me like dew water wet me a morning-time. (*Jamaican and British Guiana.*)
[Said of a selfish person.]

343. "**Manage** good" better than big wage. (*Jamaican.*)

344. The foot of the owner is **manure** for the field. (*Jamaican.*)

345. If you stand a **market** long you will owe debt. (*Jamaican.*)

346. Mean man go a **market** two time. (*Jamaican.*)

347. **Market-house** a woman court-house.

348. **Marriage** has teeth and him bite very hot. (*Jamaican.*)

349. **Marry** for love, work for money.

350. Before you **marry,** keep your two eyes open; after you marry, shut one. (*Jamaican.*)

351. **Marry** your daughter when you can, your son when you please. (*Jamaican.*)

352. You is the **mat,** me is the ground. (*Jamaican.*)
[i.e. humility.]

353. First **meal** no meal; second meal is a meal. (*Jamaican.*)

354. Counting the stars doesn't help the **meal-box.** (*American.*)

355. Dust doesn't settle on the **meal-box.** (*American.*)

356. The bottom of the **meal-box** makes mighty poor music. (*American.*)

357. When man has raw **meat** he look for fire. (*Jamaican.*)

358. Who has raw **meat,** to them look for fire. (*Jamaican.*)

359. "**Me-know-it**" never go before. (*Jamaican.*)

360. **A mile** round the road is shorter than half a mile across the field.

361. You can't take **milk** from coffee.

362. When man say him do not **mind,** then him mind. (*Jamaican.*)

363. **Mischief** come by the pound and go by the ounce. (*Jamaican.*)

364. **Misery** for two is Misery and Co. (*Louisiana and Creole.*)

365. **Misfortune** never show cloud. (*Jamaican and Trinidad.*)

366. **Mistakes** ain't haystacks, or thar'd be more fat ponies than there is.

367. When **money** done, love done. (*Jamaican.*)

368. Have **money,** have friend. (*Jamaican.*)

369. Save **money,** money save you. (*Jamaican.*)

370. More **money,** more sin. (*British Guiana.*)

371. Softly, softly ketch **monkey.** (*Jamaican.*)

372. If you back **monkey,** him will fight tiger. (*Jamaican.*)

373. Follow fashion makes **monkey** lose tail. (*West Indian.*)

374. Order **monkey,** monkey order him tail. (*Jamaican.*)
[When you order a man to do anything, he in turn orders his child to do it.]

375. **Monkey** never so drunk to go sleep in front a dog's kennel. (*Caribbean and Jamaican.*)

376. Play wid **monkey,** no play with him tail. (*Jamaican.*)

377. The full **moon** is a poor hand to keep secrets. (*American.*)

378. You cannot coax the **morning glory** to climb the wrong way round the cornstalks. (*Plantation.*)

379. Every cabin has its **mosquito.** (*West Indian.*)

380. **Mosquitoes** don't suit long prayers. (*American.*)

381. If you no have door to shut, shut your **mouth.** (*Jamaican.*)

382. Sweet **mouth** buys horses on credit. (*West Indian.*)

383. Not every open **mouth** laughs.

384. **Mouth** says "No", but eye says "Yes". (*Jamaican.*)

385. What sweet in **mouth** sometime hot in belly.

386. Just put a **mulatto** on horseback and he'll tell you his mother wasn't a negress. (*Louisiana and Creole.*)

387. **Mulattoes** fight, kids die. (*Haytian.*)

[Current proverb among slave population of St. Domingo, said to ridicule the pretensions and ambitions of the Mulatto race immediately above them, when fighting duels—never seriously undertaken, and invariably ending in a reconciliation and feast, in which kids were the chief item on the menu.]

388. A blind **mule** ain't afraid of darkness. (*American.*)

389. A fat **mule** and a straight furrow. (*American.*)

390. A **mule** can have so much goodness in his face that he don't have none left for his hind legs. (*American.*)

391. One-eyed **mule** can't be handled on the blind side. (*American.*)

392. **Mule** don't kick according to no rule. (*American.*)

393. **Mule** don't understand the wheel-barrow. (*American.*)

394. A sore-backed **mule** is a poor hand to guess the weight of a bag of meal. (*American.*)

395. It takes a heap of licks to drive a **nail** in the dark. (*American.*)

396. If you see your **neighbour's beard** on fire, water your own. (*Creole.*)

397. Dark **night** has no governor. (*Jamaican.*)

398. After **night** morning come. (*British Guiana.*)

399. **Night's** a shadder, day's a shine, gone for you catch it gwine [going].

400. Quick **ninepence** better than slow shilling. (*Jamaican.*)

401. **Nonsense-man** eat soup with fork, eat rice with pin, eat parched corn and lick him fingers. (*Jamaican.*)

402. **North wind** show the cracks in the house. (*American.*)

403. Unwilling man **nose** must bleed. (*British Guiana.*)

404. **Oil** and truth never drown. (*Jamaican.*)

405. No man too old for **old maid.** (*Jamaican.*)

406. Pretty **orange** not sweet. (*West Indian.*)

407. **Ostentation** never go to God. (*Jamaican.*)

408. It isn't one time only that the **ox** needs his tail to drive the flies away. (*Creole.*)

409. When you are given an **ox's** head to eat, don't be afraid of his eyes. (*Haytian.*)

410. **Palings** weren't fixed for climbing over. (*West Indian.*)

411. He who takes a **partner** takes a master. (*Creole.*)

412. There's a bad streak in folks that think the whole world is a **penitentiary wheel.** (*American.*)

413. Nigger that don't eat **pepper** and salt, don't trust him. (*Jamaican.*)

[i.e. he would not be normal.]

414. Father work, **picknie** spend. (*Caribbean.*)

415. Send out **picknie,** your foot rest, but your heart no rest. (*Jamaican.*)

416. **Pigs** dunno what a pen's for. (*American.*)

417. Bad family better than empty **pig-stye.** (*Jamaican.*)

418. The point of the **pin** is the easiest one to find. (*American.*)

419. If you dig a **pit** for me, you dig one for yourself.

420. **Pitcher** goes to the well every day. One day more than all it will probably leave its handle.

421. Tin **plate** don't mind dropping on the floor. (*American.*)

422. **Play-stone** kill bird. (*Jamaican.*)

423. Give a thing and take a thing, a bad man **plaything.** (*Jamaican.*)

424. All kind of **pleasure** must get one "stop-off". (*British Guiana.*)

425. It don't make much difference 'bout what sort of **plough** you use, if you just have the right sort of mule in front, and the right sort of nigger behind. (*American.*)

426. There's right smart religion in a **plough-handle.** (*American.*)

427. The **plow** point is close kin to the meal-bag.

428. Nigger with a **pocket handkerchief** better be looked after. (*American.*)

429. Some **pocket-knives** must have been made to lend out. (*American.*)

430. Man **poor,** his word poor. (*Jamaican.*)

431. **Poor** never sorry for himself. (*Jamaican.*)

432. **Poor man** never vexed. (*Jamaican.*)

433. **Poor people** entertain with the heart. (*Haytian.*)

434. Sorry for **poor thing,** poor thing kill you. (*Jamaican.*)

435. There's right sharp schooling in the tail of a **'possum,** never let go a thing long as there's a chance left. (*American.*)

436. Fire don't crack a full **pot.**

437. When man have plenty him boil **pot.** (*Jamaican.*)

438. You never see empty **pot** boil over. (*Jamaican.*)

[i.e. poor people have nothing to give away.]

439. **Pot** full, cover take half. (*Jamaican.*)

[i.e. in a rich man's house servants are well off.]

440. If you have little, put little in the **pot ;** if you have plenty, put plenty. (*Jamaican.*)

441. Quart **pot** turn down, gill pot turn up. (*Jamaican and Demarara.*)

442. If you want to lick old woman **pot,** you scratch him back. (*Jamaican.*)

443. The pint **pots** are down and the gill pots are up. (*West Indian.*)

444. **Poverty** isn't a screen, but it's a very big nail. (*Creole.*)

445. Every long **prayer** got " amen ". (*West Indian.*)

446. **Prayer** in the mouth only is no prayer. (*Jamaican.*)

447. **Prayer** needn't be long when faith's strong. (*Jamaican.*)

448. The man that's slow to **promise** sure to keep him word. (*Jamaican.*)

449. **Provocation** make dummy men talk. (*Jamaican.*)

450. The man that **puff** up soon puff down. (*Jamaican.*)

451. You can't spoil a ripe **pumpkin** by abusing it. (*American.*)

452. **Puppet-show** has their gang. (*Jamaican.*)

453. You play with **puppy,** him lick you mouth.

454. **Puppy** say he won't fret if his mumma dead, so long as afternoon rain no come. (*British Guiana, Jamaican and Caribbean.*)

455. If you play with the **puppy** you get bitten by the fleas. (*British Guiana.*)

456. When **puss** gone, rat take house. (*Jamaican.*)

457. When **puss** bellyful, rat bitter.

458. Trouble make **puss** run up prickly pear.

459. The **quagmires** don't hang out no sign. (*American.*)

460. One somebody can't **quarrel.** (*Jamaican.*)

461. Stop **quarrel** before fight come. (*Jamaican.*)

462. You want to hear how story go, wait till **quarrel** come. (*Jamaican.*)

463. Seven years is not too long for a **rabbit** to wear a rough-bosom shirt.

[Said to a boasting person who pretends he needs no help.]

464. It don't make much difference where the **rain** comes from, just so it hits the ground in the right place. (*West Indian.*)

465. The **rainbow** might be better lookin' if 'twasn't such a cheap show. (*American.*)

466. **Raindrops** can't tell broadcloth from jeans. (*American.*)

467. It **rains**, and every man feels it someday.

468. **Rat** say him would not give a hang for man who can't lose a night rest for piece of cheese. (*Jamaican.*)

[It is hard to understand a point of view different from one's own.]

469. The public road ain't free for the **rattlesnake.**

470. Grubbing a stump is a good way to whet up your **religion.** (*American.*)

471. Some niggers have got so much **religion** they want to have Sunday every day. (*American.*)

472. Saturday night help the **rheumatism** powerful. (*American.*)

473. When the **rich man** dies they say he was ill ; when the poor man dies, that he had eaten earth. (*Surinam.*)

474. **Rich man** sick, poor man drunk. (*British Guiana.*)

475. Noisy **river** never drown anybody. (*Jamaican.*)

476. Every **river** run to its mamma. (*Jamaican.*)

477. Long **road** draw sweat, short cut draw blood. (*Jamaican.*)

478. Some smart folks can't tell a **rotten rail** without sitting on it. (*West Indian.*)

479. You see somebody **run** fast, take time. (*Jamaican.*)

480. You **run** too fast, you run two time. (*Jamaican.*)

481. "Take care" the mother of **safety.** (*Jamaican.*)

482. Don't take too big a chip on a **sapling.** (*American.*)

483. Old **Satan** couldn't get along without plenty of help. (*American.*)

484. **Satan** has the Scripture in his school-house. (*American.*)

485. An hour with a **saw-buck** is more valuable than an hour with a statesman. (*American.*)

486. Hi! Where this book get all them old-time **sayings ?** (*West Indian.*)

487. Cross-road's bad place to tell **secrets.** (*American.*)

488. Better **see** somethin' before somethin' see you. (*Jamaican.*)

489. One year's weed—seven years' **seed.**

490. You **shake** man's hand, you no shake his heart. (*Jamaican.*)

491. All kind of fish eat man, only **shark** get blame. (*Jamaican.*)

492. Black **sheep** hide mighty easy in the dark. (*American.*)

493. If you have **shilling,** wash shilling, drink the water and keep the shilling. (*Jamaican.*)

494. Time wasted is **shilling** lost out of a hole in the pocket. (*American.*)

495. "Never mind" make **ship** run ashore. (*Creole and West Indian.*)

496. Only **shoe** know if stocking have hole. (*Martinique, British Guiana, Caribbean and Haytian.*)

497. The **sick,** they laugh after death. (*Jamaican.*)

498. A pimple the road for **sickness.** (*Jamaican.*)

499. **Sickness** comes horse riding, but goes away on tortoise. (*Mauritius.*)

500. **Sickness** comes horse riding ; go away foot walk. (*Jamaican.*)

501. **Sickness** comes riding upon a hare, but goes away riding upon a tortoise. (*Creole.*)

502. If there were no **sighing** in the world, the world would stifle. (*Creole.*)

503. **Silver dollar** better than family. (*Jamaican.*)

504. If you want to see your **sins,** clean up a new ground. (*American.*)

505. **Sit down** too long, serve another man. (*Jamaican.*)

506. **Skin** fit closer than shirt. (*Jamaican.*)

507. Take your own eyes to **sleep.** (*Jamaican.*)

508. **Sleep** has no master. (*Jamaican.*)

509. Man no done **sleep,** he no done dream. (*Jamaican.*)

510. If the ground is too **slippery** for man it is not slippery for frogs. (*Surinam.*)

511. If you no got **smile** on you face, no use open shop. (*West Indian.*)

512. **Snake** that want to grow up always stay in his hole. (*Jamaican.*)

513. Sweet **soup** makes man drink ants. (*Jamaican.*)

514. If you drink **soup** you love spoon. (*Jamaican.*)

[i.e. if you like success you must like what it brings to you.]

515. He who has a **spoon** often finds the soup. (*Jamaican.*)

516. If you get **spoon** you will drink soup. (*Jamaican and British Guiana.*)

517. The **squirrel** can beat the rabbit climbing a tree, but then the rabbit makes the best stew and that sort of equalizes the thing.

518. Tall tree make the **squirrel** saucy. (*American.*)

519. **Stand far,** see better. (*Jamaican.*)

520. **Steal** from a thief make God Almighty laugh. (*West Indian.*)

521. Crooked **stick,** crooked shadow. (*Jamaican.*)

522. Stand upon crooked **stick,** cut straight stick. (*Jamaican.*)

523. Lazy folks' **stomachs** don't get tired. (*Plantation.*)

524. Rock **stone** in river bottom never feel sun hot. (*Jamaican.*)

[Those in easy circumstances do not realize the hardships of others.]

525. Rock **stone** on river bottom don't know what rock stone on road feels. (*Jamaican.*)

[For explanation, see 524.]

526. **Story** no got hand, it no got foot, but it goes abroad. (*Jamaican.*)

527. Nothing can **suffice** a man except that which he has not.

528. **Sun set** mighty pretty to plough-hand. (*American.*)

529. He who goes a-**swimming** should know how to keep his clothes dry. (*Surinam.*)

530. When the **sword** sees it is long it thinks it can swallow the knife. (*Surinam.*)

531. If you afraid of **tail,** you can't eat head. (*Jamaican.*)

532. Better **" take care "** before " take care " come. (*S. Carolina.*)

533. Pleasant **tales** break the knees of the young.

534. **Talk** is the ears' food. (*Jamaican.*)

535. **Talk** some, leave some. (*Jamaican.*)

536. When a man **talk** too much, him pay him farther debt. (*Creole.*)

537. Don't bet on a **tater hill** before the grabblin' time. (*American.*)

538. If it am politics against **taters,** take the taters. (*American.*)

539. **Teeth** do not wear mourning. (*Trinidad and Creole.*)

540. There's some facts in the world that don't slide along on the **telegraph wire.** (*American.*)

541. One **time** mistake, two time purpose. (*Jamaican.*)

542. Watch man is the biggest **thief.** (*Jamaican.*)

543. When black man **thief** him steal half a bit, but when white man thief him steal a whole sugar plantation. (*Jamaican.*)

544. Every day Devil help **thief,** one day God help watch man. (*Jamaican.*)

545. Good **thief man** turn good watch man. (*British Guiana.*)

546. **" Think upon "** better than " eating done ". (*Jamaican.*)

547. The boy that's bad no worth **thrashing.** (*Jamaican.*)

548. Two cunning men can't share **three bits.** (*West Indian.*)

549. **To-day** can't catch to-morrow. (*Jamaican.*)

550. **To-day** is the elder brother of to-morrow.

551. The cheapest way to help a man along the world is to pile up flowers on his **tombstone.** (*American.*)

552. **To-morrow** is the burden of the fool. (*Jamaican.*)

553. **To-morrow** may be the carriage-driver's day for ploughing. (*American.*)

554. Padlock your **tongue,** or it lock you up. (*British Guiana.*)

555. "**Too much hurry**" get there to-morrow; "take time" get there to-day. (*Jamaican.*)

556. Poor **top,** poor bottom. (*Jamaican.*)

557. **Towel** turn tablecloth. (*Jamaican.*)

[Applied to an over-dressed person, or to one who has risen in the world.]

558. The single **tree** got to stand a heap of kickin'. (*American.*)

559. Dead limb on the **tree** shows itself when the buds come out. (*American.*)

560. **Trouble** catch man, pickney frock fit him. (*Jamaican.*)

561. **Trouble** follows sin as sure as fever follows chill.

562. **Trouble** goes on legs, scandal has wings. (*British Guiana.*)

563. **Trouble** make the man, money the monster. (*Jamaican.*)

564. **Trouble** no set like rain. (*Jamaican.*)

[In Jamaica rain is usually seen long before it comes.]

565. Never **trouble** trouble till trouble troubles you. (*Jamaican.*)

566. Too much "sit down" broke **trousers.**

567. Man with short **trousers** wear long braces. (*Jamaican.*)

568. Never **trust** what sleeps in the cold. (*Jamaican.*)

569. The green top don't measure the price of the **turnip.** (*American.*)

570. **Twelve o'clock** never in a hurry. (*American.*)

571. **Umbrella** made for rain, white man use it for sun. (*Jamaican.*)

[The adaptability of the white man.]

572. You can't take the twist out of the grape **vine** by cultivating it. (*American.*)

573. **Virtue** no go far if vanity no bear it company. (*Jamaican.*)

574. Don't fling away the empty **wallet.** (*American.*)

575. **Want** all, you lose all. (*Jamaican.*)

576. The **want** of a thing is more than its worth. (*Jamaican.*)

577. Hate people, but don't give them baskets to fetch **water** in. (*Trinidad and Haytian.*)

578. Cursin' the **weather** is mighty poor farming. (*American.*)

579. The best field has **weed.** (*West Indian.*)

580. I shall return to **weep** beneath the tree under which my husband killed his prey.

581. A man is not to be known till he takes a **wife.** (*Haytian.*)

582. Man has to take the **will** for the deed sometime. (*Jamaican.*)

583. When there is no more **wine,** friendship remains in the dregs. (*Surinam.*)

584. Patience: all God's children got **wings.**

585. The **wire-grass** [a rank weed] loves a lazy nigger. (*American.*)

586. Combination is stronger than **witchcraft.** (*Haytian.*)

587. Give your heart to a **woman** and she will kill you.

588. Beautiful **woman,** beautiful trouble. (*Jamaican.*)

589. Handsome face **woman** not be best kind of woman. (*Jamaican.*)

590. If you follow old **woman** you will eat pot bottom. (*Jamaican.*)

591. **Woman's mouth** and fowl are one. (*Jamaican.*)

592. A **woman's mouth** never takes holiday.

593. **Woman's tongue,** wasp, and tamarind-tree, the three worst things. (*Jamaican.*)

[Switches for juvenile offenders made from tamarind-tree.]

594. All **wood** is wood, but the mapon is not the cedar. (*Haytian.*)

[All things are not what they seem.]

595. What **woodpecker** say in him belly hard to answer. (*Jamaican.*)

596. The **wood pile** don't grow much on frosty nights. (*American.*)

597. The **wood pile** is afraid of the north wind. (*American.*)

598. **Words** must die, but man must live. (*Jamaican and Trinidad.*)

599. **Work** doesn't hurt—it's the eyes that are cowards. (*Creole.*)

600. The **worm** don't see nothing pretty in the robin's song. (*American.*)

601. When the ground is hot the **worm** remains in the earth. (*Surinam.*)

602. He who kills his own body works for the **worms.** (*Creole.*)

603. The new ground is the best **yardstick** to measure a strange nigger by.

NICARAGUAN

1. Have patience, **fleas,** the night is long.

PENNSYLVANIAN GERMAN

1. The **apple** does not fall far from the trunk.

[i.e. chip of the old block.]

2. **Black** is also a colour.

[Endeavouring to match dissimilar articles or reports.]

3. Cold **bones** are promised.

[Said when favours are retained for favourites.]

4. What won't **burn** needn't be blown.

5. A jolly life and a pious death spoils the **Devil's** reckoning.

6. If one gets over the **dog,** one gets over the tail.

7. Where there is enough we pepper the **dog's** soup too.

8. When one has no **flour,** one bakes cakes.

[i.e. make the best of what one has.]

9. He who has it long lets it **hang,** and he who has it longer still drags it.

[Refers to the judicious and to the extravagant use of money.]

10. Where red hair and thorns grow, there is no good **land.**

[The comparison of red hair with thorns is because a red-haired woman is usually considered a termagant and would not make a good wife; neither do thorns grow on the best-managed farms.]

11. With fat [rind of pork] the **mice** are caught.

12. The **morning hour** has gold in its mouth.

13. He who steals a **ram** is no sheep thief.

14. **Sauerkraut** and pork dispels all care.

15. Too **sharp** will not cut and too pointed will not prick.

16. That which will become a **thorn** grows sharp early.

17. Children and fools tell the **truth.**

PERUVIAN

1. Father a grocer, son a gentleman, grandson a **beggar.**
2. I may see you Tuesday unless the **bridge** falls.

   [The bridge of San Luis Rey, finest in Peru, unexpectedly fell in July, 1714.]
3. He lives by the **bridge** of San Luis Rey.

   [i.e. under the sword of Damocles.]
4. **Buzzards** do not sing in bleak regions.

   [Referring to black people who cannot stand the cold of high lands.]
5. On the **donkey's** back one must suffer lashes.
6. When going **downhill,** the stones even move along.
7. Over the **egg,** quick, quick.

   [i.e. a drink after eating an egg. Similar to Spanish "Drink wine upon figs".]
8. If you keep fit on **eggs,** don't take broth.
9. In an old **farm-yard** there is no lack of manure.
10. No warmed-up food, nor **friendship** reconciled.
11. It is better to **go round** than to roll round.
12. Don't give it to me, put it in my **hat.**
13. Put him behind you on the **horse** and he finds fault with the animal.

    [i.e. give him a helping hand and he begins to criticize.]
14. In the middle of the river do not change **horses.**
15. He who has no **Inca blood** has African.

    [Referring to half-castes.]
16. A sleeping **lobster** is carried away by the current.
17. One **olive,** and if it is good, a dozen.

    [Referring to the introduction into Peru of the olive-plant by the Spanish conquerors. Early fruit, rare, a luxury.]
18. Avoid living in **Quive.**

    [Quive is an old village in Peru which was cursed by an Archbishop.]
19. In love the **son** despises the father; in business the father despises the son.
20. He plays away the **sun** before it rises.

    [Mancio Sierra de Leguizamo, one of the Spanish conquerors of Peru, a remarkable gambler, lost in one night's play, a big golden image of the sun.]
21. Be sparing of your **visits** and you will be welcome.
22. What **will be** will be.
23. When there is a **woman** and a man, a strong wall between them.
24. **Words** lead to words.
25. What is **written** counts.

AUSTRALASIA
AND POLYNESIA

FIJIAN

1. An unimportant **day** is not to be counted.
2. No **food** was ever cooked by gay clothes and frivolity.
3. **Ignorance** is the night of the mind.
4. Let the shell of the **oyster** perish by reason of years, and to these add a thousand more, still my hatred shall be hot.
5. A **swearer** is said to be armed with teeth.

MAORI

1. Hold fast to the words of thy **ancestors** [or of thy father].
2. The **battlefield** for man ; child-birth for woman.
3. By **black** and by red it is finished.

   [i.e. when commoner and chief work together the task is done. In olden days chiefs used to anoint their faces with shark oil and red ochre.]
4. It is not good to lean upon man, for he is a moving **bolster.**
5. Return to the anchor which first held the **canoe.**

   [i.e. to your first love or wife.]
6. The stump to which the **canoe** is tied.

   [Proverbial expression for the relation of a chief to his tribe.]
7. A **child** grows, but an axe always remains small.
8. The large **chips** made by " Mr. Hardwood " fall to the lot of " Mr. Sit-still ".
9. Don't divide the **cray-fish,** give it whole.

   [i.e. a little thing.]
10. By tears and lamentation alone may [a natural] **death** be avenged.
11. Some say **delicacies** are the mainstay of life ; others that water is.
12. When the **drums** beat for the feast, see that your drum-stick is not slack.
13. You don't trouble to look at the good plate of meat before you, but the **face** you love you look at always.
14. By **feathers** alone can the bird fly ; by clouds are the heavens covered.
15. The size of your **fish** has made you disloyal.

    [i.e. too great luck has made you arrogant.]
16. Ears always listening for **food.**

    [Reproach to a glutton.]
17. The blood of man is **food,** [hence] the life of man is land.
18. Raw **food** is still possessed ; cooked, it goes to another.

    [i.e. eat your food while it is under-done ; when cooked, visitors will eat it for you.]
19. Obtaining **food** is the prized accomplishment.
20. You can always seek and gain shelter in your house, but not always so with a **friend**—death may take him.
21. When you are on **friendly** terms, settle your disputes in a friendly way ; when you are at war, redress your injuries by violence.
22. **Friends** stick to you in harvest, but fall off in summer [the season of scarcity and work].
23. A **fruit-tree** which grows on a dunghill is sure to flourish.

24. There is no warmth in the **garment** if too small.
    [Saying for a small war party; it will not be effective.]
25. You wove the **garment,** I put the border to it.
    [Said when one accuses another of that which he himself has done.]
26. The **grub** eats round the edges of the leaves.
    [Said of a greedy person, selecting tasty morsels. The metaphor is derived from a grub, a great pest, which always nibbles inwards from the edges of the Kumara leaves, eating the softer portion.]
27. At planting time one labours alone; at **harvest,** friends are all around.
28. Glad **heart** went away, bitter mind remained.
    [i.e. he who has obtained the present departs well pleased; he who has parted with it and received nothing, has bitter taste of disappointment.]
29. Let **industry** be rewarded, lest idleness gets the advantage.
30. **Journey** beneath the wing of the white hawk.
    [i.e. Those who travel with a chief fare well in the matter of food and gifts.]
31. The more you ask how far you have to go, the longer your **journey** seems.
32. I greet my only surviving parent in the world—the **land.**
33. Although the present is small, it is all **love** has to give.
34. A **mother's love,** a breast-clinging child.
35. Bale the water out of your **mouth.**
    [Rebuke to wordy, noisy antagonist.]
36. A **muscle** at home, a parrot abroad.
37. A **parrot** to travel, but a rat at home.
38. It is still a **parrot,** whether roasted or raw.
39. Eat up the green **parrots** whether roasted or raw.
    [i.e. eat your food while it is still underdone; when cooked, visitors may eat it for you.]
40. A **pigeon** at home, a parrot abroad.
    [i.e. inhospitality.]
41. Leave them to be **punished** by shame.
42. The **rat** has a double stomach.
    [Saying for a greedy fellow who is never satisfied.]
43. Broil your **rat** with its fur on lest you be disturbed by someone.
    [i.e. eat your food while it is still underdone; when cooked, visitors may eat it for you.]
44. Mind the **step,** the bottom one's the lowest.
45. Deep **throat,** shallow muscles.
    [Reproof of laziness.]
46. In **winter** a relation; in autumn a son.
    [i.e. distant relation when heavy work; after harvest when plenty of food, calls himself a son.]
47. **Women** and land destroy men.
    [i.e. causes of war.]

TAGALOG [PHILIPPINE ISLANDS]

1. There is no higher **ancestry** than Adam.
2. A **candle** in a house will illumine a street.
3. Beautiful is the **church,** but it must have its curtains [mysteries].
4. A knife will not enter a **crocodile's** back.
5. The **drummer** should beat the drum.
6. **Excesses** are rare when the heart is at rest.

7. When will you cast your **fool's** skin?
8. Make thyself a **friend** of my friend.
9. Even though naked, **gentility** will show itself.
10. Let **governors** govern.
11. Disquiet is the constant companion of **jealousy.**
12. Tell a **lie** to find a truth.
13. A sin against a **neighbour** is an offence against God.
14. The **poor** have no nurse.
15. **Sins** are the diseases of the soul.
16. Let him make a **song** or sing one. [Said to a pretender.]
17. Lift up your eyes and you will see the **stars.**
18. Trust not the disentanglement of the **threads** to a man with dirty hands.
19. If he be so **virtuous,** let him go to the wilderness [become a hermit].
20. Sing a lullaby at your **wedding.**
21. Where the **wound** is, there the plaister should be.
22. **Write** now and then; read now and then.

LINGUISTIC AND GEOGRAPHICAL INDEX

Italicized entries denote countries, districts, or territories. The proverbs of these countries, etc., are to be found under the headings which appear in brackets immediately after these entries.

All other entries denote language or dialect headings.

Abyssinia (Amharic, Galla)
Accra, see Ga, 527
Afghanistan (Pashto)

SUBJECT-MATTER INDEX

(The plural is included in the singular)

The number in brackets is the page on which the language starts, the number not in brackets is the number of the proverb.

RACE (SUB-INDEX)

[The number in brackets is the page on which the language starts, the number not in brackets is the number of the proverb.]

ALTERNATIVE CHIEF-WORD INDEX

(The plural is included in the singular)